# ORCHESTRAL MUSIC IN PRINT

## 1999 SUPPLEMENT

Edited by

**Robert W. Cho**
**F. Mark Daugherty**
**Frank James Staneck**

**Music-In-Print Series, Vol. 5u**

MUSICDATA, INC.
Philadelphia, 1999

# The Music-In-Print Series to date:

| | |
|---|---|
| Vols. 1a,b. | Sacred Choral Music In Print, Second Edition (1985) |
| Vol. 1c. | Sacred Choral Music In Print, Second Edition: Arrange |
| Vol. 1s. | Sacred Choral Music In Print: 1988 Supplement |
| Vol. 1t. | Sacred Choral Music In Print: 1992 Supplement |
| Vol. 1u. | Sacred Choral Music In Print: 1996 Supplement |
| Vol. 1x. | Sacred Choral Music In Print: Master Index 1996 |
| Vols. 2a,b. | Secular Choral Music In Print, Second Edition (1987) |
| Vol. 2c. | Secular Choral Music In Print, Second Edition: Arranger Index (1987) |
| Vol. 2s. | Secular Choral Music In Print: 1991 Supplement |
| Vol. 2t. | Secular Choral Music In Print: 1993 Supplement |
| Vol. 2u. | Secular Choral Music In Print: 1996 Supplement |
| Vol. 2x. | Secular Choral Music In Print: Master Index 1996 |
| Vol. 3. | Organ Music In Print, Second Edition (1984) |
| Vol. 3s. | Organ Music In Print: 1990 Supplement |
| Vol. 3t. | Organ Music In Print: 1997 Supplement |
| Vol. 3x. | Organ Music In Print: Master Index 1997 |
| Vol. 4. | Classical Vocal Music In Print (1976) (out of print) |
| Vol. 4s. | Classical Vocal Music In Print: 1985 Supplement |
| Vol. 4t. | Classical Vocal Music In Print: 1995 Supplement |
| Vol. 4x. | Classical Vocal Music In Print: Master Index 1995 |
| Vol. 5. | Orchestral Music In Print (1979) |
| Vol. 5s. | Orchestral Music In Print: 1983 Supplement |
| Vol. 5t. | Orchestral Music In Print: 1994 Supplement |
| Vol. 5u. | Orchestral Music In Print: 1999 Supplement |
| Vol. 5x. | Orchestral Music In Print: Master Index 1999 (in preparation) |
| Vol. 6. | String Music In Print, Second Edition (1973) |
| Vol. 6s. | String Music In Print: 1984 Supplement |
| Vol. 6t. | String Music In Print: 1998 Supplement |
| Vol. 7. | Classical Guitar Music In Print (1989) |
| Vol. 7s. | Classical Guitar Music In Print: 1998 Supplement |
| Vol. 8. | Woodwind Music In Print (1997) |
| Vols. XCa,b. | Music-In-Print Master Composer Index 1999 |
| Vol. XT. | Music-In-Print Master Title Index 1999 |

Music-In-Print Series: ISSN 0146-7883

Orchestral Music In Print: 1999 Supplement          ISBN 0-88478-051-1

Printed by Port City Press, Baltimore, Maryland

Musicdata, Inc.
P.O. Box 12380
Philadelphia, Pennsylvania 19119-0380

**Library of Congress Cataloging-in-Publication Data**

Farish, Margaret K.
    Orchestral music in print.

        (Music-in-print series; v. 5)
        1. Orchestral music--Bibliography.    I. Title.
    II. Series.
    ML128.O5F33          016.785          79-24460
    ISBN 0-88478-010-4

# Contents

# Preface

This volume is the third supplement to *Orchestral Music in Print*, published in 1979. It contains listings obtained since the second supplement published in 1994. We compiled the entries in this supplement from catalogs and lists sent by publishers from all over the world. As in *Orchestral Music in Print*, we included all works for eleven or more players except those scored solely for wind instruments. We included music for solo instruments or voices with orchestra, but we excluded works for chorus and orchestra. For information on these publications, please consult the Choral Music in Print volumes. An exception to this choral exclusionary policy exists, however, with works whose titles are usually thought of as part of the orchestral bailiwick, e.g., *Symphony No. 8* by Gustav Mahler.

In *Orchestral Music in Print* a main entry appears under the name of the composer and includes, whenever possible, the instrumentation and duration. If the work is available from more than one publisher, all editions are listed under one uniform title. We have attempted to follow this system in the present supplemental volume.

It is, of course, the publisher who is ultimately the only dependable source of information on music currently in print. Although many publishers send excellent catalogs or comprehensive listings by postal delivery or by the increasingly popular medium of electronic mail, some do not provide all of the bibliographic information needed for a complete entry. If the composer and the titles can be identified, the missing elements can sometimes be added by the editor. However, this is not always possible. Without the composer's full name and dates, it is difficult to know which member of a musical family is the composer and, even more frequently, which work is offered. For example, if "Concerto in D" by a prolific 18th century composer is listed by half a dozen publishers, it is impossible to tell whether six different concertos or six editions of one concerto are available. In these circumstances, each is listed separately with a Musicdata Identification Number (MIN) for the benefit of the computer which is programmed to treat all works with identical titles as multiple editions. A similar system is used for common titles, such as "Minuet". The repetition of identical titles indicates lack of information. The works may be the same; only an examination of the scores will provide proof.

The works of each composer are listed alphabetically by title. Because the computer-based system does not permit changes in this order, entries for collections will not always precede those for individual works, as they do in most music library files. *Symphonies* will come before *Symphony*, but *Suites* will follow *Suite*. For most titles of this nature, the English form of the plural has been used, but inevitably there are a few exceptions. The most important of these is *Concerto*. The Italian plural has been adopted in this case to accommodate the unalterable *Concerti Grossi*.

Because of the political changes that have occurred in Eastern Europe during the past decade, a great deal of music is now being made available to the world. Orchestras are discovering an important body of music that was largely unknown outside of the composer's own country. Audiences are hearing new and unfamiliar composers, and publishers are publishing their music. In some instances, the spelling of these new names has proved to be problematic, especially so if the composer's name originally was spelled using a non-Roman alphabet. The problem is further compounded by publishers who attempt to spell the name phonetically using their own language's specific symbol-as-sound conventions. We have attempted to consolidate these different spellings, choosing one as definitive (at least for the time being). In some instances the user will find a cross-reference directing him to our standard spelling, but with the newer composers this practice has not yet been consistently followed.

We wish to thank those publishers who have generously co-operated with us by providing accurate, up-to-date listings. Special thanks go to our colleague Donald T. Reese for his knowledge of the Musicdata computer system, editorial view, and constant support throughout the entire project. We also thank Musicdata staff members Kathe Jacoby and Joseph Pluciennik who assisted and encouraged us in this project with their computer expertise. Special thanks once again must go to Mark Resnick for his continued dedication to the Music-In-Print series. Finally, many thanks to Margaret Farish, whose precedent-setting work provided clear and consistent guidelines for the continuation of *Orchestral Music In Print*.

Robert W. Cho
F. Mark Daugherty
Frank James Staneck

Philadelphia, Pennsylvania
September 1999

# Guide to Use

## THE MUSIC-IN-PRINT SERIES

The Music-In-Print series is an ongoing effort to locate and catalog all music in print throughout the world. The intention is to cover all areas of music as rapidly as resources permit, as well as to provide a mechanism for keeping the information up to date.

Since 1973, Musicdata, Inc. has solicited catalogs and listings from music publishers throughout the world. Using the information supplied by co-operating publishers, the series lists specific editions which are available from a publisher either for sale or on a rental basis. The volumes in the series are basically organized by the primary performing force, instrument or instrumental family, such as Sacred Choral Music, Organ Music or String Music.

It is often difficult to define the boundaries between the various broad areas of music covered by the volumes in the series. The definition of sacred and secular choral music varies from publisher to publisher; some major choral works are no longer listed in Orchestral Music, reflecting changing editorial practice; some solo vocal music is in Orchestral Music; etc. The user is advised to consult the preface to individual volumes for greater definition of scope. The use of more than one volume may well be necessary to locate a particular edition or all editions of a work.

Editorial policy is to include as much information as the publisher supplies, within the limits of practicality. An important goal of the series is to try to bring together different editions of a composition under a single title.

## VOLUME FORMAT

The volumes of the Music-In-Print series have two basic formats: unified or structured. Reference to the editor's preface and the table of contents will assist in determining how a given volume is organized.

The unified volumes (e.g., Organ Music, Orchestral Music) are arranged in a single alphabetical interfiling of composers' names, titles of works and cross references. The title under a composer's name serves as the focus for major information on each composition. In the absence of a composer, the title in the main alphabet becomes the focal point for this information.

The structured volumes (e.g., String Music, Woodwind Music) are arranged by an imposed framework: instrumentation, time period, type of work or other categorization. Within each section, entries are alphabetized by composer name or, in the absence of a composer, by title. Entries will be repeated in all appropriate sections. A structured volume also contains a Composer/Title Index and, in some cases, other specialized indexes. The Composer/Title Index is a single alphabetical list of composers' names, composition titles and cross references, with a reference to the section(s) of the volume in which complete edition information will be found. The running heads at the top of each page of the catalog enable the user to quickly find the proper section.

## ENTRY TYPES

Two basic types of entries appear in the Music-In-Print series: normal and collection. A normal entry describes a single piece of music. A collection consists of any two or more associated pieces.

## NORMAL ENTRY CONTENT

In order to bring together all different editions of a composition under a uniform and/or structured title, many musical form titles are translated into English (so, Konzert becomes Concerto, Fantaisie becomes Fantasy, etc.). To aid in alphabetizing, initial articles in titles are rotated, as are numerals in titles. This practice is followed with English, German, French, Danish, Italian, Dutch, Spanish, Norwegian, and Swedish titles.

For each title there are two types of information: a) generic information about the composition and b) specific information pertaining to the editions which are in print. Included in the generic information category are the uniform title of the composition, a structured title for the work (e.g., Concerto No. 2 in D Minor; Cantata No. 140), a thematic catalog number or opus and number designation, the larger source from which the work was taken, and remarks.

Following the generic information about the piece is specific information about each individual edition. This information includes the arranger, the published title of the edition if different from the uniform title, the language of the text (for vocal works), instrumentation required for performance, the duration of the work in minutes (') and seconds ("), a difficulty rating assigned to the edition by the publisher or editor, the format of the publication, publisher code, publisher's number, and sale or rental information concerning the edition.

The following is an example of a typical entry under a composer:

> MOZART, WOLFGANG AMADEUS (1756-1791)
> Nozze Di Figaro, Le: Overture
> [4']
> 2.2.2.2. 2.2.0.0. timp,strings
> sc,parts RICORDI-IT rental   (M1)
> "Marriage of Figaro, The: Overture"
> sc,parts BREITKOPF-W f.s.          (M2)

In this entry under the composer, Wolfgang Amadeus Mozart, the title of an excerpt, "Overture", follows the original title of the complete work, "Nozze Di Figaro, Le". It is scored for 2 flutes, 2 oboes, 2 clarinets, 2 bassoons, 2 horns, 2 trumpets, timpani and strings. Duration is approximately 4 minutes. The code RICORDI-IT indicates the publisher of the first listed edition; score and parts are offered by this publisher on rental. The sequence number (M1) marks the end of the information on this edition. The English title

"Marriage of Figaro, The: Overture" is given for the next edition which is published by BREITKOPF-W; score and parts for this edition are for sale.

The full names and addresses of all publishers or U.S. agents are given in the publisher directory which follows the list of editions at the end of the book.

Following is an example of an entry with a structured title:

> MOZART, WOLFGANG AMADEUS (1756-1791)
> Symphony No. 25, [excerpt]
> (Gordon, Philip) 2.1.2.1.al-
> sax. ten-sax. 2.2.1.1.timp,perc,
> strings [3'] (Menuetto, [arr.])
> PRESSER sets, sc          (M3)

Here a structured title "Symphony No. 25," requires a different form of listing. The excerpt, "Menuetto", has been arranged by Philip Gordon for 2 flutes, oboe, 2 clarinets, bassoon, alto saxophone, tenor saxophone, 2 horns, 2 trumpets, trombone, tuba, timpani, percussion and strings. Duration is three minutes. The publisher, PRESSER, offers sets of parts. A separate score is available.

## INSTRUMENTATION

Instrumentation is given in the customary score order. When a work is scored for full orchestra, the number of wind players required is indicated by two groups of four numbers:

Woodwinds  (flute, oboe, clarinet, bassoon)   (1.1.1.1)
Brass        (horn, trumpet, trombone, tuba)   (1.1.1.1)

Other instruments are listed by name, or abbreviated name. A number placed before a named instrument indicates the number of players. A slash is used for alternate instrumentation.

The common auxiliary wind instruments are not mentioned by most publishers. For example, 2.2.3.3. for woodwinds indicates the work is scored for two flutes, but it may include a piccolo part which can be played by one of the flutists. Similarly, it is possible that parts for English horn, bass clarinet and contrabassoon are provided but no additional players will be required. If the publisher does specify the auxiliary instruments required, this information is given either in parentheses (the number of players is not affected) or after a plus sign (an additional player is needed).

Example:

> 2(pic).2+opt ob.3(opt bass-clar).2+contrabsn.
> 4.2.3.0+opt tuba.timp,2-3perc,harp,cel/pno,
> strings

This example is scored for 2 flutes and piccolo (played

by one of the flutists), 2 oboes plus an optional third oboe, 3 clarinets (one may play the optional bass clarinet part), 2 bassoons plus contrabassoon (additional player required), 4 horns, 2 trumpets, 3 trombones, optional tuba, timpani, percussion (2 or 3 players), harp, celeste or piano, and strings.

The term "orch" may be substituted for a detailed listing if the publisher has not provided the instrumentation for orchestral works.

Solo instrumental parts are listed following the complete orchestration of a work.

Choral parts are given as a list of voices (e.g., SATB, TTBB, etc.). The term "cor" (and similar terms) may be substituted when the publisher has not listed the specific voices.

Solo vocal parts are given as a list of voices followed by the term "solo" or "soli." The term "solo voice(s)" is used when the publisher does not specify the voice(s). (No attempt has been made to give equivalents for scale ranges listed by publishers.)

## REMARKS

The remarks are a series of codes or abbreviations giving information on the seasonal or other usage of the piece, the type of music, and the national origin and century for folk or anonymous pieces. (These codes also make it possible to retrieve, from the data base developed for the Music-In-Print series, specialized listings of music for particular seasons, types, etc.) Following this Guide to Use will be found a complete List of Abbreviations. Remarks may also include additional information about the edition as indicated by the publisher.

## SEQUENCE NUMBERS

An alphanumeric number, appearing on the right margin, has been assigned to each edition represented in this catalog. These are for the purpose of easing identification and location of specific entries.

## COLLECTION ENTRY CONTENT

An attempt has been made to provide the user with access to pieces contained within collections, while still keeping the work within reasonable bounds of time and space. Accordingly, the following practices have been adopted:

If the members of a collection are published separately, they are listed individually, regardless of the number of pieces involved. If the collection is only published as a whole, the members are listed only if they do not exceed six in number. For larger collections, a code is given indicating the number of pieces and whether or not the contents are listed in the publisher's catalog.

Example:

*CC18L indicates a collection of 18 pieces in which the titles are *listed* in the publisher's catalog
*CC101U indicates a collection of 101 pieces in which the titles are *unlisted* in the publisher's catalog
*CCU indicates a collection of an unknown number of pieces

Whenever the members of a collection are listed, they are also cross-referenced to the collection. For example, consider the following entry:

FIVE VOLUNTARIES, [ARR.]
  (Davies, Peter Maxwell) 3.3.2.1, 3.3.0.0.
  timp,perc,strings,cont   sc,parts
  SCHOTT 10994 f.s.
  contains: Attaignant, Pierre,
    Magnificat; Clarke, Jeremiah,
    King William's March; Clarke,
    Jeremiah, Serenade; Couperin,
    Louis, Sarabande; Croft, William,
    March Tune        (F1)

Published by Schott, edition number 10994, this collection edited by Peter Maxwell Davies contains five members, which are not published separately. Under each of the members there is a cross reference saying 'see FIVE VOLUNTARIES, [ARR.]'.

Collection entries also contain many of the elements of information found in normal entries. For example, the entry shown above contains arranger, instrumentation, format of publication, publisher code and publisher number.

Collections of several pieces published as a whole, but having no overall title, create another problem. In this case the complete publication information is given under the composer or title of the first piece listed, together with the comment 'contains also,' followed by titles of the other collection members.

## CROSS REFERENCES

In order to provide the user with as many points of access as possible, the Music-In-Print series has been heavily cross referenced. In the unified volumes, the cross references are interfiled with the composers' names and the titles. In the structured volumes, cross references only appear in the Composer/Title Index.

Works may be located by title, with or without knowing the name of the composer. Using the first example by Mozart above, this composition may be located under either its Italian or English title in the main alphabet, as well as under the composer. To make this possible the following cross references would exist in the main alphabet:

>    NOZZE DI FIGARO, LE: OVERTURE
>        see Mozart, Wolfgang Amadeus

>    and

>    MARRIAGE OF FIGARO, THE: OVERTURE see
>        Mozart, Wolfgang Amadeus, Nozze Di
>        Figaro, Le: Overture

and in addition, the following cross reference would be found under the composer's name:

>    Marriage of Figaro, The: Overture
>        *see Nozze Di Figaro, Le: Overture

Cross references are employed also to assist in the search for works frequently identified by popular names or subtitles, such as the "Surprise" Symphony of Haydn and the "Jupiter" Symphony of Mozart.

Numerous cross references have been made from unused and variant forms of composer names to assist the user in finding the form of the name chosen for the series.

## COLLECTION CROSS REFERENCES

Whenever the members of a collection are listed, they are cross referenced to the collection. In unified volumes, these are interfiled with composers' names and titles. In structured volumes, these cross references only occur in the Composer/Title Index.

Using the above example, FIVE VOLUNTARIES, [ARR.], a cross reference will be found under each of the composers saying 'see FIVE VOLUNTARIES, [Arr.]'. (If a collection member lacks a composer, the cross reference will occur at the title.)

When collections are also published separately, the cross references in both directions read 'see also'. If the members are only published separately (i.e., the collection were not published as a whole) then the cross reference under the collection would read 'see' and under the members, 'see from'. Thus, 'see' and 'see also' direct the user to information concerning publication, while 'see from' provides access to the collection of which a given publication is a part.

With untitled collections, which are listed under the first composer and/or title, the cross reference 'see' under each of the other collection members directs the user to the full entry under the first member, at which point complete edition information will be found.

## COMPOSER/TITLE INDEX

The Composer/Title Index is a single alphabetical listing of composer names, composition titles and cross references. This index is used to identify the location of a specific entry in a structured volume.

The actual reference is usually under the composer name, and only under a title when a work is not attributable to a person. The reference is to the chapter and/or section of the volume which contains the entry for the music sought.

For example, in String Music, IV.1 refers the user to Chapter IV, Section 1: String Quartets. Similarly, VIII refers to Chapter VIII: Music for Eight Instruments. Reference to the table of contents and the head of each page of the volume will assist the user in finding the appropriate section containing the information sought.

## ARRANGER INDEX

The Arranger Index lists in alphabetical order all arrangers and editors cited in a specific volume. The arranger's or editor's name is listed in all capital letters. In the case of multiple arrangers, the arranger names appear together, separated by semi-colons. The listing under each arranger name gives the composer and title of each arranged (edited) work, in alphabetical order. If a work has no composer, it is listed by title. In the case of uniform and translated titles, the uniform titles are the ones appearing in the index.

This arrangement allows the user to look up any desired arranger or editor and then scan for the composers and titles of desired works. Once the composer and title have been determined, the work may then be looked up in the catalog itself to obtain complete bibliographic and ordering information.

## PUBLISHER DIRECTORY

The Publisher Directory follows the body of the catalog portion of the book and any indexes that are included in the volume. This list provides full names and addresses of all publishers or U.S. agents listed within the Music-In-Print series. Publishers' names are given as codes throughout the catalog. Having recently undergone a major revision in format and content, the Publisher Directory is organized by listing codes in alphabetical order. While the codes are generally close in appearance to the actual names, in some cases the two may differ substantially. When alphabetical distance separates name and code, a cross reference has been included, directing the user to the code.

## MASTER INDEX

The Music-In-Print Master Index provides a single place to look in order to locate any composer or title listed in the Music-In-Print series. The Master Index eliminates all problems of knowing whether a specific piece of music is listed in a base volume, supplementary volumes, or not at all.

The Master Composer Index lists all composers found within the Music-In-Print series. Under each composer's name is a complete alphabetical listing of the titles of works by that composer to be found in the series. Next to each title is a number or series of numbers referring the user to the volume or volumes containing the specific piece. A key explaining these numbers and the volumes to which they correspond is to be found on the reverse side of the title page.

Once the user has located the correct volume, it is easy to find the specific piece in the volume's alphabetical sequence. In the case of structured volumes, reference should be made to the Composer/Title Index in each volume.

The Master Title Index lists in a single alphabetical listing all titles of works within the Music-In-Print series. Each title is followed by a reference number or series of numbers, directing the user to the volume or volumes containing the specific title as explained above.

Additionally, as more supplementary volumes are added to the Music-In-Print series, certain volumes may update the Master Index in a specific area from time to time, through the publication of a specialized Master Index. In this way, the user can easily locate a piece of music within the volumes dealing with a specific area.

# List of Abbreviations

The following is a general list of abbreviations developed for the Music-In-Print series. Therefore, all of the abbreviations do not necessarily occur in the present volume. Also, it should be noted that terms spelled out in full in the catalog, e.g. woodwinds, tuba, Easter, Passover, folk, Swiss, do not appear in this list.

| | | | |
|---|---|---|---|
| A | alto | db-tuba | double-bass tuba |
| acap | a cappella | dbl cor | double chorus |
| accomp | accompaniment | Ded | Dedication |
| acord | accordion | degr. | degree, 1-9 (difficulty), assigned by editor |
| Adv | Advent | | |
| Afr | African | desc | descant |
| Agnus | Agnus Dei | diag | diagram(s) |
| al-clar | alto clarinet | diff | difficult |
| al-fl | alto flute | Dounias | thematic catalog of the violin concertos of Giuseppe Tartini by Minous Dounias |
| al-sax | alto saxophone | | |
| Allelu | Alleluia | | |
| AmInd | American Indian | | |
| ampl | amplified | | |
| Anh. | Anhang (supplement) | Doxol | Doxology |
| anti | antiphonal | | |
| app | appendix, appendices | ea. | each |
| arr. | arranged | ECY | End of Church Year |
| Asc | Ascension | ed | edition |
| ASD | All Saints' Day | educ | educational material |
| aud | audience | elec | electric |
| Austral | Australian | Ember | Ember Days |
| | | Eng | English |
| | | enl | enlarged |
| B | bass | Epiph | Epiphany |
| Bald | Baldwin organ | eq voices | equal voices |
| Bar | baritone | Eur | European |
| bar horn | baritone horn | evang | evangelistic |
| bar-sax | baritone saxophone | Eve | Evening |
| bass-clar | bass clarinet | | |
| bass-fl | bass flute | | |
| bass-sax | bass saxophone | F. | thematic catalog of the instrumental works of Antonio Vivaldi by Antonio Fanna |
| bass-trom | bass trombone | | |
| bass-trp | bass trumpet | | |
| bds | boards | | |
| Belg | Belgian | f(f) | following |
| Benton | thematic catalog of the works of Ignace Pleyel by Rita Benton | f.s. | for sale |
| | | fac ed | facsimile edition |
| | | facsim | facsimile(s) |
| Bibl | Biblical | Fest | festivals |
| bk | book | film | music from film score |
| Boh | Bohemian | Finn | Finnish |
| boy cor | boys' chorus | fl | flute |
| Braz | Brazilian | Fr | French |
| Bryan | thematic catalog of the symphonies of Johann Wanhal by Paul Bryan | | |
| | | Gd.Fri. | Good Friday |
| bsn | bassoon | Ge. | thematic catalog of the works of Luigi Boccherini by Yves Gerard |
| BVM | Blessed Virgin Mary | | |
| BWV | Bach-Werke-Verzeichnis; thematic catalog of the works of J.S. Bach by Wolfgang Schmieder | | |
| | | Gen | general |
| | | Ger | German |

| | |
|---|---|
| BuxWV | Buxtehude-Werke-Verzeichnis; thematic catalog of the works of Dietrich Buxtehude by G. Kärstadt (Wiesbaden, 1974) |
| C&W | Country & Western |
| C.Landon | numbering of the keyboard sonatas of Joseph Haydn by Christa Landon |
| camb | cambiata |
| Can | Canadian |
| cant | cantata |
| Carib | Caribbean |
| CC | collection |
| CCU | collection, unlisted |
| CCUL | collection, partially listed |
| cel | celesta |
| Cen Am | Central American |
| cent | century |
| cf. | compare |
| Chin | Chinese |
| chord | chord organ |
| Circum | Circumcision |
| clar | clarinet |
| cloth | clothbound |
| cmplt ed | complete edition |
| Cnfrm | Confirmation |
| Commun | Communion |
| cong | congregation |
| Conn | Conn organ |
| cont | continuo |
| contrabsn | contrabassoon |
| copy | ed produced to order by a copy process |
| cor | chorus |
| cor pts | choral parts |
| cor-resp | choral response |
| Corpus | Corpus Christi |
| cradle | cradle song |
| cym | cymbals |
| D. | thematic catalog of the works of Franz Schubert by Otto Erich Deutsch |
| Dan | Danish |
| db | double bass |

| | | | | | |
|---|---|---|---|---|---|
| Giegling | thematic catalog of the works of Giuseppe Torelli by Franz Giegling | Kaul | thematic catalog of the instrumental works of F.A. Rosetti by Oskar Kaul | Op. Posth. | Opus Posthumous |
| girl cor | girls' chorus | kbd | keyboard | opt | optional, ad lib |
| glock | glockenspiel | Kirkpatrick | thematic catalog of the sonatas of Domenico Scarlatti by Ralph Kirkpatrick | ora | oratorio |
| gr. I-V | grades I-V, assigned by publisher | | | orch | orchestra |
| Greg | Gregorian chant | | | org | organ |
| gtr | guitar | Kor | Korean | org man | organ, manuals only |
| Gulbransen | Gulbransen organ | Krebs | thematic catalog of the works of Karl Ditters von Dittersdorf by Karl Krebs | orig | original |
| Hamm | Hammond organ | | | P., P.S. | thematic catalogs of the orchestral works of Antonio Vivaldi by Marc Pincherle |
| Harv | Harvest | | | | |
| Heb | Hebrew | | | | |
| Helm | thematic catalog of the works of C.P.E. Bach by Eugene Helm | L | listed | p(p) | page(s) |
| | | Landon | numbering of the keyboard trios of Joseph Haydn by H.C.R. Landon | Palm | Palm Sunday |
| Hill | thematic catalog of the works of F.L. Gassmann by George Hill | | | pap | paperbound |
| | | Lat | Latin | Paymer | thematic catalog of the works of G.B. Pergolesi by Marvin Paymer |
| | | liturg | liturgical | | |
| Hob. | thematic catalog of the works of Joseph Haydn by Anthony van Hoboken | Longo | thematic catalog of the sonatas of Domenico Scarlatti by Alessandro Longo | | |
| | | | | pce, pcs | piece, pieces |
| | | | | Pent | Pentecost |
| | | | | perc | percussion |
| Holywk | Holy Week | Lowery | Lowery organ | perf mat | performance material |
| horn | French horn | | | perf sc | performance score |
| hpsd | harpsichord | | | Perger | thematic catalog of the instrumental works of Michael Haydn by Lothar Perger |
| Hung | Hungarian | Magnif | Magnificat | | |
| HWC | Healey Willan Catalogue | maj | major | | |
| | | man | manualiter; on the manuals alone | pic | piccolo |
| ill | illustrated, illustrations | | | pic-trp | piccolo trumpet |
| Ind | Indian | mand | mandolin | pipe | pipe organ |
| inst | instruments | manuscript | manuscript(handwritten) | pno | piano |
| intro | introduction | med | medium | pno-cond sc | piano-conducting score |
| ipa | intrumental parts available | mel | melody | pno red | piano reduction |
| | | men cor | men's chorus | Pol | Polish |
| ipr | instrumental parts for rent | Mex | Mexican | Polynes | Polynesian |
| | | Mez | mezzo-soprano | pop | popular |
| Ir | Irish | MIN | Musicdata Identification Number | Port | Portuguese |
| Isr | Israel | | | pos | position |
| It | Italian | | | PreClass | Pre-Classical |
| | | min | minor | pref | preface |
| | | min sc | miniature score | Proces | processional |
| | | mix cor | mixed chorus | Psntd | Passiontide |
| | | Morav | Moravian | pt, pts | part, parts |
| J-C | thematic catalog of the works of G.B. Sammartini by Newell Jenkins and Bathia Churgin | Morn | Morning | | |
| | | mot | motet | quar | quartet |
| | | | | quin | quintet |
| Jap | Japanese | | | Quinqua | Quinquagesima |
| Jew | Jewish | Neth | Netherlands | | |
| jr cor | junior chorus | NJ | Name of Jesus | rec | recorder |
| Jubil | Jubilate Deo | No. | number | Reces | recessional |
| | | Nor Am | North America | Refm | Reformation |
| | | Norw | Norwegian | rent | for rent |
| | | Nos. | numbers | repr | reprint |
| | | Nunc | Nunc Dimittis | Req | Requiem |
| K. | thematic catalog of the works of W.A. Mozart by Ludwig, Ritter von Köchel; thematic catalog of the works of J.J. Fux by the same author | | | rev | revised, revision |
| | | | | Royal | royal occasion |
| | | ob | oboe | Rum | Rumanian |
| | | oct | octavo | Russ | Russian |
| | | offer | offertory | | |
| | | Op. | Opus | | |

| | |
|---|---|
| RV | Ryom-Verzeichnis; thematic catalog of the works of Antonio Vivaldi by Peter Ryom |
| S | soprano |
| s.p. | separately published |
| Sab | Sabbath |
| sac | sacred |
| sax | saxophone |
| sc | score |
| Scot | Scottish |
| sec | secular |
| Septua | Septuagesima |
| Sexa | Sexagesima |
| show | music from musical show score |
| So Am | South American |
| sop-clar | soprano clarinet |
| sop-sax | soprano saxophone |
| Span | Spanish |
| speak cor | speaking chorus |
| spir | spiritual |
| sr cor | senior chorus |
| study sc | study score |
| suppl | supplement |
| Swed | Swedish |
| SWV | Schütz-Werke-Verzeichnis; thematic catalog of the works of Heinrich Schütz by W.Bittinger (Kassel, 1960) |
| T | tenor |
| tamb | tambourine |
| temp blks | temple blocks |
| ten-sax | tenor saxophone |
| Thanks | Thanksgiving |
| Thomas | Thomas organ |
| TI | Tárrega Index; thematic catalog of the Preludes, Studies, and Excercises of Francisco Tárrega by Mijndert Jape |
| timp | timpani |
| transl | translation |
| treb | treble |
| Trin | Trinity |
| trom | trombone |
| trp | trumpet |
| TV | music from television score |
| TWV | Telemann-Werke-Verzeichnis; thematic catalog of the works of G.P. Telemann by Mencke and Ruhncke |
| U | unlisted |
| UL | partially listed |
| unis | unison |
| US | United States |

| | |
|---|---|
| vcl | violoncello |
| vibra | vibraphone |
| vla | viola |
| vln | violin |
| voc pt | vocal part |
| voc sc | vocal score |
| VOCG | Robert de Visee, Oeuvres Completes pour Guitare edited by Robert Strizich |
| vol(s) | volume(s) |
| Whitsun | Whitsuntide |
| WO | without opus number; used in thematic catalog of the works of Muzio Clementi by Alan Tyson |
| Wolf | thematic catalog of the symphonies of Johann Stamitz by Eugene Wolf |
| wom cor | women's chorus |
| WoO. | work without opus number; used in thematic catalogs of the works of Beethoven by Kinsky and Halm and of the works of J.N. Hummel by Dieter Zimmerscheid |
| Wq. | thematic catalog of the works of C.P.E. Bach by Alfred Wotquenne |
| Wurlitzer | Wurlitzer organ |
| WV | Wagenseil-Verzeichnis; thematic catalog of the works of G.C. Wagenseil by Helga Scholz-Michelitsch |
| Xmas | Christmas |
| xylo | xylophone |
| Z. | thematic catalog of the works of Henry Purcell by Franklin Zimmerman |

# ORCHESTRAL MUSIC

# A

À DEUX see Gonneville, Michel

A GONDOLAT JÁTÉKAI see Decsenyi, Janos, Giuochi Del Pensiero

A HENRY see Paganini, Niccolo

A LA CHAPELLE SIXTINE see Liszt, Franz

... À LA DUDUKI, FOR BRASS QUINTET AND ORCHESTRA see Kantscheli, Gija

À LA SOURCE D'HYPOCRENE see Burke, John

À L'AMIE PERDUE see Dupre, Marcel

A L'HEURE QUE JE VOUS see Des Prez, Josquin

A MINUIT SONNANT see Offenbach, Jacques

A MINUIT SONNANT (RONDO METELA) see Offenbach, Jacques

A PRECE SE TOCÍ see Jirasek, Jan

A ZÍTRA NASHLE... see Sodomka, Karel

AAGAARD-NILSEN, TORSTEIN (1964-   )
Concerto for Trumpet and Orchestra
2(pic).2.2(bass clar).2(contrabsn).
3.2.3(bass trom).0. 2perc,pno,
strings,trp in C solo NORSKMI
(A1)

Concerto for Trumpet and String Orchestra
string orch,trp solo [18'20"] NORSKMI
(A2)

Concerto for Violoncello and Orchestra
2(pic).2.3(bass clar).2. 4.2.2.1.
timp,2perc,strings,vcl solo [24']
NORSKMI
(A3)

Kar: Festmusikk, For Orchestra With Ocarinas
2(pic).2.2.2. 4.3.3.1. 2perc,pno,
strings, 7 ocarinas [12'] NORSKMI
(A4)

AANKOMST, DE see Ketting, Otto

AANLOOP EN KREET (VERSIE 2) see Goeyvaerts, Karel, Aquarius, No. 4 (2nd Version)

ABDELAZER see Purcell, Henry

ABEL, CARL FRIEDRICH (1723-1787)
Symphony in E flat, Op. 7, No. 6
2clar,2horn,bsn,strings [8']
((formerly known as Symphony No. 3, K. 18 by W.A. Mozart)) sc
KÜNZELMANN EKB 59P ipa
(A5)

ABEND IM HOCHGEBIRGE see Grieg, Edvard Hagerup

ABENDEMPFINDUNG see Mozart, Wolfgang Amadeus

ABENDGEBETE see Kantscheli, Gija

ABENDLÄUTEN IN CORDOBA see Trommer, Jack

ABENDLICHE SPIELE see Rakov, Nikolai

ABENDLIED see Sosen, Otto Ebel von

ABERT, JOHANN JOSEPH (1832-1915)
Frühlingssymphonie C-Dur
2.2.2.2. 4.2.3.0. timp,strings
[34'] BREITKOPF-W
(A6)

ABII NE VIDEREM see Kantscheli, Gija

ABÎMES DU RÊVE, LES see Hetu, Jacques

ABLAZE see Nelson, David

ABRAHAM LINCOLN WALKS AT MIDNIGHT see Palmer, Robert M.

ABSCHIED see Haller, Hermann see Shostakovich, Dmitri

ABSCHIED UND WIEDERKEHR see Kempkens, Arnold

ABSCHIEDSSINFONIE see Karayev, Faradzh, Tristessa I

ABSTRACTION FOR ORCHESTRA see Sundbø, Geir

ABWÄRTS WEND ICH MICH see Dittrich, Paul-Heinz

ACADEMY FESTIVAL MUSIC see Takeuchi, Kenji

ACADIAN IMAGES see Berry, Wallace

ACALANTO see Tornquist, Peter

ACANTUS FIRMUSOLYMPIADIS see Nordheim, Arne

ACCORD see Freedman, Harry

ACH ICH LIEBTE, WAR SO GLÜCKLICH see Mozart, Wolfgang Amadeus

ACH, WERD ICH IHN WOHL FINDEN see Mozart, Wolfgang Amadeus, Ah Chi Mi Dice Mai

ACHANTE ET CEPHISE: OUVERTURE see Rameau, Jean-Philippe

ACHE FOR ORCHESTRA see Sunde, Helge Havsgaard

ACHT BAGATELLEN see Finke, Fidelio Friedrich (Fritz)

1898 see Kagel, Mauricio

ACINTYAS see Sandström, Jan

ACKER, DIETER (1940-   )
Concerto for Piano and Orchestra, No. 1
2.2.3.3. 4.3.3.1. perc,harp,
strings,pno solo [35'] MOECK sc
5406 f.s., pts rent
(A7)

ACTIONS, INTERPOLATIONS AND ANALYSES: SYMPHONIES FOR AMPLIFIED BASS CLARINET SOLO, LARGE ENSEMBLE (OF REWOUND INSTRUMENTS), AND ELECTRONICS see Schaathun, Asbjørn

ACUFENOS II see Lanza, Alcides E.

AD NORDIAM HUNGARICA see Deak, Csaba

AD ORA INCERTA see Bainbridge, Simon

ADAGIETTO FOR CLARINET & STRINGS see Dix, Robert

ADAGIETTO FOR ORGAN AND STRINGS see Pinkham, Daniel

ADAGIO - ALLEGRETTO see Shostakovich, Dmitri

ADAGIO AND ALLEGRO IN A FLAT MAJOR see Schumann, Robert (Alexander), Adagio Et Allegro En La-b Majeur

ADAGIO E FUGA C-MOLL see Mozart, Wolfgang Amadeus

ADAGIO ET ALLEGRO EN LA-B MAJEUR see Schumann, Robert (Alexander)

ADAGIO ET VARIATION BRILLANTE G-DUR see Fürstenau, Anton Bernhard, Illusion, L', Op. 133

ADAGIO (IN MEMORIAM ANTON BRUCKNER), OP. 91B see Hummel, Bertold

ADAGIO UND CAPRICCIO FÜR TROMPETE, KLAVIER UND STREICHER see Hofmann, Wolfgang

ADAGIO & TEMA CON VARIAZIONI see Hummel, Johann Nepomuk

ADAGIO VON MOZART see Rypdal, Terje

ÅDALSRAPSODI see Hansgårdh, Allan

ADAM, ADOLPHE-CHARLES (1803-1856)
König von Yvetot, Le: Overture
see Roi d'Yvetot, Le: Overture

Postillon De Lonjumeau, Le: Mes Amis Écoutez l'Histoire
"Postillon Von Lonjumeau, Der: Freunde, Vernehmet Die Geschichte" 2.2.2.2. 4.2.3.0.
perc,strings,T solo,opt SATB [5']
BREITKOPF-W
(A8)

Postillon Von Lonjumeau, Der: Freunde, Vernehmet Die Geschichte see Postillon De Lonjumeau, Le: Mes Amis Écoutez l'Histoire

Roi d'Yvetot, Le: Overture
"König von Yvetot, Der: Overture"
1+pic.2.2.2. 4.2.3.0. perc,
strings [5'] (no score)
BREITKOPF-W
(A9)

ADAMIC, JOSEF
Nebeské Pastviny
"Pasturas Del Cielo, Las" string orch [15'] CESKY HUD.
(A10)

ADAMIC, JOSEF (cont'd.)

Pasturas Del Cielo, Las
see Nebeské Pastviny

Symphony No. 2
3.3.3.3. 4.3.3.1. timp,perc,strings
[22'] CESKY HUD.
(A11)

Symphony No. 3
3.3.3.3. 4.3.3.1. perc,strings
[15'] CESKY HUD.
(A12)

ADAMS, JOHN (1947-   )
Chamber Symphony
1(pic).1.2(clar in E flat,bass clar).2(contrabsn). 1.1.1.0.
perc,synthesizer,vln I,vla,vcl,db
[23'] BOOSEY-ENG rent
(A13)

Christian Zeal And Activity
1.0.1.1. 0.0.0.0. tape recorder,
harp,strings [10'] BOOSEY-ENG rent
(A14)

Concerto for Violin
2(pic,alto fl).2(English horn).2(bass clar).2. 2.1.0.0.
2perc,2synthesizer,6vln I,6vln II,4vla,4vcl,2db [32'] BOOSEY-ENG rent
(A15)

Death Of Klinghoffer, The: Aria Of The Falling Body
1+pic.2.2.2. 2.0.2.0. 2-3synthesizer,strings,Bar solo
[7'30"] BOOSEY-ENG rent
(A16)

Death Of Klinghoffer, The: The Bird Aria
1+pic.2(English horn).2(bass clar).1+contrabsn. 2.0.2.0. 2-3synthesizer,strings,Bar solo
[4'30"] BOOSEY-ENG rent
(A17)

El Dorado
3(2pic).3(English horn).3(clar in E flat,bass clar).3(contrabsn).
4.3(flügelhorn).3.1. timp,4perc,
2synthesizer,harp,strings [31']
(Part I: A Dream Of Gold; Part II: Soledades) BOOSEY-ENG rent
(A18)

Grand Pianola Score
orch sc SCHIRM.G AMP 7995 (A19)

Harmonielehre
orch sc SCHIRM.G AMP 7991 (A20)

Nixon In China: I Am Old And I Cannot Sleep
[Eng] 2(2pic).2(English horn).3(clar in E flat,2bass clar).0. soprano sax.2alto sax.baritone sax. 0.3.3.0. perc,
2elec pno,synthesizer,6vln I,6vln II,4vla,4vcl,2db,Bar solo [5']
(text by Alice Goodman) BOOSEY-ENG rent
(A21)

Nixon In China: Mr. Premier, Distinguished Guests
[Eng] 2(2pic).2(English horn).3(clar in E flat,2bass clar).0. soprano sax.2alto sax.baritone sax. 0.3.3.0. perc,
2elec pno,synthesizer,6vln I,6vln II,4vla,4vcl,2db,Bar solo [3']
(text by Alice Goodman) BOOSEY-ENG rent
(A22)

Nixon In China: News Is A Kind Of Mystery
[Eng] 2(2pic).2(English horn).3(clar in E flat,2bass clar).0. soprano sax.2alto sax.baritone sax. 0.3.3.0. perc,
2elec pno,synthesizer,6vln I,6vln II,4vla,4vcl,2db,Bar solo [7']
(text by Alice Goodman) BOOSEY-ENG rent
(A23)

Nixon In China: This Is Prophetic
[Eng] 2(2pic).2(English horn).3(clar in E flat,2bass clar).0. soprano sax.2alto sax.baritone sax. 0.3.3.0. perc,
2elec pno,synthesizer,6vln I,6vln II,4vla,4vcl,2db,S solo [9']
(text by Alice Goodman) BOOSEY-ENG rent
(A24)

ADAM'S APPLE, PRELUDE FOR ORCHESTRA see Baley, Virko

ADASKIN, MURRAY (1906-   )
Concerto for Orchestra
3(pic).2.2.2. 4.2.3.1. timp,3perc,
strings [30'] sc CANADIAN
MI 1100 A22 1 CO
(A25)

Concerto for Viola and Orchestra
3(pic).2.2.2. 4.2.3.1. timp,perc,
strings,vla solo [18'] sc
CANADIAN MI 1312 A221CO
(A26)

ADASKIN, MURRAY (cont'd.)

Concerto for Violin and Orchestra, Andante
2(pic).2.3(bass clar).2. 2.2.1.0. perc,strings,vln solo [18'] sc, solo pt CANADIAN MI 1311 A221AN
(A27)

Dance Concertante
2(pic).2.2.2. 4.3.3.1. timp,2perc, strings [15'] sc CANADIAN MI 1100 A22 1 DA
(A28)

Divertimento No. 5 for 2 Guitars and Orchestra
1.1.1.1. 1.1.1.0. timp,2perc, strings,2gtr soli [11'] sc CANADIAN MI 1415 A221DI
(A29)

March No. 3 for Orchestra
2(pic).2.2.2. 4.3.3.1. timp,perc, strings, ocarina may replace piccolo [6'] sc CANADIAN MI 1100 A22 1 M3
(A30)

Travelling Musicians, The
2(pic).2.2.2. 2.2.1.1. timp,perc, strings,narrator [25'] sc,pno red,solo pt CANADIAN MV 1400 A221TR
(A31)

ADDERLY, MARK (1960-    )
Crux
1(pic).0.1(bass clar).0. 0.1.1.0. perc,harp,strings,pno solo,med solo NORSKMI
(A32)

ADDIO. BUDVA. see Stedron, Milos

ADES, THOMAS
Chamber Symphony
fl,ob,basset horn,bass clar,horn, trp,trom,2perc,pno/acord,strings [13'] FABER
(A33)

Living Toys
fl,ob,clar,bsn,horn,trp,trom,perc, pno,strings [17'] FABER
(A34)

These Premises Are Alarmed
3.3.3.3. 4.3.3.1. 4perc,pno/cel, harp,strings [5'] FABER
(A35)

ADIEU DE LA MARIÉE see Forsyth, Malcolm

ADIEUX see Cherney, Brian

ADIRONDACK LIGHT see Tann, Hilary

ADLER, SAMUEL HANS (1928-    )
Beyond The Land
3.3.3.3. 4.3.3.1. timp,3perc,harp, kbd,strings [30'] SCHIRM.EC rent
(A36)

Concerto for Guitar and Orchestra
2.2.2.2. 2.2.0.0. timp,perc, strings,gtr solo [21'] PRESSER rent
(A37)

Concerto for Piano, No. 2
2.2.2.2. 2.2.2.1. timp,2perc,pno, strings PRESSER rent
(A38)

Concerto for Violoncello and Orchestra
3(pic).3(English horn).3(bass clar).3(contrabsn). 4.3.3(bass trom).1. timp,3perc,pno,cel, strings,vcl solo [20'] PRESSER rent
(A39)

Fixed Desire Of The Human Heart, The
2.2.2.2. 2.2.2.0. timp,2perc, strings [9'] SCHIRM.EC rent (A40)

Time In Tempest Everywhere
2.1.2.2. 2.0.0.0. perc,pno,strings, S solo (poems by W. H. Auden) PRESSER rent
(A41)

ADVENTURE IN WONDERLAND, THE see Kawasaki, Etsuo

ADVENTURES OF SEBASTIAN THE FOX, THE see Dreyfus, George

AEDON see Cunningham, Michael Gerald

AEOLIAN CAPRICES see Mills, Richard

AFFAIRE COFFIN, L' see Lauber, Anne

AFRICA see Bush, Alan [Dudley]

AFRICAINE, L': JE VOIS LA MER (NO. 21) see Meyerbeer, Giacomo

AFRICAINE, L': OVERTURE see Meyerbeer, Giacomo

AFRIKANERIN, DIE: MARSCH see Meyerbeer, Giacomo

AFRIKANERIN, DIE: OVERTURE see Meyerbeer, Giacomo

AFTER FALLEN CRUMBS see Singleton, Alvin

AFTER THE RAIN see Guy, Barry

AFTER YOU'VE GONE see Still, William Grant

AGAIN see Singleton, Alvin

AGATHA SUITE see Blake, Howard

AGITATION RAG (HAMTON) see Sieben Ragtimes Für Streichorchester: Heft 2

AGITATIONS see Wilson, Richard (Edward)

AGNÈS, DAME GALANTE see Fevrier, Henri

AGONIE: SUITE see Schnittke, Alfred

AGRÉGATS see Arcuri, Serge

AGUILA, MIGUEL DEL
Caribbean Bacchanal
3(pic).1.2.2(contrabsn).2alto sax.2tenor sax. 4.3.3.1. 5perc, banjo,gtr,elec bass,harp,pno 4-hands,strings [15'] PEER rent
(A42)

Concerto for Clarinet
1.1.1.1. 1.1.1.1. pno,2perc, strings,clar solo [15'] PEER rent
(A43)

Conga
2(pic).2.2.2. 3.2.2.1. harp,pno, 5perc,strings [11'] PEER rent
(A44)

Conga-Line In Hell
1.1.1.1. 1.1.1.1. harp,pno,perc, strings soli [11'] PEER rent
(A45)

fl,clar,pno,perc,8vcl [11'] PEER rent
(A46)

AH CHI MI DICE MAI see Mozart, Wolfgang Amadeus

AH, CORDI TRITO see Kopriva, Karel Blazej

AH, FUGGI IL TRADITOR see Mozart, Wolfgang Amadeus

AH, GROSSMUTTER, KOMM SCHNELL see Mossolov, Alexander

AH QUAL GELIDO ORROR - IL PADRE ADORATO see Mozart, Wolfgang Amadeus

AH SCOSTATI! - SMANIE IMPLACABILI see Mozart, Wolfgang Amadeus

AH! SI MON MOINE VOULAIT DANSER! see Ridout, Godfrey

AHEAD see Samuelsson, Marie

AHLBERG, GUNNAR (1942-    )
Carattere Per Orchestra
2.2.2.2. 2.2.2.0. timp,strings,pno [13'] sc STIM T-3355, H-2830
(A47)

Sottile
3(pic).2(English horn).3(bass clar).2(contrabsn). 4.4.2.1. timp,3perc,strings,pno [15'] (1. Andante 2. Poco mosso 3. Calmo) sc STIM H-2854
(A48)

AÏDA, ACT III: AIR DU NIL see Verdi, Giuseppe

AÏDA: Ô CÉLESTE AÏDA see Verdi, Giuseppe

AIM see Ed, Fredrik

AIR AND WATER see Bolcom, William Elden, Concerto No. 1 for Piano Left-Hand and Chamber Orchestra

AIR D'A. KASSIM - NO. 9 - A.II. see Auber, Daniel-François-Esprit

AIR DE LA BARONNE see Offenbach, Jacques

AIR DE LENSKI see Tchaikovsky, Piotr Ilyich

AIR DE TATIANA see Tchaikovsky, Piotr Ilyich, Scènes De La Lettre

AITKEN, HUGH (1924-    )
In Praise Of Ockeghem
strings [13'] SCHIRM.EC rent  (A49)

AITKEN, ROBERT (1939-    )
Berceuse
2.2.2.2. 2.2.1.0. timp,perc, strings,fl solo [18'] PEER rent
(A50)

AITKEN, ROBERT (cont'd.)
Shadows I: Nekuia
4.4.4.4. 6.4.4.1. 5perc,2harp, strings [8'] PEER rent      (A51)

Spiral
2.2.2.2. 2.2.0.0. perc,strings, (one of each pair of woodwinds is amplified) [16'] sc,study sc CANADIAN MI 9400 A311SP      (A52)

4 chamber groups: 1: fl, ob, 10 vln, pno; 2: clar, 3 vla, 2 trp, timp; 3: engh, 3 vcl, 2 horn, harp; 4: bsclr, bsn, trb, 2 ob [19'] PEER rent      (A53)

AJAR see Edlund, Mikael

AKCE "Z" see Knirsch,Erik

AKEDAH see Sheriff, Noam

AKPABOT, SAMUEL
Cynthia's Lament
2.0.2.2. 0.1.3.0. timp,2perc, strings,S solo [18'] OXFORD (A54)

AKROSTIKON see Scheffer, Rickard

AKTUALITY see Berkovec, Jiri

AKZENTE see Lischka, Rainer

ALAGOANA (CAPRICHOS BRASILEIROS see Zimmermann, Bernd Alois

ALAM-AL-MITHAL see Rae, Allan, Symphony No. 3

ALAN, CHARLES
Golden Romance (Romance for Viola and Chamber Orchestra)
1.1.2.1. 2.0.0.0. strings,vla solo [5'35] sc,set BUSCH HBM 020 rent
(A55)

Romance for Viola and Chamber Orchestra
see Golden Romance

ALBA: INSIEME see Eyser, Eberhard

ALBATROS see Hamel, Peter Michael

ALBERGA, ELEANOR
Roald Dahl's Snow White And The Seven Dwarfs
2(pic).2.2+bass clar.1+contrabsn. 4.3.3.1. timp,6perc,pno,strings [45'] perf sc set OXFORD 3611813 sc,pts score
(A56)

Snow White And The Seven Dwarfs
2.2.3.2. 4.3.3.1. timp,5perc,pno, harp,strings,1-3 speaking voices [42'] OXFORD
(A57)

Sun Warrior
1.1.1.1. 2.0.0.0. timp,strings [25'] (for chamber orch.) manuscript BMIC
(A58)

ALBERT, EUGÈNE FRANCIS CHARLES D' (1864-1932)
Ghismonda: Einleitung Zum 3. Aufzug
3.2+English horn.2+bass clar.3. 4.3.3.1. timp,harp,strings [3'] (no score) BREITKOPF-W      (A59)

ALBERT, STEPHEN JOEL (1941-1992)
Into Eclips
T solo,orch sc SCHIRM.G ED3806
(A60)

Treestone
ST soli,orch sc,pno red SCHIRM.G ED3868
(A61)

ALBERTA PIONEERES  *folk song
(Rae, Allan) 3.3.3.2. 4.3.3.1. timp, 3perc,strings [10'] (of many people in Alberta) sc CANADIAN MI 1100 R134AL
(A62)

ALBINONI, TOMASO (1671-1750)
Concerto A Cinque  *Op.9,No.2
ob solo,string orch (D min) KUNZELMANN 10284
(A63)

Concerto A Cinque, En Fa Majeur
see Concerto in F, Op. 9, No. 3

Concerto A Cinque, En Sol Majeur
see Concerto in G, Op. 9, No. 6

Concerto A Cinque, En Ut Majeur
see Concerto in C, Op. 9, No. 9

Concerto for Oboe and String Orchestra, Op. 7, No. 3, in B flat
ob solo,string orch sc KUNZELMANN GM 341P ipa
(A64)

Concerto for Oboe and String Orchestra, Op. 7, No. 6, in D
ob solo,string orch sc KUNZELMANN

ALBINONI, TOMASO (cont'd.)

GM 344P ipa                    (A65)

Concerto for Oboe and String
Orchestra, Op. 7, No. 9, in F
ob solo,string orch sc KUNZELMANN
GM 347P ipa                    (A66)

Concerto for Oboe and String
Orchestra, Op. 7, No. 12, in C
ob solo,string orch sc KUNZELMANN
GM 350P ipa                    (A67)

Concerto for Oboe and String
Orchestra, Op. 9, No. 2, in D
minor
ob solo,string orch sc KUNZELMANN
10284 ipa                      (A68)

Concerto for 2 Oboes and String
Orchestra, Op. 7, No. 2, in C
2ob,string orch sc KUNZELMANN
GM 340P ipa                    (A69)

Concerto for 2 Oboes and String
Orchestra, Op. 7, No. 5, in C
2ob,string orch sc KUNZELMANN
GM 343P ipa                    (A70)

Concerto for 2 Oboes and String
Orchestra, Op. 7, No. 8, in D
2ob,string orch sc KUNZELMANN
GM 346P ipa                    (A71)

Concerto for 2 Oboes and String
Orchestra, Op. 7, No. 11, in C
2ob,string orch sc KUNZELMANN
GM 349P ipa                    (A72)

Concerto for 2 Oboes and String
Orchestra, Op. 9, No. 3, in F
2ob,string orch sc KUNZELMANN
GM 357P ipa                    (A73)

Concerto for String Orchestra, Op. 7,
No. 1, in D
string orch sc KUNZELMANN GM 339P
ipa                            (A74)

Concerto for String Orchestra, Op. 7,
No. 4, in G
string orch sc KUNZELMANN GM 342P
ipa                            (A75)

Concerto for String Orchestra, Op. 7,
No. 7, in A
string orch sc KUNZELMANN GM 345P
ipa                            (A76)

Concerto for String Orchestra, Op. 7,
No. 10, in B flat
string orch sc KUNZELMANN GM 348P
ipa                            (A77)

Concerto for String Orchestra, Op.
10, No. 1, in B flat
string orch sc KUNZELMANN GM 367P
ipa                            (A78)

Concerto for Violin and Orchestra,
Op. 10, No. 5, in A
vln solo,string orch sc KUNZELMANN
GM 371P ipa                    (A79)

Concerto for Violin and String
Orchestra, Op. 5, No. 1, in B
flat
vln solo,string orch sc KUNZELMANN
GM 323P ipa                    (A80)

Concerto for Violin and String
Orchestra, Op. 5, No. 2, in F
vln solo,string orch sc KUNZELMANN
GM 324P ipa                    (A81)

Concerto for Violin and String
Orchestra, Op. 5, No. 3, in D
vln solo,string orch sc KUNZELMANN
GM 325P ipa                    (A82)

Concerto for Violin and String
Orchestra, Op. 5, No. 4, in G
vln solo,string orch sc KUNZELMANN
GM 326P ipa                    (A83)

Concerto for Violin and String
Orchestra, Op. 5, No. 5, in A
minor
vln solo,string orch sc KUNZELMANN
GM 327P ipa                    (A84)

Concerto for Violin and String
Orchestra, Op. 5, No. 6, in C
vln solo,string orch sc KUNZELMANN
GM 328P ipa                    (A85)

Concerto for Violin and String
Orchestra, Op. 5, No. 7, in D
minor
vln solo,string orch sc KUNZELMANN
GM 329P ipa                    (A86)

Concerto for Violin and String
Orchestra, Op. 5, No. 8, in F
vln solo,string orch sc KUNZELMANN

ALBINONI, TOMASO (cont'd.)

GM 330P ipa                    (A87)

Concerto for Violin and String
Orchestra, Op. 5, No. 9, in E
minor
vln solo,string orch sc KUNZELMANN
GM331P ipa                     (A88)

Concerto for Violin and String
Orchestra, Op. 5, No. 10, in A
vln solo,string orch sc KUNZELMANN
GM 332P ipa                    (A89)

Concerto for Violin and String
Orchestra, Op. 5, No. 11, in G
minor
vln solo,string orch sc KUNZELMANN
GM 333P ipa                    (A90)

Concerto for Violin and String
Orchestra, Op. 5, No. 12, in C
vln solo,string orch sc KUNZELMANN
GM 334P ipa                    (A91)

Concerto for Violin and String
Orchestra, Op. 9, No. 1, in B
flat
vln solo,string orch sc KUNZELMANN
GM 355P ipa                    (A92)

Concerto for Violin and String
Orchestra, Op. 9, No. 7, in D
vln solo,string orch sc KUNZELMANN
GM 361P ipa                    (A93)
vln solo,string orch sc KUNZELMANN
EKB 49P ipa                    (A94)

Concerto for Violin and String
Orchestra, Op. 10, No. 2, in G
minor
vln solo,string orch sc KUNZELMANN
GM 368P ipa                    (A95)

Concerto for Violin and String
Orchestra, Op. 10, No. 3, in C
vln solo,string orch sc KUNZELMANN
GM 369P ipa                    (A96)

Concerto for Violin and String
Orchestra, Op. 10, No. 4, in G
vln solo,string orch sc KUNZELMANN
GM 370P ipa                    (A97)

Concerto for Violin and String
Orchestra, Op. 10, No. 6, in D
vln solo,string orch sc KUNZELMANN
GM 372P ipa                    (A98)

Concerto for Violin and String
Orchestra, Op. 10, No. 7, in F
vln solo,string orch sc KUNZELMANN
GM 373P ipa                    (A99)

Concerto for Violin and String
Orchestra, Op. 10, No. 8, in G
minor
vln solo,string orch sc KUNZELMANN
GM 374P ipa                    (A100)

Concerto for Violin and String
Orchestra, Op. 10, No. 9, in F
vln solo,string orch sc KUNZELMANN
GM 375P ipa                    (A101)

Concerto for Violin and String
Orchestra, Op. 10, No. 10, in C
vln solo,string orch sc KUNZELMANN
GM 376P ipa                    (A102)

Concerto for Violin and String
Orchestra, Op. 10, No. 11, in G
minor
vln solo,string orch sc KUNZELMANN
GM 377P ipa                    (A103)

Concerto for Violin and String
Orchestra, Op. 10, No. 12, in B
flat
vln solo,string orch sc KUNZELMANN
GM 378P ipa                    (A104)

Concerto in C, Op. 9, No. 9
(Guyot, D.) "Concerto A Cinque, En
Ut Majeur" string orch,hpsd,2trp
soli/ob&trp soli [10'] BILLAUDOT
                               (A105)

Concerto in F, Op. 9, No. 3
(Guyot, D.) "Concerto A Cinque, En
Fa Majeur" string orch,hpsd,2trp
soli/ob&trp soli [11'] BILLAUDOT
                               (A106)

Concerto in G, Op. 9, No. 6
(Guyot, D.) "Concerto A Cinque, En
Sol Majeur" string orch,hpsd,2trp
soli/ob&trp soli [10'] BILLAUDOT
                               (A107)

Sinfonia for String Orchestra, Op. 2,
No. 4, in C minor
string orch sc KUNZELMANN GM 390P
ipa                            (A108)

Sinfonia for String Orchestra, Op. 2,
No. 11, in G minor
string orch sc KUNZELMANN GM 313P

ALBINONI, TOMASO (cont'd.)

ipa                            (A109)

Sinfonia for String Orchestra, Op. 2,
No. 12, in D
vln solo,string orch sc KUNZELMANN
GM 314P ipa                    (A110)

ALBIS see Douglas, Paul M.

ALBRIGHT, WILLIAM H. (1944-1998)
Chasm
"Symphonic Fragment" 3.3.3.3.alto
sax. 4.4.3.1. timp,3perc,pno,
harp,8vln I,7vln II,6vla,5vcl,4db
[11'] sc PETERS 04419          (A111)

Concerto for Harpsichord and Strings
8vln I,7vln II,6vla,5vcl,4db,hpsd
solo [28'] sc,solo pt PETERS
04420                          (A112)

Symphonic Fragment
see Chasm

ALBUM FOR HELENA see Rieti, Vittorio

ALCARAZ, JORDI
Fantasy for Strings and Percussion
cel,harp,pno,2vln,vla,vcl,db,3timp,
vibra,xylo, 3 crotales,
flexaphone [11'] sc ALPUERTO 1439
                               (A113)

ÁLDOZATI ZENE A LENYUGVÓ NAPHOZ see
Dukay, Barnabás, Sacrificial Music
To The Setting Sun

ALEAFONIA see Hegdal, Magne

ALEGRÍAS see Hidalgo, Manuel

ALESSANDRO see Kirkwood, Antoinette

ALESSANDRO, RAFAELE D' (1911-1959)
Concerto for Oboe, Op. 79
ob solo,orch KUNZELMANN 10065 ipr
                               (A114)

ALEXANDER EVERGREEN see Atkinson,
Condit Robert

ALEXANDER FRIEDRICH VON HESSEN
Fathûme Op. 4
2+pic.2+English horn.2+bass clar.2+
contrabsn. 4.2.3.1. timp,2perc,
harp,strings [16'] BREITKOPF-W
                               (A115)

ALFVÉN, HUGO (1872-1960)
[Bergakungen Op. 37: Svit] 1.
Besvärjelse
3(pic).3(English horn).3(bass
clar).3(contrabsn). 4.3.3.1.
timp,2perc,strings [4'] sc
GEHRMANS ED.NR 6281           (A116)

[Bergakungen Op. 37: Svit] 2.
Trollflickans Dans
3(pic).3(English horn).3(bass
clar).3. 4.3.3.1. timp,3perc,
2harp,strings,cel [5'] sc
GEHRMANS ED.NR 6282           (A117)

[Bergakungen Op. 37: Svit] 3.
Sommarregn.
4(pic).1(English horn).3(bass
clar).0.alto sax. 4.0.0.0. timp,
2perc,2harp,strings,cel [3'] sc
GEHRMANS ED.NR 6283           (A118)

[Bergakungen Op. 37: Svit] 4.
Vallflickans Dans
3(pic).3.2.3. 4.0.0.0. strings
[4'5"] sc GEHRMANS ED.NR 3599
                               (A119)

Från Havsbandet (Symphony No. 4, Op.
39)
4(pic).4(English horn).4(bass
clar).4(contrabsn). 8.4.3.1.
timp,2perc,2harp,strings,pno,cel
[45'] REIMERS ED.NR 101214 (A120)

Symphony No. 1, Op. 7, in F minor
3(pic).2(English horn).2.2.
4.2.3.1. timp,perc,strings [37']
(Version No. 2) sc GEHRMANS
ED.NR 4571                     (A121)

Symphony No. 4, Op. 39
orch study sc REIMERS 101214 (A122)
see Från Havsbandet

ALI BABA: OVERTURE see Cherubini, Luigi

ALIS, ROMAN (1931-    )
Campus Stellae *Op.98
fl,pic,ob,clar,vln,vla,vcl,db,pno,
2perc sc ALPUERTO 1211        (A123)

Somni...,El *Op.101
1+pic.1.1.1. 0.0.0.0. strings,S
solo sc ALPUERTO 1209         (A124)

ALKAN, CHARLES-HENRI VALENTIN
  (1813-1888)
  Premier Concerto Da Camera
    2.2.2.4. 4.2.3.0. timp,strings
    [13'] BILLAUDOT              (A125)

ALL IN GOOD TIME see Kolb, Barbara

ALL THE LONELY PEOPLE see Rabe, Folke

ALLA, THIERRY
  Concerto for Orchestra
    see Étoiles

  Étoiles (Concerto for Orchestra)
    1.0.1.0. 1.1.1.0. perc,pno,vln,vla,
    vcl,db [9'] pts FUZEAU 3090
                                (A126)

ALLEGORIA see Marina, Cristian

ALLEGRETTO see Godard, Benjamin Louis
  Paul

ALLEGRO IN C, FOR PIANO AND STRING
  ORCHESTRA see Tchaikovsky, Piotr
  Ilyich

ALLEGRO POSTILLIONS see Handel, George
  Frideric, Sinfonia

ALLEGRO VOLANTE, FOR XYLOPHONE AND
  ORCHESTRA see Dorff, Daniel Jay

ALLELUIA SUR LA TROMPETTE, ALLELUIA SUR
  LA CYMBALE see Messiaen, Olivier

ALLELUIAS SEREINS D'UNE ÂME QUI DÉSIRE
  LE CIEL see Messiaen, Olivier

ALLELUJA see Haydn, [Franz] Joseph,
  Symphony No. 30 in C, Hob.I: 30

ALLEMANDE see Schenker, Friedrich

ALLEN, PETER (1952-    )
  Do You Love Me
    string orch sc CANADIAN
    MI 3143 A428DO             (A127)

  Festival Overture
    2(pic).1.2.1. 3.2.2.0. timp&perc,
    perc,pno,strings, (timpani
    doubles on other percussion
    equipment) sc CANADIAN
    MI 1100 A428FE             (A128)

  'ing' Book, The
    3(pic).2.2.2. 4.2.0.1. 2perc,
    strings (Morning - Walking -
    Soaring - Jumping - Dreaming -
    Dancing - Climbing - Evening) sc
    CANADIAN MI 1100 A428IN    (A129)

  It's Fun To Be Dumb
    string orch sc CANADIAN
    MI 1500 A428IT             (A130)

  2000 Plus One
    2.2.2.2. 3.2.3.0. timp,2perc,kbd,
    harp,elec bass,strings sc
    CANADIAN MI 1100 A428TW    (A131)

ALLERS, HANS GUNTHER (1935)
  Concerto for Horn
    vln I,vln II,vla,vcl,db,timp,horn
    solo MÖSELER sc 11.453-00, pts
    11.453-01, set 11.453-09   (A132)

  Kleine Wanderzirkus, Der
    orch (five miniatures) MÖSELER
    10.468                     (A133)

ALLES FÜHLT DER LIEBE FREUDEN see
  Mozart, Wolfgang Amadeus

ALLMÄCHT'GE JUNGFRAU see Wagner,
  Richard

ALLMÄCHT'GER ZAR see Rimsky-Korsakov,
  Nikolai, Welikij Zar

ALLMÄCHTIG IST NATUR see Rimsky-
  Korsakov, Nikolai, Polna, Polna
  Tschudesj

ALL'OVERTURA see Sibelius, Jean

ALMANSOR see Reinecke, Carl

ALMOST A TREE see Ikebe, Shin-Ichiro

ALNADOS DE ESPAÑA, LOS see Still,
  William Grant

ALONE ON THE PACIFIC see Takemitsu,
  Toru

ALPENJÄGER, DER see Liszt, Franz

ALPENKÖNIG UND DER MENSCHENFEIND, DER
  see Cornell, Klaus

ALPENSINFONIE, EINE & SYMPHONIA
  DOMESTICA see Strauss, Richard

ALS FÜR EIN FREMDES LAND see Wagner,
  Richard

ALT HEIDELBERG, DU FEINE see Volbach,
  Fritz

ALTE DÄNISCHE VOLKSTÄNZE see Grondahl,
  Launy

ALTE LOK, DIE see Müller-Lampertz,
  Richard

ALTE NIEDERDEUTSCHE VOLKSTÄNZE see
  Niemann, Walter

ALTENA, MAARTEN (1943-    )
  Secret Instructions
    3.3.3.3.baritone sax. 4.3.3.0.
    2perc,marimba,pno,strings [18']
    sc DONEMUS                 (A134)

ALTERATION I see Surdin, Morris

ALTERATION II see Surdin, Morris

ALTERHAUG, BJORN (1945-    )
  Stykke Musikk Til Fest Og Ettertanke,
  Et
    2(pic).2.2.2. 4.3.3.1. 4perc,
    strings,narrator& solo voices
    NORSKMI                    (A135)

ALTERNANCE see Constant, Franz

ALTERNANCES see Michans, Carlos

ALTNORWEGISCHE ROMANZE MIT VARIATIONEN
  see Grieg, Edvard Hagerup

ALTOUMS GEBET see Busoni, Ferruccio
  Benvenuto

ALVAREZ, JAVIER
  Metro Chabacano
    string orch [7'] PEER rent  (A136)

ÅM, MAGNAR (1952-    )
  Be Quiet, My Heart
    see Kom Til Ro, Mitt Hjarte

  Gratia
    string orch,harp solo [10'] NORSKMI
                                (A137)

  Kom Til Ro, Mitt Hjarte
    "Be Quiet, My Heart"
    3(pic).2.2.3(contrabsn). 2.2.3.1.
    perc,strings [23'50] NORSKMI
                                (A138)

  My Planet, My Soul
    orch NORSK NMO 9801         (A139)

  Timeless Energy
    4(pic).1.3(bass clar).2(contrabsn).
    1.1.1.0. 2perc,pno,strings
    [7'30] NORSKMI             (A140)

AM ABEND see Keller, Hermann

AM ENDE DES ORKANS FÜR ORCHESTER see
  Cornell, Klaus

AM SPRINGQUELL see David, Ferdinand

AMANO, MASAMICHI (1957-    )
  Classic Mania
    orch,vln [7'] JAPAN         (A141)

AMDAHL, MAGNE (1943-    )
  Astrognosia Mot Mànefaser Mellom
  Stjerneregn: Orkestersuite
    2.2.2(bass clar).2. 4.3.3.0. timp,
    2perc,strings [22'] NORSKMI
                                (A142)

  Cavatina Con Dolore
    1.0.0.0. 1.0.0.0. strings,trp solo
    NORSKMI                     (A143)

  Musikk Til Feberdigte Av Knut Hamsun
    1.1.1(bass clar).1. 1.0.0.0. perc,
    pno,strings,narrator&solo voice
    [15'] NORSKMI              (A144)

  Per I Vence
    2.2(English horn).2(bass
    clar).2(contrabsn). 4.3.3.1.
    harp,synthesizer/pno,elec gtr,
    elec bass gtr,timp,2perc,strings
    NORSKMI                     (A145)

AMERICAN DANCE SUITE-BLUES see Amram,
  David Werner

AMERICAN EPITAPH see Lemeland, Aubert

AMERICAN FANTASY OVERTURE see Duffy,
  John

AMERIKANISCHES VOLKSLIED see Busch,
  Carl

AMETYST see Myska, Rudolf

AMNESTY SYMPHONY see Rossum, Frederic
  R. van

AMOROSO see Korndorf, Nicolai see
  Wahlberg, Rune

AMOS, KEITH
  Belas Knap
    string orch [15'] (suite for string
    orchestra, 3 mvts.) CMA set 198
    rent, sc 199                (A146)

  Briolette
    fl,2ob,strings [9'] CMA set 087
    rent, sc 088                (A147)

  Concertino for English Horn and
  String Orchestra
    see Princess Of The Peacocks

  Concertino for Oboe and String
  Orchestra
    see Spring In Fialta

  Concerto for Flute and Oboe
    fl,ob,string orch [18'] (3 mvts.)
    CMA set 083 rent, sc 084    (A148)

  Concerto for Violin in One Movement
    vln,string orch [17'30] CMA set
    085 rent, sc 086            (A149)

  Corbridge Lanx, The
    2.2.2.2. 4.4.3.1. pic,English horn,
    bass clar,timp,perc,strings [32']
    CMA 133 set rent, sc        (A150)

  Cortege: With Solemn Dancing And
  Bells
    2.2.2.2. 4.3.3.1. timp,perc,strings
    [25'] CMA 138 set rent, sc (A151)

  Kachinas
    2(pic).2.2.2. 4.3.3.1. timp,3perc,
    harp,strings [10'30] CMA 235 set
    rent, sc                    (A152)

  Kate Greenaway Suite
    2.2.2.2. 4.3.3.1. timp,perc,strings
    [13'50] (4 mvts.) CMA 104 set
    rent, sc                    (A153)

  Laidley Worm Of Spindleton Heugh, The
    2.2(English horn).2.2. 4.3.3.1.
    timp,perc,strings [25'] CMA 106
    set rent, sc                (A154)

  Marigold Garden
    2.2.2.2. 2.2.0.0. strings [19'] (5
    mvts.) CMA 097 set rent, sc
                                (A155)

  Peter Kirillov: Kingdom Of The White
  Waters
    2.2.2.2. 4.3.3.1. timp,perc,strings
    [25'30] CMA 105 set rent, sc
                                (A156)

  Princess Of The Peacocks (Concertino
  for English Horn and String
  Orchestra)
    [13'30] CMA set 193 rent, sc 194
                                (A157)

  Richmond Green
    2.2.2.2. 4.3.3.1. timp,perc,strings
    [12'] (3 mvts.) CMA 101 set rent,
    sc                          (A158)

  Richmond Prelude
    2.2.2.2. 4.2.2.0. timp,strings [4']
    CMA 099 set rent, sc        (A159)

  Sinfonietta
    2.2.2.2. 2.0.0.0. strings [14'] (3
    mvts.) CMA set 091 rent, sc 092
                                (A160)

  Spring In Fialta (Concertino for Oboe
  and String Orchestra)
    [16'] CMA set 195 rent, sc 196
                                (A161)

  Steadfast Tin Soldier, The
    narrator,orch [30'] CMA 149 set
    rent, sc                    (A162)

  Steadfast Tin Soldier, The: Suite No.
  1
    orch [14'30] CMA 171 set rent, sc
                                (A163)

  Steadfast Tin Soldier, The: Suite No.
  2
    orch [14'30] CMA 172 set rent, sc
                                (A164)

  Symphony, No. 1, in One Movement
    2.2.2.2. 4.2.2.0. timp,perc,strings
    [26'] CMA 107 set rent, sc (A165)

  Three Harbour Sketches
    2.2.2.2. 2.2.0.0. timp,strings
    [10'30] CMA set 089 rent, sc 090
                                (A166)

  Totonac Rain Dance
    2.2.2.2. 4.3.3.1. timp,perc,strings
    [5'40] CMA 103 set rent, sc
                                (A167)

  Tribute To Stan Kenton
    2.2.2.2. 4.4.3.1. strings, kit
    drums [18'] (3 mvts.) CMA 234 set
    rent, sc                    (A168)

AMOS, KEITH (cont'd.)

Waterhatch, The
string orch [21'] CMA set 117 rent,
sc 118 (A169)

Where The Pale Moonbeams Linger
2.2(English horn).2.2. 2.2.0.0.
timp,strings [17'30"] CMA set 095
rent, sc 096 (A170)

Wyck Rissington Green
string orch [14'] (suite, 3 mvts.)
CMA set 200 rent, sc 201 (A171)

AMRAM, DAVID WERNER (1930- )
American Dance Suite-Blues
8vln I,7vln II,6vla,5vcl,4db [5']
sc PETERS 03571 (A172)

Peer Gynt
1.1.1.1. 1.0.0.0. 2perc,vln,3vla sc
PETERS 03595 (A173)

Red River Valley: Theme & Variations
8vln I,7vln II,6vla,5vcl,4db,fl
solo [15'] sc PETERS 04429 (A174)

Shiray Neshama
see Songs Of The Soul

Songs Of The Soul
"Shiray Neshama" 2.2.2.2. 4.2.2.1.
3perc,8vln I,7vln II,6vla,5vcl,
4db sc PETERS 03523 (A175)

AMTRAK see Rathburn, Eldon

AN DEN MOND "FÜLLEST WIEDER BUSCH UND
TAL" see Schubert, Franz (Peter)

AN DER WIEGE see Grieg, Edvard Hagerup

AN DER ZUGBRÜCKE see Sibelius, Jean

AN DIE HOFFNUNG see Wildberger, Jacques

AN DIE KÜNSTLER see Liszt, Franz

AN DIE LAUTE OP. 81, NO. 2 see
Schubert, Franz (Peter)

AN DIE NACHT see Holszky, Adriana

AN DIE ZUKUNFT see Neubert, Günter

AN EINEM SOMMERTAG: 5 PIECES FOR STRING
ORCHESTRA see Rakov, Nikolai

AN HÖLDERLINS UMNACHTUNG see Huber,
Nicolaus A.

AN SCHWAGER KRONOS see Schubert, Franz
(Peter)

ANAKREON see Cherubini, Luigi

ANALYSIS see Schnebel, Dieter

ANCIENT AIRS AND DANCES, SUITE I see
Respighi, Ottorino, Antiche Danze
Ed Arie, Suite I

ANCIENT LIGHTS see Moravec, Paul

"...AND A ROLL ON THE GONG" see Parker,
Michael

AND A TIME FOR PEACE see Wernick,
Richard F.

AND DAVID WEPT see Laderman, Ezra

"...AND IT ALWAYS WILL BE" see Tittle,
Steve

AND LEFT OL' JOE A BONE, AMAZING! see
Plain, Gerald

AND THE MOUNTAINS RISING NOWHERE see
Schwantner, Joseph

AND THE UNSEEN EYEBEAM CROSSED... see
Archbold, Paul

"...AND THEN I WAS IN TIME AGAIN" see
Mansurian, Tigran

ANDANTE see Surdin, Morris

ANDANTE CANTABILE see Tchaikovsky,
Piotr Ilyich

ANDANTE CANTABILE IN B FLAT see
Tchaikovsky, Piotr Ilyich

ANDANTE& RONDO UNGARESE see Weber, Carl
Maria von

ANDANTE SOSTENUTO see Norman, Ludvig

ANDANTINO see Bizet, Georges see
Debussy, Claude

ANDERSON, JEAN (1939-    )
Concerto for Horn and String
Orchestra
[21'] sc CANADIAN MI 1632 A547CO
(A176)

Country Round, A
1.0.1.1. 1.0.0.0. strings [5'] sc
CANADIAN MI1200 A547CO (A177)

Country Round, A
1.0.1.1. 1.0.0.0. strings [6'] sc
CANADIAN MI1200 A547CO2 (A178)

Langdales (Overture)
3+pic.3+English horn.3+bass clar.3+
contrabsn. 4.3.3.1. timp,4perc,
harp,pno,strings [11'] sc
CANADIAN MI 1100 A5470V (A179)

Overture
see Langdales

Sinfonia for String Orchestra
string orch [8'] sc CANADIAN
MI 1500 A547SI (A180)

ANDERSON, JULIAN
Crazed Moon, The
3.3.3.3. 4.3.3.1. 2perc,harp,
strings [10'] FABER (A181)

Khorovod
fl,ob,clar,bsn,horn,trp,trom,2perc,
pno,strings [12'] FABER (A182)

Past Hymns
strings [10'] FABER (A183)

Three Parts Off The Ground
2fl,2clar,horn,perc,harp,mand,
strings [14'] FABER (A184)

ANDERSON, LEROY (1908-1975)
Bonnie Dundee
orch WOODBURY rent (A185)

Campbells Are Coming, The
orch WOODBURY rent (A186)

Old MacDonald Had A Farm
orch WOODBURY rent (A187)

Second Regiment Connecticut National
March
orch WOODBURY rent (A188)

ANDERSSON, MAGNUS F. (1953-    )
Overture
3(pic).3.3(bass clar).3(contrabsn).
4.3.3.1. timp,2perc,harp,strings
[9'] STIM sc H-2571, pts A-164
(A189)

ANDREAE, HANS-VOLKMAR
Concerto for Violin and Orchestra,
Op. 40
2.2.2.2. 3.2.0.0. timp,perc,strings
[14'] HUG (A190)

Li-Tai-Pe *Op.37
3.3(English horn).3(bass
clar).3(contrabsn). 4.3.3.0.
timp,perc,harp,strings,T solo
[18'] (8 chinese songs revised by
Klabund) HUG (A191)

Music for Orchestra, No. 1, Op. 35
4(pic).3(English
horn).3.3(contrabsn). 4.3.3.1.
timp,perc,pno,strings HUG (A192)

Rhapsody for Violin and Orchestra,
Op. 32
2.2.2.2. 3.2.0.0. timp,perc,strings
[14'] HUG (A193)

Sinfonia, Op. 31, in C for Orchestra
4(pic).3(English
horn).4.3(contrabsn). 4.4.3.1.
timp,perc,harp,cel,strings [25']
HUG (A194)

Sinfonische Fantasie *Op.7
3.3(English horn).3.3(contrabsn).
6.4.3.2. timp,perc,2harp,pno,
strings,org,T solo,T [25'] HUG
(A195)

ANDRIESSEN, JURRIAAN (1925-1996)
Rozenprieel, Het: In Memoriam Nico
Andriessen
string orch [10'] sc DONEMUS (A196)

ANDRIESSEN, LOUIS (1939-    )
Dances
perc,pno,harp,strings,S solo, (harp
& piano slightly amplified) [25']
BOOSEY-ENG rent (A197)

Hadewijch
see Materie, De: Part 2

Materie, De: Part 1
3.0+2English horn.5+3bass clar.0.
4.4.4.1. bass gtr,5perc,2pno,
2synthesizer,2gtr,2vln I,2vln II,
2vla,2vcl,db,T&2S&2A&2T&2B [25']
BOOSEY-ENG rent (A198)

ANDRIESSEN, LOUIS (cont'd.)

Materie, De: Part 2
"Hadewijch" 3.2+2English horn.5+
2bass clar+contrabass clar.0.
4.4.4.1. bass gtr,5perc,harp,
2pno,2synthesizer,2gtr,2vln I,
2vln II,2vla,2vcl,db,S&2S&2A&2T&
2B [25'] BOOSEY-ENG rent (A199)

Materie, De: Part 4
3.4.5+2bass clar+contrabass clar.0.
4.4.4.1. 6perc,cel,harp,2pno,
2synthesizer,2gtr,bass gtr,2vln
I,2vln II,2vla,2vcl,db, speaking
voice&2S&2A&2T&2B, speaker,
female [25'] BOOSEY-ENG rent
(A200)

Rosa: Overture
3(pic).3.0.0. tenor sax.baritone
sax. 4.3.3.1. 3perc,elec gtr,elec
bass gtr,2pno,synthesizer,2vln I,
2vln II,2vla,2vcl,db,8 solo
voices [12'] BOOSEY-ENG rent
(A201)

ANGEL DEL SOL, L' see Soler, Josep

ANGST see Krieger, Armando

ANGST: SINFONISCHE DICHTUNG NO. 2 NACH
BILDERN VON EDV. MUNCH see
Søderlind, Ragnar

ANGULO, EDUARDO
Concerto for Guitar and Orchestra,
No. 1
VOGT VF 1150 (A202)

Concerto for Guitar and Orchestra,
No. 2
VOGT VF 1184 (A203)

Dos Plegarias Für Gitarre Und
Orchester
gtr,orch VOGT VF 1 182 (A204)

ANIMA see Burrell, Diana

ANIMUS-ANIMA see Gellman, Steven

ANKUNFTSSINFONIE see Sperger, Johann
M., Sinfonia in F

ANNIVERSAIRE see Charron, Jacques

ANNIVERSARY see Carter, Elliott Cook,
Jr.

ANNIVERSARY DANCES see Mathias, William

ANON IN LOVE see Walton, [Sir] William
(Turner)

ANONYMOUS
Aria in C
(Šesták, Zdenek) "Bella Quando
Aurora" org,string orch,S solo
[9'] CESKY HUD. (A205)

Bella Quando Aurora
see Aria in C

Concerto for 2 Horns and Orchestra in
E flat
(Koukal, Bohumír) 0.2.0.0. 0.0.0.0.
strings,2horn soli [14'] CESKY
HUD. (A206)

Concerto for Trumpet, Violin, Strings
and Continuo
(Güttler, L.) strings,cont,trp&vln
soli [10'] BREITKOPF-W (A207)

Pro Beati Pauli
(Grainger, Percy Aldridge) string
orch BARDIC (A208)

ANOTHER HAPPY BIRTHDAY see Wuorinen,
Charles

ANOTHER MONDAY GIG see Freedman, Harry

ANROP; INROP; UTROP see Rehnqvist,
Karin

ANTALYA see Folie, Serge

ANTECKNINGAR FRN HESIODOS HEMKOMST see
Johansson, Johannes

ANTICHE DANZA ED ARIE PER LIUTO see
Respighi, Ottorino

ANTICHE DANZE ED ARIE, SUITE I see
Respighi, Ottorino

ANTIGONE see Brandmüller, Theo

ANTIPHONE see Yasuraoka, Akio

ANTIPHONIA II see Morthenson, Jan W.

ANTIPHONIA III see Morthenson, Jan W.

ANTOINETTE-MARSCH see Joplin, Scott

AOKI, NOBUO (1920- )
Shimoda Monogatari: Dance Suite
orch [19'] JAPAN (A209)

APERTURA see Eklund, Hans

APHRODITE: SUITE 1 see Fevrier, Henri

APHRODITE: SUITE 2 see Fevrier, Henri

APIVOR, DENIS (1916- )
Symphony, No. 5
2.2.2.2. 2.2.2.0. timp,2perc,pno/
hpsd,gtr,bass gtr,harp,strings
manuscript BMIC (A210)

APOLLYON, NICOLAY (1945- )
Transmutation
2(pic).2.2(bass clar).2(contrabsn).
4.3.3.0. timp,2perc,strings,
soundtrack, amplified alto flute
solo NORSKMI (A211)

APONTE-LEDEE, RAFAEL (1938- )
Ventana Abierta
3Mez,fl,clar,trp,2perc,pno,vln,vcl,
db SEESAW (A212)

APOTHEOSIS see Wilson, Donald M.

APPASSIONATAMENTE see Henze, Hans
Werner

APPEL DE LA NUIT see Marti, Heinz

APPLEBAUM, LOUIS (1918- )
Adagio for Clarinet and Strings
string orch,clar/alto fl solo [7']
sc,solo pt CANADIAN
MI 1623 A648AD (A213)

Dialogue With Footnotes: For Symphony
Orchestra And Jazz Band
2(pic).2(English horn).2(bass
clar).2. 4.3.3.1. timp,perc,
strings, Jazz band: 5sax, 5trp,
4trb, 2horn, gtr, pno, perc,
drum-kit, bass [13'] sc CANADIAN
MI 1450 A648DI (A214)

Fanfare And Anthem
3(pic).2.2.2. 4.4.3.1. timp,3perc,
strings, 8 heraldic trumpets
[1'40"] sc CANADIAN
MI 1431 A648FA (A215)

Harper Of The Stones, The
1(pic,alto fl).0.0.0. 0.2.1.0.
perc,pno&cel,synthesizer,
electronic tape,strings without
vcl,narrator, (flute also doubles
a tin flute and a wooden flute)
[28'] sc CANADIAN MV 1975 A648HA (A216)

Inuit: From The Eskimo
see Inunit Music: From The Eskimo

Inunit Music: From The Eskimo
"Inuit: From The Eskimo"
2(pic).2.2.2. 2.2.2.0. timp,perc,
harp,strings,solo voice [10'] (1.
North 2. At Play 3. Ice Break-Up
4. Birds 5. Quiet) sc CANADIAN
MV 1400 A648IN (A217)

APRÈS-MIDI DU DRACOULA, L' see Moran,
Robert

APRÈS UN RÊVE see Faure, Gabriel-Urbain

APRITE PRESTO, APRITE see Mozart,
Wolfgang Amadeus

AQUAMARINE see Skarecky, Jana

AQUARELLE FÜR BARITON UND ORCHESTER see
Hocke, Wolfgang

AQUARIUS, ACT I see Goeyvaerts, Karel

AQUARIUS, ACT II see Goeyvaerts, Karel

AQUARIUS, NO. 2 (2ND VERSION) see
Goeyvaerts, Karel

AQUARIUS, NO. 3 (2ND VERSION) see
Goeyvaerts, Karel

AQUARIUS, NO. 4 (2ND VERSION) see
Goeyvaerts, Karel

ARABESK see Sevius, Sven

ARAGONAISE see Proto, Frank

ARBAN, JEAN BAPTISTE (1825-1889)
Carnaval De Venise
(Herbillon, G.) 2.2.2.2. 2.2.1.0.
timp,perc,strings,trp solo [11']
BILLAUDOT (A218)

Carnival Of Venice, The: Variations
(Brooks, Arthur) string orch,horn
solo THOM ED OC1 f.s., perf mat

ARBAN, JEAN BAPTISTE (cont'd.)
rent (A219)

ARBEIDSDAG see Kvam, Oddvar S.

ARC EN CIEL see Bousch, François

ARC OF THE STARS, THE see Lumsdaine,
David

ARCADE see Keuris, Tristan

ARCHANGEL see Saylor, Bruce (Stuart)

ARCHBOLD, PAUL
And The Unseen Eyebeam Crossed...
1.2.1.2. 2.2.0.0. perc,strings
manuscript BMIC (A220)

Chiaroscuro
db,strings manuscript BMIC (A221)

ARCHETYPON II FÜR ANTON see Kelemen,
Milko

ARCHI PER ARCHI I-III see Levin, Stefan

ARCHIPELAGO S. see Takahashi, Yuji

ARCHITECTURE AND DREAMS see Powers,
Anthony

ARCHITEKTONISCHER ENTWURF see
Rosenfeld, Gerhard

ARCOLINO, FOR 24 SOLO STRINGS see
Oosterveld, Ernst

ARCTANDER: SYMPHONIE DE NUMÉRO CACHÈ
see Halmrast, Tor

ARCTOS see Bjorklund, Terje

ARCURI, SERGE (1954- )
Agrégats
3+pic.2.3+bass clar.3+contrabsn.
3.2.2.1. 3perc,harp,pno,strings
[8'] sc CANADIAN MI 1100 A657AG (A222)

ARDÉVOL, JOSÉ (1911- )
Sinfonia No. 2
2+2pic.3+English horn.3+bass
clar.3+contrabsn. 6.4.6.2. 2timp,
perc,2pno,2harp,cel,glock,
strings [35'] PEER rent (A223)

Sinfonia No. 3
2+2pic.5(2English horn).2+bass
clar.4+contrabsn.2alto sax.
8.6.6.2. 2timp,perc,2pno,opt
xylo,strings [37'] PEER rent (A224)

ARDOGINI see Eyser, Eberhard

AREA see Bohlin, Jonas

ARGENTINA (TANGO) see Thomas-Mifune,
Werner

ARGUMENTS see Bellemare, Gilles

ARIA AND SCHERZO see Buczynski, Walter

ARIA DE QUOVIS FESTO "SAEVIT MARE
SURGUNT VENTI" see Senkyr, Augustin

ARIA FOR EDWARD JOHN EYRE see
Lumsdaine, David

ARIA IN D PRO NATALI DOMINI see Brixi,
Franz Xaver, Aria in D

ARIA PASTORITIA "HUC, HUC, PASTORCULI"
see Senkyr, Augustin

ARIA PER CORDE see Kenins, Talivaldis

ARIANE: BALLET D'ARIANE see Massenet,
Jules

ARIANE: SUITE see Massenet, Jules

ARIANNA A NAXOS see Haydn, [Franz]
Joseph

ARIAS see Colgrass, Michael (Charles)

ARIAS AND BARCAROLLES see Bernstein,
Leonard

ÁRIE Z OPERY SAPPHÓ see Reicha, Anton

ARIEN DES ORPHEUS see Henze, Hans
Werner

ARIMA, REIKO (1933- )
Story Of Cats Amd Mice, The
orch,pno [9'] JAPAN (A225)

ARIOSO see Tchaikovsky, Piotr Ilyich

ARISTOFANOVSKÉ VARIACE see Hanuš, Jan

ARKIEOLOGISK SVIT see Winter, Tomas

ARKVIK, YLVA Q (1961- )
Enigma 15 - Tons
orch STIM (A226)

ARMIDA: BALLETTMUSIK see Gluck,
Christoph Willibald, Ritter von

ARMIDA: OVERTURE see Haydn, [Franz]
Joseph

ARNELL, RICHARD (1917- )
Symphony, No. 6
3.2.2.2. 4.3.3.2. timp,perc,pno,
strings manuscript BMIC (A227)

ARNOLD, ALAN
Cartoon Sketches Of The Baroque
*Suite
string orch [10'] PRESSER rent (A228)

Tour Of The Instruments Of The
Orchestra, A
see Variations On An Elizabethan
Ballad

Variations On An Elizabethan Ballad
"Tour Of The Instruments Of The
Orchestra, A" 2.2(English
horn).2.2. 4.3.3.1. timp,2perc,
strings [17'] PRESSER rent (A229)

ARNOLD, SAMUEL (1740-1802)
Macbeth: Incidental Music
(Hoskins, Robert) 2ob,2bsn,2horn,
2trp,tamb,2vln,vla,vcl,db [20']
ARTARIA AE089 (A230)

Overture, Op. 8, No. 1, in B flat
(Hoskins, Robert) 2ob,2horn,2vln,
vla,vcl,db [9'] ARTARIA AE082 (A231)

Overture, Op. 8, No. 2, in D
(Hoskins, Robert) 2ob,2horn,2vln,
vla,vcl,db [8'] ARTARIA AE083 (A232)

Overture, Op. 8, No. 3, in F
(Hoskins, Robert) 2ob,2horn,2vln,
vla,vcl,db [10'] ARTARIA AE084 (A233)

Overture, Op. 8, No. 4, in D
(Hoskins, Robert) 2ob,2horn,2vln,
vla,vcl,db [6'] ARTARIA AE085 (A234)

Overture, Op. 8, No. 5, in G
(Hoskins, Robert) 2ob,2horn,2vln,
vla,vcl,db [8'] ARTARIA AE086 (A235)

Overture, Op. 8, No. 6, in D
(Hoskins, Robert) 2ob,2horn,2vln,
vla,vcl,db [8'] ARTARIA AE087 (A236)

Polly: Overture
(Hoskins, Robert) 2ob,2horn,2vln,
vla,vcl,db [6'] ARTARIA AE088 (A237)

ARS ROMANTICA see Buczynski, Walter

ARSENEAULT, RAYNALD (1945- )
La
1.0.0.0. 0.1.0.0. 5perc,pno,hpsd,
vln,string orch/string quin,SA
soli [60'] (cantate-ballet) sc
CANADIAN MV 2400 A781JA (A238)

Quatre Miniatures Pour Orchestre
3(pic).3(English horn).3(bass
clar).3+contrabsn. 4.3.2.1. timp,
3perc,harp,pno,strings sc
CANADIAN MI 1100 A781QU (A239)

ART OF SURFING A MONSTER, THE see
Koolmees, Hans, Waters And Wortelen
- Part 2

ART POUR L'ART, L' see Suter, Robert

ARTEAGA, EDWARD (1950- )
Serenade for Flute, Harp and String
Orchestra
[16'] sc CANADIAN MI 1750 A786SE (A240)

Steps
3+pic.2.2.1. 3.2.2.1. timp,perc,
cel,strings [45'] sc CANADIAN
MI 1100 A786ST (A241)

Symphony No. 1
2+pic.2.2.2+contrabsn. 3.2.3.1.
timp,2perc,harp,strings sc
CANADIAN MI 1100 A786SY (A242)

ARTYOMOV, VYACHESLAV (1940- )
Gurische Hymne
4perc,strings,3vln soli [13'] sc
PETERS 02254 (A243)

In Memoriam
3.3.3.3. 4.3.2.1. timp,4perc,harp,
cel,pno,strings,vln solo [20']
sc,solo pt PETERS 03397 (A244)

Lamentations
3perc,org,strings,opt pno [14'] sc
PETERS 02253 (A245)

ARTYOMOV, VYACHESLAV (cont'd.)
Tristia
0.0.1.0. 0.1.0.0. 2vibra,org,
strings [17'] sc PETERS 03396
(A246)

ARVIDSSON-BREMMERS, PER (1959- )
Atertaget Drag
4(pic).3(English horn).3(bass
clar).3. 4.3.3.0. timp,4perc,
harp,strings,pno [13'] STIM sc
H-2598, pts T-198 (A247)

AS ABOVE SO BELOW see Hellstenius,
Henrik

AS FERNS see Tann, Hilary

...AS OTHERS SEE US... see Macmillan,
James

AS THE TIME PASSES BY see Grahn, Ulf

AS WE STOOD THEN see Weisgarber,
Elliott

AS YOU LIKE IT see Quilter, Roger

AS YOU LIKE IT: SUITE see Walton, [Sir]
William (Turner)

ASCENSION, L': 4 MEDITATIONS see
Messiaen, Olivier

ASCHENBRÖDEL: OVERTURE see Rossini,
Gioacchino, Cenerentola, La:
Overture

ASHEIM, NILS HENRIK (1960- )
Don Giovanni-Metamorfoser
3.3.3.3(contrabsn). 4.3.3.1. timp,
2perc,cel,strings [7'] NORSKMI
(A248)
Stemmer: Sketch For Orchestra
"Voices: Sketch For Orchestra"
2.2(English horn).2.2. 4.3.3.0.
3perc,harp,strings [3'] NORSKMI
(A249)
Voices: Sketch For Orchestra
see Stemmer: Sketch For Orchestra

ASHES see Nelson, Daniel

ASIA, DANIEL (1953- )
Concerto for Piano
3(pic).3(English horn).3(bass
clar).3(contrabsn). 4.3.2.1.
timp,3perc,harp,strings [37']
MERION rent (A250)
Gateways
4(pic,alto fl).4(English
horn).4(clar in E flat,bass
clar).4(contrabsn). 4.4.3.1.
timp,3perc,pno,strings [5']
MERION rent (A251)

ASK THE ORACLE see Geddes, Murray

ASTROGNOSIA: MÅNEFASER MELLOM
STJERNEREGN: ORKESTERSUITE see
Amdahl, Magne

ASYNDETON see Stare, Ivan

ASZTALIZENE see Farkas, Ferenc, Table
Music

AT JANUS' GATE see Kalmar, Laszlo

AT JDU VZHURU NEBO DOLU see Petr,
Zdenek

ATEM DER ERSCHÖPFTEN ZEIT, DER see
Tarnopolsky, Vladimir

ÅTERTAGET DRAG see Arvidsson-Bremmers,
Per

ATKINSON, CONDIT ROBERT (1928- )
Alexander Evergreen
2.2.3.2. 4.3.3.1. timp,3perc,harp,
strings,narrator [10'] SCHIRM.EC
rent (A252)
Dinosaur's Tale, The
2.2.3.2. 4.3.3.1. timp,3perc,harp,
strings,narrator [18'] SCHIRM.EC
rent (A253)
Musical Trip To The Zoo, A
3.3.3.2. 4.3.3.1. timp,2perc,harp,
strings,narrator [17'] SCHIRM.EC
rent (A254)

ATMEST DU NICHT MIT MIR DIE SÜSSEN
DÜFTE? see Wagner, Richard

ATMOSPHERE AS A FLUID SYSTEM, THE see
Larsen, Elizabeth B. (Libby)

ATT NALKAS STOCKHOLM see Eyser,
Eberhard

ATTACCA see Morthenson, Jan W.

AU BORD DE L'EAU see Faure, Gabriel-
Urbain

AU CHÂTEAU DE POMPAIRAIN see Mather,
Bruce

AU CIMETIÈRE see Faure, Gabriel-Urbain

AU CIRQUEL!: HUMORESQUE see Chini,
Andre

AU-DELA DU MUR DU SON see Lauber, Anne

AU TOMBEAU DU MARTYR JUIF INCONNU see
Williamson, Malcolm, Concerto for
Harp and Strings

AUBADE see Jeverud, Johan

AUBADE AND NOCTURNE see Wilson, Charles
M.

AUBADE FOR STRING ORCHESTRA see
Moravec, Paul

AUBADE POUR MORGES see Sutermeister,
Heinrich

AUBER, DANIEL-FRANÇOIS-ESPRIT
(1782-1871)
Air D'a. Kassim - No. 9 - A.II. (from
La Circassienne)
orch,solo voice BOIS (A255)
Cheval De Bronze, Le: Overture
orch BOIS (A256)
Domino Noir, Le: Overture
"Schwarze Domino, Der: Overture"
2(pic).2.2.2. 4.2.3.0. timp,perc,
strings [7'] (no score)
BREITKOPF-W (A257)
Muette Di Portici, La: Overture
"Stumme Von Portici, Die: Overture"
2+pic.2.2.2. 4.2.3.0. timp,perc,
strings, serpent [8'] BREITKOPF-W
(A258)
Muette Di Portici, La: Tarantelle
"Stumme Von Portici, Die:
Tarantelle" 1+pic.2.2.2. 4.2.3.0.
timp,strings [3'] (no score)
BREITKOPF-W (A259)
Schwarze Domino, Der: Overture
see Domino Noir, Le: Overture
Sirene, Der: Overture
see Sirène, La: Overture
Sirène, La: Overture
"Sirene, Der: Overture"
2(2pic).2.2.2. 4.2.3.0. timp,
perc,strings [8'] (no score)
BREITKOPF-W (A260)
Stumme Von Portici, Die: Overture
see Muette Di Portici, La: Overture
Stumme Von Portici, Die: Tarantelle
see Muette Di Portici, La:
Tarantelle

AUF DEM LANDE see Nicode, Jean Louis

AUF DEM SEE see Rakov, Nikolai

AUF DEM WASSER ZU SINGEN see Schubert,
Franz (Peter)

AUF DER SUCHE NACH DEM VERLORENEN TANGO
see Wahren, Karl Heinz

AUF EINER RUSSISCHEN FEIER see Tesar,
Milan

AUF FLUGELN DES GESANGES see
Mendelssohn-Bartholdy, Felix

AUF HERMANNSHÖH see Müller-Wieland, Jan

AUF KAISER FRIEDRICHS TOD see Becker,
Albert Ernst Anton

AUF ZU DEM FESTE see Mozart, Wolfgang
Amadeus, Finch' Han Dal Vino

AUFERSTANDEN AUS... see Eisler, Hanns

AUFSCHNAITER, BENEDIKT ANTON
(1665-1742)
Serenade No. 1 in G (from Concors
Discordia)
strings without db COPPENRATH sc
16.009-1, pts 16.009-21 TO 28
(A261)
Serenade No. 2 in F (from Concors
Discordia)
strings without db COPPENRATH sc
16.031-1, pts 16.031-21 TO 28
(A262)
Serenade No. 6 in B flat (from
Concors Discordia)
strings without db COPPENRATH sc

AUFSCHNAITER, BENEDIKT ANTON (cont'd.)
16.042-1, pts 16.042-21 TO 28
(A263)

AUFSCHWUNG see Röttger, Heinz

AURA see Höller, York see Koch, Dagfinn

AURA: PARÁFRASIS ORQUESTAL DE LA OPERA
see Lavista, Mario

AURE AMICHE see Reicha, Anton

AURELIA see Helbig, Michael

AURORA see Bauer, Robert

AURORA BOREALIS see Murto, Matti,
Revontulet see Schipizky, Frederick

AURORA FANFARE see Schipizky, Frederick

AUS DEM HOHELIED SALOMONIS see Zilcher,
Hermann

AUS FERNEN WELTEN see Weingartner,
(Paul) Felix von

AUS ITALIEN see Strauss, Richard

AUSSCHNITTE '80... see Flammer, Ernst-
Helmuth

AUTOBAHN see King, Reginald

AUTOMATON see Dimitrakopoulos, Apostolo

AUTOMNALE see Uy, Paul

AUTOMNE see Faure, Gabriel-Urbain

AUTOMNE ET SES ENVOLS D'ÉTOURNEAUX, L'
see Lemeland, Aubert

AUTUMN LUTE-SONG see Tan, Su Lian

AUTUMN SONATA see Musgrave, Thea

AUTUMNAL SONG see Shawn, Allen

AVALON see Cardy, Patrick

AVE MARIA see Leoncavallo, Ruggiero see
Mascagni, Pietro

AVE MARIS STELLA see Liszt, Franz

AVE REGINA see Haydn, [Johann] Michael

AVE SEIKILOS see Jiráčková, Marta

AVEC see Tremblay, Gilles

AVIGNONSKY MOST see Vodrazka, Karel

AVISON, CHARLES (1709-1770)
Concerto Grosso No. 3 in D minor
(from A Sonata By D. Scarlatti)
vln I,vln II,vla,vcl,db,2vln&vla&
vcl soli MÖSELER sc 40.151-00,
pts 40.151-01, set 40.151-09
(A264)
Concerto Grosso No. 5 in D minor
(from A Sonata By D. Scarlatti)
vln I,vln II,vla,vcl,db,2vln&vla&
vcl soli MÖSELER sc 40.155-00,
pts 40.155-01, set 40.155-09
(A265)
Concerto Grosso No. 6 in D (from A
Sonata By D. Scarlatti)
vln I,vln II,vla,vcl,db,2vln&vla&
vcl soli MÖSELER sc 40.146-00,
pts 40.146-01, set 40.146-09
(A266)
Concerto Grosso No. 10 in D minor
(from A Sonata By D. Scarlatti)
vln I,vln II,vla,vcl,db,2vln&vla&
vcl soli MÖSELER sc 40.147-00,
pts 40.147-01, set 40.147-09
(A267)

AVSHALOMOV, JACOB (1919- )
Sinfonietta
1.1.3.1. 2.2.1.0. timp,perc,kbd,
strings [17'] SCHIRM.EC rent
(A268)

AWAKENING see Gellman, Steven

AXMAN, EMIL (1887-1949)
Koncertní Predehra
2.2.1.2. 6.3.3.1. timp,perc,harp,
pno,strings [9'] CESKY HUD.
(A269)
Symphony No. 4
3.2.3.2. 6.2.2.1. timp,perc,harp,
strings [38'] CESKY HUD. (A270)

AXOLOTL see Subotnick, Morton Leon

[AYAS ÖGAL] BALETTVERK FÖR PER JONSSON:
I FÖRSPEL OCH 15 BILDER see
Sandred, Örjan

AYIN RAKSI see Saygun, Ahmed Adnan

AZ IF JÚSÁGHOZ NYITÁNY see Sárközy,
Istvan, To The Youth: Overture

AZ VZEJDOU VECI NOVÉ see Mácha, Otmar,
Sinfonietta No. 2

# B

B22 see Brott, Alexander

BABBITT, MILTON BYRON (1916-    )
Crowded Air, The
1.1.1.1. 0.0.0.0. pno,gtr,vln,vla,
vcl,db,marimba solo [10'] sc
PETERS 03614                    (B1)

BABI YAR see Martland, Steve

BABIN, VICTOR (1908-1972)
Concerto No. 2 for 2 Pianos and
Orchestra
2.2.2.2. 4.2.3.1. timp,perc,
strings,2pno soli [24'] BELAIEFF
(B2)

BÁBINCIN MARŠOVSKY VALCÍK see Kricka,
Jaroslav

BACCHAE METRES see Butler, John

BACCHANTEN-OUVERTÜRE, OP. 52 see
Bleyle, Karl

BACCHUS: SUITE see Massenet, Jules

BACCIO DI MANO, UN see Mozart, Wolfgang
Amadeus

BACH, CARL PHILIPP EMANUEL (1714-1788)
Sonata in D
(Guyot, D.) string orch,hpsd,trp
solo [11'] BILLAUDOT            (B3)

BACH, JAN MORRIS (1937-    )
Burgundy Variations
3.3.3.2. 4.3.3.1. timp,3perc,
strings [17'] SCHIRM.EC rent    (B4)

Concerto for Horn and Orchestra
horn solo,2.2.3.3. 4.3.3.1. timp,
3perc,harp,strings [35']
SCHIRM.EC rent                 (B5)

Concerto for Piano
pno solo,3.3.2.2. 4.3.3.1. timp,
2perc,harp,electronic tape,
strings [35'] SCHIRM.EC rent   (B6)

Dompes And Jompes For String
Orchestra
strings [25'] SCHIRM.EC rent   (B7)

Sprint
3.3.3.2. 4.3.3.1. timp,3perc,harp,
kbd,strings [14'] SCHIRM.EC rent
(B8)

BACH, JOHANN CHRISTIAN (1735-1782)
Ouvertüre 1
see Sinfonia, Op. 3, No. 1, in D

Sinfonia, Op. 3, No. 1, in D
(Gmür) "Ouvertüre 1" orch
KUNZELMANN ipa sc 10030A, oct
10030                          (B9)

Sinfonia, Op. 3, No. 4, in B flat
2ob,horn,strings sc KUNZELMANN
EKB 1P ipa                     (B10)

Sinfonia, Op. 6, No. 1, in G
(Gmür) 2ob,2horn,strings sc
KUNZELMANN 10029A ipa          (B11)

Sonata in E flat
(Guyot, D.) string orch,hpsd,trp
solo [10'] BILLAUDOT           (B12)

BACH, JOHANN CHRISTOPH FRIEDRICH
(1732-1795)
Four Late Sinfonias
(Nolte, Ewald V.) orch set A-R ED
ISBN 0-89579-226-5 f.s.
contains: Sinfonia in B flat, HWV
1, No. 20; Sinfonia in C, HWV
1, No. 6; Sinfonia in D, HWV 1,
No. 5; Sinfonia in E flat, HWV
1, No. 10                      (B13)

Sinfonia in B flat, HWV 1, No. 20
see Four Late Sinfonias

Sinfonia in C, HWV 1, No. 6
see Four Late Sinfonias

Sinfonia in D, HWV 1, No. 5
see Four Late Sinfonias

Sinfonia in E flat, HWV 1, No. 10
see Four Late Sinfonias

BACH, JOHANN SEBASTIAN (1685-1750)
Complete Concerti For Solo Keyboard
And Orchestra
orch,kbd solo sc DOVER 24929-8
(B14)
Complete Concertos For Two Or More
Harpsichords
orch,2hpsd, or more sc DOVER

BACH, JOHANN SEBASTIAN (cont'd.)
27136-6                        (B15)
Concerto for Oboe and Orchestra in D
ob solo,orch (E flat maj)
KUNZELMANN ipa sc 10223A, oct
10223                          (B16)

Concerto for Oboe and String
Orchestra in E flat, BWV 1034a
ob solo,string orch (originally in
D) KUNZELMANN 10223            (B17)

Concerto in F, BWV 1057
strings,cont,cembalo solo,2A rec
soli (Bach's own arrangement of
his Brandenburg Concerto No. 4)
MOSELER sc 40.033-00, solo pt
40.033-01 TO 02, pts 40.033-03,
set 40.033-09                  (B18)

Fugue in B minor (from
Woltemperierten Klavier)
(Beethoven) 2vln,vla,2vcl,db
KUNZELMANN ipa sc WW 913P, sc,pts
WW913                          (B19)

Kunst Der Fuge, Die *BWV 1080
(Collum, H.) 2.2.0.2. 0.0.0.0.
cembalo,strings [115'] BREITKOPF-
W                              (B20)

Six Brandenburg Concertos
orch sc DOVER 23376-6          (B21)

Suite Nach Dem Notenbüchlein Für Anna
Magdalena Bach
(Winkler, K.) 1.1.0.1. 0.3.0.0.
timp,strings [12'] sc,pts
BREITKOPF-W PB-OB 5226         (B22)

Three Violin Concerti
orch,vln solo sc DOVER 25124-1
(B23)

"BACH, P.D.Q." (PETER SCHICKELE)
see also SCHICKELE, PETER

Concerto for 2 Pianos and Orchestra
"Two Are Better Than One" 2.2.2.2.
2.2.3.0. timp,2perc,strings [26']
PRESSER rent                   (B24)

Two Are Better Than One
see Concerto for 2 Pianos and
Orchestra

BACH, WILHELM FRIEDEMANN (1710-1784)
Concerto for Cembalo and Strings in D
strings,cembalo solo [22']
BREITKOPF-W                    (B25)

Concerto for Cembalo and Strings in F
strings,cembalo solo [28']
BREITKOPF-W                    (B26)

Sinfonia in F
(Schneider, M.) strings,cont [13']
BREITKOPF-W                    (B27)

BACHELET, ALFRED (1864-1944)
Chère Nuit
2.2.2.2. 4.2.3.0. timp,triangle,
harp,strings LEDUC             (B28)

BACHOREK, MILAN (1939-    )
Tri Scény
strings,ob solo [12'] CESKY HUD.
(B29)

BÄCK, SVEN-ERIK (1919-1994)
Sumerki 90
orch [15'] (in 5 movements) pts
STIM T-2869                    (B30)

BACK-HAND BLUES (INSTRUMENTAL VERSION)
see Kozinski, Stefan

BACK UP BACH: VERSION 2 see Barnes,
Milton

BACKOFEN, JOHANN GEORG HEINRICH
(1768-1830)
Concerto for Basset Horn and
Orchestra
basset horn solo,orch KUNZELMANN
ipr sc 10233A, oct 10233       (B31)

BACRI, NICOLAS
Folia
orch DURAND 576-00757          (B32)
string orch,vla/vcl solo DURAND
576-00756                      (B33)

BADIAN, MAYA (1945-    )
Concertino for Piano and Orchestra
2.2.3(bass clar).2. 2.3.3.0. timp,
4perc,strings,pno solo [10'] sc
CANADIAN MI 1361 B136CON       (B34)

Concertino for 4 Timpanists, String
Orchestra and Trumpet
sc CANADIAN MI 1750 B136CO     (B35)

Concerto for Guitar and Orchestra
0.0.0.0. 2.2.2.0. timp,4perc,
strings,gtr solo sc CANADIAN

BADIAN, MAYA (cont'd.)

MI 1315 B136CO (B36)

Concerto for Marimba and Vibraphone
1(pic).1.1.0.sax. 0.1.0.0. timp,
3perc,strings,marimba&vibra solo
sc CANADIAN MI 1340 B136CO (B37)

Concerto for Violin and Orchestra
2(pic).2.3(bass clar).2. 4.3.3.1.
timp&perc,2perc,strings,vln solo
sc CANADIAN MI 1311 B136CO (B38)

Concerto for Violoncello and String
Orchestra
sc CANADIAN MI1613 B136CON (B39)

Dyptique Symphonique
2.2.2.2. 4.3.3.0. perc,strings sc
CANADIAN MI 1100 B136DY (B40)

Holocaust-In Memoriam
3.3(English horn).3(bass
clar).3(contrabsn). 4.3.3.1.
timp&perc,3perc,strings [20']
(Juifs - Extermination - Chants
Et Musique) sc CANADIAN
MI 1100 B136HO (B41)

Mouvement Symphonique
3(pic).3(English horn).3(bass
clar).3(contrabsn). 4.3.3.1.
timp,perc,strings sc CANADIAN
MI 1100 B136MO (B42)

Sinfonietta
2.2.2.2. 2.2.2.0. timp&perc,perc,
strings sc CANADIAN
MI 1100 B136SI (B43)

Toccata Et Passacaille Pour Orchestre
1(pic).1.1.0. 1.1.1.1. timp,3perc,
glock,strings sc CANADIAN
MI 1100 B136TO (B44)

Vers Les Âmes *Rum
2.2.3(bass clar).2. 0.1.1.0. perc,
18vln I,16vln II,12vla,10vcl,8db,
S solo (poetry) sc CANADIAN
MV 1400 B136VE (B45)

BAER
Meeting
4instrumental ensemble, Gruppe A-
2ob, trp, perc; Gruppe B-2clar,
horn, perc; Gruppe C-2vcl, db,
perc; Gruppe D-trb, harp, pno
MÖSELER sc 10.466.00, pts
10.466.01 TO 02, set 10.466.08
(B46)

BAGATELLEN (9) see Bredemeyer, Reiner

BAGATELLEN F.B see Bredemeyer, Reiner

BAGATELY see Lukas, Zdenek

BAIER, JIRI (1934- )
Tanecni Scherzo
2.2.2.2. 3.2.2.0. timp,perc,strings
[4'] CESKY HUD. (B47)

BAILEY, JUDITH
From Sea Paintings Of Paul Nash
0.1.1.1. 1.0.0.0. strings [10']
manuscript BMIC (B48)

Havas
2.2.2.2. 4.2.3.0. timp,perc,strings
[15'] manuscript BMIC (B49)

Voyage
2.2.2.2. 4.2.3.1. timp,perc,strings
[6'] manuscript BMIC (B50)

BAINBRIDGE, SIMON (1952- )
Ad Ora Incerta
4.3.4.1. 4.4.3.0. timp,3perc,harp,
strings,Mez solo,bsn solo [30']
NOVELLO (B51)

Caliban Fragments And Aria
1.3.3.1. 1.2.1.0. harp,2perc,
strings,Mez solo [16'] UNITED MUS
(B52)

Double Concerto
2.1.1.2. 2.2.0.0. strings,ob solo,
clar solo [17'] UNITED MUS (B53)

Song From Michelangelo
0.0.2.0. 0.0.0.0. vla,vcl,db,S solo
[3'] UNITED MUS rent (B54)

Toccata
4.3.4.3. 4.4.3.0. 3sax,4perc,elec
pno,synthesizer,strings NOVELLO
(B55)

BAJKA see Kalabis, Viktor

BAKER, MICHAEL CONWAY (1941- )
Baroque Diversions *Op.56
1.1.0.0. 1.1.0.0. strings [13'] sc
CANADIAN MI1200 B168BA (B56)

BAKER, MICHAEL CONWAY (cont'd.)

Concerto for Piano and Chamber
Orchestra, Op. 38
2(pic).2.2.2. 2.2.0.0. timp,2perc,
harp,strings,pno solo [25'] pno
red,solo pt CANADIAN
MI 1361 B168CO (B57)

Duo Concertante For Violin, Viola,
And String Orchestra
string orch,vln solo,vla solo [10']
sc,solo pt CANADIAN
MI 1717 B168DU (B58)

Encounters *Op.51
harp,pno,strings sc CANADIAN
MI1200 B168EN (B59)

Evocations *Op.57
chamber orch,fl&vln&vla&vcl soli
[18'] (1. Andante 2. March 3. Air
4. "Came a runner") sc CANADIAN
MI 1441 B168EV (B60)

Introduction And Fugue
3+pic.3+English horn.3+bass clar.3+
contrabsn. 4.3.3.1. timp,perc,
strings [4'] sc CANADIAN
MI 1100 B168IN (B61)

Okanagan Landscapes
3(pic).1.2.2. 4.3.3.1. timp,perc,
strings,pno solo [13'] sc
CANADIAN MI 1361 B168OK (B62)

Rita Joe
3(pic).3(English
horn).2.3(contrabsn). 4.3.3.1.
timp,perc,harp,pno&cel,strings,
solo voice, (an amplified english
horn may replace the voice) [18']
sc CANADIAN MV 1400 B168RI (B63)

Sinfonia Concertante, Op. 66
1(pic).1(English horn).1.1.
1.0.0.0. timp,pno,strings sc
CANADIAN MI1200 B168SI (B64)

Symphony
3(alto fl)+pic.3+English horn.3+
bass clar.3+contrabsn. 4.3.3.1.
timp,4perc,2harp,pno&cel,strings
sc CANADIAN MI 1100 B168SY (B65)

Timedancers *Op.90
3(pic).2.2.2. 4.2.3.1. timp,perc,
pno,strings,vln&clar soli sc,solo
pt CANADIAN MI 1450 B168TI (B66)

BAKKE, RUTH (1947- )
Concerto for Bassoon and Orchestra
see Illuminations

Illuminations (Concerto for Bassoon
and Orchestra)
2(pic).2(English horn).2(bass
clar).2(contrabsn). 2.0.0.0.
timp,2perc,strings NORSKMI (B67)

BAKSA, ROBERT FRANK (1938- )
Variations From The Heart
strings,clar,narrator (text by R.
Baksa) COMP.LIB. rent (B68)

BALADA A ROMANCE see Kucera, Václav

BALADA O CERVNOVÉM RÁNU see Lidl,
Václav

BALADICKÉ SOUVETI see Kucera, Premysl

BALASSA, SÁNDOR (1935- )
Concerto for Violin, Op. 3
3(pic).3(English horn).3(bass
clar).3(contrabsn). 4.3.3.1.
timp,perc,cel,strings,vln solo
[30'] EMB (B69)

Little Grape And Little Fish *Op.40
"Szölöcske És Halacska" 2.2.2.2.
2.0.0.0. timp,strings [23'] EMB
rent (B70)

Szölöcske És Halacska
see Little Grape And Little Fish

BALETNÍ HUDBA Z OPERY PRODANÁ NEVESTA
see Smetana, Bedrich

BALETNÍ MINIATURA see Petrov, Vadim

BALEY, VIRKO (1938- )
Adam's Apple, Prelude For Orchestra
2.2.2.2. 2.2.1.0. 2perc,pno&cel,
strings [3'] TROPPE TNP 1007 rent
(B71)
Concerto for Piano and Orchestra, No.
1
1.1.1(bass clar,baritone sax).1.
2.1.1.0. 3perc,harp,cel,strings,
pno solo [28'] TROPPE TNP 1006
rent (B72)

BALEY, VIRKO (cont'd.)

Concerto for Violin and Orchestra,
No. 1
2.2.2.2. 4.2.3.1. 4perc,harp,pno+
cel+amplified hpsch, str, vln
solo [26'] (quasi una fantasia)
TROPPE TNP 1004 rent (B73)
1.1.1(bass clar).1. 1.1.1.1. 2perc,
harp, pno+cel+amplified hpsch,
str, vln solo [26'] (quasi una
fantasia - chamber version)
TROPPE TNP 1003 rent (B74)

Concerto for Violin and Orchestra,
No. 2
2.2.2.2. 4.2.3.1. 3perc,pno&cel,
strings, opt. hurdy-gurdy or syn,
vln solo [29'] TROPPE TNP 1005
rent (B75)

Duma, A Soliloquy For Orchestra
2.2.2(bass clar).2. 4.2.3.1. 3perc,
strings,harp,pno,pno&cel,
amplified hpsch [13'] TROPPE
TNP 1002 rent (B76)

Orpheus Singing
strings,ob solo [12'] TROPPE
TNP 1008 rent (B77)

Partita
3.2.3(bass clar).2. 4.2.3.1. 4perc,
harp,pno&cel,strings,trom solo,
trp solo, electric vln solo [26']
(a concerto grosso for trombone,
trumpet, electric vln,
electronics and orchestra) TROPPE
TNP 1009 rent (B78)

Sacred Monuments: Symphony No. 1
1(pic,alto fl).1(English
horn).1(bass clar).1(contrabsn).
2.1.1.1. 2perc,harp,2pno&cel&
hpsd&synthesizer,strings [41']
TROPPE TNP 1010 rent (B79)

Woodcuts
string orch [8'] TROPPE TNP 1001
rent (B80)

BALKAN SUITE see Patachich, Ivan

BALLAD OF WILLIAM SYCAMORE, THE see
Biggs, John

BALLADE see Connell, Adrian

BALLADE ÉCOSSAISE see Tomasi, Henri.
Highland's Ballad

BALLADE HÉBRAÏQUE see Whettam, Graham
Dudley

BALLADE OF THE WEST see Coulthard, Jean

BALLADE POUR GEORGES see Lacour, Guy

BALLET DES AMPHORES: THREE MOVEMENTS
see Kalmar, Laszlo

BALLET DES FLEURS BLANCHES see Kalmar,
Laszlo

BALLET FOR ORCHESTRA see Bazelon, Irwin
Allen, Symphony No. 7 In Two Parts

BALLET MUSIC FROM THE MANNHEIM COURT:
PART I *ballet,18th cent
(Grave, Floyd K.) orch A-R ED
ISBN 0-89579-330-X f.s.
contains: Cannabich, Christian,
Rendes-Vous, Le, Ballet De
Chasse; Vogler, [Abbe] Georg
Joseph, Rendez-Vous De Chasse, Le
(B81)
BALLET MUSIC FROM THE MANNHEIM COURT:
PART II *ballet,18th cent
(Baker, Nicole) orch A-R ED
ISBN 0-89579-377-6 f.s.
contains: Cannabich, Christian,
Médée Et Jason; Toeschi, Carlo
Giuseppe, Mars Et Vénus (B82)

BALLET SUITE SPLEEN see Kox, Hans

BALLETTI see Pinos, Alois

BALLETTO CAMPESTRE see Paganini,
Niccolo

BALLETTSZENEN, OP. 52 see Glazunov,
Alexander Konstantinovich

BALLI TEATRALI A VENEZIA 1746-1859
(Saspories; Ruffin; Trentin) orch sc
RICORDI-IT 134867 (B83)

BALLON ET CROIX-PAS DE CIEL see
Carpenter, Patrick E.

BALSIS see Vasks, Peteris, Symphony for
Strings

BALTIN, ALEXANDER (1931- )
  Concertino for Harp and Orchestra
    INTERNAT.S. sc,pts rent, solo pt,
    pno red                (B84)

BAM DANCE see Barnes, Milton

BAMAGA DIPTYCH see Mills, Richard

BANANA-DUMP TRUCK see Mackey, Steven

BANCQUART, ALAIN (1934- )
  Symphony in Three Movements
    3.3.3.3. 4.4.3.1. 2perc,timp,pno,
    strings [24'] JOBERT     (B85)

BANG! see Picker, Tobias

BANQUET AND INVASION see Taylor,
  Matthew

BANTOCK, [SIR] GRANVILLE (1868-1946)
  Bilder Aus Dem Schottischen Hochland
    12strings [12'] (no score)
    BREITKOPF-W         (B86)

  Dramatische Tänze
    3.2.2.2. 2.2.3.1. timp,perc,harp,
    strings,vln&vla&vcl soli [13']
    BREITKOPF-W         (B87)

  Helena (Variations for Orchestra)
    2+pic.2.2.2. 4.2.3.1. timp,2perc,
    strings [18'] (no score)
    BREITKOPF-W         (B88)

  Pagan Symphony
    2+pic.1+English horn.2.2+contrabsn.
    4.3.3.0+db tuba. timp,3perc,harp,
    cel,strings [32'] sc,pts STAINER
    HL298 rent         (B89)

  Serenade
    strings [23'] (no score) BREITKOPF-
    W                (B90)

  Variations for Orchestra
    see Helena

BARA TUSEN KORTA ÅR see Robertsson,
  Karl-Olof

BARAB, SEYMOUR (1921- )
  Cantata
    see Rest Eternal

  Concerto for Viola and Orchestra
    1.1.2.1. 2.1.1.0. timp,strings,vla
    solo SEESAW         (B91)

  Moments Macabres
    solo voice,fl,ob,clar,strings [12']
    SCHIRM.EC rent       (B92)

  Rest Eternal (Cantata)
    1.1.2.1. 2.1.1.0. strings,STB soli
    SEESAW            (B93)

  Selfish Giant
    1.1.1.1. 2.0.0.0. strings,narrator
    SEESAW            (B94)

BARBE-BLEUE see Offenbach, Jacques

BARBER, SAMUEL (1910-1981)
  Symphony No. 2, Op. 19
    orch sc SCHIRM.G 50481096   (B95)

  Third Essay For Orchestra
    orch sc SCHIRM.G ED3816    (B96)

BARBER'S TIMEPIECE, THE see Woolrich,
  John

BARBIROLLI, [SIR] JOHN (1899-1970)
  Elizabethan Suite
    4horn,strings [12'] perf sc set
    OXFORD sc,pts rent     (B97)

BARCAROLE FÜR SOLO-VIOLINE UND FLÖTE
  see Kiermeir, Kurt, Bootsfahrt Mit
  Karin

BARGIEL, WOLDEMAR (1828-1897)
  Adagio for Violoncello and Orchestra
    in G, Op. 38
    2.2.2.2. 2.0.0.0. strings,vcl solo
    [11'] BREITKOPF-W     (B98)

  Prometheus: Overture *Op.16
    2+pic.2.2.2. 4.2.3.0. timp,strings
    [13'] BREITKOPF-W     (B99)

BARKER, PAUL
  Concerto for Violin and Orchestra
    2.2.2.2. 0.0.0.0. perc,strings,vln
    solo [20'] manuscript BMIC (B100)

  Malinche, La
    strings manuscript BMIC   (B101)

  Suite For Strings La Malinche
    strings manuscript BMIC   (B102)

BARKER, PAUL (cont'd.)
  Three Songs For Sylvia
    string orch,S solo manuscript BMIC
                     (B103)

  Voyage, The
    2.2.2.2. 2.2.0.0. timp,strings
    manuscript BMIC      (B104)

BARN DANCE see Weinzweig, John

BARNES, MILTON (1931- )
  Back Up Bach: Version 2
    string orch,fl solo [2'15"] sc
    CANADIAN MI 1621 B261BA   (B105)

  Bam Dance
    2.2.2.2. 4.2.3.1. timp,2perc,
    strings [2'15"] sc CANADIAN
    MI 1100 B261BA      (B106)

  Blood And Guts: Medley
    string orch,alto sax&opt soprano
    sax solo [9'] sc CANADIAN
    MI 1625 B261ME      (B107)

  Chamber Concerto
    string orch,woodwind quin soli
    [18'] sc CANADIAN MI 1726  (B108)

  Chanukah Suite No. 2
    2.2(English horn).2.2. 4.3.3.1.
    timp,3perc,strings [9'] sc
    CANADIAN MI 1100 B261 CH2 (B109)

  Concertino for Flute and String
    Orchestra
    [10'] sc,solo pt CANADIAN
    MI 1621 B261CO      (B110)

  Concerto for Double Bass and
    Orchestra
    see Song Of The Bow

  Concerto for Viola and Orchestra
    2.2.2.2. 2.2.3.0. timp,2perc,
    strings,vla solo [24'] sc
    CANADIAN MI 1312 B261CO  (B111)

  Concerto Grosso
    string orch,hpsd,vln solo, high
    trumpet [16'] (1. Ceremonial 2.
    Bacchus dance 3. Sartarello-rota
    4. Palamento 5. Fantasia 6.
    Masquerade) sc CANADIAN
    MI 1750 B261CO      (B112)

  Divertimento for Harp and String
    Quartet
    string orch,harp [18'] (1. Preamble
    2. Pavane for a live princess 3.
    Prelude and scherzo 4. Blues 5.
    Barn dance) sc,pts,solo pt
    CANADIAN MI 8506 B261DI  (B113)

  Fanfare, Prayer And Halleluyeh
    2(pic).2(English horn).2.2.
    4.2.0.0. timp,2perc,strings [15']
    sc CANADIAN MI 1100 B261FA (B114)

  Maid Of The Mist
    3+pic.2.2.2. 2.2.2.0. perc,harp,
    strings,opt timp [14'] (symphonic
    poem, On The River - Tribal Life
    - Chief Eagle - Choice Of The
    Sacrificial Maiden - Ritual
    Acceptance Dance - Over The
    Falls) sc CANADIAN MI 1100 B261MA
                     (B115)

  Odyssey, The
    2(pic).2(English horn).2.2.
    4.3.3.1. timp,3perc,strings sc
    CANADIAN MI 1100 B261OD  (B116)

  Portland Suite
    2.2.2.2. 4.4.3.0. timp,2perc,
    strings [15'] sc CANADIAN
    MI 1100 B261PO      (B117)

  Rags For String Orchestra
    string orch [4'] sc CANADIAN
    MI 1500 B261RA      (B118)

  Serenade for String Quartet and
    String Orchestra
    [6'] sc CANADIAN MI 1717 B261SE
                     (B119)

  Song Of The Bow (Concerto for Double
    Bass and Orchestra)
    2(pic).2(English horn).2.2.
    2.1.1.0. timp,harp,strings,db
    solo [22'] sc,pno red,solo pt
    CANADIAN MI 1314 B262SO  (B120)

  Symphony No. 2 for String Orchestra
    string orch [22'] sc CANADIAN
    MI 1500 B261SY      (B121)

  Three Israeli Chassidic Songs
    string orch,female solo,opt pno
    [6'] sc,solo pt,pts CANADIAN
    MV 1600 B261TH      (B122)

  Variations for Clarinet and Orchestra
    (from A Moravian Hymn Tune Of Jan
    Hus)

BARNES, MILTON (cont'd.)
    2.2.0.2. 4.2.2.0. timp,2perc,
    strings,clar solo [13'] sc
    CANADIAN MI 1323 B261VA  (B123)

BARNETT, CAROL
  Concerto
    2+pic.2.2.2. 0.2.2.1. timp,3perc,
    strings,horn solo THOM ED OC4
    f.s., perf mat rent    (B124)

BAROKNÍ PŘEDEHRA see Mácha, Otmar

BAROQUE DIVERSIONS see Baker, Michael
  Conway

BARRAUD, HENRY (1900- )
  Concerto for Strings
    8vln I,6vln II,4vla,4vcl,2db
    BOOSEY-ENG rent      (B125)

BARRETT, RICHARD (1959- )
  Ruin
    2fl,clar,bass clar,soprano sax,
    horn,2trom,tuba,3perc,strings
    [18'] UNITED MUS     (B126)

BARRIE, STUART
  Sounds From Ireland
    strings CHESTER pts CH55798, sc
    CH55797           (B127)

BARRY, GERALD (1952- )
  Flamboys
    2(pic,alto fl).2(English horn).2+
    bass clar.2+contrabsn. 4.2.3.1.
    pno,marimba,strings [9'] perf sc
    set OXFORD 3612423 sc,pts rent
                     (B128)

  Jalousie Taciturne, La
    string orch [12'] perf sc set
    OXFORD 3614170 sc,pts rent (B129)

BÁRTA, JIRÍ (1935- )
  Concerto De Camera
    strings,pno solo [17'] CESKY HUD.
                     (B130)

  Reliéfy
    3.3.3.3. 4.4.3.1. timp,perc,harp,
    strings [16'] CESKY HUD.  (B131)

BARTHOLOMEE, PIERRE
  Fredon Et Tarabusts
    4.4.4.4. 4.4.3.1. timp,perc,pno&
    cel,harp,strings [42'] BELGE
                     (B132)

  Humoresque
    3.3.3.3. 4.3.3.1. timp,perc,cel
    pno,strings [12'] BELGE  (B133)

BARTÓK, BÉLA (1881-1945)
  Két Kép *Op.10
    3(pic).2+English horn.3(bass
    clar).3(contrabsn). 4.4.3.1.
    timp,perc,2harp,cel,strings [16']
    EMB rent           (B134)

BARTON, HANUS (1960- )
  Návraty Svetla
    2.2.2.2. 4.3.3.0. timp,perc,harp,
    cel,marimba,pno,strings [20']
    CESKY HUD.        (B135)

  Otázka Bez Odpovedi
    2.2.2.2. 4.3.3.0. timp,perc,cel,
    strings,S solo [14'] CESKY HUD.
                     (B136)

  Serenade
    string orch [11'] CESKY HUD. (B137)

BARTOŠ, JAN ZDENEK (1908-1981)
  Burleska *Op.87
    string orch CESKY HUD.   (B138)

  Capriccio Concertant
    0.0.0.1. 1.0.0.0. strings,ob solo
    [6'] CESKY HUD.      (B139)

  Capriccio for Violoncello and
    Orchestra
    1.1.2.1. 2.1.1.0. timp,perc,
    strings,vcl solo [6'] CESKY HUD.
                     (B140)

  Concerto for Horn and Orchestra
    2.2.2.2. 2.2.3.1. timp,perc,
    strings,horn solo [15'] CESKY
    HUD.               (B141)

  Concerto For Three
    strings,vln&vla&vcl soli [15']
    CESKY HUD.        (B142)

  Concerto for Viola and Instrumental
    Ensemble
    2.2.3.2. 2.0.0.0. timp,perc,harp,
    strings without vln,vla,vla solo
    CESKY HUD.        (B143)

  Concerto Piccolo
    2.1.2.1. 2.2.1.0. timp,perc,
    strings,pno solo [8'] CESKY HUD.
                     (B144)

  Fantasy for Flute and Orchestra
    0.1.2.1. 2.0.0.0. timp,harp,
    strings,fl solo [20'] CESKY HUD.

BARTOŠ, JAN ZDENEK (cont'd.)

Fantasy for Organ and Strings
[11'] CESKY HUD. (B146)

Hudba Pro Smycce
string orch [5'] CESKY HUD. (B147)

Intermezzo
2.2.3.2. 4.3.3.1. perc,cel,xylo,
harp,strings [12'] CESKY HUD.
(B148)

Introdukce A Rondo
1.1.2.1. 2.2.1.0. timp,perc,
strings,vln solo [8'] CESKY HUD.
(B149)

Invention for Bass Clarinet and
String Orchestra
string orch/string quar,bass clar
solo [11'] CESKY HUD. (B150)

Jubilejní Predehra
2.2.2.2. 4.3.3.1. timp,perc,strings
[11'] CESKY HUD. (B151)

Královédvorská
see Studentská Suita

Lyrické Scény *Op.39
string orch CESKY HUD. (B152)

O Honzovi *Op.14
1.1.2.1. 2.2.1.0. timp,perc,
strings,S solo CESKY HUD. (B153)

Overture, Op. 69
see Rudy Prapor

Pochod Roku 1948
3.2.2.2. 4.3.3.1. timp,perc,strings
[5'] CESKY HUD. (B154)

Rhapsody for Violoncello and String
Orchestra
strings,vcl solo [11'] CESKY HUD.
(B155)

Rudy Prapor (Overture, Op. 69)
2.2.2.2. 4.2.3.1. timp,perc,strings
CESKY HUD. (B156)

Serenade
string orch [4'] CESKY HUD. (B157)
1.1.2.1. 2.2.1.0. timp,perc,cel,
strings,vcl solo [6'] CESKY HUD.
(B158)

Sonety O Praze
harp,strings,T&speaking voice [24']
CESKY HUD. (B159)

Studentská Suita *Op.25
"Královédvorská" string orch CESKY
HUD. (B160)

Suita Semplice
string orch CESKY HUD. (B161)

Symfonie Brevis
see Symphony No. 7

Symphonie Concertante No. 4 for Oboe
d'Amore and String Orchestra
[22'] CESKY HUD. (B162)

Symphony No. 7
"Symfonie Brevis" 2.2.2.2. 4.3.3.1.
timp,perc,harp,strings [16']
CESKY HUD. (B163)

Tarantela-Fantazie
1.1.2.1. 2.2.1.0. timp,perc,gtr,
strings,acord solo [6'] CESKY
HUD. (B164)

Tarantelle, Op. 70
2.2.2.2. 4.3.3.1. timp,perc,harp,
pno,strings CESKY HUD. (B165)

Triptych
2.2.2.2. 3.2.2.0. timp,perc,harp,
strings [18'] CESKY HUD. (B166)

Vivat Studentes *Overture
2.2.2.2. 2.2.3.1. timp,perc,strings
[9'] CESKY HUD. (B167)

BARTOŠ, JOSEF (1902-1966)
Serenade
string orch [11'] CESKY HUD. (B168)

BASCHMET-SUITE see Tchaikovsky,
Alexander

BASL, CURT
Concertino for Piano and Orchestra
see Fröhliche Episode

Fröhliche Episode (Concertino for
Piano and Orchestra)
2.1.2.1. 2.2.3.0. timp,perc,
strings,pno solo [8'] sc,set
BUSCH DM 061 rent
(B169)

BASLER, DALIBOR (1929-    )
Od Pramene
2.2.2.2. 4.2.3.1. timp,perc,strings
[5'] CESKY HUD. (B170)

BASSETT, LESLIE (1923-    )
Concerto for Orchestra
3.3.3.3. 4.3.3.1. 4perc,pno,cel,
harp,8vln I,7vln II,6vla,5vcl,4db
[28'] sc PETERS 04463 (B171)

BASTIEN UND BASTIENNE: OUVERTÜRE see
Mozart, Wolfgang Amadeus

BATÁ see Leon, Tania Justina

BATAILLE DE KERSHENEZ see Rimsky-
Korsakov, Nikolai

BÁTHROY SUITE see Horusitzky, Zoltan

BATS, CATS AND BROOMSTICKS see Huws
Jones, Edward

BATTI, BATTI, O BEL MASETTO see Mozart,
Wolfgang Amadeus

BATTLE OF BRITAIN SUITE see Walton,
[Sir] William (Turner)

BAUDIN, ERNESTINE VON
Five Études For Orchestra
3(pic).2+English horn.3.2+
contrabsn. 4.4.3.1. timp,2perc,
harp,cel,strings [22'] sc
CANADIAN (B172)

Sonata for Orchestra
3(pic).3+English horn.3+bass
clar.2. 4.3.3.1. timp,2perc,harp,
cel,strings [20'] sc CANADIAN
MI 1100 B565SO (B173)

BAUER, ROBERT (1950-    )
Aurora
3+pic.3+English horn.3+bass clar.2.
4.3.3.1. timp,2perc,strings [7']
sc CANADIAN MI 1100 B344AU (B174)

Rhapsodie En Rêve
clar,2perc,strings sc CANADIAN
MI1200 B344RH (B175)

Water Colours
string orch,2fl soli [6'] sc
CANADIAN MI 1721 B344WA (B176)

BAUHAUSMUSIK see Wenzel, Hans Jürgen

BAUMANN, HERBERT (1925-    )
Concerto for Mandolin and String
Orchestra
VOGT VF 1164 (B177)

Weihnachtskonzert, Ein
string orch VOGT VF 1156 (B178)

BAUMGESÄNGE see Schwertsik, Kurt

BAUR, JÜRG (1918-    )
Sentieri Musicali (Sinfonietta)
2(pic).2(English horn).2.2.
2.2.3.0. timp,2-3perc,harp,
strings [20'] BREITKOPF-W (B179)

Sinfonietta
see Sentieri Musicali

BAVICCHI, JOHN ALEXANDER (1922-    )
Fusions
2+pic.2.2.2. 4.4.3.1. timp,2perc,
strings,trom solo [11'] perf sc
set OXFORD sc,pts rent (B180)

BAYARDEREN-FEST see Berwald, Franz
(Adolf)

BAYER, F. (1938-    )
Propositions I
8vln I,6vln II,4vla,4vcl,2db [13']
LEDUC (B181)

BAZANT, JAROMÍR (1926-    )
Muzikantská Suita *Op.62
2.2.2.2. 3.2.2.0. timp,perc,harp,
strings [8'] CESKY HUD. (B182)

BAZANT, JIRI (1920)
Ozveny
1.0.3.0. 1.0.0.0. perc,harp,pno,
3gtr,strings,solo voice [4']
CESKY HUD. (B183)

Studie Pro Trubku
fl,sax,trom,perc,gtr,strings,trp
solo, clavinet Hohner, Yamaha
grand piano [5'] CESKY HUD.
(B184)

V Pohode
0.0.0.0.2sax. 0.1.1.0. perc,pno,
2gtr,synthesizer,strings,2acord
soli CESKY HUD. (B185)

Vzpominka
2.2.2.2. 4.3.3.0. vibra,harp,cel,
strings [4'] CESKY HUD. (B186)

BAZELON, IRWIN ALLEN (1922-1995)
Ballet For Orchestra
see Symphony No. 7 In Two Parts

Suite From Shakespeare's "The Merry
Wives Of Windsor"
1(pic).1.1(clar in E flat).1.
2.2.0.1. pno,vla,vcl [14']
PRESSER rent (B187)

Sunday Silence
see Symphony No. 9

Symphony No. 7 In Two Parts
"Ballet For Orchestra" PRESSER
416-41146 (B188)

Symphony No. 8
string orch (diff) PRESSER
416-41124 (B189)

Symphony No. 8 and Half
PRESSER 416-41135 (B190)

Symphony No. 9
"Sunday Silence" PRESSER 416-41143
(B191)

BE EMBRACED, YE MILLIONS! see Strauss,
Johann, [Jr.], Seid Umschlungen,
Millionen!

BE IN ME AS THE ETERNAL MOODS OF THE
BLEAK WINDS see Betts, Lorne M.

BE NATURAL see Singleton, Alvin

BE QUIET, MY HEART see Åm, Magnar, Kom
Til Ro, Mitt Hjarte

BEAR, THE see Foley, Daniel

BEASER, ROBERT (1954-    )
Concerto for Piano
3.3.3.2. 4.3.3.1. timp,4perc,harp,
strings,pno solo [32'] SCHOTTS
(B192)

Double Chorus
3(pic).3(English horn).3(bass
clar).3(contrabsn). 4.4.3.1.
timp,4perc,pno,strings [11']
SCHOTTS (B193)

Seven Deadly Sins, The
2(2pic).2.2.2.alto sax. 4.2.3.1.
timp,3perc,pno,harp,strings,TBar
soli [24'] (text by Hecht,
Anthony) SCHOTTS (B194)

Song Of The Bells
1(pic).2(English horn).2.2.
3.1.0.0. timp,3perc,pno,harp,
strings,fl solo [13'] SCHOTTS
(B195)

Symphony
3(pic,alto fl).3(English
horn).2(clar in E flat,bass
clar).2. 4.2.3.1. timp,perc,pno,
harp,strings [30'] (text by e. e.
cummings, William Butler Yeats,
John Fowles) SCHOTTS (B196)

BEAT ON see Dedic, Srdan

BEATAE VOCES TENEBRAE see Kenins,
Talivaldis

BÉATRIX POTTER TALES see Lanchbery,
John

BEAUX' STRATAGEM, THE see Goldberg,
Theo, Music To The Beaux' Stratagem

BECHERT, ERNST (1958-    )
"...Deutlicher
3.2.4.2. 4.3.3.1. timp,2perc,pno,
harp,8vln I,7vln II,6vla,5vcl,4db
[8'] sc PETERS 00086 (B197)

Orchesterstücke (4)
3.3.3.3. 4.3.3.1. timp,3perc,pno,
cel,harp,8vln I,7vln II,6vla,
5vcl,4db,tenor sax/soprano sax
solo [15'] sc PETERS 00087 (B198)

BECK, FRANZ (1734-1809)
Sinfonia in B flat
2ob,2horn,2vln,vla,vcl,db [12']
ARTARIA AE009 (B199)

Sinfonia in D
2ob,2horn,2vln,vla,vcl,db [12']
ARTARIA AE027 (B200)

Sinfonia in G
2ob,2horn,2vln,vla,vcl,db [14']
ARTARIA AE008 (B201)

Sinfonia, Op. 1, No. 1, in G minor
2vln,vla,vcl,db [12'] ARTARIA AE090
(B202)

Sinfonia, Op. 1, No. 2, in F
2vln,vla,vcl,db [11'] ARTARIA AE091
(B203)

Sinfonia, Op. 1, No. 3, in A
2vln,vla,vcl,db [8'] ARTARIA AE092
(B204)

BECK, FRANZ (cont'd.)

Sinfonia, Op. 1, No. 4, in E flat
2vln,vla,vcl,db [7'] ARTARIA AE093
(B205)

Sinfonia, Op. 1, No. 5, in G
2vln,vla,vcl,db [10'] ARTARIA AE094
(B206)

Sinfonia, Op. 1, No. 6, in C
2vln,vla,vcl,db [5'] ARTARIA AE095
(B207)

Sinfonia, Op. 10, No. 2, in D
2vln,vla,vcl,db [7'] ARTARIA AE006
(B208)

Sinfonia, Op. 13, No. 1, in E
2horn,2vln,vla,vcl,db [10'] ARTARIA
AE007
(B209)

BECKER, ALBERT ERNST ANTON (1834-1899)
Adagio No. 3 for Violin and
Orchestra, Op. 70
0.1.2.2. 2.0.0.0. strings,vln solo
[4'] BREITKOPF-W
(B210)

Auf Kaiser Friedrichs Tod  *Op.60,
March
2+pic.2.2+bass clar.2(contrabsn).
4.2.3.1. timp,perc,2harp,strings,
SATB [9'] (funeral) BREITKOPF-W
(B211)

Konzertstück for Violin and
Orchestra, Op. 66
2.2.2.2. 2.0.0.0. timp,strings,vln
solo [8'] BREITKOPF-W
(B212)

BECKER, GÜNTHER (1924-    )
Hard Times
1.1.2+contrabass clar.0. 2.1.1.1.
perc,pno,bsn solo [20']
BREITKOPF-W
(B213)

BECKER, JOHN
Marriage With A Space, A
"Stage Work No. 3" 3.3.2.4.
4.4.3.1. timp,4perc,2pno,2harp,
8vln I,7vln II,6vla,5vcl,4db
[50'] sc PETERS 03664
(B214)

Stage Work No. 3
see Marriage With A Space, A

BECKLER, STANWORTH R. (1923-    )
Sonata for Flute and Chamber Group
0.1.1.2sax. 1.1.1.0. pno,perc,
4strings,fl solo SEESAW
(B215)

BECKWITH, JOHN (1927-    )
Concert Of Myths, A
1(pic).2.2.2. 2.2.1.1. pno,strings,
fl solo [25'] sc CANADIAN
MI 1321 B397CO
(B216)

Peregrine
1.1.2.1. 2.1.0.0. strings,vla&perc
soli [21'] sc,solo pt CANADIAN
MI 1450 B397PE
(B217)

Round And Round
2(pic).2.2(bass clar).2.alto sax.
2.2.2.0. timp,perc,strings sc
CANADIAN MI 1100 B397RO
(B218)

BEDMAR, LUIS (1931-    )
Concerto for 2 Horns and Orchestra
sc ALPUERTO 1372
(B219)

BEDRICH, JAN (1932-    )
Symphony No. 5
3.3.3.3. 4.3.3.1. timp,perc,xylo,
harp,pno,strings [23'] CESKY HUD.
(B220)

Symphony No. 6
3.0.3.3. 3.3.0.0. timp,perc,xylo,
harp,pno,strings [26'] CESKY HUD.
(B221)

BEDTIME STORY FOR...., A see Read,
Thomas Lawrence, Sunrise Fable

BEECROFT, NORMA (1934-    )
Hemispherics
1(sax).0.1.1.tenor sax.baritone
sax. 0.1.1.0. gtr,strings,
synthesizer,2perc,vln,vcl,db sc
CANADIAN MI1200 B414HA    (B222)

BEETHOVEN, LUDWIG VAN (1770-1827)
Complete Piano Concertos By Beethoven
orch,pno solo sc DOVER 24563-2
(B223)

Concerti for Piano and Orchestra,
Nos. 4-5
(Küthen, H.W.) orch (Beethoven
Werke Series 3, Vol. 3, With
Critical Commentary) HENLE pap
4091, cloth 4092
(B224)

Concerto for Piano and Orchestra in B
flat, No. 2  *Op.19
orch (reduced string parts
available: Henle 408503) HENLE sc
408500, pts 408501:408502   (B225)

Concerto for Piano and Orchestra, No.
1, Op. 15, in C
(Lachner, V.) pno solo,string orch
KUNZELMANN sc,pts WW 903, sc

BEETHOVEN, LUDWIG VAN (cont'd.)

WW 903P        (B226)

Concerto for Piano and Orchestra, No.
4  *Op.58
orch (reduced string parts
available: Henle No. 4623) HENLE
sc 4620, pts 4621:4622      (B227)

Concerto for Piano and Orchestra, Op.
61a
2.2.2.2. 2.2.0.0. timp,pno,strings
[45'] BOCCACCINI BS. 191 rent  (B228)

Douze Menuets Posthumes
2.2.2.2. 2.2.0.0. timp,perc,strings
[25'] LEDUC         (B229)

Eroica
see Symphony No. 3 in E flat, Op.
55

Fidelio: Duet Of Leonore And
Florestan
see O Namenlose Freude

Fidelio: Duet Of Marzelline And
Jaquino
see Jetzt, Schätzchen, Jetzt Sind
Wir Allein

Fidelio: Pizarro's Aria
see Ha, Welch Ein Augenblick

Great Romantic Violin Concertos
orch,vln solo (includes violin
concerti by Beethoven,
Mendelssohn & Tchaikovsky) sc
DOVER 24989-1              (B230)

Grosse Fuge, Op. 133
(Gielen, Michael) 8vln I,7vln II,
6vla,5vcl,4db [18'] sc PETERS
04518                      (B231)
(Hidalgo, Manuel) 3.3.3.3. 4.3.3.1.
2timp,harp,strings [15']
(transcription from the string
quartet) BREITKOPF-W       (B232)

Ha, Welch Ein Augenblick
"Fidelio: Pizarro's Aria" 2.2.0.2.
2.2.0.0. timp,strings,Bar solo
[15'] BREITKOPF-W          (B233)

Jetzt, Schätzchen, Jetzt Sind Wir
Allein
"Fidelio: Duet Of Marzelline And
Jaquino" 2.2.0.0. timp,strings,
strings,ST soli [4'] BREITKOPF-W
(B234)

Largo (from Piano Sonata in E-Flat,
Op. 7)
(Schultz, J.) 0.0.1.1. 1.0.0.0.
strings [8'] BREITKOPF-W    (B235)

Nei Giorni Tuoi Felici
ST soli,orch sc KUNZELMANN EP 4833
ipa                        (B236)

O Namenlose Freude
"Fidelio: Duet Of Leonore And
Florestan" 2.2.0.2. 2.0.0.0.
strings,ST soli [3'] BREITKOPF-W
(B237)

Romance for Violin and Orchestra, No.
1, Op. 40
(Kojima, S.A.; Herttrich, E.) orch
min sc,study sc HENLE 9803
contains also: Romance for Violin
and Orchestra, No. 2, Op. 50
(B238)

Romance for Violin and Orchestra, No.
2, Op. 50
see Romance for Violin and
Orchestra, No. 1, Op. 40

Sechs Menuette  *WoO.10
(Beyer, Fr.) 2.2.2.2. 2.2.0.0.
timp,strings without vla [15']
sc,pts BREITKOPF-W PB-OB 5268
(B239)

Six Great Overtures
orch sc DOVER 24789-9      (B240)

Symphony No. 2, Op. 36, in D
(Raab, A.) orch (reduced string
parts available: Henle No. 4613)
HENLE sc 4610, pts 4611:4612
(B241)

Symphony No. 3 in E flat, Op. 55
(Hauschild) "Eroica" orch sc,pts
BREITKOPF-W PB-OB 5233     (B242)

Symphony No. 4 in B flat, Op. 60
(Hauschild) orch BREITKOPF-W sc,pts
PB-OB 5234, study sc PB 5344
(B243)

Symphony No. 5, Op. 67, in C minor
(Brown, Cl.) 2+pic.2.2.2+contrabsn.
2.2.3.0. timp,strings [36']
BREITKOPF-W sc,pts PB-OB 5235,
study sc PB 5345           (B244)

BEETHOVEN, LUDWIG VAN (cont'd.)

Symphony No. 6, Op. 68, in F
(Brown, Cl.) 2+pic.2.2.2. 2.2.2.0.
timp,strings [40'] sc,pts
BREITKOPF-W PB-OB 5236     (B245)

Symphony No. 7, Op. 92, in A
(Hauschild, P.) 2.2.2.2. 2.2.0.0.
timp,strings [38'] BREITKOPF-W
sc,pts PB-OB 5237, study sc
PB 5347                    (B246)

Symphony, Nos. 1-4
orch sc DOVER 26033-X      (B247)

Symphony, Nos. 5-7
orch sc DOVER 26034-8      (B248)

Symphony, Nos. 8-9
orch sc DOVER 26035-6      (B249)

Trauermarsch  *WoO.96 (from Leonore
Prohaska)
2.0.2.2. 4.0.0.0. strings [5']
BREITKOPF-W                (B250)

Wachtelschlag, Der  *WoO.129
(Mottl, F.) 2.2.2.2. 2.2.0.0. timp,
strings,S solo [4'] BREITKOPF-W
(B251)

Wellingtons Sieg  *Op.91
orch (reduced string parts
available: Henle 404703, Critical
Commentary 4043) HENLE sc 404700,
pts 404701:404702          (B252)

Young Prometheus, The
(Brott, Alexander) 2.2.2.2.
2.2.2.1. timp,perc,strings,
trombone may be substituted for
tuba [50'] sc CANADIAN
MI 1100 B415YO             (B253)

Zwölf Contretänze  *WoO.14
orch KUNZELMANN 10038 ipr  (B254)

Zwölf Deutsche Tänze  *WoO.8
(Kovcs) orch KUNZELMANN 10077 ipr
(B255)

Zwölf Menuette  *WoO.7
orch KUNZELMANN 10014 ipr  (B256)

BEFORE INFRARED see Ince, Kamran

BEHAR, GYORGY
Concerto for Trombone and String
Orchestra
string orch,trom solo [10'] EMB
rent                       (B257)

Három Zenekari Darab
see Three Pieces For Orchestra

Three Pieces For Orchestra
"Három Zenekari Darab" 2+pic.2+
English horn.3(bass
clar).3(contrabsn). 4.3.3.1.
timp,perc,harp,string quin [9']
EMB rent                   (B258)

BEHOLD THE SUN see Goehr, Alexander

BEHRENS, JACK (1935-    )
Declaration  *Op.43
2.2.2.2. 4.2.2.1. timp,2perc,
strings [14'] sc CANADIAN
MI 1100 B421DE             (B259)

Fantasy for String Orchestra, Op. 12
string orch [8'] sc CANADIAN
MI 1500 B421FA             (B260)

Greeting, A
2+pic.1.1.1. 1.1.1.0. 2perc,strings
[3'] sc CANADIAN MI1200 B421GR
(B261)

Introspection For String Orchestra
*Op.3
string orch [5'15"] sc CANADIAN
MI 1500 B421IN             (B262)

Occasion
string orch [9'] (Ceremony -- Games
-- Song -- Finale) sc CANADIAN
MI 1500 B421OC             (B263)

BEI DER KANONE DORT see Cornell, Klaus

BEIDEN SCHÜTZEN, DIE: OVERTURE see
Lortzing, (Gustav) Albert

BEILSCHMIDT, CURT (1886-1962)
Serenade for Chamber Orchestra in B
flat, Op. 33
1.1.1.1. 2.2.0.0. timp,strings
[18'] HEINRICH             (B264)

BEIM MÄNNERVOLK, BEI SOLDATEN see
Mozart, Wolfgang Amadeus, In
Uomini, In Soldati

BELAGERUNG VON KORINTH, DIE: OUVERTÜRE
see Rossini, Gioacchino, Siège De
Corinthe, Le: Ouverture

BELAS KNAP see Amos, Keith

BELKIN, ALAN (1951-    )
Four Emily Dickinson Songs
2(pic).2(English horn).2.2.
4.2.3.0. timp,perc,harp,strings,S
solo sc CANADIAN MV 1400 B432SY
(B265)

Nocturne
2.2(English horn).2.2. 2.2.0.0.
perc,harp,strings sc CANADIAN
MI 1100 B432NO              (B266)

Symphony No. 1
2(pic).2(English horn).2(clar in E
flat).2. 4.2.2.1. timp,2perc,
strings sc CANADIAN
MI 1100 B432SY              (B267)

Symphony No. 4
2.2.2.2. 2.2.0.0. timp,perc,harp,
strings sc CANADIAN
MI 1100 B432FO              (B268)

Symphony No. 5
2(pic).2(English horn).2.2.
4.2.3.1. timp,2perc,harp,cel,pno,
strings sc CANADIAN
MI 1100 B432SY5             (B269)

BELKIS, REGINA DI SABA see Respighi,
Ottorino

BELL, ALLAN (1953-    )
Concerto for 2 Orchestras
Orchestra 1: 1.1.1.1. 2.1.1.0.
3perc, pno; Orchestra 2: 2.2.2.2.
2.2.0.0. 2perc, kbd, strings
[15'] sc CANADIAN MI 1100 B433CO
(B270)

Drawing Down The Moon
string orch [12'] (a chamber suite.
1. Invocation 2. Lyric 3.
Benediction 4. Celebration) sc
CANADIAN MI 1500 B433DR     (B271)

Dynamus
string orch sc CANADIAN
MI 1500 B433DY             (B272)

BELLA QUANDO AURORA see Anonymous, Aria
in C

BELLA SICILIA see Mielenz, Hans

BELLE MUSIQUE, LA see Rabinowitch,
Alexandre

BELLEMARE, GILLES (1952-    )
Arguments
string orch,bsn solo [13'] sc
CANADIAN MI 1624 B439AR     (B273)

Concerto for Marimba and Orchestra
2(pic).2.2.2. 2.2.0.0. timp,harp,
strings,marimba solo (1. Préface
2. "...On Est Aussi Chez Les
Hommes..." 3. Quand Le Marimba,
Tout Bat...) sc CANADIAN
MI 1340 B439CO             (B274)

Musique Pour Neuchâtel
string orch,vln solo,ob solo sc
CANADIAN MI 1650 B439MU     (B275)

Non Piú Di Trenta
3+pic.0.2.1. 2.0.2.1. 2perc,pno,
strings [14'] sc CANADIAN
MI 1100 B439NO             (B276)

BELLINI, VINCENZO (1801-1835)
Norma: Overture
2.2.2.2. 4.2.3.1. timp,perc,
strings, serpent [5'] (no score)
BREITKOPF-W                (B277)

Romeo Und Julia: Overture
1.2.2.2. 4.2.3.1+ophicleide. timp,
perc,strings [5'] (no score)
BREITKOPF-W                (B278)

Sinfonia in E flat
2.2.2.2. 0.2.2.0. strings [10']
BOCCACCINI rent            (B279)

Tantum Ergo, For Solo Voices And
Orchestra
1.2.2.2. 2.0.0.0. strings,AT soli
[5'] BOCCACCINI BS. 156 rent
(B280)

BELLS, THE see Reaser, Ronald

BELOUNKÁ HOLUBICKO see Odstrcil, Karel

BELOVED VOICE, THE: OVERTURE see
Weinberger, Jaromir

BELTANE FIRE, THE see Davies, [Sir]
Peter Maxwell

BELTRAMI, MARCO (1966-    )
Iskios, City Of Shadows
1(pic,alto fl).1(English
horn).2(bass clar).1. 1.1.1.0.
pno,perc,2vln,vla,vcl,db [14']
PEER rent                  (B281)

BELTRAMI, MARCO (cont'd.)
Scenes From The Kingdom Of The
Dinamiten
2+pic.3(English horn).3(bass
clar).2+contrabsn. 3.4.3.1. harp,
pno/cel,3perc,timp,strings [20']
PEER rent                  (B282)

BEN-AMOTS, OFER (1955-    )
Celestial Dialogues
2perc,strings,clar solo,solo voice
[30'] sc,pts KALLISTI ipa   (B283)

BENDA, FRANZ (FRANTIŠEK) (1709-1786)
Concerto in E flat
strings,cont,vln solo [20'] CESKY
HUD.                       (B284)

BENDA, GEORG ANTON (JIŘÍ ANTONÍN)
(1722-1795)
Concerto for Cembalo and Strings in C
[18'] CESKY HUD.           (B285)

Concerto for Violin, Strings and
Continuo in B flat
[13'] CESKY HUD.           (B286)

Italské Árrie Sv. I: I.- VI. *CC6L
2.0.0.0. 2.0.0.0. cembalo,strings,
solo voice CESKY HUD. f.s. (B287)

Italské Árrie Sv. II: I.- VI. *CC6L
2.2.0.2. 2.0.0.0. cembalo,strings,
solo voice CESKY HUD. f.s. (B288)

Sinfonia in F
(Schneider, M.) 0.0.0.0. 2.0.0.0.
strings,cont [11'] BREITKOPF-W
(B289)

BENEDICT, [SIR] JULIUS (1804-1885)
Hochzeitstag, Der (Overture for
Orchestra)
(Andreas, Felix) 2.2.2.2. 4.2.3.0.
timp,perc,harp,strings [6'20"]
HEINRICH                   (B290)

Overture for Orchestra
see Hochzeitstag, Der

BENEDICTION see Bernstein, Leonard

BENGTSON, PETER (1961-    )
Orchestral Fragments
2(pic).2(English horn).2(bass
clar).2(contrabsn). 2.2.0.0.
timp,6vln I,6vln II,4vla,4vcl,2db
[14'] sc,pts STIM          (B291)

BENGUEREL, XAVIER (1931-    )
Consort Music
11 str [11'] MOECK sc 5103 f.s.,
pts rent                   (B292)

BENJAMIN, GEORGE
Sudden Time
4.3.3.3. 4.4.4.1. timp,5perc,pno,
2harp,strings [15'] FABER  (B293)

Three Inventions
2fl,ob&English horn,3clar,bsn,
2horn,trp,trom,2perc,pno&cel,
3vln,2vla,2vcl,2db [15'] FABER
(B294)

Tribute
2.1.3.1. 2.1.1.0. 2perc,pno,harp,
strings [5'] FABER         (B295)

BENNETT, RICHARD RODNEY (1936-    )
Concerto for Percussion and Orchestra
2.2.2.2. 2.2.0.0. timp,perc,strings
[22'] NOVELLO             (B296)

Concerto For Stan Getz
tenor sax,timp,strings [24']
NOVELLO                    (B297)

Variations On A Nursery Song
2.2.2.2. 4.2.3.1. timp,2perc,pno&
cel,harp,strings [15'] NOVELLO
(B298)

BENNIE THE BEAVER see Kubik, Gail

BERCEAUX, LES see Faure, Gabriel-Urbain

BERCEUSE see Sandby, Herman

BERCEUSE-RÉVERIE see Sgambati, Giovanni

BEREN AND LÚTHIEN see Buhr, Glenn

BERG, FRED JONNY (1973-    )
In The Twilight  *Op.3
3(pic).4(English horn).3(bass
clar).3. 4.2.4.0. timp,4perc,pno,
strings [5'] NORSKMI       (B299)

Lost In September  *Op.17
2.2.2.2. 4.3.3.1. timp,2perc,
strings [8'20"] NORSKMI    (B300)

People Of Blue Dimension  *Op.4b
3(pic).2.2.3(contrabsn). 4.4.3.1.
timp,3perc,harp,strings [10'30"]
NORSKMI                    (B301)

BERG, FRED JONNY (cont'd.)
Where Am I?  *Op.18
string orch,vla solo [4'30"]
NORSK                      (B302)

BERG, OLAV (1949-    )
Concerto for Clarinet and Orchestra
2.2.3(bass clar).2. 4.2.3.0. timp,
2perc,harp,strings [17'] NORSK
(B303)

Three Grieg Songs
see Tre Grieg-Sanger

Tre Grieg-Sanger
"Three Grieg Songs" string orch,S
solo (contains: "Et Håb," "Jeg
Reiste En Deilig Sommerkveld" &
"En Fuglevise") NORSKMI    (B304)

[BERGAKUNGEN OP. 37: SVIT] 1.
BESVÄRJELSE see Alfvén, Hugo

[BERGAKUNGEN OP. 37: SVIT] 2.
TROLLFLICKANS DANS see Alfvén, Hugo

[BERGAKUNGEN OP. 37: SVIT] 3.
SOMMARREGN. see Alfvén, Hugo

[BERGAKUNGEN OP. 37: SVIT] 4.
VALLFLICKANS DANS see Alfvén, Hugo

BERGE, HÅKON (1954-    )
Lavmaelt
2.2.2.2. 4.3.3(bass trom).0. timp,
2perc,strings [4'40"] NORSKMI
(B305)

Ockaia
2.2(bass clar).2. 4.3.3.0. timp,
2perc,harp,pno,strings [5'45"]
NORSKMI                    (B306)

BERGER, WILHELM (1861-1911)
Symphony in B flat, Op. 71
3(pic).2.2.2. 4.2.3.1. timp,strings
[45'] BREITKOPF-W          (B307)

BERGSMA, WILLIAM LAURENCE (1921-1994)
Changes
woodwind quin,timp,2perc,harp,
strings [9'] SCHIRM.EC rent
(B308)

Gold And The Señor Commandante:
Ballet Suite
2.1.2.2. 2.2.2.0. timp,perc,kbd,
strings [11'] SCHIRM.EC rent
(B309)

In Campo Aperto
ob solo,2bsn,strings [18']
SCHIRM.EC rent             (B310)

Sweet Was The Song The Virgin Sung
vla solo,2.2.3.2. 4.2.3.1. timp,
2perc,harp,strings [26']
SCHIRM.EC rent             (B311)

BERKELEY, MICHAEL
Concerto for Clarinet and Orchestra
2.2.2.2. 2.2.0.0. timp,strings
[20'] perf sc set OXFORD 3620456
sc,pts rent                (B312)

Concerto for Viola and Orchestra
2+pic.2+English horn.2+bass clar.2+
contrabsn. 4.3+flügelhorn.3.1.
timp,4perc,harp,strings [15']
perf sc set OXFORD 3620197 sc,pts
rent                       (B313)

Gethsemani Fragment
string orch [10'] perf sc set
OXFORD 3620545 sc,pts rent (B314)

Severn Crossing
2(pic).2(English
horn).2(contrabsn). 2.2.0.0.
timp,strings [6'] sc,pts OXFORD
362057X                    (B315)

Vision Of Piers The Ploughman, The:
Suite
2horn,pno,perc,strings [12'] perf
sc set OXFORD 3620413 sc,pts rent
(B316)

BERKOVEC, JIŘÍ (1922-    )
Aktuality
2.2.0.1. 2.0.0.0. strings [12']
CESKY HUD.                 (B317)

Miniatury
strings,fl/vln solo [10'] CESKY
HUD.                       (B318)

Rozmarné Léto (Suite for Orchestra)
3.2.2.2. 4.3.3.1. timp,perc,pno,
strings [19'] CESKY HUD.   (B319)

Slavnostní Pochod
3.2.3.2. 4.3.3.1. timp,perc,strings
[4'] CESKY HUD.            (B320)

Suite for Orchestra
see Rozmarné Léto

BERKOVEC, JIŘÍ (cont'd.)

Tavba
3.3.3.3. 4.3.3.1. perc,pno,strings
[14'] CESKY HUD.                (B321)

Variace Na Téma Adama Michny
3.2.2.2. 4.2.3.1. timp,perc,strings
[20'] CESKY HUD.                (B322)

Variace Na Téma J. A. Bendy Ve Starém
Slohu
2.0.0.1. 0.0.0.0. cembalo,strings
CESKY HUD.                      (B323)

BERLINER DIVERTIMENTO see Meyer, Ernst
Hermann

BERLINER MOMENTE II see Boudreau,
Walter

BERLIOZ, HECTOR (LOUIS) (1803-1869)
Flucht Nach Ägypten, Die: Overture
see Fuite En Egypte, La: Overture

Fuite En Egypte, La: Overture (from
L'enfance Du Christ, Op. 25)
"Flucht Nach Ägypten, Die:
Overture" 2.2.0.0. 0.0.0.0.
strings [9'] BREITKOPF-W       (B324)

March (from Symphonie Fantastique,
Op. 14)
4.4.4.4. 4.2.2.3+ophicleide. timp,
perc,harp,org,strings [6']
BREITKOPF-W                    (B325)

Rob-Roy: Overture
2.2.2.2. 4.3.3.0. timp,harp,strings
[13'] BREITKOPF-W             (B326)

Roman Carnival And Other Overtures
orch sc DOVER 28750-5          (B327)

Symphonie Fantastique & Harold In
Italy
orch sc DOVER 24657-4          (B328)

BERMEL, DEREK
Dust Dances
3(pic,alto fl).3(English
horn).3(clar in E flat,bass
clar).3(contrabsn). 4.3.3(bass
trom).1. timp,3perc,pno&cel,harp,
strings [9'50"] MARKS rent    (B329)

BERNABEI, GIUSEPPE ANTONIO (1649-1732)
Fiera, La
(Lehrndorfer, F.) "Jahrmarkt, Der"
S,A soli,fl,strings sc,pts
KUNZELMANN GM 893 ipa          (B330)

Jahrmarkt, Der
see Fiera, La

BERNAOLA, CARMELO (1929-    )
!Imita! Imita, Que Algo Queda
3.2.0.1. 3.3.0.0. 4perc,strings,
clar solo [15'] perf sc EMEC f.s.
                               (B331)

Impulsos
4.2+2English horn.3.3. 6.3.3.1.
3perc,timp,pno,2harp,strings BOIS
                               (B332)

BERNÁTEK, JAN (1950-    )
Concerto for Piano and Orchestra
2.2.3.3. 4.3.3.1. timp,perc,
strings,pno solo [22'] CESKY HUD.
                               (B333)

BERNERT, HELMUT (1896-1979)
Concerto for Violin and Orchestra
orch,vln solo BÖHM             (B334)

BERNIER, RENE (1905-1984)
C'est L'heire Aux Volets Clos
see Evasions

Évasions
2.2.2.2. 2.2.0.0. cel,bells,harp,
strings,med solo LEDUC f.s.
contains: C'est L'heire Aux
Volets Clos; Ô Muse Dont Les
Pas Dansent                    (B335)

Lettre D'Un Ami
strings,med solo [6'30"] LEDUC
                               (B336)

Ô Muse Dont Les Pas Dansent
see Évasions

BERNSTEIN, LEONARD (1918-1990)
Arias And Barcarolles
(Coughlin, Bruce) 1(pic).1(English
horn).1(clar in E flat,alto
sax).1. 2.1.0.0. 2perc,strings,
MezBar soli [31'] (text by Jennie
Bernstein, Yankev-Yitskhok Segal,
Leonard Bernstein) BOOSEY-ENG
rent                           (B337)

Benediction (from Concerto For
Orchestra)
2.2+English horn.2+bass clar.2+
contrabsn. 4.3.3.1. harp,strings,
electronic tape, or baritone solo
[8'] BOOSEY-ENG rent          (B338)

BERNSTEIN, LEONARD (cont'd.)

Candide Suite
2(pic).1(English horn).2(clar in E
flat,bass clar).1.opt soprano
sax. 2.2.2.1. timp,2perc,harp,
strings,SSMezTTBarBarB soli,cor
[50'] BOOSEY-ENG rent         (B339)

Dream With Me
(Ramin, Sid) 2.1.2+bass clar.0.
2.2.2.0. perc,harp,pno,strings,S
solo [9'] (text by Leonard
Bernstein) BOOSEY-ENG rent    (B340)

Quiet Place, A: Suite
(Ramin, Sid; Thomas, Michael
Tilson; Barrett, Michael) 3(alto
fl,pic).2+English horn.3(clar in
E flat)+bass clar.2+
contrabsn.alto sax. 4.3.3.1.
timp,5-6perc,kbd,harp,strings
[25'] BOOSEY-ENG rent         (B341)

West Side Story: Concert Suite No. 1
2.1(English horn).3(bass clar).1.
2.3.2.0. timp,2perc,elec gtr,pno&
cel,strings without vla,ST soli
[18'] (contains: Maria; One Hand,
One Heart; Somewhere; Balcony
Scene) BOOSEY-ENG rent        (B342)

West Side Story: Concert Suite No. 2
3(pic).1.4(clar in E flat,bass
clar,alto sax).1.tenor
sax.soprano sax(bass sax).
2.3.2.0. timp,4perc,gtr/elec gtr,
pno&cel,strings without vla,
SMezMezMezTBarBar soli,cor [15']
(contains: I Feel Pretty, Jet
Song, America, Tonight Quintet)
BOOSEY-ENG rent               (B343)

Wonderful Town: Selections
4trp,3trom,perc,strings, 5 groups
of woodwinds Reed I: fl, clar,
clref, saxa Reed II: clar, bsclr,
saxa, saxd, saxb Reed III: ob,
clar, saxt Reed IV: pic, fl,
bsclr, saxt Reed V: clar, saxa,
saxd, saxb, bsn BOOSEY-ENG rent
                               (B344)

BERRY, WALLACE (1928-1991)
Acadian Images
2.2.3+bass clar.3+contrabsn.
4.2.3.1. timp,2perc,strings [19']
sc CANADIAN MI 1100 B534AC    (B345)

Canto Elegiaco
3(pic).3+English horn.3+bass
clar.3+contrabsn. 4.3.4.1. timp,
2perc,harp,strings sc CANADIAN
MI 1100 B534CA                (B346)

Credo In Unam Vitam
1.0.1.2(contrabsn).baritone sax.
0.2.1.1. perc,pno,strings,T solo,
vcl solo,horn solo (1. Prologue
2. Testament 3. Epilogue) sc
CANADIAN MV 1775 B534CR       (B347)

Intonation: Victimis Hominum
Inhumanitatis In Memoriam
2.2.3+bass clar.3+contrabsn.
4.2.3.1. timp,2perc,strings sc
CANADIAN MI 1100 B534IN       (B348)

BERSERKING, THE see Macmillan, James

BERTOMEU, AGUSTIN (1929-    )
Concerto for Violoncello and
Orchestra
3.3.3.3. 4.3.3.1. timp,perc,harp,
strings,vcl solo [29'] perf sc
EMEC f.s.                      (B349)

Configuraciones Sinfonicas
2.2.3.3. 4.3.3.0. timp,cel,vibra,
pno,strings [18'] perf sc EMEC
f.s.                           (B350)

BERTONI, FERDINANDO (GIUSEPPE)
(1725-1813)
Sinfonia in C
(Müller) 2fl,2horn,strings
KUNZELMANN ipa sc 10080A, oct
10080                          (B351)

BERWALD, FRANZ (ADOLF) (1796-1868)
Bayarderen-Fest
orch REIMERS 109058 rent      (B352)

Concerto for Bassoon
REIMERS 109060 rent           (B353)

Erinnerung An Die Norwegischen Alpen
orch REIMERS 109057 rent      (B354)

Sinfonie Capricieuse
(Castegren, Nils) orch (Urtext
Edition) REIMERS 109054 rent  (B355)

Sinfonie Naïve (Symphony in E flat)
(Castegren, Nils) orch (Urtext
Edition) study sc REIMERS 109051
rent                           (B356)

BERWALD, FRANZ (ADOLF) (cont'd.)

Sinfonie Sérieuse
(Hedwall, Lennart) orch (Urtext
Edition) study sc REIMERS 109053
                               (B357)

Sinfonie Singulière
(Blomstedt, Herbert) orch (Urtext
Edition) study sc REIMERS 109050
                               (B358)

Symphony in E flat
see Sinfonie Naïve

Tema Mit Variationen
orch REIMERS 109056 rent      (B359)

Tongemälde I: Slaget Vid Leipzig;
Ernste Und Heitere Grillen;
Elfenspiel
(Hedwall, Lennart) 2(pic).2.2.2.
4.2.3.0. timp,perc,strings sc
BÄREN. ED.NR BA 4908          (B360)

Wettlauf
orch REIMERS 109059 rent      (B361)

BESIDE THE LAKE see King, Reginald

BESKYDSKÁ EPIZODA see Petrov, Vadim

BESKYDY see Oborny, Vaclav

BESOZZI, CARLO (1738-1754)
Concerto for Oboe, String Orchestra
and Harpsichord, No. 1, in C
orch KUNZELMANN ipa sc 10275A, oct
10275                          (B362)

Concerto No. 1 in D for Oboe, String
Orchestra and Harpsichord
ob solo,string orch,hpsd pno-cond
sc KUNZELMANN 10275           (B363)

BESVRJELSE see Blomberg, Erik

BETANCUR-GONZALEZ, VALENTIN (1952-    )
Concerto for Viola and Orchestra
[29'30"] sc ALPUERTO 1721     (B364)

Concerto for Violin and Orchestra
[20'-25'] sc ALPUERTO 1719    (B365)

Concerto No. 2 for Guitar and Strings
[25'-35'] sc ALPUERTO 1718    (B366)

Elegy (from Instantes)
2.2.2.2. 4.2.2.0. timp,harp/cel,
strings [9'-12'] sc ALPUERTO 1710
                               (B367)

Exhorto
"Misiva Del Plata, Una" 2pno,cym,
drums,vibra,timp,strings,speaking
voice [15'-18'] sc ALPUERTO 1720
                               (B368)

Glasperlenspiel, Das
see Sinfonia No. 1

Holocausto
see Sinfonia No. 2

Misiva Del Plata, Una
see Exhorto

Poema Mistico
orch,vln solo [14'-18'] sc ALPUERTO
1717                           (B369)

Requiem
orch,ST&narrator [58'-65'] sc
ALPUERTO 1714                 (B370)

Sinfonia No. 1
"Glasperlenspiel, Das"
3(pic).3(English horn).3(bass
clar).3(contrabsn). 4.3.3.1.
timp,snare drum,wood blocks,
temple blocks,strings [35'-45']
sc ALPUERTO 1711              (B371)

Sinfonia No. 1,First Movement
see Suite

Sinfonia No. 2
"Holocausto" 3(pic).3(3English
horn).3(bass clar).3(contrabsn).
4.3.3.1. timp,pno,harp,strings
[38'-45'] sc ALPUERTO 1713    (B372)

Steppenwolf, Der (Suite) (from El
Lobo Estepario)
orch,S&2 narrators,vla solo [25'-
35'] sc ALPUERTO 1715         (B373)

Suite (Sinfonia No. 1,First Movement)
(from Das Glasperlenspiel)
3(pic).3(English horn).3(bass
clar).3(contrabsn). 4.3.3.1.
timp,strings [7'-9'] sc ALPUERTO
1712                           (B374)
see Steppenwolf, Der

BETTS, LORNE M. (1918-1985)
Be In Me As The Eternal Moods Of The
Bleak Winds
see Five Songs For High Voice &
String Orchestra

BETTS, LORNE M. (cont'd.)

Concerto for Violoncello, Piano and
Orchestra
2.2.2.2. 4.2.2.1. perc,strings,pno
solo,vcl solo [16'] sc CANADIAN
MI 1450 B565CO                    (B375)

Corona, La
string orch,S solo [20'] sc
CANADIAN MV 1600 B565CO          (B376)

Drink Me A Skoal
see Five Songs For High Voice &
String Orchestra

Five Songs For High Voice & String
Orchestra
sc CANADIAN MV 1600 B565FI f.s.
contains: Be In Me As The Eternal
Moods Of The Bleak Winds; Drink
Me A Skoal; I Ha' Seen Them
'Mid The Clouds On The Heather;
No More For Us The Little
Sighing; Pan Is Dead         (B377)

I Ha' Seen Them 'Mid The Clouds On
The Heather
see Five Songs For High Voice &
String Orchestra

No More For Us The Little Sighing
see Five Songs For High Voice &
String Orchestra

Pan Is Dead
see Five Songs For High Voice &
String Orchestra

Suite for Chamber Orchestra
2.2.2.2. 0.0.0.0. timp,perc,strings
[11'] sc CANADIAN MI1200 B565SU
                                  (B378)
Two Sketches For Small Orchestra
2.2.2.2. 2.1.0.0. perc,harp,strings
[10'] sc CANADIAN MI1200 B565TS
                                  (B379)

BETULIA LIBERATA: OUVERTÜRE see Mozart,
Wolfgang Amadeus

BETWEEN DREAMS AND FAIRY TALES see
Wullur, Sinta

BETWEEN NIGHTBAR AND FACTORY see Kemp,
Bart De

BETWEEN TEN see Hoffman, Joel

BETWEEN YOU see Hui, Melissa

BEURDEN, BERNARD VAN (1933-    )
Concertino for Orchestra
3.3.3.3. 4.3.0.0. timp,3perc,
strings [17'] sc DONEMUS  (B380)

Symphonie À Trente
2.3.2.0.4sax. 1.1.1.1. timp,6perc,
3vln,vla,vcl,db [22'] sc DONEMUS
                                  (B381)

BEWEGT see Hedstrom, Åse

BEYOND THE LAND see Adler, Samuel Hans

BEYOND THE SOUND BARRIER see Lauber,
Anne, Au-Dela Du Mur Du Son

BEZDEK, JIRI (1961-    )
Concerto for Piano and Orchestra
3.2.2.2. 4.3.3.1. timp,perc,
strings,pno solo [23'] CESKY HUD.
                                  (B382)
Tri Vety
3.3.2.2. 4.2.2.1. perc,strings
[16'] CESKY HUD.                  (B383)

BIBALO, ANTONIO (1922-    )
Concertante: For Wind Quintet And
Orchestra
0.0.0.0. 4.3.4.0. timp,2perc,pno,
harp,strings,woodwind quin soli
[13'50"] NORSKMI                  (B384)

BICENTENNIAL SUITE see Walker, Gwyneth

BIENE, DIE see Schubert, Franz (Peter)

BIG LONELY see Symonds, Norman

BIGGS, JOHN (1932-    )
Ballad Of William Sycamore, The
orch,narrator [15'] study sc
CONSORT PR                        (B385)

Concerto for Viola, Woodwinds and
Percussion
chamber orch,vla&2fl&2clar&2bsn&
perc soli [22'] study sc CONSORT
PR CP 304                         (B386)

Concerto for Violoncello and Chamber
Orchestra
2ob,2bsn,2horn,strings [22'] study
sc CONSORT PR CP 316              (B387)

BIGGS, JOHN (cont'd.)

Pastiche
2.2.2.2. 4.3.3.1. timp,2perc,
strings [6'] study sc CONSORT PR
CP 313                            (B388)

Salutation
2.2.2.2. 4.3.3.1. timp,2perc,
strings [26'] study sc CONSORT PR
CP 314                            (B389)

Symphony No. 2
2.2.2.2. 4.3.3.1. timp,3perc,hpsd,
strings [20'] study sc CONSORT PR
CP 312                            (B390)

BIGUINE see Moross, Jerome

BILD see Blomberg, Erik

BILDER AUS DEM SCHOTTISCHEN HOCHLAND
see Bantock, [Sir] Granville

BILDER AUS DEM SÜDEN see Nicode, Jean
Louis

BILDER EINER AUSSTELLUNG see
Mussorgsky, Modest Petrovich

BILDER ZU EINEM RUSSISCHE ALPHABET see
Tcherepnin, Nikolay Nikolayevich

BILDER ZU EINEM RUSSISCHEN ALPHABET see
Tcherepnin, Nikolay Nikolayevich

BILDERSERENADE see Bredemeyer, Reiner

BILDNIS EINER FRAU see Eichhorn, Frank
Volker, Porträt

BILDNISSE III see Kirchner, Volker
David

BILLIGE LIEDER see Kaufmann, Dieter

BILLOWING FIELDS OF GOLDEN WHEAT see
Coulthard, Jean

BILLY AND THE CARNIVAL: A CHILDREN'S
GUIDE TO THE INSTRUMENTS see Dorff,
Daniel Jay

BÍLY, ANTONIN (1939-    )
Promeny Casu
2.2.3.3. 4.3.3.1. timp,perc,
strings, jazz band: fl, 3sax,
trp, trb, drums, pno, gt, db
[20'] CESKY HUD.                  (B391)

BINET, JEAN (1893-1960)
Drei Stücke
string orch min sc HUG FF 8004
                                  (B392)
Petit Concert
clar,strings [8'] HENN H 532 (B393)

BINKERD, GORDON WARE (1916-    )
Two Meditations For Strings
string orch [5'] BOOSEY-ENG rent
                                  (B394)

BIOFONIA see Homs, Joaquin

BIRD FANCYER'S DELIGHT, THE see Wilby,
Philip

BIRD NAMED BYRD, A see Stein

BIRDCAGE see Sexton, Brian

BIRDS OF LOVE see Farkas, Ferenc

BIRKENKÖTTER, JÖRG
Klänge Schatten
1(pic).1(English horn).1(bass
clar).1(contrabsn). 1.1.1.0.
3perc,harp,pno/cel,vln,vla,vcl,db
[23'] BREITKOPF-W                 (B395)

...Zur Nähe-Voran
3(2pic).3(English horn).3(bass
clar).3(contrabsn). 4.3.3.1.
timp,3perc,harp,cel&pno,strings
[17'] BREITKOPF-W                 (B396)

BIRTWISTLE, HARRISON (1934-    )
Cry Of Anubis, The
2.2.2.2. 4.2.0.0. timp,perc,harp,
strings,tuba solo [13'] BOOSEY-
ENG                               (B397)

Gawain's Journey
3.3.3.3. 4.3.3.1. euphonium,timp,
5perc,cym,harp,strings [25']
UNIVER.                           (B398)

Panic
3.3.3.3. 4.4.3.1. timp,alto sax,
perc, drum kit, [18'] BOOSEY-ENG
                                  (B399)
Ritual Fragment
fl,ob,clar,bsn,horn,trp,bass trp,
perc,bass drum,pno,strings [11']
UNIVER.                           (B400)

BISSELL, KEITH W. (1912-1992)
Canada 1967
2.2.2.2. 2.2.2.0. timp,perc,strings
pts CANADIAN MI 1100 B623CA
                                  (B401)

BIZET, GEORGES (1838-1875)
Andantino *Op.22
string orch sc,pts KUNZELMANN
WW 904 ipa                        (B402)

Fantaisie Brillante (from Carmen)
(Borne) orch sc KUNZELMANN 10260A
ipa                               (B403)
(Borne) fl solo,orch oct KUNZELMANN
10260 ipa                         (B404)
(Borne) sax solo,orch oct
KUNZELMANN 10260B ipa            (B405)

Fantasy for Flute and Orchestra
(composed with Borne)
(Meylan, Raymond) fl solo,orch
(also available in a version for
saxophone) pno-cond sc KUNZELMANN
10260                             (B406)

Kleine Orchestersuite (Kinderspiele)
*Op.22
2.2.2.2. 4.2.1.0. timp,perc,strings
[10'] BREITKOPF-W                 (B407)

BJÖRKLUND, STAFFAN (1944-    )
Concerto in G for Piano and Orchestra
2(pic),2.3(bass clar).3(contrabsn).
4.2.2.1. timp,perc,strings,pno
solo STIM                         (B408)

BJORKLUND, TERJE (1945-    )
Arctos (Concerto for Violin and
Strings)
string orch,vln solo NORSKMI (B409)

Cantio For Viola And Strings
strings,vla solo NORSKMI         (B410)

Concerto for Violin and Strings
see Arctos

BJURLING, BJÖRN (1966-    )
Infected
4vln I,4vln II,3vla,2vcl,db [7']
STIM                              (B411)

Pisodes, Les
chamber orch [12'] STIM          (B412)

BLACK, STANLEY (1915-    )
Costume Comedy Overture, A
2.2.2.2. 2.2.0.0. timp,strings [4']
BOOSEY-ENG rent                   (B413)

Percussion Fantasy
2.2.2.2. 2.2.0.0. timp,perc,strings
[6'] BOOSEY-ENG rent              (B414)

BLACK AND WHITE CONCERTO see Hallberg,
Bengt

BLACK CAT, THE see Foley, Daniel

BLACK MASKERS, THE see Sessions, Roger

BLACK STALLION'S RETURN, THE see
Delerue, Georges

BLACK SUN see Boyd, Anne

BLÁHA, OLDRICH (1930-    )
Pohlazeni
2.1.2.2. 4.2.3.1. perc,harp,
strings,English horn solo CESKY
HUD.                              (B415)

Tri Písne
2.1.3.0. 3.3.3.0. timp,perc,pno,
3gtr,strings,solo voice [8']
CESKY HUD.                        (B416)

BLAKE, DAVID (1936-    )
Concerto for Violoncello and
Orchestra
2.2.2.2. 2.2.2.0. timp,2perc,pno,
strings,vcl solo [25'] NOVELLO
                                  (B417)

Griffin's Tale, The
2(pic).1+bass clar.1. 2.1.1.0.
2perc,pno,strings,Bar solo [32']
sc UNIV.YORK 0001 f.s.            (B418)

BLAKE, HOWARD (1938-    )
Agatha Suite
2.2.2.2. 4.2.3.1. timp,perc,cel,
harp,strings [12'] FABER         (B419)

Christmas Lullaby
1.0.1.0. 0.0.0.0. strings,SMez/TBar
soli [4'] FABER                   (B420)

Concerto for Piano and Orchestra
2.2.2.2. 4.2.2.0. timp,perc,
strings,pno solo [27'] FABER
                                  (B421)
Concerto for Violin and Orchestra
2.2.2.3. 4.4.0.0. timp,perc,harp,
strings,vln solo [35'] FABER
                                  (B422)

**BLAKE, HOWARD** (cont'd.)

Month In The Country, A (Suite)
  string orch sc FABER 58043 2 f.s.
                                (B423)

Snowmam, The: Suite
  strings FABER f.s. sc,pts 51121 X,
  pts 58036 X                (B424)

Suite
  see Month In The Country, A

**BLAKE, MICHAEL**

Kwela
  2(pic).2.2.2. 2.2.0.0. perc,2vln,
  vla,vcl,db [10'] BARDIC     (B425)

Out Of The Darkness
  2(pic).1.2(clar in E flat,bass
  clar).1. 2.0.0.0. pno,perc,harp,
  2vcl,db [10'] BARDIC      (B426)

Seasons, The
  0.0.2(bass clar).0. 0.0.0.0. gtr,
  perc,vln,vcl [17'] BARDIC  (B427)

Self Delectative Songs
  0.0.1(bass clar).0.
  0.1(flügelhorn).0.0. pno,marimba&
  vibra,vln [12'30"] BARDIC  (B428)

BLAKE-BILD II see Smirnov, Dmitri,
  Jakobsleiter, Die

BLAKE-BILD IV see Smirnov, Dmitri,
  Fluss Des Lebens, Der

BLAKE SONGS see Mernier, Benoit

BLANENSKÁ SUITA see Zouhar, Zdenek

BLATÁCKÉ TANCE C. 1 A 2 see Vodrazka,
  Karel

**BLATNY, JOSEF** (1891-1980)

Overtura Seria *Op.35
  2.2.2.2. 4.2.3.1. timp,harp,strings
  [10'] CESKY HUD.        (B429)

**BLATNY, PAVEL** (1931-　　)

Hommage À Gustav Mahler
  1.1.1.1. 4.2.0.1. timp,perc,harp,
  strings [4'] CESKY HUD.   (B430)

In Modo Classico
  0.0.0.0.4sax. 0.3.3.0. perc,db,
  string quar [11'] CESKY HUD.
                              (B431)

Jubilejní Koláz
  2.2.2.2. 4.3.3.0. timp,perc,strings
  [9'] CESKY HUD.         (B432)

Jubilejni Predehra
  see Nénie Za Moji Matku

Kruh
  string orch [8'] CESKY HUD. (B433)

Nénie Za Moji Matku
  "Jubilejni Predehra" 3.2.2.2.
  4.3.3.1. timp,perc,2harp,pno,
  synthesizer,strings [13'] CESKY
  HUD.                        (B434)

Symphony
  3.2.2.2. 4.4.3.1. timp,perc,xylo,
  harp,pno,strings [30'] CESKY HUD.
                              (B435)

Zvony
  3.2.2.2. 4.3.3.1. perc,harp,pno,
  strings [11'] CESKY HUD.  (B436)

BLAUE REITER, DER see Rossum, Frederic
  R. van

**BLAZEK, ZDENEK** (1905-1988)

Concerto for Bassoon and String
  Orchestra, Op. 171
  [17'] CESKY HUD.         (B437)

Suite for Chamber Orchestra, Op. 166
  2.2.2.2. 2.2.0.0. timp,strings
  [18'] CESKY HUD.        (B438)

BLAZON see Gregson, Edward

BLESSED VIRGIN'S EXPOSTULATION, THE see
  Purcell, Henry

**BLEUSE, MARC** (1937-　　)

Char Des Ames, Le
  strings,timp,vcl solo [16']
  BILLAUDOT              (B439)

Deux Tableaux Symphoniques
  2.2.2.2. 4.2.1.1. perc,strings,S
  solo [19'] BILLAUDOT rent (B440)
  2.2.2.2. 4.2.1.1. perc,strings,clar
  solo [19'] BILLAUDOT rent (B441)

Sur Les Rives Du Trop Tard
  strings,timp,vcl solo [16']
  BILLAUDOT              (B442)

**BLEYLE, KARL** (1880-1969)

Bacchanten-Ouvertüre, Op. 52
  2.2.2.2. 3.2.0.1. timp,perc,harp,
  strings [5'] BREITKOPF-W  (B443)

Schneewittchensuite *Op.50
  2.2.2.2. 3.2.0.1. timp,harp,strings
  [15'] BREITKOPF-W      (B444)

BLISSFUL MUSIC see Raskatov, Alexander

BLISWORTH TUNNEL BLUES see Nicholson,
  George

BLITHE BELLS (J.S.BACH) see Grainger,
  Percy Aldridge

BLITZSCHLAG see Dillon, James

**BLITZSTEIN, MARC** (1905-1964)

Concerto for Piano
  2+pic.2.2.2+contrabsn. 4.2.3.1.
  strings without db [24'] BOOSEY-
  ENG rent               (B445)

Orchestra Variations
  2+pic.2+English horn.3(clar in E
  flat)+bass clar.2+contrabsn. 4.2+
  2cornet.3.1. timp,perc,pno,
  strings [15'] BOOSEY-ENG rent (B446)

Surf And Seaweed: Suite
  1.1.1.1(contrabsn). 0.1.0.0. pno,
  strings without db [16'] BOOSEY-
  ENG rent               (B447)

BLÍZÍM SE K TOBE see Precechtel, Zbynek

**BLOCH, ERNEST** (1880-1959)

Schelomo
  see Bruch, Max, Kol Nidrei

**BLODEK, VILEM (WILHELM)** (1834-1874)

V Studni. Mladá Láska
  2.2.2.2. 4.2.3.1. timp,strings,SA
  soli [3'] CESKY HUD.     (B448)

V Studni. Predehra K Opere
  2.2.2.2. 4.2.3.0. timp,perc,strings
  [7'] CESKY HUD.        (B449)

V Studni. Smes Z Opery Upravil J.
  Maly
  2.2.2.2. 3.2.3.0. timp,perc,strings
  CESKY HUD.             (B450)

V Studni. Vstupní Árie Veruny
  2.2.2.2. 4.2.0.0. timp,strings,A
  solo [4'] CESKY HUD.     (B451)

V Studni. Vychod Mesice
  2.2.2.2. 4.2.3.1. timp,perc,harp,
  strings [5'] CESKY HUD.   (B452)

V Studni. Zpev Janka
  2.2.2.2. 4.2.0.0. timp,strings,B
  solo [3'] CESKY HUD.     (B453)

**BLOMBERG, ERIK** (1922-　　)

Besvrjelse
  string orch [6'] sc STIM   (B454)

Bild
  string orch [3'] sc STIM   (B455)

Chaconne
  2.2.2.2. 2.2.2.1. strings [5'] STIM
  sc H-1629B, pts T-3385   (B456)

Dalarster
  1.1.2.1. 2.2.1.0. strings [10'] sc,
  pt STIM                (B457)

Dansscen
  2.2.2.2. 2.2.2.1. timp,strings [6']
  sc STIM                (B458)

Defilering
  2.2.2.2. 2.2.2.1. strings STIM (B459)

Efterdans
  2.2.2.2. 2.2.2.1. strings [5'] STIM
                              (B460)

Entré
  2.2.2.2. 2.2.2.1. timp,strings [5']
  STIM sc H-2838, pts T-2755 (B461)

Episod
  2.2.2.2. 2.2.2.1. strings [5'] sc
  STIM                   (B462)

Fest
  2.2.2.2. 2.2.2.1. timp,strings [7']
  sc STIM                (B463)

Frvandlingar
  string orch [7'] sc STIM   (B464)

Gåtfull Moll Och Living Moll: Två
  Stycken För Orkester
  2.2.2.2. 2.2.2.1. timp,strings
  [12'] sc,pts STIM H-2590  (B465)

Kväde 2
  2.2.2.2. 2.2.2.1. strings [7'] sc
  STIM                  (B466)

**BLOMBERG, ERIK** (cont'd.)

Kväde 3
  2.2.2.2. 2.2.2.1. timp,strings
  [5'5"] sc STIM         (B467)

Kvde 4
  string orch [3'5"] sc STIM (B468)

Lek
  2.2.2.2. 2.2.2.1. strings [5'] sc
  STIM H-1629A         (B469)

Liten Symfoni
  2.2.2.0. 2.2.2.0. strings [12'] sc
  STIM                  (B470)

Omvandlingar
  2.2.2.2. 2.2.2.1. strings [12'] sc
  STIM T-3388          (B471)

Polonaise
  2.2.2.2. 2.2.2.1. strings [5'] STIM
  sc H 2839, pts T-2755    (B472)

Sjuttonårsmelodik
  2.2.2.2. 2.2.2.1. timp,strings [5']
  sc STIM T-3369        (B473)

Strkrock
  string orch [4'] sc STIM   (B474)

Study for Viola and String Orchestra
  STIM                  (B475)

Symphony No. 8
  2.2.2.2. 2.2.2.1. timp,strings
  [23'] sc STIM H-2853    (B476)

Symphony No. 9
  2.2.2.2. 2.2.2.1. strings [23'] sc
  STIM                  (B477)

**BLOMDAHL, KARL-BIRGER** (1916-1968)

Symphony No. 1
  3.2.3.2. 4.3.3.1. timp,strings
  [26'] STIM sc T-0806, H-111, pts
  T-0807                (B478)

BLOOD AND GUTS: MEDLEY see Barnes,
  Milton

BLOOD OF SEYAVASH, THE see Ranjbaran,
  Behzad

BLOOD ON THE FLOOR see Turnage, Mark-
  Anthony

BLOWS, 56 see Singleton, Alvin

BLUE FIDDLER see Larsen, Elizabeth B.
  (Libby)

BLUE LIKE AN ORANGE see Daugherty,
  Michael

BLUE PETER see Crawley, Clifford

**BLUM, THOMAS** (1971-　　)

Overture for Orchestra, No. 2
  2.2.2.2. 3.2.3.0. timp,strings [4']
  STIM                  (B479)

Poem: Romantisk Stilstudie
  orch [10'] STIM        (B480)

Sinfonia No.1 (Symphony No. 1)
  2.2.2.2. 4.2.2.0. timp,2perc,
  strings [30'] (1. Andante Con
  Moto 2. Moderato 3. Interludium
  4. Finale) sc STIM H-2597 (B481)

Symphony No. 1
  see Sinfonia No.1

**BLYTON, CAREY** (1932-　　)

Golden Road To Samarkand, The (Suite
  for Orchestra, Op. 100, in Three
  Movements)
  2(pic).2.2.2. 4.3.3.1. timp,2perc,
  2vln,vla,vcl,db [10'] BARDIC
                              (B482)

Hobbit, The (Overture for Orchestra,
  Op. 52)
  2.1.2.1. 2.2.1.0. 2perc,2vln,vla,
  vcl,db,opt harp [5'] BARDIC
                              (B483)

On Holiday (Suite for Strings, Op.
  54, in Three Movements)
  string orch [6'30"] BARDIC  (B484)

Overture for Orchestra, Op. 52
  see Hobbit, The

Suite for Orchestra, Op. 100, in
  Three Movements
  see Golden Road To Samarkand, The

Suite for Strings, Op. 54, in Three
  Movements
  see On Holiday

BOCCADORO, CARLO (1963-    )
Adagio
1.1.1.1. 1.0.0.0. 2vln,vla,vcl,db
[9'] SONZOGNO rent            (B485)

Dulcis Memoria
string orch,clar [11'] SONZOGNO
rent                         (B486)

Movement
2.2.2.2. 2.2.0.0. timp,harp,strings
[9'] SONZOGNO rent           (B487)

BOCCHERINI, LUIGI (1743-1805)
Concerto for Violoncello and
Orchestra in A, Giegling 476
2ob,2horn,strings,vcl solo [20']
BOCCACCINI rent              (B488)

Concerto for Violoncello and
Orchestra in B flat
(Fritzsch) orch,vcl solo sc,pts
BREITKOPF-W PB-OB 5287       (B489)

Concerto for Violoncello and Strings
in D, No. 2, Ge. 479
(Pais) sc RICORDI-IT GZ 6076 (B490)

Concerto for Violoncello and Strings
in G, No. 3, Ge. 480
(Pais) sc RICORDI-IT GZ 6079 (B491)

Concerto for Violoncello, 2 Flutes
and Strings in D, No. 7, Ge. 476
(Pais) sc RICORDI-IT GZ 6057 (B492)

Concerto for Violoncello, 2 Horns and
Strings in A, No. 6, Ge. 475
(Pais) sc RICORDI-IT GZ 6117 (B493)

Concerto for Violoncello, 2 Horns and
Strings in B flat, No. 9, Ge. 482
(Pais) sc RICORDI-IT GZ 6120 (B494)

Concerto for Violoncello, 2 Horns and
Strings in C, No. 1, Ge. 477
(Pais) sc RICORDI-IT GZ 6063 (B495)

Concerto for Violoncello, 2 Horns and
Strings in C, No. 4, Ge. 481
(Pais) sc RICORDI-IT GZ 6082 (B496)

Concerto for Violoncello, 2 Oboes, 2
Horns and Strings in D, No. 8,
Ge. 478
(Pais) sc RICORDI-IT GZ 6085 (B497)

Concerto for Violoncello, 2 Oboes, 2
Horns and Strings in D, No. 10,
Ge. 483
(Pais) sc RICORDI-IT GZ 6020 (B498)

Concerto for Violoncello, 2 Oboes, 2
Horns and Strings in E flat, No.
5, Ge. 474
(Pais) sc RICORDI-IT GZ 6114 (B499)

Concerto for Violoncello, 2 Oboes,
Trumpet and Strings in C, No. 11,
Ge. 573
(Pais) sc RICORDI-IT GZ 6060 (B500)

BÖCKLIN-SYMPHONIE see Huber, Hans

BODOROVA, SYLVIE (1954-    )
Canto Di Lode
3.3.3.3. 4.4.3.1. timp,perc,harp,
strings,SMezATBarB soli [7']
CESKY HUD.                   (B501)

Concertino Doppio Con Eco
string orch,2vln&vcl soli [7']
CESKY HUD.                   (B502)

Concerto for Organ, Strings and
Percussion
see Pontem Video

Jubiloso
2.2.2.2. 2.2.0.0. perc,strings [8']
CESKY HUD.                   (B503)

Magikon
strings,ob solo [10'] CESKY HUD.
                             (B504)

Panamody
strings,fl solo [8'] CESKY HUD.
                             (B505)

Plankty
3.3.3.3. 4.4.3.1. timp,perc,harp,
pno,strings,vla solo [13'] CESKY
HUD.                         (B506)

Pontem Video (Concerto for Organ,
Strings and Percussion)
perc,strings,org solo [13'] CESKY
HUD.                         (B507)

Slunecná Svita
2.2.2.2. 4.2.2.1. timp,perc,strings
[13'] CESKY HUD.             (B508)

Tre Canzoni Da Suonare
string orch,gtr solo [6'] CESKY
HUD.                         (B509)

BOEHMER, KONRAD (1941-    )
Combattimento
vln,vcl,orch sc TONOS M-2015-4394-9
rent                         (B510)

Combattimento, Il
4.4.4.2. 4.3.4.1. 4perc,harp,pno,
strings,vln&vcl soli SEESAW  (B511)

Dr. Faustus Overture
3.3.3.2. 4.3.3.1. 5perc,strings
SEESAW                       (B512)

Dr. Faustus: Concert Overture
orch TONOS M-2015-4208-9 rent
                             (B513)

Nomos Protos
1.0.1.0. 1.1.1.0. pno,perc,string
quin SEESAW                  (B514)

BOEKLE, DIETRICH
Concerto
3.2.4.3. 4.3.3.1. timp,perc,pno,
harp,8vln I,7vln II,6vla,5vcl,4db
[12'] sc PETERS 03185        (B515)

BOESMANS, PHILIPPE (1936-    )
Doublures
2.2.2.2. 2.2.2.1. 2perc,pno,
strings,harp solo [11'] JOBERT
                             (B516)

Elément
"Extension" 1.1.1.1. 1.1.1.1.
2perc,pno,harp,gtr,strings,pno
solo [20'] JOBERT            (B517)

Extension
see Elément

Ring
1.0.1.0. 1.1.1.1. 2perc,pno,elec
org,strings,harp solo [16']
JOBERT                       (B518)

Surfing
1.1.1.1. 1.1.1.0. 2perc,harp,pno&
cel,2vln,vcl,db,vla solo [12'30"]
JOBERT                       (B519)

BOGÁR, ISTVÁN
Fuga (Hommage À J.S. Bach)
see Fugue

Fugue
"Fuga (Hommage À J.S. Bach)" 1+
pic.2.2.2.cornetto. 4.2.3.1.
perc,14vln I,12vln II,10vla,8vcl,
8db [11'] EMB rent           (B520)

BOHÁC, JOSEF (1929-    )
Concertino Pastorale
2.2.2.3. 0.3.3.1. timp,perc,harp,
strings,2horn soli [15'] CESKY
HUD.                         (B521)

Concerto for Orchestra
3.2.2.3. 4.3.3.1. timp,perc,xylo,
cel,marimba,strings [27'] CESKY
HUD.                         (B522)

Concerto for Viola and Orchestra
see Dramatické Varianty

Dramatické Varianty (Concerto for
Viola and Orchestra)
3.2.2.2. 4.3.2.0. timp,perc,vibra,
strings,vla solo [19'] CESKY HUD.
                             (B523)

Dve Symfonické Poemy
3.2.3.3. 4.3.3.1. timp,perc,strings
[22'] CESKY HUD.             (B524)

Hudba V Opere
2.2.2.2. 2.2.0.0. timp,strings
[18'] CESKY HUD.             (B525)

Komorní Koncert
2.2.2.2. 2.2.0.0. timp,vibra,
marimba,strings,vln solo [16']
CESKY HUD.                   (B526)

Meteor
3.2.3.2. 4.2.4.0. perc,xylo,strings
[5'] CESKY HUD.              (B527)

Ouvertura Bravura
2.2.2.2. 4.3.3.1. timp,strings [6']
CESKY HUD.                   (B528)

Sonata Lirica
vibra,strings,S solo [12'] CESKY
HUD.                         (B529)

Suita Capricciosa Pro Smycce
string orch [18'] CESKY HUD.  (B530)

Unorová Predehra
3.2.2.2. 4.3.3.1. timp,perc,strings
[7'] CESKY HUD.              (B531)

Vokální Poema
2.2.2.2. 2.2.0.0. timp,strings,4
solo voices [18'] CESKY HUD.
                             (B532)

BOHEMIA RAG (LAMB) see Sieben Ragtimes
Für Streichorchester: Heft 1

BOHEMICA see Drizga, Eduard, Symphony
No. 1

BOHLIN, JONAS (1963-    )
Area
2.2.2(bass clar).2. 4.2.2.1. timp,
3perc,strings,vln solo [7'5"] sc,
pts,solo pt STIM             (B533)

Oceania
4(pic).4.4(bass clar).4. 4.4.4.1.
timp,3perc,harp,strings,pno STIM
                             (B534)

Vingslag
2(pic).2.2(bass clar).2(contrabsn).
2.1.0.0. perc,strings,pno,vln
solo [11'5"] (Archaea; Exist;
Sond; Urminnen) sc,pts STIM
                             (B535)

BÖHM, GEORG (1661-1733)
Suite No. 2 in D
(Guyot, D.) string orch,hpsd,2trp
soli [10'] BILLAUDOT         (B536)

BOIELDIEU, FRANÇOIS-ADRIEN (1775-1834)
Fest Des Nachbardorfes: Overture
see Fête Du Village Voisin, La:
Overture

Fête Du Village Voisin, La: Overture
"Fest Des Nachbardorfes: Overture"
2(pic).2.2.2. 2.2.0.0. timp,perc,
strings [6'] (no score)
BREITKOPF-W                  (B537)

BOIS, ROB DU (1934-    )
Elegia
string orch,ob d'amore [17'] sc
DONEMUS                      (B538)

BOLCOM, WILLIAM ELDEN (1938-    )
Air And Water
see Concerto No. 1 for Piano Left-
Hand and Chamber Orchestra

Concerto for 2Piano Left-Hand and
Orchestra
see Gaea

Concerto No. 1 for Piano Left-Hand
and Chamber Orchestra
"Air And Water" 3(2pic).0.3(clar in
E flat,bass clar).1(contrabsn).
0.3(trp in C).3(bass trom).1.
2perc,cel,vla,pno left-hand solo
[19'] MARKS rent             (B539)

Concerto No. 2 for Piano Left-Hand
and Chamber Orchestra
"Fire And Earth" 0.3(English
horn).0.2. 4.0.0.0. 2perc,strings
without vla,pno left-hand solo
[19'] MARKS rent             (B540)

Concerto No. 3 for 2Piano Left-Hand
and Orchestra
"Fuga Galactica" 3(2pic).3(English
horn).3(clar in E flat,bass
clar).3(contrabsn). 4.3(trp in
C).3(bass trom).1. 4perc,cel,
strings,2pno left-hand soli [19']
MARKS rent                   (B541)

Fire And Earth
see Concerto No. 2 for Piano Left-
Hand and Chamber Orchestra

Fuga Galactica
see Concerto No. 3 for 2Piano Left-
Hand and Orchestra

Gaea (Concerto for 2Piano Left-Hand
and Orchestra)
MARKS rent                   (B542)

Whitman Triptych
3(pic).3(English horn).3(bass
clar).3(contrabsn). 4.3.3.1.
timp,2perc,pno&cel,harp,strings,
Mez solo (text by Walt Whitman)
MARKS rent                   (B543)

BOLLE, JAMES (1931-    )
Concerto for Oboe
2(pic).0+English horn.2(bass clar,
clar in E flat).2. 4.1.3.0. perc,
strings,ob solo [20'] PEER rent
                             (B544)

Dancing
2.2.2.2. 2.2.1.0. timp,strings
[14'] PEER rent              (B545)

BON, ANDRE (1946-    )
Concertare
6vln,3vla,3vcl [12'] JOBERT  (B546)

BON, MAARTEN (1933-    )
Boréal IV
3.3.3.3. 4.3.0.1. 2harp,strings
[6'] sc DONEMUS              (B547)

BON, MAARTEN (cont'd.)

Gut Und Böse
6.0.0.0. 0.0.0.0. 2cel,6vla [12']
sc DONEMUS       (B548)

BONDON, JACQUES (1927-    )
Sinfonia
2.2.2.3. 4.0.0.0. 2vcl,db [20']
BILLAUDOT       (B549)

BONDT, CORNELIS DE (1953-    )
Dame Blanche
2.2.2.2. 4.2.2.1. 2perc,harp,bass
gtr,pno,strings,electronic
equipment,rec solo [35'] sc
DONEMUS       (B550)

BONGARTZ, MARKUS (1963-    )
...Durch Die Reinheit Der Substanz
Ist Es, Was Es Ist, Wege Zu
Suchen... [18']
3.3.3.3. 4.3.3.1. timp,3perc,
2harp,strings
BILLAUDOT       (B551)

BONNIE DUNDEE see Anderson, Leroy

BONNY EARL O'MORAY, THE (from Folk
Songs)
(Britten, Benjamin) 2.2.2.2. 2.2.0.0.
perc,strings,high solo [2'30"]
BOOSEY-ENG rent       (B552)

BONS see Loevendie, Theo

BONS VIEUX TEMPS, LES see Strauss,
Johann, [Jr.]

BOOK OF THE HOURS see Kyr, Robert,
Symphony No. 1

BOOREN, JO VAN DEN (1935-    )
Cirkels II  *Op.90,No.2
2.2.3.2.3sax. 4.3.3.1. 2bugle,
euphonium,timp,2perc,marimba/
xylo,strings [10'] sc DONEMUS
      (B553)
Concerto No. 2 for Violin and String
Orchestra, Op. 89
[21'] sc DONEMUS       (B554)
Concerto, Op. 78
0.3.3.3. 0.2.3.1. timp,strings,fl
solo [22'] sc DONEMUS       (B555)
Meditation No. 1, Op. 80
1.1.1.1. 1.0.0.0. vibra,pno,2vln,
vla,vcl,db [20'] sc DONEMUS
      (B556)
Meditation No. 2, Op. 93
1.1.1.1. 1.0.0.0. marimba/vibra,
pno,2vln,vla,vcl,db [27'] sc
DONEMUS       (B557)
Meditation No. 3, Op. 100
1.1.1.1. 1.0.0.0. perc,2vln,vla,
vcl,db [22'] sc DONEMUS (B558)

BOOTSFAHRT MIT KARIN see Kiermeir, Kurt

BORÉAL IV see Bon, Maarten

BOREALIS see Lees, Benjamin

BORERO see Helge, Olov

BORIS GODUNOW: WARLAAMS LIED see
Mussorgsky, Modest Petrovich

BORISOVA-OLLAS, VICTORIA (1969-    )
Image: Reflection
2.2.2.2. 2.2.0.0. timp,perc,harp,
strings,pno/cel sc STIM (B559)

Schreitende Alleen
2.2.2.2. 4.2.3.0. timp,perc,strings
sc STIM       (B560)

Shadow Of The Night, A
string orch sc STIM       (B561)

Wings Of The Wind
3(pic).3.3(bass clar).0. 4.3.3.1.
timp,3perc,harp,strings,pno/cel
STIM       (B562)

BÖRJESSON, LARS-OVE (1953-    )
So What?
2.2.2.3(contrabsn). 4.3.3.1. 3perc,
strings [9'5"] STIM sc H-2835,
pts A-421       (B563)

BORODIN, ALEXANDER PORFIRIEVICH
(1833-1887)
Chanson De La Forêt Sombre
1.1.1.1. 2.1.3.0. timp,2perc,harp,
strings,med solo [3'20"] LEDUC
      (B564)
Mlada: Finale
(Rimsky-Korsakow, N.) 3.2.2.2.
4.2.3.1. timp,perc,harp,strings
[5'] study sc BELAIEFF BEL 374
      (B565)

BORODIN, ALEXANDER PORFIRIEVICH
(cont'd.)
"Polovtsian Dances" And "In The
Steppes Of Central Asia" In Full
Score
orch sc DOVER 29556-7       (B566)

BOROGYIN, A.P.
see BORODIN, ALEXANDER PORFIREVICH

BORRIS, SIEGFRIED (1906-1987)
Concerto for Horn and Orchestra, Op.
120
2.2.2. 2.2.2.0. perc,strings
[18'45"] HEINRICH       (B567)
Concerto for Strings, Op. 64a
[24'] HEINRICH       (B568)
Kammerkonzert In D  *Op.15
2.2.2.2. 2.2.0.0. strings,vcl solo
[20'] HEINRICH       (B569)

BORSTLAP, JOHN (1950-    )
Sinfonia
2.3.3.3. 2.0.0.0. strings [20'] sc
DONEMUS       (B570)

BORTOLI, STEPHANE (1956-    )
Guetteur Mélancolique, Le
1.0.1.1. 0.0.0.0. perc,vln,vla,vcl,
db,Mez solo [12'] BILLAUDOT
      (B571)
Psalm No. 22 [10']
2.2.2.2. 2.2.1.0. harp,2perc,
strings
"Psaume 22" BILLAUDOT       (B572)
Psaume 22
see Psalm No. 22

BÖRTZ, DANIEL (1943-    )
Intermezzo for Orchestra
2(pic).2(English horn).2(bass
clar).2. 2.0.0.0. strings [10']
sc STIM ED.NR 6753       (B573)
Parodos
4(pic).4(English horn).4(bass
clar).4(contrabsn). 4.4.4.1.
timp,3perc,strings [13'] sc STIM
ED.NR 6589       (B574)
Sånger Om Döden
orch,S solo GEHRMANS       (B575)
Sinfonia No. 9
3(pic).3(English horn).3(bass
clar).3(contrabsn). 4.3.3.1.
timp,perc,harp,strings,cel [25']
sc GEHRMANS ED.NR 6891       (B576)
Strindberg Suite
see Strindbergsvit
Strindbergsvit
"Strindberg Suite" 2(pic).2.3(bass
clar).2. 4.2.2.0. timp,3perc,
strings,pno [17'] sc GEHRMANS
ED.NR 7161       (B577)
Variationer Och Intermezzi
string orch [15'] sc GEHRMANS
      (B578)

BOSCHETTY, RADEK (1966-    )
Variations for Orchestra
3.3.3.3. 4.3.3.1. timp,perc,strings
[10'] CESKY HUD.       (B579)

BOSE, HANS-JÜRGEN VON (1953-    )
Concertino Per il H.W.H.
1.1.1.1. 1.1.1.0. timp,synthesizer&
pno,2vln,vla,vcl,db [3'] SCHOTTS
      (B580)
Für Lieder
1(pic).1.1(bass clar).1. 1.0.0.0.
2vln,vla,vcl,db,S solo [12'] (for
Greenpeace, text by Georg
Britting, Hans Magnus
Enzensberger) SCHOTTS       (B581)
In Hora Mortis
6vln I,5vln II,4vla,3vcl,2db,
speaking voice [20'] (text by
Thomas Bernhard) SCHOTTS (B582)
Love After Love
4.3(English horn).3(bass
clar).3(2contrabsn). 4.3.3.1.
timp,2perc,12vln I,10vln II,8vla,
6vcl,4db,S solo [6'] (text by
Derek Walcott) SCHOTTS (B583)
"...Other Echoes Inhabit The Garden"
3(pic,alto fl).2(ob d'amore,English
horn).2(basset horn,bass clar)+
contrabass clar.2(contrabsn).
2.2(piccolo trp).2(bass trom).1.
timp,3perc,2harp,8vla,6vcl,6db,ob
solo [23'] SCHOTTS       (B584)
Sappho-Gesänge
1(pic,alto fl).1.1(bass
clar).1(contrabsn). 1.1.0.0.
timp&perc,perc,pno&cel,harp,2vln,

BOSE, HANS-JÜRGEN VON (cont'd.)
2vla,2vcl,2db,Mez solo [17']
(text by Joachim Schickel)
SCHOTTS       (B585)
Scene
1(pic,alto fl).1.1(clar in E flat,
bass clar).1(contrabsn). 1.1(trp
in D).1.1. 2perc,2synthesizer&
pno,harp,2vln,2vla,2vcl,2db,
soprano sax&baritone sax&bass
clar [23'] SCHOTTS       (B586)
Three Songs
1(pic,alto fl).1(English
horn).1(clar in E flat)+bass
clar.1. 0.0.0+alto trom.0. timp&
perc,2perc,hpsd&Hamm,harp,2vla,
2vcl,db,T solo [18'] (text by
Drayton; Sidney; & Anonymous)
SCHOTTS       (B587)
Travesties In Sad Landscape
1(pic,alto fl).1(English
horn).1(bass clar).0+contrabsn.
1.1(trp in D).1.0. perc,cel,
acord&Hamm,pno,2vln,vla,vcl,db
[12'] SCHOTTS       (B588)
Two Studies
4(2pic).4(English horn).4(clar in
A,2bass clar).4(2contrabsn).
4.4.3.1. timp,2perc,12vln I,12vln
II,10vla,8vcl,6db [10'] SCHOTTS
      (B589)
Variations
12vln I,10vln II,8vla,6vcl,5db
[20'] SCHOTTS       (B590)
Werther-Szenen: Suite
2(2pic,alto fl).2(English
horn).2(clar in E flat,bass
clar).2(contrabsn). 2.2.2.0.
timp,2perc,pno,hpsd,14vln,4vla,
4vcl,3db SCHOTTS       (B591)

BÖSER KATER SITZT IN DER ECKE, EIN see
Mossolov, Alexander

BOTTENBERG, WOLFGANG (1930-    )
Prelude, Aria And Fugue
string orch [12'] sc CANADIAN
MI 1500 B751PR       (B592)

BÖTTGER, TH.
Concerto for Piano and Orchestra, No.
1
3.2.2.3. 3.2.2.1. timp,perc,cel,
harp,8vln I,7vln II,6vla,5vcl,4db
[15'] sc PETERS 03174       (B593)

BOUCHARD, LINDA (1957-    )
Frisson, La Vie
string orch/string quar,fl solo,vla
solo sc CANADIAN MI 8613 B7515FR
      (B594)

BOUDREAU, WALTER (1947-    )
Berliner Momente II
2(pic).2(English horn).2(bass
clar).2(contrabsn). 4.2.3.1.
timp,2perc,6vln I,5vln II,4vla,
3vcl,2db sc CANADIAN
MI 1100 B756BE2       (B595)
Dans Les Champs, Il Y A Des Bibittes
see Variations No. 2
Incantations Vb: Le Cercle Gnostique
see Zeniths
Tradiderunt Me In Manus Impiorum II
3(pic).3(English horn).3(bass
clar).3(contrabsn). 4.4.3.1.
timp,4perc,strings sc CANADIAN
MI 1100 B756TR       (B596)
Variations No. 2
"Dans Les Champs, Il Y A Des
Bibittes" 2(pic).2(English
horn).2(bass clar,clar in E
flat).2. 2.2.0.0. 2perc,harp,
strings,S solo, (voice in mvt. 4)
sc CANADIAN MV 1400 B756VA (B597)
Zeniths
"Incantations Vb: Le Cercle
Gnostique" 1(pic,bass
fl).1(English horn).1.0. 1.1.1.0.
perc,pno,vln,vla,vcl sc CANADIAN
MI1200 B756NE       (B598)

BOUFURI see Matsushita, Isao

BOULIANE, DENYS (1955-    )
Douze Tiroirs De Demi-Vérités Pour
Alléger Votre Descente
2(pic).2.0.2. 2.0.0.0. 2perc,
strings,pno solo [19'] sc
CANADIAN MI 1361 B763DO       (B599)

BOULOGNE, JOSEPH (CHEVALIER DE ST.-
GEORGES)
see SAINT-GEORGES, JOSEPH BOULOGNE DE

BOUNTIFUL VOYAGER see Earnest, John
David

BOUQUET OF FIELD FLOWERS see Kadosa,
Pal

BOURGEOIS GENTILHOMME, LE see Strauss,
Richard

BOURLAND, ROGER (1952-    )
Dances From The Sacred Harp
fl,clar,perc,kbd,strings [16']
SCHIRM.EC rent           (B600)

Mirabell Jam
2.2.2.2. 4.2.2.1. timp,strings
[10'] SCHIRM.EC rent     (B601)

Sweet Alchemy
2.2.2.2. 2.0.2.0. perc,kbd,strings
[15'] SCHIRM.EC rent     (B602)

BOURRÉE FANTASQUE see Chabrier,
[Alexis-] Emmanuel

BOUSCH, FRANÇOIS (1946-    )
Arc En Ciel
2.2.2.2. 2.2.2.0. timp,2perc,pno,
harp,strings,vla solo [23']
BILLAUDOT                (B603)

BOWIJAW see Lindgren, Pär

BOWMAN, KIM
Dejeune & Algunda
see Symphony No. 1

Hysteria At Penumbra Slumbers
3.3.3.3. 6.4.3.1. 5perc,harp,pno,
strings, 3 bass sax or 3 shawms
[12'] sc DONEMUS         (B604)

Symphony No. 1
"Dejeune & Algunda" 3.3.3.3.
4.4.1.1. 2bass trp,6perc,2harp,
pno,strings [18'] sc DONEMUS
                         (B605)

BOYCE, WILLIAM (1711-1779)
Peleus And Thetis: Overture
0.2.0.1. 0.0.0.0. strings [6'] pts
STAINER HL18A rent       (B606)

BOYD, ANNE
Black Sun
2+pic.2.2.2. 4.2.3.2. timp,2perc,
harp,strings [15'] sc UNIV.YORK
0110 f.s.                (B607)

Concerto for Flute
strings,fl solo [12'] sc UNIV.YORK
0112 f.s.                (B608)

Grathawai
2+pic.2.2+bass clar.2+contrabsn.
4.3.3.1. timp,2perc,harp,strings
[17'] sc UNIV.YORK 0111 f.s.
                         (B609)

BOZAY, ATTILA (1939-    )
Concertino for Horn and String
Orchestra, Op. 36
string orch,horn solo [13'] EMB
rent                     (B610)

Improvisations III. *Op.30c
"Improvizációk III." prepared pno,
strings, (5-8, 3, 2, 1) [9'] EMB
rent                     (B611)

Improvizációk III.
see Improvisations III.

Pezzo Concertato No. 3 *Op.37
2.2.2.2. 4.2.3.0. timp,perc,harp,
cel,strings,fl solo [20'] EMB
rent                     (B612)

Pezzo Sinfonico No. 2 *Op.25
1+2pic.3.3.2+contrabsn. 4.3.3.2+bass
trom.0. perc,2pno,14vln I,12vln
II,10vla,8vcl,8db [22'] EMB rent
                         (B613)

BOZZA see Kolberg, Kåre

BOZZA, EUGÈNE (1905-1991)
Cinq Chansons Niçoises
1.1.1.1. 1.0.0.0. timp,triangle,
cel,harp,strings,high solo
[5'10"] LEDUC            (B614)

BRABEC, JINDRICH (1933-    )
O Sluvko Vic
1.0.0.0.2sax. 0.1.1.0. perc,pno,
2gtr,strings,solo voice&speaking
voice [4'] CESKY HUD.    (B615)

Vecne Mladé Venuše
1.0.0.0.sax. 0.1.1.0. perc,2gtr,
synthesizer,strings,male solo,
Yamaha grand piano [5'] CESKY
HUD.                     (B616)

BRADY, TIMOTHY (1956-    )
Chamber Symphony
1.1.1.1. 2.1.0.0. strings, (all
winds double perc, conductor
doubles perc & piano, trumpet

BRADY, TIMOTHY (cont'd.)
uses resonance system) (1. Flute
music 2. Cello music 3. Solo
music-Trumpet and percussion
music) sc CANADIAN MI 9400 B812CH
                         (B617)
2.2.2.2. 2.3.0.0. strings (1. Flute
music 2. Cello music 3. Solo
music-Trumpet and percussion
music) sc CANADIAN MI 9400 B812CH
                         (B618)

Concertino for Orchestra
4(pic,alto fl).4.4(clar in E flat,
bass clar).4(contrabsn). 6.4.3.1.
2perc,harp,pno,strings [15'] sc
CANADIAN MI 1100 B812CO  (B619)

Gestures
string orch [4'-6'] (chance
compositions) sc CANADIAN
MI 1500 B812GE           (B620)

Nocturne
see Three Movements For Orchestra

Pastorale
see Three Movements For Orchestra

Three Movements For Orchestra
2(pic,alto fl).1(English horn).2+
bass clar.1. 2.2.2.0. 2perc,harp,
strings sc CANADIAN
MI 1100 B812TH ipa
contains: Nocturne; Pastorale;
Toccata                  (B621)

Toccata
see Three Movements For Orchestra

Variants
2.2.2.2. 2.2.0.0. timp,strings
[20'] sc CANADIAN MI 1100 B812VA
                         (B622)

Visions
4-55strings,inst soli, (soloists
improvise on any instrument) [7'-
30'] (aleatory music) sc CANADIAN
MI1601 B812VI            (B623)

BRAHMS, JOHANNES (1833-1897)
Complete Concerti By Brahms
orch sc DOVER 24170-X    (B624)

Complete Symphonies By Brahms
orch sc DOVER 23053-8    (B625)

Concerto for Piano and Orchestra
(from Piano Quartet Op. 25)
(Matthus, S.) 2.2.2.2. 2.2.3.1.
timp,2perc,harp,cel,strings,pno
solo BREITKOPF-W         (B626)

Danses Hongroises
(Dupin, Marc-Olivier) string orch,
vln solo [50'] BILLAUDOT (B627)

Drei Ernste Stücke *CC3U
vln I,vln II,vla,vcl,db MÖSELER
f.s. sc 40.154-00, pts 40.154-01,
set 40.154-09            (B628)

Serenade No. 1 in D, Op. 11
2.2.2.2. 4.2.0.0. timp,strings
[43'] study sc BREITKOPF-W
PB 3971                  (B629)

Serenade No. 2 in A, Op. 16
2+pic.2.2.2. 2.2.0.0. strings
without vln [30'] study sc
BREITKOPF-W PB 3972      (B630)

Symphony No. 1
orch (autograph) sc DOVER 24976-X
                         (B631)
Symphony No. 1, Op. 68, in C minor
(Pascal, R.) orch study sc HENLE
9851                     (B632)
(Pascal, R.) orch (Johannes Brahms
Werke, Series 1, Vol. 1) cloth
HENLE 6001               (B633)

Three Orchestral Works By Brahms
orch sc DOVER 24637-X    (B634)

Wiegenlied *Op.49,No.4
(Cohen, Shimon) string orch,solo
voice [1'30"] BILLAUDOT rent
                         (B635)
BRANDENBURG CONCERTO, FOR FLUTE, OBOE,
VIOLIN, STRINGS AND CEMBALO see
Jekimowski, Viktor,
Brandenburgisches Konzert

BRANDENBURGISCHES KONZERT see
Jekimowski, Viktor

BRANDMÜLLER, THEO (1948-    )
Antigone
1(pic).1(English horn).1.0.
0.0.0.0. perc,pno,vla,db [11']
(Klanggesang für Kammerensemble)
BREITKOPF-W              (B636)

BRANDMÜLLER, THEO (cont'd.)
Imaginations
1(pic).0.1(bass clar).0. 0.0.0.0.
perc,pno/cel/cembalo,db,vla solo
[20'] BREITKOPF-W        (B637)

Traumtanztango
12vln [7'] BREITKOPF-W   (B638)

Und Der Mond Heftet Ins Meer Ein
Langes Horn Aus Licht Und Tanz
4(4pic,2alto fl).4(2English
horn).4(2bass
clar).4(2contrabsn). 4.3.3.0.
5perc,13vln I,9vln II,8vla,8vcl,
5db,electronic tape,vla&vcl&db
soli [27'] BREITKOPF-W   (B639)

BRANGLE see Druckman, Jacob Raphael

BRASIL (SAMBA) see Thomas-Mifune,
Werner

BRAUEL, HENNING (1940-    )
Mercurio *Rondo
5vln,3vla,2vcl,db,vln solo [22']
SCHOTTS                  (B640)

BRAUT VON MESSINA: OVERTURE see
Schumann, Robert (Alexander)

BRAÜTIGAM, VOLKER (1939-    )
Feste Burg, Ein: Choralpartita
string orch,trp [18'] BREITKOPF-W
                         (B641)
BRAVO, MEIN GNÄDGER GEBIETER - WILL DER
HERR GRAF EIN TÄNZCHEN NUN WAGEN
see Mozart, Wolfgang Amadeus,
Bravo, Signor Padrone - Se Vuol
Ballare

BRAVO, SIGNOR PADRONE - SE VUOL BALLARE
see Mozart, Wolfgang Amadeus

BREAK OF DAY: SUITE see Dreyfus, George

BREDEMEYER, REINER (1929-1995)
Bagatellen (9)
20vln,8vla,6vcl,3db [12'] sc PETERS
03182                    (B642)

Bagatellen F.B
2.1.2.2. 2.2.2.1. timp,perc,pno,
8vln,6vla,5vcl,4db [7'] sc PETERS
00317                    (B643)

Bilderserenade (Serenade No. 4)
0.1.0.0. 0.0.1.0. perc,pno,vln,vcl
[15'] sc PETERS 03167    (B644)

Eintags-Sinfonie
see Schlagstück 6

Grosses Duett
1.2+English horn.1.1. 1.0.1.0.
perc,2pno,vln,vla,vcl,db [10'] sc
PETERS 03164             (B645)

In Memoriam Paul Dessau
5vln I,4vln II,3vla,2vcl,db [4'] sc
PETERS 03173             (B646)

Orchesterstück 2
3.2.2.3. 4.2.2.1. timp,3perc,harp,
8vln I,7vln II,6vla,5vcl,4db
[14'] sc PETERS 03183    (B647)

Schlagstück 6
"Eintags-Sinfonie" 0.0.6.4.
8.0.4.0. 4bass drum,10vcl,8db
[22'] sc PETERS 03170    (B648)

Serenade No. 4
see Bilderserenade

Sinfonia
0.1.0.0. 0.0.1.0. perc,pno,8vln I,
7vln II,6vla,5vcl,4db [14'] sc
PETERS 03162             (B649)

Sonatina for Orchestra
2.2.2.2. 2.1.1.1. timp,4perc,8vln
I,7vln II,6vla,5vcl,4db [12'] sc
PETERS 02401             (B650)

Sonatina No. 2 for Orchestra
1.3+English horn.1.1. 2.1.1.1.
3perc,8vln I,7vln II,6vla,5vcl,
4db [12'] sc PETERS 03484 (B651)
1.1.1.1. 1.1.1.1. 3perc,5vln,3vla.
3vcl,db [12'] sc PETERS 03492
                         (B652)

Sonatina No. 3 for Orchestra
3.1.1.3. 0.1.4.0. 4perc,10vln I,
8vln II,6vla,5vcl,3db [12'] sc
PETERS 03493             (B653)

Sonatina No. 4 for Orchestra
1.3+English horn.1.1. 2.0.0.1.
vibra,xylo,marimba,8vln,5vla.
3vcl,db [15'] sc PETERS 03494
                         (B654)

Sonatina No. 5 for Orchestra
2.0.1.2. 0.1.1.1. timp,perc,10vln
I,8vln II,8vla,6vcl,3db [12'] sc

BREDEMEYER, REINER (cont'd.)

   PETERS 03495         (B655)

BREGENT, MICHEL-GEORGES (1948-1993)
   Remontée d'Adanac O. Le Salmo-Salar,
     La
     2+pic.2.3+bass clar.2.tenor sax.
     4.2.3.1. 3perc,pno&cel,strings
     [8'] (epic poem for orchestra) sc
     CANADIAN MI 1100 B833RE    (B656)

BREIMO, BJØRN (1958-    )
   Canto Eterno
     2.2.2.2. 4.3.3.1. timp,2perc,
     strings [14'] NORSKMI    (B657)

   Fantasy for Strings
     string orch [13'] NORSKMI   (B658)

BRENNEND see Pröve, Bernfried

BREVIK, TOR (1932-    )
   Music for Orchestra
     2(pic).2.2.2. 2.2.0.0. timp,perc,
     strings NORSKMI    (B659)

   Sinfonia Brevik
     2(pic).2.2.2. 2.2.0.0. timp,perc,
     strings [15'] NORSKMI    (B660)

BREVISSIMA see Constant, Marius

BREWAEYS, LUC
   Laphroaig
     see Symphony No. 5

   Symphony No. 5
     "Laphroaig" Orch I: 3.3.3.3.
     4.3.2.2. timp, 5perc, piano,
     2harps, strings, 2 baritone
     saxophone. Orch II: 1.1.1.1.
     1.1.1.0. 3perc, piano, harp,
     strings [32'45] BELGE   (B661)

BRIAN, HAVERGAL (1876-1972)
   Symphony No. 2
     6(4pic).4(2English horn).4(2bass
     clar).4(contrabsn). 8.4.4.2.
     3timp,5-7perc,2harp,2pno,org,cel.
     strings, 8 more horns [40']
     UNITED MUS rent    (B662)

   Symphony No. 15
     4(pic).4(English horn).4(bass
     clar).4(contrabsn). 6.4.4.1+
     euphonium. timp,4perc,cel,2harp,
     strings [10'] UNITED MUS rent
                        (B663)

   Turandot
     3(2pic).3(English horn).4(clar in E
     flat,bass clar).3(contrabsn).
     4.4.3.1. timp,5perc,cel,2harp,
     strings [45'] (complete
     orchestral extracts) UNITED MUS
     rent    (B664)

BRICK see Torke, Michael

BRIDAL LULLABY, A "HOWARDS END THEME
   MUSIC" see Grainger, Percy Aldridge

BRIDE'S RECEPTION, THE see Gellman,
   Steven

BRIDGE, FRANK (1879-1941)
   Irish Melody, An
     "Londonderry Air" string orch [5']
     sc,pts STAINER HL296 rent  (B665)

   Londonderry Air
     see Irish Melody, An

BRIDGES IN TIME see Silverman, Faye-
   Ellen

BRIGG FAIR see Grainger, Percy Aldridge

BRILANTNÍ SCHERZO see Juchelka,
   Miroslav

BRINDLE, REGINALD SMITH
   see SMITH BRINDLE, REGINALD

BRINGS, ALLEN STEPHEN (1934-    )
   Concerto Da Camera  *No.4
     hpsd,1-5vln I,1-5vln II,1-4vla,1-
     3vcl,1-2db [12'30"] (gr. V) solo
     pt,pts MIRA    (B666)

   Serenade
     2.2.2.2. 2.2.0.0. timp,perc,strings
     [9'] (gr. IV) sc MIRA   (B667)

   Short Symphony No. 1-2
     strings [14'] (gr. IV) sc,pts MIRA
                        (B668)

   Sinfonia Da Camera
     1.1.1.1. 1.1.1.0. timp,perc,2vln,
     vla,vcl,db [18'30"] (gr. IV) sc,
     pts MIRA    (B669)

   Symphony
     2+pic.2.2.2. 4.2.3.0. timp,3perc,
     harp,cel/pno,strings [25'] (gr.
     IV) sc,study sc MIRA   (B670)

---

BRIOLETTE see Amos, Keith

BRITTEN, [SIR] BENJAMIN (1913-1976)
   Charm Of Lullabies, A  *Op.41
     (Matthews, Colin) 2.2.2(bass
     clar).2. 2.0.0.0. harp,strings,
     Mez solo [12'] (text by Blake,
     Burns, Robert Greene, Thomas
     Randolph, John Philip) BOOSEY-ENG
     rent    (B671)

   Concerto for Violin, Viola and
     Orchestra
     "Double Concerto For Violin, Viola
     And Orchestra" 2(pic).2.2.2.
     2.0.0.0. timp,perc,strings,vln&
     vla soli [21'] perf sc set OXFORD
     3622513 sc,pts rent    (B672)

   Double Concerto For Violin, Viola And
     Orchestra
     see Concerto for Violin, Viola and
     Orchestra

   King Arthur
     (Hindmarsh) 3.2.3.2. 4.3.3.1. timp,
     2perc,strings [24'] OXFORD sc
     3621754 f.s., perf sc set 3620758
     sc,pts rent    (B673)

   Now Sleeps The Crimson Petal
     horn,strings,T solo [5'] (text by
     Tennyson) BOOSEY-ENG rent (B674)

   Simple Symphony
     string orch [16'] OXFORD sc
     3619318, pts    (B675)

   Soirées Musicales  *Op.9, Suite
     2(pic).2.2.2. 4.2.3.0. timp,2perc,
     harp/pno,strings [11'] (of 5
     movements, from Rossini) BOOSEY-
     ENG rent    (B676)

     1.1.1.0. 0.1.1.0. perc,harp/pno,
     strings [11'] (of 5 movements,
     from Rossini) BOOSEY-ENG rent
                        (B677)

BRIXI, FRANZ XAVER (1732-1771)
   Aria in D
     "Aria In D Pro Natali Domini" A
     solo,2fl,2ob,2horn,strings,org
     KUNZELMANN ipa sc 10230A, oct
     10230    (B678)

   Aria In D Pro Natali Domini
     see Aria in D

   Concerto in F
     (Racek; Reienberger) org,2horn,
     2vln,vla,db,hpsd,strings
     KUNZELMANN ipa sc 10020A, oct
     10020    (B679)

BROKEN FAREWELL, THE see Killmayer,
   Wilhelm

BROKEN SYMMETRY see Matthews, Colin

BRONSART VON SCHELLENDORF, HANS
   (1830-1913)
   Frühlingsphantasie  *Op.11
     2.1.2.0. 2.2.1.0. timp,org,strings
     [26'] BREITKOPF-W    (B680)

BRONZE see Torke, Michael

BROOKLYN BRIDGE ODER MEINE ENTDECKUNG
   AMERIKAS see Tarnopolsky, Vladimir

BROTT, ALEXANDER (1915-    )
   B22 (Fantasy for Orchestra)
     2(pic).2(English horn).2+clar in E
     flat.2. 4.3.3.1. timp,3perc,
     strings, (clar in e flat and
     English horn are optional) [13']
     sc CANADIAN MI 1100 B874B2 (B681)

   E dai p milo
     string orch sc CANADIAN
     MI 1500 B874ED    (B682)

   Fantasy for Orchestra
     see B22

   Hymn II Her
     "Hymn To Her" string orch,fl solo,
     bsn solo [15'] sc CANADIAN
     MI 1726 B874HY    (B683)

   Hymn To Her
     see Hymn II Her

   Paraphrase En Polyphonie Sur Un Thème
     De Beethoven
     see Paraphrase In Polyphony: On A
     Theme By Beethoven

   Paraphrase In Polyphony: On A Theme
     By Beethoven
     "Paraphrase En Polyphonie Sur Un
     Thème De Beethoven" 3+pic.3+
     English horn.3+bass clar.3+
     contrabsn. 4.3.3.1. timp,perc,
     strings [16'] sc CANADIAN
     MI 1100 B874PA    (B684)

---

BROWN, RAYNER (1912-    )
   Concerto for Bass Trombone and
     Orchestra
     BROWN,R    (B685)

   Concerto for Harp, Violin and
     Orchestra
     BROWN,R    (B686)

   Concerto for Organ and Orchestra, No.
     8
     BROWN,R    (B687)

   Concerto for 2 Organs and Orchestra
     BROWN,R    (B688)

   Concerto for Piano and String
     Orchestra
     pno,string orch,bsn,perc BROWN,R
                        (B689)

   Concerto for Saxophone, String
     Orchestra and Percussion
     string orch,perc,soprano sax solo
     BROWN,R    (B690)

   Concerto for Violoncello and String
     Orchestra
     string orch,English horn,perc,vcl
     solo BROWN,R    (B691)

BROZ, FRANTIŠEK (1896-1962)
   Faethon  *Overture
     3.3.3.3. 4.3.3.0. timp,harp,strings
     [11'] CESKY HUD.    (B692)

   Kamycká Polka
     2.2.2.0. 1.1.0.0. perc,strings
     CESKY HUD.    (B693)

   Skrivánek
     2.2.2.2. 2.2.1.0. timp,perc,harp,
     strings,S solo [6'] CESKY HUD.
                        (B694)

BRUCH, MAX (1838-1920)
   First Violin Concerto And Scottish
     Fantasy In Full Score
     orch,vln solo sc DOVER 28295-3
                        (B695)

   Kol Nidrei
     orch,vcl solo sc DOVER f.s.
     contains also: Bloch, Ernest,
     Schelomo    (B696)

   Serenade Nach Schwedischen Melodien
     see Serenade Nach Schwedischen
     Volksliedern

   Serenade Nach Schwedischen
     Volksliedern
     "Serenade Nach Schwedischen
     Melodien" string orch KUNZELMANN
     ipa sc 10286A, oct 10286 (B697)

BRUCKNER, ANTON (1824-1896)
   Adagio for Strings
     (Almeida) string orch BOIS (B698)

   Symphonies Nos. 4 And 7
     orch sc DOVER 26262-6   (B699)

   Symphony No. 1 in C minor
     3.2.2.2. 4.2.3.0. timp,strings
     [45'] (Linzer Fassung) BREITKOPF-
     W    (B700)

   Symphony No. 2 in C minor
     2.2.2.2. 4.2.3.0. timp,strings
     [67'] ([Original version])
     BREITKOPF-W    (B701)

   Symphony No. 5 in B flat
     2.2.2.2. 4.3.3.1. timp,strings
     [80'] ([Original version])
     BREITKOPF-W    (B702)

   Symphony No. 6 in A
     2.2.2.2. 4.3.3.1. timp,strings
     [65'] ([Original version])
     BREITKOPF-W    (B703)

   Symphony No. 8 in C minor
     3.3.3.3. 4.3.3.1. timp,perc,3harp,
     strings [78'] ([Original
     version]) BREITKOPF-W   (B704)

   Symphony No. 9 in C minor
     3.3.3.3. 4.3.3.1. timp,strings
     [60'] ([Original version])
     BREITKOPF-W    (B705)

   Vier Orchesterstücke
     2.2.2.2. 2.2.3.0. timp,strings
     [12'] BREITKOPF-W    (B706)

BRÜHNS, NICHOLAUS (1665-1697)
   Jauchzet Dem Herrn Alle Welt (Psalm
     No. 100) cant
     (Walter, G.A.) strings,cont,opt
     trp,S solo [12'] BREITKOPF-W
                        (B707)

   Psalm No. 100
     see Jauchzet Dem Herrn Alle Welt

BRUMAIRE see Massenet, Jules

BRUNNEN DES LEBENS see Slavicky, Milan

BRUNS, VICTOR (1904-1996)
Concerto for English Horn and
Orchestra, Op. 61
see Edelfräulein Als Bäuerin, Das:
Suite

Edelfräulein Als Bäuerin, Das: Suite
(Concerto for English Horn and
Orchestra, Op. 61) Op.69
1.1.1.1. 2.0.0.0. perc,strings,
English horn solo [17']
BREITKOPF-W                         (B708)
3.3.2.2. 4.3.1.1. timp,perc,
strings,bsn solo [14'] BREITKOPF-
W                                   (B709)
1.1.1.1. 2.2.0.0. perc,strings,bsn
solo [20'] BREITKOPF-W             (B710)
1.1.1.1. 2.0.0.0. timp,perc,
strings,fl solo [17'] BREITKOPF-W
                                    (B711)
perc,strings,fl&English horn soli
[20'] BREITKOPF-W                  (B712)
1.2.2.1. 0.0.0.0. timp,perc,
strings,horn solo [20']
BREITKOPF-W                         (B713)
1.1.1.1. 2.0.0.0. timp,perc,
strings,clar solo [25']
BREITKOPF-W                         (B714)
strings,db solo [18'] BREITKOPF-W
                                    (B715)
strings,ob&bsn soli [20']
BREITKOPF-W                         (B716)
1.1.1.1. 3.0.1.0. timp,perc,
strings,trp solo [16'] BREITKOPF-
W                                   (B717)
1.1.1.1. 2.0.0.0. timp,perc,
strings,vla solo [25'] BREITKOPF-
W                                   (B718)
2.2.2.2. 4.2.3.1. timp,perc,
strings,vln solo [25'] BREITKOPF-
W                                   (B719)
1.1.1.1. 2.0.0.0. perc,strings,vln
solo [24'] BREITKOPF-W             (B720)
2.2.2.2. 4.2.3.1. timp,perc,
strings,vcl solo [32'] BREITKOPF-
W                                   (B721)
3(pic).2.2.2. 4.3.3.1. 2perc,
strings [25'] BREITKOPF-W          (B722)
3.2.2.2. 4.3.3.1. timp,perc,strings
[28'] BREITKOPF-W                  (B723)
timp,perc,strings,fl&ob&clar&bsn&
horn soli [22'] BREITKOPF-W
                                    (B724)
3.2.2.2. 4.3.3.1. perc,strings
[25'] BREITKOPF-W                  (B725)
3.2.2.2. 4.3.0.0. timp,perc,strings
[25'] BREITKOPF-W                  (B726)
2.1.2.1. 3.2.0.0. timp,strings
[26'] BREITKOPF-W                  (B727)

Kammersinfonie *Op.69
strings [17'] BREITKOPF-W          (B728)

Minna Von Barnhelm: Overture *Op.69
2.1.2.2. 2.2.0.0. perc,cel,strings
[6'] BREITKOPF-W                   (B729)

Orchesterstück *Op.19
3.2.2.2. 4.3.3.1. timp,perc,strings
[15'] BREITKOPF-W                  (B730)

Recht Des Herrn, Das: Suites 1 & 2
*Op.27, ballet
3.2.2.2. 4.3.3.1. timp,perc,strings
[33'] BREITKOPF-W                  (B731)

BRUSTAD, KARSTEN (1959-   )
Fragments And Shades
2(2pic).2(English horn).2(bass
clar).2(contrabsn). 4.2.2.1.
timp,2perc,harp,pno,strings [12']
NORSKMI                             (B732)

Shadows Of Light
string orch [9'] NORSKMI          (B733)

BRYARS, GAVIN
Concerto for Violoncello
2(pic).1+English horn.2(bass
clar).2(contrabsn). 2.0.0.0.
2perc,harp,strings,vcl solo [35']
SCHOTTS                             (B734)

Doctor Ox's Experiment: Epilogue
bass clar,2perc,pno,elec gtr,
strings,S solo, (double bass
amplified with effects pedals)
[22'] (text by Blake Morrison)
SCHOTTS                             (B735)

East Coast, The
bsn,2horn,harp,6vln I,6vln II,4vla,
4vcl,2db, bass oboe solo [20']
SCHOTTS                             (B736)

Green Ray, The
1(pic).1+English horn.1(bass
clar).2(contrabsn). 2.0+
flügelhorn.1.0. perc,pno,6vln I,
5vln II,4vla,4vcl,2db,soprano sax
solo [20'] study sc SCHOTTS
ED 12463                            (B737)

BRYARS, GAVIN (cont'd.)
North Shore, The
harp&pno,perc,strings,vla solo
[14'] SCHOTTS                       (B738)
harp&pno,perc,strings,vcl solo
[14'] SCHOTTS                       (B739)

BUVOS SZEKRÉNY, A see Farkas, Ferenc,
Magic Wardrobe, The: Concert
Overture

BUBALO, RUDOLPH
Spacescape For Orchestra And Tape
3.3.3.3. 4.3.3.1. timp,3perc,kbd,
electronic tape,strings [12']
SCHIRM.EC rent                      (B740)

BUBNOVÁ PAMET see Odstrcil, Karel

BUCHT, GUNNAR (1927-   )
Mouvements Sonores Et Accentués
see Symphony No. 12

Rörelser I Rummet
3(pic).2.3(pic).2. 4.4.4.1. timp,
perc,harp,strings,cel [20'] sc
STIM H-2950                         (B741)

Sinfonie Gracieuse Ou L'Apothéose De
Berwald (Symphony No. 10)
3(pic).3(English horn).3(bass
clar).3(contrabsn). 4.4.4.1.
timp,2perc,harp,strings,cel [20']
sc STIM H-2772                      (B742)

Symphony No. 9
4(pic).3(English horn).3(bass
clar).3(contrabsn). 4.4.4.1.
2timp,4perc,harp,strings,cel
[23'] sc,pts STIM H-2549     (B743)

Symphony No. 10
see Sinfonie Gracieuse Ou
L'Apothéose De Berwald

Symphony No. 11
3(pic).3(English horn).3(bass
clar).3(contrabsn). 4.4.4.1.
timp,perc,harp,strings,cel [41']
(1. In Der Schwebe 2. Festen
Schrittes 3. Zwiegespräch 4.
Abgesang) STIM sc H-2869, pts
A-520                               (B744)

Symphony No. 12
"Mouvements Sonores Et Accentués"
3(pic).3(English horn).3(bass
clar).3(contrabsn). 4.4.4.1.
timp,5perc,harp,strings,cel STIM
                                    (B745)

BUCKLIGE PFERDCHEN, DAS: SUITE NO. 1
see Shchedrin, Rodion

BUCZYNSKI, PAWEL
Fallende Blaetter
string orch TONOS M-2015-3629-3
                                    (B746)

BUCZYNSKI, WALTER (1933-   )
Aria And Scherzo
string orch [7'40"-8'20"] sc
CANADIAN MI 1500 B926ARI     (B747)

Ars Romantica
string orch [12'] sc CANADIAN
MI 1500 B926AR                      (B748)

Concerto for Piano and Orchestra
2.2.2.2. 2.2.0.0. 2perc,strings,pno
solo [27'] sc CANADIAN
MI 1361 B926CO                      (B749)

Lyric For Piano And Orchestra
2(pic).2.2.2. 2.2.2.0. timp,perc,
strings,pno solo [16'] sc
CANADIAN MI 1361 B926LY       (B750)

Lyric II For Piano And Orchestra
3(pic).3(English horn).3(bass
clar).3(contrabsn). 4.3.3.1.
timp,2perc,harp,strings,pno solo
sc CANADIAN MI 1361 B926LY2   (B751)

Lyric VI
string orch,clar solo,trp solo,
vibra/marimba solo,db solo [20']
sc CANADIAN MI 1750 B926L6 (B752)

Prayer And Dance
string orch,string quar soli,clar
solo [20'] sc CANADIAN
MI 1750 B926PR                      (B753)

Rhapsody for 2 Horns and String
Orchestra
[18'] sc CANADIAN MI 1732 B926RH
                                    (B754)

Summer Days, Summer Nights
2.2.2.2. 2.2.2.0. perc,harp,cel,
strings [11'] sc CANADIAN
MI 1100 B926SU                      (B755)

Three Serenades
1.1.1.1. 1.1.1.0. strings [16'] sc
CANADIAN MI1200 B926TH       (B756)

BUDAPESTER MARSCH
1+pic.1.2.1. 2.2.3.0. perc,pno,3vln
I,2vln II,2vla,2vcl,2db [8']
SCHOTTS CRZ 4001 perf mat rent
                                    (B757)

BUDDE, KURT (1894-1971)
Fröhlicher Abschied (Rondo, Op. 26)
Op.69
2.2.3.2. 4.3.3.1. timp,perc,strings
[14'] BREITKOPF-W                  (B758)

Rondo, Op. 26
see Fröhlicher Abschied

BUFFARDIN, PIERRE-GABRIEL
Concerto in E minor for Flute,
Strings and Continuo
cembalo,8vln I,7vln II,6vla,5vcl,
4db [15'] sc,solo pt PETERS 02402
                                    (B759)

BUHR, GLENN (1954-   )
Beren And Lúthien
3(pic).3(English horn).4(bass clar,
clar in E flat).3(contrabsn).
4.3.3.1. timp,3perc,pno&cel,harp,
strings [21'] (after the mythical
tale by j.r.r. tolkien, 1. Beren
Frchamion 2. Tinuviel 3. The Lay
Of Leithian) sc CANADIAN
MI 1100 B931BE                      (B760)

BUKOVY, WILLIAM (1932-1968)
Concerto for Violoncello and
Orchestra
5.4.5.5. 4.4.4.0. timp,perc,xylo,
vibra,cel,pno,strings,vcl solo
[21'] CESKY HUD.                   (B761)

BULIS, JIRI (1946-   )
Utrpeni Knizete Sternenhocha
3.3.3.2. 4.3.4.1. timp,perc,pno,
harp,strings [10'] CESKY HUD.
                                    (B762)

BULL, EDVARD HAGERUP (1922-   )
Concertino for Tuba and Chamber
Orchestra
see Giocoso Bucolico

Giocoso Bucolico (Concertino for Tuba
and Chamber Orchestra)
"Muse Legère, La" 1(pic).1(English
horn).0.0. 0.1.0.0. 2pno,strings,
tuba solo NORSKMI                  (B763)

Muse Legère, La
see Giocoso Bucolico

BURATINO see Odstrcil, Karel

BUREN, JOHN VAN (1952-   )
Concertino for Flute and String
Orchestra
[18'30"] PEER rent                 (B764)

BURGAN, PATRICK (1960-   )
Concertino [21']
string orch,pno
BILLAUDOT                           (B765)

Éclair...Puis La Nuit!, Un
1.1.1.1. 1.1.1.0. 2perc,harp,2vln,
vla,vcl,db LEDUC                   (B766)

BURGE, JOHN (1961-   )
Concerto for Piano and Orchestra
2.2.2.2. 4.2.2.0. timp,2perc,
strings,pno solo [35'] sc,pno red
CANADIAN MI 1361 B964CO       (B767)

BURGHAUSER, JARMIL (1921-   )
Ciaconna Per Il Fine D'Un Tempo
3.2.3.3. 4.2.3.0. timp,perc,
strings,pno solo [11'] CESKY HUD.
                                    (B768)

Strom Zivota
3.3.3.2. 4.2.3.1. timp,perc,
harp,strings [11'] CESKY HUD.
                                    (B769)

Suite in B flat
2.2.2.2. 2.2.0.0. timp,strings
[22'] CESKY HUD.                   (B770)

BURGON, GEOFFREY (1941-   )
Concerto for Trumpet and Strings
strings,trp solo [22'] CHESTER
                                    (B771)

BURGUNDY VARIATIONS see Bach, Jan
Morris

BURIAN, EMIL FRANTISEK (1904-1959)
Siréna *film/Suite
3.3.3.3. 4.3.3.1. timp,perc,pno,
harp,strings [22'] CESKY HUD.
                                    (B772)

...BURIED WITH ANY AMOUNT OF PETALS,
ALL THAT WAS BEAUTIFUL see
Ichinose, Tonika

BURKE, JOHN (1951-   )
À La Source D'Hypocrene
2fl,clar,trp in C,vln,vla,vcl,hpsd&
cel,harp,2perc [16'] sc CANADIAN
MI1200 B959AL                      (B773)

BURKE, JOHN (cont'd.)

Lament
     string orch,English horn solo sc
     CANADIAN MI 1622 B959LA          (B774)

BÜRKHOLZ, THOMAS
     Säulen Des Memnon
     2.2.1.1. 3.1.0.1. timp,perc,pno/
     synthesizer,bass gtr,drums,8vln
     I,7vln II,6vla,5vcl,4db [19'] sc
     PETERS 03186                     (B775)

BURLESCA see Coulthard, Jean

BURLESCA NR 2 see Sevius, Sven

BURLESKA see Bartoš, Jan Zdenek see
     Pravecek, Jindrich see Vacek, Miloš

BURLESQUE OUVERTUERE see Langer, Hans-
     Klaus

BURNT OFFERINGS see Gellman, Steven

BURRELL, DIANA (1948-    )
     Anima
     strings UNITED MUS               (B776)

     Concerto for Viola and Orchestra
     2.2.2.2. 2.2.0.0. perc,strings,vla
     solo [20'] UNITED MUS            (B777)

     Enchainements
     0.2.0.0. 2.0.0.0. strings [15']
     UNITED MUS                       (B778)

     Io!
     0.0.0.0. 0.3.3.0. strings [7']
     UNITED MUS rent                  (B779)

     Meer, Das So Gross Und Weit Ist, Da
     Wimmelt's Ohne Zahl, Grosse Und
     Kleine Tiere, Das
     string orch [15'] UNITED MUS rent
                                      (B780)

     Resurrection
     2.2.2.2. 2.2.0.0. perc,strings
     UNITED MUS                       (B781)

BURRITT, LLOYD (1940-    )
     Cicada
     3(pic).2.3.2. 4.3+3cornet.3.1.
     timp,perc,harp,2electronic tape,
     strings [8'] sc CANADIAN
     MI 9400 B971CI                   (B782)

     Overdose
     2.2.2.2. 2.2.0.0. perc,2electronic
     tape,strings [15'] sc CANADIAN
     MI 9400 B9710V                   (B783)

     Spectrum
     strings,pno,electronic tape [15']
     sc CANADIAN MI 9400 B971SP (B784)

     Symphonic Overture
     2(pic).2+English horn.2.1. 4.2.3.1.
     timp,perc,strings [5'] sc
     CANADIAN MI 1100 B971SY          (B785)

BURWICK, KARIN (1969-    )
     P Glnt
     2.0.2.1. 0.2.2.1. timp,2perc,
     strings,2elec gtr,elec bass,2pno
     sc STIM                          (B786)

     Speldosan: Ett Uppdragsverk
     2.2.2.2. 2.2.3.1. timp,perc,
     strings,pno sc STIM              (B787)

BUS, JAN (1961-    )
     Adagio
     string orch [7'] sc DONEMUS  (B788)

     Hel Van Het Noorden, De
     2.2.2.2.alto sax.alto sax. 2.1.1.0.
     strings [6'] sc DONEMUS          (B789)

     Quando Salta Fuori La Tonica?
     2.2.2.2. 2.2.0.0. perc,strings [6']
     sc DONEMUS                       (B790)

     Van Feesten En Angsten
     3.3.3.3. 4.3.3.0. 3perc,harp,
     strings [14'] sc DONEMUS    (B791)

BUSCH, ADOLF (1891-1952)
     Concerto for Violin and Orchestra,
     Op. 20
     (Spring, R.) 2.2.2.2. 2.2.0.0.
     timp,strings,vln solo [25']
     BREITKOPF-W                      (B792)

     Concerto, Op. 43
     2+2pic.3+English horn.3+bass
     clar.3+contrabsn.2sax. 4.2+
     2cornet.4.0. timp,4perc,strings
     [18'] BREITKOPF-W                (B793)

     Divertimento, Op. 30
     1.1.1.1. 2.1.0.0. timp,strings
     [19'] BREITKOPF-W                (B794)

BUSCH, ADOLF (cont'd.)

     Symphony in E minor, Op. 39
     2+pic.2+English horn.3+bass clar.2+
     contrabsn. 4.2.3.1. timp,perc,
     strings [27'] BREITKOPF-W        (B795)

     Variationen Über Ein Thema Von W.A.
     Mozart  *Op.41
     2.2.2.2. 3.2.0.0. timp,strings
     [20'] BREITKOPF-W                (B796)

BUSCH, CARL (1862-1943)
     Amerikanisches Volkslied
     strings [4'] BREITKOPF-W         (B797)

     Elegy in D minor, Op. 30
     strings [4'] BREITKOPF-W         (B798)

     My Old Kentucky Home
     strings [4'] BREITKOPF-W         (B799)

     Passing Of Arthur, The: Prolog
     *Op.25
     2.2.2.2. 4.2.3.1. timp,harp,strings
     [6'] BREITKOPF-W                 (B800)

BUSCH, HANS
     Im Walzerrausch
     "Valse Brillante" 2.2.2.2. 4.3.3.0.
     timp,perc,harp,strings [4'15']
     sc,set BUSCH DM 040 rent    (B801)

     Valse Brillante
     see Im Walzerrausch

BUSH, ALAN [DUDLEY] (1900-1995)
     Africa  *Op.73
     2.3.3.3. 4.3.3.1. timp,3perc,8vln
     I,7vln II,6vla,5vcl,4db,pno solo
     [25'] sc,solo pt PETERS 03156
                                      (B802)

BUSH, GEOFFREY (1920-    )
     Divertimento
     string orch [22'] sc,pts STAINER
     HL260 rent                       (B803)

BUSONI, FERRUCCIO BENVENUTO (1866-1924)
     Altoums Gebet  *Op.49,No.1
     2.1+English horn.0.2. 0.0.0.0.
     timp,strings without vln,Bar solo
     [3'] BREITKOPF-W                 (B804)

     Concerto for Piano and String
     Orchestra in D minor
     (Sitsky, Larry) (Busoni-Verz. 80)
     sc,pts BREITKOPF-W PB-OB 5160
                                      (B805)

     Concerto for Piano, Orchestra and
     Chorus, Op. 39
     3(pic)+pic.3(English horn).3(bass
     clar).3. 4.3.3.1. timp,4perc,
     strings,TTBarBarBB,pno solo [78']
     (Busoni-Verz. 247) study sc
     BREITKOPF-W PB 5104              (B806)

     Concerto for Violin and Orchestra in
     D, Op. 35a
     3(pic).2.2.2. 4.2.3.1. timp,2perc,
     strings,vln solo [24'] (Busoni-
     Verz. 243) study sc BREITKOPF-W
     PB 5270                          (B807)

BUT D: (BEHIND UTMOST DISTURBANCE) see
     Perder, Kjell

BUTLER, JOHN
     Bacchae Metres
     3.3.3.3. 4.3.3.0. perc,timp,strings
     [23'] OXFORD sc 362236X f.s.,
     perf sc set 3622343 sc,pts rent
                                      (B808)

BUTLER, MARTIN (1960-    )
     Fin Du Siècle
     2(pic).2.2(clar in E flat).2.
     4.2.3.1. timp,2perc,harp,strings
     [7'] sc,pts OXFORD 3622424 sc,pts
     rent                             (B809)

     O Rio
     3(pic).3(English horn).2+bass
     clar.3(contrabsn). 4.3.3.1.
     4perc,timp,strings [16'] OXFORD
     sc 3620995 f.s., perf sc set
     3620987 sc,pts rent              (B810)

BUTTER'S SPREAD TOO THICK, THE see
     Crawley, Clifford

BUTTING, MAX (1888-1976)
     Sieben Stücke für Orchester
     see Stationen

     Stationen  *Op.117
     "Sieben Stücke für Orchester"
     3.2.3.2. 2.3.4.0. timp,perc,gtr,
     acord,8vln I,7vln II,6vla,5vcl,
     4db [30'] sc PETERS 03155 (B811)

BUZEK, JAN (1927-    )
     Koncertantni Symfonietta
     strings,timp,2vln soli CESKY HUD.
                                      (B812)

     Symphony No. 2 for String Orchestra,
     Piano and Timpani
     [25'] CESKY HUD.                 (B813)

BUZEK, JAN (cont'd.)

     Zpevy Staré C Viny
     string orch,Mez solo [15'] CESKY
     HUD.                             (B814)

BYRNAN WOOD see Sawer, David

BYSTRÖM, BRITTA (1977-    )
     Horisontvals
     orch STIM                        (B815)

BYZANTIUM see Tippett, [Sir] Michael

# C

CABEZÓN, ANTONIO DE (1510-1566)
Prelude In The Dorian Mode
(Grainger, Percy Aldrige) strings
[4'30"] BARDIC                    (C1)

CACHUCHA GALOP see Strauss, Johann,
[Jr.]

CADENCES see Tomasi, Henri

CAESURA see Cole, Bruce

CAGE, JOHN (1912-1992)
Eighty
7alto fl,7English horn,7clar,7trp,
16vln I,14vln II,12vla,10vcl
[30'] PETERS P67467              (C2)

Fourteen
1(pic)+bass fl.0.1+bass clar.0.
1.1.0.0. 2perc,2vln,vla,vcl,db,
pno solo [15'] PETERS P67330 (C3)

Music For...
1.1.1.0. 1.1.1.0. 4perc,2pno,2vln,
vla,vcl,solo voice [30'] (title
to be completed by adding to
"Music For" the number of players
performing) pts PETERS P67040-P
                                 (C4)
108
4(pic,alto fl).5(2English
horn).5(2bass
clar).5(2contrabsn). 7.5.5.1.
5perc,18vln I,16vln II,12vla,
12vcl,8db [45'] PETERS P67414
                                 (C5)
101
4(pic,alto fl).4(English
horn).4(bass clar).4(contrabsn).
6.4.3.1. timp,4perc,pno,harp,
18vln I,16vln II,12vla,12vcl,8db
PETERS P67265                    (C6)
103
4(pic,alto fl).4(2English
horn).4(bass clar).4(contrabsn).
4.4.4.1. 2timp,2perc,strings
[90'] PETERS P67433              (C7)

Ryoanji
20inst [21'] PETERS 00248        (C8)

Seventy-Four
3.3.3.3. 4.3.3.1. 2perc,2pno,harp,
14vln I,10vln II,8vla,8vcl,6db
[12'] PETERS P67482              (C9)

Sixty-Eight
3alto fl,3English horn,5clar,5trp,
4perc,2pno,14vln I,12vln II,
10vla,10vcl [30'] PETERS P67486 (C10)
Thirteen
1.1.1.1. 0.1.1.1. 2perc,2vln I,vln
II,vla,vcl [30'] PETERS 02859   (C11)

Twenty-Eight, Twenty-Six And Twenty-
Nine
4(alto fl).4(English
horn).4.4(contrabsn). 4.4.3.1.
2timp,2perc,pno,14vln I,12vln II,
10vla,8vcl,6db [29'] PETERS
P67466                           (C12)

Twenty-Nine
2timp,2perc,pno,10vla,8vcl,6db
[29'] PETERS P67466C             (C13)

Twenty-Six
26vln [26'] PETERS P67466B       (C14)

Twenty-Three
13vln,5vla,5vcl [23'] PETERS P67228
                                 (C15)
CAJKOVSKIJ, PETR ILJIC
see TCHAIKOVSKY, PIOTR ILYICH

CALABRO, LOUIS (1926-1991)
Fugue for Strings
ELKAN-V rent                     (C16)

CALAVERAS see Gordon, Jerold James

CALENDAR see Farkas, Ferenc

CALIBAN FRAGMENTS AND ARIA see
Bainbridge, Simon

CALL OF THE MOUNTAINS, THE see Ives,
Charles

CALTABIANO, RONALD (1959-   )
Preludes, Fanfares, And Toccatas
3(pic).3(English horn).3(clar in E
flat,bass clar).3(contrabsn).
4.3.2.1. timp,3perc,pno,strings
[17'] MERION rent                (C17)

CALTABIANO, RONALD (cont'd.)
Prolegomenon
3(2pic).3(English horn).3(clar in E
flat,bass clar).3(contrabsn).
4.3.3(bass trom).1. timp,3perc,
pno,strings [5'30"] MERION rent
                                 (C18)
CALYX see Serei, Zsolt

CAMBINI, GIOVANNI GIUSEPPE (1746-1825)
Sinfonia Concertante
2.0.0.0. 2.0.0.0. strings,vln&vla
soli HUG                         (C19)

CAMBRIDGE HOCKET see Goehr, Alexander

CAMERATA MUSIC see Jarvlepp, Jan

CAMPANA, JOSE LUIS (1949-   )
Circoli Viziosi III [22']
1.1.1.1. 1.1.1.1. perc,pno,
strings
BILLAUDOT                        (C20)

CAMPANELLA, LA see Paganini, Niccolo

CAMPBELLS ARE COMING, THE see Anderson,
Leroy

CAMPO DE ESTRELLAS see Marco, Tomas

CAMPRA, ANDRÉ (1660-1744)
Tancrède: Suite Instrumentale
strings [13'] JOBERT             (C21)

CAMPUS STELLAE see Alis, Roman

CANADA 1967 see Bissell, Keith W.

CANADIAN OVERTURE see Lauber, Anne

CANADIAN SUMMER see Sherman, Norman

CANADINA see Klein, Lothar

CANAT DE CHIZY, EDITH (1950-   )
Concerto for Violin and Orchestra
see Exultet

De Noche
2.1.1.1. 1.1.1.0. perc,harp,pno,
strings [20'] JOBERT             (C22)

Exultet (Concerto for Violin and
Orchestra)
2.2.2.2. 2.2.2.0. 3perc,harp,
strings,vln solo [16'] JOBERT
                                 (C23)
Siloël
12strings [12'] JOBERT           (C24)

Yell
3.2.3.2. 4.3.2.1. 3perc,harp,pno,
strings [20'] JOBERT             (C25)

CANCAO DO POETA DO SECULO XVIII see
Villa-Lobos, Heitor

CANDIDE SUITE see Bernstein, Leonard

CANNABICH, CHRISTIAN (1731-1798)
Concerto for Flute, Oboe, Bassoon and
Orchestra in C
(Päuler) fl,ob,bsn,orch KUNZELMANN
ipa sc 10047A, oct 10047         (C26)

Sinfonia, Op. 10, No. 1, in D
(Badley, Allan) 2ob,2horn,2vln,vla,
vcl,db [10'] ARTARIA AE076       (C27)

Sinfonia, Op. 10, No. 2, in G
(Badley, Allan) 2fl,2horn,strings
[11'] ARTARIA AE077              (C28)

Sinfonia, Op. 10, No. 3, in B flat
(Badley, Allan) 2ob,2horn,2vln,vla,
vcl,db [10'] ARTARIA AE078       (C29)

Sinfonia, Op. 10, No. 4, in F
(Badley, Allan) 2ob,2horn,2vln,vla,
vcl,db [13'] ARTARIA AE079       (C30)

Sinfonia, Op. 10, No. 5, in D minor
(Badley, Allan) 2fl,2horn,2vln,vla,
vcl,db [8'] ARTARIA AE080        (C31)

Sinfonia, Op. 10, No. 6, in E
(Badley, Allan) 2fl,2horn,2vln,vla,
vcl,db [12'] ARTARIA AE081       (C32)

CANO, FRANCISCO (1940-   )
Pequeña Suite Iberoamericana
2.2.2.2. 2.0.0.0. strings,acord
solo [12'] perf sc EMEC f.s.
                                 (C33)
CANON see Sandgren, Joakim

CANONES see Schnebel, Dieter

CANTADORA see Naessen, Ray

CANTATA IN ONORE DEI SOMMO PONTEFICE
PIO NONO see Rossini, Gioacchino

CANTATE PER CONTRALTO see Vivaldi,
Antonio

CANTATE PER SOPRANO, VOL. 1 see
Vivaldi, Antonio

CANTATE PER SOPRANO, VOL. 2 see
Vivaldi, Antonio

CANTATES see Hasse, Johann Adolph

CANTAVERN see Haworth, Frank

CANTELOUBE DE MALARET, MARIE-JOSEPH
(1879-1957)
Chants Paysans: 3e Série
(Kingsley, G.) 2.1.2.1. 2.0.0.0.
harp,2perc,timp,cel,strings LEDUC
f.s.
contains: Oh Madelon, Je Dois
Partir; Quand Lou Moulinié
(Lorsque Le Meunier);
Réveillez-Vous, Belle Endormie;
Rousinholet Que Cantes
(Rossignol Qui Chante)          (C34)

Oh Madelon, Je Dois Partir
see Chants Paysans: 3e Série

Quand Lou Moulinié (Lorsque Le
Meunier)
see Chants Paysans: 3e Série

Réveillez-Vous, Belle Endormie
see Chants Paysans: 3e Série

Rousinholet Que Cantes (Rossignol Qui
Chante)
see Chants Paysans: 3e Série

CANTI see Lukas, Zdenek

CANTICLE FOR ORCHESTRA see Wallace,
William

CANTICLE II see Wallace, William

CANTICLE OF LIGHT see Nishimura, Akira

CANTICLE OF THE ISLAND see Cardy,
Patrick

CANTICO DE LA ESPOSA see Rodrigo,
Joaquín

CANTIGA see Matthews, David

CANTILENA FOR BALTIKUM see Karlsen,
Kjell Mørk

CANTILENA FOR STRING ORCHESTRA see
Saylor, Bruce (Stuart)

CANTILENA FOR STRINGS see Wallace,
William

CANTILENA INFINITA see Hobson, Bruce

CANTILENE see Durko, Zsolt

CANTIO FOR VIOLA AND STRINGS see
Bjorklund, Terje

CANTO CHE SI SPEGNE see Marti, Heinz,
Concerto for Violin, String
Orchestra and 2 Percussionists

CANTO CON PASSIONE see Edlund, Swante

CANTO DEL TEMPO see De Grandis, Renato

CANTO DELLA TERRA see De Grandis,
Renato

CANTO DI LODE see Bodorova, Sylvie

CANTO ELEGIACO see Berry, Wallace

CANTO ETERNO see Breimo, Bjørn

CANTOS see Hedstrom, Åse

CANZONA see Forsyth, Malcolm see
Salzedo, Leonard (Lopes)

CANZONA, PER KAMMERORKESTER see
Johnsen, Hallvard

CANZONA A RITORNEL see Korte, Oldrich
František

CANZONA CONCERTATA PER ARCHI see Klein,
Richard Rudolf

CANZONE see Tanejew, S.

CANZONE, FOR CLARINET AND STRING
ORCHESTRA see Taneyev, Sergey
Ivanovich

CANZONE DOLCE see Precechtel, Zbynek

CANZONE E INTERMEZZI see Peška,
Vlastimil

CANZONETTA see Liedbeck, Sixten see Nicode, Jean Louis

CANZONETTA IN E FLAT see Jonák, Zdenek

CAPLET, ANDRÉ (1878-1925)
Légende
0.1.1.1. 0.0.0.0. vln I,vln II,vla, vcl,db,alto sax solo [13'30"] pts FUZEAU 2801 (C35)

CAPRICCIO see Ideta, Keizo see Kvech, Otomar

CAPRICCIO: CLOSING SCENE see Strauss, Richard

CAPRICCIO CONCERTANT see Bartoš, Jan Zdenek

CAPRICCIO DI NICCOLO see Proto, Frank

CAPRICCIO PASTORALE see Frescobaldi, Girolamo

CAPRICCIO: SUITE NO. 1 see Lajtha, Laszlo

CAPRICCIO: SUITE NO. 2 see Lajtha, Laszlo

CAPRICCIO: SUITE NO. 3 see Lajtha, Laszlo

CAPRICCIO ÜBER EIN POLNISCHES VOLKSLIED see Finke, Fidelio Friedrich (Fritz)

CAPRICCIO ÜBER ENGLISCHE WEISEN see Tchaikovsky, Boris, Capriccio for Orchestra

CAPRICE POUR ORCHESTRE see Kingma, Piet

CAPRICHOS see Woolrich, John

CAPTAIN KIDD, JR. see Still, William Grant

CARA MIA GWEN see Singleton, Alvin

CARABALI see Leon, Tania Justina

CARATTERE PER ORCHESTRA see Ahlberg, Gunnar

CARAVANE, LA see Chausson, Ernest

CARCERI D'INVENZIONE II see Ferneyhough, Brian

CARCERI D'INVENZIONE IIA see Ferneyhough, Brian

CARDÁŠ see Dlouhy, Jaromir

CARDY, PATRICK (1953- )
Avalon
2(pic).2.2.2. 2.2.0.0. 2perc, strings [23'] sc CANADIAN MI 1100 C269AV (C36)

Canticle Of The Island
3(pic).3(English horn).3.2(contrabsn). 4.4.3.1. 6perc,pno,harp,cel,12vln I,12vln II,8vla,8vcl,4db,S solo, (voice in mvt. 3) [30'] sc CANADIAN MV 1400 C269CA (C37)

Chaconne
1.1.1.1. 1.1.0.0. 2perc,strings, marimba solo [15'] sc CANADIAN MI 1340 C269CH (C38)

Serenade for Clarinet, Bassoon and String Orchestra
(1. Prelude 2. Romance 3. Jig) sc CANADIAN MI 1626 C268SE) (C39)

Virelai
string orch,clar solo sc CANADIAN MI 1623 C269VI (C40)

CARIBBEAN BACCHANAL see Aguila, Miguel Del

CARIGNAN, NICHOLE (1952- )
Évocations
string orch [8'] sc CANADIAN MI 1500 C277EV (C41)

Mosaïques Pour Grand Orchestre
3(pic).2.4(bass clar,clar in E flat).3(contrabsn). 4.3.3.1. timp,5perc,strings sc CANADIAN MI 1100 C277MO (C42)

CARILLON see Müller-Siemens, Detlev see Northcott, Bayan see Wilson, Thomas

CARILLON, FOR ORCHESTRA, OP. 80 see Meyer, Krzysztof

CARILLON DE NOËL see Giordano, Umberto

CARLITO'S WAY see Doyle, Patrick

CARLSTEDT, JAN (1926- )
Metamorphosi Per Archi *Op.42
3vln I,3vln II,2vla,2vcl,db sc GEHRMANS (C43)

CARMEL EULOGIES see Thoresen, Lasse

CARMELA see Still, William Grant

CARMEN FANTASY, A, FOR DOUBLE BASS AND ORCHESTRA, A see Proto, Frank

CARMEN: FANTASY, FOR VIOLIN AND STRING ORCHESTRA see Sarasate, Pablo de

CARMEN FANTASY FOR JAZZ ENSEMBLE AND ORCHESTRA see Proto, Frank

CARNAVAL see Glazunov, Alexander Konstantinovich

CARNAVAL DE VENISE see Arban, Jean Baptiste see Herbillon, Giles

CARNAVAL DES ANIMAUX, LE see Saint-Saëns, Camille

CARNAVAL DES ANIMAUX FABULEUX, LE see Olofsson, Kent

CARNAVALITO see Karkoff, Ingvar

CARNEVAL DES ANIMAUX see Saint-Saëns, Camille

CARNIVAL: MOVEMENT FOR ORCHESTRA see Douglas, Clive

CARNIVAL OF THE ANIMALS see Saint-Saëns, Camille, Carnaval Des Animaux, Le

CARNIVAL OF VENICE, THE: VARIATIONS see Arban, Jean Baptiste

CARO LUIGI see Meyer, Krzysztof

CARO SASSONE, IL see Goldberg, Theo

CAROL SINGERS see Wilby, Philip

CAROLINE MATHILDE see Davies, [Sir] Peter Maxwell

CAROLÍSIMA see Davies, [Sir] Peter Maxwell

CAROLS AND CRACKERS see Wilby, Philip

CARPENTER, JOHN ALDEN (1876-1951)
Sea Drift
orch (symphonic poem, 1942 revised edition) sc SCHIRM.G ED3910 (C44)

CARPENTER, PATRICK E. (1951- )
Ballon Et Croix-Pas De Ciel
2.2.2.2. 2.1.0.0. timp,strings [13'] sc CANADIAN MI1200 C296BA (C45)

Pierres De Grise, Les
3.4+English horn.4+bass clar.3.soprano sax. 3.3.3.0. timp,perc,elec gtr,cel,strings [15'] sc CANADIAN MI 9400 C296PI (C46)

CARSON TURNER, B.
Rhapsody
strings CHESTER pts CH55839, sc CH55838 (C47)

CARTER, ELLIOTT COOK, JR. (1908- )
Anniversary
3(pic).2+English horn.2+bass clar.2+contrabsn. 4.3.3.1. timp, 2perc,pno&cel,16vln I,14vln II, 12vla,10vcl,8db [6'] BOOSEY-ENG rent (C48)
see Three Occasions For Orchestra

Celebration Of Some 100 x 150 Notes, A
see Three Occasions For Orchestra

Concerto for Violin and Orchestra
2(pic)+pic.2+English horn.2(clar in E flat,bass clar)+bass clar.2+contrabsn. 4.3.3.1. 2perc,14vln I/16vln I,12vln II/14vln II, 10vla/12vla,8vcl/10vcl,6db/8db [26'] BOOSEY-ENG rent (C49)

Double Concerto
hpsd,pno,2chamber orch sc,pts SCHIRM.G AMP96139168 (C50)

Partita
2(pic)+pic.2+English horn.2(clar in E flat)+bass clar.2+contrabsn. 4.3.3.1. timp,3-4perc,pno,harp, strings [17'] BOOSEY-ENG rent (C51)

CARTER, ELLIOTT COOK, JR. (cont'd.)
Remembrance
see Three Occasions For Orchestra

Three Occasions For Orchestra
3(2pic).2+English horn.2+contrabsn. 4.3.3.1. timp, 2perc,pno&cel,16vln I,14vln II, 12vla,10vcl,8db BOOSEY-ENG perf mat rent
contains: Anniversary; Celebration Of Some 100 x 150 Notes, A; Remembrance (C52)

Variations for Orchestra
orch sc SCHIRM.G AMP95818-150 (C53)

CARTOON SKETCHES OF THE BAROQUE see Arnold, Alan

CAS, TEN NEZASTAVÍŠ see Sedláček, Bohuslav

CASKEN, JOHN (1949- )
Concerto for Violoncello
2(2pic,alto fl).2(English horn).2(soprano sax,bass clar).0. 2.2.0.0. timp,8vln I,6vln II, 4vla,4vcl,2db,vcl solo [20'] study sc SCHOTTS ED 12394 (C54)

Concerto for Violoncello and Orchestra
2.2.2.2. 2.2.0.0. timp,strings,vcl solo [20'] SCHOTT (C55)

Darting The Skiff
strings [17'] SCHOTTS (C56)

Maharal Dreaming
2(pic).2(English horn).2.2. 2.0.0.0. perc,8vln I,6vln II, 4vla,3vcl,2db [12'] study sc SCHOTTS ED 12374 (C57)

Sortilège
3(pic).2+English horn.2+bass clar.2+contrabsn.soprano sax. 4.2+flügelhorn.3.1. timp,3perc, pno&cel,harp,strings [20'] SCHOTTS (C58)

Still Mine
3(2pic).2+English horn.2+bass clar.3(contrabsn). 4.3.3.1. timp, perc,cel,harp,strings [25'] study sc SCHOTTS ED 12419 (C59)

Tableaux Des Trois Ages
3.3.3.3. 4.3.3.1. timp,3perc, strings [18'] SCHOTTS (C60)

CASSANDRA see Firsova, Elena

CASTELNUOVO-TEDESCO, MARIO (1895-1968)
Concerto for Orchestra, No. 2, in F
FORLIVESI rent (C61)

Coplas. 11 Liriche Brevi
orch FORLIVESI rent (C62)

Ninna Nanna
pno,orch FORLIVESI rent (C63)

CASTLEMAINE ANTIPHONS see Mills, Richard

CASTLES IN THE AIR see Ince, Kamran, Symphony No. 1

CATALANI, ALFREDO (1854-1893)
Ero e Leandro
2+pic.2+English horn.2+bass clar.2. 4.0.3.1. harp,timp,strings [15'] BOCCACCINI BS. 6 rent (C64)

CATS: SUITE NO. 1 see Lloyd Webber, Andrew

CATS: SUITE NO. 2 see Lloyd Webber, Andrew

CAVALLERIA RUSTICANA: INTERMEZZO see Mascagni, Pietro

CAVALLI, (PIETRO) FRANCESCO (1602-1676)
Delizie Contente Che L'Alme Beate (Druckman, Jacob) English horn, hpsd,strings [6'] BOOSEY-ENG rent (C65)

CAVATINA see Myers, Stanley A.

CAVATINA CON DOLORE see Amdahl, Magne

CELEBRATION see Fetler, Paul see Freedman, Harry

CELEBRATION OF SOME 100 X 150 NOTES, A see Carter, Elliott Cook, Jr.

CELESTIAL DANCE see Mollicone, Henry

CELESTIAL DIALOGUES see Ben-Amots, Ofer

CELESTIAL MECHANICS see Hillborg, Anders see Hillborg, Anders, Himmelsmekanik

CELESTIAL MIRROR, THE see Howard, Brian

CÉLESTINE SUITE DE CONCERT, LA see Ohana, Maurice

CELIS, FRITS (1929- )
Concerto Grosso, Op. 31
strings,2vln&vla&vcl soli [16'30"]
BELGE                    (C66)

Contemplazioni *Op.56
strings,vla solo,opt org [18'30"]
BELGE                    (C67)

Fantasy, Op. 45b
string orch [9'] BELGE        (C68)

Ode A Claude Debussy *Op.36
2.2.2.2. 2.2.0.0. timp&vibra,
strings [12'] BELGE          (C69)

Sinfonia Concertante, Op. 59
pno,strings,alto sax solo,opt perc
[21'] BELGE                 (C70)

Sinfonia No. 4, Op. 28
3.3.3.3. 4.3.3.1. timp,perc,cel,
harp,strings [21'] BELGE     (C71)

CENERENTOLA, LA: OVERTURE see Rossini, Gioacchino

CEREMONIAL see Takemitsu, Toru

CEREMUGA, JOSEF (1930- )
Concerto for Trumpet, Piano and Orchestra
3.3.3.2. 4.2.3.1. timp,perc,
strings,trp&pno soli [20'] CESKY
HUD.                        (C72)

Concerto No. 2 for Violin and Orchestra
3.2.2.2. 4.2.3.1. timp,perc,strings
[25'] CESKY HUD.            (C73)

De Vtství
4.3.3.3. 4.3.3.1. timp,perc,harp,
strings [14'] CESKY HUD.     (C74)

Láska k Milému
3.2.2.2. 3.2.3.1. timp,perc,harp,
strings,S/T solo [15'] PANTON
                            (C75)

Slezsky Tanec c. 2 "Kuncicky"
3.3.2.2. 4.2.3.1. timp,perc,harp,
strings [5'] CESKY HUD.      (C76)

Slezsky Tanec c. 3 "Vánocní"
3.2.2.2. 4.2.3.1. timp,perc,harp,
strings [5'] CESKY HUD.      (C77)

Suite for Oboe and String Orchestra see Svetem Mládí

Svetem Mládí (Suite for Oboe and String Orchestra)
strings,ob solo [8'] CESKY HUD.
                            (C78)

Symphony No. 4
3.3.2.2. 4.2.3.1. timp,perc,
strings,pno solo [28'] CESKY HUD.
                            (C79)

CERTAIN LIGHTS REFLECTING see Gilbert, Anthony

CERVÁNKY NAD REKOU see Sedlácek, Bohuslav

CESKÁ KRAJINA see Kratochvíl, Jaromír

CESKÁ POLKA see Jeremias, Bohuslav

CESKÁ RAPSODIE see Sodomka, Karel

CESKÉ LETOKRUHY see Pinos, Alois

CESKÉ TANCE II A III see Sodomka, Karel

CESKY TANEC see Svehla, Antonin

C'EST L'HEIRE AUX VOLETS CLOS see Bernier, Rene

CESTA see Flosman, Oldrich see Petrzelka, Vilém

CESTA KE SLUNCI see Vicar, Jan

CESTA KE SVETLU see Grossmann, Jan

CESTA NA POPRAVIŠTE see Kašlik, Václav

CESTA UZDRAVENÍ see Sluka, Luboš

CESTOVÁNÍ KRAJINOU see Stepanek, Jiri

CHABRIER, [ALEXIS-] EMMANUEL (1841-1894)
Bourrée Fantasque
(Holloway, Robin) 2(pic).1.2.1.
2.2.1.0. timp,2perc,pno,strings

CHABRIER, [ALEXIS-] EMMANUEL (cont'd.)

[5'] BOOSEY-ENG rent        (C80)

Duo De L'Ouvreuse De L'Opéra Comique Et De L'Employé Du Bon Marché
(Delage, R.) 1.1.1.1. 1.1.0.0.
strings,ST soli [5'] BILLAUDOT
                            (C81)

CHACONNE AFTER MONTEVERDI see Shapero, Harold Samuel, On Green Mountain

CHACUN SA CHIMÈRE see Reimann, Aribert

CHAIKOVSKII, PETR IL'ICH
see TCHAIKOVSKY, PIOTR ILYICH

CHAILLY, LUCIANO (1920- )
Improvisation for Orchestra, No. 4
FORLIVESI rent              (C82)

Improvisation for Orchestra, No. 5
FORLIVESI rent              (C83)

Scherzo for Strings
FORLIVESI rent              (C84)

CHAITKIN, DAVID
Pacific Images (Version For 14 Players)
1.1.1.1. 1.1.1.0. 2perc,kbd,vln,
vla,vcl,db [14'] SCHIRM.EC rent
                            (C85)

CHALLAN, HENRI (1910-1977)
Concerto for Alto Saxophone
2.2.2.2. 2.2.1.0. 3timp,perc,cel&
xylo,harp,strings [20'30"] pno
red LEDUC AL 20337          (C86)

CHALUMEAU see Freedman, Harry

CHAMBER CONCERTO see Barnes, Milton see Henze, Hans Werner see Nicholson, George see Phillips, Barre see Skrowaczewski, Stanislaw see Wanek, Friedrich K.

CHAMBER CONCERTO FOR FLUTE, STRINGS AND TIMPANI, OP. 60 see Karlsen, Kjell Mørk

CHAMBER CONCERTO FOR HARPSICHORD see Diemer, Emma Lou

CHAMBER CONCERTO NO. 2 see Straesser, Joep

CHAMBER CONCERTO NO. 3 see Straesser, Joep

CHAMBER MUSIC FOR 12 NO. 1 'CLOUDS' see Ridderström, Bo, Kammarmusik För 12 Nr 1 'Moln'

CHAMBER SINFONIETTA see Swafford, Jan

CHAMBER SYMPHONY see Adams, John see Ades, Thomas see Brady, Timothy see Degen, Helmut see Korolyov, Anatoli see Kunz, Alfred see Kurtz, Eugene Allen see Wilson, Thomas

CHAMBER SYMPHONY FOR 15 SOLO INSTRUMENTS see Schoenberg, Arnold

CHAMBER SYMPHONY NO. 1 see Winter Dance

CHAMBER SYMPHONY, NO. 2 see Kraft, Leo Abraham

CHAMBER-VARIATIONS see Kalmar, Laszlo

CHAN, KA NIN (1949- )
Daughter Of Master Chin, The
3(pic).2.2.2. 4.2.3.1. 4perc,harp,
pno,strings,S solo [10'] sc
CANADIAN MV 1400 C454DA     (C87)

Ecstasy
2(pic).2(English horn).2(bass clar).2(contrabsn). 2.2.0.0.
timp&perc,perc,pno,strings sc
CANADIAN MI 1100 C454EC     (C88)

Fantastic Journey, A
2(pic).2(English horn).2.2.
4.2.3.1. timp,2perc,harp,pno,
strings [20'] sc CANADIAN
MI 1100 C454FAN             (C89)

Flower Drum Song *folk song,Chin
1(pic).2.0.2. 2.0.0.0. strings [5']
sc CANADIAN MI1200 C454FL   (C90)

Goddess Of Mercy, The
2(pic).2.2.2. 4.2.3.1. timp,perc,
strings [5'] sc CANADIAN
MI 1100 C454GO             (C91)

Liu Xiang
4horn,2perc,strings, (more percussion players may be used)
[16'] sc CANADIAN MI1200 C454LI
                            (C92)

CHAN, KA NIN (cont'd.)

Reflection
string orch [5'] sc CANADIAN
MI 1500 C454RE             (C93)

Revelation
2(pic).2(English horn).2+clar in E
flat.2(contrabsn). 2.2.1.0.
3perc,strings [24'] sc CANADIAN
MI 1100 C454R1             (C94)

Revelation For Orchestra (Version II)
3(pic).3+English horn.3(bass clar.
clar in E flat)+clar in E flat.3+
contrabsn. 4.3.3.1. 3perc,harp,
pno,strings [13'] sc CANADIAN
MI 1100 C454R2             (C95)

Revelation For Orchestra (Version III)
2(pic).2(English horn).2+clar in E
flat.2(contrabsn). 2.2.1.0. perc,
pno&cel,strings [24'] sc CANADIAN
MI 1100 C454R3             (C96)

Revelation For Orchestra (Version IV)
2(pic).2(English horn).2+clar in E
flat.2(contrabsn). 2.2.1.0.
3perc,strings [20'] sc CANADIAN
MI 1100 C454R4             (C97)

Treasured Pasture Leisure Pleasure
1(pic).1.1.1. 1.0.0.0. strings
[18'] sc CANADIAN MI1200 C454TR
                            (C98)

CHANGES see Bergsma, William Laurence

CHANNEL FIRING see Pickard, John

CHANSON DE LA BOHÉMIENNE see Tchaikovsky, Piotr Ilyich

CHANSON DE LA FORÊT SOMBRE see Borodin, Alexander Porfirievich

CHANSON DE LA GRAND-MAMAN see Pierne, Gabriel

CHANSON DE LA ROSE see DuBois, Pierre-Max

CHANSON DU PÊCHEUR see Faure, Gabriel-Urbain

CHANSON DU PETIT CORCONNIER see Forsyth, Malcolm

CHANSON MINIMALE: VARIATIONS ON A THEME BY ELGAR see Harper, Edward James

CHANSONS DE GEISHAS see Tomasi, Henri

CHANSONS DE LA GRENOUILLÈRE see Forsyth, Malcolm

CHANT see Grippe, Ragnar

CHANT DES TÉNÈBRES, LE see Escaich, Thierry

CHANT D'ORPHÉE see Ostendorf, Jens-Peter

CHANTANT, EN see Scheffer, Rickard

CHANTS CORSES see Tomasi, Henri

CHANTS ET DANSES DE LA MORT see Mussorgsky, Modest Petrovich

CHANTS PAYSANS: 3E SÉRIE see Canteloube de Malaret, Marie-Joseph

CHANUKAH SUITE NO. 2 see Barnes, Milton

CHAR DES ÂMES, LE see Bleuse, Marc

CHARIVARI see Febel, Reinhard see Trommer, Jack

CHARM OF LULLABIES, A see Britten, [Sir] Benjamin

CHARPENTIER, JACQUES (1933- )
Et Le Jour Vint
1.1.1.1.1. vln,vla,vcl,db,
perc&vibra [16'] LEDUC      (C99)

Symphony No. 8
3+pic.3+English horn.3+bass clar.3+
contrabsn. 6.6.3.1. timp,2perc,
vibra,strings LEDUC        (C100)

CHARRON, JACQUES
Anniversaire
string orch [4'53"] sc,pts FUZEAU
2835                        (C101)

CHASING THE SUN see Earnest, John David

CHASM see Albright, William H.

CHATMAN, STEPHEN (1950- )
Concerto for Piano
2.2.2.2. 4.3.2.0. timp,perc,
strings,pno solo sc CANADIAN
MI 1361 C494PI                    (C102)
2.2.2.2. 4.3.2.0. timp,perc,
strings,pno solo [17'] SCHIRM.EC
rent                             (C103)

Grouse Mountain Lullaby
2.2+English horn.2.0. 2.0.0.0.
strings [4'] sc CANADIAN
MI1200 C494GR                    (C104)

Occasions
3(pic).2.2.2. 4.3.3.1. 3perc,2harp,
cel&pno,strings (1. Sunday
daydream 2. Celebrations) sc
CANADIAN MI 1100 C4940C          (C105)

Three A.M. On Capitol Square
3(pic).2.2.2. 4.3.2.1. 3perc,2harp,
cel,strings, slide projector [6']
sc CANADIAN MI 9400 C494TH      (C106)

CHATSCHATURJAN, ARAM
see KHACHATURIAN, ARAM

CHATTER-BOX see Schultheiss, Ulrich

CHAUN, FRANTIŠEK (1921-1981)
Pet Obrázku
3.2.3.3. 4.4.3.1. timp,perc,xylo,
harp,pno,strings [17'] PANTON
                                 (C107)
Vzpominka Na Josefa Hlinomaze
2.0.0.0. 4.2.0.0. timp,perc,xylo,
pno,strings [12'] CESKY HUD.
                                 (C108)

CHAUSSON, ERNEST (1855-1899)
Caravane, La *Op.14
2+pic.2.2.2. 4.2.3.1. timp,strings
LEDUC                            (C109)

Hymne Védique
3.2.2.4. 4.2.3.1. timp,harp,strings
[12'] LEDUC                      (C110)

CHAUVE-SOURIS, LA: OVERTURE see
Strauss, Johann, [Jr.], Fledermaus,
Die: Overture

CHAVEZ, CARLOS (1899-1978)
Horsepower Suite
see Suite De Caballos De Vapor

Suite De Caballos De Vapor
"Horsepower Suite" 2+pic.2+English
horn.2+clar in E flat+bass
clar.3(contrabsn).opt soprano
sax.opt tenor sax. 4.3.3.1. timp,
3perc,strings [25'] BOOSEY-ENG
rent                             (C111)

CHAYNES, CHARLES (1925- )
Concerto No. 2 for Trumpet, String
Orchestra and Piano
pno,8vln I,7vln II,6vla,5vcl,4db,
trp solo [17'] LÉDUC             (C112)

CHE SOAVE ZEFIRETTO see Mozart,
Wolfgang Amadeus

CHEERS! see Steptoe, Roger

CHELSEA TANGO see MacCombie, Bruce

CHEMINS DE LA MILAREPA, LES see
Desjardins, Jacques

CHEN, QIGANG (1951- )
Extase [17']
2.1.2.2. 2.2.0.0. 2perc,strings,
ob solo
BILLAUDOT                        (C113)

Extase II [17']
1.1.1.1. 1.1.0.0. perc,pno,harp,
2vln,vla,vcl,db,ob solo
BILLAUDOT                        (C114)

Pétale De Lumière, Un [16']
2.2.2.2. 2.2.0.0. 2perc,strings,
fl solo
BILLAUDOT                        (C115)

Reflet d'un Temps Disparu [28']
3.3.3.3. 4.3.3.0. 3perc,pno/cel,
harp,strings,vcl solo
BILLAUDOT                        (C116)

CHEN, YI (1953- )
Ge Xu *antiphon
2.2.2.2. 4.2.3.0. timp,3perc,harp,
strings [8'] PRESSER rent  (C117)

Romance Of Hsiao And Ch'in
string orch,2vln soli [5'] PRESSER
rent                             (C118)

CHEOPS see Ketting, Otto

CHÈRE NUIT see Bachelet, Alfred

CHERNEY, BRIAN (1942- )
Adieux
3(pic).4(English horn).3(bass
clar).3+contrabsn. 6.3.3.1.
5perc,harp,cel,strings [18'] sc
CANADIAN MI 1100 C521AD     (C119)

Concerto for Oboe
2(pic).2.2.2. 2.2.0.0. 2perc,
strings,ob solo [21'] sc CANADIAN
MI 1322 C5210B                   (C120)

"...Et J'Entends La Nuit Qui Chante
Dans Cloches"
2(pic).2(English horn).2.2.
2.2.0.0. 2perc,harp,pno&cel,8vln
I,6vln II,4vla,4vcl,2db,pno solo
[21'] sc CANADIAN MI 1361 C521JE
                                 (C121)

Into The Distant Stillness
2(pic).2.2.2. 2.2.0.0. perc,pno,
8vln,3vla,3vcl,2db [16'] sc
CANADIAN MI 1100 C521INT    (C122)

Transfiguration
3(pic).2(English
horn).2.3(contrabsn). 4.3.3.1.
3perc,harp,pno&cel,12vln I,10vln
II,8vla,7vcl,5db [20'] sc
CANADIAN MI 1100 C521TR     (C123)

Variations for Orchestra
2(pic).2.2.2. 4.2.3.1. timp,harp/
pno,strings [8'] sc CANADIAN
MI 1100 C521VA                   (C124)

CHERRY see Torke, Michael

CHÉRUBIN: FRAGMENTS SYMPHONIQUES see
Massenet, Jules

CHERUBINI, LUIGI (1760-1842)
Ali Baba: Overture
1.2.2.2. 4.4.3.0+ophicleide. timp,
3perc,strings [6'] BREITKOPF-W
                                 (C125)
Anakreon
2.2.2.2. 4.3.2.0. timp,strings
[10'] BREITKOPF-W                (C126)

Elise: Overture
2.2.2.2. 4.0.0.0. timp,strings [8']
BREITKOPF-W                      (C127)

Faniska: Overture
2.2.2.2. 2.2.1.0. timp,strings [8']
BREITKOPF-W                      (C128)

Sinfonia in D
1.2.2.2. 2.0.0.0. timp,strings
[30'] BREITKOPF-W                (C129)
1.2.2.2. 2.0.0.0. timp,strings
[30'] BOCCACCINI rent            (C130)

CHEVAL DE BRONZE, LE: OVERTURE see
Auber, Daniel-François-Esprit

CHEVALIER DE SAINT-GEORGES
see SAINT-GEORGES, JOSEPH BOULOGNE DE

CHEVAUCHÉE DE NUIT: PRÉLUDES
SYMPHONIQUES see Eyser, Eberhard,
Rid I Natt

CHEVELURE, LA (ARIETTE NO.2) see Coria,
Miguel Angel

CHEVILLARD, (PAUL ALEXANDRE) CAMILLE
(1859-1923)
Fantaisie Symphonique *Op.10
2+pic.2.2.3. 4.2.3.1. timp,perc,
harp,strings [11'] BREITKOPF-W
                                 (C131)

CHI FOR ORCHESTRA see Wallin, Rolf

CHIAROSCURI see Rocca, Lodovico

CHIAROSCURO see Archbold, Paul see
Matthews, Colin

CHIASMA see Dyndahl, Petter

CHIFFRE DE CLAVECIN see Ohana, Maurice

CHIHARA, HIDEKI (1957- )
Wieder Aufzublüh'n Wirst Du Gesät
orch,fl [10'] JAPAN              (C132)

CHILCOTT, ROBERT (BOB)
Organ Dances
2perc,strings,org solo [19'] perf
sc set OXFORD 3558254 sc,pts rent
                                 (C133)

CHILD PLAY see Gellman, Steven

CHILDREN OF DON, THE: OVERTURE see
Holbrooke, Joseph

CHILD'S LONDON, A see Wilson, Richard
(Edward)

CHILI STRING see Johansen, Bertil
Palmar

CHIMAERE see Meijering, Cord

CHIMES AND CANTOS see Lutyens,
Elisabeth

CHINI, ANDRE (1945- )
Au Cirquel!: Humoresque
2(pic).2.2.2.sax. 4.2.3.1. timp,
perc,harp,strings,drums [16'] (1.
Allant; 2. Assez lent; 3. Décidé;
4.. -) STIM sc H-2784, pts A-400
                                 (C134)

Mururoa
vln,orch [24'] study sc REIMERS
101200 rent                      (C135)

CHIPPEWA: CHANT TO (T)HE FIREFLY see
Rickard, Sylvia

CHLÉB A HRY see Fried, Alexj

CHLUBNA, OSVALD (1893-1971)
Já, Potulny Sumar *cant
3.3.3.3. 4.4.3.1. timp,perc,harp,
pno,strings,T&2 speaking voices
CESKY HUD.                       (C136)

CHOIRS see Perera, Ronald Christopher

CHOPIN, FRÉDÉRIC (1810-1849)
Nocturne for Violin and Orchestra in
G minor, Op. 37, No. 1
(Wilhelmi, A.) 0.1.2.2. 2.0.0.0.
strings,vln solo [6'] BREITKOPF-W
                                 (C137)
Nocturne in E flat
(Macmillan, Ernest) 1.1.2.2.
2.0.0.0. timp,harp,strings sc
CANADIAN MI1200 C549NO           (C138)

Piano Concertos In Full Score
orch,pno solo sc DOVER 25835-1
                                 (C139)

CHORAL SYMPHONY see Cowie, Edward see
Lazarof, Henri, Symphony No. 3

CHORALVARIATIONEN see Kirchner, Volker
David

CHOREANS, LES see Delerue, Georges

CHORÉGRAPHIE II see Prevost, Andre

CHORÉGRAPHIE III see Prevost, Andre

CHOREOGRAPHIC FRESCO see Danev,
Miroslav

CHOU, WEN-CHUNG (1923- )
Concerto for Violoncello and
Orchestra
3.4.4.3. 4.3.3.1. timp,4perc,2harp,
8vln I,7vln II,6vla,5vcl,4db
[30'] sc,solo pt PETERS 04409
                                 (C140)

CHRISTE REDEMPTOR see Galuppi,
Baldassare

CHRISTIAN ZEAL AND ACTIVITY see Adams,
John

CHRISTLICHE TRILOGIE see Hamerik, Asger

CHRISTMAS see Weinberger, Jaromir

CHRISTMAS CAROL FANTASIA see McCauley,
William A.

CHRISTMAS LULLABY see Blake, Howard

CHRISTMAS MELANGE see Kozinski, Stefan

CHRISTOPHER COLUMBUS (COMPLETE) see
Walton, [Sir] William (Turner)

CHRISTOPHER COLUMBUS: SUITE see Walton,
[Sir] William (Turner)

CHRISTUS: OVERTURE see Liszt, Franz

CHROMATIC SYNCOPATIONS (THOMAS-MIFUNE)
see Sieben Ragtimes Für
Streichorchester: Heft 2

CHTEL BYSEM NAPSAT TI PSANÍ see Pauer,
Jiri

CHU-KY VII see Ton That, Tiet

CHURÁCEK, JIRI (1960)
Concerto for Bassoon and Orchestra
2.2.2.1. 2.0.0.0. timp,strings,bsn
solo [18'] CESKY HUD.       (C141)

Symphony No. 1
3.3.3.3. 4.3.3.1. timp,perc,xylo,
strings [25'] CESKY HUD.    (C142)

CHVÁLA SKROMNOSTI see Paloucek, Alois

CHVALOZPEVY MÍRU see Slezak, Pavel

CHVÍLE PRO PÍSEN TRUBKY see Petrov,
Vadim

CHVILKA S HARFOU see Sedláček, Bohuslav

CIACCONA Á 3 CHORI see Schmelzer, Johann Heinrich

CIACONA see Engelmann, Hans Ulrich, Chaconne, Op. 56

CIACONNA PER IL FINE D'UN TEMPO see Burghauser, Jarmil

CIAIKOVSKI, PIETRO
see TCHAIKOVSKY, PIOTR ILYICH

CICADA see Burritt, Lloyd

CID, DER: SIEGESMARSCH see Cornelius, Peter

CIDADE DE CAMPINAS see Prado, Almeida
see Prado, José-Antonio (Almeida)

CIGALE, LA see Massenet, Jules

CIKÁNSKÁ RAPSODIE see Macourek, Harry

CIKÁNSKÉ TANCE see Kašlik, Václav

CILENSEK, JOHANN (1913- )
Concerto for Violoncello and Orchestra
2.2.3.2. 4.2.3.1. timp,strings,vcl
solo [22'] BREITKOPF-W       (C143)

Jenaer Gesänge
3.2.3.2. 3.4.3.0. perc,harp,8vln I,
7vln II,6vla,5vcl,4db,Bar solo
[16'] sc PETERS 03134       (C144)

Konzertstück for Organ, Percussion and Strings
3perc,org,8vln I,7vln II,6vla,5vcl,
4db [22'] sc PETERS 03553   (C145)

Konzertstück for Trumpet and Orchestra
3.2.3.2. 1.1.1.0. 2perc,8vln I,7vln
II,6vla,5vcl,4db [22'] sc,solo pt
PETERS 03500                (C146)

Silhouetten
9vln,3vla,2vcl,db [15'] sc PETERS
03499                       (C147)

CIMAROSA, DOMENICO (1749-1801)
Cleopatra, La (Sinfonia)
2.2.2.2. 2.2.0.0. timp,strings [8']
BOCCACCINI BS. 149 rent     (C148)

Concerto for 2 Flutes and Orchestra in G
0.2.0.1. 2.0.0.0. 8vln I,7vln II,
6vla,5vcl,4db [18'] sc,solo pt
PETERS 02681                (C149)

Concerto for Piano and Orchestra in B flat
0.2.0.0. 2.0.0.0. strings,pno solo
[22'] BOCCACCINI BS. 164 rent (C150)

Generalprobe, Die
1.2.2.1. 2.0.0.0. timp,8vln I,7vln
II,6vla,5vcl,4db,fl&bsn&2horn&
2timp soli [20'] sc PETERS 00146 (C151)

Gloria Patri *mot
(Wojciechowski) 8vln I,7vln II,
5vcl,4db,ob solo [6'] sc PETERS
00147                       (C152)

Maître De Chapelle, Le: Overture
orch BOIS                   (C153)

Quoniam Tu Solus Sanctus *mot
8vln I,7vln II,5vcl,4db,ob solo,trp
solo [4'] sc PETERS 00149   (C154)

Sinfonia
see Cleopatra, La
see Vergine Del Sole, La

Vergine Del Sole, La (Sinfonia)
2.2.2.2. 2.2.0.0. timp,strings [8']
BOCCACCINI BS. 153 rent     (C155)

CIMMERIAN DARKNESS: MUSIC FOR STRINGS
see Olofsson, Kent

CINCO NOTICIAS see Dijk, Jan van

CINNABAR see Ward-Steinman, David

CINQ CHANSONS NIÇOISES see Bozza, Eugène

CINQ CHANSONS POUR UNE PRINCESS ERRANTE
see Glass, Paul

CINQ DANSES PROFANES ET SACRÉES see
Tomasi, Henri

5 PIÈCES POUR ORCHESTRE -CYCLES 1-2 see
Gastinel, Gérard

CINQUE LIRICHE SU VERSI DI SALVATORE
QUASIMODO see Haller, Hermann, Ed É
Subito Sera

CINQUE PICCOLI CONCERTI E RITORNELLI
see Henze, Hans Werner

CINQUINA DA CAMERA see Rieti, Vittorio

CIRCOLI VIZIOSI III see Campana, Jose
Luis

CIRCUIT II see Garant, Serge

CIRCULATION see Dmitriev, Sergej

CIRKEL AV RTT LJUS see Luthman, Arne

CIRKELS II see Booren, Jo van den

CIRKUS OF DEMOKRACY, THE see Perrin,
Glyn

CIS-TRANS FOR SINFONIETTA see Ness, Jon
Øivind

CITIZEN OF PARADISE see Floyd, Carlisle

CLAIR DE LUNE see Faure, Gabriel-Urbain
see Indy, Vincent d'

CLANG see Tenney, James C.

CLANG AND FURY see Hillborg, Anders

CLARKE, F.R.C. (1931- )
"Missa De Angelis" Fantasia
string orch,org solo [5'] sc
CANADIAN MI 1664 C592MI     (C156)

CLARKE, JIM
Phrygian Journey
3.3.3.2. 4.3.3.1. perc,pno,harp,
strings [18'] sc,pts KALLISTI ipa
                            (C157)
Portal
3.3.3.3. 4.3.3.1. 4perc,strings
[2'] sc,pts KALLISTI ipa    (C158)

Self Portrait
1.0.1.0.sax. 1.1.1.0. 2perc,kbd,
elec gtr,elec bass gtr,2vln,vcl
[10'] sc,pts KALLISTI       (C159)

CLARKE, KAMES
Maailma
3.3.3.3. 4.3.3.1. 2perc,strings
[13'] manuscript BMIC       (C160)

Pascal, Pensee 206
3.2.2.2. 4.3.3.1. timp,4perc,
strings [7'] manuscript BMIC (C161)

CLARKE, NIGEL
Venetian Mirrors
2.2.2.2. 2.2.0.0. timp,strings BMIC
                            (C162)
Winter Music
strings [12'] BMIC          (C163)

CLASSIC MANIA see Amano, Masamichi

CLASSICAL ARCADE see Kunz, Alfred

CLASSICAL VARIATIONS see Gould, Morton

CLASSICS, BOOK 1
(Steiner) PRESSER 494-01938  (C164)

CLASSICS, BOOK 2
(Steiner) PRESSER 494-01944  (C165)

CLAUDIA LEGARE: FIRST SYMPHONIC SET see
Ward, Robert Eugene

CLAWHAMMER see Plain, Gerald

CLAYTON, LAURA
Rondo for Orchestra
see Terra Lucida

Terra Lucida (Rondo for Orchestra)
3.2.2.3. 4.2.2.1. timp,3perc,pno,
harp,14vln I,10vln II,8vla,8vcl,
6db [14'] sc PETERS 03127   (C166)

CLEANING STAFF see Melnyk, Lubomyr

CLEMENZA DI TITO, LA: ECCO IL PUNTO, O
VITELLIA - NON PIÙ DI FIORI see
Mozart, Wolfgang Amadeus

CLEMENZA DI TITO, LA: SE AL VOLTO MAI
TI SENTI see Mozart, Wolfgang
Amadeus

CLEMENZA DI TITO, LA: SE ALL'IMPERO,
AMICI DEI! see Mozart, Wolfgang
Amadeus

CLEOPATRA, LA see Cimarosa, Domenico

CLEOPATRA: FANTASY see Enna, August

CLEPSIDRA see Lavista, Mario

CLOCHES POUR MICHEL see Wyre, John

CLOCKWORK '85 11' see Cornell, Klaus

CLOKUN see Habbestad, Kjell

CLOUDS see Goldschmidt, Berthold

CLOUDS ON BLUE SKY see Franzen, Olov

CLUSHOES see Sagvik, Stellan

CO JE NEJMILEJŠÍ see Sedmidubsky,
Miloslav

COEXISTENCE IV see Ichiyanagi, Toshi

COITEUX, FRANCIS
Vacances Au Névada
1.1.1.0.sax. 1.0.0.0. bells,
synthesizer,vln I,vln II,vla/vln
III,vcl,db,pno [3'] pts FUZEAU
2993                        (C167)

COLD SILENT SNOW: CONCERTO see Larsen,
Elizabeth B. (Libby), Concerto

COLE, BRUCE (1947- )
Caesura
1(pic).0.1(bass clar).0. 0.0.0.0.
perc,pno,vln,vcl [12'] BOOSEY-ENG
rent                        (C168)

COLÉBI see Dijk, Jan van

COLES, GRAHAM (1948- )
Montague Piece, The
string orch [5'] sc CANADIAN
MI 1500 C693MO              (C169)

Thesis For Orchestra
3(pic).3(English horn).3(bass
clar).3(contrabsn). 4.3.3.1.
timp,5perc,harp,strings [13'] sc
CANADIAN MI 1100 C693TH     (C170)

Variations On A Theme By Raichl
string orch [16'] sc CANADIAN
MI 1500 C693VAR             (C171)

COLGRASS, MICHAEL (CHARLES) (1932- )
Arias
2(pic,alto fl).2(English
horn).1(bass clar).2(contrabsn).
2.2.2.1. timp,3perc,pno&cel,harp,
12vln I,10vln II,8vla,6vcl,4db,
clar solo sc CANADIAN
MI 1323 C695AR              (C172)

Schubert Birds, The
2(pic).3(English horn).2(clar in E
flat,bass clar).2. 2.2.0.0. timp&
perc,strings [17'] sc CANADIAN
MI 1100 C695SC              (C173)

Snow Walker
2(pic).2.2(clar in E flat,bass
clar).2(contrabsn). 2.2.2.1.
timp,3perc,pno&cel,harp,strings,
org solo [19'] (1. Polar
Landscape 2. Throat Singing, With
Laughter 3. The Whispering Voices
Of The Spirits Who Ride With The
Lights In The Sky 4. Ice And
Light 5. Snow Walker) sc CANADIAN
MI 1364 C695SN              (C174)

COLLAGE see Dimitrakopoulos, Apostolo

COLLAGE: BOOGIE see Larsen, Elizabeth
B. (Libby)

COLLEEN BAWN see Still, William Grant

COLLEEN DHAS OR 'THE VALLEY LAY
SMILING' see Grainger, Percy
Aldridge

COLLINES D'ANACAPRI, LES see Debussy,
Claude

COLLOQUE see Fontyn, Jacqueline

COLLUM, HERBERT (1914- )
Concerto for Organ and Orchestra
2.2.0.2. 2.3.2.1. timp,3perc,8vln
I,7vln II,6vla,5vcl,4db [20'] sc,
solo pt PETERS 03131        (C175)

COLOR OF THE LAYERS NO. 1 see Kitazume,
Michio

COLORATION PROJECT X see Minami,
Satoshi

COLORES see Lidholm, Ingvar, Motus

COLOSSOS OR PANIC see Goehr, Alexander

COLOSSUS OF SOUND see Schnyder, Daniel,
Symphony No. 4

COLUMBIAD, THE: PETITE FANTASIE see Heinrich, Anton Philip

COLUMBINE see Cowie, Edward

COLUMBUS see Skroup, František

COMBATTIMENTO see Boehmer, Konrad

COMBATTIMENTO, IL see Boehmer, Konrad

COMBATTIMENTO DELLE PASSIONI UMANI, IL see Dittersdorf, Karl Ditters von

COME YOU NOT FROM NEWCASTLE? (from Folk Songs) (Britten, Benjamin) 2.2.2.2. 2.0.0.0. timp.perc.4vln,high solo,db solo [1'] BOOSEY-ENG rent      (C176)

COMEDIA see McIntyre, Paul

COMEDY CALL'D THE FUNERAL, THE: SUITE see Croft, William

COMISTA see Wanhal, Johann Baptist (Jan Krtitel)

COMMENTARY ON A VISION see Raskatov, Alexander

COMMENTS ON A THEME BY HANDEL see Soproni, Jozsef

COMPASES PARA PREGUNTAS ENSIMISMADAS see Henze, Hans Werner, Music For Viola And 22 Players

COMPLAINTE see Tomasi, Henri

COMPLETE CONCERTI BY BRAHMS see Brahms, Johannes

COMPLETE CONCERTI FOR SOLO KEYBOARD AND ORCHESTRA see Bach, Johann Sebastian

COMPLETE CONCERTI GROSSI see Corelli, Arcangelo

COMPLETE CONCERTI GROSSI IN FULL SCORE see Handel, George Frideric

COMPLETE CONCERTOS FOR TWO OR MORE HARPSICHORDS see Bach, Johann Sebastian

COMPLETE LONDON SYMPHONIES SERIES I see Haydn, [Franz] Joseph

COMPLETE LONDON SYMPHONIES SERIES II see Haydn, [Franz] Joseph

COMPLETE PIANO CONCERTOS see Tchaikovsky, Piotr Ilyich

COMPLETE PIANO CONCERTOS BY BEETHOVEN see Beethoven, Ludwig van

COMPLETE SERENADES SERIES I see Mozart, Wolfgang Amadeus

COMPLETE SERENADES SERIES II see Mozart, Wolfgang Amadeus

COMPLETE SYMPHONIES BY BRAHMS see Brahms, Johannes

COMPLETE SYMPHONIES BY SCHUMANN see Schumann, Robert (Alexander)

COMPLETE WORKS FOR PIANO AND ORCHESTRA see Mendelssohn-Bartholdy, Felix

COMPOSITIONS NO. III see Hultqvist, Anders

CON SORDINO see Korndorf, Nicolai

CONATUS see Feiler, Dror

CONCATENATIONS see Levin, Gregory

CONCERT À QUATRE see Messiaen, Olivier

CONCERT ARIA see Lutyens, Elisabeth

CONCERT ARIA ("DIALOGO") see Lutyens, Elisabeth

CONCERT ASIATIQUE see Tomasi, Henri

CONCERT AVEC PLUSIEURS INSTRUMENTS NO. 7 see Dittrich, Paul-Heinz

CONCERT AVEC PLUSIEURS INSTRUMENTS NO. 8 see Dittrich, Paul-Heinz

CONCERT CAROUGEOIS NO. 4 see Marescotti, André François

CONCERT CLASSIQUE see Pilsl, Fritz

CONCERT DE CHAMBRE see Milhaud, Darius

CONCERT MUSIC see Ward, Robert Eugene

CONCERT MUSIC V see Karlins, M. William

CONCERT OF MYTHS, A see Beckwith, John

CONCERT OVERTURE IN C MINOR see Strauss, Richard

CONCERT SYMPHONIQUE; IN MEMORIAM GYULA KRUDY see Vécsey, Jeno

CONCERT VARIATIONS see Reutter, Hermann

CONCERT VARIATIONS, FOR BAJAN AND ORCHESTRA see Nagai, Akira

CONCERT VOOR 3 KLOKKEN, ALTVIOOL EN ORKEST see Holt, Klaas Ten

CONCERTANTE see Eyser, Eberhard, Sinfonietta No. 3 for Chamber Orchestra see Paulus, Stephen Harrison see Spitta, Heinrich

CONCERTANTE A FÜR 2 VIOLINEN UND ORCHESTER see Spohr, Ludwig (Louis)

CONCERTANTE FOR 2 WINDS see Rainier, Priaulx

CONCERTANTE FOR HARP, VIOLIN & ORCHESTRA see Spohr, Ludwig (Louis)

CONCERTANTE FOR STRING QUARTET AND ORCHESTRA see Davidovsky, Mario

CONCERTANTE: FOR WIND QUINTET AND ORCHESTRA see Bibalo, Antonio

CONCERTANTE MUSIC NO. 3 see Pinkham, Daniel

CONCERTANTE NO. 1 see Pinkham, Daniel

CONCERTANTE NO. 1 IN G see Spohr, Ludwig (Louis)

CONCERTANTE PER PIANOFORTE E ORCHESTRA D'ARCHI see Kalmar, Laszlo, Toccata

CONCERTANTE QUARTET IN B-FLAT see Stamitz, Carl

CONCERTANTE QUARTET IN G see Stamitz, Carl

CONCERTARE see Bon, Andre

CONCERTI FOR WIND INSTRUMENTS see Mozart, Wolfgang Amadeus

CONCERTINA NOVELLA see Rieti, Vittorio

CONCERTINO see Dalbavie, Marc-Andre

CONCERTINO AI DUE BOEMI see Lucky, Stepan

CONCERTINO BRILLANTE "RAUTILIO", FOR STRING ORCHESTRA see Racevicius, Aleksas-Rimvydas

CONCERTINO BUFFO, FOR CHAMBER ORCHESTRA see Petrov, Andrei P.

CONCERTINO DOPPIO CON ECO see Bodorova, Sylvie

CONCERTINO FACILE see Smutny, Jiri

CONCERTINO FOR CASTANETS AND ORCHESTRA see Proto, Frank, Viva Lucero

CONCERTINO FOR CIMBALOM AND ORCHESTRA see Patachich, Ivan, Presentazioni

CONCERTINO FOR ELECTRIC STRING QUARTET AND STRING ORCHESTRA see Weinstangel, Sasha

CONCERTINO GROSSO see Lemeland, Aubert

CONCERTINO IM RUSSISCHEN STIL see Janschinow, A.

CONCERTINO PASTORALE see Bohac, Josef

CONCERTINO PER DIVERTIMENTO see Gullberg, Olof

CONCERTINO PER IL H.W.H. see Bose, Hans-Jurgen Von

CONCERTINO PRO KLAVÍR A MALY SMYCCOVY ORCHESTR see Jirasek, Ivo

CONCERTINO PRO SAN LUCA see Rieti, Vittorio

CONCERTINO RHYTHMIKOSMOS see Reise, Jay

CONCERTINO RUSTICO see Farkas, Ferenc

CONCERTINO SEMPLICE see Fischer, Jan F. see Stanek, Pavel

CONCERTO, FOR BAJAN (ACCORDION) AND ORCHESTRA see Tschaikin, Nikolaj, Concerto for Accordion and Orchestra in B flat

CONCERTO, FOR PIANO AND ORCHESTRA "KREUZTONARTEN" (SHARP KEYS) see Shchedrin, Rodion, Concerto for Piano and Orchestra, No. 4

CONCERTO, FOR PIANO AND ORCHESTRA WITH SOLO TRUMPET see Sergejewa, Tatjana, Concerto for Piano and Orchestra, No. 2, Op. 18

CONCERTO A 15 see Jelinek, Stanislav

CONCERTO A CINQUE see Albinoni, Tomaso

CONCERTO A CINQUE, EN FA MAJEUR see Albinoni, Tomaso, Concerto in F, Op. 9, No. 3

CONCERTO A CINQUE, EN SOL MAJEUR see Albinoni, Tomaso, Concerto in G, Op. 9, No. 6

CONCERTO A CINQUE, EN UT MAJEUR see Albinoni, Tomaso, Concerto in C, Op. 9, No. 9

CONCERTO ARDENTE see Whettam, Graham Dudley

CONCERTO BREVE see Graap, Lothar see Loudova, Ivana see Schibler, Armin

CONCERTO BREVE NR.1 see Kraft, Karl

CONCERTO BURLESCO see Válek, Jiri

CONCERTO CALDO see Harrison, Jonty

CONCERTO-CANTATA see Gorecki, Henryk Mikolaj

CONCERTO CONCERTANT IN D see Reicha, Joseph

CONCERTO CONCISO see Whettam, Graham Dudley

CONCERTO CONCITATO I see Leistner-Mayer, Roland

CONCERTO CONCITATO III see Leistner-Mayer, Roland

CONCERTO CONCITATO IV see Leistner-Mayer, Roland

CONCERTO CORALE see Nabokov, Nicolas

CONCERTO DA CAMERA see Brings, Allen Stephen see Hipman, Silvester see Houdy, Pierick see Jelinek, Stanislav see Michans, Carlos

CONCERTO DA CAMERA FÜR CEMBALO UND KLEINES ORCHESTER see Moeschinger, Albert

CONCERTO DA CAMERA IN D MAJOR see Takemitsu, Toru

CONCERTO DA REQUIEM POUR COR EN FA ET ORCHESTRE see Rønnes, Robert

CONCERTO DA VERONA (CONCIERTO DE LA SENDA NO. 3) see Seco De Arpe, Manuel

CONCERTO DE CAMERA see Bárta, Jiri see Kubik, Ladislav

CONCERTO DE CHAMBRE NO. 1 see Nodaira, Ichiro

CONCERTO DE CHAMBRE NO. 2 see Nodaira, Ichiro

CONCERTO DE L'ADIEU see Delerue, Georges

CONCERTO DE PRINTEMPS see Tomasi, Henri

CONCERTO DELLO SPIRITO see Gougeon, Denis

CONCERTO DI CAMERA see Kenins, Talivaldis

CONCERTO DI CAMERA NO. 2 see Kenins, Talivaldis

CONCERTO DI FLAUTI see Marcello, Alessandro, Concerto

CONCERTO E-G PER PIANOFORTE ED ORCHESTRA see Kapr, Jan

CONCERTO FACILE see Klein, Richard Rudolf

CONCERTO FESTIVO see Obrovská, Jana

CONCERTO FOR BRASS CHOIR AND ORCHESTRA see Lees, Benjamin

CONCERTO FOR CLARINET
"Procrustean Concerto For The B Flat Clarinet" 3.2.3.2.3sax. 2.4.2.3. 4perc,strings,clar solo [17'] sc, pts KALLISTI ipa (C177)

CONCERTO FOR DOUBLE BRASS see Harbison, John

CONCERTO FOR ELECTRIC GUITAR, ORCHESTRA AND CHOIR, OP.14B see Rypdal, Terje

CONCERTO FOR FLÜGELHORN AND ORCHESTRA WITH OBLIGATO TRUMPETS AFTER J. A. HASSE see Goldberg, Theo, Caro Sassone, Il

CONCERTO FOR FLÜGELHORN AND STRING ORCHESTRA see Hagen, Daron

CONCERTO FOR HARP AND CHAMBER ORCHESTRA IN E FLAT MINOR
INTERNAT.S. sc,pts rent, solo pt,pno red (C178)

CONCERTO FOR HARP AND SMALL ORCHESTRA see Hamilton, Iain

CONCERTO FOR HURDY GURDY AND PERCUSSION see Skempton

CONCERTO FOR KOTO AND CHAMBER ORCHESTRA see Ichiyanagi, Toshi

CONCERTO FOR OBOE AND ECHOES OF OTHERS see Dragstra, Willem

CONCERTO FOR ORCHESTRA see Horwood, Michael

CONCERTO FOR PIANO, OP. 90
2.2.2.2. 4.2.0.0. timp,strings [40'] SCHOTTS perf mat rent (C179)

CONCERTO FOR PIANO, STRING ORCHESTRA, AND DRUMS see Gardiner, Mary

CONCERTO FOR SACKBUT AND ORCHESTRA see Mason, Benedict

CONCERTO FOR SHAKUHACHI 20-STR. KOTO AND ORCHESTRA see Terashima, Rikuya

CONCERTO FOR STAN GETZ see Bennett, Richard Rodney

CONCERTO FOR STEEL BAND AND SYMPHONY ORCHESTRA see Rathburn, Eldon, Steelhenge

CONCERTO FOR THREE see Bartoš, Jan Zdenek

CONCERTO FOR THREE GROUPS see Hobson, Bruce

CONCERTO FOR VIOLA SECTION AND ORCHESTRA see Mason, Benedict

CONCERTO FURVUS FOR TUBA AND ORCHESTRA see Karlsen, Kjell Mørk

CONCERTO GIANETTO see Rieti, Vittorio

CONCERTO GIOCOSO see Válek, Jiri

CONCERTO GROSSO 3 X 3 see Sekiai, Satoshi

CONCERTO GROSSO FOR JAZZ QUINTET AND ORCHESTRA see Symonds, Norman

CONCERTO GROSSO IN MEMORIAM ANTON WEBERN see Karayev, Faradzh

CONCERTO GROSSO ÜBER DAS THEMA B-A-C-H see Ulmann, Helmut von, Concerto Grosso for String Orchestra, Op. 21

CONCERTO HONGROIS IN F see Djabadary, Heraclius

CONCERTO IN B-FLAT MAJOR (A-WGM, Q 16467 [NO. 4]) see Mysliveczek, Joseph

CONCERTO IN D MAJOR (A-WGM, Q 16467 [NO. 5]) see Mysliveczek, Joseph

CONCERTO IN D MAJOR (CS-PNM, XXXVIII F 158) see Mysliveczek, Joseph

CONCERTO IN HONOREM BALDVINI REGIS see Verhaegen, Marc

CONCERTO IN MEM. P. CASALS see Lason, Aleksander

CONCERTO LIRICO see Faltus, Leos

CONCERTO MILITAIRE, FOR CELLO see Offenbach, Jacques

CONCERTO NACH EINER VIOLONCELLO-SONATE E-MOLL see Vivaldi, Antonio, Concerto for Violoncello and String Orchestra

CONCERTO "PABLO CASALS IN MEMORIAM" see Lason, Aleksander

CONCERTO PASTORALE see Miller, Franz R.

CONCERTO PER PIANOFORTE ESTEMPORANEO see Glass, Paul

CONCERTO PICCOLO see Bartoš, Jan Zdenek see Linde, Bo, Liten Konsert see Obrovská, Jana see Thilman, Johannes Paul

CONCERTO PICCOLO FÜR KLAVIER UND ORCHESTER see Pick, Carl Heinz

CONCERTO PICCOLO ÜBER B-A-C-H, FOR TRUMPET, STRING ORCHESTRA, HARPSICHORD AND PIANO see Pärt, Arvo

CONCERTO PRIMAVERILE, FOR VIOLIN AND STRING ORCHESTRA see Slonimsky, Sergey, Concerto for Violin and String Orchestra

CONCERTO PROFANO see Stadlmair, Hans

CONCERTO RECITATIVO see Vackar, Tomas

CONCERTO RITMICO see Neubert, Günter

CONCERTO ROMANTICO see Dubrovay, Laszlo

CONCERTO RUSTICO see Domazlicky, Frantisek

CONCERTO SEMPLICE see Hidas, Frigyes see Lendvay, Kamillo see Obrovská, Jana

CONCERTO SERENO: FÜR TROMPETE UND KAMMERORCHESTER (BLÄSER AD LIB.) see Klein, Richard Rudolf

CONCERTO SYMPHONIQUE POUR HARPE ET ORCHESTRE see Ma'ayani, Ami

CONCERTO TRIPLO FOR VIOLIN, VIOLA AND PIANO see Rieti, Vittorio

CONCERTOS D'ORGUE, LES see Corrette, Michel

CONCIERTO ANDALUZ see Rodrigo, Joaquín

CONCIERTO DE CASTILLA see Moreno Torroba, Federico

CONCIERTO DE LA LUZ Y LAS TINIEBLAS see Goethals, Lucien

CONCIERTO PASTORAL see Rodrigo, Joaquín

CONCIERTO ROMANTICO see Ponce, Manuel Maria

CONCRETE JUNGLE see Daugherty, Michael

CONDUCTUS see Wilson, Charles M.

CONFESSION OF ISOBEL GOWDIE, THE see Macmillan, James

CONFESSIONI see Sárközy, Istvan

CONFIDENCIAS see Groba, Rogelio

CONFIGURACIONES SINFONICAS see Bertomeu, Agustin

CONGA see Aguila, Miguel Del

CONGA-LINE IN HELL see Aguila, Miguel Del

CONGEDO (FAREWELL) see Rieti, Vittorio

CONNELL, ADRIAN
Ballade
0.2.0.0. 2.0.0.0. timp,strings,vln solo [11'] manuscript BMIC (C180)

Concerto for Violin and Orchestra
0.2.0.0. 2.0.0.0. timp,strings,vln solo [33'] manuscript BMIC (C181)

In Paradisum
strings [12'] manuscript BMIC (C182)

Spring Song
strings [12'] manuscript BMIC (C183)

Symphonia Romantica
3.3.3.3. 4.3.3.1. timp,3perc,harp, strings,opt pno,opt org, opt 3-9

CONNELL, ADRIAN (cont'd.)
off-stage trp [55'] manuscript BMIC (C184)

CONNEXUS see Wyre, John

CONOSZENA see Stendel, Wolfgang

CONQUERING THE FURY OF OBLIVION see Thomas, Augusta Read

CONSOLATIO PHILOSOPHIAE see Sutermeister, Heinrich

CONSORT MUSIC see Benguerel, Xavier

CONSTANT, FRANZ (1910- )
Alternance *Op.132
3.3.3.2. 4.3.3.1. timp,perc, strings,clar solo [10'15"] BELGE (C185)

Primavera [18']
fl,ob,horn,perc,strings,gtr solo BILLAUDOT (C186)

CONSTANT, MARIUS (1925- )
Brevissima (Symphony in Four Movements)
3(alto fl,pic).3(English horn).4(clar in E flat,bass clar).3(contrabsn). 4.3.3.1. timp,3perc,harp,strings [10'] DURAND rent (C187)

Symphony in Four Movements see Brevissima

CONSTANZE! CONSTANZE! O WIE ÄNGSTLICH, O WIE FEURIG see Mozart, Wolfgang Amadeus

CONSTELLATIONS see Doi, Yoshiyuki

CONSTELLATIONS OF TIME see Matsunaga, Michiharu

CONTE, DAVID
Hymn To The Nativity
1(pic).1+English horn.0.0. 2.0.0.0. perc,harp,kbd,strings [10'] SCHIRM.EC rent (C188)

Masque Of The Red Death, The
3(1pic).2+1English horn.3(1bass clar).2(1contrabsn). 4.3.3.1. timp,perc,harp,kbd,strings SCHIRM.EC rent (C189)

CONTE DE L'OISEAU, LE see Prevost, Andre

CONTEMPLAZIONI see Celis, Frits

CONTENTED HOUSE see Coulthard, Jean

CONTES D'HOFFMANN, LES see Offenbach, Jacques, Tales Of Hoffmann

CONTINUE see Vaage, Knut

CONTINUO: A PARTIRE DA PACHELBEL see Hambraeus, Bengt

CONTRA see Morthenson, Jan W.

CONTRAFLOW see Matthews, Colin

CONTRAPROVISATIONS see Ellis, David

CONTRASTS see Maros, Rudolf

CONVERGENCE OF THE TWAIN, THE see Nicholson, George

CONVERSAZIONI CONCERTANTI see Suter, Robert

CONWAY, JOE
Sad Tuned Tale, A
string quar,string orch [12'] BARDIC (C190)

Three Folk Tales
string orch [15'] BARDIC (C191)

COPLAND, AARON (1900-1990)
Heiress Suite, The
(Freed, Arnold) 3(2alto fl, pic).1(English horn).3.1. 4.3.3.1. 2perc,harp,pno&cel, strings [8'] BOOSEY-ENG rent (C192)

Jubilee Variation
2+pic.2+English horn.2+bass clar.2+ contrabsn. 4.3.3.1. timp,perc, pno,strings [2'] BOOSEY-ENG rent (C193)

Sonata for Violin and Orchestra
(Elias, Gerald) 2(pic)+opt alto fl.2(English horn).2(clar in E flat)+bass clar.2+contrabsn. 2.2.1.1. timp,4perc,pno&cel,harp, strings [19'] BOOSEY-ENG rent (C194)

COPLAS. 11 LIRICHE BREVI see
Castelnuovo-Tedesco, Mario

COR JESU see Emmert, Frantisek,
Symphony No. 9

CORALE, VARIAZIONI E FINALE see Rieti,
Vittorio

CORBETT, SIDNEY
Concerto for Trombone and Orchestra
2.2.2.2. 4.2.2.1. perc,harp,
strings,trom solo [20'] MOECK sc
5495 f.s., pts rent        (C195)

Symphony, No. 1
3.3.3.3. 4.3.3.1. perc,harp,strings
[20'] MOECK sc 5487 f.s., pts
rent                       (C196)

CORBRIDGE LANX, THE see Amos, Keith

CORE see Kono, Atsuro

CORE VI DONO BELL' IDOLO MIO, IL see
Mozart, Wolfgang Amadeus

CORELLI, ARCANGELO (1653-1713)
Complete Concerti Grossi
orch sc DOVER 25606-5       (C197)

Concerto in F
(Guyot, D.) string orch,hpsd,trp
solo [9'] BILLAUDOT         (C198)

Pastorale (from Concerto Grosso Op.
6, No. 8)
(Schering) 8vln I,7vln II,6vla,
5vcl,pno/org,2vln soli,vcl solo
[4'] sc KAHNT 02765         (C199)

CORGHI, AZIO (1937-    )
...Fero Dolore
[It/Lat] ob d'amore,perc,strings,
female solo sc RICORDI-IT 136439
                            (C200)

CORIA, MIGUEL ANGEL (1937-    )
Chevelure, La (Ariette No.2)
(Bandelaire, Charles) 3.2.2.2.
4.0.0.0. cel,harp,strings,solo
voice [6'] perf sc EMEC f.s.
                            (C201)

Verra La Morte (Ariette No.3)
(Pavese, Cesare) 2.3.2.2. 4.0.0.0.
pno,harp,strings,solo voice
[5'30"] perf sc EMEC f.s.   (C202)

CORIGLIANO, JOHN (1938-    )
Gazebo Dances
strings sc SCHIRM.G ED3916   (C203)

Symphony No. 1
orch sc SCHIRM.G ED3864      (C204)

Tournaments
orch sc SCHIRM.G ED3854      (C205)

CORIOLIS see Larsen, Elizabeth B.
(Libby)

CORNELIA see Kubelik, Rafael

CORNELIUS, PETER (1824-1874)
Cid, Der: Siegesmarsch
2+pic.2+English horn.2+bass clar.2.
4.3.3.1. timp,strings [6']
BREITKOPF-W                  (C206)

Gunlöd: Gunlöd, Wie Seh' Ich Dich
Strahlend Geschmückt
3.2+English horn.2+bass clar.3.
4.3.3.1. timp,harp,strings,MezT
soli [13'] BREITKOPF-W       (C207)

Gunlöd: Hidolf, Der Recke, Und Erna,
Sein Weib
3(pic).2+English horn.2+bass
clar.3. 4.3.3.1. timp,harp,
strings,Mez solo [10'] BREITKOPF-
W                            (C208)

Sechs Weinachtslieder *Op.8
(Molin) 2.2.2.2. 2.1.0.0. timp,
perc,cel,harp,8vln I,7vln II,
6vla,5vcl,4db,solo voice [12'] sc
PETERS 02785                 (C209)

CORNELL, KLAUS (1932-    )
Alpenkönig Und Der Menschenfeind, Der
2(pic).0.3(bass clar).0. 0.3.3.0.
1perc,gtr,harp,xylo&vibra,vln,
vcl,db MULL & SCH rent       (C210)

Am Ende Des Orkans Für Orchester
2(pic).1(English horn).2(bass
clar).2. 3.3.3.1. perc,harp,
strings,solo voice MULL & SCH
rent                         (C211)

Bei Der Kanone Dort
see Vier Gesänge Aus Brechts
"Schweyk"

Clockwork '85 11'
1(pic).1.1(bass clar).0. 1.1.0.0.
perc,gtr,2pno,2synthesizer,vln,

CORNELL, KLAUS (cont'd.)
vla,vcl,db, the horn may be
replaced by alto sax or trb MULL
& SCH rent                   (C212)

Concerto for Chamber Group
see Spiel Der Elfen Mit Den Zwölfen

Deutsche Miserere, Das
see Vier Gesänge Aus Brechts
"Schweyk"

Erik Esö Kolozssvarban  *folk song,
Hung
string orch MULL & SCH rent  (C213)

Gewitter
see Weinstock, Der: Zyklus Für
Violoncello Und Streichorchester

Herbst
see Weinstock, Der: Zyklus Für
Violoncello Und Streichorchester

Kälbermarsch
see Vier Gesänge Aus Brechts
"Schweyk"

Lied Von Der Moldau
see Vier Gesänge Aus Brechts
"Schweyk"

Nocturnes
1(pic).1.1.1. 1.0.0.0. strings
(orchestration of nocturnes for
piano) MULL & SCH rent       (C214)

Raimundiana 71: Ein Scherzo-
Kaleidoskop
1(pic).0.2(bass clar).0. 0.3.3.0.
2perc,gtr,mand,harp,pno,cel,
strings (homage to Ferdinand
Daymund) MULL & SCH rent     (C215)

Rebschnitt
see Weinstock, Der: Zyklus Für
Violoncello Und Streichorchester

Remember Kolozsvar
string orch [30'] (Transylvanian
sketches) MULL & SCH rent    (C216)

Sombreval
vln I,vln II,vla,vcl,db,org solo
MULL & SCH rent              (C217)

Sombreval II
3(pic).2(English horn).3(bass
clar).2.tenor sax. 3.2.3.0. timp,
perc,harp,strings [16'] MULL &
SCH rent                     (C218)

Sommer
see Weinstock, Der: Zyklus Für
Violoncello Und Streichorchester

Spiel Der Elfen Mit Den Zwölfen
(Concerto for Chamber Group)
fl,2perc,harp,pno&org,strings,Mez
solo, pan flute, lotos flöte,
zuspielbänder [8'] MULL & SCH
rent                         (C219)

Tod Im Rebberg
see Weinstock, Der: Zyklus Für
Violoncello Und Streichorchester

Vier Gesänge Aus Brechts "Schweyk"
(Eisler; Cornell) orch MULL & SCH
f.s.
contains: Bei Der Kanone Dort;
Deutsche Miserere, Das;
Kälbermarsch; Lied Von Der
Moldau                       (C220)

Weinstock, Der: Zyklus Für
Violoncello Und Streichorchester
vln I,vln II,vla,vcl,db,vcl solo
MULL & SCH f.s.
contains: Gewitter; Herbst;
Rebschnitt; Sommer; Tod Im
Rebberg                      (C221)

CORONA see Sandred, Örjan see Telemann,
Georg Philipp, Concerto Grosso for
2 Flutes, Bassoon, Strings and
Continuo in E minor

CORONA, LA see Betts, Lorne M.

CORONATION FANFARE see Goossens, [Sir]
Eugene

CORPUS see Malmborg-Ward, Paula Af

CORRETTE, MICHEL (1709-1795)
Concerto No. 7
see Servante Au Bon Tabac, La

Concertos D'orgue, Les
orch,org BOIS               (C222)

Servante Au Bon Tabac, La (Concerto
No. 7)
2.2.0.1. 1.0.0.0. timp,strings,

CORRETTE, MICHEL (cont'd.)
solo voices BOIS            (C223)

CORTEGE see Matthews, Colin

CORTÈGE SOLENNEL see Glazunov,
Alexander Konstantinovich

CORTEGE: WITH SOLEMN DANCING AND BELLS
see Amos, Keith

CORYN, R.
Concerto, Op. 54
3.3.3.3.2sax. 4.3.3.1. strings,
vibra solo,xylo solo,glock solo,
marimbaphone solo [27'23"] BELGE
                            (C224)

Vijf Concertpreluden, Op. 44
2+pic.2.12+clar in A, sop-clar in E
flat, 2bass clar, contrabass
clar, sop-sax, 2al-sax, 2ten-sax,
bar-sax, bass-sax. 2bsn+
contrabsn. 4.4+corn.4+bass-
trom.2euph. 4bass tuba. vcl, db,
perc, cel, pno, ob solo [10'30"]
BELGE                        (C225)

COSI DUNQUE TRADISCI see Mozart,
Wolfgang Amadeus

COSÌ FAN TUTTE: AH GUARDA, SORELLA see
Mozart, Wolfgang Amadeus

COSMIC LANDSCAPE see Murakumo, Ayako

COSMIC TREE, THE see Niimi, Tokuhide

COSMOSTROPHE QUAN-QUEN & SAI-BA-RAQ see
Ito, Ken

COSTUME COMEDY OVERTURE, A see Black,
Stanley

COTEK, PAVEL (1922-    )
Glosa Pro Orchestr
4.3.4.3. 4.3.3.1. timp,perc,pno,
harp,strings [12'] CESKY HUD.
                            (C226)

COULEURS POUR ORCHESTRE see Jentzsch,
Wilfried

COULTHARD, JEAN (1908-    )
Ballade Of The West
chamber orch,pno solo [12'] sc
CANADIAN MI 1361 C855BA     (C227)

Billowing Fields Of Golden Wheat
see Introduction And Three Folk
Songs

Burlesca
string orch,pno solo [15'] sc
CANADIAN MI 1661 C855BU     (C228)

Contented House
see Introduction And Three Folk
Songs

I Often Wonder
see Stand Swaying, Slightly

Introduction And Three Folk Songs
2(pic).2(English horn).2.2.
2.1.1.0. timp&perc,harp/pno,
strings sc CANADIAN
MI 1100 C855IN ipa
contains: Billowing Fields Of
Golden Wheat; Contented House;
Lullaby For A Snowy Night;
Mam'zelle Québécoise        (C229)

Lullaby For A Snowy Night
see Introduction And Three Folk
Songs

Lyric Symphony (Symphony No. 3)
3.1.2.1. 2.0.0.0. timp,perc,
strings,bsn solo [25'] sc,pno
red,solo pt CANADIAN
MI 1324 C855LY              (C230)

Mam'zelle Québécoise
see Introduction And Three Folk
Songs

Song For Fine Weather: Of The Haida
Indians
1.1.2.1. 2.2.1.0. timp,perc,
strings,S solo [4'] sc CANADIAN
MV 1400 C855SO              (C231)

Stand Swaying, Slightly
string orch,low solo CANADIAN
MV 1600 C855CY contains also: I
Often Wonder; There Is No
Darkness                     (C232)

Symphony No. 3
see Lyric Symphony

There Is No Darkness
see Stand Swaying, Slightly

COUNTERPOISE see Druckman, Jacob
Raphael

COUNTRY GARDENS see Grainger, Percy
Aldridge

COUNTRY ROUND, A see Anderson, Jean

COUNTRY ROUND, A see Anderson, Jean

COURSING see Knussen, Oliver

COUVERTURE see Öjebo, Pär

COWBOY FANTASY see Goossens, [Sir]
Eugene

COWELL, HENRY DIXON (1897-1965)
Ensemble
  string orch sc SCHIRM.G 50482072
                             (C233)

COWEN, [SIR] FREDERIC HYMEN (1852-1935)
Idyllische Symphonie E-Dur Nr. 6
  see Symphony in E, No. 6

Symphony in E, No. 6
  "Idyllische Symphonie E-Dur Nr. 6"
  3.2.3.2. 4.2.3.1. 3timp,2perc,
  strings [35'] BREITKOPF-W (C234)

COWIE, EDWARD (1943- )
Choral Symphony
  2.2.2.3. 4.2.3.1. timp,3perc,harp,
  strings,mix cor,Bar solo [45']
  (text by J. W. M. Turner, T.
  Hook) SCHOTTS (C235)

Columbine
  1.1.1.1. 1.1.0.0. perc,pno,harp,
  gtr,strings,coloratura sop [30']
  SCHOTTS (C236)

Concerto for Orchestra
  1+pic+alto fl.2.3.3. 4.3.3.1. timp,
  3perc,cel&hpsd,pno,harp,strings
  [35'] SCHOTTS (C237)

Concerto for Piano
  2(pic,alto fl).2(English horn).2.2.
  2.0.0.0. cel,harp,strings,pno
  solo [35'] SCHOTTS (C238)

Fifteen Minute Australia
  2+pic.2+English horn.2+bass clar.2.
  4.3.3.1. timp,2perc,pno,harp,
  strings [15'] SCHOTTS (C239)

Leonardo *Op.20
  2(pic,alto fl).2(English
  horn).2(clar in E flat,bass
  clar).2. 2.0.0.0. strings [25']
  SCHOTTS (C240)

Or De La Trompette D'Été, L'
  8vln I,8vln II,8vla,8vcl,4db [20']
  SCHOTTS (C241)

Prima Vera, La
  1(pic,alto fl).2(English
  horn).2(alto sax,bass clar).2.
  2.0.0.0. 6vln I,5vln II,3vla,
  3vcl,db,harp solo [35'] SCHOTTS
                             (C242)

Symphony
  3.2.3.3.soprano sax.tenor sax.
  4.3.3.1. timp,2perc,pno&cel,harp,
  strings [35'] ("The American")
  SCHOTTS (C243)

CRAWFORD, PAUL (1947- )
Lyric Piece For Orchestra
  4.4.4.4+contrabsn. 6.4.4.0. 2perc,
  harp,strings [15'] sc CANADIAN
  MI 1100 C899LY (C244)

CRAWLEY, CLIFFORD (1929- )
Blue Peter
  string orch [10'] sc CANADIAN
  MI 3134 C911BL (C245)

Butter's Spread Too Thick, The
  see "...Of Cabbages And Kings"

Concertino for Piano and Orchestra
  3(pic).2.2.2. 4.2.3.1. timp,4perc,
  strings,pno solo [10'] sc
  CANADIAN (C246)
  1.0.2.0. 2.1.0.0. timp,3perc,
  strings,pno solo [10'] sc
  CANADIAN (C247)

Curiouser And Curiouser!
  see "...Of Cabbages And Kings"

"Fritter My Wig!"
  see "...Of Cabbages And Kings"

Koleda *Xmas,Overture
  3+pic.3.opt English horn.3.opt bass
  clar.3.opt contrabsn. 4.3.3.1.
  timp,3perc,strings,opt harp [6']
  sc CANADIAN MI 1100 C911KO (C248)

Loyalists Suite, The
  3(pic).2.2.2. 4.2.3.1. timp,3perc,
  strings [15'] sc CANADIAN

CRAWLEY, CLIFFORD (cont'd.)
  MI 1100 C911LO (C249)
  2(pic).1.2.1. 2.2.0.0. timp,3perc,
  pno/org,strings [15'] sc CANADIAN
  MI 1100 C911LO (C250)

"...Of Cabbages And Kings"
  2(pic).1.2.1. 2.1.1.0. timp,perc,
  pno,strings, timpani may double
  percussion in lieu of percussion
  part sc CANADIAN MI 1100 C911OF
  f.s. five quotations from lewis
  carroll
  contains: Butter's Spread Too
  Thick, The; Curiouser And
  Curiouser!; "Fritter My Wig!";
  Off With Her Head!; Will You,
  Won't You, Will You, Won't You,
  Will You Join The Dance? (C251)

Off With Her Head!
  see "...Of Cabbages And Kings"

Overture, Air, And Dances
  string orch [12'] sc CANADIAN
  MI 1500 C911OV (C252)

Overture On A Canadian Theme (Or Two)
  3+pic.2.2.2. 2.2.2.0. timp,perc,
  strings [6'] sc CANADIAN
  MI 1100 C911OV (C253)

Pavane And Galliard
  string orch sc CANADIAN
  MI 8903 C911PA (C254)

Serenade for Violoncello and
Orchestra
  sc,pno red,solo pt CANADIAN
  MI 1313 C911SE (C255)

Star-Ship Twinkle
  2(pic).2.2.2. 4.2.3.1. timp,4perc,
  harp/kbd,strings,2 narrators,
  suzuki strings, (horns, 3rd trb,
  and tuba are optional) CANADIAN
  MV 2400 C911ST (C256)

Tyendinaga: Legend For Orchestra
  2(pic).2.2.2. 4.3.3.1. timp,3-
  4perc,harp,cel/pno,strings [9']
  sc CANADIAN MI 1100 C911TY (C257)

Will You, Won't You, Will You, Won't
You, Will You Join The Dance?
  see "...Of Cabbages And Kings"

CRAWLING UP THE WALL see Emmer, Huib

CRAZED MOON, THE see Anderson, Julian

CREAKY DOOR, THE (HALLOWEEN OVERTURE)
  see Kozinski, Stefan

CREATION OF THE MAYA WORLD, THE see
  Ginastera, Alberto, Popol Vuh

CREDO IN UNAM VITAM see Berry, Wallace

CRÉPUSCULE see Massenet, Jules

CREW OF THE LONG SERPENT see Grainger,
  Percy Aldridge

CRIMSON see Saunders, Rebecca see
  Torke, Michael

CROFT, WILLIAM (1678-1727)
Comedy Call'd The Funeral, The: Suite
  (Platt) string orch,hpsd [10'] sc,
  pts OXFORD 3624184 sc,pts rent
                             (C258)

CRONOGRAMME 1 see Wittinger, Robert

CROQUEFER: NO. 4 see Offenbach, Jacques

CROSS-CURRENTS see Lerdahl, Fred

CROSS LANE FAIR see Davies, [Sir] Peter
  Maxwell

CROSS WATER ROADS see Ichiyanagi,
  Toshi, Concerto for Piano, No. 3

CROSSE, GORDON (1937- )
Demon Of Adachigahara: Suite
  2.2.2.2. 4.3.2.1. timp,3-5perc,pno,
  strings [14'] sc,pts OXFORD
  3624885 sc,pts rent (C259)

Story Of Vasco: Suite No.1
  3(2pic).2+English horn.2+bass
  clar.3. 4.3.3.1. timp,3perc,harp,
  cimbalom,pno&cel,strings [20']
  perf sc set OXFORD 3624680 sc,pts
  rent (C260)

CROSSING THE BORDER see Martland, Steve

CROSSING THE MERIDIAN see Phillips,
  Barre

CROSSLEY, LAWRENCE
Symphonic Essay
  2+alto fl.2+English horn.2.2.
  4.3.3.1. timp,perc,harp,pno&cel,
  strings [7'] sc CANADIAN
  MI 1100 C949SY (C261)

CROW-CRY see Gilbert, Anthony

CROWDED AIR, THE see Babbitt, Milton
  Byron

CRUDEL! PERCHÈ FINORA FARMI LANGUIR
  COSI see Mozart, Wolfgang Amadeus

CRUDELE? - NON MI DIR see Mozart,
  Wolfgang Amadeus

CRUMB OF MUSIC FOR GEORGE CRUMB, A see
  Karayev, Faradzh

CRUSELL, BERNHARD HENRIK (1775-1838)
Concerto for Clarinet and Orchestra,
  Op. 1, in E flat
  sc REIMERS 107025 rent (C262)

Concerto for Clarinet and Orchestra,
  Op. 5, in F minor
  sc REIMERS 107026 rent (C263)

Concerto for Clarinet and Orchestra,
  Op. 11, in B flat
  sc REIMERS 107027 rent (C264)

CRUX see Adderly, Mark

CRUZ DE CASTRO, CARLOS (1941- )
De Nativitate Domini
  1(pic).1.1.1. 0.0.0.0. 2vln,vla,
  vcl,perc,S,Mez/A soli [20'] sc
  ALPUERTO 1365 (C265)

CRY OF ANUBIS, THE see Birtwistle,
  Harrison

CRYPT see Ohana, Maurice

CRYSTALLISATIO see Tüür, Erkki-Sven

CSÁRDÁS see Strauss, Johann, [Jr.]

CSEMICZKY, M.
Laterna Magica
  1(pic).1(English horn).1.1.
  1.1.1.0. pno,strings [20'] EMB
  rent (C266)

CTYRI DRAMATICKÉ STUDIE see Jirasek,
  Ivo

CTYRI KUSY see Foltyn, Jaroslav see
  Kocáb, Michael

CTYRI LIDOVÉ PÍSNE see Vodrazka, Karel

CTYRI SCÉNY Z FAUSTA see Jirasek, Ivo

CTYRI SYMFONICKÁ PRELUDIA see Kopecky,
  Pavel

CTYRI SYMFONICKÉ OBRAZY see Fiala, Petr

CTYRI VETY see Kanák, Milan

CU-HU-MU: ALEF; BET; GIMEL; DALET see
  Lindroth, Peter

CUCKOO AND THE NIGHTINGALE, THE see
  Handel, George Frideric, Concerto
  for Organ, No. 13, in F, HWV 295

CUNNINGHAM, MICHAEL GERALD (1937- )
Aedon
  1.1.1.1. 2.0.0.0. strings,tamb
  SEESAW (C267)

CUR see Palmér, Catharina

CURIOUSER AND CURIOUSER! see Crawley,
  Clifford

CURTAIN TUNE, A see Woolrich, John

CUSTER, LAURENZ
Vier Canzonen
  string orch [12'] sc,pts MULL & SCH
  ESM 10'009 f.s. (C268)

CYCLE OF LIFE, THE see Kvam, Oddvar S.

CYDALISE ET LE CHÈVRE-PIED: L'ÉCOLE DES
  AEGIPANS see Pierne, Gabriel

CYMBOA see Hidas, Frigyes

CYNTHIA'S LAMENT see Akpabot, Samuel

# D

DA GIOVINE REGINA LA LUNA MAESTOSA see
Hamerik, Asger

DA ICH NICHT HOFFE (IN MEMORIAM IGOR
STRAWINSKY) see Mansurian, Tigran

DADAK, JAROMIR (1930-    )
Concerto for Tuba and Chamber
Orchestra
2.1.1.1. 1.0.0.0. timp,strings,tuba
solo [15'] CESKY HUD.          (D1)

Sonata Corta Per Orchestra Da Camera
D'Archi
string orch [14'] CESKY HUD.   (D2)

DAEDALUS REMEMBERS see Holt, Simon

DAHL, INGOLF (1912-1970)
Hymn
(Morton, Lawrence) 3.3.3.3.
4.3.3.1. timp,5perc,pno&cel,harp,
strings [5'] SCHOTTS perf mat
rent                           (D3)

Symphony Concertante
3(pic).2.0.2. 2.2.2.1. 2perc,harp,
strings,2clar soli [27'] SCHOTTS
perf mat rent                  (D4)

DAHLGREN, EVA (1960-    )
Jorden Är Ett Litet Rum
(Hillborg, Anders) 2.2.2.1.
4.0.0.0. strings,solo voice,pno
STIM                           (D5)

DAIGNEAULT, ROBERT
North Shore #5 *Op.160
string orch [6'] sc CANADIAN
MI 1500 D132NO                 (D6)

Soliloquy No. 1 *Op.144
string orch,fl solo [7'] sc,solo pt
CANADIAN MI 1621 D132SO        (D7)

DÁL NEZ JÁ see Soukup, Ondrej

DAL RODENO AL RENO see Martin, Frank,
Zwischen Rhone Und Rhein

DALA-RONDO see Koch, Erland von

DALARSTER see Blomberg, Erik

DALBAVIE, MARC-ANDRE (1961-    )
Concertino [14']
2.2.0.1. 2.0.0.0. hpsd,strings
BILLAUDOT                      (D8)

Concerto for Violin and Orchestra
[24']
3.2.3.2. 4.3.4.1. perc,timp,harp,
2pno,strings,vln solo
BILLAUDOT                      (D9)

Diadèmes
2.1.2.1. 0.0.0.0. 2perc,pno,elec
org,3vln,db,vla solo, 2 Dx7 [25']
JOBERT                         (D10)

Miroirs Transparents, Les
3.2.3.2. 4.3.3.1. 2perc,harp,pno,
strings [17'] JOBERT           (D11)

DALBY, MARTIN (1942-    )
John Clare's Vision
strings,S solo [25'] manuscript
BMIC                           (D12)

Mary Bean, The
3.3.3.3. 4.3.3.1. timp,3perc,harp,
strings [16'] NOVELLO          (D13)

DALCIKLUS see Kazacsay, Tibor, Pro
Memoria

DALECARLIAN RONDO see Koch, Erland von,
Dala-Rondo

D'ALESSANDRO, RAFAELE
see ALESSANDRO, RAFAELE D'

D'ALLER see Leroux, Philippe

DAMASE, JEAN-MICHEL (1928-    )
Concerto for Trumpet and String
Orchestra
[9'30"] pts FUZEAU 4287        (D14)

DAME BLANCHE see Bondt, Cornelis de

DANCE see Nobis, Herbert

DANCE CONCERTANTE see Adaskin, Murray

DANCE EPISODES see Swack, Irwin

DANCE FANTASY see Perle, George see
Zilcher, Hermann

DANCE MUSIC see Wishart, Trevor

DANCE MUSIC 3 see Wishart, Trevor

DANCE MUSIC 4 see Wishart, Trevor

DANCE OF DEATH see Liszt, Franz

DANCE OF THE MASKS see Prokofiev, Serge

DANCE PIECE see Larsen, Elizabeth B.
(Libby), Ghosts Of An Old Ceremony

DANCE SCENES see Maw, Nicholas

DANCE SUITE see Spinks, Charles

DANCE SYMPHONY IN 3 MOVEMENTS, A see
Kyr, Robert, Symphony No. 4

DANCE-TRANCE see Jastrzebska, Anna

DANCES see Andriessen, Louis

DANCES FROM THE SACRED HARP see
Bourland, Roger

DANCIN
(Berg, Sebastian) pic,ob,bass clar,
bsn,trom,perc,strings [6'] sc,pts
STIM                           (D15)

DANCING see Bolle, James

DANCING ON WINGS OF THE FIRE see
Hiscott, James

DANEV, MIROSLAV
Choreographic Fresco
3.3.3.2. 4.3.3.1. timp,perc,harp,
pno,strings SEESAW             (D16)

Suite for Flute and Orchestra
0.2.2.2. 2.1.0.0. harp,strings,fl
solo SEESAW                    (D17)

Via Dolorosa
3.3.3.3. 6.3.3.1. timp,3perc,harp,
strings SEESAW                 (D18)

DANIEL, OMAR (1960-    )
Masque Of The Red Death
string orch, violin obbligato [17']
sc CANADIAN MI1611 D184MA      (D19)

DANIEL-LESUR
see LESUR, DANIEL

DANIELPOUR, RICHARD (1956-    )
Concerto for Chamber Orchestra in One
Movement
see First Light

First Light (Concerto for Chamber
Orchestra in One Movement)
chamber orch sc SCHIRM.G AMP8019
                               (D20)

DANS LES CHAMPS, IL Y A DES BIBITTES
see Boudreau, Walter, Variations
No. 2

DANS LES RUINES D'UNE ABBAYE see Faure,
Gabriel-Urbain

DANSE AGRESTE see Tomasi, Henri

DANSE BARBARE see Donaldson, Will

DANSE DE PUCK, LA see Debussy, Claude

DANSE GUERRIÈRE see Tomasi, Henri

DANSE NUPTIALE see Tomasi, Henri

DANSE PROFANE see Tomasi, Henri

DANSE SACRÉE see Tomasi, Henri

DANSES see Debussy, Claude

DANSES CAUCASIENNES see Djabadary,
Heraclius

DANSES HONGROISES see Brahms, Johannes

DANSSCEN see Blomberg, Erik

DANZA see Still, William Grant

DANZA CRIOLLA see Piazzolla, Astor

DANZA RITUAL DEL FUEGO see Falla,
Manuel de

DANZAS SINFONICAS see Orbon, Julian

DANZI, FRANZ (1763-1826)
Concerto for Flute and Orchestra, No.
2, in D minor, Op. 31
(Förster) fl solo,orch pno-cond sc
KUNZELMANN 10079 ipr          (D21)

DANZI, FRANZ (cont'd.)
Concerto for Flute and Orchestra, No.
4, Op. 43
(Förster) fl solo,orch pno-cond sc
KUNZELMANN 10069 ipr          (D22)

DANZÓN NO. 2 see Márquez, Arturo

DANZÓN NO. 3 see Márquez, Arturo

DAPHNE: CLOSING SCENE see Strauss,
Richard

DAPHNIS AND CHLOE (IN FULL SCORE) see
Ravel, Maurice

DARGOMYZHSKY, ALEXANDER SERGEYEVICH
(1813-1869)
Steinerne Gast, Der: Overture
(Rimsky-Korsakov, N.; Cui, C.)
2.2.2.2. 4.2.3.0. timp,strings
[10'] BREITKOPF-W             (D23)

DARK MADONNA see Donaldson, Will

DARK SONG see Herbolsheimer, Bern

DARK SUN see Montague, Stephen

DARTING THE SKIFF see Casken, John

DARVAS, GÁBOR (1911-    )
Fantasy for Piano and Chamber
Orchestra
pno,1.1.1.1. 1.1.0.0. perc,harp,
string quin [14'] EMB rent    (D24)

DAUGHERTY, MICHAEL (1954-    )
Blue Like An Orange
1(pic).1.1+bass clar.0. 1.1.1.0.
kbd,3perc,strings, (strings - one
each or small complements) [10']
PEER rent                     (D25)

Concrete Jungle
3.3.3.3. 4.4.3.1. timp,4perc,
synthesizer,pno,strings, or
amplified string quartet &
acoustic basses [20'] PEER rent
                              (D26)

Flamingo
1+pic.1.1.1. 1.1.1.0. 2perc,pno,
strings, opt 2nd horn [9'] PEER
rent                          (D27)

Krypton
see Metropolis Symphony

Lex
see Metropolis Symphony

Metropolis Symphony
3(pic).3.3(clar in E flat,bass
clar).3(contrabsn). 4.4.3.1.
timp,4perc,pno,synthesizer,
strings PEER perf mat rent
contains: Krypton; Lex; Mxyzptlk;
Oh, Lois!; Red Cape Tango (D28)

Mxyzptlk
see Metropolis Symphony

Oh, Lois!
see Metropolis Symphony

Red Cape Tango
see Metropolis Symphony

Snap
1(pic).1.1+bass clar.0. 1.1.1.0.
kbd,3perc,strings, (strings - one
each or small complements) [7']
PEER rent                     (D29)

Tombeau De Liberace, Le
1(pic).1.1.1. 2.1.1.1. 2perc,
strings, (strings - one each or
small complements) [15'] PEER
rent                          (D30)

What's That Spell?
1(pic).1.1.1.alto sax. 1.1.1.0.
perc,strings, SS soli amplified
[13'] PEER rent               (D31)

DAUGHTER OF MASTER CHIN, THE see Chan,
Ka Nin

DAVELUY, RAYMOND (1926-    )
Concerto in E for Organ and Orchestra
2.2.2.3(contrabsn). 2.2.3.1. timp,
strings,org solo sc CANADIAN
MI 1364 D246CO                (D32)

DAVID, FERDINAND (1810-1873)
Am Springquell *Op.39,No.6
(Scharwenka, Ph.) 2.0.2.2. 2.0.0.0.
strings,vln solo [4'] BREITKOPF-W
                              (D33)

DAVID, THOMAS CHRISTIAN (1925-    )
Divertimento, Op. 7
strings [23'] BREITKOPF-W     (D34)

DAVID AND BATHSHEBA see Duffy, John

DAVIDOVSKY, MARIO (1934-    )
  Concertante For String Quartet And
    Orchestra
    3.2.3.1. 4.3.3.1. 3perc,pno,harp,
    8vln I,7vln II,6vla,5vcl,4db,
    string quar soli [20'] sc PETERS
    04412                           (D35)

  Concertino
    2.2.2.2. 2.0.0.0. 5vln I,4vln II,
    3vla,3vcl,db,vln solo [12'] sc
    PETERS 04650                    (D36)

  Shulamit's Dream
    3.2.3.1. 4.3.3.1. timp,2perc,pno,
    harp,8vln I,7vln II,6vla,5vcl,4db
    [16'] sc PETERS 04414           (D37)

DAVIES, [SIR] PETER MAXWELL (1934-    )
  Ballade for Chamber Orchestra
    see Cross Lane Fair

  Beltane Fire, The
    3.3.3.3. 4.3.3.1. 6perc,cel,harp,
    strings [30'] BOOSEY-ENG        (D38)

  Caroline Mathilde
    orch [33'] CHESTER              (D39)

  Carolísima
    1(pic).1.1+bass clar.1(contrabsn).
    1.1.1.0. perc,strings [17'] study
    sc SCHOTTS SL 12491 perf mat rent
                                    (D40)

  Cross Lane Fair (Ballade for Chamber
    Orchestra)
    orch, northumbrian small pipes
    [16'] CHESTER                   (D41)

  Ojai Festival Overture
    2(pic).2(English horn).2.2.
    2.2.0.0. timp,strings [6']
    BOOSEY-ENG rent                 (D42)

  Sir Charles His Pavan
    2+alto fl.2.2+bass clar.2+
    contrabsn. 4.2.3.1. timp,perc,
    harp,strings [4'] study sc
    SCHOTTS ED 12438 perf mat rent
                                    (D43)

  Spell For Green Corn
    2.2.2.2. 2.2.2.0. perc,strings,vln
    solo [20'] CHESTER              (D44)

  Strathclyde Concerto No. 3 For Horn,
    Trumpet And Orchestra
    2(alto fl).2(English horn).2(bass
    clar).2(contrabsn). 0.0.0.0.
    timp,strings [28'] BOOSEY-ENG
    rent                            (D45)

  Strathclyde Concerto No. 4
    2.2.1.2. 2.0.0.0. perc,strings,clar
    solo [30'] CHESTER              (D46)

  Strathclyde Concerto No. 5 For
    Violin, Viola And String
    Orchestra
    strings,vln&vla soli [35'] BOOSEY-
    ENG rent                        (D47)

  Strathclyde Concerto No. 6
    0.0.2.1. 2.2.0.0. timp,perc,
    strings,fl solo [25'] CHESTER
                                    (D48)

  Strathclyde Concerto No. 7 For Double
    Bass And Orchestra
    2(alto fl).2(English horn).1+bass
    clar.2(contrabsn). 2.0.0.0.
    strings [21'] BOOSEY-ENG rent
                                    (D49)

  Strathclyde Concerto No. 8
    2.0.2.1. 2.0.0.0. timp,strings,bsn
    solo [25'] CHESTER              (D50)

  Strathclyde Concerto No. 9
    pic,alto fl,English horn,clar in E
    flat,bass clar,contrabsn,strings
    [26'] CHESTER                   (D51)

  Strathclyde Concerto No.10
    2.2.2.2. 2.2.0.0. timp,strings
    [31'] BOOSEY-ENG                (D52)

  Symphony, No. 5
    3.3.3.3. 4.3.3.1. timp,5perc,cel,
    harp,strings [26'] BOOSEY-ENG
                                    (D53)

  Turn Of The Tide, The  *educ
    2.2.2.2. 2.2.3.1. timp,perc,cel,
    harp,strings,opt cor [25']
    CHESTER                         (D54)

  Vanitas (from A Fragment By Johan
    Ban)
    string orch [3'] (only to be
    performed with Strathclyde
    Concerto No. 5) BOOSEY-ENG rent
                                    (D55)

DAVIES, VICTOR (1939-    )
  From Harmony
    2(pic).2.2.2. 4.2.3.1. timp,2perc,
    strings,narrator [7'] sc CANADIAN
    MV 1400 D257FR                  (D56)

DAVIES, VICTOR (cont'd.)
  Pulsations
    3.2.2.2. 4.3.3.1. timp,2perc,drums,
    pno,elec pno,bass gtr,elec gtr,
    strings, electric violin solo
    [33'] (1. Wheel of fire 2. Sunday
    afternoon 3. Between the planets)
    sc CANADIAN MI 9400 D257PU      (D57)

DAVIS, CARL
  Duck's Diary, A
    2.2.2.2. 2.1.1.0. perc,harp,
    strings,speaking voice [16']
    FABER                           (D58)

  Grand National From "Champions"
    study sc FABER f.s.             (D59)

  Keystone Kops Theme
    orch study sc FABER f.s.        (D60)

  Town Fox, The
    3.3.3.3. 4.4.4.3.1. timp,3perc,pno,
    harp,strings,speaking voice FABER
                                    (D61)

DAWN ON THE CHAO PRAYA see Gifford,
  Keith

DE GRANDIS, RENATO (1927-    )
  Canto Del Tempo
    2.2.2.2. 4.3.3.1. perc,harp,pno,
    strings SEESAW                  (D62)

  Canto Della Terra (Symphony No. 1)
    3.3.3.3. 4.3.3.1. perc,timp,harp,
    strings SEESAW                  (D63)

  Memory Of The Fire
    3.3.2.3. 4.3.4.0. 3perc,harp,pno,
    strings SEESAW                  (D64)

  Sinfonia No. 2
    2.2.2.2. 4.3.3.1. perc,timp,harp,
    pno,strings SEESAW              (D65)

  Symphony No. 1
    see Canto Della Terra

  Tre Preludi Sinfonici
    2.2.2.2. 4.2.1.0. harp,hpsd,2perc,
    strings SEESAW                  (D66)

DE NATIVITATE DOMINI see Cruz de
  Castro, Carlos

DE NOCHE see Canat De Chizy, Edith

DE PABLO, LUIS
  see PABLO, LUIS DE

DE PAZ, XAVIER
  Sentado Sobre Un Golfo De Sombra
    ob,trp,perc,vln,vla,vcl,db EMEC
    554-01021                       (D67)

DE PROFUNDIS see Liszt, Franz see
  Ryelandt, Joseph see Somers-Cocks,
  John

DE PROFUNDIS: PSALM, FOR ORCHESTRA see
  Kverndokk, Gisle

DE ST-MALO À BOURGES PAR BOUFFÉMONT see
  Longtin, Michel

DE VOS MALAN, JACQUES
  Irana's Changing Face
    1.0+English horn.1.1. 1.0.0.0.
    perc,2pno,vln,vla,vcl SEESAW
                                    (D68)

DE VTSTVÍ see Ceremuga, Josef

DEAK, CSABA (1932-    )
  Ad Nordiam Hungarica
    1(pic).1(English horn).1(bass
    clar).1. 1.0.0.0. 2vln,vla,vcl,
    db,pno [12'] sc,pts STIM        (D69)

DEAL see Mackey, Steven

DEATH AND FIRE see Tan, Dun

DEATH OF KLINGHOFFER, THE: ARIA OF THE
  FALLING BODY see Adams, John

DEATH OF KLINGHOFFER, THE: BIRD ARIA
  see Adams, John

DEBUSSY, CLAUDE (1862-1918)
  Andantino (String Quartet in G minor,
    Third Movement)
    (Perna, Dana Paul) string orch [8']
    BARDIC                          (D70)

  Collines d'Anacapri, Les
    see Fünf Préludes

  Danse De Puck, La
    see Fünf Préludes

  Danses
    8vln I,7vln II,6vla,5vcl,4db [15']
    sc,study sc,solo pt PETERS 00335
                                    (D71)

DEBUSSY, CLAUDE (cont'd.)
  Des Pas Sur La Neige
    see Fünf Préludes

  Fünf Préludes
    (Zender, Hans) 2(pic,2alto
    fl).2(English horn).2(bass
    clar).1(contrabsn). 1.1.1.0.
    3perc,timp,harp,strings, optional
    lotos flute BREITKOPF-W f.s.
    [18']
    contains: Collines d'Anacapri,
    Les; Danse De Puck, La; Des Pas
    Sur La Neige; "Général Lavine",
    Eccentric; Voiles               (D72)

  "Général Lavine", Eccentric
    see Fünf Préludes

  Images, Jeux And The Martyrdom Of St.
    Sebastian
    orch sc DOVER 27101-3           (D73)

  Prélude à l'après-midi d'un faune
    orch BOIS                       (D74)
    (Reinisch) sc,pts BREITKOPF-W
    PB-OB 5169                      (D75)

  Sinfonia in B minor
    3.3.2.2. 4.2.3.1. timp,2perc,harp,
    8vln I,7vln II,6vla,5vcl,4db
    [18'] sc PETERS 00165           (D76)

  String Quartet in G minor,Third
    Movement
    see Andantino

  Three Great Orchestral Works
    orch sc DOVER 24441-5           (D77)

  Voiles
    see Fünf Préludes

DECLARATION see Behrens, Jack

DECSENYI, JANOS (1927-    )
  A Gondolat Játékai
    see Giuochi Del Pensiero

  Divertimento for Harpsichord and
    Chamber Orchestra
    2.0.2.0. 1.0.0.0. timp,perc,strings
    [20'] EMB rent                  (D78)

  Giuochi Del Pensiero  *cant
    "A Gondolat Játékai" 1.1.1.1.
    1.0.0.0. timp,perc,harp,pno,
    strings,S solo [11'] EMB rent
                                    (D79)

  Harmadik, A
    see Third, The

  Sinfonietta
    strings [13'] EMB rent          (D80)

  Symphony
    2.2.2.2. 4.3.3.0. timp,perc,strings
    EMB rent                        (D81)

  Third, The
    "Harmadik, A" 15strings [12'] EMB
    rent                            (D82)

  Variációk Zenekarra Obligát
    Zongorával
    see Variations For Orchestra With
    Piano Obbligato

  Variations
    see Variations For Orchestra With
    Piano Obbligato

  Variations For Orchestra With Piano
    Obbligato (Variations)
    "Variációk Zenekarra Obligát
    Zongorával" 3(2pic).3.3(bass
    clar).3(contrabsn). 4.4.4.0.
    timp,perc,cembalo,pno,12vln I,
    12vln II,10vla,8vcl,8db [14'] EMB
    rent                            (D83)

DEDIC, SRDAN
  Beat On
    3.3.3.3. 4.3.3.1. timp,3perc,glock,
    harp,strings [12'] sc DONEMUS
                                    (D84)

DEDICATION see Wilson, Donald M.

DEDICATIONS see Stahmer, Klaus H.

DEDIKACE see Neumann, Veroslav

DEEP FLIGHT see Ince, Kamran

DEEP SUMMER MUSIC see Larsen, Elizabeth
  B. (Libby)

DEFAYE, JEAN MICHEL (1932-    )
  Performance
    1.1.2.1. 4.4.4.0. pno,perc,strings,
    trp&trp in C solo [17'30"] pno
    red LEDUC AL 24879              (D85)

DEFILERING see Blomberg, Erik

DEGAZIO, BRUNO (1958-    )
  Variations On Ave Maris Stella
    2.2.2.2. 2.2.2.1. timp,2perc,
    synthesizer,strings [7']
    (Fractual Etude 6) sc CANADIAN
    MI 1100 D317VA                    (D86)

DEGE, PETER
  Orchestermusik I
    3.2.2.2. 0.3.3.0. timp,perc,8vln I,
    7vln II,6vla,5vcl,4db [9'] sc
    PETERS 03114                      (D87)

DEGEN, HELMUT (1911-    )
  Chamber Symphony (Symphony No. 2)
    2(pic).1.0.1. 2.1.0.0. strings
    [21'] study sc SCHOTTS ED 3542
    perf mat rent                     (D88)

  Symphony No. 2
    see Chamber Symphony

DEH VIENI ALLA FINESTRA see Mozart,
  Wolfgang Amadeus

DEHNERT, MAX (1893-1972)
  Divertimento
    2.2.2.2. 2.2.0.0. strings [17']
    BREITKOPF-W                       (D89)

  Festliche Musik
    2.2.2.2. 4.2.2.0. timp,strings [6']
    BREITKOPF-W                       (D90)

DEIN LIEBESFEUER see Wolf, Hugo,
  Seufzer

DEINE LIEBE IST MEIN GANZES LEBEN see
  Mattes, Willy

DEINE SCHÖNHEIT see Weingartner, (Paul)
  Felix von

DEJEUNE & ALGUNDA see Bowman, Kim,
  Symphony No. 1

...DEL AMOR OSCURO see Surtel, Maarten

DEL TREDICI, DAVID (1937-    )
  Interlude And Ecstatic Alice (from In
    Memory Of A Summer Day (Child
    Alice, Part I))
    3(pic).3(English horn).3(clar in E
    flat)+bass clar.3(contrabsn).
    4.3.3.1. timp,5perc,2harp,cel,
    strings,S solo, (soprano
    amplified) (text by Lewis
    Carroll) BOOSEY-ENG rent          (D91)

  Steps
    4(2pic).3(English horn).3(bass
    clar)+clar in E
    flat.3(contrabsn). 4.4.4.1. timp,
    perc,cel,harp,strings [31']
    BOOSEY-ENG rent                   (D92)

  Triumphant Alice (from In Memory Of A
    Summer Day (Child Alice, Part I))
    3(2pic).3(English horn).2+clar in E
    flat+bass clar.2+contrabsn.
    4.3.3.1. timp,5perc,2harp,cel,
    strings [16'] BOOSEY-ENG rent     (D93)

DELERUE, GEORGES (1925-1992)
  Black Stallion's Return, The
    orch,solo voice BOIS              (D94)

  Choreans, Les
    orch,solo voice BOIS              (D95)

  Concerto De L'Adieu (from Diên Biên
    Phû) film
    2.1.2.2. 3.0.0.0. timp,strings
    [9'50"] pno red LEDUC            (D96)

  Concerto for 4 Guitars
    2.1+English horn.2.2. 2.0.0.0.
    harp,strings [13'30"] pno red
    LEDUC AL29097                     (D97)

  Concerto for 4 Guitars and Orchestra
    2.2+English horn.2.2. 2.0.0.0.
    harp,strings,4gtr soli [17'] BOIS
                                      (D98)

  Concerto for Violin
    2.2.2.2. 2.2.0.0. perc,harp,strings
    [24'] pno red LEDUC AL29094 (D99)
    2.2+English horn.2.2. 2.0.0.0.
    harp,3timp,strings,vln solo [24']
    BOIS                             (D100)

  Dialogue Concertant
    timp,strings,trp&trom soli [16']
    BILLAUDOT                        (D101)

  Hommage À François Truffaut
    2.1.2.1. 3.1.1.0. harp,strings
    [14'] BOIS                       (D102)

  Mouvement Concertant
    2+pic+English horn.2+bass clar.2+
    contrabsn. 6.4.3.1. timp,perc,
    2harp,strings [13'30"] LEDUC
                                     (D103)

DELERUE, GEORGES (cont'd.)
  Nuit Americaine, La
    orch,solo voice BOIS             (D104)

  Platoon
    orch,solo voice BOIS             (D105)

  Première suite cinématographique
    1.2+English horn.1.1. 3.2+piccolo
    trp.0.0. 4timp,pno,harp,strings
    [25'] BOIS                       (D106)

  Salvador
    orch,solo voice BOIS             (D107)

  Sept Maupilliers, Les
    orch,solo voice BOIS             (D108)

  Sinfonia Concertante for Piano
    2+pic.2+English horn.3+bass clar.2+
    contrabsn. 4.3.3.1. timp,perc,
    strings [27'] LEDUC solo pt rent,
    pno red rent                     (D109)

  Stellaire
    orch,solo voice BOIS             (D110)

  Symphonie Concertante for Piano and
    Orchestra
    2+pic.2+English horn.2.2+contrabsn.
    0.3.3.1. 4timp,perc,harp,pno,
    strings [27'] BOIS               (D111)

  Trois Mousquetaires, Les: Suite
    Épique
    2+pic.2+English horn.2.2. 4.4.3.1.
    5timp,3perc,2harp,strings [38']
    BOIS                             (D112)

  Variations libres pour un libre
    penseur musical
    3+pic.2+English horn.2+bass clar.2+
    contrabsn. 4.3.3.1. 5timp,3perc,
    harp,strings [7'] (on the name of
    L.V. Beethoven) BOIS             (D113)

DELIBES, LÉO (1836-1891)
  Lakmé: La Cabane
    2.2.2.2. 4.2.3.0. timp,harp,strings
    LEDUC                            (D114)

  Roi S'Amuse, Le: Passepied (Extrait
    No. 6)
    2.2.2.2. 2.0.0.0. tamb,strings [2']
    (extrait no. 6) LEDUC            (D115)

  Sylvia: Les Pizzicati
    2.2.2.2. 2.2.3.0. timp,harp,strings
    [1'35"] sc,pts LEDUC             (D116)

  Sylvia: Pas Des Esclaves (from the
    suite Sylvia)
    2.2.2.2. 4.0.3.0. 2timp,3perc,
    strings LEDUC                    (D117)

  Sylvia: Valse Lente
    2.2.2.2. 2.2.0.0. timp,harp,strings
    [3'] sc,pts LEDUC                (D118)

DELIRIO DELLI COMPOSITORI, OSSIA IL
  GUSTO D'OGGIDI, IL see Dittersdorf,
  Karl Ditters von

DELIUS, FREDERICK (1862-1934)
  Everglades, The (from The Magic
    Fountain) Suite
    (Palmer, Christopher) 2(alto fl)+
    pic.3(English horn).4+bass
    clar.3+contrabsn. 4.3.3.0. timp,
    2harp,strings BOOSEY-ENG rent
                                     (D119)

  Five Little Pieces
    (Fenby, Eric) 1.1.2.1. 2.1.0.0. opt
    timp,strings [7'] BOOSEY-ENG rent
                                     (D120)

  Four Songs (From The Danish)
    BOOSEY-ENG rent
    contains: In The Garden Of The
    Seraglio (2.2.2.2. 4.0.0.0.
    perc,harp,strings,med solo)
    [3']; Irmelin Rose (2.2.2.2.
    4.2.0.0. timp,strings,med solo,
    vln solo) [4']; Silken Shoes
    (2.2.2.2. 4.1.0.0. timp,perc,
    harp,strings,med solo) [2'];
    Violet, The (1.1.2.2. 4.0.0.0.
    strings,med solo) [3']  (D121)

  Idylle de Printemps
    3.2.2.2. 4.0.0.0. timp,harp,strings
    BOOSEY-ENG rent                  (D122)

  In The Garden Of The Seraglio
    see Four Songs (From The Danish)

  Irmelin Rose
    see Four Songs (From The Danish)

  Maud  *song cycle
    3(pic).2+English horn.2+bass
    clar.2. 4.2.2.1. timp,harp,
    strings,T solo [20'] (text by
    Tennyson) BOOSEY-ENG rent (D123)

DELIUS, FREDERICK (cont'd.)
  On Hearing The First Cuckoo In Spring
    (Beecham, Sir Thomas) 1.1.2.2.
    2.0.0.0. strings [6'] sc,pts
    STAINER HL286 rent               (D124)

  Quadroone, La
    "Rhapsodie Floridienne" 2+pic.2+
    English horn.2.2. 4.2.3.1. timp,
    perc,harp,strings BOOSEY-ENG rent
                                     (D125)

  Rhapsodie Floridienne
    see Quadroone, La

  Scherzo
    2+pic.2+English horn.2.2. 4.2.2.0.
    timp,perc,harp,strings BOOSEY-ENG
    rent                             (D126)

  Silken Shoes
    see Four Songs (From The Danish)

  Summer Night On The River
    (Beecham, Sir Thomas) 2.1.2.2.
    2.0.0.0. strings [6'] sc,pts
    STAINER HL287 rent               (D127)

  Violet, The
    see Four Songs (From The Danish)

DELIZIE CONTENTE CHE L'ALME BEATE see
  Cavalli, (Pietro) Francesco

DELUGE, THE see Goehr, Alexander

DELVAUX, ALBERT (1913-    )
  Sinfonia No. 4
    3.3.3.3. 4.3.3.1. timp,perc,cel,
    harp,strings [28'] BELGE   (D128)

DEMILLAC, F.-P. (1917-    )
  Concertino for Flute and String
    Orchestra
    [14'] LEDUC                      (D129)

DEMON OF ADACHIGAHARA: SUITE see
  Crosse, Gordon

DEMON'S ISLE see Giron, Arsenio

DEMOS see Druckman, Jacob Raphael

DEMURE CHARM see Komorous, Rudolf

DEN TATEN DER NEUEN BILDHAUER see
  Engelmann, Hans Ulrich, Strukturen

DENISOV, EDISON VASILIEVICH (1929-1996)
  Concerto for Flute and Harp
    2ob,2horn,strings,fl&harp soli
    [27'] BILLAUDOT                  (D130)

  Concerto for 2 Violas
    string orch,hpsd,2vla soli [32']
    BILLAUDOT                        (D131)

  Happy End
    string orch,2vln&vcl&db soli [7']
    BILLAUDOT                        (D132)

  Sonne Die Inkas, Der
    1.1.1.0. 1.1.0.0. timp,perc,2pno,
    strings,S&3 speaking voices [18']
    (poem by Gabriela Mistral) EMB
    rent                             (D133)

  Symphony
    LEDUC 576-00735                  (D134)

  Symphony for Orchestra
    4.4.4+bass clar.4(contrabsn).
    6.4.4.1. cel,timp,6perc,2vibra,
    2harp,strings [50'] LEDUC (D135)

  Symphony No. 2
    3.3.3.3. 6.4.4.1. 2harp,cel,pno,
    4perc,9vln I,8vln II,7vla,6vcl,
    5db [30'] LEDUC                  (D136)

DENN BLEIBEN IST NIRGENDS see Reimann,
  Aribert

DENSITIES see Surdin, Morris

DÉPARTS see Morel, Francois d'Assise

DÉPLORATION see Kokaji, Kunitaka

DÉPLORATION SUR LA MORT DE JOHANN
  OCKEGHEM see Des Prez, Josquin

...DER DIE GESÄNGE ZERSCHLUG see
  Ruzicka, Peter

DEREINST, GEDANKE MEIN see Grieg,
  Edvard Hagerup

DERIVACION see Homs, Joaquin

DERNIER SOMMEIL, DANSE GALILÉENNE see
  Massenet, Jules, Vierge, La

DERUNGS, MARTIN (1943-    )
Concertino for Recorder, Double Bass,
Percussion, Cembalo and Strings
[14'] HUG                        (D137)

Concerto for Recorder, Double Bass,
Cembalo and Strings
[19'] HUG                        (D138)

Concerto for Violin and Orchestra
3.3.3(bass clar,contrabass
clar).2(contrabsn). 4.3(bass
trp).3.1. harp,cel,harmonium,
4perc,12vln I,10vln II,8vla,8vcl,
6db,vln solo [35'] HUG           (D139)

Etude Pointillistique
2(pic).2.2.2. 2.2.1.0. harp,2perc,
strings HUG                      (D140)

DES KINDES SCHEIDEN see Weingartner,
(Paul) Felix von

DES PAS SUR LA NEIGE see Debussy,
Claude

DES PREZ, JOSQUIN (ca. 1440-1521)
A L'Heure Que Je Vous
(Grainger, Percy Aldridge) strings
BARDIC                           (D141)

Déploration Sur La Mort De Johann
Ockeghem
(Vries, Klaas De) 1.0.2.1. 1.0.0.0.
perc,harp,vln,2vla,2vcl [5'] sc
DONEMUS                          (D142)

DESERT FLOWERS BLOOM see Ung, Chinary,
Grand Spiral

DESERT LANDSCAPE WITH FIGURES see
Healey, Derek

DESIGN FOR STRING ORCHESTRA see
Feldman, Barbara Monk

DESJARDINS, JACQUES (1962-    )
Chemins De La Milarepa, Les
2(pic).2.2(clar in E flat).2.
4.3.3.1. timp,4perc,pno,cel,harp,
strings sc CANADIAN
MI 1100 D459CH                   (D143)

Nuit De Bleue
1(pic,alto fl).1(English horn,ob
d'amore).2(clar in E flat,bass
clar).1(contrabsn). 1.1.1.0.
timp&perc,pno&cel,strings sc
CANADIAN MI1200 D459NU           (D144)

Regards Et Jeux Dans L'Espace
string orch sc CANADIAN
MI 1500 D459RE                   (D145)

DESJOYEAUX, N.
Suite for Violin
2.2.2.2. 4.2.3.0. timp,strings
LEDUC                            (D146)

DESPRES, JOSQUIN
see DES PREZ, JOSQUIN

DESSAU, PAUL (1894-1979)
5 Kanons Aus "Musikalisches Opfer"
Von Johann Sebastian Bach
3.4.0.1. 2.3.2.0. timp,strings,SATB
soli [12'] PETERS                (D147)

Music for Orchestra, No. 3
2.2.2.2. 4.4.3.0. timp,pno,strings,
mix cor&jr cor [18'] PETERS
                                 (D148)

DEŠTNÍK Z PICCADILLY see Hanuš, Jan

DESTRUCTION see Oguri, Katsuhiro

DETSKÁ SVITA see Havelka, Svatopluk

DETSKÉ CONCERTINO see Pexidr, Karel

DETSKY KONCERT NO. 1 see Odstrcil,
Karel

DETSKY KONCERT NO. 3 see Odstrcil,
Karel

DETSKY KONCERT PRO 2 KLARINETY A
ORCHESTR see Odstrcil, Karel,
Concerto for 2 Clarinets and
Orchestra

DETSKY VALCÍK see Vodrazka, Karel

"...DEUTLICHER see Bechert, Ernst

DEUTSCH, PETER (1910-1965)
Gay Nineties, The
see Glücklichen 90er

Glücklichen 90er
"Gay Nineties, The" string orch,pno
solo [2'50"] pno-cond sc,pts
BUSCH                            (D149)

DEUTSCHE MISERERE, DAS see Cornell,
Klaus

DEUTSCHE SINFONIE see Eisler, Hanns

DEUTSCHER TANZ see Mozart, Wolfgang
Amadeus

DEUTSCHLAND (STUBEN-MUSI) see Thomas-
Mifune, Werner

DEUTSCHLANDSBERGER MOHRENTANZ NOS. 1-2
see Henze, Hans Werner

DEUX BERCEUSES see Perna, Dana Paul

DEUX BRÈVES ET UNE LONGUE see Louvier,
Alain

DEUX CONCERTOS INÉDITS P. VIOLON ET
CORD see Vivaldi, Antonio

DEUX TABLEAUX SYMPHONIQUES see Bleuse,
Marc

DEUX TAPISSERIES see Gellman, Steven

2 DÉCEMBRE see Wal-Berg, Concertino for
Piano and Orchestra

DEUXIEME SYMPHONIE see Lajtha, Laszlo,
Symphony No. 2, Op. 27

DEVA ET ASURA see Vivier, Claude

DEVANT LA MADONE see Massenet, Jules

DEVÁTY, ANTONÍN (1903-1984)
Concerto for Horn and Orchestra
2.2.2.2. 3.2.3.0. timp,perc,
strings,horn solo [19'] CESKY
HUD.                             (D150)

Intermezzo
see Pro Potešení

Kontrasty
perc,pno,string orch,clar solo
CESKY HUD.                       (D151)

Mirová Predehra
3.3.3.2. 4.3.3.1. timp,perc,harp,
pno,strings [12'] CESKY HUD.     (D152)

Olešnické Hory. Pochod: 1. Verze
1.1.1.1. 0.0.1.0. perc,strings
CESKY HUD.                       (D153)

Olešnické Hory. Pochod: 2. Verze
2.2.2.2. 4.3.3.0. perc,strings
CESKY HUD.                       (D154)

Pro Potešení (Intermezzo)
1.1.2.1. 2.2.1.0. perc,pno/
harmonium,strings CESKY HUD.
                                 (D155)

Radostné Mládí  *Overture
3.2.2.1. 4.3.3.0. timp,perc,xylo,
strings CESKY HUD.               (D156)

Serenade
2.2.2.2. 2.2.1.0. timp,perc,harp,
strings,vcl solo CESKY HUD.
                                 (D157)

V Tichu Podvecera
2.1.1.1. 4.2.0.1. euphonium,xylo,
strings,vcl solo CESKY HUD.
                                 (D158)

Vítezná
2.2.2.2. 0.3.3.1. timp,perc,harp,
strings CESKY HUD.               (D159)

DEVIENNE, FRANÇOIS (1759-1803)
Concerto for 2 Clarinets and
Orchestra, Op. 25
(Balassa) 2clar,orch KUNZELMANN ipa
sc 10145A, oct 10145             (D160)

Sinfonia Concertante No. 2
(Mariassy) ob/clar,bsn,orch
KUNZELMANN ipa sc 10096A, oct
10096                            (D161)

DEVIN DU VILLAGE, LE: OUVERTURE see
Rousseau, Jean-Jacques

DEVOS, G. (1927-    )
Sinfonietta for Strings
[17'] LEDUC                      (D162)

DEXTERA DOMINI see Franck, Cesar

DEYIS see Saygun, Ahmed Adnan

D'HOEDT, HENRY GEORGE
Narcusse
4.3.3.3. 4.3.3.1. timp,perc,cel,
harp,carillon,strings [31']
(symphonic legend) BELGE         (D163)

DIABLE DANS LE BEFFROI, LE: PRÉLUDE ET
DANSE FINALE see Inghelbrecht,
Désiré Émile

DIABLE DANS LE BELFROI, LE see
Vallerand, Jean

DIADÈMES see Dalbavie, Marc-Andre

DIAGONALEN see Koenig, Gottfried
Michael

DIALOG see Schweinitz, Wolfgang von see
Staidl, Ladislav

DIALOG FÜR KLAVIER UND ORCHESTER see
Ramovs, Primoz

DIALOGHI ATTRAVERSO LO SPAZIO see
Wildberger, Jacques

DIALOGUE AVEC LA NATURE see Ton That,
Tiet

DIALOGUE CONCERTANT see Delerue,
Georges

DIALOGUE FOR STRINGS see Eaton, Darryl

DIALOGUE WITH FOOTNOTES: FOR SYMPHONY
ORCHESTRA AND JAZZ BAND see
Applebaum, Louis

DIALOGUE WITH PAUL KLEE see Tan, Dun,
Death And Fire

DIALOGUES see Gougeon, Denis see Tull,
Fisher Aubrey

DIALOGUES FOR VIOLIN, CELLO AND
ORCHESTRA see Ward, Robert Eugene

DIAMOND, DAVID (1915-    )
Symphony No. 11
3(2pic).2+English horn.0+clar in E
flat+2bass clar.2+contrabsn. 4.3+
piccolo trp+bass trp.3.1. 2timp,
4perc,pno/cel,harp,strings [46']
PEER rent                        (D164)

Tom: Orchestral Suite No. 1
2+pic.2+English horn.2+bass clar.2+
contrabsn. 4.3.3.1. timp,perc,
pno/cel,harp,strings [30'] PEER
rent                             (D165)

DIAPASON see Schnebel, Dieter

DIAPHONIE see Goeyvaerts, Karel

DIASPALMATA see Larsson, Hokan

DIASTASE see Pröve, Bernfried

DICE ARE LOADED, THE see Hatch, Peter

DICTA IN THREE MOVEMENTS see Falk,
Karl-Axel

DICTS DU LUNANTHROPE, LES see Gagné,
Marc, Concerto for Chamber
Orchestra

DICTUM see Saygun, Ahmed Adnan, Deyis

DIEBEL, W.
Fantasy for Harp, Flute and Strings
INTERNAT.S. sc,pts rent, solo pt,
pno red                          (D166)

DIED FOR LOVE see Grainger, Percy
Aldridge

DIEMER, EMMA LOU (1927-    )
Chamber Concerto For Harpsichord
2.2.3.2. 4.1.1.0. perc,strings,hpsd
solo SEESAW                      (D167)

DIEPENBROCK, ALPHONS (1862-1921)
Lydische Nacht
2.3.3.2. 4.3.3.0. timp,perc,harp,
strings [18'] sc DONEMUS         (D168)

Muziek Voor Elektra
2.2.3.0. 0.3.3.0. timp,perc,harp,
strings [22'] sc DONEMUS         (D169)

DIES IRAE & LACRIMOSA see Gondai,
Atsuhiko

DIJK, C. VAN
Higgajon IV  *Op.799,No.4
1.1.2.0. 0.1.0.0. harmonium,strings
[5'] sc DONEMUS                  (D170)

DIJK, JAN VAN (1918-    )
Andante for Organ and String
Orchestra, Op. 866
[8'] sc DONEMUS                  (D171)

Cinco Noticias
see Three Symphonic Pieces

Colébi  *Op.429a
3.2.2.2.alto sax. 3.3.3.0. timp,
perc,strings [8'] (version for
orchestra) sc DONEMUS            (D172)

DIJK, JAN VAN (cont'd.)

Concerto for Violin and Orchestra,
Op. 893
2.2.2.2.alto sax. 2.2.1.0. timp,
perc,strings,vln solo [13'] sc
DONEMUS (D173)

Drie Choralen *Op.900a
1.1.3.1.alto sax. 2.0.0.0. strings
[5'] sc DONEMUS (D174)

Flirt Aux Fleurs
see Trois Pieces Pour Piano Et
Orchestre

Higgajon IV *Op.799,No.4
1.1.2.0. 0.1.0.0. harmonium,strings
[5'] sc DONEMUS (D175)

Hymne Et Fugue
see Zes Stukken Voor Strijkorkest

Nocturne
see Trois Pieces Pour Piano Et
Orchestre

Ouverture D Gr. T.
see Zes Stukken Voor Strijkorkest

Partita Piccola
see Zes Stukken Voor Strijkorkest

Petite Fantaisie
see Trois Pièces Pour Orchestre À
Cordes
see Zes Stukken Voor Strijkorkest

Prelude, Counterpoint And March
see Zes Stukken Voor Strijkorkest

Ronde Des Causses
see Trois Pieces Pour Piano Et
Orchestre

Rondine
see Trois Pièces Pour Orchestre À
Cordes

Sagrada Familia
see Three Symphonic Pieces

Serenade
see Zes Stukken Voor Strijkorkest

Sévérac
see Three Symphonic Pieces

Six Bagatelles
see Trois Pièces Pour Orchestre À
Cordes

Three Symphonic Pieces
3.2.3.2.alto sax. 2.2.2.1. timp,
3perc,harp,pno,strings sc DONEMUS
f.s.
contains: Cinco Noticias, Op.848;
Sagrada Familia, Op.845;
Sévérac, Op.871 (D176)

Trois Pièces Pour Orchestre À Cordes
string orch sc DONEMUS f.s.
contains: Petite Fantaisie,
Op.672,No.2; Rondine, Op.742;
Six Bagatelles, Op.878 (D177)

Trois Pièces Pour Piano Et Orchestre
3.2.3.2. 3.2.1.0. timp,2perc,
strings,pno solo sc DONEMUS f.s.
contains: Flirt Aux Fleurs,
Op.827; Nocturne, Op.886; Ronde
Des Causses, Op.617 (D178)

Zes Stukken Voor Strijkorkest
string orch sc DONEMUS f.s.
contains: Hymne Et Fugue, Op.833;
Ouverture D Gr. T., Op.831;
Partita Piccola, Op.815; Petite
Fantaisie, Op.672; Prelude,
Counterpoint And March, Op.836;
Serenade, Op.664 (D179)

DIJK, RUDI MARTINUS VAN
Concerto for Piano and Orchestra
3.3.3.3. 4.3.3.1. timp,7perc,harp,
strings,pno solo [24'] DONEMUS
(D180)

DIJKSTRA, LOWELL
Towards Summer
3.3.3.3. 4.3.3.1. 4perc,harp,
strings [18'] sc DONEMUS (D181)

DIKTAN: VERS 1 see Sandberg, Lars

DILLON, JAMES (1950- )
Blitzschlag
"German Tryptichon Part 3" 2.2.3.3.
3.2.2.1. timp,4perc,pno,cel,harp,
22vln,8vla,6vcl,4db,fl solo sc
PETERS 04548 (D182)

German Tryptichon Part 2
see Helle Nacht

DILLON, JAMES (cont'd.)

German Tryptichon Part 3
see Blitzschlag

Helle Nacht
"German Tryptichon Part 2" 3.3.3.3.
4.3.3.1. 5perc,pno,harp,30vln,
12vla,10vcl,8db [28'] sc PETERS
(D183)

Ignis Noster
4.4.4.4. 6.5.4.1. 2timp,4perc,pno,
harp,8vln I,7vln II,6vla,5vcl,4db
[22'] sc PETERS 03940 (D184)

Introitus
6vln,2vla,2vcl,2db,electronic tape,
synthesizer [28'] sc PETERS
EP 7408 (D185)

Nine Rivers
electronic tape,6vln I,2vln II,
2vla,2vcl,2db [28'] sc PETERS
02855 (D186)

Vernal Showers
1.1.0.0. 0.0.0.0. perc,cembalo,
harp,gtr,vla,vcl,db,vln solo,mand
solo [14'] sc PETERS 04543 (D187)

Windows And Canopies
2.2.0.1. 2.0.0.0. perc,7vln,2vla,
2vcl,db [25'] sc PETERS EP 7319
(D188)

DIMBOOLA WATER MUSIC AND WALTZ see
Dreyfus, George

DIMITRAKOPOULOS, APOSTOLO (1955- )
Automaton
1.1.1.1. 1.1.1.0. 3perc,harp,2vln,
vcl,db [8'] sc,pts STIM (D189)

Collage
2(pic).2.2(bass clar).2. 4.2.2.0.
timp,2perc,harp,strings,pno/cel
STIM sc H-2791, pts A-430 (D190)

Divertimento for Strings
string orch [9'] sc STIM (D191)

Schreckensutopien
2.2(English horn).2(bass
clar).2(contrabsn). 4.2.2.0.
timp,3perc,strings,pno
(Schreckensutopien 1-3) sc STIM
(D192)

DIMLER, ANTON (1753-1819)
Concerto for Clarinet and Orchestra
in B flat
(Balassa; Fodor) clar solo,orch
KUNZELMANN ipa sc 10064A, oct
10064 (D193)

DINDONS, LES: SUITE see Djabadary,
Heraclius

DINICU, GRIGORAS (1889-1949)
Hora Staccato
(Brooks, Arthur) string orch,horn
solo THOM ED OC2 f.s., perf mat
rent (D194)

DINNER ROLLS see Horwood, Michael

DINOSAUR'S TALE, THE see Atkinson,
Condit Robert

DION, DENIS (1957- )
Kant
1.1.1(bass clar).1. 1.0.0.0. 2perc,
harp,strings,gtr solo [15'] sc
CANADIAN MI 1315 D592KA (D195)

Vers 210 Milliards De Souvenirs En
Quête De Bois De Rose
3(pic).3(English horn).3(bass
clar).3. 4.3.3.1. 4perc,harp,
12vln I,10vln II,8vla,8vcl,6db sc
CANADIAN MI 1100 D592VE (D196)

DIONYSOS UND APOLLO see Zechlin, Ruth

DIPLIPITO see Kantscheli, Gija

DIPTYCH see Kalabis, Viktor

DIRGE see Morawetz, Oskar

DIS-TANZ see Ungvari, Tamas

DISCANTUS see Morthenson, Jan W.

DISCHARGE
4.4.4.3. 4.3.3.1. timp,4perc,pno,
strings [6'] (contains: "Does This
System Work?" by Huba De Graaff;
"Cries Of Help" by Rijnhard
Bokelmann, & "Life's Destruction"
by Arthur Sauer) sc DONEMUS (D197)

DISMAL SWAMP see Still, William Grant

DISPELLING THE FEARS see Turnage, Mark-
Anthony

DISSOLVED WINDOW see Edlund, Mikael,
Upplst Fnster

DISTRIBUTION 2 see Myatt, Tony

DITES LUI see Offenbach, Jacques

DITTERSDORF, KARL DITTERS VON
(1739-1799)
Combattimento Delle Passioni Umani,
Il (Sinfonia in D)
2ob,2horn,2vln,vla,vcl,db [25']
ARTARIA AE035 (D198)

Concerto for Violoncello and
Orchestra in D
vcl solo,orch KUNZELMANN ipa sc
10249A, oct 10249 (D199)

Delirio Delli Compositori, Ossia Il
Gusto D'Oggidi, Il (Sinfonia in A
minor)
2ob,2horn,2vln,vla,vcl,db [19']
ARTARIA AE033 (D200)

Nazionale Nel Gusto Di Cinque
Nazioni' (Sinfonia in A)
2ob,2horn,2vln,vla,vcl,db [21']
ARTARIA AE034 (D201)

Sinfonia in A
see Nazionale Nel Gusto Di Cinque
Nazioni'

Sinfonia in A minor
see Delirio Delli Compositori,
Ossia Il Gusto D'Oggidi, Il

Sinfonia in D
see Combattimento Delle Passioni
Umani, Il

Sinfonia in D minor
2ob,2horn,2vln,vla,vcl,db [12']
ARTARIA AE037 (D202)

Sinfonia in F
2ob,2horn,2vln,vla,vcl,db [12']
ARTARIA AE036 (D203)

Sinfonia in G minor
fl,2ob,2horn,2vln,vla,vcl,db [26']
ARTARIA AE038 (D204)

DITTICO see Rocca, Lodovico

DITTICO (DIPTYCH) FOR VIOLIN AND
ORCHESTRA see Rieti, Vittorio

DITTRICH, PAUL-HEINZ (1930- )
Abwärts Wend Ich Mich
2.1.3.1. 2.2.2.0. 3perc,pno,
strings,7 female soli [60']
BREITKOPF-W (D205)

Concert Avec Plusieurs Instruments
No. 7 (Concerto for Oboe,
Trombone, Violoncello, 4 Voices
and Orchestra, No. 7)
"Leipziger Konzert" 0.2.0.0.
0.1.2.1. 4perc,2pno,4vcl,4
speaking voices,ob&trom&vcl soli
[28'] BREITKOPF-W (D206)

Concert Avec Plusieurs Instruments
No. 8 (Concerto for Violoncello,
3Solo Voices and Orchestra, No.
8)
3.0.4.3.2sax. 2.3+cornet.3.0.
2perc,2vln,2vla,vcl,db,3S,vcl
solo [20'] BREITKOPF-W (D207)

Concerto for Instruments, No. 6
1.0.1.0. 2.0.2.0. 2perc,3vln,2vla,
2vcl,db,ob&inst soli [22'] sc,
solo pt PETERS 03436 (D208)

Concerto for Oboe, Trombone,
Violoncello, 4 Voices and
Orchestra, No. 7
see Concert Avec Plusieurs
Instruments No. 7

Concerto for Violoncello, 3Solo
Voices and Orchestra, No. 8
see Concert Avec Plusieurs
Instruments No. 8

Etym
3.3.3.3.tenor sax. 6.4.4.1. timp,
9perc,pno,cel,hpsd,harp,8vln,
6vla,5vcl,4db [26'] sc PETERS
02405 (D209)

Hymnischer Entwurf I
3.3.3.3. 6.4.4.1. timp,4perc,hpsd,
harp,vibra,tubular bells,12vln I,
12vln II,12vla,10vcl,8db,speaking
voice [27'] sc PETERS 02886
(D210)

Hymnischer Entwurf II
3.3.3.3. 6.4.4.1. timp,4perc,hpsd,
harp,12vln I,12vln II,12vla,

DITTRICH, PAUL-HEINZ (cont'd.)

10vcl,8db,Bar solo [35'] sc
PETERS 02887 (D211)

Leipziger Konzert
see Concert Avec Plusieurs
Instruments No. 7

Sprachlandschaft
1.0.2.0. 2.0.2.0. 2perc,3vln,2vla,
2vcl,db [22'] sc,solo pt PETERS
03438 (D212)

DIVAN I SHAMS I TABRIZ see Schafer, R.
Murray

DÍVAT SE DO JARA see Precechtel, Zbynek

DIVERTIMENTO CONCERTANTE see Meyer,
Ernst Hermann

DIVERTIMENTO CORSICA see Tomasi, Henri

DIVERTIMENTO INVERSO see Glaser, Werner
Wolf

DIVERTIMENTO SEMPLICE see Zamecnik,
Evzen

DIX, ROBERT (1917-    )
Adagietto For Clarinet & Strings
clar,strings [5'] (one movement)
DRK (D213)

Concertino for Chamber Orchestra and
Piano in Three Movements
1.1.1.1. 2.1.1.0. pno,strings [9']
DRK (D214)

Concertino for Viola and String
Orchestra in One Movement
strings,vla solo [12'] DRK (D215)

Symphony No. 1 in Three Movements
3.3.3.2. 4.3.3.1. timp,3perc,
strings [23'] DRK (D216)

Three Movements For Orchestra
3.3.3.2. 4.2.3.1. timp,2perc,
strings [15'] DRK (D217)

DIXIE: PRELUDE AND FUGUE see
Weinberger, Jaromir

DIXIT DOMINUS see Martinez, Marianne Di

DJABADARY, HERACLIUS
Concerto Hongrois In F
pno,orch [29'] BOIS (D218)

Concerto No. 1 in C
pno,orch [35'] BOIS (D219)

Concerto No. 3 in A
pno,orch BOIS (D220)

Danses Caucasiennes
pno,orch BOIS (D221)

Dindons, Les: Suite
orch BOIS (D222)

Légende Géorgienne
orch BOIS (D223)

Lekouri: Danse Géorgienne
orch [2'] BOIS (D224)

Mazurka in G minor for Orchestra
orch BOIS (D225)

Mélopée Du Serpent, La
2.2.2.0. 0.0.0.0. strings,fl solo
[4'] BOIS (D226)

Tiflisiana
orch BOIS (D227)

DJANGO see Laman, Wim

DLOUHY, JAROMIR (1929-    )
Cardáš
1.0.2.0. 1.3.3.0. perc,harp,pno,
2gtr,strings [6'] CESKY HUD.
(D228)

Concerto Grosso for 2 Orchestras
3.2.2.2. 4.3.3.1. timp,perc,
strings, Orchestra 2: 4sax, 3trp,
3trb, perc, pno, gt [15'] CESKY
HUD. (D229)

Koncertrock
2.2.1.2.sax. 4.2.2.1. timp,perc,
harp,strings [4'] CESKY HUD.
(D230)

Letní Rapsodie
2.1.2.1. 2.3.3.0. timp,perc,strings
[7'] CESKY HUD. (D231)

Lunapark
2.2.2.2. 3.2.2.0. perc,xylo,strings
CESKY HUD. (D232)

DLOUHY, JAROMIR (cont'd.)

Májová Predehra
2.2.2.2. 4.2.3.1. timp,perc,strings
[4'] CESKY HUD. (D233)

Poetické Scherzo
2.2.2.2. 4.2.0.0. timp,perc,harp,
strings,vln solo [5'] CESKY HUD.
(D234)

Rapsodická Fantazie
2.0.2.0. 2.3.0.0. timp,perc,bass
gtr,strings,pno solo [5'] CESKY
HUD. (D235)

Rapsodická Polka
2.2.2.2. 4.3.3.1. timp,perc,
strings,vln solo [6'] CESKY HUD.
(D236)

DMITRIEV, SERGEJ (1964-    )
Circulation
1(pic).2(English horn).2.2.
2.2.2.0. perc,strings,pno,marimba
[11'] sc,pts STIM (D237)

Magnifico
3(pic).3(English horn).3(bass
clar).3(contrabsn). 4.3.0.1.
timp,2perc,harp/pno,synthesizer,
strings [11'] STIM sc H-2808, pts
T-3161 (D238)

DMITRIYEV, GEORGI (1942-    )
Concerto in Two Movements for Violin
and Orchestra
3.2.3.2.2sax. 4.3.3.0. 4perc,cel,
harp,elec gtr,8vln I,7vln II,
6vla,5vcl,4db [26'] sc PETERS
02841 (D239)

Kiew
3.3.3.3. 4.3.3.1. 5perc,8vln I,7vln
II,6vla,5vcl,4db [11'] sc PETERS
02840 (D240)

Sibylle
0.2.0.0. 2.0.0.0. 2perc,pno,cel,
cembalo,8vln I,7vln II,6vla,5vcl,
4db,fl solo [21'] sc PETERS 02842
(D241)

DNES UZ VIM see Marat, Zdenek

DO YOU LOVE ME see Allen, Peter

DOBIÁŠ, DANIEL (1946-    )
Nez Srdce Opustíme
perc,pno,2gtr,strings,solo voice,
polymoog CESKY HUD. (D242)

DOBROWOLSKI, ANDRZEJ (1921-1990)
Music for Oboe and Orchestra
2.0.2.2. 4.4.4.0. 4perc,cel,
strings,ob solo [15'] MOECK sc
5312 f.s., pts rent (D243)

DOCELA PROSTÁ PÍSNICKA see Smékal,
Mojmir

DR. FAUSTUS OVERTURE see Boehmer,
Konrad

DOCTOR OX'S EXPERIMENT: EPILOGUE see
Bryars, Gavin

DODES'KA-DEN see Takemitsu, Toru

DODGSON, STEPHEN (1924-    )
Concerto for Flute and Strings
strings,fl solo [17'] manuscript
BMIC (D244)

Rising Of Job, The
2.2.2.2. 2.2.0.0. timp,strings [9']
manuscript BMIC (D245)

DODICETTO see Rieti, Vittorio

DODICI CONCERTI - OPERA TERZA: HEFT I
see Manfredini, Francesco

DODICI CONCERTI - OPERA TERZA: HEFT II
see Manfredini, Francesco

DODICI CONCERTI - OPERA TERZA: HEFT III
see Manfredini, Francesco

DODICI CONCERTI - OPERA TERZA: HEFT IV
see Manfredini, Francesco

DÖHL, FRIEDHELM (1936-    )
Sommerreise
2.1.1.1. 1.2.1.1. perc,strings,pno
[22'] MOECK rent sc 5308, pts
(D246)

DOI, YOSHIYUKI (1944-    )
Constellations
9vln,4vla,2vcl,2db [10'] JAPAN
(D247)

Fuyu Ni...
orch,fl [11'] JAPAN (D248)

Permutation
orch [11'] JAPAN (D249)

DR. FAUSTUS: CONCERT OVERTURE see
Boehmer, Konrad

DR. MABUSE, DER SPIELER, PART 1: DER
GROSSE SPIELER. EIN BILD DER ZEIT
see Obst, Michael

DR. MABUSE, DER SPIELER, PART 2:
INFERNO. MENSCHEN DER ZEIT see
Obst, Michael

DOLIN, SAMUEL (1917-    )
Symphony No. 3
2(pic).2.2.2. 4.2.2.0. timp,perc,
strings [20'] sc,study sc
CANADIAN MI 1100 D664S3 (D250)

DOLOR, FOR STRINGS AND HARP see
Hukvari, Jeno

DOLOR NASCENS ET EFFLUENS see Nevonmaa,
Kimmo

DOLORES see Waldteufel, Emile

DOMAZLICKY, FRANTISEK (1913-    )
Concerto for Clarinet and Strings,
Op. 50
[16'] CESKY HUD. (D251)

Concerto for Trumpet and Orchestra,
Op. 60
2.2.2.2. 2.0.0.0. timp,strings,trp
solo [13'] CESKY HUD. (D252)

Concerto for Tuba and Strings, Op. 53
strings,db tuba solo [13'] CESKY
HUD. (D253)

Concerto for 2 Violins and Strings,
Op. 51
strings,2vln soli [15'] CESKY HUD.
(D254)

Concerto No. 2 for Violin and String
Orchestra, Op. 47
[22'] CESKY HUD. (D255)

Concerto Rustico *Op.55
strings,db solo [13'] CESKY HUD.
(D256)

Forotto
strings [5'] CESKY HUD. (D257)

Suita Danza Per Archi *Op.52
string orch [17'] CESKY HUD. (D258)

Valcík
string orch [3'] CESKY HUD. (D259)

DOMES see Ince, Kamran

DOMHARDT, GERD (1945-    )
Moire
5vln I,5vln II,2vla,2vcl,db [9'] sc
PETERS 03412 (D260)

Prometheus
2.2.2.2. 3.3.3.0. timp,2perc,pno,
8vln I,7vln II,6vla,5vcl,4db,
speaking voice [19'] sc PETERS
03108 (D261)
2.2.2.2. 3.3.3.0. timp,2perc,pno,
8vln I,7vln II,6vla,5vcl,4db,
speaking voice [15'] sc PETERS
03110 (D262)

DOMINE NON SECUNDUM see Franck, Cesar

DOMINO NOIR, LE: OVERTURE see Auber,
Daniel-François-Esprit

DOMPES AND JOMPES FOR STRING ORCHESTRA
see Bach, Jan Morris

DON GIOVANNI-METAMORFOSER see Asheim,
Nils Henrik

DON GIOVANNI: OUVERTÜRE see Mozart,
Wolfgang Amadeus

DON JUAN: FOUR DANCES see Gluck,
Christoph Willibald, Ritter von

DON JUAN: VIER SÄTZE see Gluck,
Christoph Willibald, Ritter von

DON QUICHOTTE: SYMPHONIC VARIATIONS see
Nabokov, Nicolas

DON QUIXOTE TANZT FANDANGO see Ullmann,
Viktor

DONALDSON, WILL
Danse Barbare
(Still, William Grant)
2(pic).2.2.2.2sax. 4.2.3.1. perc,
banjo,5strings,T solo pno-cond sc
STILL (D263)

Dark Madonna
(Still, William Grant)
2.2.2.2.3sax. 4.2.3.1. timp,perc,
drums,banjo,5strings,T solo STILL
(D264)

DONATI
Preghiera A S. Sergio
FORLIVESI rent                        (D265)

DONATONI, FRANCO (1927-    )
Tema Per 12 Strumenti
see Theme For 12 Instruments

Theme For 12 Instruments
"Tema Per 12 Strumenti" chamber
orch sc RICORDI-IT 133236   (D266)

DONIZETTI, GAETANO (1797-1848)
Concertino for Clarinet and Orchestra
(Pauler) clar solo,orch KUNZELMANN
ipa sc 10040A, oct 10040    (D267)

Sinfonia in E for Orchestra
(Meylan) 3.2.2.2. 4.2.3.1. timp,
strings [32']  PETERS        (D268)

DONNE MIE, LA FATE A TANTI see Mozart,
Wolfgang Amadeus

DOOLITTLE, QUENTIN (1925-    )
Divertimento in Two Movements
string orch [10'] sc CANADIAN
MI 1500 D691DI              (D269)

Music For Oedipus
2.2.2.2. 2.2.2.1. timp,perc,pno,
strings [9'] sc CANADIAN
MI 1100 D691MU             (D270)

Seven Mysteries Of Life, The
string orch,Bar solo [22'] sc,solo
pt CANADIAN MV 1600 D691SE (D271)

DOPO, FOR CELLO OG STRYKEORKESTER see
Kleiberg, Ståle

DOPPEL KONZERT FÜR SHAKUHACHI UND KUGO
see Yamamoto, Junnosuke

DOPPELKAMMERVARIATIONEN see Jekimowski,
Viktor

DOPPELKONZERT, FOR VIOLIN, CLARINET &
CHAMBER ORCHESTRA, OP. 65 see
Lobanov, Vassily

DOPPELKONZERT G-DUR see Hummel, Johann
Nepomuk

DOPPELKONZERT: NOVELLE see Eichhorn,
Frank Volker

D'ORESTE, D'AJACE see Mozart, Wolfgang
Amadeus

DORFF, DANIEL JAY (1956-    )
Allegro Volante, For Xylophone And
Orchestra
2.2.2.2. 4.3.3.1. 3perc,timp,harp,
strings [5'] PRESSER sc f.s., pts
perf mat rent              (D272)

Billy And The Carnival: A Children's
Guide To The Instruments
2(pic).2.2.2. 2.2.1.0. 2perc,timp,
strings,narrator [14'] PRESSER
pts perf mat rent, sc f.s. (D273)

Concerto for Contrabassoon
0.0.1.0. 1.0.0.0. strings,contrabsn
solo [12'] MMB sc f.s., pts f.s.,
perf mat rent             (D274)

Concerto for Percussion and Orchestra
2.2.2.2. 4.3.3(euphonium).1. 3perc,
timp,harp,strings [20'] PRESSER
sc f.s., pts perf mat rent, solo
pt f.s.                    (D275)

Fanfare Overture
2.2.2.2. 4.3.3.1. 3perc,harp,
strings [3'] MMB sc f.s., pts
perf mat rent             (D276)

Fast Walk
2.2.2+bass clar.2. 4.3.3.1. 3perc,
timp,strings [3'] MMB sc f.s.,
pts perf mat rent         (D277)

Lamentations
string orch [5'] PRESSER sc f.s.,
pts perf mat rent         (D278)

Philly Rhapsody
2+pic.2.2+bass clar.2. 4.3.3.1.
4perc,timp,harp,pno,strings [11']
PRESSER sc f.s., pts perf mat
rent                      (D279)

Summer Solstice
string orch,clar solo [19'] MMB sc
f.s., pts perf mat rent, solo pt
f.s.                      (D280)

Sunburst
string orch,vln solo [3'30']
PRESSER pts perf mat rent, sc
f.s., solo pt f.s.        (D281)

DORFF, DANIEL JAY (cont'd.)
Tortoise And The Hare, The
1.1.1.1+contrabsn. 1.1.1.0. 2perc,
harp,strings,narrator [5'30']
PRESSER                   (D282)

DORFMAN, JOSEPH (1940-    )
Concerto for Violin and Orchestra
2.2.2.2. 2.2.2.0. 4perc,pno,2harp,
strings,vln solo [32'] PEER rent
(D283)

Concerto for Violoncello and
Orchestra
0.0.4.1. 0.0.0.0. timp,cimbalom,
strings,vcl solo [29'] PEER rent
(D284)

Metamorphosis Of Themes By Mozart
string orch [14'] PEER rent  (D285)

DORIAN GRAY SUITE see Kox, Hans

DORIAN PRELUDE see Maggio, Robert

DOS PLEGARIAS FÜR GITARRE UND ORCHESTER
see Angulo, Eduardo

DOTEKY see Ištvan, Miloslav

DOUBLE CHORUS see Beaser, Robert

DOUBLE CONCERTO see Bainbridge, Simon
see Carter, Elliott Cook, Jr. see
Francaix, Jean see Jacob, Gordon
see Keuris, Tristan see Kurtag,
György see Müller-Siemens, Detlev
see Paulus, Stephen Harrison see
Sydeman, William J.

DOUBLE CONCERTO FOR EUPHONIUM AND TUBA
AND ORCHESTRA see Owens, David

DOUBLE CONCERTO FOR OBOE, VIOLA AND
STRING ORCHESTRA see Parker, Alice

DOUBLE CONCERTO FOR TENOR AND BASS
TROMBONE AND SYMPHONIC ORCHESTRA
see Hidas, Frigyes

DOUBLE CONCERTO FOR TWO CONTRABASSI AND
CHAMBER ORCHESTRA see Foley, Daniel

DOUBLE CONCERTO FOR TWO ELECTRIC
GUITARS AND SYMPHONY ORCHESTRA see
Rypdal, Terje

DOUBLE CONCERTO FOR VIOLA, CELLO AND
ORCHESTRA see Hoffman, Joel

DOUBLE CONCERTO FOR VIOLIN, VIOLA AND
ORCHESTRA see Britten, [Sir]
Benjamin, Concerto for Violin,
Viola and Orchestra

DOUBLE CONCERTO, OP. 68 see Holloway,
Robin, Concerto for Clarinet,
Saxophone and 2 Chamber Orchestras,
Op. 68

DOUBLE DEALER, THE see Purcell, Henry

DOUBLEPORTRAIT FOR CONCERTANTE VIOLIN,
4 INSTRUMENTAL GROUPS AND LIVE
ELECTRONICS see Schaathun, Asbjørn

DOUBLURES see Boesmans, Philippe

DOUBRAVKA see Rimón, Jan

DOUBRIDGE see Shimoyama, Hifumi

DOUBTING LIGHT, THE see Williams,
Adrian

DOUGLAS, CLIVE (1903-1977)
Carnival: Movement For Orchestra
2.2.2.2. 4.2.3.1. timp,perc,harp,
strings [3'] ALLANS        (D286)

Divertimento for Piano and Orchestra,
No. 2
2.2.2.2. 2.2.0.0. timp,harp,strings
ALLANS                    (D287)

Essay For Strings
strings ALLANS            (D288)

Five Pastels For Soprano And Ensemble
strings,cel,S solo ALLANS  (D289)

DOUGLAS, PAUL M. (1936-    )
Albis
3+pic.2.2.2. 4.2.3.1. timp,perc,
strings [7'] sc CANADIAN
MI 1100 D735AL             (D290)

Rigi: In Memoria A Friend
orch [6'] sc CANADIAN MI1200 D735RI
(D291)

DOUGLAS, ROY (1907-    )
Nowell Sequence, A
string orch [6'] sc OXFORD 3629488
f.s., ipa                  (D292)

DOUSA, EDUARD (1951-    )
Concertino for Trumpet and Orchestra
1.1.1.1. 1.0.0.0. timp,perc,
strings,trp solo [16'] CESKY HUD.
(D293)

Podzimní Kolonáda
1.1.1.1. 1.0.0.0. perc,strings,
acord solo [6'] CESKY HUD. (D294)

Rapsodická Ouvertura
3.3.3.3. 4.3.3.1. timp,perc,xylo,
harp,strings [8'] CESKY HUD.
(D295)

Variace Na Barokní Téma
string orch [13'] CESKY HUD. (D296)

DOUZE MENUETS POSTHUMES see Beethoven,
Ludwig van

DOUZE MINIATURES see Rossum, Frederic
R. van

DOUZE TIROIRS DE DEMI-VÉRITÉS POUR
ALLÉGER VOTRE DESCENTE see
Bouliane, Denys

DOVE see Hrabánek, Pavel

DOVE DESCENDING, THE see Tsontakis,
George

DOVE SON? - SOAVE SIA IL VENTO see
Mozart, Wolfgang Amadeus

DOWNES, ANDREW (1950-    )
Symphony No. 3
3.2.3.3. 4.3.3.1. timp,perc,strings
LYNWOOD                   (D297)

Towards A New Age
4.2.2.3. 4.2.3.1. timp,perc,strings
LYNWOOD                   (D298)

DOWNEY, JOHN WILHAM (1927-    )
For Those Who Suffered
"Yad Vashem" 1(pic).1(English
horn).1.0. 1.1.0.0. 2perc,pno,
acord,strings PRESSER rent (D299)

Yad Vashem
see For Those Who Suffered

DOYLE, PATRICK
Carlito's Way
2(pic).2.3(bass clar).2. 3.3.3.1.
timp,4perc,drums,pno,synthesizer,
harp,strings MCA rent      (D300)

DRAAK, HET HUIS, DE ZON, DE BOOM EN DE
VIJVER, DE see Wagemans, Peter-Jan

DRAEGER, WALTER (1888-1976)
Concerto for Piano and Orchestra
2.2.2.2. 4.3.3.1. timp,strings,pno
solo [28'] BREITKOPF-W     (D301)

DRAESEKE, FELIX (1835-1913)
Jubelouvertüre  *Op.65
2+pic.2.3.2. 4.4.4.4. timp,4perc,
2harp,strings [7'] BREITKOPF-W
(D302)

DRAGONS DE VILLARS, LES see Maillart,
Louis Aime

DRAGONS OF ALCALA, THE see Proto, Frank

DRAGSTRA, WILLEM
Concerto For Oboe And Echoes Of
Others
0.0.0.0. 2.0.0.0. perc,harp,
strings,ob/English horn solo
[18'] DONEMUS             (D303)

Ricercare
2.2.2.2. 4.2.2.1. 4perc,harp,opt
org,pno/cel,strings [18'] sc
DONEMUS                   (D304)

DRAMATICKÁ PREDEHRA see Svatos,
Vladimir

DRAMATICKÉ VARIANTY see Bohác, Josef

DRAMATISCHE MUSIK see Katzer, Georg

DRAMATISCHE TÄNZE see Bantock, [Sir]
Granville

DRAPKIN, MICHAEL (1957-    )
Sinfonietta No. 2
2.2.2.2. 2.2.0.0. timp,strings
[10'] BMIC                 (D305)

Symphony, No. 13
3.3.3.3. 4.3.3.0. timp,7perc,
strings [25'] BMIC         (D306)

DRAWING DOWN THE MOON see Bell, Allan

DREAM WITH ME see Bernstein, Leonard

DREAMCALLER see Schwantner, Joseph

DREAMERY see Grainger, Percy Aldridge

DREAMS see Martinsson, Rolf

DREAMS ABOUT DANCING see Tittle, Steve

DREAMS (WHAT DID THE LAST DINOSAUR DREAM OF?) see Wagemans, Peter-Jan

DREAMSCAPE see Hiraishi, Hirokazu

DREI ARABESKEN, OP. 70 see Kneip, Gustav

DREI ASKO STUECKE see Koenig, Gottfried Michael

DREI DIVERTIMENTI see Mozart, Wolfgang Amadeus

DREI ERNSTE STÜCKE see Brahms, Johannes

DREI GESÄNGE see Trexler, Georg

DREI GESÄNGE: ABGESANG see Kirchner, Volker David

DREI HYMNEN AN DIE NACHT see Hausegger, Siegmund von

DREI KINDERSZENEN, FOR SOLO VOICE AND CHAMBER ORCHESTRA, OP. 18 see Mossolov, Alexander

DREI KIRCHENARIEN see Galuppi, Baldassare

DREI LÄNDLER FÜR ORCHESTER see Hess, Willy

DREI LIEBESLIEDER see Holliger, Heinz

DREI MÄRCHEN see Genzmer, Harald

DREI MENUETTE see Mozart, Wolfgang Amadeus

DREI MONOLOGE DES EMPEDOKLES see Reutter, Hermann

DREI MOZART'SCHE ORGELSONATEN see Henze, Hans Werner

DREI ORCHESTERSTÜCKE see Hartmann, Karl Amadeus see Henze, Hans Werner see Lampson, Elmar

DREI ORCHESTERSTÜCKE, OP. 3 see Paul, Berthold

DREI PALMEN, DIE see Spendiarov, Alexander

DREI PINTOS: ARIETTA see Weber, Carl Maria von

DREI PRÄLUDIEN UND TOCCATA see Tamberg, Eino, Concerto for Trumpet and Orchestra, No. 2, Op. 100

DREI RAGTIMES see Joplin, Scott

DREI RAGTIMES see Joplin, Scott

DREI SONATEN see Scarlatti, Domenico

DREI STÜCKE see Binet, Jean see Huber, Nicolaus A.

DREI STÜCKE FÜR STREICHORCHESTER UND HARFE, OP. 53 see Kienzl, Wilhelm

DREJSL, RADIM (1923-1953)
Rozkvetly Den
2.2.2.2. 3.2.3.0. timp,perc,harp,
strings [3'] CESKY HUD. (D307)

DRESDNER SUITE: DER FRIEDE see Gerster, Ottmar

DRESSLER, RUDOLF (1932- )
Zwölf Gershwin-Impressionen
2.2.0.1. 2.0.0.0. strings [22']
BREITKOPF-W (D308)

DREYFUS, GEORGE (1928- )
Adventures Of Sebastian The Fox, The
*Suite
1.1.1.1. 1.1.1.0. timp,bass drum,
snare drum,cym,tom-tom,tam-tam,
triangle,wood blocks,glock,
strings,narrator, (two
percussionists + timpanist) [8']
(of eight descriptive pieces)
ALLANS (D309)
string orch [8'] (of eight
descriptive pieces) ALLANS (D310)

Break Of Day: Suite
2.2.2.2. 4.2.3.1. timp,triangle,
glock,snare drum,cym,tamb,harp,
pno/cel,strings, (one
percussionist + timpanist) [12']
ALLANS (D311)

Dimboola Water Music And Waltz
2.2.2.2. 4.2.3.1. timp,snare drum,
bass drum,cym,tubular bells,

DREYFUS, GEORGE (cont'd.)
strings, (one percussionist +
timpanist) [8'] ALLANS (D312)

Folk Music With Large Orchestra
4.4.6.4. 6.4.4.1. timp,snare drum,
bongos,tom-tom,strings, (one
percussionist + timpanist) [14']
ALLANS (D313)

Grand Ridge Road
1.1.1.1. 3.1.1.0. timp,snare drum,
bass drum,tamb,cym,tam-tam,
tubular bells,vibra,strings, (one
percussionist + timpanist) [21']
ALLANS (D314)

Great Expectations
2.2.2.2. 4.2.3.1. timp,perc,strings
[5'] ALLANS (D315)

Larino, Safe Haven
strings,fl/ob solo [3'] ALLANS
(D316)

Let The Balloon Go
2.2.2.2. 4.2.3.1. timp,harp,pno,
strings [6'] ALLANS (D317)

Lighthouse
string orch [5'] ALLANS (D318)

Love Your Animal
0.2.0.0. 2.0.0.0. strings [6']
ALLANS (D319)

Marion
0.0.2.2. 0.1.3.0. harp,strings [3']
ALLANS (D320)

Mary Gilmore Goes To Paraguay
0.0.0.0. 4.3.3.1. timp,snare drum,
bass drum,tamb,cym,tubular bells,
xylo,marimba,strings, (one
percussionist + timpanist) [14']
ALLANS (D321)

Peace
2.1.2.1. 4.2.3.1. harp,strings [4']
ALLANS (D322)

Rush
(Butcher, M.; James, A.F.) 2.2.2.2.
4.2.3.1. timp,cym,tamb,strings
[3'] ALLANS (D323)
(Butcher, M.; James, A.F.) 0.2.2.2.
4.2.3.1. timp,cym,tamb,strings,fl
solo [3'] ALLANS (D324)
(Butcher, M.; James, A.F.) string
orch [3'] ALLANS (D325)
(Butcher, M.; James, A.F.) 12vcl
[3'] ALLANS (D326)

Serenade For Small Orchestra
2.1.2.1. 1.1.1.0. snare drum,bass
drum,cym,tubular bells,wood
blocks,castanets,glock,xylo,
strings, (three percussionists)
[8'] ALLANS (D327)

Sound Sculptures From Rathenau
3.3.3.3. 4.3.3.1. timp,perc,
strings,snare drum&trom soli,
didjeridu+suono+zampônas soli
[15'] ALLANS (D328)

Steam Train Passes, A
2.2.2.2. 4.2.3.1. timp,glock,harp,
pno,strings [10'] ALLANS (D329)

Tender Mercies
strings,horn solo [3'] ALLANS
(D330)

Waterfront
2.2.2.2. 4.2.3.1. timp,snare drum,
bass drum,tamb,cym,strings, (one
percussionist + timpanist) [5']
ALLANS (D331)

DRIE CHORALEN see Dijk, Jan van

DRINK ME A SKOAL see Betts, Lorne M.

DRIZGA, EDUARD (1944- )
Bohemica
see Symphony No. 1

Sinfonia Piccola
2.2.2.2. 2.0.0.0. strings [15']
CESKY HUD. (D332)

Symphony No. 1
"Bohemica" 3.2.3.2. 4.3.3.1. timp,
perc,pno,strings [33'] CESKY HUD.
(D333)

DRONES AND DANCES see Rolnick, Neil B.

DROUET, JEAN-PIERRE (1935- )
Mi-Clos
string orch,horn,perc
[15'] BILLAUDOT (D334)

DROWNED OUT see Turnage, Mark-Anthony

DRUCKMAN, JACOB RAPHAEL (1928-1996)
Brangle
3(pic,alto fl).2+English horn.2+
bass clar.2. 4.3.3.1. timp,3perc,
harp,pno,strings [20'] BOOSEY-ENG
rent (D335)

Counterpoise
[Eng/Fr] 2(pic)+alto fl.2+English
horn.2+bass clar.2. 4.3.3.1.
timp,3perc,harp,pno,strings,S
solo [19'] (text by Emily
Dickinson & Apollinaire) BOOSEY-
ENG rent (D336)

Demos
3(pic).2+English horn.2+bass
clar.2. 4.3.3.1. timp,3perc,harp,
pno,strings [18'] BOOSEY-ENG rent
(D337)

New York, New York: Variations
see Variations On Bernstein's "New
York, New York"

Nor Spell Nor Charm
1(alto fl).2.2(bass clar).2.
2.0.0.0. pno&synthesizer,strings
[15'] BOOSEY-ENG rent (D338)

Seraphic Games
3(2pic).2+English horn.2+bass clar+
contrabass clar.2. 4.4.3.1.
4perc,harp,pno,strings [9']
BOOSEY-ENG rent (D339)

Shog
3(pic,alto fl).2+English
horn.2(clar in E flat)+bass
clar.2. 4.3.3.1. timp,3perc,harp,
pno,strings [20'] BOOSEY-ENG rent
(D340)

Summer Lightning
3(pic,alto fl).2+English horn.2+
bass clar+contrabass clar.2.
4.4.3.1. 4perc,pno,harp,strings
[8'] BOOSEY-ENG rent (D341)

That Quickening Pulse (from Brangle)
2(pic)+alto fl.2+English horn.2+
bass clar.2. 4.3.3.1. timp,3perc,
harp,pno,strings [8'] (3rd
movement) BOOSEY-ENG rent (D342)

Variations On Bernstein's "New York,
New York"
"New York, New York: Variations" 1+
pic+alto fl.2+English horn.2+bass
clar.2. 4.0.3.1. 4perc,harp,pno,
strings [2'] BOOSEY-ENG rent
(D343)

DRUSCHETZKY, GEORG (1745-1819)
Concerto for Oboe and Orchestra in F
ob solo,orch KUNZELMANN ipa sc
10160A, oct 10160 (D344)

Concerto for Oboe, 2 Horns and
Strings in B flat
ob,2horn,strings pno-cond sc
KUNZELMANN 10125 (D345)

DRUZECKY, JIRÍ
Concerto for Oboe and Orchestra in C
(Adamus, Jan) 0.0.2.2. 0.2.0.0.
timp,strings,ob solo [25'] CESKY
HUD. (D346)
(Koukal, Bohumír) 0.0.2.2. 0.2.0.0.
timp,strings,ob solo [25'] CESKY
HUD. (D347)

Concerto for Timpani, Oboe and
Orchestra
(Kopriva, Martin) 0.0.2.2. 0.2.0.0.
strings,timp&ob soli [23'] CESKY
HUD. (D348)

DRUZECKY, JOSEF (1745-1819)
Partita in C
(Kopriva, Martin) 0.2.0.0. 2.0.0.0.
strings,timp soli [10'] CESKY
HUD. (D349)

DRYADE see Sibelius, Jean

DU ÄRMSTE KANNST WOHL NIE ERMESSEN see
Wagner, Richard

DU BIST EIN KIND see Weingartner,
(Paul) Felix von

DU BIST ES! DU! see Streicher, Theodore

DU BOIS, ROB
see BOIS, ROB DU

DU DENKST MIT EINEM FÄDCHEN see Wolf,
Hugo

DU HOLDE KUNST see Wildberger, Jacques

DUAL PERSONALITY I see Kawashima,
Motoharu

DUBBEL CONCERTO see Verbesselt, Auguste

DUBOIS, PIERRE-MAX (1930-1995)
Chanson De La Rose
see Étoiles Brûlées

Concerto for Saxophone and Orchestra,
No. 2 [20']
2.2.2.2. 2.2.1.0. 2perc,cel,
strings,sax solo
BILLAUDOT                    (D350)

Étoiles Brûlées
2.1.2.2. 2.1.1.0. timp,perc,harp/
pno,strings,T solo LEDUC f.s. 5
melodies to the poems by Maurice
Fombeure
contains: Chanson De La Rose;
Poussivité; Variations Pour Une
Trompette De Cavalerie;
Vieilles Chansons; Voyage En
Tortillard                    (D351)

Poussiyité
see Étoiles Brûlées

Suite De Danse
string orch,opt harp,vla solo [8']
LEDUC                         (D352)

Variations Pour Une Trompette De
Cavalerie
see Étoiles Brûlées

Vieilles Chansons
see Étoiles Brûlées

Voyage En Tortillard
see Étoiles Brûlées

DUBROVAY, LASZLO (1943-    )
Concerto for Piano, Synthesizer and
Orchestra
2.2.2.2. 4.3.3.1. timp,perc,harp,
strings,pno solo,synthesizer solo
[23'] EMB rent                (D353)

Concerto for Violin and Orchestra
1.1.1.1. 1.1.1.1. perc,harp,cel,
strings,vln solo [13'] EMB rent
                              (D354)

Concerto Romantico
2+pic.2+English horn.2+bass clar.2+
contrabsn. 4.4.3.1. timp,perc,
2harp,cel,strings,pno solo [27']
EMB rent                      (D355)

Tripelkocert
2.2.2.2. 4.3.3.1. timp,perc,
strings,trp&trom&tuba soli [12']
EMB rent                      (D356)

Verificazione
3(alto fl).2+English horn.3.2+
contrabsn. 4.3.3.1. timp,perc,
harp,cel,strings,S solo, or alto
fl solo [8'] EMB rent         (D357)

DUCHAC, MILOSLAV (1924-    )
Nemel Jsem Te Rád
clar,perc,pno,gtr,strings,solo
voice CESKY HUD.              (D358)

DUCK'S DIARY, A see Davis, Carl

DUE CANTI E FINALE see Rainier, Priaulx

DUE PER OTTONI ED ARCHI see Obrovská,
Jana

DUE PICCOLO COMPOSIZIONE see Perna,
Dana Paul

DUE SINFONIE see Laube, Antonin

DUE SONETTI see Wanek, Friedrich K.

DUET see Reich, Steve

DUFAY, GUILLAUME (ca. 1400-1474)
Jour S'Endort, Le
(Grainger, Percy Aldridge) strings
BARDIC                        (D359)

DUFFY
Symphony No. 1
see Utah

Time For Remembrance
orch study sc EUR.AM.MUS. EA00752
                              (D360)

Utah (Symphony No. 1)
orch study sc EUR.AM.MUS. EA00689X
                              (D361)

DUFFY, JOHN
American Fantasy Overture
2(pic).2.2.2. 4.2.3.0. timp,2perc,
pno,harp,strings [4'] SCHOTTS
perf mat rent                 (D362)

David And Bathsheba
2(pic).2(English horn).2.2.
4.2.3.1. 2perc,pno,harp,strings
[5'] SCHOTTS perf mat rent    (D363)

Heritage Waltz
2.2.1.2. 4.2.3.1. timp,2perc,pno&
cel,harp,strings [4'] SCHOTTS

DUFFY, JOHN (cont'd.)

perf mat rent                 (D364)

Three Jewish Portraits
2(pic).2.2.2. 4.2.3.1. timp,2perc,
pno&cel,harp,strings [9'] SCHOTTS
perf mat rent                 (D365)

Two Jewish Dances
2(pic).2.2.2. 4.2.3.1. timp,2perc,
pno&cel,harp,strings [8'] SCHOTTS
perf mat rent                 (D366)

DUFOURT, HUGUES (1943-    )
Surgir
4.4.4.4. 4.4.4.1. 5perc,timp,2harp,
strings [30'] JOBERT          (D367)

DUHAMEL, ANTOINE (1925-    )
Concerto for Viola and Chamber
Orchestra
see Lamento-Mémoire

Lamento-Mémoire (Concerto for Viola
and Chamber Orchestra)
1.1.2.1. 2.1.0.0. harp,mand,
strings,vla solo [20'] LEDUC
                              (D368)

DUHOVY VALCÍK see Strasek, Emil

DUKAY, BARNABÁS
Áldozati Zene A Lenyugvó Naphoz
see Sacrificial Music To The
Setting Sun

Sacrificial Music To The Setting Sun
"Áldozati Zene A Lenyugvó Naphoz"
12inst, without indication of the
instrument EMB rent           (D369)

DULCIS MEMORIA see Boccadoro, Carlo

DUM NÁŠ see Jonák, Zdenek

DUMA see Kálik, Vaclav

DUMA, A SOLILOQUY FOR ORCHESTRA see
Baley, Virko

DUMBARTON OAKS see Stravinsky, Igor

DUNSTABLE, JOHN (ca. 1385-1453)
Veni Sancte Spiritus
orch/strings BARDIC           (D370)

DUO CONCERTANTE see Szekely, Endre

DUO CONCERTANTE FOR VIOLIN, VIOLA, AND
STRING ORCHESTRA see Baker, Michael
Conway

DUO DE "FLEURETTE", LE see Offenbach,
Jacques

DUO DE L'OUVREUSE DE L'OPÉRA COMIQUE ET
DE L'EMPLOYÉ DU BON MARCHÉ see
Chabrier, [Alexis-] Emmanuel

DUO DE ROMÉO ET JULIETTE see
Tchaikovsky, Piotr Ilyich

DUPÁK see Krízek, Zdenek

DUPIN, MARC-OLIVIER (1954-    )
Variations Sur La Traviata De Verdi
string orch,vln solo [18']
BILLAUDOT                     (D371)

DUPONT, JACQUES (JAQUE-DUPONT)
(1906-1985)
Concerto for Violin, Op. 6
2+pic.2+English horn.2+bass clar.2+
contrabsn. 4.3.3.0. timp,2perc,
strings [19'] LEDUC           (D372)

DUPRE, MARCEL (1886-1971)
À L'Amie Perdue  *CC7U
1.1.1.1. 2.1.0.0. timp,3perc,harp,
strings,med solo LEDUC f.s.
                              (D373)

Concerto for Organ in E minor
3(pic).3(English horn).3(bass
clar).3(contrabsn). 4.3.3(bass
trom).0. 3timp,cel,glock,harp,
strings, A tuba may replace the
bass trombone [23'] LEDUC     (D374)

DURANTE, FRANCESCO (1684-1755)
Huit Concerti  *CC8L
string orch,cont. (harpsichord) sc
LEDUC f.s. HE 32106, LP. 26
                              (D375)

DURCH ALLES see Singleton, Alvin

...DURCH DIE REINHEIT DER SUBSTANZ IST
ES, WAS ES IST, WEGE ZU SUCHEN...
see Bongartz, Markus

DURCH ZÄRTLICHKEIT UND SCHMEICHELN see
Mozart, Wolfgang Amadeus

DURKO, ZSOLT (1934-    )
Cantilene
4(4pic,alto fl).1(English
horn).3(bass clar).2+contrabsn.
4.3.3+bass trom.1. timp,perc,
harp,cel,strings,pno solo [14']
EMB rent                      (D376)

Ludus Stellaris
3.0.2.0. 1.0.2.0. timp,perc,pno,
strings [13'] EMB rent        (D377)

Rapsodia (Second Version)
3(alto fl,pic).3(English
horn).3(clar in E flat,bass
clar).3(contrabsn). 4.3(piccolo
trp).3.1. timp,perc,2harp,cel&
glock,pno,strings [38'] (in four
movements) EMB rent           (D378)

Three English Verses
1(pic).1.1.1. 1.0.0.0. harp,pno,
strings,Mez solo [20'] (poems by
W. Wordsworth, W. Blake & T.S.
Eliot) EMB rent               (D379)

DUSATKO, TOMAS (1952-    )
Traces Of Becoming
2.2.2.2. 2.2.0.0. perc,pno,strings
sc CANADIAN MI 1100 D971TR    (D380)

DUŠEK, FRANTISEK XAVER
see DUSSEK, FRANZ

DUSÍK, JAN LADISLAV
see DUSSEK, JOHANN LADISLAUS

DUSSEK, FRANZ (1731-1799)
Concerto for Piano and Orchestra in D
strings,2horn,pno solo [21'] CESKY
HUD.                          (D381)

Serenade in E flat
0.2.2.0. 2.0.0.0. strings [20']
CESKY HUD.                    (D382)

Sinfonia in A
2ob,2horn,2vln,vla,vcl,db [11']
ARTARIA AE099                 (D383)

Sinfonia in B flat
2ob,2horn,2vln,vla,vcl,db [23']
ARTARIA AE075                 (D384)

Sinfonia in B flat, MIN 1
2ob,2horn,2vln,vla,vcl,db [23']
ARTARIA AE0102                (D385)

Sinfonia in C
0.2.0.0. 2.0.0.0. strings [8']
CESKY HUD.                    (D386)

Sinfonia in E flat
2ob,2horn,2vln,vla,vcl,db [23']
ARTARIA AE073                 (D387)

Sinfonia in F
2ob,2horn,2vln,vla,vcl,db [23']
ARTARIA AE072                 (D388)

Sinfonia in G
2ob,2horn,2vln,vla,vcl,db [20']
ARTARIA AE074                 (D389)

Sinfonia in G, MIN 1
2ob,2horn,2vln,2vla,vcl,db [11']
ARTARIA AE098                 (D390)

DUSSEK, JOHANN LADISLAUS (1760-1812)
Concerto for Harp and Orchestra
0.2.0.1. 2.0.0.0. strings
INTERNAT.S. sc,pts rent, solo pt,
pno red                       (D391)

Concerto for Harp and Orchestra, Op.
15
0.2.0.0. 2.0.0.0. strings,harp solo
[23'] CESKY HUD.              (D392)

DUST DANCES see Bermel, Derek

DUTILLEUX, HENRI (1916-    )
Mystère De L'Instant
pic,4timp,2cym,gong,tam-tam,
48strings, (2 percussionists)
[15'] LEDUC                   (D393)

DUVERNOY, CHARLES (1766-1845)
Concerto for Clarinet, No. 3, in B
flat
clar solo,orch pno-cond sc
KUNZELMANN 10131              (D394)

DUVOSEL, LIEVEN (1877-1956)
Leiezyklus Nr. 1
see Morgen, Der

Morgen, Der
"Leiezyklus Nr. 1" 2+pic.2+English
horn.2+bass clar.2. 4.3.3.1.
timp,4perc,harp,strings [8']
BREITKOPF-W                   (D395)

DVA FRAGMENTY see Hlavacek, Libor

DVA GRAFICKÉ ZNAKY see Malek, Jan, Concerto for Piano and Chamber Orchestra

DVA SVETY see Kalabis, Viktor

DVE CHODSKÉ PÍSNE see Vodrazka, Karel

DVE PÍSNE see Saudek, Vojtech

DVE RONDA see Parsch, Arnost

DVE SYMFONICKÉ POEMY see Bohác, Josef

DVOJKONCERT PRO HOUSLE, KLAVIR A ORCHESTR see Rehor, Bohuslav, Concerto for Violin, Piano and Orchestra

DVOJMONOLOG see Gahér, Jozef

DVORÁCEK, JIRÍ (1928- )
Concerto for Organ and Orchestra, No. 2
0.0.0.0. 2.2.2.0. timp,perc,vibra, strings,org solo [23'] CESKY HUD.
(D396)

Giubilo
3.3.3.3. 6.4.4.0. timp,perc,harp, strings [7'] CESKY HUD. (D397)

Suite Concertante
3.3.3.3. 6.3.3.1. timp,perc,cel, xylo,harp,strings [23'] CESKY HUD. (D398)

Symphony
3.3.2.2. 4.3.3.1. timp,perc,harp, strings [25'] CESKY HUD. (D399)

DVORÁK, ANTONÍN (1841-1904)
Concerto for Violin and Orchestra, Op. 53, in A minor
2.2.2.2. 2.2.2.0. timp,strings,vln solo [32'] BREITKOPF-W (D400)

Concerto for Violoncello and Orchestra in B minor, Op. 104 (Döge, Klaus; Schiff, Heinrich) sc, pts BREITKOPF-W PB-OB 5290 (D401)

From The New World
see Symphony No. 9, Op. 95, in E minor

Slavonic Dances
orch sc DOVER 25394-5 (D402)

Slawische Tänze *Op.46
(Döge, K.) 2+pic.2.2.2. 4.2.3.0. timp,perc,strings [35'] sc,pts BREITKOPF-W PB-OB 5273 (D403)

Symphony No. 9, Op. 95, in E minor (Riedel, Chr. R.) "From The New World" 2(pic).2+English horn.2.2. 4.2.3.1. timp,perc,strings [45'] study sc BREITKOPF-W PB 5229
(D404)

Symphony, Nos. 6-7
orch sc DOVER 28026-8 (D405)

Symphony, Nos. 8-9
orch sc DOVER 24749-X (D406)

DVORSKÉ TANCE see Kašlik, Václav

DWARF AND THE GIANT, THE see Polgar, Tibor

DYNAMUS see Bell, Allan

DYNDAHL, PETTER (1957- )
Chiasma
3(pic).3(English horn).3(bass clar).3(contrabsn). 4.3.3.1. timp,3perc,harp,strings [12'30"] NORSKMI (D407)

DYPTIQUE SYMPHONIQUE see Badian, Maya

DYZ SEM see Vodrazka, Karel

DZUKISCHE VARIATIONEN see Kutavicius, Bronius

## E

E DAI P MILO see Brott, Alexander

...E QUINDI USCIMMO A RIVEDER LE STELLE see Hedstrom, Ase

EAGLE, DAVID (1955- )
Precipice
3(pic).2.2.2. 2.2.2.1. timp,perc, strings [4'] sc CANADIAN MI 1100 E11PR (E1)

EARLY ONE MORNING see Grainger, Percy Aldridge

EARNEST, JOHN DAVID
Bountiful Voyager
2.2.2.2. 2.2.0.0. perc,harp,strings [12'] SCHIRM.EC rent (E2)

Chasing The Sun (Scherzo for Orchestra)
3.2.2.2. 4.3.3.1. timp,3perc,harp, strings [6'] SCHIRM.EC rent (E3)

In After Time
3.3.3.3. 4.3.3.1. timp,2perc,harp, kbd,strings [12'] SCHIRM.EC rent (E4)

Scherzo for Orchestra
see Chasing The Sun

EAST COAST, THE see Bryars, Gavin

EASTER ORISONS see Harvey, Jonathan

EASTERN INTERMEZZO see Grainger, Percy Aldridge

EASY WINNERS, THE (JOPLIN) see Sieben Ragtimes Für Streichorchester: Heft 1

EATING GREENS see Mackey, Steven

EATON, DARRYL (1940- )
Dialogue For Strings
string orch [11'] (in three untitled movements) sc CANADIAN MI 1500 E14DI (E5)

Reflections
group a: 1.1.1.1. 1.1.0.0. 2perc, pno, sqar; group b: 1.1.1.1. 1.1.0.0. 2perc, sqar (includes graphic notation) sc CANADIAN MI 1100 E14RE (E6)

EBB see McPherson, Gordon

EBULLIENT SHADOWS see Ince, Kamran

ECHANGES PER 16 STRUMENTALISTI see Glass, Paul

ECHOES OF NORMANDY see Lees, Benjamin

ECHOI see Lutyens, Elisabeth

ECHO'S see Franssens, Joep

ECKHARDT-GRAMATTE, SOPHIE CARMEN (1899-1974)
Concerto for Piano and Orchestra, No. 1
2(pic).2(English horn).2.2. 4.2.4.0. timp,3perc,harp,strings, pno solo sc CANADIAN MI 1361 E19CO (E7)

Concerto for Trumpet and Chamber Orchestra
2.2.2.2. 2.1.0.0. strings,trp solo [14'] sc CANADIAN MI 1331 E19CO (E8)

Konzertstück for Violoncello and Orchestra
0.0.0.2. 2.2.0.0. strings without vcl,vcl solo sc,solo pt CANADIAN MI 1313 E19KO (E9)

Molto Sostenuto: E131
string orch [11'] sc CANADIAN MI 1500 E19MO (E10)

Passacaglia Und Fuge
3+pic.2(English horn).2.2. 4.3.3.1. timp,perc,harp,strings [15'] sc CANADIAN MI 1100 E19PA (E11)

ÉCLAIR...PUIS LA NUIT!, UN see Burgan, Patrick

ÉCLAIRS SUR L'AU-DELA: VOLUME 1 see Messiaen, Olivier

ÉCLAIRS SUR L'AU-DELA: VOLUME 2 see Messiaen, Olivier

ECSTASY see Chan, Ka Nin

ED, FREDRIK (1964- )
Aim
5vln I,4vln II,3vla,2vcl,db [10'] STIM (E12)

Hyss
3(pic).3.3(bass clar).3. 4.3.2.0. timp,2perc,strings [8'] STIM sc H-2936, pts (E13)

Still
1(pic).1.1.0. 2.0.0.0. 2perc,string quar [12'] sc STIM (E14)

Stryk
6vln I,5vln II,4vla,3vcl,2db [6'] sc STIM (E15)

Vid
3(pic).3(English horn).3(bass clar).3(contrabsn). 4.3.3.1. timp,4perc,strings,elec gtr [20'] sc STIM (E16)

ED É SUBITO SERA see Haller, Hermann

EDELFRÄULEIN ALS BÄUERIN, DAS: SUITE see Bruns, Victor

EDITH see Hallin, Margareta

EDLUND, MIKAEL (1950- )
Ajar
3(pic).3.3(bass clar).3(contrabsn). 4.3.3.1. timp,3perc,harp,pno/cel, strings [11'] STIM sc H-2637, pts (E17)

Dissolved Window
see Upplst Fnster

Upplst Fnster
"Dissolved Window" 6vln I,6vln II, 4vla,3vcl,2db [16'] sc,pts STIM (E18)

EDLUND, SWANTE (1946- )
Canto Con Passione *Op.38
string quin/string orch,pno,vcl solo STIM (E19)

EDMONTON SUITE see Nicholson, G. Gordon

EDN, MATS (1957- )
Vackra Dalkullan: Dansdrama Kring Ett Kvinnode
clar,horn,acord,perc,strings, 12 dancers [60'] STIM (E20)

EDWARDS, ROSS (1943- )
Symphony Da Pacem Domine
2+pic.2+English horn.3.2+contrabsn. 4.3.3.1. timp,perc,cel,harp,16vln I,14vln II,12vla,10vcl,8db [29'] BOOSEY-ENG rent (E21)

EEAST see Rebne, Rune, Feast

EFE see Minami, Satoshi

EFFECTIVE MYTHOLOGIES see McPherson, Gordon

EFFET DE NUIT see Lazzari, Silvio

EFTER-KLANG (VER ETT FRAGMENT UR ADAGIO H-MOLL KV 540 AV W A MOZART): VERSION 3 see Sandberg, Lars

EFTER-KLANG: VERSION 4 see Sandberg, Lars

EFTERDANS see Blomberg, Erik

EGLOGA see Lang, Istvan

EGYPTIAN NIGHTS see Prokofiev, Serge

EGYPTIAN PRINCESS see Still, William Grant

EHMANN, HEINRICH (1938- )
Hommage
orch MÖSELER 10.472 rent (E22)

EI PARTE - PER PIETÀ, BEN MIO, PERDONA see Mozart, Wolfgang Amadeus

EICHHORN, FRANK VOLKER
Bildnis Einer Frau
see Porträt

Doppelkonzert: Novelle
1.0.0.0. 0.2.0.4. perc,8vln I,7vln II,6vla,5vcl,4db,vcl solo,harp solo [10'] sc PETERS 03103 (E23)

Porträt
"Bildnis Einer Frau" 3.3.1.2. 0.0.0.0. 4vln I,4vln II,4vla, 4vcl,2db [15'] sc PETERS 03102 (E24)

Reflexionen
3.3.3.3. 4.3.3.1. 4perc,8vln I,7vln II,6vla,5vcl,4db [15'] sc PETERS 03101 (E25)

EIDESIS V see Lanza, Alcides E.

EIDESIS VI see Lanza, Alcides E.

EIDETICS see Nilsson, Ivo

EIGHT HOUSES OF THE I CHING, THE see Kasemets, Udo

1812 OVERTURE, MARCHE SLAVE AND FRANCESCA DA RIMINI see Tchaikovsky, Piotr Ilyich

1812 OVERTURE see Tchaikovsky, Piotr Ilyich, Ouverture Solennelle Es-Dur, Op. 49

...EIGHTH AUTHOR, THE see Thommessen, Olav Anton

EIGHTY see Cage, John

EINDKRAK (II) see Meijering, Chiel

EINDRUCK-AUSDRUCK II: (HOMMAGE) À KANDINSKY see Tarnopolsky, Vladimir

EINES TAGES AUS DEM LEBEN DES GOTTES BRAHMA see Lönner, Oddvar

EINFACHE LIEDER see Korngold, Erich Wolfgang

EINFACHE MUSIK see Hidalgo, Manuel

EINTAGS-SINFONIE see Bredemeyer, Reiner, Schlagstück 6

EINZUG DER GÖTTER IN WALHALL see Wagner, Richard

EIRÉNÉ see Mácha, Otmar

EISBRENNER, WERNER (1908-1981)
Lieder Unserer Heimat (Rhapsody) folk song,Ger
2.2(English horn).2.1. 3.2.3.0.
timp,perc,harp,strings [11'40"]
sc,set BUSCH DM 039 rent    (E26)

Rhapsody
see Lieder Unserer Heimat

Valse Moderato
see Vergessene Melodie

Vergessene Melodie
"Valse Moderato" 2.1(English horn).3(bass clar).1. 3.0.3.0.
gtr,bongos,drums,strings [4'45"]
sc,set BUSCH DM 055 rent    (E27)

EISLER, HANNS (1898-1962)
Auferstanden Aus... *hymn
2.2.2.2. 3.3.3.1. timp,perc,8vln I,
7vln II,6vla,5vcl,4db [5'] sc
PETERS 04002    (E28)

Deutsche Sinfonie
2.2.2.3. 4.3.2.1. timp,perc,
strings,MezBar&2 speaking voices,
SATB [70'] DEUTSCHER    (E29)

Niemands Land Marsch
(Bauer, E.) 2.2.2.2. 4.2.3.0. timp,
perc,pno,harmonium,strings [5']
PETERS    (E30)

Solidaritätslied
0.0.3.0.alto sax.4tenor sax.
0.2.1.1. perc,banjo,pno,4vcl,2db
[3'] PETERS    (E31)

EJIRI, SAKAE (1947- )
Ginga Tetsudo No Koibitotachi
orch [130'] JAPAN    (E32)

EKLIN, SALOMON (1756-1803)
Sju Danser
(Hedwall, Lennart) string orch (1.
Polonesse; 2. Menuetto; 3.
Menuetto; 4. Menuetto; 5.
Polonesse; 6. Menuetto; 7.
Polonois) sc STIM    (E33)

EKLUND, HANS (1927- )
Apertura
1.1.1.1. 1.0.0.0. strings [9'] sc
STIM    (E34)

Freschi
see Sinfonia 12

Hotch-Potch
"Kleine Spassmusik, Eine" string
orch sc STIM    (E35)

Kleine Spassmusik, Eine
see Hotch-Potch

Mesto Per Archi
string orch [7'] sc GEHRMANS (E36)

Serenata, La
see Symphony No. 7

EKLUND, HANS (cont'd.)
Sine Nomine
see Sinfonia 10

Sinfonia 10 (Symphony No. 10)
"Sine Nomine" 3(pic).2.2.2.
4.2.3.1. timp,2perc,strings (1.
Andante desolato; 2. Allegro
Arrabiato; 3. Fine: Adagio) sc
STIM    (E37)

Sinfonia 12 (Symphony No. 12)
"Freschi" 3(pic).2.2.2. 4.2.3.1.
timp,3perc,strings sc STIM    (E38)

Sinfonia Introvertita
see Symphony No. 9

Sinfonia Piccola
see Symphony No. 10

Symphony No. 7
"Serenata, La" 3(pic).2.2.2.
4.2.3.1. timp,3perc,strings,pno
sc,pts STIM H-2705    (E39)

Symphony No. 9
"Sinfonia Introvertita"
3(pic).2.2.2. 4.2.3.1. timp,
2perc,strings [20'-25'] sc,pts
STIM    (E40)

Symphony No. 10
"Sinfonia Piccola" 3(pic).2.2.2.
4.2.3.1. timp,3perc,strings sc
STIM    (E41)
see Sinfonia 10

Symphony No. 12
see Sinfonia 12

Toccata Ostinata
3(pic).2.2.2. 4.2.3.1. timp,2perc,
strings sc STIM    (E42)

EKSTASIS see Jeverud, Johan

EKSTRÖM, LARS (1956- )
Fond Sombre, Un
5vln I,4vln II,3vla,2vcl,db,vcl
solo [17'] sc,pts SUECIA    (E43)

Genom Prisman Ave En Skrva: Musik
Komponerad Efter August
Strindbergs Mleri
1(pic).1(English horn).2(bass
clar).1(contrabsn). 1.1.2.1.
2perc,2vln I,2vln II,2vla,vcl,db,
pno [45'-50'] (Kustlandskap II;
Sol gr ned uti hav; Staden;
Svartsjukans natt; Ovder;
Golgata; Underlandet; Den ensama
tisteln) sc,pts STIM    (E44)

Genom Skärvan Av En Prisma
"Musik Komponerad Efter August
Strindbergs Måleri"
3(pic).2(English horn).3(bass
clar).2(contrabsn). 4.2.3.1.
timp.2perc,strings,pno [45'-50']
STIM sc H-2885, pts    (E45)

Musik För Orkester
2(pic).2(English horn).1.1.
2.2.2.0. timp,2perc,strings pts
STIM T-1202    (E46)

Musik Komponerad Efter August
Strindbergs Måleri
see Genom Skärvan Av En Prisma

Världen Genom Världar
3(pic).3(English horn).3(bass
clar).3(contrabsn). 4.3.3.1.
timp,2perc,strings,pno [22'] STIM
sc H-2915, pts    (E47)

Word, Crystal Circles And The World
7vln I,6vln II,4vla,6vcl,2db sc,pts
STIM    (E48)

EKTENIA see Glass, Paul

EL-DABH, HALIM (1921- )
Vision At The Cross Road
3.2.2.2. 2.2.2.0. timp,3perc,8vln
I,7vln II,6vla,5vcl,4db [8'] sc
PETERS 03804    (E49)

EL DORADO see Adams, John see Mozetich,
Marjan

ELANCIA SUITE see Haworth, Frank

ELECTRIZATION see Schenker, Friedrich

ELEGANT JOURNEY WITH STOPPING POINTS OF
INTEREST see Moran, Robert

ELEGIA see Bois, Rob du see Hayashi,
Hikaru see Kocsar, Miklos, Elegy
for Bassoon and Chamber Orchestra
see Zuckert, Leon

ELEGIAC SERENADE see Williams, Adrian

ÉLÉGIE see Harman, Chris

ELÉGIE À LA MÉMOIRE DE SAMUEL BARBER
see Lemeland, Aubert

ELEGIE NA ODCHODNOU see Raichl,
Miroslav

ELEGY see Knox, Roger see Ranjbaran,
Behzad

ELEGY FOR OUR TIME see Heard, Alan

ELEGY OF THE FLOWERS see Lutyens,
Elisabeth

ELÉMENT see Boesmans, Philippe

ELF LIEDER see Jolas, Betsy

ELGAR, [SIR] EDWARD (WILLIAM)
(1857-1934)
Enigma Variations And Pomp And
Circumstance Marches Nos. 1-4
orch sc DOVER 27342-3    (E50)

Sospiri *Op.70
harp/pno,strings,opt harmonium/org
[6'] sc,pts BREITKOPF-W
PB-OB 5271    (E51)

ELIAS: SEI STILLE DEM HERRN see
Mendelssohn-Bartholdy, Felix

ELIAS: SO IHR MICH VON GANZEM HERZEN
SUCHET see Mendelssohn-Bartholdy,
Felix

ELIASSON, ANDERS (1947- )
Sinfonia Da Camera
chamber orch [14'] sc REIMERS
101099 rent    (E52)

Symphony No. 1
3(pic).3(English horn).3(bass
clar).3(contrabsn). 4.3.3.1.
timp,6perc,strings,cel/pno [30']
sc,pts STIM H-2357    (E53)

ELISE: OVERTURE see Cherubini, Luigi

ELIZABETHAN SUITE see Barbirolli, [Sir]
John

ELLENTÉTEK see Maros, Rudolf, Contrasts

ELLINGHAM MARSHAS see Holland, Theodore

ELLIPSIS see Sackman, Nicholas

ELLIS, DAVID
Contraprovisations
3.3.3.3. 4.3.3.1. timp,3perc,cel,
harp,strings [14'] manuscript
BMIC    (E54)

Two Fantasias
strings [12'] DA CAPO    (E55)

ELMEHED, RUNE (1925- )
Variationer Över En Fransk Folkmelodi
marimba,fl,ob,string orch STIM
(E56)

ELOQUENCES see Rossum, Frederic R. van

ELVERHÖI, SYMFONISCH GEDICHT see
Wagenaar, Johan

EMBER see Feiler, Dror

EMMER, HUIB (1951- )
Crawling Up The Wall
1.1.1.1. 1.1.1.1. perc,harp,pno,
2vln,vla,vcl,db [12'] sc DONEMUS
(E57)

Pulse Palace
2.2.2.2. 2.2.1.1. vibra,strings
[10'] sc DONEMUS    (E58)

EMMERIK, IVO VAN (1961- )
Ventriloquist
2.1.1.2. 2.0.1.0. perc,harp,strings
[10'] sc DONEMUS    (E59)

EMMERT, FRANTISEK (1940- )
Concerto for Violoncello and Chamber
Orchestra
2.1.1.1. 4.2.0.1. euphonium,xylo,
strings,vcl solo [14'] CESKY HUD.
(E60)

Cor Jesu
see Symphony No. 9

Hudba Pro Komorní Orchestr (Music for
String Orchestra)
string orch [9'] CESKY HUD.    (E61)

Komorní Koncert Pro Smyccovy Orchestr
A Koncertantní Housle
string orch,vln solo [12'] CESKY
HUD.    (E62)

EMMERT, FRANTISEK (cont'd.)

Music for String Orchestra
see Hudba Pro Komorní Orchestr

Symphony No. 7
4.3.3.4. 4.5.5.1. timp,perc,2harp,
strings [27'] CESKY HUD.     (E63)

Symphony No. 8
4.5.4.4. 4.6.6.2. timp,perc,2harp,
strings [35'] CESKY HUD.     (E64)

Symphony No. 9
"Cor Jesu" 3.3.3.3. 4.4.5.1. 1-
4timp,perc,harp,strings,3vln I&
3vln II&3vla&3vcl soli [17']
CESKY HUD.     (E65)

EMPEROR'S SONG see Sandström, Jan

EMPFANGE, GELIEBTE, DIES HERZ HIER ZU
EIGEN see Mozart, Wolfgang Amadeus,
Core Vi Dono Bell' Idolo Mio, Il

EMPFINDSAMES KONZERT, EIN see
Schwertsik, Kurt, Concerto for
Double Bass, Op. 56

EMPT, WILHELM
Suite for Strings
MÖSELER sc 10.463-00, pts
10.463-01, set 10.463-09     (E66)

EMPTY STABLE, THE see Kirkwood,
Antoinette

EMURA, TETSUJI (1960-  )
Concerto for Violin and Orchestra,
No. 2
see Intéxtérieur, L'

Intéxtérieur, L' (Concerto for Violin
and Orchestra, No. 2)
[17'] JAPAN     (E67)

Lydian
chamber orch [15'] JAPAN     (E68)

Primavera
orch,S solo [31'] JAPAN     (E69)

EN AL LUISTEREND... see Verbugt, Eric

EN PASSANT L'EAU see Stscherbatcheff,
Nikolai

EN PRIÈRE see Faure, Gabriel-Urbain

ENCANTADAS, THE see Picker, Tobias

ENCHAINEMENTS see Burrell, Diana

ENCORE see Killmayer, Wilhelm

ENCOUNTERS see Baker, Michael Conway
see Musto, John

ENCOUNTERS WITH DYLAN THOMAS see
Lazarof, Henri

ÉNEKSZÓ see Kodály, Zoltán

ENGELMANN, HANS ULRICH (1921-  )
Chaconne, Op. 56
"Ciacona" 1.0.0+bass clar.0.
0.0.0.0. vibra,pno,strings [14']
BREITKOPF-W     (E70)

Ciacona
see Chaconne, Op. 56

Concerto for Violoncello and String
Orchestra, Op. 2b
strings,vcl solo [12'] BREITKOPF-W
(E71)

Den Taten Der Neuen Bildhauer
see Strukturen

Ezra Pound Music *Op.21
1(pic).1+English horn.0.1. 0.0.1.0.
4perc,4vcl,4db [9'] BREITKOPF-W
(E72)

Kaleidoskop
1.1.1.1.sax. 0.3.3.0. timp,2perc,
strings [10'] BREITKOPF-W     (E73)

Leopoldskron
1.1.1(sax).1. 0.1.1.1. timp,4perc,
harp,cel,pno,strings [15']
BREITKOPF-W     (E74)

Magog: Fünf Orchesterstücke *Op.16b
2+pic.2.2.2+contrabsn.sax. 4.4.3.1.
timp,5perc,harp,cel,pno,strings
[15'] BREITKOPF-W     (E75)

Music for Strings, Brass and
Percussion, Op. 3a
0.0.0.0. 4.3.3.1. timp,3perc,
strings [10'] BREITKOPF-W     (E76)

Noche De Luna *Op.18b
1.0.0.0.soprano sax. 0.1.1.0.
3perc,harp,elec gtr,cembalo,
strings without db [15']

ENGELMANN, HANS ULRICH (cont'd.)

(pantomime for 2 female and 2
male dancers.) BREITKOPF-W     (E77)

Nocturne, Op. 18a
1.0.0.0.soprano sax. 0.1.1.0.
3perc,harp,elec gtr,cembalo,
strings without db,S solo [15']
BREITKOPF-W     (E78)

Orchester-Fantasie, Op. 6 (Sinfonia,
Op. 6)
2.2.2.2+contrabsn. 4.3.3.1. timp,
4perc,harp,cel,pno,strings [15']
BREITKOPF-W     (E79)

Partita, Op. 12
0.0.0.0. 0.3.0.0. timp,3perc,
strings [12'] BREITKOPF-W     (E80)

Polifonica *Op.17
1.0+English horn.0.1.sax. 1.1.1.0.
4perc,harp,elec gtr,strings
without db [8'] BREITKOPF-W     (E81)

Sinfonia, Op. 6
see Orchester-Fantasie, Op. 6

Strukturen *Op.15
"Den Taten Der Neuen Bildhauer"
1.1.1.1. 1.1.1.0. timp,4perc,
harp,pno,strings without db [12']
BREITKOPF-W     (E82)

Trias *Op.24
1.1.1.1. 1.1.1.1. 3perc,strings,
electronic tape,pno solo [22']
BREITKOPF-W     (E83)

ENGLISH DANCE see Grainger, Percy
Aldridge

ENGLISHBY, PAUL
Last Clarinet, The
1(pic).1.1.1. 1.1.1.1. perc,pno,
strings,narrator [25'] perf sc
set OXFORD 3564122 sc,pts rent
(E84)

ENGSTRÖM, TORBJÖRN (1963-  )
Orkestersvit
2.2.2.2. 2.0.2.0. strings [10'] sc
STIM     (E85)

Pangea
see Symphony No. 1

Symphony No. 1
"Pangea" 3(pic).3(English
horn).3(bass clar).3(contrabsn).
4.2.3.0. timp,2perc,strings [22']
sc STIM H-2847     (E86)

Symposion
3.3.3.3. 4.3.3.1. timp,perc,strings
[10'] sc,pts STIM H-2560     (E87)

ENHARMONIC VARIATIONS see Rieti,
Vittorio

ENIGMA see Müller-Siemens, Detlev

ENIGMA 15 - TONS see Arkvik, Ylva Q

ENIGMA SINFONICO see Rieti, Vittorio

ENIGMA VARIATIONS AND POMP AND
CIRCUMSTANCE MARCHES NOS. 1-4 see
Elgar, [Sir] Edward (William)

ENNA, AUGUST (1859-1939)
Cleopatra: Fantasy (Fantasy) (from
Cleopatra)
(Sandré, G.) 2.2.2.2. 4.0.3.1.
timp,3perc,harp,strings [13']
BREITKOPF-W     (E88)

Fantasy
see Cleopatra: Fantasy

Hans Christian Andersen: Overture
3(pic).2.2.2. 4.2.2.1. timp,strings
[11'] (no score) BREITKOPF-W
(E89)

Märchen
3.2.2.2. 4.2.2.1. timp,perc,harp,
strings [28'] BREITKOPF-W     (E90)

Streichholzmädel, Das: Overture
2.2.2.2. 4.2.3.0. timp,perc,harp,
strings [7'] BREITKOPF-W     (E91)

ENSEMBLE see Cowell, Henry Dixon

ENSEMBLEKONZERT II see Goldmann,
Friedrich

ENTERTAINER, THE see Joplin, Scott

ENTFERNE DICH! - FURCHTBARE QUALEN IHR
see Mozart, Wolfgang Amadeus, Ah
Scostati! - Smanie Implacabili

ENTFÜHRUNG AUS DEM SERAIL, DIE:
OUVERTÜRE see Mozart, Wolfgang
Amadeus

ENTRATA see Orff, Carl

ENTRÉ see Blomberg, Erik

ENTREE ET SCHERZO INGENU see
Moeschinger, Albert

ENTYMOLOGY see Strindberg, Henrik

EOS see Lutyens, Elisabeth

EÖTVÖS, JÓSZEF (1962-  )
Revisor, Der
1(pic).2.1.1. 2.2.1.0. timp,3perc,
pno,harp,strings,trp solo [17']
(concert suite) SCHOTTS perf mat
rent     (E92)

Variationen Über Ein Altes Wiener
Strophenlied
2.2.2.2. 2.2.0.0. pno,harp,strings,
coloratura sop [7'] pno red
SCHOTTS ED 3788 perf mat rent
(E93)

Verlobung In San Domingo, Die
2(pic).2.2.2. 4.3.3.0. timp,2perc,
pno,strings,MezT soli (3 pieces,
text by Werner Egk after Heinrich
von Kleist) SCHOTTS perf mat rent
(E94)

Waltzer Für Orchester
2+pic.3.3.2+contrabsn. 4.3.3.1.
perc,strings SCHOTTS perf mat
rent     (E95)

EÖTVÖS, PÉTER (1944-  )
Steine, Für Ensemble
1(pic).1(English horn).1+bass
clar.1(contrabsn). 2.2.2.1. perc,
cym solo,harp,cel,strings [10']
EMB rent     (E96)

EPICKÁ CIACONNA see Stárek, Jiri

EPICLESIS see Macmillan, James

EPILOG see Korndorf, Nicolai

EPIMETHEUS USA see Gutchë, Gene

EPISOD see Blomberg, Erik

EPISODEN see Haller, Hermann

EPISODY see Foltyn, Jaroslav

EPITAPH see Erdmann, Dietrich see
Koprowski, Peter Paul

EPITAPH FÜR OPHELIA see Reutter,
Hermann

EPITAPH UND POLYPHONIE see Zechlin,
Ruth, Musik Zu Bach

EPITAPHE see Rossum, Frederic R. van

EPITAPHE DE LA 2E SYMPHONIE see Fiala,
George

ER EI SLIK NATT, DET see Søderlind,
Ragnar

ER FLIEHET - O VERZEIH', VERZEIH',
GELIEBTER see Mozart, Wolfgang
Amadeus, Ei Parte - Per Pietà, Ben
Mio, Perdona

ER WEISS ES BESSER see Weingartner,
(Paul) Felix von

ERASMUS see Kalach, Jiri

ERAT ERIT EST: FOR 15 INSTRUMENTS see
Ore, Cecilie

ERBARMEN see Nicode, Jean Louis

ERDMANN, DIETRICH (1917-  )
Epitaph
clar,bass clar,mand,gtr,vln,vla,vcl
[12'] BREITKOPF-W     (E97)

Konzertstück for Alto Saxophone and
Chamber Orchestra
2horn,perc,strings,alto sax solo
[6'] BREITKOPF-W     (E98)

Reminiscences Für Orchester
sc RIES 51092 perf mat rent     (E99)

ERHEBE DICH, GENOSSIN MEINER SCHMACH
see Wagner, Richard

ERIK ESÖ KOLOZSSVARBAN see Cornell,
Klaus

ERIKSON, ÅKE (1937-  )
Spel
2(pic).2(English horn).2(bass
clar).2(contrabsn). 4.2.2.0.
timp,perc,strings [12'] STIM sc
H-2763, pts     (E100)

ERINNERUNG AN DIE NORWEGISCHEN ALPEN
see Berwald, Franz (Adolf)

ERKEL, FRANZ (FERENC) (1810-1893)
"Palotache" (from László Hunyadi)
2+pic.2.2.2. 4.2.3.1. timp,perc,
strings [6'] (Hungarian ballroom
dance) EMB rent          (E101)

ERMINIA: REZITATIVE UND ARIE see
Scarlatti, Alessandro

ERMIONE, SINFONIA WITH CHORUS see
Rossini, Gioacchino

ERNTETANZ see Hamerik, Asger

ERO E LEANDRO see Catalani, Alfredo

ERÖFFNUNG UND ZERTRÜMMERUNG see Huber,
Nicolaus A.

EROICA see Beethoven, Ludwig van,
Symphony No. 3 in E flat, Op. 55
see Schulhoff, Erwin, Symphony No.
7

EROS see Finke, Fidelio Friedrich
(Fritz)

EROS AND DEATH see Theodorakis, Mikis

ERRATIQUE see Moeschinger, Albert

ERSCHAFFUNG DER WELT, DIE: SUITE NO. 1
see Petrov, Andrei P.

ERSCHAFFUNG DER WELT, DIE: SUITE NO. 2
see Petrov, Andrei P.

ERSCHEINUNG IM PARK, DIE see Gefors,
Hans

ERYS see Ibarrondo, Felix

ES ERHOB SICH EIN GESCHREI see Ruzicka,
Peter

ES WAREN ZWEI KÖNIGSKINDER see Volbach,
Fritz

ESCAICH, THIERRY (1965-    )
Chant Des Ténèbres, Le [15']
string orch,sax solo
BILLAUDOT          (E102)

Concerto for Organ and Orchestra
2.2.2.2. 2.2.2.0. timp,2perc,
strings [27'] LEDUC          (E103)

Symphony No. 1  *Kyrie
2(pic).2(English horn).2(bass
clar).2(contrabsn). 4.3.2.0.
2timp,2perc,harp,10vln I,9vln II,
8vla,6vcl,3db [25'] (of an
imaginary Mass) LEDUC          (E104)

Threni  *Op.22
3.3.4.3. 6.4.4.1. timp,5perc,pno&
cel,strings,S solo [25']
BILLAUDOT rent          (E105)

ESCAPE ME NEVER see Walton, [Sir]
William (Turner)

ESCAPE ME NEVER: SUITE see Walton,
[Sir] William (Turner)

ESCENAS GRANADINAS: SUITE DE BALLET
ESPAÑOL see Zuckert, Leon

ESCHATOS: BALLETT FÜR ORCHESTER see
Glass, Paul

ESCHATOS: SUITE NO. 1 see Glass, Paul

ESCHATOS: SUITE NO. 2 Glass, Paul

ESCHER, RUDOLF GEORGE (1912-1980)
Largo (from Sinfonia In Memoriam
Maurice Ravel)
4.3.4.4.sax.sax.sax. 3.2.2.1. timp,
2perc,cel,2harp,strings [8'] sc
DONEMUS          (E106)

Passacaglia
4.4.4.4.2sax. 4.5.3.1. timp,4perc,
cel,2harp,org,strings [13'] sc
DONEMUS          (E107)

Symphony No. 1
4.4.4.4.sax. 4.4.3.1. 2timp,perc,
cel,2harp,strings [26'] sc
DONEMUS          (E108)

ESMERALDA see Hilmar, František

ESPACE DE SENTIMENT CONTINU, L' see
Safronov, Anton

ESPADA see Massenet, Jules

ESPAÑA see Waldteufel, Emile

ESPERA, LA see Rodrigo, Joaquín

ESQUISSE SYMPHONIQUE see Zuckert, Leon,
Symphonic Sketch

ESSAY FOR ORCHESTRA see Kulesha, Gary

ESSAY FOR STRINGS see Douglas, Clive

ESSL, KARL HEINZ (1960-    )
...Et Consumimur Igni
0.0.0.0. 2.2.2.0. 3perc,strings
[16'] BREITKOPF-W          (E109)

In Girum. Imus. Nocte
4(2pic,3alto fl).4(2English
horn).4(4bass clar,contrabass
clar).4(contrabsn). 4.4.4.2.
8perc,harp,pno,12vln I,10vln II,
8vla,4vcl,db [15'] BREITKOPF-W
          (E110)

Met Him Pike Trousers
4.4.4.4. 4.4.4.2. 6perc,harp,pno,
strings SEESAW          (E111)
orch sc TONOS M-2015-4287-4 rent
          (E112)

ESTE A TÁBORBAN see Vass, Lajos,
Evening In The Camp

ESTLÄNDSKA BILDER see Lundin, Dag

ESTONIAN PICTURES see Lundin, Dag,
Estländska Bilder

...ET CONSUMIMUR IGNI see Essl, Karl
Heinz

ET IN TERRA PAX see Nobis, Herbert

"...ET J'ENTENDS LA NUIT QUI CHANTE
DANS CLOCHES" see Cherney, Brian

ET LE JOUR VINT see Charpentier,
Jacques

ETERNAL EARTH, THE see Louie, Alexina

ETERNAL MEMORY see Tavener, John

ÉTOILE DU BERGER, L' see
Stscherbatcheff, Nikolai

ÉTOILES see Alla, Thierry

ÉTOILES BRÛLÉES see DuBois, Pierre-Max

ETUDE D'EXÖCUTION TRANSCENDANTE see
Febel, Reinhard

ETUDE POINTILLISTIQUE see Derungs,
Martin

ÉTUDES FÜR GROSSES ORCHESTER see Kagel,
Mauricio

ETYM see Dittrich, Paul-Heinz see
Ruzicka, Peter

ETYMOLOGY see Strindberg, Henrik

EU-MUSIK NR. 1 see Wohlgemuth, Gerhard

EUFONIA see Glass, Paul

EUMÉNIDES, LES: LE FINAL see Milhaud,
Darius

EUMÉNIDES, LES: OVERTURE TO ACT III see
Milhaud, Darius

EUPHONIA I see Lenners, Claude

EURYDICE see Kovach, Andor

EUTERPÉ see Peška, Vlastimil

EVA see Mraczek, Joseph Gustav

EVANGELIO DE NAVIDAD see Turina,
Joaquín

EVANGELISTA, JOSE (1943-    )
Piano Concertante
1(pic).1.1.1. 1.1.1.0. vibra,
strings,pno solo sc CANADIAN
MI 1361 E92P          (E113)

ÉVASIONS see Bernier, Rene

EVEN TOMORROW see Singleton, Alvin

EVENING IN A RUSSIAN VILLAGE see
Zuckert, Leon

EVENING IN THE CAMP see Vass, Lajos

EVENING LAND see Schwantner, Joseph

EVENTS OF NOVEMBER 10, 1812, THE see
Sherman, Norman

EVERGLADES, THE see Delius, Frederick

EVOCATIONS see Baker, Michael Conway
see Carignan, Nichole

EVOKACE see Mateju, Zbynek

EX-ANIMO see Schut, Vladislav see Shut,
Vladislav

EXEGI MONUMENTUM see Silvestrov,
Valentin

EXHORTO see Betancur-Gonzalez, Valentin

EXISTENCE see Ichiyanagi, Toshi

EXKURSION see Goldmann, Friedrich

EXORCISM OF RIO SUMPÚL, THE see
Macmillan, James

EXPENSIVE EMBARRASSMENT SUITE, AN see
Gougeon, Denis

EXSULTATE, JUBILATE see Mozart,
Wolfgang Amadeus

EXTASE see Chen, Qigang

EXTASE II see Chen, Qigang

EXTEMPORE see Vackár, Dalibor Cyril

EXTENSION see Boesmans, Philippe,
Elément

EXTENSION-CONTRACTION (MUSIQUE
ÉLÉGIAQUE) see Haller, Hermann

EXULTET see Canat De Chizy, Edith

EXZENTRISCHEN, DIE see Trommer, Jack

EYBLER, JOSEPH (1765-1846)
Concerto for Clarinet and Orchestra
in B flat
(Weinmann) clar solo,orch
KUNZELMANN 10132          (E114)

EYE ON GENESIS II see Yuasa, Joji

EYERLY, SCOTT
Variations On A Theme By Honegger
3.3.3.3. 4.3.3.1. timp,4perc,harp,
8vln I,7vln II,6vla,5vcl,4db
[30'] sc PETERS 03126          (E115)

EYKEN, ERNEST VAN DER
Poem
string orch [8'] BELGE          (E116)

EYSER, EBERHARD (1932-    )
Alba: Insieme
string orch [15'] sc,pts STIM
          (E117)

Ardogini
2.2.2.2. 2.2.0.0. timp,strings
[15'] sc STIM          (E118)

Att Nalkas Stockholm
chamber orch [15'] CON B          (E119)

Chevauchée De Nuit: Préludes
Symphoniques
see Rid I Natt

Concertante
see Sinfonietta No. 3 for Chamber
Orchestra

Heldenleben: Ein Traum
string orch/string quin [20'] sc,
pts STIM          (E120)

Itaból
2.2.2.2. 2.2.3.0. perc,strings
[10'5"] sc STIM          (E121)

Lustspelsuvertyr
see Trägen Vinner

Macbeth
2(pic).2(English horn).4(bass
clar).2. 4.2.3.1. timp,perc,
strings [12'5"] (concert
overture) sc STIM          (E122)

Passacaglia
2(pic).2(English horn).3(bass
clar).2. 2.2.3.1. timp,perc,
strings [12'5"] sc STIM          (E123)

Rid I Natt
"Chevauchée De Nuit: Préludes
Symphoniques" 3(pic).3(English
horn).3(bass clar).3(contrabsn).
4.3.3.1. timp,perc,strings [13']
STIM          (E124)

Sinfonietta No. 3 for Chamber
Orchestra
"Concertante" 1.1.1.1. 1.0.0.0.
strings [15'] sc STIM A-444
          (E125)

Stoccasta  *Op.57
4(pic).4.5(bass clar).4. 4.2.3.1.
timp,2perc,strings [11'5"] sc
STIM          (E126)

**EYSER, EBERHARD** (cont'd.)

Stragano
  string orch/string quin [11'5"]
  STIM (E127)

Trägen Vinner
  "Lustspelsuvertyr" 2.1(English
  horn).2.2. 2.2.3.1. timp,3perc,
  strings [9'5"] sc,pts STIM
  ED.NR 309A (E128)

EZRA POUND MUSIC see Engelmann, Hans
  Ulrich

# F

F TO BE see Rossé, Francois

FABEL see Støyva, Njål Gunnar

FACADE: SUITE NO.3 see Walton, [Sir]
  William (Turner)

FACE OF THE NIGHT, THE HEART OF THE
  DARK, THE see Peterson, Wayne
  Turner

FACE-TO-FACE see Kox, Hans

FACKELTANZ NR. 1 B-DUR see Meyerbeer,
  Giacomo

FAETHON see Broz, František

FAGYONGY see Farkas, Ferenc, Mistletoe

FAIRY QUEEN, THE: TWO SUITES see
  Purcell, Henry

FAIRY TALE IN MUSIC, A see Polgar,
  Tibor, Dwarf And The Giant, The

**FALCNÍK, STANISLAV** (1961- )
  Concerto Grosso
  1.2.0.2. 0.2.0.0. strings [10']
  CESKY HUD. (F1)

**FALK, KARL-AXEL** (1958- )
  Dicta In Three Movements
  fl,clar,timp,perc,pno,strings
  without db [9'48"] NORSKMI (F2)

**FALLA, MANUEL DE** (1876-1946)
  Danza Ritual Del Fuego
  (Cohen, Shimon) string orch [3']
  (for USA and Canada only) PRESSER
  rent (F3)

  Three-Cornered Hat In Full Score
  orch sc DOVER 29647-4 (F4)

FALLENDE BLAETTER see Buczynski, Pawel

FALSE TREE, A see Sandgren, Joakim

**FALTUS, LEOS** (1937- )
  Concerto Lirico
  strings,bsn solo [9'] CESKY HUD.
  (F5)

  Harmonia Mundi - Res Humana
  see Symphony No. 4

  Hudba Pro Smycce
  "Mundstockiana" string orch CESKY
  HUD. (F6)

  Mundstockiana
  see Hudba Pro Smycce

  Serenata Inconsonante
  strings,timp [15'] CESKY HUD. (F7)

  Symphony No. 4
  "Harmonia Mundi - Res Humana"
  3.3.2.2. 4.3.3.1. timp,perc,harp,
  strings [14'] CESKY HUD. (F8)

FAMILY TREE see Takemitsu, Toru

FANAL see Höller, York

FANAL SPANIEN 1936 see Schenker,
  Friedrich

FANDANGO, ANDANTE UND REZITATIV see
  Mozart, Wolfgang Amadeus

FANFARE AND ANTHEM see Applebaum, Louis

FANFARE FOR CINCINNATI see Stucky,
  Steven Edward

FANFARE FOR LOS ANGELES see Stucky,
  Steven Edward

FANFARE FOR ORCHESTRA see
  Skrowaczewski, Stanisław

FANFARE FOR THE FAMILY FARM see Walker,
  Gwyneth

FANFARE INAUGURALE see Gilson, Paul

FANFARE OF PRIDE AND JOY see Polgar,
  Tibor

FANFARE OVERTURE see Dorff, Daniel Jay

FANFARE, PRAYER AND HALLELUYEH see
  Barnes, Milton

FANFARE REGALE see Søderlind, Ragnar

FANFARES see Wolfe, Lawrence

FANFARES AND CANZONA see Kunz, Alfred

FANFARES FOR A NEW DAY see McIntyre,
  Paul

FANFARES FOR ORCHESTRA see Klein,
  Lothar

FANFARES FOR PERCUSSION AND ORCHESTRA
  see Mills, Richard

FANISKA: OVERTURE see Cherubini, Luigi

FANTAISIE BRILLANTE see Bizet, Georges

FANTAISIE DE CONCERT see Tchaikovsky,
  Piotr Ilyich

FANTAISIE SYMPHONIQUE see Chevillard,
  (Paul Alexandre) Camille

FANTASIA CONCERTANTE see Szekely, Endre

FANTASIA DA CONCERTO see Jira, Milan

FANTASIA ON A THEME BY THOMAS TALLIS
  see Vaughan Williams, Ralph

FANTASIA ON A TWELVE-TONE SYSTEM see
  Fridolfson, Ruben, Fantasia On A
  Twelvetone System

FANTASIA ON A TWELVETONE SYSTEM see
  Fridolfson, Ruben

FANTASIA ON "GREENSLEEVES" see Vaughan
  Williams, Ralph

FANTASÍA PARA CASTAÑUELAS Y ORQUESTA
  see Llacer "Regoli", E.

FANTASIA PARA UN GENTILHOMBRE see
  Rodrigo, Joaquín

FANTASIA SAKAIMINATO see Toyama, Yuzo

FANTASIA SOPRA "LO SDEGNO DEL MARE" see
  Henze, Hans Werner,
  Appassionatamente

FANTASIES AND VARIATIONS ON A CHANSON
  BY ORLANDO DI LASSO see Levi, Paul
  Alan, Transformations Of The Heart

FANTASIESTÜCK see Schlemm, Gustav Adolf

FANTASMA-CANTOS see Takemitsu, Toru

FANTASMA-CANTOS II see Takemitsu, Toru

FANTASTIC JOURNEY, A see Chan, Ka Nin

FANTASTIC PANTOMIMES see Mills, Richard

FANTASY AND POLKA see Rorem, Ned

FANTASY AND VARIATIONS see Wilson,
  Richard (Edward)

FANTASY IN BLUE see Pütz, Eduard

FANTASY ON A THEME see Jones, Kelsey

FANTASY ON MR. HYDE'S SONG see
  Grantham, Donald

FANTASY-PIECES (ON THE HEINE
  "LIEDERKREIS" OF SCHUMANN) see
  Holloway, Robin

FAR FROM THESE THINGS FOR CHAMBER
  ORCHESTRA see Lennon, John Anthony

FARAMONDO: OVERTURE see Handel, George
  Frideric

FARBEN see Frischknecht, Hans Eugen

FARBEN UND RHYTHMEN see Schmidt,
  Hansjürgen, Sinfonia No. 2

FARBENSPIEL see Schuller, Gunther

FAREWELL FROM THE BIRDS OF PASSAGE see
  Raskatov, Alexander

**FARIS, ALEXANDER**
  Upstairs Downstairs
  (Frazer, Alan) strings sc,pts
  CRAMER 90437 f.s. (F9)

**FARKAS, FERENC** (1905- )
  Asztalizene
  see Table Music

  Birds Of Love
  2.1.2.1. 0.0.0.0. harp,strings,solo
  voice [3'] (cycle of songs to
  poems by Ferenc Kazinczy & Mihály
  Csokonai Vitéz) EMB rent (F10)

  Buvos Szekrény, A
  see Magic Wardrobe, The: Concert
  Overture

**FARKAS, FERENC (cont'd.)**

Calendar
"Naptár" 1.1.1.1. 1.0.0.0. harp,
strings,ST soli [15'] (12
miniatures to poems by Miklós
Radnóti) EMB rent                     (F11)

Concertino for Piano and Orchestra
2(pic).2(English
horn).2.2(contrabsn). 4.2.3.0.
timp,perc,strings,pno solo [15']
EMB rent                              (F12)

Concertino No. 5
strings [12'] EMB rent                (F13)

Concertino Rustico
string orch, Alphorn solo [10'] EMB
rent                                  (F14)

Divertimento
2(pic).2.2.2. 2.2.0.0. timp,perc,
strings [15'] EMB rent                (F15)

Fagyongy
see Mistletoe

Kárpáti Rapszódia
see Rhapsodia Carpathiana

Két Magyar Tánc
see Two Hungarian Dances

Klasszikus Variációk
see Variazioni Classiche

Magic Wardrobe, The: Concert Overture
"Buvos Szekrény, A" 2.2.2.2.
4.3.3.1. timp,perc,harp,cel,opt
vibra,strings [6'] EMB rent  (F16)

Mistletoe
"Fagyongy" 2(pic).1+English
horn.2(bass clar).1. 2.1.0.0.
harp,cel,strings,solo voice [6']
(cycle of songs to poems by
Lörinc Szabó) EMB rent               (F17)

Musica Pentatonica
"Toccata, Aria E Fuga" strings
[10'] EMB rent                        (F18)

Naptár
see Calendar

Pastorali
0.1.2.1. 2.1.1.0. strings,female
solo [8'] EMB rent                    (F19)

Rhapsodia Carpathiana
"Kárpáti Rapszódia" 1.1(English
horn).2.1. 2.2.1.0. timp,perc,
harp,strings [10'] EMB rent (F20)

Scherzo Sinfonico
2.2.2.2. 2.2.0.0. timp,perc,harp,
strings [9'] EMB rent                 (F21)

Table Music
"Asztalizene" 1.1.2.1. 2.1.1.0.
strings [9'] EMB rent                 (F22)

Toccata, Aria E Fuga
see Musica Pentatonica

Two Hungarian Dances
"Két Magyar Tánc" 2.1.2.1. 2.2.1.0.
timp,harp,strings [8'] EMB rent
                                      (F23)
Variazioni Classiche (from Melodie Di
Carillon) 19th cent.
"Klasszikus Variációk"
2(pic).2.2.2. 4.3.3.0. timp,perc,
cel&opt pno,strings [18'] EMB
rent                                  (F24)

**FARRENC, LOUISE (1804-1875)**
Overture for Orchestra
(Pickett, Susan) HILDEGARD 09757
rent                                  (F25)

**FASCH, JOHANN FRIEDRICH (1688-1758)**
Concerto for Flute, Oboe and String
Orchestra in E minor
(Braun) fl,ob,string orch
KUNZELMANN ipa sc 10091A, oct
10091                                 (F26)

Concerto for Flute, Oboe, Strings and
Continuo in E minor
vln I,vln II,vla,vcl,db,fl&ob soli
MÖSELER sc 40.159-00, pts
40.159-01, set 40.159-09   (F27)

Concerto for Oboe and String
Orchestra in A minor
(Braun) ob solo,string orch
KUNZELMANN ipa sc 10092A, oct
10092                                 (F28)

Concerto for Oboe, Strings and
Continuo in D minor
vln I,vln II,vla,vcl,db,ob solo
MÖSELER sc 40.157-00, pts
40.157-01, set 40.157-09   (F29)

**FASCH, JOHANN FRIEDRICH (cont'd.)**

Concerto for Violin, 2 Flutes, 2
Oboes, Bassoon, Strings and
Continuo in D
2.2.0.1. 0.0.0.0. vln I,vln II,vla
I,vla II,vcl,db,vln solo MÖSELER
sc 40.158-00, solo pt 40.158-01,
pts 40.158-02 TO 03, set
40.158-09                             (F30)

Concerto for Violin, Strings and
Continuo in A
vln I,vln II,vla,vcl,db,vln solo
MÖSELER sc 40.160-00, pts
40.160-01, set 40.160-09   (F31)

Concerto in G
(Scheck, Helmut) strings,cont,ob/
vln solo BÖHM                         (F32)

Suite for Orchestra in B flat
(Riemann, H.) 0.2.0.1. 0.0.0.0.
strings,cont [41'] BREITKOPF-W
                                      (F33)

FASCHINGSBILDER see Nicode, Jean Louis

FASCINACE see Klug, J.

FAST ERSTARRTE UNRUHE...2 see Goldmann,
Friedrich

FAST ERSTARRTE UNRUHE...3 see Goldmann,
Friedrich

FAST WALK see Dorff, Daniel Jay

FATHÔME OP. 4 see Alexander Friedrich
Von Hessen

FAULE KROKODILE (BLUES) see Thomas-
Mifune, Werner

**FAURE, GABRIEL-URBAIN (1845-1924)**
Après Un Rêve
(Busser, H.) 1.1.1.1. 1.0.0.0.
strings,high solo/med solo [3']
LEDUC                                 (F34)

Au Bord De L'Eau
(Mignan, É) 1.1.2.1. 2.0.0.0. harp,
strings,high solo [3'] LEDUC
                                      (F35)
Au Cimetière
(Busser, H.) 1.1.1.1. 1.1.0.0.
timp,strings,high solo/med solo
[4'15"] LEDUC                         (F36)

Automne
(Busser, H.) 1.1.1.1. 1.0.0.0.
strings,high solo/med solo
[2'30"] LEDUC                         (F37)

Berceaux, Les
(Brunel, O.) 2.2+English horn.2.2.
4.0.3.0. timp,harp,strings,high
solo/med solo [3'] LEDUC             (F38)

Chanson Du Pêcheur
2.1.0.1. 0.0.0.0. harp,strings,high
solo/med solo [3'15"] LEDUC (F39)

Clair De Lune
2.0.1.1. 1.0.0.0. harp,strings,high
solo/med solo [3'] LEDUC             (F40)

Dans Les Ruines D'Une Abbaye
1.1.2.1. 2.0.0.0. harp,strings,high
solo, (horns in g) [2'30"] LEDUC
                                      (F41)
En Prière
2.1.2.1. 4.0.0.0. harp,strings,high
solo/med solo [2'15"] LEDUC (F42)

Fée Aux Chansons, La
1.1.1.1. 1.0.0.0. harp,strings,high
solo [1'30"] LEDUC                    (F43)

Fleur Jetée
(Busser, H.) 2.2.2.2. 2.2.0.0.
timp,strings,high solo [1'30"]
LEDUC                                 (F44)

Mandoline
(Schmitt, Fl.) 1.1.2.2. 2.0.0.0.
harp,strings,high solo/med solo
[1'45"] LEDUC                         (F45)

Mélisande's Song
(Koechlin, Ch.) [Eng] 2.0+English
horn+ob d'amore.2.1. 2.0.0.0.
strings,high solo/med solo [3']
LEDUC                                 (F46)

Nell
(Rasse, F.) 1.1.1.1. 1.0.0.0.
strings,high solo/med solo [2']
LEDUC                                 (F47)

Nocturne (from Shylock)
(Badenes, G.) strings [2'40"] LEDUC
                                      (F48)
Notre Amour
(Busser, H.) 1.1.1.1. 1.0.0.0.
harp,strings,high solo [2'] LEDUC
                                      (F49)

**FAURE, GABRIEL-URBAIN (cont'd.)**

O Salutaris
2horn,harp,strings,high solo [3']
LEDUC                                 (F50)

Papillon Et La Fleur, Le
(Rosenthal, M.) 1.1.1.1. 1.0.0.0.
harp,strings,high solo [2'] LEDUC
                                      (F51)
Parfum Impérissable, Le
(Busser, H.) 1.1.1.1. 1.0.0.0.
harp,strings,high solo&med solo
[2'15"] LEDUC                         (F52)

Plus Doux Chemin, Le
(Samuel, M.; Rousseau) 1.1.2.1.
1.0.0.0. harp,strings,high solo
[1'20"] LEDUC                         (F53)

Prison
(Schmith, Fl.) 1.1.2.2. 2.0.0.0.
timp,perc,harp,strings,med solo
[2'] LEDUC                            (F54)

Rançon, La
(Doin, G.) pno,strings,med solo
[2'15"] LEDUC                         (F55)

Romance for Violoncello, Op. 69
(Busser, H.) 2.1.2.1. 2.0.0.0.
harp,strings [4'] LEDUC     (F56)

Roses D'Ispahan, Les
2.1.2.2. 2.0.0.0. harp,strings,high
solo&med solo [3'] LEDUC   (F57)

Secret, Le
(Rasse, F.) 1.1.1.1. 0.0.0.0. harp,
strings,high solo/med solo [2']
LEDUC                                 (F58)

Soir
(Aubert, L.) 2.1.2.2. 2.0.0.0.
harp,strings,high solo/med solo
[3'30"] LEDUC                         (F59)

Voyageur, Le
(Mignan, É) 2.2.2.2. 4.2.3.0. timp,
strings,med solo [2'] LEDUC (F60)

FAUST: BALLETMUSIK see Gounod, Charles
François

FAUST-QUADRILLE, OP. 112 see Strauss,
Josef

FAUST-SYMPHONIE, EINE see Liszt, Franz

FAUST-SZENEN: OVERTURE see Schumann,
Robert (Alexander)

FAUX PAS DE QUATRE see Hurník, Ilja

FAVORITE, THE see Joplin, Scott

FEAST see Rebne, Rune

**FEBEL, REINHARD (1952- )**
Charivari
1.1.1.1. 1.1.1.0. 2perc,harp,cel,
strings [15'] MOECK sc 5233 f.s.,
pts rent                              (F61)

Etude D'exöcution Transcendante
2.0.2.0. 1.1.1.0. perc,pno,strings
[13'] MOECK sc 5234 f.s., pts
rent                                  (F62)

**FEDELI, DENISE**
Miraggi
2.2.2.2. 2.0.2.0. 2perc,cel,pno,
harp,strings [9'] sc MULL & SCH
M&S 1166 rent                         (F63)

FÉE AUX CHANSONS, LA see Faure,
Gabriel-Urbain

FÉERIE LAOTIENNE: SUITE see Tomasi,
Henri

FEIERMUSIK II see Herrmann, Hugo,
Concerto Grosso

**FEILER, DROR (1951- )**
Conatus
1(pic).1.2(bass clar).1(contrabsn).
1.1.1.0. 2perc,2harp,strings
[30'] sc,pts STIM                     (F64)

Ember
3(pic).3(English horn).3(bass
clar).0. 4.3.3.1. timp,2perc,
strings, amplification STIM (F65)

Knutna Nven, Den
electronic tape,electronic
equipment, 10 instrumentalists,
computer STIM                         (F66)

Music For Dead Europeans
1(pic).1.1(bass
clar).1(contrabsn).sax. 1.1.1.0.
2perc,strings,pno/harmonium,
electronic tape [30'] sc,pts STIM
                                      (F67)

FEILER, DROR (cont'd.)

Sham Mayim
1.1.2(bass clar).1. 1.1.1.0. 2perc,
vln,vla,vcl,2pno [15'] sc,pts
STIM                          (F68)

Sparagmos
1(pic).1.1(bass clar).1(contrabsn).
1.1.1.0. 2perc,strings,electronic
equipment,vln solo STIM        (F69)

FEINSLIEBCHEN, KOMM ANS FENSTER see
Mozart, Wolfgang Amadeus, Deh Vieni
Alla Finestra

FELCIANO, RICHARD (1930-    )
Orchestra
3.3.3.3. 4.3.3.1. timp,4perc,harp,
2kbd,strings [20'] SCHIRM.EC rent
                              (F70)

FELD, JINDRICH (1925-    )
Concerto for Harp and Orchestra
INTERNAT.S. sc,pts rent, solo pt
                              (F71)
2.2.2.2. 2.2.0.0. perc,strings,harp
solo [25'] CESKY HUD.          (F72)

Serenade for String Orchestra
string orch [11'] CESKY HUD.  (F73)

FELDER, DAVID (1953-    )
Inner Sky
1(pic).0.0.0. 0.0.0.0. 2perc,kbd,
strings, computer MERION rent
                              (F74)

Pressure Triggering Dreams, A
3(pic,alto fl,bass fl).3(English
horn).3(clar in E flat,bass clar,
contrabass clar).3(contrabsn).
4.3(piccolo trp,trp in D).3(bass
trom).1. timp,3perc,electronic
equipment,elec bass,harp,kbd,
strings [19'] MERION rent    (F75)

Three Pieces For Orchestra
3(pic,alto fl).3(English
horn).3(clar in E flat,bass clar,
contrabass clar).3(contrabsn).
4.3(piccolo trp,trp in D).3(bass
trom).1. timp,3perc,kbd,harp,elec
bass,strings [19'30"] MERION rent
                              (F76)

FELDMAN, BARBARA MONK
Design For String Orchestra
string orch sc CANADIAN
MI 1500 F312DE                (F77)
string orch [12'] COLLERAN   (F78)

Northern Shore, The
chamber orch/orch,pno solo,perc
solo [30'] COLLERAN          (F79)

FELDMAN, MORTON (1926-1987)
Rabbi Akiba
fl,English horn,horn,trp,trom,tuba,
perc,pno/cel,vcl,db,S solo perf
sc PETERS P6957              (F80)

FELIX, VÁCLAV (1928-    )
Concerto for Trumpet and Orchestra,
Op. 63
2.2.2.2. 2.0.2.0. timp,perc,
strings,trp solo [22'] CESKY HUD.
                              (F81)
Concerto for Violoncello, Piano and
Orchestra, Op. 50
perc,strings,vcl/bass clar solo,pno
solo [22'] CESKY HUD.         (F82)

Na Devátého Máje
3.2.3.2. 4.3.3.1. timp,perc,harp,
strings,Bar solo [7'] CESKY HUD.
                              (F83)

Romance Letního Dne  *Op.54
2.2.2.2. 4.2.3.1. timp,perc,harp,
strings,clar solo [10'] CESKY
HUD.                          (F84)

Slavnostni
see Symphony No. 4, Op. 70

Symphony No. 2, Op. 59
2.2.2.2. 2.2.2.0. timp,perc,strings
[23'] CESKY HUD.              (F85)

Symphony No. 4, Op. 70
"Slavnostni" 3.3.3.3. 4.3.3.1.
timp,perc,strings [15'] CESKY
HUD.                          (F86)

Symphony No. 5 for Chamber Orchestra,
Op. 71
2.2.2.2. 2.2.0.0. perc,strings
[22'] CESKY HUD.              (F87)

FEM ORKESTERSTYCKEN see Uppström, Tore

FEMININUM see Odstrcil, Karel

FENIX see Karkoff, Ingvar

FERIENREISE, ESPAÑA
(Thomas-Mifune, W.) string orch sc,
pts KUNZELMANN GM 1714A ipa  (F88)

---

FERN VOM MEER NOCH FÜHL ICH'S see
Mozart, Wolfgang Amadeus, Fuor Del
Mar Ho Un Mar In Seno

FERNE -LANDSCHAFT I see Hosokawa,
Toshio

FERNE -LANDSCHAFT II see Hosokawa,
Toshio

FERNEYHOUGH, BRIAN (1943-    )
Carceri d'Invenzione II
0.2(English horn).2(clar in E flat,
bass clar).1. 2.0.0.0. 8vln,2vla,
2vcl,db,fl solo [14'] PETERS
study sc P-7292 f.s., set rent
                              (F89)
Carceri D'Invenzione IIa
0.2.2.1. 2.0.0.0. strings,fl solo
[14'] sc PETERS EP 7292A      (F90)

FERNOLD, JOHAN (1969-    )
Hö
orch STIM                     (F91)

FERNSTRÖM, JOHN (1897-1961)
Suite No. 2 (from Music To The Ballet
"Nisi-Pleng" Op. 87b)
2(pic).2(English horn).2(bass
clar).2. 2.2.1.1. timp,perc,harp,
strings,pno,cel,xylo STIM    (F92)

FERNUNG - HORIZONT - NAEHE see Pröve,
Bernfried

...FERO DOLORE see Corghi, Azio

FERRABOSCO, ALFONSO (I) (1543-1588)
Four Note Pavan
(Grainger, Percy Aldridge) strings
BARDIC                        (F93)

FERRO CANTO see Heyn, Volker

FEST see Blomberg, Erik

FEST DES NACHBARDORFES: OVERTURE see
Boieldieu, François-Adrien, Fête Du
Village Voisin, La: Overture

FEST-OUVERTURE see Tamas, Janos

FEST-OUVERTURE OP. 25 see Hegar,
Friedrich

FESTAL OVERTURE see Ridout, Godfrey

FESTE AMOROSE, LE see Filas, Juraj,
Symphony No. 1

FESTE BURG, EIN: CHORALPARTITA see
Braütigam, Volker

FESTE ROMANE see Respighi, Ottorino

FESTIVAL CONCERTINO see Gibbs, Alan

FESTIVAL FANTASY see Nakajima, Katsuma

FESTIVAL MUSIC, (1994 VERSION), OP. 46B
see Plagge, Wolfgang

FESTIVAL OVERTURE see Allen, Peter see
Rice, Thomas N.

FESTIVAL TRIPTYCH FOR NARRATOR AND
ORCHESTRA see Ward, Robert Eugene

FESTIVE OVERTURE see Fiala, George see
Okabe, Fujio see Still, William
Grant

FESTIVE POEM "THIRTY YEARS" see
Prokofiev, Serge

FESTIVO see Patterson, Paul

FESTIVO (BOLERO) see Sibelius, Jean

FESTLICHE MUSIK see Dehnert, Max see
Finke, Fidelio Friedrich (Fritz)
see Zipp, Friedrich

FESTLICHES POEM FÜR ORCHESTER see
Prokofiev, Serge

FESTLIG DANS, EN see Larsson, Folke

FESTMARSCH see Necksten, Gärt

FESTMUSIK FÜR STREICHER see Kazandjiev,
Vassil

FESTOUVERTÜRE FÜR GROSSES ORCHESTER see
Thilman, Johannes Paul

FESTUVERTYR GRÄNNA-BRAHE see Johansson,
Sven Eric

FÊTE CHEZ THÉRÈSE, LA: SUITE NO. 2 see
Hahn, Reynaldo

FÊTE DU VILLAGE VOISIN, LA: OVERTURE
see Boieldieu, François-Adrien

---

FÉTIS, FRANÇOIS-JOSEPH (1784-1871)
Concerto for Flute and Orchestra in B
minor
fl solo,orch KUNZELMANN 10155 ipr
                              (F94)

FETLER, PAUL (1920-    )
Celebration
3(pic).3(English horn).3(bass
clar).3(contrabsn). 4.3.3.1.
timp,perc,cel,strings [24'] study
sc SCHOTTS EA 429 perf mat rent
                              (F95)

FEU D'ARTIFICE see Stravinsky, Igor

FEUERSCHUH UND WINDSANDALE see
Fujiwara, Yutaka

FEUERWEHR-MAMBO see Thomas-Mifune,
Werner

FEVRIER, HENRI (1875-1957)
Agnès, Dame Galante  *Suite
1.1.2.1. 0.0.0.0. timp,bells,harp,
strings [17'] (ancient style
dance) LEDUC                 (F96)

Aphrodite: Suite 1
1.1.2.1. 0.1.1.0. perc,pno,strings
[11'] (4 numbers) LEDUC      (F97)

Aphrodite: Suite 2
1.1.2.1. 0.1.1.0. perc,pno,strings
[9'] (3 numbers) LEDUC       (F98)

Gismonda (Interlude for String
Orchestra)
string orch [1'50"] LEDUC    (F99)

Interlude for String Orchestra
see Gismonda

FIALA, GEORGE (1922-    )
Concertino for Piano, Trumpet,
Timpani and String Orchestra, Op.
2
[14'] sc CANADIAN MI 1750 F438CO
                             (F100)
Epitaphe De La 2e Symphonie
2.3.3.2. 4.2.3.1. timp,perc,cel,
harp,strings sc CANADIAN
MI 1100 F438EP               (F101)

Festive Overture
3+pic.2.2.2. 4.2.2.1. timp,2perc,
harp,strings [14'] sc CANADIAN
MI 1100 F438FE               (F102)

Kurelek Suite, The
3+pic.2(English horn).2.2.alto sax.
4.3.2.1. timp,3perc,harp,pno&cel,
strings [20'] (1. The Maze 2.
Arctic Madonna 3. Ukrainian
Christmas 4. Fields 5. I Spit On
Life.) sc CANADIAN MI 1100 F438KU
                             (F103)

Overtura Buffa  *Overture
3+pic.2.2.2. 4.2.2.1. timp,2perc,
strings sc CANADIAN
MI 1100 F438OV               (F104)

Sinfonico
3+pic.3+English horn.3+bass clar.3+
contrabsn. 4.2.3.1. timp,perc,
harp,pno,strings [15'] sc
CANADIAN MI 1100 F438SI      (F105)

FIALA, JAROMÍR (1892-    )
Concerto for Bassoon and Orchestra in
C
bsn solo,orch KUNZELMANN ipa sc
10277A, oct 10277            (F106)

FIALA, JIRÍ JULIUS (1892-1974)
O Praze
3.3.3.3. 4.3.3.1. timp,perc,harp,
cel,org,strings [9'] CESKY HUD.
                             (F107)
Tri Melodramy
2.2.2.2. 4.2.3.0. timp,perc,harp,
strings,speaking voice CESKY HUD.
                             (F108)
Vcera-Dnes-Zítra
3.3.3.3. 4.3.3.1. timp,perc,harp,
cel,strings [20'] CESKY HUD.
                             (F109)

FIALA, JOSEPH (1748-1816)
Concerto for 2 Horns and String
Orchestra in E flat
(Koukal, Bohumír) strings,2horn
[13'] CESKY HUD.             (F110)

Concerto for Oboe and Orchestra in B
flat
2.0.0.0. 2.0.0.0. strings,ob solo
CESKY HUD.                   (F111)

Concerto for Violoncello and
Orchestra in G
(Koukal, Bohumír) 2.0.0.0. 2.0.0.0.
strings,vcl solo [14'] CESKY HUD.
                             (F112)

FIALA, PETR (1943-    )
Concerto for Accordion and Orchestra
1.0.0.0. 2.2.2.1. timp,perc,vibra,
strings,acord solo [20'] CESKY
HUD.                         (F113)

FIALA, PETR (cont'd.)

Concerto for Trumpet and String
Orchestra
strings,snare drum,trp solo [16']
CESKY HUD.                        (F114)

Concerto for Wind Quintet and Chamber
Orchestra
1.1.1.1. 1.1.1.0. strings,wind quin
soli [17'] CESKY HUD.           (F115)

Ctyri Symfonické Obrazy
2.3.3.2. 4.3.3.1. perc,strings
[20'] CESKY HUD.                 (F116)

Hudba Pro Trombón A Smyccovy Orchestr
(Music for Trombone and String
Orchestra)
perc,strings,trom solo [15'] CESKY
HUD.                             (F117)

Music for Trombone and String
Orchestra
see Hudba Pro Trombón A Smyccovy
Orchestr

Musica Da Concerto
string orch,vla solo [10'] CESKY
HUD.                             (F118)

Poselství
see Symphony No. 3

Suite for String Orchestra
string orch [12'] CESKY HUD. (F119)

Symphony No. 3
"Poselství" 2.2.2.2. 4.5.3.1. perc,
pno,strings,Bar solo [22'] CESKY
HUD.                             (F120)

FIBER OF THE BREATH see Saruya, Toshiro

FICCIONES see Lavista, Mario

FICHER, JACOBO (1896-    )
Overture Don Segundo
2+pic.2+English horn.2+bass clar.2.
4.3.3.1. timp,perc,strings PEER
rent                             (F121)

FIDDLER OF THE REELS, THE see Harper,
Edward James

FIDDLERS, THE see Murto, Matti,
Soittoniekat

FIDELIO: DUET OF LEONORE AND FLORESTAN
see Beethoven, Ludwig van, O
Namenlose Freude

FIDELIO: DUET OF MARZELLINE AND JAQUINO
see Beethoven, Ludwig van, Jetzt,
Schätzchen, Jetzt Sind Wir Allein

FIDELIO: PIZARRO'S ARIA see Beethoven,
Ludwig van, Ha, Welch Ein
Augenblick

FIDLOVACKA see Skroup, František

FIELD, JOHN (1782-1837)
Concerto for Piano and Orchestra, No.
2, in A flat
1.0.2.2. 2.2.0.0. timp,strings,pno
solo [34'] (no score) BREITKOPF-W
(F122)
Concerto for Piano and Orchestra, No.
3, in E flat
2.2.2.2. 2.2.0.0. timp,strings,pno
solo [32'] (no score) BREITKOPF-W
(F123)
Concerto for Piano and Orchestra, No.
4, in E flat
1.0.2.2. 2.2.0.0. timp,strings,pno
solo [28'] (no score) BREITKOPF-W
(F124)
Concerto for Piano and Orchestra, No.
5, in C
1.0.2.2. 2.2.1.0. timp,strings,pno
solo [28'] (no score) BREITKOPF-W
(F125)
Concerto for Piano and Orchestra, No.
6, in C
1.2.2.2. 2.2.1.0. timp,strings,pno
solo [35'] (no score) BREITKOPF-W
(F126)
Concerto for Piano and Orchestra, No.
7, in C minor
2.2.2.2. 2.2.1.0. timp,strings,pno
solo [30'] (no score) BREITKOPF-W
(F127)

FIERA, LA see Bernabei, Giuseppe
Antonio

FIESTA see Korbar, Leopold

FIFTEEN MINUTE AUSTRALIA see Cowie,
Edward

FIFTH SEASON, THE see Kyr, Robert,
Symphony No. 3

FIFTY-SIX BLOWS see Singleton, Alvin
see Singleton, Alvin, Blows, 56

FIGARO IN AFRIKA see Thomas-Mifune,
Werner

FIGURE IN A LANDSCAPE see Kucharzyk,
Henry

FILAR IL TUONO see Lake, Larry

FILAS, JURAJ (1955-    )
Feste Amorose, Le
see Symphony No. 1

Freska
0.0.0.0. 4.4.3.1. timp,perc,vibra,
pno,strings [17'] CESKY HUD.
(F128)

Overtura Popolosa
2.2.2.2. 2.2.0.0. timp,strings
[13'] CESKY HUD.                 (F129)

Palpito
3.3.3.3. 4.4.4.1. timp,perc,xylo,
vibra,cel,pno,strings [14'] CESKY
HUD.                             (F130)

Symfonie Komorní, 1.
2.0.0.0. 0.0.0.0. pno,strings [14']
CESKY HUD.                       (F131)

Symfonie Komorní, 2.
2.2.2.2. 2.2.0.0. timp,strings
[21'] CESKY HUD.                 (F132)

Symphonia "Vampa"
"Vyhna" 4.3.3.3. 4.6.4.1. timp,
perc,vibra,cel,2harp,strings
[30'] CESKY HUD.                 (F133)

Symphony No. 1
"Feste Amorose, Le" 3.2.4.3.
4.6.4.1. timp,perc,vibra,cel,
harp,strings [25'] CESKY HUD.
(F134)

Vyhna
see Symphonia "Vampa"

FILHARMONICKÉ VARIACE see Flosman,
Oldrich

FILM-OUVERTÜRE, EINE see Schröder, Kurt

FILMMUSIK see Nordgren, Erik

FILS, [JOHANN] ANTON (1733-1760)
Sinfonia in D
string orch CESKY HUD.        (F135)

FILTZ, ANTON (ANTONÍN)
see FILS, [JOHANN] ANTON

FIN DU SIÈCLE see Butler, Martin

FINALE see Flosman, Oldrich see
Hvoslef, Ketil

FINALE FESTOSO see Lukas, Zdenek

FINALE MIT KAMMERENSEMBLE see Kagel,
Mauricio

FINALE WITH ORCHESTRA see Kagel,
Mauricio, Finale Mit Kammerensemble

FINCH' HAN DAL VINO see Mozart,
Wolfgang Amadeus

FINDING OF LOVE, THE see Mather, Bruce

FINITE INFINITY see Reimann, Aribert

FINKE, FIDELIO FRIEDRICH (FRITZ)
(1891-1968)
Acht Bagatellen
2.2.2.2. 2.2.3.0. timp,perc,strings
[15'] BREITKOPF-W              (F136)

Capriccio Über Ein Polnisches
Volkslied
2.2.2.3. 4.3.3.1. timp,perc,
strings,pno solo [15'] BREITKOPF-
W                                (F137)

Eros   *cant
3.3.3.3. 4.3.3.0. timp,perc,harp,
strings,ST soli [40'] BREITKOPF-W
(F138)

Festliche Musik
2.1.1.2. 1.2.2.0. timp,perc,strings
[8'] BREITKOPF-W               (F139)

Pan
4.3.3.4. 6.3.3.1. timp,perc,harp,
cel,strings [24'] BREITKOPF-W
(F140)

Suite No. 2
2.2.2.3. 4.3.3.1. timp,perc,harp,
strings [25'] BREITKOPF-W (F141)

Suite No. 3
3.3.3.3. 4.3.3.1. timp,perc,harp,
strings [28'] BREITKOPF-W (F142)

FINKE, FIDELIO FRIEDRICH (FRITZ)
(cont'd.)

Suite No. 7
3.2.3.3. 4.3.3.1. timp,perc,strings
[17'] BREITKOPF-W              (F143)

FINNISCHE FANTASIE see Glazunov,
Alexander Konstantinovich

FINNISCHE VOLKSLIEDER see Godzinsky,
George De

FINNISSY, MICHAEL (1946-    )
Glad Day
2fl/2rec,2trp,harp,org,strings
[13'] perf sc set OXFORD sc,pts
rent                             (F144)

Plain Harmony
orch [12'] perf sc set OXFORD
3632101 sc,pts rent           (F145)

Speak Its Name!
2.2.2.2. 2.2.1.0. timp,2vibra,harp,
strings, quarter-tone keyboard
[24'] perf sc set OXFORD 3564599
sc,pts rent                      (F146)

FINZI, GERALD (1901-1956)
Five Bagatelles  *Op.23a
(Ashmore, Lawrence) clar,strings
[14'] BOOSEY-ENG rent         (F147)

FIORILLO, FEDERIGO (1755-1823)
Concerto for Violin and Orchestra,
No. 1, in F
(Mezö) vln solo,orch KUNZELMANN ipa
sc 10277A, oct 10277            (F148)

Sinfonia Concertante for 2 Oboes and
Orchestra in F
2ob,orch KUNZELMANN 10124 ipr
(F149)

FIRE AND EARTH see Bolcom, William
Elden, Concerto No. 2 for Piano
Left-Hand and Chamber Orchestra

FIRE MUSIC see Hagen, Daron

FIRE ON THE EARTH see Franke-Blom, Lars
Åke, Symphony No. 3

FIREBIRD see Stravinsky, Igor

FIREBIRD-BALLET 1910 see Stravinsky,
Igor

FIREWORKS see Plain, Gerald

FIRSOVA, ELENA (1950-    )
Cassandra  *Op.60
1+pic.2.2(clar in E flat,bass
clar).2+contrabsn. 4.3.3.1. perc,
cel,harp,strings [12'] BOOSEY-ENG
rent                             (F150)

FIRST BLUE HOURS see Koehne, Graeme

FIRST DUENNESE ELEGY see Reimann,
Aribert, Denn Bleiben Ist Nirgends

FIRST LIGHT see Danielpour, Richard

FIRST-PIECES see Sandred, Örjan

FIRST VIOLIN CONCERTO AND SCOTTISH
FANTASY IN FULL SCORE see Bruch,
Max

FISCHER, EDUARD (1930-    )
Music for Percussion and Orchestra
3.2.2.3. 4.3.3.1. pno,strings,perc
solo [35'] CESKY HUD.         (F151)

Partita in A
2.2.2.3. 2.2.2.0. timp,perc,pno,
strings [19'] CESKY HUD.      (F152)

Prolog
3.2.2.3. 4.2.3.1. timp,perc,strings
[19'] CESKY HUD.              (F153)

Teo Toriate  *Variations
string orch,vcl solo [19'] CESKY
HUD.                             (F154)

Tiché Písne
pno,3vln I,3vln II,2vla,2vcl,S
solo [18'] CESKY HUD.         (F155)

Variacní Fantazie Na Téma G. Ph.
Telemanna
string orch [12'] CESKY HUD. (F156)

FISCHER, JAN F. (1921-    )
Concertino Semplice
1.0.2.0. 0.0.0.0. gtr,strings,pno
solo [10'] CESKY HUD.         (F157)

Concerto for Orchestra in E flat
3.3.4.3. 4.3.3.1. timp,perc,harp,
pno,strings [19'] CESKY HUD.
(F158)

FISCHER, JAN F. (cont'd.)

O Radosti
see Obrazy III

Obrazy III
"O Radosti" 3.3.3.3. 4.4.3.1. timp,
perc,vibra,cel,harp,pno,strings
[15'] CESKY HUD.          (F159)

Partita in C
string orch [13'] PANTON     (F160)

Valcík Pro Orchestr
3.3.3.3. 4.3.3.1. timp,perc,harp,
pno,strings [10'] CESKY HUD.
(F161)

FISCHER, JOHANN CHRISTIAN (1733-1800)
Concerto in G for Trumpet and
Orchestra
(Guyot, D.) 1.1.0.2. 2.0.0.0.
strings,trp solo [18'] BILLAUDOT
(F162)

FISHER'S BOARDING HOUSE see Grainger,
Percy Aldridge

FISICA see Hidalgo, Manuel

FITZENHAGEN, WILHELM (1848-1890)
Concerto No. 1 for Violoncello and
Orchestra, Op. 2, in B minor
2.2.2.2. 2.2.3.0. timp,strings,vcl
solo [14'] (no score) BREITKOPF-W
(F163)
Concerto No. 2 for Violoncello and
Orchestra, Op. 4, in A minor
2.2.2.2. 2.2.1.0. timp,strings,vcl
solo [14'] BREITKOPF-W    (F164)

Resignation (Geistliches Lied Ohne
Worte) *Op.8
1.1.2.2. 2.0.0.0. vcl,db,vcl solo
[4'] BREITKOPF-W         (F165)

FIVE BAGATELLES see Finzi, Gerald &
Walton, [Sir] William (Turner)

FIVE: CONCERTO FOR AMPLIFIED CELLO AND
ORCHESTRA see Wuorinen, Charles

FIVE CONTRASTS see Zador, Eugene (Jenö)

FIVE EASY PIECES see Karkoff, Ingvar

FIVE ÉTUDES FOR ORCHESTRA see Baudin,
Ernestine Von

FIVE FIRES see Levinson, Gerald

FIVE FOLK SONGS FOR STRINGS see Raitio,
Väinö, Viisi Hämäläistä
Kansanlaulua Jousiork

FIVE HAIKU see Thomas, Augusta Read

FIVE LITTLE PIECES see Delius,
Frederick

FIVE MINIATURES FOR BASS TROMBONE, HARP
AND STRINGS see McCauley, William
A.

FIVE ORCHESTRAL PIECES & PELLEAS UND
MELISANDE see Schoenberg, Arnold

FIVE PASTELS FOR SOPRANO AND ENSEMBLE
see Douglas, Clive

FIVE PIECES IN THE FORM OF A SUITE FOR
HARMONICA AND STRING ORCHESTRA see
Jacob, Gordon

FIVE-PLUS see Pentland, Barbara

FIVE SHADES OF BRASS see Surdin, Morris

FIVE SKETCHES see Pfister

FIVE SONGS FOR HIGH VOICE & STRING
ORCHESTRA see Betts, Lorne M.

FIVE SUMMER SONGS see Phillips, Barre

FIVE TIMES FIVE. 4 VARIATIONS ON A
FIVE-PART THEME see Ward, Robert
Eugene

FIXED DESIRE OF THE HUMAN HEART, THE
see Adler, Samuel Hans

FLAMBOYS see Barry, Gerald

FLAME AND SHADOW see Nishimura, Akira

FLAMINGO see Daugherty, Michael

FLAMMER, ERNST-HELMUTH (1949-    )
Ausschnitte '80...
1.0.2.0. 1.0.1.0. 2harp,2vln,vla,
vcl,db,cembalo solo [14'] sc
PETERS 02410            (F166)

FLARES see Müller, Thomas

FLEDERMAUS, DIE: OVERTURE see Strauss,
Johann, [Jr.]

FLENDER, REINHARD DAVID (1953-    )
Concerto for Piano and Orchestra
2.1.3.1.alto sax. 1.1.2.1. timp,
2perc,harp,strings,pno solo
[17'25"] PEER rent       (F167)

Threnos II
2.1.1.2.alto sax. 1.0.0.0. timp,
perc,cel,4vcl,3db,2pno&vln soli
[15'] PEER rent          (F168)

FLEUR JETÉE see Faure, Gabriel-Urbain

FLICKAN KOM IFRÅN SIN ÄLSKLINGS MÖTE
see Sibelius, Jean

FLIEGE SUMM-SUMM, DIE see Tishchenko,
Boris, Mucha-Zokotucha

FLIEGENDE HOLLÄNDER, DER: MIT GEWITTER
UND STURM see Wagner, Richard

FLIGHT OF ICARUS, THE see Pickard, John

FLIRT AUX FLEURS see Dijk, Jan van

FLJD: FYRA ORKESTERSKISSER see
Sandberg, Lars

FLODIN, ANDERS (1961-    )
Konsert Över Fragment Till En Piano-
Konsert I H-Moll Av E Grieg
3(pic).2.2.2. 4.3.3.0. timp,2perc,
strings,pno/synthesizer solo STIM
(F169)
Sinfonia (Symphony)
2.2.2.2. 4.2.3.1. timp,2perc,harp,
strings [28'] sc STIM    (F170)

Symphony
see Sinfonia

FLOH-WALZER (SAMBA) see Thomas-Mifune,
Werner

FLORENTZ, JEAN-LOUIS (1947)
Jardins D'Amènta, Les *Op.13
4.3.3.3. 4.4.3.0. timp,4perc,cel,
2harp,16vln I,14vln II,12vla,
12vcl,10db [32'] (symphonic tale)
LEDUC                   (F171)

Second Chant De Nyandarua *Op.11
12vcl/8vcl [16'] sc LEDUC AL 29025
(F172)

Songe De Lluc Alcari, Le
1(pic,alto fl)+pic.2+English
horn.2+bass clar.2+contrabsn.
4.4.3.0. timp,3perc,cel,2harp,
16vln I,14vln II,12vla,12vcl,8db,
vcl solo [35'] pno red LEDUC
AL 28920                (F173)

Ténéré-Incantation Sur Un Verset
Coranique
2.2.2.2. 2.0.0.0. strings [20']
LEDUC                   (F174)

Ti-Nde
2(2pic,alto fl).1+English horn.2.1.
0.0.0.0. xylo,marimba,vibra,
temple blocks,3vln,2vcl,db,vla
solo [10'] LEDUC        (F175)

FLORES FOR PIANO AND STRING ORCHESTRA
see Hedstrom, Åse

FLORI SUITE see Panufnik, Roxanna

FLORIDA BLUES see Phillips, William

FLOSMAN, OLDRICH (1925-    )
Cesta *Overture
3.3.3.2. 4.3.3.1. timp,perc,xylo,
pno,strings [13'] CESKY HUD.
(F176)
Concerto for Bass Clarinet, Piano and
Orchestra
2.2.2.2. 2.2.0.0. timp,strings,bass
clar&pno soli [23'] CESKY HUD.
(F177)
Filharmonické Variace
3.3.3.3. 4.3.3.1. timp,perc,xylo,
cel,strings [10'] CESKY HUD.
(F178)
Finale
3.2.2.2. 4.3.3.1. timp,perc,strings
[6'] CESKY HUD.          (F179)
Fraternità
timp,strings,2trp soli [8'] CESKY
HUD.                    (F180)
Ohne V Horách *Overture
3.3.3.3. 4.3.3.1. timp,perc,strings
[10'] CESKY HUD.         (F181)
Plzensky Mateník
3.2.3.2. 4.2.3.1. timp,perc,strings
[4'] CESKY HUD.          (F182)

FLOSMAN, OLDRICH (cont'd.)
Sen O Houslích
3.2.3.2. 4.2.2.1. timp,perc,
strings,vln solo [8'] CESKY HUD.
(F183)
Serenade for 3 Horns and Strings
[11'] CESKY HUD.         (F184)
Symfonická Fuga
3.3.3.3. 4.3.3.1. timp,perc,xylo,
cel,strings [13'] CESKY HUD.
(F185)
Symfonické Vyprávení
3.3.3.2. 4.3.3.1. timp,perc,xylo,
strings [26'] CESKY HUD.  (F186)
Tance Pro Harfu A Smyccovy Orchestr
string orch,harp solo [13'] CESKY
HUD.                    (F187)
Variace Na Starou Francouzskou Písen
string orch [10'] CESKY HUD. (F188)
Zásnubní Tance Karla IV
2.2.2.2. 2.2.0.0. timp,perc,
strings,pno solo [15'] CESKY HUD.
(F189)

FLÖTENSINFONIE see Schenker, Friedrich

FLOTHUIS, MARIUS (1914-    )
Poem, Op. 96
1.0.0.0.alto sax. 0.0.0.0. perc,
strings,harp solo [11'] DONEMUS
(F190)

FLOTOW, FRIEDRICH VON (1812-1883)
Nancy! Julia! Verweile! Blickt Sein
Auge... Letzte Rose, Wie Magst Du
So Einsam (from Martha)
2(pic).2.2.2. 4.2.3.1. timp,harp,
strings [5'] BREITKOPF-W  (F191)

FLOURISH WITH FIREWORKS see Knussen,
Oliver

FLOURISHES see Floyd, Carlisle

FLOWER DRUM SONG see Chan, Ka Nin

FLOWINGS see Malmlöf-Forssling, Carin

FLOYD, CARLISLE (1926-    )
Citizen Of Paradise
2(pic).2(English horn).2(bass
clar).2. 2.1.1.0. timp,perc,pno&
cel,strings,Mez solo [34'] (text
by Emily Dickinson) BOOSEY-ENG
rent                    (F192)

Flourishes
3(pic).2.3.2. 4.3.3.1. timp,perc,
pno,strings [4'] BOOSEY-ENG rent
(F193)

FLUCHT NACH ÄGYPTEN, DIE: OVERTURE see
Berlioz, Hector (Louis), Fuite En
Egypte, La: Overture

FLÜGELLOS see Kantscheli, Gija

FLUSS DES LEBENS, DER see Smirnov,
Dmitri

FOCKE, WILLY
Concerto for Basset Horn and
Orchestra
3.0.0.0. 0.0.0.0. perc,cel,marimba,
vibra,harp,10vla,8vcl,6db [18']
sc PETERS 03091          (F194)

FOCUS AND FADE see Grange, Philip

FODI, JOHN (1944-    )
Adagio for String Orchestra, Op. 62
string orch [7'] sc CANADIAN
MI 1500 F653AD          (F195)

FOERSTER, JOSEF BOHUSLAV (1859-1951)
Písne Na Slova Jaroslava Vrchlického
2.2.2.2. 4.0.0.0. timp,perc,harp,
strings CESKY HUD.      (F196)

FOJTÍK, BOHUMIL (1925-    )
Suite for String Orchestra
string orch [15'] CESKY HUD. (F197)

FOLEY, DANIEL (1952-    )
Bear, The
see Menagerie

Black Cat, The
see Menagerie

Double Concerto For Two Contrabassi
And Chamber Orchestra
2(pic).1.3(clar in E flat).0.
2.0.0.0. timp,3perc,harp,pno&cel,
strings sc,solo pt CANADIAN
MI 1414 F663DO          (F198)

Menagerie
1(pic).1(English horn).1.1.
1.0.0.0. strings sc CANADIAN
MI1200 F663ME f.s.
contains: Bear, The, "Ours, L'";
Black Cat, The, "Chat Noir,
Le"; Monkey, The, "Singe, Le";

FOLEY, DANIEL (cont'd.)
    Mouse, The, "Ouris, La";
    Nightingale, The, "Rossignol,
    Le                          (F199)

    Monkey, The
    see Menagerie

    Mouse, The
    see Menagerie

    Nightingale, The
    see Menagerie

FOLGET DER HEISSGELIEBTEN see Mozart,
    Wolfgang Amadeus, Mio Tesoro
    Intanto, Il

FOLIA see Bacri, Nicolas

FOLIE, SERGE
    Antalya
    2.2.2+English horn.1.soprano
    sax.alto sax. 2.3.3.1. perc,harp,
    pno,8vln I,8vln II,6vla,4vcl,2db
    [25'] FUZEAU sc 2051, pts 2257
                                (F200)

FOLIES MAZARGUAISES, LES see Tomasi,
    Henri

FOLK MUSIC WITH LARGE ORCHESTRA see
    Dreyfus, George

FOLKSONGS OF EASTERN CANADA see Ridout,
    Godfrey

FOLLIA see Mihalovici, Marcel

FOLLIA, LA see Jansson, Johannes

FOLTYN, JAROSLAV (1927-    )
    Ctyri Kusy *Op.240
    string orch [10'] CESKY HUD. (F201)

    Episody *Op.241
    string orch [5'] CESKY HUD. (F202)

FOND SOMBRE, UN see Ekström, Lars

FONTAINE, LA (5 FABLES) see Rieti,
    Vittorio, Suite for Orchestra

FONTANE DI ROMA see Respighi, Ottorino

FONTE DOS AMORES "UM INEZ WEINTEN" see
    Streicher, Theodore

FONTYN, JACQUELINE (1930-    )
    Colloque
    1.1.1.1. 1.0.0.0. strings [13']
    PEER rent                   (F203)

    In The Green Shade
    3(pic).2.2+bass clar.2(contrabsn).
    4.3.3.1. 3perc,strings [15'] PEER
    rent                        (F204)

FOOTBALL see Smetácek, Rudolf, Kvapík
    Sportovcu

FOR MADMEN ONLY see Steven, Donald

FOR ORKESTER see Hegdal, Magne

FOR THE VICTIMS OF WARS AND VIOLENCE OF
    OUR TIME see Kasemets, Udo, Requiem
    Renga

FOR THOSE WHO SUFFERED see Downey, John
    Wilham

FOR TWELVE STRINGS (RISING) see Tenney,
    James C.

FORBES, SEBASTIAN (1941-    )
    Sinfonia 3
    3.2.3.3. 4.3.3.1. timp,3perc,harp,
    strings manuscript BMIC      (F205)

FORCE DE GRIS see Rossé, Francois

FORD, CLIFFORD (1947-    )
    Little Romance, A
    string orch,pno sc,pts CANADIAN
    MI 3245 F699LI              (F206)

    Metamorphose II
    1.1.1.1. 0.0.0.0. pno,string orch/
    string quin [15'] sc CANADIAN
    MI1200 F699ME              (F207)

FORD, RONALD (1959-    )
    Orfeo Fast Forward
    3.3.3.3. 4.4.3.1. strings [12'] sc
    DONEMUS                     (F208)

FOREST see Weir, Judith

FOREST AND SKY see Symonds, Norman

FORMASJONER FOR CELLO OG ORKESTER MED
    OBLIGAT KLAVER see Koch, Dagfinn

FOROTTO see Domazlicky, Frantisek

FORRETT see Kruse, Bjørn Howard

FORSBERG, ROLAND (1939-    )
    Koraluvertyr *Op.152
    2.2.2.2. 2.2.0.0. timp,strings STIM
                                (F209)

    Malungsvit *Op.135b
    clar,string orch STIM       (F210)

    Sommarkoral *Op.161
    1.1.1.1. 2.2.0.0. 3vln,vla,vcl/db
    STIM                        (F211)

FORSYTH, MALCOLM (1936-    )
    Adieu De La Mariée
    see Three Métis Songs From
    Saskatchewan

    Canzona *vocalise
    3(pic).2.3(bass clar).2. 4.3.3.1.
    timp,2perc,harp,strings,high
    solo/low solo [8'45"] sc,pts,solo
    pt CANADIAN MV 1400 F735CA (F212)

    Chanson Du Petit Corconnier
    see Three Métis Songs From
    Saskatchewan

    Chansons De La Grenouillère
    see Three Métis Songs From
    Saskatchewan

    Concerto for Piano
    2(pic).2.2.2. 4.2.3.1. timp,2perc,
    strings,pno solo, (tuba & 2nd
    percussion optional) [25'] sc
    KERBY MI 1361 F735CO        (F213)

    Concerto Grosso No. 3
    see Salpinx, The

    Host Of Nomads, A (Symphony No. 2)
    2(pic).2.2.2. 2.2.0.0. timp,perc,
    10vln I,8vln II,6vla,6vcl,4db
    [20'] sc,min sc CANADIAN
    MI 1100 F735S2              (F214)

    Images Of Night
    2(pic).2(English horn).2.2.
    4.2.3.0. timp,2perc,harp,strings,
    opt tuba [15'] sc CANADIAN
    MI 1100 F735IM             (F215)

    Rhapsody for 14 Strings
    4vln I,4vln II,3vla,2vcl,db [16']
    sc CANADIAN MI 1500 F735RH (F216)

    Salpinx, The (Concerto Grosso No. 3)
    2.2.2.2. 2.0.0.0. timp,perc,
    strings,string quar soli [21'] sc
    CANADIAN MI 1417 F735SA     (F217)

    Symphony No. 2
    see Host Of Nomads, A

    Three Métis Songs From Saskatchewan
    [Fr] 2.0.2.1. 0.0.0.0. harp,
    strings,Mez solo CANADIAN
    MV 1400 F735TH f.s.
    contains: Adieu De La Mariée,
    "Bride's Farewell, A"; Chanson
    Du Petit Corconnier, "Song Of
    The Little Shoemaker"; Chansons
    De La Grenouillère, "Song Of
    The Frog Plain"             (F218)

    Valley Of A Thousand Hills
    0.2.0.2. 2.0.0.0. timp&perc,strings
    [19'] sc CANADIAN MI1200 F735VA
                                (F219)

FORTNER, JACK (1935-    )
    Spring
    1.0.0.1.sax. 0.0.0.0. vibra,pno,
    harp,strings,S solo [9'] (text by
    e. e. cummings) JOBERT       (F220)

FORTNER, WOLFGANG (1907-    )
    Klangvariation
    3(pic).2+English horn.2+bass
    clar.2+contrabsn. 3.3.3.1. timp,
    perc,harp,6vla,5vcl,4db,4vla soli
    [12'] (to the "Impromtus")
    SCHOTTS perf mat rent       (F221)

FOUGSTEDT, NILS-ERIC (1910-1961)
    Passacaglia, Op. 21
    2.2.2.2. 4.3.3.1. timp,perc,strings
    [11'] BREITKOPF-W           (F222)

FOUR see Lindroth, Peter

FOUR DANCES FROM SAHDJI see Still,
    William Grant

FOUR EMILY DICKINSON SONGS see Belkin,
    Alan

FOUR FOLK SONGS FOR STRINGS see Raitio,
    Väinö, Neljä Hämäläistä
    Kansanlaulua Jousiork

405 see Vidovszky, Laszlo

FOUR INDIAN SONGS see Rickard, Sylvia

FOUR LATE SINFONIAS see Bach, Johann
    Christoph Friedrich

FOUR NOTE PAVAN see Ferrabosco, Alfonso
    (I)

FOUR ORCHESTRAL WORKS see Prokofiev,
    Serge see Ravel, Maurice

FOUR PAINTINGS OF SALVADOR DALI see
    Rae, Allan, Concerto for Double
    Bass

FOUR PIECES FOR STRING ORCHESTRA see
    Hiscott, James

FOUR SCENES AFTER PICASSO see Proto,
    Frank

FOUR SCENES FROM "THE TRUMPET MAJOR"
    see Hoddinott, Alun, Trumpet Major,
    The: Four Scenes

FOUR SEASONS see Vivaldi, Antonio

FOUR SEASONS, THE see Vivaldi, Antonio,
    Quattro Stagioni, Le

FOUR SKETCHES see Karkoff, Maurice

FOUR SONGS see Schubert, Franz (Peter)

FOUR SONGS (FROM THE DANISH) see
    Delius, Frederick

FOUR SONGS OF THE NIGHT see Lees,
    Benjamin

FOUR SYMPHONIES CONCERTANTES FOR
    HARPSICHORD AND PIANO WITH
    ORCHESTRA AD LIBITUM see Tapray,
    Jean-François

FOUR SYMPHONIES IN FULL SCORE see
    Schubert, Franz (Peter)

FOUR WALT WHITMAN SONGS see Weill, Kurt

FOURTEEN see Cage, John

FOURTH CHAMBER CONCERTO: FOR BRASS
    CONCERTANTE, WOODWINDS, STRINGS AND
    PERCUSSION see Kulesha, Gary

FOURTH OF JULY, THE see Ives, Charles

FRAGMENT see Maros, Rudolf see
    Shostakovich, Dmitri

FRAGMENT FOR CELLO SOLO AND ORCHESTRA
    see Janson, Alfred

FRAGMENTS see Vidovszky, Laszlo

FRAGMENTS AND SHADES see Brustad,
    Karsten

FRAGMENTS FROM "LEAR" see Reimann,
    Aribert

FRAGMENTS OF A CIRCLE see Lindgren, Pär

FRAMES: A SYMPHONIC IMPRESSION see
    Kjaernes, Bjorn Morten

FRÅN HAVSBANDET see Alfvén, Hugo

FRANCAIX, JEAN (1912-    )
    Concerto for Accordion and Orchestra
    2(2pic).2.2.2(contrabsn). 2.0.0.0.
    strings,acord solo [20'] SCHOTTS
    perf mat rent study sc ED 8582,
    pno red ED 8225             (F223)

    Double Concerto
    0.2.0.2(contrabsn). 2.0.0.0.
    strings,fl&alto fl&pic solo,clar&
    clar in E flat&bass clar solo
    [16'] SCHOTTS perf mat rent sc
    ED 8180, pts,pno red,solo pt
    ED 8078                     (F224)

    Mesures Et Un Da Capo, 85
    2.0.0.1.alto sax.tenor sax.
    0.2.1.0. perc,3vln,vla,vcl [3']
    SCHOTTS perf mat rent       (F225)

    "Noel Nouvelet" Et "Il Est Né, Le
    Divin Enfant"
    12vcl (two improvisations) SCHOTTS
    sc ED 7557, pts ED 7613     (F226)

    Triade De Toujours
    1.1.1.1. 1.0.0.0. harp,2vln,vla,
    vcl,db,SBar soli [20'] voc sc
    SCHOTTS ED 7964 perf mat rent
                                (F227)

FRANCHOMME, A
    Concerto for Violoncello and
    Orchestra, Op. 33
    vcl solo,orch KUNZELMANN 10236 ipr
                                (F228)

FRANCK, CESAR (1822-1890)
Dextera Domini  *Lent,Offer
2.2.2.2. 4.2.3.0. timp,strings,STB
soli LEDUC                    (F229)

Domine Non Secundum  *Adv/Lent,Offer
(Wright, J.) 1.1.1.1. 2.0.0.0.
timp,strings LEDUC            (F230)

Panis Angelicus
(Michelot) 2.2.2.2. 2.0.0.0. 2harp,
strings,T solo LEDUC         (F231)
(Michelot) 2.2.2.2. 2.0.0.0. 2harp,
strings,vln solo LEDUC       (F232)
(Sandré) 2.2.2.2. 2.0.0.0. strings,
T solo LEDUC                 (F233)
(Sandré) 2.2.2.2. 2.0.0.0. strings,
vln solo LEDUC               (F234)

Procession, La
2.1.1.1. 2.0.0.0. timp,strings,
harp,high solo&low solo [5'30"]
(poem by Ch. Brizeux) LEDUC
(F235)

Sinfonische Variationen
2.2.2.2. 4.2.0.0. timp,strings,pno
solo [27'] BREITKOPF-W       (F236)

Symphony in D minor
orch sc DOVER 25373-2        (F237)
(Jost) 2.3.3.2. 4.2+2cornet.3.1.
timp,harp,strings [28']
BREITKOPF-W PB-OB 5328       (F238)

Zwölf Miniaturen (from L'Organiste)
vln I,vln II,vla,T rec,vcl,db
MÖSELER sc,perf sc 40.164-00, pts
40.164-01, set 40.164-09     (F239)

FRANCL, JAROSLAV (1906-  )
Meditace A Scherzo
string orch [6'] CESKY HUD.  (F240)

Podzimní Hudba (Suite for Strings)
string orch [16'] CESKY HUD. (F241)

Suite for Strings
see Podzimní Hudba

FRANCO, CESARE
see FRANCK, CESAR

FRANKE, BERND (1959-  )
Music for Trumpet, Harp, Violin and
Orchestra
3.3.3.3. 4.3.3.1. timp,4perc,
strings,trp&harp&vln soli [28']
BREITKOPF-W                  (F242)

FRANKE-BLOM, LARS ÅKE (1941-  )
Fire On The Earth
see Symphony No. 3

Lustamas Trädgård
see Symphony No. 2

Symphony No. 2
"Lustamas Trädgård" orch [26'] STIM
sc H-2852, pts               (F243)

Symphony No. 3
"Fire On The Earth" 3(pic).3.3(bass
clar).3(contrabsn). 4.3.3.1.
timp,3perc,harp,strings,pno [25']
sc STIM                      (F244)

FRANKIE AND JOHNNY, BALLET SUITE see
Moross, Jerome

FRANSSENS, JOEP (1955-  )
Echo's
4.3.0.0. 0.3.0.0. vibra,marimba,
strings [25'] sc DONEMUS     (F245)

Sanctus
3.3.4.3. 4.2.0.0. timp,pno,strings
[19'] sc DONEMUS             (F246)

FRANZEN, OLOV (1946-  )
Adagio
see Clouds On Blue Sky

Clouds On Blue Sky (Adagio)
2(pic).2.2.2. 2.2.0.0. perc,strings
[9'] STIM sc H-2899, pts     (F247)

FRANZISKUS: TRAUERMARSCH see Tinel,
Edgar

FRATERNITÀ see Flosman, Oldrich

FRAZELLE, KENNETH
Elegy for String Orchestra
[11'] PEER rent              (F248)

FREDON ET TARABUSTS see Bartholomee,
Pierre

FREE MUSIC NO. 1 see Grainger, Percy
Aldridge

FREEDMAN, HARRY (1922-  )
Accord
3(pic&pic).2(English horn).3.2.
4.3.2.1. timp,perc,strings,vln
solo [11'] sc CANADIAN

FREEDMAN, HARRY (cont'd.)
MI 1311 F853AC               (F249)

Another Monday Gig
clar,soprano sax,tenor sax,baritone
sax,bsn,trp,trom,vln,vcl,kbd,gtr,
db,perc,drums sc CANADIAN
MI1200 F8563AN               (F250)

Celebration
3(pic).0.3.0. 4.3.3.0. 3perc,harp,
strings,soprano sax&baritone sax
solo [23'] sc CANADIAN
MI 1325 F853CE               (F251)

Chalumeau
string orch,clar solo [17'] sc
CANADIAN MI 1623 F853CH      (F252)

Concerto for Orchestra
3+pic.3+English horn.3(bass
clar).3(contrabsn). 4.3.3.1.
timp,4perc,harp,strings [35'] sc
CANADIAN MI 1100 F853CO      (F253)

Concerto Grosso for Brass Quintet and
Orchestra
see Royal Flush

Graphic 6: Town
2(pic).2.2.2. 2.2.2.0. 2perc,pno&
cel,harp,strings sc CANADIAN
MI 1100 F853G6               (F254)

Passacaglia for Band and Orchestra
2(pic).2.2.2. 4.3.3.1. timp,perc,
harp,strings, band (5trp, 2horn,
5trb, 5sax, electric piano, gt,
bass, drumset, and perc) [14'] sc
CANADIAN MI 1100 F853PA      (F255)

Rose Latulippe: Suite
2(pic).2.2.2. 2.2.1.0. timp,perc,
strings [45'] sc CANADIAN
MI 1100 F853SU               (F256)

Royal Flush (Concerto Grosso for
Brass Quintet and Orchestra)
2(pic).3(English horn).2.2.
0.0.0.0. timp,3perc,harp,strings,
brass quin soli [15'] sc CANADIAN
MI 1430 F853RO               (F257)

Strands Of Blue
1.1.1.1. 1.1.0.0. perc,harp,vln,
vla,vcl [11'] sc CANADIAN
MI1200 F853ST                (F258)

Symphony No. 3
3(pic).3+English horn.3(bass
clar).3+contrabsn. 4.3.3.1. timp,
3perc,harp,strings [31'] sc
CANADIAN MI 1100 F853TH      (F259)

Touchings
2(pic).2(English horn).2(bass
clar).2. 2.2.2.0. harp,strings sc
CANADIAN MI 1441 F853TO      (F260)

Town
2(pic).2.2.2. 2.2.2.0. 3perc,pno,
cel,harp,strings sc CANADIAN
MI 1100 F853TO               (F261)

Voice Lines
string orch,S solo [14'] (1. Nuages
2. Déjeuner du matin 3. Page
d'écriture) sc CANADIAN
MV 1600 F853VO               (F262)

FREEFALL see Wolfe, Lawrence

FREEFLIGHT see Schwantner, Joseph

FREISCHÜTZ, DER: EINST TRÄUMTE see
Weber, Carl Maria von

FREISCHÜTZ, DER: HIER IM IRD'SCHEN
JAMMERTAL see Weber, Carl Maria von

FREISCHÜTZ, DER: KOMMT EIN SCHLANKER
BURSCH GEGANGEN see Weber, Carl
Maria von

FREISCHÜTZ, DER: LIED DES CASPAR see
Weber, Carl Maria von

FREISCHÜTZ, DER: NEIN, LÄNGER TRAG ICH
NICHT DIE QUALEN see Weber, Carl
Maria von

FREISCHÜTZ, DER: ROMANZE UND ARIE see
Weber, Carl Maria von

FREISCHÜTZ, DER: UND OB DIE WOLKE see
Weber, Carl Maria von

FRENETTE, CLAUDE (1955-  )
Mouvements Provisoires 2
3(pic).3+English horn.3(bass
clar).2. 4.2.2.1. timp,2perc,
harp,pno&cel,strings [12'] sc
CANADIAN MI 1100 F878MO      (F263)

FRESCHI see Eklund, Hans, Sinfonia 12

FRESCO see Schroyens, Daniël

FRESCOBALDI, GIROLAMO (1583-1643)
Capriccio Pastorale
strings,opt fl BÖHM          (F264)

FRESCOES see Trafford, Edmund

FRESKA see Filas, Juraj

FRESKY see Slimacek, Milan

FREUDENLEERE GEDANKEN, FOR VIOLONCELLO
AND ORCHESTRA see Kantscheli, Gija,
Simi

FREUDENTHAL, OTTO (1934-  )
Fantasy
string orch STIM             (F265)

Höst
see Orkesterförspel

Orkesterförspel
"Höst" 2.2.2.2. 2.2.3.0. timp,
strings [9'] STIM sc H-2872, pts
(F266)

FREUNDE AUS UNSERN KINDERJAHREN see
Wellejus, Henning

FRIBERG, TOMAS (1962-  )
Word Without A Word, The
string orch [10'] sc STIM    (F267)

FRICKER, PETER RACINE (1920-1990)
Fantasy
2.2.2.2. 2.2.0.0. timp,strings [3']
(on a theme of Mozart) SCHOTTS
perf mat rent                (F268)

Symphony No. 5, Op. 74
2+pic.3.3.3. 4.3.3.1. timp,3perc,
org,strings [20'] SCHOTTS perf
mat rent                     (F269)

FRIDOLFSON, RUBEN (1933-  )
Fantasia On A Twelve-Tone System
see Fantasia On A Twelvetone System

Fantasia On A Twelvetone System
"Fantasia On A Twelve-Tone System"
2.2.3(bass clar).2. 4.3.3.1.
timp,perc,harp,strings [4'5"]
STIM sc H-2757, pts          (F270)

Fantasy No. 2
2.2.2.2. 4.3.3.1. timp,perc,strings
[4'5"] STIM sc H-2868, pts   (F271)

Musik För Orkester
2.2.2.2. 4.3.3.0. timp,perc,strings
[14'] (1. Allegro moderato; 2.
Andante sostenuto) sc,pts STIM
(F272)

Prelude for Chamber Orchestra
woodwind quin,string orch [7'] sc,
pts STIM                     (F273)

Prelude, Pastorale And Fugue
fl,ob,clar,bsn,horn,trp,trom,timp,
pno,vcl,db sc,pts STIM       (F274)

Suite for Strings
string orch sc,pts STIM      (F275)

Three Movements On A Twelve-Tone
System
3(pic).3(English horn).3(bass
clar).3(contrabsn). 4.3.3.1.
timp,perc,harp,strings [14'] sc,
pts STIM                     (F276)

FRIED, ALEXJ (1922-  )
Chléb A Hry
"Panem Et Circenses" 2.2.2.2.
4.3.4.0. timp,perc,pno,elec gtr,
synthesizer,strings,fl&soprano
sax&horn soli [19'] CESKY HUD.
(F277)

Concertino for Oboe, Clarinet,
Bassoon and Orchestra
perc,strings,ob&clar&bsn soli [14']
CESKY HUD.                   (F278)

Concerto No. 2 for Clarinet and
Orchestra
2.2.2.2. 4.3.3.1. timp,perc,
strings,clar solo [20'] CESKY
HUD.                         (F279)

Kasace
2.2.2.2. 2.2.0.0. perc,strings
[15'] CESKY HUD.             (F280)

Panem Et Circenses
see Chléb A Hry

FRIEDENSLIED see Weismann, Wilhelm,
Concerto for Solo Voice, Chorus,
Organ and Orchestra

FRISCHKNECHT, HANS EUGEN (1939-   )
Farben
3.3.3.3. 4.3.3.0. perc,timp,harp, strings MULL & SCH rent   (F281)

Orgorchestra
2.2.2.2. 2.2.2.2. 2perc,strings,org solo MULL & SCH rent   (F282)

FRISSON, LA VIE see Bouchard, Linda

FRISSONS see Naulais, Jerome

"FRITTER MY WIG!" see Crawley, Clifford

FRÖHLICHE EPISODE see Basl, Curt

FRÖHLICHER ABSCHIED see Budde, Kurt

FROM A DARK MILLENNIUM see Schwantner, Joseph

FROM A DIFFERENT COUNTRY see Turner, Robert [Comrie]

...FROM AFAR see Schwantner, Joseph

FROM HARMONY see Davies, Victor

FROM SEA PAINTINGS OF PAUL NASH see Bailey, Judith

FROM SEA TO SKY see Matthews, David

FROM SILENCE see Rosen, Robert

FROM THE EYE OF THE WIND see Symonds, Norman

FROM THE JOURNAL OF A WANDERER see Still, William Grant

FROM THE NEW WORLD see Dvořák, Antonín, Symphony No. 9, Op. 95, in E minor

FROM UNDER THE OVERTURE see Schipizky, Frederick

FROST AT MIDNIGHT see Holloway, Robin

FRÜHLINGS-SYMPHONIE see Schumann, Robert (Alexander), Symphony No. 1 in B flat, Op. 38

FRÜHLINGSPHANTASIE see Bronsart Von Schellendorf, Hans

FRÜHLINGSSYMPHONIE C-DUR see Abert, Johann Joseph

FRÜHLINGSTIMMEN see Strauss, Johann, [Jr.]

FRUIT DES VIEILLES HABITUDES see Offenbach, Jacques

FRVANDLINGAR see Blomberg, Erik

FRYDA, JAN (1913-1984)
Idylka G-Dur
2.2.2.2. 3.2.2.0. timp,perc,strings [4'] CESKY HUD.   (F283)

Intermezzo
see U Léčivého Vrídla

U Léčivého Vrídla (Intermezzo)
2.2.2.2. 3.2.2.0. timp,perc,strings [4'] CESKY HUD.   (F284)

V Zadumání
2.2.3.0. 3.2.3.0. timp,perc,harp, strings CESKY HUD.   (F285)

FSTEN O FALL see Isaksson, Madeleine

FU SHI (DIE GESTALT DES WINDES) see Ishii, Maki

FUCHS, PETER (FUX, PIETRO) (1753-1831)
Concerto in E flat for Horn and Orchestra
(Koukal, Bohumír) 0.2.0.0. 2.0.0.0. strings,horn solo [16'] CESKY HUD.   (F286)

FUCIK, JULIUS (1872-1916)
Stary Brucoun
2.2.2.0. 3.2.3.0. perc,strings,bsn solo CESKY HUD.   (F287)

FUGA GALACTICA see Bolcom, William Elden, Concerto No. 3 for 2Piano Left-Hand and Orchestra

FUGA (HOMMAGE À J.S. BACH) see Bogár, István, Fugue

FUGOVÁ SUITA, 1. D-MOLL see Smolka, Jaroslav

FUGUE FANTASIA FÜR GROSSES ORCHESTER see Zador, Eugene (Jenö)

FUGUE ON THE NOTES OF THE FOURTH PSALM see Goehr, Alexander

FUITE EN EGYPTE, LA: OVERTURE see Berlioz, Hector (Louis)

FUJIL, SONOKO (1941-   )
Kooghe
orch [15'] JAPAN   (F288)

FUJIWARA, YUTAKA (1960-   )
Feuerschuh Und Windsandale
orch,pno [15'] JAPAN   (F289)

Haru No Yo No Yume
orch [25'] JAPAN   (F290)

FUKEI JUNGINMOZAIKU FROM SOSHITE ICHIMEN NO NANOHANA see Ichinose, Tonika

FUKKO ENO INORI see Yanagi, Hirosi

FUNERAL MUSIC see Takemitsu, Toru

FÜNF ASPEKTE see Haller, Hermann

FÜNF FRAGMENTE ZU BILDERN VON HIERONYMUS BOSCH see Schnittke, Alfred

FÜNF PRÉLUDES see Debussy, Claude

FÜNF STÜCKE AUS DER FILMMUSIK "KÖNIG LEAR" see Shostakovich, Dmitri, King Lear: Five Pieces

5 KANONS AUS "MUSIKALISCHES OPFER" VON JOHANN SEBASTIAN BACH see Dessau, Paul

FUOR DEL MAR HO UN MAR IN SENO see Mozart, Wolfgang Amadeus

FÜR CLARA see Kaufmann, Dieter

FÜR DIE JUGEND see Scharwenka, Philipp

FÜR LIEDER see Bose, Hans-Jurgen Von

FÜR LIVERPOOL see Schnittke, Alfred

FÜR 16 see Willi, Herbert

FURER, ARTHUR (1924-   )
Concertino for Oboe and String Orchestra
string orch/string quar,ob solo [15'] pts MULL & SCH M&S 1209   (F291)

Concerto for Violin, No. 1
strings,timp,vln solo [21'] MULL & SCH rent   (F292)

Concerto for Violin, No. 3
2(pic).2.2.2(contrabsn). 3.3.2.0. timp,perc,strings,vln solo [30'] MULL & SCH rent   (F293)

Divertimento
strings,pno&clar soli [17'] MULL & SCH rent   (F294)

Klavierfantasie
1.1.1.1. 1.0.0.0. strings,pno solo [16'30"] MULL & SCH rent   (F295)

Sinfonia in E minor
2(pic).2(English horn).2.2(contrabsn). 2.2.2.1. 4timp,perc,strings [30'] MULL & SCH rent   (F296)

FURGERI, BIANCA MARIA
Levia
string orch EMB rent   (F297)

FURIN NO KYO see Zender, Hans

FURIOSO see Spahlinger, Mathias

FÜRSTENAU, ANTON BERNHARD (1792-1852)
Adagio Et Variation Brillante G-Dur see Illusion, L', Op. 133

Illusion, L', Op. 133
"Adagio Et Variation Brillante G-Dur" 2.0.2.2. 2.2.0.0. timp, strings,fl solo [12'] (no score) BREITKOPF-W   (F298)

FUSION see Trochu, Pierre

FUSIONS see Bavicchi, John Alexander

FUTURUM EXACTUM see Ore, Cecilie

FUYU NI... see Doi, Yoshiyuki

FYRA RSTIDSPASTORALER: 1. VRPASTORAL see Koch, Erland von

FYRA RSTIDSPASTORALER: 2. SOMMARPASTORAL see Koch, Erland von

FYRA RSTIDSPASTORALER: 3. HSTPASTORAL see Koch, Erland von

FYRA RSTIDSPASTORALER: 4. VINTERPASTORAL see Koch, Erland von

# G

G AND E ON A see Saunders, Rebecca

G-STRING MAMBO see Zuidam, Rob

GAAL, JENÖ (1906-    )
Sinfonia No. 2
strings [22'] EMB rent          (G1)

GAATHAUG, MORTEN (1955-    )
Concerto for Oboe and Orchestra, Op.
45
1.0.2.1. 2.0.0.0. pno,strings,ob
solo [25'] NORSKMI          (G2)

Symfonisk Introduksjon Til En Sang Av
Brahms *Op.43a
(Heyse, Paul) "Symphonic
Introduction To A Song By Brahms"
[Norw] 3(pic).3(English
horn).3(bass clar).3(contrabsn).
4.3.3(bass trom).0. timp,perc,
pno&cel,2harp,strings,cor NORSKMI
(G3)
Symphonic Introduction To A Song By
Brahms
see Symfonisk Introduksjon Til En
Sang Av Brahms

GABORIAU TOUPIN FERRON ET LES AUTRES
see Longtin, Michel

GADE, NIELS WILHELM (1817-1890)
Hamlet *Op.37
3.2.2.2. 4.2.3.1. timp,strings [8']
(concert overture) BREITKOPF-W
(G4)

Holbergiana *Op.61, Suite
2(pic).2.2.2. 4.2.3.1. timp,
triangle,strings [23'] BREITKOPF-
W          (G5)

GAEA see Bolcom, William Elden

GAGNÉ, MARC (1939-    )
Concerto for Chamber Orchestra
"Dicts Du Lunanthrope, Les" chamber
orch [20'] sc CANADIAN
MI1200 G135CO          (G6)

Dicts Du Lunanthrope, Les
see Concerto for Chamber Orchestra

GAGNON, ALAIN (1938-    )
Suite Chorégraphique *Op.30
2(pic,alto fl).2(English horn).2.2.
4.3.3.1. timp,perc,pno,harp,
strings sc CANADIAN
MI 1100 G135SU          (G7)

GAHÉR, JOZEF (1934-    )
Dvojmonolog
3.3.3.3. 4.3.3.1. perc,strings
[29'] CESKY HUD.          (G8)

Na Pochodu Se Neumírá
3.3.3.3. 4.3.3.1. perc,harp,org,
strings [30'] CESKY HUD.          (G9)

GAL, HANS (1890-1987)
Servian Songs *Op.36
1.1.2.1. 2.2.1.0. perc,harmonium,
strings (orchestral arrangement
of the 4 Servian Dances, Op. 3)
BOOSEY-ENG rent          (G10)

GALANTE, CARLO (1959-    )
Concerto for Violin and Orchestra
see Yeliel

Giocatore D'Anime
clar,trp,bsn,string orch [20']
SONZOGNO rent          (G11)

Yeliel (Concerto for Violin and
Orchestra)
2.2.2.2. 2.2.0.0. timp,perc,strings
[22'] SONZOGNO rent          (G12)

GALGENLIEDER see Lang, Walter

GALLINA, JAN ADAM ( ? -1773)
Sinfonia in A
(Sesták, Zdenek) 0.2.0.1. 2.0.0.0.
strings [15'] CESKY HUD.          (G13)

Sinfonia in C
(Sesták, Zdenek) 0.2.0.2. 2.0.0.0.
strings [14'] CESKY HUD.          (G14)

GALLO, GERARD
Serenade for Violin and Orchestra
(from Epingle Noire)
BOIS          (G15)

GALLOIS MONTBRUN, RAYMOND (1918-1994)
Trois Mélodies
1.1.1.1. 1.1.0.0. timp,2perc,
strings,harp,med solo [10'20"]
(poems by J. Mariat, No. 1.

GALLOIS MONTBRUN, RAYMOND (cont'd.)
Lorsque Tu Dors No. 3. Mélodies)
LEDUC          (G16)

GALOP ARTISTU see Sodomka, Karel

GALOP INDIEN see Strauss, Johann, [Jr.]

GALUPPI, BALDASSARE (1706-1785)
Christe Redemptor
see Drei Kirchenarien

Drei Kirchenarien
KUNZELMANN GM 1173 f.s.
contains: Christe Redemptor (S
solo,string orch); Pastores
Mecum Omnes Venite Adoramus (S
solo,string orch); Pfingst-
Hymnus: Veni Creator Spiritus
(S solo,2fl,string orch)          (G17)

Pastores Mecum Omnes Venite Adoramus
see Drei Kirchenarien

Pfingst-Hymnus: Veni Creator Spiritus
see Drei Kirchenarien

Regina Coeli
S solo,string orch sc,pts
KUNZELMANN GM 1116 ipa          (G18)

Zwei Sonaten Für Orchester
orch KUNZELMANN ipa sc 10213A, oct
10213          (G19)

GAMELODION see Kyr, Robert

GAMLE DANSKE FOLKEDANSE see Grondahl,
Launy, Alte Dänische Volkstänze

GAMSTORP, GÖRAN (1957-    )
Growings
4(pic).4(English horn).4(bass
clar).4(contrabsn). 6.4.4.2.
2timp,4perc,strings,electronic
tape [60'] STIM sc H-2802, pts
(G20)
Puls III
string orch [15'] sc,pts STIM (G21)

GÄNGE see Jahn, Thomas

GANZ ALLERLIEBST see Waldteufel, Emile

GARALL, PERCIVAL
Three Dance Miniatures *Op.57
1.1.1.1. 0.0.0.0. 8vln I,7vln II,
6vla,5vcl,4db [5'] sc PETERS
04617          (G22)

GARANT, SERGE (1929-1986)
Circuit II
2fl,clar,vln,vla,trp,horn,trom,
harp,2pno,3perc [14'] sc CANADIAN
MI1200 G212C2          (G23)

GARDELLI, LAMBERTO
Concerto for Orchestra
2+pic.2+English horn.2+bass clar.2+
contrabsn. 6.4.3.1. timp,perc,
org,cel,strings [20'] EMB rent
(G24)
Divertimento for Piano and Orchestra
see Italia

Italia (Divertimento for Piano and
Orchestra)
1.1.1.1. 2.3.2.1. timp,perc,
strings,pno solo EMB rent          (G25)

Johannes Portrait
1(pic).0.0.0. 4.0+2trp in C.3.0.
perc,pno,cel,strings [28'] EMB
rent          (G26)

Piccola Suite
strings [15'] EMB rent          (G27)

Quattro Momenti Musicali (Sinfonia)
2(2pic).2.0+2clar in C.2+contrabsn.
6.4.3.1. timp,perc,harp,cel,pno,
strings [32'] EMB rent          (G28)

Sinfonia
see Quattro Momenti Musicali

GARDEN OF EARTHLY DELIGHTS, A see
Lumsdaine, David

GARDINER, MARY (1932-    )
Concerto For Piano, String Orchestra,
And Drums
[12'] (1. Con energico 2. Tempo
comodo 3. Allegro vivo) sc,pno
red CANADIAN MI 1661 G223CO          (G29)

GARDNER, JOHN LINTON (1917-    )
It's This Island
2.2.2.2. 4.0.3.1. harp,strings,Bar
solo [6'] perf sc set OXFORD
3632292 sc,pts rent          (G30)

GARDNER, R. NEIL
Concertino for Oboe d'Amore and
Strings
strings,ob d'amore solo [10']
manuscript BMIC          (G31)

Waltzes
strings [10'] manuscript BMIC (G32)

GARTEN LIEDER I see Hosokawa, Toshio

GARWOOD, MARGARET (1927-    )
Japanese Songs
clar,harp,perc,strings,S solo study
sc,pts HILDEGARD 09549 rent (G33)

GAŠPAROVICOVÁ, MARIE
Hudba Pro Smyccovy Orchestr
string orch [10'] CESKY HUD.  (G34)

Symfonická Svita
3.2.2.2. 4.3.3.1. timp,perc,cel,
harp,pno,strings [15'] CESKY HUD.
(G35)

GASTINEL, GÉRARD
5 Pièces Pour Orchestre -Cycles 1-2
2.1.2+clar in E flat.soprano
sax.2alto sax.0. 0.3.0.0. 3perc,
pno,vln I,vln II,vln III,vcl I,
vcl II,db FUZEAU sc 1399, pts
2695          (G36)

Concertino for Orchestra
[12'] FUZEAU sc 2837, pts 3106
(G37)
Overture No. 1 for Orchestra
2.0.2.0.2sax. 0.2.0.0. bass drum,
tam-tam,pno 4-hands,vln I,vln II,
vla,vcl I,vcl II pts FUZEAU 1408
(G38)
Petit Louveteau Gris, Le
2.2.2.1.alto sax.tenor sax.
3.2.1.0. 2perc,harp,vln I,vln II,
vln III,vla,vcl,db FUZEAU sc
1436, pts 2693          (G39)

Petite Valse
2.0.2.0.2alto sax. 0.0+2trp in
C.0.0. vln,vla,vcl pts FUZEAU
1411          (G40)

Satie's Faction
fl,harp,gtr,vln I,vln II,vln III,
vla,vcl I,vcl II/db pts FUZEAU
1407          (G41)

GATEWAYS see Asia, Daniel

GÅTFULL MOLL OCH LIVING MOLL: TVÅ
STYCKEN FÖR ORKESTER see Blomberg,
Erik

GAWAIN'S JOURNEY see Birtwistle,
Harrison

GAY NINETIES, THE see Deutsch, Peter,
Glücklichen 90er

GAYFER, JAMES MCDONALD (1916-    )
Symphony No. 1 in B flat
3(pic).3+English horn.3+bass
clar.2. 4.3.3.1. timp,perc,
strings [21'] sc CANADIAN
MI 1100 G286S1          (G42)

Variations For Orchestra On A. E. G.
3(pic).2+English horn.3+bass
clar.3. 4.3.3.1. timp,perc,harp,
strings [15'] sc CANADIAN
MI 1100 G286VA          (G43)

GAZEBO DANCES see Corigliano, John

GAZZA LADRA, LA: OVERTURE see Rossini,
Gioacchino

GE XU see Chen, Yi

GEBAUER, ADOLF
Concerto for Violin and Orchestra
2.2.2.2. 2.1.1.0. timp,perc,harp,
pno,strings,vln solo [26'] MOECK
sc 5355 f.s., pts rent          (G44)
3.2.2.2. 2.1.1.0. timp,perc,harp,
pno,strings,vln solo [24'] CESKY
HUD.          (G45)

GEBHARD, A.M.
Salve Regina
(Münster) S/T solo,fl solo,string
orch sc KUNZELMANN GM 254 ipa
(G46)
GEDANKEN see Stendel, Wolfgang, Pensees

GEDATSU see Ishii, Maki

GEDDES, MURRAY (1950-    )
Ask The Oracle
2(alto fl).2.2(bass clar).2.
4.2.3.1. 3perc,harp,strings [15']
sc CANADIAN MI 1100 G295AS (G47)

GEDENKEN "HABE IN DEN HERBST HINAUS"
see Streicher, Theodore

GEERTENS, GERDA (1955- )
Heartland
3.3.3.3. 4.4.3.1. 6perc,strings
[11'] sc DONEMUS          (G48)

Leave It Alone, An Audioclip
1.1.1.1. 1.1.1.0. perc,harp,pno,
2vln,vla,vcl,db [15'] sc DONEMUS
                          (G49)

GEFILDE DER SELIGEN, DAS see
Weingartner, (Paul) Felix von

GEFORS, HANS (1952- )
Erscheinung Im Park, Die (Music, No.
4 for Orchestra)
2(pic).2(English horn).2(bass
clar).2(contrabsn).2sax. 2.3+
cornet.3.1+Wagner tuba. 4perc,
2synthesizer,strings,Bar solo,
two more oboes [30'] STIM sc
H-2593, pts            (G50)

Music, No. 4 for Orchestra
see Erscheinung Im Park, Die

GEGEN HERBST see Sköld, Sven

GEHEIMES see Schubert, Franz (Peter)

GEISSLER, FRITZ (1921-1984)
Concerto for Flute, Strings, Harp and
Timpani
1.0.0.0. 0.0.0.0. timp,harp,8vln I,
7vln II,6vla,5vcl,4db [15'] sc,
solo pt PETERS 03073      (G51)

Concerto for Organ, Timpani,
Percussion and Strings
timp,perc,org,8vln I,7vln II,6vla,
5vcl,4db [35'] sc,solo pt PETERS
03075                     (G52)

Concerto for Violoncello and
Orchestra
2.2.2.2. 4.3.2.1. timp,perc,pno,
harp,8vln I,7vln II,6vla,5vcl,4db
[20'] sc PETERS 03071     (G53)

Liebenden, Die
1.1.1.1. 0.0.0.0. vibra,vln,vla,
4vcl [12'] sc PETERS 03067 (G54)

Offenbach-Metamorphosen
3.3.3.3. 4.3.3.1. timp,2perc,
strings [18'] PETERS      (G55)

Solo Für Lehrer Sperling
1.1.1.0. 1.1.1.0. timp,perc,pno,
harp,8vln I,7vln II,6vla,5vcl,4db
sc PETERS 03066           (G56)

GEISTHARDT, HANS-JOACHIM (1925- )
Triptychon
5vln I,4vln II,3vla,2vcl,db [21']
sc PETERS 04386           (G57)

GEISTLICHE MUSIK see Koch, Markus

GELB UND GRÜN: SUITE see Zimmermann,
Bernd Alois

GELIEBTE STIMME, DIE: OVERTURE see
Weinberger, Jaromir, Beloved Voice,
The: Overture

GELLMAN, STEVEN (1947- )
Andante for String Orchestra
string orch [12'] sc CANADIAN
MI 1500 G319AN            (G58)

Animus-Anima *vocalise
3(pic,alto fl).3(English
horn).3(bass clar).2. 4.2(trp in
D).3.1. perc,harp,strings,SSS
soli [22'] sc CANADIAN
MV 3400 G319AN            (G59)

Awakening
4(pic,alto fl).4+English horn.4+
bass clar.4+contrabsn. 4.3.3(bass
trom).1. timp,3perc,harp,strings
[13'] sc CANADIAN MI 1100 G319AW
                          (G60)

Bride's Reception, The
3(pic,alto fl).2.3(clar in E flat,
bass clar).3(contrabsn). 4.3.3.1.
timp,3perc,pno,harp,strings,
English horn solo,vla solo [25']
sc CANADIAN MI 1450 G319BR (G61)

Burnt Offerings
string orch sc CANADIAN
MI 1500 G319BU            (G62)

Child Play *Suite
1.1.1.1. 0.1.0.0. strings (for
children) CANADIAN MI1200 G319CH
                          (G63)

Deux Tapisseries
2(pic).2.2+bass clar.2. 2.2.1.1.
2perc,harp,pno&cel,strings sc
CANADIAN MI 1100 G319DE f.s.
contains: Lightning Tapestry
"Tapisserie D'Eclair"; Twilight
Tapestry, "Tapisserie De
Crépuscule"               (G64)

GELLMAN, STEVEN (cont'd.)
Lightning Tapestry
see Deux Tapisseries

Twilight Tapestry
see Deux Tapisseries

GEMINI see Gutché, Gene

GEMINIANI, FRANCESCO (1687-1762)
Concerto Grosso, Op. 2, No. 2
strings,cembalo BÖHM       (G65)

GEMROT, JIRI (1957- )
Concerto for Oboe, Bassoon and
Orchestra
1.0.2.0. 2.0.0.0. strings,ob&bsn
soli [18'] CESKY HUD.      (G66)

Concerto for Piano and Orchestra
3.2.3.2. 3.3.3.1. timp,perc,cel,
strings,pno solo [20'] CESKY HUD.
                          (G67)

Concerto for Violoncello and
Orchestra
3.2.2.3. 4.3.3.0. timp,perc,
strings,vcl solo [16'] CESKY HUD.
                          (G68)

Pocty
3.2.2.2. 4.3.3.1. perc,harp,strings
[20'] CESKY HUD.          (G69)

Predehra
3.2.2.2. 4.2.3.0. timp,perc,strings
[7'] CESKY HUD.           (G70)

Sentence
string orch [12'] CESKY HUD. (G71)

Tance A Reflexe
3.2.2.2. 4.3.3.1. timp,perc,strings
[16'] CESKY HUD.          (G72)

GEN see Noda, Ryo

"GÉNÉRAL LAVINE", ECCENTRIC see
Debussy, Claude

GENERALPROBE, DIE see Cimarosa,
Domenico

GENESIS see Kasparov, Youri

GENESIS II: CANTI STRUMENTALI see
Gorecki, Henryk Mikolaj

GENESIS III: MONODRAMMA see Gorecki,
Henryk Mikolaj

GENGE, ANTHONY (1952- )
Music for String Orchestra
string orch sc CANADIAN
MI 1500 G329MU            (G73)

River In Summer, The
1.0+English horn.1.1. 1.0.0.0.
perc,pno,vln,vla,vcl,db [10'] sc
CANADIAN MI1200 G329RI    (G74)

GENGHIS KHAN see Gutché, Gene

GENOM PRISMAN AVE EN SKRVA: MUSIK
KOMPONERAD EFTER AUGUST STRINDBERGS
MLERI see Ekström, Lars

GENOM SKÄRVAN AV EN PRISMA see Ekström,
Lars

GENZMER, HARALD (1909- )
Concerto for Clarinet and Orchestra
2.1.0.2. 2.2.1.0. timp,perc,harp,
strings,clar solo [22'] PETERS
                          (G75)

Concerto for Flute, Harp and Strings
[18'] PETERS             (G76)

Concerto for 2 Guitars and Orchestra
1.1.1.1. 1.0.0.0. strings,2gtr soli
[24'] PETERS             (G77)

Concerto for 2 Pianos and Orchestra
2.2.2.2. 2.2.0.0. timp,perc,8vln I,
7vln II,6vla,5vcl,4db,2pno soli
[24'] sc,solo pt PETERS 02588
                          (G78)

0.0.0.2. 0.0.0.0. timp,perc,
strings,2pno soli [5'] PETERS
                          (G79)

Concerto for Trumpet, Organ and
Strings
[18'] PETERS             (G80)

Drei Märchen
PETERS f.s.
contains: Kleine Hässliche Raupe,
Die (2.2.2.2. 2.1.0.0. timp,
perc,harp,strings,speaking
voice) [8']; Springer, Der
(2.2.2.2. 2.1.0.0. timp,perc,
harp,strings,speaking voice)
[8']; Trommler, Der (2.2.2.2.
2.1.1.1. timp,perc,harp,
strings,speaking voice) [20']
                          (G81)

GENZMER, HARALD (cont'd.)
Hölderlin Fragmente I-V (Music for
Orchestra)
2.2.2.2. 4.2.1.0. timp,2perc,harp,
9vln I,8vln II,7vla,6vcl,5db
[31'] sc PETERS 04634     (G82)

Kammerkonzert
8vln I,7vln II,6vla,5vcl,4db,vla
solo [14'] sc,solo pt PETERS
00419                     (G83)

Kleine Hässliche Raupe, Die
see Drei Märchen

Music for Orchestra
see Hölderlin Fragmente I-V

Music for Orchestra, No. 2
2.2.2.2. 3.2.1.0. timp,2perc,harp,
8vln I,7vln II,6vla,5vcl,4db [6']
sc PETERS 00432           (G84)

Music for Orchestra, No. 3
2.2.2.2. 4.2.1.0. timp,perc,8vln I,
7vln II,6vla,5vcl,4db [3'] sc
PETERS 00431              (G85)

Music for Orchestra, No. 4
2.1.2.2. 4.0.0.0. timp,2perc,8vln
I,7vln II,6vla,5vcl,4db [3'] sc
PETERS 00433              (G86)

Music for Orchestra, No. 5
2.2.2.2. 4.2.1.0. timp,2perc,8vln I,
7vln II,6vla,5vcl,4db [8'] sc
PETERS 00434              (G87)

Prolog II Für Orchester
2.2.2.2. 2.2.2.1. timp,perc,strings
[8'] PETERS              (G88)

Sinfonia No. 4 for Orchestra
3.3.3.2. 3.2.2.1. timp,perc,strings
[24'] PETERS             (G89)

Sinfonietta for String Orchestra, No.
2
SCHOTTS sc CON 246, pts CON 246-70
                          (G90)

Sinfonietta No. 2
strings SCHOTTS perf mat rent sc
CON 246, pts 246-70       (G91)

Springer, Der
see Drei Märchen

Trommler, Der
see Drei Märchen

GEPARD see Kosut, Michal

GERHARD, FRITZ CHRISTIAN (1911- )
Ode
orch MÖSELER 10.471 rent   (G92)

GERHARD, ROBERTO (1896-1970)
Pandora: Suite
1(pic).1(English horn).2(contrabass
clar).1. 2.1.1.0. 3perc,harp,pno&
cel,strings [26'] BOOSEY-ENG rent
                          (G93)

Sis Cançons Populars Catalanes
see Six Catalan Folksongs

Six Catalan Folksongs
"Sis Cançons Populars Catalanes"
2(pic).2.2.2. 2.2.2.1. timp,
2perc,harp,pno,cel,vln I,2vln II,
vla,vcl,db,solo voice [13']
BOOSEY-ENG rent           (G94)

Symphony No. 2
1+pic.1+English horn.2(bass
clar).2(contrabsn). 4.2.2.1.
timp,7perc,pno,acord,harp,strings
[28'] BOOSEY-ENG rent     (G95)

Three Canciones Toreras
[Span] 2(pic).2(English horn).2.2.
4.2.3.1. 2perc,harp,strings,med
solo [9'] (text by Juan
Serrallonga (pseudonym)) BOOSEY-
ENG rent                  (G96)

GERMAN TRYPTICHON PART 2 see Dillon,
James, Helle Nacht

GERMAN TRYPTICHON PART 3 see Dillon,
James, Blitzschlag

GERMETEN, GUNNAR (1947- )
Utslätt
2horn,perc,strings, hardange fiddle
solo [8'30"] NORSKMI      (G97)

GERSTER, OTTMAR (1897-1969)
Concerto for Violin and Orchestra
2.2.2.2. 4.2.2.1. timp,perc,8vln I,
7vln II,6vla,5vcl,4db,vln solo
[31'] sc,pno-cond sc,solo pt
PETERS 03488              (G98)

GERSTER, OTTMAR (cont'd.)

Dresdner Suite: Der Friede
2.2.3.3. 4.3.3.1. timp,perc,8vln I,
7vln II,6vla,5vcl,4db [5'] sc
PETERS 03058 (G99)

GESANG, FOR ORCHESTRA see Plakidis,
Petr

GESANG EINER GEFANGENEN AMSEL see
Kofron, Petr

GESCHICHTE EINES UNBEKANNTEN
SCHAUSPIELERS, DIE: SUITE see
Schnittke, Alfred

GESCHICHTEN AUS DEM WIENERWALD see
Strauss, Johann, [Jr.]

GESCHWIND DIE TÜR GEÖFFNET see Mozart,
Wolfgang Amadeus, Aprite Presto,
Aprite

GESEGNETE, DAS VERFLUCHTE, DAS see
Ruzicka, Peter

GESTURES see Brady, Timothy

GESUALDO DI VENOSA: SIX MADRIGALS see
Skrowaczewski, Stanislaw

GETHSEMANI FRAGMENT see Berkeley,
Michael

GEWALTIG WIE DER TOD see Neubert,
Günter

GEWICKSMANN, VITALI
Concerto for Cembalo, Recorder and
Strings
cembalo,8vln I,7vln II,6vla,5vcl,
4db,rec solo sc PETERS 02488
(G100)

GEWITTER see Cornell, Klaus

GEYSEN, FRANS
Staalkaarten Voor Een Hoboconcert
4.4.4.4. 6.4.3.1. timp,perc,harp,
strings,ob solo [20'] BELGE
(G101)

GHISMONDA: EINLEITUNG ZUM 3. AUFZUG see
Albert, Eugène Francis Charles d'

GHOST IN MACHINE see Proto, Frank

GHOST IN THE MACHINE, THE see Woolrich,
John

GHOSTS OF AN OLD CEREMONY see Larsen,
Elizabeth B. (Libby)

GIBBS, ALAN
Festival Concertino
0.2.0.0. 2.0.0.0. 5vln I,4vln II,
2vla,3vcl,db [13'] BARDIC (G102)

Reflections On A Life
2.2.2.2. 2.2.3.1. timp,perc,harp,
strings,vln solo [19'] BARDIC
(G103)

Viendra l'Aube
string orch [12'] BARDIC (G104)

GIFFORD, KEITH
Dawn On The Chao Praya
4.4.4.4. 6.4.3.1. timp,4perc,2harp,
strings [20'] manuscript BMIC
(G105)

Scarf Of White Stream, A
2perc,pno,strings [21'] manuscript
BMIC (G106)

GIFT FROM THE SEA see Turner, Robert
[Comrie], Symphony in One Movement

GIFT OF THANKSGIVING, THE see Symonds,
Norman

GIFTS see Melnyk, Lubomyr

GILBERT, ANTHONY (1934- )
Certain Lights Reflecting
2(2pic).2(ob d'amore,English
horn).2(bass clar).2(contrabsn).
4.2.3.0. timp,3perc,cel,harp,
strings [19'] SCHOTTS perf mat
rent (G107)
Mez solo,orch [22'] SCHOTT (G108)

Crow-Cry *Op.27
1(pic).1.1(bass clar).1. 1.1.1(bass
trom).0. perc,elec pno,vln,vla,
vcl,db [20'] SCHOTTS perf mat
rent (G109)

Igorochki
2perc,cimbalom,gtr,strings,rec solo
[17'] SCHOTTS perf mat rent
(G110)

Mozart Sampler With Ground
2(pic).2.1+bass clar.2. 2.0.0.0.
2vln,vla,vcl,db [10'] (after KV
550) SCHOTTS perf mat rent (G111)

GILBERT, ANTHONY (cont'd.)

Tree Of Singing Names
1(pic).1(English horn).1(bass
clar).1(contrabsn). 2.1.0.0.
perc,6vln,6vla,4vcl,2db [15']
SCHOTTS perf mat rent (G112)

GILSON, PAUL (1865-1942)
Fanfare Inaugurale
3(pic).2.2.2. 6.3.3.1. timp,4perc,
harp,strings [7'] BREITKOPF-W
(G113)

GINASTERA, ALBERTO (1916-1983)
Creation Of The Maya World, The
see Popol Vuh

Popol Vuh *Op.44
"Creation Of The Maya World, The"
3(2pic).3(English horn).3(clar in
E flat,bass clar).3(contrabsn).
4.4.4.1. timp,4perc,2harp,pno/
cel,strings [26'] BOOSEY-ENG rent
(G114)

GINGA TETSUDO NO KOIBITOTACHI see
Ejiri, Sakae

GIOCATORE D'ANIME see Galante, Carlo

GIOCOSO BUCOLICO see Bull, Edvard
Hagerup

GIOH see Ishii, Maki

GIORDANO, UMBERTO (1867-1948)
Carillon De Noël
(Zani, Giacomo) 1.1.1.1. 1.0.0.0.
timp,strings,solo voice [2'30"]
SONZOGNO rent (G115)

GIOVANNA D'ARCO: SINFONIA see Verdi,
Giuseppe

GIRARD, ANTHONY (1959- )
Préludes, 24 [25']
2.2.2.2. 2.2.0.0. timp,strings
BILLAUDOT (G116)

GIRL OF THE MOUNTAIN, THE see Qu, Xiao-
Song

GIRON, ARSENIO (1932- )
Concerto for Violoncello and
Orchestra
2(pic).1.1.0. 1.0.0.0. perc,strings
without db,vcl solo [13'] sc
CANADIAN MI 1313 G527CO (G117)

Demon's Isle
2(pic).0.2.2. 2.1.0.0. timp&perc,
perc,strings [10'] (1. Arrival 2.
The Fallen 3. Tragic Dance) sc
CANADIAN MI 1100 G527DE (G118)

Sinfonia Concertante for Clarinet,
Piano and Chamber Orchestra
see Sinfonia No. 3

Sinfonia No. 1
2+pic.0.2.0. 2.0.0.0. 2perc,harp,
cel,strings without db [15'] sc
CANADIAN MI1200 G527S1 (G119)

Sinfonia No. 2
1(pic).1.2.1. 2.2.1.0. 4perc,
strings [19'] sc CANADIAN
MI 1100 G527S2 (G120)

Sinfonia No. 3 (Sinfonia Concertante
for Clarinet, Piano and Chamber
Orchestra)
1.0.1.1. 0.0.0.0. perc,strings,clar
solo,pno solo [24'] (Intrada -
Dirge - Scherzo I - Berceuse -
Scherzo I - Finale) sc CANADIAN
MI 1450 G527SI (G121)

GISMONDA see Fevrier, Henri

GISTELINCK, ELIAS
Symphony, Op. 53
3.3.3.3. 4.3.3.1. timp,perc,strings
[25'] BELGE (G122)

GIUBILO see Dvoráček, Jiri

GIUFFRE, GAETANO (1918- )
New York Concerto
2.2.2.2. 4.3.3.0. timp,perc,harp,
strings,pno solo SEESAW (G123)

GIUOCHI DEL PENSIERO see Decsenyi,
Janos

GLACIAL FRAGMENTS see Prezament, Wendy

GLAD DAY see Finnissy, Michael

GLANS, FREDRIK (1966- )
Music for Strings
see Musik För Stråker

Musik För Stråker (Music for Strings)
string orch [20'] NORSKMI (G124)

GLANVILLE-HICKS, PEGGY (1912-1990)
Saul And The Witch Of Endor
0.1.0.0. 0.0.0.0. 3perc,8vln I,7vln
II,6vla,5vcl,4db [20'] sc PETERS
03874 (G125)

GLASER, WERNER WOLF (1910- )
Divertimento Inverso
2.2.1.1. 1.0.0.0. strings,opt bsn/
baritone sax [40'] sc,pts STIM
(G126)

Musica Seria
fl,clar,org,string orch STIM (G127)

Symphony No. 13
2.2.2.2. 4.2.3.1. timp,3perc,
strings [30'] sc STIM (G128)

GLASPERLENSPIEL, DAS see Betancur-
Gonzalez, Valentin, Sinfonia No. 1

GLASS, PAUL
Cinq Chansons Pour Une Princess
Errante
2(pic).2(English horn).2(bass
clar).2(contrabsn). 4.3.2.1.
timp,2perc,harp,pno,strings,Bar
solo [9'] sc,pno red MULL & SCH
M&S 1215- rent (G129)

Concerto for Violoncello
2.2.2.2. 2.2.1.0. timp,2perc,harp,
strings,vcl solo [15'] MULL & SCH
rent (G130)

Concerto Per Pianoforte Estemporaneo
3.3.3.3. 4.4.3.1. harp,4perc,
strings,pno solo [17'] MULL & SCH
rent (G131)

Echanges Per 16 Strumentalisti
1.1.1+bass clar.1. 1.1.1.1. perc,
harp,pno,vln,vcl,db [16'] MULL &
SCH rent (G132)

Ektenia
2.1(English horn).2(bass
clar).2(contrabsn). 4.2.3.1.
timp,2perc,harp,strings [2'30"]
MULL & SCH rent (G133)

Eschatos: Ballett Für Orchester
1.1.1.1. 1.1.1.0. perc,6vln I,6vln
II,4vla,4vcl,2db [20'] MULL & SCH
rent (G134)

Eschatos: Suite No. 1
1.1.1.1. 1.1.1.0. perc,6vln I,6vln
II,4vla,4vcl,2db [7'] MULL & SCH
rent (G135)

Eschatos: Suite No. 2
1.1.1.1. 1.1.1.0. perc,6vln I,6vln
II,4vla,4vcl,2db [8'] MULL & SCH
rent (G136)

Eufonia
string orch [4'] sc,pts MULL & SCH
M&S 1249- (G137)

Lamento Dell'Acqua
2.2.2.2. 2.2.0.0. perc,pno,7-12vln
I,7-10vln II,5-8vla,4-6vcl,3-4db
[20'] sc MULL & SCH M&S 1219-
rent (G138)

Sinfonia No. 1
3.3.2(bass clar).2(contrabsn).
4.3.3.1. timp,perc,harp,strings
[17'] MULL & SCH rent (G139)

Sinfonia No. 2
see Symphonic Suite

Sinfonia No. 3
2.2.2.2.sax. 2.2.1.0. timp,3perc,
harp,strings [38'30"] sc MULL &
SCH M&S 1103 rent (G140)

Sinfonia No. 4
3(pic).3(English horn).3(soprano
clar in E flat,bass
clar).3(contrabsn). 4.4.3.1.
timp,3perc,harp,pno/cel,strings
[24'] sc MULL & SCH M&S rent
(G141)

Symphonic Suite (Sinfonia No. 2)
3.2(English horn).2(bass
clar).2(contrabsn). 4.4.3.1.
4timp,4perc,pno,cel,harp,strings
[18'] MULL & SCH rent (G142)

GLAZUNOV, ALEXANDER KONSTANTINOVICH
(1865-1936)
Ballettszenen, Op. 52
3.2.3.2. 4.3.3.1. timp,6perc,harp,
8vln I,7vln II,6vla,5vcl,4db
[30'] sc BELAIEFF 01555 (G143)

Carnaval (Overture, Op. 45)
(Hartmann) 2.1.2.1. 2.2.2.0. timp,
pno,harp,5vln I,3vln II,vla,3vcl,
db [9'] BELAIEFF 01558 (G144)

GLAZUNOV, ALEXANDER KONSTANTINOVICH
(cont'd.)

Cortège Solennel *Op.91
3.2.3.2. 4.3.3.1. timp,perc,harp,
strings [6'] BELAIEFF            (G145)
3.2.3.2. 4.3.3.1. timp,2perc,8vln
I,7vln II,6vla,5vcl,4db [6'] sc
BELAIEFF                         (G146)

Finnische Fantasie *Op.88
3.3.3.3. 4.3.3.2. timp,perc,harp,
strings [12'] BELAIEFF           (G147)
3.3.3.3. 4.3.3.2. timp,perc,harp,
8vln I,7vln II,6vla,5vcl,4db
[12'] sc BELAIEFF 01578          (G148)

Idylle
2.2.2.2. 4.0.0.0. harp,8vln I,7vln
II,6vla,5vcl,4db [10'] sc
BELAIEFF 01668                   (G149)

Jahreszeiten, Die *Op.67
3.2.2.2. 4.2.3.1. timp,6perc,pno,
cel,harp,8vln I,7vln II,6vla,
5vcl,4db [35'] sc,study sc
BELAIEFF 01584                   (G150)

Konzertwalzer Nr. 1 D-Dur *Op.47
3.2.3.2. 4.2.3.0. timp,5perc,harp,
8vln I,7vln II,6vla,5vcl,4db
[13'] sc PETERS 01593            (G151)

Konzertwalzer Nr. 2 F-Dur *Op.51
3.2.2.2. 4.2.3.0. timp,3perc,harp,
8vln I,7vln II,6vla,5vcl,4db
[10'] sc PETERS 01594            (G152)

Liebeslist
see Ruses D'Amour

- Musikalisches Bild
3.2.2.2. 4.2.3.1. timp,harp,strings
[10'] BELAIEFF                   (G153)

Nocturne, Op. 15, No. 1 (from
Chopiniana (Les Sylphides))
3.2.2.2. 4.2.3.0. timp,3perc,8vln
I,7vln II,6vla,5vcl,4db [3']
BELAIEFF 01568                   (G154)

Overture, Op. 45
see Carnaval

Polonaise, Op. 40, No. 1 (from
Chopiniana (Les Sylphides))
3.2.2.2. 4.2.3.0. timp,3perc,8vln
I,7vln II,6vla,5vcl,4db [3']
BELAIEFF 01567                   (G155)

Raymonda Akt I: Adagio
3.2.3.2. 4.3.3.1. timp,harp,8vln I,
7vln II,6vla,5vcl,4db [5'] sc
BELAIEFF 01619                   (G156)

Raymonda Akt I: Grand Valse
3.2.3.2. 4.3.3.1. timp,4perc,harp,
8vln I,7vln II,6vla,5vcl,4db
[10'] sc BELAIEFF 01630          (G157)

Raymonda Akt I: Valse Fantastique
3.2.3.2. 4.2.0.0. timp,perc,harp,
cel,8vln I,7vln II,6vla,5vcl,4db
[5'] sc BELAIEFF 01636           (G158)

Raymonda Akt I: Valse Fantastique
(S.O.)
2.1.2.1. 2.2.2.0. timp,harmonium,
2vln I,vln II,vla,vcl,4db [5'] sc
BELAIEFF 01637                   (G159)

Raymonda Akt I: Variation III "bis"
3.2.2.2. 2.0.0.0. perc,harp,cel,
8vln I,7vln II,6vla,5vcl,4db [2']
sc BELAIEFF 01639                (G160)

Raymonda Akt II: Danse Garcons Arabes
3.2.3.2. 4.3.0.0. timp,4perc,2vln,
vla,vcl,db [5'] sc BELAIEFF 01620 (G161)

Raymonda Akt II: Grand Pas Espagnol
3.2.3.2. 4.3.3.1. timp,perc,harp,
8vln I,7vln II,6vla,5vcl,4db
[10'] sc BELAIEFF 01628          (G162)

Raymonda Akt III: Coda
3.2.3.2. 4.3.3.1. timp,harp,8vln I,
7vln II,6vla,5vcl,4db [5'] sc
BELAIEFF 01622                   (G163)

Raymonda Akt III: Danse Des Enfants
3.2.3.2. 4.3.3.1. timp,harp,8vln I,
7vln II,6vla,5vcl,4db [5'] sc
BELAIEFF 01621                   (G164)

Raymonda Akt III: Entree & Pas
Clas.Hon.
3.2.3.2. 4.3.3.1. timp,harp,8vln I,
7vln II,6vla,5vcl,4db [5'] sc
BELAIEFF 01623                   (G165)

Raymonda Akt III: Galop
3.2.3.2. 4.3.3.1. timp,harp,8vln I,
7vln II,6vla,5vcl,4db [4'] sc
BELAIEFF 01624                   (G166)

GLAZUNOV, ALEXANDER KONSTANTINOVICH
(cont'd.)

Raymonda Akt III: Pas De Dix
3.2.3.2. 4.3.3.1. timp,6perc,pno,
harp,8vln I,7vln II,6vla,5vcl,4db
[10'] sc BELAIEFF 01633          (G167)

Raymonda Akt III: Variation IV
3.2.2.2. 2.0.0.0. pno,8vln I,7vln
II,6vla,5vcl,4db [5'] sc BELAIEFF
01641                            (G168)

Raymonda: Ballett-Suite Op. 57a
3.2.3.2. 4.3.3.1. timp,6perc,harp,
cel,8vln I,7vln II,6vla,5vcl,4db
[40'] sc,study sc BELAIEFF 01642 (G169)

Raymonda: Garden Party
2.2.2.2. 4.2.3.0. timp,3perc,harp,
8vln I,7vln II,6vla,5vcl,4db
[29'] sc BELAIEFF 01625          (G170)

Raymonda: Grand Pas D'Action
3.2.3.2. 4.3.3.1. timp,3perc,harp,
8vln I,7vln II,6vla,5vcl,4db
[10'] sc BELAIEFF 01627          (G171)

Raymonda: Grand Pas Hongrois
3.2.3.2. 4.3.3.1. timp,perc,cel,
harp,8vln I,7vln II,6vla,5vcl,4db
[10'] sc BELAIEFF 01629          (G172)

Raymonda: Grande Adagio
3.2.3.2. 4.2.3.1. timp,harp,8vln I,
7vln II,6vla,5vcl,4db [5'] sc,
pno-cond sc BELAIEFF 01626       (G173)
(McCanley) 1.1.1.1. 1.1.2.0. perc,
pno,8vln I,7vln II,6vla,5vcl,4db
[5'] sc BELAIEFF 00537           (G174)

Raymonda: Grande Pas D'Action
(Agostini) 2.2.2.1. 1.2.3.0. timp,
perc,8vln I,7vln II,6vla,5vcl,4db
[5'] BELAIEFF 01320              (G175)

Raymonda: Grande Valse
(McCanley) 1.1.1.1. 1.1.2.0. perc,
pno,gtr,8vln I,7vln II,6vla,5vcl,
4db [5'] sc BELAIEFF 01643       (G176)

Raymonda: Pas De Deux
3.2.3.2. 4.3.3.1. timp,4perc,8vln
I,7vln II,6vla,5vcl,4db [10'] sc
BELAIEFF 01631                   (G177)

Raymonda: Pas De Deux No. 2
3.2.3.2. 4.3.3.1. timp,2perc,harp,
8vln I,7vln II,6vla,5vcl,4db
[10'] sc BELAIEFF 01632          (G178)

Raymonda: Pizzicato
(McCanley) 1.1.2.1. 1.1.2.0. perc,
cel,gtr,8vln I,7vln II,6vla,5vcl,
4db [5'] sc BELAIEFF 01644       (G179)

Raymonda: Reprise De La Valse
(McCanley) 1.1.1.1. 1.1.2.0. pno,
gtr,8vln I,7vln II,6vla,5vcl,4db
[5'] sc BELAIEFF 01645           (G180)

Raymonda: Tänze
3.2.3.2. 4.3.3.1. timp,perc,8vln I,
7vln II,6vla,5vcl,4db [23'] sc,
study sc BELAIEFF 01635          (G181)

Raymonda: Variation II
(Agostini) 2.2.2.1. 1.2.3.0. timp,
perc,8vln I,7vln II,6vla,5vcl,4db
[5'] sc BELAIEFF 01638           (G182)

Raymonda: Variation III: Coda
(Agostini) 2.2.2.1. 1.2.3.0. timp,
perc,8vln I,7vln II,6vla,5vcl,4db
[5'] sc BELAIEFF 01640           (G183)

Raymonda: Variation IV
(Agostini) 2.2.2.1. 0.0.0.0. harp,
8vln I,7vln II,6vla,5vcl,4db [5']
sc BELAIEFF 01646                (G184)

Reverie for Horn and Orchestra, Op.
24
2.1.2.2. 0.0.0.0. timp,2harp,8vln
I,7vln II,6vla,5vcl,4db [3'] sc,
solo pt BELAIEFF 01648           (G185)
(Robinson) 3.3.3.3. 4.3.3.1. timp,
harp,8vln I,7vln II,6vla,5vcl,4db
[3'] sc BELAIEFF 01649           (G186)

Romance, Op. 67 (from Die
Jahreszeiten)
1.1.2.1. 2.2.1.0. perc,2pno,2vln I,
vln II,vla,vcl,db [5'] sc
BELAIEFF 01609                   (G187)

Ruses D'Amour *Op.61
"Liebeslist" 3.2.2.2. 4.2.3.1.
timp,7perc,cel,harp,8vln I,7vln
II,6vla,5vcl,4db [47'] sc
BELAIEFF 01650                   (G188)

Salome: Introduktion Und Tanz *Op.90
3.3.2.3. 4.2.3.1. timp,5perc,harp,
8vln I,7vln II,6vla,5vcl,4db
[13'] sc BELAIEFF 01652          (G189)

GLAZUNOV, ALEXANDER KONSTANTINOVICH
(cont'd.)

Serenade Espagnole Op. 20
2.2.2.2. 2.0.0.0. harp,8vln I,7vln
II,6vla,5vcl,4db [5'] sc BELAIEFF
03477                            (G190)

Strophes De Petrarque, 2
3.2.3.2. 4.2.0.0. timp,harp,8vln I,
7vln II,6vla,5vcl,4db [8']
BELAIEFF 01667                   (G191)

Tarantelle, Op. 43 (from Chopiniana
(Les Sylphides))
3.2.2.2. 4.2.3.0. timp,3perc,8vln
I,7vln II,6vla,5vcl,4db [3']
BELAIEFF 01571                   (G192)

Theme and Variations for String
Orchestra, Op. 72
8vln I,7vln II,6vla,5vcl,4db [13']
sc BELAIEFF 02904                (G193)

Theme and Variations, Op. 72 for
Strings
[13'] BELAIEFF                   (G194)

Variationen Über Ein Russisches Thema
3.2.2.2. 4.2.3.1. timp,2perc,harp,
8vln I,7vln II,6vla,5vcl,4db
[25'] sc BELAIEFF 01865          (G195)

Variationen Über Ein Russisches
Volkslied
8vln I,7vln II,6vla,5vcl,4db [5']
study sc BELAIEFF 01867          (G196)

Waltz No. 1 in D, Op. 47
3.2.3.2. 4.2.3.0. timp,perc,harp,
strings [13'] BELAIEFF           (G197)

Waltz No. 2 in F, Op. 51
3.2.2.2. 4.2.3.0. timp,perc,harp,
strings [10'] BELAIEFF           (G198)

Waltz, Op. 64, No. 2 (from Chopiniana
(Les Sylphides))
3.2.2.2. 4.2.3.0. timp,perc,8vln I,
7vln II,6vla,5vcl,4db [9']
BELAIEFF 01570                   (G199)

GLENZ see Jeths, Willem

GLICK, SRUL IRVING (1934-    )
Concerto for Piano and Orchestra
"Song Of Joy" 2.2.2.2. 2.0.0.0.
perc,strings,pno solo [22'] sc
CANADIAN MI 1361 G559CO          (G200)

Concerto for Viola and String
Orchestra in One Movement
[27'] sc,solo pt CANADIAN
MI1612 G559CO                    (G201)

Concerto for Violin and Orchestra
"Song Of Ascension" 2.2.2.2.
2.2.2.0. timp,2perc,strings,vln
solo [27'] sc CANADIAN
MI 1311 G559CO                   (G202)

Sonata for Orchestra in One Movement
2(opt pic).2(English horn).2.2.
3.2.1.0. timp,perc,strings [15']
sc CANADIAN MI 1100 G559SO       (G203)

Song Of Ascension
see Concerto for Violin and
Orchestra

Song Of Joy
see Concerto for Piano and
Orchestra

GLICKMAN, SYLVIA (1932-    )
Walls Are Quiet Now, The
2.2.2.2. 2.2.0.0. timp,perc,strings
[14'] (holocaust remembrance)
HILDEGARD 09433A study sc f.s.
sc,pts rent                      (G204)
2.2.2.2. 4.2.2.1. timp,3perc,
strings [14'] (holocaust
remembrance) HILDEGARD 09433B
study sc f.s., sc,pts rent       (G205)

GLIÈRE, REINHOLD MORITZOVICH
(1875-1956)
Syrènes, Les *Op.33
4.4.4.3. 6.3.3.1. timp,perc,cel,
strings [15'] study sc BELAIEFF
EP 528                           (G206)

GLIMMER BROKE see Underhill, Owen

GLINKA, MIKHAIL IVANOVICH (1804-1857)
Leben Für Den Zaren, Ein: Arie D.
Sussanin
2.2.2.2. 2.0.2.1. 8vln I,7vln II,
6vla,5vcl,4db [5'] BELAIEFF 01692 (G207)

Leben Für Den Zaren, Ein: Arie Des
Wanja
2.2.2.2. 4.2.3.1. timp,harp,8vln I,
7vln II,6vla,5vcl,4db [5']
BELAIEFF 02468                   (G208)

GLINKA, MIKHAIL IVANOVICH (cont'd.)

Leben Für Den Zaren, Ein: Mazurka Und
Finale
2.2.2.2. 4.2.3.0. timp,pno,8vln I,
7vln II,6vla,5vcl,4db [5']
BELAIEFF 01691                    (G209)

Leben Für Den Zaren, Ein: Overture
2.2.2.2. 4.2.3.0. timp,strings
[10'] BREITKOPF-W                 (G210)

Valse-Fantaisie
2.2.2.2. 2.2.1.0. timp,perc,strings
[8'] BREITKOPF-W                  (G211)

GLOBO see Ingvaldsen, Didrick

GLOBOKAR, VINKO (1934-    )
Standpunkte
4.4.4.4. 6.4.4.1. timp,3perc,
strings,instrumental ensemble
soli, solo voices,cor [100']
PETERS                            (G212)

GLÖCKCHEN DES EREMITEN, DAS see
Maillart, Louis Aime, Dragons De
Villars, Les

GLORIA PATRI see Cimarosa, Domenico

GLOSA PRO ORCHESTR see Cotek, Pavel

GLOSSY-LEAVED FOREST, THE see Ikebe,
Shin-Ichiro

GLUCK, CHRISTOPH WILLIBALD, RITTER VON
(1714-1787)
Armida: Ballettmusik
1.2.2.2. 2.0.0.0. strings [15']
BREITKOPF-W                       (G213)

Concerto for Flute
orch,fl solo BOIS                 (G214)

Don Juan: Four Dances
(Mozart, Leopold; Eisen, Cliff)
2ob,2bsn,2horn,2vln,vla,vcl,db
[7'] ARTARIA AE169                (G215)

Don Juan: Vier Sätze
2.2.0.2. 2.2.1.0. strings [20']
BREITKOPF-W                       (G216)

Gavotte for Strings
see Iphigénie En Aulide

Iphigénie En Aulide (Gavotte for
Strings)
strings [2'50"] LEDUC             (G217)

Menuet d'Orphée
fl,strings BOIS                   (G218)

Parida Ed Elena: Balletmusik
0.2.2.0. 2.2.3.0. timp,strings
[19'] BREITKOPF-W                 (G219)

GLÜCKLICHEN 90ER see Deutsch, Peter

GNGLT see Larsson, Hokan

GO AHEAD see Huber, Nicolaus A.

GOD SAVE THE KING see Paganini, Niccolo

GODAM UN BRIVIBAI see Kenins,
Talivaldis, Honour And Freedom

GODARD, BENJAMIN LOUIS PAUL (1849-1895)
Allegretto *Waltz
(Cohen, Shimon) "Idylle" string
orch,fl solo [10'] PRESSER rent
(G220)
Idylle
see Allegretto

GODDESS OF MERCY, THE see Chan, Ka Nin

GODS GO A BEGGING, THE see Handel,
George Frideric

GODS GO A-BEGGING SUITE see Handel,
George Frideric

GODZINSKY, GEORGE DE
Finnische Volkslieder (Suite No. 3)
harp,string orch,vln solo [18'40"]
sc,pts BUSCH HBM 058 rent (G221)

Polka
see Säkkijärven-Polka

Rhapsodie Romantique (Rhapsody for
Piano and Orchestra)
2(pic).1.2.1. 4.2.3.1. timp,perc,
strings,pno solo [12'30"] sc,set
BUSCH HBM 009 rent                (G222)

Rhapsody for Piano and Orchestra
see Rhapsodie Romantique

Romance for Violin and Orchestra
see Weisse Nächte Im Norden


GODZINSKY, GEORGE DE (cont'd.)

Säkkijärven-Polka (Polka) Finn
2(pic).1.2(bass clar).1. 3.3.3.1.
timp,perc,harp,strings [3'40"]
sc,set BUSCH HBM 035 rent (G223)

Sechs Finnische Volkslieder (Suite
No. 1)
harp,string orch,vln solo [11'20"]
sc,pts BUSCH DM 031 rent (G224)

Suite No. 1
see Sechs Finnische Volkslieder

Suite No. 2
see Volksmelodien Und Tänze Aus
Finnland

Suite No. 3
see Finnische Volkslieder

Trompeten In Tirol (Waltz for 3
Trumpets and Orchestra)
2.1.2.1. 4.0.3.1. timp,perc,
strings,3trp soli [4'25"] sc,set
BUSCH HBM 035 rent                (G225)

Volksmelodien Und Tänze Aus Finnland
(Suite No. 2)
harp,string orch,vln solo [18'5"]
sc,pts BUSCH DM 035 rent (G226)

Waltz for 3 Trumpets and Orchestra
see Trompeten In Tirol

Weisse Nächte Im Norden (Romance for
Violin and Orchestra)
2.2(English horn).2.2. 4.0.0.0.
timp,perc,harp,cel,strings,vln
solo [4'] sc,set BUSCH DM 062
rent                              (G227)

GOEHR, ALEXANDER (1932-    )
Behold The Sun *Op.44a
1.1.1.1. 1.1.1.0. vibra,pno,2vln,
vla,db [15'] (concert aria)
SCHOTTS perf mat rent             (G228)

Cambridge Hocket *Op.57
3(pic).2+English horn.3.3. 0.2.3.0.
2perc,pno,strings,4horn solo [8']
SCHOTTS perf mat rent             (G229)

Colossos Or Panic *Op.55
3(alto fl).2+English horn.3(clar in
E flat)+bass clar.3. 4.3.3.1.
perc,pno,harp,strings [25'] study
sc SCHOTTS ED 11847 perf mat rent
(G230)

Deluge, The *Op.7
1.0.0.0. 1.1.0.0. harp,vln,vla,vcl,
db,SA soli [16'] (text after
Leonardo da Vinci) study sc
SCHOTTS ED 10703 perf mat rent
(G231)

Fugue On The Notes Of The Fourth
Psalm *Op.38b
strings [16'] study sc SCHOTTS
ED 11403 perf mat rent            (G232)

...A Musical Offering (J.S.B.
1985)... *Op.46
1.0.2(bass clar).0. 1.1.1.0. perc,
pno,3vln,2vla,db study sc SCHOTTS
ED 12257 perf mat rent            (G233)

Romanza On The Notes Of The Fourth
Psalm *Op.38c
strings,2vln&2vla soli [20'] study
sc SCHOTTS ED 11109 perf mat rent
(G234)

Still Lands
2(alto fl).1.2(bass clar).1.
2.1.1.0. timp,strings [15']
SCHOTTS perf mat rent             (G235)

GOENS, DANIEL VAN
Concerto for Violoncello
2.1.1.1. 1.0.0.0. timp,strings,vcl
solo [18'] LEDUC                  (G236)

GOEPFERT, KARL ANDREAS (1768-1818)
Concerto for Clarinet and Orchestra
clar solo,orch KUNZELMANN 10248 ipr
(G237)

GOETHALS, LUCIEN (1931-    )
Concierto De La Luz Y Las Tinieblas
1.1.1.1. 1.1.1.1. 2perc,strings
without vla,org solo [26'] BELGE
(G238)

GOEYVAERTS, KAREL (1923-1993)
Aanloop En Kreet (Versie 2)
see Aquarius, No. 4 (2nd Version)

Aquarius, Act I
3.3.3.3. 4.3.3.1. timp,perc,cel,
pno,strings,8S&8Bar BELGE (G239)

Aquarius, Act II
3.3.3.3. 4.3.3.1. timp,perc,cel,
pno,strings,8S&8Bar BELGE (G240)

Aquarius, No. 2 (2nd Version)
"Zang Van Aquarius, De (Versie 2)"
3.3.3.3. 4.3.3.0. pno,cel,strings


GOEYVAERTS, KAREL (cont'd.)

[9'] BELGE                        (G241)

Aquarius, No. 3 (2nd Version)
"Opbouw (Versie 2)" 3.3.3.3.
4.3.3.1. timp,perc,pno,strings
[12'] BELGE                       (G242)

Aquarius, No. 4 (2nd Version)
"Aanloop En Kreet (Versie 2)"
3.3.3.3. 4.3.3.1. timp,perc,pno,
strings [14'18"] BELGE            (G243)

Diaphonie
2.3.5.2. 3.1.5.1. pno&hpsd,harp,
24vln,12db [15'] BELGE            (G244)

Heilige Stad, De
1.1.1.0. 1.1.1.0. timp,perc,strings
[13'30"] BELGE                    (G245)

Opbouw (Versie 2)
see Aquarius, No. 3 (2nd Version)

Opus 6 Met 180 Klankvoorwerpen
1.1.2.0. 1.1.0.0. xylo,cel,pno,
harp,gtr,vln,vla,vcl,db [11'30"]
BELGE                             (G246)

Zang Van Aquarius, De (Versie 2)
see Aquarius, No. 2 (2nd Version)

GOGOL-SUITE see Schnittke, Alfred

GOLD AND THE SEÑOR COMMANDANTE: BALLET
SUITE see Bergsma, William Laurence

GOLDBERG, THEO (1921-    )
Beaux' Stratagem, The
see Music To The Beaux' Stratagem

Caro Sassone, Il
"Concerto For Flügelhorn And
Orchestra With Obligato Trumpets
After J. A. Hasse" timp,harp,
strings,flügelhorn solo, 2
obligato trumpets [15'] sc
CANADIAN MI 1435 G618CA           (G247)

Concerto For Flügelhorn And Orchestra
With Obligato Trumpets After J.
A. Hasse
see Caro Sassone, Il

Music To The Beaux' Stratagem
"Beaux' Stratagem, The" 2.2.2.2.
4.2.0.0. timp,harp,strings (1.
Sinfonia 2. Trifle 3. Ballet
Entr'acte 4. Second Trifle To The
Tune 5. Final Tableau) sc
CANADIAN MI 1100 G618MU           (G248)

GOLDEN see Plain, Gerald

GOLDEN HEART see Warner, Scott

GOLDEN ROAD TO SAMARKAND, THE see
Blyton, Carey

GOLDEN ROMANCE see Alan, Charles

GOLDMANN, FRIEDRICH (1941-    )
Ensemblekonzert II
1.1(English horn).1.1. 1.1.1.0.
2perc,harp,2vln,vla,vcl,db [18']
sc PETERS EP 10362                (G249)

Exkursion
3+pic.2+English horn.2+bass clar.2.
4.3.3.0. timp,2perc,gtr,strings
[25'] (music for orchestra with
Henrico Sagittario) PETERS (G250)

Fast Erstarrte Unruhe...2
1.0.1.0. 0.0.1.0. pno,vibra,2vln,
vla,vcl [11'] sc PETERS 04484
(G251)

Fast Erstarrte Unruhe...3
1.0.1.0. 1.0.1.0. pno,gtr,vibra,
2vln,vla,vcl,db [13'] sc PETERS
04561                             (G252)

In Memoriam Paul Dessau
5vln I,4vln II,3vla,2vcl,db [5'] sc
PETERS 02911                      (G253)

Klangszenen 1
3.2.3.2. 3.2.2.1. 3perc,2harp,10vln
I,8vln II,6vla,6vcl,4db,
Saalmusik: pic, ob, eorg, 2vln
[18'] sc PETERS 02190             (G254)

Klangszenen 2
3.3.3.3. 4.3.3.1. 3perc,2harp,8vln
I,7vln II,6vla,5vcl,4db [20'] sc
PETERS 02598                      (G255)

Querstrebige Verbindungen
3.0.2+bass clar.0. 0.0.0.0. 3perc,
pno,vln,vla,vcl [30'] sc PETERS
03515                             (G256)

Schweriner Serenade
2.1.2.1. 1.1.1.0. timp,perc,8vln,
6vla,5vcl,4db [18'] sc PETERS

GOLDMANN, FRIEDRICH (cont'd.)

03063                                    (G257)

Sinfonia No. 3
3.2.3.2. 3.2.2.1. timp,2perc,pno,
harp,8vln I,7vln II,6vla,5vcl,4db
[28'] sc PETERS 02651            (G258)

Sinfonia No. 4
4.4.3.3. 4.3.3.1. 5perc,harp,8vln
I,7vln II,6vla,5vcl,4db [43'] sc
PETERS 02287                     (G259)

Sonata A Quattro
1.1.1.1. 1.1.1.1. 4perc,vln,vla,
vcl,db [21'] PETERS              (G260)

Spannungen Eingegrenzt
3.3.3.3. 4.3.3.1. timp,perc,harp,
strings [18'] PETERS            (G261)

GOLDMARK, KARL (1830-1915)
Im Frühling  *Op.36, Overture
3.2.2.2. 4.3.3.1. timp,strings
[10'] BREITKOPF-W               (G262)

GOLDREGEN see Waldteufel, Emile

GOLDSCHMIDT, BERTHOLD (1903-1996)
Clouds
2(pic).1+English horn.2.2. 2.2.0.0.
timp,strings,solo voice [4']
(text by Rupert Brooke) BOOSEY-
ENG rent                        (G263)

Concerto for Clarinet
2(pic).2(English horn).0+bass
clar.2(contrabsn). 2.2.0.0. timp,
perc,harp,strings,clar solo [21']
BOOSEY-ENG rent                 (G264)

Concerto for Violin
2(pic).2(English horn).2.2.
2.2.0.0. timp,perc,strings,vln
solo [24'] BOOSEY-ENG rent      (G265)

Concerto for Violoncello
2(pic).2(English horn).2.2.
2.2.3.0. timp,perc,harp,strings,
vcl solo [20'] BOOSEY-ENG rent
                                (G266)

Greek Suite  *folk song,Greek
2(pic).2.2.2. 2.2.2.0. timp,perc,
strings [13'] BOOSEY-ENG rent   (G267)

Marche Militaire
2(pic).2.2.2. 4.2.3.1. timp,perc,
strings [6'] BOOSEY-ENG rent
                                (G268)

Mediterranean Songs
2.2(English horn).2(bass clar).2.
4.2.0.0. timp,3perc,harp,strings,
T solo [20'] (text by Byron,
James Stephens, Lawrence Durrell,
Bernard Spencer, James Elroy
Flecker, and Shelley) BOOSEY-ENG
rent                            (G269)

GOLGATHA see Kirchner, Volker David

GOLOVIN MUSIC, THE see Roman, Johan
Helmich, Golovinmusiken

GOLOVINMUSIKEN see Roman, Johan Helmich

GOLVIN-MUSIKEN BERI 1 see Roman, Johan
Helmich

GOMEL LE'ISH HASSID see Sheriff, Noam

GONDAI, ATSUHIKO (1965-    )
Dies Irae & Lacrimosa
orch [18'] JAPAN                (G270)

Seven Choral Variations To Silence
orch [16'] JAPAN                (G271)

GONNEVILLE, MICHEL (1950-    )
À Deux
2orch, Orchestra 1: 1.1.1.1.
1.1.0.0. timp, strings (4-4-3-2-
1): Orchestra 2: 1.1.1.1.
1.1.0.0. timp, strings (4-4-3-2-
1) [13'] sc CANADIAN
MI 1100 G639AD                  (G272)

GOOD KING WENCESLAS see Mayer, William
Robert

GOORMANS, RAF
Requiem Per La Morte Di Un Povero
strings,horn solo [18'] BELGE
                                (G273)

GOOSSENS, [SIR] EUGENE (1893-1962)
Coronation Fanfare
3(pic).2(English horn).2(bass
clar).2(contrabsn). 4.4.3.1.
perc,harp,strings BOOSEY-ENG rent
                                (G274)

Cowboy Fantasy  *Op.61, film
1(pic).1(English horn).1.1.
1.1.0.0. perc,harp,strings
BOOSEY-ENG rent                 (G275)

GORDON, JEROLD JAMES
Calaveras
3.3.3.3. 4.3.3.1. timp,2perc,harp,
strings [19'] LENGNICK          (G276)

GORECKI, HENRYK MIKOLAJ (1933-    )
Concerto-Cantata  *Op.65
4(pic).4.4.4. 6.4.3.1. perc,harp,
16-18vln I,14-16vln II,12-14vla,
10-12vcl,8-10db,fl&alto fl solo
[22'] BOOSEY-ENG rent           (G277)

Concerto for Harpsichord and String
Orchestra, Op. 40
6vln I,6vln II,4vcl,4vcl,2db,hpsd
solo [9'] BOOSEY-ENG rent       (G278)
16vln I.14vln II,12vla,10vcl,8db,
pno solo [9'] BOOSEY-ENG rent
                                (G279)

Genesis II: Canti Strumentali
*Op.19,No.2
pic,fl,trp,mand,gtr,pno 4-hands,
2perc,3vln,3vla [8'] BOOSEY-ENG
rent                            (G280)

Genesis III: Monodramma  *Op.19,No.3
13perc,6db,S solo [10'] (text by
the composer) BOOSEY-ENG rent
                                (G281)

Kleines Requiem Für Eine Polka
*Op.66
1.1.1.1. 1.1.1.0. perc,pno,2vln,
vla,vcl,db [25'] BOOSEY-ENG rent
                                (G282)

GORGON see Rouse, Christopher

GOSSEC, FRANÇOIS JOSEPH (1734-1829)
Sinfonia in B flat
2ob,2horn,2vln,vla,vcl,db [12']
ARTARIA AE009                   (G283)

Sinfonia in G
2ob,2horn,2vln,vla,vcl,db [14']
ARTARIA AE008                   (G284)

Tambourin
(Cohen, Shimon) string orch,fl solo
[1'30"] PRESSER rent            (G285)

GOTISCHES POEM see Montvilas, Vytautas

GÖTTERDÄMMERUNG: SCHLUSSGESANG DER
BRÜNNHILDE see Wagner, Richard

GOTTRON, A.
Händelsche Orgelkonzerte
strings,fl,harmonium,opt 2ob&bsn
BÖHM                            (G286)

GÖTZE, HEINRICH (1836-1906)
Serenade No. 2 in G, Op. 23
strings [11'] BREITKOPF-W       (G287)

GOUGEON, DENIS (1951-    )
Concerto Dello Spirito
3+pic.2.2.2. 2.2.3.1. 4perc,pno,
strings sc CANADIAN
MI 1100 G691CO                  (G288)

Dialogues
2.2.2.2. 2.2.2.0. 8vln I,6vln II,
5vla,4vcl,2db,marimba solo sc
CANADIAN MI 1340 G691DI         (G289)

Expensive Embarrassment Suite, An
1.1.1.1. 2.2.1.1. timp&perc,strings
sc CANADIAN MI1200 G691EX       (G290)

GOULD, MORTON (1913-1996)
Classical Variations
orch sc SCHIRM.G ED3773         (G291)

Jogger And The Dinosaur
narrator,orch sc SCHIRM.G ED3915
                                (G292)

Minute Plus Waltz Rag
orch set SCHIRM.G ED3848        (G293)

Notes Of Remembrance
orch sc SCHIRM.G ED3812         (G294)

Stringmusic
orch sc SCHIRM.G ED3979         (G295)

GOUNOD, CHARLES FRANÇOIS (1818-1893)
Faust: Balletmusik
2.2.2.2. 4.2+2cornet.3.1. timp,
perc,4harp,strings [9']
BREITKOPF-W                     (G296)

GRAAP, LOTHAR (1933-    )
Concerto Breve
2.1.0.1. 0.1.0.0. timp,strings
[14'] sc,pts BREITKOPF-W
PB-OB 4056L                     (G297)

GRABNER, HERMANN (1886-1969)
Perkeo (Suite for Winds) Op.15
2.2.2.3. 4.0.0.0. strings [16']
KAHNT                           (G298)

Suite for Winds
see Perkeo

GRABOVSKY, LEONID (1935-    )
Meditation
see Zwei Stücke, For Strings

Pathetisches Rezitativ
see Zwei Stücke, For Strings

Vier Inventionen, For Chamber
Orchestra
1.1.1.alto sax. 1.1.1.1. timp,
perc,elec gtr,cel&hpsd&pno,harp,
strings [5'] SIKORSKI perf mat
rent                            (G299)

Zwei Stücke, For Strings
SIKORSKI perf mat rent
contains: Meditation;
Pathetisches Rezitativ          (G300)

GRADATION AND OBELISK see Okita,
Daisuke

GRAHAM, PETER (1952-    )
Concerto for Horn, Violin, Piano and
Orchestra
4.2.2.2. 0.3.3.1. perc,org,strings,
horn&vln&pno soli, cornamusa
[23'] CESKY HUD.                (G301)

GRAHN, ULF (1942-    )
As The Time Passes By
2(pic).2.2.2. 2.2.1.0. timp,harp,
strings [8'] sc STIM            (G302)

Morning Rush (from Three Orchestra
Pieces)
orch [2'] STIM                  (G303)

Morning Whisper (from Three Orchestra
Pieces)
orch [3'] STIM                  (G304)

Pezzo
2(pic).2.2.2. 2.2.2.1. timp,perc,
harp/pno,strings [10'] sc STIM
                                (G305)

Pieces For The Nieces
2.2.2.2. 2.2.1.0. perc,harp,strings
[12'] (Entrance to the land of
dreams; Dream at the seashore;
The dreamlight of the horizon;
Dance of..; Clouds of dreamland;
The dreambird's lullaby; Exit)
STIM                            (G306)

Tale, A
2(pic).2.2.2. 2.2.2.1. timp,perc,
harp,strings [8'] sc STIM       (G307)

GRAINGER, ELLA
Honey Pot Bee
1.0.1.0.soprano sax. 0.0.0.0. harp,
pno,harmonium,vibra/marimba,2vln,
vla,vcl,db,solo voice [3'] BARDIC
                                (G308)

To Echo
1+pic.0.2+bass clar.1.alto
sax.tenor sax. 0.0.0.0. vibra/
harp/pno,vla,vcl,db,opt vln,solo
voice [2'30"] BARDIC            (G309)

GRAINGER, PERCY ALDRIDGE (1882-1961)
Blithe Bells (J.S.Bach)
2.1.2.1.alto sax. 1.1.1.0. perc,
pno,strings [5'] SCHOTTS perf mat
rent                            (G310)

Bridal Lullaby, A "Howards End Theme
Music"
(Gibbs, Alan) strings,harp/pno,opt
T solo,opt SSATBB [6'] BARDIC
                                (G311)
(Pickard, John) 2.2.2.1. 2.0.0.0.
pno,2vln,vla,vcl,db [2'30"]
BARDIC                          (G312)

Brigg Fair
(Conway, Joseph) strings,T solo
[3'45"] BARDIC                  (G313)

Colleen Dhas Or 'The Valley Lay
Smiling'
fl,English horn,gtr/harp,2vln,vla,
vcl,db [30'] BARDIC             (G314)

Country Gardens
(King, Reginald) 3vln,vla,vcl,pno
[3'] BARDIC                     (G315)
(Ould, Barry Peter) 1.1.1.1.alto
sax. 1.1.0.0. harmonium,pno,perc,
2vln,vla,vcl,db [3'] BARDIC     (G316)

Crew Of The Long Serpent
orch [4'35"] BARDIC             (G317)

Died For Love
string orch/strings without db [2']
BARDIC                          (G318)

Dreamery
2.2.2+bass clar.2.2alto sax.tenor
sax.baritone sax. 4.3.3.1. org,
vibra,marimba,pno,3vln,2vla,2vcl,
db,Bar solo [6'] BARDIC         (G319)
string orch [6'] BARDIC         (G320)

GRAINGER, PERCY ALDRIDGE (cont'd.)

Early One Morning
2.0.0.1+contrabsn. 1.1.0.1. 4vln,
2vla,2-3vcl,2db,S/Bar solo
[3'30"] BARDIC                    (G321)
string orch [1'30"] BARDIC        (G322)

Eastern Intermezzo (from Youthful
Suite)
2+pic.2.2.2. 4.1.3.1. timp,perc,
cel,pno,harp,org,strings [2']
SCHOTTS perf mat rent             (G323)

English Dance
pipe/elec org,harmonium,pno,
strings/strings without db,solo
voice [10'] BARDIC                (G324)

Fisher's Boarding House
2.2.2.2. 2.0.0.0. strings [7']
BARDIC                            (G325)

Free Music No. 1
string orch/string quar [30']
BARDIC                            (G326)

Handel In The Strand
1.1.1.1. 1.1.0.0. harmonium,pno,
perc,strings [4'30"] BARDIC
                                  (G327)

Harvest Hymn
1.1.2+bass clar.2.alto sax.soprano
sax.tenor sax.
1.1.1(euphonium).0. org&
harmonium,pno,strings,opt cor
[4'] SCHOTTS perf mat rent (G328)

Hill-Song No. 2
3+pic.3+English horn.3+bass clar.2+
contrabsn. 2.3.0.0. euphonium/
baritone horn,cym,strings [5'30"]
BARDIC                            (G329)

Irish Tune From County Derry
1.1.0.0. 0.1.0.0. cym,harmonium,
strings,solo voice [4'] BARDIC
                                  (G330)

Kleines Variationen-Form
2.2.2.2. 2.2.0.0. strings BARDIC
                                  (G331)

Lonely Desert Man Sees The Tents Of
The Happy Tribes, The
0.0.2.2.alto sax. 1.1.0.0. 2gtr,
2marimba,vibra/harp,pno,strings
[2'30"] BARDIC                    (G332)
2gtr,2marimba,vibra/harp,pno,
strings,STBar soli [2'30"] BARDIC
                                  (G333)

Lord Maxwell's Goodnight
string orch,solo voice,2vln&2vla&
2vcl soli [3'30"] BARDIC (G334)
2+pic.2.2+bass clar.2. 2.2.2.0.
strings [3'30"] BARDIC            (G335)
strings,unis men cor [3'30"] BARDIC
                                  (G336)
string orch/string quar,high solo
[3'30"] BARDIC                    (G337)

Lord Peter's Stable Boy
0.0.1.0.soprano sax.alto sax.tenor
sax. 1.1.1.0+euphonium. timp,
perc,pno&pno 4-hands,harmonium&
org,strings [3'] SCHOTTS perf mat
rent                              (G338)

Love Song Of Har Dyal, The
0.1.0.1. 0.0.0.0. harp,harmonium,
pno,strings,S solo [2'30"] BARDIC
                                  (G339)

Merry King, The
1+pic.0.2+bass clar.2+
contrabsn.baritone sax.bass sax.
1.1.0.0. pno,harmonium,strings
[3'45"] BARDIC                    (G340)

Mock Morris
1+pic.1.1.1. 1.1.0.1. pno,
harmonium,strings [3'30"] BARDIC
                                  (G341)

Near Woodstock Town
(Ould, Barry Peter) string orch
[2'30"] BARDIC                    (G342)

Nightingale And The Two Sisters, The
2+pic.2.4+bass clar.2+
contrabsn.4sax. 4.3.3.1. timp,
perc,org,harmonium,pno,2harp,
strings [4'] SCHOTTS perf mat
rent                              (G343)

Power Of Love, The
harmonium,pno,strings,opt 2horn,opt
solo voices [3'15"] BARDIC (G344)

Power Of Rome And The Christian
Heart, The
2+2pic.2+English horn.3+clar in E
flat+bass clar.2.soprano sax.alto
sax.tenor sax. 4.3.3.0.
euphonium,baritone horn,perc,
strings [12'] BARDIC              (G345)

Proud Vesselil
see Stalt Vesselil

GRAINGER, PERCY ALDRIDGE (cont'd.)

Scherzo for String Orchestra
BARDIC                            (G346)

Sea-Song
pipe/harmonium/pno,strings [1'25"]
BARDIC                            (G347)
string orch [1'25"] BARDIC        (G348)

Shoemaker From Jerusalem, The
1.0.0.0. 0.1.0.0. pno 4-hands,
strings [4'] BARDIC               (G349)

Six Dukes Went A-Fishin'
(Bedford, Steuart) strings,solo
voice [2'45"] BARDIC              (G350)

Stalt Vesselil
(Tall, David) "Proud Vesselil" fl,
English horn,strings [2'30"]
BARDIC                            (G351)

Thanksgiving Song
1+pic.0.2+bass clar.1.alto sax.
1.1.0.1. 4perc,harmonium,strings
BARDIC                            (G352)

There Were Three Friends
2.0.2.2. 2.0.0.0. strings [2']
BARDIC                            (G353)

Train Music
(Rathburn, Eldon) 3+pic.3+English
horn.3+bass clar.3+contrabsn.
4.3.2+bass trom.0. strings
[2'30"] BARDIC                    (G354)

Under En Bro
1.0.1.0. 0.1.0.0. 2xylo,2marimba,
3tubular bells,2pno,strings
[3'30"] BARDIC                    (G355)

We Were Dreamers
2.2.2.2. 4.0.0.0. strings [4']
BARDIC                            (G356)

Ye Banks And Braes O'Bonnie Doon
1+pic.1.3+clar in E flat+2bass
clar.2.2sax. 2.2.2.1. harmonium/
org,strings [3'] SCHOTTS perf mat
rent                              (G357)

Youthful Rapture
fl,clar/trp/soprano sax,horn/alto
sax,glock,harmonium/org,pno,harp,
strings,vcl solo [6'] SCHOTTS
perf mat rent                     (G358)

Youthful Suite
2+pic.2+English horn.2+bass clar.2+
contrabsn. 4.3.3.1. timp,perc,
harmonium,pno,harp,strings [26']
SCHOTTS perf mat rent             (G359)

GRANADA SCENES: SPANISH BALLET SUITE
see Zuckert, Leon, Escenas
Granadinas: Suite De Ballet Español

GRAND LINE see Hagen, Daron

GRAND NATIONAL FROM "CHAMPIONS" see
Davis, Carl

GRAND PIANOLA SCORE see Adams, John

GRAND RIDGE ROAD see Dreyfus, George

GRAND SPIRAL see Ung, Chinary

GRANDERT, JOHNNY (1939-    )
Staccato
string orch [15'] sc,pts STIM
                                  (G360)

Symphony No. 7
4(pic).3(English horn).3(bass
clar).3(contrabsn).baritone sax.
4.4.4.1. timp,2perc,strings [40']
sc STIM                           (G361)

GRANDIS, RENATO DE
see DE GRANDIS, RENATO

GRANDJANY, MARCEL (1891-1975)
Concerto for Harp, Horn and Orchestra
see Symphonic Poem

Symphonic Poem (Concerto for Harp,
Horn and Orchestra)
INTERNAT.S. sc,pts rent, solo pt,
pno red                           (G362)

GRANGE, PHILIP
Focus And Fade
3.3.3.3. 4.3.3.1. timp,5perc,harp,
strings [20'] BMIC                (G363)

GRANT, STEWART (1948-    )
Landscapes
2(pic).2(English horn).2.2.
4.2.3(bass trom).1. timp,2perc,
pno,strings [20'] PRESSER rent
                                  (G364)

Spring Came Dancing
string orch PRESSER rent          (G365)

GRANT, STEWART (cont'd.)

Symphony "Et In Terra"
2.2(English horn).2.2. 4.2.3(bass
trom).1. timp,strings PRESSER
rent                              (G366)

GRANTHAM, DONALD (1947-    )
Fantasy On Mr. Hyde's Song
2(pic).2.2(bass clar).2. 2.2.1.0.
2perc,pno&cel,strings [7'] PEER
rent                              (G367)

To The Wind's Twelve Quarters
2+pic.2.2.2+contrabsn. 4.3.3.1.
timp,3perc,pno&cel,harp,strings
[7'] PEER rent                    (G368)

GRAPHIC 6: TOWN see Freedman, Harry

GRATHAWAI see Boyd, Anne

GRATIA see Ám, Magnar

GRÄTZER WALZER see Schubert, Franz
(Peter)

GRAUN, JOHANN GOTTLIEB (1703-1771)
Concerto for Violin, Viola and String
Orchestra in C minor
(Janetzky; Richter) string orch,
cont,vln&vla soli [23']
BREITKOPF-W                       (G369)

Sinfonia in D
(Schneider, M.) 2.0.0.2. 2.3.0.0.
timp,strings,cont [16']
BREITKOPF-W                       (G370)

GRAUPNER, CHRISTOPH (1683-1760)
Concerto
2trp,4trom,strings,cont KUNZELMANN
ipa sc 10165A, oct 10165 (G371)

Concerto for 2 Flutes and String
Orchestra, No. 35, in E minor
(Braun) 2fl,string orch KUNZELMANN
ipa sc 10090A, oct 10090   (G372)

Concerto for Trumpet, Strings and
Continuo, No. 14
strings,cont,trp solo [15']
DEUTSCHER                         (G373)

Concerto for Viola d'Amore, Strings
and Continuo
strings,cont,vla d'amore/vla solo
MÖSELER 400.165                   (G374)

Concerto for Viola, Strings and
Continuo
vln I,vln II,vla,vcl,db,cont,vla
solo MÖSELER sc 40.134-00, solo
pt 40.134-01, pts 40.134-02, set
40.134-09                         (G375)

Concerto No. 2 in D
trp in D,string orch,cont
KUNZELMANN ipa sc 10172A, oct
10172                             (G376)

GRAY GLOVE see Underhill, Owen

GREAT EXPECTATIONS see Dreyfus, George

GREAT LITTLE TRAIN OF WALES, A see
Rathburn, Eldon

GREAT MOON, THE see Raminsh, Imant,
Sahali

GREAT ORGAN CONCERTI, OPP. 4 & 7 see
Handel, George Frideric

GREAT OVERTURES BY WEBER IN FULL SCORE
see Weber, Carl Maria von

GREAT PROCESSION, THE see Wuorinen,
Charles

GREAT ROMANTIC CELLO CONCERTOS BY
SCHUMANN, SAINT-SAENS, AND DVORAK
orch,vcl solo sc DOVER 24584-5 (G377)

GREAT ROMANTIC VIOLIN CONCERTOS see
Beethoven, Ludwig van

GREAT VIOLIN CONCERTOS
orch,vln solo (Sibelius et al) sc
DOVER                             (G378)

GREAT WALTZES IN FULL SCORE see
Strauss, Johann

GREAT WORKS FOR PIANO AND ORCHESTRA see
Schumann, Robert (Alexander)

GREATING OF KODÁLY see Kodály, Zoltán

GREEK SUITE see Goldschmidt, Berthold
see Turnage, Mark-Anthony

GREEN see Torke, Michael

GREEN RAY, THE see Bryars, Gavin

GREETING, A see Behrens, Jack

GREETINGS TO WK 89 THE DEMOCRATIC
ORCHESTRA see Wallin, Peter

GREGOR, CESTMÍR (1926-    )
Concerto for Piano and Orchestra
3.3.3.2. 4.3.3.1. timp,perc,
strings,pno solo [25'] CESKY HUD.
(G379)

Já Na Vojnu Se Dal
"Variations On An Old French
Ballade" 2.1.2.1. 2.2.1.0. timp,
perc,strings [12'] CESKY HUD.
(G380)

Symfonické Matamorfózy
3.3.4.1.3sax. 4.4.4.1. timp,perc,
xylo,harp,cel,strings [20'] CESKY
HUD.
(G381)

Variations On An Old French Ballade
see Já Na Vojnu Se Dal

GREGSON, EDWARD
Blazon
3.3.3.3. 4.3.3.1. timp,3perc,pno,
harp,strings [10'] BMIC      (G382)

GRÉTRY, ANDRÉ ERNEST MODESTE
(1741-1813)
Concerto for Flute
orch,fl solo BOIS          (G383)

Menuet À La Reine
(Walter, C.) 2.2.2.2. 4.2.3.0.
timp,perc,strings [3'] BREITKOPF-
W
(G384)

GRIEG, EDVARD HAGERUP (1843-1907)
Abend Im Hochgebirge
see Zwei Lyrische Stücke Aus Op. 68

Altnorwegische Romanze Mit
Variationen *Op.51
3.2.2.2. 4.2.3.1. timp,perc,harp,
strings [22'] PETERS      (G385)

An Der Wiege
see Zwei Lyrische Stücke Aus Op. 68

Dereinst, Gedanke Mein
see Sechs Deutsche Lieder, Op. 48

Gruss
see Sechs Deutsche Lieder, Op. 48

Klokke-Klang *Op.54,No.6
2.2.2.2. 4.2.3.1. timp,perc,harp,
8vln I,7vln II,6vla,5vcl,4db [7']
sc PETERS 02826           (G386)

Lauf Der Welt
see Sechs Deutsche Lieder, Op. 48

Menuett Aus Der Klaviersonate Op. 7
(Henriques, R.) 2(pic).2.2.2.
4.2.3.1. timp,strings BREITKOPF-W
(G387)

Peer Gynt Suites Nos. 1 And 2 In Full
Score
orch sc DOVER 29582-6      (G388)

Piano Concerto In Full Score
orch sc DOVER 27931-6      (G389)

Sechs Deutsche Lieder, Op. 48
(Söderlind, Ragnar) 3(pic).2.2.2.
4.2.3.1. timp,perc,harp,strings,
solo voice NORSKMI perf mat rent
contains: Dereinst, Gedanke Mein;
Gruss; Lauf Der Welt; Traum,
Ein; Verschwiegende Nachtigall,
Die; Zur Rosenzeit          (G390)

Suite Lyrique
orch BOIS                  (G391)

Three Lyric Pieces Op. 12 (Nos. 2, 4
& 5)
(Grainger, Percy) 2.2.3.2. 2.2.0.0.
strings [6'] BARDIC        (G392)

Traum, Ein
see Sechs Deutsche Lieder, Op. 48

Verschwiegende Nachtigall, Die
see Sechs Deutsche Lieder, Op. 48

Wedding Day At Troldhaugen
orch BOIS                  (G393)

Zur Rosenzeit
see Sechs Deutsche Lieder, Op. 48

Zwei Lyrische Stücke Aus Op. 68
PETERS f.s.
contains: Abend Im Hochgebirge
(ob,horn,strings) [3']; An Der
Wiege (strings) [3']       (G394)

GRIESBACH, KARL-RUDI (1916-    )
Konzertante Musik
2.2.0.0. 0.0.0.0. perc,strings,pno
solo [10'] BREITKOPF-W    (G395)

Ostinati
2.2.2.2. 2.3.3.0. perc,strings
[15'] sc BREITKOPF-W PB 4074
(G396)

Sinfonia
4.3.3.3. 4.3.3.1. timp,perc,pno,
strings [12'] BREITKOPF-W  (G397)

GRIFFES, CHARLES TOMLINSON (1884-1920)
Pleasure Dome For Kubla Khan, The
orch sc SCHIRM.G ED3920    (G398)

GRIFFIN'S TALE, THE see Blake, David

GRIMM, JULIUS OTTO (1827-1903)
Träumerei *Op.2,No.3
strings [4'] BREITKOPF-W   (G399)

GRIPPE, RAGNAR (1951-    )
Chant
3(pic).2(English horn).3(bass
clar).3(contrabsn). 4.3.3.1.
timp,5perc,strings,xylo sc STIM
(G400)

Symphonie Des Deux Continents
3(pic).2(English horn).2(bass
clar).2(contrabsn). 4.3.3.1.
timp,4perc,harp,strings sc,study
sc STIM                    (G401)

GRISÉLIDIS: FRAGMENTS see Massenet,
Jules

GROBA, ROGELIO (1934-    )
Confidencias
orch,vln solo [41'30"] sc ALPUERTO
1746                       (G402)

GRONDAHL, LAUNY (1886-1960)
Alte Dänische Volkstänze
"Gamle Danske Folkedanse" fl,clar,
string orch [9'] sc,pts BUSCH
(G403)

Gamle Danske Folkedanse
see Alte Dänische Volkstänze

GROPP, JOHANN-MARIA (1954-    )
Lamentoso
3.3.3.3. 4.0.0.0. 8vln I,7vln II,
6vla,5vcl,4db sc PETERS 00953
(G404)

Maestoso
3.3.3.3. 4.3.3.1. timp,2perc,8vln
I,7vln II,6vla,5vcl,4db [15'] sc
PETERS 02832              (G405)

Orchesterlieder, 3
4.4.4.4. 4.2.0.0. 8vln I,7vln II,
6vla,5vcl,4db,Mez solo [14'] sc
PETERS 02833             (G406)

Scherzo
orch [10'] PETERS 00952    (G407)

Scherzo Fantastique
3.3.3.3. 4.3.3.0. timp,2perc,cel,
harp,8vln I,7vln II,6vla,5vcl,4db
[10'] sc PETERS 02851      (G408)

GROSSE FUGE, OP. 133 see Beethoven,
Ludwig van

GROSSES DUETT see Bredemeyer, Reiner

GROSSMANN, JAN (1949-    )
Cesta Ke Svetlu
3.2.2.3.sax. 4.2.3.1. xylo,harp,
strings [9'] CESKY HUD.    (G409)

Concertino for Violin and Orchestra
2.2.2.2. 2.2.2.0. timp,perc,pno,
strings,vln solo [13'] CESKY HUD.
(G410)

Concerto for Harp and Orchestra
3.2.2.3.2sax. 4.2.3.0. perc,cel,
strings,harp solo [20'] CESKY
HUD.                       (G411)

GROUND BREAKER see Paulus, Stephen
Harrison

GROUP OF SEVEN, A see Turner, Robert
[Comrie]

GROUSE MOUNTAIN LULLABY see Chatman,
Stephen

GROV, MAGNE (1938-    )
Symphony
3(pic).2.2.2. 4.2.3(bass trom).1.
timp,2perc,harp,strings [40']
NORSKMI                    (G412)

GROVEN, SIGMUND (1946-    )
Aria
(Wright, Gordon) 2.2.2.2. 2.2.0.0.
timp,strings,harmonica solo
NORSKMI                    (G413)

GROVEN, SIGMUND (cont'd.)
Siesta
(Farnon, Robert) 2.2(English
horn).2(bass clar).2. 4.3.3.0.
2perc,strings,harmonica solo
NORSKMI                    (G414)

GROWINGS see Gamstorp, Göran

GRÜNAUER, INGOMAR (1938-    )
Sinfonietta
2+pic.2+English horn.2.0+contrabsn.
4.3.3.0+db tuba. timp,strings
(text by Franz Kafka) SCHOTTS
perf mat rent              (G415)

GRUND-DRAG: VERS 2 see Sandberg, Lars

GRÜNE GESICHT, DAS: SUITE see Kox, Hans

GRUPPE AUS DEM TARTARUS see Schubert,
Franz (Peter)

GRUSS see Grieg, Edvard Hagerup see
Mendelssohn-Bartholdy, Felix

GUADIANA see Marco, Tomas

GUETTEUR MÉLANCOLIQUE, LE see Bortoli,
Stephane

GUILLARD, RÉMI
Concertino No. 1, Op. 61
1.0.1.0.3sax. 0.0.0.0. harp,vln,vcl
I,vcl II,pno solo [20'] pts
FÜZEAU 2986               (G416)

GUILLAUME TELL: BALLET MUSIC see
Rossini, Gioacchino

GUINJOAN, JOAN (1931-    )
Concerto for Guitar and Orchestra
EMEC 576-00777            (G417)
2.2.2.2. 4.2.0.0. 2perc,strings,gtr
solo [28'] perf sc EMEC f.s.
(G418)

Concerto for Violin and Orchestra,
No. 1
2.2.2.2. 4.2.2.0. 3perc,harp,
strings,vln solo [25'] perf sc
EMEC f.s.                  (G419)

Improvisacion I
fl,pic,ob,clar,pno,strings,perc
[10'] sc ALPUERTO 1098     (G420)

GULLBERG, OLOF (1931-    )
Concertino Per Divertimento
1.1.2(bass clar).0. 1.1.0.0. 4vln
I,4vln II,4vla,3vcl,2db,pno [10']
sc STIM                    (G421)

Lyrisk Svit
2(pic).1.2.1. 1.0.0.0. strings,pno
[10'] (Prelude; Sarabande; Valse;
Postlude) sc STIM          (G422)

Preludium - Berceuse - Menuet
fl,ob,clar,bsn,horn,pno,strings
[8'] sc STIM               (G423)

Strofe
1.0.1.1. 2.0.0.0. strings,pno STIM
(G424)

Svit Suite Champtre
1.1.1.1. 1.0.0.0. strings,pno [10']
(Entre; Danse champtre;
Ritournele; Chant d'amour;
Ritournele; Valse) sc STIM
(G425)

Tor Zum Verlassenen Garten
(Variations)
1.1.2(pic).0. 1.1.1.0. 6vln I,6vln
II,4vla,3vcl,2db,pno [8'] sc STIM
(G426)

Tre Intermezzi: I. Segnali E Canto
1.1.2(bass clar).0. 1.1.0.0.
strings,pno [5'] sc STIM   (G427)

Tre Intermezzi: II. Autunnale
1.1.2(bass clar).0. 1.1.0.0.
strings,pno [4'] sc STIM   (G428)

Tre Intermezzi: III. Serenata Con
Interruzioni
1.1.2(bass clar).0. 1.1.0.0.
strings,pno [3'] sc STIM   (G429)

Variations
see Tor Zum Verlassenen Garten

GUNLÖD: GUNLÖD, WIE SEH' ICH DICH
STRAHLEND GESCHMÜCKT see Cornelius,
Peter

GUNLÖD: HIDOLF, DER RECKE, UND ERNA,
SEIN WEIB see Cornelius, Peter

GUNSENHEIMER, GUSTAV (1934-    )
Concertino No. 2 for Instruments and
String Orchestra
string orch,S rec/ob solo VOGT
VF 1010                    (G430)

# H

GUNSENHEIMER, GUSTAV (cont'd.)
Concertino No. 3 for Saxophone and
String Orchestra
sax/clar,string orch VOGT VF 1029
(G431)
Concertino No. 4 for Recorder and
Orchestra
sopranino rec/fl/soprano sax,string
orch VOGT VF 1049 (G432)

Concerto No. 1
pno/hpsd,timp,string orch VOGT
VF 1004 (G433)

GURISCHE HYMNE see Artyomov, Vyacheslav

GÜRSCHING, ALBRECHT (1934- )
Concerto for Bassoon and Strings
4vln I,4vln II,3vla,3vcl,db,bsn
solo [18'50"] PEER rent (G434)

Concerto for Flute and Strings
[17'] PEER rent (G435)

Concerto No. 2
2.2.2.2. 2.2.1.0. strings,pno solo
[17'] PEER rent (G436)

Portrait
2.2.2.2. 4.3.3.1. harp,strings
[9'30"] PEER rent (G437)

GUT UND BÖSE see Bon, Maarten

GUTCHË, GENE (1907- )
Concertino for Orchestra, Op. 28
1.1.1.1. 1.1.1.1. 2perc,strings
[19'] SCHIRM.EC rent (G438)

Epimetheus USA *Op.46
3.3.3.3. 4.3.3.1. alto sax,timp,
3perc,strings [8'] SCHIRM.EC rent
(G439)

Gemini *Op.41
pno 4-hands solo,3.3.3.3. 4.3.3.1.
timp,3perc,strings [15']
SCHIRM.EC rent (G440)

Genghis Khan *Op.37
3.3.4.3. 4.4.2.1. 2perc,db [8']
SCHIRM.EC rent (G441)

Raquel *Op.38
3.3.3.3. 4.4.3.1. timp,2perc,
strings [8'] SCHIRM.EC rent
(G442)

Timpani Concertante *Op.31
timp solo,3.3.3.3. 4.3.3.1. perc,
strings,opt clar in E flat [7']
SCHIRM.EC rent (G443)

GUTEN MORGEN see Rakov, Nikolai

GUTIÉRREZ HERAS, JOAQUÍN (1927- )
Postludio
string orch [11'] PEER rent (G444)

GUTTORMSEN, GUTTORM (1950- )
Terje Vigen
2.2.2.2. 4.2.3.1. timp,perc,cel,
harp,strings,B solo [35'] NORSKMI
(G445)

GUY, BARRY (1947- )
After The Rain
strings [25'] NOVELLO (G446)

GYMNOPEDIE 1 see Satie, Erik

GYMNOPEDIE 2 see Satie, Erik

GYMNOPEDIE 3 see Satie, Erik

GYROWETZ, ADALBERT (JIROVEC)
(1763-1850)
Concerto for Piano and Orchestra, Op.
49
(Štefan, Jiří) 1.2.2.2. 2.2.0.0.
strings,pno solo [25'] CESKY HUD.
(G447)
Symphonie Concertante for Oboe and
Orchestra, Op. 9
0.2.0.0. 2.0.0.0. strings,ob solo
CESKY HUD. (G448)

GYULAI GAAL, JÁNOS
Concertino for Piano and Orchestra
2(pic).2.2.2. 4.2.2.0. timp,harp,
cel,strings,pno solo [14'] EMB
rent (G449)

H'UN (LACERATIONS): IN MEMORIAM see
Sheng, Bright

HA, WELCH EIN AUGENBLICK see Beethoven,
Ludwig van

HAAR see McPherson, Gordon

HAAS, JOSEPH (1879-1960)
Lyrisches Intermezzo
2.2.2.2. 4.2.3.0. timp,harp,strings
[7'] SCHOTTS perf mat rent (H1)
1.1.2.1. 2.2.1.0. timp,strings [7']
SCHOTTS perf mat rent (H2)

HÁBA, MIROSLAV (1935- )
Království Slunce
2.2.2.1. 1.1.1.1. perc,strings [7']
CESKY HUD. (H3)

HABANERA see Proto, Frank

HABBESTAD, KJELL (1955- )
Clokun
[Eng] 3(pic).2.2.3(2contrabsn).
4.3.3(bass trom).1. timp,2perc,
harp,pno,strings,S solo [5'40"]
NORSKMI (H4)

HABICHT, GÜNTER (1916- )
Sinfonietta
2.2.2.2. 2.0.0.0. timp,triangle,
strings [11'] BREITKOPF-W (H5)

HABISREUTINGER-KONZERT see Schibler,
Armin, Concerto Breve

HAB'S VERSTANDEN, GNÄDGER HERR see
Mozart, Wolfgang Amadeus, Ho
Capito, Signor, Si

HACIA EL COMIENZO see Lavista, Mario

HADEWIJCH see Andriessen, Louis,
Materie, De: Part 2

HAEC AURORA GRATIOSA see Lokaj, Jakub

HAGEN, DARON
Concerto For Flügelhorn And String
Orchestra
flügelhorn solo,string orch [15']
SCHIRM.EC rent (H6)

Fire Music
3.3.3.3. 4.4.3.1. timp,3perc,harp,
kbd,strings [16'] SCHIRM.EC rent
(H7)

Grand Line
2.2.2.2. 2.2.0.0. timp,perc,kbd,
strings [13'] SCHIRM.EC rent (H8)

Heliotrope
2.2.2.2. 2.2.2.0. timp,perc,harp,
kbd,strings [11'] SCHIRM.EC rent
(H9)

Heliotrope Bouquet (Theatre Orchestra
Version)
2.2.2.2. 2.1.1.0. perc,kbd,strings
[4'] SCHIRM.EC rent (H10)

Interior (Ballet Music)
fl,ob,clar,bsn,kbd,strings [19']
SCHIRM.EC rent (H11)

Occasional Notes. Suite For Eleven
Players
1.1.1.1. 1.1.0.0. perc,string quar
[18'] SCHIRM.EC rent (H12)

Philharmonia (A Fanfare)
3.4.4.4. 6.4.3.1. timp,3perc,harp,
kbd,strings [8'] SCHIRM.EC rent
(H13)

Romance for Piano and Orchestra
pno solo,2.1.2.1. 2.1.1.0. strings,
marimba [11'] SCHIRM.EC rent
(H14)

Short Symphony
see Symphony No. 1

Stanzas For Cello And Chamber
Orchestra
vcl solo,1.0.1.1. 1.0.0.0. kbd,
strings [12'] SCHIRM.EC rent
(H15)

Stillness At Appomattox, A
2.0.2.2. 2.2.2.0. timp,2perc,harp,
strings [9'] SCHIRM.EC rent (H16)

Symphony No. 1
"Short Symphony" 3.3.3.3. 4.3.3.1.
timp,2perc,harp,kbd,strings [28']
SCHIRM.EC rent (H17)

Symphony No. 2
3.3.3.3. 4.3.3.1. timp,3perc,harp,
kbd,strings [34'] SCHIRM.EC rent
(H18)

HAGERUP BULL, EDVARD
see BULL, EDVARD HAGERUP

HAGOROMO see Lumsdaine, David

HAHN, REYNALDO (1875-1947)
Fête Chez Thérèse, La: Suite No. 2
4.2.2.4. 4.4.3.0. timp,2perc,2harp,
pno,alto sax,strings [14'20"]
LEDUC (H19)

HAINDL, FRANZ SEBASTIAN (1725-1812)
Sinfonia in G
2horn,strings without db,cont
COPPENRATH sc 16.047-01, kbd pt
16.047-03, pts 16.047-21, pts
16.047-43 (H20)

HAJDU, MIHALY (1909- )
Divertimento in D
2.2.2.0. 2.2.1.0. strings EMB rent
(H21)

HAJDÚTÁNC see Ranki, György, Heyduck
Dance

HÁJEK, ALEŠ (1937- )
Fantasy for Strings
string orch [12'] CESKY HUD. (H22)

Sinfonietta No. 2
2.2.2.2. 2.3.0.0. timp,strings
[16'] CESKY HUD. (H23)

HAJI, HIROSHI (1953- )
Concerto for Clarinet and Strings
string orch,clar solo [25'] JAPAN
(H24)
Serenade for Strings
string orch [15'] JAPAN (H25)

HÁJKU, MICHAL
Concerto for Guitar and Strings
[16'] CESKY HUD. (H26)

HÁLA, JAN (1956- )
Concertino for Marimba, Guitar, Flute
and String Orchestra
[12'] CESKY HUD. (H27)

Sinfonietta
3.2.2.2. 4.3.3.1. timp,perc,harp,
cel,strings [13'] CESKY HUD.
(H28)

HALA, VLASTIMIL (1924-1985)
Rudolfovo Cislo
0.0.0.0.2sax. 0.1.1.0. perc,
synthesizer,2gtr,strings [5']
CESKY HUD. (H29)

HALÁL TÁNC see Liszt, Franz, Dance Of
Death

HALÁSZ, KÁLMÁN
Concertino
strings [16'] EMB rent (H30)

HALÉVY, JACQUES (1799-1862)
Jüdin, Die: Overture
see Juive, La: Overture

Juive, La: Overture
"Jüdin, Die: Overture" 2+pic.2.2.2.
4.4.3.1. timp,perc,strings [13']
(no score) BREITKOPF-W (H31)

Königin Von Zypern, Die: Overture
see Reine De Chypre, La: Overture

Reine De Chypre, La: Overture
(Hoffmann, F.) "Königin Von Zypern,
Die: Overture" 2(pic).2.2.2.
4.4.3.1. timp,perc,strings [9']
(no score) BREITKOPF-W (H32)

HALL, CARL-AXEL (1947- )
Sense Of Place, A
3.3.3.3(contrabsn). 3.3.3.1. timp,
perc,strings,pno,cel [10'] STIM
sc H-2843, pts (H33)

HALLBERG, BENGT (1932- )
Black And White Concerto (Concerto
for Piano and Orchestra)
2(pic).2.2(bass clar).2(contrabsn).
2.2.1.0. timp,perc,strings,pno
solo STIM (H34)

Concerto for Piano and Orchestra
see Black And White Concerto

HALLELUJAH I, A SYMPHONY OF THE NORTH
see Vriend, Jan N.M.

HALLER, HERMANN (1914- )
Abschied
string orch,S solo [13'] HEINRICH
(H35)

Cinque Liriche Su Versi Di Salvatore
Quasimodo
see Ed É Subito Sera

Ed É Subito Sera
"Cinque Liriche Su Versi Di
Salvatore Quasimodo" 3.2.2.2.
4.2.3.0. timp,perc,harp,strings,
Bar solo [27'] HEINRICH (H36)

**HALLER, HERMANN (cont'd.)**

Episoden
1.1.1.1. 2.0.0.0. strings,vla solo
[14'] HEINRICH (H37)

Extension-Contraction (Musique
Élégiaque)
vcl,orch [17'] HEINRICH (H38)

Fünf Aspekte
orch [18'] HEINRICH (H39)

Resonances
2ob,2horn,string orch,vln solo
[18'] HEINRICH (H40)

Variations for Orchestra
3.3(English horn).3(bass
clar).3(contrabsn). 4.3.3(bass
trom).1. timp,perc,harp,strings
[20'] HEINRICH (H41)

**HALLGRIMSSON, HAFLIDI (1941- )**
Herma
strings,vcl solo CHESTER (H42)

**HALLIN, MARGARETA**
Edith
1.2(English horn).1.0. 0.0.0.0.
perc,harp,strings,SB soli STIM (H43)

**HALLNÄS, EYVIND (1937- )**
Tre Orkesterstycken
3(pic).2.2.2. 4.2.3.1. timp,2perc,
strings [8'] sc STIM (H44)

**HALMRAST, TOR (1951- )**
Arctander: Symphonie De Numéro Cachè
2(pic,alto fl).2.2(bass
clar).2(contrabsn). 4.3.3.0.
2perc,strings, plastic bags [15']
NORSKMI (H45)

**HAMABE NO ARASHI see Proto, Frank**

**HAMARY, ANDRÁS**
Timor
4.2.3.3. 4.4.3.1. 4timp,pno,strings
[12'30"] MOECK sc 5274 f.s., pts
rent (H46)

**HAMBRAEUS, BENGT (1928- )**
Concerto for Organ and String
Orchestra, Op. 16
string orch,org solo [20'] sc
CANADIAN MI 1664 H199CO (H47)

Continuo: A Partire Da Pachelbel
3(pic).3.3.3(contrabsn). 6.4.4.1.
3perc,strings,org solo [31'] sc
CANADIAN MI 1364 H199CO (H48)

Nocturnals
1(pic).1(English
horn).1.1(contrabsn).baritone
sax. 1.1.1.0. timp&perc,harp,
strings [22'] (Incantation -
Figures fugitives - Choros) sc
CANADIAN MI1200 H199NO (H49)

Recitativ Och Koral *Op.25,No.1
(Ek, Hans) vln,string orch,pno STIM (H50)

Ricordanza
2(pic).3.2.2(contrabsn). 3.2.1.0.
timp,2perc,pno,strings [20'] sc
CANADIAN MI 1100 H199RI (H51)

**HAMBURG, JEFF (1956- )**
Prayer And A Dance, A
string orch [11'] sc DONEMUS (H52)

Schuylkill
string orch [22'] sc DONEMUS (H53)

Symphony in E flat
2.2.2.2. opt 2alto sax. 2.1.1.0.
perc,strings [15'] sc DONEMUS (H54)

**HAMEL, MICHA**
Wintergezicht
3.3.3.3. 4.2.3.1. 4perc,cel,harp,
pno,strings [23'] sc DONEMUS (H55)

**HAMEL, PETER MICHAEL (1947- )**
Albatros
3(pic,alto fl).3(English
horn).3(bass
clar).1(contrabsn).2alto sax.
3.2.4.1+db tuba. timp,3perc,cel,
12-14vln I,8-10vln II,6-9vla,6-
9vcl,3-5db, improvisation group
[25'] SCHOTTS perf mat rent (H56)

**HAMELIN: DREI KLANGBILDER see Hiller,
Wilfried**

**HAMERIK, ASGER (1843-1923)**
Christliche Trilogie *Op.31
3(pic).2.2.2. 4.2.3.1. timp,perc,
harp,org,strings [46'] BREITKOPF-
W (H57)

**HAMERIK, ASGER (cont'd.)**

Da Giovine Regina La Luna Maestosa
(Nocturne)
1.0.0.0. 0.0.0.0. strings,Mez solo
[6'] BREITKOPF-W (H58)

Erntetanz *Op.37
2.2.2.2. 2.0.0.0. timp,strings,SSAA
[12'] BREITKOPF-W (H59)

Jüdische Trilogie *Op.19
2.2.2.2. 4.2.3.0. timp,perc,strings
[18'] (no score) BREITKOPF-W (H60)

Nocturne
see Da Giovine Regina La Luna
Maestosa

Symphonie Sérieuse (Nr. 5) g-moll
*Op.36
3(pic).2.2.2. 4.2.3.1. timp,strings
[42'] (no score) BREITKOPF-W (H61)

Vierte Nordische Suite *Op.25
2.2.2.2. 4.2.3.1. timp,2perc,harp,
strings [36'] BREITKOPF-W (H62)

**HAMILTON, IAIN (1922- )**
Concerto For Harp And Small Orchestra
1(pic).1(English horn).1(bass
clar).1. 1.1.0.0. perc,strings
[25'] PRESSER rent (H63)

Transit Of Jupiter, The
2(pic).2(English horn).2(bass
clar).2. 4.3.3(bass trom).1.
2perc,harp,strings [17'] PRESSER
rent (H64)

**HAMILTON CONCERTO see Weinstangel,
Sasha**

**HAMLET see Gade, Niels Wilhelm see
Joachim, Joseph**

**HAMLET: INCIDENTAL MUSIC see Prokofiev,
Serge**

**HAMLET, NÁŠ SOUCASNÍK see Válek, Jirí**

**HAMLETIANA see Slavicky, Milan**

**HAMMERTH, JOHAN (1953- )**
Slagverkskonsert
2.2.2.2(contrabsn). 4.2.3.1. timp,
perc,harp,strings STIM (H65)

**HAMPSHIRE SUITE, A see Holst, Gustav**

**HAN GEINOU MANDALA see Imai,Shigeyuki**

**HAND-PRINTS OF SORCERERS see Maggio,
Robert**

**HANDEL, GEORGE FRIDERIC (1685-1759)**
Allegro Postillions
see Sinfonia

Complete Concerti Grossi In Full
Score
orch sc DOVER 24187-4 (H66)

Concerto for Harp in B flat
(Lenzewski) harp,strings sc,pts
INTERNAT.S. (H67)

Concerto for Harp in B flat, MIN 1
harp,strings sc,pts INTERNAT.S. (H68)

Concerto for 2 Horns, 2 Oboes,
Bassoon and Strings in F
(Gmür) 2horn,2ob,bsn,strings
KUNZELMANN 10180 (H69)

Concerto for Organ, No. 13, in F, HWV
295
(Koopman, Ton) "Cuckoo And The
Nightingale, The" orch,org solo
sc,pts BREITKOPF-W PB-OB 5250 (H70)

Concerto for Organ, No. 14, in A, HWV
296a
(Koopman, Ton) orch,org solo sc,pts
BREITKOPF-W PB-OB 5251 (H71)

Concerto Grosso No. 19 in C minor,
Op. 6, HWV 326
string orch,cont,2vln&vcl soli
[16'] BREITKOPF-W (H72)

Concerto in B flat
(Thilde, J.) string orch,2trp soli
[8'] BILLAUDOT (H73)

Concerto No. 9 for Organ, Op. 7, No.
3, in B flat *HWV308
(Koopman, T.) 0.2.0.1. 0.0.0.0.
strings,cont,org solo [14'] sc,
pts BREITKOPF-W PB-OB 5213 (H74)

Concerto No. 10 for Organ, Op. 7, No.
4, in D minor *HWV309
(Seiffert, M.) 0.2.0.2. 0.0.0.0.
strings,cont,org solo [20'] sc,
pts BREITKOPF-W PB-OB 5214 (H75)

**HANDEL, GEORGE FRIDERIC (cont'd.)**

Concerto No. 11 for Organ, Op. 7, No.
5, in G minor *HWV310
(Seiffert, M.) 0.2.0.1. 0.0.0.0.
strings,cont,org solo [15'] sc
pts BREITKOPF-W PB-OB 5215 (H76)

Concerto No. 12 for Organ, Op. 7, No.
6, in B flat *HWV311
(Seiffert, M.) 0.2.0.1. 0.0.0.0.
strings,cont,org solo [13'] sc,
pts BREITKOPF-W PB-OB 5216 (H77)

Cuckoo And The Nightingale, The
see Concerto for Organ, No. 13, in
F, HWV 295

Faramondo: Overture
orch sc KUNZELMANN EKB 54P ipa (H78)

Gods Go A Begging, The (from various
operas) Suite
(Beecham, Thomas) 2.2.2.2. 4.2.0.0.
timp,hpsd,strings [19'] BOOSEY-
ENG rent (H79)

Gods Go A-Begging Suite
(Beecham, Sir Thomas) 2.2.2.2.
4.2.0.0. timp,harp,strings [19']
CRAMER rent (H80)

Great Organ Concerti, Opp. 4 & 7
orch,org solo sc DOVER 24462-8 (H81)

Julius César: Air De Cléopatre Et Air
De César
(Malgloire) orch,solo voice BOIS (H82)

Meine Liebliche Platane
see Xerxes: Frondi Tenere

Messiah: Overture *HWV56
(Mozart, W.A.) 0.0.0.2. 2.0.3.0.
strings BREITKOPF-W (H83)

Messiah: Pifa
(Mozart, W.A.) 2(pic).2.2.2.
2.0.0.0. strings [3'] BREITKOPF-W (H84)

Overture in B flat
(Frotscher, Gotthold) vln I/ob,vln
II/ob,vla/vln III,vcl/db/bsn HUG
sc PE 853, pts PE 853-30 (H85)

Rodelinda: Overture
(Müller) orch KUNZELMANN 10105 f.s.
contains also: Terpsicore: Suite (H86)

Rodrigo, Der: Fünf Arien
(Müller, Hermann) string orch,cont,
opt 2ob,S/T solo HUG (H87)

Sinfonia
"Allegro Postillions" 0.2.0.0.
0.0.0.0. strings,cont [3']
BREITKOPF-W (H88)

Suite in D, HWV 341
0.2.0.0. 0.0.0.0. strings,cont,trp
solo [8'] DEUTSCHER (H89)

Terpsicore: Suite
see Rodelinda: Overture

Water Music And Royal Fireworks
orch sc DOVER 25070-9 (H90)

Xerxes: Frondi Tenere *HWV40
(Mottl, F.) "Meine Liebliche
Platane" 0.1.2.2. 2.0.0.0. harp,
strings,S solo [5'] BREITKOPF-W (H91)

Xerxes: Overture And Sinfonia
orch sc KUNZELMANN EKB 58P ipa (H92)

**HANDEL IN THE STRAND see Grainger,
Percy Aldridge**

**HÄNDELSCHE ORGELKONZERTE see Gottron,
A.**

**HANNIG, PETR (1946- )**
Symphony
3.2.3.3. 4.3.4.1. timp,perc,xylo,
3gtr,pno,synthesizer,strings
[45'] CESKY HUD. (H93)

**HANS CHRISTIAN ANDERSEN: OVERTURE see
Enna, August**

**HANS HEILING: AN JENEM TAG see
Marschner, Heinrich (August)**

**HANS HEILING: ARIA OF HANS see
Marschner, Heinrich (August), Hans
Heiling: An Jenem Tag**

**HÄNSCHEN KLEIN see Spohr, Mathias**

**HANSEN, KRISTER (1966- )**
Retrospektiv Metamorfos
see Till Minnet

HANSEN, KRISTER (cont'd.)

Tidsmusik
2.2.2(bass clar).2. 4.3.2.1. timp,
2perc,strings [12'] sc STIM (H94)

Till Minnet
"Retrospektiv Metamorfos" orch
[13'] STIM (H95)

HANSGÅRDH, ALLAN (1926- )
Ådalsrapsodi
2.2(English horn).2.2. 2.2.2.0.
timp,perc,strings [7'] sc,pts
STIM H-2486 (H96)

Capriccio
2(pic).2.2(bass clar).2. 2.2.2.0.
timp,2perc,strings [7'] STIM sc
H-2905, pts (H97)

HANSSON, MATS O. (1960- )
Moo
1.1(English horn).1(bass clar).1.
1.0.0.0. perc,strings STIM (H98)

HANUŠ, JAN (1915- )
Aristofanovské Variace
2.2.2.2. 2.2.1.0. perc,strings,pno
solo [21'] CESKÝ HUD. (H99)

Concerto for Violin and Orchestra,
Op. 112
"Tre Pezzi Concertante" 2.2.2.2.
2.2.0.0. perc,cel/pno,strings
[26'] CESKÝ HUD. (H100)

Deštník Z Piccadilly *Op.103
3.3.3.2. 4.3.3.1. timp,perc,vibra,
harp,cel,strings,B solo [26']
CESKÝ HUD. (H101)

Passacaglia Concertante *Op.102
strings,2vcl&cel soli [14'] CESKY
HUD. (H102)

Tre Pezzi Concertante
see Concerto for Violin and
Orchestra, Op. 112

Tri Dantovská Preludia (from Baletu
"Labyrint" Op. 98a)
3.3.3.2.sax. 4.3.3.1. timp,perc,
xylo,vibra,harp,pno,gtr,strings
[12'] CESKÝ HUD. (H103)

Variace A Koláze *Op.99
3.3.3.2. 4.3.3.1. timp,perc,harp,
pno,strings [20'] CESKÝ HUD.
(H104)

HAPPY BIRTHDAY: VARIATIONS, FOR
ORCHESTRA see Heidrich, Peter

HAPPY END see Denisov, Edison
Vasilievich

HARBISON, JOHN (1938- )
Concerto For Double Brass
cor,orch sc SCHIRM.G AMP8048 (H105)

Symphony No. 2
orch sc SCHIRM.G AMP8061 (H106)

HARD TIMES see Becker, Günther

HARFENSINFONIE see Voigtländer, Lothar

HARGRAVE, HENRY
Concerto for Bassoon, String
Orchestra and Continuo in F
bsn solo/vcl solo,string orch,cont
KUNZELMANN ipa sc 10245A, oct
10245 (H107)

HARK THE ECHOING AIR see Purcell, Henry

HARLEY, JAMES (1959- )
Windprints
2(pic).2.2.2(contrabsn). 4.2.2.1.
timp&perc,2perc,pno,strings [15']
sc CANADIAN MI 1100 H285WI (H108)

HARMADIK, A see Decsenyi, Janos, Third,
The

HARMAN, CHRIS (1970- )
Élégie
string orch,pno solo [15'] sc
CANADIAN MI 1661 H287EL (H109)

Fantasy for Strings
4vln I,4vln II,2vla,2vcl,db [9'] sc
CANADIAN MI 1500 H287FA (H110)

Iridescence
8vln I,6vln II,4vla,4vcl,2db [12']
sc CANADIAN MI 1500 H287IR (H111)

Irisation
8vln I,6vln II,4vla,4vcl,2db [16']
sc CANADIAN MI 1500 H287IRI
(H112)

HARMONIA MUNDI - RES HUMANA see Faltus,
Leos, Symphony No. 4

HARMONIELEHRE see Adams, John

HARMOONIA: SUITE see Paulus, Stephen
Harrison

HÁROM BALETT-KÉP see Horusitzky,
Zoltan, Three Ballet Pictures

HÁROM SZIMFONIKUS KÉP see Kalmar,
Laszlo, Three Symphonic Pictures

HÁROM SZIMFONIKUS TÉTEL see Kalmar,
Laszlo, Hermes: Three Symphonic
Movements see Kalmar, Laszlo,
Horae: Three Symphonic Movements

HÁROM TÉTEL see Hidas, Frigyes, Three
Movements

HÁROM TÉTEL ZENEKARRA see Kalmar,
Laszlo, Ballet Des Amphores: Three
Movements

HÁROM ZENEKARI DARAB see Behar, Gyorgy,
Three Pieces For Orchestra see
Soproni, Jozsef, Three Pieces For
Orchestra

HARPER, EDWARD JAMES (1941- )
Chanson Minimale: Variations On A
Theme By Elgar
2.2.2.2. 2.2.2.0. timp,perc,strings
[6'] perf sc set OXFORD 3641569
sc,pts rent (H113)

Concerto for Clarinet and Orchestra
2(pic).2.2(clar in E flat,bass
clar).2. 4.2.3.1. harp,strings,
clar solo [18'] perf sc set
OXFORD 363919X sc,pts rent (H114)

Fantasy No. 4
0.2.2.2. 2.2.0.0. strings,vln&pno
soli [16'] sc OXFORD 3639173
f.s., sc,pts rent (H115)

Fantasy No. 5
2(pic).2.2(bass clar).2. 2.2.0.0.
timp,strings [15'] perf sc set
OXFORD 3639181 sc,pts rent (H116)

Fiddler Of The Reels, The
string orch [8'] perf sc set OXFORD
364150X sc,pts rent (H117)

Homage To Thomas Hardy
2.2.2.2. 2.2.0.0. perc,bells,
strings,Bar solo [27'] OXFORD
(H118)

In Memoriam
2.2.2.2. 2.2.0.0. timp,perc,harp,
pno,strings,vcl solo [18'] perf
sc set OXFORD 3568977 sc,pts rent
(H119)

Overture for Chamber Orchestra
2.2.2.2. 2.2.0.0. perc,timp,strings
[10'] perf sc set OXFORD 3641550
sc,pts rent (H120)

HARPER OF THE STONES, THE see
Applebaum, Louis

HARRIS, DONALD (1931- )
Mermaid Variations
2.1.2(bass clar).1. 2.1.1.0. timp,
strings [10'13"] PRESSER rent
(H121)

HARRISON, JONTY (1952- )
Concerto Caldo
4vln,2vla,2vcl,db,harp,2vln soli
[15'] (for amplified strings) sc
UNIV.YORK 0011 f.s. (H122)

Paroles Plus Hérétiques
1.1.1. 1.1.1.0. pno,harp,vibra,
2vln,vla,vcl,db,S solo [18'] sc
UNIV.YORK 0014 f.s. (H123)

HARRISON, LOU (1917- )
New First Suite For Strings
string orch [16'] PEER rent (H124)

Parade, A
4(pic).4(English horn).4(bass
clar).4(contrabsn). 4.4.4.1.
6perc,cel,pno,harp,strings [7']
PEER rent (H125)

Symfony In Free Style
4.0.0.0. 0.0.1.0. 2perc,pno,cel,
5harp,8vla,opt vibra [5'] sc
PETERS 03883 (H126)

Symphony No. 4
3(pic).3(English horn).3(bass
clar).3(contrabsn). 4.3.3.1.
4perc,cel,prepared pno,harp,
strings,Bar solo [37'] PEER rent
(H127)

HARTLEY, WALTER SINCLAIR (1927- )
Symphony No. 3
3.3.3.3. 4.3.3.1. timp,2perc,
strings [14'] SCHIRM.EC rent
(H128)

HARTMANN, KARL AMADEUS (1905-1963)
Drei Orchesterstücke
(Henze, Hans Werner) 3(2pic,alto
fl).2+English horn+Heckelphone.2+
bass clar.2+contrabsn. 4.3.3.1.
timp,3perc,cel,pno,harp,strings,
alto sax&tenor sax [20'] (on the
2nd version of the Piano Sonata
"27. April 1945") SCHOTTS perf
mat rent (H129)

Klagegesang
3(3pic).3(English
horn).3.3(contrabsn). 4.3.3.1.
timp,4perc,cel,harp,strings [23']
study sc SCHOTTS ED 7887 perf mat
rent (H130)

HARTMANN, PETER (1940- )
Adagio
3(pic).2+2English horn.1+clar in E
flat+bass clar.2+contrabsn.alto
sax. 4.2.3.0. timp,perc,cel,pno,
2harp,strings,euphonium/tuba,
bombardon or tuba [14'] SCHOTTS
perf mat rent (H131)

HARTWELL, HUGH
Sonata for Orchestra
4(pic.2alto fl).4(English
horn).4(clar in E flat,2bass
clar).4(2contrabsn). 8.5.3.1.
timp,6perc,2harp,strings sc
CANADIAN MI 1100 H337SO (H132)

HARU NO YO NO YUME see Fujiwara, Yutaka

HARVEST HYMN see Grainger, Percy
Aldridge

HARVEY, JONATHAN (1939- )
Concerto for Percussion and Orchestra
3.2.3.3. 4.3.3.1. perc,pno,harp,
strings [15'] FABER (H133)

Concerto for Violoncello and
Orchestra
3.3.3.3. 4.3.3.1. 2perc,strings,vcl
solo [21'] FABER (H134)

Easter Orisons
chamber orch sc FABER 50821 9 f.s.
(H135)

Hidden Voice
pic,fl,ob,clar,bsn&contrabsn,2horn,
perc,2vln,vla,2vcl,db [7'] FABER
(H136)

HASE UND DIE SCHILDKRÖTE, DER see Shi,
Zhen-Rong

HASELBACH, JOSEF (1936- )
Hegareske
3.2(English horn).3.3. 3.3.0.0.
strings [6'] HUG (H137)

Monodien
T solo,harp,string orch [15'] HUG
(H138)

Sinfonia Concertante for Clarinet,
Saxophone, Trumpet and String
Orchestra
[18'] HUG (H139)

...Und Verstreut Gedichte...
1.1.2.1. 1.1.1.0. 2harp,3perc,
strings [12'] HUG (H140)

HASHAGEN, KLAUS (1924- )
Melodie I (Neufassung 93)
1.1.1.0. 1.1.0.0. 2perc,harp,8vln,
4vla,4vcl,2db [15'] sc PETERS
03539 (H141)

HASSE, JOHANN ADOLPH (1699-1783)
Cantates
2.2.0.0. 2.0.0.0. strings,cont,
female solo LEDUC (H142)

Concerto for Flute and String
Orchestra
fl solo,string orch KUNZELMANN
10244 (H143)

Concerto for Flute in F
(Jeney; Müller) fl solo,orch
KUNZELMANN ipa sc 10051A, oct
10051 (H144)

Concerto for Flute, String Orchestra
and Continuo in G
fl solo,string orch KUNZELMANN ipa
sc 10245A, oct 10245 (H145)

HASSE, KARL (1883-1960)
Suite In A minor for Strings, Op. 36a
8vln I,7vln II,6vla,5vcl,4db [10']
sc PETERS 00629 (H146)

HASSID'S REWARD, THE see Sheriff, Noam,
Gomel Le'ish Hassid

HATCH, PETER (1957- )
Dice Are Loaded, The
3sax,bass clar,bsn,vln,vcl,trp,
trom,gtr,pno,db,drums,perc sc
CANADIAN MI1200 H361DI (H147)

HATIKVAH
(Weill, Kurt) 3.2.3.2. 4.3.3.1. timp,
perc,harp,strings [4'] EUR.AM.MUS.
perf mat rent                          (H148)

HAUG, HALVOR (1952-   )
Insignia
2.2(English horn).2.2. 2.2.0.0.
timp,strings [14'30"] NORSKMI     (H149)

Norske Aspekter
2(pic).2.2.2. 4.3.3.0. timp,2perc,
strings [7'45"] NORSKMI           (H150)

Sinfonietta
orch NORSK NMO 9873                    (H151)

Symphony No. 1
orch NORSK NMO 9882                    (H152)

Symphony No. 3
"Symphony No. 3: The Inscrutable
Life" 3(pic).3(English
horn).3(bass clar).3(contrabsn).
4.3.3.1. timp,3perc,harp,
electronic tape,strings [37']
NORSKMI                                (H153)

Symphony No. 3: The Inscrutable Life
see Symphony No. 3

HAUGTUSSA see Hundsnes, Svein

HAUSEGGER, SIEGMUND VON (1872-1948)
Drei Hymnen An Die Nacht
KAHNT f.s. after the text by
Gottfried Keller
contains: Stille Der Nacht
(3.2.3.2. 3.0.0.0. harp,
strings,Bar solo); Unruhe Der
Nacht (3.3.3.3. 4.2.3.1. timp,
perc,strings,Bar solo); Unter
Sternen (3.3.3.3. 4.3.2.1.
timp,harp,strings,Bar solo)
                                       (H154)

Stille Der Nacht
see Drei Hymnen An Die Nacht

Unruhe Der Nacht
see Drei Hymnen An Die Nacht

Unter Sternen
see Drei Hymnen An Die Nacht

HAVAS see Bailey, Judith

HAVCLAAR, ANTON
Reis, De
3.3.3.2. 3.3.3.1. 5perc,harp,pno/
cel,strings [25'] sc DONEMUS
                                       (H155)

HAVELKA, SVATOPLUK (1925-   )
Detská Svita
3.3.4.2. 4.3.0.0. perc,harp,pno/
cel,strings [24'] CESKY HUD.
                                       (H156)

Prípad Lupínek (Jednou nebudeme mali)
2.2.2.2. 3.2.3.0. perc,strings
CESKY HUD.                             (H157)

HAVRAN see Plachy, Zdenek

HAWAIIAN HOLIDAY see Proto, Frank

HAWKINS, JOHN (1944-   )
Prelude And Prayer
3(pic).3(English horn).3(clar in E
flat,bass clar).3(contrabsn).
4.3.3.1. timp,5perc,harp,pno&cel,
strings,T solo [16'] sc CANADIAN
MV 1400 H393PR                         (H158)

HAWKINS, MALCOLM
Concerto for Piano and Orchestra
"Rasmandala (Theme, Variations And
Fugue)" pno solo,3.3.3.3.
4.3.3.1. timp,3perc,harp,kbd,
strings SCHIRM.EC rent                 (H159)

Rasmandala (Theme, Variations And
Fugue)
see Concerto for Piano and
Orchestra

HAWORTH, FRANK (1905-   )
Cantavern
2.2.2.2. 2.2.2.0. timp,strings
[3'5"] sc CANADIAN MI 1100 H397CA
                                       (H160)

Elancia Suite
string orch/string quin,A rec solo
[8'] sc CANADIAN MI 1620 H397EL
                                       (H161)

Maventa Suite
string orch [6'] sc,pts CANADIAN
MI 1500 H397MA                         (H162)

Trevelua Suite
string orch [6'] sc,pts CANADIAN
MI 1500 H397TR                         (H163)

Vairey Suite
string orch [6'] sc CANADIAN
MI 1500 H397VA                         (H164)

HAWTHORN see Sackman, Nicholas

HAYASHI, HIKARU (1931-   )
Concerto for Viola
see Elegia

Elegia (Concerto for Viola)
string orch,vla solo [35'] ZEN-ON
                                       (H165)

HAYDN, [FRANZ] JOSEPH (1732-1809)
Alleluja
see Symphony No. 30 in C, Hob.I: 30

Arianna A Naxos  *Hob.XXXIb:2, cant
(Hodges, Paul) S solo,strings
DOBLINGER DM 1200                      (H166)

Armida: Overture (Overture, Hob.Ia:
14) Hob.XXVIIa:12
1.2.0.2. 2.0.0.0. strings [7']
BREITKOPF-W                            (H167)

Complete London Symphonies Series I
orch sc DOVER 29754-3                  (H168)

Complete London Symphonies Series II
orch sc DOVER                          (H169)

Concerto for Oboe and Orchestra in C
(Rothwell) 2ob,2horn,2trp,timp,
strings,ob solo [21'] perf sc set
OXFORD 364214X sc,pts rent     (H170)

Concerto for Violin, Hob.VIIa: 3, in
B flat
strings,cont,vln solo [25']
BREITKOPF-W                            (H171)

Concerto for Violin, Hob.XVIII: 6, in
F
string orch,cont,vln solo [11']
BREITKOPF-W                            (H172)

Concerto for Violin, No. 1, in C
vln solo,orch perf sc KUNZELMANN
ETP 1202 ipa                           (H173)

Concerto for Violoncello and
Orchestra, Op. 101
(Schönzeler) orch perf sc
KUNZELMANN ETP 769 ipa                 (H174)

Joseph Haydn Werke, Series 1, Volume
3: Sinfonien 1761-1763
(Braun, J; Gerlach, S.) orch HENLE
sc,pap 5011, sc,cloth 5012     (H175)

Merkur
see Symphony No. 43 in E flat,
Hob.I: 43

Notturno No. 1, Hob.II: 25, in C
1.1.0.0. 2.0.0.0. strings, (viola
divisi) [8'] BREITKOPF-W        (H176)

Notturno No. 2, Hob.II: 26, in C
2.0.0.0. 2.0.0.0. strings, (viola
divisi) [8'] BREITKOPF-W        (H177)

Overture, Hob.Ia: 14
see Armida: Overture

Roxelane, La
see Symphony No. 63 in C

Schulmeister, Der
see Symphony No. 55 in E flat

Symphony No. 3
2ob,2horn,strings sc KUNZELMANN
EKB 12P ipa                            (H178)

Symphony No. 12 in E
2ob,2horn,strings sc KUNZELMANN
EKB 2P ipa                             (H179)

Symphony No. 30 in C, Hob.I: 30
"Alleluja" 1.2.0.0. 2.0.0.0.
strings [11'] BREITKOPF-W       (H180)

Symphony No. 43 in E flat, Hob.I: 43
"Merkur" 0.2.0.2. 2.0.0.0. strings
[20'] BREITKOPF-W                      (H181)

Symphony No. 44
(Trauer;Landon) orch sc KUNZELMANN
GM 750 ipa                             (H182)

Symphony No. 55 in E flat
"Schulmeister, Der" 2ob,2horn,bsn,
vla,vcl/db,vln I,vln II
KUNZELMANN ipa ETP 518, EKB 26P
                                       (H183)

Symphony No. 63 in C
"Roxelane, La" fl,2ob,2horn,bsn,
string orch sc KUNZELMANN EKB 11P
ipa                                    (H184)

Symphony No. 70 in D
fl,2ob,bsn,2horn,2trp,timp,string
orch sc KUNZELMANN EKB 25P ipa
                                       (H185)

Symphony No. 75 in D, Hob.I: 75
1.2.0.2. 2.0.0.0. timp,strings
[20'] BREITKOPF-W                      (H186)

HAYDN, [FRANZ] JOSEPH (cont'd.)
Symphony No. 81 in G, Hob.I: 81
1.2.0.2. 2.0.0.0. strings [24']
BREITKOPF-W                            (H187)

Symphony No. 90 in C, Hob.I: 90
1.2.0.2. 2.0.0.0. strings [23']
BREITKOPF-W                            (H188)

Symphony No. 91 in E flat, Hob.I: 91
1.2.0.2. 2.0.0.0. strings [18']
BREITKOPF-W                            (H189)

Symphony, Nos. 88-92
orch sc DOVER 24445-8                  (H190)

HAYDN, [JOHANN] MICHAEL (1737-1806)
Ave Regina
(Münster) B solo,vla solo,string
orch sc,pts KUNZELMANN GM 30 ipa
                                       (H191)

Concerto for 2 Clarinets and
Orchestra
2clar,orch KUNZELMANN ipa sc
10283A, oct 10283                      (H192)

Concerto for Violin and String
Orchestra, Perger 53
vln solo,orch KUNZELMANN ipa sc
10232A, oct 10232                      (H193)

Concerto in D
2ob,2horn,strings,horn solo [16']
HEINRICH sc 6219, pts 6220     (H194)

Concerto No. 1 in C for Violin
vln solo,orch min sc KUNZELMANN
ETP 1202                               (H195)

Wir Beten Dich Unendlich Wesen
(Münster) S,A soli,string orch,cont
sc,pts KUNZELMANN GM 207        (H196)

HAYES, GARY (1948-   )
Nuances Du Nord
2.2.2.1. 2.2.1.0. perc,strings
[13'] sc CANADIAN MI 1100 H417NU
                                       (H197)

Two Studies In Strings
string orch [12'] sc CANADIAN
MI 1500 H417TW                         (H198)

HAZELL, CHRIS
Shining Brightly: A Christmas
Fantasia
2(pic).2.2.2. 4.2.3.1. timp,2-
4perc,opt org,strings [9']
(fantasia on "I Saw Three Ships",
"Good Christian Men Rejoice", "In
The Bleak Midwinter") pts STAINER
HL294 rent                             (H199)

HAZLEHURST, RONNIE
Last Of The Summer Wine
instrumental ensemble sc,pts FABER
51302 6 f.s.                           (H200)

HEADINGTON, CHRISTOPHER (1930-1996)
Concerto for Violin
2.2.2.2. 4.2.3.1. timp,2perc,harp,
strings,vln solo [33'] BARDIC
                                       (H201)

HEADLESS HORSEMAN, THE see Walker,
Gwyneth

HEALEY, DEREK (1936-   )
Desert Landscape With Figures
(Fantasy for Orchestra, Op. 49)
2.2.2.2. 2.2.1.0. 2perc,harp,acord/
elec org,strings [12'] sc
CANADIAN                               (H202)

Fantasy for Orchestra, Op. 47
see Sweet Prospect

Fantasy for Orchestra, Op. 49
see Desert Landscape With Figures

Music For A Small Planet
see Symphony No. 3

Oregon Fancy  *Op.52
2.2.0.2. 2.0.0.0. harp,strings [5']
sc CANADIAN MI1200 H434OR       (H203)

Romany Variations  *Op.22
string orch,perc,org [15'] (a
diversion) sc CANADIAN
MI 1750 H434RO                         (H204)

Salal: An Idyll For Orchestra  *Op.71
2.1.2.2. 2.0.0.0. timp&perc,pno/
harp,strings [8'] sc CANADIAN
MI1200 H434SA                          (H205)

Shape-Note Symphony, A
2.2.2.2. 2.2.1.0. perc,strings
[28'] (Tribulation and the
morning - Sweet prospect -
Primrose in paradise) sc CANADIAN
MI 1100 H434SH                         (H206)

Sweet Prospect (Fantasy for
Orchestra, Op. 47) (from A Shape
Note Symphony (Part 2))

**HEALEY, DEREK (cont'd.)**

2.2.2.2. 2.2.1.0. perc,strings (on a shape note hymn) sc CANADIAN MI 1100 H434SW (H207)

Symphony No. 3 "Music For A Small Planet" 3+pic.3.3.3+contrabsn. 4.3.3.1. 4perc,harp,strings (1. Ancient Songs 2. Shouts And Dances 3. Bells) sc CANADIAN MI 1100 H434S3 (H208)

Tribulation And The Morning Trumpet (from A Shape Note Symphony (Part 1)) 2.2.2.2. 2.2.1.0. perc,strings sc CANADIAN MI 1100 H434TR (H209)

HEAR MY PRAYER, OH LORD see Purcell, Henry

**HEARD, ALAN (1942-    )**
Concerto for Clarinet and Orchestra 4(pic,alto fl).4(English horn).0.4(contrabsn).2alto sax.baritone sax.bass sax. 4.3.4.1. 6perc,2harp,pno&cel, strings,clar&clar in E flat&clar in A&bass clar solo [24'] sc CANADIAN MI 1323 H435CO (H210)

Elegy For Our Time 3(pic).3(English horn).3(clar in E flat).2. 4.3.3.1. timp,2perc, strings [15'] sc CANADIAN MI 1100 H435EL (H211)

Partita Barocca 0.3(English horn).0.2. 2.0.0.0. hpsd,strings [12'] (1. Praeludium 2. Double I: Allemande 3. Double II: Courante 4. Double III: Sicilienne 5. Double IV: Gigue) sc CANADIAN MI1200 H435PA (H212)

Sinfonia Nello Stile Antico 4(pic,alto fl).3+English horn.4(alto clar in E flat,bass clar).3+contrabsn. 4.3.3.1. timp, perc,strings [33'] sc CANADIAN MI 1100 H435SI (H213)

Symphonic Etude 2.2.2.2. 2.2.0.0. timp,strings [13'] sc CANADIAN MI 1100 H435SYM (H214)

Symphonic Variations 4(alto fl)+pic.3+English horn.4(bass clar)+clar in E flat.3+contrabsn. 4.3+2cornet.3.0. 3perc,harp,pno&cel, strings [25'] sc CANADIAN MI 1100 H435SY (H215)

HEARTLAND see Geertens, Gerda

HEART'S ASSURANCE, THE see Tippett, [Sir] Michael

HEAVENLY MAIDEN IN DEFORMATION, THE & WEAVER STAR see Isaji, Sunao

HEBRAIC SCENES see Zinn, William

HECHIZOS see Leon, Tania Justina

**HEDELIN, FREDRIK (1965-    )**
Hip Hop Hurra! 3.3.3.3(contrabsn). 4.3.3.1. 4perc, strings,pno [7'5"] STIM sc H-2743, pts (H216)

Oad 3trp,3trom,strings [7'5"] sc,pts STIM (H217)

Vingel 1.1.1.1. 1.1.1.0. strings sc STIM (H218)

Zveke Nummer Tv 1.1.1.1. 1.1.1.0. 2vln,vla,vcl,db [4'] sc,pts STIM (H219)

**HEDSTROM, ÅSE (1950-    )**
Bewegt fl,ob,clar/bass clar,horn,trom, 2perc,2vln,vla,vcl [10'40"] NORSKMI (H220)

Cantos 2(pic).2.2.2. 4.3.3.1. timp,4perc, strings [15'] NORSKMI (H221)

...E Quindi Uscimmo A Riveder Le Stelle 2.2.2.2. 4.3.3.0. timp,2perc, strings [4'15"] NORSKMI (H222)

Flores For Piano And String Orchestra [12'] NORSKMI (H223)

Nenia orch NORSK NMO 10180 (H224)

**HEDWALL, LENNART (1932-    )**
Concerto for Flute and String Orchestra STIM (H225)

Jul Igen En Liten Tid "Lätt Säsongsbetonad Rapsodi, En" 2(pic).2.2.2. 2.2.3.0. timp,perc, strings [18'] STIM sc H-2771, pts (H226)

Lätt Säsongsbetonad Rapsodi, En see Jul Igen En Liten Tid

**HEGAR, FRIEDRICH (1841-1927)**
Fest-Ouverture Op. 25 2.2.2.2. 4.2.3.1. 3timp,strings [14'] HUG (H227)

HEGARESKE see Haselbach, Josef

**HEGDAL, MAGNE (1944-    )**
Aleafonia see For Orkester

Fantasy see For Orkester

For Orkester 3(pic).3(English horn).3(bass clar).3(contrabsn). 4.2.3.1. timp,strings NORSKMI perf mat rent contains: Aleafonia; Fantasy; Sinfonia (H228)

Sinfonia see For Orkester

HEH! VOLTAIRE! see McPherson, Gordon

**HEIDER, WERNER (1930-    )**
Modelle 1.1.1.1.sax. 1.1.1.0. 4perc,pno, harp,8vln I,7vln II,6vla,5vcl, 4db,vln solo [20'] sc PETERS 00676 (H229)

Musik-Geschichte 2.2.2.2. 4.2.2.0. 3perc,strings,pno [23'] MOECK sc 5269 f.s., pts rent (H230)

Schoene Aussichten strings,horn [16'] MOECK sc 5492 f.s., pts rent (H231)

**HEIDRICH, PETER (1935-    )**
Happy Birthday: Variations, For Orchestra 3.2.2.2. 4.2.3.0. timp,perc,gtr, harp,strings [7'] SIKORSKI (H232)

HEILIGE OPFER, DAS see Knaifel, Alexander

HEILIGE STAD, DE see Goeyvaerts, Karel

**HEILMANN, HARALD (1924-    )**
Fantasy for Violoncello and Orchestra 2.2.2.2. 2.2.1.0. timp,strings [15'] HEINRICH (H233)

Trauerode (from Psalmenkantate) English horn,string orch [8'] HEINRICH (H234)

Trauerode: Für Posaune Und Tiefe Streicher (from Psalmenkantate) trom,vla I,vla II,vcl I,vcl II,db [8'] HEINRICH (H235)

HEIMKEHR, DIE see Vustin, Alexander

**HEINICHEN, JOHANN DAVID (1683-1729)**
Concerto for 4 Flutes and String Orchestra strings,cont,4fl soli [9'] BREITKOPF-W (H236)

Concerto for 2 Horns and Orchestra (Janetzky) 2horn,orch KUNZELMANN ipa sc 10214A, oct 10214 (H237)

Ouvertüre G-Dur see Suite in G

Suite in G (Winschermann, Helmut) "Ouvertüre G-Dur" 2ob,bsn,strings,cont [14'] SIKORSKI perf mat rent (H238)

**HEINRICH, ANTON PHILIP (1781-1861)**
Columbiad, The: Petite Fantasie chamber orch,1.0.2.1. 2.1.0.0. 2vln,2vla,vcl,db sc,pts KALLISTI (H239)

Otetto fl,triangle,string orch [4'] sc,pts KALLISTI (H240)

War Of The Elements, The 4+2pic.2.2.2. 4.4.3.0. 6perc, strings [8'] sc,pts KALLISTI ipa (H241)

**HEINRICH, ANTON PHILIP (cont'd.)**

Wildwood Spirit's Chant, The 3.2.4.3. 4.4.3.1. 2cornet,basset horn,ophicleide,6perc,org, strings, serp KALLISTI (H242)

HEIRESS SUITE, THE see Copland, Aaron

HEISSGELIEBTER, WENN AUF'S NEUE see Mozart, Wolfgang Amadeus, Idol Mio, Se Ritroso Altro

**HEKSTER, WALTER (1937-    )**
Relief No. 2 timp,5perc,elec gtr,strings,bsn solo [10'] DONEMUS (H243)

HEL VAN HET NOORDEN, DE see Bus, Jan

**HELBIG, MICHAEL**
Aurelia "Walzerimpression" fl,ob,2clar, horn,cel&pno,perc,gtr,harp, strings [2'35"] sc,pts BUSCH DM 065 rent (H244)

Walzerimpression see Aurelia

HELDENLEBEN: EIN TRAUM see Eyser, Eberhard

HELENA see Bantock, [Sir] Granville

**HELGASON, HALLGRIMUR (1914-    )**
Intrada Und Canzona strings [7'] BREITKOPF-W (H245)

Suita Arctica *folk song,Icelandic strings [12'] (6 songs) BREITKOPF-W (H246)

**HELGE, OLOV (1950-    )**
Borero 2(pic).2.2(bass clar).2(contrabsn). 2.0.0.0. timp,strings [6'] sc,pts STIM (H247)

Ovazione No. 2 2.2.3(bass clar).2. 4.4.3.1. timp, 2perc,harp,strings [6'] sc STIM (H248)

HELICES see Matsudaira, Yori-Aki

HÉLIO-TROPE see Padilla, Antoine

HELIOTROPE see Hagen, Daron

HELIOTROPE BOUQUET (JOPLIN) see Sieben Ragtimes Für Streichorchester: Heft 2

HELIOTROPE BOUQUET (THEATRE ORCHESTRA VERSION) see Hagen, Daron

**HELLAN, ARNE (1953-    )**
Serenade For Mezzosopran Og Strykere see Serenade for Solo Voice and Strings

Serenade for Solo Voice and Strings "Serenade For Mezzosopran Og Strykere" string orch,Mez solo NORSKMI (H249)

**HELLAWELL, PIERS**
Quadruple Elegy 2.2.2.2. 2.2.0.0. vln,perc,strings [25'] BMIC (H250)

HELLE BACH, DER: SUITE see Shostakovich, Dmitri

HELLE NACHT see Dillon, James

**HELLER, JOHN (1898-1969)**
Divertimento for Chamber Orchestra 2(pic).1(English horn).1(bass clar).1. 2.1.1.1. timp,perc, strings [12'] HEINRICH (H251)

**HELLMAN, IVAR (1891-1994)**
Symfonisk Svit 2(pic).2.2.2. 4.2.3.0. timp,harp, strings,pno [20'] (Entrata; Andante; Scherzo; Allegro moderato) sc,pts SUECIA (H252)

**HELLSTENIUS, HENRIK (1963-    )**
As Above So Below 3(pic).3(English horn).3(bass clar).3(contrabsn). 4.3.3.1. 3perc,harp,pno&cel,strings NORSKMI (H253)

Tre Bevegelser For Strykeorkester string orch NORSKMI (H254)

HEMISPHERICS see Beecroft, Norma

HEMLAND: MENUETT see Larsson, Hokan

HEMLIGHETER see Winter, Tomas

HEMPEL, MAX (1877-1959)
Laridah-Marsch
chamber orch BÖHM          (H255)

HENGARTNER, MAX (1894-1958)
Kleine Suite
string orch min sc KUNZELMANN
EES 445P          (H256)

HENKE, CLAES (1960-    )
Mellan Dalarö Och Utö
see Symphonisk Fantasi Nr 3 Op. 14

Symphonisk Fantasi Nr 3 Op. 14
"Mellan Dalarö Och Utö" 2.2.2.2.
4.2.3.1. timp,perc,strings STIM
(H257)

HENRY V: A SHAKESPEARE SCENARIO see
Walton, [Sir] William (Turner)

HENSEL, FANNY MENDELSSOHN (1805-1847)
Overture in C
2.2.2.2. 4.2.0.0. timp,strings
HILDEGARD 09646 study sc f.s.,
perf sc rent          (H258)

HENSELT, ADOLPH VON (1814-1889)
Variations for Piano and Orchestra,
Op. 11
2.2.2.2. 2.2.3.0. timp,strings,pno
solo [20'] (no score) BREITKOPF-W
(H259)

HENZE, HANS WERNER (1926-    )
Appassionatamente
"Fantasia Sopra "Lo Sdegno Del
Mare"" 3(2pic,alto fl).1+English
horn.0+2bass clar(contrabass
clar).3(contrabsn).soprano sax.
4.3.4.0. timp,5perc,cel,pno,
2harp,strings [12'] study sc
SCHOTTS ED 8428 perf mat rent
(H260)

Arien Des Orpheus
gtr,harp,hpsd,strings [25'] SCHOTTS
perf mat rent          (H261)

Chamber Concerto
strings,pno solo,fl solo [12'] pts
SCHOTTS ED 7161 (SOLI) perf mat
rent          (H262)

Cinque Piccoli Concerti E Ritornelli
2(2pic,alto fl).1(English horn,
Heckelphone).2(clar in E flat,
clar in A,bass clar,contrabass
clar).2(contrabsn). 2.1.1.0.
timp,3perc,cel,pno,harp,6vln I,
4vln II,3vla,3vcl,db [20']
SCHOTTS perf mat rent          (H263)

Compases Para Preguntas Ensimismadas
see Music For Viola And 22 Players

Deutschlandsberger Mohrentanz Nos. 1-
2
S rec,A rec,T rec,B rec,5perc,gtr,
strings,string quar soli SCHOTTS
perf mat rent sc CON 203, pts
CON 203-01 (-06)          (H264)

Drei Mozart'sche Orgelsonaten
alto fl,bass fl,ob d'amore,English
horn,bass clar,bsn,harp,gtr,vla
d'amore,2vla,2vcl,db [14']
SCHOTTS perf mat rent          (H265)

Drei Orchesterstücke
(Hartmann, Karl Amadeus) 3(2pic,
alto fl).2+English horn+
Heckelphone.2+bass clar.2+
contrabsn.alto sax(tenor sax).
4.3.3.1. timp,3perc,cel,pno,harp,
strings [20'] (on the 2nd version
of the Piano Sonata "27.April
1945") SCHOTTS perf mat rent
(H266)

Fantasia Sopra "Lo Sdegno Del Mare"
see Appassionatamente

Introduktion, Thema Und Variationen
harp,strings,vcl solo [10'] sc
SCHOTTS ED 8298 perf mat rent
(H267)

Liebeslieder
2(pic)+alto fl.2+English horn.2+
bass clar.3(contrabsn). 4.3.2+
bass trom.1. timp,3perc,cel,pno,
harp,strings,vcl solo [25'] pts
SCHOTTS ED 7418 (SOLO) perf mat
rent          (H268)

Music For Viola And 22 Players
"Compases Para Preguntas
Ensimismadas" 1(pic,alto
fl).1(English horn).1(bass
clar).1. 1.0.0.0. 2perc,hpsd,pno&
cel,A rec&T rec,harp,6vln,4vcl,db
[26'] SCHOTTS perf mat rent
(H269)

Orpheus - Concert Version
2(2pic,alto fl,bass fl).3(ob
d'amore,English horn,
Heckelphone).2(clar in E flat,
bass clar,
Heckelphone).2(contrabsn).soprano
sax(alto sax,tenor sax,baritone

HENZE, HANS WERNER (cont'd.)
sax,bass clar). 6.3.3.1. 4perc,
cel,pno,hpsd,org,harp,gtr,9vln,
4vla,4vcl,3db,speaking voice
[120'] (text by Edward Bond)
SCHOTTS perf mat rent          (H270)
2(2pic,alto fl,bass fl).4(ob
d'amore,2English horn,
2Heckelphone).2(clar in E flat,
bass clar,
Heckelphone).2(contrabsn).sax.so-
prano sax(alto sax,tenor sax,
baritone sax,bass sax). 6.3.3.1.
6perc,cel,pno,hpsd,org,2harp,
2gtr,9vln,4vla,4vcl,3db,speaking
voice [120'] (text by Edward
Bond) SCHOTTS perf mat rent
(H271)

Orpheus: Dramatic Scenes No. 1
2(2pic).3(ob d'amore,English horn,
Heckelphone).2(clar in E flat,
bass clar).2(contrabsn).sax(alto
sax,bass clar). 6.3.3.1. 4perc,
cel,pno,hpsd,org,harp,9vln,4vla,
4vcl,3db [50'] SCHOTTS perf mat
rent          (H272)

Orpheus: Dramatic Scenes No. 2
2(2pic,alto fl,bass fl).3(ob
d'amore,English horn,
Heckelphone).2(clar in E flat,
bass clar).2(contrabsn).sax(alto
sax,tenor sax,baritone sax,bass
clar). 6.3.3.1. 4perc,cel,pno,
hpsd,org,harp,gtr,9vln,4vla,4vcl,
3db [50'] SCHOTTS perf mat rent
(H273)

Paraphrasen Über Dostojewski
1(pic).0.1.1. 0.1.1.0. perc,pno,
vln,vla,vcl,db,speaking voice
[32'] (text by Ingeborg Bachmann,
voiced for Prince Myshkin)
SCHOTTS perf mat rent          (H274)

Requiem
2(2pic,alto fl).1+English
horn.1(clar in E
flat).1(contrabsn). 2.2.2.0.
timp,3perc,cel,harp,soprano sax&
alto sax&baritone sax,4vln,3vla,
3vcl,db,trp solo,pno solo, bass
trombone+contrabass trombone
[90'] (9 sacred concerti) study
sc SCHOTTS ED 8198 perf mat rent
(H275)

Selva Incantata, La
2(pic).2(English horn).2(bass
clar).2(contrabsn). 3.2.2.0.
timp,2perc,pno,8vln I,7vln II,
6vla,5vcl,4db [11'] SCHOTTS perf
mat rent          (H276)

Sentimenti Di Carl Philipp Emanuel
Bach, I
4vln,2vla,2vcl,db,fl solo,harp solo
(transcription of the Clavier-
Fantasie) SCHOTTS perf mat rent
(H277)
strings,string quar soli
(transcription of the Clavier-
Fantasie) SCHOTTS perf mat rent
(H278)

Sonata No. 2 for Strings
strings [9'] SCHOTTS perf mat rent
(H279)

Symphony No. 8
2(pic,alto fl).2(English
horn).2(bass clar).2(contrabsn).
4.2.1+bass trom.1. timp,3perc,
cel,pno,harp,strings [25'] study
sc SCHOTTS ED 8276 perf mat rent
(H280)

Tancredi
1(pic).1+English horn.1+bass
clar.1+contrabsn. 4.2.2.1. timp,
3perc,cel,pno,harp,strings,
trautonium [17'] (ballet-suite)
SCHOTTS perf mat rent          (H281)

Tanz- Und Salonmusik, From "The
Idiot"
1(pic).0.1.1. 0.1.1.0. 3perc,pno,
vln,vla,vcl,db [18'] SCHOTTS perf
mat rent          (H282)

Three Sacred Concertos (from Requiem)
2(2pic,alto fl).1+English
horn.1(clar in E
flat).1(contrabsn). 2.2.1.0.
timp,3perc,cel,harp,alto sax&
baritone sax,4vln,3vla,3vcl,db,
trp solo, bass trombone+
contrabass trombone [28'] SCHOTTS
perf mat rent          (H283)

Voie Lactée Ô Soeur Lumineuse
*toccata
1(pic).0.1.1. 1.1.1.0. timp,3perc,
vibra,marimba,cel,pno,2vln,vla,
vcl,db [8'] SCHOTTS perf mat rent
(H284)

HEPHAESTUS FORGE see Olofsson, Kent

HERBILLON, GILES (1962-    )
Carnaval De Venise
2.2.2.2. 2.2.1.0. timp,perc,
strings,cornet solo [11']
BILLAUDOT rent          (H285)

HERBOLSHEIMER, BERN
Dark Song
2.3.2.2. 4.2.2.0. timp,2perc,kbd,
strings [20'] SCHIRM.EC rent
(H286)

In Mysterium Tremendum
horn,trp,trom,perc,kbd,strings
[12'] SCHIRM.EC rent          (H287)

Symphony No. 1
2.2.2.2. 4.3.3.0. timp,perc,kbd,
strings [20'] SCHIRM.EC rent
(H288)

HERBST see Cornell, Klaus

HERBSTWEISEN see Waldteufel, Emile

HERCHET, JÖRG (1943-    )
Kantate Zum Ersten Sonntag Nach
Neujahr
0.1.1.0. 1.0.0.0. 3perc,cembalo,
5vcl,T solo [20'] PETERS          (H289)

Komposition, Für Sopran, Bariton Und
Instrumente
1.1.1.1. 1.1.1.0. 2perc,harp,vln,
vcl,SBar soli [30'] sc PETERS
01257          (H290)

Komposition Nach Böhme: Silesius
1.1.1.1. 1.1.1.0. 2perc,harp,vln,
vcl [30'] sc PETERS 03446 (H291)

Komposition No. 1
4.4.5.4. 6.4.4.1. 5perc,cel,harp,
8vln I,7vln II,6vla,5vcl,4db
[35'] sc PETERS 03062          (H292)

Komposition No. 2
4.3.4.3.alto sax. 6.3.3.1. 5perc,
pno,harp,8vln I,7vln II,6vla,
5vcl,4db [21'] sc PETERS 00695
(H293)

Komposition No. 3
2.2.3.2. 4.3.3.0. timp,2perc,pno,
harp,10vln I,8vln II,6vla,5vcl,
4db [33'] sc PETERS 02176 (H294)

HERE THE CLIFFS see Tann, Hilary

HERITAGE WALTZ see Duffy, John

HERMA see Hallgrimsson, Haflidi

HERMANSON, ÅKE (1923-1996)
Ultima *Op.13
2.2.2.2. 4.2.3.1. 6perc,strings,pno
[13'] REIMERS ED.NR 105          (H295)

HERMANSON, CHRISTER (1943-    )
Musikalisk Sammankomst
see Runion Musicale

Runion Musicale
"Musikalisk Sammankomst" string
orch [8'] perf sc STIM          (H296)

HERMES: THREE SYMPHONIC MOVEMENTS see
Kalmar, Laszlo

HÉRÓ A LEANDROS see Hlavác, Miroslav

HERO OF OUR TIME, A see London, Edwin

HEROIC STROKES OF THE BOW see Weir,
Judith

HEROISCHE-SYMPHONIE see Huber, Hans

HEROLD, LOUIS-JOSEPH-FERDINAND
(1791-1833)
Zampa: Overture
2.2.2.2. 4.2.3.0+ophicleide. timp,
perc,strings [8'] BREITKOPF-W
(H297)

HEROS ET SON MIROIR, L' see Kelemen,
Milko, Spiegel, Der

HERRMANN, HUGO (1896-1967)
Concerto Grosso
"Feiermusik II" 2.2.2.2. 3.2.3.1.
timp,perc,harp,strings,vln&vcl
soli [12'] SIKORSKI perf mat rent
(H298)

Feiermusik II
see Concerto Grosso

HERTEL, JOHANN WILHELM (1727-1789)
Sinfonia in G
(Schneider, M.) 2.2.0.2. 2.0.0.0.
strings,cont [9'] BREITKOPF-W
(H299)

HERTL, FRANTIŠEK (1906-1973)
Concertino for Trumpet and Orchestra
harp,strings,trp solo [15'] CESKY
HUD.          (H300)

Concertino for Trumpet, Piano and
Orchestra
harp,strings,trp&pno soli CESKY

HERTL, FRANTIŠEK (cont'd.)

   HUD.                          (H301)

HERZBRUNNEN, DER see Jochum, Otto

HERZOGENBERG, HEINRICH VON (1843-1900)
   Symphony No. 2 in B flat
     2.2.2.2. 4.2.3.0. timp,strings
     [38'] PETERS                 (H302)

HESPERIDÁK see Kalmar, Laszlo,
   Hesperides

HESPERIDES see Kalmar, Laszlo

HESS, DANIEL
   Concerto for 2 Pianos and Chamber
     Group
     1(alto fl).1(English horn).1.1.
     0.0.0.0. vln,vla,vcl [16'] MULL &
     SCH ESM 10'005             (H303)

   Jerusalem (Sinfonia No. 1)
     2(pic).2(English horn).2.2.
     4.3.3.1. 3perc,timp,pno,strings
     [18'] MULL & SCH ESM 10'001
                                (H304)

   Sinfonia No. 1
     see Jerusalem

HESS, ERNST (1912-1968)
   Concerto for Horn and Chamber
     Orchestra, Op. 24
     [20'] HUG                  (H305)

   Concerto for Viola, Violoncello and
     Chamber Orchestra, Op. 20
     HUG                        (H306)

   Concerto for Violin and Orchestra,
     Op. 27
     2.2.2.2. 3.2.2.1. timp,perc,harp,
     strings [30'] HUG          (H307)

   Divertimento for String Orchestra,
     Clarinet and Horn, Op. 11
     [5'] HUG                   (H308)

   Kleine Sinfonia
     see Sinfonia Accademica

   Sinfonia Accademica *Op.22
     "Kleine Sinfonia" 2.1.1.1. 1.1.1.0.
     perc,strings HUG           (H309)

HESS, WILLY (1906-   )
   Drei Ländler Für Orchester
     1.1.2.2. 2.0.0.0. strings [14']
     MULL & SCH ESM 10'037      (H310)

HETEROPHONY see Roosendael, Jan Rokus
   van

HETU, JACQUES (1938-   )
   Abîmes Du Rêve, Les *Op.36
     [Fr] 4(pic).4(English horn).4(bass
     clar).4(contrabsn). 4.4.3.1.
     timp,4perc,harp,cel,strings,B
     solo sc CANADIAN MV 1400 H591AB
     f.s.
     contains: Je Veux M'Éluder -
     Interlude; Romance Du Vin, La;
     Ténèbres; Vaisseau D'Or, Le
                                (H311)

   Concerto for Bassoon and Chamber
     Orchestra
     2(pic).2(English horn).2(bass
     clar).2. 2.1.0.0. timp,strings,
     bsn solo [18'] sc CANADIAN
     MI 1324 H591CO             (H312)

   Concerto for Clarinet
     2.2(English horn).2.2. 2.0.0.0.
     strings,clar solo [15'] sc
     CANADIAN MI 1323 H591CO    (H313)

   Concerto for Ondes Martenot, Op. 49
     2(pic).2.2.2. 4.2.0.0. timp,2perc,
     strings,Ondes Martenot solo [23']
     sc CANADIAN MI 1301 H591CO (H314)

   Concerto, Op. 51
     1.2.2.2. 2.2.0.0. timp&perc,
     strings,fl solo [16'] pno red,
     solo pt CANADIAN MI 1321 H591CO
                                (H315)

   Fantasy for Piano and Orchestra, Op.
     21
     4(pic).3(English horn).3(bass
     clar).2. 4.3.3.1. timp,3perc,
     strings,pno solo [8'] sc CANADIAN
     MI 1361 H591FA             (H316)

   Je Veux M'Éluder - Interlude
     see Abîmes Du Rêve, Les

   Mirages (Suite for Chamber Orchestra)
     Op.34
     2(pic).2(English horn).2(bass
     clar).2. 2.2.0.0. timp&perc,
     strings [16'] (1. Vision 2.
     Tourbillon 3. Hymne 4. Cortège 5.
     Final) sc CANADIAN MI1200 H591MI
                                (H317)

HETU, JACQUES (cont'd.)
   Mouvement Symphonique
     see Tombeau De Nelligan, Le

   Romance Du Vin, La
     see Abîmes Du Rêve, Les

   Suite for Chamber Orchestra
     see Mirages

   Ténèbres
     see Abîmes Du Rêve, Les

   Tombeau De Nelligan, Le *Op.52
     "Mouvement Symphonique" 3(pic).2+
     English horn.3(bass
     clar).3(contrabsn). 4.3.3.1.
     timp,perc,strings [12'] sc
     CANADIAN MI 1100 H591TO    (H318)

   Vaisseau D'Or, Le
     see Abîmes Du Rêve, Les

HEUBERGER, RICHARD (1850-1914)
   Nachtmusik *Op.7
     orch KUNZELMANN ipa sc WW 909P, sc,
     pts WW 909                 (H319)

HEWITT-JONES, TONY (1926-   )
   Whirligig
     strings CHESTER pts CH55567, sc
     CH55566                    (H320)

HEYDUCK DANCE see Ranki, György

HEYN, VOLKER (1938-   )
   Ferro Canto
     2+pic.3(English horn).2+bass clar+
     2contrabass clar.1+
     2contrabsn.bass sax. 4.4.4.0.
     5perc,2pno,org,8vln I,7vln II,
     6vla,5vcl,4db, sopranino sax
     [30'] study sc BREITKOPF-W
     PB 5406                    (H321)

HIDALGO, MANUEL (1956-   )
   Alegrías (Concerto for Piano and
     Chamber Orchestra)
     2(pic,bass fl).0.2(bass clar).0.
     0.1.1.0. 2perc,harp,2vln I,2vla,
     2vcl,2db,AA soli,pno solo [13']
     study sc BREITKOPF-W PB 5404
                                (H322)

   Concerto for Piano and Chamber
     Orchestra
     see Alegrías

   Concerto for Saxophone and
     Instrumental Ensemble
     see Romance De Le Chatelier

   Einfache Musik
     strings [12'] BREITKOPF-W  (H323)

   Fisica
     3(3pic).3(English horn).2+bass
     clar.0+2contrabsn. 4.3.3.1.
     3perc,acord,12vln I,12vln
     II,8vla,8vcl,8db [14'] BREITKOPF-
     W                          (H324)

   Gloria for 6 Voices and Orchestra
     2(pic).2.1+bass clar.2(contrabsn).
     2.0.1.1. 3perc,harp,strings,
     SSAABarBar soli [15'] BREITKOPF-W
                                (H325)

   Nuut
     0+pic.1.1+bass clar.1. 1.1.1.0.
     2perc,harp,pno,2vln I,2vla,2vcl,db,
     acord solo [16'] BREITKOPF-W
                                (H326)

   Romance De Le Chatelier (Concerto for
     Saxophone and Instrumental
     Ensemble)
     2.0.1+bass clar.1. 0.1.1.0. 2perc,
     harp,pno,2vln I,2vla,2vcl,db,
     baritone sax solo [13']
     BREITKOPF-W                (H327)

HIDAS, FRIGYES (1928-   )
   Adagio (from The Ballet "The Cedar")
     "Pleasure-Ride At The Seaside And
     Pas De Deux" 2+pic.2+English
     horn.3+bass clar.2+contrabsn.
     4.3.3.1. timp,perc,harp,cel,
     strings [12'] EMB rent    (H328)

   Concerto for Harp and Orchestra
     string orch,cel,vibra,harp solo
     [19'] EMB rent             (H329)

   Concerto for Trombone and Orchestra
     timp,perc,strings,trom solo [15']
     EMB rent                   (H330)

   Concerto for Trombone, No. 2
     2.2.3.2. 3.2.3.1. timp,3perc,harp,
     cel,strings,trom solo [14'] EMB
     rent                       (H331)

   Concerto for Violin and Orchestra
     2.2.2+bass clar.2. 3.2.0.0. timp,
     perc,harp,strings,vln solo [13']
     EMB rent                   (H332)

HIDAS, FRIGYES (cont'd.)
   Concerto Semplice
     string orch,clar solo [19'] EMB
     rent                       (H333)

   Cymboa
     cimbalom,ob,strings, (5, 4, 3, 3,
     2) [11'] EMB rent          (H334)

   Double Concerto For Tenor And Bass
     Trombone And Symphonic Orchestra
     2+pic.2.2+bass clar.2. 4.2.0.0.
     timp,perc,harp,cel,strings,trom&
     bass trom soli [18'] EMB rent
                                (H335)

   Három Tétel
     see Three Movements

   Pleasure-Ride At The Seaside And Pas
     De Deux
     see Adagio

   Quintetto Concertante
     brass quin,2.2.2.2. 3.2.1.1. timp,
     perc,cel,horn solo,strings [19']
     EMB rent                   (H336)

   Sinfonia
     2+2pic.3+English horn.3+clar in E
     flat+bass clar.3. 4.5.4.1. harp,
     cel&pno,strings [22'] EMB rent
                                (H337)

   Széchenyi Concerto
     3(pic).3(English horn).4(bass
     clar).2. 4.3.3.1. timp,perc,
     strings [10'] EMB rent     (H338)

   Three Movements
     "Három Tétel" 2+pic.2+English
     horn.3+bass clar.2+contrabsn.
     4.3.3.1. timp,perc,cel,strings
     [26'] EMB rent             (H339)

HIDDEN VARIABLES see Matthews, Colin

HIDDEN VOICE see Harvey, Jonathan

HIER SOLL ICH DICH DENN SEHEN,
   CONSTANZE! see Mozart, Wolfgang
   Amadeus

HIGGAJON IV see Dijk, C. Van see Dijk,
   Jan van

HIGH ANXIETY see Marina, Cristian

HIGHLAND'S BALLAD see Tomasi, Henri

HILL-SONG NO. 2 see Grainger, Percy
   Aldridge

HILLBORG, ANDERS (1954-   )
   Celestial Mechanics
     8vln,4vla,3vcl,2db,perc [20'] sc
     NORDISKA                   (H340)
     see Himmelsmekanik

   Clang And Fury
     4(pic).4.5(bass clar).1(contrabsn).
     6.4.3.1. 4perc,strings [27'] sc
     STIM H-2612                (H341)

   Himmelsmekanik
     "Celestial Mechanics" string orch,
     perc [18'] sc STIM         (H342)

   Introduktion
     see Lava

   Lava
     "Introduktion" 3.3.3.0. 4.3.3.1.
     strings [1'5"] sc STIM     (H343)

   Liquid Marble
     3(pic).3(English horn).2.2.
     4.3.3.0. strings [11'] STIM sc
     H-2898, pts               (H344)

   Meltdown Variations
     1.1.3(pic).2(contrabsn). 1.1.1.1.
     perc,strings sc,pts STIM   (H345)

   Worlds
     3xylo&claves,3marimba,elec gtr,
     2harp,2pno,16vln I,16vln II,
     12vla,10vcl,8db [11'5"] sc
     NORDISKA ED.NR 10566       (H346)

HILLER, FERDINAND (1811-1885)
   Traum In Der Christnacht, Ein
     *Overture
     1.2.2.2. 4.2.3.0. timp,strings [7']
     BREITKOPF-W                (H347)

HILLER, LEJAREN ARTHUR (1924-1994)
   Time Of The Heathen: Suite
     1.1.1.1. 2.2.1.1. 2perc,strings
     without vln [25'] sc,pts KALLISTI
     ipa                        (H348)

HILLER, WILFRIED (1941-   )
   Hamelin: Drei Klangbilder (from Der
     Rattenfänger)
     timp,3perc,pno&opt cel,harp,strings
     [14'] SCHOTTS perf mat rent

HILLER, WILFRIED (cont'd.)
                                              (H349)

Hintergründige Gedanken Des
    Erzbischöflichen Salzburger
    Compositeurs Heinrich Ignaz Franz
    Biber Beim Belauschen Eines
    Vogelkonzerts
    strings [15'] SCHOTTS perf mat rent
                                              (H350)

München
    1(alto fl)+pic.2.2.2. 4.2.2.1.
    timp,perc,cel,pno,harp,strings
    [20'] (dance suite) SCHOTTS perf
    mat rent                                  (H351)

Pegasus 51 *Concerto
    2(pic).2.2.2.alto sax. 4.3.3.1.
    timp,3perc,harp,strings, jazz
    percussion solo [16'] SCHOTTS
    perf mat rent                             (H352)

Veitstanz
    3(pic).2.0.2+contrabsn. 4.3.3.1.
    3timp,3perc,cel,harp,strings,clar
    solo [18'] SCHOTTS perf mat rent
                                              (H353)

HILMAR, FRANTIŠEK (1803-1881)
    Esmeralda (Polka)
    (Smetáček) 2.2.2.2. 4.2.3.0. perc,
    strings CESKY HUD.                        (H354)

Polka
    see Esmeralda

HIMALAYA see Kruyf, Ton de

HIMMELSMEKANIK see Hillborg, Anders

HINDEMITH, PAUL (1895-1963)
    In Sturm Und Eis
    1(pic).1.1.0. 0.1.1.0. timp,perc,
    pno,harmonium,strings SCHOTTS
    perf mat rent                             (H355)

Ludus Tonalis (Suite No. 1 for
    Orchestra)
    (Santos, Joao Oliver dos) 3(2pic,
    alto fl).3(ob d'amore,English
    horn).2+clar in E flat+bass
    clar.2(contrabsn).tenor sax.
    4.3(piccolo trp).3.1. 2timp,
    5perc,pno&cel,2harp,16vln I,14vln
    II,12vla,10vcl,8db,bass trp&
    euphonium [63'] (studies in
    counterpoint) SCHOTTS perf mat
    rent                                      (H356)
    (Santos, Joao Oliver dos) 3(2pic,
    alto fl).3+English horn.2+clar in
    E flat+bass clar.2(contrabsn).
    4.3.3.1. timp,5perc,pno&cel,
    2harp,16vln I,14vln II,12vla,
    10vcl,8db [20'] SCHOTTS perf mat
    rent                                      (H357)

Schulwerk, Op. 4: 5pieces4, No. 4
    strings [10'] SCHOTTS perf mat rent
                                              (H358)
Schulwerk, Op. 44, No. 2: 8 Canons
    strings [6'] SCHOTTS perf mat rent
                                              (H359)
Schulwerk, Op. 44, No. 3: 8 Pieces
    strings [8'] SCHOTTS perf mat rent
                                              (H360)
Sing- Und Spiel-Musiken: Ein Jäger
    Aus Kurpfalz *Op.45,No.3
    winds,strings [5'] SCHOTTS perf mat
    rent                                      (H361)

Suite No. 1 for Orchestra
    see Ludus Tonalis

HINDUMÄDCHEN, DAS see Reinecke, Carl

HINTERGRÜNDIGE GEDANKEN DES
    ERZBISCHÖFLICHEN SALZBURGER
    COMPOSITEURS HEINRICH IGNAZ FRANZ
    BIBER BEIM BELAUSCHEN EINES
    VOGELKONZERTS see Hiller, Wilfried

HIP HOP HURRA! see Hedelin, Fredrik

HIPMAN, SILVESTER (1893-1974)
    Concerto Da Camera
    strings,clar [18'] CESKY HUD.
                                              (H362)

HIPPENSCOMBE VALLEY 'FANTASY' see
    Somers-Cocks, John

HIRAI V (RIVISION) see Matsuo, Masataka

HIRAISHI, HIROKAZU (1948-    )
    Dreamscape
    orch [22'] JAPAN                          (H363)

HIROSE, RYOHEI (1930-    )
    Sinfonia Kyoto
    orch [21'] JAPAN                          (H364)

HIROSHIMA REQUIEM: I. PRELUDIO -
    "NIGHT" see Hosokawa, Toshio

HIROSHIMA REQUIEM: III. "DAWN" see
    Hosokawa, Toshio

HIRSCHBERGER, ALBERICUS (1709-1745)
    Concerto No. 1 in C
    see Raitenhaslacher Konzert Nr. 1

Concerto No. 2 in G
    "St. Alberici" 2horn,2vln,cont
    COPPENRATH sc 16.001-01, kbd pt
    16.001-03, pts 16.001-21, pts
    16.001-43                                 (H365)

Raitenhaslacher Konzert Nr. 1
    (Concerto No. 1 in C)
    2trp,timp,strings,hpsd/org sc
    KÜNZELMANN GM 67 ipa                      (H366)

St. Alberici
    see Concerto No. 2 in G

HISADA, NORIKO (1963-    )
    Pursuit
    string orch,vcl solo [12'] JAPAN
                                              (H367)

HISATOME, TOMOYUKI (1955-    )
    Pensiero Del Bosco, Il
    orch [17'] JAPAN                          (H368)

HISCOTT, JAMES (1948-    )
    Dancing On Wings Of The Fire
    1.1.1.1. 1.1.1.0. perc,strings,
    acord solo sc CANADIAN
    MI 1366 H673DA                            (H369)

Four Pieces For String Orchestra
    string orch [14'] sc CANADIAN
    MI 1500 H673FO                            (H370)

Limitation
    6vln,4vla,2vcl [13'] sc CANADIAN
    MI 1500 H673LI                            (H371)

Moss Growing On Ruins
    1(alto fl).1(English horn).1(bass
    clar).1. 4.0.0.0. perc,2vln,vla,
    2vcl [20'] sc CANADIAN
    MI1200 H673MO                             (H372)

Planes
    2(pic).2.2(bass clar).2(contrabsn).
    4.3.3.1. timp,3perc,strings [13']
    sc CANADIAN MI 1100 H673PL                (H373)

HISTORIE MÉHO SRDCE see Jelinek,
    Stanislav

HLAS NEJSLADŠÍ see Jirák, Karel
    Boleslav

HLAVÁC, MIROSLAV (1923-    )
    Concerto for Violin and Orchestra
    3.2.2.2. 4.3.3.1. timp,perc,xylo,
    harp,strings,vln solo [25'] CESKY
    HUD.                                      (H374)

Héró A Leandros
    3.2.2.3. 4.3.3.1. timp,perc,harp,
    strings [25'] CESKY HUD.                  (H375)

Serenade for String Orchestra
    string orch [8'] PANTON                   (H376)

Sinfonietta for String Orchestra
    string orch [13'] CESKY HUD.              (H377)

Vychodoslovenské Lidové Písne
    string orch/string quar [20'] CESKY
    HUD.                                      (H378)

HLAVACEK, LIBOR (1928-    )
    Concerto for Violin and Orchestra
    0.2.0.0. 0.1.0.0. perc,pno,strings,
    vln solo [20'] CESKY HUD.                 (H379)

Dva Fragmenty
    strings,timp,perc [14'] CESKY HUD.
                                              (H380)

Koncertni Valcík
    2.2.2.2. 4.1.3.0. timp,perc,harp,
    strings [12'] CESKY HUD.                  (H381)

Pochod Socialismu
    1.2.2.2. 4.3.3.1. timp,perc,strings
    [5'] CESKY HUD.                           (H382)

Poema O Ceskomoravské Vysocine
    2.2.2.2. 2.2.0.0. timp,strings,Bar
    solo [13'] CESKY HUD.                     (H383)

Pomnik Neznámého Vojína
    2.0.1.0. 2.1.0.0. timp,perc,pno,
    strings,speaking voice,vln solo
    [15'] CESKY HUD.                          (H384)

Tarantelle for Orchestra
    2.2.2.2. 4.2.3.1. timp,perc,harp,
    strings [5'] CESKY HUD.                   (H385)

HLOBIL, EMIL (1901-1987)
    Concerto for Marimba and Orchestra
    3.3.3.2. 0.3.3.0. timp,perc,
    strings,marimba solo [16'] CESKY
    HUD.                                      (H386)

Concerto for Violoncello and
    Orchestra, Op. 106
    3.2.2.2. 0.3.3.0. timp,perc,harp,
    strings,vcl solo [22'] CESKY HUD.

HLOBIL, EMIL (cont'd.)
                                              (H387)

HÖ see Fernold, Johan

HO CAPITO, SIGNOR, SI see Mozart,
    Wolfgang Amadeus

HOBBIT, THE see Blyton, Carey

HOBSON, BRUCE (1943-    )
    Cantilena Infinita [20']
    1.1.1.0. 1.1.1.0. 2perc,strings
    (diff) manuscript EQUINOX f.s., pts
    rent                                      (H388)

Concerto for Orchestra [17']
    4.4.5.3. 4.2.2.1. 2perc,strings
    (diff) manuscript EQUINOX f.s., pts
    rent                                      (H389)

Concerto For Three Groups [16']
    Group 1: 2horn, 2trp, 2trom;
    Group 2: clar in E flat, clar,
    trp, pno, perc; Group 3:
    baritone horn, tuba, cel, pno,
    2perc
    (diff) manuscript EQUINOX f.s., pts
    rent                                      (H390)

Three For Two Trumpets And Orchestra
    [18']
    3.3.3.0. 3.0.2.1. 2perc,strings
    without vla
    (diff) EQUINOX f.s., ipa              (H391)

HOC EST HOKUS POKUS see Jansson, Reine

HOCHEL, STANISLAV (1950-    )
    Musica Pathetica
    2.2.2.2. 4.3.3.1. perc,harp,
    strings,pno solo [11'] CESKY HUD.
                                              (H392)

Naše Doba
    3.3.4.3. 4.2.2.1. perc,strings,
    speaking voice,pno solo [21']
    CESKY HUD.                                (H393)

HÖCHSTES VERTRAUN HAST DU MIR SCHON ZU
    DANKEN see Wagner, Richard

HOCHZEIT DER SCHÄFERIN, DIE see
    Lahusen, Christian

HOCHZEITSTAG, DER see Benedict, [Sir]
    Julius

HOCKE, WOLFGANG
    Aquarelle Für Bariton Und Orchester
    orch,Bar solo VOGT VF 1209 (H394)

Metamorphosen Für Orchester
    orch VOGT VF 1197                         (H395)

HODDINOTT, ALUN (1929-    )
    Concerto for Clarinet and Orchestra,
    No. 2
    2.1.2.1. 3.0.0.0. timp,perc,strings
    [21'] perf sc set OXFORD 3644134
    sc,pts set                                (H396)

Concerto for Orchestra
    3.3.3.3. 4.3.3.1. timp,3perc,harp,
    strings [22'] LENGNICK             (H397)

Concerto for Piano and Orchestra, No.
    3
    3(pic).2.2+bass clar.2. 4.3.3.0.
    timp,3perc,harp,cel,strings,pno
    solo [24'] perf sc set OXFORD
    3645262 sc,pts rent                       (H398)

Four Scenes From "The Trumpet Major"
    see Trumpet Major, The: Four Scenes

Trumpet Major, The: Four Scenes
    "Four Scenes From "The Trumpet
    Major"" 3(pic).0.2+bass clar.2+
    contrabsn. 4.2.3.0. timp,3perc,
    harp,pno&cel,strings [20'] perf
    sc set OXFORD 3644541 sc,pts rent
                                              (H399)

HODGSON, IVOR JAMES
    Concerto for Contrabassoon
    2.2.2.2. 2.1.2.1. timp,perc,
    strings,contrabsn solo [30'] (4
    mvts.) CMA 206 set rent, sc
                                              (H400)

Theme and Variations
    1.2.2.2. 2.1.0.0. timp,perc,harp,
    strings,pno [30'] CMA perf mat
    rent kbd pt 141, sc 136           (H401)

HOFFMAN, JOEL
    Between Ten
    3.3.3.3. 4.3.3.1. timp,3perc,
    strings [12'] SCHIRM.EC rent      (H402)

Concerto for Violin
    vln solo,3.3.3.3. 4.3.3.1. timp,
    2perc,harp,strings [37']
    SCHIRM.EC rent                            (H403)

Concerto for Violin, Viola,
    Violoncello and Orchestra
    vln solo,vla solo,vcl solo,2.2.3.3.

HOFFMAN, JOEL (cont'd.)
4.2.3.1. timp,perc,strings [26']
SCHIRM.EC rent (H404)

Double Concerto For Viola, Cello And Orchestra
vla solo,vcl solo,3.2.2.2. 2.2.2.0. timp,2perc,harp,kbd,strings [31']
SCHIRM.EC rent (H405)

HOFFMANN
Serenade for Flute and Strings
BOIS (H406)

HOFFMANN, LEOPOLD (HOFMANN) (1730-1793)
Concerto for Flute and String Orchestra in D
fl solo,string orch KUNZELMANN ipa sc 10278A, oct 10278 (H407)

Concerto in D for Flute, 2 Horns, Strings and Continuo
(Burmeister) strings,cont,opt 2horn,fl solo [25'] (formerly attributed to Joseph Haydn)
PETERS (H408)

Concerto in G for Flute, Strings and Continuo
(Burmeister) [16'] PETERS (H409)

HOFFMEISTER, FRANZ ANTON (1754-1812)
Concerto for Clarinet and Orchestra in B flat
(Balassa, Hajdu) 2ob,2horn,strings, clar solo [15'] EMB rent (H410)
(Balasza) 2ob,2horn,strings,orch KUNZELMANN ipa sc 10115A, oct 10115 (H411)

Concerto for Clarinet, Bassoon and Orchestra
2ob,2horn,strings,clar&bsn soli KUNZELMANN ipa sc 10179A, oct 10179 (H412)

Concerto for Piano and Orchestra in D, Op. 24
pno solo,orch sc KUNZELMANN EKB 27P ipa (H413)

Concerto for Viola and Orchestra in D
vla solo,orch KUNZELMANN ipa sc 10185A, oct 10185 (H414)

Concerto No. 1 in D, Op. 64
(Müller) 2fl,2ob,2horn,string orch KUNZELMANN ipa sc 10203A, oct 10203 (H415)

Sinfonia Concertante for Clarinet, Bassoon and String Orchestra
clar,bsn,string orch KUNZELMANN 10271 (H416)

HOFFSTETTER, JOH. U.
Sinfonia for 2 Oboes, 2 Horns, Strings and Continuo in D
0.2.0.0. 0.0.0.0. vln I,vln II,vla, vcl,db,cont,opt 2horn MOSELER sc 40.133-00, pts 40.133-01 TO 02, set 40.133-09 (H417)

HOFMANN, HEINRICH (1852-1902)
Konzertstück in G minor, Op. 98
2.2.2.2. 4.2.0.0. timp,strings,fl solo [11'] BREITKOPF-W (H418)

HOFMANN, LEOPOLD (1738-1793)
Concertino for Violoncello in C
2ob,2horn,2vln,vla,vcl,db,2vcl soli [14'] ARTARIA AE067 (H419)

Concerto for Flute in A
2vln,vla,vcl,db,fl solo [13'] ARTARIA AE143 (H420)

Concerto for Flute in D
2horn,2vln,vla,vcl,db,fl solo [18'] ARTARIA AE142 (H421)

Concerto for Flute in D, MIN 1
2vln,vla,vcl,db,fl solo [16'] ARTARIA AE139 (H422)

Concerto for Flute in D, MIN 2
2horn,2vln,vla,vcl,db,fl solo [18'] ARTARIA AE144 (H423)

Concerto for Flute in D, MIN 3
2horn,2vln,vla,vcl,db,fl solo [12'] ARTARIA AE141 (H424)

Concerto for Flute in E minor
2horn,2vln,vla,vcl,db,fl solo [14'] ARTARIA AE138 (H425)

Concerto for Flute in G
2vln,vla,vcl,db,fl solo [20'] ARTARIA AE145 (H426)

Concerto for Flute in G, MIN 1
2horn,2vln,vla,vcl,db,fl solo [12'] ARTARIA AE140 (H427)

HOFMANN, LEOPOLD (cont'd.)
Concerto for Oboe and Cembalo in C
2vln,vla,vcl,db,ob&cembalo soli [22'] ARTARIA AE070 (H428)

Concerto for Oboe and Cembalo in F
2horn,2vln,vla,vcl,db,ob&cembalo soli [20'] ARTARIA AE071 (H429)

Concerto for Oboe in C
2horn,2vln,vla,vcl,db,ob solo [16'] ARTARIA AE068 (H430)

Concerto for Oboe in G
2horn,2vln,vla,vcl,db,ob solo [12'] ARTARIA AE069 (H431)

Concerto for Violin and Violoncello in G
2vln,vla,vcl,db,vln&vcl soli [21'] ARTARIA AE028 (H432)

Concerto for Violin in A
2vln,vla,vcl,db,vln solo [19'] ARTARIA AE031 (H433)

Concerto for Violin in B flat
2vln,vla,vcl,db,vln solo [16'] ARTARIA AE032 (H434)

Concerto for Violoncello in C
2horn,2vln,vla,vcl,db,vcl solo [15'] ARTARIA AE029 (H435)

Concerto for Violoncello in C, MIN 1
2horn,2vln,db,vcl solo [21'] ARTARIA AE064 (H436)

Concerto for Violoncello in C, MIN 2
2vln,db,vcl solo [12'] ARTARIA AE001 (H437)

Concerto for Violoncello in C, MIN 3
2vln,db,vcl solo [11'] ARTARIA AE065 (H438)

Concerto for Violoncello in D
2vln,vla,vcl,db,vcl solo [13'] ARTARIA AE063 (H439)

Concerto for Violoncello in D, MIN 1
2horn,2vln,vla,vcl,db,vcl solo [12'] ARTARIA AE066 (H440)

Concerto for Violoncello in D, MIN 2
2horn,2vln,vla,vcl,db,vcl solo [19'] ARTARIA AE030 (H441)

Sinfonia in B flat
2ob,2vln,vla,vcl,db [9'] ARTARIA AE024 (H442)

Sinfonia in C
2ob,2horn,2vln,vla,vcl,db [17'] ARTARIA AE025 (H443)

Sinfonia in D
2ob,2horn,2vln,vla,vcl,db [12'] ARTARIA AE022 (H444)

Sinfonia in F
2vln,vla,vcl,db [14'] ARTARIA AE023 (H445)

Sinfonia in F, MIN 1
2ob,2horn,2vln,vla,vcl,db [11'] ARTARIA AE026 (H446)

HOFMANN, WOLFGANG (1922-   )
Adagio Und Capriccio Für Trompete, Klavier Und Streicher
strings [8'] sc PETERS 00709 (H447)

Concerto for Viola and String Orchestra
"Konzert" string orch,vla solo HEINRICH (H448)

Intermezzo (from Der Mond)
"Mond, Der: Intermezzo" 0.0.1.0. 2.0.1.0. perc,pno,strings [6']
PETERS (H449)

Konzert
see Concerto for Viola and String Orchestra

Mond, Der: Furioso
0.1.1.1. 2.1.1.0. perc,pno,8vln I, 7vln II,6vla,5vcl,4db [3'] sc PETERS 00737 (H450)

Mond, Der: Intermezzo
0.0.1.0. 2.0.1.0. perc,pno,8vln I, 7vln II,6vla,5vcl,4db [6'] PETERS 00736 (H451)
see Intermezzo

Mond, Der: Sinfonia Brevis
0.1.0.1. 0.1.1.0. perc,pno,8vln I, 7vln II,6vla,5vcl,4db [7'] sc PETERS 00735 (H452)

HOHELIED see Zechlin, Ruth

HOHENSEE, WOLFGANG (1927-   )
Tre Bozze
orch [17'] BREITKOPF-W (H453)

HOHL, HÖHLE see Ruzicka, Peter

HOIBY, LEE (1926-   )
Serpent, The
2(pic).1.1+bass clar.1. 0.0.0.1. perc,harp,strings,med solo [4']
PEER rent (H454)

HOLAB, WILLIAM
Symphony for Strings
8vln I,7vln II,6vla,5vcl,4db [14'] sc PETERS 03900 (H455)

HOLBERGIANA see Gade, Niels Wilhelm

HOLBROOKE, JOSEPH (1878-1958)
Children Of Don, The: Overture *Op.5
3.3.3.3. 4.3.3.1. timp,3perc,2harp, 8vln I,7vln II,6vla,5vcl,4db sc PETERS 04619 (H456)

HOLD, TREVOR
Concerto for Piano and Orchestra
3.3.3.3. 4.2.3.1. timp,2perc, strings,pno solo [30'] manuscript BMIC (H457)

HOLD MLÁDÍ see Lukas, Zdenek

HÖLDERLIN FRAGMENTE I-V see Genzmer, Harald

HÖLDERLIN-GESÄNGE see Thiele, Siegfried

HOLIDAY IN BRAZIL see McCauley, William A.

HOLKA MODROOKÁ see Sevcik, Otakar

HOLLAND, THEODORE (1878-1947)
Ellingham Marshas
2.2.2.2. 4.2.3.0. timp,perc,8vln I, 7vln II,6vla,5vcl,4db,vla solo [19'] sc,solo pt PETERS 04621 (H458)

HOLLAND ANZIKSZ see Vajda, János, Picture Postcard From Holland

HÖLLER, YORK (1944-   )
Aura
4(2pic).3(English horn).3(bass clar).3(contrabsn). 4.3.3.1. 5perc,harp,2kbd,14vln I,12vln II, 10vla,8vcl,6db [20'] BOOSEY-ENG rent (H459)

Fanal
2.2(English horn).2(bass clar).2(contrabsn). 2.1.2.1. 2perc,harp,3vln,2vla,2vcl,db,trp solo [17'] BOOSEY-ENG rent (H460)

Margaritas Traum (from Der Meister Und Margarita) scena
3(3pic,alto fl).3(English horn).3(clar in E flat,bass clar).3(contrabsn).alto sax. 4.4.3.1. 6-7perc,harp,gtr&elec gtr,cel,pno,2synthesizer, electronic tape,14vln I,12vln II, 10vla,8vcl,6db,S solo [30'] BOOSEY-ENG rent (H461)

Pensées *Req
3(pic).2+English horn.2+bass clar.2+contrabsn. 4.3.3.1. timp, 5-6perc,harp,synthesizer, electronic equipment,electronic tape,14vln I,12vln II,10vla,8vcl, 6db,pno solo, computer (Mac) [25'] BOOSEY-ENG rent (H462)

HOLLIGER, HEINZ (1939-   )
Concerto for Violin
3(3pic,alto fl).3(English horn).4(2bass clar).2. 3.3.3(tenor sax,baritone sax).0. timp,5perc,cym,cel,harp,6vln I, 6vln II,4vla,4vcl,3db [24'] (hommage à Louis Soutter) SCHOTTS perf mat rent (H463)

Drei Liebeslieder
2(pic).2(English horn).2(bass clar).2(contrabsn). 2.4.2.0. timp,perc,cel,pno,harp,gtr, strings,A solo [9'] (text by Georg Trakl) SCHOTTS perf mat rent (H464)

Ostinato Funebre (from Scardanelli Zyklus)
2(2pic).2.2(bass clar)+contrabass clar.2. 2.1.1.0. timp,3perc,2vln, 2vla,2vcl,db [8'] SCHOTTS perf mat rent (H465)

(S)Irató
3(2pic).3(English horn).2+2bass clar+contrabass clar.3(contrabsn). 4.3.4.1. timp, 5perc,pno,cel,cym,harp,14vln I,

HOLLIGER, HEINZ (cont'd.)

12vln II.10vla,10vcl,6vcl [15']
study sc SCHOTTS ED 8439 perf mat
rent　　　　(H466)

Schaufelrad (from Scardanelli Zyklus)
0+alto fl.0+ob d'amore+English
horn.1.2.2alto sax. 1.1.1.0. vln,
vla,vcl,4-5 female soli [8']
SCHOTTS perf mat rent　　(H467)

Zwei Lieder
3(2alto fl).2(2English horn).3(bass
clar)+bass clar.2. 4.4.2.1. timp,
4perc,cel,pno,harp,gtr,14vln I,
12vln II,10vla,8vcl,6db,A solo
[14'] (text by Georg Trakl)
SCHOTTS perf mat rent　　(H468)

HOLLÓS, MÁTÉ
Sinfonietta
1.0.1.1. 0.1.0.0. harp,marimba,vln,
vla,vcl [10'] EMB rent　　(H469)

HOLLOWAY, ROBIN (1943-　)
Concerto for Clarinet, Saxophone and
2 Chamber Orchestras, Op. 68
"Double Concerto, Op. 68" 2(alto
fl,pic).1+English horn.1(bass
clar).2(contrabsn). 1.1.1.1.
timp&cym,2perc,harp,pno&cel,4vln,
2vla,2vcl,2db,clar solo,sax solo
[22'] BOOSEY-ENG rent　　(H470)

Concerto for Violin and Orchestra
3.2.2.2. 2.2.1.0. 3perc,cel,pno,
harp,strings,vln solo [38']
BOOSEY-ENG　　(H471)

Concerto for Violin, Op. 70
3(2pic,alto fl).2(English
horn).2(clar in E flat).2.
2.2.1.0. 3perc,harp,cel,pno,8vln
I,8vln II,8vla,8vcl,4db [24']
BOOSEY-ENG rent　　(H472)

Double Concerto, Op. 68
see Concerto for Clarinet,
Saxophone and 2 Chamber
Orchestras, Op. 68

Fantasy-Pieces (On The Heine
"Liederkreis" Of Schumann)
*Op.16
2.1.1.1. 1.1.0.0. pno,2vln,vla,vcl,
db [28'] BOOSEY-ENG rent　(H473)

Frost At Midnight
2.2.0.2. 0.2.0.0. perc,strings
BOOSEY-ENG　　(H474)

Scenes From Schumann　*Op.13
"Seven Paraphrases For Orchestra"
3(pic,alto fl).2(English
horn).2(bass clar).2(contrabsn).
2.2.1.0. harp,pno,strings [22']
BOOSEY-ENG rent　　(H475)

Serenade for Strings in E, Op. 73
[20'] BOOSEY-ENG rent　　(H476)

Seven Paraphrases For Orchestra
see Scenes From Schumann

Third Idyll: Frost At Midnight
*Op.78
2(2pic).2(English horn).0.2.
0.2.0.0. perc,7vln I,6vln II,
4vla,3vcl,2db [12'] BOOSEY-ENG
rent　　(H477)

Wagner Nights (from Parsifal)
2(pic).2+English horn.2(clar in E
flat)+bass clar.2(contrabsn).
3.2.3.0. timp,2perc,harp,strings
[20'] BOOSEY-ENG rent　　(H478)

HOLLYOAK, SIDNEY
Welsh Suite
2.2.2.2. 2.2.3.0. timp,pno,8vln I,
7vln II,6vla,5vcl,4db [6'] sc
PETERS 04622　　(H479)

HOLMAN, DEREK (1931-　)
Serenade for Clarinet and String
Orchestra
sc,solo pt CANADIAN MI 1623 H747SE
　　(H480)

HOLOCAUST-IN MEMORIAM see Badian, Maya

HOLOCAUSTO see Betancur-Gonzalez,
Valentin, Sinfonia No. 2

HOLST, GUSTAV (1874-1934)
Hampshire Suite, A　*Op.28,No.2
(Jacob, Gordon) 2(pic).2.2.2.
4.2.3.1. timp,2perc,strings [11']
BOOSEY-ENG rent　　(H481)

Planets
orch sc DOVER 29277-0　　(H482)

Saint Paul's Suite
BROUDE BR.　　(H483)

HOLSTAMP see Lovén, Birgitta

HOLSZKY, ADRIANA (1953)
An Die Nacht
orch [15'] BREITKOPF-W　　(H484)

Lichtflug
3(pic,alto fl).3(English
horn).3(clar in E flat,bass
clar).3+contrabsn. 3.3(trp in
C).3.1. 4perc,24vln,6db,vln&fl
soli [15'] BREITKOPF-W　　(H485)

HOLT, KLAAS TEN
Concert Voor 3 Klokken, Altviool En
Orkest
2.1.2.2. 2.1.2.0. 5perc,harp,elec
gtr,pno,strings,vla solo [20']
DONEMUS　　(H486)

HOLT, PATRICIA BLOMFIELD (1910-　)
Short Sketch On A Theme
1.1.1.1. 0.3.3.0. pno,strings [4']
sc CANADIAN MI1200 H758SH　(H487)

HOLT, SIMON (1958-　)
Daedalus Remembers
2horn,flügelhorn,perc,cimbalom,
harp,3vla,4vcl,2db,vcl solo [17']
CHESTER　　(H488)

Icarus Lamentations
2clar,cimbalom,harp, 11 str [16']
UNIVER.　　(H489)

Walking With The River's Roar
3.2.3.1. 2.3.0.1. 2perc,harp,vla,
strings [19'] UNIVER.　　(H490)

HOLZBAUER, IGNAZ JAKOB (1711-1783)
Concerto for Viola, Violoncello and
String Orchestra
(Drüner) vla,vcl,string orch
KUNZELMANN ipa sc 10109A, oct
10109　　(H491)

HOLZSCHNITTE, 3 see Sachse, Hans
Wolfgang

HOMAGE, A see Zuckert, Leon

HOMAGE TO TBILISI see Smith, Michael

HOMAGE TO THOMAS HARDY see Harper,
Edward James

HOMAGE TO WAGNER see Horwood, Michael

HOME see MacIntyre, David

HOMENAJE A GABRIEL G. MARQUEZ see Jung,
Helge

HOMENAJE A LA TONADILLA see Orbon,
Julian

HOMMA, MASAO (1930-　)
Sound Shift No. 5
orch [21'] JAPAN　　(H492)

Tonal Landscape - Isawa
orch [17'] JAPAN　　(H493)

HOMMAGE see Ehmann, Heinrich

HOMMAGE, UN see Zuckert, Leon, Homage,
A

HOMMAGE À BEETHOVEN see Vustin,
Alexander

HOMMAGE À EULER see Longtin, Michel

HOMMAGE À FRANÇOIS TRUFFAUT see
Delerue, Georges

HOMMAGE À GRIEG see Schnittke, Alfred

HOMMAGE À GUSTAV MAHLER see Blatny,
Pavel

HOMMAGE À JEAN RIVIER see Lemeland,
Aubert

HOMMAGE À SAINT EXUPÉRY see Slavicky,
Milan

HOMMAGE À SIBELIUS see Yuasa, Joji

HOMMAGE À VASARELY see Rea, John

HOMO ET FATUM see Moeschinger, Albert

HOMS, JOAQUIN (1906-　)
Biofonia
3.2.4.2. 2.2.2.1. timp,2perc,harp,
cel,strings [12'] perf sc EMEC
f.s.　　(H494)

Derivacion
1+pic.1.1.1. 1.1.1.0. timp,perc,
pno,strings [11'30"] sc ALPUERTO
1749　　(H495)

HOMS, JOAQUIN (cont'd.)

Memoralia
2+2pic.2.2.1. 2.1.1.1. timp,2perc,
strings [12'30"] (symphonic
movement) sc ALPUERTO 1742 (H496)

HONEY POT BEE see Grainger, Ella

HONOUR AND FREEDOM see Kenins,
Talivaldis

HONZA KRÁLEM see Maršik, Otakar

HOPKINS, ANTHONY (1921-　)
John And The Magic Music-Man
2(pic).2(English horn).2.2.
4.2.3.1. timp,harp,pno,3perc,
strings,opt pno,narrator, opt fl
III [24'] BARDIC　　(H497)

HOPKINS, JAMES FREDERICK (1939-　)
Songs Of Eternity
2.2(English horn).2(bass clar).2.
4.3.3.1. perc,harp,kbd,strings
[25'] SCHIRM.EC rent　　(H498)

HÖR-SPIEL NR. 2 see Muller-Weinberg,
Achim

HÖR-SPIEL NR. 3 see Muller-Weinberg,
Achim

HORA STACCATO see Dinicu, Grigoras

HORAE see Koenig, Gottfried Michael

HORAE: THREE SYMPHONIC MOVEMENTS see
Kalmar, Laszlo

HORIKOSHI, RYUICHI (1949-　)
Pavane For Open Strings
string orch [4'] (revision) JAPAN
　　(H499)

HORISONTVALS see Byström, Britta

HORIZONS see Naulais, Jerome

HORKY, FRANTIŠEK (1943-　)
Sinfonietta
3.2.2.3. 4.4.3.1. timp,perc,xylo,
cel,strings [11'] CESKY HUD.
　　(H500)

HORKY, KAREL (1909-1988)
Slavnostní Pochod
3.2.2.2. 4.4.3.1. timp,perc,strings
[6'] CESKY HUD.　　(H501)

HORMS, HUGO
Hungarian Dance
2(pic).2.2.2. 4.0.3.0. timp,perc,
harp,strings SCHOTTS perf mat
rent　　(H502)

HORNE, DAVID (1970-　)
Concerto for Piano
2(alto fl,pic).2.2(bass clar).1+
contrabsn. 2.2.2.1. 2perc,cel,
harp,strings [22'] BOOSEY-ENG
rent　　(H503)

Northscape
1.1.1.1. 1.0.0.0. harp,3vln I,3vln
II,2vla,2vcl,db,opt jr cor [12']
BOOSEY-ENG rent　　(H504)

Persistence
1(pic,alto fl).1(English
horn).1(bass clar).1(contrabsn).
1.1.1.0. 2perc,strings [13']
BOOSEY-ENG rent　　(H505)

HOROVITZ, JOSEPH (1926-　)
Concerto for Oboe and Orchestra
1.0.2.1. 2.0.0.0. strings,ob solo
[19'] manuscript BMIC　　(H506)

HORSEPOWER SUITE see Chavez, Carlos,
Suite De Caballos De Vapor

HORTUS MAGICUS see Kirchner, Volker
David

HORUSITZKY, ZOLTAN (1903-　)
Báthroy Suite
3(pic).2+English horn.3(bass
clar).2+contrabsn. 4.3.3.1. timp,
perc,harp,strings [15'] EMB rent
　　(H507)

Concerto for Piano and Orchestra, No.
1
2.0.2.0. 0.3.0.0. timp,perc,
strings,pno solo [18'] EMB rent
　　(H508)

Concerto for Piano and Orchestra, No.
2
2+pic.2.2.2. 4.3.3.1. timp,perc,
harp,strings,pno solo [24'] EMB
rent　　(H509)

Három Balett-Kép
see Three Ballet Pictures

Three Ballet Pictures
"Három Balett-Kép" 2+pic.2.2.3+
contrabsn. 4.3.3.1. timp,perc,

**HORUSITZKY, ZOLTAN** (cont'd.)

xylo,harp,pno,strings [29'] EMB
rent (H510)

**HORWOOD, MICHAEL** (1947- )
Concerto for Double Bass and String
Orchestra
[13'] sc,solo pt CANADIAN
MI1614 H824CO (H511)

Concerto For Orchestra
see Six Chromosomes

Dinner Rolls
see Six Chromosomes

Homage To Wagner
see Six Chromosomes

National Park Suite
3(pic).2(English horn).2.2.
4.2.3.1. timp,2perc,harp,strings
(1. Forillon National Park,
Québec 2. Bryce Canyon National
Park, Utah 3. Fathom Five Marine
Park, Ontario 4. Yellowstone
National Park, Wyoming 5. Jasper
National Park, Alberta) sc
CANADIAN MI 1100 H824NA (H512)

Return Of Death With A Slap In The
Face, The
see Six Chromosomes

Rondo
see Six Chromosomes

Six Chromosomes
2+pic.2+English horn.2+clar in E
flat+bass clar.2+contrabsn.
5.3.3.1. timp,3perc,strings sc
CANADIAN MI 1100 H824SI f.s.
contains: Concerto For Orchestra;
Dinner Rolls; Homage To Wagner;
Return Of Death With A Slap In
The Face, The; Rondo; Timber
Timbre (H513)

Timber Timbre
see Six Chromosomes

Women Of Trachis *incidental music
1(pic).1.1.0. 1.1.0.0. 2perc,pno,
strings,opt mand sc CANADIAN
MI1200 H824WO (H514)

**HOSOKAWA, TOSHIO** (1955- )
Concerto for Flute
"Per-Sonare" 2(pic).2.2(bass
clar).0+contrabsn. 2.2.1.1.
3perc,harp,12vln I,10vln II,8vla,
6vcl,4db,fl&pic&alto fl&bass fl
solo, Echo I: Fl+Pic, Horn, Trp,
Trb, Perc; Echo II: Ob, Horn,
Trp, Trb, Perc [25'] SCHOTTS perf
mat rent (H515)

Ferne -Landschaft I
3(2pic,alto fl).3.2+bass clar.2+
contrabsn. 4.3.2.1. 4perc,harp,
14vln I,12vln II,10vla,8vcl,6db,
Echo I: trp, trb; Echo II: trp,
trb [15'] study sc SCHOTTS
SJ 1079 perf mat rent (H516)

Ferne -Landschaft II
3(2pic,alto fl).3.3.2+contrabsn.
4.5.5.1. 4perc,pno,harp,14vln I,
12vln II,10vla,8vcl,6db [15']
SCHOTTS perf mat rent (H517)

Garten Lieder I
1(pic,alto fl).1(English
horn).2(bass clar).1(contrabsn).
2.1.0.0. 2perc,pno,strings [14']
SCHOTTS perf mat rent (H518)

Hiroshima Requiem: I. Preludio -
"Night"
3(2pic,alto fl).3.2+bass clar.2+
contrabsn. 4.3.3.1. 4perc,pno,
cel,harp,strings, Echo I: horn,
trp, trb; Echo I: horn, trp, trb
[14'] SCHOTTS perf mat rent
(H519)

Hiroshima Requiem: III. "Dawn"
2(2pic).2.2(bass clar).1+contrabsn.
4.2.2.1. 2perc,strings [11']
SCHOTTS perf mat rent (H520)

In Die Tiefe Der Zeit
acord,4vln I,4vln II,3vla,2vcl,2db,
vcl solo [18'] SCHOTTS perf mat
rent (H521)

Landscape III
2(2pic).2.2(bass
clar).2(contrabsn). 2.2.2.1.
4perc,harp,strings,vln solo [19']
SCHOTTS perf mat rent (H522)

Landscape VI: Cloudscapes
1(pic,alto fl).1(English
horn).1(bass clar)+clar in
A.1(contrabsn). 1.1.0.0. perc,

**HOSOKAWA, TOSHIO** (cont'd.)

harp,strings [16'] SCHOTTS perf
mat rent (H523)

Medea Fragments I *Overture
1(pic,alto fl).1(English
horn).2(bass clar).0. 0.0.1.0.
2perc,2vln,vla,vcl,db [8']
SCHOTTS perf mat rent (H524)

Per-Sonare
see Concerto for Flute

Super Flumina Babylonis
1(pic,alto fl).1(English
horn).2(bass clar).1(contrabsn).
2.1.1.0. 3perc,harp,strings,SA
soli [18'] SCHOTTS perf mat rent
(H525)

Utsurohi-Nagi
Group A: vln, vla, db; Group B:
2vln, vcl; Right: 2perc, harp,
10vln, 4vla, 3vcl; Left: 2perc,
cel, 10vln, 4vla, 3vcl, 2db, shô
solo [17'] SCHOTTS perf mat rent
(H526)

HÖST see Freudenthal, Otto,
Orkesterförspel

HOST OF NOMADS, A see Forsyth, Malcolm

HÖSTHORN: FÖRSPEL see Koch, Erland von

HOT, RED, COLD, VIBRANT see Ince,
Kamran

HOT-SONATE see Schulhoff, Erwin

HOTCH-POTCH see Eklund, Hans

**HOUDY, PIERICK** (1929- )
Concerto Da Camera
string orch,vln solo,pno solo
CANADIAN sc MI 1750 H836CO, pno
red MI 1750 H836CA (H527)

HOUSES IN MOTION see Larsson, Mats

**HOVE, LUC VAN**
Stacked Time *Op.26
3.3.3.3. 4.4.3.1. timp,2perc,pno,
harp,strings,elec gtr solo [15']
BELGE (H528)

Strings *Op.33
string orch [22'] BELGE (H529)

Symphony No. 1, Op. 25
3.3.3.3. 4.6.3.1. timp,4perc,pno,
harp,strings [17'] BELGE (H530)

Triptiek *Op.29
2.2.2.2. 2.2.1.0. timp,perc,harp,
strings,ob solo [18'] BELGE
(H531)

HOVERING OF CELESTIAL FORMS see Ishii,
Maki, Ode To The Hiten

**HOVHANESS, ALAN** (1911- )
Concerto for Viola and String
Orchestra
see Talin

Talin (Concerto for Viola and String
Orchestra)
set SCHIRM.G 50242260 (H532)

**HOVLAND, EGIL** (1924- )
Concerto for Oboe and Orchestra, Op.
150
3.0.3.3. 4.0.3.1. timp,perc,harp,
pno,strings,ob solo [23'] NORSKMI
(H533)

HOW SLOW THE WIND see Takemitsu, Toru

**HOWARD, BRIAN** (1951- )
Celestial Mirror, The
3(pic).2(English horn).2.1+
contrabsn. 4.3.3.1. 3perc,strings
[25'] BOOSEY-ENG rent (H534)

Sun And Steel
7vln,2vla,2vcl,db [10'] BOOSEY-ENG
rent (H535)

Temple Of The Golden Pavilion, The
2(pic).1(English horn).3(clar in E
flat,bass clar).1(contrabsn).
2.2.3.1. 3perc,2harp,strings
[13'] BOOSEY-ENG rent (H536)

Tramonto Della Luna, Il
3(pic).2+English horn.2+bass
clar.2+contrabsn. 4.3.3.0. 4perc,
cel,harp,14vln I,12vln II,10vla,
8vcl,6db [16'] BOOSEY-ENG rent
(H537)

Wildbird Dreaming
2.2.2.2. 4.3.1.0. 2perc,harp,
strings [15'] BOOSEY-ENG rent
(H538)

**HOYER, KARL** (1891-1936)
Introduction Und Chaconne
3.2.2.2. 2.2.2.1. timp,perc,
strings,org solo [17'] BREITKOPF-
W (H539)

**HOYER, RALF** (1950)
Sinfonietta
4.3.3.4. 0.0.0.0. strings [12']
PETERS (H540)

Sonata Fragile
14vln I,6vla,5vcl,3db [13'] sc
PETERS 03049 (H541)

Study No. 1 for 28 Strings
sc PETERS 03038 (H542)

**HOYLAND, VICTOR** (1945- )
Vixen (A-Vixen-A)
2(pic,alto fl).2+English horn.2+
bass clar.2+contrabsn. 4.4.3.1.
4perc,2harp,strings,electronic
tape [30'] sc UNIV.YORK 0119 f.s.
(H543)

HRA SVETLA A STÍNU see Rimón, Jan

**HRABÁNEK, PAVEL** (1946- )
Concerto for Horn, Piano and String
Orchestra
strings,horn&pno soli [13'] CESKY
HUD. (H544)

Concerto for Trumpet and Orchestra
3.3.4.3. 4.3.3.1. timp,perc,harp,
pno,strings,trp solo [14'] CESKY
HUD. (H545)

Dove *Symphony
3.3.4.3. 4.3.3.1. timp,perc,2harp,
cel,strings [26'] CESKY HUD.
(H546)

Music for Strings
see Symfonie Pro Smyccové Nástroje

Symfonie Pro Smyccové Nástroje (Music
for Strings)
string orch [30'] CESKY HUD. (H547)

HRÁTKY S HOUSLEMI see Machek, Miloš

HRUBÍNOVY POHÁDKY see Mácha, Otmar

**HRUBY, VICTOR** (1894- )
Variationen Über Ein Eigenes Thema
2(pic).2(English horn).2.2.
4.2.3.1. timp,8perc,strings [21']
BREITKOPF-W (H548)

**HRUŠKA, JAROMÍR** (1880-1954)
O Zlatem Klíci A Zivé Vode
1.2.2.0. 2.0.0.0. strings [10']
CESKY HUD. (H549)

**HRUŠKA, JAROMÍR LUDVÍK** (1910-1984)
Tri Vety
1.2.0.0. 2.0.0.0. strings [20']
CESKY HUD. (H550)

HRY see Ištvan, Miloslav

HUAN see Qu, Xiao-Song

**HUBER, HANS** (1852-1921)
Böcklin-Symphonie (Symphony No. 2 in
E minor, Op. 115)
3(pic).2.2.3(contrabsn). 4.2.3.1.
timp,perc,strings [40'] HUG
(H551)

Concerto for Piano and Orchestra in B
flat, No. 4
3(pic).2.2.2. 4.2.3.0. timp,perc,
strings [20'] HUG (H552)

Concerto for Piano and Orchestra, Op.
36, in C minor
2.2.2.2. 2.2.3.0. timp,perc,
strings,pno solo [32'] BREITKOPF-
W (H553)

Heroische-Symphonie (Symphony No. 3
in C, Op. 118)
3(pic).2.2.2. 4.3.3.1. timp,perc,
strings [37'] HUG (H554)

Schweizerische-Symphonie (Symphony
No. 7 in D minor)
3.3(English horn).3(bass
clar).3(contrabsn). 6.3.3.1.
timp,perc,cel,harp,strings [45']
HUG (H555)

Serenade No. 2 for Orchestra
see Winternächte

Symphony No. 2 in E minor, Op. 115
see Böcklin-Symphonie

Symphony No. 3 in C, Op. 118
see Heroische-Symphonie

Symphony No. 7 in D minor
see Schweizerische-Symphonie

HUBER, HANS (cont'd.)

  Winternächte (Serenade No. 2 for
      Orchestra)
      2.2.2.2. 2.2.0.0. timp,perc,strings
      [25'] HUG                        (H556)

HUBER, KLAUS (1924-    )
  "...Ohne Grenze Und Rand..."
      3.2(2ob d'amore).1+bass clar.0.
      2.3.0.0. 3perc,strings,
      (3.0.0.2.1) [12'] SCHOTTS perf
      mat rent                         (H557)

HUBER, NICOLAUS A. (1939-    )
  An Hölderlins Umnachtung
      1(pic).1.1.1. 1.1.1.0. 2perc,harp,
      pno,vln,vla,vcl,db [19'] study sc
      BREITKOPF-W PB 5414              (H558)

  Drei Stücke
      2(pic).2.2(contrabass
      clar).2(contrabsn). 2.2.2.0.
      timp,3perc,harp,cel,14vln I,12vln
      II,10vla,8vcl,10db,solo voice,pno
      [31'] study sc BREITKOPF-W
      PB 5410                          (H559)

  Eröffnung Und Zertrümmerung
      0.1.1.0. 0.1.1.0. 2perc,acord,pno,
      vln,vcl,db,electronic tape,
      electronic equipment [21']
      BREITKOPF-W                      (H560)

  Go Ahead
      2(pic).2(English horn).2(contrabass
      clar).3(contrabsn). 3.2.2.0.
      timp,3perc,harp,cel,pno,13vln I,
      10vln II,8vla,6vcl,5db, Group A:
      1.1.1.0. 0.0.0.0. vln, vla, vcl,
      db Group B: 0.0.0.0. 1.1.1.0.
      Group C: 2vln, vla, vcl [30']
      study sc BREITKOPF-W PB 5413    (H561)

  Tote Metren
      0.0.1(contrabass
      clar).1(contrabsn). 1.0.0.0.
      perc,pno,2vln,vla,vcl,db,B solo
      [7'] BREITKOPF-W                 (H562)

HÜBLER, KLAUS-K. (1955-    )
  Kryptogramm
      2pno 4-hands,harp,bsn,vcl,2db,2perc
      [6'] BREITKOPF-W                 (H563)

HÜBNER, WILHELM (1915-    )
  Kalenderblatt-Sinfonie
      strings [23'] BREITKOPF-W        (H564)

HUCKLEBERRY FINN: FIVE SONGS see Weill,
  Kurt

HUDBA PRO KOMORNÍ ORCHESTR see Emmert,
  Frantisek see Kovarícek, František

HUDBA PRO SMYCCE see Bartoš, Jan Zdenek
  see Faltus, Leos see Matys, Jirí

HUDBA PRO SMYCCE A TYMPÁNY see Vicar,
  Jan

HUDBA PRO SMYCCOVY ORCHESTR see
  Gašparovicová, Marie

HUDBA PRO TROMBÓN A SMYCCOVY ORCHESTR
  see Fiala, Petr

HUDBA V OPERE see Boháč, Josef

HUDEC, JIRÍ (1923-    )
  Humoreska
      2.2.2.2. 4.2.3.0. timp,harp,strings
      [4'] CESKY HUD.                  (H565)

  Kaleidoskop *Overture
      2.1.3.1. 2.3.3.0. timp,perc,xylo,
      harp,pno,2gtr,strings [5'] CESKY
      HUD.                             (H566)

  Koncertni Valcík
      2.2.2.2. 4.2.3.0. timp,perc,
      marimba,harp,strings [5'] CESKY
      HUD.                             (H567)

  Lyrické Intermezzo
      2.2.2.2. 3.2.2.0. timp,perc,harp,
      strings [3'] CESKY HUD.          (H568)

  Podzimní Meditace
      2.2.2.2. 4.2.3.0. timp,perc,harp,
      strings [4'] CESKY HUD.          (H569)

  Poetická Polka
      2.1.2.1. 3.2.3.0. perc,cel,strings
      [3'] CESKY HUD.                  (H570)

  Polka in G minor
      2.2.2.2. 4.2.3.0. timp,perc,strings
      [4'] CESKY HUD.                  (H571)

  Scherzo in F
      2.2.2.2. 4.3.3.0. timp,perc,harp,
      strings [4'] CESKY HUD.          (H572)

HUDEC, JIRÍ (cont'd.)
  Tempo, Tempo
      2.2.2.2. 4.2.3.1. timp,perc,xylo,
      strings [3'] CESKY HUD.          (H573)

  Uspávanka Pro Martínku
      1.0.1.0. 1.0.0.0. bells,harp,cel,
      strings [7'] CESKY HUD.          (H574)

  Zpod Javoriny
      2.2.2.2. 4.2.3.0. timp,perc,harp,
      strings [5'] CESKY HUD.          (H575)

HUDECEK, RADOVAN (1945-    )
  Upplandia
      1.1.1.1.2sax. 1.1.1.0. timp,
      strings,pno,drums STIM           (H576)

HUDSON VALLEY SUITE see Starer, Robert

HUGENOTTEN, DIE: IHR EDLEN HERRN
  ALLHIER see Meyerbeer, Giacomo,
  Huguenots, Les: Cavatina Of Urban

HUGENOTTEN, DIE: IHR WANGENPAAR see
  Meyerbeer, Giacomo, Huguenots, Les:
  Romance Of Raoul

HUGENOTTEN, DIE: OVERTURE see
  Meyerbeer, Giacomo, Huguenots, Les:
  Overture

HUGENOTTEN, DIE: ZIGEUNERTANZ see
  Meyerbeer, Giacomo

HUGUENOTS, LES: CAVATINA OF URBAN see
  Meyerbeer, Giacomo

HUGUENOTS, LES: OVERTURE see Meyerbeer,
  Giacomo

HUGUENOTS, LES: ROMANCE OF RAOUL see
  Meyerbeer, Giacomo

HUI, MELISSA (1966-    )
  Between You
      3(pic).3(English horn).3(contrabass
      clar).3(contrabsn). 4.3.3.1.
      timp,2perc,16vln I,14vln II,
      12vla,10vcl,6db [16'] sc CANADIAN
      MI 1200 H899B                    (H577)

  Shadow Play
      1.1.1.1. 1.0.0.0. strings [10'] sc
      CANADIAN MI1200 H899SH           (H578)

  Two Sides To The Wind
      2.2.2.0.2tenor sax. 2.2.1.0. 2perc,
      pno,6vln I,6vln II,5vla,4vcl,2db
      [9'-12'] sc CANADIAN
      MI 1331 H899TW                   (H579)

HUIT CONCERTI see Durante, Francesco

HUIT POÉSIES DE MALLARMÉ see Killmayer,
  Wilhelm

HUKVARI, JENO (1935-    )
  Dolor, For Strings And Harp
      [3'55"] NORSKMI                  (H580)

HULLÁMMOZGÁSOK see Szekely, Endre, Wave
  Motions

HULTQVIST, ANDERS (1955-    )
  Compositions No. III
      chamber orch STIM                (H581)

  Skog I
      string orch [4'] sc,pts STIM     (H582)

  Skog II
      string orch [5'] perf sc STIM
                                       (H583)

  Skog III
      string orch [5'] sc,pts STIM (H584)

  Time And The Bell
      3(pic).3(English horn).3(bass
      clar).3(contrabsn). 4.3.3.1.
      timp,4perc,strings,pno [15']
      SUECIA pts H-2508, sc            (H585)

  Vatten
      2.2.2. 0.2.2.0. 3perc,strings
      [8'] STIM sc H-2726, pts         (H586)

  Vintertrdgrden
      "Wintergarden, The" string orch
      [12'] sc,pts STIM                (H587)

  Wintergarden, The
      see Vintertrdgrden

HUMEL, GERALD (1931-    )
  Lepini
      4(3pic,alto fl).2+English horn.1+
      clar in E flat.2+contrabsn. 4.3+
      bass trp.2+bass trom.1. timp,
      4perc,harp,strings [26'] SCHOTTS
      perf mat rent                    (H588)

HUMMEL, BERTOLD (1925-    )
  Adagio (In Memoriam Anton Bruckner),
      Op. 91b
      orch BÖHM                        (H589)

  Kontraste *Op.50
      strings [18'] SCHOTTS perf mat rent
                                       (H590)

  Konzertante Musik *Op.89
      gtr,string orch VOGT VF 1060 (H591)

  Visionen *Op.73
      3(pic).2+English horn.2+bass
      clar.2+contrabsn. 4.3.3.1. timp,
      4perc,harp,strings [22'] SCHOTTS
      perf mat rent                    (H592)

HUMMEL, JOHANN NEPOMUK (1778-1837)
  Adagio & Tema Con Variazioni
      (Steinbeck) ob solo,orch KUNZELMANN
      10006 ipr                        (H593)

  Concerto for Piano, Violin and
      Orchestra in G, Op. 17
      (Wojciechowski) 2.2.0.2. 2.0.0.0.
      8vln I,7vln II,6vla,5vcl,4db
      [24'] sc,solo pt PETERS 00752
                                       (H594)

      see Doppelkonzert G-Dur

  Doppelkonzert G-Dur (Concerto for
      Piano, Violin and Orchestra in G,
      Op. 17) Op.17
      (Wojciechowski) 2.2.0.2. 2.0.0.0.
      strings [24'] PETERS             (H595)

HUMMEL, JOSEPH FRIEDRICH (1841-1919)
  Berceuse for Clarinet and String
      Orchestra
      harp,strings,clar solo [3']
      BREITKOPF-W                      (H596)

  Concerto for Clarinet and Orchestra,
      No. 1, in E flat
      2.2.0.2. 2.2.1.0. timp,strings,clar
      solo [18'] BREITKOPF-W           (H597)

  Tarantelle for Clarinet and Orchestra
      1.1.1.1. 3.2.0.0. timp,strings,clar
      solo [3'] BREITKOPF-W            (H598)

HUMORESK see Sevius, Sven

HUMORESKA see Hudec, Jirí see Rimón,
  Jan

HUMORESQUE see Bartholomee, Pierre

HUNDSNES, SVEIN (1951-    )
  Haugtussa
      "Orchestral Songs By The Edge Of
      Romanticism" [Norw] 2.1.1.1.
      1.2.3(bass trom).1. 3perc,
      strings,S solo [48'] NORSKMI
                                       (H599)

  Orchestral Songs By The Edge Of
      Romanticism
      see Haugtussa

  Symphonie Rendez-Vous
      2.2.2.2. 4.3.3.0. timp,perc,elec
      gtr,elec bass,kbd,drums,strings
      NORSKMI                          (H600)

HUNGARIA, QUATROS LIRICAS see Ogando

HUNGARIAN DANCE see Horms, Hugo

HUNGARIAN DANCES FROM THE 16TH CENTURY
  see Ranki, György

HUNGARIAN RHAPSODY NO. 6 see Liszt,
  Franz

HUNGARIAN RONDO see Kodály, Zoltán

HUNGARIAN SKETCHES see Volkmann, Robert

HUNGARIAN SUITE see Patachich, Ivan

HUNISUCCLE see Kondo, Jo

HUNT, RICHARD (1930-    )
  Nimbus
      2+pic.2+English horn.2+bass clar.2+
      contrabsn. 2.2.1.0. strings [12']
      sc CANADIAN MI1200 H942NI        (H601)

HURLEBUSCH, KONRAD FRIEDRICH
      (1696-1765)
  Concerto
      0.2.0.1. 0.0.0.0. 2cembalo,strings
      [12'] BREITKOPF-W                (H602)

HURNÍK, ILJA (1922-    )
  Concertino for Piano and String
      Orchestra
      strings,pno solo [11'] PANTON (H603)

  Concertino for 2 Violins and Chamber
      Orchestra
      strings,2vln soli [12'] CESKY HUD.
                                       (H604)

  Concertino in A for Violin and
      Strings
      [9'] CESKY HUD.                  (H605)

HURNÍK, ILJA (cont'd.)

Faux Pas De Quatre
2.2.2.2. 0.2.2.0. perc,harp,pno,
strings [16'] CESKY HUD. (H606)

Klicperovská Predehra
2.2.2.2. 2.2.2.0. timp,perc,strings
CESKY HUD. (H607)

Malá Svita
2.2.2.2. 2.1.0.0. timp,perc,harp,
strings [13'] CESKY HUD. (H608)

HUSA, KAREL (1921- )
Concerto for Violoncello
vcl,orch sc SCHIRM.G AMP 50482581
(H609)

Reflections Symphony No. 2
orch sc SCHIRM.G AMP8036 (H610)

Symphonic Suite
orch sc SCHIRM.G AMP8056 (H611)

HUWS JONES, EDWARD
Bats, Cats And Broomsticks
strings CHESTER pts CH55939, sc
CH55938 (H612)

HUZELLA, ELEK (1915-1971)
Rapsodia
see Rhapsody

Rhapsody
"Rapsodia" pno,timp,strings [7']
EMB rent (H613)

HUZULEN-TRIPTYCHON see Skoryk, Myroslav

HVILKET SKULLE BEVISES see Rypdal,
Terje, Q.E.D. [Quod Erat
Demonstrandum]

HVOSLEF, KETIL (1939- )
Concertino for Trumpet in C
3(pic).3.3(bass clar).3. 4.3.2.0.
timp,perc,pno,strings,trp solo
NORSKMI (H614)

Concerto for Piano and Orchestra
3(pic).2.2(bass clar).2(contrabsn).
3.2.2.0. pno,timp,perc,strings
[31'30"] NORSKMI (H615)

Concerto for Violin, Violoncello,
Piano and Orchestra
"Trippelkonsert" 3(pic).3(English
horn).3(bass clar).3(contrabsn).
4.3(trp in C).3.1. 3perc,strings,
vln&vcl&pno soli [32'] NORSKMI
(H616)
Finale
2(pic).2.2(bass clar).2(contrabsn).
3.2.2(bass trom).0. timp,2perc,
harp/pno,strings,vcl solo
[11'35"] NORSKMI (H617)

Serenade for Strings
"Serenata Per Archi" string orch
[15'] NORSK (H618)
see Serenata Per Archi

Serenata Per Archi (Serenade for
Strings)
[15'] NORSKMI (H619)
see Serenade for Strings

Trippelkonsert
see Concerto for Violin,
Violoncello, Piano and Orchestra

HYMN see Dahl, Ingolf

HYMN FOR ORCHESTRA see Sundin, Haokan

HYMN II HER see Brott, Alexander

HYMN TO HER see Brott, Alexander, Hymn
II Her

HYMN TO THE EARTH see Sibelius, Jean

HYMN TO THE NATIVITY see Conte, David

HYMNE ET FUGUE see Dijk, Jan van

HYMNE NR. 2 see Korndorf, Nicolai

HYMNE VÉDIQUE see Chausson, Ernest

HYMNISCHER ENTWURF I see Dittrich,
Paul-Heinz

HYMNISCHER ENTWURF II see Dittrich,
Paul-Heinz

HYMNOS see Whettam, Graham Dudley

HYMNUS see Schnebel, Dieter

HYMNUS III see Korndorf, Nicolai

HYMNUS ORGANI see Thyrestam, Gunnar

HYPERBOLA: SUITE see Lang, Istvan

HYPERIONS SONG OF DESTINY see Sary,
Laszlo

HYPERION SORSDALA see Sary, Laszlo,
Hyperions Song Of Destiny

HYPERTROPHIES POUR ENSEMBLE see
Schaathun, Asbjørn

HYSS see Ed, Fredrik

HYSTERIA AT PENUMBRA SLUMBERS see
Bowman, Kim

# I

I see Macmillan, James

I DEN LÅNGA VÄNTANS SKOG [4] see
Naessen, Ray

I DEN LNGA VNTANS SKOG [2] see Naessen,
Ray

I DEN LNGA VNTANS SKOG [3] see Naessen,
Ray

I DEN LNGA VNTANS SKOG: EN BETRAKTELSE
see Naessen, Ray

I GRÖNSKAN SKALL DU FINNA RO see
Larsson, Martin

I HA' SEEN THEM 'MID THE CLOUDS ON THE
HEATHER see Betts, Lorne M.

I KDYBY SE ROZPLAKALY RÍMSY see
Wittmann, Max

I OFTEN WONDER see Coulthard, Jean

I TRÄD see Strindberg, Henrik

IBARRA, FEDERICO (1943- )
Sinfonia No. 1
2.2.2.2. 2.0.0.0. timp,strings
[12'] PEER rent (I1)

IBARRONDO, FELIX (1943- )
Concerto for Violin and Orchestra
2.2.2.2. 2.2.2.0. 3perc,harp,8vln
I,6vln II,5vla,4vcl,2db,vln solo
[17'] JOBERT (I2)

Erys
3.3.3.3. 4.3.3.1. 3perc,harp,
strings [20'] JOBERT (I3)

Nayan
12vln,4vla,3vcl,db,vla solo [13']
JOBERT (I4)

IBERG, HELGE (1954)
Motor For Symfoniorkester Og Tape
"Ouvertyre Til Norsk Esso's 100 Års
Jubileum" 3(pic).3.3(bass
clar).3(contrabsn).2sax.
4.3.3(bass trom).1. timp,4perc,
harp,pno/synthesizer,strings,
electronic tape NORSKMI (I5)

Opptog: Blomstenes Inntogmarsj
3(pic).2.2.2. 4.3.3(bass trom).1.
timp,3perc,harp,pno&cel,strings
NORSKMI (I6)

Ouvertyre Til Norsk Esso's 100 Års
Jubileum
see Motor For Symfoniorkester Og
Tape

IBERT, JACQUES (1890-1962)
Trois Chansons
1.1.1.1. 1.1.1.0. timp,3perc,harp,
strings,pno,solo voice [10'30"]
(to the poems by Charles Vildrac,
No. 3. Comme Elle A Les Yeux
Bandés) LEDUC (I7)

ICARUS LAMENTATIONS see Holt, Simon

ICE see Jarvlepp, Jan

ICE FIELDS see Paulus, Stephen Harrison

ICH BAUE GANZ AUF DEINE STÄRKE see
Mozart, Wolfgang Amadeus

ICH GEHE, DOCH RATE ICH DIR see Mozart,
Wolfgang Amadeus

ICH GRAUSAM? - SAG MIR NICHT see
Mozart, Wolfgang Amadeus, Crudele?
- Non Mi Dir

ICH REISE WEIT see Sutermeister,
Heinrich, Romeo And Juliet:
Juliet's Aria

ICH SEHE HINAUF see Ruzicka, Peter

ICH WEISS EIN MITTEL see Mozart,
Wolfgang Amadeus, Vedrai, Carino

ICHI see Toyama, Yuzo

ICHIBA, KOSUKE (1910- )
Symphony No. 2
orch [20'] JAPAN (I8)

ICHINOSE, TONIKA (1970- )
...Buried With Any Amount Of Petals,
All That Was Beautiful
chamber orch,fl [15'] JAPAN (I9)

ICHINOSE, TONIKA (cont'd.)

Fukei Junginmozaiku From Soshite
Ichimen No Nanohana
"Three Images By The Poems Of Bocho
Yamamura" orch,S/Mez/countertenor
[5'] JAPAN　　　　　　　　　　(I10)

Three Images By The Poems Of Bocho
Yamamura
see Fukei Junginmozaiku From
Soshite Ichimen No Nanohana

ICHIYANAGI, TOSHI (1933-　)
Coexistence IV
orch,Ondes Martenot [7'] JAPAN　(I11)

Concerto For Koto And Chamber
Orchestra
"Origin, The" 2(pic).2.2.2.
2.2.0.0. 2perc,pno,8vln I,6vln
II,4vla,4vcl,2db, koto solo [17']
SCHOTTS perf mat rent　　　　(I12)

Concerto for Piano, No. 1
"Reminiscence Of Spaces" 2+pic.2+
English horn.2.2+contrabsn.
4.2.2+bass trom.0. 4perc,14vln I,
12vln II,10vla,10vcl,8db,pno solo
[14'] SCHOTTS perf mat rent (I13)

Concerto for Piano, No. 2
"Winter Portrait" 2+pic.3.3.2.
4.3.2+bass trom.0. 5perc,14vln I,
12vln II,10vla,8vcl,6db,pno solo
[15'] SCHOTTS perf mat rent (I14)

Concerto for Piano, No. 3
"Cross Water Roads"
2(pic).2(English horn).2.2+
contrabsn. 2.2.0+bass trom.0.
2perc,strings,pno solo [17']
SCHOTTS perf mat rent　　　　(I15)

Cross Water Roads
see Concerto for Piano, No. 3

Existence
3(pic).2+English horn.2+bass
clar.2+contrabsn. 4.3.2+bass
trom.0. 4perc,harp,14vln I,12vln
II,10vla,8vcl,6db,org solo [12']
SCHOTTS perf mat rent　　　　(I16)

In The Reflection Of Lighting Image
1+pic.2.1+clar in E flat.2. 4.2.1+
bass trom.1. pno&cel,harp,12vln
I,10vln II,8vla,8vcl,6db,perc
solo [23'] SCHOTTS perf mat rent
(I17)
Inner Communication (Symphony No. 3)
orch [20'] JAPAN　　　　　　(I18)

Interplay
10vln,4vla,3vcl,2db,fl solo [20']
SCHOTTS perf mat rent　　　　(I19)

Luminous Space
3(pic).3.3.2+contrabsn. 4.3.2+bass
trom.0. timp,3perc,pno&cel,16vln
I,14vln II,12vla,10vcl,8db,Ondes
Martenot solo, shô solo [23']
SCHOTTS perf mat rent　　　　(I20)

Origin, The
see Concerto For Koto And Chamber
Orchestra

Paganini Personal
2+pic.2.2.2. 4.2.2+bass trom.0.
4perc,pno,14vln I,12vln II,10vla,
10vcl,8db,marimba solo [13']
SCHOTTS perf mat rent　　　　(I21)

Reminiscence Of Spaces
see Concerto for Piano, No. 1

Sapporo
15inst [20'] sc PETERS EP 6632
(I22)
Symphonic Movement "Kyoto"
2+pic+alto fl.2.2.2+contrabsn.
4.3.2+bass trom.0. 4perc,pno,
harp,16vln I,14vln II,12vla,
10vcl,8db [10'] SCHOTTS perf mat
rent　　　　　　　　　　　　(I23)

Symphony for Chamber Orchestra
see Time Current

Symphony No. 3
see Inner Communication

Time Current (Symphony for Chamber
Orchestra)
1.1.1.1. 1.1.1.0. 2perc,pno,2vln,
vla,vcl,db [20'] SCHOTTS perf mat
rent　　　　　　　　　　　　(I24)

Time Surrounding
2+pic.3.3.2+contrabsn. 4.3.3.1.
8perc,pno,12vln I,10vln II,8vla,
8vcl,6db [12'] SCHOTTS perf mat
rent　　　　　　　　　　　　(I25)

ICHIYANAGI, TOSHI (cont'd.)

Voices From The Environment
3(pic).3.3.2+contrabsn. 4.3.2+bass
trom.1. timp,4perc,pno,strings
[12'] SCHOTTS perf mat rent (I26)

Winter Portrait
see Concerto for Piano, No. 2

ICONOGRAPHY see Olofsson, Kent,
Hephaestus Forge

IDEAL CANZONE, L' see Tosti, Francesco
Paolo

IDEE IST EIN STUECK STOFF, EINE see
Singleton, Alvin

IDETA, KEIZO (1955-　)
Capriccio (Concertino for Piano)
orch,pno [8'] JAPAN　　　　(I27)

Concertino for Piano
see Capriccio

IDOL MIO, SE RITROSO ALTRO see Mozart,
Wolfgang Amadeus

IDOMENEO: MARCIA see Mozart, Wolfgang
Amadeus

IDYLKA G-DUR see Fryda, Jan

IDYLL see Konkoh, Iwao see Whettam,
Graham Dudley

IDYLLE see Glazunov, Alexander
Konstantinovich see Godard,
Benjamin Louis Paul, Allegretto see
Jansson, Torbjörn

IDYLLE DE PRINTEMPS see Delius,
Frederick

IDYLLISCHE SYMPHONIE E-DUR NR. 6 see
Cowen, [Sir] Frederic Hymen,
Symphony in E, No. 6

IGLO, MILAN
Variace A Fuga Pro Maly Smyccovy
Orchestr Na Téma Národní Písne
string orch [11'] CESKY HUD. (I28)

IGNIS NOSTER see Dillon, James

IGOROCHKI see Gilbert, Anthony

IHR VERWEGNEN! - WIE DER FELSEN see
Mozart, Wolfgang Amadeus, Temerari
- Come Scoglio

IKAROS see Mellnäs, Arne see Mellnäs,
Arne, Symphony No. 1

IKEBE, SHIN-ICHIRO (1943-　)
Almost A Tree (Concerto for
Violoncello and Orchestra)
orch,vcl solo [20'] ZEN-ON　(I29)

Concerto for Violoncello and
Orchestra
see Almost A Tree

Glossy-Leaved Forest, The
strings [9'] ZEN-ON　　　　(I30)

IKRAMOWA, ANNA (1966-　)
Concerto for Violin and Orchestra
3.3.3.2. 2.0.0.0. timp,perc,harp,
cel,strings [17'] SIKORSKI perf
mat rent　　　　　　　　　　(I31)

I'LL GIVE MY LOVE AN APPLE see Ridout,
Godfrey

ILLUMINATIONS see Bakke, Ruth see
Saroun, Jaroslav, Svetla

ILLUSION, L', OP. 133 see Fürstenau,
Anton Bernhard

IM FRÜHLING see Goldmark, Karl

IM MORGENLAND GEFANGEN see Mozart,
Wolfgang Amadeus

IM WALZERRAUSCH see Busch, Hans

IMAGE: REFLECTION see Borisova-Ollas,
Victoria

IMAGE-TEMPS see Rens, Jean-Marie

IMAGES, JEUX AND THE MARTYRDOM OF ST.
SEBASTIAN see Debussy, Claude

IMAGES OF NIGHT see Forsyth, Malcolm

IMAGINARY DANCES see Maggio, Robert

IMAGINATIONS see Brandmüller, Theo

IMAGINED FABLE, AN see Wilby, Philip

IMAGO I see Steinbrenner, Wilfried

IMAI,SHIGEYUKI (1933-　)
Han Geinou Mandala
orch, tegun, chango, 20-gen,
japanese percussion [30'] JAPAN
(I32)
!IMITA! IMITA, QUE ALGO QUEDA see
Bernaola, Carmelo

IMMER ODER NIMMER see Waldteufel, Emile

IMPRESSION see Martinsson, Rolf

IMPRESSIONI UNGHERESI see Weiner, Leo,
Divertimento No. 3, Op. 25

IMPROVISACION I see Guinjoan, Joan

IMPROVISATIONS III. see Bozay, Attila

IMPROVISO TRIPARTITO see Rieti,
Vittorio

IMPROVIZÁCIÓK III. see Bozay, Attila,
Improvisations III.

IMPULSE see Thilman, Johannes Paul

IMPULSOS see Bernaola, Carmelo

IN A PERSIAN GARDEN see Lehmann, Liza

IN AFTER TIME see Earnest, John David

IN ARCADIA see Mathias, William

IN CAMPO APERTO see Bergsma, William
Laurence

IN DEN STUNDEN DES NEUMONDS see
Roslavetz, Nicolas, V Casy
Novolunija

IN DIE TIEFE DER ZEIT see Hosokawa,
Toshio

IN DULCI JUBILO see Naessen, Ray

IN EPICENTRUM see Vanek, Stanislav

IN EXTASIBUS VIGILIBUS see Naessen, Ray

IN GIRUM. IMUS. NOCTE see Essl, Karl
Heinz

IN HORA MORTIS see Bose, Hans-Jurgen
Von

IN LUMINE LUMEN see Looten, Christophe

IN MEMORIAM see Artyomov, Vyacheslav
see Harper, Edward James see
Petrov, Andrei P. see Schnittke,
Alfred

IN MEMORIAM ANNE FRANK see Ridout,
Godfrey

IN MEMORIAM BORIS KLUSNER see Vustin,
Alexander

IN MEMORIAM DIMITRI SHOSTAKOVICH see
Raaff, Robin De

IN MEMORIAM - JUMBO see Rathburn, Eldon

IN MEMORIAM KAROL SZYMANOWSKI see
Koprowski, Peter Paul

IN MEMORIAM PAUL DESSAU see Bredemeyer,
Reiner see Goldmann, Friedrich see
Schenker, Friedrich

IN MODO CLASSICO see Blatny, Pavel

IN MYSTERIUM TREMENDUM see
Herbolsheimer, Bern

IN PARADISUM see Connell, Adrian

IN PRAISE OF OCKEGHEM see Aitken, Hugh

IN PROCESS OF TIME see Mori, Kurodo

IN PURSUIT OF SONG FOR BABYLON see
Moriya, Yuko

IN SILENCE, IN MEMORY see Nelson, Larry

IN STATU NASCENDI see Stare, Ivan

IN STURM UND EIS see Hindemith, Paul

IN THE FOREST OF THE LONG WAIT [3] see
Naessen, Ray, I Den Lnga Vntans
Skog [3]

IN THE GARDEN OF THE SERAGLIO see
Delius, Frederick

IN THE GREEN SHADE see Fontyn,
Jacqueline

...IN THE NIGHT BEFORE THE TOWN-CRIER BEGIN TO CRY see Kverndokk, Gisle

IN THE REFLECTION OF LIGHTING IMAGE see Ichiyanagi, Toshi

IN THE TWILIGHT see Berg, Fred Jonny

IN THE WOODS see Kondo, Jo

IN TRANSII see Sharman, Rodney

IN UOMINI, IN SOLDATI see Mozart, Wolfgang Amadeus

INCANTATIONS VB: LE CERCLE GNOSTIQUE see Boudreau, Walter, Zeniths

INCE, KAMRAN (1960- )
Before Infrared
3.2.3.3. 4.3.3.1. timp,3perc,harp, strings [10'] SCHOTTS perf mat rent                (I33)

Castles In The Air
see Symphony No. 1

Concerto for Piano
3.2.2.3. 4.2.3.1. timp,3perc, strings,pno solo [19'] SCHOTTS perf mat rent              (I34)

Deep Flight
1.1.1.1. 2.2.3.1. timp,perc,pno, strings [11'] SCHOTTS perf mat rent                (I35)

Domes
orch study sc EUR.AM.MUS. EA00742                                     (I36)
3(pic,alto fl).3(English horn).3(bass clar).3(contrabsn). 4.3.3.1. 3perc,pno,harp,strings [12'] study sc SCHOTTS EA 742 perf mat rent              (I37)

Ebullient Shadows
orch (special order) EUR.AM.MUS. EA00615                        (I38)
4.3.4.4. 4.3.3.1. timp,3perc,pno, harp,strings [14'] study sc SCHOTTS EA 615X perf mat rent      (I39)

Hot, Red, Cold, Vibrant
2(pic).3(English horn).3(clar in E flat,bass clar).2. 4.3.3.0. 3perc,pno,harp,strings [10'] SCHOTTS perf mat rent           (I40)

Infrared
orch study sc EUR.AM.MUS. EA00778                                     (I41)

Infrared Only
3.2.3.3. 4.3.3.1. timp,3perc,harp, strings [10'] SCHOTTS perf mat rent                (I42)

Lipstick
2(pic).2.2(clar in E flat,bass clar).2.4sax. 1.2.2.0. 3perc,pno, synthesizer,harp,strings [22'] SCHOTTS perf mat rent           (I43)

Plexus
1(pic).0.1.0.4sax. 0.2.2.0. synthesizer,pno,elec gtr,elec bass,strings, drum machine [23'] SCHOTTS perf mat rent           (I44)

Symphony No. 1
"Castles In The Air" 3.3.3.3. 4.3.3.1. timp,3perc,pno,strings [28'] SCHOTTS perf mat rent (I45)

INDIANA BALLET SUITE see Rieti, Vittorio

INDICATIF 1 see Roland, Claude Robert

INDIGENA see Leon, Tania Justina

INDULÓ A ZÁSZLÓK BEVONULÁSÁHOZ see Vidovszky, Laszlo, March To The Procession Of Flags

INDY, VINCENT D' (1851-1931)
Clair De Lune
2.2.2.2. 4.2.3.0. strings,med solo LEDUC                       (I46)

Sauge Fleurie
2+pic.2.3.4. 4.4+2cornet.3.1. timp, perc,harp,strings [17'] LEDUC                 (I47)

INFECTED see Bjurling, Björn

INFRARED see Ince, Kamran

INFRARED ONLY see Ince, Kamran

'ING' BOOK, THE see Allen, Peter

INGHAM, STEPHEN
Concerto for Piano and Orchestra
2.2.2(bass clar).2. 2.2.0.0. timp, perc,8vln I,8vln II,6vla,4vcl,2db KEYS sc f.s., set rent          (I48)

INGHELBRECHT, DÉSIRÉ ÉMILE (1880-1965)
Diable Dans Le Beffroi, Le: Prélude Et Danse Finale *ballet
2.2.2.2. 4.2.3.1. timp,perc,harp, sax,strings [12'] LEDUC             (I49)

INGVALDSEN, DIDRICK (1960- )
Globo
2.2.2.2. 4.2.3.1. 2perc,strings, juvenile orchestra, 130 children [12'50"] NORSKMI            (I50)

INITIASJON see Kverndokk, Gisle

INITIATION see Kverndokk, Gisle, Initiasjon

INNER AND OUTER STRINGS see Mayer, William Robert

INNER COMMUNICATION see Ichiyanagi, Toshi

INNER SKY see Felder, David

INSIDE LOOKING OUT see Parmerud

INSIGNIA see Haug, Halvor

INSULA DESERTA see Tüür, Erkki-Sven

INTER see Schnebel, Dieter

INTERFACE see Marez Oyens, Tera de

INTERIOR (BALLET MUSIC) see Hagen, Daron

INTERLUDE AND ECSTATIC ALICE see Del Tredici, David

INTERLUDIO see Lundin, Morgan

INTERMEDIUM 1: FROM SIEFRIED-IDYLL (WAGNER) TO KONSERT OP. 24 (WEBERN) see Valkare, Gunnar

INTERMEDIUM 2: FROM KONSERT OP.24 (WEBERN) TILL UR HISTOIRE DU SOLDAT (STRAVINSKIJ) see Valkare, Gunnar

INTERMEZZO see Proto, Frank

INTERMEZZO SCHERZOSO see Rimón, Jan

INTERMEZZO: STJRNSKUGGOR see Karkoff, Ingvar

INTERNA see Morthenson, Jan W.

INTERPLAY see Ichiyanagi, Toshi

INTERVIEW AVEC D. see Kagel, Mauricio

INTÉXTÉRIEUR, L' see Emura, Tetsuji

INTIMATE GAMES see Mellnäs, Arne

INTO ECLIPS see Albert, Stephen Joel

INTO THE DISTANT STILLNESS see Cherney, Brian

INTONATION: VICTIMIS HOMINUM INHUMANITATIS IN MEMORIAM see Berry, Wallace

INTONAZIONE see Mernier, Benoit

INTRADA ET DANCERIE see Leduc, Jacques

INTRADA UND CANZONA see Helgason, Hallgrimur

INTRODUCTION AND ALLEGRO see Nicholson, G. Gordon

INTRODUCTION AND FUGUE see Baker, Michael Conway

INTRODUCTION AND FUNK see Wallin, Peter

INTRODUCTION AND NATIONAL ANTHEM see Walton, [Sir] William (Turner)

INTRODUCTION AND PASSACAGLIA see Wallace, William

INTRODUCTION AND SCHERZO-IMPETUOSO-BENVENUTO CELLINI see Whettam, Graham Dudley

INTRODUCTION AND THREE FOLK SONGS see Coulthard, Jean

INTRODUCTION, CHANSON ET RONDE see Thiriet, Maurice

INTRODUCTION ET SCHERZO see Lalo, Edouard

INTRODUCTION UND CHACONNE see Hoyer, Karl

INTRODUKCE A ALLEGRO see Reiner, Karel

INTRODUKCE A RONDO see Bartoš, Jan Zdenek

INTRODUKTION see Hillborg, Anders, Lava

INTRODUKTION, THEMA UND VARIATIONEN see Henze, Hans Werner

INTRODUZIONE CON VARIAZIONI see Salieri, Giramolo

INTRODUZIONE E SCHERZO see Trexler, Georg

INTRODUZIONE-MOVIMENTO-RAPIDO see Toda, Kunio

INTRODUZIONE SEMPLICE see Pauer, Jiri

INTROIT see Matthews, David

INTROITUS see Dillon, James

INTROSPECTION FOR STRING ORCHESTRA see Behrens, Jack

INUIT: FROM THE ESKIMO see Applebaum, Louis, Inunit Music: From The Eskimo

INUNIT MUSIC: FROM THE ESKIMO see Applebaum, Louis

INVENTION see Larsson, Folke

INVENZIONI see Reimann, Aribert

INVITURA see Lundin, Bengt

IO! see Burrell, Diana

IO TI LASCIO see Mozart, Wolfgang Amadeus

IPHIGÉNIE EN AULIDE see Gluck, Christoph Willibald, Ritter von

IRANA'S CHANGING FACE see De Vos Malan, Jacques

IRENINY MELODIE see Maršik, Otakar

IRIDESCENCE see Harman, Chris

IRISATION see Harman, Chris

IRISCHE RHAPSODIE NR. 1 see Stanford, [Sir] Charles Villiers

IRISH MELODY, AN see Bridge, Frank

IRISH TUNE FROM COUNTY DERRY see Grainger, Percy Aldridge

IRKANDA 4 see Sculthorpe, Peter [Joshua]

IRMELIN ROSE see Delius, Frederick

IS-SLOTTET see Karlsen, Kjell Mørk, Symphony No. 3

ISAJI, SUNAO
Heavenly Maiden In Deformation, The & Weaver Star
orch [20'] JAPAN                     (I51)

ISAKSSON, MADELEINE (1950- )
Fsten Ó Fall
2(pic).2(English horn).3(bass clar).2(contrabsn). 2.0.0.0. strings [10'] sc,pts STIM       (I52)

Tillstnd - Avstnd
alto fl,alto sax,horn,flügelhorn/ trp,trom,tuba,acord,2perc,harp, pno,vln,vla,vcl,db sc,pts STIM               (I53)

ISHII, MAKI (1936- )
Fu Shi (Die Gestalt Des Windes)
3.3.3.3. 6.3.3.1. 6perc,2harp,cel, pno,strings [18'] MOECK sc 5463 f.s., pts rent              (I54)

Gedatsu *Op.63
2.2.2.2. 4.2.1.0. 5perc,harp,cel, strings [17'] MOECK sc 5308 f.s. pts rent              (I55)

Gioh
2.2.2.2. 4.2.1.0. 5perc,harp,cel, strings,fl solo [23'] MOECK sc 5309 f.s., pts rent           (I56)

Hovering Of Celestial Forms
see Ode To The Hiten

ISHII, MAKI (cont'd.)

Lost Sounds III
2.2.2.2. 4.2.2.1. 4perc,harp,pno,
strings,vln solo [14'] MOECK sc
5206 f.s., pts rent                    (I57)

Ode To The Hiten  *Op.106
"Hovering Of Celestial Forms" orch,
erhé [17'] JAPAN                       (I58)

Saidoki (D-Mon)
3.3.3.3. 6.3.3.1. 5perc,2harp,pno,
cel,strings [13'] MOECK sc 5479
f.s., pts rent                         (I59)

Schlagzeugkonzert Süden-Feuer-Sommer
2.2.2.2. 4.2.2.0. perc,pno,strings
[15'] MOECK sc 5482 f.s., pts
rent                                   (I60)

Sho Myo Kokyo I  *Op.105
orch, ryu [37'] JAPAN                  (I61)

Sho Myo Kokyo II  *Op.105b
orch, shomyo, gagaku (bugaku),
ballet [37'] JAPAN                     (I62)

ISKIOS, CITY OF SHADOWS see Beltrami,
Marco

ISLA DE LAS CALMAS, LA see Valen,
Fartein

ISLANDS see Lutyens, Elisabeth

ISRAELJAN, MARTIN (1938-    )
Capriccio for 14 Instruments
1.1.1.1. 1.1.1.0. perc,pno,2vln,
vla,vcl,db [10'] SIKORSKI perf
mat rent                               (I63)

Concerto for Chamber Orchestra
1.2.0.0. 2.0.0.0. pno,strings [30']
SIKORSKI perf mat rent                 (I64)

IŠTVAN, MILOSLAV (1928-1990)
Doteky
2.3.2.2. 3.2.2.1. perc,pno,strings
[8'] CESKY HUD.                        (I65)

Hry
3.3.3.3. 3.3.2.1. timp,perc,2harp,
pno,strings [18'] CESKY HUD.           (I66)

Partita for Strings
16strings CESKY HUD.                   (I67)

Variace Na Renesancní Téma
1.1.1.0. 0.0.0.0. perc,vibra,
cembalo,strings,2 speaking voices
[17'] CESKY HUD.                       (I68)

Vokální Symfonie
4.1.4.3. 4.3.2.1+euphonium. perc,
cel,elec bass gtr,strings,SB&
speaking voice [22'] CESKY HUD.        (I69)

IT IS MIDNIGHT, DR. SCHWEITZER see
Woolrich, John

ITABÓL see Eyser, Eberhard

ITALIA see Gardelli, Lamberto

ITALIENISCHE AMSELN see Kötscher,
Edmund

ITALSKÉ ÁRRIE SV. I: I.- VI. see Benda,
Georg Anton (Jirí Antonín)

ITALSKÉ ÁRRIE SV. II: I.- VI. see
Benda, Georg Anton (Jirí Antonín)

ITINÉRAIRES D'OUTRE-RÊVE see Louvier,
Alain

ITO, KEN
Cosmostrophe Quan-Quen & Sai-Ba-Rag
orch JAPAN                             (I70)

ITO, YASUHIDE (1960-    )
Melodies
strings [9'] JAPAN                     (I71)

IT'S FUN TO BE DUMB see Allen, Peter

IT'S THIS ISLAND see Gardner, John
Linton

IVAN THE TERRIBLE: ORCHESTRAL SUITE see
Prokofiev, Serge

IVANOVS, JANIS (1906-    )
Latschplesis
3.3.3.3. 4.3.3.1. timp,harp,strings
[16'] SIKORSKI perf mat rent           (I72)

IVES, CHARLES (1874-1954)
Call Of The Mountains, The (from
String Quartet No. 2)
(Dore, J.) string orch [11'] PEER
rent                                   (I73)

IVES, CHARLES (cont'd.)

Fourth Of July, The
orch sc SCHIRM.G AMP8057               (I74)

Orchestral Set No. 2
(Sinclair, J.) 2(pic).0.3.2.
1.3.3.1. timp,perc,2pno,cel/
bells,harp,org,acord, zither,
strings, opt unis cor [21'] PEER
rent                                   (I75)

Universe Symphony
(Austin, Larry) 2+2pic+alto fl.2+
English horn.3+bass clar.2+
contrabsn. 4.4.4.1. 24perc,2pno,
cel,harp,strings [36'30"] PEER
rent                                   (I76)
(Reinhard, Johnny) 9.2.3(bass
clar).5(2contrabsn). 4.5.4.2.
12perc,pno/cel,org,strings,
overtone machine [63'] PEER rent       (I77)

Universe Symphony: Prelude, Section
A, And Coda Of Section C
(Porter, David G.) Earth group:
1.2.3.3. 4.4.4.2. strings; Perc
ensemble: 11 players; Heavens
group: 3.1.1.0. 0.0.0.0. pno,
strings [14'] PEER rent                (I78)

IVY see Rossé, Francois

# J

JA! see Korndorf, Nicolai

JÁ NA VOJNU SE DAL see Gregor, Cestmír

JÁ, POTULNY ŠUMAR see Chlubna, Osvald

JABADAO see Tomasi, Henri

JACK AND THE BEANSTALK see Pelecis,
George

JACOB, GORDON (1895-1984)
Concerto for Bassoon, Percussion and
String Orchestra
2perc,strings,bsn solo [15']
STAINER solo pt,pno red 2627
f.s., sc,pts HL112                     (J1)

Double Concerto
clar,trp,strings [12'] BOOSEY-ENG
rent                                   (J2)

Five Pieces In The Form Of A Suite
For Harmonica And String
Orchestra
strings,harmonica [12'] STAINER
solo pt,pno red 2632 f.s., sc,pts
HL139                                  (J3)

Noyse Of Minstrells, A
2+pic.2+English horn.2+bass clar.2.
4.3.3.1. timp,4perc,harp,strings
[6'] perf sc set OXFORD 3650398
sc,pts rent                            (J4)

Overture: Funfare
2.3(opt English horn).2(opt bass
clar).2(opt contrabsn). 4.3.3.1.
timp,2-4perc,opt xylo,opt harp,
strings [5'] perf sc set OXFORD
3649640 sc,pts rent                    (J5)

Rhapsody For Cor Anglais Or E Flat
Saxophone And String Orchestra
strings,English horn/alto sax solo
[9'] STAINER solo pt,pno red H187
f.s., sc,pts HL132                     (J6)

JACOBI, WOLFGANG (1894-1972)
Concerto for Cembalo and Orchestra
2.1.1.2. 0.1.0.0. timp,perc,8vln I,
7vln II,6vla,5vcl,4db sc,solo pt
KAHNT 04798                            (J7)

JACOB'S LADDER see Smirnov, Dmitri

JADASSOHN, SOLOMON (1831-1902)
Johannisnacht  *Op.58, ballet
2+pic.2.2.2. 2.2.0.0. timp,2perc,
strings [16'] BREITKOPF-W            (J8)

Kavatine  *Op.120
2.0.2.2. 2.0.0.0. strings,vcl solo
[10'] BREITKOPF-W                     (J9)

Symphony No. 4, Op. 101, in C minor
2.2.2.2. 4.2.3.0. timp,harp,strings
[27'] BREITKOPF-W                     (J10)

JAGD, DIE (OUVERTÜRE) see Sibelius,
Jean

JAGD NACH DEM GLÜCK, DIE see Nicode,
Jean Louis

JAGER, ROBERT EDWARD (1939-    )
Kokopelli Dances
timp,4perc,pno/cel,harp,strings,fl
solo [15'] MARKS rent                 (J11)

Wall, The
3(pic).3(English horn).3(bass
clar).3(contrabsn).alto sax.
4.3.3(bass trom).1. timp,2perc,
pno,harp,strings [14'30"] MARKS
rent                                  (J12)

JAHN, THOMAS (1940-    )
Gänge
3(pic,alto fl).3(English
horn).3(clar in E flat,bass
clar).3(contrabsn). 4.4.3.1.
3perc,2pno,hpsd,cel,harp,strings
[110'] PEER rent                      (J13)

JAHR 1917, DAS see Shostakovich,
Dmitri, Sinfonia No. 12, Op. 112

JAHRESZEITEN, DIE see Glazunov,
Alexander Konstantinovich

JAHRMARKT, DER see Bernabei, Giuseppe
Antonio, Fiera, La

J'AI CUEILLI LA BELLE ROSE see Ridout,
Godfrey

J'AIME LES MILITAIRES see Offenbach, Jacques

JAJAMEN see Smedeby, Sune

JAK MILÉ, ROZKOŠNÉ see Ryba, Jan Jakub Simon

JAKO Z POHÁDKY see Stanek, Pavel

JAKOBSLEITER, DIE see Smirnov, Dmitri

JALOUSIE TACITURNE, LA see Barry, Gerald

JAMBOREE see Lundin, Dag

JAN HOUSLISTA see Šesták, Zdeněk

JAN SANTINI AICHEL see Kosut, Michal

JANÁCEK-MOMENT see Schnebel, Dieter

JANNOCH, HANS-PETER (1933-    )
Divertimento
0.2.0.1. 2.0.0.0. strings [15']
BREITKOPF-W                    (J14)

Pneuma
3.2.3.2. 4.3.3.1. cembalo,2vln,vcl,
db sc PETERS 03762             (J15)

JANSCHINOW, A.
Concertino Im Russischen Stil *Op.35
8vln I,7vln II,6vla,5vcl,4db PETERS
                              (J16)

JANSON, ALFRED (1937-    )
Fragment For Cello Solo And Orchestra
3(pic).2.3.3(contrabsn). 4.3.3.1.
timp,3perc,harp,strings,vcl solo
NORSKMI                        (J17)

JANSSEN, GUUS (1951-    )
Passevite
1.1.2.1. 1.0.0.0. perc,pno,2vln,
vla,vcl,db [13'] sc DONEMUS (J18)

Verstelwerk
2.2.2.2. 2.2.1.0. perc,strings,
tenor sax&pno&perc soli [15']
DONEMUS                        (J19)

Zaterdageditie, De
1.0.1.1. 0.1.0.0. perc,acord,pno,
strings, actor [5'] sc DONEMUS (J20)

Zoek
string orch,hpsd,pic [12'] DONEMUS
                              (J21)

JANSSON, GUNNAR (1944-    )
Soundscape
2.2.2.2. 2.2.1.1. timp,perc,harp,
strings [10'] STIM            (J22)

JANSSON, JOHANNES (1950-    )
Follia, La
3(pic).3(English horn).3(bass
clar).3(contrabsn). 4.3.3.1.
timp,2perc,strings [15'] STIM sc
H-2910, pts                    (J23)

Sogno, Il
1.2.1.1. 2.0.0.0. harp,strings
[30'] (1. Sommerso nella terra 2.
L'infanzia del mare 3. Le
impronte dell'infinito 4. Su
sirio ci sono bambini) sc,pts
SUECIA                         (J24)

JANSSON, REINE (1960-    )
Hoc Est Hokus Pokus
1.0.1(bass clar).1(contrabsn).
0.0.1.0. perc,string quar&perc,
MezB soli, dancers [25'] (text by
Trollformel) sc STIM           (J25)

Lge
woodwind quin,string orch [13']
STIM                           (J26)

Om Att Cykla
2(pic).1.2(bass clar).1. 0.0.0.0.
2perc,strings,pno [12'] sc,pts
STIM                           (J27)

JANSSON, TORBJÖRN (1961-    )
Idylle
3.4(English horn).3(bass clar).3.
4.3.3.0. timp,2perc,strings sc
STIM                           (J28)

Scherzo For Bida
3.3.3.3. 4.2.2.0. timp,2perc,harp,
strings sc STIM                (J29)

Symphony in D
3.3.3.3. 2.3.3.0. timp,perc,strings
sc STIM                        (J30)

JANUS KAPUJÁBAN see Kalmar, Laszlo, At Janus' Gate

JAPANESE SONGS see Garwood, Margaret

JAPPART, JEAN
Nenciozza Mia
(Grainger, Percy Aldridge) strings
(G maj) BARDIC                 (J31)
(Grainger, Percy Aldridge) strings
(F maj) BARDIC                 (J32)

JAQUE-DUPONT
see DUPONT, JACQUES

JARDIN DES OLIVIERS, LE see Provost, Serge

JARDINS D'AMÈNTA, LES see Florentz, Jean-Louis

JARNÍ see Krízek, Zdenek

JARO A MLÁDÍ see Krízek, Zdenek

JARO V PRAZE see Petr, Zdenek

JARRE, MAURICE (1924-    )
Concertino, No. 11 (from Divertimento
Für Mozart)
2.2.2+2basset horn.2. 2.2.2.0.
4timp,perc,strings [3'] SCHOTTS
perf mat rent                  (J33)

JARVLEPP, JAN (1953-    )
Camerata Music
2(pic).2.2.2. 2.2.2.0. 2perc,
strings [8'] sc CANADIAN
MI 1100 J38CA                  (J34)

Ice
string orch,vibra, fender electric
piano, and 2 metal percussion
[15'] sc CANADIAN MI 1750 J38IC
                              (J35)

JASTRZEBSKA, ANNA (1950-    )
Dance-Trance
2(pic).1.1.1. 2.1.1.0. 3perc,pno,
strings [18'] NORSKMI          (J36)

JAUBERT, MAURICE (1900-1940)
Saisir
string orch,harp,pno,S solo [12']
BILLAUDOT                      (J37)

JAUCHZET DEM HERRN ALLE WELT see Brühns, Nicholaus

JAZZ POEM FOR PIANO AND ORCHESTRA, A
see Thompson, Randall

JE T'ADORE, BRIGAND see Offenbach, Jacques

JE VEUX M'ÉLUDER - INTERLUDE see Hetu, Jacques

JEKIMOWSKI, VIKTOR (1947-    )
Brandenburg Concerto, For Flute,
Oboe, Violin, Strings And Cembalo
see Brandenburgisches Konzert

Brandenburgisches Konzert
"Brandenburg Concerto, For Flute,
Oboe, Violin, Strings And
Cembalo" string orch,hpsd,fl&ob&
vln soli [12'] SIKORSKI perf mat
rent                           (J38)

Doppelkammervariationen
1.1.1.1. 1.1.1.0. 2vln,vla,vcl,db
[10'] SIKORSKI                 (J39)

Kammervariationen
"Komposition 15, For 13 Players"
1.1.1.1. 1.1.1.0. perc,harp,vln,
vla,vcl,db [8'] SIKORSKI perf mat
rent                           (J40)

Komposition 15, For 13 Players
see Kammervariationen

Sinfonische Tänze, For Piano And
Orchestra
3.3.3.3. 4.3.3.1. 5perc,2pno,
strings,pno solo [15'] SIKORSKI
perf mat rent                  (J41)

Tripelkammervariationen
1.1.2.1. 2.1.1.1. 2vln,vla,vcl,db
[20'] SIKORSKI                 (J42)

JELINEK, STANISLAV (1945-    )
Concerto A 15
fl,2clar,bsn,2horn,3vln,3vla,3vcl,
db [12'] CESKY HUD.            (J43)

Concerto Da Camera
1.0.1.0. 0.0.0.0. perc,cembalo,
strings,vln solo [18'] CESKY HUD.
                              (J44)

Concerto for Oboe and Orchestra
0.0.2.2. 0.0.0.0. strings,ob solo
[17'] CESKY HUD.               (J45)

Historie Mého Srdce
1.0.1.0. 0.0.0.0. perc,pno,strings,
Bar solo [19'] CESKY HUD.      (J46)

JELINEK, STANISLAV (cont'd.)

Partita for English Horn and Strings
[16'] CESKY HUD.               (J47)

Suite Concertante for Violin and
Chamber Orchestra
strings,vln solo [12'] CESKY HUD.
                              (J48)

Tre Episodi
2.2.2.2. 2.2.0.0. timp,strings
[15'] CESKY HUD.               (J49)

JENAER GESÄNGE see Cilensek, Johann

JENEY, ZOLTAN (1943-    )
Laude
3(pic).2.3.3. 4.3.3.1. harp,6vln I,
6vln II,4vla,4vcl,2db [20'] EMB
rent                           (J50)

JENNEFELT, THOMAS (1954-    )
Musik Vid Ett Berg
3(pic).3.3.3(contrabsn). 3.3.3.1.
timp,2perc,strings [13'] sc STIM
                              (J51)

JENOM NE STRACH see Smolka, Jaroslav

JENSEITS DER EWIGEN RUHE see Kasparov, Youri

JENTZSCH, WILFRIED (1941-    )
Couleurs Pour Orchestre
3.2.2.0. 2.2.2.0. timp,perc,pno,
cel,cembalo,harp,8vln I,7vln II,
6vla,5vcl,4db [9'] sc PETERS
01255                          (J52)

JERABEK, PAVEL (1948-    )
Musica Giocosa
2.2.2.0. 2.0.0.0. timp,perc,strings
[8'] PANTON                    (J53)

JEREMIAS, BOHUSLAV (1859-1918)
Ceská Polka
2.2.2.2. 4.2.3.0. timp,perc,strings
[3'] CESKY HUD.                (J54)

JERUSALEM see Hess, Daniel

JÉRUSALEM: ENTRACTES see Massenet, Jules

JESSONDA: OVERTURE see Spohr, Ludwig (Louis)

JEŠTE SE VRÁTÍM see Sedlácek, Bohuslav

JESU, DEINE TIEFEN WUNDEN: CHORALE
PRELUDE see Tarnopolsky, Vladimir

JESU, DEINE TIEFEN WUNDEN:
CHORALVORSPIEL see Tarnopolsky, Vladimir

JESUS, MESSIAS, ERRETTE UNS! see
Ustvolskaya, Galina, Symphony No. 3

JETHS, WILLEM (1959-    )
Glenz
string orch,vln solo [22'] DONEMUS
                              (J55)
Meander
2.2.3.3. 4.4.3.1. timp,4perc,harp,
strings [15'] sc DONEMUS       (J56)
Pianoconcerto
4.2.3.3. 6.4.3.1. timp,6perc,
strings,pno solo [22'] DONEMUS
                              (J57)
Throb
3.3.3.3. 4.4.3.1. timp,8perc,2harp,
org,strings [17'] sc DONEMUS   (J58)

JETZT, SCHÄTZCHEN, JETZT SIND WIR
ALLEIN see Beethoven, Ludwig van

JEU DE CARTES see Stravinsky, Igor

JEVERUD, JOHAN (1962-    )
Aubade
string orch [9'] sc,pts STIM   (J59)

Concerto for Alto Saxophone
2(pic).2.2.2. 2.2.2.0. strings,alto
sax solo STIM                  (J60)

Concerto for Orchestra
see Konsert För Orkester

Concerto No. 2 for Orchestra
see Konsert Nr. 2 För Orkester

Ekstasis
string orch [11'] sc,pts STIM (J61)

Kammarkonsert
chamber orch STIM              (J62)

Konsert För Orkester (Concerto for
Orchestra)
2(pic).2.2.2. 4.3.3.1. strings
[25'] sc STIM                  (J63)

JEVERUD, JOHAN (cont'd.)

Konsert Nr. 2 För Orkester (Concerto
   No. 2 for Orchestra)
   2(pic).2.2.2. 4.2.0.0. strings
   [17'] sc,pts STIM            (J64)

Musiks Anatomi
   2(pic).2.2.2. 2.2.3.0. 4perc,
   strings,pno [20'] STIM sc H-2611,
   pts                          (J65)

Orchestral Variations
   see Orkestervariationer

Orkestervariationer
   "Orchestral Variations"
   2(pic).2.2(bass clar).2. 2.2.2.1.
   perc,strings,pno [20'] (1. Bleck;
   2. Stråkar; 3. Träblås; 4. Tutti)
   sc,pts STIM ED.NR 435        (J66)

Pastorale
   2.2.2.2. 2.0.0.0. strings [11'5"]
   sc,pts STIM                  (J67)

Svit Ur Tolv Främda Mn
   1(pic).1(English horn).1.0.
   1.0.1.0. perc,2vln,vla,vcl,db,pno
   [21'] sc,pts STIM            (J68)

13 Variations
   see 13 Variationer Över En Sonat Av
   Scarlatti

Tolv Främda Mn: Filmmusikaliska
   Porträtt
   1(pic).1(English horn).1.0.
   1.0.1.0. perc,2vln,vla,vcl,db,pno
   [40'] STIM                   (J69)

13 Variationer Över En Sonat Av
   Scarlatti
   "13 Variations" 2.2.2.2. 4.2.3.0.
   strings STIM                 (J70)

Tv Ballader
   "Two Ballads" string orch [17'5"]
   sc,pts STIM                  (J71)

Två Symfoniska Etyder
   2(pic).0.3(bass clar).2. 2.2.2.1.
   2perc,strings,pno [27'] sc SUECIA
                                (J72)

Two Ballads
   see Tv Ballader

Vinterresa
   2.2.2.2. 2.2.2.1. timp,strings STIM
                                (J73)

JEVTIC, IVAN (1947-    )
Concerto for Piano, No. 2
   2+pic.2.2.2. 4.3(trp in C).2+bass
   trom.1. timp,xylo,2perc,strings
   [17'] pno red LEDUC AL 28981
                                (J74)

JIHOCESKOU KRAJINOU see Strasek, Emil

JINDRA, ALFONS (1908-1978)
Vosí Hnízdo
   2.2.2.1. 3.3.3.1. timp,perc,harp,
   strings CESKY HUD.           (J75)

JINGLE see Larsson, Mats

JIRA, MILAN (1935-    )
Concerto for Violin and Orchestra
   2.2.2.2. 4.2.2.0. timp,perc,
   strings,vln solo [23'] CESKY HUD.
                                (J76)

Fantasia Da Concerto
   3.2.2.2. 4.2.2.0. timp,perc,cel,
   strings,fl solo [15'] CESKY HUD.
                                (J77)

Sinfonietta
   2.2.2.2. 4.2.2.0. timp,perc,strings
   [15'] CESKY HUD.             (J78)

Symphony No. 7
   3.2.2.2. 4.2.2.1. timp,perc,strings
   [30'] CESKY HUD.             (J79)

JIRÁCKOVÁ, MARTA (1932-    )
Ave Seikilos
   strings,tam-tam,bass drum [11']
   CESKY HUD.                   (J80)

Motylí Efekt
   perc,strings,vcl solo [12'] CESKY
   HUD.                         (J81)

JIRÁK, KAREL BOLESLAV (1891-1972)
Hlas Nejsladší *Op.49,No.1
   3.2.2.2. 4.2.0.0. timp,harp,
   strings,med solo CESKY HUD.  (J82)

Legenda *Op.74
   2.2.2.2. 4.2.3.1. timp,harp,strings
   [10'] CESKY HUD.             (J83)

Tri Zpevy Domova
   2.3.3.0. 4.2.0.0. timp,perc,harp,
   cel,strings,med solo [12'] CESKY
   HUD.                         (J84)

JIRASEK, IVO (1920-    )
Concertino for Cembalo and 11 Strings
   3vln I,3vln II,2vla,2vcl,db,cembalo
   solo [15'] CESKY HUD.        (J85)

Concertino for Chamber Orchestra
   see Mozartiana

Concertino Pro Klavír A Maly Smyccovy
   Orchestr
   pno,strings, (without vla & db)
   [12'] PANTON                 (J86)

Ctyri Dramatické Studie
   3.2.4.3. 4.3.3.1. timp,perc,xylo,
   harp,strings [19'] CESKY HUD.
                                (J87)

Ctyri Scény Z Fausta
   3.2.3.4. 4.3.3.1. timp,perc,xylo,
   vibra,harp,strings [21'] CESKY
   HUD.                         (J88)

Malá Koncertní Hudba
   3.2.2.2. 2.2.1.0. timp,perc,
   strings,synthesizer solo [16']
   CESKY HUD.                   (J89)

Mozartiana (Concertino for Chamber
   Orchestra)
   2.2.2.2. 2.2.0.0. timp,strings
   [20'] CESKY HUD.             (J90)

Podvecerní Hudba
   string orch,English horn solo [16']
   CESKY HUD.                   (J91)

JIRASEK, JAN (1955-    )
A Prece Se Tocí
   2.2.2.2. 4.3.3.1. bells,
   2synthesizer,strings [14'] CESKY
   HUD.                         (J92)

Variace Na Rockové Téma
   3synthesizer,pno,strings [14']
   CESKY HUD.                   (J93)

JIROVEC, VOJTECH MATEJ
   see GYROWETZ, ADALBERT

JÍZDA NOVYMI ALEJEMI 1848 see Koštál,
   Arnošt

JOACHIM, JOSEPH (1831-1907)
Concerto for Violin and Orchestra,
   Op. 3, in G minor
   2.2.2.2. 4.2.3.0. timp,strings,vln
   solo [15'] (no score) BREITKOPF-W
                                (J94)

Hamlet *Op.4, Overture
   2.2.2.2. 4.2.3.0. timp,strings
   [17'] BREITKOPF-W            (J95)

JOCHUM, OTTO (1898-1969)
Herzbrunnen, Der *Op.49
   chamber orch BÖHM            (J96)

JOGGER AND THE DINOSAUR see Gould,
   Morton

JOHANN ERNST, PRINZ VON SACHSEN-WEIMAR
   (1696-1715)
Concerto for Violin and Strings in G
   strings,cont,vln solo [16']
   BREITKOPF-W                  (J97)

JOHANNES PORTRAIT see Gardelli,
   Lamberto

JOHANNISNACHT see Jadassohn, Solomon

JOHANN'S GIFT TO CHRISTMAS see Turner,
   Robert [Comrie]

JOHANSEN, BERTIL PALMAR (1954-    )
Chili String
   string orch NORSKMI          (J98)

Concerto for 2 Violins and String
   Orchestra
   NORSKMI                      (J99)

Olympus Mons
   3(pic).3(English horn).3(bass
   clar).3(contrabsn). 4.3.3.1.
   timp,2perc,harp,pno,strings [28']
   NORSKMI                      (J100)

Olympus Mons Part 2
   see Tharsis Variations

Tharsis Variations
   "Olympus Mons Part 2"
   3(pic).3(English horn).3(bass
   clar).3(contrabsn). 4.3.3.1.
   timp,2perc,harp,pno/cel,strings
   [15'] NORSKMI                (J101)

JOHANSSON, JOHANNES
Anteckningar Frn Hesiodos Hemkomst
   fl,clar,bass clar,string quar,db,
   perc,pno,electronic tape [12']
   STIM                         (J102)

JOHANSSON, SVEN ERIC (1919-1997)
Festuvertyr Gränna-Brahe
   2(pic).2.2.2. 2.2.2.0. timp,perc,
   strings [10'-11'] STIM sc H-2741,
   pts                          (J103)

Sinfonia d'autunno (Symphony No. 11)
   3(pic).3(English
   horn).2.3(contrabsn). 4.2.3.1.
   timp,4perc,harp,strings [25'] sc,
   pts STIM                     (J104)

Symphonie Chez Nous (Symphony No. 10)
   4(pic).3(English horn).4(bass
   clar).4(contrabsn).alto sax.
   6.4.4.1. timp,6perc,harp,strings
   [23'] sc,pts SUECIA ED.NR 410
                                (J105)

Symphony No. 10
   see Symphonie Chez Nous

Symphony No. 11
   see Sinfonia d'autunno

JOHN AND THE MAGIC MUSIC-MAN see
   Hopkins, Anthony

JOHN CLARE'S VISION see Dalby, Martin

JOHNS
Symphony No. 12
   chamber orch (Sinfonia da camera,
   Arnold Schoenberg in memoriam)
   sc,pts STIM                  (J106)

JOHNSEN, HALLVARD (1916-    )
Canzona, Per Kammerorkester *Op.116
   string orch NORSKMI          (J107)

Concerto for Violin and Chamber
   Orchestra, Op. 28
   1.0.1.1. 2.0.0.0. strings,vln solo
   NORSKMI                      (J108)

Oceano
   see Symphony No. 19, Op. 115

Pastorale E Coral: In Memoriam
   *Op.117
   2.2.2.2. 2.2.2.1. timp,perc,strings
   NORSKMI                      (J109)

Symphony No. 18, Op. 111
   2(pic).2.2.3(contrabsn). 4.2.2.2.
   timp,perc,pno,cel,strings [26']
   NORSKMI                      (J110)

Symphony No. 19, Op. 115
   "Oceano" 2.2.2.2. 4.3.2.1. timp,
   perc,strings NORSKMI         (J111)

Symphony No. 20, Op. 120
   3(pic).3(English horn).2.2.
   4.3.2.1. timp,perc,cel,strings
   NORSKMI                      (J112)

JOHNSON, GEIR (1953-    )
Sentimental Journey: Hommage À Ringo
   Starr
   2.1.2(bass clar).1. 2.2.2.0. perc,
   strings, sampler NORSKMI     (J113)

JOHNSTON, RICHARD (1917-    )
Poem for Orchestra
   2(pic).2(English horn).2(clar in E
   flat).2. 4.3(piccolo trp).3.1.
   timp,3perc,harp,strings [14'] sc
   CANADIAN MI 1100 J73PO       (J114)

JOIE DE VIVRE see Killmayer, Wilhelm

JOLAS, BETSY (1926-    )
Elf Lieder
   2.2.2.3. 2.2.1.0. 3perc,harp,pno,
   5strings soli,trp solo [15']
   LEDUC                        (J115)

Liring Ballade [22']
   3.3.3.3. 4.3.3.2. 4perc,pno,
   strings,Bar solo
   BILLAUDOT                    (J116)

Lumor [25']
   2.2.3.2. 2.2.2.1. timp,4perc,pno,
   strings,sax solo
   BILLAUDOT                    (J117)

Petite Symphonie Concertante [12']
   2.2.2.2. 2.2.0.0. timp,perc,pno,
   strings,vln solo
   BILLAUDOT                    (J118)

Points D'Or [23']
   2clar,bass clar,2trp,2trom,pno,
   2perc,2vla,2vcl,db,sax solo
   BILLAUDOT                    (J119)

Sigrancia Ballade [25']
   3.3.3.3. 4.3.3.1. 4perc,timp,
   harp,pno,strings,Bar solo
   BILLAUDOT                    (J120)

Stance
   3(pic).2.3.7+contrabsn. 4.2.2.1.
   3perc,drums,harp,cel,strings,pno
   solo [21'] min sc LEDUC HE 32587,

JOLAS, BETSY (cont'd.)

PH 306 (J121)

Well Met
7vln,2vla,2vcl,db [15'] LEDUC (J122)

JOMMELLI, NICCOLO (1714-1774)
Zwei Veni Sponsa Christi
S solo,string orch,cont sc,pts
KUNZELMANN GM 1214 ipa (J123)

JONAH: DANCE OF THE NINEVITES (ACT 2)
see Owens, David

JONAH: ENTR'ACTE (ACT 3) see Owens,
David

JONAH: FOUR ORCHESTRAL PIECES see
Owens, David

JONAH: PRELUDE (ACT 1) see Owens, David

JONAH: STORM SCENE (ACT 1) see Owens,
David

JONÁK, ZDENEK (1917- )
Canzonetta In E Flat
3.0.3.2. 4.2.3.1. timp,perc,harp,
pno,strings,trp solo [6'] CESKY
HUD. (J124)

Dum Náš
2.2.2.2. 4.2.3.1. timp,perc,harp,
strings,B solo CESKY HUD. (J125)

Melody for Trumpet and Orchestra
2.1.2.1. 3.1.2.0. perc,harp,
strings,trp solo [6'] CESKY HUD.
(J126)

Na Bratrství
3.2.2.2. 4.2.3.1. timp,perc,harp,
strings [6'] CESKY HUD. (J127)

Rokoková Serenáda
2.1.2.1. 3.2.3.0. timp,perc,harp,
strings [4'] CESKY HUD. (J128)

Ver Temto Dnúm
3.2.3.2. 4.3.3.1. timp,perc,strings
CESKY HUD. (J129)

JONES, KELSEY (1922- )
Fantasy On A Theme
2.3+English horn.2.2. 4.2.3.1.
timp,perc,strings [18'] sc
CANADIAN MI 1100 J77FA (J130)

JONSSON, JOSEF [PETRUS] (1887-1969)
Nordland (Symphony No. 1, Op. 23)
2.3.2.3. 4.2.3.0. timp,perc,harp,
strings [55'] SUECIA sc H-253,
pts (J131)

Symphony No. 1, Op. 23
see Nordland

JONSSON, REINE (1960- )
Symfoni, En
3(pic).3(English horn).3(bass
clar).3(contrabsn). 4.3.3.2.
timp,3perc,harp,strings,cel [18']
STIM sc H-2602, pts (J132)

JOPLIN, SCOTT (1868-1917)
Antoinette-Marsch
see Drei Ragtimes

Drei Ragtimes
string orch sc,pts KUNZELMANN
GM 1258 f.s., ipa
contains: Antoinette-Marsch;
Entertainer, The; Strenuous
Life, The (J133)

Drei Ragtimes
(Beyer, F.) string orch sc,pts
KUNZELMANN GM 1258B f.s., ipa
contains: Favorite, The; Ragtime
Dance, The; Ragtime Two-Step, A
(J134)

Entertainer, The
(Frazer, Alan) 2.1.2.1. 2.2.1.0.
pno,perc,strings sc,pts CRAMER
90435 f.s. (J135)
see Drei Ragtimes

Favorite, The
see Drei Ragtimes

Ragtime Dance, The
see Drei Ragtimes

Ragtime Two-Step, A
see Drei Ragtimes

Strenuous Life, The
see Drei Ragtimes

JORDEN ÄR ETT LITET RUM see Dahlgren,
Eva

JOSEPH HAYDN WERKE, SERIES 1, VOLUME 3:
SINFONIEN 1761-1763 see Haydn,
[Franz] Joseph

JOSEPH: OVERTURE see Méhul, Étienne-
Nicolas

JOSIPOVIC, IVO
Samba Da Camera
13strings TONOS sc M-2015-3744-3
rent, pts M-2015-3743-6 rent
(J136)

JOSJÖ, MÅRTEN (1969- )
På Öppen Gata
orch STIM (J137)

JOSQUIN
see DES PREZ, JOSQUIN

JOUR S'ENDORT, LE see Dufay, Guillaume

JOURNEY THROUGH SACRED TIME see Satoh,
Somei

JOURNEY TO LOVE see Karayev, Faradzh

JOYFUL NOISE see Perera, Ronald
Christopher

JUAN: SYMFONICKÁ SVITA Z BALETU see
Kašlík, Václav

JUBELOUVERTÜRE see Draeseke, Felix

JUBILATION see Ward, Robert Eugene see
Zwilich, Ellen Taaffe

JUBILEE VARIATION see Copland, Aaron

JUBILEJNÍ see Vackár, Dalibor Cyril,
Sinfonietta No. 2

JUBILEJNÍ KOLÁZ see Blatny, Pavel

JUBILEJNÍ PREDEHRA see Bartoš, Jan
Zdenek see Blatny, Pavel, Nénie Za
Moji Matku see Mácha, Otmar

JUBILOSO see Bodorova, Sylvie

JUCHELKA, MIROSLAV (1922- )
Brilantní Scherzo
2.2.2.2. 4.2.3.1. timp,perc,xylo,
harp,strings [4'] CESKY HUD.
(J138)

Concerto for Piano and Orchestra
2.2.2.2. 4.2.3.1. timp,perc,
strings,pno solo [24'] CESKY HUD.
(J139)

Elegy for Violoncello and Orchestra
2.2.2.2. 4.2.3.1. timp,perc,
strings,vcl solo [5'] CESKY HUD.
(J140)

No Pasaran
3.2.2.3. 4.3.3.1. timp,perc,xylo,
harp,strings CESKY HUD. (J141)

Poetická Polka
2.2.2.2. 4.2.3.0. timp,perc,strings
[4'] CESKY HUD. (J142)

Romance
2.2.2.2. 4.0.0.1. timp,perc,harp,
strings,trp solo [4'] CESKY HUD.
(J143)

Sarba
2.1.2.1. 3.3.3.0. timp,perc,xylo,
harp,strings,opt org [4'] CESKY
HUD. (J144)

Slavnostní Pochod 6. Petiletky
3.2.2.2. 4.4.4.1. timp,perc,xylo,
strings [5'] CESKY HUD. (J145)

Tarantella Festiva
2.2.2.2. 4.2.3.1. timp,perc,strings
[5'] CESKY HUD. (J146)

To Je Má Zem
3.2.2.2. 4.2.3.1. timp,perc,harp,
strings,male solo [5'] CESKY HUD.
(J147)

Úsmevy A Slzy
2.2.2.2. 4.2.3.1. timp,perc,harp,
strings [8'] CESKY HUD. (J148)

Zámecká Serenáda
2.2.2.2. 4.0.0.0. perc,harp,strings
[5'] CESKY HUD. (J149)

JUDGEMENT OF PARIS, THE see Weill, Kurt

JÜDIN, DIE: OVERTURE see Halévy,
Jacques, Juive, La: Overture

JÜDISCHE TRILOGIE see Hamerik, Asger

JUGEND-MUSIK see Philipp, Franz

JUGENDALBUM: SUITE NO. 1 see
Tchaikovsky, Piotr Ilyich

JUGENDALBUM: SUITE NO. 2 see
Tchaikovsky, Piotr Ilyich

JUGENDMUSIK see Reinhold, Otto

JUIVE, LA: OVERTURE see Halévy, Jacques

JUL IGEN EN LITEN TID see Hedwall,
Lennart

JULIUS CÉSAR: AIR DE CLÉOPATRE ET AIR
DE CÉSAR see Handel, George
Frideric

JULY REMEMBRANCES see Shore, Clare

JUNG, HELGE (1943- )
Concertino for Piano and Orchestra,
Op. 30a
2.0.2.2. 2.1.2.0. timp,perc,8vln I,
7vln II,6vla,5vcl,4db [21'] sc
PETERS 03030 (J150)

Concerto for Piano, No. 2, Op. 30
2.0.2.2. 2.1.2.0. timp,perc,cel,
8vln I,7vln II,6vla,5vcl,4db
[21'] sc PETERS 03029 (J151)

Concerto for Violin, Op. 61
1.1.1.1. 1.0.0.0. perc,harp,8vln,
3vla,3vcl,db,vln solo [23'] sc
PETERS 04374 (J152)

Concerto No. 2 for 15 Strings
8vln I,3vla,3vcl,db [23'] sc PETERS
04486 (J153)

Divertimento for Orchestra, Op. 13
2.1.2.1. 2.2.2.0. timp,perc,8vln I,
7vln II,6vla,5vcl,4db [14'] sc
PETERS 03026 (J154)

Homenaje A Gabriel G. Marquez *Op.47
3.3.3.3. 4.3.3.0. timp,4perc,8vln
I,7vln II,6vla,5vcl,4db [11'] sc
PETERS 03032 (J155)

Und Fürchten Sie Nicht Den...
1.1.1.1. 1.1.1.0. 2perc,pno,harp,
electronic tape,2vln,vla,vcl,db
[60'] sc PETERS 04356 (J156)

JUNGE GARDE, DIE: SUITE see
Shostakovich, Dmitri

JUST FOR FUN see Silverman, Faye-Ellen

JUST LISTEN TO THOSE VIOLINS! see
Lindroth, Peter

JUZELIUNAS, JULIUS (1916- )
Symphony No. 4
3.3.3.3. 4.3.3.1. timp,perc,strings
[35'] SIKORSKI perf mat rent
(J157)

# K

K CÍLI BLÍZ see Strasek, Emil

KABALEVSKY, DMITRI BORISOVICH
(1904-1987)
Concerto for Violin in C, Op. 48
1.1.2.1. 2.1.1.0. timp,perc,
strings,vln solo [20'] PETERS
(K1)

KACHINAS see Amos, Keith

KADOSA, PAL (1903-1983)
Bouquet Of Field Flowers *Op.42a
"Mezei Csokor" 2.2.2.2. 2.0.0.0.
timp,perc,strings [7'] (Suite for
small orchestra) EMB rent    (K2)

Merry Music
"Vidám Zene" 2.2.2.2. 2.2.0.0.
timp,strings [4'] EMB rent   (K3)

Mezei Csokor
see Bouquet Of Field Flowers

Nádi Hegedu
see Peasant Fiddle

Peasant Fiddle *Op.16b
"Nádi Hegedu" 1.1.1.1. 2.1.1.0.
timp,strings [8'] (Suite of
folksongs for small orchestra)
EMB rent    (K4)

Sinfonia In Tre Movimento
2(pic).2(English horn).2(clar in
D).2+contrabsn.alto sax. 2.0+trp
in D.1.0. timp,perc,pno,strings,
trumpet in a EMB rent    (K5)

Vidám Zene
see Merry Music

KAGEL, MAURICIO (1931-    )
1898
1.0.1+bass clar.0. 0.1.0.1. 2perc,
harp,pno,vln,vla,vcl,db,wom cor/
jr cor [35'] PETERS    (K6)

Étude No. 1
see Études Für Grosses Orchester

Étude No. 2
see Études Für Grosses Orchester

Étude No. 3
see Études Für Grosses Orchester

Étude, Nos. 1-3
4.4.4.4. 4.4.3.1. timp,4perc,pno,
cel,harp,8vln I,7vln II,6vla,
5vcl,4db [14'] sc PETERS 02889
(K7)

Études Für Grosses Orchester
4.4.4.4. 4.4.3.1. timp,4perc,harp,
cel,pno,strings sc PETERS EP 8767
f.s.
contains: Étude No. 1 [7'30"];
Étude No. 2 [10']; Étude No. 3
[7'30"]    (K8)

Finale Mit Kammerensemble
"Finale With Orchestra" 1(pic).1.1+
bass clar.1. 1.1.1.1. perc,pno,
strings [22'] sc PETERS EP 8599
(K9)
Finale With Orchestra
see Finale Mit Kammerensemble

Interview Avec D.
[Fr] 3.3.4.2. 4.2.2.0. perc,harp,
pno&cel,strings,speaking voice
[26'] (text by Claude Debussy) sc
PETERS EP 8842    (K10)

Konzertstück for Orchestra
see Opus 1.991

Konzertstück for Timpani and
Orchestra
4(2alto fl).4(English horn).3+bass
clar.3(contrabsn). 4.3.3.1.
3perc,strings,5timp solo, (one
timpanist) [19'] PETERS    (K11)

Opus 1.991 (Konzertstück for
Orchestra)
4(2alto fl).4(English horn).3+bass
clar.3(contrabsn). 4.3.3.1.
3perc,strings [16'30"] sc PETERS
EP 8839    (K12)

Orchestrion-Straat
2.0.2.0.alto sax. 0.2.0.2. 2perc,
acord,pno,2vln,2vcl,2db [23']
PETERS    (K13)

KAGURA see Marsh, Roger

KAI see Turnage, Mark-Anthony

KAISER-MARSCH see Wagner, Richard

KAJANUS, ROBERT (1856-1933)
Marsch Karls XII.
2.2.2.2. 4.2.3.1. 3perc,strings
[2'] BREITKOPF-W    (K14)

KAKADU see Sculthorpe, Peter [Joshua]

KALABIS, VIKTOR (1923-    )
Bajka
2.2.2.2. 2.1.0.0. strings [12']
CESKY HUD.    (K15)

Concerto No. 2 for Violin and
Orchestra
2.2.2.2. 4.2.3.1. timp,perc,
strings,vln solo [15'] CESKY HUD.
(K16)

Diptych
13strings [15'] CESKY HUD.    (K17)

Dva Svety
4.4.3.3. 4.3.3.1. timp,perc,harp,
pno,strings [22'] (Baletní hudba)
CESKY HUD.    (K18)

Sinfonia Concertante for Viola and
Strings, Op. 56
see Tristium

Symphony No. 5, [excerpt]
3.3.3.3. 4.3.3.1. timp,perc,strings
[15'] PANTON    (K19)

Tristium (Sinfonia Concertante for
Viola and Strings, Op. 56)
strings,vla solo [11'] CESKY HUD.
(K20)

KALACH, JIRI (1934-    )
Concerto for Orchestra
3.3.3.3. 4.4.3.1. timp,perc,xylo,
harp,strings [20'] CESKY HUD.
(K21)
Concerto for 2 Violins and Orchestra
2.2.2.2. 2.2.0.0. perc,cel,strings
[18'] CESKY HUD.    (K22)

Concerto Grosso for Violin, Viola,
Violoncello and String Orchestra
strings,vln&vla&vcl soli [15']
CESKY HUD.    (K23)

Erasmus (Meditation for Violin and
Orchestra)
3.3.3.3. 0.3.3.0. timp,perc,harp,
cel/pno,strings without vln,vln
solo [18'] CESKY HUD.    (K24)

Meditation for Violin and Orchestra
see Erasmus

Partita for Orchestra
3.3.3.3. 4.3.3.1. timp,perc,harp,
strings [17'] CESKY HUD.    (K25)

Symphony No. 3
3.3.3.3. 4.3.3.1. timp,perc,harp,
cel,strings [24'] CESKY HUD.
(K26)
Symphony No. 4
3.3.3.3. 4.3.3.1. timp,perc,pno,
strings [19'] CESKY HUD.    (K27)

Symphony No. 5
3.3.3.3. 4.3.3.1. timp,perc,xylo,
harp,cel,strings [22'] CESKY HUD.
(K28)
Tiše
string orch,high solo [20'] CESKY
HUD.    (K29)

KÄLBERMARSCH see Cornell, Klaus

KALEIDOSCOPE see Maros, Rudolf see
Wishart, Trevor

KALEIDOSCOPE, BALLET FOR SMALL
ORCHESTRA see Rieti, Vittorio

KALEIDOSKOP see Engelmann, Hans Ulrich
see Hudec, Jiri

KALEIDOSZKÓP see Maros, Rudolf,
Kaleidoscope

KALENDERBLATT-SINFONIE see Hübner,
Wilhelm

KALI DANCES see Lumsdaine, David

KALIF STORCH see Lindner, Torsten

KÁLIK, VACLAV (1891-1951)
Duma
2.2.2.2. 4.0.0.0. timp,harp,
strings,Bar solo CESKY HUD. (K30)

Fantasy for Orchestra
3.2.2.2. 4.3.0.0. timp,perc,strings
CESKY HUD.    (K31)

KÁLIK, VACLAV (cont'd.)
More
3.2.2.3. 6.4.3.1. timp,harp,strings
CESKY HUD.    (K32)

Venezia
string orch CESKY HUD.    (K33)

KALIVODA, JAN KRTITEL
see KALLIWODA, JOHANN WENZEL

KALLIWODA, JOHANN WENZEL (1801-1866)
Koncertní Skladba Pro Klarinet
*Op.229
(Smetácek, Václav) 2.2.0.2.
2.0.0.0. strings,clar solo CESKY
HUD.    (K34)

Symphony No. 1 in F minor, Op. 7
2.2.2.2. 2.2.1.0. timp,strings
[26'] CESKY HUD.    (K35)

Symphony No. 2 in E flat, Op. 17
2.2.2.2. 2.2.1.0. timp,strings
CESKY HUD.    (K36)

Symphony No. 3 in D minor, Op. 32
2.2.2.2. 4.2.1.0. timp,strings
CESKY HUD.    (K37)

Symphony No. 4 in C minor, Op. 60
2.2.2.2. 2.2.3.0. timp,strings
CESKY HUD.    (K38)

Symphony No. 5 in B minor, Op. 106
2.2.2.2. 2.2.1.0. timp,strings
CESKY HUD.    (K39)

Symphony No. 6 in F, Op. 132
2.2.2.2. 2.2.1.0. timp,strings
[30'] CESKY HUD.    (K40)

KALMAR, LASZLO (1931-    )
At Janus' Gate
"Janus Kapujában" 3.2+English
horn.3.3(contrabsn). 4.3.3.1.
harp,strings [20'] (Two movements
for orchestra) EMB rent    (K41)

Ballet Des Amphores: Three Movements
"Három Tétel Zenekarra" 2.1.2(bass
clar).1. 2.1.1.0. pno solo,
strings [20'] EMB rent    (K42)

Ballet Des Fleurs Blanches
string orch EMB rent    (K43)

Chamber-Variations
"Kamaraváltozatok" 2.0.1+bass
clar.0. 2.0.0.0. strings [14']
(Hommage à Johannes Brahms) EMB
rent    (K44)

Concertante Per Pianoforte E
Orchestra D'Archi
see Toccata

Concerto for Piano, No. 2
3.2+English horn.3(bass
clar).3(contrabsn). 4.3.3.1.
strings,pno solo (in memoriam S.
Rachmaninov) EMB rent    (K45)

Három Szimfonikus Kép
see Three Symphonic Pictures

Három Szimfonikus Tétel
see Hermes: Three Symphonic
Movements
see Horae: Three Symphonic
Movements

Három Tétel Zenekarra
see Ballet Des Amphores: Three
Movements

Hermes: Three Symphonic Movements
"Három Szimfonikus Tétel" 3.2+
English horn.3+bass clar.3+
contrabsn. 4.3.3.1. harp,strings
EMB rent    (K46)

Hesperidák
see Hesperides

Hesperides
"Hesperidák" 3.2+English horn.3+
bass clar.3+contrabsn. 4.3.3.1.
pno,strings [14'] (Variations Of
An Antique Theme) EMB rent  (K47)

Horae: Three Symphonic Movements
"Három Szimfonikus Tétel" 3(pic).2+
English horn.3+bass clar.3+
contrabsn. 4.3.3.1. harp,strings
[21'] EMB rent    (K48)

Janus Kapujában
see At Janus' Gate

Kamaraváltozatok
see Chamber-Variations

KALMAR, LASZLO (cont'd.)

Memoriale (In Memoriam S.F.)
timp,perc,strings,6A,6B [12'] EMB
rent                             (K49)

Notturno No. 1 for 15 Instruments
0.0.3.0. 3.0.0.0. harp,elec org,
vibra,3vla,2vcl,db [8'] EMB rent
(K50)

Three Symphonic Pictures
"Három Szimfonikus Kép" 4.2+English
horn.3+bass clar.3+contrabsn.
6.4.3.1. 18vln I,16vln II,14vla,
12vcl,8db EMB rent              (K51)

Toccata
"Concertante Per Pianoforte E
Orchestra D'Archi" string orch,
pno solo [12'] EMB rent         (K52)

KALMAR NYCKEL see Lees, Benjamin,
Symphony No. 5

KALOUS, (JAN?) (fl. ca. 1750?)
Concerto for Clarinet and Orchestra
in E flat
0.2.0.0. 2.0.0.0. strings,clar solo
[11'] PANTON                    (K53)

KALSON, ROMUALD (1936-    )
Concerto for Violoncello and
Orchestra
3.2.3.2. 2.2.0.0. timp,perc,cel,
strings,vcl solo [25'] SIKORSKI
perf mat rent                   (K54)

Symphony for Chamber Orchestra
strings,hpsd, flexatone [17']
SIKORSKI perf mat rent          (K55)

Vor Dem Verlassen
3.3.3.3. 4.4.3.1. timp,perc,harp,
cel,strings [20'] SIKORSKI perf
mat rent                        (K56)

KAMARAVÁLTOZATOK see Kalmar, Laszlo,
Chamber-Variations

KAMEKE, ERNST-ULRICH VON (1926-    )
Concerto for Organ and Orchestra
2.3.2.2. 4.2.3.1. timp,2perc,
strings,org solo [33'] SIKORSKI
perf mat rent                   (K57)

KAMINSKI, HEINRICH (1886-1946)
Concerto for Orchestra and Piano
1.1.0.1. 1.1.0.0. strings,pno solo
[26'] SCHOTTS perf mat rent (K58)

KAMMARKONSERT see Jeverud, Johan

KAMMARMUSIK FÖR 12 NR 1 'MOLN' see
Ridderström, Bo

KAMMERKONZERT see Genzmer, Harald see
Lason, Aleksander

KAMMERKONZERT II see Kratzschmar,
Wilfried

KAMMERKONZERT IN D see Borris,
Siegfried

KAMMERMUSIK NR. 8 see Linke, Robert

KAMMERMUSIK V see Lason, Aleksander

KAMMERSINFONIE see Bruns, Victor see
Lohse, Fred see Meyer, Ernst
Hermann see Plate, Anton see
Shostakovich, Dmitri

KAMMERSINFONIE NR. 2 see Zechlin, Ruth

KAMMERSINFONIE NR. 4 see Schut,
Vladislav

KAMMERSINFONIE, OP. 34 see Kangro,
Raimo, Tuuru

KAMMERVARIATIONEN see Jekimowski,
Viktor

KAMOGAWA see Toyama, Yuzo

KAMYCKÁ POLKA see Broz, František

KANADISCHE RHAPSODIE see Mackenzie,
[Sir] Alexander Campbell

KANÁK, MILAN (1955-    )
Ctyri Vety
3.3.3.3. 4.3.3.1. timp,perc,harp,
pno,strings [18'] CESKY HUD.
(K59)

Koncertní Hudba
2.2.3.2. 2.1.1.1. timp,perc,vibra,
cel,pno,marimba,strings,vln&db
soli [23'] CESKY HUD.           (K60)

KANEKO, SHIN-ICHI (1937-    )
Wan Chai
orch [7'] JAPAN                 (K61)

---

KANETA, TCHOJI (1948-    )
Metempsychose III
string orch,bsn solo [15'] JAPAN
(K62)

Shikisokuzekuu II
orch, shaku [20'] JAPAN         (K63)

KANGRO, RAIMO (1949-    )
Concerto for 2 Pianos, Brass, Strings
and Percussion, No. 3, Op. 47
0.0.0.0. 2.2.0.0. 3perc,strings,
2pno soli [31'] SIKORSKI perf mat
rent                            (K64)

Concerto for 2 Pianos, Percussion and
Strings, No. 1, Op. 22
string orch,perc,2pno soli [19']
SIKORSKI perf mat rent          (K65)

Concerto for Violin and Orchestra,
No. 2, Op. 19
3.2.2.2. 2.2.2.1. timp,perc,harp,
pno,strings,vln solo [17']
SIKORSKI perf mat rent          (K66)

Kammersinfonie, Op. 34
see Tuuru

Leichte Sinfonie, Op. 18
1.0.1.1. 1.0.0.0. perc,pno,strings
[13'] SIKORSKI perf mat rent
(K67)

Tuuru
"Kammersinfonie, Op. 34" 1.1.0.0.
1.0.0.0. timp,perc,mand,gtr,pno,
strings [18'] SIKORSKI perf mat
rent                            (K68)

KANKA, JAN NEPOMUK (1772-1865)
Sinfonia in E flat
(Stefan, Jiri) 3.2.2.2. 2.2.0.0.
timp,perc,strings CESKY HUD.
(K69)

KANNO, YOSHIHIRO (1953-    )
Mythical Implosion, A
orch [30'] JAPAN                (K70)

KANT see Dion, Denis

KANTATE "NACHT UND MORGEN": ADAGIO UND
PASSACAGLIA see Schumann, Gerhard

KANTATE ZUM ERSTEN SONNTAG NACH NEUJAHR
see Herchet, Jörg

KANTILÉNA see Pinos, Alois

KANTSCHELI, GIJA (1935-    )
... A La Duduki, For Brass Quintet
And Orchestra
3.3.3.3. 0.0.0.0. 4perc,harp,pno,
strings,brass quin soli [25']
SIKORSKI perf mat rent          (K71)

Abendgebete
1.1.0.0. 1.2.2.1. 3perc,bass gtr,
pno,strings [20'] SIKORSKI sc
1910 f.s., sc,pts perf mat rent
(K72)

Abii Ne Viderem
strings,alto fl,pno,bass gtr [25']
SIKORSKI perf mat rent      (K73)
strings,pno,bass gtr,vla solo [22']
SIKORSKI sc 1929 f.s., sc,pts
perf mat rent                   (K74)

Diplipito
perc,gtr,bass gtr,pno,strings,vcl
solo,countertenor [28'] SIKORSKI
perf mat rent                   (K75)

Flügellos
"Wingless" 3.3.3.3. 4.3.3.1. 5perc,
bass gtr,pno,strings [28']
RICORDI-IT perf mat rent    (K76)

Freudenleere Gedanken, For
Violoncello And Orchestra
see Simi

Lament: Trauermusik Im Gedenken An
Luigi Nono
4.1.0.0. 4.4.4.1. 7perc,cel,pno,
spinett, strings, violin solo &
soprano solo [48'] SIKORSKI perf
mat rent                        (K77)

Largo Und Allegro
string orch,pno,timp [15'] SIKORSKI
perf mat rent                   (K78)

Morgengebete
alto fl,bass gtr,pno,strings,tape
recorder, pre-recorded boy's
voice & organ [23'] SIKORSKI sc
1902 f.s., sc,pts perf mat rent
(K79)

Nachtgebete
soprano sax,strings,tape recorder
[23'] SCHIRM.G perf mat rent
(K80)

Noch Einen Schritt...
2.2.2.2. 4.3.3.1. 3perc,harp,pno,
strings, offstage viola solo
[17'] SIKORSKI perf mat rent
(K81)

---

KANTSCHELI, GIJA (cont'd.)

Simi
"Freudenleere Gedanken, For
Violoncello And Orchestra"
3.2.2.3. 4.4.3.1. 6perc,harp,pno,
strings,vcl solo [30'] SIKORSKI
perf mat rent                   (K82)

Symphony No. 7
4.3.3.3. 6.6.4.1. 7perc,bass gtr,
harp,pno, spinett, strings [33']
SIKORSKI sc 1865 f.s., sc,pts
perf mat rent                   (K83)

Tagesgebete
1.1.0.1. 1.2.3.1. 3perc,bass gtr,
pno,vln,vla,vcl,db,clar solo,boy
solo [24'] SIKORSKI sc 1909 f.s.,
sc,pts perf mat rent            (K84)

Trauerfarbenes Land
3.2.2.2. 4.4.4.1. timp,6perc,bass
gtr,harp,pno,strings [37']
SIKORSKI perf mat rent          (K85)

V & V
string orch,vln solo,tape recorder
[10'] SCHIRM.G perf mat rent
(K86)

Valse Boston
string orch,pno [24'] SIKORSKI perf
mat rent                        (K87)

Wingless
see Flügellos

KANZONE see Zechlin, Ruth

KAPESNÍ VESMÍR see Vostrák, Zbynek

KAPR, JAN (1914-1988)
Concerto E-G Per Pianoforte Ed
Orchestra
3.2.2.2. 4.3.3.1. timp,perc,xylo,
cel,strings,pno solo [28'] CESKY
HUD.                            (K88)

Concerto for Accordion and Strings
[18'] CESKY HUD.                (K89)

Lanzhotská
see Symphony No. 10

Symphony No. 10
"Lanzhotská" 3.3.2.2. 4.3.3.1.
timp,perc,2harp,gtr,strings,MezT
soli [50'] CESKY HUD.           (K90)

KAR: FESTMUSIKK, FOR ORCHESTRA WITH
OCARINAS see Aagaard-Nilsen,
Torstein

KARABITS, IVAN (1945-    )
Concerto for Orchestra, No. 2
3.3.3.3. 4.3.3.1. timp,perc,harp,
cel,hpsd,strings [16'] SIKORSKI
perf mat rent                   (K91)

KARAYEV, FARADZH (1943-    )
Abschiedssinfonie
see Tristessa I

Concerto Grosso for Chamber Orchestra
see Concerto Grosso In Memoriam
Anton Webern

Concerto Grosso In Memoriam Anton
Webern (Concerto Grosso for
Chamber Orchestra)
1.2.0.1. 2.0.0.0. pno,strings [18']
SIKORSKI perf mat rent          (K92)

Crumb Of Music For George Crumb, A
1.1.1.1. 1.1.1.0. 2perc,harp,pno,
2vln,vla,vcl,db [15'] SIKORSKI
perf mat rent                   (K93)

Journey To Love  *scena
1.0.1.0. 0.0.0.0. 2glock,vibra/pno,
prepared pno,acord,elec gtr,bass
gtr,drums,elec pno,strings [38']
SIKORSKI perf mat rent          (K94)

Tristessa I
"Abschiedssinfonie" 2fl,clar,2horn,
3perc,pno,org, amplified
harpsichord & prepared piano,
strings [42'] SIKORSKI perf mat
rent                            (K95)

KARAYEV, KARA (1918-1982)
Wiegenlied (from Auf Dem Pfade Des
Donners)
1.1.2.1. 0.0.0.0. harp,cel,strings
[8'] SIKORSKI perf mat rent (K96)

KAREL, RUDOLF (1880-1945)
Fantasy, Op. 8
4.2.2.2. 4.2.3.1. timp,perc,harp,
strings CESKY HUD.              (K97)

KARIKATUREN FÜR STREICHORCHESTER see
Thomas-Mifune, Werner

KARKOFF, INGVAR (1958-    )
Carnavalito
1.1.1.1. 1.1.1.0. perc,strings [8']
sc,pts STIM                        (K98)

Concerto for Mandolin and Chamber
Orchestra
1(pic).1.1.1. 1.1.1.0. harp,
strings,cel,mand solo STIM    (K99)

Fenix
3(pic).2.3(bass clar).2. 4.2.3.1.
timp,2perc,harp,strings [15']
STIM sc H-2745, pts          (K100)

Five Easy Pieces
2(pic).1.1.1. 2.1.1.0. 2perc,
strings [20'] (1. Prelude; 2.
Hymn I; 3. The Doll's House; 4.
Barcarole; 5. Hymn II) STIM sc
H-2561, pts                  (K101)

Intermezzo: Stjrnskuggor
string orch [9'] sc,pts STIM (K102)

Oregon
2.2.2.2. 2.2.2.0. perc,strings,pno
[7'] STIM sc H-2677, pts     (K103)

Symphony No. 1
3(pic).2(English horn).3(bass
clar).2. 2.2(piccolo trp).2.0.
2perc,harp,strings [26'] STIM sc
H-2902, pts                  (K104)

Three Orchestral Movements
2(pic).1(English horn).2(bass
clar).1. 2.1.1.0. 2perc,strings
[21'] (1. Positive and sensitive;
2. Slow and expressive; 3.
Precisely rhythmical) sc STIM
                             (K105)

KARKOFF, MAURICE (1927-    )
Four Sketches *Op.171
string orch [16'] (Preludio;
Intermezzo 1; Intermezzo 2;
Finale) sc,pts STIM          (K106)

Sinfonia Da Camera Op. 128
see Symphony No. 7, Op. 128

Sinfonia Della Vita
see Symphony No. 11, Op. 202

Sinfonia Semplice
see Symphony No. 12, Op. 206

Sinfonietta No. 5, Op. 170
2(pic).1.1.1. 2.1.1.0. 3perc,
strings [17'] sc,pts STIM H-2564
                             (K107)

Suite, Op. 67 for Strings and
Harpsichord
DA CAPO                      (K108)

Symphony No. 7, Op. 128
"Sinfonia Da Camera Op. 128"
2(pic).2(English horn).2(bass
clar).2(contrabsn). 2.2.1.0.
timp,2perc,strings,cel [12'] sc,
pts SUECIA ED.NR 376         (K109)

Symphony No. 11, Op. 202
"Sinfonia Della Vita" 3(pic).1.1.1.
3.2.0.1. 3perc,strings [16'] STIM
sc H-2335, pts               (K110)

Symphony No. 12, Op. 206
"Sinfonia Semplice" 3(pic).1.1.1.
2.2.1.0. timp,3perc,strings [16']
sc STIM H-2927               (K111)

KARKOSCHKA, ERHARD (1923-    )
Kollektives Improvisieren
chamber orch TONOS M-2015-3746-7
                             (K112)

KARLINS, M. WILLIAM (1932-    )
Concert Music V
3.3.3.3.3sax. 4.4.2.2. 5perc,timp,
pno,strings SEESAW           (K113)

KARLSEN, KJELL MØRK (1947-    )
Cantilena For Baltikum
string orch NORSKMI          (K114)

Chamber Concerto For Flute, Strings
And Timpani, Op. 60
[13'20"] NORSK               (K115)

Concerto for Trombone and Strings,
Op. 83
NORSK NMO 10320              (K116)

Concerto for Tuba and Orchestra, Op.
97
see Concerto Furvus For Tuba And
Orchestra

Concerto Furvus For Tuba And
Orchestra (Concerto for Tuba and
Orchestra, Op. 97) Op.97
2(pic).2.2.2. 4.3.3.1. timp,3perc,
strings,tuba solo [17'] NORSKMI
                             (K117)

KARLSEN, KJELL MØRK (cont'd.)

Is-Slottet
see Symphony No. 3

Norwegian Suite For String Orchestra
[10'] NORSKMI                (K118)

Sinfonia Da Requiem
see Symphony No. 2, Op. 73

Sinfonia Piccola For Small Orchestra,
Op. 69
2.1.2.1. 2.2.0.0. strings [11']
NORSK                        (K119)

Sinfonia Romantica
see Symphony No. 5

Symphony No. 2, Op. 73
"Sinfonia Da Requiem" 3(pic).2.2.2.
4.4.3.1. 3timp,2perc,org,strings,
SATB [38'] NORSKMI           (K120)

Symphony No. 3
"Is-Slottet" orch NORSK NMO 10300
                             (K121)

Symphony No. 5 *Op.99b
"Sinfonia Romantica" 2.2.2.2.
4.3.3.1. 2perc,strings [42']
NORSKMI                      (K122)

KARNEVAL DER TIERE, DER see Saint-
Saëns, Camille, Carnaval Des
Animaux, Le

KARNEVAL SVETA see Kvech, Otomar

KAROLYI, PAL (1934-    )
Monodia
string orch,vcl solo [11'] EMB rent
                             (K123)

KÁRPÁTI RAPSZÓDIA see Farkas, Ferenc,
Rhapsodia Carpathiana

KARPATSKY KONCERT see Slezak, Pavel

KASACE see Fried, Alexj

KASANDIEFF, WASSIL
see KAZANDJIEV, VASSIL

KASANDSHIEV, VASSIL
see KAZANDJIEV, VASSIL

KASCHLAJEW, MURAD (1931-    )
Studenten
see Suite No. 3

Suite No. 3 (from Gorjanka)
"Studenten" 3.2.3.3. 4.4.4.1. timp,
perc,harp,strings [16'] SIKORSKI
perf mat rent                (K124)

KASEMETS, UDO (1919-    )
Eight Houses Of The I Ching, The
12strings sc CANADIAN MI 1500 K19EI
                             (K125)

For The Victims Of Wars And Violence
Of Our Time
see Requiem Renga

Requiem Renga
"For The Victims Of Wars And
Violence Of Our Time" 2perc,
15strings [41'] sc CANADIAN
MI1200 K19RE                 (K126)

KAŠLIK, IVAN (1947-    )
Concerto for Piano, Strings and
Timpani
strings,timp,pno solo [21'] CESKY
HUD.                         (K127)

Concerto for Strings, Piano and
Timpani
[21'] CESKY HUD.             (K128)

KAŠLIK, VÁCLAV (1917-1989)
Cesta Na Popraviste
3.3.3.2. 4.3.3.1. timp,perc,harp,
pno,strings [6'] CESKY HUD.
                             (K129)
Cikánské Tance (Suite for Violin and
Orchestra) (from Baletu Jánošik)
3.3.3.2. 4.3.3.1. timp,perc,harp,
2mand,pno,strings,vln solo [12']
CESKY HUD.                   (K130)

Dvorské Tance (from Baletu Jánošik)
3.3.3.2. 4.3.3.1. timp,perc,harp,
vibra,cel,cimbalom,pno,strings
[20'] CESKY HUD.             (K131)

Juan: Symfonická Svita Z Baletu
3.3.3.3. 4.3.3.1. timp,perc,harp,
cel,2pno,org/harmonium,strings
[40'] CESKY HUD.             (K132)

Masopustní - Tanec Smrti (from Baletu
Prazsky Karneval)
3.2.3.3. 4.3.3.1. timp,perc,xylo,
vibra,harp,cel,pno,gtr,cimbalom,
strings, cornamusa [16'] CESKY
HUD.                         (K133)

KAŠLIK, VÁCLAV (cont'd.)

Milostny Tanec
3.2.2.2. 4.3.4.0. vibra,2mand,harp,
pno,strings [3'] CESKÝ HUD.
                             (K134)
Slavnosti
3.3.3.3. 4.4.4.1. timp,perc,acord,
org,strings [15'] CESKÝ HUD.
                             (K135)
Suite for Violin and Orchestra
see Cikánské Tance

Tance Kejklíru (from Baletu Kouzelník
Zito)
3.3.3.3. 4.3.3.1. timp,perc,xylo,
harp,cel,gtr,mand,strings,
cornamusa, 2rumba [4'] CESKÝ HUD.
                             (K136)
Tance Pred Branou (from Baletu
Kouzelnik Zito)
3.2.2.3. 4.3.3.1. timp,perc,xylo,
harp,pno,acord,gtr,strings [4']
CESKÝ HUD.                   (K137)
Zbojnické Tance (from Baletu Jánošik)
Suite
3.3.3.2. 4.3.3.1. perc,harp,pno,
strings [18'] CESKÝ HUD.     (K138)

KAŠPÁREK see Vodrazka, Karel, Klaun

KASPAROV, YOURI (1955-    )
Genesis
2.2.2.2. 2.2.2.0. 3perc,harp,cel&
pno,strings [6'] CHANT perf mat
rent                         (K139)

Jenseits Der Ewigen Ruhe
1.1.1.0. 1.1.1.0. 2perc,pno,2vln,
vla,vcl,db,bsn solo [10'] CHANT
perf mat rent                (K140)

Teufelstriller
1.1.1.1. 1.1.1.0. 2perc,harp,cel/
pno,strings [8'] SIKORSKI perf
mat rent                     (K141)

KASSANDRA see Tarnopolsky, Vladimir

KAST see Rehnqvist, Karin

KATE GREENAWAY SUITE see Amos, Keith

KATEDRÁLA see Válek, Jirí

KATERINA ISMAILOWA see Shostakovich,
Dmitri

KÄTHCHEN VON HEILBRONN, DAS see
Naumann, Emil

KATHEDRALE see Lason, Aleksander

KATSU see Strindberg, Henrik

KATZER, GEORG (1935-    )
Concerto for Flute and Orchestra
2.2.2.2. 4.2.2.0. timp,3perc,harp,
pno,10vln I,8vln II,6vla,6vcl,
5db,fl&pic&alto fl solo [20'] sc
PETERS 02951                 (K142)

Concerto for Oboe and Orchestra
3.3.3.3. 4.3.3.1. 3perc,harp,cel,
strings,ob solo [30'] sc PETERS
02289                        (K143)

Concerto for Orchestra, No. 2
3.3.3.2. 4.3.3.1. 3perc,harp,pno,
strings [21'] sc PETERS 02432
                             (K144)
Concerto for Orchestra, No. 3
"Schwarze Vögel" 3.3.3.3. 4.3.3.1.
timp,4perc,harp,strings [26'] sc
PETERS 02952                 (K145)

Concerto for Violoncello and
Orchestra
3.3.3.3. 4.2.2.1. 3perc,harp,
strings,vcl solo [18'] sc PETERS
02288                        (K146)

Dramatische Musik
3.2.3.2. 4.2.3.1. timp,perc,harp,
cel,pno,strings [24'] sc PETERS
01326                        (K147)

Offene Landschaft
2.2.2.2. 2.2.1.0. 3perc,strings
[22'] sc PETERS 02189        (K148)

Schwarze Vögel
see Concerto for Orchestra, No. 3

Sonata for Orchestra
3.3.3.3. 4.3.3.1. timp,3perc,harp,
2pno,strings [14'] sc PETERS
01325                        (K149)

KAUDER, HUGO (1888-1972)
Passacaglia
2.2.2.2. 4.2.3.0. strings (1961)
SEESAW                       (K150)

KAUDER, HUGO (cont'd.)

Symphony No. 2
2.2.2.2. 3.2.0.0. timp,strings
(1939) SEESAW                    (K151)

KAUFMANN, DIETER (1941-    )
Billige Lieder  *Ger
chamber orch,electronic tape,solo
voice,speaking voice [30'] (text
by Gert Jonke) sc REIMERS 101139
rent                             (K152)

Für Clara
pno,orch REIMERS sc 101100 rent,
rent                             (K153)

KAVATINE see Jadassohn, Solomon

KAWASAKI, ETSUO (1959-    )
Adventure In Wonderland, The
orch,pno [12'] JAPAN             (K154)

KAWASHIMA, MOTOHARU (1972-    )
Dual Personality I
orch,perc [11'] JAPAN            (K155)

KAZACSAY, TIBOR (1892-    )
Concerto for Bassoon and Orchestra
2.2.2.0. 2.2.1.0. timp,perc,harp/
pno,strings,bsn solo [15'] EMB
rent                             (K156)

Dalciklus
see Pro Memoria

Pro Memoria  *Op.122
"Dalciklus" 2.2.2.2. 2.2.0.0. timp,
perc,harp,cel,strings,Bar solo
[15'] (song cycle) EMB rent      (K157)

KAZANDJIEV, VASSIL (1934-    )
Festmusik Für Streicher
"Psalmen Und Rituale" strings [10']
study sc PETERS EP 8228          (K158)

Psalmen Und Rituale
see Festmusik Für Streicher

Sinfonia No. 3
3.3.4.3. 4.3.3.1. 4timp,4perc,pno,
harp,8vln I,7vln II,6vla,5vcl,4db
sc JUS-AUTOR 02179               (K159)

KDYZ PLÁCE TRÁVA see Volejnicek,
Drahoslav

KEANE, DAVID (1943)
Meridies
string orch [8'] sc CANADIAN
MI 3148 K24MR                    (K160)

Orbis
string orch,4vln soli [12'] sc
CANADIAN MI 1711 K24OR           (K161)

Ortus
2.2.2.2. 4.0+3cornet.3.1. strings,
12 herald trumpets [2'35"] sc
CANADIAN MI 1100 K24OR           (K162)

Tombeau De Lester Pearson
2.2.2.2. 4.2.2.1. strings [12'] sc
CANADIAN MI 1100 K24TO           (K163)

KEEP THE CHANGE see Melin, Sten

KEISHO see Narita, Kazuko

KEJSARVISAN see Sandström, Jan,
Emperor's Song

KELEMEN, MILKO (1924-    )
Archetypon II Für Anton
4.4.4.4. 6.4.3.5(tenor tuba,db
tuba). 2timp,3perc,harp,cel/hpsd/
pno,strings [20'] SIKORSKI perf
mat rent                         (K164)

Heros Et Son Miroir, L'
see Spiegel, Der

Neue Mieter, Der
3.0.3.0. 3.3.2.1. 4perc,pno,cel,
harp,1-12vln,1-6vla,1-4db,
xylorimba [30'] sc PETERS 00856  (K165)

Spiegel, Der
"Heros Et Son Miroir, L'" 1.0.0.0.
0.3.0.0. timp,4perc,vibra,pno,
8vln I,7vln II,6vla,5vcl,4db
[23'] sc,pno-cond sc PETERS 00863 (K166)

Symphonic Music 1957
2.2.2.2. 4.2.3.1. timp,perc,strings
[20'] SCHOTTS perf mat rent      (K167)

Visions
3.3.3.3. 4.3.3.1. timp,perc,strings
[11'] SIKORSKI perf mat rent     (K168)

KELEN, H.
Tragic Prelude
"Tragikus Elöjáték" 2.1.2.1.
2.2.3.0. timp,perc,strings [6']
EMB rent                         (K169)

KELEN, H. (cont'd.)

Tragikus Elöjáték
see Tragic Prelude

KELLER, HERMANN
Am Abend
3.2.2.2. 2.3.3.0. timp,perc,pno,
8vln I,6vla,5vcl,4db [14'] sc
PETERS 03033                     (K170)

Bagatelle for 15 Strings
5vln I,4vln II,3vla,2vcl,db [8'] sc
PETERS 04371                     (K171)

Concerto for Piano and Orchestra
3.3.3.3. 4.3.3.1. timp,2perc,8vln
I,7vln II,6vla,5vcl,4db,pno solo
[22'] sc,solo pt PETERS 01322    (K172)

Momentaufnahmen
2.2.0.2. 4.2.3.0. timp,perc,8vln I,
7vln II,6vla,5vcl,4db,ob solo,vcl
solo sc PETERS 04372             (K173)

Sonata for 2 Orchestras
5.4.5.4. 5.4.4.1. timp,3perc,pno,
harp,24vln I,12vla,9vcl,7db sc
PETERS 01323                     (K174)

KEMP, BART DE
Between Nightbar And Factory
1.1.1.1. 1.1.1.0. 2perc,pno,strings
[15'] sc DONEMUS                 (K175)

Paperclip Music
1.1.1.1.alto sax. 1.1.1.0. perc,
pno,strings [10'] sc DONEMUS     (K176)

KEMPFF, WILHELM (1895-1991)
Symphony No. 2, Op. 19, in D minor
2+pic.2+English horn.2+bass clar.2+
contrabsn. 6.4.3.1. perc,org,
strings [30'] BREITKOPF-W        (K177)

KEMPKENS, ARNOLD
Abschied Und Wiederkehr
3.2.2.2. 4.3.3.1. harp,3perc,
strings SEESAW                   (K178)
orch TONOS M-2015-3557-9 rent    (K179)

Spiegel, Der  *ballet
orch TONOS M-2-15-3558-6 rent    (K180)

3.2.2.2. 4.4.3.1. harp,2perc,
strings SEESAW                   (K181)

KENESSEY, STEFANIA MARIA DE (1956-    )
Summer Nights
1.0.1.1. 0.0.0.0. pno,strings
SEESAW                           (K182)

KENINS, TALIVALDIS (1919-    )
Aria Per Corde
string orch [8'] sc,pts CANADIAN
MI 3143 K33AR                    (K183)

Beatae Voces Tenebrae
3+pic.3+English horn.3+bass clar.2.
4.3.3.1. timp,3perc,harp,strings
[13'] sc,study sc CANADIAN
MI 1100 K33BE                    (K184)

Concerto Di Camera
string orch,clar,pno,fl solo [16']
sc CANADIAN MI 8815 K33CO        (K185)

Concerto Di Camera No. 2
string orch,horn,trp,perc,fl solo
[22'] sc,pts,solo pt CANADIAN
MI 8973 K33CO                    (K186)

Concerto for 14 Instruments
1.1.1.1. 1.1.0.0. strings [25'] sc,
pts CANADIAN MI1200 K33CO        (K187)

Concerto for 5 Percussionists and
Orchestra
3(pic).3(English horn).3(bass
clar).3(contrabsn). 4.3.3.1.
harp,pno&cel,strings,5perc soli
[20'] sc CANADIAN MI 1441 K33CO  (K188)

Concerto for Piano, String Orchestra
and Percussion
[17'] (Molto vivace -- Largo quasi
una passacaglia -- Presto-
prestissimo) sc CANADIAN
MI 1661 K33CO                    (K189)

Godam Un Brivibai
see Honour And Freedom

Honour And Freedom
"Godam Un Brivibai"
2(pic).2.2.2(contrabsn). 4.3.3.1.
timp,2perc,strings [10']
(symphonic prologue) sc CANADIAN
MI 1100 K33HO                    (K190)

Partita for Strings
string orch [20'] (on Lutheran
chorales, 1. Sinfonia 2. Corrente
3. Pastorale 4. Variazioni sopra
il 'Pater Noster' 5. Epilogo) sc
CANADIAN MI 1500 K33PA           (K191)

KENINS, TALIVALDIS (cont'd.)

Sinfonia Ad Fugam (Symphony No. 6)
2(pic).2(English horn).2(bass
clar).2(contrabsn).2(bass
trp).0.0. perc,strings [18']
(based on the c sharp minor fugue
of Book I Of The Well-Tempered
Clavier By J. S. Bach) sc
CANADIAN MI1200 K33SI            (K192)

Suite En Concert
string orch,2gtr soli [13'] sc,pts
CANADIAN MI 8606 K33SU           (K193)

Symphony In The Form Of Passacaille
see Symphony No. 7

Symphony No. 5
2(pic).2(English horn).2.2.
4.3.3.1. timp,2perc,harp,strings
[21'] sc CANADIAN MI 1100 K33FI  (K194)

Symphony No. 6
see Sinfonia Ad Fugam

Symphony No. 7
"Symphony In The Form Of
Passacaille" 2(pic).2(English
horn).2(bass clar).2(contrabsn).
4.3.3.1. timp,2perc,harp,strings,
Mez solo [26'] (text in English
and Latvian, Introduction --
Passacaglia and fugue -- Aria:
Song of destiny -- Epilogue)
CANADIAN MV 1400 K33SY           (K195)

KERMESSE, LA see Melchers, H. Melcher

KERSTERS, WILLEM (1929-    )
Concerto for Violin, Op. 86
2.2.2.2. 4.2.2.1. timp,3perc,harp,
strings,vln solo [28'] BELGE     (K196)

KÉT KÉP see Bartók, Béla

KÉT MAGYAR TÁNC see Farkas, Ferenc, Two
Hungarian Dances

KÉT RONDÓ see Kokai, Rezsö, Two Rondos

KÉT ZENEKARI DARAB see Szönyi, Erzsebet
(Elizabeth), Two Pieces For
Orchestra

KETTING, OTTO (1935-    )
Aankomst, De
1.2.1.1. 2.0.0.1. perc,strings
[16'] sc DONEMUS                 (K197)

Adagio
3.3.3.3. 4.4.3.1. timp,4perc,harp,
pno/cel,strings [11'] sc DONEMUS (K198)

Capriccio
1.1.2.1. 1.0.0.0. marimba,pno,
strings,vln solo [16'] DONEMUS   (K199)

Cheops
4.0.0.0. 0.2.2.1. perc,harp,
strings,horn solo [15'] DONEMUS  (K200)

Kom, Over De Zeeën
"Vem Sobre Os Mares" 3.3.3.3.
4.3.3.1. 3perc,harp,pno/cel,
strings [18'] sc DONEMUS         (K201)

Medusa
2.0.0.0.4sax. 1.4.4.0. drums,harp,
pno,strings,alto sax solo [9']
DONEMUS                          (K202)

Overtocht, De
"Passage, The" 1.0.1.0. 0.1.1.0.
perc,harp,gtr,mand,pno,strings
[17'] sc DONEMUS                 (K203)

Passage, The
see Overtocht, De

Provincie, De: Muziek Uit De Film Van
Jan Bosdriesz
0.1.0.0. 1.0.0.0. pno,strings [21']
sc DONEMUS                       (K204)

Vem Sobre Os Mares
see Kom, Over De Zeeën

KEULEN, GEERT VAN (1943-    )
Tympan
5.4.5.4. 6.5.5.1. timp,4perc,vibra,
2harp,pno,synthesizer,strings
[18'] sc DONEMUS                 (K205)

KEULER, JENÖ
Overture
2(pic).2.2.2. 4.2.2.1. perc,
strings, tuba is optional [11']
EMB rent                         (K206)

KEURIS, TRISTAN (1946-    )
Arcade
3.3.4.3. 4.3.3.1. 3perc,harp,
strings [15'] sc DONEMUS         (K207)

KEURIS, TRISTAN (cont'd.)
Aria
3.2.3.2. 4.0.0.0. 2perc,cel,harp,
strings,fl solo [8'] sc DONEMUS
(K208)

Concerto for Organ and Orchestra
3.3.3.2. 4.3.0.0. timp,perc,harp,
strings,org solo [22'] sc DONEMUS
(K209)

Concerto No. 2 for Violin
3.2.3.2. 4.2.0.0. perc,harp,
strings,vln solo [33'] sc DONEMUS
(K210)

Double Concerto
4.3.4.0. 4.0.0.0. timp,3perc,harp,
pno,strings,2vcl soli [21'] sc
NOVELLO
(K211)

Symphony in D
2.2.2.2. 2.2.0.0. timp,strings
[27'] sc DONEMUS
(K212)

Three Preludes
3.3.4.3. 4.3.3.1. timp,3perc,harp,
strings [8'] sc DONEMUS
(K213)

KEYSTONE KOPS THEME see Davis, Carl

KHACHATURIAN, ARAM ILYICH (1903-1978)
Concerto for Piano and Orchestra
2.2.3.2. 4.2.3.1. timp,perc,
strings,pno solo [36'] BREITKOPF-
W
(K214)

KHOROVOD see Anderson, Julian

KHOROVODY-REIGEN see Shchedrin, Rodion

KIDS' STUFF see Ridout, Godfrey

KIEL, FRIEDRICH (1821-1885)
Waltz, Op. 73
string orch sc,pts KUNZELMANN
WW 104B ipa
(K215)

KIENZL, WILHELM (1857-1941)
Drei Stücke Für Streichorchester Und
Harfe, Op. 53
harp,string orch INTERNAT.S. rent
(K216)

KIERMEIR, KURT
Barcarole Für Solo-Violine Und Flöte
see Bootsfahrt Mit Karin

Bootsfahrt Mit Karin
"Barcarole Für Solo-Violine Und
Flöte" fl,3vln,vla,vcl,db,harp,
cel&pno,vln solo [2'50"] sc,pts
BUSCH DM 048 rent
(K217)

KIEW see Dmitriyev, Georgi

KIKUCHI, YUKIO (1964-    )
Ballade
orch [15'] JAPAN
(K218)

Yohen
pno,orch JAPAN
(K219)

KILLMAYER, WILHELM (1927-    )
Broken Farewell, The
1.1.1.1. 1.0.0.0. strings,trp solo
[5'] SCHOTTS perf mat rent (K220)

Divertissement
2+pic.2.2.2. 2.2.3.1. timp,perc,
glock,xylo,cel,pno,harp,strings
[14'] SCHOTTS perf mat rent
(K221)

Encore
"Schnellpolka" 2+pic.2.2.2.
3.3.3.1. timp,3perc,pno,strings
[3'] SCHOTTS perf mat rent (K222)

Huit Poésies De Mallarmé
2(pic,alto fl,bass fl).1.2(bass
clar,alto sax).1. 2.1.0.0. 2perc,
pno,elec org&hpsd,harp,strings,S
solo [17'] (text by Stephane
Mallarmé) voc sc SCHOTTS ED 8317
perf mat rent
(K223)

Joie De Vivre
0.2.0.1. 2.0.0.0. 6vln,vla,vcl,db
[14'] SCHOTTS perf mat rent
(K224)

Schnellpolka
see Encore

Zittern Und Wagen *Waltz
2(pic,rec).2.2.1. 2.2.3.1. timp,
perc,harp,strings [4'] SCHOTTS
perf mat rent
(K225)

KINEMA see Valkare, Gunnar

KING, REGINALD (1904-    )
Autobahn
(Green, Roy) 1.1.1.0. 0.2.1.0. pno,
perc,strings [3'] BARDIC (K226)

Beside The Lake
1.2.1.1. 2.2.0.0. harp,cel,strings
[3'] BARDIC
(K227)

KING, REGINALD (cont'd.)
Lilacs In The Rain
2.1.2.1. 2.2.2.0. harp,perc,strings
[4'30"] BARDIC
(K228)

Pierrette On The Balcony
1.1.1.1. 0.0.0.0. timp,harp,glock,
strings [3'30"] BARDIC
(K229)

Plantation Mood
1.1.2.1. 2.2.2.0. harp,perc,gtr,
strings [3'] BARDIC
(K230)

Sentimental Interlude
see Summer Haze

String Cascade
2.1.2.1. 0.2.1.0. harp,perc,strings
BARDIC
(K231)

Summer Haze
"Sentimental Interlude" 1.1.1.0.
0.2.1.0. pno,perc,strings [3']
BARDIC
(K232)

Twilight On The Waters
1.1.2.1. 2.2.2+bass trom.0. harp,
perc,strings [3'45"] BARDIC
(K233)

KING ARTHUR see Britten, [Sir] Benjamin

KING LEAR: FIVE PIECES see
Shostakovich, Dmitri

KINGMA, PIET (1926-    )
Caprice Pour Orchestre
3.2.2.2. 4.3.3.1. timp,2perc,2harp,
strings sc DONEMUS
(K234)

Poème Symphonique
3.2.2.2. 2.2.2.0. timp,perc,strings
[20'] sc DONEMUS
(K235)

KINOSHITA, MAKIKO (1956-    )
Sinfonietta
string orch [15'] ONGAKU
(K236)

KIRCHNER, LEON (1919-    )
Music For Orchestra
orch sc SCHIRM.G AMP8045
(K237)

KIRCHNER, VOLKER DAVID (1942-    )
Bildnisse III
1.2(English horn).0+bass clar+
2basset horn.0+contrabsn.
2.0.0.0. perc,strings [15'] study
sc SCHOTTS ED 8181 perf mat rent
(K238)

Choralvariationen
7vln,4vla,3vcl,db [10'] study sc
SCHOTTS ED 7880 perf mat rent
(K239)

Concerto for Violin
3(pic).3(English horn).3(clar in E
flat,bass clar).2+contrabsn.
4.3.3.1. 2timp,perc,strings,vln
solo [25'] pno red SCHOTTS
ED 7939 perf mat rent
(K240)

Drei Gesänge: Abgesang
3(pic).3(English horn).3(bass
clar).3(contrabsn).
8(4tuba).4.4.1+db tuba. 2timp,
3perc,cel,pno,mand,2harp,16vln I,
14vln II,12vla,10vcl,8db,low solo
SCHOTTS perf mat rent
(K241)

Golgatha
pic,fl,ob,2English horn&ob da
caccia,bsn,drums,6vla,4vcl,2db
[10'] (text from the Bible)
SCHOTTS perf mat rent
(K242)

Hortus Magicus
3(pic)+pic.2+English horn.3(bass
clar).2+contrabsn. 4.3.3.1. timp,
3perc,cel,harp,strings [10']
SCHOTTS perf mat rent
(K243)

Kondukt *funeral
1.2(English horn).0+2basset horn.0+
contrabsn. 2.0.0.0. perc,strings
[5'] SCHOTTS perf mat rent (K244)

Musikalisches Hor d'Oeuvre, Ein
see Souper Des Monsieur Papagenor,
Das

Mythen
see Symphony No. 2

Orphischer Gesang
string orch/2vln&2vla&2vcl [10']
SCHOTTS perf mat rent
(K245)

Poème Concertante
see Schibboleth

Schattengesang
strings [15'] SCHOTTS perf mat rent
(K246)

Schibboleth
"Poème Concertante" 3.3.3.3.
4.4.4.2. timp,perc,cel,pno 4-
hands,12vln I,10vln II,8vla,6vcl,

KIRCHNER, VOLKER DAVID (cont'd.)
4db,vla solo [10'] pno red
SCHOTTS ED 7809 perf mat rent
(K247)

Souper Des Monsieur Papagenor, Das
"Musikalisches Hor d'Oeuvre, Ein"
2(pic).2(English
horn).2(contrabsn). 2.2.0.0.
perc,strings, lotos flute doubled
by a flutist [4'] SCHOTTS perf
mat rent
(K248)

Symphony No. 1
"Totentanz" 4(pic).3.3(clar in E
flat)+bass clar.3+contrabsn.
8(4tuba).4.4.0+db tuba. 2timp,
8perc,cel,pno,mand,2harp,16vln I,
14vln II,12vla,10vcl,8db [20']
SCHOTTS perf mat rent
(K249)

Symphony No. 2
"Mythen" 4(3pic).3(English
horn).3(clar in E flat).2+
contrabsn. 4.3.3.1. 2timp,5perc,
cel&pno&org,harp,14vln I,12vln
II,10vla,8vcl,5db,electronic tape
[40'] SCHOTTS perf mat rent
(K250)

Totentanz
see Symphony No. 1

Trauung, Die: Three Fragments
3(pic).3(English horn).3(bass
clar).3(contrabsn). 4.4.4.2.
timp,4perc,pno&cel.2harp,strings,
(10.10.7-8.6.5) SCHOTTS perf mat
rent
(K251)

KIRKWOOD, ANTOINETTE
Alessandro *Op.12, ballet
3+pic.3.3.2+contrabsn. 4.4.3.1.
timp,2perc,pno,harp,strings [58']
BARDIC
(K252)

Empty Stable, The *Op.10
0.1.0.0. 0.0.0.0. gtr,pno,strings,
SSS soli, Chinese drum [21']
BARDIC
(K253)

Fantasy No. 1, Op. 13
2.1.2.1. 2.2.1.0. timp,harp,strings
[4'30"] BARDIC
(K254)

Fantasy No. 2, Op. 14
2.1.2.1. 2.2.1.0. timp,harp,strings
[4'30"] BARDIC
(K255)

Fantasy No. 3, Op. 18
2.1.2.1. 2.2.1.0. timp,harp,strings
[4'30"] BARDIC
(K256)

Kroenung *Op.17,No.2
strings,high solo [4'30"] (words by
Heinrich Heine) BARDIC (K257)

Musa The Saint *Op.16, ballet
2+pic.1.2.1. 2.2.1.0. timp,pno,
harp,strings [30'] BARDIC (K258)

Must She Go? *Op.9,No.1
strings,Bar solo [5'] (words by
James Forsyth) BARDIC (K259)

Schiffbruechige, Der *Op.15
strings,high solo [7'30"] (words by
Heinrich Heine) BARDIC (K260)

Suite for Strings, Op. 5
string orch [18'] BARDIC (K261)

Symphony No. 1, Op. 8
2.2.2.2. 4.3.3.1. timp,perc,strings
[32'] BARDIC
(K262)

KITAZUME, MICHIO (1948-    )
Color Of The Layers No. 1
chamber orch [15'] JAPAN (K263)

Side By Side
perc,orch [10'] JAPAN (K264)

Side By Side (Version II)
perc,chamber orch [11'] JAPAN
(K265)

KIVIUQ: AN INUIT LEGEND see McIntosh,
Diana

KJAER, VILFRED
Concerto in G minor for Accordion and
Orchestra, in Three Movements
2.2.2.2. 2.3.2.0. timp,perc,cel,
strings,acord solo [16'25"] sc,
set BUSCH rent
(K266)

KJAERE MOZART! see Skouen, Synne

KJAERNES, BJORN MORTEN
Frames: A Symphonic Impression
2.2.2.2. 4.3.3.0. timp,5perc,
strings [30'] NORSKMI (K267)

KLAGE see Zilcher, Hermann

KLAGEGESANG see Hartmann, Karl Amadeus

KLÄNGE SCHATTEN see Birkenkötter, Jörg

KLANGSZENEN 1 see Goldmann, Friedrich

KLANGSZENEN 2 see Goldmann, Friedrich

KLANGVARIATION see Fortner, Wolfgang

KLASICKÁ see Válek, Jirí, Symphony No. 2

KLASSZIKUS VARIÁCIÓK see Farkas, Ferenc, Variazioni Classiche

KLAUN see Vodrazka, Karel

KLAVIERFANTASIE see Furer, Arthur

KLEBE, GISELHER (1925-  )
Symphony No. 1, Op. 12
12vln I,10vln II,8vla,6vcl,6db
[26'] SCHOTTS perf mat rent
(K268)

Symphony No. 2, Op. 16
2(pic).2(English horn).2(bass
clar).2(contrabsn). 4.2.0.1.
2timp,harp,12vln I,10vln II,8vla,
6vcl,6db [18'] SCHOTTS perf mat
rent                           (K269)

KLEGA, MIROSLAV (1926-  )
Príbehy A Zázraky
3.2.3.3. 4.3.3.1. timp,perc,xylo,
harp,cel,pno,strings [50'] CESKY
HUD.                           (K270)

KLEIBERG, STÅLE (1958-  )
Dopo, For Cello Og Strykeorkester
string orch,vcl solo [10'] NORSKMI
(K271)

Klokkeskjaeret (Symphony No. 1)
2(pic).2.2.2. 4.2.3.0. timp,2perc,
harp,strings [24'] NORSKMI (K272)

Rosevinduet: Musikk For 12
Instrumenter Og Resitatør
[Norw] 1.1.1.0. 0.0.0.0. perc,harp,
cel,org,2vln,vla,vcl,db,narrator
(text by Stein Mehren) NORSKMI
(K273)

Symphony No. 1
see Klokkeskjaeret

KLEIN, LOTHAR (1932-  )
Canadina *Suite
"Reflets Du Passé" 3(pic).2.2.2.
4.2.2.1. timp,2perc,harp,cel,
strings (ballet) sc CANADIAN
MI 1100 K64CA                  (K274)

Fanfares For Orchestra
3(3pic).3+English horn.2(clar in E
flat).3(contrabsn). 4.3.3.1.
timp,3perc,harp,pno,strings [3']
sc CANADIAN                    (K275)

Masque Of Orianna: Suite
2(pic).2(English horn).2(bass
clar).2. 2.2.0.0. timp,3perc,
harp,hpsd,strings [14'] (Prelude
- Madrigal - Fantastic Sprites)
sc CANADIAN MI 1100 K64MA      (K276)

Music For Kids
2(pic).2.2.2. 2.2.0.0. perc,
strings,narrator,pno solo [12']
sc CANADIAN MV 1400 K64MU      (K277)

Music On Themes Of Paganini
3(pic).2.3(clar in E flat,bass
clar).2. 4.2.2.0. timp,2perc,
strings,vln solo [18'] sc
CANADIAN MI 1311 K64PA         (K278)

Reflets Du Passé
see Canadina

Trésor Des Dieux, Le
2(2pic).1(English horn).1(bass
clar).0. 1.0.0.0. harp,perc,
strings,gtr solo [15'] (1.
Ricercare 2. Affen Tanz (Monkey's
Dance) 3. Aric D'Orphée 4.
Doubles) sc CANADIAN
MI 1315 K64TR                  (K279)

Two Scenes For Timpani And Strings
string orch,timp solo [9'] (1.
Evocation 2. Drum language) sc
CANADIAN MI 1640 K64TW         (K280)

KLEIN, RICHARD RUDOLF (1921-  )
Canzona Concertata Per Archi
string quar,string orch MÖSELER sc
10.469.00, pts 10.469.01 TO 02,
set 10.469.09                  (K281)

Concerto Facile
pno,orch MÖSELER 11.456        (K282)

Concerto Sereno: Für Trompete Und
Kammerorchester (Bläser Ad Lib.)
1.0.1.2. 2.0.0.0. strings,trp solo
sc,pts HEINRICH 2069           (K283)

KLEIN, RICHARD RUDOLF (cont'd.)
Partita No. 3 for Brass, Percussion
and Strings
MÖSELER 10.467 rent            (K284)

KLEINE ERÖFFNUNGSMUSIK see Meyer, Ernst
Hermann

KLEINE GESCHICHTE see Sieber

KLEINE "HAMMER-KLAPPER" MUSIK, EINE:
EIN MUSIKALISCHER SPASS see Surdin,
Morris

KLEINE HÄSSLICHE RAUPE, DIE see
Genzmer, Harald

KLEINE NACHT MUSIK, EINE see Mozart,
Wolfgang Amadeus

KLEINE ORCHESTERSUITE (KINDERSPIELE)
see Bizet, Georges

KLEINE SINFONIA see Hess, Ernst,
Sinfonia Accademica

KLEINE SINFONIE, EINE, OP. 49A see
Shostakovich, Dmitri

KLEINE SINFONIE, FOR STRING ORCHESTRA
see Rakov, Nikolai

KLEINE SPASSMUSIK, EINE see Eklund,
Hans, Hotch-Potch

KLEINE SUITE see Hengartner, Max see
Trexler, Georg

KLEINE SUITE FÜR STREICHORCHESTER see
Schipizky, Frederick

KLEINE SUITE NACH ALTEN WEISEN see
Lohse, Fred

KLEINE TRAGÖDIEN: SUITE see Schnittke,
Alfred

KLEINE WANDERZIRKUS, DER see Allers,
Hans Gunther

KLEINES KONZERT see Orff, Carl

KLEINES REQUIEM FÜR EINE POLKA see
Gorecki, Henryk Mikolaj

KLEINES VARIATIONEN-FORM see Grainger,
Percy Aldridge

KLEIST-BRIEFE, FÜR BARITON UND
ORCHESTER see Rosenfeld, Gerhard

KLEMPÍR, JAROMIR (1944-  )
Modry Vítr Nad Rekou
fl,clar,trp,trom,perc,pno,2gtr,
strings,2 solo voices, electric
strings [3'] CESKY HUD.        (K285)

Nejhodnejší
fl,sax,perc,2gtr,synthesizer,
strings,S solo, Yamaha grand
piano CESKY HUD.               (K286)

KLENGEL, JULIUS (1859-1933)
Concerto for Violin, Violoncello and
Orchestra, Op. 61
2(pic).2.2.2. 4.2.3.0. timp,perc,
strings,vln&vcl soli [22']
BREITKOPF-W                    (K287)

Concerto for 2 Violoncelli and
Orchestra, Op. 45, in E minor
2.2.2.2. 4.2.3.0. timp,strings,2vcl
soli [25'] BREITKOPF-W         (K288)

Concerto for Violoncello and
Orchestra, Op. 4, in A minor
2.2.2.2. 2.2.0.0. timp,strings,vcl
solo [22'] BREITKOPF-W         (K289)

Concerto for Violoncello and
Orchestra, Op. 37, in B minor
2.2.2.2. 2.2.0.0. timp,strings,vcl
solo [26'] BREITKOPF-W         (K290)

Serenade, Op. 24, in F
strings [26'] BREITKOPF-W      (K291)

KLENOVICKÁ POLKA see Strasek, Emil

KLEY, ERICH (1914-  )
Music for Chamber Orchestra, Op. 85
strings [18'] BREITKOPF-W      (K292)

KLICPEROVSKÁ PREDEHRA see Hurník, Ilja

KLOKKE-KLANG see Grieg, Edvard Hagerup

KLOKKESKJAERET see Kleiberg, Ståle

KLOPPERS, JACOBUS (1937-  )
Concerto for Organ, Strings and
Timpani
sc,pno red CANADIAN MI 1664 K66CO
(K293)

KLUG, J.
Fascinace
strings,perc,pno [11'] CESKY HUD.
(K294)

KLUSÁK, JAN (1934-  )
Invention No. 7
"Peškova" 2.4.0.2.2sax. 4.2.1.1.
perc,harp,strings [15'] CESKY
HUD.                           (K295)

Partita for Strings
string orch [12'] CESKY HUD.   (K296)

Peškova
see Invention No. 7

Šest Malych Preludií
2.2.2.2. 2.2.2.0. timp,perc,harp,
strings CESKY HUD.             (K297)

Smutecni Monodie
2.3.2.2.sax. 2.1.2.1. perc,harp,
strings [15'] CESKY HUD.       (K298)

Tvár. 4 Básne Františka Halase
2.2.2.3. 0.2.1.0. harp,perc,strings
CESKY HUD.                     (K299)

KNAIFEL, ALEXANDER (1943-  )
Heilige Opfer, Das
5vln I,5vln II,3vla,2vcl,db [60']
sc BELAIEFF 03454              (K300)

Nike
17db [140'] SIKORSKI perf mat rent
(K301)

Passione
4.4.4.4. 8.4.4.2. 4timp,4perc,vln,
vla,vcl,db,4sax&4rec&6horn soli
sc BELAIEFF 02624             (K302)

Vera
2harp,hpsd,string orch [25']
SIKORSKI perf mat rent         (K303)

KNEIP, GUSTAV (1905-1992)
Drei Arabesken, Op. 70
vibra,pno,string orch [11']
SIKORSKI perf mat rent         (K304)

Moritat Vom Schinderhannes, Die:
Suite
2.2.2.2. 4.3.3.1. timp,perc,pno,
strings [15'] SIKORSKI perf mat
rent                           (K305)

KNIPPER, LEV KONSTANTINOVICH
(1898-1974)
Maku
2.1.1.1. 2.1.1.1. timp,perc,strings
[24'] SIKORSKI perf mat rent
(K306)

KNIRSCH,ERIK (1928-  )
Akce "Z"
2.2.2.2. 4.3.3.1. timp,perc,xylo,
2gtr,strings [3'] CESKY HUD.
(K307)

KNOPF, DER see Lhotka-Kalinski, Ivo

KNORR, IVAN (1853-1916)
Variationen Über Ein Ukrainisches
Volkslied *Op.7
2.2.2.2. 2.2.0.0. timp,strings
[16'] BREITKOPF-W             (K308)

KNOX, ROGER
Elegy
2.2.2.2. 4.2.3.1. timp,perc,pno,
harp,strings [16'] sc CANADIAN
MI 1100 K74EL                  (K309)

KNUSSEN, OLIVER (1952-  )
Coursing
chamber orch sc FABER 50790 5 f.s.
(K310)

Flourish With Fireworks
orch sc FABER 51459 6 f.s.     (K311)

Music For A Puppet Court
2chamber orch (puzzle pieces) sc
FABER 50865 0 f.s.             (K312)

Scriabin Settings
instrumental ensemble [8'] FABER
(K313)

Songs And A Sea Interlude
orch,S solo sc FABER 50706 9 f.s.
(K314)

Symphony, No. 2
chamber orch,S solo sc FABER
50747 6 f.s.                   (K315)

Symphony, No. 3
orch sc FABER 50639 9 f.s.     (K316)

Two Organa
chamber group sc FABER 51624 6 f.s.
(K317)

2fl,ob,English horn,2clar,bsn,
2horn,trp,trom,2perc,cel,
harmonium,pno,harp,strings [6']
FABER                          (K318)

Way To Castle Yonder, The
3.2.3.3. 4.0.3.0. 4perc,cel,pno,
harp,strings [8'] FABER        (K319)

KNUSSEN, OLIVER (cont'd.)

Whitman Settings
3.2.3.3. 4.2.0.0. 4perc,cel,harp,
strings,S solo [12'] FABER (K320)

KNUTNA NVEN, DEN see Feiler, Dror

KOCÁB, MICHAEL (1954-    )
Ctyri Kusy
string orch CESKY HUD.        (K321)

KOCH, DAGFINN (1964-    )
Aura
string orch NORSKMI           (K322)

Formasjoner For Cello Og Orkester Med
Obligat Klavér
2(pic).1.2.1.rec. 2.1.1.0. cel,
3perc,pno,strings,vcl solo [12']
NORSKMI                       (K323)

KOCH, ERLAND VON (1910-    )
Cantata, Op. 36, Prelude
see Hösthorn: Förspel

Concerto for Violoncello
2.1.2.1. 4.3.3.1. timp,perc,strings
[19'] PEER rent               (K324)

Dala-Rondo
"Dalecarlian Rondo"
2(pic).2(English horn).2.2.
2.2.2.0. timp,2perc,strings
[9'5] STIM sc H-2773, pts (K325)

Dalecarlian Rondo
see Dala-Rondo

Fyra Rstidspastoraler: 1. Vrpastoral
1.1.1.1. 1.0.0.0. strings [5'] sc
GEHRMANS                      (K326)

Fyra Rstidspastoraler: 2.
Sommarpastoral
1.1.1.1. 1.0.0.0. strings [5'] sc
GEHRMANS                      (K327)

Fyra Rstidspastoraler: 3. Hstpastoral
1.1.1.1. 1.0.0.0. strings [5'] sc
GEHRMANS                      (K328)

Fyra Rstidspastoraler: 4.
Vinterpastoral
1.1.1.1. 1.0.0.0. strings [5'] sc
GEHRMANS                      (K329)

Hösthorn: Förspel (Cantata, Op. 36,
Prelude)
2.2.2.2. 2.2.2.0. timp,perc,strings
STIM                          (K330)

Lamento Ver Estonia-Katastrofen
2.2.2.2. 2.0.0.0. timp,perc,strings
[5'] (composed after the Estonia
catastrophe September 28, 1994)
sc STIM                       (K331)

Musik Ur Ingmar Bergman-Filmer 1-6
2(pic).2(English horn).2(bass
clar).2. 2.2.1.0. timp,perc,
strings,opt harp,opt cel [25']
(1. Kris; 2. Det regnar på vår
kärlek; 3. Skepp til Indialand;
4. Hamstad; 5. Fängelse; 6. Musik
i mörker) sc STIM             (K332)

Rauna
"Variations On A Lappish Melody"
1.1.2.1. 1.0.0.0. strings [7'] sc
STIM                          (K333)

Rondo Giocoso
2(pic).2.2.2. 2.2.1.0. timp,perc,
strings STIM                  (K334)

Salvare La Terra
see Symfoni Nr 6

Sinfonia Dalecarlica
see Symphony No. 2

Sinfonia No. 6
see Symfoni Nr 6

Symfoni Nr 6 (Sinfonia No. 6)
"Salvare La Terra" 3(pic).3(English
horn).3(bass clar).3(contrabsn).
4.3.3.1. timp,2perc,strings [16']
sc STIM H-2738                (K335)

Symphony No. 2  *Op.30
"Sinfonia Dalecarlica" 2.2.2.2.
4.2.3.1. timp,perc,strings STIM
(K336)

Variations On A Lappish Melody
see Rauna

Virvelpolska
"Whirl Dance" 3(pic).2.2.2.
3.2.1.0. timp,perc,strings [3']
sc,pts STIM                   (K337)

Whirl Dance
see Virvelpolska

KOCH, FRIEDRICH E. (1862-1927)
Romantische Suite  *Op.37
3.2.2.3. 3.3.0.0. timp,perc,strings
[29'] sc KAHNT                (K338)

KOCH, MARKUS (1879-1948)
Geistliche Musik  *Op.67
strings,org BOHM              (K339)

KOCSAR, MIKLOS (1933-    )
Elegia
see Elegy for Bassoon and Chamber
Orchestra

Elegy for Bassoon and Chamber
Orchestra
"Elegia" hpsd,harp,perc,strings,bsn
solo [14'] EMB rent           (K340)

Serenade
strings [15'] EMB rent        (K341)

KODÁLY, ZOLTÁN (1882-1967)
Adagio for Viola and Strings
strings,vla solo [9'] BOOSEY-ENG
rent                          (K342)
(Sulyok) strings,vla solo [9'] EMB
rent                          (K343)

Adagio for Violin and Chamber
Orchestra
(Sulyok) 1.1.1.1. 1.0.0.0. strings,
vln solo [9'] EMB rent        (K344)

Énekszó  *Op.1
(Székely) 1.1.1.1. 1.0.0.0. harp,
strings,solo voice [28'] EMB rent
(K345)

Greating Of Kodály
(Farkas, Ferenc) "Kodály-
Koszonto" 3(pic).3(English
horn).3(bass clar,alto
sax).3(contrabsn). 4.3.3.1. timp,
perc,harp,cel,pno,strings [25']
EMB rent                      (K346)

Hungarian Rondo (from An Old
Hungarian Soldiers' Tune)
0.0.2.2. 0.0.0.0. strings [8']
BOOSEY-ENG rent               (K347)
"Magyar Rondó" 2clar,2bsn,string
orch [15'] EMB rent           (K348)

Kodály-Koszonto
see Greating Of Kodály

Magyar Rondó
see Hungarian Rondo

Two Songs Op. 5
[Hung/Ger] 3(pic).2+English horn.2+
bass clar.3(contrabsn). 4.2.3.1.
timp,perc,harp,strings,B solo
[18'] (text by Berzsenyi & Ady)
BOOSEY-ENG rent               (K349)

Two Songs Op. 14, Nos. 1 & 3
[Hung/Ger] 2.2.2.2. 2.0.0.0. timp,
perc,strings,S solo [6'] (text by
Berzsenyi & anon) BOOSEY-ENG rent
(K350)
KODÁLY-KOSZONTO see Kodály, Zoltán,
Greating Of Kodály

KOECHLIN, CHARLES
Sonata No. 1, Op. 85 for Clarinet and
Chamber Orchestra
BILLAUDOT 576-00722           (K351)

KOEHLER, EMIL (1849-1902)
Optimismus  *Waltz
2.2.2.2. 2.2.2.0. timp,perc,strings
SCHOTTS perf mat rent         (K352)

KOEHNE, GRAEME (1956-    )
Capriccio for Piano and Strings
pno,string orch [20'] BOOSEY-ENG
rent                          (K353)

First Blue Hours
3.2.3(bass clar).2. 2.2.3.0.
strings [6'] BOOSEY-ENG rent
(K354)

Nearly Beloved  *ballet
fl,clar,trp,trom,perc,pno,string
quin [90'] BOOSEY-ENG rent (K355)

Once Around The Sun: Suite  *ballet
2.2.2.2. 2.2.0.0. strings [20']
BOOSEY-ENG rent               (K356)

Powerhouse
2+pic.3.2+bass clar.3. 4.3.3.1.
timp,4perc,pno,strings [12']
BOOSEY-ENG rent               (K357)

Rain Forest
3(pic).3.3(bass clar).2. 4.3.3.1.
3perc,harp,cel,strings [13']
BOOSEY-ENG rent               (K358)

Rhythmic Birds Of The Antipodes
3(pic).2.0+bass clar.2. 4.3.3.1.
3perc,cel/pno,harp,strings [20']
BOOSEY-ENG rent               (K359)

KOEHNE, GRAEME (cont'd.)

Riverrun...
3.3.3.3. 4.3.3.1. harp,2perc,
strings [13'] BOOSEY-ENG rent
(K360)

Selfish Giant, The: Visions Of
Paradise  *Suite
2.2.2.2. 4.3.3.1. 2perc,harp,cel,
strings [22'] BOOSEY-ENG rent
(K361)

Three Nocturnes (from Gallery) ballet
3.3.3.3. 4.3.3.1. 3perc,harp,cel,
strings [20'] BOOSEY-ENG rent
(K362)

Three Poems Of Byron
6vln I,4vln II,3vla,3vcl,db,Mez
solo [20'] BOOSEY-ENG rent (K363)

To His Servant Bach, God Grants A
Final Glimpse: The Morning Star
string orch [5'] BOOSEY-ENG rent
(K364)

Unchained Melody
3(pic).3.3(bass clar).3. 4.3.3.1.
4perc,pno,strings [10'] BOOSEY-
ENG rent                      (K365)

KOENIG, GOTTFRIED MICHAEL (1926-    )
Concerto for Chamber Orchestra
1.1.1.1. 0.1.1.0. perc,pno,strings
SEESAW                        (K366)
sc TONOS M-2015-4400-7 rent (K367)

Concerto for Flute
0.2.0.2. 2.1.0.0. 3perc,harp,
strings,fl solo SEESAW        (K368)

Concerto for Flute and Chamber
Orchestra
sc TONOS M-2015-4399-4 rent (K369)

Concerto for Harpsichord, 2 Flutes
and Strings
sc TONOS M-2015-4406-9 rent (K370)

Diagonalen
orch sc TONOS M-2015-4402-1 rent
(K371)
2.2.2.2. 2.2.2.2. 2perc,pno,strings
SEESAW                        (K372)

Drei Asko Stuecke
1.0.2.1.sax. 0.0.2.0. marimba,pno,
string quin SEESAW            (K373)

Fantasy for Orchestra
3.2.3.2. 1.3.1.0. perc,2pno,strings
SEESAW                        (K374)
sc TONOS M-2015-4398-7 rent (K375)

Horae
orch sc TONOS M-2015-4397-0 rent
(K376)
3.2.3.2. 4.4.3.1. timp,perc,pno,
strings SEESAW                (K377)

Komposition Fuer 26 Instrumente
2.2.2.3. 1.1.1.0. 3perc,pno,strings
SEESAW                        (K378)
26inst sc TONOS M-2015-4403-8 rent
(K379)

Orchesterstueck 1
orch sc TONOS M-2015-4404-5 rent
(K380)
4.2.4.4.sax. 4.4.4.2. perc,2harp,
3pno,strings SEESAW           (K381)

Orchesterstueck 3
1.2.2.1.sax. 2.2.2.0. perc,pno,
strings SEESAW                (K382)
orch sc TONOS M-2015-4405-2 rent
(K383)

Zwei Orchesterstuecke
orch sc TONOS M-2015-4401-4 rent
(K384)
3.2.3.3. 3.5.3.1. 3perc,pno,strings
SEESAW                        (K385)

KOERPPEN, ALFRED (1926-    )
Silvanus: Scene, For Orchestra
orch MÖSELER 10.477 rent      (K386)

Sinfonia for Orchestra
MÖSELER 10.474                (K387)

KOETSIER, JAN (1911-    )
Concerto for Brass Quintet and
Orchestra, Op. 133
"Konzert Für Blechbläser-Quintett
Und Orchester, Op. 133" 2.2.2.2.
2.2.0.0. timp,perc,strings,horn&
2trp&trom&tuba soli [18'] sc
DONEMUS                       (K388)

Konzert Für Blechbläser-Quintett Und
Orchester, Op. 133
see Concerto for Brass Quintet and
Orchestra, Op. 133

Konzertantes Rondo, Für Klavier Und
Streichorchester  *Op.123
string orch,pno solo [15'] sc
DONEMUS                       (K389)

KOFRON, PETR (1955- )
Gesang Einer Gefangenen Amsel
3.3.3.3. 4.2.2.1. timp,strings,S
solo [5'] CESKY HUD. (K390)

KOHJIBA, TOMIKO (1952- )
Piano Concerto "Do" - For Children
orch,pno solo [5'] JAPAN (K391)

KÖHLER, SIEGFRIED (1927- )
Concerto for Piano and Orchestra, Op. 46
2.2.2.2. 4.3.3.1. strings [24'] sc
PETERS 02971 (K392)

Concerto for Violin and Orchestra, Op. 64
2.2.2.2. 4.3.3.0. timp,perc,harp, pno,strings [27'] sc,solo pt
PETERS 02436 (K393)

KOHOUT, JOSEF (1736-1793)
Overture
see Sinfonia

Sinfonia
(Ondráček, Stanislav) "Overture"
CESKY HUD. (K394)

KOHOUTEK, CTIRAD (1929- )
Zrození Cloveka
2.2.2.2. 2.2.0.0. timp,perc,pno, strings,ST soli [18'] CESKY HUD.
(K395)

KOKAI, REZSÖ (1906-1962)
Két Rondó
see Two Rondos

Two Rondos
"Két Rondó" 2.2.2.2. 2.2.0.0. timp, perc,harp,cel,pno,strings [10']
EMB rent (K396)

KOKAJI, KUNITAKA (1955- )
Déploration
orch [7'] JAPAN (K397)

Song Of Love
string orch [7'] JAPAN (K398)

KOKOPELLI DANCES see Jager, Robert Edward

KOL NIDREI see Bruch, Max

KOLB, BARBARA (1939- )
All In Good Time
2+pic.2+English horn.2+clar in E flat+bass clar.2+ contrabsn.soprano sax. 4.3.3.1. timp,4perc,strings [10'] BOOSEY-ENG rent (K399)

Voyants
1+pic.1.1.1. 1.1.1.0. perc,2vln, vla,vcl,db,pno solo [18'] BOOSEY-ENG rent (K400)

KOLBERG, KÅRE (1936- )
Bozza
3(pic).3.3(bass clar).3(contrabsn). 4.3.3(bass trom).1. timp,3perc, pno,strings [15'] NORSKMI (K401)

Nå Da?
2.2.2.2. 4.2.2.0. timp,2perc, strings NORSKMI (K402)

Takomil
2.2.2.2. 4.2.2.0. timp,2perc, strings NORSKMI (K403)

KOLEDA see Crawley, Clifford

KOLLEKTIVES IMPROVISIEREN see Karkoschka, Erhard

KOLLERT, JIRI (1943- )
Concerto for Violin and Orchestra
3.3.3.3. 4.3.3.1. timp,perc,xylo, vibra,2harp,cel,pno,strings,vln solo CESKY HUD. (K404)

Pueblo Unido, El
3.3.3.3. 4.3.3.1. timp,perc,xylo, harp,cel,pno,strings [20'] CESKY HUD. (K405)

Symphony No. 2
4.0.0.1. 0.3.3.0. perc,pno,elec gtr,synthesizer,strings, electric violin [16'] CESKY HUD. (K406)

KOLONÁDA see Spanily, Petr

KOLONÁDNÍ MOTIVY see Krízek, Zdenek

KOLOŠ, VIT (1962- )
Concerto for Horn and Orchestra
2.2.2.2. 0.0.0.0. timp,perc,harp, strings,horn solo [13'] CESKY HUD. (K407)

Concerto for Piano and Orchestra
1.2.0.1. 0.0.0.0. timp,perc,xylo, strings,pno solo [17'] CESKY HUD.

KOLOŠ, VIT (cont'd.)
(K408)

KOM, OVER DE ZEEËN see Ketting, Otto

KOM TIL RO, MITT HJARTE see Åm, Magnar

KOMMENTÁROK EGY HANDEL-TÉMÁHOZ see Soproni, Jozsef, Comments On A Theme By Handel

KOMORNÍ KONCERT see Bohác, Josef

KOMORNÍ KONCERT PRO SMYCCOVY ORCHESTR A KONCERTANTNÍ HOUSLE see Emmert, Frantisek

KOMORNÍ SUITA see Peška, Vlastimil

KOMORNÍ SYMFONIE see Stárek, Jiri

KOMORNÍ VETY PRO KLAVÍR, KLARINET A SMYCCE see Rehor, Bohuslav

KOMOROUS, RUDOLF (1931- )
Demure Charm
string orch,bsn solo, flute obbligato [15'] sc,solo pt
CANADIAN MI 1726 K81DE (K409)

Serenade for Strings
string orch [12'] sc CANADIAN MI 1500 K81SE (K410)

Twenty-Three Poems About Horses
2(pic).2.2.2. 2.2.0.0. strings [16'] sc CANADIAN MV 1243 K81TW (K411)

KOMPOSITION, FÜR SOPRAN, BARITON UND INSTRUMENTE see Herchet, Jörg

KOMPOSITION 15, FOR 13 PLAYERS see Jekimowski, Viktor, Kammervariationen

KOMPOSITION FUER 26 INSTRUMENTE see Koenig, Gottfried Michael

KOMPOSITION NACH BÖHME: SILESIUS see Herchet, Jörg

KOMPOSITION NO. 1 see Herchet, Jörg

KOMPOSITION NO. 2 see Herchet, Jörg

KOMPOSITION NO. 3 see Herchet, Jörg

KONCERT-FANTAZIE PRO HOUSLE, HARFU A ORCHESTR see Teml, Jiri

KONCERT-SYMFONIE see Zemek, Pavel

KONCERTANTNÍ FANTAZIE see Lucky, Štepán

KONCERTANTNÍ SYMFONIETTA see Buzek, Jan

KONCERTNÍ HUDBA see Kanák, Milan see Lukas, Zdenek

KONCERTNÍ KUS see Viskup, Anton

KONCERTNÍ PREDEHRA see Axman, Emil

KONCERTNÍ SKLADBA PRO KLARINET see Kalliwoda, Johann Wenzel

KONCERTNI VALCÍK see Hlavacek, Libor see Hudec, Jiri

KONCERTROCK see Dlouhy, Jaromir

KONDO, JO (1947- )
Hunisuccle
fl,ob,clar,bsn,horn,trp,2trom,pno, 2vln,vla,vcl,db [8'] SONIC ARTS 1326 sc f.s., sc,pts rent (K412)

In The Woods
4.4.4.4. 4.4.6.0. 3perc,strings [12'] SONIC ARTS 1304 sc f.s., sc,pts rent (K413)

Pastorale
3.3.3.3. 3.3.8.0. pno,strings [14'] SONIC ARTS 1303 sc f.s., sc,pts rent (K414)

Quickstep And Slow Ending
strings [10'] JAPAN (K415)
string orch [9'] SONIC ARTS 1367 sc f.s., sc,pts rent (K416)

Res Sonorae
fl,clar,bsn,horn,trp,trom,pno,perc, 2vln,vcl,db,ob solo,vla solo [14'] SONIC ARTS 1340 sc f.s. sc,pts rent (K417)

Serenata Secca Con Obbligato
fl,ob,clar,bsn,horn,trp,trom,perc, 2vln,vla,vcl,db,fl solo [11'] SONIC ARTS 1349 sc f.s., sc,pts rent (K418)

KONDO, JO (cont'd.)
Serotinous, The
fl,clar,horn,trp,2vln,vla,vcl,db, pno solo [8'] SONIC ARTS 1334 sc f.s., sc,pts rent (K419)

Shape Of Time, A
3.2.4.3. 3.3.2.1. strings,pno solo [18'] SONIC ARTS 1302 sc f.s. sc,pts rent (K420)

To The Headland
orch [13'] JAPAN (K421)
2.2.2.2. 2.2.0.0. 2perc,strings [13'] SONIC ARTS 1361 sc f.s. sc,pts rent (K422)

When The Wind Blew
1.1.1.1. 1.0.0.0. perc,pno,strings [14'] SONIC ARTS 1301 sc f.s. sc,pts rent (K423)

KONDUKT see Kirchner, Volker David

KONEC VÁLKY see Podešva, Jaromír

KÖNIG UND SEIN FLOH see Werdin, Eberhard

KÖNIG VON YVETOT, DER: OVERTURE see Adam, Adolphe-Charles, Roi d'Yvetot, Le: Overture

KÖNIG WITICHIS' WERBUNG see Scharwenka, Xaver

KÖNIGIN VON ZYPERN, DIE: OVERTURE see Halévy, Jacques, Reine De Chypre, La: Overture

KÖNIGSKINDER see Löhr, Hanns

KONKOH, IWAO (1933- )
Idyll
chamber orch [12'] JAPAN (K424)

KONO, ATSURO (1952- )
Core
string orch [10'] JAPAN (K425)

KONRAD TOMMELFINGER: SOME NIGHTMAREMUSIC see Moland, Eirik

KONSERT D-DUR see Zschotzscher, Johan Christian, Concerto in D

KONSERT FÖR ORKESTER see Jeverud, Johan

KONSERT NR. 2 FÖR ORKESTER see Jeverud, Johan

KONSERT ÖVER FRAGMENT TILL EN PIANO-KONSERT I H-MOLL AV E GRIEG see Flodin, Anders

KONSERTANT MUSIK see Linde, Bo

KONSTELLATION FÜR BALLETT see Zechlin, Ruth, Vita, La

KONTRAPUNKTUS see Liebermann, Lowell

KONTRASTE see Hummel, Bertold

KONTRASTY see Deváty, Antonín

KONZERT see Hofmann, Wolfgang, Concerto for Viola and String Orchestra

KONZERT-ELEGIE, FOR STRINGS see Sograbjan, Aschot

KONZERT FÜR BLECHBLÄSER-QUINTETT UND ORCHESTER, OP. 133 see Koetsier, Jan, Concerto for Brass Quintet and Orchestra, Op. 133

KONZERT FÜR VOLKSMUSIKINSTRUMENTE UND KAMMERORCHESTER see Schweizer, Alfred

KONZERT-RONDO see Mozart, Wolfgang Amadeus

KONZERT-RONDO ES-DUR see Mozart, Wolfgang Amadeus

KONZERTANTE MUSIC: FÜR 2 INSTRUMENTALCHÖRE see Werdin, Eberhard

KONZERTANTE MUSIK see Griesbach, Karl-Rudi see Hummel, Bertold see Werdin, Eberhard

KONZERTANTE SINFONIE IN D see Stamitz, Anton

KONZERTANTE SZENEN see Wildberger, Jacques

KONZERTANTES RONDO, FÜR KLAVIER UND STREICHORCHESTER see Koetsier, Jan

KONZERTFANTASIE, FOR CLARINET AND
ORCHESTRA see Rakov, Nikolai

KONZERTOUVERTÜRE C-DUR see Wagner,
Richard

KONZERTOUVERTÜRE D-MOLL see Wagner,
Richard

KONZERTSATZ F-MOLL see Schumann, Clara
(Wieck)

KONZERTSUITE A-DUR see Telemann, Georg
Philipp

KONZERTWALZER NR. 1 D-DUR see Glazunov,
Alexander Konstantinovich

KONZERTWALZER NR. 2 F-DUR see Glazunov,
Alexander Konstantinovich

KOOGHE see Fujil, Sonoko

KOOLMEES, HANS
Art Of Surfing A Monster, The
see Waters And Wortelen - Part 2

Cantata
5.5.5.5.soprano sax. 4.4.4.1. timp,
5perc,harp,2pno,strings [9'] sc
DONEMUS                          (K426)

Waters And Wortelen - Part 2
"Art Of Surfing A Monster, The"
0.2.0.0. 2.2.2.0. strings [11']
sc DONEMUS                       (K427)

KOPECKY, PAVEL (1949-    )
Concerto for Clarinet and Strings
see On A Oni

Concerto for Horn and Strings
[16'] CESKY HUD.                 (K428)

Concerto for Piano and Orchestra
2.2.2.2. 4.3.3.1. timp,perc,
strings,pno solo [18'] CESKY HUD.
                                 (K429)

Ctyri Symfonická Preludia
"Moskevská" 3.2.2.2. 4.3.3.1. timp,
perc,xylo,vibra,pno,strings [15']
CESKY HUD.                       (K430)

Moskevská
see Ctyri Symfonická Preludia

On A Oni (Concerto for Clarinet and
Strings)
[12'] CESKY HUD.                 (K431)

KOPRETINY see Korbar, Leopold

KOPRIVA, JAN JACHYM (1734-1792)
Mass in D,Benedictus
(Sesták, Zdenek) orch,strings,S
solo [6'] CESKY HUD.             (K432)

KOPRIVA, KAREL BLAZEJ (1756-1785)
Ah, Cordi Trito (Aria in D flat)
(Sesták, Zdenek) [Lat] 0.2.0.0.
2.0.0.0. org,strings,S solo [6']
CESKY HUD.                       (K433)

Aria in B flat
see Siste Ultricem Dexteram

Aria in D flat
see Ah, Cordi Trito
see Quod Pia Voce Cano

Concerto in D flat for Organ and
Orchestra
(Sesták Zdenek) 0.0.0.0. 2.0.0.0.
cembalo,strings [18'] CESKY HUD.
                                 (K434)

Motet in D
see Veni Sponsa Christi

Qui Tollis (from Missa Solemnis In D
Flat: Gloria)
(Sesták, Zdenek) [Lat] 0.2.0.0.
2.0.0.0. org,strings,A solo [4']
CESKY HUD.                       (K435)

Quod Pia Voce Cano (Aria in D flat)
(Sesták, Zdenek) [Lat] 0.2.0.0.
2.0.0.0. org,strings,B solo [7']
CESKY HUD.                       (K436)

Siste Ultricem Dexteram (Aria in B
flat)
(Sesták, Zdenek) [Lat] 0.2.0.0.
2.0.0.0. org,strings,S solo CESKY
HUD.                             (K437)

Veni Sponsa Christi (Motet in D)
(Sesták, Zdenek) [Lat] 0.2.0.1.
2.0.0.0. org,strings,SATB soli
[6'] CESKY HUD.                  (K438)

KOPROWSKI, PETER PAUL (1947-    )
Concerto for Flute
3(pic).3(English horn).3(clar in E
flat,bass clar).3(contrabsn).
4.3.3.1. timp,3perc,pno&cel,16vln
I,14vln II,12vla,10vcl,8db,fl

KOPROWSKI, PETER PAUL (cont'd.)

solo [27'] sc,solo pt CANADIAN
                                 (K439)

Concerto for Horn and Orchestra
3(pic).3(English horn).3(bass
clar).3(contrabsn). 2.2.1.1.
3perc,strings,horn solo [20'] sc
CANADIAN MI 1332 K83CO           (K440)

Epitaph
string orch,string quar soli [11']
sc CANADIAN MI 1717 K83EP        (K441)

In Memoriam Karol Szymanowski
2(alto fl).2+English horn.2(bass
clar).2. 2.2.0.0. timp,strings
[20'] (1. Chorale 2. Interlude 3.
Elegy 4. Finale (Funèbre)) sc,
study sc CANADIAN MI 1100 K83IN  (K442)

Peripeteia
4(pic).4+English horn.4+bass
clar.4+contrabsn. 6.4.3.1. timp,
perc,harp,strings [32'] (1.
Prologue 2. Episodes 3. Epilogue)
sc CANADIAN MI 1100 K83PE        (K443)

Psalm 42
2(pic,alto fl).2(English
horn).2(bass clar).2(contrabsn).
2.2.1.1. 2perc,strings,Bar solo
[12'] sc CANADIAN MV 1400 K83PS
                                 (K444)

Souvenirs De Pologne
2(pic).2(English horn).2.2.
2.2.0.0. timp,strings,pno solo
[24'] sc CANADIAN MI 1361 K83SO
                                 (K445)

Sweet Baroque
2(pic).2.2.2. 2.2.0.0. timp,strings
[12'] (1. Pompous Overture
(Hercules) 2. Mischievous
Allemande (Columbine) 3.
Capricious Courante (Columbina)
4. Sombre Sarabande(Pierrot) 5.
Merry Gigue (Pierrette) 6. Dotty
Finale (Harlequin)) sc CANADIAN
MI 1100 K83SW                    (K446)

KORALUVERTYR see Forsberg, Roland

KORBAR, LEOPOLD (1917-    )
Fiesta
2.0.3.0. 1.3.3.0. timp,perc,harp,
2gtr,bass gtr,strings [4'] CESKY
HUD.                             (K447)

Kopretiny
(Rimon, J.) 2.2.2.2. 4.3.3.1. perc,
strings [4'] CESKY HUD.          (K448)

Valse Triste
2.2.2.2. 3.2.2.0. timp,perc,harp,
strings [5'] CESKY HUD.          (K449)

KORELACE see Vorlová, Sláva

KORNDORF, NICOLAI (1947-    )
Amoroso
1.1.1.0. 2.0.0.0. 2perc,harp/cel,
vla,vcl,db [20'] PETERS          (K450)
1.1.1.0. 2.0.0.0. 2perc,harp/cel,
vla,vcl,db [20'] SIKORSKI perf
mat rent                         (K451)

Con Sordino
8vln I,7vln II,6vla,5vcl,4db,opt
cembalo [15'] sc PETERS 03383    (K452)
8vln,3vla,3vcl,2db,opt hpsd [14']
SIKORSKI perf mat rent           (K453)

Epilog
3.3.3.3. 4.3.3.1. timp,3perc,harp,
8vln I,7vln II,6vla,5vcl,4db
[15'] sc PETERS 03541            (K454)

Hymne Nr. 2
4.3.3.4. 8.5.4.1. timp,perc,vibra,
strings [26'] sc PETERS 03384    (K455)

Hymnus III
4.4.4.3. 4.4.4.1. timp,6perc,bass
gtr,strings, 2 off-stage trumpets
[15'] SIKORSKI sc 1928 f.s., sc,
pts perf mat rent                (K456)

Ja!
0..0+English horn.1.1. 2.2.2.0.
2perc,strings,STT soli [40']
SIKORSKI perf mat rent           (K457)

Let The Earth Bring Forth
1.1.2.1. 2.1.1.0. 2perc,pno,cel,
cembalo,harp,8vln I,7vln II,6vla,
5vcl,4db,elec bass [33'] sc
PETERS 04668                     (K458)

Prolog
4.4.4.4. 6.4.4.1. timp,perc,strings
[15'] sc PETERS 03380            (K459)

Symphony No. 2 for Orchestra
4.3.3.3. 6.3.3.1. timp,perc,2harp,
pno,strings [35'] PETERS         (K460)

KORNDORF, NICOLAI (cont'd.)

Symphony No. 3
4.4.4.4.4sax. 8.5.4.1. timp,9perc,
elec gtr,bass gtr,cel,org,pno,
strings,speaking voice,men cor&jr
cor, 6 trumpets in the hall [90']
PETERS                           (K461)

Victor
3.3.3.3. 4.4.3.1. timp,6perc,8vln
I,7vln II,6vla,5vcl,4db [37'] sc
PETERS 04669                     (K462)

KORNGOLD, ERICH WOLFGANG (1897-1957)
Einfache Lieder  *Op.9
2.2(English horn).2.2. 2.2.0.0.
timp,perc,cel,pno,harp,strings,
solo voice [23'] voc sc SCHOTTS
ED 8306 perf mat rent            (K463)

Lieder Des Abschieds  *Op.14
3.2(English horn).2+bass clar.2.
4.0.0.0. timp,perc,cel,harp,
strings,A solo [12'] SCHOTTS perf
mat rent sc BSS 30745, pno red
ED 2032                          (K464)

Military March
2.2.2.2. 4.2.3.0. timp,perc,harp,
strings [8'] SCHOTTS perf mat
rent                             (K465)

Straussiana
2+opt pic.1.2.1. 2.2.2.0. timp,
perc,pno,harp,2vln,vla,vcl,db
[6'] SCHOTTS perf mat rent       (K466)

Sursum Corda
see Symphonic Overture

Symphonic Overture  *Op.13
"Sursum Corda" 3(pic).2+English
horn.3+bass clar.2+contrabsn.
4.3+bass trp.3.1. timp,perc,pno,
2harp,14vln I,8vln II,8vln III,
6vla II,6vcl I,6vcl II,8db
[18'] sc SCHOTTS BSS 30495 perf
mat rent                         (K467)

KOROLYOV, ANATOLI (1949-    )
Chamber Symphony (Symphony for
Chamber Group)
1.0.1.0. 0.1.1.0. perc,harp,org/
elec org,vln,vla,vcl,db,speaking
voice [25'] SIKORSKI perf mat
rent                             (K468)

Symphony for Chamber Group
see Chamber Symphony

KORTE, OLDRICH FRANTISEK (1926-    )
Canzona A Ritornel
3.1.1.1. 0.0.0.0. harp,cembalo,
lute,strings [6'] CESKY HUD.     (K469)

Concerto Grosso for 2 Flutes, 2
Trumpets, Piano and Strings
[25'] CESKY HUD.                 (K470)

KOSMOS see Rohwer, Jens

KOSTÁL, ARNOST (1920-    )
Jízda Novymi Alejemi 1848
3.2.3.2. 3.3.3.1. timp,perc,acord,
strings,SMezATBarB soli [26']
CESKY HUD.                       (K471)

Pohnutá Idyla
2.1.3.1. 3.2.2.0. timp,perc,strings
[9'] CESKY HUD.                  (K472)

Sloky Odvahy
2.1.3.2. 3.3.3.1. timp,perc,harp,
pno,strings [16'] CESKY HUD.
                                 (K473)

KOSTECK, GREGORY WILLIAM (1937-1991)
Memento (Tchernobil 86)
3+pic.2+English horn.3+bass clar.2+
contrabsn. 4.3.3.1. timp,perc,
elec org,gtr,2harp,vibra,glock,
cimbalom,harmonium,cel,xylo,
acord,pno,10vln I,8vln II,8vla,
8vcl,8db, hurdy-gurdy [19'] EMB
rent                             (K474)

KOSUT, MICHAL (1954-    )
Concertino for Cembalo and Strings
strings,cembalo solo [8'] CESKY
HUD.                             (K475)

Gepard
3.3.3.3. 0.0.0.0. harp,cembalo,
synthesizer,strings [12'] CESKY
HUD.                             (K476)

Jan Santini Aichel
3.3.3.2. 4.3.3.1. timp,perc,vibra,
harp,cel,pno,org,strings [16']
CESKY HUD.                       (K477)

Portrét Básníka  *Fantasy
3.3.3.2. 4.3.3.1. timp,perc,harp,
cel,pno,cembalo,strings [10']
CESKY HUD.                       (K478)

KOSUT, MICHAL (cont'd.)

Zvony Z Chatyne
2.2.2.1. 2.2.0.0. timp,perc,strings
[8'] CESKY HUD. (K479)

KÖTSCHER, EDMUND (1909-1990)
Italienische Amseln (composed with
Eberhard, Wolfgang)
2.2.2.2. 2.2.2.0. timp,perc,gtr,
strings [4'] SIKORSKI perf mat
rent (K480)

KOU EN see Yamamoto, Junnosuke,
Prominence

KOUGUELL, ARKADIE (1898-    )
Intermezzo for Harp and Strings
sc,solo pt,pts INTERNAT.S. (K481)

KOUZELNÉ NOCI see Martinu, Bohuslav
(Jan)

KOVACH, A.
Sinfonietta
strings KUNZELMANN 10112 ipr (K482)

KOVACH, ANDOR
Eurydice *Overture
2+pic.2+English horn.2+bass clar.2+
contrabsn. 4.3.2.1. timp,perc,
pno,harp,strings SCHOTTS perf mat
rent (K483)

Musique Concertante
perc,strings,marimba solo [20']
SCHOTTS perf mat rent (K484)

Pallas Athene: Symphony
2(pic).2.2(bass clar).2. 4.2.2.0.
timp,3perc,cel,pno,harp,strings
[22'] (co-produced with Universal
Ed.) study sc SCHOTTS ED 5006
perf mat rent (K485)

KOVARÍCEK, FRANTIŠEK (1924-    )
Hudba Pro Komorní Orchestr
2.2.2.2. 2.2.0.0. timp,perc,strings
[23'] CESKY HUD. (K486)

KOX, HANS (1930-    )
Ballet Suite Spleen
0.1.1.0. 1.3.2.0. timp,2perc,
strings [17'] sc DONEMUS (K487)

Concerto for Alto Saxophone and
String Orchestra
see Face-To-Face

Concerto No. 3
1.1.1.1. 2.2.0.0. strings,vln solo
[23'] sc DONEMUS (K488)

Dorian Gray Suite
2.2.2.0. 2.2.0.0. timp,2perc,harp,
strings [15'] sc DONEMUS (K489)

Face-To-Face (Concerto for Alto
Saxophone and String Orchestra)
string orch,alto sax solo [20'] sc
DONEMUS (K490)

Grüne Gesicht, Das: Suite
"Orchester-Suite Aus Der Oper Das
Grüne Gesicht" 2.2.2.2. 4.3.3.1.
timp,perc,strings [19'] sc
DONEMUS (K491)

Orchester-Suite Aus Der Oper Das
Grüne Gesicht
see Grüne Gesicht, Das: Suite

KOYAMA, KAORU (1955-    )
Requiem
1.0.1.0. 0.0.0.0. harp,5perc,2vln,
vla,vcl,S solo [20'] JAPAN (K492)

Sinfonia Concertante
orch,pic solo,ob solo,clar solo,
harp solo [14'] JAPAN (K493)

KOZDERKA, LADISLAV
Scherzo for Trumpet and Orchestra
2.0.3.0. 2.2.3.0. perc,pno,strings,
trp solo [4'] CESKY HUD. (K494)

KOZELUCH, LEOPOLD ANTON (1747-1818)
Concerto for Clarinet and Orchestra
in E flat
clar solo,orch KUNZELMANN ipa sc
10106A, oct 10106 (K495)

Sinfonia in B flat
(Bilková, Alena) 0.2.0.1. 2.0.0.0.
strings [21'] CESKY HUD. (K496)

KOZELUHA, LUBOMIR (1918-    )
Portréty
3.3.3.3. 4.4.3.1. timp,perc,xylo,
strings,pno solo [22'] CESKY HUD.
(K497)

Tri Obelisky
3.3.2.3. 4.3.3.1. timp,perc,xylo,
harp,pno,strings [22'] CESKY HUD.
(K498)

KOZINSKI, STEFAN
Back-Hand Blues (Instrumental
Version)
2.1.2.0.5sax. 3.4.3.1. timp,perc,
harp,elec bass,strings SCHIRM.EC
rent (K499)

Christmas Melange
3.2.2.2. 4.3.3.1. timp,2perc,harp,
synthesizer,strings,opt handbells
SCHIRM.EC rent (K500)

Creaky Door, The (Halloween Overture)
3.2.2.2. 4.2.3.1. timp,3perc,
synthesizer,strings [3']
SCHIRM.EC rent (K501)

KRAFT, KARL (1908-1978)
Concerto Breve Nr.1 *Op.77
strings,org (A min) BÖHM (K502)

Partita for String Orchestra, No. 1,
in G minor
BÖHM (K503)

KRAFT, LEO ABRAHAM (1922-    )
Chamber Symphony, No. 2
1.1.1.1. 0.1.0.0. strings SEESAW
(K504)

Concerto No. 2 for 12 Instruments
1.1.1.1. 1.1.1.0. perc,vln,vla,vcl,
db SEESAW (K505)

Symphonic Prelude
2.2.2.2.sax. 4.2.2.0. timp,perc,
strings SEESAW (K506)

KRÁLOVÉDVORSKÁ see Bartoš, Jan Zdenek,
Studentská Suita

KRÁLOVÉHRADECKY see Šimicek, Jan,
Concerto for Piano and Orchestra,
Op. 19

KRÁLOVSTVÍ SLUNCE see Hába, Miroslav

KRAMAR, FRANTISEK
see KROMMER, FRANZ

KRAMAR-KROMMER
see KROMMER, FRANZ

KRATOCHVÍL, JAROMÍR (1924-    )
Ceská Krajina
3.2.3.2. 4.4.0.0. timp,perc,harp,
strings [12'] CESKY HUD. (K507)

Lento (from Symphony No. 1)
4.3.3.3.3sax. 0.0.0.0. timp,perc,
2harp,cel,pno,strings [9'] CESKY
HUD. (K508)

Romantická Suita
1.1.1.0. 0.0.0.0. timp,pno,strings
[5'] CESKY HUD. (K509)

KRATZSCHMAR, WILFRIED (1944-    )
Capriccio for Orchestra
2.2.2.2. 3.2.2.0. perc,8vln I,7vln
II,6vla,5vcl,4db [15'] sc PÉTERS
02981 (K510)

Kammerkonzert II
5vln I,4vln II,3vla,2vcl,db [15']
sc PÉTERS 04373 (K511)

KRAUS, EBERHARD (1931-    )
Concertino for String Orchestra
vln I,vln II,vla,vcl,db,2vln&vla&
vcl soli MÖSELER sc 11.457-00,
solo pt 11.457-01, pts 11.457-02,
set 11.457-09 (K512)

KRAUS, P. LAMBERT, OSB (1729-1790)
Sinfonia No. 10 in G
2horn,strings COPPENRATH sc
16.049-01, pts 16.047-21 TO 29,
pts 16.049-43 (K513)

KRCEK, JAROSLAV (1939-    )
Concerto for Oboe, Harp and Chamber
Group
2.1.1.1. 0.0.0.0. harp,2vln,vla,db,
ob&harp soli [11'] CESKY HUD.
(K514)

Concerto for Violin and Orchestra
2.1.1.1. 2.1.3.0. perc,harp,
strings,vln solo [16'] CESKY HUD.
(K515)

Majestas Carolina
2.1.0.1. 0.0.0.0. harp,cimbalom,
strings,solo voice [23'] CESKY
HUD. (K516)

Tri Tance Ve Starém Slohu
strings,perc [14'] PANTON (K517)

KREBS, JOACHIM (1952-    )
Slow-Mobile
1(pic).1(English horn).1+bass
clar.1+contrabsn. 2.0.0.0. harp,
2perc,vln,vla,vcl,db [21'] PEER
rent (K518)

KREISEL IST KAPUTT, DER see Mossolov,
Alexander

KREISLER, FRITZ (1875-1962)
Praeludium Und Allegro (composed with
Pugnani, Gaetano)
(Cohen, Shimon) string orch [3']
PRESSER rent (K519)

Trille Du Diable, Le (composed with
Tartini, Giuseppe)
(Dupin, M.O.) string orch,vln solo
[12'] BILLAUDOT rent (K520)

Variationen Uber Ein Thema Von
Corelli (composed with Tartini,
Giuseppe)
(Cohen, Shimon) strings [2']
PRESSER rent (K521)

KREUTZER, KONRADIN (1780-1849)
Schütz Bin Ich, Ein (from Das
Nachtlager Von Granada)
1.2.2.2. 4.2.0.0. timp,strings,Bar
solo [4'] (no score) BREITKOPF-W
(K522)

KRICKA, JAROSLAV (1882-1969)
Bábincin Maršovsky Valcík
1.2.2.2.3sax. 4.2.3.0. perc,acord,
strings,solo voice CESKY HUD.
(K523)

KRIEGER, ARMANDO (1940-    )
Angst
2.2.2.2. 4.3.3.1. 3perc,pno,strings
SEESAW (K524)
chamber orch TONOS M-2015-3774-0
rent (K525)

Metamorfosis d'Apres
1.1.1.1. 1.1.1.0. 2perc,strings,pno
solo SEESAW (K526)

Metamorfosis D'Après Une Lecture De
Kafka
"Metamorfosis D'AprÒs Une Lecture
De Kafka" chamber orch,pno solo
TONOS M-2015-3771-9 rent (K527)

Metamorfosis D'AprÒs Une Lecture De
Kafka
see Metamorfosis D'Après Une
Lecture De Kafka

KRISTALLE see Zechlin, Ruth

KRISTALLENE GUSLI see Shchedrin, Rodion

KRISTALLISATION see Zechlin, Ruth

KRIVINKA, GUSTAV (1928-    )
Concerto Grosso No. 2 for String
Quartet and Chamber Orchestra
string orch,string quar soli [20']
CESKY HUD. (K528)

Legenda O Velkém Hríšníkovi
0.1.0.0. 2.2.3.1. perc,harp,strings
[20'] CESKY HUD. (K529)

KRÍZEK, MILAN (1926-    )
Concerto for Chamber Orchestra
2.2.2.2. 2.2.0.0. timp,perc,harp,
strings [18'] CESKY HUD. (K530)

Variace Na Téma Albana Berga
2.2.2.2. 2.2.0.0. strings [15']
CESKY HUD. (K531)

KRÍZEK, ZDENEK (1927-    )
Capriccio for Oboe and Strings
[3'] CESKY HUD. (K532)

Dupák
2.2.2.2. 4.3.3.1. timp,perc,xylo,
harp,strings [3'] CESKY HUD.
(K533)

Jarní
2.1.2.1. 3.2.2.0. timp,perc,harp,
strings,S solo [4'] CESKY HUD.
(K534)

Jaro A Mládí *Overture
2.2.2.2. 4.3.3.0. timp,perc,harp,
strings [7'] CESKY HUD. (K535)

Kolonádní Motivy *Overture
2.2.2.2. 3.2.3.0. timp,perc,xylo,
harp,strings [8'] CESKY HUD.
(K536)

Májové Rondo
2.2.2.2. 4.3.3.0. timp,perc,strings
[3'] CESKY HUD. (K537)

Melancholické Intermezzo
2.1.2.1. 3.0.2.0. timp,perc,harp,
strings [4'] CESKY HUD. (K538)

Písen Rodné Reci
2.1.2.1. 3.0.2.0. timp,perc,
strings,Bar solo [4'] CESKY HUD.
(K539)

Radostnym Dnum
2.2.2.2. 4.3.3.1. timp,perc,harp,
strings [3'] CESKY HUD. (K540)

KRÍZEK, ZDENEK (cont'd.)

Ráno Po Sedmé
2.1.2.1. 3.3.3.0. perc,pno,2gtr,
strings [3'] CESKY HUD.    (K541)

Šedomodré Nokturno
2.0.3.0. 1.3.3.0. perc,harp,pno,
2gtr,strings [5'] CESKY HUD.    (K542)

Španelsky Tanec
2.0.3.0. 3.3.3.0. perc,harp,pno,
2gtr,strings [4'] CESKY HUD.    (K543)

Strahovsky Valcík
2.2.2.2. 4.3.3.1. perc,harp,strings
[4'] CESKY HUD.    (K544)

Vzpomínka Na Balcik
2.2.2.2. 3.3.0.0. timp,perc,harp,
strings [3'] CESKY HUD.    (K545)

KROENUNG see Kirkwood, Antoinette

KROMMER, FRANZ (1759-1831)
Concertino for Clarinet and Orchestra
in E flat
(Koukal, Bohumír) 1.2.0.2. 2.2.0.0.
strings,clar solo [13'] CESKY
HUD.    (K546)

Concertino, Op. 65
(Müller, H.) fl,ob,2horn,strings
sc,solo pt KUNZELMANN GM 1246 ipa    (K547)

Concerto for Clarinet and Orchestra,
Op. 36, in E flat
(Berlasz) clar solo,orch KUNZELMANN
ipa sc 10095A, oct 10095    (K548)

Concerto for 2 Clarinets and
Orchestra, Op. 91
(Padrta, Karel) 1.2.0.2. 2.0.0.0.
timp,strings,2clar soli [16']
CESKY HUD.    (K549)

Concerto for Violin
vln solo,vln I,vln II,2vla,db,2ob,
2horn sc KUNZELMANN ipr 10285A,
10285    (K550)

KROUMATA SYMPHONY see Lundquist,
Torbjörn, Symphony No. 8

KROUSE, IAN
Concerto for Bass Clarinet and
Orchestra
4(2pic,alto fl).3+English
horn.3(clar in E flat,clar in A,
bass clar).3+contrabsn. 4.4(opt
piccolo trp,opt bass trp).2.1.
timp,5-6perc,harp,cel,strings,
bass clar solo [21'] PEER rent    (K551)

Rhapsody for Violin and Orchestra
2(2pic).2.2.2. 2.2.2.0. timp,perc,
harp,strings,vln solo [22'] PEER
rent    (K552)

Tientos
string orch,fl solo [21'] PEER rent    (K553)

KRUH see Blatny, Pavel

KRUISBRINK, ANNETTE
Sgraffito
1.1.2.1.alto sax. 0.0.0.0. perc,
harp,pno,strings [3'] sc DONEMUS    (K554)

KRUMPHOLTZ, JOHANN BAPTIST (1742-1790)
Concerto for Harp and Orchestra, Op.
4, No. 2, in B flat
(Schroeder) harp solo,orch
KUNZELMANN ipa sc 10019A, oct
10019    (K555)

KRUSE, BJØRN HOWARD (1946- )
Forrett
1(pic).1.1.1. 1.0.0.0. strings [7']
NORSKMI    (K556)

KRUYF, TON DE (1937- )
Himalaya
2.2.2.2.2sax. 2.2.2.1. 4perc,harp,
pno,strings [67'] sc DONEMUS    (K557)

KRYPTOGRAMM see Hübler, Klaus-K.

KRYPTON see Daugherty, Michael

KRYSTALY see Strasek, Emil see Vostrák,
Zbynek

KUBELIK, RAFAEL (1914-1996)
Cornelia (Suite for Orchestra)
2.2.3.2. 4.3.3.1. timp,3perc,pno,
cel,cembalo,harp,8vln I,7vln II,
6vla,5vcl,4db [10'] sc PETERS
03832    (K558)

Sinfonia in One Movement
3.3.4.2. 4.3.3.1. timp,6perc,harp,
8vln I,7vln II,6vla,5vcl,4db
[27'] sc,study sc PETERS 00888    (K559)

KUBELIK, RAFAEL (cont'd.)

Suite for Orchestra
see Cornelia

KUBICKA, MIROSLAV (1951- )
Concerto No. 2 for Piano and
Orchestra
3.2.2.3. 4.3.3.1. timp,perc,xylo,
cel,harp,strings,pno solo [17']
CESKY HUD.    (K560)

Písne Citové A Zertovné
2.1.2.2. 2.1.1.0. harp,xylo,vibra,
strings,S solo [13'] CESKY HUD.    (K561)

Prolog
3.2.3.3. 4.3.3.1. timp,perc,strings
[8'] CESKY HUD.    (K562)

Symphony
3.3.3.3. 4.3.3.1. timp,perc,cel,
strings [20'] CESKY HUD.    (K563)

KUBIK, GAIL (1914-1984)
Bennie The Beaver
1(pic).1.1.1. 1.1.0.0. pno,vla,vcl,
narrator,perc solo [7'] PEER rent    (K564)

KUBIK, LADISLAV (1946- )
Concerto De Camera
strings,vln&pno soli [15'] CESKY
HUD.    (K565)

Concerto Grosso for Violin, Piano,
Percussion and Strings
[20'] CESKY HUD.    (K566)

Pocta Majakovskému *Overture
4.4.4.4. 6.4.4.2. timp,perc,xylo,
vibra,cel,marimba,pno,strings
[8'] CESKY HUD.    (K567)

Slova
2.2.2.2. 2.0.0.0. timp,strings,Mez
solo [14'] CESKY HUD.    (K568)

Symphony
3.3.3.3. 4.3.3.1. timp,perc,pno,
strings [18'] CESKY HUD.    (K569)

KUBÍN, RUDOLF (1909-1973)
Concerto for Violoncello and
Orchestra
3.3.3.3. 4.2.3.1. timp,perc,harp,
cel,strings,vcl solo [24'] PANTON    (K570)

KUCERA, PREMYSL (1960- )
Baladické Souveti
3.3.3.3. 4.3.3.1. timp,perc,vibra,
marimba,strings [28'] CESKY HUD.    (K571)

KUCERA, VÁCLAV (1929- )
Balada A Romance
2.2.2.2. 2.0.0.0. perc,strings
[17'] CESKY HUD.    (K572)

Operand
1.1.1.1. 2.1.0.0. perc,strings [9']
CESKY HUD.    (K573)

KUCHARZYK, HENRY (1953- )
Figure In A Landscape (Suite for
Orchestra)
2.2.2(bass clar).2. 2.2.0.0. timp&
perc,harp,pno,strings,vln
solo sc CANADIAN MI 1311 K95FI    (K574)

Suite for Orchestra
see Figure In A Landscape

Walk The Line
string orch,perc solo [18'] sc
CANADIAN MI 1640 K95WA    (K575)

KUCHYNKA, VOJTA (1871-1942)
Duo for Violin and Double Bass
1.1.2.1. 2.2.2.0. perc,strings,vln&
db soli [5'] CESKY HUD.    (K576)

KÜFFNER, JOSEPH (1776-1856)
Polonaise
trp solo,orch KUNZELMANN 10263 ipr    (K577)

KÜHNL, CLAUS (1957- )
Visionen
12vln,3vla,3vcl,2db [10']
BREITKOPF-W    (K578)

KUKIYAMA, NAOSHI (1958- )
Mori
string orch [10'] JAPAN    (K579)

KULENTY, HANNA
Concerto for Violin, No. 2
4.4.4.4. 6.4.4.1. timp,2perc,harp,
pno,strings,vln solo [38'] sc
DONEMUS    (K580)

Sinequan Forte A
4.4.4.4. 6.4.4.1. 3perc,pno,
strings,vcl solo [17'] (cello
amplified & delay) sc DONEMUS    (K581)

KULENTY, HANNA (cont'd.)

Sinequan Forte B
2.2.2.2. 2.2.2.0. 3perc,pno,
strings,vcl solo [17'] (cello
amplified & delay) sc DONEMUS    (K582)

KULESHA, GARY (1954- )
Concerto for Marimba, Bass Clarinet
and Chamber Orchestra
0.2.0.0. 2.0.0.0. strings,marimba
solo,bass clar solo [24'] sc
CANADIAN MI 1450 K96CO    (K583)

Divertimento for String Orchestra in
Five Movements
string orch [9'] sc CANADIAN
MI 1500 K96DI    (K584)

Essay For Orchestra
2(pic).2.2(bass clar).2. 4.2.3.1.
timp,3perc,pno,strings [10'] sc
CANADIAN MI 1100 K96ES    (K585)

Fourth Chamber Concerto: For Brass
Concertante, Woodwinds, Strings
And Percussion
1.1.1.1. 2.2.1.1. perc,strings
[26'] sc CANADIAN    (K586)

Midnight Road, The
"Third Essay For Orchestra"
2.2.2.2. 4.2.3.1. timp,2perc,
strings [11'] sc CANADIAN    (K587)

Nocturne for Chamber Orchestra
1(alto fl).1.1.1. 1.1.0.0. perc,
4vln I,3vln II,2vla,2vcl,db [12']
sc CANADIAN MI1200 K96N    (K588)

Third Essay For Orchestra
see Midnight Road, The

KUNIEDA, HARUE (1958- )
Reflection III
orch [10'] JAPAN    (K589)

KUNST DER FUGE, DIE see Bach, Johann
Sebastian

KUNTZEN, ADOLPH CARL (1720-1781)
Sinfonia in D minor
(Schneider, M.) 0.2.0.0. 0.0.0.0.
strings,cont [11'] BREITKOPF-W    (K590)

KUNZ, ALFRED (1929- )
Chamber Symphony
1.1.1.1. 2.1.1.0. timp,perc,strings
[27'] sc CANADIAN MI1200 K965CH    (K591)

Classical Arcade
2.2.2.0. 2.2.0.0. perc,strings sc
CANADIAN MI1200 K965CL    (K592)

Fanfares And Canzona
3(pic).2.2.2. 4.3.3.1. timp,perc,
strings, (fanfares for brass
ensemble only) sc CANADIAN
MI 1100 K965FA    (K593)

Overture For Fun
3(pic).2.2.2. 4.3.2.1. timp,perc,
strings [8'] sc,study sc CANADIAN
MI 1100 K965OV    (K594)

Spring Into Summer
2.2.2.2. 2.2.0.0. perc,strings sc
CANADIAN MI1200 K965SP    (K595)

Three Pieces For Clarinet And Strings
string orch,clar solo [15'] sc
CANADIAN MI 1623 K965TH    (K596)

Winterlude
3+pic.2.2.2. 4.3.3.1. timp,perc,
harp,strings sc CANADIAN
MI 1100 K965WI    (K597)

KUPKA, KAREL (1927-1985)
Concerto for Bassoon and Chamber
Orchestra
2.0.0.0. 0.0.0.0. timp,perc,xylo,
pno,strings,bsn solo [28'] CESKY
HUD.    (K598)

Paraboly
[18'] CESKY HUD.    (K599)

KURACHI, TATSUYA (1962- )
Music For City Opera
orch, solo voices [6'] JAPAN (K600)

KURELEK SUITE, THE see Fiala, George

KURTAG, GYÖRGY (1926- )
Double Concerto *Op.27,No.2
pno solo,vcl solo,2chamber orch,
[Vcl Group: 1(alto fl)+tenor
recorder. 1(english horn).1(clar
in E flat)+bass clar. 1(contra
bsn). 1.1.1.1. timp, perc, harp,
cel, pno, cimbalom, strings; Pno
Group: 1(alto fl, pic)+tenor
recorder.1(english horn). 1(clar
in E flat)+bass clar. 1(contra
bsn). 1.1.1.1. timp, perc, harp,

KURTAG, GYÖRGY (cont'd.)

    cel, cimbalom, strings] [16'] EMB
rent               (K601)

    Messages Of The Late R.V. Troussova
     *Op.17
     0.1.1(clar in E flat).0. 1.0.0.0.
     perc,mand,harp,cel,pno,cimbalom,
     vln,vla,db,S solo [27'] (poems by
     Rimma Dalos) EMB rent   (K602)

KURTZ, EUGENE ALLEN (1923- )
   Chamber Symphony
    2vln,2vla,2vcl,pno,cel,2perc [12']
    JOBERT            (K603)

KURZ, IVAN
   Naklonená Rovina
    3.3.3.3. 4.3.3.1. timp,perc,Ondes
    Martenot,cel,strings [17'] CESKY
    HUD.              (K604)

   Podobenství
    3.3.3.3. 4.3.3.1. timp,perc,xylo,
    2harp,cel,org,strings [14'] CESKY
    HUD.              (K605)

   Symphony No. 3
    3.2.3.3. 4.3.3.1. timp,perc,xylo,
    cel,strings [25'] CESKY HUD.
                  (K606)

   Vzlínáni
    3.3.3.3. 4.3.3.1. timp,perc,strings
    [23'] CESKY HUD.    (K607)

KURZBACH, PAUL (1902- )
   Concerto for Double Bass and
    Orchestra
    1.1.1. 1.0.0.0. perc,cembalo,db
    solo [17'] sc,solo pt BREITKOPF-W
    PB 3967L         (K608)

   Serenade No. 3
    2.2.2.2. 2.2.2.0. timp,perc,strings
    [22'] BREITKOPF-W   (K609)

   Serenade No. 6 for String Orchestra
    strings [16'] BREITKOPF-W (K610)

KUTAVICIUS, BRONIUS (1932- )
   Dzukische Variationen
    pno,strings,tape recorder, pre-
    recorded women's choir [13']
    SIKORSKI perf mat rent  (K611)

   Uhren Der Vergangenheit II
    1.1.1.1. 1.1.1.0. pno,2vln,vla,vcl,
    db [10'] CHANT perf mat rent
                 (K612)

KUTZER, ERNST (1918- )
   Concertino for Trumpet and Strings,
    Op. 96
    see Morgenglanz Der Ewigkeit

   Morgenglanz Der Ewigkeit (Concertino
    for Trumpet and Strings, Op. 96)
    trp,strings,opt speaking voice BÖHM
                 (K613)

KUUTAMO JUPITERISSA see Raitio, Väinö

KUZMENKO, LARYSA
   Concertino for Vibraphone and Marimba
    1.1.1.1. 1.1.0.0. perc,strings,
    vibra solo sc CANADIAN
    MI 1340 K97CO     (K614)

KVÄDE 2 see Blomberg, Erik

KVÄDE 3 see Blomberg, Erik

KVADRUPPELKONSERT, FOR FLUTE, OBOE,
   CLARINET, BASSOON AND ORCHESTRA see
   Lerstad, Terje B., Concerto Grosso
   No. 3, Op. 200

KVAM, ODDVAR S. (1927- )
   Arbeidsdag
    see Tre Gloselund-Sanger, Op. 56c

   Concerto for Violin and Orchestra,
    Op. 96
    "Neptunus" 2.2.2.2. 2.2.2.0. timp,
    3perc,strings,vln solo [16']
    NORSKMI          (K615)

   Cycle Of Life, The *Op.87
    2(pic).2(English horn).2(bass
    clar).2(contrabsn). 4.3.3.0.
    timp,2perc,strings [12'] NORSKMI
                 (K616)

   Neptunus
    see Concerto for Violin and
    Orchestra, Op. 96

   Sangens Makt
    see Tre Gloselund-Sanger, Op. 56c

   Student Gloselund
    see Tre Gloselund-Sanger, Op. 56c

   Towards The End *Op.82
    3.3.3.3. 4.3.3.0. timp,3perc,harp,
    strings [10'] NORSKMI  (K617)

KVAM, ODDVAR S. (cont'd.)

   Tre Gloselund-Sanger, Op. 56c
    [Norw] string orch,pno,Mez/Bar solo
    NORSKMI f.s.
    contains: Arbeidsdag; Sangens
    Makt; Student Gloselund (K618)

KVANDAL, JOHAN (1919- )
   Concerto for 2 Pianos and Orchestra,
    Op. 77
    2(pic).2.2.2. 4.2.3.0. timp,perc,
    strings,2pno soli NORSKMI (K619)

   Sonata for Strings, Op. 79
    string orch NORSKMI   (K620)

KVAPÍK SPORTOVCU see Smetácek, Rudolf

KVAPIL, JAROSLAV (1892-1958)
   Concerto for Violin and Orchestra,
    No. 1
    3.3.3.3. 4.3.3.1. timp,perc,harp,
    strings,vln solo [36'] CESKY HUD.
                 (K621)

KVDE 4 see Blomberg, Erik

KVECH, OTOMAR (1950- )
   Capriccio (Concerto for Piano,
    Violin, Violoncello and
    Orchestra)
    3.2.2.2. 4.2.3.1. timp,perc,harp,
    cel,strings,pno&vln&vcl soli
    [22'] CESKY HUD.   (K622)

   Concerto for Piano, Violin,
    Violoncello and Orchestra
    see Capriccio

   Karneval Sveta *Overture
    3.2.2.2. 4.2.3.1. timp,perc,xylo,
    strings [11'] CESKY HUD. (K623)

   Olympijsky Pochod
    2.2.2.2. 2.3.2.4.0. timp,perc,strings
    [4'] CESKY HUD.    (K624)

   Passacaglia
    see R.U.R.

   Predehra
    2.2.2.2. 2.2.3.1. timp,perc,strings
    [9'] CESKY HUD.    (K625)

   Promena (Sinfonietta for Violin and
    Chamber Orchestra)
    string orch,vln solo [12'] CESKY
    HUD.              (K626)

   R.U.R. (Passacaglia) (from Podnetu
    Hry Karla Capka)
    3.3.3.2. 4.2.3.1. timp,perc,strings
    [14'] CESKY HUD.   (K627)

   Sinfonietta for Violin and Chamber
    Orchestra
    see Promena

   Symphony in D
    2.2.2.2. 2.2.0.0. timp,strings
    [22'] CESKY HUD.   (K628)

   Symphony in E flat
    3.3.3.3. 4.3.3.1. timp,perc,pno,
    strings [27'] CESKY HUD. (K629)

   V Krajine Vzpomínáni
    strings,high solo [14'] CESKY HUD.
                 (K630)

KVERNDOKK, GISLE (1967- )
   Concerto for Oboe and Orchestra
    3(pic).1.3(bass clar).3(contrabsn).
    4.3.3(bass trom).1. timp,3perc,
    harp,pno,strings, obbligato
    string sextett: 2 violins, 2
    violas & 2 violoncelli [20']
    NORSKMI          (K631)

   De Profundis: Psalm, For Orchestra
    3(pic).2.2.4.2soprano sax. 3.3(trp
    in C).1.0. timp,2perc,harp,hpsd,
    pno,org,strings, 6 off stage
    trombones NORSKMI   (K632)

   ...In The Night Before The Town-Crier
    Begin To Cry
    [Eng] 3(pic).2.2.2. 4.3.3.1. 2perc,
    harp,pno,strings,narrator NORSKMI
                 (K633)

   Initiasjon
    "Initiation" 3(pic).2(English
    horn).2(bass clar).2(contrabsn).
    4.2.3.1. timp,4perc,harp,pno,
    synthesizer,strings [11'] NORSK
                 (K634)

   Initiation
    see Initiasjon

   Selene For Orchestra
    3(pic).3(English horn).3(bass
    clar).3(contrabsn). 4.3.3.1.
    timp,2perc,cel,harp,pno,strings
    [28'] NORSKMI    (K635)

KVETINOVÉ SCHERZO see Rimón, Jan

KVITSUNN see Søderlind, Ragnar,
   Sinfonia No. 5, Op. 60

KWAKIUTL: PRAYER TO THE YOUNG CEDAR see
   Rickard, Sylvia

KWELA see Blake, Michael

KWERNADSE, BIDSINA (1928- )
   Symphony for String Orchestra
    [24'] SIKORSKI perf mat rent (K636)

KYLLÖNEN, TIMO-JUHANI (1955- )
   Sarja Jousiorkesterille (Suite for
    String Orchestra, Op. 27)
    sc,pts MODUS M94   (K637)

   Sinfonia (Symphony No. 1, Op. 8)
    3.2.3.3. 4.3.3.1. timp,3perc,cel,
    vibra,harp,strings sc MODUS M47
                 (K638)

   Suite for String Orchestra, Op. 27
    see Sarja Jousiorkesterille

   Symphony No. 1, Op. 8
    see Sinfonia

KYR, ROBERT
   Book Of The Hours
    see Symphony No. 1

   Dance Symphony In 3 Movements, A
    see Symphony No. 4

   Fifth Season, The
    see Symphony No. 3

   Gamelodion
    2.2.2.2. 4.3.2.1. timp,4perc,harp,
    strings [15'] SCHIRM.EC rent
                 (K639)

   Lovers' Almanac, The
    S solo,fl,clar,pno,vln,vcl,marimba
    [21'] SCHIRM.EC rent  (K640)

   Maelstrom For Soprano And Chamber
    Orchestra
    S solo,fl,clar,2perc,kbd,vln,vcl
    [40'] SCHIRM.EC rent  (K641)

   Signal In The Land, A
    narrator,3.2.3.2. 4.3.3.1. timp,
    3perc,strings [40'] SCHIRM.EC
    rent             (K642)

   Symphony No. 1
    "Book Of The Hours" S/countertenor/
    Mez solo,2.2.2.2. 4.2.2.1. harp,
    kbd,marimba,vibra,strings [35']
    SCHIRM.EC rent    (K643)

   Symphony No. 3
    "Fifth Season, The" 4.4.4.4.
    4.4.3.1. perc,2harp,2kbd,strings
    [40'] SCHIRM.EC rent  (K644)

   Symphony No. 4
    "Dance Symphony In 3 Movements, A"
    2.2.2.2. 4.2.2.1. strings [33']
    SCHIRM.EC rent    (K645)

KYTICKA NA MOHYLU see Matej, Jozka
   (Josef)

KYU-NO-KYOKU see Miki, Minoru

# L

LA see Arseneault, Raynald

LA BARRE, MICHEL DE (ca. 1674-ca. 1744)
  Suite for 2 Trumpets in D
    (Guyot, D.) hpsd,string orch,2trp
    soli [9'] pno red BILLAUDOT rent
                                    (L1)

  Suite in D
    (Guyot, D.) string orch,hpsd,2trp
    soli [9'] BILLAUDOT         (L2)

LABIRINTO ARMONICO, IL see Locatelli,
  Pietro

LABURDA, JIRI (1931-   )
  Concertino for Trumpet and String
    Orchestra
    [24'] CESKY HUD.           (L3)

  Concerto for Accordion and Strings
    [24'] CESKY HUD.           (L4)

  Divertimento in D for String
    Orchestra
    [13'] CESKY HUD.           (L5)

  Pastorale for Flute and String
    Orchestra
    [13'] CESKY HUD.           (L6)

  Petits Riens, Les
    2.2.2.2. 4.2.1.1. timp,perc,xylo,
    cel,pno,strings [27'] (baletní
    scény) CESKY HUD.          (L7)

  Slavnostní Predehra
    2.2.2.2. 4.4.3.1. timp,perc,strings
    [6'] CESKY HUD.            (L8)

  Symphony No. 1
    2.2.2.2. 4.4.3.1. perc,pno,strings
    [30'] CESKY HUD.           (L9)

LACHENMANN, HELMUT FRIEDRICH
  (1935-   )
  Air for Orchestra and Percussion
    4(pic).0.4.2+contrabsn. 6.3.3.1.
    4perc,harp,gtr,pno,Hamm,14vln I,
    12vln II,10vla,8vcl,7db [20']
    study sc BREITKOPF-W PB 5420
                                    (L10)

  Notturno for Violoncello and Chamber
    Orchestra
    2(pic).0.0.0. 0.1.0.0. timp,3perc,
    harp,strings,vcl solo [15'] study
    sc BREITKOPF-W PB 5405    (L11)

  Staub
    2(alto fl)+pic.2.2.2+contrabsn.
    4.2.3.0. 3perc,6vln I,6vln II,
    5vla,4vcl.8db [23'] study sc
    BREITKOPF-W PB 5177        (L12)

  Tableau
    4(pic).4.3+bass clar.3+contrabsn.
    8.4.4.0. timp,4perc,harp,pno,
    12vln I,12vln II,10vla,8vcl,8db
    [10'] study sc BREITKOPF-W
    PB 5416                    (L13)

  "...Zwei Gefühle...", Musik Mit
    Leonardo
    alto fl,bass fl,English horn,bass
    clar,contrabass clar,contrabsn,
    2trp,trom,tuba,2perc,harp,gtr,
    pno,vln,vla,vcl,db,2 speaking
    voices [20'] study sc BREITKOPF-W
    PB 5419                    (L14)

LACOUR, GUY (1932-   )
  Ballade Pour Georges
    string orch,sax solo [15']
    BILLAUDOT                  (L15)

LACRYMOSA see Lavista, Mario

LADERMAN, EZRA (1924-   )
  And David Wept
    1.1.1.1. 1.1.0.0. timp,2perc,pno,
    harp,strings PRESSER rent  (L16)

  Concerto for Orchestra
    see Satire

  Satire (Concerto for Orchestra)
    3(pic).3(English horn).3(bass
    clar).3(contrabsn). 4.3.3.1.
    timp,2perc,cel,harp,strings
    PRESSER rent               (L17)

LADY FROM COLORADO: SECOND SYMPHONIC
  SET see Ward, Robert Eugene

LADY MACBETH VON MZENSK, ZWISCHENSPIELE
  see Shostakovich, Dmitri

LADY MACBETH VON MZENSK: SINFONISCHE
  SUITE see Shostakovich, Dmitri

---

LAGERSBEWRGS-SVIT see Lundin, Dag

LAGIDSE, REWAS (1921-   )
  Satschidao
    3(pic).2.2.2. 4.3.3.1. timp,perc,
    strings [3'] SIKORSKI perf mat
    rent                       (L18)

LAGUNEN-WALZER see Strauss, Johann,
  [Jr.]

LAHUSEN, CHRISTIAN (1886-1975)
  Hochzeit Der Schäferin, Die *ballet
    1.0.1.1. 1.0.0.0. harp,strings
    [30'] BREITKOPF-W          (L19)

LAIDLEY WORM OF SPINDLETON HEUGH, THE
  see Amos, Keith

LAJTHA, LASZLO (1891-1963)
  Capriccio: Suite No. 1
    2.2.2.2. 2.1+cornet.2.1. timp,perc,
    harp,cel,strings [26'] EMB rent
                                    (L20)

  Capriccio: Suite No. 2
    2.2.2.2. 2.1+cornet.2.1. timp,perc,
    harp,cel,strings [26'] EMB rent
                                    (L21)

  Capriccio: Suite No. 3
    2.2.2.2. 2.1+cornet.2.1. timp,perc,
    harp,cel,strings [27'] EMB rent
                                    (L22)

  Deuxieme Symphonie
    see Symphony No. 2, Op. 27

  Primavera, La
    see Sinfonia No. 4

  Recruiting Dance Of Kossuth
    3clar,3cimbalom,strings,solo voice
    [5'] EMB rent              (L23)

  Sinfonia No. 4
    "Primavera, La" 1+pic.1+English
    horn.2.1+contrabsn. 4.1+
    cornet.0.0. timp,perc,harp,cel,
    strings [18'] EMB rent     (L24)

  Symphony No. 2, Op. 27
    "Deuxieme Symphonie" 2(pic).2.2.2.
    4.2.0.0. timp,perc,harp,pno,
    strings [30'] EMB rent     (L25)

LAKE, LARRY (1943-   )
  Filar Il Tuono
    clar,alto sax,tenor sax,baritone
    sax,trp,trom,marimba,elec gtr,
    bass gtr,pno, amplified bassoon,
    electric violin, electric cello
    sc CANADIAN MI 9377 L192FI (L26)

LAKMÉ: LA CABANE see Delibes, Léo

LALO, EDOUARD (1823-1892)
  Introduction Et Scherzo
    2.2.2.2. 4.2+cornet.2.0. timp,perc,
    strings [13'] LEDUC        (L27)

  Symphonie Espagnole *Op.21
    2+pic.2.2.2. 4.2.3.0. timp,perc,
    harp,strings,vln solo [35'] sc,
    pts BREITKOPF-W PB 2836-OB 2578L
                                    (L28)

    orch,vln solo sc DOVER 29532-X
                                    (L29)

  Valse De La Cigarette
    2.2.2.2. 4.0.0.0. timp,strings
    LEDUC                      (L30)

LAMAN, WIM (1946-   )
  Django
    1.1.2.0. 0.0.0.0. perc,harp,2gtr,
    pno,strings [8'] sc DONEMUS (L31)

LAMENT see Burke, John see Maros,
  Rudolf see Zuckert, Leon

LAMENT FOR STRINGS see Sculthorpe,
  Peter [Joshua]

LAMENT: TRAUERMUSIK IM GEDENKEN AN
  LUIGI NONO see Kantscheli, Gija

LAMENTATIONS see Artyomov, Vyacheslav
  see Dorff, Daniel Jay

LAMENTO see Nobis, Herbert see Ollone,
  Max d' see Rehnqvist, Karin see
  Sinigaglia, Leone see Zuckert,
  Leon, Lament

LAMENTO DELL'ACQUA see Glass, Paul

LAMENTO-MÉMOIRE see Duhamel, Antoine

LAMENTO-RYTMEN AV EN RÖST see
  Rehnqvist, Karin

LAMENTO VER ESTONIA-KATASTROFEN see
  Koch, Erland von

LAMENTOSO see Gropp, Johann-Maria

LAMENTU D'U TRENU see Tomasi, Henri

---

LAMPSON, ELMAR
  Drei Orchesterstücke
    2.2.2.2. 2.2.2.1. timp,perc,strings
    [15'] PEER rent            (L32)

  Sinfonietta Für Solistenensemble
    0.2.2.2. 1.1.0.0. vibra,marimba,
    timp,perc,pno,harp,vln,vcl,3db
    [23'] PEER rent            (L33)

LANAIA I - VI see Nickel, Volker

LANCHBERY, JOHN
  Béatrix Potter Tales
    orch (excerpt from the film) BOIS
                                    (L34)

LAND OF PEOPLE, THE see Slavicky, Milan

LANDL, ERNST
  Skandinavisches Idyll
    "Sketch" 2.1.2.1. 2.0.0.0. timp,
    perc,harp,cel,strings [3'25"] sc,
    set BUSCH DM 063 rent      (L35)

  Sketch
    see Skandinavisches Idyll

LANDSCAPE see Matthews, Colin, Sonata
  No. 5 see Matthews, Michael

LANDSCAPE III see Hosokawa, Toshio

LANDSCAPE VI: CLOUDSCAPES see Hosokawa,
  Toshio

LANDSCAPES see Grant, Stewart

LANDSCHAFT NACH DER SCHLACHT see
  Tarnopolsky, Vladimir

LANDSCHAPPEN 5 see Westerlinck,
  Wilfried

LANDSCHAPPEN II see Westerlinck,
  Wilfried

LANE, PHILIP (1950-   )
  Three Christmas Pictures
    3.2.2.2. 4.2.2.1. perc,cel,harp,
    strings [10'] sc OXFORD 3652943
    f.s., sc,pts rent          (L36)

LANG, ISTVAN (1933-   )
  Egloga
    2.1.0.0. 2.0.0.0. timp&castanets,
    pno,strings EMB rent       (L37)

  Hyperbola: Suite
    1(pic).1.1.1. 1.1.0.0. timp,perc,
    harp,pno,8vln I,6vln II,4vla,
    4vcl,3db [15'] EMB rent    (L38)

  Pezzo Lirico
    string orch,ob solo [13'] EMB rent
                                    (L39)

  Variazioni E Allegro
    2(pic).2.2+clar in E flat+bass
    clar.2. 4.3.3.0. timp,perc,harp,
    pno,strings [10'] EMB rent (L40)

LANG, JOHANN GEORG (1724-1794)
  Concerto for Violin and Strings in D
    strings,vln solo MOSELER 40.165
                                    (L41)

LANG, WALTER (1896-1966)
  Concerto for Piano and Orchestra, Op.
    34
    2.2.2.2. 2.2.2.0. timp,perc,strings
    [19'] HUG                  (L42)

  Galgenlieder *Op.27
    1(pic).1(English horn).1.1.alto
    sax. 1.1.0.0. harp,pno,2perc,
    strings,B solo [30'] (text by
    Christian Morgenstern) HUG (L43)

  Poem, Op. 41
    fl,string orch [11'] HUG   (L44)

LANGDALES see Anderson, Jean

LANGER, HANS-KLAUS (1903-   )
  Burlesque Ouvertuere
    orch sc TONOS M-2015-4548-6 (L45)

LÅNGSTRÖM, OLLE (1952-   )
  Vivant Westmanniae
    2.2.2.2. 4.2.3.1. timp,2perc,
    strings [19'] (symphonic
    variations) STIM           (L46)

LANN, VANESSA
  Madness And The Moonwoman
    2.3.3.3. 4.2.2.1. perc,harp,strings
    [14'] sc DONEMUS           (L47)

LANZA, ALCIDES E. (1929-   )
  Acufenos II
    winds,perc,kbd,strings,electronic
    equipment [12'] BOOSEY-ENG rent
                                    (L48)

  Eidesis V
    1.1.2(bass clar).0. 1.1.1.0. 2perc,
    pno,strings without vln, (graphic
    notation included) [15'] sc
    CANADIAN MI1200 L297EI     (L49)

LANZA, ALCIDES E. (cont'd.)

Eidesis VI
4vln I,4vln II,3vla,3vcl,2db,pno
solo [14'] sc CANADIAN
MI 1661 L297EI
(L50)

LANZHOTSKÁ see Kapr, Jan, Symphony No.
10

LAPHROAIG see Brewaeys, Luc, Symphony
No. 5

LAPORTE, ANDRE (1931-    )
Fantasy
2.2.3.3. 4.1.0.1. timp,perc,cel,
pno,harp,strings,vln solo [8'30"]
(rondino con tempa reale) BELGE
(L51)

LAQUAI, REINHOLD (1894-1957)
Ouverture Zu Einer Alten Komödie
3.3.3.3(contrabsn). 4.3.3.1. perc,
harp,strings [10'] HUG    (L52)

LARGHETTO see Lekeu, Guillaume see
Tamas, Janos

LARGO see Perna, Dana Paul

LARGO & ALLEGRO, FOR FLUTE AND STRING
ORCHESTRA see Tchaikovsky, Piotr
Ilyich

LARGO E PASSACAGLIA CROMATICA see
Schilling, Hans Ludwig

LARGO-SINFONIE see Schut, Vladislav

LARGO UND ALLEGRO see Kantscheli, Gija

LARIDAH-MARSCH see Hempel, Max

LARINO, SAFE HAVEN see Dreyfus, George

LARMES DE JACQUELIN, LES see Offenbach,
Jacques

LARSEN, EILERT LINDORFF
see LINDORFF-LARSEN, EILERT

LARSEN, ELIZABETH B. (LIBBY)
(1950-    )
Atmosphere As A Fluid System, The
fl,perc,strings [12'] perf sc set
OXFORD sc,pts rent    (L53)

Blue Fiddler
3(pic).2.2+bass clar.2. 4.3.3.1.
timp,3perc,pno,strings [12'] perf
sc set OXFORD 3860333 sc,pts rent
(L54)

Cold Silent Snow: Concerto
see Concerto

Collage: Boogie
3.2.3.2. 4.3.3.1. timp,3perc,kbd,
strings,pno, amplified [6']
SCHIRM.EC rent    (L55)

Concerto
"Cold Silent Snow: Concerto"
2.2.2.2. 2.0.0.0. 2perc,strings,
fl solo,harp solo [22'] SCHIRM.EC
rent    (L56)

Concerto for Marimba
"Marimba Concerto: After Hampton"
2.2.2.2. 4.3.3.1. timp,2perc,
harp,kbd,strings,marimba solo
[23'] SCHIRM.EC rent    (L57)

Concerto for Piano
"Piano Concerto: Since Armstrong"
3.3.3.2. 4.2.3.1. timp,3perc,
strings [25'] SCHIRM.EC rent
(L58)

Concerto for Trumpet and Orchestra
2.2.2.2. 4.2.3.1. 3perc,kbd,
strings,trp in C solo [19']
SCHIRM.EC rent    (L59)

Coriolis
3.2.3.3. 4.2.3.1. timp,3perc,2kbd,
strings [11'] SCHIRM.EC rent
(L60)

Dance Piece
see Ghosts Of An Old Ceremony

Deep Summer Music
2.2.1.2. 4.1.3.0. timp,2perc,
strings [8'] SCHIRM.EC rent (L61)

Ghosts Of An Old Ceremony
"Dance Piece" 3.1.2.1. 4.3.3.0.
timp,3perc,2kbd,strings [29']
SCHIRM.EC rent    (L62)

Marimba Concerto: After Hampton
see Concerto for Marimba

Mary Cassatt
3(pic).2.2.2. 4.2.0.1. timp,2perc,
harp,strings,trom solo,Mez solo
[30'] perf sc set OXFORD sc,pts
rent    (L63)

LARSEN, ELIZABETH B. (LIBBY) (cont'd.)

Overture For The End Of A Century
2+pic.2.2.2. 4.3.3.1. timp,3perc,
pno,strings [6'] OXFORD sc
3859696 f.s., pts 385970X f.s.
(L64)

Overture: Parachute Dancing
2.2.2.2. 4.2.3.1. timp,3perc,kbd,
strings [7'] SCHIRM.EC rent (L65)

Piano Concerto: Since Armstrong
see Concerto for Piano

Pinions For Chamber Orchestra
1.1.1.1. 1.0.0.0. kbd,strings,vln
solo [15'] SCHIRM.EC rent (L66)

Ring Of Fire
2+pic.2.3.2. 4.3.3.1. timp,2perc,
harp,strings [12'] perf sc set
OXFORD 3860228 sc,pts rent (L67)

Sonnets From The Portuguese
1.1.2.1. 0.0.0.0. harp,perc,
strings,S solo [20'] perf sc set
OXFORD 3859823 sc,pts rent (L68)

Symphony
"Symphony: Water Music" 3.2.3.3.
4.3.3.1. timp,3perc,harp,kbd,
strings [21'] SCHIRM.EC rent
(L69)

Symphony No. 3
"Symphony No. 3: Lyric" 3.3.3.3.
4.3.3.1. timp,3perc,harp,kbd,
strings [26'] SCHIRM.EC rent
(L70)

Symphony No. 3: Lyric
see Symphony No. 3

Symphony: Water Music
see Symphony

Tom Twist For Narrator And Orchestra
2.1.2.2.alto sax. 1.1.0.0. 2perc,
harp,kbd,strings,narrator [8']
SCHIRM.EC rent    (L71)

Weaver's Song And Jig
1.1.1.1. 1.0.0.0. perc,strings,
mand,gtr,db,pno, fiddl [10']
SCHIRM.EC rent    (L72)

What The Monster Saw
1.1.1.1. 1.1.0.0. 2perc,kbd,
synthesizer,strings [10']
SCHIRM.EC rent    (L73)

LARSON, CHRICHAN (1956-    )
Lissages
1(pic).1+English horn.2(2bass
clar).2. 2.2(piccolo trp).0.0.
mand,mandola,gtr,cimbalom,3vln,
2vla,2vcl,db [9'] sc,pts STIM
(L74)

LARSON, MARTIN (1967-    )
Orchestral Music 1 "E Il Librö
3(pic).3(English horn).3(bass
clar).3(contrabsn). 4.4.3.1.
timp,3perc,harp,strings,pno,cel,
cembalo STIM    (L75)

LARSSON, FOLKE (1924-    )
Festlig Dans, En  *Op.53d
1.1.2.1. 2.2.1.0. perc,3vln I,2vln
II,2vla,2vcl,db [2'] sc,pts STIM
(L76)

Invention  *Op.54a
1.1.2.1. 2.2.1.0. timp,3vln I,2vln
II,2vla,2vcl,db [4'5"] sc STIM
(L77)

Romans  *Op.53c
1.1.2.1. 2.2.1.0. timp,perc,strings
[3'] sc,pts STIM    (L78)

Stillhet  *Op.54b
1.1.2.1. 2.2.1.0. 3vln I,2vln II,
2vla,2vcl,db [4'] sc STIM   (L79)

Symfonisk Dikt Bergslagen  *Op.53b
1.1.2.1. 2.2.1.0. timp,3vln I,2vln
II,2vla,2vcl,db [5'] sc STIM
(L80)

LARSSON, HOKAN (1959-    )
Diaspalmata
string orch STIM    (L81)

Gnglt
string orch [10'] sc STIM    (L82)

Hemland: Menuett
string orch [5'-6'] sc STIM   (L83)

Overture for String Orchestra
string orch [8'] STIM    (L84)

Rapsodi Miniatyr
fl,ob,clar,bsn,horn,strings [5'-6']
sc STIM    (L85)

Sinfonietta
1.1.1(bass clar).1. 1.1.1.0. perc,
strings,pno [19'] sc STIM   (L86)

LARSSON, HOKAN (cont'd.)

Symphony No. 1
3(pic).3(English horn).3(bass
clar).3(contrabsn). 4.3.3.1.
timp,perc,harp,strings,pno [30']
sc STIM    (L87)

Vid En Vg: Musik
1.1.1.1. 1.1.1.0. timp,perc,2vln,
vla,vcl,db,pno [8'-10'] sc STIM
(L88)

Vintermusik
2.2.2.2. 2.2.2.0. 2perc,strings,pno
[10'] sc STIM    (L89)

LARSSON, LARS-ERIK (1908-1986)
Sinfonietta, Op. 10
string orch [18'] UNIVER.    (L90)

LARSSON, MARTIN (1967-    )
Concerto for Bass Trombone and
Orchestra
2.2(English horn).2(bass
clar).2(contrabsn). 2.1.1.0.
timp,2perc,harp,strings,cel,bass
trom solo STIM    (L91)

Concerto for Violin and Orchestra
2(pic).2(English horn).2(bass
clar).2(contrabsn). 2.1.1.0.
timp,2perc,harp,strings,cel/
bells,vln solo STIM    (L92)

I Grönskan Skall Du Finna Ro
3(pic).3(English horn).3(bass
clar).3(contrabsn).sax. 4.1+
cornet.3.1. timp,2perc,harp,
strings,vln solo, flicorno STIM
(L93)

LARSSON, MATS (1965-    )
Concerto for Piano and Chamber
Orchestra
2(pic).2(English horn).2.2.
2.2.0.0. timp,strings,pno solo
STIM    (L94)

Houses In Motion
2(pic).2.2.2. 4.3.3.1. timp,2perc,
pno,strings [9'] STIM sc H-2812,
pts    (L95)
orch [9'] sc REIMERS 101222 rent
(L96)

Jingle
1.1.1.1. 1.1.1.0. perc,strings,pno
[1'] sc STIM    (L97)

Lugubre
3(pic).3(English horn).3(bass
clar).3(contrabsn). 4.3.3.1.
timp,2perc,strings,pno [6'] sc,
pts STIM    (L98)

Mixing Memories And Desires
see Symphony No. 1

Symphony No. 1
"Mixing Memories And Desires"
3(pic).3(English horn).4(bass
clar).3(contrabsn). 4.3.3.1.
3perc,harp,strings,pno,cel,opt
org [30'] sc STIM    (L99)

LÁSKA K MILÉMU see Ceremuga, Josef

LÁSKO POSMUTNELÁ see Ondrácek, Bohuslav

LASON, ALEKSANDER (1951-    )
Concerto In Mem. P. Casals
2.2.2.0. 3.2.2.0. perc,pno,strings,
vcl solo SEESAW    (L100)

Concerto "Pablo Casals In Memoriam"
orch,vcl solo TONOS sc
M-2015-3797-9 rent, pts
M-2015-3798-6 rent    (L101)

Kammerkonzert
ob,string orch TONOS M-2015-3790-0
rent    (L102)

Kammermusik V
0.0.1.0. 0.0.1.0. 5vln,3vla,2vcl
SEESAW    (L103)

Kathedrale
orch sc TONOS M-2015-3802-0 (L104)
3.3.3.3. 4.3.3.0. 5perc,pno,strings
SEESAW    (L105)

Sinfonia No. 2
4.3.3.3. 4.4.4.1. 5perc,strings,pno
solo SEESAW    (L106)
orch,pno solo TONOS M-2015-3794-8
(L107)

LASS MEIN LIEBES KIND DICH NENNEN see
Mozart, Wolfgang Amadeus, Riconosci
In Questo Amplesso

LASSONDE, CLAUDE (1955-    )
Noème - Au Seuil Des Mémoires
D'Avenir
2(pic,alto fl).0.2(bass clar,
contrabass clar).0. 2.1.0+2bass
trom.0. 4perc,pno&cel&hpsd,2harp,
2vcl,db, soprano sax&bass sax

LASSONDE, CLAUDE (cont'd.)

[14'] sc CANADIAN MI1200 L347AU
(L108)

LAST CLARINET, THE see Englishby, Paul

LAST DIARY, THE see Torstensson, Klas

LAST JUDGEMENT, THE see Moross, Jerome

LAST OF THE SUMMER WINE see Hazlehurst,
Ronnie

LAST PARADISE, THE see Xiaogang, Ye

LATAKIA; BY THE WATER'S EDGE see Ware,
Peter

LATE AUGUST see Swafford, Jan

LATER SYMPHONIES (NOS. 35-41) see
Mozart, Wolfgang Amadeus

LATERNA MAGICA see Csemiczky, M.

LATSCHPLESIS see Ivanovs, Janis

LÄTT SÄSONGSBETONAD RAPSODI, EN see
Hedwall, Lennart, Jul Igen En Liten
Tid

LATTICES - GUITAR CONCERTO see Orton,
Richard, Concerto for Guitar

LAUBE, ANTONIN (1718-1784)
Due Sinfonie
(Havlik, Jaromir) 2.0.0.0. 2.0.0.0.
strings CESKY HUD. f.s.
contains: Sinfonia in D [7'];
Sinfonia in G [13']      (L109)

Sinfonia in D
see Due Sinfonie

Sinfonia in G
see Due Sinfonie

LAUBER, ANNE (1943-    )
Affaire Coffin, L'
2.2.2.2. 4.2.3.0. timp,perc,
strings,pno solo [30'] sc
CANADIAN MI 1361 L366AF    (L110)

Au-Dela Du Mur Du Son
"Beyond The Sound Barrier" [Eng/Fr]
2(pic).2(English horn).2.2.
4.2.2.1. timp,2perc,strings,2
narrators [35'] sc CANADIAN
MV 2400 L366AU        (L111)

Beyond The Sound Barrier
see Au-Dela Du Mur Du Son

Canadian Overture
"Ouverture Canadienne"
2(pic).2.2.2. 4.2.2.1. timp,
2perc,strings [9'] sc CANADIAN
MI 1100 L366OU        (L112)

Concerto for Piano
2(pic).2.2.2. 4.2.3.0. timp,
strings,pno solo [28'] sc,pno red
CANADIAN MI 1361 L366CO  (L113)

Concerto for Violin and Orchestra
2(pic).2.2.2. 4.2.3.0. timp,
strings,vln solo sc,pno red,solo
pt CANADIAN MI 1311 L366CO (L114)

Divertimento for Strings
string orch [9'] sc CANADIAN
MI 1500 L366DI        (L115)

Osmose
see Pièce Symphonique No. II

Ouverture Canadienne
see Canadian Overture

Pièce Symphonique No. II
"Osmose" 3(pic).3.3(bass
clar).3(contrabsn). 0.0.0.0.
timp,3perc,strings [20'] sc
CANADIAN MI 1100 L366OS  (L116)

Poèm Pour Une Métamorphose
2.2.2.2. 2.2.3.0. perc,strings [7']
sc CANADIAN MI 1100 L366PO (L117)

Valse Concertante Pour Piano Et
Orchestre
2(pic,alto fl).2(English horn).2.2.
2.2.2.0. timp,2perc,strings,pno
solo [19'] sc,pno red CANADIAN
MI 1361 L366VA        (L118)

LAUDA see Vasks, Peteris

LAUDE see Jeney, Zoltan

LAUF DER WELT see Grieg, Edvard Hagerup

LAUFER, EDWARD C. (1938-    )
Divertimento
2+pic.2+English horn.2+bass clar.2.
2.1.0.0. timp,strings [8'] sc
CANADIAN MI1200 L373DI    (L119)

LAVA see Hillborg, Anders

LAVISTA, MARIO (1943-    )
Aura: Paráfrasis Orquestal De La
Opera
"Orchestral Paraphrase From The
Opera 'Aura'" 2+pic.2+English
horn.2+bass clar.2+contrabsn.
4.2.3.1. timp,perc,cel,harp,
strings [15'] PEER rent    (L120)

Clepsidra
2+pic.2+English horn.2+bass clar.2.
4.2.2.0. tam-tam,cel,harp,strings
[10'] PEER rent          (L121)

Ficciones
2+pic.2+English horn.2+bass clar.2+
contrabsn. 4.3.2.1. timp,perc,
harp,pno,strings [8'] PEER rent
(L122)

Hacia El Comienzo
"Toward The Beginning" 2.2+English
horn.2+bass clar.2. 4.2.2.0.
harp,strings [9'] (text by
Octavio Paz) PEER rent    (L123)

Lacrymosa
0.2.1.1+contrabsn. 0.0.4.0. timp,
4perc,strings [12'30"] PEER rent
(L124)

Lyhannh
2+pic.2+English horn.2+bass clar.3+
contrabsn. 4.3.3.1. perc,pno,
harp,strings [8'] PEER rent
(L125)

Orchestral Paraphrase From The Opera
'Aura'
see Aura: Paráfrasis Orquestal De
La Opera

Reflections Of The Night
see Reflejos De La Noche

Reflejos De La Noche
"Reflections Of The Night" string
orch [10'30"] PEER rent  (L126)

Toward The Beginning
see Hacia El Comienzo

LAVMAELT see Berge, Håkon

LAZAROF, HENRI (1932-    )
Choral Symphony
see Symphony No. 3

Concerto for Oboe and Chamber
Orchestra
2.0.2.2. 2.0.0.0. strings without
db,ob solo [18'40"] study sc
MERION rent              (L127)
PRESSER 446-41096        (L128)

Encounters With Dylan Thomas
chamber group,S solo PRESSER
446-41086                (L129)

Fantasy for Horn and Orchestra
3.3.3.3. 4.3.3(bass trom).1. timp,
3perc,harp,strings,horn solo
[18'] study sc MERION rent (L130)

Preludes And Interludes To A Drama
1.1.2(bass clar).1. 1.1.0.0. perc,
vln,vla,vcl [20'] study sc MERION
rent                    (L131)

Rhapsody for Viola
3(alto fl).3(English horn).3(bass
clar).3. 4.3.3(bass trom).1.
timp,3perc,pno&cel,harp,strings
study sc MERION rent    (L132)

Symphony No. 3
"Choral Symphony" orch,ABar soli,
SATB PRESSER 446-41082    (L133)

Three Pieces For Orchestra
3.3(English horn).3(bass
clar).3(contrabsn). 4.3.3(bass
trom).1. timp,3perc,pno&cel,harp,
strings [18'] MERION rent (L134)

LÁZENSKY KARNEVAL see Sodomka, Karel

LÁZENSKY VALCÍK see Precechtel, Zbynek

LAZZARI, SILVIO (1857-1944)
Effet De Nuit
3(pic).2+English horn.2+bass
clar.3(contrabsn). 4.3.3.1. timp,
drums,triangle,strings [15'25"]
LEDUC                    (L135)

LEADEN ECHO AND THE GOLDEN ECHO see
MacCombie, Bruce

LEAVE IT ALONE, AN AUDIOCLIP see
Geertens, Gerda

LEBEN FÜR DEN ZAREN, EIN: ARIE D.
SUSSANIN see Glinka, Mikhail
Ivanovich

LEBEN FÜR DEN ZAREN, EIN: ARIE DES
WANJA see Glinka, Mikhail Ivanovich

LEBEN FÜR DEN ZAREN, EIN: MAZURKA UND
FINALE see Glinka, Mikhail
Ivanovich

LEBEN FÜR DEN ZAREN, EIN: OVERTURE see
Glinka, Mikhail Ivanovich

LEBWOHL see Pavlyenko, Sergei

LECLAIR, JEAN MARIE (1697-1764)
Concerto in D, Op. 10, No. 3
see Three Concerti For Violin

Concerto in F, Op. 10, No. 4
see Three Concerti For Violin

Concerto, Op. 10, No. 5
see Three Concerti For Violin

Scylla Et Glaucus: Suite
(Boulay, Laurence) strings [22']
BOOSEY-ENG rent          (L136)

Three Concerti For Violin
(Blanchard) orch,vln solo BOIS f.s.
contains: Concerto in D, Op. 10,
No. 3; Concerto in F, Op. 10,
No. 4; Concerto, Op. 10, No. 5
(L137)

LEDENJOV, ROMAN (1930-    )
Sieben Stimmungen
1.1.1.1. 1.1.0.0. pno,strings [5']
PETERS                  (L138)

LEDUC, JACQUES (1932-    )
Intrada Et Dancerie  *Op.75b
string orch [4'30"] BELGE  (L139)

LEE, WILLIAM FRANKLIN (1929-    )
Veri
3(pic).3.3(bass clar).3. 4.3.3.1.
4perc,harp,synthesizer,strings
[24'] PEER rent          (L140)

LEES, BENJAMIN (1924-    )
Borealis
3(pic).3.3(bass clar).3(contrabsn).
4.3.3.1. timp,3perc,harp,strings
[8'] BOOSEY-ENG rent    (L141)

Concerto For Brass Choir And
Orchestra
3(2pic).0.0.0. 4.3.3.1. timp,perc,
cel,strings, solo group [20']
BOOSEY-ENG rent          (L142)

Concerto for Horn and Orchestra
3(2pic).3.3.3(contrabsn). 4.3.3.1.
timp,perc,cel,strings [26']
BOOSEY-ENG rent          (L143)

Echoes Of Normandy
3(2pic).3.3.3(contrabsn). 4.3.3.1.
timp,4perc,electronic tape,org,
strings,T solo [25'] (text by
Richard Nickson, Louis Simpson,
Henry Wadsworth Longfellow)
BOOSEY-ENG rent          (L144)

Four Songs Of The Night
1.1.1.1. 1.1.0.0. timp,cel,2vln,
vla,vcl,db,S solo [8'] (text by
Richard Nickson) BOOSEY-ENG rent
(L145)

Kalmar Nyckel
see Symphony No. 5

Symphony No. 5
"Kalmar Nyckel" 3(2pic).3.3(bass
clar).3(contrabsn). 4.3.3.1.
timp,perc,harp,strings [26']
BOOSEY-ENG rent          (L146)

LEGALLIENNE, DORIAN (1916-1963)
Overture in E flat
2.2.2.2. 4.2.3.1. perc,harp,strings
[8'] ALLANS              (L147)

LEGEND OF CHUNG 'AH, THE see Romero,
Manly

LEGEND OF HEIMDALL, THE see Raum,
Elizabeth

LEGENDA see Jirák, Karel Boleslav

LEGENDA O VELKÉM HRÍSNÍKOVI see
Krivinka, Gustav

LÉGENDE see Caplet, André

LÉGENDE GÉORGIENNE see Djabadary,
Heraclius

LEGENDE VON DER UNSICHTBAREN STADT
KITESCH, DIE: SUITE see Rimsky-
Korsakov, Nikolai

LÉGENDES I. WATER
2(pic).0+ob d'amore+English horn.2+
bass clar.2. 4.3.2+bass trom.0.
3perc,pno&cel,harp,8vln I,8vln II,
6vla,6vcl,4db [25'] (4 symphonic
meditations, text by Jean-Luc
Parant) SCHOTTS perf mat rent
(L148)

LEHMANN, LIZA (1862-1918)
In A Persian Garden
2.2.2.2. 2.0+2cornet.0.0. timp,
perc,harp,strings CRAMER rent
(L149)

LEICHTE SINFONIE, OP. 18 see Kangro,
Raimo

LEICHTLING, ALAN (1947-    )
Concerto for Chamber Orchestra
1.0.1+bass clar.0. 1.1.1.0. 4perc,
strings SEESAW          (L150)

My Lady Anita's Songbook
S solo,orch SEESAW      (L151)

Psalm No. 37
2vln/vla,vcl,harp,pno,cel,4perc,Mez
solo SEESAW            (L152)

LEIEZYKLUS NR. 1 see Duvosel, Lieven,
Morgen, Der

LEIPZIGER KONZERT see Dittrich, Paul-
Heinz, Concert Avec Plusieurs
Instruments No. 7

LEISE ZIEHT DURCH MEIN GEMÜT see
Mendelssohn-Bartholdy, Felix

LEISTNER-MAYER, ROLAND (1945-    )
Ballade, Op. 72
orch VOGT VF 1216      (L153)

Concerto Concitato I  *Op.30
orch VOGT VF 1208      (L154)

Concerto Concitato III  *Op.78
10vln,pno VOGT VF 1181 (L155)

Concerto Concitato IV  *Op.90
VOGT VF 1177           (L156)

Concerto for Piano and Orchestra, Op.
89
VOGT VF 1222           (L157)

Concerto for Violin and Orchestra,
Op. 21
VOGT VF 1223           (L158)

Interlude, Op. 61
VOGT VF 1175           (L159)

Music for Double Bass and Orchestra,
Op. 38
VOGT VF 1200           (L160)

Ratibor Op. 58
VOGT VF 1101           (L161)

Rhapsody No. 1, Op. 27
orch VOGT VF 1237      (L162)

Symphony No. 1, Op. 14
VOGT VF 1120           (L163)

Symphony No. 2, Op. 31
VOGT VF 1148           (L164)

Symphony No. 3 for Solo Voices,
Chorus and Orchestra
see Weisse Requiem

Weisse Requiem (Symphony No. 3 for
Solo Voices, Chorus and
Orchestra)
VOGT VF 1189           (L165)

Zwei Verlorenen Trompeten Und Das
Konzert, Die  *Op.41
orch,2trp soli VOGT VF 1202 (L166)

LEK see Blomberg, Erik

LEKEU, GUILLAUME (1870-1894)
Larghetto
0.0.0.1. 2.0.0.0. strings,vcl solo
[9'50"] BELGE          (L167)

LEKOURI: DANSE GÉORGIENNE see
Djabadary, Heraclius

LÉMANIC 70 see Zbinden, Julien-François

LEMELAND, AUBERT (1932-    )
American Epitaph  *Op.147
orch,vln&vla&vcl soli [14']
BILLAUDOT              (L168)

Automne Et Ses Envols D'Étourneaux,
L'  *Op.145
string orch,English horn,harp
[11'] BILLAUDOT        (L169)

LEMELAND, AUBERT (cont'd.)
Concertino Grosso  *Op.127 [15']
string orch,fl solo
BILLAUDOT              (L170)

Concerto for Harp and String
Orchestra, Op. 150 [17']
string orch,harp solo
BILLAUDOT              (L171)

Concerto for Viola and String
Orchestra, Op. 139
string orch,vla solo [15']
BILLAUDOT              (L172)

Concerto for Violin and Orchestra,
Op. 131 [14']
3.3.3.3. 4.3.2.1. timp,2perc,
strings,vln solo
BILLAUDOT              (L173)

Concerto for Violin and String
Orchestra, Op. 128 [20']
string orch,vln solo
BILLAUDOT              (L174)

Concerto for Violin and String
Orchestra, Op. 148 [15']
string orch,vln solo
BILLAUDOT              (L175)

Concerto for Violin and String
Orchestra, Op. 151 [12']
string orch,vln solo
BILLAUDOT              (L176)

Elégie À La Mémoire De Samuel Barber
*Op.125
string orch [7'] BILLAUDOT  (L177)

Hommage À Jean Rivier  *Op.134
string orch [7'] BILLAUDOT  (L178)

Songs For The Dead Soldiers
string orch,horn,harp,S solo [32']
BILLAUDOT              (L179)

LENDVAY, KAMILLO (1928-    )
Chaconne
3(pic).3(English horn).3(bass
clar).3(contrabsn). 4.3.3.1.
timp,perc,elec bass gtr,vln solo,
strings [14'] EMB rent (L180)

Concerto Semplice
string orch,cimbalom solo [10'] EMB
rent                  (L181)

Rhapsody
string orch,vln solo [9'] EMB rent
(L182)

Scenes From Tetralogy "Joseph And His
Brothers" By Thomas Mann  *cant
4(alto fl,3pic).3(English
horn).krummhorn.3(bass
clar).3(contrabsn). 4.3.3.1.
timp,perc,harp,cel,strings,S,B/
Bar soli [24'] EMB rent (L183)

Travestia, For 11 Instruments
fl,ob,clar,bsn,horn,pno,glock,vln,
vla,vcl,db [15'] EMB rent (L184)

LENNERS, CLAUDE (1956-    )
Euphonia I
1.1.1.1. 0.2.2.0. 2pno,2perc,2vln,
vla,vcl [15'] LEMOINE rent (L185)

LENNON, JOHN ANTHONY (1950-    )
Concerto for Guitar and Orchestra
"Zingari" gtr solo,3.3.3.2.
4.3.1.0. timp,3perc,harp,strings
[18'] SCHIRM.EC rent   (L186)

Far From These Things For Chamber
Orchestra
1.1.1.1. 1.1.1.0. timp,kbd,strings
[15'] SCHIRM.EC rent   (L187)

Metapictures
1.1.1.1. 2.1.1.0. timp,perc,harp,
2kbd,strings [15'] SCHIRM.EC rent
(L188)

Spectra
3.2.2.2. 4.3.2.1. timp,4perc,harp,
2kbd,strings [24'] SCHIRM.EC rent
(L189)

Suite Of Fables For Narrator And
Orchestra
3.2.2.2. 4.3.2.1. timp,2perc,harp,
2kbd,strings,narrator [15']
SCHIRM.EC rent         (L190)

Zingari
see Concerto for Guitar and
Orchestra

LENORE, BALLADE VOM BÜRGER see Liszt,
Franz

LENT, VAGUE, INDÉCIS see Wagenaar,
Diderik

LENTO see Kratochvíl, Jaromír see
Skempton

LENZ, DER see Lindorff-Larsen, Eilert

LEO, LEONARDO (ORTENSIO SALVATORE DE)
(1694-1744)
Sant' Elena Al Calvario: Sinfonia
(Kretzschmar, H.) 2.2.2.2. 2.0.0.0.
strings [6'] BREITKOPF-W  (L191)

LEON, TANIA JUSTINA (1944-    )
Batá
orch PEER min sc 61886-856 f.s.
pts rent              (L192)

Carabali
3(pic).2+English horn.2+bass
clar.2+contrabsn. 4.3.3.1. timp,
3perc,harp,pno&cel,strings [17']
PEER rent             (L193)

Hechizos
1(pic).1.1(clar in A)+bass
clar.0. soprano sax.tenor sax.
1.1.1.0. gtr,2perc,vln,vla,vcl,db
[13'] PEER rent       (L194)

Indigena
"Native" 1.1.1.1. 1.1.0.0. perc,
pno,vln I,vln II,vla,vcl,db [8']
PEER rent             (L195)

Native
see Indigena

Para Viola Y Orquesta
2(pic,alto fl).2.2(bass
clar).2(contrabsn). 2.2.1.0.
timp,2perc,cel,strings,vla solo
[18'] PEER rent       (L196)

LEONARDO see Cowie, Edward

LEONCAVALLO, RUGGIERO (1858-1919)
Ave Maria
(Zani, Giacomo) strings,harp/pno,
solo voice [4'] SONZOGNO rent
(L197)

Serenade Française
(Zani, Giacomo) strings,solo voice
[3'] SONZOGNO rent    (L198)

Serenade Napolitaine
(Zani, Giacomo) strings,opt fl,solo
voice [4'] SONZOGNO rent  (L199)

LEOPOLDSKRON see Engelmann, Hans Ulrich

LEPINI see Humel, Gerald

LERDAHL, FRED (1943-    )
Cross-Currents
3(pic).3.3.3. 4.2.3.1. 4perc,pno,
harp,strings [10'] sc,pts JERONA
rent                  (L200)

Waves
2.2.2.2. 2.0.0.0. strings [15'] sc,
pts JERONA rent       (L201)

LEROUX, PHILIPPE (1959-    )
D'Aller
2.1.2.0. 1.1.0.1. perc,pno,harp,
string quin,vln solo [17']
BILLAUDOT             (L202)

LERSTAD, TERJE B. (1955-    )
Concerto Grosso No. 3, Op. 200
"Kvadruppelkonsert, For Flute,
Oboe, Clarinet, Bassoon And
Orchestra" 2(2pic).1(English
horn).0.1(contrabsn). 4.2.3.1.
timp,2perc,pno,strings [25']
NORSKMI               (L203)

Kvadruppelkonsert, For Flute, Oboe,
Clarinet, Bassoon And Orchestra
see Concerto Grosso No. 3, Op. 200

LESUR, DANIEL (1908-    )
Variations for Piano and Orchestra
2.2.2.2. 2.2.3.0. timp,strings,pno
solo [25'] JOBERT     (L204)

LET SULLEN DISCORD SMILE see Purcell,
Henry

LET THE BALLOON GO see Dreyfus, George

LET THE EARTH BRING FORTH see Korndorf,
Nicolai

LETNÍ RAPSODIE see Dlouhy, Jaromir

LETNÍ VÍTR see Rimón, Jan

LETTRE D'ÉTIENNE Á JACQUES see Longtin,
Michel

LETTRE D'UN AMI see Bernier, Rene

LETZTEN TAGE VON ST. PETERSBURG, DIE:
SUITE see Schnittke, Alfred

LETZTER TANZ see Weingartner, (Paul)
Felix von

LETZTER WALZER see Schubert, Franz
(Peter)

LEUCHTTURM AM ENDE DER WELT, DER see
Plate, Anton

LEUTWILER, TONI (1923-    )
Concertino for Horn and Orchestra
2.2.2.2. 3.3.3.0. timp,perc,harp,
strings,opt cel,horn solo [4'5']
HEINRICH sc 3165, pts 3205 (L205)

LEVI, PAUL ALAN (1941-    )
Fantasies And Variations On A Chanson
By Orlando Di Lasso
see Transformations Of The Heart

Transformations Of The Heart
"Fantasies And Variations On A
Chanson By Orlando Di Lasso"
2.2.2.2. 2.2.2.0. 2perc,harp,
strings [12'] JERONA sc B12450
f.s., pts rent            (L206)

LEVIA see Furgeri, Bianca Maria

LEVIN, GREGORY (1943-    )
Concatenations
1.1.1.1. 1.1.1.0. strings sc
CANADIAN MI1200 L665CO     (L207)

LEVIN, STEFAN (1964-    )
Archi Per Archi I-III
string orch STIM           (L208)

LEVINSON, GERALD (1951-    )
Five Fires
3(2pic).3.4(clar in E
flat).3(contrabsn). 4.3.3.1.
timp,3perc,pno&cel,harp,strings
[9'] MERION rent           (L209)

Symphony No. 2
5(2pic,alto fl).4(English
horn).4(clar in E flat,bass clar,
contrabass clar).4(contrabsn).
4.4(trp in C).4.1. timp,4-5perc,
cel,pno,harp,strings [40'] MERION
rent                       (L210)

LEWIS, PETER SCOTT (1953-    )
Where The Heart Is Pure
1.1(English horn).1(bass clar).0.
0.0.0.0. strings,Mez solo [16']
(text by Robert Sund) PRESSER
rent                       (L211)

LEWIS, ROBERT HALL (1926-1996)
Scena
strings PRESSER rent       (L212)

LEX see Daugherty, Michael

LEYENDECKER, ULRICH (1946-    )
Concerto for Violin and Orchestra
3(pic,alto fl).2(English
horn).3(clar in E flat,bass
clar).3(contrabsn).alto sax.
4.2.2.0. timp,5perc,harp,cel,
strings [20'] SIKORSKI sc 1953
f.s., sc,pts f.s.          (L213)

Notturno for Solo Voice and Orchestra
2.2.3(bass clar).0+contrabsn.
0.2.2.0. 2perc,cel,pno,strings
[12'] SIKORSKI perf mat rent (L214)

Symphony No. 3
4(pic,alto fl).3(ob d'amore,English
horn).4(clar in E flat,bass
clar).3(contrabsn).soprano
sax.alto sax.tenor sax.
4.3(piccolo trp,flügelhorn).3.1.
timp,5perc,mand,elec gtr,2harp,
cel,pno,strings [32'] SIKORSKI sc
1900 f.s., sc,pts perf mat rent (L215)

Symphony No. 4
4(pic,alto fl).2(English
horn).4(clar in E flat,bass
clar).3(contrabsn). 4.2.2(bass
trom).1. 3-5perc,harp,cel,pno,
strings [11'] SIKORSKI sc 1968
f.s., sc,pts perf mat rent (L216)

LGE see Jansson, Reine

LHOTKA-KALINSKI, IVO (1913-    )
Knopf, Der
2.1.2.1. 2.2.1.0. timp,perc,8vln I,
7vln II,6vla,5vcl,4db [25'] sc
PETERS 02014              (L217)

LI-TAI-PE see Andreae, Hans-Volkmar

LIADOV, ANATOL KONSTANTINOVICH
(1855-1914)
Verzauberte See, Der *Op.62
3.2.3.2. 4.0.0.0. timp,perc,harp,
cel,strings [6'] study sc
BELAIEFF BEL 329          (L218)

LIATOSHINSKY, BORIS (1895-1968)
Slawische Suite
see Suite, Op. 68

Suite, Op. 68
"Slawische Suite" 3.3.3.3. 4.4.3.1.
timp,perc,harp,cel,strings [28']
SIKORSKI perf mat rent     (L219)

LIBERTY BELL MARCH, THE see Sousa, John
Philip

LIBUŠIN SOUD see Smetana, Bedrich

LICHT DES MONDES, DAS see Meijering,
Cord

LICHTEN ET FRICHTE: FANTASY see
Offenbach, Jacques

LICHTENBERGER KONZERT see Thilman,
Johannes Paul

LICHTFLUG see Holszky, Adriana

LIDHOLM, INGVAR (1921-    )
Colores
see Motus

Motus
"Colores" 2(pic).2(English
horn).3(bass clar).2(contrabsn).
2.2.2.1. 8perc,harp,strings,mand,
gtr,cel/glock [15'5'] sc,pts
SUECIA ED.NR 279          (L220)

Riter: Ballet And Concert Suite
2(pic).2(English horn).2(bass
clar).2(contrabsn). 4.3.3.1.
timp,4perc,harp,strings [30'] (I.
Rituelle Tänze; II. Intermezzo;
III. Prozession; IV. Opfertanz 1;
V. Opfertanz 2; VI. Epiloge) sc
UNIVER. ED.NR 13255       (L221)

Ritornello
2(pic).2(English horn).2(bass
clar).2(contrabsn). 2.2.2.1.
timp,4perc,harp,strings [17'] sc
UNIVER. ED.NR 12892       (L222)

Toccata E Canto
1(pic).1.1.1. 0.0.0.0. strings
[14'] sc GEHRMANS          (L223)

Verk
orch STIM                  (L224)

LÍDL, VÁCLAV (1922-    )
Balada O Cervnovém Ránu
3.3.3.3. 4.3.3.1. timp,perc,strings
[13'] CESKY HUD.          (L225)

Concerto for Trumpet
2.2.2.2. 4.1.3.1. timp,perc,
strings,trp solo [18'] CESKY HUD.
(L226)

Radostná Predehra
3.3.3.3. 4.3.3.1. timp,perc,strings
[5'] CESKY HUD.           (L227)

Rapsodia Romantica
2.2.2.2. 4.3.3.1. timp,perc,harp,
strings,pno solo [14'] CESKY HUD.
(L228)

Renata (Waltz for String Orchestra)
string orch [5'] CESKY HUD. (L229)

Serenade for String Orchestra
[13'] CESKY HUD.           (L230)

Suita Rustica
2.2.1.2. 2.2.0.0. timp,strings
[14'] CESKY HUD.          (L231)

Symphony No. 3
2.2.2.2. 4.3.3.1. timp,perc,pno,
strings [20'] CESKY HUD.   (L232)

Waltz for String Orchestra
see Renata

LIEBE HIMMLISCHES GEFÜHL, DER see
Mozart, Wolfgang Amadeus

LIEBENDEN, DIE see Geissler, Fritz

LIEBERMANN, LOWELL
Concerto for Flute, Harp and
Orchestra, Op. 48
0.2.0.0. 2.0.0.0. timp,marimba,
vibra,pno&cel,strings,fl solo,
harp solo [20'] PRESSER rent
(L233)

Concerto for Piccolo and Orchestra,
Op. 50
2.2.2.2. 2.2(trp in C).0.0. timp,
perc,harp,pno,strings,pic solo
[20'] PRESSER rent         (L234)

Kontrapunktus
3(pic).3(English horn).3(bass
clar).3(contrabsn). 4.3.3.0.
timp,4perc,strings, 3 Japanese
drums [15'] PRESSER rent   (L235)

LIEBERMANN, LOWELL (cont'd.)

Revelry  *Op.47
3(pic).2.2.2. 4.3.3.1. timp,3perc,
strings [7'] PRESSER rent  (L236)

LIEBESLIEDER see Henze, Hans Werner

LIEBESLIST see Glazunov, Alexander
Konstantinovich, Ruses D'Amour

LIEBLICHE, HEITERE SOMMERZEIT, DIE see
Lindorff-Larsen, Eilert

LIED DER GHAWAZE see Weingartner,
(Paul) Felix von

LIED DER TÄNZERIN "WECKET DIE FLAMMEN
AUF" see Streicher, Theodore

LIED VOM GEFEITEN OLEG see Rimsky-
Korsakov, Nikolai

LIED VON DER ERDE, DAS see Mahler,
Gustav

LIED VON DER MOLDAU see Cornell, Klaus

LIEDBECK, SIXTEN (1916-    )
Canzonetta
fl,string orch STIM        (L237)

Symfoniska Episoder
2(pic).2(English horn).2.2.
4.2.3.1. timp,perc,harp,strings
[12'] sc STIM             (L238)

LIEDCHEN VON DER SEE, EIN see Röntgen,
Julius

LIEDER DES ABSCHIEDS see Korngold,
Erich Wolfgang

LIEDER UND BALLADEN see Weismann,
Wilhelm

LIEDER UNSERER HEIMAT see Eisbrenner,
Werner

LIFE see Morthenson, Jan W.

LIGETI, GYÖRGY (1923-    )
Mysteries Of The Macabre
2.3(English horn).2(bass
clar).2(contrabsn). 4.2.1.1.
2perc,cel,pno,elec org,harp,mand,
strings,S solo,trp solo [9']
study sc SCHOTTS ED 8205 perf mat
rent                       (L239)

(Howarth, Elgar) 1(pic).1.1(bass
clar).1(contrabsn). 1.1.1.0.
2perc,pno&cel,mand,2vln,vla,vcl
[9'] study sc SCHOTTS ED 8210
perf mat rent              (L240)

LIGHT FANTASTIC, THE see Skempton

LIGHT OF THREE MORNINGS, THE see
Walker, Gwyneth

LIGHTHOUSE see Dreyfus, George see
Tüür, Erkki-Sven

LIGHTNING TAPESTRY see Gellman, Steven

LIKE A SPRING RAIN see Mostad, Jon

LILACS IN THE RAIN see King, Reginald

LILJEHOLM, THOMAS (1944-    )
Tetrachordon
5vln I,4vln II,3vla,2vcl,db [13'5']
sc,pts STIM               (L241)

LILLEBJERKA, SIGMUND (1931-    )
Liten Serenade
string orch [9'] NORSKMI   (L242)

Marmaelen Danser, Der
string orch,timp,perc [15'] NORSKMI
(L243)

Pezzo Umoristico
string orch NORSKMI        (L244)

LIMITATION see Hiscott, James

LINDAHL, THOMAS (1953-    )
Sunes Sommar
orch [30'] STIM            (L245)

Sunes Sommar: En Nämndemans Död
2(pic).2.2.2. 2.1.1.0. timp,perc,
harp,strings [8'] (film music)
sc,pts STIM               (L246)

LINDE, BO (1933-1970)
Concerto Piccolo
see Liten Konsert

Konsertant Musik *Op.27
"Musica Concertante" 2(pic).2.2.2.
2.1.0. timp,perc,strings,xylo
[24'] sc,pts SUECIA        (L247)

LINDE, BO (cont'd.)

Liten Konsert *Op.35
"Concerto Piccolo" woodwind quin,
string orch [17'] sc,pts SUECIA
(L248)

Musica Concertante
see Konsertant Musik

LINDE, HANS-MARTIN (1930-    )
Concerto for Recorder and String
Orchestra
A rec/sopranino rec/B rec solo,
string orch SCHOTTS sc CON 247,
pts CON 247-70          (L249)

LINDGREN, PÄR (1952-    )
Bowijaw
6vln I,6vln II,4vla,3vcl,2db [13']
sc,pts SUECIA          (L250)

Fragments Of A Circle
4(pic).4.5(bass clar).3(contrabsn).
4.4.4.0. 4perc,harp,strings,pno
[28'] STIM sc H-2770, pts  (L251)

Lines & Figurations
see Oaijé

Oaijé
"Lines & Figurations"
3(pic).3(English
horn).3.3(contrabsn). 4.0.3.1.
3perc,strings [15'] SUECIA sc
H-2733, pts          (L252)

Tutu
chamber orch STIM          (L253)

Wing
string orch [11'] sc,pts STIM
(L254)

LINDH, BJÖRN J. (1944-    )
Slapstick And Sweet Sorrows *Suite
2(pic).2.2.2. 2.2.1.1. timp,perc,
strings,pno solo STIM     (L255)

LINDNER, TORSTEN (1968-    )
Kalif Storch *Op.3
2.2.2.2. 2.0.0.0. timp,perc,strings
[30'] SIKORSKI perf mat rent
(L256)

LINDORFF-LARSEN, EILERT (1902-    )
Concerto for Piano and Chamber
Orchestra
see Sommernachtskonzert

Lenz, Der (Overture)
2(pic).2.2.2. 4.3.2.0. timp,perc,
harp,strings [7'] sc,set BUSCH
rent          (L257)

Liebliche, Heitere Sommerzeit, Die
*Variations
"Yndig Og Frydefuld Sommertid, En"
string orch [5'] (on a Danish
folk song) sc,pts BUSCH   (L258)

Overture
see Lenz, Der

Romance for Violin and Orchestra in E
pno,strings,vln solo,opt fl,opt
clar [5'30"] pno-cond sc,pts
BUSCH          (L259)

Sommarnattkonsert
see Sommernachtskonzert

Sommernachtskonzert (Concerto for
Piano and Chamber Orchestra)
"Sommarnattkonsert" 1.1.2.1.
2.0.0.0. timp,strings,pno solo
[7'45"] pno-cond sc,pts BUSCH
rent          (L260)

Yndig Og Frydefuld Sommertid, En
see Liebliche, Heitere Sommerzeit,
Die

LINDPAINTER, PETER JOSEPH (1791-1856)
Sinfonia Concertante, Op. 36, in B
flat for Flute, Oboe, Clarinet,
Horn and Bassoon
(Förster) fl,ob,clar,horn,bsn,orch
KUNZELMANN 10204 ipr     (L261)

LINDROTH, PETER (1950-    )
CU-HU-MU: alef; bet; gimel; dalet
1(pic).1(English horn).1(bass
clar).1. 1.1.1.0. perc,strings,
org/pno [7'-8'] sc,pts STIM
(L262)

Four
3(pic).1.3(bass clar).3(contrabsn).
3.1.3.1. timp,3perc,strings,
harmonium sc STIM     (L263)

Just Listen To Those Violins!
string orch [12'] sc STIM  (L264)

Rite Now
strings,perc,opt electronic tape
[12'5"] pts REIMERS      (L265)

LINDROTH, PETER (cont'd.)

Three
3(pic).3.3(bass clar).3(contrabsn).
4.3.3.1. 3perc,strings,pno [13']
STIM sc H-2809, pts      (L266)

LINE AND TEXTURE see Sexton, Brian

LINES AND LABYRITHS see Palmér,
Catharina

LINES & FIGURATIONS see Lindgren, Pär,
Oaijé

LINIEN see Zechlin, Ruth

LINIEN II see Zechlin, Ruth

LINKA, ARNE (1938-    )
Sinfonietta
3.3.3.3. 4.4.3.1. timp,perc,2harp,
pno,org,cembalo,strings [17']
CESKY HUD.          (L267)

LINKA DUVERY see Odstrcil, Karel

LINKE, ROBERT
Kammermusik Nr. 8
"Tod Des Hasen, Der" 1.0+English
horn.0+bass clar.0. 0.2.0.0.
perc,electronic tape,2vln,2vcl,
2db [13'] sc PETERS 04375 (L268)

Tod Des Hasen, Der
see Kammermusik Nr. 8

LINZER SYMPHONY see Mozart, Wolfgang
Amadeus, Symphony in C, K. 425

LIPSTICK see Ince, Kamran

LIQUID MARBLE see Hillborg, Anders

LIRING BALLADE see Jolas, Betsy

LISCHKA, RAINER (1942-    )
Akzente
3.3.3.3. 4.3.3.1. timp,3perc,harp,
8vln I,7vln II,6vla,5vcl,4db
[22'] sc PETERS 02988     (L269)

LISSAGES see Larson, Chrichan

LISZT, FRANZ (1811-1886)
A La Chapelle Sixtine (from Miserere
of Allegri and Mozart's Ave Verum
Corpus)
2.2.2.2. 4.2.3.1. timp,perc,strings
EMB rent          (L270)

Alpenjäger, Der
2.2.2.2. 2.2.3.0. timp,8vln I,7vln
II,6vla,5vcl,4db [5'] sc KAHNT
04793          (L271)

An Die Künstler
2.2.2.2. 4.4.3.1. timp,perc,harp,
8vln I,7vln II,6vla,5vcl,4db,TTBB
soli [20'] sc KAHNT 01909 (L272)

Ave Maris Stella
(Hahn, A.) 2.2.2.2. 2.2.2.1. timp,
harp,8vln I,7vln II,6vla,5vcl,4db
[10'] sc KAHNT 01910     (L273)

Christus: Overture
3.3.2.2. 4.3.3.1. timp,perc,harp,
org,strings [10'] PETERS  (L274)

Dance Of Death
"Halál Tánc" 2+pic.2.2.2. 2.2.3.1.
timp,perc,strings,pno solo [16']
(paraphrase on dies irae) EMB
rent          (L275)

De Profundis
(Ács, J.) 2.2.2.2. 2.2.3.0. timp,
strings,pno solo [25'] BREITKOPF-
W          (L276)

Faust-Symphonie, Eine
3.2.2.2. 4.2.3.1. timp,perc,org,
strings [70'] KAHNT      (L277)

Halál Tánc
see Dance Of Death

Hungarian Rhapsody No. 6
(Farkas) "Magyar Rapszódia No. 6"
2(pic).2.2.2. 4.2.3.1. timp,perc,
harp,strings [7'] EMB rent (L278)

Lenore, Ballade Vom Bürger
(Woldert) 2.2.2.2. 4.0.3.0. timp,
perc,8vln I,7vln II,6vla,5vcl,4db
[6'] KAHNT 01961     (L279)

Lyon
2(pic).2.2.2. 4.2.3.1. timp,perc,
strings [9'] EMB rent     (L280)

Magyar Rapszódia No. 6
see Hungarian Rhapsody No. 6

LISZT, FRANZ (cont'd.)

Malédiction
pno,orch BOIS          (L281)

Piano Concerti By Liszt (In Full
Score)
orch sc DOVER 25221-3     (L282)

Preludes, Les And Other Symphonic
Poems
orch sc DOVER 28322-4     (L283)

Stanislaus: Salve Polonia
2.2.2.2. 4.2.3.1. timp,8vln I,7vln
II,6vla,5vcl,4db [6'] sc KAHNT
02531          (L284)

Symphony To Danteus "Divina
Commedia", A
3(pic).2+English horn.2+bass
clar.2. 4.2.3.1. timp,perc,2harp&
pno,harmonium,strings,wom cor
[45'] EMB rent          (L285)

Szózat And Hungarian Hymn
"Szózat És Magyar Himnusz" 2.2.2.2.
4.2.3.1. timp,perc,harp,strings
EMB rent          (L286)

Szózat És Magyar Himnusz
see Szózat And Hungarian Hymn

Wilhelm Tell: 3 Lieder
2.2.2.2. 2.2.3.0. timp,8vln I,7vln
II,6vla,5vcl,4db [15'] sc KAHNT
04790          (L287)

LITANIA see Raskatov, Alexander

LITANIAE LAURETANAE see Mozart,
Wolfgang Amadeus

LITEN KONSERT see Linde, Bo

LITEN SERENADE see Lillebjerka, Sigmund

LITEN SYMFONI see Blomberg, Erik

LITTLE CHACONNE see Matthews, David

LITTLE CONCERT see Maw, Nicholas

LITTLE CONCERTINOS see Palas, Rainer,
Pienoiskonserttoja

LITTLE CONQUEROR see Still, William
Grant

LITTLE GRAPE AND LITTLE FISH see
Balassa, Sándor

LITTLE RED RIDING HOOD see Patterson,
Paul

LITTLE ROMANCE, A see Ford, Clifford

LITTLE SIR WILLIAM (from Folk Songs)
(Britten, Benjamin) 2.2.2.2. 2.2.0.0.
timp,strings,high solo [2'30"]
BOOSEY-ENG rent          (L288)

LITTLE SONG THAT WANTED TO BE A
SYMPHONY, THE see Still, William
Grant

LIU, TIES-HAN
Tanz Der Nationalen Minderheiten
3.2.2.2. 4.2.3.1. timp,perc,8vln I,
7vln II,6vla,5vcl,4db [7'] sc
PETERS 00909          (L289)

LIU XIANG see Chan, Ka Nin

LIVERPOOL SUITE see McCartney, Sir
[John] Paul

LIVING TOYS see Ades, Thomas

LLACER "REGOLI", E.
Fantasia Para Castañuelas Y Orquesta
3(pic).2.3(bass clar).2. 4.3.3.1.
timp,3-4perc,strings [9'] PRESSER
rent          (L290)

LLOYD, JONATHAN (1948-    )
Marching To A Different Song
1(pic).1.1(bass clar).1. 1.1.1.0.
perc,2vln,vla,vcl,db,S solo [12']
(text by the composer) BOOSEY-ENG
rent          (L291)

There
string orch,gtr [8'] BOOSEY-ENG
rent          (L292)

Tolerance
4(alto fl,pic).3(English
horn).3(clar in E flat)+bass
clar.3+contrabsn. 6.4(trp in
D).3.1. timp,4perc,strings [20']
BOOSEY-ENG rent          (L293)

Wa Wa Mozart
2.2.2(bass clar).2. 2.0.0.0. pno,
10vln I,8vln II,6vla,4vcl,2db

LLOYD, JONATHAN (cont'd.)

  [5'] (concertante) BOOSEY-ENG
  rent            (L294)

LLOYD WEBBER, ANDREW (1949- )
  Cats: Suite No. 1
    strings FABER f.s. sc,pts 51163 5,
    pts 51213 5         (L295)

  Cats: Suite No. 2
    strings FABER f.s. sc,pts 51165 1,
    pts 51214 3         (L296)

  Memory
    instrumental ensemble sc,pts FABER
    51172 4 f.s.        (L297)

LOBANOV, VASSILY (1947- )
  Concerto for Piano and Chamber
    Orchestra, Op. 35
    3.2.3.3.alto sax. 4.3.3.1. timp,
    3perc,harp,strings [25'] SIKORSKI
    perf mat rent      (L298)

  Concerto for Viola and String
    Orchestra, Op. 52
    [20'] SIKORSKI perf mat rent (L299)

  Concerto for Violin, Clarinet and
    Chamber Orchestra, Op. 65
    see Doppelkonzert, For Violin,
    Clarinet & Chamber Orchestra, Op.
    65

  Concerto for Violin, Violoncello,
    Piano and Chamber Orchestra, Op.
    27
    see Tripelkonzert, For Violin,
    Violoncello, Piano & Chamber
    Orchestra, Op. 27

  Doppelkonzert, For Violin, Clarinet &
    Chamber Orchestra, Op. 65
    (Concerto for Violin, Clarinet
    and Chamber Orchestra, Op. 65)
    2.0.0.2. 2.0.0.0. strings,vln&clar
    soli [20'] SIKORSKI perf mat rent
               (L300)

  Sinfonietta for Chamber Orchestra,
    Op. 47
    1.1.1.1. 1.1.1.0. timp,glock,2vln,
    vla,vcl,db [20'] SIKORSKI perf
    mat rent        (L301)

  Symphony for Chamber Orchestra, No.
    1, Op. 22
    4fl,trp,3perc,harp,cel,hpsd,strings
    [25'] SIKORSKI perf mat rent
               (L302)

  Tripelkonzert, For Violin,
    Violoncello, Piano & Chamber
    Orchestra, Op. 27 (Concerto for
    Violin, Violoncello, Piano and
    Chamber Orchestra, Op. 27)
    1.1.1.1. 1.1.1.1. timp,perc,
    strings,vln&vcl&pno soli [20']
    SIKORSKI perf mat rent  (L303)

LOBGESANG see Mendelssohn-Bartholdy,
  Felix, Symphony No. 2, Op. 52, in B
  flat

LOCATELLI, PIETRO (1695-1764)
  Concerto Grosso, Op. 1, No. 11, in C
    minor
    (Géczy) orch KUNZELMANN 10063
               (L304)

  Concerto No. 1 in D (from L'Arte del
    Violino)
    strings,cont,vln solo [20']
    BOCCACCINI BS. 178 rent  (L305)

  Concerto No. 2 in C minor (from
    L'Arte del Violino)
    strings,cont,vln solo [20']
    BOCCACCINI BS. 179 rent  (L306)

  Concerto No. 3 in F (from L'Arte del
    Violino)
    strings,cont,vln solo [20']
    BOCCACCINI BS. 180 rent  (L307)

  Concerto No. 4 in E (from L'Arte del
    Violino)
    strings,cont,vln solo [20']
    BOCCACCINI BS. 181 rent  (L308)

  Concerto No. 5 in C (from L'Arte del
    Violino)
    strings,cont,vln solo [20']
    BOCCACCINI BS. 182 rent  (L309)

  Concerto No. 6 in G minor (from
    L'Arte del Violino)
    strings,cont,vln solo [20']
    BOCCACCINI BS. 183 rent  (L310)

  Concerto No. 7 in B flat (from L'Arte
    del Violino)
    strings,cont,vln solo [20']
    BOCCACCINI BS. 184 rent  (L311)

  Concerto No. 8 in E minor (from
    L'Arte del Violino)
    strings,cont,vln solo [20']

LOCATELLI, PIETRO (cont'd.)

  BOCCACCINI BS. 185 rent   (L312)

  Concerto No. 9 in G (from L'Arte del
    Violino)
    strings,cont,vln solo [20']
    BOCCACCINI BS. 186 rent  (L313)

  Concerto No. 10 in F (from L'Arte del
    Violino)
    strings,cont,vln solo [20']
    BOCCACCINI BS. 187 rent  (L314)

  Concerto No. 11 in A (from L'Arte del
    Violino)
    strings,cont,vln solo [20']
    BOCCACCINI BS. 188 rent  (L315)

  Concerto No. 12 in D
    see Labirinto Armonico, Il

  Labirinto Armonico, Il (Concerto No.
    12 in D) (from L'Arte del
    Violino)
    strings,cont,vln solo [20']
    BOCCACCINI BS. 189 rent  (L316)

  Weihnachtskonzert *Op.1,No.8
    org,string orch sc,pts KUNZELMANN
    GM 1308 ipa      (L317)

LOCKE, MATTHEW (1630-1677)
  Tempest, The: Incidental Music
    (Dennison) string orch,cont [24']
    perf sc set OXFORD 3653516 (L318)

  Vier Suiten
    8vln I,7vln II,6vla,5vcl,4db [20']
    sc PETERS 02648    (L319)

LOEVENDIE, THEO (1930- )
  Bons
    pic,bass clar,2perc,pno,harp,2vln,
    vla,vcl,db, improviser (any
    instr.) [8'] PEER rent  (L320)

  Concerto for Piano and Orchestra
    2(pic).2(English horn).2(bass
    clar).1+contrabsn. 2.1.1.0.
    3perc,strings,pno solo [20'] PEER
    rent           (L321)

LÖHR, HANNS (1892-1979)
  Königskinder *Waltz
    2.2.2.2. 4.2.2.0. perc,strings,opt
    acord [10'] pts PETERS LICO 86
               (L322)

LOHSE, FRED (1908- )
  Concerto for Clarinet, Trumpet,
    Piano, Timpani, Percussion and
    Strings
    0.0.1.0. 0.1.0.0. timp,perc,pno,
    8vln I,7vln II,6vla,5vcl,4db
    [20'] sc PETERS 02989  (L323)

  Concerto for Trumpet and Orchestra
    2.3.2.2. 2.3.0.0. timp,perc,8vln I,
    7vln II,6vla,5vcl,4db [20'] sc,
    solo pt PETERS 02993  (L324)

  Kammersinfonie
    1.1.1.1. 1.0.0.0. perc,pno,8vln I,
    7vln II,6vla,5vcl,4db [17'] sc
    PETERS 02992     (L325)

  Kleine Suite Nach Alten Weisen
    1.1.1.1. 2.1.0.0. timp,perc,8vln I,
    7vln II,6vla,5vcl,4db [6'] sc
    PETERS 02437     (L326)

  Sinfonia No. 3
    2.2.2.2. 2.2.2.0. timp,perc,pno,
    harp,8vln I,7vln II,6vla,5vcl,4db
    [17'] sc PETERS 04376  (L327)

LOKAJ, JAKUB (1752- ? )
  Aria in D flat
    see Haec Aurora Gratiosa

  Haec Aurora Gratiosa (Aria in D flat)
    (Sesták, Zdenek) [Lat] 0.2.0.0.
    2.0.0.0. org,strings,S solo [5']
    CESKY HUD.       (L328)

LOKOMOTIVE VON MOMBASA, DIE see Thomas-
  Mifune, Werner

LOKSCHIN,ALEXANDER (1920-1987)
  Margarete
    [Ger/Russ] 1.1.2.2. 1.1.1.0. timp,
    perc,harp,strings,S solo [19']
    SIKORSKI perf mat rent  (L329)

  Sinfonia Stretta
    see Symphony No. 4

  Sinfonie (Requiem) (Symphony No. 1)
    [Lat] 3.3.3.3.soprano sax.2alto
    sax.tenor sax. 4.3.3.1. timp,
    perc,2harp,pno/cel,strings,cor
    [30'] CHANT perf mat rent  (L330)

  Symphony No. 1
    see Sinfonie (Requiem)

LOKSCHIN,ALEXANDER (cont'd.)

  Symphony No. 4
    "Sinfonia Stretta" 3.3.4.3.
    4.4.4.0. timp,perc,2harp,strings
    [20'] SIKORSKI perf mat rent
               (L331)

  Symphony No. 5
    [Eng/Russ] string orch,harp,Bar
    solo [15'] SIKORSKI perf mat rent
               (L332)

  Three Scenes From Goethe's Faust
    1.0+English horn.2(clar in E flat)+
    bass clar.2(contrabsn). 1.1.1.0.
    timp,perc,harp,strings,S solo
    [38'] sc SCHOTTS KIN 1002 perf
    mat rent         (L333)

LONDON, EDWIN (1929- )
  Hero Of Our Time, A
    4.3.4.3. 4.4.3.1. timp,4perc,pno,
    harp,8vln I,7vln II,6vla,5vcl,4db
    [17'] sc PETERS 04433  (L334)

  Peter Quince At The Clavier
    3.2.3.2. 4.3.3.1. 3perc,harp,pno&
    cel,10vln I,8vln II,6vla,5vcl,
    3db,T solo [30'] sc PETERS 04014
               (L335)

  Two A'Marvell's For Words
    2.1.3.0. 2.1.1.0. 2perc,harp,pno/
    cel,strings [25'] sc PETERS
    EP 67391        (L336)

LONDON SYMPHONY see Vaughan Williams,
  Ralph

LONDONDERRY AIR see Bridge, Frank,
  Irish Melody, An

LONELY DESERT MAN SEES THE TENTS OF THE
  HAPPY TRIBES, THE see Grainger,
  Percy Aldridge

LONGTIN, MICHEL (1946- )
  De St-Malo À Bourges Par Bouffémont
    3(pic).3(English horn).3(clar in E
    flat,bass clar).3(contrabsn).
    4.4(piccolo trp).3.1. 5perc,
    strings sc CANADIAN
    MI 1100 L857DE    (L337)

  Gaboriau Toupin Ferron Et Les Autres
    2.2.2(bass clar,tenor sax).2.alto
    sax. 3.1.1.0. 3perc,3pno,strings
    sc CANADIAN MI 1100 L857GA (L338)

  Hommage À Euler
    2(pic).2.2.2. 2.2.2.0. timp&perc,
    perc,7vln I,7vln II,5vla,5vcl,4db
    sc CANADIAN MI 1100 L857HO (L339)

  Lettre d'Étienne À Jacques
    2(pic).2.2.2. 2.2.2.0. 2perc,
    strings [20'] sc CANADIAN
    MI 1100 L857LE    (L340)

  Migration Vers L'Automne
    2perc,6vln I,5vln II,4vla,4vcl,2db
    [10'] sc CANADIAN MI1200 L857MI
               (L341)

  Pohjatuuli
    clar&perc,2horn,trp&perc,trom,
    3perc,2vcl,2db [30'] (homage to
    Sibelius) sc,pts CANADIAN
    MI1200 L857PO     (L342)

LÖNNER, ODDVAR (1954- )
  Eines Tages Aus Dem Leben Des Gottes
    Brahma
    2(pic).1(English horn).2(bass
    clar).2(contrabsn). 2.2.1.1.
    perc,harp,strings [20'] NORSKMI
               (L343)

LOOTEN, CHRISTOPHE (1958- )
  In Lumine Lumen [26']
    3.3.3.3. 4.3.3.0. 4perc,timp,
    harp,strings,vln solo
    BILLAUDOT        (L344)

  Mains Ailées, Les [20']
    3.3.3.3. 4.3.2.0. 2perc,harp,vla,
    vcl,db,vln solo
    BILLAUDOT        (L345)

  Palpitaret Haerens [18']
    0.1.1.1. 1.1.1.0. 2perc,harp,vln,
    vla,vcl
    BILLAUDOT        (L346)

LORCA see Theodorakis, Mikis

LORCA REVISITED: PRELUDE AND FOUR
  SCENES see Rosenman, Leonard

LORD MAXWELL'S GOODNIGHT see Grainger,
  Percy Aldridge

LORD PETER'S STABLE BOY see Grainger,
  Percy Aldridge

LORTZING, (GUSTAV) ALBERT (1801-1851)
  Beiden Schützen, Die: Overture
    (Lohse, O.) 2+pic.2.2.2. 4.2.1.0.
    timp,strings [7'] BREITKOPF-W
               (L347)

LORTZING, (GUSTAV) ALBERT (cont'd.)

Opernprobe, Die: Overture
2.2.2.2. 2.2.0.0. timp,strings [5']
BREITKOPF-W (L348)

Undine: Balletmusik
1+pic.2.2.2. 4.2.3.0. timp,2perc,
strings [9'] BREITKOPF-W (L349)

Undine: Hinweg! Hinweg! ...Mir Schien
Der Morgen Aufgegangen
2.2.2.2. 4.2.3.0. timp,strings,T
solo [8'] BREITKOPF-W (L350)

Undine: Overture
2.2.2.2. 4.2.3.1. timp,perc,strings
[9'] BREITKOPF-W (L351)

Waffenschmied, Der: Bringt Eilig Hut
Und Mantel Mir
"Waffenschmied, Der: Stadinger's
Aria" 2.2.2.2. 4.2.3.0. timp,
perc,strings,B solo [7']
BREITKOPF-W (L352)

Waffenschmied, Der: Marie's Aria
see Waffenschmied, Der: Wir Armen,
Armen Mädchen

Waffenschmied, Der: Stadinger's Aria
see Waffenschmied, Der: Bringt
Eilig Hut Und Mantel Mir

Waffenschmied, Der: Wir Armen, Armen
Mädchen
"Waffenschmied, Der: Marie's Aria"
2.2.0.2. 2.0.0.0. strings,S solo
[3'] BREITKOPF-W (L353)

Wildschütz, Der: Komm, Liebes
Gretchen, Bekenne Frei
"Wildschütz, Der: Terzett" 2.2.2.2.
2.0.0.0. strings,STB soli [4']
BREITKOPF-W (L354)

Wildschütz, Der: Terzett
see Wildschütz, Der: Komm, Liebes
Gretchen, Bekenne Frei

Zar Und Zimmermann: Darf Eine Niedere
Magd Es Wagen
"Zar Und Zimmermann: Duet Of Marie
And Iwanow" 2.0.2.2. 4.0.0.0.
strings,ST soli [8'] BREITKOPF-W
(L355)

Zar Und Zimmermann: Duet Of Marie And
Iwanow
see Zar Und Zimmermann: Darf Eine
Niedere Magd Es Wagen

LOS AND ORC: VERK I VI SATSER see
Naessen, Ray

LOST IN SEPTEMBER see Berg, Fred Jonny

LOST LOVE see Mather, Bruce

LOST SOUNDS III see Ishii, Maki

LOTUSBLUME, DIE see Schumann, Robert
(Alexander)

LOUDOVA, IVANA (1941-    )
Concerto Breve
2.0.0.0. 0.0.0.0. timp,perc,xylo,
strings,fl/vln solo [11'] CESKY
HUD. (L356)

Nocturne for Viola and Strings
strings,vla solo [10'] CESKY HUD.
(L357)

LOUEL, JEAN (1914-    )
Concerto
2.2.2.2. 4.3.3.1. timp,perc,cel,
harp,strings,clar solo [17']
BELGE (L358)

LOUIE, ALEXINA (1949-    )
Eternal Earth, The
3(pic,alto fl).3(English
horn).3(bass clar).2+contrabsn.
4.3.3.1. timp,4perc,harp,strings
(1. Summoning The Earth Spirit 2.
To The Ends Of The Earth 3. The
Radiant Universe) sc CANADIAN
MI 1100 L 888ET (L359)

O Magnum Mysterium
string orch [17'] (in memoriam
Glenn Gould) sc CANADIAN
MI 1500 L8880M (L360)

Songs Of Paradise
2(pic).2.2.2. 4.2.2.0. timp,2perc,
strings [14'] sc CANADIAN
MI 1100 L888SO (L361)

LOUTKY see Martinu, Bohuslav (Jan)

LOUVIER, ALAIN (1945-    )
Deux Brèves Et Une Longue
16vcl,vcl solo [4'30"] LEDUC (L362)

LOUVIER, ALAIN (cont'd.)

Itinéraires D'Outre-Rêve
2(pic).0.1+bass clar.0. 1.0.1.1.
3perc,harp,2kbd,vln,vla,vcl,pno
solo LEDUC (L363)

Tutti, Pour Grand Orchestre
Partie I - violins, violas,
percussion I; Partie II - flutes,
oboes, trumpets, percussion II;
Partie III - horns, saxophones,
clarinettes, percussion III;
Partie IV - bassoons, trombones,
tubas, cellos, double basses,
percussion IV LEDUC (L364)

LOVE AFTER LOVE see Bose, Hans-Jurgen
Von

LOVE SONG see Panufnik, Andrzej

LOVE: SONG CYCLE NO.1 see Poynter,
Arthur R.

LOVE SONG OF HAR DYAL, THE see
Grainger, Percy Aldridge

LOVE YOUR ANIMAL see Dreyfus, George

LOVELY ROSALIND, THE see Lumby, Herbert

LOVÉN, BIRGITTA (1933-    )
Holstamp
"Trollpolska" orch STIM (L365)

Trollpolska
see Holstamp

LØVENSKJOLD, HERMAN SEVERIN
Sylphide, La
(Lanchbery) 2+pic.2.2.2. 4.3.2+bass
trom.1. timp,3perc,harp
[70'] perf sc set OXFORD 3653753
sc,pts rent (L366)

LOVERS' ALMANAC, THE see Kyr, Robert

LOWE, WESLEY (1953-    )
Trichrus Musica
3+pic.2.3+bass clar.2. 4.3.3.1.
timp,3perc,cel,strings sc
CANADIAN MI 1100 L913TR (L367)

LOYALISTS SUITE, THE see Crawley,
Clifford

LUCKY, ŠTEPÁN (1919-    )
Concertino Ai Due Boemi
strings,bass clar&pno soli [13']
CESKY HUD. (L368)

Concerto for Bass Clarinet, Piano and
Strings
see Koncertantní Fantazie

Concerto for Orchestra
3.3.3.3. 4.3.3.1. timp,perc,xylo,
harp,strings [17'] CESKY HUD.
(L369)

Koncertantní Fantazie (Concerto for
Bass Clarinet, Piano and Strings)
[8'] CESKY HUD. (L370)

LUDAS MATYI see Szabo, Ferenc

LUDUS STELLARIS see Durko, Zsolt

LUDUS TONALIS see Hindemith, Paul

LUEDEKE, RAYMOND (1944-    )
Concerto for Violin and Orchestra
2(pic).2.(English
horn).2.2(contrabsn). 4.2.3.1.
timp,2perc,pno,strings,opt harp,
vln solo [32'] sc,pno red,solo pt
CANADIAN MI 1311 L948CO (L371)

North Wind's Gift, The
2(pic).2(English horn).2(bass
clar).2(contrabsn). 4.2.3.1.
timp,2perc,pno,strings sc
CANADIAN MI 1100 L948NO (L372)

LUENING, OTTO (1900-1996)
Fantasy for String Orchestra
strings [7'] SCHIRM.EC rent (L373)

Serenade for Flute and Strings
fl solo,strings [8'] SCHIRM.EC rent
(L374)

Serenade for 3 Horns and Strings
3horn,strings [8'] SCHIRM.EC rent
(L375)

Songs, Poem And Dance
fl,strings [10'] SCHIRM.EC rent
(L376)

Two Mexican Serenades
2.2.2.1. 1.0.0.0. 2perc,db [11']
SCHIRM.EC rent (L377)

LUGUBRE see Larsson, Mats

LUKAS, ZDENEK (1928-    )
Bagately
2.2.2.2. 2.2.0.0. timp,perc,strings
[16'] CESKY HUD. (L378)

Canti
[21'] CESKY HUD. (L379)

Concerto for Bassoon and Orchestra
2.2.2.0. 4.2.3.1. timp,perc,pno,
strings,bsn solo [19'] CESKY HUD.
(L380)

Concerto for Cembalo and Strings
strings,cembalo solo [22'] CESKY
HUD. (L381)

Concerto for Flute and Orchestra
0.0.0.0. 3.3.0.1. timp,perc,
strings,fl solo [22'] CESKY HUD.
(L382)

Concerto for Piano and Orchestra
3.2.2.0. 4.2.3.1. timp,perc,
strings,pno solo [22'] CESKY HUD.
(L383)

Concerto for Viola and Orchestra
2.2.2.2. 2.2.0.0. perc,strings,vla
solo [22'] CESKY HUD. (L384)

Concerto for Violin and Orchestra
3.2.2.2. 4.2.3.1. timp,perc,harp,
strings,vln solo [26'] CESKY HUD.
(L385)

Concerto for Violoncello and
Orchestra
3.2.2.2. 4.3.3.1. timp,perc,
strings,vcl solo [23'] CESKY HUD.
(L386)

Concerto Grosso No. 3 for 6 Violins
and Chamber Orchestra
2.2.2.2. 2.0.0.0. strings,6vln soli
[20'] CESKY HUD. (L387)

Finale Festoso
3.2.2.2. 4.2.3.1. timp,perc,strings
[11'] CESKY HUD. (L388)

Hold Mládí
3.2.2.2. 4.2.3.1. timp,perc,
strings, 4(4horn, 3trp, 3trb,
tba) [11'] CESKY HUD. (L389)

Koncertní Hudba
string orch,harp solo [14'] CESKY
HUD. (L390)

Ouvertura Boema
4.2.2.2. 4.3.3.1. timp,perc,strings
[10'] CESKY HUD. (L391)

Preludio E Rondo
string orch,vln solo [9'] CESKY
HUD. (L392)

Promeny
2.1.2.1. 1.1.1.0. timp,strings,pno
solo [20'] CESKY HUD. (L393)

Suite Concertante
0.0.0.0. 1.2.2.0. strings [18']
CESKY HUD. (L394)

Zasadit Strom
string orch,low solo [14'] CESKY
HUD. (L395)

LULLABY FOR A SNOWY NIGHT see
Coulthard, Jean

LULLY, JEAN-BAPTISTE (LULLI)
(1632-1687)
Te Deum  *Overture
2.2.0.2. 0.2.0.0. timp,org,strings
LEDUC (L396)

LUMBY, HERBERT
Lovely Rosalind, The  *Op.11
8vln I,7vln II,6vla,5vcl,4db [4']
sc PETERS 04624 (L397)

LUMINANCE see Saint-Marcoux, Micheline
Coulombe

LUMINATIONS see Wallace, William

LUMINOUS SPACE see Ichiyanagi, Toshi

LUMOR see Jolas, Betsy

LUMSDAINE, DAVID (1931-    )
Arc Of The Stars, The
string orch [22'] sc UNIV.YORK 0081
f.s. (L398)

Aria For Edward John Eyre
chamber orch,electronic tape,
electronic equipment,db solo,S&
narrator [57'] sc UNIV.YORK 0082
f.s. (L399)

Garden Of Earthly Delights, A
3(pic).3(English horn).3(bass
clar).3(contrabsn). 4.4.3.1.
harp,4perc,strings [32'] sc
UNIV.YORK 0028 f.s. (L400)

LUMSDAINE, DAVID (cont'd.)

Hagoromo
  3(pic,alto fl).3(English
  horn).3(clar in E flat,bass
  clar).3(contrabsn). 4.4.3.1.
  6perc,harp,pno,strings [30']
  (harp amplified) sc UNIV.YORK
  0079 f.s.                   (L401)

Kali Dances
  1.1.1.0. 0.1.0.1. pno,vibra,vln,
  vla,vcl,db [21'] sc UNIV.YORK
  0033 f.s.                   (L402)

Mandala 5
  3(pic).3(English horn).3(clar in E
  flat).3(contrabsn). 4.4.3.1.
  harp,4perc,strings [23'] sc
  UNIV.YORK 0037 f.s.         (L403)

Salvation Creek With Eagle
  1.1.1.1. 1.1.1.0. perc,pno,strings
  [18'] sc UNIV.YORK 0077 f.s.
                              (L404)

Shoalhaven
  2.1.2.1. 2.2.2.0. timp,3perc,
  strings [16'] sc UNIV.YORK 0080
  f.s.                        (L405)

Sunflower
  1.1+English horn.1+bass clar.2.
  2.0.0.0. strings [22'] sc
  UNIV.YORK 0078 f.s.         (L406)

LUNAPARK see Dlouhy, Jaromir

LUNDIN, BENGT (1945-    )
Invitura
  3(pic).2.3(bass clar).2(contrabsn).
  4.3.3.1. timp,4perc,strings,pno
  sc,pts STIM                 (L407)

LUNDIN, DAG (1943-    )
Concerto No. 2 for Alto Saxophone and
  Chamber Orchestra
  timp/perc,strings,alto sax solo
  STIM                        (L408)

Concerto No. 2 for Flute
  2.2.2.2. 3.0.0.0. timp,perc,
  strings,fl solo STIM        (L409)

Estländska Bilder
  "Estonian Pictures"
  3(pic).3(English horn).3(bass
  clar).3. 4.3.3.1. timp,4perc,
  harp,strings [61'] (orchestral
  rhapsody in three parts, 1.
  Sommarmorgon; 2. Afton; 3.
  Skördefest) sc STIM         (L410)

Estonian Pictures
  see Estländska Bilder

Jamboree
  1(pic).2.2.2. 3.3.3.1. timp,2perc,
  harp,strings,pno (symphonic
  suite) STIM                 (L411)

Lagersbewrgs-Svit
  2(pic).2.2(bass clar).2. 4.3.3.1.
  timp,3perc,strings sc STIM  (L412)

Sigurd Fafnesbane
  3(pic).3.3(bass clar).3(contrabsn).
  4.4.3.1. timp,4perc,harp,strings
  (symfonisk orkestersvit över
  sörmländsk hällristning) sc STIM
                              (L413)

Till Strkorkesterns Lov  *Suite
  string orch (1. Ostinato; 2.
  Lamentoso 3. Giocoso) sc STIM
                              (L414)

LUNDIN, MORGAN (1926-    )
Interludio
  string orch [3'] sc,pts STIM (L415)

LUNDQUIST, TORBJÖRN (1920-    )
Kroumata Symphony
  see Symphony No. 8

Survival
  see Symphony No. 9 in One Movement

Symphony No. 8
  "Kroumata Symphony"
  3(pic).3(English horn).3(bass
  clar).3(contrabsn). 4.3.3.1.
  timp,4perc,2harp,strings,pno
  [30'] STIM sc H-2732, solo pt
                              (L416)

Symphony No. 9 in One Movement
  "Survival" 2.2.2.2(contrabsn).sax.
  4.3.3.1. timp,3perc,harp,strings,
  pno [20'] sc STIM           (L417)

LUSTAMAS TRÄDGÅRD see Franke-Blom, Lars
  Åke, Symphony No. 2

LUSTIGEN WEIBER VON WINDSOR, DIE:
  BALLETMUSIK see Nicolai, Otto

LUSTSPELSUVERTYR see Eyser, Eberhard,
  Trägen Vinner

LUSTSPIELSUITE see Zilcher, Hermann

LUTHMAN, ARNE (1954-    )
Cirkel Av Rtt Ljus
  fl,ob,string orch [10'] sc,pts STIM
                              (L418)

LUTYENS, ELISABETH (1906-1983)
Cantata  *Op.130
  1(alto fl).1.1(bass clar).0.
  1.1.1.0. harp,perc,vln,vla,vcl,
  db,S solo [16'] sc UNIV.YORK 066
  f.s.                        (L419)
  ob,clar,pno,cel,perc,vln,vla,vcl,
  SABar soli [13'] sc UNIV.YORK 067
  f.s.                        (L420)

Chimes And Cantos  *Op.86
  0.0.0.0. 0.2.2.0. perc,4vln,4db,Bar
  solo [7'] sc UNIV.YORK 059 f.s.
                              (L421)

Concert Aria  *Op.112
  3.2.2.2. 2.2.2.0. harp,pno,cel,
  mand,gtr,timp,2perc,strings,
  female solo [12'] sc UNIV.YORK
  061 f.s.                    (L422)

Concert Aria ("Dialogo")  *Op.142
  1(alto fl).1.1.1. 1.1.3.0. harp,
  timp,perc,strings,S solo [13'] sc
  UNIV.YORK 069 f.s.          (L423)

Echoi  *Op.129
  3.2+English horn.2.0. 2.2.4.0.
  harp,pno,cel,3perc,strings,Mez
  solo [13'] sc UNIV.YORK 065 f.s.
                              (L424)

Elegy Of The Flowers  *Op.127
  1(alto fl).0.1(bass clar).0.
  2.0.2.0. perc,2vln,2vla,vcl,db,T
  solo [13'] sc UNIV.YORK 064 f.s.
                              (L425)

Eos  *Op.108
  1.1.2.1. 2.2.3.0. pno,2perc,strings
  [10'] sc UNIV.YORK 012 f.s.
                              (L426)

Islands  *Op.80
  instrumental ensemble,ST&narrator
  [26'] sc UNIV.YORK 056 f.s.
                              (L427)

Music for Orchestra, No. 4, Op. 152
  1(alto fl).1.1(bass clar).0.
  2.2.2.0. pno,2perc,strings
  without vln [13'] sc UNIV.YORK
  018 f.s.                    (L428)

Novenaria  *Op.67,No.1
  3.3.3.2. 4.4.3.1. harp,perc,strings
  [12'] sc UNIV.YORK 0010 f.s.
                              (L429)

Plenum II  *Op.92
  ob,13inst [23'] sc UNIV.YORK 033
  f.s.                        (L430)

Rapprochement  *Op.144
  1(alto fl).1.1(bass clar).0.
  0.0.0.0. pno,cel,2perc,vln,vla,
  vcl,horn solo,harp solo [12'] sc
  UNIV.YORK 044 f.s.          (L431)

Rondel  *Op.108
  3.2.2.1. 4.2.3.1. harp,pno,cel,
  timp,perc,strings [15'] sc
  UNIV.YORK 013 f.s.          (L432)

Six Bagatelles  *Op.113
  2.1.2.1. 2.2.1.0. harp,pno&cel,
  perc,strings [14'] sc UNIV.YORK
  014 f.s.                    (L433)

Tears Of Night, The  *Op.82
  3instrumental ensemble,
  countertenor&6S [13'] sc
  UNIV.YORK 058 f.s.          (L434)

Tides  *Op.124
  0.0.0+bass clar.0. 3.3.3.0. harp,
  pno&cel,3perc,strings [13'] sc
  UNIV.YORK 016 f.s.          (L435)

Wild Decembers  *Op.149
  0.0.0.0. 2.2.3.0. pno&cel,2perc,
  strings [12'] sc UNIV.YORK 017
  f.s.                        (L436)

Winter Of The World, The  *Op.98
  orch [16'] sc UNIV.YORK 011 f.s.
                              (L437)

LUTZOW-HOLM, OLE (1954-    )
Sounding: Silver In The Wake
  1(pic).1(English horn).1(bass
  clar).1(contrabsn). 1.1.1.0.
  perc,harp,3vln,2vla,2vcl,db [12']
  sc,pts SUECIA               (L438)

Wandering Rocks
  3(pic).3(English horn).3(bass
  clar).3(contrabsn). 4.4.2.2.
  timp,3perc,strings [3'] sc,pts
  STIM                        (L439)

LUX INTIMA FOR CHAMBER ORCHESTRA see
  Nevonmaa, Kimmo

LUZÁNKY see Petr, Zdenek

LYDIAN see Emura, Tetsuji

LYDISCHE NACHT see Diepenbrock, Alphons

LYHANNH see Lavista, Mario

LYON see Liszt, Franz

LYRIC FOR PIANO AND ORCHESTRA see
  Buczynski, Walter

LYRIC II FOR PIANO AND ORCHESTRA see
  Buczynski, Walter

LYRIC INTERMEZZO FOR 15 PLAYERS see
  Perle, George

LYRIC PIECE FOR ORCHESTRA see Crawford,
  Paul

LYRIC SERENADE see Wallace, William

LYRIC SYMPHONY see Coulthard, Jean see
  Stokes, Harvey J.

LYRIC VI see Buczynski, Walter

LYRIC WALTZ see Pitfield, Thomas Baron

LYRICAL STORY see Rossum, Frederic R.
  van

LYRICKÁ SYMFONIE see Srnka, Jiri

LYRICKÉ DIALOGY see Machek, Miloš

LYRICKÉ INTERMEZZO see Hudec, Jiri

LYRICKÉ SCÉNY see Bartoš, Jan Zdenek

LYRICKY POCHOD see Rimón, Jan

LYRISCHES INTERMEZZO see Haas, Joseph

LYRISK SVIT see Gullberg, Olof

# M

MA BERGÈRE see Nivelet

MÁ LÁSKA VELIKÁ see Petr, Zdenek

MAAILMA see Clarke, Kames

MA'AYANI, AMI (1936-   )
Concertino for Harp and String
Orchestra
INTERNAT.S. sc,pts rent, solo pt,
pno red                          (M1)

Concerto Symphonique Pour Harpe Et
Orchestre
harp,orch INTERNAT.S. sc,pts rent,
solo pt,pno red                  (M2)

Sinfonietta On Hebrew Themes
2(pic).2.2.2. 2.2.0.0. timp,perc,
strings [27'] ISRAELI rent       (M3)

MACBETH see Eyser, Eberhard

MACBETH A CARODEJNICE see Smetana,
Bedrich

MACBETH: INCIDENTAL MUSIC see Arnold,
Samuel

MCCARTNEY, SIR [JOHN] PAUL (1942-   )
Liverpool Suite
(Davis, Carl) strings sc,pts FABER
51348 4 f.s.                     (M4)

Standing Stone
3(pic,alto fl).2+English
horn.3(bass clar).2+contrabsn.
4.3.3.1. timp,4perc,pno&cel,harp,
strings,SATB [75'] FABER         (M5)

MCCAULEY, WILLIAM A. (1917-   )
Christmas Carol Fantasia
3(pic).3+English horn.3+bass
clar.2. 4.3.2.1. timp,3perc,harp,
strings [12'] sc CANADIAN
MI 1100 M117CH                   (M6)

Concerto for Piano, No. 1
3(pic).3(English horn).3(bass
clar).3(contrabsn). 4.3.3.1.
timp,3perc,harp,strings,pno solo
sc CANADIAN MI 1361 M123PI       (M7)

Five Miniatures For Bass Trombone,
Harp And Strings
string orch,bass trom,harp [10']
(4th degr., 1. Powerful 2.
Peaceful 3. Prankish 4. Pensive
5. Progressive) sc CANADIAN
MI 1750 M123FI                   (M8)

Holiday In Brazil
4(pic).3+English horn.3+bass
clar.3+contrabsn. 4.3.3.1. timp,
5perc,harp,strings sc CANADIAN
MI 1100 M123HO                   (M9)

Rhapsody for Alto Flute
3(pic).3(English horn).3(bass
clar).3(contrabsn). 4.3.3.1.
timp,2perc,harp,strings,alto fl
solo, (3rd flute optional) sc
CANADIAN MI 1321 M123RH          (M10)

Wilderness
1(alto fl).1+English horn.1.0.
0.0.0.0. perc,harp,acord,strings
without vla [23'] sc CANADIAN
MI 1200 M123WI                   (M11)

MACCOMBIE, BRUCE (1943-   )
Chelsea Tango
orch study sc EUR.AM.MUS. EA00743
                                 (M12)
3(pic).3(English horn).3(bass
clar).3(contrabsn). 4.3.3.1.
timp,3perc,pno,strings [11']
study sc SCHOTTS EA 743 perf mat
rent                             (M13)

Elegy
chamber group study sc EUR.AM.MUS.
EA00765                          (M14)

Leaden Echo And The Golden Echo
orch study sc EUR.AM.MUS. EA00686
                                 (M15)
1.1.1.0. 1.1.1.0. perc,pno,strings,
S solo [16'] (text by Gerard
Manley Hopkins) study sc SCHOTTS
EA 686 perf mat rent             (M16)

Nightshade Rounds
strings,gtr [10'] SCHOTTS perf mat
rent                             (M17)

MCDOUGALL, IAN (1938-   )
Concerto for Clarinet and String
Orchestra
[20'] sc CANADIAN MI 1623 M137CO
                                 (M18)

Ojistoh
2(pic).2.2(bass clar).2. 2.2.1.0.
timp,6vln I,6vln II,4vla,4vcl,
2db,S/Mez solo [26'] sc CANADIAN
MV 1400 M1370J                   (M19)

MACDOWELL, EDWARD ALEXANDER (1861-1908)
Sarazenen, Die; Die Schöne Alda
*Op.30
2+pic.2.2.2. 4.2.3.1. timp,perc,
strings [8'] (two fragments after
the Rolandslied) BREITKOPF-W
                                 (M20)

MÁCHA, OTMAR (1922-   )
Az Vzejdou Veci Nové
see Sinfonietta No. 2

Barokní Predehra
3.3.3.3. 4.3.4.0. timp,perc,strings
[9'] CESKY HUD.                  (M21)

Concerto for Violin and Orchestra
2.2.2.2. 3.3.3.0. timp,perc,
strings,vln solo [20'] CESKY HUD.
                                 (M22)

Concerto Grosso
3.3.3.3. 4.3.3.1. timp,perc,
strings,SMezATBarB soli [20']
CESKY HUD.                       (M23)

Eiréné (Fantasy for Oboe and Strings)
strings,ob solo [10'] CESKY HUD.
                                 (M24)

Fantasy for Oboe and Strings
see Eiréné

Hrubínovy Pohádky
3.2.3.2. 2.2.2.1. timp,perc,harp,
strings,narrator [22'] CESKY HUD.
                                 (M25)

Jubilejní Predehra
0.0.0.0. 4.3.3.1. timp,perc,strings
[8'] CESKY HUD.                  (M26)

Plác Saxofonu
2.1.2.1. 0.0.0.0. tam-tam,strings,
sax solo [7'] CESKY HUD.         (M27)

Putování Jana Amose: Suite
3.2.2.3. 4.4.4.1. timp,perc,harp,
pno,gtr,strings [18'] CESKY HUD.
                                 (M28)

Sinfonietta No. 2
"Az Vzejdou Veci Nové" 3.3.3.3.
4.3.3.1. timp,perc,strings [16']
CESKY HUD.                       (M29)

MACHAULT MON CHOU see Wuorinen, Charles

MACHAUT, GUILLAUME DE (ca. 1300-1377)
Ballade No. 17
(Grainger, Percy Aldridge) strings
BARDIC                           (M30)

Sept Ballades D'Amour
(Wagemans, Peter-Jan) string orch
[18'] sc DONEMUS                 (M31)

MACHAVARIANI, ALEXEI (1913-1995)
Othello: Suite No. 3
see Suite No. 3

Suite No. 3
"Othello: Suite No. 3"
3(pic).3(English horn).3(bass
clar).3(contrabsn).alto sax.
4.3.3.1. timp,perc,2harp,cel,pno,
strings [36'] SIKORSKI perf mat
rent                             (M32)

Symphony No. 2
3(pic).3(English horn).4(clar in E
flat,bass clar).3(contrabsn).
4.3.3.1. timp,perc,2harp,cel,pno,
strings [42'] SIKORSKI perf mat
rent                             (M33)

MACHEK, MILOŠ (1923-   )
Hrátky S Houslemi
2.2.2.2. 4.3.3.1. timp,perc,strings
[4'] CESKY HUD.                  (M34)

Lyrické Dialogy
2.2.2.2. 4.2.3.0. timp,perc,harp,
strings [5'] CESKY HUD.          (M35)

Písen A Tanec
2.2.2.2. 4.0.0.0. timp,perc,harp,
strings,vln solo [4'] CESKY HUD.
                                 (M36)

Svátek Písne *Overture
2.2.2.2. 4.2.3.1. timp,perc,harp,
strings CESKY HUD.               (M37)

Zpev Slavíka
2.2.2.2. 4.2.3.1. timp,perc,harp,
strings,vln solo [3'] CESKY HUD.
                                 (M38)

MACHINES AND DREAMS see Matthews, Colin

MACHONCHY, ELIZABETH
Serenade
see Serenata

Serenata (Serenade)
2.2.2.2. 4.3.3.1. timp,perc,harp,
strings,vln solo [23'] perf sc
set OXFORD 3655411 sc,pts rent
                                 (M39)

MCINTOSH, DIANA (1937-   )
Kiviuq: An Inuit Legend
1(pic).1(English horn).1.1.
0.0.0.0. 2perc,strings,tenor sax&
baritone sax sc CANADIAN
MI 1200 M152KI                   (M40)

MACINTYRE, DAVID (1952-   )
Home
string orch,horn solo sc CANADIAN
MI 1632 M1522HO                  (M41)

MCINTYRE, PAUL (1931-   )
Comedia
2+pic.2.2.2. 2.2.0.0. perc,opt
harp,strings [17'] (based on
musical ideas from Jean-Baptiste
Lully and on the song "Au clair
de la lune") sc CANADIAN
MI 1100 M1525CO                  (M42)

Concertino for Piano and Chamber
Orchestra
see Pieces Of Four

Fanfares For A New Day
3(pic).2.2.3(contrabsn). 4.2.3.1.
timp,perc,strings sc CANADIAN
MI 1100 M1525FA                  (M43)

Pieces Of Four (Concertino for Piano
and Chamber Orchestra)
1.1.1.1. 1.0.0.0. perc,strings,pno
solo (1. Entrance Piece 2. Party
Piece 3. Think Piece 4. Exit
Piece) sc CANADIAN MI 1361 M172PI
                                 (M44)

MACKENZIE, [SIR] ALEXANDER CAMPBELL
(1847-1935)
Kanadische Rhapsodie *Op.67
2.3.2.2. 4.2.3.0. timp,4perc,
strings [17'] BREITKOPF-W        (M45)

MACKEY, STEVEN (1956-   )
Banana-Dump Truck
2(pic).2.2(bass clar).2. 2.2.2.0.
3perc,pno,harp,6vln I,6vln II,
4vla,4vcl,2db,vcl solo [23']
BOOSEY-ENG rent                  (M46)

Deal
1(pic).1(English horn).1(bass
clar).1. 1.1.1.0. perc,harp,
electronic tape,2vln,vla,vcl,db,
elec gtr solo,opt drums solo
[20'] BOOSEY-ENG rent            (M47)

Eating Greens
3(2pic).3(English horn).2+bass
clar(contrabass clar).2+
contrabsn.tenor sax(baritone
sax). 4.3.3.1. timp,harp,pno&cel&
harmonium,strings [18'] BOOSEY-
ENG rent                         (M48)

Tilt
3(2pic).3(English horn).3(alto sax,
contrabass clar).3(contrabsn).
4.3.3.1. timp,4perc,harp,pno,
strings [12'] BOOSEY-ENG rent
                                 (M49)

MACMILLAN, JAMES (1959-   )
...As Others See Us...
1(pic).0.1(bass clar).1(contrabsn).
0.1.0.0. perc,vln,vla,vcl,db
[20'] BOOSEY-ENG rent            (M50)

Berserking, The (Concerto for Piano
and Orchestra)
3(pic).3(English horn).3(bass
clar).3(contrabsn). 4.3.2+bass
trom.1. timp,3perc,cel,harp,14vln
I,12vln II,10vla,8vcl,8db [30']
BOOSEY-ENG rent                  (M51)

Concerto for Percussion and Orchestra
see Veni, Veni, Emmanuel

Concerto for Piano and Orchestra
see Berserking, The

Concerto for Trumpet and Orchestra
see Epiclesis

Confession Of Isobel Gowdie, The
2.2.2.2. 4.3.3.1. timp,2perc,
strings [22'] BOOSEY-ENG rent
                                 (M52)

Epiclesis (Concerto for Trumpet and
Orchestra)
3(pic).3(English horn).3(bass
clar).2+contrabsn. 6.3.3.1. timp,
4perc,14vln I,12vln II,10vla,
8vcl,8db [20'] BOOSEY-ENG rent
                                 (M53)

MACMILLAN, JAMES (cont'd.)

Exorcism Of Rio Sumpúl, The
  1.2.2.1. 2.0.0.0. perc,strings
  [25'] BOOSEY-ENG rent           (M54)

I
  strings,perc,tubular bells,
  thundersheet, steel pans BOOSEY-
  ENG                             (M55)

Sinfonietta
  0(pic)+alto fl.0+English
  horn.0(bass clar)+clar in E
  flat.0+contrabsn.soprano sax.
  1.0+piccolo trp.1.1. 2perc,harp,
  pno,6vln I,6vln II,4vla,4vcl,2db
  [20'] BOOSEY-ENG rent           (M56)

Veni, Veni, Emmanuel (Concerto for
  Percussion and Orchestra)
  2(pic).2(English horn).2(bass
  clar).2(contrabsn). 2.2.1+bass
  trom.0. timp,strings,perc solo
  [25'] BOOSEY-ENG rent           (M57)

Visitatio Sepulchri
  2(pic).2(English horn).2(bass
  clar).2(contrabsn). 2.2.2(bass
  trom).0. timp,perc,strings,SSATTB
  soli, male speaker [40'] BOOSEY-
  ENG rent                        (M58)

MACOUREK, HARRY (1923-    )
  Cikánská Rapsodie
  2.2.2.2. 4.3.3.0. timp,perc,strings
  [5'] CESKY HUD.                 (M59)

  Prázdninová Predehra  *Op.74
  2.2.2.2. 4.3.3.1. timp,perc,strings
  [6'] CESKY HUD.                 (M60)

  Prazská Nokturna  *Op.81
  string orch [13'] CESKY HUD.    (M61)

  Serenade for Guitar and String
  Orchestra, Op. 73
  [13'] CESKY HUD.                (M62)

MCPEEK, BENJAMIN D. (1934-1981)
  Concerto for Piano, No. 1
  2(pic).3(English horn).2.2.
  4.3.3.1. timp,3perc,harp,strings,
  pno solo [30'] sc CANADIAN
  MI 1361 MI72PI                  (M63)

MCPHERSON, GORDON
  Ebb
  timp,5perc,harp,cel,strings perf sc
  set OXFORD 357799 sc,pts rent   (M64)

  Effective Mythologies
  orch,vln solo perf sc set OXFORD
  3657589 sc,pts rent             (M65)

  Haar
  timp,perc,harp,strings,vla solo
  [20'] perf sc set OXFORD 3657570
  sc,pts rent                     (M66)

  Heh! Voltaire!
  1.1.1.1. 1.2.2.0. 2sax,2perc,pno,
  elec bass gtr,2vln,vla,vcl,db
  [15'] perf sc set OXFORD 3578069
  sc,pts rent                     (M67)

MAD HORSE, A see Sandgren, Joakim

MADAME CHRYSANTHÈME: BALLET MUSIC see
  Rawsthorne, Alan

MÄDCHEN KAM VOM STELLDICHEIN see
  Sibelius, Jean, Flickan Kom Ifrån
  Sin Älsklings Möte

MÄDCHEN NINETTE, DAS: SCÈNES DE BALLET
  see Schaefers, Anton

MÄDCHEN, SO TREIBT IHR'S MIT ALLEN see
  Mozart, Wolfgang Amadeus, Donne
  Mie, La Fate A Tanti

MADJERA, GOTTFRIED (1905-1980)
  Fantasy for Orchestra
  see Petersburger Skizzen

  Petersburger Skizzen (Fantasy for
  Orchestra)
  2(pic).2.2.2. 3.2.3.1. timp,perc,
  strings [14'] SIKORSKI perf mat
  rent                            (M68)

MADNESS AND THE MOONWOMAN see Lann,
  Vanessa

MADRIGALESCO see Vivaldi, Antonio,
  Concerto for String Orchestra in D
  minor, Op. 54, No. 1, P. 86

MADSEN, TRYGVE (1940-    )
  Concerto for Bassoon and Orchestra
  2(pic).2(English horn).2(bass
  clar).1. 0.0.0.0. timp,2perc,
  strings,bsn solo NORSKMI        (M69)

MADSEN, TRYGVE (cont'd.)

Salvador Dali: A Symphonic Portrait
  see Salvador Dali: Et Symfonisk
  Portrett

Salvador Dali: Et Symfonisk Portrett
  *Op.77
  "Salvador Dali: A Symphonic
  Portrait" 3(pic).2.2.2.
  4.3.3(bass trom).1. timp,2perc,
  strings MUSIKK                  (M70)

Symphony No. 2, Op. 66
  3(pic).2.2.2. 4.2.3.1. 2perc,
  strings MUSIKK                  (M71)
  3(pic).2.2.2. 4.2.3.1. 2perc,
  strings NORSKMI                 (M72)

MAELSTROM FOR SOPRANO AND CHAMBER
  ORCHESTRA see Kyr, Robert

MAESTOSA SUONATA SENTIMENTALE see
  Paganini, Niccolo

MAESTOSO see Gropp, Johann-Maria

MAEYER, JAN DE
  Concertino for Clarinet and Strings,
  Op. 30a
  [13'] BELGE                     (M73)

  Concerto Grosso, Op. 23
  see Tricromia Arcangelica

  Tricromia Arcangelica (Concerto
  Grosso, Op. 23)
  2.1.2.2. 4.2.3.1. timp,2perc,harp,
  strings,ob&clar&bsn soli [23'30"]
  BELGE                           (M74)

MAGE, LE: AIRS DE BALLET see Massenet,
  Jules

MAGGIO, ROBERT (1964-    )
  Dorian Prelude
  3(pic).2.2(clar in E flat).3.
  4.3.3.1. timp,3perc,pno,strings
  [10'] PRESSER rent              (M75)

  Hand-Prints Of Sorcerers
  2(pic).2.2.2. 4.3.3.1. timp,2perc,
  strings [12'] PRESSER rent      (M76)

  Imaginary Dances
  3(pic).3.3(bass clar).3. 4.3.3.1.
  timp,4perc,pno&cel,harp,strings
  [34'] PRESSER rent              (M77)

  Symphony Of Memory, A
  3(pic).3(English horn).3(clar in E
  flat,bass clar).3(contrabsn).
  4.3.3.1. 3perc,pno&cel,harp,
  strings [32'] PRESSER rent      (M78)

  Tragicomedy
  1(pic).1.1(bass clar).1. 1.1.1.0.
  2perc,pno,2vln,vla,vcl,db [22']
  PRESSER rent                    (M79)

MAGI, FORTUNATO
  Preludio
  2+pic.2.2.2. 4.0.3.1. timp,strings
  KUNZELMANN ipa sc 10279A, oct
  10279                           (M80)

MAGIC WARDROBE, THE: CONCERT OVERTURE
  see Farkas, Ferenc

MAGIKON see Bodorova, Sylvie

MAGJAR VIGADÒ
  2.2.2.2. 4.2.3.1. timp,perc,pno,harp,
  strings [4'] SCHOTTS perf mat rent
                                  (M81)

MAGNIFICO see Dmitriev, Sergej

MAGOG: FÜNF ORCHESTERSTÜCKE see
  Engelmann, Hans Ulrich

MAGYAR RAPSZÓDIA NO. 6 see Liszt,
  Franz, Hungarian Rhapsody No. 6

MAGYAR RONDÓ see Kodály, Zoltán,
  Hungarian Rondo

MAGYAR SZVIT see Patachich, Ivan,
  Hungarian Suite

MAGYAR TÁNCOK A XVI. SZÁZADBÓL see
  Ranki, György, Hungarian Dances
  From The 16th Century

MAHARAL DREAMING see Casken, John

MAHLER, GUSTAV (1860-1911)
  Lied Von Der Erde, Das
  orch,solo voice sc DOVER 25657-X
                                  (M82)
  (Riehn, Rainer) "Song Of The Earth"
  1+pic.1+English horn.1+clar in E
  flat.1. 1.0.0.0. 2perc,harmonium&
  cel,pno,vln I,vln II,vla,vcl,db,
  AT soli [60'] BELMONT           (M83)

MAHLER, GUSTAV (cont'd.)

Song Of The Earth
  see Lied Von Der Erde, Das

Songs Of Wayfarer And
  Kindertotenlieder
  orch,solo voice sc DOVER 26318-5
                                  (M84)

Symphony, No. 7
  (facsimile, documentation) FABER
  51591 6 f.s.                    (M85)
  orch (in full score) sc DOVER
  27339-3                         (M86)

Symphony No. 8
  orch sc DOVER 26022-4           (M87)

Symphony No. 9
  orch (in full score) sc DOVER
  27492-6                         (M88)

Symphony, Nos. 1-2
  orch sc DOVER 25473-9           (M89)

Symphony, Nos. 3-4
  orch sc DOVER 26166-2           (M90)

Symphony, Nos. 5-6
  orch sc DOVER 26888-8           (M91)

MAID OF THE MIST see Barnes, Milton

MAILLART, LOUIS AIME (1817-1871)
  Dragons De Villars, Les  *Overture
  "Glöckchen Des Eremiten, Das"
  2.2.2.2. 4.2+2cornet.3.0. timp,
  perc,strings [4'] (no score)
  BREITKOPF-W                     (M92)

  Glöckchen Des Eremiten, Das
  see Dragons De Villars, Les

MAINS AILÉES, LES see Looten,
  Christophe

MAÎTRE DE CHAPELLE, LE: OVERTURE see
  Cimarosa, Domenico

MAÎTRE PERONILLA: OVERTURE see
  Offenbach, Jacques

MAJDALENKA A VÍTR see Marík, A.F.

MAJESTAS CAROLINA see Krcek, Jaroslav

MAJESTÉ DU CHRIST DEMANDANT SA GLOIRE À
  SON PÈRE see Messiaen, Olivier

MAJOR ORCHESTRAL WORKS see Mendelssohn-
  Bartholdy, Felix

MÁJOVÁ PREDEHRA see Dlouhy, Jaromir

MÁJOVÉ RONDO see Krízek, Zdenek

MAKU see Knipper, Lev Konstantinovich

MALÁ INSTRUMENTÁLNÍ ETUDA see Malásek,
  Jirí

MALÁ KONCERTNÍ HUDBA see Jirasek, Ivo

MALÁ PROCHÁZKA see Svehla, Antonin

MALÁ SERENÁDA see Svatos, Vladimír

MALÁ SUITA see Palkovsky, Oldrich

MALÁ SVITA see Hurník, Ilja

MALAGUENA, FOR VIOLIN AND ORCHESTRA see
  Sarasate, Pablo de

MÄLAR-OAR see Winter, Tomas

MALÁSEK, JIRÍ (1927-1983)
  Malá Instrumentální Etuda
  2.0.3.0. 0.2.0.0. perc,harp,pno,
  2gtr,strings,tenor sax solo [4']
  CESKY HUD.                      (M93)

  Setkání Ve Snech
  fl,perc,strings,pno solo [5'] CESKY
  HUD.                            (M94)

MALAT, JAN (1843-1915)
  Slavnostní Pochod Národní
  2.2.2.2. 4.3.3.0. perc,strings [6']
  CESKY HUD.                      (M95)

  Z Ceskych Zpevu  *Overture
  2.2.2.2. 4.2.3.0. timp,perc,strings
  CESKY HUD.                      (M96)

MALCÁT, JOSEF (1723-1760)
  Symphony in D
  (Trojan, Jan) strings,cont CESKY
  HUD.                            (M97)

  Symphony in G
  (Trojan, Jan) strings,cont CESKY
  HUD.                            (M98)

MALDERE, PIERRE VAN (1729-1768)
Six Symphonies A Più Strumenti, Opus 4
(Lister, Craig) 0.2.0.0. 2.0.0.0.
vln I,vln II,vla,db,cont set A-R
ED ISBN 0-89579-248-6 f.s.
contains: Symphony in B flat, Op.
4, No. 3; Symphony in C, Op. 4,
No. 2; Symphony in D, Op. 4,
No. 6; Symphony in E flat, Op.
4, No. 5; Symphony in G minor,
Op. 4, No. 1; Symphony in G,
Op. 4, No. 4 (M99)

Symphony in B flat, Op. 4, No. 3
see Six Symphonies A Più Strumenti,
Opus 4

Symphony in C, Op. 4, No. 2
see Six Symphonies A Più Strumenti,
Opus 4

Symphony in D, Op. 4, No. 6
see Six Symphonies A Più Strumenti,
Opus 4

Symphony in E flat, Op. 4, No. 5
see Six Symphonies A Più Strumenti,
Opus 4

Symphony in G minor, Op. 4, No. 1
see Six Symphonies A Più Strumenti,
Opus 4

Symphony in G, Op. 4, No. 4
see Six Symphonies A Più Strumenti,
Opus 4

MALÉ ETUDY PRO MALÉHO DIRIGENTA see
Smutny, Jirí

MALÉDICTION see Liszt, Franz

MALEK, JAN (1938- )
Concerto for Piano and Chamber
Orchestra
"Dva Grafické Znaky" 2.1.2.1.
1.1.1.0. timp,strings,pno solo
[20'] CESKY HUD. (M100)

Divertimento for Strings
see Páví Pero

Divertimento No. 2
"Quasi Concertante" 0.0.2.0.
0.2.0.0. strings [13'] CESKY HUD. (M101)

Dva Grafické Znaky
see Concerto for Piano and Chamber
Orchestra

Páví Pero (Divertimento for Strings)
[12'] CESKY HUD. (M102)

Quasi Concertante
see Divertimento No. 2

Sinfonia Su Una Cantilena
3.3.3.3. 6.3.3.0. timp,perc,xylo,
harp,pno,strings [24'] CESKY HUD. (M103)

Symphony No. 2
1.2.0.1. 2.0.0.0. strings [33']
CESKY HUD. (M104)

MALER, WILHELM (1902-1976)
Concerto for Violin in A
2(pic).2(English horn).2(bass
clar).2(contrabsn). 4.2.3.1.
timp,strings,vln solo SCHOTTS
perf mat rent (M105)

Concerto Grosso, Op. 11
"Orchesterspiel II" 4vln I,4vln II,
3vla,2vcl,db,fl&pic solo,bsn
solo,pno&vln&vla&vcl soli SCHOTTS
perf mat rent (M106)

Concerto, Op. 10
1(pic).1(English horn).1.1.
1.0.0.0. perc,strings,hpsd&pno
solo [18'] SCHOTTS perf mat rent (M107)

Orchesterspiel II
see Concerto Grosso, Op. 11

MALIGE, FRED (1895- )
Über Oder Und Neisse
3.2.2.2. 5.2.3.1. timp,perc,8vln I,
7vln II,6vla,5vcl,4db [15'] sc
PETERS 02996 (M108)

MALINCHE, LA see Barker, Paul

MALMBORG-WARD, PAULA AF (1962- )
Corpus
2(pic).2.3(bass clar).2(contrabsn).
4.2.3.1. timp,2perc,harp,strings
[6'] sc,pts STIM (M109)

Tnk Om Man Hade En Tidsmaskin
string orch [5'] sc,pts STIM (M110)

MALMLÖF-FORSSLING, CARIN (1916- )
Flowings
4.4.4.4. 4.4.3.1. timp,3perc,harp,
strings [9'5"] STIM sc H-2280,
pts (M111)

Release
string orch [9'] (1. Andante; 2.
Allegro con spirito; 3. Adagio
funebre) sc,pts STIM (M112)

Shanti, Shanti
2.2.2.2. 2.2.2.1. timp,2perc,
strings,S solo [12'5"] STIM sc
H-2586, pts (M113)

MALOVÁNÍ PRO SMYCCE see Rimón, Jan

MALUNGSVIT see Forsberg, Roland

MAMA LIKES POYOPOYO-ZAURS see Maruyama,
Kazunori

MÁME ZELENOU see Strasek, Emil

MAMLOK, URSULA (1928- )
Concertino
1.1.1.1. 1.0.0.0. perc,2vln,vla,
vcl,db [11'] sc PETERS 04042 (M114)

MAM'ZELLE QUÉBÉCOISE see Coulthard,
Jean

MANAS see Montgomery, James

MANDALA 5 see Lumsdaine, David

MANDOLINE see Faure, Gabriel-Urbain

MANFREDINI, FRANCESCO (1680-1748)
Concerti, Nos. 1-3
see Dodici Concerti - Opera Terza:
Heft I

Concerti, Nos. 4-6
see Dodici Concerti - Opera Terza:
Heft II

Concerti, Nos. 7-9
see Dodici Concerti - Opera Terza:
Heft III

Concerti, Nos. 10-12
see Dodici Concerti - Opera Terza:
Heft IV

Concerto
1-2trp,2vln,vla,vcl,db,hpsd
KUNZELMANN ipa sc 10218A, oct
10218 (M115)

Dodici Concerti - Opera Terza: Heft I
2vln,cont,strings MULL & SCH f.s.
contains: Concerti, Nos. 1-3 (M116)

Dodici Concerti - Opera Terza: Heft
II
2vln,cont,strings MULL & SCH f.s.
contains: Concerti, Nos. 4-6 (M117)

Dodici Concerti - Opera Terza: Heft
III
2vln,cont,strings MULL & SCH f.s.
contains: Concerti, Nos. 7-9 (M118)

Dodici Concerti - Opera Terza: Heft
IV
2vln,cont,strings MULL & SCH f.s.
contains: Concerti, Nos. 10-12 (M119)

Weihnachtskonzert
pno,8vln I,7vln II,6vla,5vcl,4db,
2vln soli [12'] sc KAHNT 04510 (M120)

MANGROVE see Sculthorpe, Peter [Joshua]

MANHATTAN CONCERTO FOR ORCHESTRA see
Matthus, Siegfried

MANHATTAN SINFONIETTA see Paulus,
Stephen Harrison

MANITOBA MEMOIR see Turner, Robert
[Comrie]

MANN, LESLIE (1923- )
My Master Hath A Garden *Op.141,
cant
1.1.1. 1.0.0.0. harp,string orch/
string quin,high solo [18'] (1.
Prelude (Instrumental) 2. My
Master Hath A Garden 3. Allegro
Giusto (Instrumental) 4. Even
Such Is Time - Sir Walter Raleigh
5. Drop, Drop Slow Tears -
Phineas Fletcher) sc CANADIAN
MV 1246 M281MY (M121)

Weep You No More Sad Fountains
*Op.36
2.2.2.2. 2.1.1.0. timp,perc,
strings,solo voice [19'] (7 songs
to elizabethan poems) sc CANADIAN
MV 1273 M281WE (M122)

MANON LESCAUT, PRELUDIO ATTO II see
Puccini, Giacomo

MANSURIAN, TIGRAN (1939- )
"...And Then I Was In Time Again"
5vln I,5vln II,4vla,3vcl,db,vla
solo [20'] sc,solo pt BELAIEFF
04508 (M123)

Da Ich Nicht Hoffe (In Memoriam Igor
Strawinsky)
1.1.1.1. 1.1.1.0. 2perc,cel/pno,
2vln,vla,vcl [10'] SIKORSKI perf
mat rent (M124)

Postlude for Clarinet, Violoncello
and Strings
strings,clar solo,vcl solo [12']
BELAIEFF (M125)

MANTRA FÜR STREICHORCHESTER MIT "VIOLON
FOU" see Schweizer, Alfred

MANUEL, ROLAND
see ROLAND-MANUEL, ALEXIS

MANUELA see Svehla, Antonin

MARAT, ZDENEK (1931- )
Dnes Uz Vim (from Musical "Pohádka
Mého Zivota")
2.2.2.2. 4.3.3.0. perc,harp,
strings,S solo [3'] CESKY HUD. (M126)

Na Nádvorí (Polonaise for Orchestra)
2.2.2.2. 4.2.3.0. timp,perc,harp,
strings [4'] CESKY HUD. (M127)

Polonaise for Orchestra
see Na Nádvorí

Serenade for Trumpet
2.2.2.2. 3.0.3.0. timp,perc,harp,
strings,trp solo [4'] CESKY HUD. (M128)

MARATHON, LE see Petitgirard, Laurent

MARCELLO, ALESSANDRO
(ca. 1684-ca. 1750)
Concerto
"Concerto Di Flauti" 2S rec&2vln/2A
rec&vla/2T rec&vla,bass fl,vcl,
cont sc,pts KUNZELMANN GM 1265
ipa (M129)

Concerto Di Flauti
see Concerto

Concerto for Oboe, Strings and
Continuo
[9'] PETERS (M130)

MARCH: HISTORY OF THE ENGLISH SPEAKING
PEOPLES see Walton, [Sir] William
(Turner)

MARCH PAST OF THE KITCHEN UTENSILS see
Vaughan Williams, Ralph

MARCH TO THE PROCESSION OF FLAGS see
Vidovszky, Laszlo

MARCHANT SUITE see Rieti, Vittorio

MARCHE FUNÉBRE POUR LE GÉNÉRAL HOCHE
see Paisiello, Giovanni

MARCHE MILITAIRE see Goldschmidt,
Berthold

MÄRCHEN see Enna, August

MÄRCHEN, EIN see Nicode, Jean Louis

MÄRCHEN VOM POPEN UND SEINEM KNECHT
BALDA, DAS: SUITE see Shostakovich,
Dmitri

MÄRCHEN VON FANFERLIESCHEN
SCHÖNEFÜSSCHEN, DAS:
VERWANDLUNGSMUSIK see Schwertsik,
Kurt

MARCHING IN see Perera, Ronald
Christopher

MARCHING TO A DIFFERENT SONG see Lloyd,
Jonathan

MARCIA FUNEBRE see Suter, Robert

MARCO, TOMAS (1942- )
Campo De Estrellas
3.3.3.3. 4.3.3.1. timp,3perc,harp,
strings [11'] perf sc EMEC f.s. (M131)

Concerto for Guitar and String
Orchestra
see Guadiana

Guadiana (Concerto for Guitar and
String Orchestra)
4vln,2vla,2vcl,db [14'] sc ALPUERTO
1199 (M132)

MARCO, TOMAS (cont'd.)

Sinfonia, No. 5
3.3.3.3. 4.3.3.1. timp,3perc,harp,
cel,strings [32'] perf sc EMEC
f.s.　　　　　　　　　　　　(M133)

MARESCOTTI, ANDRÉ FRANÇOIS (1902-　　)
Concert Carougeois No. 4
strings [22'] JOBERT　　　　(M134)

MAREZ OYENS, TERA DE (1932-1996)
Concerto for Alto Saxophone
3.3.2.2. 4.3.3.1. timp,3perc,
strings,alto sax solo [20'] sc
DONEMUS　　　　　　　　　　(M135)

Interface
string orch [12'] sc DONEMUS (M136)

Unison
2.2.3.2. 4.3.3.1. timp,3perc,harp,
strings [20'] sc DONEMUS　(M137)

MARGARETE see Lokschin,Alexander

MARGARITAS TRAUM see Höller, York

MÁRGUEZ, ARTURO (1950)
Danzón No. 2
2.2.2.2. 4.2.3.1. 4perc,pno,strings
[10'30"] PEER rent　　　　(M138)

Danzón No. 3
0.0.2.0. 2.0.0.0. 2perc,strings,fl&
gtr soli [13'] PEER rent　(M139)

Paisajes Bajo El Signo De Cosmos
"Passages Under The Sign Of Cosmos"
2.2.2.2. 4.2.3.1. 5perc,harp,
strings [10'] PEER rent　(M140)

Passages Under The Sign Of Cosmos
see Paisajes Bajo El Signo De
Cosmos

MARIGOLD GARDEN see Amos, Keith

MARÍK, A.F. (1921-　　)
Majdalenka A Vítr
3.2.2.2. 2.2.3.1. timp,perc,
strings,speaking voice [10']
CESKY HUD.　　　　　　　　(M141)

Polka Jede
3.2.2.2. 2.2.1.0. timp,perc,
strings,speaking voice [4'] CESKY
HUD.　　　　　　　　　　　　(M142)

Romance o Karlu IV
2.2.2.1. 2.3.1.0. timp,perc,
strings,speaking voice [5'] CESKY
HUD.　　　　　　　　　　　　(M143)

MARIMBA CONCERTO: AFTER HAMPTON see
Larsen, Elizabeth B. (Libby),
Concerto for Marimba

MARINA, CRISTIAN (1965-　　)
Allegoria
4(pic).3.4(bass
clar).4(contrabsn).4sax. 4.3.3.1.
timp,3perc,harp,strings,pno/
cembalo [9'5"] sc STIM　　(M144)

High Anxiety
1(pic).1(English horn).1(bass
clar).1. 1.1.1.0. 2perc,harp,
strings,pno/cel [8'] sc STIM
　　　　　　　　　　　　　　(M145)

Mirabilis
1(pic).1(bass clar).1.sax.
1.1.1.0. timp,2perc,strings,pno/
cel [10'] sc,pts STIM　　(M146)

MARION see Dreyfus, George

MARK OF CAIN, THE see Stevens, Bernard
George

MARKEVITCH, IGOR (1912-1983)
Psaume-Tehillim
2+pic.1+clar in E
flat.2(contrabsn). 1.1+
flügelhorn.1.1. timp,4perc,cel,
pno,4vln,4vla,3vcl,2db,S solo,
optional unison chorus of 6
sopranos [22'] BOOSEY-ENG rent
　　　　　　　　　　　　　　(M147)

MARKYZA DE POMPADOUR see Vacek, Miloš

MARMAELEN DANSER, DER see Lillebjerka,
Sigmund

MAROS, RUDOLF (1917-1982)
Concertino for Bassoon and Orchestra
2(pic).2.2.2. 4.2.2.0. timp,perc,
harp,strings,bsn solo [15'] EMB
rent　　　　　　　　　　　　(M148)

Contrasts
"Ellentétek" 1.1.1+bass clar.1.
0.0.0.0. perc,harp,strings [9']
EMB rent　　　　　　　　　　(M149)

MAROS, RUDOLF (cont'd.)

Ellentétek
see Contrasts

Fragment
"Töredék" 2(pic).2.2.2. 4.2.2.1.
timp,perc,harp,strings [8'] EMB
rent　　　　　　　　　　　　(M150)

Kaleidoscope
"Kaleidoszkóp" 1.1.2(bass clar).1.
1.0.0.0. perc,cimbalom,harp,hpsd,
strings [6'] EMB rent　　(M151)

Kaleidoszkóp
see Kaleidoscope

Lament
1(alto fl).1.1.1. 0.0.0.0. perc,
harp,strings,S solo [3'] EMB rent
　　　　　　　　　　　　　　(M152)

Töredék
see Fragment

MARRIAGE WITH A SPACE, A see Becker,
John

MARS see Pichl, Wenzel (Vaclav),
Sinfonia in D

MARSCH DER PRIESTER see Mozart,
Wolfgang Amadeus

MARSCH KARLS XII. see Kajanus, Robert

MARSCHNER, HEINRICH (AUGUST)
(1795-1861)
Hans Heiling: An Jenem Tag　*Op.80
"Hans Heiling: Aria Of Hans"
2.2.2.2. 4.0.0.0. strings,Bar
solo [4'] (no score) BREITKOPF-W
　　　　　　　　　　　　　　(M153)

Hans Heiling: Aria Of Hans
see Hans Heiling: An Jenem Tag

Vampir, Der: Overture　*Op.42
2.2.2.2. 4.2.3.0. timp,strings [8']
(no score) BREITKOPF-W　　(M154)

MARSH, ROGER (1949-　　)
Kagura
(13 instruments) NOVELLO　　(M155)

Stepping Out
4.3.4.3. 4.4.3.1. 3perc,harp,pno,
strings [12'] NOVELLO　　(M156)

MARSIK, EMANUEL (1875-1936)
Studentská Láska　*Overture
2.2.2.2. 3.3.3.0. timp,perc,strings
[6'] CESKY HUD.　　　　　　(M157)

Symphony in D minor,Scherzo
3.2.2.2. 4.3.3.1. timp,perc,harp,
strings CESKY HUD.　　　　(M158)

MARŠÍK, OTAKAR (1913-　　)
Honza Králem
2.2.2.2. 2.2.0.0. timp,perc,strings
[8'] CESKY HUD.　　　　　　(M159)

Ireniny Melodie
2.2.2.2. 3.2.2.0. timp,perc,harp,
strings [10'] CESKY HUD.　(M160)

MÅRTENSSON, PER (1967-　　)
Till-Flykt
2(pic).2.2(bass clar).2. 2.2.0.0.
timp,6vln I,5vln II,4vla,3vcl,2db
[13'] sc,pts STIM　　　　(M161)

Undervegetation
2(pic).2.2(bass clar).2. 2.2.0.0.
2perc,strings [7'5"] sc,pts STIM
　　　　　　　　　　　　　　(M162)

MARTERN ALLER ARTEN see Mozart,
Wolfgang Amadeus

MARTI, HEINZ (1934-　　)
Appel De La Nuit
2.1.2(bass clar).2. 0.0.2.0. timp,
perc,harp,strings,horn solo [12']
solo pt,pno red HUG GH 11564
　　　　　　　　　　　　　　(M163)

Canto Che Si Spegne
see Concerto for Violin, String
Orchestra and 2 Percussionists

Concerto for Organ, String Orchestra,
Trumpet, Timpani and Percussion
[13'] HUG　　　　　　　　　(M164)

Concerto for Violin, String Orchestra
and 2 Percussionists
"Canto Che Si Spegne" [17'] HUG
　　　　　　　　　　　　　　(M165)

Mask Für 3 Orchestergruppen
1.0+English horn.1.1. 1.1.1.0.
2perc,harp,6vln I,6vln II,6vln
III,6vla,5vcl,2db [12'] HUG
　　　　　　　　　　　　　　(M166)

Nuit D'Insomnie
perc,string orch/11strings soli
[13'] HUG　　　　　　　　　(M167)

MARTI, HEINZ (cont'd.)

Reflections
strings [10'] (four movements) HUG
　　　　　　　　　　　　　　(M168)

Wachsende Bedrohung
3.3(English horn).3.3. 4.3.3.1.
timp,perc,strings [12'] HUG
　　　　　　　　　　　　　　(M169)

MARTIN, FRANK (1890-1974)
Dal Rodeno Al Reno
see Zwischen Rhone Und Rhein

Zwischen Rhone Und Rhein
"Dal Rodeno Al Reno"
2(pic).2(English
horn).3.3(contrabsn).alto sax.
4.3.3.1. timp,perc,drums,strings
HUG　　　　　　　　　　　　(M170)

MARTINET, JEAN-LOUIS (1916-　　)
Prométhée
3.3.3.3. 4.3.3.1. timp,perc,harp,
cel,pno,strings [25'] LEDUC
　　　　　　　　　　　　　　(M171)

Sept Poèmes De René Char
2.2.2.2. 2.1.2.1. perc,xylo,cel,
harp,alto sax,strings,4 solo
voices [25'] LEDUC　　　　(M172)

Trois Poèmes De René Char
2.1.2.1. 1.1.0.0. 2perc,harp,pno,
strings,female solo [10'] LEDUC
　　　　　　　　　　　　　　(M173)

MARTINEZ, MARIANNE DI (1744-1812)
Concerto for Piano and Orchestra in A
HILDEGARD 09647 sc f.s., perf sc,
pts rent　　　　　　　　　(M174)

Dixit Dominus　*18th cent
(Godt, Irving) 2.2.0.0. 0.2.0.0.
timp,vln I,vln II,vla,cont set A-
R ED ISBN 0-89579-384-9　(M175)

MARTINEZ, MIGUEL ANGEL GOMÉZ
Suite Burlesca
3.3.3.3. 4.2.3.1. timp,pno,perc,
strings [22'] perf sc EMEC f.s.
　　　　　　　　　　　　　　(M176)

MARTINI, [PADRE] GIOVANNI BATTISTA
(1706-1784)
Concerto in D
vcl,2trp,string orch,cont
KUNZELMANN ipa sc 10229A, oct
10229　　　　　　　　　　　(M177)

Gavotte in F
(Kranz, Albert) 1.1.2.1. 2.0.1.0.
perc,strings [3'] HEINRICH (M178)

MARTINI, GIOVANNI
see MARTINI, JEAN PAUL EGIDE

MARTINI, JEAN PAUL EGIDE
(SCHWARZENDORF) (1741-1816)
Plaisir D'amour
[Fr/It] orch,solo voice BOIS (M179)

MARTINOV, VLADIMIR (1946-　　)
Passionslieder Und Passionsgesänge
fl,perc,vln,hpsd,strings,S solo
[57'] SIKORSKI perf mat rent
　　　　　　　　　　　　　　(M180)

MARTINSSON, ROLF (1956-　　)
Dreams
orch [25'] (symphonic scenes) sc,
pts STIM　　　　　　　　　(M181)

Impression
2(pic).2.2.2. 2.0.0.0. timp,strings
[18'5"] sc,pts STIM　　　(M182)

MARTINU, BOHUSLAV (JAN) (1890-1959)
Kouzelné Noci
4.3.2.2. 2.2.0.0. perc,harp,cel,
strings,S solo [16'] CESKY HUD.
　　　　　　　　　　　　　　(M183)

Loutky
2.2.2.2. 2.2.0.0. timp,perc,harp,
strings [14'] CESKY HUD.　(M184)

Nipponari
4fl,English horn,triangle,tam-tam,
harp,cel,pno,strings,S solo [24']
PANTON　　　　　　　　　　(M185)

Zaloba Proti Neznámému
3.2.3.2. 4.2.3.1. timp,perc,pno,
strings [15'] PANTON　　　(M186)

MARTLAND, STEVE (1959-　　)
Babi Yar
1+2pic.1+English horn.2+bass
clar.2.alto sax.tenor sax.
4.3.3.1. 7perc,pno,synthesizer,
elec gtr,bass gtr,32vln,8vla,
10vcl,8db [35'] SCHOTTS perf mat
rent　　　　　　　　　　　(M187)

Crossing The Border
8vln I,8vln II,4vla,4vcl,2db [25']
study sc SCHOTTS ED 12402 perf
mat rent　　　　　　　　　(M188)
strings [24'] SCHOTT　　(M189)

MARTLAND, STEVE (cont'd.)

Principia
instrumental ensemble [3'] SCHOTT
(M190)

MARUYAMA, KAZUNORI (1959- )
Mama Likes Poyopoyo-Zaurs
[60'] JAPAN (M191)

MARX, HANS-JOACHIM (1923- )
Sinfonietta
3.3.3.3. 4.3.3.1. timp,3perc,harp,
pno,strings [40'] SIKORSKI perf
mat rent (M192)

MARX, KARL (1897-1985)
Passacaglia, Op. 19
2.2.3.3. 4.3.3.1. timp,perc,strings
[18'] BREITKOPF-W (M193)

MARY BEAN, THE see Dalby, Martin

MARY CASSATT see Larsen, Elizabeth B.
(Libby)

MARY GILMORE GOES TO PARAGUAY see
Dreyfus, George

MASCAGNI, PIETRO (1863-1945)
Ave Maria
(Zani, Giacomo) harp,strings,solo
voice [3'] SONZOGNO rent (M194)
(Zani, Giacomo) orch,solo voice
[3'] SONZOGNO rent (M195)

Cavalleria Rusticana: Intermezzo
4.1.2.0. 0.0.0.0. harp,org,strings
[2'45"] LEDUC (M196)

MASK FÜR 3 ORCHESTERGRUPPEN see Marti,
Heinz

MASON, BENEDICT
Concerto For Sackbut And Orchestra
strings, sackbut-trb-horn
manuscript BMIC (M197)

Concerto For Viola Section And
Orchestra
3.3.3.3. 4.3.3.1. timp,6perc,pno&
cel,synthesizer,2harp,strings,SB
soli, viola section [28'] CHESTER
(M198)

MASOPUSTNÍ - TANEC SMRTI see Kašlik,
Václav

MASQUE OF ORIANNA: SUITE see Klein,
Lothar

MASQUE OF THE RED DEATH see Daniel,
Omar

MASQUE OF THE RED DEATH, THE see Conte,
David

MASSENET, JULES (1842-1912)
Ariane: Ballet d'Ariane
3.3.3.3. 4.3.6.1. timp,3perc,2harp,
strings [15'] LEDUC (M199)

Ariane: Suite
orch [21'] LEDUC (M200)

Bacchus: Suite
3.3.3.3. 4.3.6.1. timp,perc,harp,
strings [22'] (contains: "Le
triomphe de Bacchus" "La bataille
simiesque" "Les mystères
dionysiaques") LEDUC (M201)

Brumaire *Overture
3.3.3.3. 4.3.3.1. timp,perc,2harp,
org,strings LEDUC (M202)

Chérubin: Fragments Symphoniques
*Interlude/Overture
3.2.2.2. 4.3.3.1. 2perc,harp,
strings [9'] LEDUC (M203)

Cigale, La (Divertissement)
3.3.2.2. 4.3.3.1. timp,perc,2harp,
strings [30'] LEDUC (M204)

Crépuscule
string orch,fl&vln&vcl soli [10']
LEDUC (M205)

Dernier Sommeil, Danse Galiléenne
see Vierge, La

Devant La Madone
1.1.1.0. 0.0.0.0. strings [6']
LEDUC (M206)

Divertissement
see Cigale, La
see Rosati, Les

Espada *Suite
3.2.2.2. 4.3.3.1. timp,perc,2harp,
strings [25'] LEDUC (M207)

Fantasy for Violoncello
2.2.2.2. 4.2.3.0. timp,perc,harp,
strings [14'] LEDUC (M208)

MASSENET, JULES (cont'd.)
Grisélidis: Fragments
3.3.2.2. 4.0.0.0. timp,perc,harp,
strings [6'] (entracte, idylle,
valse des esprits) LEDUC (M209)

Jérusalem: Entractes
3.3.3.3. 4.3.3.1. timp,2perc,harp,
strings [8'] LEDUC (M210)

Mage, Le: Airs De Ballet
3.3.3.3. 4.3.3.1. timp,perc,harp,
strings [7'] LEDUC (M211)

Panurge (Excerpts)
2.2.2.2. 4.2.3.0. 3perc,strings
[9'] (contains: Intermède de
l'île des lanternes, Parade
militaire) LEDUC (M212)

Roi De Lahore, Le: 4 Morceaux
2.2.2.2. 4.4.3.1. timp,2perc,bells,
harp,strings [27'] LEDUC (M213)

Roma *Overture
3.3.3.3. 4.3.3.1. timp,perc,2harp,
strings [8'] LEDUC (M214)

Rosati, Les (Divertissement)
2.2.2.2. 4.2.3.1. timp,perc,harp,
cel,strings [21'] LEDUC (M215)

Sarabande Espagnole Du XVIe Siècle
1.1.0.1. 0.2.0.0. perc,strings
[10'] LEDUC (M216)

Scènes De Féerie
see Suite for Orchestra, No. 6

Scènes Hongroises
see Suite for Orchestra, No. 2

Suite for Orchestra, No. 2
"Scènes Hongroises" 3.2.2.2.
4.4.3.1. timp,perc,harp,strings
[18'] LEDUC (M217)

Suite for Orchestra, No. 6
"Scènes De Féerie" 2.2.2.2.
4.2.3.1. timp,perc,strings [24']
LEDUC (M218)

Suite for Orchestra, No. 8
"Suite Théâtrale" 3.3.3.3. 4.3.3.1.
timp,perc,2harp,hpsd,harmonium,
strings [24'] LEDUC (M219)

Suite for Orchestra, No. 9
"Suite Parnassienne" 3.3.3.3.
4.2.3.1. timp,perc,xylo,harp,
strings [21'] (posthumous) LEDUC
(M220)

Suite Parnassienne
see Suite for Orchestra, No. 9

Suite Théâtrale
see Suite for Orchestra, No. 8

Thérèse: La Chute Des Feuilles
timp,strings [2'] LEDUC (M221)

Vierge, La
"Dernier Sommeil, Danse Galiléenne"
strings [6'] LEDUC (M222)

MASSEUS, JAN (1913- )
Concerto, Op. 81
3.2.3.3. 4.3.2.1. timp,4perc,
strings,pno solo [18'] sc DONEMUS
(M223)

MASTER JACOB PÅ AFVEJE see Wellejus,
Henning, Meister Jakob Auf Abwegen

MATEJ, JOZKA (JOSEF) (1922-1992)
Concerto for Bassoon, String
Orchestra and Piano
pno,strings,bsn solo [20'] CESKY
HUD. (M224)

Kyticka Na Mohylu
3.3.3.2. 4.3.3.1. timp,perc,strings
[18'] CESKY HUD. (M225)

MATEJU, ZBYNEK (1958- )
Concerto for Violin and Orchestra
1.1.1.1. 0.0.0.0. timp,perc,harp,
strings,vln solo [12'] CESKY HUD.
(M226)

Evokace (Symphony No. 1)
2.2.2.2. 4.2.3.1. timp,perc,pno,
strings [24'] CESKY HUD. (M227)

Okna S Andely (Symphony for String
Orchestra)
[18'] CESKY HUD. (M228)

Sinfonia Brevis
2.2.2.2. 4.2.3.1. timp,perc,pno,
strings [18'] CESKY HUD. (M229)

Symphony for String Orchestra
see Okna S Andely

MATEJU, ZBYNEK (cont'd.)

Symphony No. 1
see Evokace

MATERIE, DE: PART 1 see Andriessen,
Louis

MATERIE, DE: PART 2 see Andriessen,
Louis

MATERIE, DE: PART 4 see Andriessen,
Louis

MATHER, BRUCE (1939- )
Au Château De Pompairain *vocalise
2(pic).2.2.2. 2.2.0.0. 2perc,harp,
10vln I,8vln II,6vla,5vcl,4db,Mez
solo [13'] sc CANADIAN
MV 1400 M427AU (M230)

Concerto for Piano and Chamber
Orchestra
1.1.1.1. 1.0.0.0. strings without
db,pno solo [7'] sc CANADIAN
MI 1361 427CO (M231)

Finding Of Love, The
string orch,S solo [13'] sc
CANADIAN MV 1600 M427FI (M232)

Lost Love
string orch,S solo sc CANADIAN
MV 1600 M427LO (M233)

Musigny
2+pic.2+English horn.2+bass clar.2.
4.3.3.1. 4perc,2harp,pno,strings
sc CANADIAN MI 1100 M427MU (M234)

Travaux De Nuit
1(pic).1.2(bass clar).1. 1.1.0.0.
perc,pno&synthesizer,strings,Bar
solo sc CANADIAN MV 1400 M427TR
(M235)

Two Songs For Bass-Baritone And
Orchestra
2.2.2.2. 2.2.0.0. timp,perc,harp,
strings,Bar solo [7'] sc CANADIAN
MV 1400 M427TW (M236)

MATHIAS, WILLIAM (1934-1992)
Anniversary Dances
3(pic).2.2.2+contrabsn. 4.3.3.1.
timp,3perc,harp/cel,strings [23']
perf sc set OXFORD 3655578 sc,pts
rent (M237)

Concerto for Flute and Strings
[14'] perf sc set OXFORD 3655950
sc,pts rent (M238)

Concerto for Violin and Orchestra
2.2.2.2+contrabsn. 4.2.3.0. timp,
2perc,cel,harp,strings [36'] perf
sc set OXFORD 3656922 sc,pts rent
(M239)

In Arcadia
3.2.2.3. 4.3.3.1. timp,perc,cel
strings [17'] OXFORD sc 3655926
f.s., perf sc set 365590X sc,pts
rent (M240)

Symphony No. 3
3.3.3.3. 4.3.3.1. timp,3perc,harp,
cel,pno,strings [35'] OXFORD sc
3656515 f.s., perf sc set 3656531
sc,pts rent (M241)

Threnos
string orch OXFORD (M242)

MATOUSEK, LUKAS (1943- )
Promeny Ticha
[10'] CESKY HUD. (M243)

Radices Temporis
2.2.3.3. 4.2.3.1. timp,perc,strings
[15'] CESKY HUD. (M244)

Sonata for Double Bass and Chamber
Group
1.1.1.1. 1.0.0.0. 2vln,vla,vcl,db
solo [12'] CESKY HUD. (M245)

MATOUŠEK, VLASTISLAV (1948- )
Sázeni Hrušky *Fantasy
3.2.3.3. 3.3.3.1. timp,perc,xylo
strings [19'] CESKY HUD. (M246)

Symphony
3.2.3.3. 4.3.3.1. timp,perc,strings
[32'] CESKY HUD. (M247)

MATSUDAIRA, YORI-AKI (1931- )
Helices
orch [12'] JAPAN (M248)

Recollection
2.1.1.1. 2.1.1.0. perc,harp,pno,
strings [15'] MOECK sc 5453 f.s.
pts rent (M249)

Remembrance
pno,orch [12'] JAPAN (M250)

MATSUNAGA, MICHIHARU (1927-    )
Constellations Of Time
   pno,orch [17'] JAPAN     (M251)

MATSUO, MASATAKA (1959-    )
Hirai V (Rivision)
   orch,clar solo,pno solo [20'] JAPAN
          (M252)

Phonosphere I (Revision)
   orch, shaku [24'] JAPAN   (M253)

MATSUSHITA, ISAO (1951-    )
Boufuri
   chamber orch, kyogen [25'] (kyogen
   opera) JAPAN       (M254)

Concertino for Viola
   see To The Air Of A Dream

Midsummer Night's Dream, A
   chamber orch, kyogen [30'] (kyogen
   opera) JAPAN       (M255)

To The Air Of A Dream (Concertino for
   Viola)
   chamber orch,vla solo [10'] JAPAN
          (M256)

MATTES, WILLY (1916-    )
Deine Liebe Ist Mein Ganzes Leben
   2.1.3(bass clar).0. 2.0.0.0. timp,
   perc,strings,T solo [3'] SIKORSKI
   perf mat rent      (M257)

MATTHEWS, COLIN (1946-    )
Broken Symmetry
   3.3.5.3. 6.4.3.1. timp,4perc,pno,
   harp,strings [22'] FABER   (M258)

Chiaroscuro
   2.2.2.2. 2.1.0.0. perc,cel,harp,
   strings [16'] FABER    (M259)

Concerto for Violoncello and
   Orchestra
   orch,vcl solo sc FABER 50836 7 f.s.
          (M260)

Concerto for Violoncello and
   Orchestra, No. 2
   2.2.3.3. 4.2.3.1. timp,3perc,harp,
   strings,vcl solo [27'] FABER
          (M261)

Contraflow
   1.1.1.1. 1.1.1.0. perc,pno,strings
   [12'] FABER       (M262)

Cortege
   orch sc FABER 51291 7 f.s.  (M263)

Divertimento
   2string orch sc FABER 50719 0 f.s.
          (M264)

Hidden Variables
   chamber orch (15 players) sc FABER
   51187 2 f.s.      (M265)
   3.3.3.2. 4.2.3.0. timp,2perc,pno&
   synthesizer,harp,strings [13']
   FABER        (M266)

Landscape
   see Sonata No. 5

Machines And Dreams  *educ
   3.3.3.3. 4.3.3.1. timp,3perc,pno,
   harp,strings, & toy orchestra
   [15'] FABER     (M267)

Memorial
   3.3.3.3. 4.3.3.1. timp,4perc,pno,
   harp,strings [20'] FABER  (M268)

M50
   3.3.3.3. 4.3.3.1. timp,2perc,harp,
   strings [4'] sc FABER 51612 2
          (M269)

Monody
   orch sc FABER 51061 2 f.s.  (M270)

Night Music
   chamber orch sc FABER 50534 1 f.s.
          (M271)

Sonata No. 5
   "Landscape" orch sc FABER 50658 5
   f.s.         (M272)

Through The Glass
   alto fl,ob&English horn,clar,bass
   clar&clar in E flat,bsn&
   contrabsn,2horn,trp,perc,pno,
   harp,strings [16'] FABER  (M273)

To Compose Without ...
   instrumental ensemble [10'] FABER
          (M274)

MATTHEWS, DAVID (1943-    )
Cantiga
   chamber orch,S solo sc FABER
   51290 9 f.s.     (M275)

Capriccio
   0.0.0.0. 2.0.0.0. strings [10']
   FABER        (M276)

Chaconne
   orch sc FABER 51146 5 f.s.  (M277)

MATTHEWS, DAVID (cont'd.)
Concerto for Oboe and Orchestra
   orch,ob solo [18'] FABER  (M278)

From Sea To Sky
   0.2.0.0. 2.0.0.0. strings [4']
   FABER        (M279)

Introit
   2trp,strings sc FABER 50741 7 f.s.
          (M280)

Little Chaconne
   strings [10'] FABER   (M281)

Music Of Dawn, The
   4.4.4.4. 6.3.3.1. timp,4perc,2harp,
   strings [30'] sc FABER 51220 8
          (M282)

Romanza
   2.2.2.2. 2.0.0.0. strings,vcl solo
   [12'] FABER      (M283)

Scherzo Capriccioso
   2.2.2.2. 2.2.1.0. 2perc,pno,strings
   [8'] FABER      (M284)

Symphony, No. 2
   orch sc FABER 50810 3 f.s.  (M285)

Symphony, No. 3
   orch sc FABER 50991 6 f.s.  (M286)

Symphony, No. 4
   1.2.0.2. 2.0.0.0. strings [25']
   FABER        (M287)

Vision And A Journey, A
   3.3.3.3. 4.3.3.1. timp,3perc,cel,
   harp,strings [20'] FABER  (M288)

MATTHEWS, MICHAEL (1950-    )
Landscape
   4vln I,4vln II,3vla,2vcl,db,pno
   solo [15'] (1. Rock on Rock 2.
   Perpetual water) sc CANADIAN
   MI 1661 M441LA    (M289)

MATTHUS, SIEGFRIED (1934-    )
Concerto for Piano and Orchestra
   (from Brahms's Piano Quartet, Op.
   25)
   2.2.2.2. 2.2.3.1. timp,2perc,harp,
   cel,strings,pno solo [50']
   DEUTSCHER      (M290)

Manhattan Concerto For Orchestra
   3.3.3.3. 4.3.3.1. timp,3perc,harp,
   cel,strings [30'] DEUTSCHER
          (M291)

Sarmatische Lieder
   3.2.3.2. 2.2.2.1. timp,3perc,harp,
   pno,cel,strings,S/T solo [20']
   BREITKOPF-W     (M292)

MATTON, ROGER (1929-    )
Mouvement Symphonique IV
   3(pic).3(English horn).3(bass
   clar).3(contrabsn). 4.3.3.1.
   timp,4perc,harp,strings [15']
   (concertant) sc CANADIAN
   MI 1100 M444MO4    (M293)

MATYS, JIŘÍ (1927-    )
Hudba Pro Smyčce
   [12'] ČESKÝ HUD.   (M294)

Naléhavost Času
   3.2.2.2. 4.2.3.1. timp,perc,pno,
   strings,speaking voice,vla solo
   [15'] ČESKÝ HUD.   (M295)

MAUD see Delius, Frederick

MAUSFALLEN SPRÜCHLEIN see Wolf, Hugo

MAVENTA SUITE see Haworth, Frank

MAW, NICHOLAS (1935-    )
Concerto for Violin and Orchestra
   2.2.2.2. 4.2.0.1. timp,perc,harp,
   strings,vln solo [42'] FABER
          (M296)

Dance Scenes
   3.2.2.3. 4.3.3.0. timp,perc,strings
   FABER        (M297)

Little Concert
   chamber orch,ob solo sc FABER
   51100 7 f.s.     (M298)

Shahnama
   1.1.1.1. 1.1.1.0. pno,strings [28']
   FABER        (M299)

Sonata Notturna
   string orch,vcl solo sc FABER
   51030 2 f.s.     (M300)

Spring Music
   orch sc FABER 50815 4 f.s.  (M301)

Summer Dances
   orch sc FABER 50712 3 f.s.  (M302)

MAW, NICHOLAS (cont'd.)
Variations
   2.2.2.3. 4.3.3.1. timp,2perc,harp,
   strings FABER     (M303)

MAXWELL DAVIES, PETER
see DAVIES, PETER MAXWELL

MAYER, WILLIAM ROBERT (1925-    )
Good King Wenceslas
   2(pic).2.2.2. 2.2.1.1. timp,perc,
   pno,strings,narrator,opt SATB
   [15'] (text by A.A. Milne)
   PRESSER rent     (M304)

Inner And Outer Strings
   string orch,string quar soli [9']
   JERONA sc B13200 f.s., pts rent
          (M305)

MAYR, RUPERT IGNAZ (1646-1712)
Suite No. 1 in F
   strings without db,cont COPPENRATH
   sc 16.044-01, kbd pt 16.044-03A,
   pts 16.044-21A, 24A  (M306)

Suite No. 7 in B flat
   string orch,cont COPPENRATH sc
   16.048-01, pts 16.048-21 TO 29
          (M307)

MAYR, [JOHANN] SIMON (1763-1845)
Concerto for Bassoon and Orchestra
   2ob,2horn,strings,bsn solo [15']
   BOCCACCINI rent    (M308)

Concerto for Piccolo, Flute,
   Clarinet, Basset Horn and
   Orchestra
   0.0.2.1. 1.2.0.0. timp,strings,pic
   solo,fl solo,clar solo,basset
   horn solo [20'] BOCCACCINI rent
          (M309)

MAZEPPA: AIR D'ANDRÉ (NO. 16) see
Tchaikovsky, Piotr Ilyich

MÉ KAMENICI NAD LIPOU see Vacek, Miloš

ME L'A DIT QU'À LA MOISSON, IL see
Migot, Georges

MEALE, RICHARD (1932-    )
Scenes From Mer De Glace
   3(pic).3(English horn).3(clar in E
   flat,bass clar).3(2contrabsn).
   4.3.3.1. 3perc,cel,harp,strings
   [16'] BOOSEY-ENG rent  (M310)

Symphony
   3(2pic).2+English horn.3(clar in E
   flat,bass clar).3(contrabsn).
   4.3.3.1. timp,3perc,harp,cel,
   strings [25'] BOOSEY-ENG rent
          (M311)

MEANDER see Jeths, Willem

MECHAYE HAMETIM see Sheriff, Noam

MEDEA FRAGMENTS I see Hosokawa, Toshio

MEDEK, TILO (1940-    )
Concerto for Timpani and Orchestra
   2.2.2.2. 4.4.4.1. strings,timp solo
   [21'] MOECK sc 5358 f.s., pts
   rent        (M312)

Concerto for Trumpet and Orchestra
   3.3.3.3. 4.4.4.1. perc,strings,trp
   solo [30'] MOECK sc 5405 f.s.,
   pts rent     (M313)

Concerto for Violin and Orchestra
   2.2.2.2. 4.1.1.0. 2perc,trp,
   strings,vln solo [30'] MOECK sc
   5272 f.s., pts rent  (M314)

Concerto for Violoncello and
   Orchestra, No. 2
   2.2.2.2. 2.2.2.0. trp,strings,vcl
   solo [22'] MOECK sc 5288 f.s.,
   pts rent     (M315)

Concerto for Violoncello and
   Orchestra, No. 3
   2.2.2.2. 0.0.0.0. 3perc,harp,cel,
   trp,strings,vcl solo [30'] MOECK
   sc 5477 f.s., pts rent  (M316)

Symphony, No. 1
   3.3.3.3. 3.3.3.1. perc,pno,org,trp,
   strings [40'] MOECK sc 5281 f.s.,
   pts rent     (M317)

Symphony, No. 2
   2.2.2.2. 4.3.3.1. perc,trp,strings
   [22'] MOECK sc 5364 f.s., pts
   rent        (M318)

MEDIA VITA see Thiel, Wolfgang

MEDITACE A SCHERZO see Francl, Jaroslav

MEDITATION see Grabovsky, Leonid

MEDITERRANEAN SONGS see Goldschmidt,
Berthold

MEDUSA see Ketting, Otto

MEER, DAS SO GROSS UND WEIT IST, DA
WIMMELT'S OHNE ZAHL, GROSSE UND
KLEINE TIERE, DAS see Burrell,
Diana

MEETING see Baer

MEETING OF THE VOLGA AND THE DON, THE
see Prokofiev, Serge

MEHRTENS, JANINE
Concerto
1.1.1.1. 1.1.0.0. timp,perc,cel,
harp,strings,pno solo [12'] sc
DONEMUS                          (M319)

MÉHUL, ÉTIENNE-NICOLAS (1763-1817)
Joseph: Overture
2.2.2.1. 2.2.0.0. timp,strings
[3'30"] BREITKOPF-W            (M320)

Symphony No. 1
(Petit, J.-L.) orch BOIS        (M321)

MEIJERING, CHIEL (1954-    )
Eindkrak (II)
2.2.2.2. 2.1.1.0. 2perc,strings,vcl
solo [15'] sc DONEMUS          (M322)

Nice Guys Always Finish Last
2.2.2.2.2alto sax. 2.1.1.0. perc,
strings [34'] sc DONEMUS       (M323)

P.W. And His Skillet Lickers
string orch,perc,vcl solo [13'] sc
DONEMUS                          (M324)

Rekkelijken En De Preciesen, De
2.2.2.2.2sax. 2.1.1.0. perc,
strings, drum computer-rhythmbox
[6'] sc DONEMUS                (M325)

Schleimige Last, Die
string orch,hpsd, theorbo [5'] sc
DONEMUS                          (M326)

Who's Hot And Who's Not
1.1.0.0. 0.0.0.0. perc,3gtr,strings
[17'] sc DONEMUS               (M327)
fl,ob,perc,2string quar,db,3gtr
[17'20"] DONEMUS rent          (M328)

MEIJERING, CORD (1955-    )
Chimaere
Mez solo,fl,clar,horn,perc,harp,
gtr,2vln,vla,vcl,db [32'] MOECK
sc 5392 f.s., pts rent         (M329)

Licht Des Mondes, Das
3.3.4.3. 4.3.3.1. Mez solo,2perc,
harp,pno,trp,strings [26'] MOECK
sc 5336 f.s., pts rent         (M330)

Symphony, No. 2
3.3.3.3. 4.3.3.1. perc,harp,pno,
strings [31'] MOECK sc 5467 f.s.,
pts rent                        (M331)

Voice Of The Winter, The
3.3.3.3. 4.3.3.1. 3perc,harp,trp,
strings [15'] MOECK sc 5337 f.s.,
pts rent                        (M332)

MEINE LIEBLICHE PLATANE see Handel,
George Frideric, Xerxes: Frondi
Tenere

MEISTER JAKOB AUF ABWEGEN see Wellejus,
Henning

MEISTER UND MARGARITA, DER see Petrov,
Andrei P.

MEISTER UND MARGARITA: SUITE see
Schnittke, Alfred

MELANCHOLICKÉ INTERMEZZO see Krízek,
Zdenek

MELCHERS, H. MELCHER
Kermesse, La
orch (symphonic poem after the
picture of Rubens) STIM        (M333)

MELIN, STEN (1957-    )
Keep The Change
1.1.2(bass clar).1(contrabsn).
1.1.1.0. 2perc,harp,strings,2gtr,
2pno [20'] sc,pts STIM         (M334)
1.1.2(pic).1(contrabsn). 1.1.1.0.
2perc,harp,strings,mand,gtr,pno
[20'] STIM                     (M335)

MÉLISANDE'S SONG see Faure, Gabriel-
Urbain

MELLAN DALARÖ OCH UTÖ see Henke, Claes,
Symphonisk Fantasi Nr 3 Op. 14

MELLNÄS, ARNE (1933-    )
Ikaros (Symphony No. 1)
3(pic).3(English horn).3(bass
clar).3(contrabsn). 4.3.3.1.
timp,4perc,harp,strings,cel [26']

MELLNÄS, ARNE (cont'd.)
sc REIMERS ED.NR 101152        (M336)
see Symphony No. 1

Intimate Games
fl,chamber orch [18'] study sc
REIMERS 101201 rent            (M337)

Symphony No. 1
"Ikaros" orch [26'] sc REIMERS
101152 rent                    (M338)
see Ikaros

MELNYK, LUBOMYR (1948-    )
Cleaning Staff
3(pic).3(English horn).3(bass
clar).3(contrabsn). 4.1+
cornet.2.1. timp,13vln I,11vln
II,9vla,9vcl,6db,2pno&string quar
soli sc CANADIAN MI 1450 M527CL
(M339)
Gifts
string orch,pno solo [20'] sc,solo
pt CANADIAN MI 1661 M527GI (M340)

Once
string orch,2pno soli [51'-68'] sc
CANADIAN MI 8605 M5270N        (M341)

MÉLODIE EN FA see Rubinstein, Anton

MELODIE I (NEUFASSUNG 93) see Hashagen,
Klaus

MELODIES see Ito, Yasuhide

MÉLOPÉE DU SERPENT, LA see Djabadary,
Heraclius

MELOS AURA see Nishimura, Akira

MELTDOWN VARIATIONS see Hillborg,
Anders

MEMENTO see Neubert, Günter

MEMENTO: HOMMAGE A SCHOSTAKOWITSCH see
Voigtländer, Lothar

MEMENTO (TCHERNOBIL 86) see Kosteck,
Gregory William

MEMNON see Schubert, Franz (Peter)

MEMORALIA see Homs, Joaquin

MEMORIAL see Matthews, Colin

MEMORIALE (IN MEMORIAM S.F.) see
Kalmar, Laszlo

MEMORY see Lloyd Webber, Andrew

MEMORY OF THE FIRE see De Grandis,
Renato

MENAGERIE see Foley, Daniel

MENDELSSOHN, FANNY
see HENSEL, FANNY MENDELSSOHN

MENDELSSOHN-BARTHOLDY, FELIX
(1809-1847)
Auf Flugeln Des Gesanges
(Cohen, Shimon) string orch,solo
voice [1'30"] PRESSER rent (M342)

Complete Works For Piano And
Orchestra
orch,pno sc DOVER 29032-8      (M343)

Concert Piece, Op. 113-114 for
Clarinet, Basset Horn and Strings
see Zwei Konzertstücke, Op. 113 &
114

Concerto for Piano and Orchestra in A
minor
(Hellmundt) sc,pts BREITKOPF-W
PB-OB 5331                      (M344)

Elias: Sei Stille Dem Herrn *Op.70
1.0.0.0. 0.0.0.0. strings,A solo
[4'] BREITKOPF-W               (M345)

Elias: So Ihr Mich Von Ganzem Herzen
Suchet *Op.70
1.0.2.2. 0.0.0.0. strings,T solo
[3'] BREITKOPF-W               (M346)

Gruss
(Cohen, Shimon) string orch,solo
voice [1'] PRESSER rent        (M347)

Konzertstück No. 1 in F minor, Op.
113
2.2.0.2. 2.2.0.0. timp,strings,
clar&basset horn/2clar soli sc,
pts BREITKOPF-W PB-OB 5191 (M348)

Konzertstück No. 2 in D minor, Op.
114
clar,basset horn,orch sc,pts
BREITKOPF-W PB-OB 5327         (M349)

MENDELSSOHN-BARTHOLDY, FELIX (cont'd.)
Leise Zieht Durch Mein Gemüt (from 12
Songs For High Voice & Orchestra)
(Matthus, Siegfried) 2.2.2.2.
2.0.0.0. timp,perc,harp,strings,
S/T solo [32'] BREITKOPF-W (M350)

Lobgesang
see Symphony No. 2, Op. 52, in B
flat

Major Orchestral Works
orch sc DOVER 23184-4          (M351)

Paulus: Gott Sei Mir Gnädig
0.1.0.1. 2.0.3.0. strings,B solo
[6'] BREITKOPF-W               (M352)

Paulus: Jerusalem, Die Du Tötest Die
Propheten (from Paulus Op. 36)
1.0.2.2. 1.0.0.0. org,strings,S
solo [3'30"] BREITKOPF-W   (M353)

Paulus: Overture *Op.36
2.2.2.2. 2.2.3.0. timp,strings,
serpent or contra bassoon [10']
BREITKOPF-W                     (M354)

Reformation Symphony
see Symphony No. 5

Scottish Symphony
see Symphony No. 3 in A minor, Op.
56

Sinfonia No. 1 in C
(Wolff, H. Chr.) strings [10'] sc,
pts BREITKOPF-W DV 1761-2761
(M355)

Sinfonia No. 2 in D
(Wolff, H. Chr.) strings [9'] sc,
pts BREITKOPF-W DV 1762-2762
(M356)

Sinfonia No. 3 in E minor
(Wolff, H. Chr.) strings [8'] sc,
pts BREITKOPF-W DV 1763-2763
(M357)

Sinfonia No. 4 in C minor
(Wolff, H. Chr.) strings [9'] sc,
pts BREITKOPF-W DV 1764-2764
(M358)

Sinfonia No. 5 in B flat
(Wolff, H. Chr.) strings [11'] sc,
pts BREITKOPF-W DV 1765-2765
(M359)

Sinfonia No. 6 in E flat
(Wolff, H. Chr.) strings [12'] sc,
pts BREITKOPF-W DV 1766-2766
(M360)

Sinfonia No. 7 in D minor
(Wolff, H. Chr.) strings [19'] sc,
pts BREITKOPF-W DV 1767-2767
(M361)

Sinfonia No. 10 in B minor
(Wolff, H. Chr.) strings [11'] sc,
pts BREITKOPF-W DV 1770-2770
(M362)

Sinfonia No. 12 in G minor
(Wolff, H. Chr.) strings [18'] sc,
pts BREITKOPF-W DV 1772-2772
(M363)

Symphony No. 2, Op. 52, in B flat
(Konold, W.) "Lobgesang" 2.2.2.2.
4.2.3.0. timp,org,strings,SST
soli,SSAATTBB [64'] sc,pts
BREITKOPF-W PB-OB 5102         (M364)

Symphony No. 3 in A minor, Op. 56
"Scottish Symphony" BROUDE BR.
(M365)

Symphony No. 5
"Reformation Symphony" orch sc
DOVER 27875-1                  (M366)

Symphony No. 8 in D for Strings
string orch BOIS               (M367)

Symphony No. 11 in F for Strings
string orch BOIS               (M368)

Tanz Von Rüpeln, Ein (from Ein
Sommernachtstraum Op. 61)
2.2.2.2. 2.0.0.0+ophicleide. perc,
strings [2'] BREITKOPF-W       (M369)

Zwei Konzertstücke, Op. 113 & 114
(Concert Piece, Op. 113-114 for
Clarinet, Basset Horn and
Strings)
strings,clar,basset horn/clar study
sc PETERS EP 8595A             (M370)

MÉNÉTRIER, LE see Ollone, Max d'

MENGELBERG, MISJA (1935-    )
Concerto for Saxophone and Orchestra
3.3.3.2. 2.2.2.1. 2perc,strings,
alto sax solo [13'] sc DONEMUS
(M371)

Zeekip Ahoy
2.2.2.1.alto sax. 2.1.1.1. perc,
pno,strings [11'] sc DONEMUS
(M372)

MENOTTI, GIAN CARLO (1911-    )
Concerto for Violin and Orchestra
orch,vln solo sc SCHIRM.G ED3869
(M373)

Nocturne
S solo,harp,strings sc,pts SCHIRM.G
ED-3552
(M374)

MENTIA L'AVVISO see Puccini, Giacomo

MENTRE TI LASCIO, O FIGLIA see Mozart,
Wolfgang Amadeus

MENUET À LA REINE see Grétry, André
Ernest Modeste

MENUET D'ORPHÉE see Gluck, Christoph
Willibald, Ritter von

MENUET SUR LE NOM D'HAYDN see Ravel,
Maurice

MENUETT AUS DER KLAVIERSONATE OP. 7 see
Grieg, Edvard Hagerup

MERCADANTE, G. SAVERIO (1795-1870)
Concerto for Flute and Orchestra in E
minor
2.2.2.2. 2.2.1.0. timp,strings,fl
solo [28'] (original version for
grand orchestra) BOCCACCINI
BS. 155 rent
(M375)

Variations for Flute and Strings in F
[10'] BOCCACCINI BS. 160 rent
(M376)

MERCURIO see Brauel, Henning

MERIDIES see Keane, David

MERKUR see Haydn, [Franz] Joseph,
Symphony No. 43 in E flat, Hob.I:
43

MERMAID VARIATIONS see Harris, Donald

MERNIER, BENOIT (1964-    )
Blake Songs
1.0.1.0. 1.0.1.0. 2perc,harp,pno,
2vln,vla,vcl,db,female solo [27']
BILLAUDOT
(M377)

Intonazione [17']
3.3.3.3. 4.3.3.1. 3perc,pno/cel,
harp,strings
BILLAUDOT
(M378)

MERRY KING, THE see Grainger, Percy
Aldridge

MERRY MARCH see Szervanszky, Endre

MERRY MUSIC see Kadosa, Pal see Vass,
Lajos

MERRY OUVERTURE see Vincze, Ottó

MESSAGE see Vasks, Peteris, Vestijums

MESSAGES OF THE LATE R.V. TROUSSOVA see
Kurtag, György

MESSIAEN, OLIVIER (1908-1992)
Alleluia Sur La Trompette, Alleluia
Sur La Cymbale
see Ascension, L': 4 Meditations

Alleluias Sereins d'une Âme Qui
Désire Le Ciel
see Ascension, L': 4 Meditations

Ascension, L': 4 Meditations
3.2+English horn.2+bass clar.3.
4.3.3.1. 3timp,triangle,cym,bass
drum,tamb,8vln I,8vln II,7vla,
6vcl,5db LEDUC f.s. sc AL 20523,
min sc AL 20720
contains: Alleluia Sur La
Trompette, Alleluia Sur La
Cymbale; Alleluias Sereins
d'une Âme Qui Désire Le Ciel;
Majesté Du Christ Demandant Sa
Gloire À Son Père; Prière Du
Christ Montant Vers Son Père
(M379)

Concert À Quatre
4+pic.3+English horn.3+soprano clar
in E flat+bass clar.3+contrabsn.
4.3+trp in D.3.1. 7perc,marimba,
xylo,xylorimba,cel,glock,strings
LEDUC
(M380)

Éclairs Sur L'Au-Dela: Volume 1
*CC6L
6+3pic+alto fl.3+English horn.6+
2soprano clar in E flat+bass
clar+contrabass clar.3+contrabsn.
6.0+2trp in D+3trp in C.3.2+db
tuba. 10perc,glock,xylo,
xylorimba,marimba,16vln I,16vln
II,14vla,12vcl,10db, crotales,
(The double basses are five-
stringed) sc LEDUC AL 28226 f.s.
(M381)

MESSIAEN, OLIVIER (cont'd.)

Éclairs Sur L'Au-Dela: Volume 2
*CC5L
6+3pic+alto fl.3+English horn.6+
2soprano clar in E flat+bass
clar+contrabass clar.3+contrabsn.
6.0+2trp in D+3trp in C.3.2+db
tuba. 10perc,glock,xylo,
xylorimba,marimba,16vln I,16vln
II,14vla,12vcl,10db, crotales,
(The double basses are five-
stringed) sc LEDUC AL 28842 f.s.
(M382)

Majesté Du Christ Demandant Sa Gloire
À Son Père
see Ascension, L': 4 Meditations

Prière Du Christ Montant Vers Son
Père
see Ascension, L': 4 Meditations

Sourire, Un
3+pic.3+English horn.3.3. 4.1.0.0.
2perc,16vln I,16vln II,14vla,
12vcl [10'] sc LEDUC AL 28156
(M383)

MESSIAH: OVERTURE see Handel, George
Frideric

MESSIAH: PIFA see Handel, George
Frideric

MESSNER, JOSEPH (1893-1969)
Symphonische Festmusik *Op.45
orch BÖHM
(M384)

MESTO PER ARCHI see Eklund, Hans

MESURES ET UN DA CAPO, 85 see Francaix,
Jean

MET HIM PIKE TROUSERS see Essl, Karl
Heinz

META-MUSIC see Silvestrov, Valentin

META-MUSIK see Schweizer, Alfred

METAMORFOSIS D'APRES see Krieger,
Armando

METAMORFOSIS D'APRÈS UNE LECTURE DE
KAFKA see Krieger, Armando

METAMORFOSIS D'APRÒS UNE LECTURE DE
KAFKA see Krieger, Armando,
Metamorfosis D'Après Une Lecture De
Kafka

METAMORPHOSE II see Ford, Clifford

METAMORPHOSEN DES OVID ODER DIE
BEWEGUNG VON DEN RÄNDERN ZUR MITTE
HIN UND UMGEKEHRT see Schnebel,
Dieter

METAMORPHOSEN FÜR ORCHESTER see Hocke,
Wolfgang

METAMORPHOSEN ÜBER EIN KLANGFELD VON
JOSEPH HAYDN see Ruzicka, Peter

METAMORPHOSENMUSIK see Schnebel, Dieter

METAMORPHOSI PER ARCHI see Carlstedt,
Jan

METAMORPHOSIS OF THEMES BY MOZART see
Dorfman, Joseph

METAPHORA see Sodomka, Karel

METAPICTURES see Lennon, John Anthony

METCALF, JOHN W.
Concerto for Marimba and Orchestra
orch,perc,marimba solo [17']
manuscript BMIC
(M385)

Variations
orch [25'] manuscript BMIC
(M386)

METEMPSYCHOSE III see Kaneta, Tchoji

METEOR see Bohác, Josef

METRO CHABACANO see Alvarez, Javier

METROPOLIS SYMPHONY see Daugherty,
Michael

METSK, JURO
Psychogramme
3.2.3.2.sax. 2.2.3.1. timp,5perc,
harp,cel,xylo,pno,strings [13']
sc PETERS 03018
(M387)

METZLER, FRIEDRICH (1910-1979)
Sinfonia No. 5 for Orchestra
MÖSELER rent
(M388)

MEUDE-MONPAS, J.J.O., CHEVALIER DE
(ca. 1786)
Concerto in D for Violin and
Orchestra
(Hijleh, Mark D.) 2ob,2horn,
strings,vln solo [18'30"] PRESSER
rent
(M389)

MEXIKANISCHES PASTELL see Pütz,
Johannes

MEYER, CARL HEINRICH
Concertino for Bass Trombone and
Orchestra
1.0.2.2. 2.2.1.0. timp,strings
[13'] sc,solo pt PETERS 02700
(M390)

MEYER, ERNST HERMANN (1905-1988)
Berliner Divertimento
3.3.3.3. 4.3.3.0. timp,perc,strings
[25'] sc PETERS 03090
(M391)

Concerto for Violoncello and
Orchestra
2.1.1.1. 4.2.1.0. timp,harp,8vln I,
7vln II,6vla,5vcl,4db [10'] sc
PETERS 03525
(M392)
2.1.1.1. 4.2.1.0. timp,harp,8vln I,
7vln II,6vla,5vcl,4db [15'] sc
PETERS 03505
(M393)

Divertimento Concertante
2.3.3.2. 4.3.3.0. timp,perc,harp,
strings [20'] BREITKOPF-W (M394)

Kammersinfonie
5vln I,4vln II,3vla,2vcl,db [16']
sc PETERS 03016
(M395)

Kleine Eröffnungsmusik
string orch,clar solo [14']
BREITKOPF-W
(M396)

Poem for Viola and Orchestra
2.2.2.2. 4.2.1.0. timp,perc,harp,
strings,vla solo [14'] BREITKOPF-
W
(M397)

Sinfonische Widmung
"Symphonic Dedication" 3.2.2.3.
4.3.3.1. timp,perc,4harp,8vln I,
7vln II,6vla,5vcl,4db,org solo
[15'] sc PETERS 03017 (M398)

Symphonic Dedication
see Sinfonische Widmung

MEYER, KRZYSZTOF (1943-    )
Carillon, For Orchestra, Op. 80
3(pic,alto fl).3.3(clar in E
flat).3. 3.3.0.0. 6perc,2harp,
pno,strings [14'] SIKORSKI perf
mat rent
(M399)

Caro Luigi *Op.73
string orch,4vcl soli [10']
SIKORSKI min sc 1586 f.s., sc,pts
perf mat rent
(M400)

Concerto for Alto Saxophone and
String Orchestra, Op. 79
[17'] SIKORSKI min sc 1596 f.s.,
sc,pts perf mat rent
(M401)

Concerto for Piano and Orchestra, Op.
46
3(pic).2.2(clar in E
flat).1(contrabsn). 2.2.2.0.
4perc,harp,cel,pno,strings,pno
solo [29'] SIKORSKI pno red 1591
f.s., sc,pts perf mat rent (M402)

Concerto for Violoncello and
Orchestra, No. 2, Op. 85
2.0.1.2(contrabsn). 0.0.0.0. 6perc,
harp,cel,pno,strings,vcl solo
[25'] SIKORSKI perf mat rent
(M403)

MEYERBEER, GIACOMO (1791-1864)
Africaine, L': Je Vois La Mer (No.
21)
orch,solo voice BOIS
(M404)

Africaine, L': Overture
BREITKOPF-W
(M405)

Afrikanerin, Die: Marsch
2+pic.2.2+bass clar.2. 4.2.3.1.
timp,perc,harp,strings [9'] (no
score) BREITKOPF-W
(M406)

Afrikanerin, Die: Overture
2+pic.2+English horn.2+bass clar.3.
4.2+2cornet.3.1. timp,perc,harp,
strings [5'] BREITKOPF-W (M407)

Fackeltanz Nr. 1 B-Dur
(Hoffmann, F.) 1+pic.2.2.2.
4.2.3.1. timp,perc,strings [4']
(no score) BREITKOPF-W (M408)

Hugenotten, Die: Ihr Edlen Herrn
Allhier
see Huguenots, Les: Cavatina Of
Urban

**MEYERBEER, GIACOMO (cont'd.)**

Hugenotten, Die: Ihr Wangenpaar
see Huguenots, Les: Romance Of
Raoul

Hugenotten, Die: Overture
see Huguenots, Les: Overture

Hugenotten, Die: Zigeunertanz
2+pic.2.2.2. 4.4.3.1. timp,perc,
strings [5'] (no score)
BREITKOPF-W (M409)

Huguenots, Les: Cavatina Of Urban
"Hugenotten, Die: Ihr Edlen Herrn
Allhier" 2.2.2.2. 4.2.0.0.
strings,S solo [5'] BREITKOPF-W
(M410)

Huguenots, Les: Overture
"Hugenotten, Die: Overture" 2+
pic.2+English horn.2.2. 4.4.3.0+
ophicleide. timp,perc,strings
[6'] BREITKOPF-W (M411)

Huguenots, Les: Romance Of Raoul
"Hugenotten, Die: Ihr Wangenpaar"
2.2.2.2. 4.2.0.0. timp,strings,T
solo,vla solo [6'] (no score)
BREITKOPF-W (M412)

Polonaise
see Struensee: Zweiter Entreact

Prophet, Der: Ach! Mein Sohn, Segen
Dir!
see Prophète, Le: Arioso Of Fides

Prophet, Der: O Gebt, Errettet Einen
Armen
see Prophète, Le: Romance Of Fides

Prophète, Le: Arioso Of Fides
"Prophet, Der: Ach! Mein Sohn,
Segen Dir!" 2+pic.2.2.2. 4.0.0.0.
strings,A solo [5'] (no score)
BREITKOPF-W (M413)

Prophète, Le: Balletmusic
2+pic.2.2.2. 4.4.3.1. timp,perc,
strings [12'] (no score)
BREITKOPF-W (M414)

Prophète, Le: Romance Of Fides
"Prophet, Der: O Gebt, Errettet
Einen Armen" 2.2.2.2. 4.0.0.0.
strings,A solo [4'] BREITKOPF-W
(M415)

Robert Der Teufel: Robert, Robert,
Mein Geliebter
2.1+English horn.2.2. 4.2.3.0+
ophicleide. timp,2harp,strings,S
solo [6'] (no score; cavatina of
Isabelle) BREITKOPF-W (M416)

Robert Le Diable: Balletmusic
3.2.2.2. 4.2.3.1. timp,perc,strings
[12'] (no score) BREITKOPF-W
(M417)

Robert Le Diable: Overture And
Bacchanale
2+pic.2.2.2. 4.2.3.1. timp,perc,
strings [9'] (no score)
BREITKOPF-W (M418)

Struensee: Overture
3(pic).2.2.2. 4.2.3.1. timp,harp,
strings [14'] (no score)
BREITKOPF-W (M419)

Struensee: Zweiter Entreact
(Polonaise)
(Hoffmann, F.) 2+pic.2.2.2.
4.2.3.1. timp,strings (no score)
BREITKOPF-W (M420)

**MEYERS, RANDALL**
Telegraphist, The: Overture
3(pic).3(English horn).3(bass
clar).3(contrabsn). 4.2.3.1.
cimbalom,timp,harp,pno,strings
[6'] NORSKMI (M421)

Zannata For Oboe Solo And Chamber
Orchestra
1.1(English horn).1.1. 1.1.0.0.
timp,pno,strings,ob solo NORSKMI
(M422)

MEZEI CSOKOR see Kadosa, Pal, Bouquet
Of Field Flowers

M50 see Matthews, Colin

MI-CLOS see Drouet, Jean-Pierre

**MICA, JAN ADAM FRANTISEK (1746-1811)**
Concertino in F for Cembalo and Oboe
0.2.0.0. 2.0.0.0. strings,cembalo&
ob soli CESKY HUD. (M423)

**MICHANS, CARLOS (1950- )**
Alternances
string orch,4sax [13'] sc DONEMUS
(M424)

**MICHANS, CARLOS (cont'd.)**

Concerto Da Camera
1.1.1.1. 1.1.1.0. perc,pno,strings,
vln solo [16'] sc DONEMUS (M425)

Sinfonia Concertante for Violin,
Violoncello and Orchestra, No. 2
2.2.2.2. 2.0.0.0. harp,strings,vln&
vcl soli [24'] sc DONEMUS (M426)

**MICHEL, PAUL-BAUDOUIN (1930- )**
Parcours Mosan
1.1.1.0. 0.0.0.0. strings [11'30"]
BELGE (M427)

MICHELANGELO-SINFONIE see Schenker,
Friedrich

**MICKA, VIT**
Concertino for Piano, Strings, 2
Trumpets and Timpani
[17'] CESKY HUD. (M428)

MICROSYMPHONY see Wuorinen, Charles

MIDNIGHT ROAD, THE see Kulesha, Gary

MIDNIGHT SUN, THE see Yuasa, Joji,
Hommage À Sibelius

MIDSOMMARVISA
(Burwick, Karin) 1.1.2.1.alto sax.
1.1.2.0. strings sc STIM (M429)

MIDSUMMER NIGHT'S DREAM, A see
Matsushita, Isao

MIDSUMMER NIGHT'S DREAM (INCIDENTAL
MUSIC) see Shawn, Allen

**MIELENZ, HANS**
Bella Sicilia (Tarantelle)
2.1.2.1. 3.3.3.0. perc,harp,cel,
strings [3'] sc,set BUSCH DM 050
rent (M430)

Tarantelle
see Bella Sicilia

MIGNON: OUVERTÜRE see Thomas, Ambroise

**MIGOT, GEORGES (1891-1976)**
Me L'A Dit Qu'À La Moisson, Il (from
Deux Chants, Sur 2 Poèmes De G.
Ville)
orch,high solo [6'] LEDUC (M431)

Ne Demandons À L'Avenir
see Trois Chants

Printemps
see Trois Chants

Symphony No. 4
2.2.2.2. 2.2.0.0. strings [22']
LEDUC (M432)

Trois Chants
orch,3 high soli, (nos. 1 & 3 only
with orchestra) LEDUC f.s.
contains: Ne Demandons À
L'Avenir; Printemps (M433)

MIGRATION VERS L'AUTOMNE see Longtin,
Michel

**MIHAJLOVIC**
Preludio, Aria E Finale
3.3.3.3. 4.4.4.1. timp,perc,pno,
cel,harp,8vln I,7vln II,6vla,
5vcl,4db [14'] sc PETERS 03021
(M434)

**MIHALOVICI, MARCEL (1898-1985)**
Follia *Op.106
3.2.3.3. 4.3.4.0. timp,perc,pno,
cel,harp,strings [21']
(paraphrase for grand orchestra)
min sc LEDUC HE 32585, PH 304
(M435)

Refrains
3.3.3.3. 4.3.3.1. 2timp,7perc,pno,
strings [14'] LEDUC (M436)

**MIKI, MINORU (1930- )**
Kyu-No-Kyoku *Symphony
"Symphony For Two Worlds" 3.3.3.3.
4.3.3.1. timp,perc,strings [33']
(for European or Japanese
orchestra) PETERS EP 8766 (M437)
"Symphony For Two Worlds" orch, of
Japanese ethnic instruments [33']
(for European or Japanese
orchestra) PETERS EP 8766 (M438)

Symphony For Two Worlds
see Kyu-No-Kyoku

MILD UND LEISE WIE ER LÄCHELT see
Wagner, Richard

**MILFORD, ROBIN (1903-1959)**
Nightpiece
8vln I,7vln II,6vla,5vcl,4db [8']
sc PETERS 04719 (M439)

**MILHAUD, DARIUS (1892-1974)**
Concert De Chambre *Op.389
wind quin,string quin,pno ESCHIG
554-01013 (M440)

Euménides, Les: Le Final
2.2.4.4.4sax. 2.4.3.0. timp,7perc,
strings, 4 saxhorns LEDUC (M441)

Euménides, Les: Overture To Act III
2.2.3.4.4sax. 2.2.3.0. timp,4perc,
strings, 4 saxhorns (to Act Iv)
LEDUC (M442)

Quatre Chansons De Ronsard *Op.233
[Fr/Eng] 2(pic).2.2(alto sax).2.
2.2.2.0. timp,perc,strings,S solo
[10'] (text by Ronsard) BOOSEY-
ENG rent (M443)

Suite Anglaise *Op.234
2.2.2.2. 2.2.2.1. timp,perc,
strings,harmonica/vln/acord solo
[17'] BOOSEY-ENG rent (M444)

MILITARY MARCH see Korngold, Erich
Wolfgang

**MILLER, ELMA (1954- )**
Concerto for Percussion and Orchestra
2(pic).2(English horn).2.2.
4.2.1.0. timp&perc,strings,perc
solo sc CANADIAN MI 1340 M647CO
(M445)

Striding Folly
1.1.1.1. 1.0.0.0. strings [25'] (1.
Five Red Herrings 2. Tweedledee
3. Gaudy Night: Folly Bridge 4.
Tweedledum 5. And Then There Were
None) sc CANADIAN MI 1200 M647ST
(M446)

"...To Light One Candle..."
string orch,acord solo sc CANADIAN
MI 1666 M647TO (M447)

**MILLER, FRANZ R. (1926- )**
Concerto Pastorale
1.1.1.1. 1.0.0.0. harp,xylo,glock,
triangle,strings BÖHM (M448)

Trio Giocoso
strings BÖHM (M449)

**MILLER, MICHAEL R. (1932- )**
Sonata for String Orchestra
"To Mother Earth And Father Time"
string orch [24'] sc CANADIAN
MI 1500 M649SO (M450)

To Mother Earth And Father Time
see Sonata for String Orchestra

**MILLER, PHILIP (1961- )**
Symphony
3(pic).2.3(bass clar).3(contrabsn).
4.3.3.1. timp,2perc,strings [18']
sc STIM (M451)

Symphony No. 1
3(pic).3(English horn).3(bass
clar).3(contrabsn).sax. 4.3.3.1.
timp,3perc,harp,strings [30']
STIM sc H-2934, pts (M452)

**MILLS, RICHARD (1949- )**
Aeolian Caprices
2+pic.2+English horn.2+bass clar.2+
contrabsn. 4.3.3.1. timp&tubular
bells&wood blocks,3perc,harp,pno,
strings [6'] BOOSEY-ENG rent
(M453)

Bamaga Diptych
2+2pic.2+English horn.2+clar in E
flat+bass clar.2+contrabsn. 4.3+
piccolo trp.4.1. timp&cym,4perc,
harp,pno,cel,strings [18']
BOOSEY-ENG rent (M454)

Castlemaine Antiphons
2+pic.2.3(bass clar). 2+contrabsn.
4.3.3.1. timp&cym,4perc,harp,
strings, brass band [10'] BOOSEY-
ENG rent (M455)

Concerto for Flute
2(pic).1+English horn.2(clar in E
flat,bass clar).2. 2.2.3.0. timp,
4perc,harp,pno,strings,fl solo
[19'] BOOSEY-ENG rent (M456)

Concerto for Trumpet
2(pic).2.2.2. 2.2.3.0. timp,2perc,
harp,pno&cel,strings,trp solo
[23'] BOOSEY-ENG rent (M457)

Concerto for Violin
2(pic,alto fl).2(English
horn).2(bass clar).2(contrabsn).
2.2.1.0. perc,harp,pno&cel,8vln
I,8vln II,6vla,4vcl,2db,vln solo
[20'] BOOSEY-ENG rent (M458)

Concerto for Violoncello
2(alto fl,pic).1+English
horn.2(bass clar)+bass clar.2+
contrabsn. 4.2(flügelhorn).3.1.

MILLS, RICHARD (cont'd.)

    timp,2perc,harp,pno,strings,vcl
    solo [20'] BOOSEY-ENG rent (M459)

Fanfares For Percussion And Orchestra
    2.2.2.2. 4.2.3.0. 2perc,strings
    [2'] BOOSEY-ENG rent          (M460)

Fantastic Pantomimes
    2(pic).2.2.2+contrabsn.
    4.3(2piccolo trp).3.1. timp&cym,
    4perc,harp,strings,fl&ob&clar&
    horn&trp soli [17'] BOOSEY-ENG
    rent                          (M461)

Music for Strings
    string orch [25'] BOOSEY-ENG rent (M462)

Overture With Fanfares
    2(pic).2.2.2. 4.3.3.1. timp,3perc,
    strings [10'] BOOSEY-ENG rent (M463)

Sappho Monologues
    2+pic.2(English horn).3(clar in E
    flat,bass clar).2. 4.2.3.0.
    3perc,pno,2harp,cel,strings [20']
    BOOSEY-ENG rent               (M464)

Seaside Dances
    6vln I,4vln II,4vla,3vcl,db [20']
    BOOSEY-ENG rent               (M465)

Sequenzas Concertante
    2(pic).2.2.2. 2.2.0.0. timp,2perc,
    strings [18'] BOOSEY-ENG rent (M466)

Snugglepot And Cuddlepie Suite
    2+pic.+English horn.3(clar in E
    flat,bass clar).2+contrabsn.
    4.3(piccolo trp).3.1. timp,3perc,
    harp,pno,strings [20'] BOOSEY-ENG
    rent                          (M467)

Soundscapes For Percussion And
    Orchestra
    2+pic.2+English horn.2+bass clar.2+
    contrabsn. 4.3.3.1. timp,4perc,
    harp,pno&cel,strings [21']
    BOOSEY-ENG rent               (M468)

Tenebrae
    3(pic,alto fl).2+English
    horn.3(bass clar).3(contrabsn).
    4.3.3.1. 2timp,3perc,2harp,cel,
    pno,strings [18'] BOOSEY-ENG rent
                                  (M469)

MILOSTNY TANEC see Kašlik, Václav

MINAMI, SATOSHI (1955-    )
    Coloration Project X  *Op.17,No.10
    orch,pno [38'] JAPAN          (M470)

    Efe  *Op.35
    pno,orch [16'] JAPAN          (M471)

MINIATUREN FÜR STREICHORCHESTER see
    Schnyder, Daniel

MINIATURY see Berkovec, Jirí see
    Precechtel, Zbynek

MINNA VON BARNHELM: OUVERTURE see Bruns,
    Victor

MINNELIED see Sibelius, Jean

MINUTE PLUS WALTZ RAG see Gould, Morton

MIO TESORO INTANTO, IL see Mozart,
    Wolfgang Amadeus

MIRABELL JAM see Bourland, Roger

MIRABILIS see Marina, Cristian

MIRACROSE see Trochu, Pierre

MIRAGE see Parmerud

MIRAGES see Hetu, Jacques

MIRAGGI see Fedeli, Denise

MIRJAMS SIEGESGESANG see Reinecke, Carl

MIROGLIO, FRANCIS (1924-    )
    Reseaux For Harp And Orchestra
    harp,orch sc INTERNAT.S.      (M472)

MIROIRS TRANSPARENTS, LES see Dalbavie,
    Marc-Andre

MIROVÁ PREDEHRA see Deváty, Antonín

MIRROR OF GALADRIEL see Rae, Allan

MIRROR OF MIST, A see Nishimura, Akira

MISCELLANEOUS SHORTER WORKS see Walton,
    [Sir] William (Turner)

MISERERE see Raskatov, Alexander

MISERO ME see Mozart, Wolfgang Amadeus

MISIVA DEL PLATA, UNA see Betancur-
    Gonzalez, Valentin, Exhorto

"MISSA DE ANGELIS" FANTASIA see Clarke,
    F.R.C.

MIST see Qu, Xiao-Song

MISTERIUM see Sitsky, Larry

MISTLETOE see Farkas, Ferenc

MIT DEN RIESENSTIEFELN see Schwertsik,
    Kurt

MITSCHURIN: WALTZES see Shostakovich,
    Dmitri

MITTERNACHTSPOLKA see Waldteufel, Emile

MIXING MEMORIES AND DESIRES see
    Larsson, Mats, Symphony No. 1

MJØSDRONNINGEN see Vea, Ketil

MLADA: FINALE see Borodin, Alexander
    Porfirievich

MLÉCNÁ DRÁHA see Stepanek, Jiri

MMMATTER
    (Berg, Sebastian) English horn,perc,
    strings [2'5"] sc,pts STIM    (M473)

MOCHIZUKI, MISATO (1969-    )
    One Glance In Spiros' Backyard
    chamber orch [9'] JAPAN       (M474)

MOCK MORRIS see Grainger, Percy
    Aldridge

MODELLE see Heider, Werner

MODER JORD see Winter, Tomas

MODLITBA ZA VODU see Sedlácek, Bohuslav

MODR, ANTONÍN (1898-1983)
    Variations for Orchestra, Op. 17
    3.2.2.2. 4.3.3.1. timp,perc,harp,
    cel,org,strings CESKY HUD.    (M475)

MODRY VÍTR NAD REKOU see Klempír,
    Jaromir

MODULES see Powell, Mel

MODUS VIVENDI see Skog, Ylva see
    Wendelboe, Jens

MOESCHINGER, ALBERT (1897-    )
    Concerto Da Camera Für Cembalo Und
    Kleines Orchester
    1.1.1.1. 1.0.0.0. strings MULL &
    SCH rent                      (M476)

    Concerto for Piano and Chamber
    Orchestra, No. 2, Op. 23
    MULL & SCH rent               (M477)

    Concerto for Piano and Chamber
    Orchestra, No. 3, Op. 42
    MULL & SCH rent               (M478)

    Concerto for Piano and Orchestra, Op.
    77
    2.1.2.2. 4.2.2.1. timp,perc,strings
    MULL & SCH rent               (M479)

    Entree Et Scherzo Ingenu
    orch MULL & SCH rent          (M480)

    Erratique  *Op.104
    2.2.2.2. 4.2.1.0. pno,harp,cel,
    perc,strings MULL & SCH rent
                                  (M481)

    Homo Et Fatum
    2.2.2.2. 4.2.1.0. timp,perc,cel,
    pno,strings MULL & SCH rent
                                  (M482)

    Sargasmes  *Op.101
    2.2.2.2. 2.1.0.0. harp,cel,pno,
    perc,strings MULL & SCH rent
                                  (M483)

    Symphony, Op. 71
    orch (to the glory of...) MULL &
    SCH rent                      (M484)

    Tre Caprichos
    2.2.2.2. 2.2.2.0. timp,perc,cel,
    pno,harp,strings [12'] MULL & SCH
    rent                          (M485)

MOEVS, ROBERT WALTER (1921-    )
    Symphonic Piece No. 6
    3(pic).3(English horn).3(bass
    clar).3(contrabsn). 4.3.3.1.
    timp,4perc,strings PRESSER rent
                                  (M486)

MOHLER, PHILIPP (1908-1982)
    Vagabundenlieder, Op. 36
    2.2.2.2. 4.3.3.1. timp,perc,harp,
    strings,Bar solo [12'] (texts by
    Hermann Hesse) SIKORSKI perf mat

MOHLER, PHILIPP (cont'd.)

    rent                          (M487)

MOHR VON VENEDIG, DER: OUVERTÜRE see
    Rossini, Gioacchino, Otello:
    Ouverture

MOIRE see Domhardt, Gerd

MOJZIS, VOJTECH (1949-    )
    Vinicné Sumice
    3.3.3.3. 8.4.4.1. perc,harp,pno,
    strings [7'] CESKY HUD.       (M488)

MOLAND, EIRIK (1959-    )
    Konrad Tommelfinger: Some
    Nightmaremusic
    [Norw] 1(pic).1.1(pic).1. 0.0.2.0.
    timp,3perc,strings,Bar solo [6']
    (text by Heinrich Hoffmann &
    Sofie Foss) NORSKMI          (M489)

"MOLDAU" AND OTHER WORKS see Smetana,
    Bedrich

MOLDOVAN RHAPSODY see Szabo, Ferenc

MOLIQUE, (WILHELM) BERNHARD (1802-1869)
    Concerto for Flute and Orchestra in D
    minor, Op. 69
    fl solo,orch KUNZELMANN 10234 ipr
                                  (M490)

    Concerto No. 2 for Violin and
    Orchestra, Op. 9, in A
    1.2.2.2. 2.2.0.0. timp,strings,vln
    solo [18'] (no score) BREITKOPF-W
                                  (M491)

MOLLICONE, HENRY (1946-    )
    Celestial Dance
    3.3.3.2. 4.3.3.1. timp,4perc,harp,
    2kbd,strings [7'] SCHIRM.EC rent
                                  (M492)

MOLLY'S SONG 1 see Saunders, Rebecca,
    Crimson

MOLTO SOSTENUTO: E131 see Eckhardt-
    Gramatte, Sophie Carmen

MOMENTAUFNAHMEN see Keller, Hermann

MOMENTE see Poulheim, Bert

MOMENTS MACABRES see Barab, Seymour

MOMENTS MUSICAUX see Vlach-Vruticky,
    Josef

MOMENTUM see Turnage, Mark-Anthony

MONADE see Pepin, Clermont

MOND, DER: FURIOSO see Hofmann,
    Wolfgang

MOND, DER: INTERMEZZO see Hofmann,
    Wolfgang see Hofmann, Wolfgang,
    Intermezzo

MOND, DER: SINFONIA BREVIS see Hofmann,
    Wolfgang

MONDAY AND TUESDAY see Torke, Michael

MONKEY, THE see Foley, Daniel

MONN, GEORG MATTHIAS (1717-1750)
    Concerto for Violoncello and Strings
    vcl solo,strings KUNZELMANN ipa sc
    10007A, oct 10007            (M493)

MONODIA see Karolyi, Pal

MONODIEN see Haselbach, Josef

MONODY see Matthews, Colin

MONODY FOR ORCHESTRA see Nishimura,
    Akira

MONOLOG JULIE see Zahradník, Zdenek

MONOLOG JULIE II see Zahradník, Zdenek

MONOLOGE see Uspensky, Vladislav

MONSIEUR ET MADAME DENIS: OVERTURE see
    Offenbach, Jacques

MONTAGGIO see Wittinger, Robert

MONTAGUE, STEPHEN (1943-    )
    Dark Sun
    orch,1-2pno UNITED MUS        (M494)

    Snakebite
    0.2.0.0. 2.0.0.0. strings [14']
    UNITED MUS rent               (M495)

MONTAGUE PIECE, THE see Coles, Graham

MONTANYAS DEL ROSELLO see Roget,
    Henriette Puig

MONTBRUN, RAYMOND GALLOIS
see GALLOIS MONTBRUN, RAYMOND

MONTE GELBOE see Orbon, Julian

MONTGOMERY, JAMES (1943-    )
Manas
3+pic.1.4(bass clar,clar in E
flat).2(contrabsn). 2.2.3.1.
3perc,strings [15'] sc CANADIAN
MI 1100 M787MA            (M496)

Reconnaissance
string orch [12'] sc CANADIAN
MI 1500 M787RE            (M497)

MONTH IN THE COUNTRY, A see Blake,
Howard

MONTRAL, PIERRE
Concertino
fl,harp,strings sc TONOS
M-2015-3833-4             (M498)

Concerto for Percussion and
Orchestra, No. 1
TONOS M-2015-3817-4 rent  (M499)

Variations D'Concertantes
chamber orch sc TONOS M-2015-3821-1
                         (M500)
MONTVILAS, VYTAUTAS
Gotisches Poem
2.2.2.2. 4.3.3.0. timp,perc,strings
[11'] SIKORSKI perf mat rent
                         (M501)
MONTY PYTHON'S FLYING CIRCUS see Sousa,
John Philip, Liberty Bell March,
The

MOO see Hansson, Mats O.

MOONLIGHT ON JUPITER see Raitio, Väinö,
Kuutamo Jupiterissa

MORAN, ROBERT (1937-    )
Après-Midi Du Dracoula, L'
orch [13'] SCHOTTS perf mat rent
                         (M502)
Elegant Journey With Stopping Points
Of Interest
chamber orch,opt perc SCHOTTS perf
mat rent                 (M503)

MORAVEC, PAUL
Ancient Lights
2.2.2.2. 2.2.1.0. timp,perc,kbd,
strings [15'] SCHIRM.EC rent
                         (M504)
Aubade For String Orchestra
strings [15'] SCHIRM.EC rent (M505)

Spiritdance
3.3.3.2. 3.2.2.1. timp,perc,kbd,
strings [10'] SCHIRM.EC rent
                         (M506)
Streamline
2.2.2.2. 2.2.1.0. timp,perc,strings
[14'] SCHIRM.EC rent     (M507)

MORAWETZ, OSKAR (1917-    )
Concerto for Harp and Orchestra
2(pic).2.2.2. 2.2.0.0. timp,perc,
strings,harp solo [27'] sc
CANADIAN MI 1316 M831CO   (M508)

Dirge (from Symphony No. 1)
3+pic.2.2.2. 4.3.3.1. timp,perc,
harp,strings [32'] sc,min sc
CANADIAN MI 1100 M831DI   (M509)

Fantasy (from Symphony No. 1)
3+pic.2.2.2. 4.3.3.1. timp,perc,
harp,strings [32'] sc CANADIAN
MI 1100 M831FA            (M510)

Psalm 22 - My God Why Have You
Forsaken Me?
orch,med solo [14'] CANADIAN
MV 1400 M831PS            (M511)

Symphonic Scherzo (Symphony No. 1,
Third Movement)
2+pic.2.2.2. 4.3.3.1. timp,perc,
harp,strings sc CANADIAN
MI 1100 M831SC            (M512)

Symphony No. 1,Third Movement
see Symphonic Scherzo

MORCEAU DE CONCERT, OP. 154 see Saint-
Saëns, Camille

MORE see Kálik, Vaclav

MOREL, FRANCOIS D'ASSISE (1926-    )
Départs
2perc,harp,gtr,strings [10'] sc
CANADIAN MI 1100 M839DE_A (M513)

Paraphrase Sur Des Airs De Nöel
3+pic.2.2.2. 4.3.3.1. timp,perc,
harp,strings [6'] sc CANADIAN
MI 1100 M839PA            (M514)

MOREL, FRANCOIS D'ASSISE (cont'd.)
Rituel dec l'espace
3(pic).2(English horn).2(bass
clar).2. 2.2.2.1. 4perc,pno&cel,
4vcl,4db [19'] sc CANADIAN
MI 1100 M839RI            (M515)

Trajectoire
3(pic).2(English horn).3(bass
clar).2(contrabsn). 4.4.4.1.
timp,2perc,harp,pno&cel,strings,
narrator [11'] sc CANADIAN
MI 1100 M839TR            (M516)

MORENO TORROBA, FEDERICO (1891-1982)
Concerto for Guitar and Orchestra
see Concierto De Castilla

Concierto De Castilla (Concerto for
Guitar and Orchestra)
1.1.2.1. 0.1.0.0. timp,harp,cel,
strings,gtr solo [15'] SIKORSKI
pno red 669K f.s., sc,pts perf
mat rent                 (M517)

MORGAN, DAVID (1933-    )
Threnody
string orch sc CANADIAN
MI 1500 M847TH            (M518)

MORGEN, DER see Duvosel, Lieven

MORGENGEBETE see Kantscheli, Gija

MORGENGLANZ DER EWIGKEIT see Kutzer,
Ernst

MORI see Kukiyama, Naoshi

MORI, KURODO (1950-    )
In Process Of Time
2.2.2.2. 3.2.3.0. harp,cel,7vln I,
6vln II,5vla,4vcl,3db [13']
SCHOTTS perf mat rent    (M519)

Premier Beau Matin De Mai
1.1.1.1. 1.1.1.0. pno,vln,vla,vcl,
db [12'] SCHOTTS perf mat rent
                         (M520)
MORITAT VOM SCHINDERHANNES, DIE: SUITE
see Kneip, Gustav

MORIYA, YUKO (1969-    )
In Pursuit Of Song For Babylon
orch,vcl [12'] JAPAN      (M521)

MORNING RUSH see Grahn, Ulf

MORNING WHISPER see Grahn, Ulf

MOROSS, JEROME (1913-1983)
Biguine [4'25"]
3(pic).3.2(bass clar).2. 4.4.3.1.
perc,pno,strings
SOROM                    (M522)

Frankie And Johnny, Ballet Suite
[21'0"]
2.2.3(bass clar).2. 2.2.2(bass
trom).0. 5perc,pno,strings,SSA
soli
SOROM                    (M523)

Last Judgement, The [21'8"] ballet
2(2pic).1(English horn).2(bass
clar).1. 2.2.1.0. perc,harp,
pno,cel,strings
(contains 10 dances) SOROM (M524)

Symphony No. 1 [20'18"]
3(pic).3(English horn).3(clar in
E flat,bass clar).3(contrabsn).
4.3(trp in D).2+bass trom.1. 2-
3perc,pno,cel,strings
SOROM                    (M525)

Tall Story For Orchestra, A [9'12"]
3(pic).2.3(bass clar).2. 4.3.2+
bass trom.1. 3perc,strings
SOROM                    (M526)

Variations On A Waltz [14'0"]
3(pic).3(English horn).3(bass
clar).3(contrabsn). 4.3.3(bass
trom).1. 5perc,harp,cel,strings
SOROM                    (M527)

MORTARI, VIRGILIO (1902-1993)
Variazioni Sul Carnevale Di Venezia
orch FORLIVESI rent       (M528)

MORTHENSON, JAN W. (1940-    )
Antiphonia II
orch perf sc REIMERS 101181 rent
                         (M529)
Antiphonia III
orch REIMERS 101182 rent  (M530)

Attacca
string orch,electronic tape sc
REIMERS 101043 rent      (M531)

Contra
1(pic).1(English horn).1(bass
clar).1.alto sax. 1.1.1.0. perc,

MORTHENSON, JAN W. (cont'd.)
strings [17'] REIMERS study sc
101184, sc rent          (M532)

Discantus
chamber orch sc REIMERS 101203 rent
                         (M533)
Interna
orch [45'] sc REIMERS 101230 rent
                         (M534)
orch [33'] REIMERS        (M535)

Life
chamber group,orch, one actor [17']
sc REIMERS 101014 rent   (M536)

MOSAIC, FOR WIND QUINTET, BRASS
QUINTET, STRING QUARTET, PERCUSSION
AND STRING ORCHESTRA see Sunde,
Helge Havsgaard, Mosaikk

MOSAIKK see Sunde, Helge Havsgaard

MOSAÏQUES POUR GRAND ORCHESTRE see
Carignan, Nichole

MOSKEVSKÁ see Kopecky, Pavel, Ctyri
Symfonická Preludia

MOSS GROWING ON RUINS see Hiscott,
James

MOSSOLOV, ALEXANDER (1900-1973)
Ah, Grossmutter, Komm Schnell
see Drei Kinderszenen, For Solo
Voice And Chamber Orchestra, Op.
18

Böser Kater Sitzt In Der Ecke, Ein
see Drei Kinderszenen, For Solo
Voice And Chamber Orchestra, Op.
18

Drei Kinderszenen, For Solo Voice And
Chamber Orchestra, Op. 18
(Denissow, Edison) [Russ] 1.1.1.1.
1.1.1.0. perc,harp,pno,vln,vla,
vcl,db,solo voice SIKORSKI perf
mat rent
contains: Ah, Grossmutter, Komm
Schnell; Böser Kater Sitzt In
Der Ecke, Ein; Kreisel Ist
Kaputt, Der             (M537)

Kreisel Ist Kaputt, Der
see Drei Kinderszenen, For Solo
Voice And Chamber Orchestra, Op.
18

Symphony No. 5
2+pic.2+English horn.2+bass clar.2+
contrabsn. 4.3.3.1. timp,6perc,
cel&pno,harp,strings [35']
sc SCHOTTS KIN 1001 perf mat rent
                         (M538)
MOSTAD, JON (1942-    )
Concerto for Violoncello and
Orchestra
2(pic).1.2(bass clar).1. 2.1.1.0.
2perc,pno,strings,vcl solo [22']
NORSKMI                  (M539)

Like A Spring Rain
2.2.2.2. 4.3.3.1. timp,2perc,harp,
strings [5'] NORSKMI      (M540)

MOTOR FOR SYMFONIORKESTER OG TAPE see
Iberg, Helge

MOTUS see Lidholm, Ingvar

MOTYLÍ EFEKT see Jirácková, Marta

MOUNTAIN, THE see Qu, Xiao-Song

MOURNING THE LOSS OF OUR DEMONS see
Tittle, Steve

MOUSE, THE see Foley, Daniel

MOUSSORGSKY, MODEST PETROVITCH
see MUSSORGSKY, MODEST PETROVICH

MOUTON, CHARLES
Concerti, Nos. 5-7
strings,cont MÖSELER      (M541)

MOUVEMENT CONCERTANT see Delerue,
Georges

MOUVEMENT SYMPHONIQUE see Badian, Maya
see Hetu, Jacques, Tombeau De
Nelligan, Le

MOUVEMENT SYMPHONIQUE IV see Matton,
Roger

MOUVEMENTS PROVISOIRES 2 see Frenette,
Claude

MOUVEMENTS SONORES ET ACCENTUÉS see
Bucht, Gunnar, Symphony No. 12

MOVEMENT see Boccadoro, Carlo

MÖWE, DIE: SUITE see Shchedrin, Rodion

MOZART see Toovey, Andrew

MOZART, LEOPOLD (1719-1787)
Concerto for Trombone and Orchestra
(Weinmann) trom solo/vla,2ob,
2horn,2trp,timp,strings
KUNZELMANN ipa sc 10139A, oct
10139                        (M542)

Concerto for Trumpet and Orchestra in
D
(Weinmann) trp solo,orch KUNZELMANN
ipa sc 10138A, oct 10138    (M543)

Musikalische Schlittenfahrt
2ob,2bsn,2cornet,2trp in C,timp,
strings, sleigh bells and whip
KUNZELMANN ipa sc 10222A, oct
10222                        (M544)

Sinfonia in A
(Eisen, Cliff) 2vln,vla,vcl,db [7']
ARTARIA AE167                (M545)

Sinfonia in D
(Eisen, Cliff) 2horn,2vln,vla,vcl,
db [12'] ARTARIA AE166       (M546)

Sinfonia in D, MIN 1
(Eisen, Cliff) 2horn,2vln,vla,vcl,
db [14'] ARTARIA AE168       (M547)

Sinfonia in G
(Eisen, Cliff) 2ob,2horn,2vln,vla,
vcl,db [13'] ARTARIA AE165 (M548)

Sinfonia Pastorale
corno pastoriccio (Alp-, Hirten-,
Jagd-, Wald-, Ventilhorn),
strings KUNZELMANN ipa sc 10159A,
oct 10159                    (M549)

MOZART, WOLFGANG AMADEUS (1756-1791)
Abendempfindung  *K.523
(Mottl, F.) 1.1.1.1. 1.0.0.0.
strings,S solo [4'30"] BREITKOPF-
W                            (M550)

Ach Ich Liebte, War So Glücklich
*K.384 (from Die Entführung Aus
Dem Serail)
0.2.2.2. 2.0.0.0. strings,S solo
[5'] (aria of Constanze)
BREITKOPF-W                  (M551)

Ach, Werd Ich Ihn Wohl Finden
see Ah Chi Mi Dice Mai

Adagio E Fuga C-Moll  *K.546
strings study sc,set,pts SCHOTT
                             (M552)

Adagio in E, K. 261
solo voice,orch sc KUNZELMANN
EKB 41P ipa                  (M553)

Ah Chi Mi Dice Mai  *K.527 (from Don
Giovanni)
"Ach, Werd Ich Ihn Wohl Finden"
0.0.2.2. 2.0.0.0. strings,SBarB
soli [4'] (aria-trio of Elvira,
Don Giovanni, and Leporello)
BREITKOPF-W                  (M554)

Ah, Fuggi Il Traditor  *K.527 (from
Don Giovanni)
"Oh Flieh, Betrogne, Flieh"
strings,S solo [2'] (aria of
Donna Elvira) BREITKOPF-W (M555)

Ah Qual Gelido Orror - Il Padre
Adorato  *K.366 (from Idomeneo,
Re Di Creta)
"Welche Schreckliche Nacht - Ich
Finde Den Vater" 1.1.0.1.
2.0.0.0. strings,T solo [3']
(recitative & aria of Idamantes)
BREITKOPF-W                  (M556)

Ah Scostati! - Smanie Implacabili
*K.588 (from Così Fan Tutte)
"Entferne Dich! - Furchtbare Qualen
Ihr" 2.0.2.2. 2.0.0.0. strings,
Mez solo [3'30"] (recitative &
aria of Dorabella) BREITKOPF-W
                             (M557)

Alles Fühlt Der Liebe Freuden  *K.620
(from Die Zauberflöte)
1+pic.0.2.2. 0.0.0.0. strings,B
solo [2'] (aria of Monostatos)
BREITKOPF-W                  (M558)

Aprite Presto, Aprite  *K.492 (from
Le Nozze Di Figaro)
"Geschwind Die Tür Geöffnet"
strings,SS soli [3'] (duettino of
Susanna & Cherubino) BREITKOPF-W
                             (M559)

Auf Zu Dem Feste
see Finch' Han Dal Vino

MOZART, WOLFGANG AMADEUS (cont'd.)

Baccio Di Mano, Un  *K.541
orch,solo voice BOIS         (M560)

Bastien Und Bastienne: Ouvertüre
*K.50
0.2.0.0. 2.0.0.0. strings [2']
BREITKOPF-W                  (M561)

Batti, Batti, O Bel Masetto  *K.527
(from Don Giovanni)
"Schmäle, Schmäle, Lieber Junge"
1.1.0.1. 2.0.0.0. strings,S solo
[4'] (aria of Zerlina) BREITKOPF-
W                            (M562)

Beim Männervolk, Bei Soldaten
see In Uomini, In Soldati

Betulia Liberata: Ouvertüre  *K.118
0.2.0.2. 4.2.0.0. strings [5']
BREITKOPF-W                  (M563)

Bravo, Mein Gnädger Gebieter - Will
Der Herr Graf Ein Tänzchen Nun
Wagen
see Bravo, Signor Padrone - Se Vuol
Ballare

Bravo, Signor Padrone - Se Vuol
Ballare  *K.492 (from Le Nozze Di
Figaro)
"Bravo, Mein Gnädger Gebieter -
Will Der Herr Graf Ein Tänzchen
Nun Wagen" 0.2.0.2. 2.0.0.0.
strings,B solo [5'] (recitative
and cavatina of Figaro)
BREITKOPF-W                  (M564)

Che Soave Zefiretto  *K.492 (from Le
Nozze Di Figaro)
"Wenn Die Sanften Abendwinde"
0.1.0.1. 0.0.0.0. strings,SS soli
[4'] (duet of Susanna & The
Countess) BREITKOPF-W        (M565)

Clemenza Di Tito, La: Ecco Il Punto,
O Vitellia - Non Più Di Fiori
"Titus: Jetzt, Vitellia! Schlägt
Die Stunde - Nie Soll Mit Rosen"
strings,S solo [8'] (recitative
and rondo of Vitellia) BREITKOPF-
W                            (M566)

Clemenza Di Tito, La: Se Al Volto Mai
Ti Senti
"Titus: Wir Bald Ein Leises
Lüftchen" 0.2.2.0. 2.0.0.0.
strings,SSB soli [4'] (trio of
Vitellia, Sesto, and Publio)
BREITKOPF-W                  (M567)

Clemenza Di Tito, La: Se All'Impero,
Amici Dei!  *K.621
"Titus: Soll Die Strenge, Ihr
Güt'gen Götter" 2.2.0.2. 2.0.0.0.
strings,T solo [5'] (aria of
Titus) BREITKOPF-W           (M568)

Complete Serenades Series I
orch sc DOVER 26565-X        (M569)

Complete Serenades Series II
orch sc DOVER 26566-8        (M570)

Concerti for Piano, Nos. 11-16
orch,pno solo sc DOVER 25468-2
                             (M571)

Concerti for Piano, Nos. 17-22
orch,pno solo sc DOVER 23599-8
                             (M572)

Concerti for Piano, Nos. 23-27
orch,pno solo sc DOVER 23600-5
                             (M573)

Concerti For Wind Instruments
orch,winds solo sc DOVER 25228-0
                             (M574)

Concerto for Basset Horn, K. 621b, in
G
2.0.0.2. 2.0.0.0. strings,basset
horn solo [12'] LEDUC        (M575)

Concerto for Flute and Orchestra, K.
622, in G
(Müller, A.E.; Förster, D.H.) fl
solo,orch (Clarinet Concerto (K.
622) re-worked for flute) sc
KUNZELMANN GM 920 ipa        (M576)

Concerto for Horn and Orchestra, K.
412, in D
(Beyer, F.) orch (with Rondo)
KUNZELMANN ipa sc 10241A, oct
10241                        (M577)

Concerto for Oboe and Orchestra, K.
293
(Levin) 0.0.2.2. 2.0.0.0. 8vln I,
7vln II,6vla,5vcl,4db [7']
(fragment) sc,solo pt PETERS
02532                        (M578)

Concerto for Piano and Orchestra, K.
382, in D
see Konzert-Rondo

MOZART, WOLFGANG AMADEUS (cont'd.)

Concerto for Piano in A, K. 414
(Hinze-Reinhold) strings,opt 2ob,
opt 2horn,pno solo [24'] (new
issue by Wolf & Zacharias EP
8812) PETERS sc EP 9027, pts,kbd
pt                           (M579)

Concerto for Piano in C, K. 415
(Hinze-Reinhold) strings,opt 2ob,
opt 2bsn,opt 2horn,opt 2trp,timp,
pno solo [25'] (new issue by Wolf
& Zacharias EP 8813) PETERS sc
EP 9079, pts,kbd pt          (M580)

Concerto for Piano in E flat, K. 449
(Hinze-Reinhold) strings,opt 2ob,
opt 2horn,pno solo [22'] (new
issue by Wolf & Zacharias EP
8814) PETERS sc EP 4602, pts,kbd
pt                           (M581)

Concerto for Piano in F, K. 413
(Hinze-Reinhold) strings,opt 2ob,
opt 2horn,pno solo [21'] (new
issue by Wolf & Zacharias EP
8811) PETERS sc EP 9045, pts,kbd
pt                           (M582)

Concerto for Piano, No. 9, K. 271, in
E flat
(Busoni, F.) 0.2.0.0. 2.0.0.0.
strings,pno solo [35'] (two
cadenzas) BREITKOPF-W EB 8577
                             (M583)

Concerto for Piano, No. 17, K. 453,
in G
(Busoni, F.) 1.2.0.2. 2.0.0.0.
strings,pno solo [30'] (two
cadenzas) BREITKOPF-W EB 8577
                             (M584)

Concerto for Piano, No. 19, K. 459,
in F
(Busoni, F.) 1.2.0.2. 2.0.0.0.
strings,pno solo [24'] (two
cadenzas) BREITKOPF-W EB 8577
                             (M585)

Concerto for Piano, No. 20, K. 466,
in D minor
(Busoni, F.) 1.2.0.2. 2.2.0.0.
timp,strings,pno solo [32'] (two
cadenzas) BREITKOPF-W EB 8578
                             (M586)

Concerto for Piano, No. 21, K. 467,
in C
(Busoni, F.) 1.2.0.2. 2.2.0.0.
timp,strings,pno solo [30']
(three cadenzas) BREITKOPF-W
EB 8578                      (M587)

Concerto for Piano, No. 22, K. 482,
in E flat
(Busoni, F.) 1.0.2.2. 2.2.0.0.
timp,strings,pno solo [32'] (two
cadenzas) BREITKOPF-W EB 8579
                             (M588)

Concerto for Piano, No. 23, K. 488,
in A
(Busoni, F.) 1.0.2.2. 2.0.0.0.
strings,pno solo [26'] (cadenza)
BREITKOPF-W EB 8579          (M589)

Concerto for Piano, No. 24, K. 491,
in C minor
(Busoni, F.) 1.2.2.2. 2.2.0.0.
timp,strings,pno solo [28']
(three cadenzas) BREITKOPF-W
EB 8579                      (M590)

Concerto for Piano, No. 25, K. 503,
in C
(Busoni, F.) 1.2.0.2. 2.2.0.0.
timp,strings,pno solo [33']
(cadenza) BREITKOPF-W EB 8579
                             (M591)

Concerto for Piano, No. 26
orch,pno solo (autograph score) sc
DOVER 26747-4                (M592)

Concerto for 3 Pianos, K. 241, in F
(Badura-Skoda) 3pno soli,orch
KUNZELMANN 10050             (M593)

Concerto for Violoncello in B flat,
K. 191
(Seiffert, M.) orch,vcl/bsn solo
BOIS                         (M594)

Concerto in E flat for Oboe
(Thilde, J.) 0.2.0.0. 2.0.0.0.
hpsd,strings,ob solo [18'] solo
pt BILLAUDOT rent            (M595)

Constanze! Constanze! O Wie
Angstlich, O Wie Feurig  *K.384
(from Die Entführung Aus Dem
Serail)
1.1.0.1. 2.0.0.0. strings,T solo
[5'] (recitative & aria of
Belmonte) BREITKOPF-W        (M596)

Core Vi Dono Bell' Idolo Mio, Il
*K.588 (from Così Fan Tutte)
"Empfange, Geliebte, Dies Herz Hier
Zu Eigen" 0.2.2. 2.0.0.0.

MOZART, WOLFGANG AMADEUS (cont'd.)

strings,MezBar soli [5'] (duet of
Dorabella & Guglielmo) BREITKOPF-
W                                    (M597)

Cosi Dunque Tradisci  *K.432
orch,solo voice BOIS                 (M598)

Così Fan Tutte: Ah Guarda, Sorella
*K.588 (from Così Fan Tutte)
"O Sieh Doch Nur, Schwester"
0.0.2.2. 2.0.0.0. strings,SMez
soli [4'30"] (duet of Fiordiligi
& Dorabella) BREITKOPF-W    (M599)

Crudel! Perchè Finora Farmi Languir
Cosi  *K.492 (from Le Nozze Di
Figaro)
"Warum Gabst Du Bis Heute Nie
Meinem Flehn Gehör?" 2.0.0.2.
2.0.0.0. strings,SBar soli [4']
(duet of Susanna & Count)
BREITKOPF-W                          (M600)

Crudele? - Non Mi Dir  *K.527 (from
Don Giovanni)
"Ich Grausam? - Sag Mir Nicht"
1.0.2.2. 2.0.0.0. strings,S solo
[2'] (recitative & aria of Donna
Anna) BREITKOPF-W                    (M601)

Deh Vieni Alla Finestra  *K.527 (from
Don Giovanni)
"Feinsliebchen, Komm Ans Fenster"
strings,mand,Bar solo [2']
(canzonetta of Don Giovanni)
BREITKOPF-W                          (M602)

Deutscher Tanz
see Sechs Deutsche Tänze

Don Giovanni: Ouvertüre  *K.527
(Blomhert, B.) 2.2.2.2. 2.2.0.0.
timp,strings [6'] sc,pts
BREITKOPF-W PB-OB 5267               (M603)

Donne Mie, La Fate A Tanti  *K.588
(from Così Fan Tutte)
"Mädchen, So Treibt Ihr's Mit
Allen" 2.2.0.2. 2.0.0.0. strings,
Bar solo [3'00"] (aria of
Guglielmo) BREITKOPF-W               (M604)

D'Oreste, d'Ajace  *K.366 (from
Idomeneo, Re Di Creta)
"Orestes und Ajas" 2.2.0.2.
4.2.0.0. timp,strings,Mez solo
[7'] (aria of Elektra) BREITKOPF-
W                                    (M605)

Dove Son? - Soave Sia Il Vento
*K.588 (from Così Fan Tutte)
"Sind Sie Fort? - Weht Leiser, Ihr
Winde" 2.0.2.2. 2.0.0.0. strings,
SMezB soli [4'] (recitative &
trio of Fiordiligi, Dorabella,
and Don Alfonso) BREITKOPF-W         (M606)

Drei Divertimenti  *K.136-138
(Herrmann) strings PETERS f.s.
study sc EP 4266A, kbd pt
EP 4266, pts                         (M607)

Drei Menuette  *K.363
0.2.0.2. 2.2.0.0. timp,strings
without vla [3'] BREITKOPF-W         (M608)

Durch Zärtlichkeit Und Schmeicheln
*K.384 (from Die Entführung Aus
Dem Serail)
strings,S solo [4'] (aria of
Blondchen) BREITKOPF-W               (M609)

Ei Parte - Per Pietà, Ben Mio,
Perdona  *K.588 (from Così Fan
Tutte)
"Er Fliehet - O Verzeih', Verzeih',
Geliebter" 2.0.2.2. 2.0.0.0.
strings,S solo [10'30"]
(recitative & rondo of
Fiordiligi) BREITKOPF-W              (M610)

Empfange, Geliebte, Dies Herz Hier Zu
Eigen
see Core Vi Dono Bell' Idolo Mio,
Il

Entferne Dich! - Furchtbare Qualen
Ihr
see Ah Scostati! - Smanie
Implacabili

Entführung Aus Dem Serail, Die:
Ouvertüre  *K.384 (from Don
Giovanni)
(Blomhert, B.) 1(pic).2.2.2.
2.2.0.0. timp,3perc,strings [5']
BREITKOPF-W                          (M611)
(Busoni, F.) 1(pic).2.2.2. 2.2.0.0.
timp,3perc,strings [5']
BREITKOPF-W                          (M612)

Er Fliehet - O Verzeih', Verzeih',
Geliebter
see Ei Parte - Per Pietà, Ben Mio,

MOZART, WOLFGANG AMADEUS (cont'd.)

Perdona

Exsultate, Jubilate  *K.165, mot
(Mandyczewski, E.; Riedel, Chr. R.)
0.2.0.1. 2.0.0.0. org,strings,S
solo [15'] sc,pts BREITKOPF-W
PB-OB 5228                           (M613)

Fandango, Andante Und Rezitativ
*K.492 (from Le Nozze Di Figaro)
1.1.0.1. 2.0.0.0. strings,BarB soli
[3'] (duet of Count & Figaro)
BREITKOPF-W                          (M614)

Feinsliebchen, Komm Ans Fenster
see Deh Vieni Alla Finestra

Fern Vom Meer Noch Fühl Ich's
see Fuor Del Mar Ho Un Mar In Seno

Finch' Han Dal Vino  *K.527 (from Don
Giovanni)
"Auf Zu Dem Feste" 2.2.2.2.
2.0.0.0. strings,Bar solo [5']
(champagne aria of Don Giovanni)
BREITKOPF-W                          (M615)

Folget Der Heissgeliebten
see Mio Tesoro Intanto, Il

Fuor Del Mar Ho Un Mar In Seno
*K.366 (from Idomeneo, Re Di
Creta)
"Fern Vom Meer Noch Fühl Ich's"
2.2.0.2. 2.2.0.0. timp,strings,T
solo [7'] (aria of Idomeneo)
BREITKOPF-W                          (M616)

Geschwind Die Tür Geöffnet
see Aprite Presto, Aprite

Hab's Verstanden, Gnädger Herr
see Ho Capito, Signor, Si

Heissgeliebter, Wenn Auf's Neue
see Idol Mio, Se Ritroso Altro

Hier Soll Ich Dich Denn Sehen,
Constanze!  *K.384 (from Die
Entführung Aus Dem Serail)
0.0.2.2. 2.0.0.0. strings,T solo
[3'] (aria of Belmonte)
BREITKOPF-W                          (M617)

Ho Capito, Signor, Si  *K.527 (from
Don Giovanni)
"Hab's Verstanden, Gnädger Herr"
2.0.0.2. 2.0.0.0. strings,B solo
[2'] (aria of Masetto) BREITKOPF-
W                                    (M618)

Ich Baue Ganz Auf Deine Stärke
*K.384 (from Die Entführung Aus
Dem Serail)
2.0.2.2. 2.0.0.0. strings,T solo
[7'] (aria of Belmonte)
BREITKOPF-W                          (M619)

Ich Gehe, Doch Rate Ich Dir  *K.384
(from Die Entführung Aus Dem
Serail)
0.2.0.0. 2.0.0.0. strings,SB soli
[4'] (duet of Blondchen & Osmin)
BREITKOPF-W                          (M620)

Ich Grausam? - Sag Mir Nicht
see Crudele? - Non Mi Dir

Ich Weiss Ein Mittel
see Vedrai, Carino

Idol Mio, Se Ritroso Altro  *K.366
(from Idomeneo, Re Di Creta)
"Heissgeliebter, Wenn Auf's Neue"
strings,Mez solo [5'] (aria of
Elektra) BREITKOPF-W                 (M621)

Idomeneo: Marcia  *K.366 (from
Idomeneo, Re Di Creta)
2.2.2.2. 2.2.0.0. strings [2']
BREITKOPF-W                          (M622)

Ihr Verwegnen! - Wie Der Felsen
see Temerari - Come Scoglio

Im Morgenland Gefangen  *K.384 (from
Die Entführung Aus Dem Serail)
strings,T solo [3'] (romance of
Pedrillo) BREITKOPF-W                (M623)

In Uomini, In Soldati  *K.588 (from
Così Fan Tutte)
"Beim Männervolk, Bei Soldaten"
1.1.0.1. 0.0.0.0. strings,S solo
[3'] (aria of Despina) BREITKOPF-
W                                    (M624)

Io Ti Lascio  *K.245
orch,solo voice BOIS                 (M625)

Kleine Nacht Musik, Eine (Serenade
for Strings, K. 525, in G)
strings SCHOTTS study sc ETP 218,
set EO 218, pt EO 218-10      (M626)

MOZART, WOLFGANG AMADEUS (cont'd.)

Konzert-Rondo (Concerto for Piano and
Orchestra, K. 382, in D)
(Lachner, V.) pno solo,string orch
sc KUNZELMANN WW 902 ipa   (M627)

Konzert-Rondo Es-Dur  *K.371
0.2.0.0. 2.0.0.0. strings,horn solo
[6'] BREITKOPF-W                     (M628)

Lass Mein Liebes Kind Dich Nennen
see Riconosci In Questo Amplesso

Later Symphonies (Nos. 35-41)
orch sc DOVER 23052-X                (M629)

Liebe Himmlisches Gefühl, Der  *K.119
(Beyer, F.) 0.2.0.0. 2.0.0.0.
strings,S solo [7'] (aria)
BREITKOPF-W                          (M630)

Linzer Symphony
see Symphony in C, K. 425

Litaniae Lauretanae  *K.109
0.0.0.0. 0.0.3.0. strings without
vla,SATB soli [10'] BREITKOPF-W
                                     (M631)

Mädchen, So Treibt Ihr's Mit Allen
see Donne Mie, La Fate A Tanti

Marsch Der Priester  *K.620 (from Die
Zauberflöte)
1.0.2+basset horn.2. 2.2.3.0.
strings [4'] BREITKOPF-W   (M632)

Martern Aller Arten  *K.384 (from Die
Entführung Aus Dem Serail)
1.1.2.2. 2.2.0.0. timp,strings,S
solo,vln&vcl solo [10'] (aria of
Constanze) BREITKOPF-W               (M633)

Mentre Ti Lascio, O Figlia  *K.513
orch,solo voice BOIS                 (M634)

Mio Tesoro Intanto, Il  *K.527 (from
Don Giovanni)
"Folget Der Heissgeliebten"
0.0.2.2. 2.0.0.0. strings,T solo
[5'] (aria of Don Ottavio)
BREITKOPF-W                          (M635)

Misero Me  *K.77
0.2.0.2. 2.0.0.0. strings,S solo,
(viola divisi) [15'] (recitative
& aria) BREITKOPF-W                  (M636)

Müsst Ich Auch Durch Tausend Drachen
*K.435
(Beyer, Fr.) 1.1.1.2. 2.2.0.0.
timp,strings,T solo [6']
BREITKOPF-W                          (M637)

Nicht Worte Können Sagen
see Spiegarti Non Poss'io

Nozze Di Figaro, Le: Eight Variant
Versions
(Tyson) 2.2.0.2. 2.2.0.0. timp,
strings,solo voice OXFORD sc
3376288 f.s., perf sc set 3376296
sc,pts rent                          (M638)

O Sieh Doch Nur, Schwester
see Così Fan Tutte: Ah Guarda,
Sorella

O Temerario Arbace  *K.74
orch,solo voice BOIS                 (M639)

O, Wie Will Ich Triumphieren  *K.384
(from Die Entführung Aus Dem
Serail)
0+pic.2.2.2. 2.0.0.0. strings,B
solo [4'] (aria of Osmin)
BREITKOPF-W                          (M640)

Oh Flieh, Betrogne, Flieh
see Ah, Fuggi Il Traditor

Ombra Felice  *K.255
2ob,2horn,strings,A solo sc,pts
KUNZELMANN EKB 13P                   (M641)

Orestes und Ajas
see D'Oreste, d'Ajace

Ouvertüre Und Drei Kontretänze
*K.106
0.2.0.2. 2.0.0.0. strings without
vla [5'] BREITKOPF-W                 (M642)

Pantalon Und Colombine: Musik Zu
Einer Pantomime  *K.466
(Beyer, F.) orch KUNZELMANN ipa sc
10113A, oct 10113                    (M643)

Per Quel Paterno
orch,solo voice BOIS                 (M644)

Per Questa Bella Mano  *K.612
orch,solo voice BOIS                 (M645)

MOZART, WOLFGANG AMADEUS (cont'd.)

Quando Avran - Padre, Germani *K.366
(from Idomeneo, Re Di Creta)
"Wann Werden Je, Ihr Götter -
Vater, Geschwister" 0.2.0.2.
2.0.0.0. strings,S solo [8']
(recitative and aria of Ilia)
BREITKOPF-W                    (M646)

Riconosci In Questo Amplesso *K.492
(from Le Nozze Di Figaro)
"Lass Mein Liebes Kind Dich Nennen"
2.2.0.2. 2.0.0.0. strings,
SMezTBarBB soli [7'] (sextet of
Susanna, Marcellina, Don Curzio,
Conte, Bartolo, Figaro)
BREITKOPF-W                    (M647)

Rondo (from Concerto For Horn And
Orchestra, K. 412 In D)
(Beyer, F.) orch KUNZELMANN ipa sc
10241A, oct 10241          (M648)

Rondo for Flute, 2 Oboes, 2 Horns and
Strings, K. 373, in D
0.2.0.0. 2.0.0.0. vln I,vln II,vla,
vcl,db,fl solo MÖSELER sc
40.161-00, pts 40.161-01, set
40.161-09                      (M649)

Rondo for Horn and Orchestra in E
flat, K. 371
(Beyer, F.) horn solo,orch
KUNZELMANN ipa sc 10266A, oct
10266                          (M650)

Rondo for Violoncello and String
Orchestra, K. 373
(Thomas-Mifune, W.) vcl solo,string
orch sc,pts KUNZELMANN GM 1192
ipa                            (M651)

Schmäle, Schmäle, Lieber Junge
see Batti, Batti, O Bel Masetto

Schon Lacht Der Holde Frühling
*K.580
(Beyer, Fr.) 0.0.2.2. 2.0.0.0.
strings,S solo [9'] BREITKOPF-W
                               (M652)

Schuldigkeit Des Ersten Gebotes, Die
*K.35, Overture
0.2.0.2. 2.0.0.0. strings [5']
BREITKOPF-W                    (M653)

Se Il Padre Perdei *K.366 (from
Idomeneo, Re Di Creta)
"Verlor Ich Den Vater" 1.1.0.0.
1.0.0.0. strings,S solo [6']
(aria of Ilia) BREITKOPF-W (M654)

Sechs Deutsche Tänze
(Soldan) 3.2.0.2. 2.2.0.0. timp,
perc,strings PETERS f.s. sc
EP 3941, pts,kbd pt
contains: Deutscher Tanz, K.600,
No.1; Deutscher Tanz, K.600,
No.2; Deutscher Tanz, K.602,
No.5; Deutscher Tanz, K.605,
No.3; Deutscher Tanz, K.605,
No.2; Deutscher Tanz, K.605,
No.3                           (M655)

Sechs Kontretänze *K.462
0.2.0.0. 2.0.0.0. strings [6']
BREITKOPF-W                    (M656)

Sechs Mailannder Sinfonien: Folge 1
*K.156-157,K.159, CC3L
vln II,vln II,vla,vcl,db MÖSELER
f.s. sc 40.162-00, pts 40.162-01,
set 40.162-09                  (M657)

Sechs Mailannder Sinfonien: Folge 2
*K.155,K.158,K.160, CC3L
vln II,vln II,vla,vcl,db MÖSELER
f.s. sc 40.163-00, pts 40.163-01,
set 40.163-09                  (M658)

Serenade for Strings, K. 525, in G
see Kleine Nacht Musik, Eine

Seventeen Divertimenti
orch sc DOVER 23862-8      (M659)

Sind Sie Fort? - Weht Leiser, Ihr
Winde
see Dove Son? - Soave Sia Il Vento

Sinfonia Concertante, K. 297b
(Bopp, J.) orch pts KUNZELMANN
EKB 200 rent                   (M660)

Sogno Di Scipione, Il *K.126,
Overture
2.2.0.2. 2.2.0.0. timp,strings [6']
BREITKOPF-W                    (M661)

Solche Hergelaufne Laffen *K.384
(from Die Entführung Aus Dem
Serail)
0.2.0.0. 2.0.0.0. strings,B solo
[5'] (aria of Osmin) BREITKOPF-W
                               (M662)

MOZART, WOLFGANG AMADEUS (cont'd.)

Soll Ich Dich, Teurer, Nicht Mehr
Sehn? *K.620 (from Die
Zauberflöte)
0.2.0.2. 0.0.0.0. strings,STB soli
[4'] (trio of Pamina, Tamino, and
Sarastro) BREITKOPF-W     (M663)

Sonata No. 12 in C, K. 278
0.2.0.0. 0.2.0.0. timp,org,strings
without vla [4'] BREITKOPF-W
                               (M664)

Sonata No. 14 in C, K. 329
0.2.0.0. 2.2.0.0. timp,org,strings
without vla [4'] BREITKOPF-W
                               (M665)

Spiegarti Non Poss'io *K.489 (from
Idomeneo, Re Di Creta)
"Nicht Worte Können Sagen" 0.2.0.0.
2.0.0.0. strings,ST soli [3']
(duet of Idomeneo & Ilia)
BREITKOPF-W                    (M666)

Süsse Rache
see Vendetta, Oh, La Vendetta, La

Symphony in C, K. 425
(Eisen, C.) "Linzer Symphony"
0.2.0.2. 2.2.0.0. timp,strings
[30'] sc PETERS EP 7332    (M667)

Symphony No. 4 in D, K. 19
0.2.0.0. 2.0.0.0. strings [9']
BREITKOPF-W                    (M668)

Symphony No. 11 in D, K. 84
0.2.0.0. 2.0.0.0. strings [13']
BREITKOPF-W                    (M669)

Symphony No. 12 in G, K. 110
2.2.0.2. 2.0.0.0. strings [15']
BREITKOPF-W                    (M670)

Symphony No. 20 in D, K. 133
0.2.0.0. 2.2.0.0. strings [20']
BREITKOPF-W                    (M671)

Symphony Nos. 22-34
orch sc DOVER 26675-3      (M672)

Temerari - Come Scoglio *K.588 (from
Così Fan Tutte)
"Ihr Verwegnen! - Wie Der Felsen"
0.2.2.2. 2.0.0.0. strings,S solo
[5'30"] (recitative and aria of
Fiordiligi) BREITKOPF-W   (M673)

Titus: Jetzt, Vitellia! Schlägt Die
Stunde - Nie Soll Mit Rosen
see Clemenza Di Tito, La: Ecco Il
Punto, O Vitellia - Non Più Di
Fiori

Titus: Soll Die Strenge, Ihr Güt'gen
Götter
see Clemenza Di Tito, La: Se
All'Impero, Amici Dei!

Titus: Wir Bald Ein Leises Lüftchen
see Clemenza Di Tito, La: Se Al
Volto Mai Ti Senti

Vedrai, Carino *K.527 (from Don
Giovanni)
"Ich Weiss Ein Mittel" 2.0.2.2.
2.0.0.0. strings,S solo [4']
(aria of Zerlina) BREITKOPF-W
                               (M674)

Vendetta, Oh, La Vendetta, La *K.492
(from Le Nozze Di Figaro)
"Süsse Rache" 2.2.0.2. 2.2.0.0.
timp,strings,B solo [4'] (aria of
Bartolo) BREITKOPF-W      (M675)

Verlor Ich Den Vater
see Se Il Padre Perdei

Vier Kontretänze *K.267
1.2.0.1. 2.0.0.0. strings without
vla [7'] BREITKOPF-W      (M676)

Vier Menuette *K.601
2+pic.2.2.2. 2.2.0.0. timp,strings
without vla, lyre [11']
BREITKOPF-W                    (M677)

Violin Concerti And Sinfonia
Concertante
orch,vln solo sc DOVER 25169-1
                               (M678)

Wann Werden Je, Ihr Götter - Vater,
Geschwister
see Quando Avran - Padre, Germani

Warum Gabst Du Bis Heute Nie Meinem
Flehn Gehör?
see Crudel! Perchè Finora Farmi
Languir Cosi

Welch Ein Geschick - Meinetwegen
Soll't Du Sterben *K.384 (from
Die Entführung Aus Dem Serail)
2.0.2.2. 2.0.0.0. strings,ST soli
[9'] (recitative and duet of
Constanze & Belmonte) BREITKOPF-W

MOZART, WOLFGANG AMADEUS (cont'd.)
                               (M679)

Welche Schreckliche Nacht - Ich Finde
Den Vater
see Ah Qual Gelido Orror - Il Padre
Adorato

Wenn Die Sanften Abendwinde
see Che Soave Zefiretto

Wer Ein Liebchen Hat Gefunden *K.384
(from Die Entführung Aus Dem
Serail)
1.2.0.2. 2.0.0.0. strings,TB soli
[7'] (lied and duet of Belmonte &
Osmin) BREITKOPF-W        (M680)

Zu Hilfe, Zu Hilfe *K.620 (from Die
Zauberflöte)
2.2.2.2. 0.2.0.0. timp,strings,T
solo [7'] (introduction of
Tamino) BREITKOPF-W       (M681)

MOZART A NOVE ANNI see Sciarrino,
Salvatore

MOZART-MOMENT see Schnebel, Dieter

MOZART SAMPLER WITH GROUND see Gilbert,
Anthony

MOZART UND SALIERI: INTERMEZZO UND
FUGHUE see Rimsky-Korsakov, Nikolai

MOZART-VARIATIONEN, FOR ORCHESTRA, OP.
47 see Smirnov, Dmitri

MOZARTIANA see Jirasek, Ivo see
Tchaikovsky, Piotr Ilyich

MOZETICH, MARJAN (1948-    )
El Dorado
string orch,harp solo [16'] sc,solo
pt CANADIAN MI1616 M939EL  (M682)

Romantic Rhapsody, A (Symphony No. 1,
Third Movement)
2.2.2(clar in A).2. 2.2.2.0.
strings sc CANADIAN
MI 1100 M939SY1                (M683)

Symphony No. 1
2.2.2(clar in A).2. 2.2.2.0.
strings [25'] sc CANADIAN
MI 1100 M939SY1                (M684)

Symphony No. 1,Third Movement
see Romantic Rhapsody, A

MRACZEK, JOSEPH GUSTAV (1878-1944)
Eva
3.3(English horn).3(bass
clar).3(contrabsn). 4.4.3.1.
timp,perc,2harp,cel,strings [26']
HEINRICH                       (M685)

MUCHA-ZOKOTUCHA see Tishchenko, Boris

MUETTE DI PORTICI, LA: OVERTURE see
Auber, Daniel-François-Esprit

MUETTE DI PORTICI, LA: TARANTELLE see
Auber, Daniel-François-Esprit

MULDOWNEY, DOMINIC (1952-    )
Concerto for Oboe and Orchestra
3.1.3.3. 4.2.2.1. 4perc,harp,
strings,ob solo [25'] FABER
                               (M686)
Concerto for Percussion and Orchestra
1.2.1.2. 2.2.0.0. perc,strings
[20'] FABER                    (M687)

Concerto for Trumpet and Orchestra
2.2.2.2. 2.0.0.0. pno,strings,trp
solo [20'] FABER               (M688)

Polka
3.3.3.3. 4.4.3.1. timp,3perc,
strings [3'] FABER             (M689)

Three Pieces For Orchestra
3.2.1.2. 2.3.3.1. 2alto sax,4perc,
strings [22'] FABER            (M690)

MÜLLER, SIGFRID WALTHER (1905-1946)
Concerto Grosso in D, Op. 23
2.2.2.2. 4.4.3.0. timp,strings,pno
solo [30'] BREITKOPF-W    (M691)

Divertimento in F, Op. 34
1.1.1.1. 1.1.1.0. timp,perc,strings
[25'] BREITKOPF-W              (M692)

MÜLLER, THOMAS
Flares
3.3.4.3. 4.3.3.1. timp,perc,pno,
harp,16vln I,14vln II,12vla,
10vcl,8db [10'] sc PETERS 02444
                               (M693)

Picture For Orchestra
3.2.3.2. 4.3.3.1. timp,3perc,harp,
vibra,18vln I,8vla,8vcl,6db [10']
sc PETERS 03050                (M694)

MÜLLER, THOMAS (cont'd.)

Spuren
3.3.3.3. 4.4.3.1. timp,3perc,pno,
harp,elec gtr,16vln I,14vln II,
12vla,6vcl,6db [10'] sc PETERS
02789 (M695)

MÜLLER-LAMPERTZ, RICHARD (1910-1982)
Alte Lok, Die
3.3.3.2. 4.3.3.1. timp,perc,harp,
cel,strings,B solo [7'] SIKORSKI
perf mat rent (M696)

Urlauber, Der
3.3.3.2. 4.3.3.1. timp,perc,harp,
cel,org,strings,B solo [5']
SIKORSKI perf mat rent (M697)

MÜLLER-MEDEK, TILO
see MEDEK, TILO

MÜLLER-SIEMENS, DETLEV (1957-  )
Carillon
3(3pic).3(English horn).3(bass
clar).3(contrabsn). 4.3.3.1. pno,
strings [20'] SCHOTTS perf mat
rent (M698)

Concerto for Horn
2+pic.2.2+bass clar.2+contrabsn.
2.2.2.1. perc,12vln I,10vln II,
8vla,6vcl,4db,horn solo [20']
study sc SCHOTTS AVV 321 perf mat
rent (M699)

Concerto for Piano
3.3.3.3. 4.3.3.0. perc,elec org,
strings,pno solo [20'] SCHOTTS
perf mat rent (M700)

Double Concerto
2(pic).2(English horn).2(bass
clar).2(contrabsn). 2.2.0.0.
perc,strings,vln solo,vla solo
[24'] SCHOTTS perf mat rent
(M701)

Enigma
1.1.1. 1.1.1.0. perc,pno,strings
[12'] SCHOTTS perf mat rent
(M702)

Passacaglia
3+pic.3.3.3(contrabsn). 4.3.3.1.
timp,strings [17'] SCHOTTS perf
mat rent (M703)

Pavan
3.3.3.3. 4.2.3.0. 2perc,strings
[8'] SCHOTTS perf mat rent (M704)

Phoenix 1
1.1.1(bass clar).1. 1.1.1(bass
trom).0. pno,strings [14']
SCHOTTS perf mat rent (M705)

Phoenix 2
1.1.1(bass clar).1. 1.1.1(bass
trom).0. pno,strings [14']
SCHOTTS perf mat rent (M706)

Phoenix 3
1.1.1.1. 1.1.1.0. pno,strings
SCHOTTS perf mat rent (M707)

Quatre Passages
3(pic).3.3.3. 4.2.3.0. perc,strings
[24'] SCHOTTS perf mat rent
(M708)

Songs And Pavanes
3(pic).2+English horn.3(bass
clar).3(contrabsn). 4.3(trp in
D).3.1. strings,T solo [35']
(text Franz Kafka) SCHOTTS perf
mat rent (M709)

Symphony No. 1
3+pic.3.3.3(contrabsn). 4.3.3.1.
timp,perc,strings [45'] SCHOTTS
perf mat rent (M710)

Tom-A-Bedlam
1(pic).1(English horn).1(bass
clar).1(contrabsn). 1.0.0.0.
strings,SSMezTBarB soli [27']
SCHOTTS perf mat rent (M711)
1(pic).1(English horn).1(bass
clar).1(contrabsn).soprano
sax.alto sax.tenor sax. 1.0+
flügelhorn.1.0+euphonium. strings
[27'] SCHOTTS perf mat rent
(M712)

Under Neonlight 1
1.1.1.1. 1.1.1.0. perc,pno,strings,
opt elec org [15'] study sc
SCHOTTS AVV 315 perf mat rent
(M713)

MULLER-WEINBERG, ACHIM
Concerto for Strings
4vln I,3vln II,3vla,2vcl,db [18']
sc PETERS 03083 (M714)

Hör-Spiel Nr. 2
0.0.0.0. 0.3.3.0. pno,harp,6vln I,
3vla,3vcl [15'] sc,solo pt PETERS
03052 (M715)

MULLER-WEINBERG, ACHIM (cont'd.)

Hör-Spiel Nr. 3
2.2.2.2. 0.3.3.0. timp,3perc,6vla,
3db,vln&vcl&pno soli [16'] sc
PETERS 03053 (M716)

Sinfonia No. 1
"Zeitzeichen" 3.2.3.2. 4.3.3.0.
timp,4perc,8vln I,7vln II,6vla,
5vcl,4db [25'] sc PETERS 03084
(M717)

Sinfonia No. 2
3.3.3.3. 4.4.4.1. timp,2perc,harp,
harp,vibra,8vln I,7vln II,6vla,
5vcl,4db [28'] sc PETERS 03687
(M718)

Zeitzeichen
see Sinfonia No. 1

MÜLLER-WIELAND, JAN (1966-  )
Auf Hermannshöh (Serenade for String
Orchestra)
[8'] SIKORSKI perf mat rent (M719)

Concerto for Marimba and Strings
15 solo strings, marimbaphone solo
[17'] SIKORSKI perf mat rent
(M720)

Concerto for Vibraphone and Orchestra
1(pic).1(bass clar).1. 1.1.1.0.
harp,cel/pno,strings,vibra solo
[19'] SIKORSKI perf mat rent (M721)

Concerto for Violoncello and
Orchestra
3(pic).3.3.3. 4.3.3.1. timp,2perc,
harp,pno,strings,vcl solo [30']
SIKORSKI perf mat rent (M722)

Poem Des Morgens
4(2pic).3(English horn,
Heckelphone).3(bass clar,
contrabass
clar).2(2contrabsn).soprano
sax.alto sax.tenor sax.baritone
sax. 4+2flügelhorn.6(2piccolo
trp,2bass trp).6(bass trom).1.
10perc,2harp,cel,pno,acord,
strings SIKORSKI perf mat
rent (M723)

Revolutionsplatz, Der
1(pic).2(English horn).1(bass
clar).1. 1.1.1.0. 2perc,pno,
strings [11'] SIKORSKI perf mat
rent (M724)

Serenade for String Orchestra
see Auf Hermannshöh

Symphony No. 1
3(3pic).2(English horn).3(bass
clar).2(contrabsn). 4.4.3.1.
3perc,harp,cel/pno,strings [25']
SIKORSKI perf mat rent (M725)

Symphony No. 2
3(pic).2(English horn).3(bass
clar).2. 4.3.3.1. 3perc,harp,cel,
pno,strings [36'] SIKORSKI perf
mat rent (M726)

Symphony No. 3
2(pic).2.3(bass clar).2(contrabsn).
4.3.3.1. 3perc,harp,cel,strings,
pno solo,S solo [35'] SIKORSKI
perf mat rent (M727)

Symphony No. 4
2.2.2(bass clar).2. 4.3.3.1. timp,
2perc,strings [30'] SIKORSKI perf
mat rent (M728)

Zwei Stücke, Für Kammerorchester
1(pic).1.1.1. 1.1.1.0. perc,harp,
cel,strings [9'] SIKORSKI perf
mat rent (M729)

MÜLLER-ZÜRICH, PAUL (1898-1993)
Psalmenmusik
S solo,string orch KUNZELMANN
GM 982 (M730)

Sinfonietta No. 1, Op. 66
orch KUNZELMANN 10086 ipr (M731)

MULTIPLICITÉ see Suzuki, Jummei

MÜNCHEN see Hiller, Wilfried

MUNDSTOCKIANA see Faltus, Leos, Hudba
Pro Smycce

MURAKUMO, AYAKO (1949-  )
Cosmic Landscape
orch [17'] JAPAN (M732)

MURTO, MATTI (1947-  )
Aurora Borealis
see Revontulet

Concertino for Violin and Strings
sc,pts MODUS M29A (M733)

MURTO, MATTI (cont'd.)

Fiddlers, The
see Soittoniekat

Prelude for Orchestra
see Revontulet

Revontulet (Prelude for Orchestra)
"Aurora Borealis" 3.2.2.2. 4.3.3.1.
timp,2perc,strings MODUS M23
(M734)

Soittoniekat (Suite for Strings)
"Fiddlers, The" MODUS sc M5, pts
M5C (M735)

Suite for Strings
see Soittoniekat

MURUROA see Chini, Andre

MUSA THE SAINT see Kirkwood, Antoinette

MUSE LEGÈRE, LA see Bull, Edvard
Hagerup, Giocoso Bucolico

MUSGRAVE, THEA (1928-  )
Autumn Sonata
2.2.2.2. 3.2.2.0. timp,perc,
strings,bass clar solo [20']
NOVELLO (M736)

MUSIC AT NIGHT see Skrowaczewski,
Stanislaw

MUSIC FOR... see Cage, John

MUSIC FOR A MERRY CHRISTMAS NO. 1
(ADESTE...) see Pinkham, Daniel

MUSIC FOR A MERRY CHRISTMAS NO. 2
(ANGEL VO.) see Pinkham, Daniel

MUSIC FOR A MERRY CHRISTMAS NO. 3 (ALL
MY H.) see Pinkham, Daniel

MUSIC FOR A MERRY CHRISTMAS NO. 4 (THE
BIRDS) see Pinkham, Daniel

MUSIC FOR A MERRY CHRISTMAS NO. 6 (DECK
THE HALL) see Pinkham, Daniel

MUSIC FOR A MERRY CHRISTMAS NO. 7 (THE
FIRST) see Pinkham, Daniel

MUSIC FOR A MERRY CHRISTMAS NO. 9 (GOOD
KING) see Pinkham, Daniel

MUSIC FOR A MERRY CHRISTMAS NO. 10
(GREENS) see Pinkham, Daniel

MUSIC FOR A MERRY CHRISTMAS NO. 11 (THE
HOLLY) see Pinkham, Daniel

MUSIC FOR A MERRY CHRISTMAS NO. 13 (JOY
TO..) see Pinkham, Daniel

MUSIC FOR A MERRY CHRISTMAS NO. 14
(MARCH OF) see Pinkham, Daniel

MUSIC FOR A MERRY CHRISTMAS NO. 15 (O
TANNE) see Pinkham, Daniel

MUSIC FOR A MERRY CHRISTMAS NO. 16
(SILENT.) see Pinkham, Daniel

MUSIC FOR A MERRY CHRISTMAS NO. 17
(SING WE) see Pinkham, Daniel

MUSIC FOR A MERRY CHRISTMAS NO. 18
(WASSAIL) see Pinkham, Daniel

MUSIC FOR A MERRY CHRISTMAS NO. 19 (WE
THREE) see Pinkham, Daniel

MUSIC FOR A PUPPET COURT see Knussen,
Oliver

MUSIC FOR A SMALL PLANET see Healey,
Derek, Symphony No. 3

MUSIC FOR CELEBRATION see Schuller,
Gunther

MUSIC FOR CHILDREN: GALOP - FINALE see
Walton, [Sir] William (Turner)

MUSIC FOR CITY OPERA see Kurachi,
Tatsuya

MUSIC FOR DEAD EUROPEANS see Feiler,
Dror

MUSIC FOR FLUTE AND ORCHESTRA see
Perera, Ronald Christopher

MUSIC FOR GYÖR see Vidovszky, Laszlo

MUSIC FOR JAPAN see Sculthorpe, Peter
[Joshua]

MUSIC FOR KIDS see Klein, Lothar

MUSIC FOR OEDIPUS see Doolittle,
Quentin

MUSIC FOR ORCHESTRA see Kirchner, Leon

MUSIC FOR RADIO NO. 1: OUR CANADA see Weinzweig, John

MUSIC FOR SAXOPHONES AND STRINGS see Stucky, Steven Edward

MUSIC FOR VIOLA AND 22 PLAYERS see Henze, Hans Werner

MUSIC FROM A HOUSE OF CROSSED DESIRES see Woolrich, John

MUSIC-HALL see Oosten, Roel van

MUSIC OF AMBER see Schwantner, Joseph

MUSIC OF DAWN, THE see Matthews, David

MUSIC OF TRAINING AND REST see Takemitsu, Toru

MUSIC ON THEMES OF PAGANINI see Klein, Lothar

MUSIC TO THE BEAUX' STRATAGEM see Goldberg, Theo

MUSIC, UNTANGLED see Weir, Judith

MUSICA CONCERTANTE see Linde, Bo, Konsertant Musik see Vackár, Dalibor Cyril

MUSICA COUCERTANTE see Vackár, Dalibor Cyril, Musica Concertante

MUSICA DA CONCERTO see Fiala, Petr

MUSICA DOLOROSA see Sograbjan, Aschot

MUSICA FESTIVA see Reznicek, Petr

MUSICA GIOCOSA see Jerabek, Pavel see Pololánik, Zdenek see Žouhar, Zdenek

MUSICA LAMENTOSA see Zamecnik, Evzen

MUSICA NEOCLASSICA see Palkovsky, Pavel

MUSICA PATHETICA see Hochel, Stanislav

MUSICA PENTATONICA see Farkas, Ferenc

MUSICA SERIA see Glaser, Werner Wolf

MUSICAL FLIGHT see Yasumura, Yoshihiro

...A MUSICAL OFFERING (J.S.B. 1985)... see Goehr, Alexander

MUSICAL TRIP TO THE ZOO, A see Atkinson, Condit Robert

MUSICAL VERSES FOR YOUNG PEOPLE see Takemitsu, Toru, Family Tree

MUSIGNY see Mather, Bruce

MUSIK AUS "UBU REX" see Penderecki, Krzysztof

MUSIK FÖR ORKESTER see Ekström, Lars see Fridolfson, Ruben

MUSIK FÖR STRÄKER see Glans, Fredrik

MUSIK FÜR 7 SAITENINSTRUMENTE see Stephan, Rudi

MUSIK FÜR ORCHESTER (1979) see Suter, Robert, Art Pour L'Art, L'

MUSIK-GESCHICHTE see Heider, Werner

MUSIK IN NORWEGISCHEN TONLEITERN FÜR ORCHESTER see Tveitt, Geirr, Prillar I G-Lydisk

MUSIK KOMPONERAD EFTER AUGUST STRINDBERGS MÅLERI see Ekström, Lars, Genom Skärvan Av En Prisma

MUSIK TILL FACKLORNA: EN FILM I TRE AVSNITT FÖR TV see Sandred, Örjan

MUSIK UR INGMAR BERGMAN-FILMER 1-6 see Koch, Erland von

MUSIK VID ETT BERG see Jennefelt, Thomas

MUSIK ZU BACH see Zechlin, Ruth

MUSIK ZU SHAKESPEARES WINTERMÄRCHEN see Zilcher, Hermann

MUSIK ZU TURANDOT see Weber, Carl Maria von

MUSIKALISCHE SCHLITTENFAHRT see Mozart, Leopold

- MUSIKALISCHES BILD see Glazunov, Alexander Konstantinovich

MUSIKALISCHES HOR D'OEUVRE, EIN see Kirchner, Volker David, Souper Des Monsieur Papagenor, Das

MUSIKALISK SAMMANKOMST see Hermanson, Christer, Runion Musicale

MUSIKK TIL FEBERDIGTE AV KNUT HAMSUN see Amdahl, Magne

MUSIKS ANATOMI see Jeverud, Johan

MUSIQUE CONCERTANTE see Kovach, Andor

MUSIQUE POUR NEUCHÂTEL see Bellemare, Gilles

MUSIQUE SATT TILL EN FESTIN... see Roman, Johan Helmich, Golvinmusiken BeRI 1

MUSSORGSKY, MODEST PETROVICH (1839-1881)
Bilder Einer Ausstellung
(Gortschakow, S.) 3.3.4(soprano sax).3. 4.3.3.2. timp,perc,harp, cel,strings [29'] PETERS　(M737)
(Leonardi, Leonidas) 3(pic).2+ English horn.2+bass clar.0+ 2contrabsn.soprano sax.2alto sax.3tenor sax. 8.6.3.2. 2harp, pno,glock,cel,strings [31'] BREITKOPF-W　(M738)
(Ravel, Maurice) "Pictures At An Exhibition" orch min sc KUNZELMANN ETP 1303　(M739)

Boris Godunow: Warlaams Lied (Rimsky-Korsakov, N.) 2+pic.2.2+ bass clar.2. 4.2.3.1. timp,3perc, strings,B solo [3'] BREITKOPF-W　(M740)

Chants Et Danses De La Mort orch,solo voice BOIS　(M741)

Night On Bare Mountain (Lloyd-Jones) OXFORD sc 3660962, perf sc set 3660970 sc,pts rent　(M742)

Pictures At An Exhibition (Naoumoff, Emile) 3(pic,alto fl).2+ English horn.2(clar in A,clar in E flat)+bass clar.2+contrabsn. 4.3.3.0. timp,perc,strings,pno solo [40'] SCHOTTS perf mat rent　(M743)
see Bilder Einer Ausstellung

MÜSST ICH AUCH DURCH TAUSEND DRACHEN see Mozart, Wolfgang Amadeus

MUST SHE GO? see Kirkwood, Antoinette

MUSTO, JOHN
Encounters
2(pic).2(English horn).2(bass clar).2(contrabsn). 2.2.2.0. timp,perc,harp,cel,pno,strings,T solo [22'] PEER rent　(M744)

MUTUAL RECOGNITION see Saruya, Toshiro

MUUMIMAISUUKSIA see Wessman, Harri

MUZIEK IV see Wagemans, Peter-Jan

MUZIEK VOOR ELEKTRA see Diepenbrock, Alphons

MUZIKANTSKÁ SUITA see Bazant, Jaromír

MW see Sollima, Giovanni

MXYZPTLK see Daugherty, Michael

MY DOG HAS FLEAS see Walker, Robert

MY LADY ANITA'S SONGBOOK see Leichtling, Alan

MY MASTER HATH A GARDEN see Mann, Leslie

MY OLD KENTUCKY HOME see Busch, Carl

MY PLANET, MY SOUL see Ám, Magnar

MYATT, TONY (1963-　)
Distribution 2
3(3pic).2+English horn.2(bass clar).2. 4.4.3.1. 4perc,strings [23'] sc UNIV.YORK 0039 f.s.　(M745)

MYERS, STANLEY A. (1908-1994)
Cavatina
(Frazer, Alan) 2.1.2.1. 2.0.0.0. perc,harp/pno,strings sc,pts CRAMER 90436 f.s.　(M746)

MYSKA, RUDOLF (1922-　)
Ametyst *Waltz
2.2.2.2. 4.2.3.1. timp,perc,harp, strings [6'] CESKY HUD.　(M747)

Concertino for Trumpet and Orchestra
2.2.2.2. 4.2.3.0. timp,perc, strings,trp solo [6'] CESKY HUD.　(M748)

Intermezzo
see Stastnou Cestu

Pod Modrou Oblohou
3.2.2.2. 4.2.3.1. timp,perc,harp, strings [7'] CESKY HUD.　(M749)

Pohlednice Z Tarenta (Tarantelle for Orchestra)
3.2.2.2. 4.2.3.0. timp,perc,harp, strings [7'] CESKY HUD.　(M750)

Pozdrav Prátelum
2.2.2.2. 4.2.3.1. timp,perc,strings [5'] CESKY HUD.　(M751)

Štastnou Cestu (Intermezzo)
2.2.2.2. 4.2.3.1. timp,perc,harp, strings [5'] CESKY HUD.　(M752)

Tarantelle for Orchestra
see Pohlednice Z Tarenta

V Hudební Síni
2.2.2.2. 4.2.3.0. perc,strings,SS soli [8'] CESKY HUD.　(M753)

V Lázenském Parku *Waltz
2.2.2.2. 4.2.3.0. timp,perc,strings [6'] CESKY HUD.　(M754)

Z Polabské Krajiny
3.2.2.2. 4.2.3.1. timp,perc,harp, strings [6'] CESKY HUD.　(M755)

Zámecké Ozveny
2.2.2.2. 4.2.3.0. timp,perc,harp, strings [6'] CESKY HUD.　(M756)

Zárivy Den
3.2.2.2. 4.2.3.1. timp,perc,harp, strings [4'] CESKY HUD.　(M757)

MYSLIVECZEK, JOSEPH (1737-1781)
Concerto for 2 Clarinets and Orchestra in E flat
(Hóly, F.) 2clar,orch KUNZELMANN ipa sc 10282A, oct 10280　(M758)

Concerto for Violin and Orchestra in A
0.2.0.0. 2.0.0.0. strings,vln solo [18'] CESKY HUD.　(M759)

Concerto for Violin and Orchestra in B flat
(Hercl, Josef; Thuri, F. X.) 0.2.0.0. 2.0.0.0. strings,vln solo [21'] CESKY HUD.　(M760)

Concerto for Violin and Orchestra in G
0.2.0.0. 2.0.0.0. strings,vln solo CESKY HUD.　(M761)

Concerto for Violoncello and Orchestra in C
(Pulkert, Oldrich) 0.2.0.0. 4.0.0.0. strings,vcl solo CESKY HUD.　(M762)

Concerto In B-Flat Major (A-Wgm, Q 16467 [no. 4])
see Three Violin Concertos

Concerto In D Major (A-Wgm, Q 16467 [no. 5])
see Three Violin Concertos

Concerto In D Major (CS-Pnm, XXXVIII F 158)
see Three Violin Concertos

Sinfonia
0.2.0.0. 2.0.0.0. strings CESKY HUD.　(M763)

Sinfonia in B flat
0.2.0.0. 2.0.0.0. strings [8'] CESKY HUD.　(M764)

Sinfonia in D
2ob,2horn,strings KUNZELMANN ipa sc 10081A, oct 10181　(M765)

Sinfonia No. 1 in D
2ob,2horn,strings KUNZELMANN ipa sc 10157A, oct 10157　(M766)

Three Violin Concertos
(White, Chappell) A-R ED ISBN 0-89579-290-7 f.s.
contains: Concerto In B-Flat Major (A-Wgm, Q 16467 [no. 4]) (0.2.0.0. 2.0.0.0. vln I,vln II,vla,db,vln solo); Concerto In D Major (A-Wgm, Q 16467 [no.

MYSLIVECZEK, JOSEPH (cont'd.)

5]) (vln I,vln II,vla,db,vln
solo); Concerto In D Major (CS-
Pnm, XXXVIII F 158) (0.2.0.0.
2.0.0.0. vln I,vln II,vla,db,
vln solo)                    (M767)

MYSTÈRE DE L'INSTANT see Dutilleux,
Henri

MYSTERIES OF THE MACABRE see Ligeti,
György

MYTHEN see Kirchner, Volker David,
Symphony No. 2

MYTHICAL IMPLOSION, A see Kanno,
Yoshihiro

MYTHS see Reynolds, Roger, Sinfonia

# N

NA BRATRSTVÍ see Jonák, Zdenek

NÅ DA? see Kolberg, Kåre

NA DEVÁTÉHO MÁJE see Felix, Václav

NA MORAVSKOU NOTU see Sedlácek,
Bohuslav

NA NÁDVORÍ see Marat, Zdenek

NA PASEKÁCH see Sternwald, Jiri

NA POCHODU SE NEUMÍRÁ see Gahér, Jozef

NA PRÁTELSTVÍ see Strniste, Jiri

NA TOM NAŠEM DVORE -- HUSAR see
Vodrazka, Karel

NABESHIMA, KAORI (1960-    )
Sparkling Waves For 21 Players
marimba,trp,horn,bsn,trom,tuba,fl,
clar,ob,strings [17'] JAPAN  (N1)

NABOKOV, NICOLAS (1903-1978)
Concerto Corale
strings,fl solo,pno solo [17']
PETERS                       (N2)

Don Quichotte: Symphonic Variations
3.3.3.3. 4.3.3.1. timp,perc,harp,
cel,pno,strings [38'] PETERS (N3)

NACHT UND TRÄUME see Ruoff, Axel D.

NACHTGEBETE see Kantscheli, Gija

NACHTGESANG see Trümpy, Balz

NACHTMUSIK see Heuberger, Richard

NACHTSTÜCK (-AUFGEGEBENES WERK) see
Ruzicka, Peter

NACHTVLINDER see Vandevorst, Toon

NADEJE see Slavicky, Milan

NADERMANN, FRANCOIS-JOSEPH (1773-1835)
Trois Pieces
(Rosenthal) harp,chamber orch solo
pt,pno red INTERNAT.S.      (N4)

NÁDI HEGEDU see Kadosa, Pal, Peasant
Fiddle

NAESSEN, RAY (1950-    )
Cantadora
3(pic).3(English horn).3(bass
clar).3(contrabsn). 5.4.4.1.
timp,perc,strings STIM       (N5)

Concerto for Bassoon and Strings in
Four Movements
see In Extasibus Vigilibus

I Den Långa Väntans Skog [4]
string orch STIM             (N6)

I Den Lnga Vntans Skog [2]
string orch [5'] sc,pts STIM (N7)

I Den Lnga Vntans Skog [3]
"In The Forest Of The Long Wait
[3]" string orch [4'5] sc,pts
STIM                         (N8)

I Den Lnga Vntans Skog: En
Betraktelse
string orch [5'] sc STIM     (N9)

In Dulci Jubilo
woodwind quin,timp,string orch
[7'5] sc,pts STIM            (N10)

In Extasibus Vigilibus (Concerto for
Bassoon and Strings in Four
Movements)
"Vaken Hänryckning" strings,bsn
solo STIM                    (N11)

In The Forest Of The Long Wait [3]
see I Den Lnga Vntans Skog [3]

Los And Orc: Verk I VI Satser
woodwind quin,strings [20'] sc,pts
STIM                         (N12)

Music for Strings
string orch [10'] sc STIM    (N13)

Vaken Hänryckning
see In Extasibus Vigilibus

NAGAI, AKIRA
Concert Variations, For Bajan And
Orchestra
timp,perc,strings, bajan solo [12']
SIKORSKI perf mat rent      (N14)

Symphonic Poem "Shinano"
orch [26'] JAPAN            (N15)

NAITO AKEMI (1956-    )
Strings And Time III
strings [4'] JAPAN          (N16)

NAKAGAWA, TOSHIO (1958-    )
Symphonique Concerto
JAPAN                       (N17)

NAKAJIMA, KATSUMA (1958-    )
Festival Fantasy
string orch [10'] JAPAN     (N18)

NAKLONENÁ ROVINA see Kurz, Ivan

NÁLADY Z PLÁTNA I see Sternwald, Jiri

NÁLADY Z PLÁTNA II see Sternwald, Jiri

NÁLADY Z PLÁTNA III see Sternwald, Jiri

NALÉHAVOST CASU see Matys, Jiri

NAMI NO BON see Takemitsu, Toru

NANCARROW, CONLON (1912-    )
Study No. 1
(Mikhashoff, Yvar) 0+
pic.1.1.1.soprano sax(bass clar).
1.1.1.0. timp,perc,pno,hpsd&cel,
synthesizer,strings,opt gtr
SCHOTTS perf mat rent       (N19)

Study No. 2
(Mikhashoff, Yvar) 1.1(English
horn).1+bass clar.1.soprano sax.
1.1.1.0. perc,cel&hpsd,strings,
(1.0.1.1.1) SCHOTTS perf mat rent
(N20)

Study No. 5
(Mikhashoff, Yvar) pic,ob/clar,bass
clar/tenor sax,bsn/bass clar,
3trp/3trp in C,xylo,marimba,2pno,
2vln,vla/vcl,vcl/db,db/vcl
SCHOTTS perf mat rent       (N21)

Study No. 6
(Mikhashoff, Yvar) 1.1(English
horn).1(bass clar).0. 1.0.0.0.
glock,marimba,cel,2pno,2vln,vla,
2db SCHOTTS perf mat rent   (N22)

Study No. 7
(Mikhashoff, Yvar) 0+pic.1.2(clar
in E flat,bass clar,alto sax,
tenor sax).1. 1.1.1.0. xylo,
marimba,pno,hpsd&cel,strings
SCHOTTS perf mat rent       (N23)

Study No. 9
(Mikhashoff, Yvar) 0+pic.1.1+clar
in E flat+bass clar.1. 1.1.1.0.
xylo,marimba,pno&cel,hpsd,
strings, (1.0.1.1.1) SCHOTTS perf
mat rent                    (N24)

Study No. 12
(Mikhashoff, Yvar) 0+pic.1(English
horn).1(clar in E flat)+bass
clar(alto sax).1. 1.1.0.0.
marimba&xylo&vibra,acord,pno&cel,
hpsd,gtr,2vln&mand,vla,vcl,db
SCHOTTS perf mat rent       (N25)

NANCY! JULIA! VERWEILE! BLICKT SEIN
AUGE... LETZTE ROSE, WIE MAGST DU
SO EINSAM see Flotow, Friedrich von

NANNA, BERCEUSE see Tomasi, Henri

NAOUMOFF, EMILE (1962-    )
Concerto for Piano, No. 2
2.2.2.2. 2.2.2.0. strings,pno solo
[25'] SCHOTTS perf mat rent (N26)

Triptyque
strings,vln solo [12'] SCHOTTS perf
mat rent                    (N27)

NAPOLEON see Paganini, Niccolo

NAPTÁR see Farkas, Ferenc, Calendar

NARCUSSE see D'hoedt, Henry George

NARDINI, PIETRO (1722-1793)
Concerto for Violin and String
Orchestra in G
(Nagy ; Ney) vln solo,string orch
KUNZELMANN ipa sc 10054A, oct
10054                       (N28)

NARITA, KAZUKO (1957-    )
Concerto, Op. 51
see Keisho

NARITA, KAZUKO (cont'd.)

Keisho (Concerto, Op. 51)
string orch, 20 gen, koto solo
[16'] JAPAN                        (N29)

NÁRODNÍ TANCE I-XII see Vlach-Vruticky,
Josef

NARROW ROAD INTO THE DEEP NORTH; BASHO,
THE see Yuasa, Joji see Yuasa,
Joji, Symphonic Suite

NAŠE DOBA see Hochel, Stanislav

NASSIDSE, SULCHAN (1927-    )
Concerto for Violin, Violoncello and
Chamber Orchestra
strings,hpsd,vln&vcl soli [17']
SIKORSKI perf mat rent            (N30)

NATIONAL PARK SUITE see Horwood,
Michael

NATIVE see Leon, Tania Justina,
Indigena

NATIVITY ACCORDING TO ST. LUKE: LULLABY
see Thompson, Randall

NATIVITY ACCORDING TO ST. LUKE:
MAGNIFICAT see Thompson, Randall

NATSUDA, MASAKAZU (1968-    )
Solition
chamber orch [7'] JAPAN           (N31)

Variations Sur Le Thème De "La
Truite" De Schubert
chamber orch [2'] JAPAN           (N32)

NATTLIG MADONNA see Strindberg, Henrik

NATURE, HERD AND RELATIVES see Rabe,
Folke, Naturen, Flocken Och Släkten

NATUREN, FLOCKEN OCH SLÄKTEN see Rabe,
Folke

NAULAIS, JEROME (1951-    )
Frissons [11']
2.2.2.2. 2.2.0.0. timp,strings,
alto sax solo
BILLAUDOT                         (N33)

Horizons [15']
2.2.2.2. 2.2.0.0. timp,strings,
trp solo
BILLAUDOT                         (N34)

NAUMANN, EMIL (1827-1888)
Käthchen Von Heilbronn, Das  *Op.40,
Overture
2+pic.2.2.2. 4.2.3.0. timp,strings
[10'] BREITKOPF-W                 (N35)

NAUMANN, ERNST (1832-1910)
Pastorale in F, Op. 16
1.2.2.2. 2.0.0.0. strings [10']
BREITKOPF-W                       (N36)

NÁVRAT, JAROMÍR (1967-    )
Symfonické Vety
2.2.2.2. 4.2.3.1. timp,perc,xylo,
harp,pno,strings [18'] CESKY HUD.
                                  (N37)

NÁVRATY SVETLA see Barton, Hanus

NAYAN see Ibarrondo, Felix

NAYLOR, BERNARD (1907-1986)
Overture In The Form Of Variations
2.2.2.2. 2.2.0.0. timp,perc,strings
[8'] sc CANADIAN                  (N38)

NAZIONALE NEL GUSTO DI CINQUE NAZIONI'
see Dittersdorf, Karl Ditters von

NE DEMANDONS À L'AVENIR see Migot,
Georges

NEAR THE COMETHEAD see Thommessen, Olav
Anton, Ved Komethodet

NEAR WOODSTOCK TOWN see Grainger, Percy
Aldridge

NEARLY BELOVED see Koehne, Graeme

NEBESKÉ PASTVINY see Adamic, Josef

NEBULA see Rossnes, Dagfinn

NECKSTEN, GÄRT (1934-    )
Festmarsch
"Vivat Carlscrona" orch [4'] STIM
ED.NR 0601                        (N39)

Vivat Carlscrona
see Festmarsch

NEDBAL, OSKAR (1874-1930)
Suite Mignonne  *Op.15
3.2.2.2. 4.2.0.0. timp,perc,harp,
strings [10'] CESKY HUD.          (N40)

NEEF, WILHELM (1916-    )
Shakespeareana  *ballet/Suite
2.2.2.2. 2.3.3.0. timp,perc,pno,
cembalo,cel,strings, jazz
instruments soli BREITKOPF-W
                                  (N41)

NEI GIORNI TUOI FELICI see Beethoven,
Ludwig van

NEIDHÖFER, CHRISTOPH (1967-    )
Transitio [14']
2.2.2.2. 2.2.0.0. perc,pno,
strings
BILLAUDOT                         (N42)

NEIN, DAS IST WIRKLICH DOCH ZU KECK see
Nicolai, Otto

NEJHODNEJŠÍ see Klempír, Jaromir

NELHYBEL, VACLAV (1919-1996)
Oratio I
piccolo trp,chimes,strings
EUR.AM.MUS. set EA00362BS, pts
EA00362AS, sc EA00362FS           (N43)

NELJÄ HÄMÄLÄISTÄ KANSANLAULUA JOUSIORK
see Raitio, Väinö

NELL see Faure, Gabriel-Urbain

NELLESSEN, HERMANN JOSEF (1923-    )
Divertimento
strings [9'] BREITKOPF-W          (N44)

NELSON, DANIEL (1965-    )
Ashes
fl,clar,bsn,pno,strings,vln solo
STIM                              (N45)

Neon-O-Matic
1.1.1.1. 1.1.1.0. strings STIM
                                  (N46)

Rondo Neuroica
string orch [7'] sc,pts STIM      (N47)

NELSON, DAVID (1965-    )
Ablaze (Concerto for Violin and
String Orchestra)
string orch,vln solo STIM         (N48)

Concerto for Violin and String
Orchestra
see Ablaze

NELSON, LARRY
In Silence, In Memory
1.1.1.1. 1.1.1.0. perc,pno,strings
[18'] PRESSER rent                (N49)

NEMEL JSEM TE RÁD see Duchac, Miloslav

NENCIOZZA MIA see Jappart, Jean

NENIA see Hedstrom, Åse

NÉNIE ZA MOJI MATKU see Blatny, Pavel

NEON-O-MATIC see Nelson, Daniel

NEPTUNUS see Kvam, Oddvar S., Concerto
for Violin and Orchestra, Op. 96

NERUDA, JOHANN BAPTIST (JAN KRTITEL)
(ca. 1707-1780)
Concerto in E flat for Orchestra
(Koukal, Bohumír) strings,horn solo
[16'] CESKY HUD.                  (N50)

NESS, JON ØIVIND (1968-    )
Cis-Trans For Sinfonietta
1.1.1.1.soprano sax. 1.1.1.1. pno,
perc,vln,vla,vcl,db [13'] NORSKMI
                                  (N51)

Schatten For Chamber Orchestra
2(pic,alto fl).2.2(bass
clar).2(contrabsn). 2.1.1.1.
2perc,pno/synthesizer,strings,
soprano sax/baritone sax NORSKMI
                                  (N52)

NETZ-WERK 1 see Wüthrich-Mathez, Hans

NETZ-WERK 2 see Wüthrich-Mathez, Hans

NETZ-WERK 3 see Wüthrich-Mathez, Hans

NEUBAUER, FRANZ CHRISTOPH (1760-1795)
Concerto for Violin and Chamber
Orchestra in B flat
(Slivanská, A.) PANTON            (N53)

NEUBERT, GÜNTER (1936-    )
An Die Zukunft
8vln I,7vln II,6vla,5vcl,4db,alto
fl/vln solo,English horn/vla solo
[9'] sc PETERS 03078              (N54)

Concerto Ritmico
2.2.2.2. 3.2.2.0. perc,pno,8vln I,
7vln II,6vla,5vcl,4db [23'] sc,
solo pt PETERS 03079              (N55)

Gewaltig Wie Der Tod
3.3.3.2. 3.3.3.1. timp,2perc,pno,
2harp,vibra,marimba,8vln I,7vln
II,6vla,5vcl,4db [19'] sc,pno-

NEUBERT, GÜNTER (cont'd.)

cond sc PETERS 01296              (N56)

Memento
1.1.1.1. 1.1.1.0. 2perc,pno,harp,
2vln,vla,vcl,db [33'] sc PETERS
03616                             (N57)

Neue Jahrhundert, Das
3.2.3.3. 4.4.3.1. timp,3perc,cel,
2harp,8vln I,7vln II,6vla,5vcl,
4db,Bar solo [25'] sc PETERS
03405                             (N58)

Sinfonia Infernale (Sinfonia No. 2)
3.2.3.3. 4.3.3.1. timp,3perc,8vln
I,7vln II,6vla,5vcl,4db [17'] sc
PETERS 03089                      (N59)

Sinfonia No. 2
see Sinfonia Infernale

Von Menschlichen Schwächen
2.2.0.1. 2.1.1.0. 8vln I,7vln II,
6vla,5vcl,4db [20'] sc PETERS
03088                             (N60)

NEUE JAHRHUNDERT, DAS see Neubert,
Günter

NEUE MIETER, DER see Kelemen, Milko

NEUMANN, VEROSLAV (1931-    )
Concerto for Trumpet, Strings and
Electronic Tape
[15'] CESKY HUD.                  (N61)

Dedikace
2.2.2.1. 2.2.0.0. timp,perc,strings
[8'] CESKY HUD.                   (N62)

Symfonické Tance
3.3.3.2. 4.3.3.0. timp,perc,harp,
cel,pno,strings [25'] CESKY HUD.
                                  (N63)

NEUN STÜCKE FÜR ORCHESTER see Reimann,
Aribert

NEVERTHELESS see Pelecis, George

NEVONMAA, KIMMO (1960-    )
Dolor Nascens Et Effluens (Sinfonia
for String Orchestra, Percussion
and Harp)
MODUS M59                         (N64)

Lux Intima For Chamber Orchestra
1.1.1.1. 1.1.1.0. 2perc,strings sc
MODUS M60                         (N65)

Sinfonia for String Orchestra,
Percussion and Harp
see Dolor Nascens Et Effluens

NEW FIRST SUITE FOR STRINGS see
Harrison, Lou

NEW SEASONS, THE see Proto, Frank

NEW YEAR SUITE see Tippett, [Sir]
Michael

NEW YORK CONCERTO see Giuffre, Gaetano

NEW YORK, NEW YORK: VARIATIONS see
Druckman, Jacob Raphael, Variations
On Bernstein's "New York, New York"

NEWFIE BULLET, THE: A NEWFOUNDLAND
JOURNEY see Sexton, Brian

NEZ SRDCE OPUSTÍME see Dobiáš, Daniel

NICE GUYS ALWAYS FINISH LAST see
Meijering, Chiel

NICHELMANN, CHRISTOPH (1717-1762)
Sinfonia in E flat
(Schneider, M.) 2.2.0.0. 2.0.0.0.
strings,cont [8'] BREITKOPF-W
                                  (N66)

NICHOLSON, G. GORDON (1942-    )
Edmonton Suite
string orch,S rec,2A rec,T rec,B
rec [18'] (a musical collage: 1.
Skyline 2. Churchill square 3.
Planetarium 4. Children's climber
in Mayfair Park 5. Oil 6.
Skyline) sc CANADIAN
MI 1720 N625ED                    (N67)

Introduction And Allegro
2(pic).2(English horn).2(bass
clar). 2. 4.3.3.1. 2timp,perc,
strings sc CANADIAN               (N68)

NICHOLSON, GEORGE (1949-    )
Blisworth Tunnel Blues
2(pic).2(ob d'amore).3(3bass clar,
alto sax,tenor sax).1(contrabsn).
2.0.1.0. harp,pno&cel,2perc,2vln,
vla,vcl,db,S solo [38'] sc
UNIV.YORK 0054 f.s.               (N69)

NICHOLSON, GEORGE (cont'd.)

Chamber Concerto
1(pic,alto fl).1(English horn).1.0.
1.1.0.0. harp,pno&cel,perc,vln,
vla,vcl,db [20'] sc UNIV.YORK
0048 f.s.                          (N70)

Concerto for Flute and Orchestra
3(pic,alto fl).3(English
horn).3(bass clar,clar in E
flat).3(contrabsn). 4.3.3.1.
harp,3perc,strings,fl solo [30']
sc UNIV.YORK 0045 f.s.             (N71)

Concerto for Violoncello and
Orchestra
3(pic,alto fl).3(English
horn).3(bass clar).3(contrabsn).
4.3.3.1. harp,pno&cel,timp,3perc,
strings,vcl solo [30'] sc
UNIV.YORK 0044 f.s.                (N72)

Convergence Of The Twain, The
2(pic).2(English horn).2(bass
clar).2. 2.2.0.0. timp,strings
[17'] sc UNIV.YORK 0043 f.s.       (N73)

Sea Change
strings [21'] sc UNIV.YORK 0053
f.s.                               (N74)

NICHT WORTE KÖNNEN SAGEN see Mozart,
Wolfgang Amadeus, Spiegarti Non
Poss'io

NICKEL, VOLKER (1970-    )
Lanaia I - VI
orch BÖHM                          (N75)

NICODE, JEAN LOUIS (1853-1919)
Auf Dem Lande
see Zwei Stücke, Op. 32

Bilder Aus Dem Süden *Op.29
(Pohle, M.) 2.2.2.2. 4.2.3.1. timp,
3perc,harp,strings [27'] (1.
Bolero 2. Maurisches Tanzlied 3.
Serenade 4. Andalusienne 5.
Provençalisches Märchen 6. In der
Taberna) BREITKOPF-W             (N76)

Canzonetta *Op.13,No.2
2.2.2.2. 2.0.0.0. timp,strings [6']
BREITKOPF-W                        (N77)

Erbarmen *Op.33, hymn
2.2.2.2. 4.2.3.0. timp,strings,A/
Mez solo [10'] BREITKOPF-W         (N78)

Faschingsbilder *Op.24
3.2.2.2. 4.2.3.0. timp,perc,harp,
strings [35'] (1. Maskenzug 2.
Liebesgeständnis 3. Seltsamer
Traum 4. Humoreske) BREITKOPF-W
                                   (N79)

Jagd Nach Dem Glück, Die *Op.11
2(pic).2.2.2. 4.2.3.0. timp,strings
[9'] BREITKOPF-W                   (N80)

Märchen, Ein
see Zwei Stücke, Op. 32

Romance for Violin and Orchestra, Op.
14
2.2.2.2. 2.0.0.0. timp,strings,vln
solo [6'] BREITKOPF-W              (N81)

Symphonische Variationen c-Moll
*Op.27
2.2.2.2. 4.2.3.0. timp,perc,strings
[22'] BREITKOPF-W                  (N82)

Zwei Stücke, Op. 32
0.2.0.0. 2.0.0.0. strings
BREITKOPF-W f.s.
contains: Auf Dem Lande; Märchen,
Ein                                (N83)

NICOLAI, OTTO (1810-1849)
Lustigen Weiber Von Windsor, Die:
Balletmusik
1+pic.2.2.2. 4.2.3.0. timp,perc,
strings [10'] BREITKOPF-W          (N84)

Nein, Das Ist Wirklich Doch Zu Keck
(from Die Lustigen Weiber von
Windsor)
2.2.2.2. 2.0.0.0. timp,strings,SMez
soli [7'] (duet of Frau Fluth and
Frau Reich) BREITKOPF-W            (N85)

Nun Eilt Herbei (from Die Lustigen
Weiber von Windsor)
2(pic).2.2.2. 2.0.0.0. timp,
strings,S solo [7'] (aria and
recitative of Frau Fluth)
BREITKOPF-W                        (N86)

Wohl Denn, Gefasst Ist Der Entschluss
(from Die Lustigen Weiber von
Windsor)
2.2.2.2. 2.0.0.0. strings,S solo
[7'] (aria of Anna Reich)
BREITKOPF-W                        (N87)

NIELSEN, CARL (1865-1931)
Sinfonia Espansiva Nr. 3 Op. 27
3.3.3.3. 4.3.3.1. timp,8vln I,7vln
II,6vla,5vcl,4db,SBar soli [38']
sc,study sc KAHNT 01882            (N88)

NIEMANDS LAND MARSCH see Eisler, Hanns

NIEMANN, WALTER (1876-1953)
Alte Niederdeutsche Volkstänze
1.1.1.1. 2.2.0.0. timp,perc,strings
[13'] KAHNT                        (N89)

Pompeji (Suite for 2 Flutes and
Strings)
[14'] PETERS                       (N90)

Suite for 2 Flutes and Strings
see Pompeji

NIEMINEN, KAI (1953-    )
Viacoli In Ombra
orch sc MODUS M102A                (N91)

NIGGUN II see Permont, Haim

NIGHT MUSIC see Matthews, Colin

NIGHT ON BARE MOUNTAIN see Mussorgsky,
Modest Petrovich

NIGHT SPEECH see Paulus, Stephen
Harrison

NIGHTINGALE, THE see Foley, Daniel

NIGHTINGALE AND THE TWO SISTERS, THE
see Grainger, Percy Aldridge

NIGHTPIECE see Milford, Robin

NIGHTSHADE ROUNDS see MacCombie, Bruce

NIIMI, TOKUHIDE (1947-    )
Cosmic Tree, The
orch, 20 gen [25'] ZEN-ON         (N92)

NIKE see Knaifel, Alexander

NIKIPROWETZKY, TOLIA (1916-    )
Concerto for Violin and Orchestra
2.2.2.2. 2.2.2.0. perc,timp,harp,
strings,vln solo [20'] JOBERT
                                   (N93)

NILSSON, ANDERS (1954-    )
Concerto for Piano and Orchestra
2(pic).2.2(bass clar).2. 2.2.0.0.
timp,strings,pno solo STIM         (N94)

Sinfonietta
2(pic).2.2.2. 1.2.2.1. strings
[18'] (I-II. Ouverture e Scherzo
III-IV. Canto e Finale) STIM sc
H-2674, pts                        (N95)

NILSSON, BO (1937-    )
Spirit's Whisper, A: In Swedenborg's
Gazebo *film
12vln I,12vln II,10vla,8vcl,6db,
synthesizer/pno,electronic tape,
coloratura sop STIM                (N96)

NILSSON, IVO (1966-    )
Eidetics
0.1.1.1.baritone sax. 0.1.1.0.
2perc,electronic equipment,vln,
vla,vcl,db [10'] sc,pts STIM
                                   (N97)

Totentanz
1(pic).1(English horn).1(bass
clar).0.sax. 1.1.1.0. timp,2vln,
vla,vcl,db [15'] sc,pts STIM
                                   (N98)

Udda eller jämt?
2.2.2.2. 2.2.2.0. 3perc,strings
[7'] STIM sc H-2955, pts           (N99)

NILSSON, TORBJÖRN (1955-    )
Toccata for String Orchestra
STIM                               (N100)

NILSSON, TORSTEN (1920-    )
On The Threshold
see Steget Över Tröskeln

Steget Över Tröskeln
"On The Threshold" pno,perc, wind
inst. [25'] sc REIMERS 101087
rent                               (N101)

NIMBUS see Hunt, Richard

NINE LEVELS BY ZE-AMI see Yuasa, Joji

NINE RIVERS see Dillon, James

NINNA NANNA see Castelnuovo-Tedesco,
Mario

NINOMIYA, TSUYOSHI (1972-    )
Seduced By Evening Cicadas
cembalo,string orch [16'] JAPAN
                                   (N102)

NIPPONARI see Martinu, Bohuslav (Jan)

NISHIMURA, AKIRA (1953-    )
Canticle Of Light
orch [21'] ZEN-ON                  (N103)

Concerto for Viola
see Flame And Shadow

Flame And Shadow (Concerto for Viola)
orch,vla solo [23'] ZEN-ON         (N104)

Melos Aura
orch [22'] ZEN-ON                  (N105)

Mirror Of Mist, A
strings,vln solo [14'] ZEN-ON
                                   (N106)

Monody For Orchestra
orch [18'] ZEN-ON                  (N107)

Vision In Twilight
orch [16'] ZEN-ON                  (N108)

Zeami *ballet
orch [75'] ZEN-ON                  (N109)

NIVELET
Ma Bergère
1.1.1.1. 1.1.1.0. perc,strings
[3'30"] (A maj, Tyrolienne) LEDUC
                                   (N110)

NIXON IN CHINA: I AM OLD AND I CANNOT
SLEEP see Adams, John

NIXON IN CHINA: MR. PREMIER,
DISTINGUISHED GUESTS see Adams,
John

NIXON IN CHINA: NEWS IS A KIND OF
MYSTERY see Adams, John

NIXON IN CHINA: THIS IS PROPHETIC see
Adams, John

NO MEAN CITY: SCENES FROM CHILDHOOD see
Ridout, Godfrey

NO MORE FOR US THE LITTLE SIGHING see
Betts, Lorne M.

NO PASARAN see Juchelka, Miroslav

NOBIS, HERBERT (1941-    )
Dance
2.2.3.2. 4.2.2.1. perc,strings
[5'30"] MOECK sc 5457 f.s., pts
rent                               (N111)
2.2.3.2. 4.2.2.1. 2perc,trp,strings
[10'] MOECK sc 5461 f.s., pts
rent                               (N112)

Et In Terra Pax
3.2.3.2. 4.2.3.1. perc,strings
[11'] MOECK sc 5462 f.s., pts
rent                               (N113)

Lamento
0.0.1.1. 0.0.0.0. perc,strings,org
[11'] MOECK sc 5419 f.s., pts
rent                               (N114)

NOCES DE CENDRES, LES see Tomasi, Henri

NOCH EINEN SCHRITT... see Kantscheli,
Gija

NOCHE DE LUNA see Engelmann, Hans
Ulrich

NOCTURNAL MADONNA see Strindberg,
Henrik, Nattlig Madonna

NOCTURNALS see Hambraeus, Bengt

NOCTURNE see Dijk, Jan van see Tomasi,
Henri

NOCTURNES see Cornell, Klaus

NOCTURNES FOR PIANO AND CHAMBER
ORCHESTRA see Shawn, Allen

NOCTURNOS DE ANDALUCÍA see Paisiello,
Giovanni see Palomo, Lorenzo

NODA, RYO (1948-    )
Concerto for Alto Saxophone
see Gen

Gen (Concerto for Alto Saxophone)
pno,cel,xylo,marimba,timp,4perc,
strings [15'] LEDUC                (N115)

NODAIRA, ICHIRO (1953-    )
Concerto De Chambre No. 1
orch [11'] LEMOINE                 (N116)

Concerto De Chambre No. 2
chamber orch [10'] LEMOINE         (N117)

"NOEL NOUVELET" ET "IL EST NÉ, LE DIVIN
ENFANT" see Francaix, Jean

NOÈME - AU SEUIL DES MÉMOIRES D'AVENIR
see Lassonde, Claude

NOMOS-GEGEBILD see Völker, Toni

NOMOS-GEGENBILD see Völker, Toni

NOMOS PROTOS see Boehmer, Konrad

NON PIÚ DI TRENTA see Bellemare, Gilles

NON PIÙ MESTA see Paganini, Niccolo

NOOTKA LOVE SONG see Rickard, Sylvia

NOR SPELL NOR CHARM see Druckman, Jacob
Raphael

NORDEN, MAARTEN VAN
Two Worlds
[20'] sc DONEMUS        (N118)

NORDGREN, ERIK (1913- )
Filmmusik
orch STIM        (N119)

NORDHEIM, ARNE (1931- )
Acantus Firmusolympiadis
string orch,trp,electronic tape,
hardangerfiddle NORSKMI     (N120)

NORDLAND see Jonsson, Josef [Petrus]

NORDLANDET FOR SOPRAN SOLO, RESITASJON
OG ORKESTER see Vea, Ketil

NORMA: OVERTURE see Bellini, Vincenzo

NORMAN, LUDVIG (1831-1885)
Andante Sostenuto
string orch [6'] sc GEHRMANS (N121)

NORSKE ASPEKTER see Haug, Halvor

NORTH SHORE, THE see Bryars, Gavin

NORTH SHORE #5 see Daigneault, Robert

NORTH WIND'S GIFT, THE see Luedeke,
Raymond

NORTHCOTT, BAYAN
Carillon
1(pic).1.1.1: 1.1.1.0. 1perc,pno,
strings [5'] sc,pts STAINER HL292
rent        (N122)

NORTHERN SHORE, THE see Feldman,
Barbara Monk

NORTHSCAPE see Horne, David

NORTHUMBRIAN ELEGY, A see Weisgarber,
Elliott

NORWEGIAN SUITE FOR STRING ORCHESTRA
see Karlsen, Kjell Mørk

NOT ALL MY TORMENTS see Purcell, Henry

NOTES OF REMEMBRANCE see Gould, Morton

NOTRE AMOUR see Faure, Gabriel-Urbain

NOTTURNO see Verbey, Theo

NOVÁK, JIRÍ F. (1913- )
Concerto for Bass Clarinet and
Orchestra
3.3.0.3. 4.2.3.1. timp,perc,harp,
cel,strings,bass clar solo [21']
CESKY HUD.        (N123)

Serenade for String Orchestra, Op. 60
[23'] CESKY HUD.        (N124)

NOVAK, VITEZSLAV (1870-1949)
Quartet No. 3, Op. 66
[28'] CESKY HUD.        (N125)

Südböhmische Suite *Op.64
3.3.3.3. 4.3.3.1. timp,perc,harp,
pno,cel,strings [30'] BREITKOPF-W
       (N126)

NOVEMBER 17 see Vacek, Miloš, 17.
Lostopad

NOVENARIA see Lutyens, Elisabeth

NOVENKO, MICHAL (1962- )
Concerto for Violin and Orchestra
2.2.2.2. 2.2.0.0. perc,strings,vln
solo [18'] CESKY HUD.    (N127)

NOVOKLASICKÁ OUVERTURA see Smolka,
Jaroslav

NOVOSAD, LUBOMIR (1922- )
Satyr A Dívka
1.0.3.0. 1.3.3.0. perc,harp,3gtr,
strings [10'] CESKY HUD.   (N128)

Sólová Návšteva
2.0.1.0. 1.3.3.0. timp,perc,harp,
3gtr,strings,clar solo [7'] CESKY
HUD.        (N129)

NOW SLEEPS THE CRIMSON PETAL see
Britten, [Sir] Benjamin

NOW THE TRUMPET SUMMONS US AGAIN see
Pinkham, Daniel

NOWELL SEQUENCE, A see Douglas, Roy

NOWKA, DIETER (1924- )
Sinfonia No. 2
2.2.2.2. 4.2.3.0. timp,perc,harp,
strings [30'] BREITKOPF-W (N130)

Sinfonia No. 4
2.3.2.2. 3.2.3.0. timp,perc,harp,
8vln I,7vln II,6vla,5vcl,4db
[27'] sc PETERS 03098    (N131)

Sinfonia No. 5 for Strings
8vln I,7vln II,6vla,5vcl,4db [29']
sc PETERS 03099        (N132)

NOYSE OF MINSTRELLS, A see Jacob,
Gordon

NOZZE DI FIGARO, LE: EIGHT VARIANT
VERSIONS see Mozart, Wolfgang
Amadeus

NUANCES DU NORD see Hayes, Gary

NUIT AMERICAINE, LA see Delerue,
Georges

NUIT BLANCHE: DRINKING SONG see
Offenbach, Jacques

NUIT DE BLEUE see Desjardins, Jacques

NUIT D'INSOMNIE see Marti, Heinz

NUIT OBSCURE DE SAINT JEAN DE LA CROIX,
LA see Tomasi, Henri

NUITS DE PROVENCE see Tomasi, Henri

NUN EILT HERBEI see Nicolai, Otto

NUN LASS UNS FRIEDEN SCHLIESSEN see
Wolf, Hugo

NUN SEI BEDANKT, MEIN LIEBER SCHWAN see
Wagner, Richard

NUNC ET NUNC see Ore, Cecilie

NUTCRACKER SUITE see Tchaikovsky, Piotr
Ilyich

NUUT see Hidalgo, Manuel

NYMAN, MICHAEL
Piano For Strings, The
strings CHESTER        (N133)

Where The Bee Dances
1.2.1.2. 2.1.1.0. pno,strings,
soprano sax solo [20'] CHESTER
       (N134)

NYSTEDT, KNUT (1915- )
Concerto for Horn and Orchestra, Op.
114
NORSK NMO 10287B        (N135)

Spenningens Land *Op.19
3.2.3.2. 4.3.3.1. timp,perc,strings
[9'] PETERS        (N136)
3.2.3.2. 4.3.3.1. timp,perc,8vln I,
7vln II,6vla,5vcl,4db [9'] sc,
study sc LYCHE 02081    (N137)

# O

O CAN YE SEW CUSHIONS? (from Folk
Songs)
(Britten, Benjamin) 2.1+English
horn.1+bass clar.2. 2.0.0.0. harp,
high solo [2'] BOOSEY-ENG rent (O1)

O HONZOVI see Bartoš, Jan Zdenek

O MAGNUM MYSTERIUM see Louie, Alexina

Ô MUSE DONT LES PAS DANSENT see
Bernier, Rene

O NAMENLOSE FREUDE see Beethoven,
Ludwig van

O PRAZE see Fiala, Jirí Julius

O, QUAE MUTATIO RERUM see Rossnes,
Dagfinn

O QUAM CARAE ET QUAM BEATAE SILVAE see
Sacchini, Antonio (Maria Gasparo
Gioacchino)

O RADOSTI see Fischer, Jan F., Obrazy
III

O RIO see Butler, Martin

O SALUTARIS see Faure, Gabriel-Urbain

O SIEH DOCH NUR, SCHWESTER see Mozart,
Wolfgang Amadeus, Così Fan Tutte:
Ah Guarda, Sorella

O SLUVKO VIC see Brabec, Jindrich

O TEMERARIO ARBACE see Mozart, Wolfgang
Amadeus

O WALY, WALY (from Folk Songs)
(Britten, Benjamin) "Water Is Wide,
The" strings,high solo [3'] BOOSEY-
ENG rent        (O2)

O, WIE WILL ICH TRIUMPHIEREN see
Mozart, Wolfgang Amadeus

O ZLATEM KLÍCI A ZIVÉ VODE see Hruška,
Jaromír

OAD see Hedelin, Fredrik

OAIJÉ see Lindgren, Pär

OBOE CONCERTANTE see Vackár, Dalibor
Cyril

OBORNY, VACLAV
Beskydy *Op.47
2.3.2.2. 3.3.3.1. strings [17']
CESKY HUD.        (O3)

Sachty *Op.40
3.2.3.1. 3.3.2.1. timp,perc,strings
[20'] CESKY HUD.        (O4)

Sinfonietta No. 3, Op. 48
3.3.3.2. 3.2.3.1. timp,perc,strings
[29'] CESKY HUD.        (O5)

OBRAZ PRO ORCHESTR see Smetana, Radim

OBRAZY III see Fischer, Jan F.

OBROVSKÁ, JANA (1930-1987)
Concertino for Violin, Viola, Double
Bass and Strings
[15'] CESKY HUD.        (O6)

Concerto Festivo
1.1.1.1. 2.0.2.0. timp,perc,strings
[13'] CESKY HUD.        (O7)

Concerto for 2 Guitars and Orchestra
2.1.1.1. 2.3.2.0. perc,xylo,harp,
cel,strings,2gtr soli [18'] CESKY
HUD.        (O8)

Concerto Piccolo
strings,fl solo [13'] CESKY HUD.
       (O9)

Concerto Semplice
strings,vln solo [13'] CESKY HUD.
       (O10)

Due Per Ottoni Ed Archi
0.0.0.0. 4.3.3.0. strings CESKY
HUD.        (O11)

Fantasy for Viola and Chamber
Orchestra
see Smutek Sluší Viole

Fantasy for Violoncello and Strings
strings,vcl solo [13'] CESKY HUD.
       (O12)

OBROVSKÁ, JANA (cont'd.)

Smutek Sluší Viole (Fantasy for Viola
and Chamber Orchestra)
2.2.2.2. 0.0.0.0. timp,harp,
strings,vla solo [13'] CESKY HUD.
(013)

Suite for String Orchestra
[13'] CESKY HUD.                        (014)

OBST, MICHAEL (1955-    )
Dr. Mabuse, Der Spieler, Part 1: Der
Grosse Spieler. Ein Bild Der Zeit
2(2alto fl).1+English horn.2+bass
clar.1. 0.2.2.0. 3perc,harp,2pno,
4vln,2vla,2vcl [165'] BREITKOPF-W
(015)

Dr. Mabuse, Der Spieler, Part 2:
Inferno. Menschen Der Zeit
1(alto fl).1.3(bass
clar).1(contrabsn). 1.2.1.0.
3perc,harp,pno&cel,strings [120']
BREITKOPF-W                             (016)

Poèmes
4(2pic).4.4+bass clar.2(contrabsn).
6.4.4.1. 4perc,harp,pno,strings
[30'] BREITKOPF-W                       (017)

OCCASION see Behrens, Jack

OCCASIONAL NOTES. SUITE FOR ELEVEN
PLAYERS see Hagen, Daron

OCCASIONS see Chatman, Stephen

OCEANIA see Bohlin, Jonas

OCEANO see Johnsen, Hallvard, Symphony
No. 19, Op. 115

OCKAIA see Berge, Håkon

O'CONNER, FREDERICK
Old House, The
string orch,solo voice CRAMER rent
(018)

OD PRAMENE see Basler, Dalibor

ODE see Gerhard, Fritz Christian

ODE A CLAUDE DEBUSSY see Celis, Frits

ODE TO THE HITEN see Ishii, Maki

ODI ET AMO see Panufnik, Roxanna

ODIN SOM SCHAMAN see Winter, Tomas

ODSTRCIL, KAREL (1930-    )
Belounká Holubicko
2.1.2.1. 2.2.1.0. timp,perc,
strings,S solo [14'] CESKY HUD.
(019)

Bubnová Pamet  *Suite
[36'] CESKY HUD.                        (020)

Buratino
2.2.3.2. 4.2.2.1. timp,perc,xylo,
vibra,strings [17'] CESKY HUD.
(021)

Concerto for 2 Clarinets and
Orchestra
"Detsky Koncert Pro 2 Klarinety A
Orchestr" 0.0.0.0. 6.0.0.0. perc,
vibra,strings,2horn soli [17']
CESKY HUD.                              (022)

Concerto for 2 Clarinets and
Orchestra in B flat
see Detsky Koncert No. 1

Concerto for Piano and Orchestra, No.
3
see Detsky Koncert No. 3

Detsky Koncert No. 1 (Concerto for 2
Clarinets and Orchestra in B
flat)
0.0.0.0. 4.0.0.0. perc,vibra,
strings,2clar soli [17'] (B flat
maj) CESKY HUD.                         (023)

Detsky Koncert No. 3 (Concerto for
Piano and Orchestra, No. 3)
timp,perc,2gtr,strings,pno solo
[13'] CESKY HUD.                        (024)

Detsky Koncert Pro 2 Klarinety A
Orchestr
see Concerto for 2 Clarinets and
Orchestra

Femininum
3.3.2.2.3sax. 3.3.1.1. timp,perc,
vibra,harp,cel,strings [9'] CESKY
HUD.                                    (025)

Linka Duvery
strings,ob&clar&bsn soli [9'] CESKY
HUD.                                    (026)

Podoba Cloveka
3.3.3.3. 4.4.3.1. timp,perc,xylo,
pno,strings [21'] CESKY HUD.
(027)

ODSTRCIL, KAREL (cont'd.)
Radegast
3.2.2.2. 4.3.2.1. timp,perc,strings
[24'] CESKY HUD.                        (028)

ODYSSEY see Reynolds, Roger

ODYSSEY, THE see Barnes, Milton

"...OF CABBAGES AND KINGS" see Crawley,
Clifford

OF THE WING OF MADNESS see Taub, Bruce
J.H.

OFF WITH HER HEAD! see Crawley,
Clifford

OFFENBACH, JACQUES (1819-1880)
A Minuit Sonnant (from Vie
Parisienne)
(Rosenthal) orch,solo voice BOIS
(029)

A Minuit Sonnant (Rondo Metela) (from
Vie Parisienne)
orch,solo voice BOIS                    (030)

Air De La Baronne (from Vie
Parisienne)
orch,solo voice BOIS                    (031)

Barbe-Bleue  *Overture
2.1.2.1. 2.2.1.0. timp,perc,strings
LEDUC                                   (032)

Concerto Militaire, For Cello
(Clément) 2.2.2.2. 4.2.3.0. timp,
perc,strings,vcl solo [28'] BOIS
(033)

Contes D'Hoffmann, Les
see Tales Of Hoffmann

Croquefer: No. 4
orch,solo voice BOIS                    (034)

Dites Lui (from Gérolstein)
(Rosenthal) orch,solo voice BOIS
(035)

Duo De "Fleurette", Le
(Lajoignie) orch, solo voices BOIS
(036)

Fruit Des Vieilles Habitudes (from
Roi Cartte)
(Rosenthal) orch,solo voice BOIS
(037)

J'aime Les Militaires (from
Gérolstein)
orch,solo voice BOIS                    (038)

Je T'Adore, Brigand (from Périchole)
(Rosenthal) orch,solo voice BOIS
(039)

Larmes De Jacquelin, Les  *Op.76,No.2
vcl solo,string orch sc,pts
KUNZELMANN GM 1234 ipa                  (040)

Lichten Et Frichte: Fantasy
orch BOIS                               (041)

Maître Peronilla: Overture
orch BOIS                               (042)

Monsieur Et Madame Denis: Overture
orch BOIS                               (043)

Nuit Blanche: Drinking Song
orch,solo voice BOIS                    (044)

Offenbachiana
(Rosenthal) 2.2.2.2. 4.2.3.1. timp,
2perc,harp,strings [35'] BOIS
(045)

On Va Courir (from Vie Parisienne)
orch,solo voice BOIS                    (046)

Orphée Aux Enfers: Quadrille
(composed with Strauss, Johann,
[Jr.])
1.2.2.2. 4.1+2cornet.3.1. timp,
perc,strings pno red LEDUC rent
(047)

2.2.2.2. 4.1+2cornet.3.1. timp,
2perc,strings pno-cond sc LEDUC
(048)

Orphée Aux Enfers: Quadrille (Galop)
orch BOIS                               (049)

Orphée Aux Enfers (Version En 4
Actes): Ouverture
2.2.2.2. 4.2.3.1. timp,harp,strings
LEDUC                                   (050)

Papillon, Le  *Suite
(Lanchbery) 3.2.2.2. 4.3.3.1. perc,
timp,harp,strings [22'] BOIS
(051)

Périchole, La: Quadrille Et Fantaisie
orch BOIS                               (052)

Rhein Nixen, Die: Overture
orch BOIS                               (053)

Robinson Crusoé: No. 12
orch,solo voice BOIS                    (054)

OFFENBACH, JACQUES (cont'd.)
Roi Carotte: Overture
orch BOIS                               (055)

Sa Robe Fait Frou Frou (from Vie
Parisienne)
(Rosenthal) orch,solo voice BOIS
(056)

Si Vous Croyez Que Je Vais Dire (from
Ch. Fortunio)
orch,solo voice BOIS                    (057)

Six Fables De La Fontaine
string orch,fl,clar,S solo [25']
BILLAUDOT                               (058)

Souvenir d'Aix-Les-Bains  *Suite
1+pic.1.1.1. 1.1.1.0. timp,perc,
strings (of 3 waltzes) BOIS            (059)

Tales Of Hoffmann
"Contes D'Hoffmann, Les" orch
(concert version) CRAMER rent
(060)

Trébizonde: Brindisi Et Galop
orch,solo voice BOIS                    (061)

Trombalcazar: Trio
orch, solo voices BOIS                  (062)

Vie Parisienne, La: Overture
orch (short and long versions) BOIS
(063)

Vie Parisienne, La: Quadrille
(Strauss) orch BOIS                     (064)

Voici Le Notaires (from Périchole)
(Rosenthal) orch,solo voice BOIS
(065)

Voyage Dans La Lune, Le
2.2.2.2. 2.2.3.0. timp,2perc,
strings [8'] BOIS perf mat rent
(066)

Voyage Dans La Lune: Overture
orch BOIS                               (067)

Whittington: No. 25
orch,solo voice BOIS                    (068)

OFFENBACH-METAMORPHOSEN see Geissler,
Fritz

OFFENBACHIANA see Offenbach, Jacques

OFFENE LANDSCHAFT see Katzer, Georg

OFTEN FATAL MALADY, AN see Taub, Bruce
J.H.

OGANDO
Hungaria. Quatros Liricas
orch FORLIVESI rent                     (069)

OGURI, KATSUHIRO (1962-    )
Concertino for Violoncello and
Chamber Orchestra
chamber orch,vla solo [15'] JAPAN
(070)

Concerto for Viola
orch,vla solo [17'] JAPAN               (071)

Destruction
orch [17'] JAPAN                        (072)

OH FLIEH, BETROGNE, FLIEH see Mozart,
Wolfgang Amadeus, Ah, Fuggi Il
Traditor

OH, LOIS! see Daugherty, Michael

OH MADELON, JE DOIS PARTIR see
Canteloube de Malaret, Marie-Joseph

OHANA, MAURICE (1914-1992)
Célestine Suite De Concert, La
2.3.3.3. 2.2.3.0. 3perc,hpsd,pno,
strings,SSMezABar soli,cor [42']
BILLAUDOT rent                          (073)

Chiffre De Clavecin
1.1.2.1. 2.1.1.0. 3perc,harp,
strings,hpsd solo [17'] JOBERT
(074)

Concerto for Violoncello and
Orchestra
2.2.3.2. 2.2.2.1. 2perc,harp,
strings,vcl solo [20'] JOBERT
(075)

Crypt
strings [7'30"] JOBERT                  (076)

"... OHNE GRENZE UND RAND..." see
Huber, Klaus

OHNE V HORÁCH see Flosman, Oldrich

OHNIVÁ KREV see Strasek, Emil

OHSE, REINHARD (1930-    )
Serenade
strings [18'] BREITKOPF-W               (077)

OJAI FESTIVAL OVERTURE see Davies,
[Sir] Peter Maxwell

ÖJEBO, PÄR (1940-   )
Couverture
2.2.2.2. 2.2.2.1. timp,2perc,
strings [10'] sc STIM        (078)

OJIBWAY: DRUMS OF MY FATHER see
Rickard, Sylvia

OJISTOH see McDougall, Ian

OKABE, FUJIO (1947-   )
Festive Overture
orch [2'] JAPAN             (079)

OKADA, SHODAI (1929-   )
Symphonic Poem, A
orch [45'] JAPAN            (080)

OKANAGAN LANDSCAPES see Baker, Michael
Conway

OKASAKA, KEIKI (1940-   )
Sketch
see Sobyo

Sobyo
"Sketch" orch [10'] JAPAN   (081)

OKITA, DAISUKE (1958-   )
Gradation And Obelisk
orch [12'] JAPAN            (082)

OKNA S ANDELY see Mateju, Zbynek

OLD AND LOST RIVERS see Picker, Tobias

OLD HOUSE, THE see O'Conner, Frederick

OLD MACDONALD HAD A FARM see Anderson,
Leroy

OLD POLISH MUSIC see Panufnik, Andrzej

OLD RUSSIAN CIRCUS MUSIC see Shchedrin,
Rodion

OLEŠNICKÉ HORY. POCHOD: 1. VERZE see
Deváty, Antonín

OLEŠNICKÉ HORY. POCHOD: 2. VERZE see
Deváty, Antonín

OLIAS, LOTHAR (1913-1990)
Sahara
2.2.2.2. 2.2.2.0. timp,perc,harp,
strings [13'] pno-cond sc
SIKORSKI perf mat rent      (083)

OLIVER CROMWELL (from Folk Songs)
(Britten, Benjamin) 1+pic.2.2.2.
2.2.0.0. timp,strings,high solo
[30"] BOOSEY-ENG rent       (084)

OLLONE, MAX D' (1875-1959)
Lamento
2+pic.2.2+bass clar.2. 4.3.3.1.
timp,bass drum,2harp,strings [8']
LEDUC                       (085)

Ménétrier, Le (Poem for Violin and
Orchestra)
2+pic.2+English horn.2.2. 4.2.3.1.
timp,perc,harp,strings,vln solo
[25'] LEDUC                 (086)

Poem for Violin and Orchestra
see Ménétrier, Le

OLOFSSON, KENT (1962-   )
Carnaval Des Animaux Fabuleux, Le
(Variations)
2.2.2.2. 2.2.3.1. timp,2perc,
strings,pno [8'5"] (12
variations) STIM sc H-2592, pts
(087)
Cimmerian Darkness: Music For Strings
string orch [15'] pts STIM  (088)

Hephaestus Forge
"Iconography" 3.2.2.2. 4.2.3.0.
2perc,harp,strings,pno STIM  (089)

Iconography
see Hephaestus Forge

Variations
see Carnaval Des Animaux Fabuleux,
Le

OLTHUIS, KEES (1940-   )
Parade
2.2.2.2. 2.2.0.0. 2perc,strings
[13'] sc DONEMUS            (090)

Scenes De Ballet
3.3.3.2. 3.2.2.0. timp,2perc,
strings [20'] sc DONEMUS    (091)

OLYMPIJSKY POCHOD see Kvech, Otomar

OLYMPUS MONS see Johansen, Bertil
Palmar

OLYMPUS MONS PART 2 see Johansen,
Bertil Palmar, Tharsis Variations

OM ATT CYKLA see Jansson, Reine

OMASIS see Wranitzky, Anton

OMBRA FELICE see Mozart, Wolfgang
Amadeus

OMVANDLINGAR see Blomberg, Erik

ON A ONI see Kopecky, Pavel

ON AN EMERALD SEA see Symonds, Norman

ON GREEN MOUNTAIN see Shapero, Harold
Samuel

ON HEARING THE FIRST CUCKOO IN SPRING
see Delius, Frederick

ON HOLIDAY see Blyton, Carey

ON THE SNOWY HILL OF THE RAINBOW see
Sugár, M.

ON THE THRESHOLD see Nilsson, Torsten,
Steget Över Tröskeln

ON VA COURIR see Offenbach, Jacques

ONCE see Melnyk, Lubomyr

ONCE AROUND THE SUN: SUITE see Koehne,
Graeme

ONDRÁCEK, BOHUSLAV (1932-   )
Lásko Posmutnelá
sax,perc,2gtr,strings,solo voice,
Yamaha pno [4'] CESKY HUD.   (092)

ONE GLANCE IN SPIROS' BACKYARD see
Mochizuki, Misato

108 see Cage, John

101 see Cage, John

103 see Cage, John

ONE IN HEART see Owens, David

OOSTEN, ROEL VAN (1958-   )
Music-Hall
3.3.3.3. 4.3.3.1. timp,3perc,harp,
pno,strings [12'] sc DONEMUS
(093)
Square (version for large orchestra)
4.4.4.4. 8.5.3.2. timp,4perc,2harp,
strings [12'] sc DONEMUS    (094)

Square (version for orchestra)
3.3.3.3. 4.3.3.1. timp,3perc,harp,
strings [12'] sc DONEMUS    (095)

OOSTERVELD, ERNST (1951-   )
Arcolino, For 24 Solo Strings
14vln,4vla,4vcl,2db [11'] sc
DONEMUS                     (096)

OPBOUW (VERSIE 2) see Goeyvaerts,
Karel, Aquarius, No. 3 (2nd
Version)

OPEN THE DOOR. ORCHESTRAL OVERTURE see
Walker, Gwyneth

OPERAND see Kucera, Václav

OPERNPROBE, DIE: OVERTURE see Lortzing,
(Gustav) Albert

OPPOSITE OF ONE, THE see Wendelboe,
Jens

OPPOSITIONS MULTIPLES see Rens, Jean-
Marie

OPPTOG: BLOMSTENES INNTOGMARSJ see
Iberg, Helge

OPTIMISMUS see Koehler, Emil

OPUS 1.991 see Kagel, Mauricio

OPUS 6 MET 180 KLANKVOORWERPEN see
Goeyvaerts, Karel

OPUS LABYRINTHUM LEGO see Zeeland, Cees
Van

OR DE LA TROMPETTE D'ÉTÉ, L' see Cowie,
Edward

ORATIO I see Nelhybel, Vaclav

ORB AND SCEPTRE: CORONATION MARCH see
Walton, [Sir] William (Turner)

ORBIS see Keane, David

ORBON, JULIAN (1925-1991)
Danzas Sinfonicas
2+pic.2.2.2. 4.3.0.0. timp,perc,
cel,2harp,pno,strings [18'] PEER
rent                        (097)

ORBON, JULIAN (cont'd.)

Homenaje A La Tonadilla
4+pic.4+English horn.4+bass clar.3+
contrabsn. 4.3.3.1. timp,perc,
cel,glock,harp,strings [16'] PEER
rent                        (098)

Monte Gelboe
2.2.2(bass clar).2. 4.3.0.0. timp,
perc,harp,cel,strings,T&narrator
[18'] (text from the Bible: II
Samuel) PEER rent           (099)

Partita No. 4
"Symphonic Movement For Piano And
Orchestra" 2.2.2(bass clar).2.
4.3.3.0. timp,3perc,strings,pno
solo PEER rent             (0100)

Symphonic Movement For Piano And
Orchestra
see Partita No. 4

Three Symphonic Versions
see Tres Versiones Sinfonicas

Tres Versiones Sinfonicas
"Three Symphonic Versions" 4.2.4.4.
4.4.3.1. timp,perc,cel,harp,pno,
strings [23'] PEER rent    (0101)

ORCHESTER-FANTASIE, OP. 6 see
Engelmann, Hans Ulrich

ORCHESTER-SUITE AUS DER OPER DAS GRÜNE
GESICHT see Kox, Hans, Grüne
Gesicht, Das: Suite

ORCHESTERBALLADE see Thilman, Johannes
Paul

ORCHESTERLIEDER, 3 see Gropp, Johann-
Maria

ORCHESTERMUSIK I see Dege, Peter see
Stöckigt, Michael

ORCHESTERMUSIK II see Schmidt,
Christfried

ORCHESTERMUSIK IV see Stöckigt, Michael

ORCHESTERSPIEL II see Maler, Wilhelm,
Concerto Grosso, Op. 11

ORCHESTERSTÜCK see Bruns, Victor

ORCHESTERSTÜCK 2 see Bredemeyer, Reiner

ORCHESTERSTÜCK NR. 1 "...CIELO
AZZURRO..." see Schweizer, Alfred

ORCHESTERSTÜCK NR. 2 "DANSES" see
Schweizer, Alfred

ORCHESTERSTÜCK NR. 3 see Schweizer,
Alfred

ORCHESTERSTÜCKE (4) see Bechert, Ernst

ORCHESTERSTUECK 1 see Koenig, Gottfried
Michael

ORCHESTERSTUECK 3 see Koenig, Gottfried
Michael

ORCHESTRA see Felciano, Richard

ORCHESTRA: SYMPHONIC MUSIC FOR MOBILE
MUSICIAN see Schnebel, Dieter

ORCHESTRA VARIATIONS see Blitzstein,
Marc

ORCHESTRAL FRAGMENTS see Bengtson,
Peter

ORCHESTRAL MUSIC 1 "E IL LIBRÖ see
Larson, Martin

ORCHESTRAL MUSIC IN SALZBURG, 1750-1780
*CC8L
(Eisen, Cliff) 0.2.0.0. 2.2.0.0.
timp,vln I,vln II,vla,vcl/db, (No
piece uses all the instruments)
sets A-R ED ISBN 0-89579-287-7 f.s.
seven symphonies and one parthia by
Seidl, Christelli, Eberlin, Leopold
Mozart, Hebelt, Paris, Hafeneder,
and Scheicher               (0102)

ORCHESTRAL PARAPHRASE FROM THE OPERA
'AURA' see Lavista, Mario, Aura:
Paráfrasis Orquestal De La Opera

ORCHESTRAL QUARTET IN B-FLAT see
Stamitz, Carl

ORCHESTRAL QUARTET IN C see Stamitz,
Carl

ORCHESTRAL QUARTET IN D see Stamitz,
Carl

ORCHESTRAL QUARTET IN E-FLAT see
Stamitz, Carl

ORCHESTRAL QUARTET IN F see Stamitz,
Carl

ORCHESTRAL QUARTET IN F see Stamitz,
Carl

ORCHESTRAL QUARTET IN G see Stamitz,
Carl

ORCHESTRAL SET NO. 2 see Ives, Charles

ORCHESTRAL SONGS BY THE EDGE OF
ROMANTICISM see Hundsnes, Svein,
Haugtussa

ORCHESTRAL TRIO IN A see Stamitz,
Johann Wenzel Anton

ORCHESTRAL TRIO IN B-FLAT see Stamitz,
Johann Wenzel Anton

ORCHESTRAL TRIO IN C see Stamitz,
Johann Wenzel Anton

ORCHESTRAL TRIO IN D see Stamitz,
Johann Wenzel Anton

ORCHESTRAL TRIO IN E see Stamitz,
Johann Wenzel Anton

ORCHESTRAL TRIO IN F see Stamitz,
Johann Wenzel Anton

ORCHESTRAL TRIO IN G see Stamitz,
Johann Wenzel Anton

ORCHESTRAL VARIATIONS see Jeverud,
Johan, Orkestervariationer

ORCHESTRALES see Visman, Bart

ORCHESTRÁLNÍ TRIO F-DUR see Stamitz,
Carl

ORCHESTRATION OF ALEC ROWLEY'S "PAVAN"
see Roseingrave

ORCHESTRION-STRAAT see Kagel, Mauricio

ORDONEZ, CARLO D' (1734-1786)
Sinfonia in A
2ob,2horn,2vln,vla,vcl,db [10']
ARTARIA AE119              (O103)

Sinfonia in B minor
2ob,2horn,2vln,vla,vcl,db [13']
ARTARIA AE118              (O104)

Sinfonia in C
2ob,2horn,2vln,vla,vcl,db,vln&vcl
soli [11'] ARTARIA AE061   (O105)

Sinfonia in C, MIN 1
2ob,2horn,2vln,vla,vcl,db [9']
ARTARIA AE117              (O106)

Sinfonia in C, MIN 2
2ob,2horn,2trp,timp,2vln,vla,vcl,db
[8'] ARTARIA AE120         (O107)

Sinfonia in D
2ob,2horn,2vln,vla,vcl,db [6']
ARTARIA AE062              (O108)

Sinfonia in E
2ob,2horn,2vln,vla,vcl,db [10']
ARTARIA AE058              (O109)

Sinfonia in F minor
2vln,vla,vcl,db [13'] ARTARIA AE059
                          (O110)
Sinfonia in G minor
2ob,2vln,vla,vcl,db [14'] ARTARIA
AE060                      (O111)

Sinfonia in G minor, MIN 1
2ob,2horn,2vln,vla,vcl,db [14']
ARTARIA AE116              (O112)

ORDWAY OVERTURE see Paulus, Stephen
Harrison

ORE, CECILIE (1954-    )
Erat Erit Est: For 15 Instruments
1(pic).1(English horn).1(bass
clar).1. 2.1.1.0. 3perc,2vln,vla,
vcl, amplification NORSKMI (O113)

Futurum Exactum
amplified string orchestra [15'30"]
NORSKMI                    (O114)

Nunc Et Nunc
3(pic).3(English horn).3(2bass
clar).3. 4.4.4.0. 3perc,strings
[29'30"] NORSKMI           (O115)

OREGON see Karkoff, Ingvar

OREGON FANCY see Healey, Derek

ORESTES UND AJAS see Mozart, Wolfgang
Amadeus, D'Oreste, d'Ajace

ORFEO FAST FORWARD see Ford, Ronald

ORFF, CARL (1895-1982)
Entrata
6.4+2English horn.0.2+contrabsn.
6.9.4.2. 4timp,perc,2cel,4pno,
org,2harp,strings, 2more trumpets
[12'] SCHOTTS perf mat rent (O116)

(Wagner, Robert) 4.4(2English
horn).0.2+contrabsn. 4.8.3.1.
2timp,perc,pno 4-hands&cel&glock,
org,2harp,strings [12'] SCHOTTS
perf mat rent             (O117)
(Wagner, Robert) 3.3(2English
horn).0.2+contrabsn. 4.6.3.1.
2timp,perc,pno 4-hands&cel&glock,
org,2harp,strings [12'] SCHOTTS
perf mat rent             (O118)

Kleines Konzert
1(pic).2.0.2. 2.1.1.0. timp,2perc,
cel,harp,strings [13'] SCHOTTS
perf mat rent             (O119)

Tanzende Faune  *Op.21
4.2+English horn.3.3. 4.2.0.0.
timp,perc,cel&pno 4-hands,2harp,
8vln I,8vln II,4vla,4vcl,2db
[15'] (orchestral play) SCHOTTS
perf mat rent             (O120)

Uf Dem Anger (from Carmina Burana)
3.2+English horn.2+clar in E
flat.2. 4.3.3.0. timp,perc,
strings [2'] SCHOTTS perf mat
rent                      (O121)

ORGAN DANCES see Chilcott, Robert (Bob)

ORGAN SYMPHONY see Saint-Saëns,
Camille, Symphony No. 3

ORGELSINFONIE (SALZAUER SINFONIE) see
Voigtländer, Lothar, Sinfonia No. 3

ORGORCHESTRA see Frischknecht, Hans
Eugen

ORIGIN, THE see Ichiyanagi, Toshi,
Concerto For Koto And Chamber
Orchestra

ORION see Vivier, Claude

ORKESTERFÖRSPEL see Freudenthal, Otto

ORKESTERSVIT see Engström, Torbjörn

ORKESTERVARIATIONER see Jeverud, Johan

ORKESTSTUK MET PIANO, K. 27 see Pijper,
Willem

ORLANDO FURIOSO see Orton, Richard

ORNAMENTE see Thilman, Johannes Paul

ORPHÉE AUX ENFERS: QUADRILLE see
Offenbach, Jacques

ORPHÉE AUX ENFERS: QUADRILLE (GALOP)
see Offenbach, Jacques

ORPHÉE AUX ENFERS (VERSION EN 4 ACTES):
OUVERTURE see Offenbach, Jacques

ORPHEUS - CONCERT VERSION see Henze,
Hans Werner

ORPHEUS: DRAMATIC SCENES NO. 1 see
Henze, Hans Werner

ORPHEUS: DRAMATIC SCENES NO. 2 see
Henze, Hans Werner

ORPHEUS SINGING see Baley, Virko

ORPHISCHER GESANG see Kirchner, Volker
David

ORTON, RICHARD
Concerto for Guitar
"Lattices - Guitar Concerto"
2.1.1.0. 1.1.0.1. marimba,vibra,
strings,2vcl solo,gtr solo [20']
sc UNIV.YORK 0059 f.s.     (O122)

Lattices - Guitar Concerto
see Concerto for Guitar

Orlando Furioso
1.1.1.1. 1.1.1.0. harp,perc,2vln,
vla,vcl,db, DX7 kbd. [12'] sc
UNIV.YORK 0061 f.s.        (O123)

Stellations
15 solo strings [10'] sc UNIV.YORK
0098 f.s.                  (O124)

ORTUS see Keane, David

OSAMELY MOREPLAVEC see Vacek, Miloš

OSBORNE, NIGEL (1948-    )
Concerto for Violin and Orchestra
2.2.2.2. 3.2.2.0. 2perc,pno,harp,
strings,vln solo [22'] UNIVER.
                          (O125)

Sun Of Venice, The
3.3.3.3. 3.3.2.1. 3perc,cel,pno,
harp,strings, (2 concertante
groups) [27'] UNIVER.     (O126)

OSMOSE see Lauber, Anne, Pièce
Symphonique No. II see Trochu,
Pierre

OSPALD, KLAUS (1956-    )
Schöne Welt, Schöne Welt
1.2.4.1. 0.2.1.1. 3perc,harp,gtr,
cel,pno,2vln,2vla,2vcl,db,female
solo&female solo&female solo&
speaking voice [25'] BREITKOPF-W
                          (O127)

"...und die Erd ist kalt..."
1.2.2.1. 1.0.0.0. 2perc,harp,2pno,
db [20'] BREITKOPF-W      (O128)

OSTEN-SACKEN, MAXIMILIAN D'
Berceuse
8vln I,7vln II,6vla,5vcl,4db [5']
sc BELAIEFF 02939         (O129)

OSTENDORF, JENS-PETER (1944-    )
Chant D'Orphée
perc,20strings soli,T solo [12']
SIKORSKI perf mat rent    (O130)

OSTERGAARD, EDVIN (1959-    )
Reminiscence For 17 Musicians
2(pic,alto fl).1.1(bass clar).1.
1.1.1.0. 3perc,pno,2vln,vla,vcl,
db [18'] NORSKMI          (O131)

OSTINATI see Griesbach, Karl-Rudi

OSTINATO see Papineau-Couture, Jean

OSTINATO FUNEBRE see Holliger, Heinz

OSTRAVSKÁ see Podešva, Jaromír,
Symphony No. 8

OSTRCIL, OTAKAR (1879-1935)
Polka, Op. 109
2.2.2.2. 4.2.3.1. timp,perc,strings
[3'] CESKY HUD.           (O132)

OSVALD, MILOSLAV (1946-    )
Concerto Grosso
3.3.3.2. 2.2.0.0. timp,perc,strings
[15'] CESKY HUD.          (O133)

OTÁZKA BEZ ODPOVEDI see Barton, Hanus

OTELLO: OUVERTURE see Rossini,
Gioacchino

OTETTO see Heinrich, Anton Philip

OTHELLO: SUITE NO. 3 see Machavariani,
Alexei, Suite No. 3

OTHER ECHOES see Tsontakis, George

"...OTHER ECHOES INHABIT THE GARDEN"
see Bose, Hans-Jurgen Von

OTTO, VALERIUS (fl. ca. 1600-1625)
Parthia Isabella
(Burghauser, Jarmil) strings,gtr
[15'] CESKY HUD.          (O134)

OUT OF THE DARKNESS see Blake, Michael

OUVERTURA BOEMA see Lukas, Zdenek

OUVERTURA BRAVURA see Bohác, Josef

OUVERTURE see Trommer, Jack

OUVERTÜRE 1 see Bach, Johann Christian,
Sinfonia, Op. 3, No. 1, in D

OUVERTURE CANADIENNE see Lauber, Anne,
Canadian Overture

OUVERTURE D GR. T. see Dijk, Jan van

OUVERTURE DANOISE see Tchaikovsky,
Piotr Ilyich

OUVERTÜRE G-DUR see Heinichen, Johann
David, Suite in G

OUVERTURE SOLENNELLE ES-DUR, OP. 49 see
Tchaikovsky, Piotr Ilyich

OUVERTÜRE UND DREI KONTRETÄNZE see
Mozart, Wolfgang Amadeus

OUVERTURE ZU EINER ALTEN KOMÖDIE see
Laquai, Reinhold

OUVERTYRE TIL NORSK ESSO'S 100 ÅRS
JUBILEUM see Iberg, Helge, Motor
For Symfoniorkester Og Tape

OVAZIONE NO. 2 see Helge, Olov

OVERDOSE see Burritt, Lloyd

OVERTOCHT, DE see Ketting, Otto

OVERTURA BUFFA see Fiala, George

OVERTURA POPOLOSA see Filas, Juraj

OVERTURA SERIA see Blatny, Josef

OVERTURE see Kohout, Josef, Sinfonia

OVERTURE, AIR, AND DANCES see Crawley, Clifford

OVERTURE CONCERTANTE see Pinkham, Daniel

OVERTURE ... DE ORIGEN VOLCÁNICO see Vriend, Jan N.M.

OVERTURE DON SEGUNDO see Ficher, Jacobo

OVERTURE FOR FUN see Kunz, Alfred

OVERTURE FOR THE END OF A CENTURY see Larsen, Elizabeth B. (Libby)

OVERTURE: FUNFARE see Jacob, Gordon

OVERTURE: HALLÉ see Rawsthorne, Alan

OVERTURE IN THE FORM OF VARIATIONS see Naylor, Bernard

OVERTURE ON A CANADIAN THEME (OR TWO) see Crawley, Clifford

OVERTURE: PARACHUTE DANCING see Larsen, Elizabeth B. (Libby)

OVERTURE TO A KNIGHTLY PLAY see Weinberger, Jaromir

OVERTURE TO A MARIONETTE PLAY see Weinberger, Jaromir

OVERTURE TO SERENADE CONCERTANTE see Waxman, Donald

OVERTURE WITH FANFARES see Mills, Richard

OVERTURES AND PRELUDES see Wagner, Richard

OWENS, DAVID
  Double Concerto For Euphonium And
    Tuba And Orchestra
    2.2.2.2. 3.2.3.0. timp,snare drum,
    bass drum,glock,tamb,xylo,strings
    [20'] (in four movements) ANDREA
                                    (0135)

  Jonah: Dance Of The Ninevites (Act 2)
    see Jonah: Four Orchestral Pieces

  Jonah: Entr'acte (Act 3)
    see Jonah: Four Orchestral Pieces

  Jonah: Four Orchestral Pieces
    2.2.2.2. 3.2.3.1. timp,snare drum,
    bass drum,tamb,cym,xylo,harp,
    strings ANDREA f.s.
    contains: Jonah: Dance Of The
      Ninevites (Act 2); Jonah:
      Entr'acte (Act 3); Jonah:
      Prelude (Act 1); Jonah: Storm
      Scene (Act 1)            (0136)

  Jonah: Prelude (Act 1)
    see Jonah: Four Orchestral Pieces

  Jonah: Storm Scene (Act 1)
    see Jonah: Four Orchestral Pieces

  One In Heart  *Proces,March
    3.3.3.2. 4.2.3.1. timp,snare drum,
    bass drum,tamb,cym,glock,
    triangle,harp,strings [7'] ANDREA
                                    (0137)

OXFORD SINFONIA see Twa, Andrew

OYENS, TERA DE MARZ
  see MAREZ OYENS, TERA DE

OZIVENÁ KRAJINA see Slavicky, Milan

OZVENY see Bazant, Jiri see Precechtel, Zbynek

# P

P GLNT see Burwick, Karin

P.W. AND HIS SKILLET LICKERS see Meijering, Chiel

PÅ KVELDSHØGDA see Søderlind, Ragnar

PÅ ÖPPEN GATA see Josjö, Mårten

PABLO, LUIS DE (1930- )
  Polar
    chamber orch TONOS M-2015-3878-5
                                    (P1)

PACHMUTOVA, ALEXANDRA (1929- )
  Concerto for Orchestra
    3.2.2.2. 4.4.3.1. timp,perc,harp,
    pno,strings [15'] SIKORSKI perf
    mat rent                        (P2)

PACIFIC IMAGES (VERSION FOR 14 PLAYERS)
  see Chaitkin, David

PADDING, MARTIJN
  Scharf Abreissen
    4.5.4.4. 6.5.4.1. 4perc,2harp,pno,
    strings [24'] sc DONEMUS        (P3)

PADILLA, ANTOINE (1940- )
  Hélio-Trope
    1.0.0.1. 2.1.1.0. perc,harp,Ondes
    Martenot,string orch/string quin,
    S solo [23'] sc CANADIAN
    MV 1973 P123HE_A                (P4)

  Symphonie De Chambre
    2(pic).2.2.2. 2.0.0.0. 2perc,harp,
    strings sc CANADIAN
    MI 1200 P123SY                  (P5)

PAGAN SYMPHONY see Bantock, [Sir] Granville

PAGANINI, NICCOLO (1782-1840)
  A Henry
    2+pic.2.2.2. 2.2.3.0. timp,perc,
    strings,bsn&horn soli [25']
    BOCCACCINI BS. 59 rent          (P6)

  Balletto Campestre
    (Spada) 2.2.2.2. 2.2.0.0. timp,
    perc,strings [16'] BOCCACCINI
    BS. 113 rent                    (P7)

  Campanella, La
    (Cohen, Shimon) string orch,vln
    solo [3'30"] PRESSER rent       (P8)

  Concerto for Violin and Orchestra in
    D, Op. 6, No. 1
    2.2.2.1+contrabsn. 2.2.3.0. timp,
    2perc,strings,vln solo [35']
    study sc BREITKOPF-W PB 5260    (P9)

  Concerto No. 2 in B minor
    (Petruci, G.L.) 1.2.2.2. 2.2.2.0.
    strings,fl solo [31'] BILLAUDOT
                                    (P10)

  Concerto No. 2 in E minor for Flute
    (Petruci, G.L.) 1.2.2.2. 2.2.2.0.
    strings,fl solo [31'] sc,solo pt
    BILLAUDOT rent                  (P11)

  God Save The King
    2.2.2.2. 2.2.3.0. timp,perc,
    strings,vln solo [15'] BOCCACCINI
    BS. 94 rent                     (P12)

  Maestosa Suonata Sentimentale
    2.2.2.2. 2.2.3.0. perc,strings
    [18'] BOCCACCINI BS. 132 rent   (P13)

  Napoleon
    2.2.2.2. 2.2.3.0. timp,perc,
    strings,vln solo [15'] BOCCACCINI
    BS. 197 rent                    (P14)

  Non Più Mesta
    1.2.2.2. 2.2.3.0. strings,vln solo
    [12'] BOCCACCINI rent           (P15)

  Palpiti, I
    2.2.2.2. 2.2.1.0. timp,perc,strings
    [15'] BOCCACCINI BS. 63 rent    (P16)

  Perpetuela
    strings,vln solo [6'] BOCCACCINI
    BS. 198 rent                    (P17)

  Polacca Con Variazioni
    (Spada) 2.2.2.2. 2.2.0.0. timp,
    perc,strings,vln solo [15']
    BOCCACCINI BS. 195 rent         (P18)

  Primavera, La
    (Spada) 2.2.2.2. 2.2.0.0. timp,
    strings [18'] BOCCACCINI BS. 48
    rent                            (P19)

PAGANINI, NICCOLO (cont'd.)

  Sonata A Preghiera
    strings,vln solo [14'] BOCCACCINI
    rent
    (Fiore) strings,vln solo [14']
    BOCCACCINI BS. 42 rent          (P20)
                                    (P21)

  Sonata Maria Luisa
    (Spada) 2.2.2.2. 2.2.0.0. timp,
    strings [15'] BOCCACCINI BS. 123
    rent                            (P22)

  Sonata Per La Gran Viola
    (Fiore) 2+pic.2.2.2. 2.2.3.0. timp,
    6perc,strings,vla solo [29']
    BOCCACCINI BS. 199 rent         (P23)

  Streghe, Le
    2+pic.2.2.2. 4.2.3.0. timp,perc,
    strings,vln solo [15'] BOCCACCINI
    BS. 196 rent                    (P24)

  Suonata Varsavia
    (Spada) 2.2.2.2. 2.2.0.0. timp,
    strings [18'] BOCCACCINI BS. 124
    rent                            (P25)

  Variationen Auf Einer Saite Nach
    Einem Thema Von Rossini
    (Thomas-Mifune, W.) vcl solo,string
    orch sc,pts KUNZELMANN GM 1177
    ipa                             (P26)

PAGANINI PERSONAL see Ichiyanagi, Toshi

PAGES FROM A MOTHER'S DIARY (LITTLE RED
  SCHOOLHOUSE) see Still, William
  Grant

PAIDSOMENEST see Sagvik, Stellan

PAINE, JOHN KNOWLES (1839-1906)
  Shakespeares Sturm
    2+pic.2.2.2. 4.2.3.1. timp,harp,
    strings [25'] BREITKOPF-W       (P27)

  Symphony No. 1, Op. 23
    2.2.2.2. 4.2.3.0. timp,strings
    [38'] BREITKOPF-W               (P28)

  Was Ihr Wollt  *Op.28, Overture
    2+pic.2.2.2. 4.2.3.0. timp,strings
    [11'] BREITKOPF-W               (P29)

PAISAJES BAJO EL SIGNO DE COSMOS see
  Márquez, Arturo

PAISIBLE, JAMES (JACQUES)
  (ca. 1650-1721)
  Sonata No. 10 in D
    (Platt) 2trp/2ob,strings,hpsd [10']
    OXFORD sc 3662604 f.s., perf sc
    set 3662612 sc,pts rent         (P30)

PAISIELLO, GIOVANNI (1740-1816)
  Concerto for Cembalo and Orchestra,
    No. 1, in C
    2.0.0.0. 2.0.0.0. strings,cembalo
    solo [15'] BOCCACCINI BS. 51 rent
                                    (P31)

  Concerto for Cembalo and Orchestra,
    No. 2, in F
    2.0.0.0. 2.0.0.0. strings,cembalo
    solo [15'] BOCCACCINI BS. 53 rent
                                    (P32)

  Concerto in B flat for Violin and
    Strings
    [15'] BOCCACCINI rent           (P33)

  Marche Funébre Pour Le Général Hoche
    0.2.0.0. 2.0.0.0. strings [12']
    BOCCACCINI BS. 200 rent         (P34)

  Nocturnos De Andalucía
    "Suite Concertante For Guitar And
    Orchestra" 2(pic).2(English
    horn).2.2. 4.2.3.1. timp,perc,
    strings [37'] sc PRESSER rent   (P35)

  Suite Concertante For Guitar And
    Orchestra
    see Nocturnos De Andalucía

PALAS, RAINER (1933- )
  Little Concertino
    see Pienoiskonserttoja

  Pienoiskonserttoja
    "Little Concertinos" sc,pts MODUS
    M37                             (P36)

PÁLENÍCEK, JOSEF (1914-1991)
  Concerto for Piano, Strings and
    Timpani in C
    [30'] CESKY HUD.                (P37)

  Quetzal Coatl
    4.3.3.3. 4.3.3.1. timp,perc,xylo,
    vibra,harp,cel,pno,marimba,
    strings,ABar soli [34'] CESKY
    HUD.                            (P38)

PALKOVSKY, OLDRICH (1907-1983)
Malá Suita *Op.76
2.3.3.2. 4.3.3.1. timp,perc,strings
[12'] CESKY HUD. (P39)

Sinfonietta, Op. 69
3.3.3.3. 4.3.3.1. timp,perc,strings
[15'] CESKY HUD. (P40)

Sonata for Chamber Orchestra, Op. 56
1.1.2.2. 2.1.0.0. strings [13']
CESKY HUD. (P41)

PALKOVSKY, PAVEL (1939- )
Musica Neoclassica
[11'] CESKY HUD. (P42)

PALLAS ATHENE: SYMPHONY see Kovach,
Andor

PALMÉR, CATHARINA (1963- )
Cur
3.2.3(bass clar).3(contrabsn).
4.3.3.1. timp,2perc,strings [16']
sc STIM (P43)

Lines And Labyriths
15inst [12'] STIM (P44)

PALMER, ROBERT M. (1915- )
Abraham Lincoln Walks At Midnight
3.2(English horn).2.2. 4.3.3.1.
timp,strings [12'] (text by V.
Lindsay) PEER rent (P45)

PALOMO, LORENZO (1938- )
Nocturnos De Andalucia
2.2.2.2. 4.2.3.1. perc,strings,gtr
solo [37'] perf sc EMEC f.s.
(P46)
"PALOTACHE" see Erkel, Franz (Ferenc)

PALOUCEK, ALOIS (1931-1986)
Chvála Skromnosti
1.0.3.0. 2.3.3.0. perc,2gtr,strings
[4'] CESKY HUD. (P47)

Serenade for Violin and Orchestra
2.2.2.1. 2.2.2.0. timp,perc,
strings,vln solo CESKY HUD. (P48)

Tomášovská Polka
2.2.2.1. 4.2.3.0. perc,strings,bsn
solo [4'] CESKY HUD. (P49)

Valcík (Waltz for Trumpet and
Orchestra)
2.2.2.2. 4.0.3.0. timp,perc,
strings,trp solo CESKY HUD. (P50)

Waltz for Trumpet and Orchestra
see Valcík

PALPITARET HAERENS see Looten,
Christophe

PALPITI, I see Paganini, Niccolo

PALPITO see Filas, Juraj

PAMET see Šesták, Zdeněk

PAMIETAM see Wilson, Richard (Edward)

PAN see Finke, Fidelio Friedrich
(Fritz)

PAN IS DEAD see Betts, Lorne M.

PANAMODY see Bodorova, Sylvie

PANDORA: SUITE see Gerhard, Roberto

PANEM ET CIRCENSES see Fried, Alexj,
Chléb A Hry

PANGEA see Engström, Torbjörn, Symphony
No. 1

PANIC see Birtwistle, Harrison

PANIS ANGELICUS see Franck, Cesar

PANNETON, ISABELLE (1955- )
Trois Fois Passera
string orch sc CANADIAN
MI 1500 P194TR (P51)

PANTALON UND COLOMBINE: MUSIK ZU EINER
PANTOMIME see Mozart, Wolfgang
Amadeus

PANUFNIK, ANDRZEJ (1914-1991)
Concerto for Violoncello
2fl,2clar,perc,8-12vln I,6-10vln
II,4-8vla,3-6vcl,1-4db,vcl solo
[19'] BOOSEY-ENG rent (P52)

Concerto for Violoncello and
Orchestra
0.2.2.0. 1.0.0.0. perc,strings,vcl
solo [23'] BOOSEY-ENG (P53)

Love Song
harp/pno,strings,Mez solo [5']
(text by Sir Philip Sidney)

PANUFNIK, ANDRZEJ (cont'd.)

BOOSEY-ENG rent (P54)

Old Polish Music
5horn,4trp,4trom,8vln I,8vln II,
8vla,8vcl,8db [23'] (includes 3
pieces) BOOSEY-ENG rent (P55)

Sinfonia Di Speranza
see Symphony No. 9

Symphony No. 9
"Sinfonia Di Speranza" 3.2.2+bass
clar.2+contrabsn. 4.3.3.1. timp,
strings [38'] BOOSEY-ENG rent
(P56)
PANUFNIK, ROXANNA
Flori Suite
A rec,hpsd,strings, 2 theorbos
[10'] KALMUS,A (P57)

Odi Et Amo
English horn,bass clar,trp,perc,
pno,gtr,harp,2vln,2vla,vcl,db
[24'] KALMUS,A (P58)

Virtue
strings,Mez solo [6'] manuscript
BMIC (P59)

PANURGE (EXCERPTS) see Massenet, Jules

PAPERCLIP MUSIC see Kemp, Bart De

PAPILLON, LE see Offenbach, Jacques

PAPILLON ET LA FLEUR, LE see Faure,
Gabriel-Urbain

PAPINEAU-COUTURE, JEAN (1916- )
Ostinato
string orch [2'30"] sc CANADIAN
MI 1500 P2170S (P60)

PARA VIOLA Y ORQUESTA see Leon, Tania
Justina

PARABEL see Schmidt, Hansjürgen

PARABOLA PRO ORCHESTR see Vostrák,
Zbynek

PARABOLES ET CATASTROPHES see Thibault,
Alain

PARABOLY see Kupka, Karel

PARADE see Olthuis, Kees

PARADE, A see Harrison, Lou

PARADISE LOST: ADAGIETTO see
Penderecki, Krzysztof

PARALLELEGY see Sexton, Brian

PARAPHRASE see Prevost, Andre

PARAPHRASE EN POLYPHONIE SUR UN THÈME
DE BEETHOVEN see Brott, Alexander,
Paraphrase In Polyphony: On A Theme
By Beethoven

PARAPHRASE IN POLYPHONY: ON A THEME BY
BEETHOVEN see Brott, Alexander

PARAPHRASE SUR DES AIRS DE NÖEL see
Morel, Francois d'Assise

PARAPHRASEN ÜBER DOSTOJEWSKI see Henze,
Hans Werner

PARCHMAN, GEN LOUIS (1929- )
Concerto for Marimba
2.3.3.3. 4.4.3.2. timp,3perc,
strings,marimba solo SEESAW (P61)

Concerto for Timpani
3.3.3.3. 4.4.3.1. strings,timp solo
SEESAW (P62)

Symphony For Chorus
3.2.3.3. 4.4.3.1. harp,perc,
strings,SATB SEESAW (P63)

Symphony No. 5
2.2.2.2. 2.2.0.0. timp,perc,strings
SEESAW (P64)

PARCOURS MOSAN see Michel, Paul-
Baudouin

PARFUM IMPÉRISSABLE, LE see Faure,
Gabriel-Urbain

PARIDA ED ELENA: BALLETMUSIK see Gluck,
Christoph Willibald, Ritter von

PARKER, ALICE (1925- )
Double Concerto For Oboe, Viola And
String Orchestra
ob solo,vla solo,strings [20']
SCHIRM.EC rent (P65)

PARKER, MICHAEL (1948- )
"...And A Roll On The Gong" (Concerto
for Percussion and Orchestra, Op.
36)
2(pic).2.2.2. 4.2.3.1. timp,
strings,perc solo sc CANADIAN
MI 1340 P242AN (P66)

Concerto for Percussion and
Orchestra, Op. 36
see "...And A Roll On The Gong"

PARMERUD (1953- )
Inside Looking Out
chamber orch SUECIA (P67)

Mirage
1(pic).0.1(bass clar).0. 0.0.1.0.
2perc,strings,pno solo, computer
STIM (P68)

PARODOS see Börtz, Daniel

PARODY FROM J.S. BACH see Tangiwa,
Tadihiro

PAROLES PLUS HÉRÉTIQUES see Harrison,
Jonty

PARROTT, IAN (1916- )
Pensieri
8vln I,7vln II,6vla,5vcl,4db [16']
sc PETERS 04721 (P69)

PARSCH, ARNOST (1936- )
Dve Ronda
[10'] CESKY HUD. (P70)

Fantasy for 2 String Orchestras
see Poselství

Poema-Koncert
3.3.3.3. 4.3.3.1. perc,2harp,
strings,cym solo [21'] CESKY HUD.
(P71)
Poselství (Fantasy for 2 String
Orchestras)
2string orch [14'] CESKY HUD. (P72)

Pro Futuro
4.3.4.3. 4.3.3.1. timp,perc,harp,
cel,pno,strings [10'] CESKY HUD.
(P73)
Prométheus *Rondo
3.3.5.3. 4.4.3.1. perc,strings,vln
solo [13'] CESKY HUD. (P74)

Sonata for Chamber Orchestra
fl,clar,horn,perc,vibra,cel,pno,
cembalo,vln,vla,vcl,electronic
tape [11'] CESKY HUD. (P75)

Symfonie-Koncert
3.3.4.3. 4.3.3.1. timp,perc,cel,
harp,strings,horn [18'] CESKY
HUD. (P76)

PÄRT, ARVO (1935- )
Concerto Piccolo Über B-A-C-H, For
Trumpet, String Orchestra,
Harpsichord And Piano
[8'] SIKORSKI min sc 1931 f.s., sc,
pts perf mat rent (P77)

Sinfonia No. 3
3.3.4.3. 4.4.4.1. timp,perc,cel,
strings [21'] study sc PETERS
EP 5775 (P78)
3.3.4.3. 4.4.4.1. timp,perc,cel,
8vln I,7vln II,6vla,5vcl,4db [5']
sc,study sc PETERS 01099 (P79)

PARTHIA IN D see Rössler-Rosetti,
Frantisek Antonin

PARTHIA IN F see Rössler-Rosetti,
Frantisek Antonin

PARTHIA ISABELLA see Otto, Valerius

PARTITA BAROCCA see Heard, Alan

PARTITA DANZANTE see Slimácek, Jan

PARTITA PICCOLA see Dijk, Jan van see
Thilman, Johannes Paul

PASACALLE 1992 see Salzedo, Leonard
(Lopes)

PASCAL, PENSEE 206 see Clarke, Kames

PASEABASE, THE MOORISH KING see
Pisador, Diego

PASEO DE LOS TRISTES see Román, José
García

PASSACAGLIA CONCERTANTE see Hanuš, Jan

PASSACAGLIA IMMAGINARIA see
Skrowaczewski, Stanislaw

PASSACAGLIA, TOCCATA A FUGA see Sokola,
Milos

PASSACAGLIA UND FUGE see Eckhardt-Gramatte, Sophie Carmen

PASSAGE see Spahlinger, Mathias

PASSAGE, THE see Ketting, Otto, Overtocht, De

PASSAGES UNDER THE SIGN OF COSMOS see Márquez, Arturo, Paisajes Bajo El Signo De Cosmos

PASSENGER, THE see Thompson, Randall

PASSEVITE see Janssen, Guus

PASSING OF ARTHUR, THE: PROLOG see Busch, Carl

PASSING OF BEATRICE see Wallace, William

PASSIONE see Knaifel, Alexander

PASSIONSLIEDER UND PASSIONSGESÄNGE see Martinov, Vladimir

PAST HYMNS see Anderson, Julian

PASTICHE see Biggs, John

PASTORAL DREAM see Rieti, Vittorio

PASTORAL OVERTURE see Rice, Thomas N.

PASTORALE see Jeverud, Johan

PASTORALE E CORAL: IN MEMORIAM see Johnsen, Hallvard

PASTORALES PROVENÇALES see Tomasi, Henri

PASTORALI see Farkas, Ferenc

PASTORALOUVERTÜRE see Siegl, Otto

PASTORES MECUM OMNES VENITE ADORAMUS see Galuppi, Baldassare

PASTURAS DEL CIELO, LAS see Adamic, Josef, Nebeské Pastviny

PATACHICH, IVAN (1922-　)
　Balkan Suite
　　2.2.2.2. 4.3.3.0. timp,perc,harp,
　　　strings [13'] EMB rent　　(P80)

　Concertino For Cimbalom And Orchestra
　　see Presentazioni

　Concerto for Organ and Chamber
　　Orchestra
　　timp,perc,harp,strings,org solo
　　[17'] EMB rent　　(P81)

　Concerto for Percussion
　　2.2.2.2. 3.2.3.0. timp,harp,cel,
　　　strings,perc solo [14'] EMB rent
　　　　　　　　(P82)
　Hungarian Suite
　　"Magyar Szvit" 2(pic).2.2.2.
　　　4.3.3.0. timp,perc,strings [12']
　　　EMB rent　　(P83)

　Magyar Szvit
　　see Hungarian Suite

　Presentazioni
　　"Concertino For Cimbalom And
　　Orchestra" 1(pic).1(English
　　horn).1(bass clar).1. 1.0.0.0.
　　perc,strings,cimbalom solo [13']
　　EMB rent　　(P84)

PATCHWORK FÜR KLAVIER UND ORCHESTER see Werner, Rudolf

PATHETISCHES REZITATIV see Grabovsky, Leonid

PATTERNS CIRCUS PATTERNS see Wienhorst, Richard

PATTERSON, PAUL (1947-　)
　Concerto for Violin and String
　　Orchestra
　　string orch,vln solo [18']
　　WEINBERGER　　(P85)

　Festivo
　　2.2.2.2. 4.2.3.1. timp,3perc,harp,
　　　strings [10'] WEINBERGER　(P86)

　Little Red Riding Hood  *educ
　　2.2.2.2. 4.2.3.1. timp,3perc,harp,
　　　strings,3 speaking voices [28']
　　　WEINBERGER　　(P87)

PAUER, JIRÍ (1919-　)
　Chtel Bysem Napsat Ti Psani
　　2.2.3.2. 2.2.2.1. timp,perc,xylo,
　　　harp,strings,male solo [16']
　　　CESKY HUD.　　(P88)

---

PAUER, JIRÍ (cont'd.)

　Concerto for Marimba and String
　　Orchestra
　　[15'] CESKY HUD.　　(P89)

　Introduzione Semplice  *Overture
　　2.2.2.2. 2.2.0.0. timp,strings [9']
　　　CESKY HUD.　　(P90)

　Písen O Lásce
　　2.2.2.2. 2.0.0.0. perc,harp,cel,
　　　strings,male solo [14'] CESKY
　　　HUD.　　(P91)

　Smutecní Hudba
　　string orch,trp solo [15'] CESKY
　　　HUD.　　(P92)

　Suite for Orchestra
　　3.3.2.2. 4.3.3.1. timp,perc,xylo,
　　　harp,cel,pno,strings [25'] CESKY
　　　HUD.　　(P93)

　Zuzana Vojírová  *Overture
　　3.3.3.3. 4.3.3.1. timp,perc,2harp,
　　　cel,strings [5'] CESKY HUD. (P94)

PAUK, ALEX (1945-　)
　Solari
　　2.2.2.2. 2.2.1.1. 2perc,strings
　　　[16'] sc CANADIAN MI 1100 P323SO
　　　　　　　　(P95)
PAUL, BERTHOLD (1948-　)
　Drei Orchesterstücke, Op. 3
　　2.0.2.2. 2.2.2.0. timp,strings
　　　[10'] SIKORSKI perf mat rent
　　　　　　　　(P96)
PAULUS, STEPHEN HARRISON (1949-　)
　Concertante
　　orch (special order) EUR.AM.MUS.
　　　EA00678X　　(P97)
　　3(pic).3.3.3. 4.3.2+bass trom.1.
　　　timp,3perc,pno,strings [11']
　　　SCHOTTS perf mat rent　(P98)

　Concerto for Organ
　　timp,perc,strings,org solo [21']
　　　pts,solo pt SCHOTTS EA 767 perf
　　　mat rent　　(P99)

　Concerto for Trumpet
　　3.3.3.3. 4.3.3.1. timp,3perc,pno/
　　　cel,harp,strings,trp solo [25']
　　　SCHOTTS perf mat rent　(P100)

　Concerto for Violin, No. 1
　　3.3.3.3. 4.3.2.1. timp,3perc,pno,
　　　harp,strings,vln solo [25']
　　　SCHOTTS perf mat rent　(P101)

　Concerto for Violin, No. 2
　　2.2.2.2. 2.2.1.0. timp,2perc,pno,
　　　harp,strings,vln solo [21']
　　　SCHOTTS perf mat rent　(P102)

　Divertimento
　　1.1.1.1. 0.0.0.0. timp,perc,6vln I,
　　　6vln II,4vla,4vcl,2db,harp solo
　　　[12'] SCHOTTS perf mat rent
　　　　　　　　(P103)
　Double Concerto
　　3(pic).3(English horn).3(bass
　　　clar).3. 4.3.2+bass trom.1. timp,
　　　3perc,pno/cel,harp,strings,vln
　　　solo,vcl solo [25'] SCHOTTS perf
　　　mat rent　　(P104)

　Ground Breaker
　　2(pic).2.2.2. 4.3.2+bass trom.1.
　　　timp,perc,strings, 4 workers with
　　　power tools [7'] SCHOTTS perf mat
　　　rent　　(P105)

　Harmoonia: Suite
　　2.2.2.2. 4.3.2.1. timp,3perc,pno,
　　　harp,strings,speaking voice [5']
　　　(text by Michael Dennis Browne)
　　　SCHOTTS perf mat rent　(P106)

　Ice Fields
　　2.2.2.2. 4.2.2.1. timp,2perc,
　　　strings,gtr solo [20'] SCHOTTS
　　　perf mat rent　　(P107)

　Manhattan Sinfonietta
　　orch study sc EUR.AM.MUS. EA00769
　　　　　　　　(P108)
　Night Speech
　　3(pic).3.3.3. 4.3.2+bass trom.1.
　　　timp,3perc,pno,harp,strings,Bar
　　　solo [20'] SCHOTTS perf mat rent
　　　　　　　　(P109)
　Ordway Overture
　　orch (special order) study sc
　　　EUR.AM.MUS. EA00669X　(P110)
　　3(pic).3.3.3. 4.3.3.1. timp,2perc,
　　　strings [5'] study sc SCHOTTS
　　　EA 669X perf mat rent　(P111)

　Postman Always Rings Twice, The:
　　Suite
　　3(pic).3.3.3.alto sax. 4.3.2+bass
　　　trom.1. timp,3perc,pno,harp,
　　　strings [22'] SCHOTTS perf mat
　　　rent　　(P112)

---

PAULUS, STEPHEN HARRISON (cont'd.)

　Reflections: 4 Movements On A Theme
　　Of Wallace Stevens
　　1.2.1.2. 2.1.0.0. timp,perc,pno,
　　　strings [22'] SCHOTTS perf mat
　　　rent　　(P113)

　Seven Short Pieces For Orchestra
　　3(pic).3.3(bass clar).3(contrabsn).
　　　4.3.2+bass trom.1. timp,3perc,
　　　pno/cel,harp,strings [13']
　　　SCHOTTS perf mat rent　(P114)

　Sinfonietta
　　3.3.3(bass clar).3. 4.3.2+bass
　　　trom.1. timp,3perc,harp,strings
　　　[15'] SCHOTTS perf mat rent
　　　　　　　　(P115)
　Street Music
　　2.2.2.2. 4.3.3.1. timp,2perc,
　　　strings [4'] SCHOTTS perf mat
　　　rent　　(P116)

　Symphony for Strings
　　strings [22'] SCHOTTS perf mat rent
　　　　　　　　(P117)
　Symphony in Three Movements
　　orch (special order) study sc
　　　EUR.AM.MUS. EA00581X　(P118)
　　3(pic).3.3.3. 4.3.3.1. timp,3perc,
　　　pno&cel,harp,strings [30']
　　　SCHOTTS perf mat rent　(P119)

　Translucent Landscapes
　　2.1.2.1. 2.1.1.0. timp,perc,pno,
　　　harp,8vln I,6vln II,5vla,4vcl,2db
　　　[18'] SCHOTTS perf mat rent
　　　　　　　　(P120)
　Voices From The Gallery
　　1.1.1.1. 1.1.0.0. timp,perc,
　　　strings,speaking voice [30']
　　　SCHOTTS perf mat rent　(P121)

PAULUS: GOTT SEI MIR GNÄDIG see Mendelssohn-Bartholdy, Felix

PAULUS: JERUSALEM, DIE DU TÖTEST DIE PROPHETEN see Mendelssohn-Bartholdy, Felix

PAULUS: OVERTURE see Mendelssohn-Bartholdy, Felix

PAVANE AND GALLIARD see Crawley, Clifford

PAVANE FOR OPEN STRINGS see Horikoshi, Ryuichi

PAVANE OUBLIÉE see Verbey, Theo

PÁVÍ PERO see Malek, Jan

PAVLYENKO, SERGEI (1952-　)
　Lebwohl
　　string orch [15'] SIKORSKI perf mat
　　　rent　　(P122)

　Sinfonia Humana, For Piano And String
　　Orchestra
　　[40'] SIKORSKI perf mat rent (P123)

PAYNE, ANTHONY (1936-　)
　Time's Arrow
　　3.3.3.3. 6.4.3.1. timp,2perc,harp,
　　　strings [27'] CHESTER　(P124)

PAYSAGE see Spahlinger, Mathias, Passage see Tomasi, Henri

PEACE see Dreyfus, George

PEASABLE, JAMES
　see PAISIBLE, JAMES (JACQUES)

PEASANT FIDDLE see Kadosa, Pal

PEASLEE, RICHARD (1930-　)
　Suite for Guitar and Strings
　　gtr,strings SCHIRM.EC rent　(P125)

　Suite From "Marat-Sade"
　　2.2.2.2. 4.3.3.1. timp,perc,harp,
　　　strings [18'] SCHIRM.EC rent
　　　　　　　　(P126)
PEER GYNT see Amram, David Werner

PEER GYNT SUITES NOS. 1 AND 2 IN FULL SCORE see Grieg, Edvard Hagerup

PEGASUS 51 see Hiller, Wilfried

PEIKO, NIKOLAI (1916-1995)
　Concerto for Oboe and Chamber
　　Orchestra
　　perc,strings,ob solo [20'] SIKORSKI
　　　perf mat rent　　(P127)

　Symphony No. 4
　　3(pic).3(English horn).3(clar in E
　　　flat).2. 4.3.3.1. 5perc,cel/pno,
　　　strings [24'] SIKORSKI perf mat
　　　rent　　(P128)

PEKING DRUM see Zhou, Long

PEKNY DEN see Svehla, Antonin

PELECIS, GEORGE (1947- )
Concerto for Trumpet and Orchestra
2.2.2.2. 4.2.3.1. timp,perc,
strings,trp solo [40'] SIKORSKI
perf mat rent (P129)

Concerto for Violin, Piano and String
Orchestra
see Nevertheless

Jack And The Beanstalk
2.2.2.0. 4.2.3.1. timp,perc,8vln I,
7vln II,6vla,5vcl,4db,soprano
sax/2alto sax,2tenor sax/baritone
sax [30'] sc PETERS 04722 (P130)

Nevertheless (Concerto for Violin,
Piano and String Orchestra)
[15'] SIKORSKI perf mat rent (P131)

PELEUS AND THETIS: OVERTURE see Boyce,
William

PELIKÁN, MIROSLAV (1922- )
Suite for String Orchestra
[24'] CESKY HÚD. (P132)

PENDERECKI, KRZYSZTOF (1933- )
Canon
24vln,8vla,8vcl,6db,electronic tape
[10'] study sc SCHOTTS ED 6342
perf mat rent (P133)

Concerto for Flute and Chamber
Orchestra
2(pic).2(English horn).2(bass
clar).2(contrabsn). 2.2.0.0.
2perc,cel,8vln I,6vln II,4vla,
4vcl,2db,fl/clar solo [25'] pno
red SCHOTTS ED 8108 perf mat rent (P134)

Concerto for Violin, No. 2
2(pic).2(English horn).2(bass
clar).2(contrabsn). 4.2.3.0.
timp,3perc,cel,strings,vln solo
[15'] pno red SCHOTTS ED 8451
perf mat rent (P135)

Musik Aus "Ubu Rex"
(Brauel, Henning) 2+pic.2+English
horn.2+clar in E flat+bass
clar.2+contrabsn. 4.3.3.1. timp,
4perc,cel,strings [25'] SCHOTTS
perf mat rent (P136)

Paradise Lost: Adagietto
2.2(English horn).2.2(contrabsn).
4.3.3.1. timp,perc,strings [5']
study sc SCHOTTS ED 6902 perf mat
rent (P137)

Sinfonietta for Strings
[12'] study sc SCHOTTS ED 8117 perf
mat rent (P138)

Sinfonietta No. 2
strings,clar solo [20'] study sc
SCHOTTS ED 8343 perf mat rent (P139)

Symphony No. 3
2+pic.2+English horn.3(clar in E
flat,clar in A)+bass clar.3+
contrabsn. 5.3+bass trp.4.1.
timp,3perc,cel,strings [50']
SCHOTTS perf mat rent (P140)

Symphony No. 4, Adagio
2+pic.2+English horn.2+clar in E
flat+bass clar.2+contrabsn.
5.3.4.1. timp,2perc,strings, 3trp
in the back stage [33'] study sc
SCHOTTS ED 8064 perf mat rent (P141)

Symphony No. 5
4(pic).4(English horn).4(clar in E
flat)+bass clar.3+contrabsn.
5.3.4.1. timp,4perc,cel,16vln I,
14vln II,12vla,12vcl,10db [35']
SCHOTTS perf mat rent (P142)

PENDLETON, EDMOND (1905-1987)
Concerto [15']
1.1.1.1. 2.2.0.0. timp,perc,
strings,vla solo
BILLAUDOT (P143)

PENSÉES see Höller, York see Stendel,
Wolfgang

PENSIERI see Parrott, Ian

PENSIERO DEL BOSCO, IL see Hisatome,
Tomoyuki

PENSIVE OVERTURE, A see Schryer, Claude

PENTHESILEA see Wolf, Hugo

PENTLAND, BARBARA (1912- )
Five-Plus
string orch [6'] (1. Largo 2.
Andante 3. Grave e molto
sostenuto 4. Presto 5. Andante)
sc CANADIAN MI 1500 P419FI (P144)

Res Musica
string orch [15'] sc CANADIAN
MI 1500 P419RE (P145)

PEOPLE OF BLUE DIMENSION see Berg, Fred
Jonny

PEPIN, CLERMONT (1926- )
Monade
14strings [9'] sc CANADIAN
MI 1500 P422M1 (P146)

PEPPING, ERNST (1901-1981)
Invention
2.2.2.2. 2.2.0.0. strings [4']
SCHOTTS perf mat rent (P147)

Prelude
2.3.3.3. 4.3.2.1. strings [6']
SCHOTTS perf mat rent (P148)

PEPUSCH, JOHN CHRISTOPHER (1667-1752)
Concertino in D for Trumpet, Strings
and Continuo
[10'] PETERS (P149)

Concerto in D for Trumpet, Strings
and Continuo
0.0.0.1. 0.0.0.0. hpsd,8vln I,7vln
II,6vla,5vcl,4db [10'] sc,pno-
cond sc,solo pt PETERS 02704 (P150)

PEQUEÑA SUITE IBEROAMERICANA see Cano,
Francisco

PER I VENCE see Amdahl, Magne

PER QUEL PATERNO see Mozart, Wolfgang
Amadeus

PER QUESTA BELLA MANO see Mozart,
Wolfgang Amadeus

PER-SONARE see Hosokawa, Toshio,
Concerto for Flute

PERCUSSION FANTASY see Black, Stanley

PERDER, KJELL (1954- )
But D: (Behind Utmost Disturbance)
woodwind quin,trp,trom,perc,string
quar [5'5"] sc,pts STIM (P151)

PEREGRINA II see Schoeck, Othmar

PEREGRINE see Beckwith, John

PERERA, RONALD CHRISTOPHER (1941- )
Choirs
see Saints, The: Three Pieces For
Orchestra (With Optional Audience
Participation)

Joyful Noise
see Saints, The: Three Pieces For
Orchestra (With Optional Audience
Participation)

Marching In
see Saints, The: Three Pieces For
Orchestra (With Optional Audience
Participation)

Music For Flute And Orchestra
3.3.3.3. 4.3.3.1. 2perc,harp,pno,
strings,fl solo [10'] sc,pts
JERONA rent (P152)

Saints, The: Three Pieces For
Orchestra (With Optional Audience
Participation)
2.2.2(soprano sax).2.alto sax.tenor
sax. 2.2.2.1. timp,perc,pno,
strings,electronic tape,opt banjo
sc,pts JERONA rent
contains: Choirs; Joyful Noise;
Marching In (P153)

PERFALL, KARL (1824-1907)
Schlummerlied Der Melusine (from
Raimondin)
2.2.2.2. 3.0.0.0. strings,S solo
[3'] BREITKOPF-W (P154)

PERFORMANCE see Defaye, Jean Michel

PERGOLESI, GIOVANNI BATTISTA
(1710-1736)
Concerto for Violin and Strings in B
flat
strings,vln solo [15'] BOCCACCINI
BS. 201 rent (P155)

Salve Regina
A solo,strings KUNZELMANN ipa sc
10093A, oct 10093 (P156)

PERGOLESI, GIOVANNI BATTISTA (cont'd.)
Stabat Mater
S,A soli,string orch KUNZELMANN ipa
sc 10173A, oct 10173 (P157)

PÉRICHOLE, LA: QUADRILLE ET FANTAISIE
see Offenbach, Jacques

PERIODIC TABLE OF THE ELEMENTS, A see
Stiller, Andrew

PERIPETEIA see Koprowski, Peter Paul

PERKEO see Grabner, Hermann

PERLE, GEORGE (1915- )
Adagio for Orchestra
4.4.4.4. 4.4.4.1. timp,harp,kbd,
strings [15'] SCHIRM.EC rent (P158)

Concerto No. 1 for Piano and
Orchestra
4.4.4.4. 4.4.3.1. timp,3perc,harp,
kbd,strings,pno solo [25']
SCHIRM.EC rent (P159)

Concerto No. 2 for Piano and
Orchestra
2.2.2.2. 4.2.0.0. timp,2perc,
strings,pno solo [18'] SCHIRM.EC
rent (P160)

Dance Fantasy
3.3.3.3. 4.3.3.1. timp,3perc,harp,
2kbd,marimba,strings [10']
SCHIRM.EC rent (P161)

Lyric Intermezzo For 15 Players
1.1.1.1. 1.1.1.0. perc,harp,2vln,
vla,vcl [16'] SCHIRM.EC rent (P162)

Serenade No. 1 for Viola and Chamber
Orchestra
vla solo,1.1.1.1. 1.1.1.0. perc,
alto sax,db [13'] SCHIRM.EC rent (P163)

Sinfonietta No. 1
1.2.1.2. 2.1.0.0. perc,strings
[14'] SCHIRM.EC rent (P164)

Sinfonietta No. 2
2.2.2.2. 2.2.1.0. timp,3perc,harp,
xylo,strings [15'] SCHIRM.EC rent (P165)

PERMONT, HAIM (1950- )
Niggun II
string orch,harp [24'] ISRAELI rent (P166)

PERMUTATION see Doi, Yoshiyuki

PERNA, DANA PAUL
Deux Berceuses
orch,fl solo [10'] BARDIC (P167)

Due Piccolo Composizione
2+pic.2+English horn.2+bass clar.2.
3.3.3.1. timp,perc,strings [5']
BARDIC (P168)

Largo
string orch [5'] BARDIC (P169)

Nocturne, Op. 63b
strings,vla solo [7'] BARDIC (P170)

Prout's Neck
2+pic.2+English horn.2+bass clar.2.
4.3.3.1. pno,harp,4perc,strings
[8'] BARDIC (P171)

Riconoscenza Per Bernard Herrmann
strings,harp,vln solo,vla/vla
d'amore solo,vcl solo [2'30"]
BARDIC (P172)

Riconoscenza Per Jean Martinon
strings,vln solo,harp solo [3']
BARDIC (P173)

Riconoscenza Per Leonard Bernstein
string orch [1'] BARDIC (P174)

Structures
2+pic.1+English horn.2+bass clar.2+
contrabsn. 4.3.3.1. 4-5perc,
strings [7'] BARDIC (P175)

Symphony No. 1
2+pic.2+English horn.2+bass clar.2+
contrabsn. 4.3.3.1. harp,4-5perc,
strings [17'] (in one continuous
movement) BARDIC (P176)

Tapestry
2+pic.2+English horn.2+bass clar.2+
contrabsn. 4.3.3.1. 4-5perc,
strings [8'] BARDIC (P177)

Visages Oubliees
2+pic.1.2.2. 2.1.2.1. harp/pno,
3perc,strings [10'] BARDIC (P178)

PERPETUELA see Paganini, Niccolo

PERRIN, GLYN (1955-    )
Cirkus Of Demokracy, The
3(pic).2+English horn.2+bass
clar.3. 4.3.3.1. 4perc,strings,
opt electronic tape [16'] sc
UNIV.YORK 0100 f.s.          (P179)

Tu, Même
3(pic).3(English horn).3(soprano
sax,alto sax,bass
clar).3(contrabsn). 4.3.3.1.
prepared pno,harp,3perc,strings
[30'] sc UNIV.YORK 0099 f.s.
(P180)

PERSISTENCE see Horne, David

PEŠKA, VLASTIMIL (1954-    )
Canzone E Intermezzi
strings,fl solo [12'] CESKY HUD.
(P181)

Euterpé
2.3.2.2. 3.3.1.1+2euphonium. perc,
harp,pno,strings [20'] CESKY HUD.
(P182)

Komorní Suita
strings,vla solo [12'] CESKY HUD.
(P183)

PEŠKOVA see Klusák, Jan, Invention No.
7

PET OBRÁZKU see Chaun, František

PÉTALE DE LUMIÈRE, UN see Chen, Qigang

PETER KIRILLOV: KINGDOM OF THE WHITE
WATERS see Amos, Keith

PETER QUINCE AT THE CLAVIER see London,
Edwin

PETERSBURGER SKIZZEN see Madjera,
Gottfried

PETERSON, WAYNE TURNER (1927-    )
Face Of The Night, The Heart Of The
Dark, The
3.3.3.3. 4.3.3.1. timp,3perc,harp,
pno/cel,strings [19'] PETERS
(P184)

PETERSON-BERGER, (OLOF) WILHELM
(1867-1942)
Schwedische Miniaturen (Suite in Five
Movements)
2.1(English horn).2.2. 2.2.3.0.
timp,perc,strings,opt harp [14']
sc,set BUSCH rent          (P185)

Suite in Five Movements
see Schwedische Miniaturen

PETEY see Still, William Grant

PETIT CONCERT see Binet, Jean

PETIT LOUVETEAU GRIS, LE see Gastinel,
Gérard

PETITE FANTAISIE see Dijk, Jan van

PETITE SUITE RÉACTIONNAIRE see Rossum,
Frederic R. van

PETITE SYMPHONIE CONCERTANTE see Jolas,
Betsy

PETITE VALSE see Gastinel, Gérard

PETITGIRARD, ALAIN (1940-    )
Rosebud Suite
pno,orch [20'] BOIS          (P186)

PETITGIRARD, LAURENT
Concerto for Violoncello and
Orchestra
2(pic).2(English horn).3(bass
clar).3(contrabsn). 4.3.3.1.
timp,3perc,harp,strings,vcl solo
[25'] DURAND rent          (P187)

Marathon, Le
"Suite Symphonique" 2.2.2.2.
3.2.2.1. 4perc,cel,2harp,strings
[20'] DURAND rent          (P188)

Suite Symphonique
see Marathon, Le

PETITS RIENS, LES see Laburda, Jiri

PETR, ZDENEK
At Jdu Vzhuru Nebo Dolu (from Zly
Jelen)
2.1.2.1. 2.0.2.0. perc,harp,
strings,male solo [3'] CESKY HUD.
(P189)

Jaro V Praze
2.2.2.2. 4.3.3.1. timp,perc,
strings,T solo [3'] CESKY HUD.
(P190)

Luzánky  *Waltz
2.2.2.2. 4.2.3.1. timp,perc,harp,
strings [4'] CESKY HUD.   (P191)

Má Láska Veliká
2.0.3.0. 1.3.3.0. timp,perc,harp,
gtr,strings [4'] CESKY HUD.

PETR, ZDENEK (cont'd.)
(P192)

Písen O Ruzi
2.1.2.1. 3.3.0.0. timp,perc,harp,
strings,male solo [3'] CESKY HUD.
(P193)

Prípitek
2.2.2.2. 4.3.3.0. timp,perc,
strings,solo voice,pno solo [5']
CESKY HUD.          (P194)

Ráz-Dva-Tri-Ctyri
2.2.2.2. 4.3.3.0. perc,harp,strings
[3'] CESKY HUD.          (P195)

Škádlení
2.2.2.2. 4.3.3.0. timp,strings [4']
CESKY HUD.          (P196)

Tri Duby
2.0.3.0. 3.3.3.0. harp,strings [4']
CESKY HUD.          (P197)

V Meste Kromerízi
2.2.2.2. 4.2.3.0. timp,perc,harp,
strings [4'] CESKY HUD.   (P198)

Vyletel Sokol
2.2.2.2. 4.2.3.1. timp,perc,harp,
strings [4'] CESKY HUD.   (P199)

PETRINI, FRANZ
Concerto for Harp, No. 4, in E flat
sc,solo pt INTERNAT.S.          (P200)

PETROV, ANDREI P. (1930-    )
Concertino Buffo, For Chamber
Orchestra
1.1.1.1. 1.0.0.0. perc,hpsd,strings
[10'] SIKORSKI perf mat rent
(P201)

Erschaffung Der Welt, Die: Suite No.
1
3.3.3.3. 4.4.3.1. timp,perc,harp,
hpsd,pno,acord,strings [20']
SIKORSKI perf mat rent     (P202)

Erschaffung Der Welt, Die: Suite No.
2
[Russ] 3.3.3.3. 4.4.3.1. timp,perc,
harp,hpsd,pno,strings,jr cor
[23'] SIKORSKI perf mat rent
(P203)

In Memoriam
1.1.1.1. 1.0.0.0. strings [10']
SIKORSKI perf mat rent     (P204)

Meister Und Margarita, Der
3.3.3.3. 4.4.3.1. timp,perc,bass
gtr,harp,pno,org,strings [28']
SIKORSKI perf mat rent     (P205)

Romantische Variationen, For
Orchestra
2.2.2.2. 2.2.0.0. perc,strings
[14'] SIKORSKI perf mat rent
(P206)

PETROV, VADIM (1932-    )
Baletní Miniatura  *Op.64
2.2.2.2. 4.3.3.0. timp,perc,vibra,
harp,strings [8'] CESKY HUD.
(P207)

Beskydská Epizoda  *Op.63
2.2.2.2. 4.3.3.1. timp,perc,xylo,
strings [6'] CESKY HUD.   (P208)

Chvíle Pro Písen Trubky
2.2.2.2. 3.2.2.0. timp,perc,harp,
strings,trp solo [5'] CESKY HUD.
(P209)

Prazské Ornamenty  *Op.68
3.2.2.2. 4.3.3.1. timp,perc,strings
[6'] CESKY HUD.          (P210)

Principálka  *Op.69
2.2.2.2. 4.3.3.1. timp,perc,xylo,
harp,strings [6'] CESKY HUD.
(P211)

Rhapsody for Guitar, Piano and
Orchestra
2.0.2.0. 3.3.3.0. timp,perc,
strings,gtr&pno soli [7'] CESKY
HUD.          (P212)

Tarantelle for Orchestra, Op. 67
2.2.2.2. 4.2.3.1. timp,perc,strings
[4'] CESKY HUD.          (P213)

Valašské Intermezzo  *Op.71
2.2.2.2. 4.0.0.0. timp,perc,xylo,
harp,strings [5'] CESKY HUD.
(P214)

PETROVA, ELENA (1929-    )
Slunecnice: Suite
3.2.3.2. 4.3.3.1. timp,perc,2harp,
strings [22'] CESKY HUD.   (P215)

PETROVICS, EMIL (1930-    )
Concertino for Trumpet and Orchestra
2.2(clar).2. 2.0.0.0. timp,perc,
harp,strings,trp solo [20'] EMB
rent          (P216)

PETRUSHKA see Stravinsky, Igor

PETRZELKA, VILÉM (1889-1967)
Cesta  *Op.14
2.2.2.2. 4.0.0.0. timp,perc,harp,
cel,strings,solo voice [11']
CESKY HUD.          (P217)

Partita for String Orchestra, Op. 31
[31'] CESKY HUD.          (P218)

Pochod Bohému
3.2.2.2. 4.2.3.1. timp,perc,strings
CESKY HUD.          (P219)

Symphony in Three Movements, Op. 13
see Vecny Narat

Vecny Narat (Symphony in Three
Movements, Op. 13)
4.3.3.3. 4.4.3.1. timp,perc,2harp,
cel,strings [44'] CESKY HUD.
(P220)

Zivly  *Op.7
3.3.3.3. 4.3.3.1. timp,perc,harp,
strings,Bar solo [12'] CESKY HUD.
(P221)

PETTERSSON, ALLAN (1911-1980)
Symphony No. 9
3(pic).2.3(bass clar).3(contrabsn).
4.3.3.1. timp,5perc,strings [65']
sc NORDISKA ED.NR 10649   (P222)

Symphony No. 10
3(pic).2.3(bass clar).3(contrabsn).
4.3.3.1. timp,2perc,strings [25']
sc NORDISKA ED.NR 10681   (P223)

Symphony No. 11
3(pic).2.3(bass clar).3(contrabsn).
4.3.3.1. timp,5perc,strings [24']
sc NORDISKA ED.NR 10684   (P224)

Symphony No. 14
3(pic).2.3(bass clar).3(contrabsn).
4.3.3.1. timp,4perc,strings [48']
sc NORDISKA ED.NR 10685   (P225)

Symphony No. 15
3(pic).2.3(bass clar).3(contrabsn).
4.3.3.1. timp,4perc,strings [31']
sc NORDISKA ED.NR 10686   (P226)

PEXIDR, KAREL (1929-    )
Concertino for Piano, Strings and
Percussion
see Detské Concertino

Concerto for Piano and Orchestra
3.2.2.2. 4.2.3.1. timp,perc,
strings,pno solo [21'] CESKY HUD.
(P227)

Concerto for Piano and Orchestra, No.
2
2.2.2.2. 2.2.2.0. timp,perc,
strings,pno solo [20'] CESKY HUD.
(P228)

Detské Concertino (Concertino for
Piano, Strings and Percussion)
perc,strings,pno solo [12'] CESKY
HUD.          (P229)

PEZZO see Grahn, Ulf

PEZZO CONCERTATO NO. 3 see Bozay,
Attila

PEZZO LIRICO see Lang, Istvan

PEZZO SINFONICO NO. 2 see Bozay, Attila

PEZZO UMORISTICO see Lillebjerka,
Sigmund

PFEIFFER, FRANZ ANTON (1752-1787)
Concerto for Basset Horn and
Orchestra in B flat
(Beyer, S.) basset horn solo/bsn
solo,orch KUNZELMANN 10247 ipr
(P230)

PFINGST-HYMNUS: VENI CREATOR SPIRITUS
see Galuppi, Baldassare

PFISTER
Five Sketches
perc,orch min sc KUNZELMANN GM 110P
ipr          (P231)

PFISTER, HUGO (1914-1969)
Tre Pezzi Concertanti
chamber orch,pno KUNZELMANN 10042
ipr          (P232)

PHAEDRA see Theodorakis, Mikis

PHAÉTON see Saint-Saëns, Camille

PHANTOM SCREEN see Sharman, Rodney

PHILHARMONIA (A FANFARE) see Hagen,
Daron

PHILIPP, FRANZ (1890-1972)
Jugend-Musik *Op.47
orch BOHM                              (P233)

Symphonischer Prolog *Op.11
orch,org,harp BOHM                     (P234)

PHILIPPINISCHES TAGEBUCH see Straume,
Egils

PHILIPPOT, MICHEL PAUL (1925-1996)
Meditation
1.1.1.1. 1.1.1.0. string quin [16']
BILLAUDOT                              (P235)

PHILLIPS, BARRE (1934-    )
Chamber Concerto
brass quin,2.1.2.1. 1.1.1.0. 2perc,
kbd [19'] SCHIRM.EC rent               (P236)

Crossing The Meridian
T solo,fl,clar,perc,kbd,vln,vla,vcl
[20'] SCHIRM.EC rent                   (P237)

Five Summer Songs
perc,harp,kbd,strings [12']
SCHIRM.EC rent                         (P238)

White Whale, The. Theater Music
Bar solo,1.1.2.2. 1.1.1.0. 2perc,
harp,kbd,strings [30'] SCHIRM.EC
rent                                   (P239)

PHILLIPS, WILLIAM
Florida Blues
(Still, William Grant) 1.0.1.0.
0.2(cornet).1.0. drums,cym,
triangle,wood blocks,pno,strings
STILL                                  (P240)

PHILLY RHAPSODY see Dorff, Daniel Jay

PHOENIX 1 see Müller-Siemens, Detlev

PHOENIX 2 see Müller-Siemens, Detlev

PHOENIX 3 see Müller-Siemens, Detlev

PHONOSPHERE I (REVISION) see Matsuo,
Masataka

PHRYGIAN JOURNEY see Clarke, Jim

PIANISSIMO, FOR ORCHESTRA see
Schnittke, Alfred

PIANO AMERICANO see Tutino, Marco

PIANO CONCERTANTE see Evangelista, Jose

PIANO CONCERTI BY LISZT (IN FULL SCORE)
see Liszt, Franz

PIANO CONCERTO "DO" - FOR CHILDREN see
Kohjiba, Tomiko

PIANO CONCERTO IN FULL SCORE see Grieg,
Edvard Hagerup

PIANO CONCERTO: SINCE ARMSTRONG see
Larsen, Elizabeth B. (Libby),
Concerto for Piano

PIANO CONCERTOS IN FULL SCORE see
Chopin, Frédéric

PIANO CONCERTOS NOS. 2 AND 4 see Saint-
Saëns, Camille

PIANO FOR STRINGS, THE see Nyman,
Michael

PIANOCONCERTO see Jeths, Willem

PIANOPHONIE see Serocki, Kazimierz

PIAZZOLLA, ASTOR (1921-1992)
Danza Criolla
1(pic).1.1.1. 2.2.1.0. timp,perc,
harp,pno,strings PEER rent (P241)

PICCOLA SUITE see Gardelli, Lamberto

PICCOLO CONCERTO see Pinkham, Daniel,
Concerto for Piccolo

PICHL, WENZEL (VACLAV) (1741-1805)
Mars
see Sinfonia in D

Sinfonia in D
(Myslik, Antonin) "Mars" 0.2.0.0.
2.0.0.0. strings [16'] CESKY HUD.
(P242)

Sinfonia No. 4 in E flat
orch KUNZELMANN ipa sc 10199A, oct
10199                                  (P243)

Symphony No. 1
0.2.0.0. 2.0.0.0. strings CESKY
HUD.                                   (P244)

Symphony No. 2
0.2.0.0. 2.0.0.0. strings CESKY
HUD.                                   (P245)

PICHL, WENZEL (VACLAV) (cont'd.)

Symphony No. 3
0.2.0.0. 2.0.0.0. strings CESKY
HUD.                                   (P246)

Symphony No. 4
2.0.0.0. 2.0.0.0. strings CESKY
HUD.                                   (P247)

Symphony No. 5
0.2.0.0. 2.0.0.0. strings CESKY
HUD.                                   (P248)

PICK, CARL HEINZ (1929-    )
Concerto for Violin and Orchestra
2.2.2.2. 3.2.0.0. timp,perc,8vln I,
7vln II,6vla,5vcl,4db [20'] sc
PETERS 04488                           (P249)

Concerto Piccolo Für Klavier Und
Orchester
2.2.2.1. 3.2.2.0. timp,perc,pno,
harp,gtr,bass gtr,drums,8vln I,
7vln II,6vla,5vcl,4db [15'] sc
pno-cond sc PETERS 03119    (P250)

PICKARD, JOHN
Channel Firing
2+pic.2+English horn.2+bass clar.2+
contrabsn. 4.3.3.1. timp,3perc,
strings [26'] BARDIC          (P251)

Flight Of Icarus, The
2+2pic.2+English horn.2+bass
clar.2+contrabsn. 4.3.3.1. timp,
3perc,strings [18'] BARDIC (P252)

Partita for Strings
string orch [23'] BARDIC      (P253)

Sea-Change
2+pic.2.2.2. 4.3.3.1. timp,3perc,
strings [18'] BARDIC          (P254)

Serenata Concertata
horn,trom,pno,strings,fl solo [23']
BARDIC                         (P255)

Symphony No. 2
2+pic.2+English horn.2+bass clar.2+
contrabsn. 4.3.3.1. timp,3perc,
strings [22'] BARDIC          (P256)

Symphony No. 3
2(pic)+pic.3(English horn).2+clar
in E flat+bass clar.2+contrabsn.
4.4.3.1. timp,4perc,strings [37']
BARDIC                         (P257)

PICKER, TOBIAS (1954-    )
Bang!
3.2.3.3. 4.3.4.1. timp,perc,cel,
harp,strings,pno solo [4']
SCHOTTS perf mat rent          (P258)

Concerto for Piano, No. 1
2(pic,alto fl).2(English
horn).2(bass clar).2. 4.2.4.1.
timp,strings,pno solo [20']
SCHOTTS perf mat rent          (P259)

Concerto for Piano, No. 3
3.3.3.3. 4.3.4.1. timp,perc,2harp,
strings,pno solo [24'] (Kilauea)
SCHOTTS perf mat rent          (P260)

Concerto for Violin
2.2(English horn).3(bass clar).2.
4.2.3.1. timp,pno,harp,strings,
vln solo [22'] SCHOTTS perf mat
rent                           (P261)

Encantadas, The
2(pic).2(English horn).2(bass
clar).2. 4.2.3.1. timp,perc,pno,
harp,strings,speaking voice [27']
(text by Herman Melville) SCHOTTS
perf mat rent                  (P262)
2(pic).2(English horn).2(bass
clar).2. 2.2.0.0. timp,perc,pno,
harp,strings,speaking voice [27']
(text by Herman Melville) SCHOTTS
perf mat rent                  (P263)

Old And Lost Rivers
3(pic).2.3(bass clar).3. 6.3.0.1.
timp,perc,pno,harp,strings [6']
study sc SCHOTTS EA 673 perf mat
rent                           (P264)

Romances And Interludes
2.1(English horn).2.2. 4.0.0.0.
timp,perc,pno/cel,harp,strings,ob
solo [25'] SCHOTTS perf mat rent
(P265)

Seance-Homage A Sibelius
4.1+English horn.2.3. 4.0.3.0.
timp,perc,pno,strings [4']
SCHOTTS perf mat rent          (P266)

Symphony No. 1
3(pic).3(English horn).3(bass
clar).3. 4.2.3.1. timp,perc,pno,
2harp,strings [28'] SCHOTTS perf
mat rent                       (P267)

PICKER, TOBIAS (cont'd.)

Symphony No. 2
3(pic).3(English horn).3(bass
clar).3(contrabsn). 4.3.3.1.
timp,2perc,pno,harp,strings,S
solo [30'] (Aussöhnung) SCHOTTS
perf mat rent                  (P268)

Symphony No. 3
strings [24'] SCHOTTS perf mat rent
(P269)

Two Fantasies
3.2.2.3. 4.3.3.1. timp,perc,pno,
strings [11'] SCHOTTS perf mat
rent                           (P270)

PICTURE FOR ORCHESTRA see Müller,
Thomas

PICTURE POSTCARD FROM HOLLAND see
Vajda, János

PICTURES AT AN EXHIBITION see
Mussorgsky, Modest Petrovich see
Mussorgsky, Modest Petrovich,
Bilder Einer Ausstellung

PIÈCE CONCERTANTE POUR PIANO ET
ORCHESTRE see Prevost, Andre,
Variations Et Thème

PIÈCE EN FORME DE HABANERA see Ravel,
Maurice

PIÈCE NOIRE see Platz, Robert

PIÈCE SYMPHONIQUE NO. II see Lauber,
Anne

PIECE WITH TRANSPOSING HARMONICS
orch [7'] KALLISTI solo pt, set
(P271)

PIÈCES BRÈVES, 4 see Wanek, Friedrich
K.

PIECES FOR THE NIECES see Grahn, Ulf

PIECES OF FOUR see McIntyre, Paul

PIECES OF PIECES see Sandred, Örjan

PIENOISKONSERTTOJA see Palas, Rainer

PIERNE, GABRIEL (1863-1937)
Chanson De La Grand-Maman
strings without db [2'30"] LEDUC
(P272)

Cydalise Et Le Chèvre-Pied: L'École
Des Aegipans
(Mouton, H.) 2.2.2.1. 2.2.3.0.
perc,strings [1'45"] LEDUC (P273)

Konzertstück for Harp and Orchestra
INTERNAT.S. sc,pts rent, solo pt,
pno red                        (P274)

Scènes Franciscaines
2+pic.2+English horn.3.2+contrabsn.
4.2+2cornet.3.1. timp,perc,cel,
bells,2harp,strings [16'] LEDUC
(P275)

PIERRES DE GRISE, LES see Carpenter,
Patrick E.

PIERRETTE ON THE BALCONY see King,
Reginald

PIEZA PARA ORQUESTA see Revueltas,
Silvestre

PIEZAS INFANTILES, 5 see Rodrigo,
Joaquín

PIJPER, WILLEM (1894-1947)
Orkeststuk Met Piano, K. 27
3.2.3.2. 4.3.0.0. timp,2perc,harp,
strings,pno solo [13'] sc DONEMUS
(P276)

PILSL, FRITZ
Concert Classique
gtr,mand,orch VOGT VF 1181   (P277)

Concertino for Mandolin and String
Orchestra
VOGT VF 1146                   (P278)

Concerto for Orchestra, No. 2
[26'40"] VOGT VF 1133         (P279)

Concerto for Orchestra, No. 3
VOGT VF 1174                   (P280)

Concerto for String Orchestra, No. 1
[18'] VOGT VF 1131            (P281)

PINI DI ROMA see Respighi, Ottorino

PINIONS FOR CHAMBER ORCHESTRA see
Larsen, Elizabeth B. (Libby)

PINKHAM, DANIEL (1923-    )
Adagietto For Organ And Strings
org,8vln I,7vln II,6vla,5vcl,4db
[6'] sc PETERS 04435          (P282)

PINKHAM, DANIEL (cont'd.)

Concertante Music No. 3
perc,8vln I,7vla II,6vla,5vcl,4db,
gtr solo,cembalo solo [12'] sc
PETERS 04091                        (P283)

Concertante No. 1
vln solo,strings,hpsd [10']
SCHIRM.EC rent                      (P284)

Concerto for Piccolo
"Piccolo Concerto" pic solo,strings
[9'] SCHIRM.EC rent                 (P285)

Concerto for Violin
vln solo,2ob,2horn,harp,kbd,strings
[18'] SCHIRM.EC rent                (P286)

Divertimento for Oboe and Strings
ob/S rec,strings [8'] SCHIRM.EC
rent                                (P287)

Music For A Merry Christmas No. 1
(Adeste...)
0.0.0.0. 0.2.2.0. timp,perc,org,
2ob,bsn,opt strings [3'] sc
PETERS 04095                        (P288)

Music For A Merry Christmas No. 2
(Angel Vo.)
0.2.0.1. 0.0.0.0. org,harp,8vln I,
7vln II,6vla,5vcl,4db [2'] sc
PETERS 04096                        (P289)

Music For A Merry Christmas No. 3
(All My H.)
0.2+English horn.0.1. 0.0.0.0. org,
8vln I,7vln II,6vla,5vcl,4db [4']
sc PETERS 04097                     (P290)

Music For A Merry Christmas No. 4
(The Birds)
0.2.0.1. perc,org,cel/pno,
8vln I,7vln II,6vla,5vcl,4db [1']
sc PETERS 04098                     (P291)

Music For A Merry Christmas No. 6
(Deck The Hall)
0.2.0.1. 0.2.2.0. timp,perc,org,
8vln I,7vln II,6vla,5vcl,4db [1']
sc PETERS 04100                     (P292)

Music For A Merry Christmas No. 7
(The First)
0.2.0.1. 0.2.2.0. timp,org,8vln I,
7vln II,6vla,5vcl,4db,opt perc&
harp [3'] sc PETERS 04105  (P293)

Music For A Merry Christmas No. 9
(Good King)
0.2.0.1. 0.0.0.0. org,8vln I,7vln
II,6vla,5vcl,4db,opt harp [2'] sc
PETERS 04107                        (P294)

Music For A Merry Christmas No. 10
(Greens)
0.2.0.1. 0.0.0.0. timp,perc,org,
harp,8vln I,7vln II,6vla,5vcl,4db
[2'] sc PETERS 04108                (P295)

Music For A Merry Christmas No. 11
(The Holly)
0.2.0.1. 0.2.2.0. timp,perc,org,
8vln I,7vln II,6vla,5vcl,4db [2']
sc PETERS 04109                     (P296)

Music For A Merry Christmas No. 13
(Joy To..)
0.0.0.0. 0.2.2.0. timp,perc,org,
8vln I,7vln II,6vla,5vcl,4db,opt
2ob&bsn&harp [1'] sc PETERS 04111
                                    (P297)

Music For A Merry Christmas No. 14
(March Of)
0.0.0.0. 0.2.2.0. timp,perc,org,
8vln I,7vln II,6vla,5vcl,4db,opt
ob&English horn&bsn&cym, optional
third trumpet [2'] sc PETERS
04112                               (P298)

Music For A Merry Christmas No. 15 (O
Tanne)
0.2.0.1. 0.0.0.0. org,8vln I,7vln
II,6vla,5vcl,4db,opt 2trp&2trom,
opt cel/pno [2'] sc PETERS 04113
                                    (P299)

Music For A Merry Christmas No. 16
(Silent..)
0.2.0.1. 0.0.0.0. cel/pno,org/harp,
8vln I,7vln II,6vla,5vcl,4db [2']
sc PETERS 04114                     (P300)

Music For A Merry Christmas No. 17
(Sing We)
0.2.0.1. 0.2.2.0. perc,cel/pno,8vln
I,7vln II,6vla,5vcl,4db [2'] sc
PETERS 04115                        (P301)

Music For A Merry Christmas No. 18
(Wassail)
0.2.0.1. 0.2.1.0. perc,cel,org,
harp,8vln I,7vln II,6vla,5vcl,
4db, optional second trombone
[1'] sc PETERS 04116                (P302)

PINKHAM, DANIEL (cont'd.)

Music For A Merry Christmas No. 19
(We Three)
0.2.0.1. 0.2.2.0. 2perc,org,8vln I,
7vln II,6vla,5vcl,4db [3'] sc
PETERS 04117                        (P303)

Now The Trumpet Summons Us Again
3.3.3.2. 4.3.3.1. timp,perc,harp,
8vln I,7vln II,6vla,5vcl,4db [5']
sc PETERS 04118                     (P304)

Overture Concertante
3.3.3.2. 4.3.2.1. timp,perc,cel,
8vln I,7vln II,6vla,5vcl,4db,org
solo [10'] sc PETERS 04391     (P305)

Piccolo Concerto
see Concerto for Piccolo

Sinfonia No. 4
3.2.2.2. 2.3.2.0. timp,3perc,cel,
harp,8vln I,7vln II,6vla,5vcl,4db
[15'] sc PETERS 04436               (P306)

Three Songs From Ecclesiastes
high solo,strings [5'] SCHIRM.EC
rent                                (P307)

Up And At It! (Curtain Raiser)
2bsn,2horn,strings [4'] SCHIRM.EC
rent                                (P308)

PINOS, ALOIS (1925- )
Balletti
1.0.1.1.2sax. 0.1.1.0. perc,pno,
strings [17'] CESKY HUD.       (P309)

Ceské Letokruhy
4.4.4.4.4sax. 4.4.4.1. perc,2harp,
pno,cembalo,strings [12'] CESKY
HUD.                                (P310)

Concerto for Harp and String
Orchestra
[16'] CESKY HUD.                    (P311)

Concerto for Organ and Orchestra
PANTON 039-90                       (P312)
3.3.3.0. 4.3.3.0. perc,strings
[18'] CESKY HUD.                    (P313)

Divertimento
3.3.3.3. 4.3.2.1. perc,harp,pno,
strings [16'] CESKY HUD.       (P314)

Kantiléna
strings,vln&vcl soli [11'] CESKY
HUD.                                (P315)

PINTURAS DE TAMAYO see Stucky, Steven
Edward

PIROGOW: SUITE see Shostakovich, Dmitri

PISADOR, DIEGO (ca. 1508-1557)
Paseabase, The Moorish King
(Grainger, Percy Aldridge) orch
BARDIC                              (P316)

PÍSECKÉ DIVERTIMENTO see Teml, Jiri

PÍSEN A TANEC see Machek, Miloš

PÍSEN O LÁSCE see Pauer, Jiri

PÍSEN O RUZI see Petr, Zdenek

PÍSEN RODNÉ RECI see Krízek, Zdenek

PISHNY-FLOYD, MONTE KEENE (1941-    )
Sonorities For Sixty Seasons
2+pic.2.2.1+contrabsn. 4.2.3.1.
3perc,strings (expanded version)
sc CANADIAN MI 1100 P677SO (P317)

Suite For Small Orchestra
1.1.1.1. 0.1.0.0. strings, (horn
may replace trumpet) sc CANADIAN
                                    (P318)

PÍSNE CITOVÉ A ZERTOVNÉ see Kubicka,
Miroslav

PÍSNE NA SLOVA JAROSLAVA VRCHLICKÉHO
see Foerster, Josef Bohuslav

PISODES, LES see Bjurling, Björn

PITFIELD, THOMAS BARON (1903-     )
Concerto for Piano, No. 1
2+pic.2.2.2. 4.2.3.0. timp,2perc,
pno,strings [25'] BARDIC      (P319)

Concerto for Piano, No. 2
"Student, The" 2.2.2.2. 4.2.3.0.
timp,perc,pno,strings [10']
BARDIC                              (P320)

Concerto for Recorder
glock,strings, treble recorder solo
[14'] BARDIC                        (P321)

Lyric Waltz
string orch [4'] BARDIC        (P322)

PITFIELD, THOMAS BARON (cont'd.)

Student, The
see Concerto for Piano, No. 2

PIZZARRO, PABLO
Intrada for String Orchestra
see Shalom

Shalom (Intrada for String Orchestra)
[6'] sc,pts BUSCH DM 043       (P323)

Tarantelle for Violin and Orchestra,
Op. 35
2.2.2.2. 2.2.0.0. harp,strings,vln
solo [3'45] sc,set BUSCH DM 051
rent                                (P324)

PLÁC SAXOFONU see Mácha, Otmar

PLACE see Subotnick, Morton Leon

PLACHY, ZDENEK (1961-    )
Havran
2.0.1.0.sax. 0.0.0.0. vibra,
strings,B&2 speaking voices,
salterio [18'] CESKY HUD.      (P325)

PLAGGE, WOLFGANG (1960-    )
Concerto for Accordion and Orchestra,
Op. 81
2(pic).2(English horn).2.2.
4.2.3.0. timp,2perc,strings,acord
solo [20'] NORSKMI                  (P326)

Concerto for Trumpet and Orchestra,
Op. 80
2.2.2.2. 2.0.2.0. timp,perc,
strings,trp solo [17'] NORSKMI
                                    (P327)

Concerto for Violin and Orchestra,
Op. 55
3(pic).3(English
horn).2.3(contrabsn). 4.2.3.1.
timp,perc,harp,strings,vln solo
[31'30] NORSKMI                     (P328)

Concerto No. 2 for Piano and
Orchestra, Op. 60
3(pic).2.2.3(contrabsn). 4.2.3.1.
timp,2perc,strings,pno solo [14']
NORSKMI                             (P329)

Festival Music, (1994 Version), Op.
46b
2(pic).2(English horn).2.2.
4.3.3(bass trom).1. 4timp,3perc,
strings [13'] NORSKMI          (P330)

PLAIN, GERALD
And Left Ol' Joe A Bone, AMAZING!
2+pic.2+English horn.2+bass clar.2+
contrabsn. 4.3.3.1. timp,4perc,
pno,strings [18'] perf sc set
OXFORD 3860252 sc,pts rent (P331)

Clawhammer
2(pic).2.2.2. 2.1.1.0. 2perc,harp,
elec pno,strings [12'] perf sc
set OXFORD 3859610 sc,pts rent
                                    (P332)

Fireworks
2+pic.2+English horn.2+bass clar.2+
contrabsn. 4.4.3.1. timp,3perc,
pno,strings [4'] perf sc set
OXFORD 3859831 sc,pts rent (P333)

Golden
3(pic).3(English horn).3(bass
clar).2+contrabsn. 4.3.3.0.
3perc,harp,synthesizer,strings
[10'] perf sc set OXFORD 386021X
sc,pts rent                         (P334)

Portrait I: Sally Goodin
2(pic)+pic.2(English horn).2(bass
clar).2(contrabsn). 4.2.1.0.
3perc,harp,elec pno,strings [14']
perf sc set OXFORD 3860244 sc,pts
rent                                (P335)

Portrait II: Pretty Polly
2.1.1.2. 2.1.0.1. 4perc,2harp,pno&
cel,strings [19'] perf sc set
OXFORD 3860260 sc,pts rent (P336)

PLAIN HARMONY see Finnissy, Michael

PLAISIR D'AMOUR see Martini, Jean Paul
Egide (Schwarzendorf)

PLAKIDIS, PETR (1947-    )
Gesang, For Orchestra
3.3.3.3. 6.4.3.1. timp,2perc,bass
gtr,2harp,strings [20'] SIKORSKI
perf mat rent                       (P337)

PLANES see Hiscott, James

PLANETS see Holst, Gustav

PLANKTY see Bodorova, Sylvie

PLANTATION MOOD see King, Reginald

PLATE, ANTON (1950- )
Kammersinfonie
trp,bells,pno,strings [30'] MOECK
sc 5331 f.s., pts rent          (P338)

Leuchtturm Am Ende Der Welt, Der
2.2.2.2. 4.3.3.1. perc,strings,vln
[35'] MOECK sc 5485 f.s., pts
rent                            (P339)

PLATÉE: DIVERTIMENTO see Rameau, Jean-
Philippe

PLATÉE: OVERTURE see Rameau, Jean-
Philippe

PLATONIUM see Rossé, Francois

PLATOON see Delerue, Georges

PLATTI, GIOVANNI BENEDETTO (1690-1763)
Concerto in A
see Two Keyboard Concertos

Concerto in F
see Two Keyboard Concertos

Two Keyboard Concertos
(Freeman, Daniel E.) vln I,vln II,
vla,vcl,kbd solo set A-R ED
ISBN 0-89579-260-5 f.s.
contains: Concerto in A; Concerto
in F                            (P340)

PLATZ, ROBERT (1951- )
Pièce Noire
0+alto fl+bass fl.1.1(contrabass
clar).0. 1.1.1.0. pno,vln,vla,
vcl,db,electronic tape [20']
BREITKOPF-W                     (P341)

Schreyahn
1.0+English horn.1.1.tenor sax.
2.2.2.2. 2pno,vcl solo [25']
BREITKOPF-W                     (P342)

PLAY NEXT see Valkare, Gunnar

PLAY OF SHADOWS, A see Schwantner,
Joseph

PLEASURE DOME FOR KUBLA KHAN, THE see
Griffes, Charles Tomlinson

PLEASURE-RIDE AT THE SEASIDE AND PAS DE
DEUX see Hidas, Frigyes, Adagio

PLENUM II see Lutyens, Elisabeth

PLEXUS see Ince, Kamran

PLEYEL, IGNACE JOSEPH (1757-1831)
Concerto for Clarinet and Orchestra
in B flat
(Balasza) clar solo,orch KUNZELMANN
ipa sc 10114A, oct 10114  (P343)

Concerto for Violoncello and
Orchestra in C
vcl solo/fl solo/clar solo,orch
KUNZELMANN ipa sc 10212A, oct
10212                           (P344)

PLUS DOUX CHEMIN, LE see Faure,
Gabriel-Urbain

PLZENSKY MATENÍK see Flosman, Oldrich

PNEUMA see Jannoch, Hans-Peter

POCHOD see Smetácek, Václav see
Vodrazka, Karel

POCHOD BOHÉMU see Petrzelka, Vilém

POCHOD NÁRODNÍ GARDY see Smetana,
Bedrich

POCHOD PRÁTELSTVÍ see Vacek, Miloš

POCHOD ROKU 1948 see Bartoš, Jan Zdenek

POCHOD SOCIALISMU see Hlavacek, Libor

POCHOD STUDENTSKÉ LEGIE see Smetana,
Bedrich

POCTA HÄNDLOVI see Teml, Jiri

POCTA MAJAKOVSKÉMU see Kubik, Ladislav

POCTA VÁCLAV JANU STICHOVI PUNTOVI see
Smolka, Jaroslav

POCTY see Gemrot, Jiri

POD MODROU OBLOHOU see Myska, Rudolf

POD PYRENEJEMI see Rimón, Jan

PODEŠVA, JAROMÍR (1927- )
Concerto for Clarinet and Orchestra
2.2.1.2. 4.2.1.1. timp,strings,clar
solo [23'] CESKY HUD.          (P345)

PODEŠVA, JAROMÍR (cont'd.)
Concerto for String Orchestra
[22'] CESKY HUD.               (P346)

Concerto for Viola and Orchestra
2.2.2.3. 2.2.2.0. timp,strings,vla
solo [21'] CESKY HUD.          (P347)

Konec Války
3.3.3.3. 4.3.3.1. timp,perc,vibra,
strings [16'] CESKY HUD.       (P348)

Ostravská
see Symphony No. 8

Slavnosti Snezenek
3.3.3.3. 4.3.3.1. timp,perc,xylo,
vibra,harp,pno,strings [23']
CESKY HUD.                     (P349)

Symfonietta Festiva
[17'] CESKY HUD.               (P350)

Symphony No. 7
3.3.3.3. 4.4.3.1. vibra,gtr,strings
[26'] CESKY HUD.               (P351)

Symphony No. 8
"Ostravská" 4.3.3.3. 4.3.3.1. timp,
perc,harp,pno,elec gtr,strings
[27'] CESKY HUD.               (P352)

PODOBA CLOVEKA see Odstrcil, Karel

PODOBENSTVÍ see Kurz, Ivan

PODVECERNÍ HUDBA see Jirasek, Ivo

PODZIMNÍ HUDBA see Francl, Jaroslav

PODZIMNÍ KOLONÁDA see Dousa, Eduard

PODZIMNÍ MEDITACE see Hudec, Jiří

POEM DES MORGENS see Müller-Wieland,
Jan

"POEM OF ECSTASY" & "PROMETHEUS" see
Scriabin, Alexander

POÈM POUR UNE MÉTAMORPHOSE see Lauber,
Anne

POEM: ROMANTISK STILSTUDIE see Blum,
Thomas

POEMA-KONCERT see Parsch, Arnost

POEMA MISTICO see Betancur-Gonzalez,
Valentin

POEMA O CESKOMORAVSKÉ VYSOCINE see
Hlavacek, Libor

POÈME see Schultheiss, Ulrich

POÈME CONCERTANTE see Kirchner, Volker
David, Schibboleth

POÈME SYMPHONIQUE see Kingma, Piet

POÈMES see Obst, Michael

POEMS FROM TANG see Zhou, Long

POETICKÁ HUMORESKA see Strasek, Emil

POETICKÁ POLKA see Hudec, Jiří see
Juchelka, Miroslav

POETICKÉ SCHERZO see Dlouhy, Jaromir

POHJATUULI see Longtin, Michel

POHLAZENI see Bláha, Oldrich

POHLEDNICE Z TARENTA see Myska, Rudolf

POHNUTÁ IDYLA see Koštál, Arnošt

POINTS D'OR see Jolas, Betsy

POJDTE S NÁMI see Svehla, Antonin

POKUŠENÍ A CIN see Riedlbauch, Vaclav

POLACCA CON VARIAZIONI see Paganini,
Niccolo

POLAR see Pablo, Luis de

POLGAR, TIBOR (1907-1993)
Dwarf And The Giant, The
"Fairy Tale In Music, A" 1.2.2.2.
2.2.0.0. timp,perc,harp,strings,
pic solo,tuba solo [4'35"] sc
CANADIAN MI 1450 P765DW       (P353)

Fairy Tale In Music, A
see Dwarf And The Giant, The

Fanfare Of Pride And Joy
3(pic).2.2.2. 4.2.3.1. timp,4perc,
harp,org,strings, 12 fanfare
trumpets sc CANADIAN

POLGAR, TIBOR (cont'd.)
MI 1431 P765FA                 (P354)

Puszta, A: Egy Nap A Magyar Puszta
Életébol
"Puszta, Die: Ein Tag Aus Dem Leben
Der Ungarischen Puszta"
1(pic).1(English horn).1.1.
1.0.0.0. timp,perc,harp,2vln,vla,
vcl,db [35'] sc CANADIAN
MI 1200 P765PU                 (P355)

Puszta, Die: Ein Tag Aus Dem Leben
Der Ungarischen Puszta
see Puszta, A: Egy Nap A Magyar
Puszta Életébol

Souvenir
2.2.2.2. 4.2.3.0. timp,perc,harp,
strings [7'] sc CANADIAN
MI 1100 P765SO                 (P356)

Suite No. 2
3(pic).2.2.2. 4.3.3.1. timp,perc,
harp,pno,cel,strings [25'] sc
CANADIAN MI 1100 P765SZ       (P357)

POLIFONIA see Yasuraoka, Akio

POLIFONÍAS see Raxach, Enrique

POLIFONICA see Engelmann, Hans Ulrich

POLKA see Muldowney, Dominic

POLKA JEDE see Marík, A.F.

POLKA SLÁNSKYCH ABITURIENTU see
Smetácek, Rudolf

POLLY: OVERTURE see Arnold, Samuel

POLNA, POLNA TSCHUDESJ see Rimsky-
Korsakov, Nikolai

POLOLÁNÍK, ZDENEK (1935- )
Concertino for Piano and Strings
[26'] CESKY HUD.               (P358)

Concerto Grosso for Clarinet, Bassoon
and Strings
[22'] CESKY HUD.               (P359)

Musica Giocosa
2.2.3.2. 2.0.0.0. perc,pno,db,vln
solo [15'] CESKY HUD.          (P360)

Proglas
0.0.0.0. 1.0.0.0. perc,cembalo,
strings,S solo [17'] CESKY HUD.
                               (P361)

Sinfonietta
3.3.3.3. 4.3.3.1. timp,perc,pno,
strings [22'] CESKY HUD.       (P362)

Symphony No. 1
3.3.3.3. 4.3.3.1. timp,perc,harp,
pno,strings [35'] CESKY HUD.
                               (P363)

Toccata for Double Bass
0.0.0.0. 4.3.3.1. timp,perc,2harp,
pno,strings,db solo [7'] CESKY
HUD.                           (P364)

POLONIA: OVERTURE see Wagner, Richard

"POLOVTSIAN DANCES" AND "IN THE STEPPES
OF CENTRAL ASIA" IN FULL SCORE see
Borodin, Alexander Porfirievich

POLSON, ARTHUR (1934- )
Concertino for Violin and String
Orchestra in Three Movements
string orch,vln solo sc,solo pt
CANADIAN MI1611 P778CO         (P365)

Concerto for Flute, Strings, Timpani
and Percussion
string orch,timp,2perc,fl solo,
string quar soli,db solo [16'] sc
CANADIAN MI 1750 P778CO       (P366)

POLYKROM see Sandred, Örjan

POLYPHONIE FOR 28 INSTRUMENTS see Sary,
Laszlo

POLYPHONISCHER TANGO see Schnittke,
Alfred

POLYPTYQUE see Rossum, Frederic R. van

POMNIK NEZNÁMÉHO VOJÍNA see Hlavacek,
Libor

POMPEJI see Niemann, Walter

PONCE, MANUEL MARIA (1882-1948)
Concierto Romantico
2.1+English horn.2.2. 2.2.3.1.
timp,strings,pno solo [19'] PEER
rent                           (P367)

PONTEM VIDEO see Bodorova, Sylvie

POOT, MARCEL (1901-1988)
Symphony No. 2
3.3.3.3. 4.3.3.1. timp,perc,harp,
strings [24'30"] (symphonic
triptyque) BELGE                    (P368)

POPELKA, VLADIMIR (1932-    )
Vzpomínka Na J. M.
tenor sax,trp,trom,perc,2gtr,
3synthesizer,strings,soprano sax&
pno soli [4'] CESKY HUD.            (P369)

POPOL VUH see Ginastera, Alberto

PORPORA, NICOLA ANTONIO (1686-1768)
Semiramide: Introduction
(Divall, R.) 0.2.0.2. 2.2.0.0.
strings [6'] ALLANS                 (P370)

Symphony No. 3 for Strings
(Blanchard) string orch [8'] BOIS
                                    (P371)

PORT ESSINGTON see Sculthorpe, Peter
[Joshua]

PORTAL see Clarke, Jim

PORTLAND SUITE see Barnes, Milton

PORTRAIT see Gürsching, Albrecht see
Zechlin, Ruth

PORTRAIT I: SALLY GOODIN see Plain,
Gerald

PORTRAIT II: PRETTY POLLY see Plain,
Gerald

PORTRÄT see Eichhorn, Frank Volker

PORTRÉT BÁSNÍKA see Kosut, Michal

PORTRÉTY see Kozeluha, Lubomir

POSELSTVÍ see Fiala, Petr, Symphony No.
3 see Parsch, Arnost

POSTEL, CHRISTIAN HEINRICH
Concerto in B flat for Oboe, Strings
and Continuo
8vln I,7vln II,6vla,5vcl,4db,hpsd,
ob solo [10'] sc,solo pt PETERS
02705                               (P372)
(Mühne, Chr.) [10'] PETERS          (P373)

POSTILLON DE LONJUMEAU, LE: MES AMIS
ÉCOUTEZ L'HISTOIRE see Adam,
Adolphe-Charles

POSTILLON VON LONJUMEAU, DER: FREUNDE,
VERNEHMET DIE GESCHICHTE see Adam,
Adolphe-Charles, Postillon De
Lonjumeau, Le: Mes Amis Écoutez
l'Histoire

POSTLUDIO see Gutiérrez Heras, Joaquín

POSTMAN ALWAYS RINGS TWICE, THE: SUITE
see Paulus, Stephen Harrison

POSTVOGNEN RULLER see Wellejus,
Henning, Postwagen Rollt, Der

POSTWAGEN ROLLT, DER see Wellejus,
Henning

POULHEIM, BERT (1952-    )
Momente
2.2.2.2. 2.2.2.1. timp,perc,vibra,
8vln I,7vln II,6vla,5vcl,4db
[15'] sc PETERS 03120               (P374)

POUSSIVITÉ see DuBois, Pierre-Max

POVEZ MI MÁ LÁSKO see Smékal, Mojmir

POVÍDKA see Riedlbauch, Vaclav

POWELL, MEL (1923-    )
Modules
orch sc SCHIRM.G AMP3778            (P375)

POWER OF LOVE, THE see Grainger, Percy
Aldridge

POWER OF ROME AND THE CHRISTIAN HEART,
THE see Grainger, Percy Aldridge

POWERHOUSE see Koehne, Graeme

POWERS, ANTHONY (1953-    )
Architecture And Dreams
1(pic,alto fl).1(English
horn).1(bass clar).1(contrabsn).
1.0.0.0. perc,harp,strings [19']
perf sc set OXFORD 3365766 sc,pts
rent                                (P376)

Concerto for Horn and Orchestra
3.3.3.3. 4.3.3.1. timp,3perc,harp,
cel,strings [24'] perf sc set
OXFORD 3665832 sc,pts rent (P377)

POWERS, ANTHONY (cont'd.)
Concerto for Violoncello and
Orchestra
2.2.2.2. 2.1.1.0. timp,2perc,pno,
mand,strings,vcl solo [24']
OXFORD sc 3665867 f.s., perf sc
set 3665859 sc,pts rent            (P378)

Symphony
2(alto fl)+pic.2+English horn.2+
bass clar.2+contrabsn.alto sax.
4.3.3.1. timp,4perc,harp,pno&cel,
strings [40'] perf sc set OXFORD
3665921 perf mat rent             (P379)

Terrain
3.3.3.3. 4.3.3.1. timp,3perc,2harp,
pno/cel,strings OXFORD sc 3665913
f.s., perf sc set 3665913 sc,pts
rent                               (P380)

POYNTER, ARTHUR R. (1913-1981)
Love: Song Cycle No.1
3(pic,alto fl).2(English horn).2.2.
4.3.3.1. timp,perc,2harp,strings,
S solo [26'] (text by
Rabindranath Tagore: Away From
The Sight Of Thy Face -- The Song
That I Came To Sing -- I Am Only
Waiting For Love -- Light, Light,
O Where Is The Light? -- Let Only
That Little Be Left Of Me -- That
I Want Thee) sc CANADIAN
MV 1400 P892L0                     (P381)

POZDRAV PRÁTELUM see Myska, Rudolf

PRADO, ALMEIDA
Cidade De Campinas
1.1.3.2. 4.3.3.1. perc,pno,strings
SEESAW                             (P382)

Sinfonia Dos Orixas
2.2.2.2. 5.3.3.1. timp,perc,harp,
strings SEESAW                     (P383)

Sinfonia No. 1
2.2.2.2. 4.2.3.1. pno,4perc,strings
SEESAW                             (P384)

PRADO, JOSÉ-ANTONIO (ALMEIDA)
(1943-    )
Cidade De Campinas
orch TONOS M-2015-4112-9 rent      (P385)

Sinfonia Dos OrixÃs
orch TONOS sc M-2015-4099-3 rent,
pts M-2015-4096-2 rent             (P386)

Sinfonia No. 1
orch sc TONOS M-2015-4095-5 rent
                                   (P387)

Suite Das OrixÃs
orch TONOS M-2015-4069-6           (P388)

PRAELUDIUM UND ALLEGRO see Kreisler,
Fritz

PRAGER VISION see Zechlin, Ruth

PRAVECEK, JINDRICH (1909-    )
Burleska
2.2.2.2. 4.2.3.0. timp,perc,
strings,clar solo [3'] CESKY HUD.
                                   (P389)
Capriccio for Violin and Orchestra
2.2.2.2. 4.2.3.0. timp,perc,
strings,vln solo [5'] CESKY HUD.
                                   (P390)
Invention for Trumpet and Orchestra
2.2.2.2. 4.2.3.0. timp,perc,
strings,trp solo [4'] CESKY HUD.
                                   (P391)
Promenádní Pochod
2.2.2.2. 4.3.3.0. timp,perc,strings
[4'] CESKY HUD.                    (P392)
Usmevavá Polka
2.2.2.2. 4.2.3.0. timp,perc,strings
[4'] CESKY HUD.                    (P393)

PRAYER AND A DANCE, A see Hamburg, Jeff

PRAYER AND DANCE see Buczynski, Walter

PRÁZDNINOVÁ PREDEHRA see Macourek,
Harry

PRAZSKÁ NOKTURNA see Macourek, Harry

PRAZSKÉ ORNAMENTY see Petrov, Vadim

PRAZSKÉ PROMENÁDY see Strasek, Emil

PRECECHTEL, ZBYNEK (1916-    )
Blízím Se K Tobe
2.2.2.2. 4.3.3.1. timp,perc,harp,
strings,female solo [4'] CESKY
HUD.                               (P394)

Canzone Dolce
2.2.2.2. 3.2.2.0. perc,vibra,harp,
strings [4'] CESKY HUD.            (P395)

PRECECHTEL, ZBYNEK (cont'd.)
Dívat Se Do Jara
2.2.2.2. 4.2.2.1. perc,harp,strings
[5'] CESKY HUD.                    (P396)

Lázensky Valcík
2.2.2.2. 4.2.3.0. perc,harp,strings
[4'] CESKY HUD.                    (P397)

Miniatury (Suite for String
Orchestra)
string orch [11'] CESKY HUD. (P398)

Ozveny
1.1.3.0. 3.3.3.0. timp,perc,strings
[4'] CESKY HUD.                    (P399)

Poem
2.2.2.2. 4.2.2.1. timp,perc,harp,
strings [5'] CESKY HUD.            (P400)

Serenade for Orchestra
2.2.2.2. 4.2.3.1. perc,harp,strings
[3'] CESKY HUD.                    (P401)

Suite for String Orchestra
see Miniatury

PRECIOSA AND THE WIND: BALLET ON A
THEME BY FEDERICO GARCIA LORCA see
Zuckert, Leon, Preciosa Y El
Viento: Ballet Sobre Un Tema De
Federico Garcia Lorca

PRECIOSA Y EL VIENTO: BALLET SOBRE UN
TEMA DE FEDERICO GARCIA LORCA see
Zuckert, Leon

PRECIPICE see Eagle, David

PREDEHRA see Gemrot, Jiri see Kvech,
Otomar see Svehla, Antonin

PREGHIERA A S. SERGIO see Donati

PREGHIERA PER I MORTI see Santoliquido,
Francesco

PRÉLUDE À LA NOUVELLE JOURNÉE see
Vermeulen, Matthijs, Symphony No. 2

PRÉLUDE À L'APRÈS-MIDI D'UN FAUNE see
Debussy, Claude

PRELUDE AND PRAYER see Hawkins, John

PRELUDE, ARIA AND FUGUE see Bottenberg,
Wolfgang

PRELUDE, COUNTERPOINT AND MARCH see
Dijk, Jan van

PRÉLUDE ET ALLEGRO see Pugnani, Gaetano

PRELUDE IN THE DORIAN MODE see Cabezón,
Antonio de

PRELUDE, PASTORALE AND FUGUE see
Fridolfson, Ruben

PRELUDE TO ACT I see Proto, Frank

PRÉLUDES, 24 see Girard, Anthony

PRELUDES, LES AND OTHER SYMPHONIC POEMS
see Liszt, Franz

PRELUDES AND INTERLUDES TO A DRAMA see
Lazarof, Henri

PRELUDES, FANFARES, AND TOCCATAS see
Caltabiano, Ronald

PRELUDIO see Magi, Fortunato

PRELUDIO, ADAGIO E FUGA see Szöllösy,
Andras

PRELUDIO, ARIA E FINALE see Mihajlovic

PRELUDIO DECISO see Zamecnik, Evzen

PRELUDIO E FUGA see Szönyi, Erzsebet
(Elizabeth)

PRELUDIO E RONDINO GIOCOSO see Srnka,
Jiri

PRELUDIO E RONDO see Lukas, Zdenek

PRELUDIO FILARMONICO see Zamecnik,
Evzen

PRELUDIO PARA UN POEMA A LA ALHAMBRA
see Rodrigo, Joaquín

PRELUDIUM - BERCEUSE - MENUET see
Gullberg, Olof

PRELUDIUM K JUBILEU see Zamecnik, Evzen

PREMIER BEAU MATIN DE MAI see Mori,
Kurodo

PREMIER CONCERTO DA CAMERA see Alkan, Charles-Henri Valentin

PREMIÈRE SUITE CINÉMATOGRAPHIQUE see Delerue, Georges

PRESENTAZIONI see Patachich, Ivan

PRESSER, WILLIAM HENRY (1916-    )
Three Songs Of Love And Woe
pno,string quar/string orch,Mez
solo TENUTO rent                    (P402)

PRESSURE TRIGGERING DREAMS, A see Felder, David

PREVOST, ANDRE (1934-    )
Chorégraphie II
3(pic,alto fl).2+English
horn.2(clar in E flat)+bass
clar.2+contrabsn. 4.3.3.1. timp,
3perc,2harp,cel,pno,12vln I,10vln
II,6vla,6vcl,4db [21'] sc
CANADIAN MI 1100 P944CH2      (P403)

Chorégraphie III
3(pic,alto fl).3(English
horn).3(bass clar).3(contrabsn).
4.4(2trp in D).3.1. timp,5perc,
2harp,cel,pno,strings [18'] sc
CANADIAN MI 1100 P944CH3      (P404)

Concerto for Violoncello and
Orchestra
3(pic,alto fl).3(English
horn).3(bass clar,clar in E
flat).3(contrabsn). 4.4.3.1.
timp,perc,harp,cel,pno,strings,
vcl solo [28'] sc,solo pt
CANADIAN MI 1313 P944CO      (P405)

Conte De L'Oiseau, Le
"Tale Of The Bird" [Eng/Fr] 3(alto
fl).3(English horn).3(clar in E
flat).3(contrabsn). 4.3.3.1.
timp,5perc,strings,2 narrators
[30'] sc,solo pt CANADIAN
MV 2400 P944CO               (P406)

Paraphrase
2(pic,alto fl).2(English
horn).2(bass clar).2. 2.2.0.0.
timp,3perc,cel,strings,string
quar soli [16'] sc CANADIAN
MI 1417 P944PA              (P407)

Pièce Concertante Pour Piano Et
Orchestre
see Variations Et Thème

Tale Of The Bird
see Conte De L'Oiseau, Le

Theme and Variations
see Variations Et Thème

Variations Et Thème (Theme and
Variations)
"Pièce Concertante Pour Piano Et
Orchestre" 2(pic).2.2.2. 4.2.3.1.
timp,2perc,strings,pno solo sc
CANADIAN MI 1361 P944VA     (P408)

PREZAMENT, WENDY (1955-    )
Glacial Fragments
2.2.2.2. 2.2.0.0. 2perc,strings
[8'] sc CANADIAN MI 1100 P9445GL
                               (P409)

PRI SLUNCI A JEHO JASU see Zahradník, Zdenek

PRÍBEH O PETI KAPITOLÁCH see Vackár, Dalibor Cyril

PRÍBEHY A ZÁZRAKY see Klega, Miroslav

PRIÈRE DU CHRIST MONTANT VERS SON PÈRE see Messiaen, Olivier

PRÍHODA see Riedlbauch, Vaclav

PRILLAR I G-LYDISK see Tveitt, Geirr

PRIMA VERA, LA see Cowie, Edward

PRIMAL SONG see Raskatov, Alexander, Urlied

PRIMAVERA see Constant, Franz see Emura, Tetsuji

PRIMAVERA, LA see Lajtha, Laszlo, Sinfonia No. 4 see Paganini, Niccolo

PRINCESS OF THE PEACOCKS see Amos, Keith

PRINCIPÁLKA see Petrov, Vadim

PRINCIPIA see Martland, Steve

PRINTEMPS see Migot, Georges

PRÍPAD LUPÍNEK (JEDNOU NEBUDEME MALÍ) see Havelka, Svatopluk

PRÍPITEK see Petr, Zdenek

PRISON see Faure, Gabriel-Urbain

PRO BEATI PAULI see Anonymous

PRO FUTURO see Parsch, Arnost

PRO JUVENTUTE see Vackár, Dalibor Cyril, Symphony No. 5

PRO MEMORIA see Kazacsay, Tibor

PRO ORCHESTR see Šrom, Karel

PRO POTEŠENÍ see Deváty, Antonín

PRO SOMNO IGORIS STRAVINSKY QUIETO see Szöllösy, Andras

PROCESSION, LA see Franck, Cesar

PROCESSIONAL MARCH see Ward, Robert Eugene

PROCRUSTEAN CONCERTO FOR THE B FLAT CLARINET see Concerto for Clarinet

PROGLAS see Pololáník, Zdenek

PROHASKA, CARL (1869-1927)
Passacaglia, Op. 22
4.3.4.3. 4.3.3.1. perc,2harp,
strings [30'] BREITKOPF-W (P410)

Serenade, Op. 20
2.2.2+bass clar.2. 4.2.0.0. timp,
perc,strings [40'] BREITKOPF-W
                               (P411)

PROKOFIEV, SERGE (1891-1953)
Concerto for Flute
(Palmer, Christopher) 0.1(English
horn).2(bass clar).1. 2.1.0.0.
timp,2perc,pno&cel,harp,8vln I,
6vln II,4vla,4vcl,3db [24']
(Flute Sonata in D orchestrated)
BOOSEY-ENG rent             (P412)

Dance Of The Masks (from The Duenna
(Betrothal In A Monastery) Op.
86)
2+pic.2+English horn.2+bass clar.2+
contrabsn. 4.3.3.1. timp,perc,
harp,strings [14'] BOOSEY-ENG
rent                         (P413)

Egyptian Nights *Op.61
2+pic.2+English horn.2+bass clar.2+
contrabsn.tenor sax. 4.2.3.1.
timp,3perc,harp,pno,strings [18']
(symphonic suite) BOOSEY-ENG rent
                               (P414)

Festive Poem "Thirty Years" *Op.113
2.2.2.2. 4.2.3.1. timp,perc,pno,
strings [15'] BOOSEY-ENG rent
                               (P415)

Festliches Poem Für Orchester
*Op.113
2.2.2.2. 2.4.3.1. timp,perc,pno,
strings [15'] PETERS         (P416)

Four Orchestral Works
orch sc DOVER 20279-8        (P417)

Hamlet: Incidental Music *Op.77
[Russ] 1.1.1.1. 2.1.1.0. perc,
acord,opt pno,strings,sBar soli
[30'] BOOSEY-ENG rent        (P418)

Ivan The Terrible: Orchestral Suite
*Op.116a
(Palmer, Christopher) 2(pic)+pic.2+
English horn.3+bass clar.3+
contrabsn.alto sax.tenor sax.bass
sax. 4.5.3.2. timp,perc,2harp,
pno,strings [25'] BOOSEY-ENG rent
                               (P419)

Meeting Of The Volga And The Don, The
*Op.130
3.3.3.3. 4.3.3.1. timp,perc,cel,
harp,pno,strings [16'] BOOSEY-ENG
rent                         (P420)

Summer Night *Op.123 (from The
Duenna (Betrothal In A Monastery)
Op. 86)
2+pic.2+English horn.2+bass clar.2+
contrabsn. 4.3.3.1. timp,perc,
harp,strings [20'] (symphonic
suite) BOOSEY-ENG rent       (P421)

Year 1941, The *Op.90, Suite
2+pic.2+English horn.2+bass clar.2+
contrabsn. 4.2.2.1. timp,perc,
harp,strings [12'] BOOSEY-ENG
rent                         (P422)

Zwei Puschkin-Walzer *Op.120
2.3.3.2. 4.2.3.1. timp,perc,strings
[12'] PETERS                 (P423)

PROLEGOMENON see Caltabiano, Ronald

PROLOG see Fischer, Eduard see
Korndorf, Nicolai see Kubicka,
Miroslav

PROLOG II FÜR ORCHESTER see Genzmer, Harald

PROLOGO Y NARRACIÓN see Still, William Grant

PROLOGOS see Reuter, Willi Albrecht

PROMENA see Kvech, Otomar see Stepanek, Jiri

PROMENÁDNÍ POCHOD see Pravecek, Jindrich

PROMENÁDNÍ PREDEHRA see Zamecnik, Evzen

PROMENY see Lukas, Zdenek

PROMENY CASU see Bíly, Antonin

PROMENY TICHA see Matousek, Lukas

PROMÉTHÉE see Martinet, Jean-Louis

PROMETHEUS see Domhardt, Gerd see
Parsch, Arnost

PROMETHEUS: OVERTURE see Bargiel, Woldemar

PROMINADENFLIRT see Ronelli, Bob

PROMINENCE see Yamamoto, Junnosuke

PROPHET, DER: ACH! MEIN SOHN, SEGEN
DIR! see Meyerbeer, Giacomo,
Prophète, Le: Arioso Of Fides

PROPHET, DER: O GEBT, ERRETTET EINEN
ARMEN see Meyerbeer, Giacomo,
Prophète, Le: Romance Of Fides

PROPHÈTE, LE: ARIOSO OF FIDES see
Meyerbeer, Giacomo

PROPHÈTE, LE: BALLETMUSIC see
Meyerbeer, Giacomo

PROPHÈTE, LE: ROMANCE OF FIDES see
Meyerbeer, Giacomo

PROPOSITIONS I see Bayer, F.

PROTO, FRANK (1941-    )
Aragonaise
see Carmen Fantasy For Jazz
Ensemble And Orchestra

Capriccio Di Niccolo
"Variations On A Theme Of Paganini
For Trumpet And Orchestra" 2+
pic.1+English horn.2+bass clar.2.
4.3.3.1. timp,3perc,harp,strings,
trp solo [12'] LIBEN        (P424)

Carmen Fantasy, A, For Double Bass
And Orchestra, A
1+pic.1+English horn.1+bass clar.0.
0.0.0.0. 2perc,harp,pno/cel,
strings,db solo [25'] LIBEN
                               (P425)

Carmen Fantasy For Jazz Ensemble And
Orchestra
2+pic.2.2+English horn.2+contrabsn.
4.3.3.1. timp,2perc,harp,strings,
solo group: trumpet, reed 1 (alto
sax, soprano sax, flute, alto
flute, piccolo), reed 2 (baritone
sax, clarinet),
trombone, piano or electric
piano, bass or electric bass,
drums, percussion LIBEN f.s.
contains: Aragonaise; Dragons Of
Alcala, The; Habanera;
Intermezzo; Prelude To Act I;
Verse To The Toreador Song
                               (P426)

Concertino For Castanets And
Orchestra
see Viva Lucero

Concerto for Double Bass and
Orchestra, No. 3
see Four Scenes After Picasso

Concerto for Violin, Double Bass and
Orchestra in One Movement
2.2+English horn.3+bass clar.2+
contrabsn. 4.3.3.1. timp,4perc,
harp,pno/cel,strings,vln&db soli
[14'] LIBEN                  (P427)

Dragons Of Alcala, The
see Carmen Fantasy For Jazz
Ensemble And Orchestra

Four Scenes After Picasso (Concerto
for Double Bass and Orchestra,
No. 3)
1+pic.2.1+bass clar.1. 0.0.0.0.

PROTO, FRANK (cont'd.)

2perc,harp,pno/cel,strings,db
solo [28'] LIBEN                    (P428)

Ghost In Machine
2+pic.2+English horn.3+bass clar.2+
contrabsn. 4.4.4.1. timp,5perc,
banjo,harp,2pno/pno&cel,strings,
soprano sax/tenor sax,female
solo&narrator [70'] LIBEN   (P429)

Habanera
see Carmen Fantasy For Jazz
Ensemble And Orchestra

Hamabe No Arashi
2+pic.2+English horn.2+bass
clar.2.opt alto sax. 4.3.3.1.
timp,3perc,harp,pno/cel,elec
bass,strings [6'30"] LIBEN (P430)

Hawaiian Holiday
3+pic.2.2.2. 4.3.3.1. timp,4perc,
harp,pno/cel,elec pno,elec bass,
strings [7'] LIBEN          (P431)

Intermezzo
see Carmen Fantasy For Jazz
Ensemble And Orchestra

New Seasons, The (Sinfonia
Concertante for Tuba, 2
Percussionists, 4 Flutes and
Strings)
[30'] LIBEN                 (P432)

Prelude To Act I
see Carmen Fantasy For Jazz
Ensemble And Orchestra

Sinfonia Concertante for Tuba, 2
Percussionists, 4 Flutes and
Strings
see New Seasons, The

Variations On A Theme Of Paganini For
Trumpet And Orchestra
see Capriccio Di Niccolo

Variations On An Old American Melody
see Voyage That Johnny Never Knew,
The

Verse To The Toreador Song
see Carmen Fantasy For Jazz
Ensemble And Orchestra

Viva Lucero
"Concertino For Castanets And
Orchestra" 1+pic.2.1+bass clar.1.
0.1.0.0. 2perc,strings,castanets
solo [12'] LIBEN            (P433)

Voyage That Johnny Never Knew, The
"Variations On An Old American
Melody" 2+pic.2+English horn.2+
bass clar.1+contrabsn. 4.3.3.1.
timp,3perc,pno/cel,strings [8']
LIBEN                       (P434)

PROUD VESSELIL see Grainger, Percy
Aldridge, Stalt Vesselil

PROUT'S NECK see Perna, Dana Paul

PRÖVE, BERNFRIED (1963-    )
Brennend
3.3.3.3. 4.3.3.1. 6perc,harp,cel,
pno,strings [10'] MOECK sc 5446
f.s., pts rent              (P435)

Diastase
3.2.3.3. 4.2.3.2. 4perc,harp,pno,
strings [17'] MOECK sc 5452 f.s.,
pts rent                    (P436)

Fernung - Horizont - Naehe
4.3.4.3. 4.4.4.1. perc,harp,pno,
strings [12'30"] MOECK sc 5486
f.s., pts rent              (P437)

PROVINCIE, DE: MUZIEK UIT DE FILM VAN
JAN BÖSDRIESZ see Ketting, Otto

PROVOST, SERGE (1952-    )
Jardin Des Oliviers, Le
fl,trp,3perc,2vln,vla,vcl,cel,
harmonium [11'] BILLAUDOT   (P438)

PRVOSENKA see Vodrazka, Karel

PSALM see Saxton, Robert, Song Of
Ascents, A

PSALM 22 - MY GOD WHY HAVE YOU FORSAKEN
ME? see Morawetz, Oskar

PSALM 42 see Koprowski, Peter Paul

PSALM NO. 8 see Swack, Irwin

PSALM NO. 22 see Bortoli, Stephane

PSALM NO. 37 see Leichtling, Alan

PSALM NO. 100 see Brühns, Nicholaus,
Jauchzet Dem Herrn Alle Welt

PSALMEN UND RITUALE see Kazandjiev,
Vassil, Festmusik Für Streicher

PSALMENMUSIK see Müller-Zürich, Paul

PSAUME 22 see Bortoli, Stephane, Psalm
No. 22

PSAUME-TEHILLIM see Markevitch, Igor

PSYCHOGRAMME see Metsk, Juro

PUCCINI, GIACOMO (1858-1924)
Manon Lescaut, Preludio Atto II
2.2+English horn.2.2. 2.0.0.0.
timp,harp,strings [5'] BOCCACCINI
BS. 202 rent                (P439)

Mentia L'Avviso  *scena
(Boccadoro, Carlo) strings,T solo
[5'30"] (lyric) SONZOGNO rent
(P440)

Segreta Voce, La
(Boccadoro, Carlo) strings,T solo
[16'30"] (7 romances) SONZOGNO
rent                        (P441)

Villi, Le, Tregenda
2+pic.2.2.2. 4.0.3.1. timp,perc,
strings [15'] BOCCACCINI BS. 203
rent                        (P442)

PUEBLO UNIDO, EL see Kollert, Jiri

PUGNANI, GAETANO (1731-1798)
Prélude Et Allegro (composed with
Kreisler, Fritz)
vln,string orch [6'] FUZEAU 2883
(P443)

PUIG-ROGET, HENRIETTE
see ROGET, HENRIETTE

PULS III see Gamstorp, Göran

PULSATIONS see Davies, Victor

PULSE PALACE see Emmer, Huib

PUNKTE, LINIEN, VOLUMINA II...KANDINSKY
see Tarnopolsky, Vladimir

PURCELL, HENRY (1658 or 59-1695)
Abdelazer  *incidental music
strings FABER f.s. sc 50811 1, pts
50812 X                     (P444)

Blessed Virgin's Expostulation, The
(Rosenthal) 2.1.0.2. 2.0.0.0. timp,
harp,strings,solo voice [12']
BILLAUDOT                   (P445)

Double Dealer, The
strings FABER f.s. pts 50814 6, sc
50813 8                     (P446)

Fairy Queen, The: Two Suites
"Two Suites From The Fairy Queen"
string orch KUNZELMANN ipa sc
10181A, oct 10181           (P447)

Hark The Echoing Air
see Three Songs From "Orpheus
Britannicus"

Hear My Prayer, Oh Lord
(Perna, Dana Paul) double string
orchestra [2'30"] BARDIC   (P448)

Let Sullen Discord Smile
see Suite Of Six Songs From
"Orpheus Britannicus"

Not All My Torments
see Three Songs From "Orpheus
Britannicus"

Sechs Fantasien
(Gülke, P.) 3.3.1.2. 0.3.2.0.
strings [20'] PETERS        (P449)

So When The Glittering Queen Of Night
see Suite Of Six Songs From
"Orpheus Britannicus"

Sound Fame Thy Brazen Trumpet
see Suite Of Six Songs From
"Orpheus Britannicus"

Suite in D
(Guyot, D.) string orch,2trp soli
[11'] BILLAUDOT             (P450)

Suite Of Six Songs From "Orpheus
Britannicus"
(Britten, Benjamin) 2.2.0.1.
0.1.0.0. strings,high solo
BOOSEY-ENG f.s.
contains: Let Sullen Discord
Smile; So When The Glittering
Queen Of Night; Sound Fame Thy
Brazen Trumpet; Thou Tunest The

PURCELL, HENRY (cont'd.)

World; T'is Holiday; Why Should
Me Quarrel                 (P451)

Take Not A Woman's Anger
see Three Songs From "Orpheus
Britannicus"

Thou Tunest The World
see Suite Of Six Songs From
"Orpheus Britannicus"

Three Songs From "Orpheus
Britannicus"
(Britten, Benjamin) 2(pic).2.0.2.
0.0.0.0. strings,high solo
BOOSEY-ENG f.s.
contains: Hark The Echoing Air;
Not All My Torments; Take Not A
Woman's Anger             (P452)

T'is Holiday
see Suite Of Six Songs From
"Orpheus Britannicus"

Two Suites From The Fairy Queen
see Fairy Queen, The: Two Suites

Why Should Me Quarrel
see Suite Of Six Songs From
"Orpheus Britannicus"

PURPLE FOG & WHITE POPPY see Xiaogang,
Ye

PURSUIT see Hisada, Noriko

PUSCHMANN, JOSEF (ca. 1740-1794)
Concerto for Viola and Orchestra in C
0.2.0.0. 2.2.0.0. timp,cembalo,
strings,vla solo [18'] CESKY HUD.
(P453)

PUST, ET, FOR OBOE AND STRINGS see
Wiese, Jan

PUSZTA, A: EGY NAP A MAGYAR PUSZTA
ÉLETÉBOL see Polgar, Tibor

PUSZTA, DIE: EIN TAG AUS DEM LEBEN DER
UNGARISCHEN PUSZTA see Polgar,
Tibor, Puszta, A: Egy Nap A Magyar
Puszta Életébol

PUTOVÁNÍ JANA AMOSE: SUITE see Mácha,
Otmar

PÜTZ, EDUARD (1911-    )
Fantasy In Blue
orch SCHOTTS sc CON 245, augmented
set CON 245-50, set CON 245-60
(P454)

3(pic).2.2+bass clar.2.alto
sax.baritone sax. 4.4.3.1. timp,
2perc,elec pno,harp,elec gtr,
strings [10'] SCHOTTS perf mat
rent sc CON 245, pts
CON 245-50-60              (P455)

PÜTZ, JOHANNES
Mexikanisches Pastell
"Sketch" 2.1.3(bass clar).1.
4.3.3.0. perc,gtr,cel,vibra,harp,
strings [2'50"] sc,set BUSCH
DM 049 rent               (P456)

Sketch
see Mexikanisches Pastell

PYROGRAVURES see Rossum, Frederic R.
van

# Q

Q.E.D. [QUOD ERAT DEMONSTRANDUM] see Rypdal, Terje

QU, XIAO-SONG (1952- )
Concerto for Violoncello
2(2pic)+pic.2.2.2+contrabsn.
4.3.3.1. timp,perc,harp,pno,
strings,vcl solo [19'30"] PEER
rent                            (Q1)

Girl Of The Mountain, The
2(pic)+pic.2.2(bass clar).2.
4.2.3.1. timp,perc,cel,harp,
strings,vln solo [12'] PEER rent
                                (Q2)

Huan
3(2pic).3.3.3. 4.3.3.1. timp,perc,
pno,strings [18'] PEER rent   (Q3)
40strings,pno [18'] PEER rent (Q4)
17strings,pno [18'] PEER rent (Q5)

Mist
1.1.1.0. 0.0.0.0. perc,pno,mand,
gtr,strings,SBar soli [19'30"]
PEER rent                       (Q6)

Mountain, The
3(pic).3.3(bass clar).2+contrabsn.
4.3.3.1. perc,harp,strings
[16'30"] PEER rent              (Q7)

String Symphony
string orch,perc [21'] PEER rent
                                (Q8)
Symphony No. 1
3(pic).3.3.2+contrabsn. 4.3.3.1.
timp,perc,strings [23'] PEER rent
                                (Q9)

QUADROONE, LA see Delius, Frederick

QUADRUPLE ELEGY see Hellawell, Piers

QUAKER READER, A see Rorem, Ned

QUAND LOU MOULINIÉ (LORSQUE LE MEUNIER)
see Canteloube de Malaret, Marie-Joseph

QUANDO AVRAN - PADRE, GERMANI see
Mozart, Wolfgang Amadeus

QUANDO SALTA FUORI LA TONICA? see Bus,
Jan

QUANTZ, JOHANN JOACHIM (1697-1773)
Concerto for Flute, Strings and
Continuo in G
(Augsbach, H.) strings,cont,fl solo
[15'] sc,pts BREITKOPF-W
PB-OB 5219                     (Q10)

Concerto for Horn, String Orchestra
and Continuo in E flat
(Delius, N.) horn solo,string orch,
cont KUNZELMANN ipa sc 10227A,
oct 10227                      (Q11)

Concerto in B minor for Flute,
Strings and Continuo
8vln I,7vln II,6vla,5vcl,4db,
cembalo [19'] sc,solo pt PETERS
02746                          (Q12)
(Augsbach) [18'] PETERS        (Q13)

QUARTET IN A see Stamitz, Carl

QUARTET IN D see Stamitz, Carl

QUASI CONCERTANTE see Malek, Jan,
Divertimento No. 2

QUASI UNA SINFONIA see Salbert, Dieter

QUATRE BAGATELLES see Werner, Jean-Jacques

QUATRE CHANSONS DE RONSARD see Milhaud,
Darius

QUATRE MINIATURES POUR ORCHESTRE see
Arseneault, Raynald

QUATRE PASSAGES see Müller-Siemens,
Detlev

QUATRE PSAUMES see Schütz, Heinrich

QUATTRO INTERMEZZI see Slimácek, Jan

QUATTRO MOMENTI MUSICALI see Gardelli,
Lamberto

QUATTRO OPERE DI ANDY WARHOL see
Sollima, Giovanni

QUATTRO STAGIONI, LE see Vivaldi,
Antonio see Vivaldi, Antonio,
Concerto for Violin, Strings and
Continuo, Op. 8, Nos. 1-4

QUEENS TOUCHÉ, THE see Yngwe, Jan

QUERSTREBIGE VERBINDUNGEN see Goldmann,
Friedrich

QUEST, THE: COMPLETE BALLET MUSIC see
Walton, [Sir] William (Turner)

QUETZAL COATL see Pálenícek, Josef

QUI TOLLIS see Kopriva, Karel Blazej

QUICKSTEP AND SLOW ENDING see Kondo, Jo

QUIET EVE see Schipizky, Frederick

QUIET PLACE, A: SUITE see Bernstein,
Leonard

QUILTER, ROGER (1877-1953)
As You Like It *Op.21, Suite
1.1.2.1. 2.2.1.0. timp,perc,harp,
strings [9'] BOOSEY-ENG rent
                               (Q14)

QUINT OF CAROLS, A see Waxman, Donald

QUINTETTO CONCERTANTE see Hidas,
Frigyes

QUIS CUSTODIET CUSTODIES? see
Singleton, Alvin, Fifty-Six Blows

QUISLOWCK see Werner, Rudolf

QUIT DAT FOOL'NISH see Still, William
Grant

QUOD PIA VOCE CANO see Kopriva, Karel
Blazej

QUONIAM TU SOLUS SANCTUS see Cimarosa,
Domenico

QUOTATION OF DREAM see Takemitsu, Toru

# R

R.U.R. see Kvech, Otomar

RAAFF, ROBIN DE
Concerto for Flute
1.1.1.0. 1.1.0.0. 2perc,harp,gtr,
mand,pno,strings,fl&pic&alto fl
solo [18'] sc DONEMUS          (R1)

In Memoriam Dimitri Shostakovich
2.2.2.2. 0.0.2.0. timp,perc,
strings,2horn&2trp soli [18'] sc
DONEMUS                        (R2)

RAATS, JÄÄN (1932- )
Concerto for String Orchestra, No. 2,
Op. 78
[16'] SIKORSKI perf mat rent   (R3)

RABBI AKIBA see Feldman, Morton

RABE, FOLKE (1935- )
All The Lonely People
trom,chamber orch [14'] sc REIMERS
101177 rent                    (R4)

Concerto for Trumpet and Orchestra
see Sardinsarkofagen

Nature, Herd And Relatives
see Naturen, Flocken Och Släkten

Naturen, Flocken Och Släkten
"Nature, Herd And Relatives" horn,
string orch [16'] study sc
REIMERS 101189 rent            (R5)

Sardine Sarcophagus
see Sardinsarkofagen

Sardinsarkofagen (Concerto for
Trumpet and Orchestra)
REIMERS                        (R6)
"Sardine Sarcophagus" trp, and
sinfonietta sc REIMERS 101228
rent                           (R7)

RABINOWITCH, ALEXANDRE (1945- )
Belle Musique, La
3.3.3.3. 4.3.3.1. timp,perc,harp,
pno,strings,opt cel [20'] sc
BELAIEFF BEL 532               (R8)

RACEVICIUS, ALEKSAS-RIMVYDAS
(1935- )
Concertino Brillante "Rautilio", For
String Orchestra
[21'] SIKORSKI perf mat rent   (R9)

RACHMANINOFF, SERGEY VASSILIEVICH
(1873-1943)
Concerti for Piano, Nos. 1-3
orch,pno solo sc DOVER 26350-9
                               (R10)
Concerto for Piano, No. 1, in F sharp
minor, Op. 1
2.2.2.2. 4.2.3.1. timp,strings,pno
solo [25'] PETERS              (R11)

Romance for String Orchestra
string orch KUNZELMANN f.s. sc
WW 999P, sc,pts WW 999 contains
also: Scherzo for String
Orchestra                      (R12)

Scherzo for String Orchestra
see Romance for String Orchestra

Vocalise *Op.34,No.14
(Brooks, Arthur) 2.2+English
horn.2.2. 2.0.0.0.+strings,horn
solo THOM ED OC3 f.s., perf mat
rent                           (R13)

RACINE FRICKER, PETER
see FRICKER, PETER RACINE

RÁDA, RÁDA see Vodrazka, Karel

RADEGAST see Odstrcil, Karel

RADICES TEMPORIS see Matousek, Lukas

RADOST Z ÚSPECHU see Strasek, Emil

RADOSTNÁ PREDEHRA see Lídl, Václav

RADOSTNÉ MLÁDÍ see Deváty, Antonín

RADOSTNYM DNUM see Krízek, Zdenek

RADULESCU, HORATIO (1942- )
Thirteen Dreams Ago
33strings [33'] JOBERT        (R14)

RAE, ALLAN (1942- )
Alam-Al-Mithal
see Symphony No. 3

RAE, ALLAN (cont'd.)

Concerto for Double Bass
"Four Paintings Of Salvador Dali"
3vln I,3vln II,3vla,vcl,db,db
solo [20'] (1. Dali, At The Age
Of Six. . . 2. The Dream Of
Christopher Columbus 3. Sleep 4.
Resurrection Of The Flesh) sc
CANADIAN MI1614 R124CO        (R15)

Concerto for Harp and String
Orchestra in D flat
string orch,harp solo [16'] sc
CANADIAN MI1616 R134DF        (R16)

Concerto for Piano in D minor
3vln I,3vln II,2vla,2vcl,db,4perc,
pno solo [30'] sc CANADIAN
MI 1750 R134DM               (R17)

Concerto for Violin
2vln I,3vln II,2vla,2vcl,db,vln
solo [30'] sc CANADIAN
MI1611 R134CO               (R18)

Four Paintings Of Salvador Dali
see Concerto for Double Bass

Mirror Of Galadriel (Suite for
Orchestra)
3(pic,alto fl).3(English
horn).3(bass clar).3(contrabsn).
4.3.3.1(euphonium). 4perc,harp,
pno,strings [30'] (1. Mirror Of
Gladriel 2. Passage Of The
Marshes 3. The Road Goes Ever On
And On 4. Fog On Barrow Downs 5.
Gathering Of The Ents) sc
CANADIAN MI 1100 R134MIR     (R19)

Sonata for Bass Clarinet and String
Orchestra
[13'] sc CANADIAN MI 1620 R134SO
                            (R20)

Suite for Orchestra
see Mirror Of Galadriel

Symphony No. 2
"Winds Of Change" 2(pic,alto
fl).2(English horn).2(bass
clar).2(contrabsn). 2.2.2.1.
timp,3perc,harp,cel,pno,strings
[32'] sc CANADIAN MI 1100 R134S2
                            (R21)

Symphony No. 3
"Alam-Al-Mithal" 2(pic,alto
fl).2(English horn).2(bass
clar).2(contrabsn). 2.2.2.1.
timp,3perc,harp,cel,pno,strings
[30'] sc CANADIAN MI 1100 R134S3
                            (R22)

Winds Of Change
see Symphony No. 2

RAG CONCERTINA
(Fagin, Gary) 1(pic).1.2.1.alto
sax.tenor sax.baritone sax.
2.2.2.1. banjo,drums,strings PEER
perf mat rent
contains: Joplin, Scott, Bethena;
Northup, Joseph, Cannonball, The;
Turpin, Tom, St. Louis Rag, The
                            (R23)

RAGS FOR STRING ORCHESTRA see Barnes,
Milton

RAGTIME DANCE, THE see Joplin, Scott

RAGTIME TWO-STEP, A see Joplin, Scott

RAICHL, MIROSLAV (1930-    )
Divertimento for Chamber Orchestra
2.2.2.2. 2.3.0.0. timp,perc,strings
[14'] CESKY HUD.             (R24)

Elegie Na Odchodnou
2.2.2.2. 2.2.0.0. perc,harp,pno,
strings,S solo [16'] CESKY HUD.
                            (R25)

RAIMUNDIANA 71: EIN SCHERZO-KALEIDOSKOP
see Cornell, Klaus

RAIN FOREST see Koehne, Graeme

RAINFOREST 3 see Willcocks, Jonathan

RAINIER, PRIAULX (1903-    )
Concertante For 2 Winds
2.1.0.1. 2.2.2.0. timp,2perc,
strings,ob solo,clar solo [18']
study sc SCHOTTS ED 12082 perf
mat rent                    (R26)

Due Canti E Finale
3.3.2.2. 2.2.0.1. timp,perc,
strings,vln solo [23'] study sc
SCHOTTS ED 12132 perf mat rent
                            (R27)

RAITENHASLACHER KONZERT NR. 1 see
Hirschberger, Albericus

RAITHEL, HUGO (1932-    )
Sinfonietta, Op. 18
2.1.1.2. 2.2.2.0. timp,perc,strings
[24'] BREITKOPF-W           (R28)

RAITIO, VÄINÖ (1891-1945)
Five Folk Songs For Strings
see Viisi Hämäläistä Kansanlaulua
Jousiork

Four Folk Songs For Strings
see Neljä Hämäläistä Kansanlaulua
Jousiork

Kuutamo Jupiterissa  *Op.24
"Moonlight On Jupiter" 3.3.3.3.
4.4.3.1. timp,3perc,2harp,cel,
strings sc MODUS M49        (R29)

Moonlight On Jupiter
see Kuutamo Jupiterissa

Neljä Hämäläistä Kansanlaulua
Jousiork (Suite No. 1)
"Four Folk Songs For Strings" MODUS
M53                         (R30)

Poem for Violoncello and Orchestra,
Op. 7
see Runoelma Sellolle Ja
Orkesterille

Runoelma Sellolle Ja Orkesterille
(Poem for Violoncello and
Orchestra, Op. 7)
2.2.2.1. 2.0.0.0. perc,strings,vcl
solo MODUS M50              (R31)

Suite No. 1
see Neljä Hämäläistä Kansanlaulua
Jousiork

Suite No. 2
see Viisi Hämäläistä Kansanlaulua
Jousiork

Viisi Hämäläistä Kansanlaulua
Jousiork (Suite No. 2)
"Five Folk Songs For Strings" MODUS
M54                         (R32)

RAK, STEPÁN (1945-    )
Renesancní Koncert
timp,string orch,marimba solo [18']
CESKY HUD.                  (R33)

RAKOV, NIKOLAI (1908-1990)
Abendliche Spiele
see An Einem Sommertag: 5 Pieces
For String Orchestra

An Einem Sommertag: 5 Pieces For
String Orchestra
SIKORSKI perf mat rent
contains: Abendliche Spiele; Auf
Dem See; Guten Morgen;
Sportlermarsch; Über Die Wiese
Ziehen Wir                  (R34)

Auf Dem See
see An Einem Sommertag: 5 Pieces
For String Orchestra

Guten Morgen
see An Einem Sommertag: 5 Pieces
For String Orchestra

Kleine Sinfonie, For String Orchestra
[10'] SIKORSKI perf mat rent (R35)

Konzertfantasie, For Clarinet And
Orchestra
0.0.0.0. 4.3.1.0. harp,strings,clar
solo [15'] SIKORSKI perf mat rent
                            (R36)

Sportlermarsch
see An Einem Sommertag: 5 Pieces
For String Orchestra

Über Die Wiese Ziehen Wir
see An Einem Sommertag: 5 Pieces
For String Orchestra

RAMEAU, JEAN-PHILIPPE (1683-1764)
Achante Et Cephise: Ouverture
(Fajon, R.) 2.0.2.2. 2.2.0.0. timp,
strings,countertenor [6']
BILLAUDOT                   (R37)

Platée: Divertimento
0.1.0.1. 0.0.0.0. strings [5'30"]
LEDUC                       (R38)

Platée: Overture
2.2.0.2. 0.0.0.0. strings [3'30"]
LEDUC                       (R39)

Suite (from Concerts En Sextuor)
(Thilde, J.) string orch,trp solo
[8'] BILLAUDOT              (R40)

RAMINSH, IMANT (1943-    )
Great Moon, The
see Sahali

RAMINSH, IMANT (cont'd.)

Sahali (Suite for Orchestra)
"Great Moon, The" 2.2.2.1. 2.2.1.0.
timp,strings [18'] (1. Invocation
2. Dawn 3. Horizon 4. Homecoming)
sc CANADIAN MI 1100 R137SA  (R41)

Suite for Orchestra
see Sahali

RAMOVS, PRIMOZ (1921-    )
Dialog Für Klavier Und Orchester
2.2.2.2. 3.3.3.1. timp,3perc,8vln
I,7vln II,6vla,5vcl,4db [23'] sc,
solo pt PETERS 03196        (R42)

RANÇON, LA see Faure, Gabriel-Urbain

RANDS, BERNARD (1935-    )
Tre Canzoni Senza Parole
orch study sc EUR.AM.MUS. EA00753
                            (R43)

RANJBARAN, BEHZAD
Blood Of Seyavash, The
3(pic).3(English horn).2.2.
4.3.3(bass trom).1. timp,perc,
cel,harp,strings PRESSER rent
                            (R44)

Concerto for Violin
3(pic).3(English horn).2.2.
4.2.2.0. timp,perc,cel,harp,
strings,vln solo [26'] pno red
PRESSER rent                (R45)

Elegy
strings [7'] PRESSER rent   (R46)

Seemorgh
3(pic).3(English horn).3(bass
clar).3(contrabsn). 4.3.2.1.
timp,3perc,cel,harp,strings [20']
PRESSER rent                (R47)

Symphony No. 1
3(pic).3(English horn).2.4.
4.2.2(bass trom).0. timp,perc,
cel,harp,strings [20'] PRESSER
rent                        (R48)

RANKI, GYÖRGY (1907-    )
Concertino for Violoncello and
Orchestra
timp,perc,strings,vcl solo [13']
EMB rent                    (R49)

Hajdútánc
see Heyduck Dance

Heyduck Dance
"Hajdútánc" 3(pic).2(English
horn).2.2. 4.2.3.1. timp,perc,
strings [10'] EMB rent      (R50)

Hungarian Dances From The 16th
Century
"Magyar Táncok A XVI. Századból"
1.1.2.1. 2.0.0.0. gtr,opt pno/
harp,cimbalom,strings [9'] EMB
rent                        (R51)

Magyar Táncok A XVI. Századból
see Hungarian Dances From The 16th
Century

RÁNO PO SEDMÉ see Krízek, Zdenek

RAPHAEL, GÜNTHER (1903-1960)
Concertino for Viola and Orchestra in
D
1.1.1.1. 1.1.1.0. perc,strings,vla
solo [9'] BREITKOPF-W       (R52)

RAPPROCHEMENT see Lutyens, Elisabeth

RAPSODI MINIATYR see Larsson, Hokan

RAPSODIA see Huzella, Elek, Rhapsody

RAPSODIA CONCERTANTE see Szekely, Endre

RAPSODIA ROMANTICA see Lídl, Václav

RAPSODIA (SECOND VERSION) see Durko,
Zsolt

RAPSODICKÁ FANTAZIE see Dlouhy, Jaromir

RAPSODICKÁ OUVERTURA see Dousa, Eduard

RAPSODICKÁ POLKA see Dlouhy, Jaromir

RAPSODISK OUVERTURE see Tarp, Svend
Erik, Rhapsodiesche Ouvertüre

RAQUEL see Gutchë, Gene

RASCH, KURT (1902-1986)
Sinfonietta, Op. 28
3.3.2.4. 4.3.3.1. timp,perc,strings
[22'] BREITKOPF-W           (R53)

RASKATOV, ALEXANDER (1953- )
Blissful Music
0.0.0.0. 2.0.0.0. perc,6vln,3vla,
3vcl,db,vcl&pno soli BELAIEFF
(R54)

Commentary On A Vision
0.0.3.3.tenor sax.baritone sax.
4.0.4.1. 4perc,pno,cel,org,harp,
12vla,12vcl,8db,perc solo [32']
BELAIEFF
(R55)

Concerto for Oboe and 15 Strings
[20'] SIKORSKI perf mat rent (R56)

Farewell From The Birds Of Passage
perc,8vln,2vla,2vcl,db,alto sax
solo [17'] BELAIEFF (R57)

Litania
1.1.1.1. 1.1.1.0. 2perc,pno,harp,
vln,vla,vcl,db [20'] BELAIEFF
(R58)

Miserere
0.2.0.0. 2.0.0.0. perc,strings,vla&
vln solo,vcl solo [40'] BELAIEFF (R59)

Primal Song
see Urlied

Sechs Psalmodien
harp,15strings,vla solo [17']
SIKORSKI perf mat rent (R60)

"66", Für Sopran Und 12 Instrumente
""66", For Soprano And 12
Instruments" 1.0.1.0. 0.1.1.0.
perc,pno,harp,vln,vcl,db,S solo
[12'] (sonnett by William
Shakespeare) BELAIEFF (R61)

Sentimental Sequences
1.1.1.1. 1.1.1.0. 2perc,cembalo,
vla,vcl,db [18'] BELAIEFF (R62)

Sentimentale Sequenzen
1.1.1.1. 1.1.1.0. 2perc,hpsd,vla,
vcl,db [14'] SIKORSKI perf mat
rent (R63)

"66", For Soprano And 12 Instruments
see "66", Für Sopran Und 12
Instrumente

Urlied
"Primal Song" 8vln,3vla,3vcl,db,vla
solo [17'] BELAIEFF (R64)

Xenia
2.0.2.0. 2.0.0.0. 2perc,pno,cel,
harp,8vln I,3vla,3vcl,db [25'] sc
BELAIEFF 04613 (R65)

RASMANDALA (THEME, VARIATIONS AND
FUGUE) see Hawkins, Malcolm,
Concerto for Piano and Orchestra

RATHBURN, ELDON (1916- )
Amtrak
see Six Railroad Preludes

Concerto For Steel Band And Symphony
Orchestra
see Steelhenge

Great Little Train Of Wales, A
see Six Railroad Preludes

In Memoriam - Jumbo
see Six Railroad Preludes

Six Railroad Preludes
3(pic).2.2.2. 4.3.3.1. timp&perc,
2perc,pno,harp,strings sc
CANADIAN MI 1100 R234SI f.s.
contains: Amtrak; Great Little
Train Of Wales, A; In Memoriam
- Jumbo; Spiral Tunnel Boogie;
Thoreau's Train; Tiddles Of
Paddington (R66)

Spiral Tunnel Boogie
see Six Railroad Preludes

Steelhenge
"Concerto For Steel Band And
Symphony Orchestra" orch, Steel
band: high tenor (ping pong),
double tenor, double seconds,
cellos (triple and double), bass,
and percussion [13'] pno red
CANADIAN MI 1441 R234ST (R67)

Thoreau's Train
see Six Railroad Preludes

Tiddles Of Paddington
see Six Railroad Preludes

RATHGEBER, VALENTIN (1682-1750)
Concerto in E flat, Op. 6, No. 15
2trp,2vln,vcl/db,org,cont sc
KUNZELMANN EKB 36P ipa (R68)

RATIBOR OP. 58 see Leistner-Mayer,
Roland

RAUM, ELIZABETH (1945- )
Legend Of Heimdall, The
2(pic).2.2.2. 3.3.3.0. timp,2perc,
strings,tuba solo [22'] (1.
Heimdall's Gjallarhorn 2. Tale Of
The Bard, The 3. Attack On
Asgard, The) sc,pno red,solo pt
CANADIAN MI 1334 R246LE (R69)

RÄUME see Willi, Herbert

RAUNA see Koch, Erland von

RAVEL, MAURICE (1875-1937)
Daphnis And Chloe (In Full Score)
orch sc DOVER 25826-2 (R70)

Four Orchestral Works
orch sc DOVER 25962-5 (R71)

Menuet Sur Le Nom d'Haydn
(Perna, Dana Paul) 2.1.2.2.
2.0.0.0. harp,strings [2'] BARDIC
(R72)

Pièce En Forme De Habanera *vocalise
1.1.2.1. 1.0.0.0. timp,tamb,
strings,high solo&med solo LEDUC
(R73)

Prelude
(Perna, Dana Paul) strings,harp
[2'] BARDIC (R74)

Tzigane
2.2.2.2. 2.1.0.0. perc,harp,cel,
strings,vln solo [7'] PETERS
(R75)

Vallee Des Cloches, La
(Grainger, Percy Aldridge) perc,pno
4-hands,harp,cel,strings,
dulcitone or pno II or harp II
[5'30"] BARDIC (R76)

Valse, La
orch sc DOVER 29591-5 (R77)

RAWSTHORNE, ALAN (1905-1971)
Concerto for Piano, Strings and
Percussion, No. 1
[20'] perf sc set OXFORD 3670283
sc,pts rent (R78)

Madame Chrysanthème: Ballet Music
3.1.0.2. 2.3.0.0. timp,2perc,harp,
strings,Mez solo [40'] perf sc
set OXFORD 3670011 sc,pts rent
(R79)

Overture: Hallé
2.2.2.2. 4.3.3.1. timp,2perc,
strings [8'] perf sc set OXFORD
366979X sc,pts rent (R80)

RAXACH, ENRIQUE (1932- )
Concertino for Piano and Orchestra
3.3.3.3. 4.3.3.1. 5perc,harp,
strings,pno solo [28'] sc DONEMUS
(R81)

Polifonías
string orch [17'] sc DONEMUS (R82)

RAYMONDA AKT I: ADAGIO see Glazunov,
Alexander Konstantinovich

RAYMONDA AKT I: GRAND VALSE see
Glazunov, Alexander Konstantinovich

RAYMONDA AKT I: VALSE FANTASTIQUE see
Glazunov, Alexander Konstantinovich

RAYMONDA AKT I: VALSE FANTASTIQUE
(S.O.) see Glazunov, Alexander
Konstantinovich

RAYMONDA AKT I: VARIATION III "BIS" see
Glazunov, Alexander Konstantinovich

RAYMONDA AKT II: DANSE GARCONS ARABES
see Glazunov, Alexander
Konstantinovich

RAYMONDA AKT II: GRAND PAS ESPAGNOL see
Glazunov, Alexander Konstantinovich

RAYMONDA AKT III: CODA see Glazunov,
Alexander Konstantinovich

RAYMONDA AKT III: DANSE DES ENFANTS see
Glazunov, Alexander Konstantinovich

RAYMONDA AKT III: ENTREE & PAS
CLAS.HON. see Glazunov, Alexander
Konstantinovich

RAYMONDA AKT III: GALOP see Glazunov,
Alexander Konstantinovich

RAYMONDA AKT III: PAS DE DIX see
Glazunov, Alexander Konstantinovich

RAYMONDA AKT III: VARIATION IV see
Glazunov, Alexander Konstantinovich

RAYMONDA: BALLETT-SUITE OP. 57A see
Glazunov, Alexander Konstantinovich

RAYMONDA: GARDEN PARTY see Glazunov,
Alexander Konstantinovich

RAYMONDA: GRAND PAS D'ACTION see
Glazunov, Alexander Konstantinovich

RAYMONDA: GRAND PAS HONGROIS see
Glazunov, Alexander Konstantinovich

RAYMONDA: GRANDE ADAGIO see Glazunov,
Alexander Konstantinovich

RAYMONDA: GRANDE PAS D'ACTION see
Glazunov, Alexander Konstantinovich

RAYMONDA: GRANDE VALSE see Glazunov,
Alexander Konstantinovich

RAYMONDA: PAS DE DEUX see Glazunov,
Alexander Konstantinovich

RAYMONDA: PAS DE DEUX NO. 2 see
Glazunov, Alexander Konstantinovich

RAYMONDA: PIZZICATO see Glazunov,
Alexander Konstantinovich

RAYMONDA: REPRISE DE LA VALSE see
Glazunov, Alexander Konstantinovich

RAYMONDA: TÄNZE see Glazunov, Alexander
Konstantinovich

RAYMONDA: VARIATION II see Glazunov,
Alexander Konstantinovich

RAYMONDA: VARIATION III: CODA see
Glazunov, Alexander Konstantinovich

RAYMONDA: VARIATION IV see Glazunov,
Alexander Konstantinovich

RÁZ-DVA-TRI-CTYRI see Petr, Zdenek

REA, JOHN (1944- )
Hommage À Vasarely
3(pic).3.3(bass clar).3. 2.3.3.0.
2perc,16vln I,12vln II,12vla,
10vcl,6db [13'] sc CANADIAN
MI 1100 R281HO (R83)

Time And Again
2.2.2.2. 2.2.0.0. 2perc,pno,6vln I,
6vln II,4vla,4vcl,2db [12'] sc
CANADIAN MI 1100 R281TI (R84)

Vanishing Points: A Tableau For
Orchestra
2.2.2.2. 2.2.0.0. perc,strings
[14'] sc CANADIAN MI 1200 R281VA
(R85)

READ, THOMAS LAWRENCE (1938- )
Bedtime Story For.... A
see Sunrise Fable

Sunrise Fable
"Bedtime Story For..., A" 3.2.2.2.
4.2.3.1. timp,2perc,8vln I,7vln
II,6vla,5vcl,4db [18'] sc PETERS
04186 (R86)

REAL TIME see Rolnick, Neil B.

REASER, RONALD
Bells, The
2.0.2+2clar in E flat.2. 2.2.2+bass
trom.0. 4timp,perc,strings,
narrator [13'] PEER rent (R87)

REBNE, RUNE (1961- )
Eeast
see Feast

Feast
"Eeast" 3(pic).2(English
horn).2.3(contrabsn). 4.3(trp in
C).3.1. timp,2perc,strings [9']
NORSKMI (R88)

REBSCHNITT see Cornell, Klaus

RECHT DES HERRN, DAS: SUITES 1 & 2 see
Bruns, Victor

RECITATIV OCH KORAL see Hambraeus,
Bengt

RECOLLECTION see Matsudaira, Yori-Aki

RECONNAISSANCE see Montgomery, James

RECONTRES see Sugár, M.

RECRUITING DANCE OF KOSSUTH see Lajtha,
Laszlo

RED see Torke, Michael

RED CAPE TANGO see Daugherty, Michael

RED RIVER VALLEY: THEME & VARIATIONS
see Amram, David Werner

REDMAN, REGINALD (1892- )
Nocturne
2.2.2.2. 4.2.3.1. timp,perc,cel,
harp,8vln I,7vln II,6vla,5vcl,4db
sc PETERS 04626 (R89)

Rhapsody On Somerset Folk Songs
2.1.2.1. 2.2.3.0. timp,perc,harp,
8vln I,7vln II,6vla,5vcl,4db,SATB
soli [8'] sc PETERS 04627 (R90)

REFLECTION see Chan, Ka Nin

REFLECTION II see Suzuki, Hideaki

REFLECTION III see Kunieda, Harue

REFLECTIONS see Eaton, Darryl see
Marti, Heinz

REFLECTIONS: 4 MOVEMENTS ON A THEME OF
WALLACE STEVENS see Paulus, Stephen
Harrison

REFLECTIONS OF THE NIGHT see Lavista,
Mario, Reflejos De La Noche

REFLECTIONS ON A LIFE see Gibbs, Alan

REFLECTIONS SYMPHONY NO. 2 see Husa,
Karel

REFLEJOS DE LA NOCHE see Lavista, Mario

REFLET D'UN TEMPS DISPARU see Chen,
Qigang

REFLETS DU PASSÉ see Klein, Lothar,
Canadina

REFLEXIONEN see Eichhorn, Frank Volker
see Röttger, Heinz

REFORMATION SYMPHONY see Mendelssohn-
Bartholdy, Felix, Symphony No. 5

REFRAINS see Mihalovici, Marcel

REGARDS ET JEUX DANS L'ESPACE see
Desjardins, Jacques

REGEN ÜBER PARIS see Trommer, Jack

REGER, MAX (1873-1916)
Variationen Und Fuge Über Ein Thema
Von J. Adam Hiller *Op.100
2.2.2.3. 4.2.3.1. timp,harp,strings
[48'] PETERS (R91)

Variationen Und Fuge Über Ein Thema
Von Mozart *Op.132
(Weil, B.) 3.2.2.2. 4.2.0.0. timp,
harp,strings [25'] study sc
BREITKOPF-W PB 5272 (R92)

REGER-VARIATIONEN, FÜR STREICHQUARTET
UND ORCHESTER see Rosenfeld,
Gerhard

REGINA COELI see Galuppi, Baldassare

REHNQVIST, KARIN (1957- )
Anrop; Inrop; Utrop
1(pic).1(English horn).1.1.sax.
1.1.1.0. perc,harp,string quin
STIM (R93)

Kast
strings [11'] sc REIMERS 101164
rent (R94)

Lamento
"Rytmen Av En Röst"
3(pic).3(English horn).4(bass
clar).3(contrabsn). 4.3.3.1.
timp,3perc,harp,strings [16'] sc
STIM ED.NR 101210 (R95)

Lamento-Rytmen Av En Röst
orch [14'] REIMERS 101210 rent
(R96)

Rytmen Av En Röst
see Lamento

Senhst - Senhst: Lek Med Vivaldi
15strings, in two groups [2'5"]
STIM (R97)

Skrin (composed with Ahlbäck, Sven)
vln,orch [32'] study sc REIMERS
101173 rent (R98)

Solsågen
"Sunsong" solo voice,2 speaking
voices,chamber orch [32'] sc
REIMERS 101226 rent (R99)

Sunsong
see Solsågen

Taromirs Tid
"Time Of Taromir" 13strings/
11strings&fl&clar sc REIMERS
101165 rent (R100)

REHNQVIST, KARIN (cont'd.)

Time Of Taromir
see Taromirs Tid

REHOR, BOHUSLAV (1938- )
Concerto for Clarinet and Orchestra
2.1.0.0. 3.3.2.0. timp,perc,vibra,
marimba,strings,clar solo [15']
CESKY HUD. (R101)

Concerto for English Horn and Strings
[19'] CESKY HUD. (R102)

Concerto for 2 Horns and Strings
[12'] CESKY HUD. (R103)

Concerto for Violin, Piano and
Orchestra
"Dvojkoncert Pro Housle, Klavir A
Orchestr" 2.2.2.2. 4.4.3.1. timp,
perc,strings,vln&pno soli [23']
CESKY HUD. (R104)

Concerto Grosso for Strings
[12'] CESKY HUD. (R105)

Dvojkoncert Pro Housle, Klavir A
Orchestr
see Concerto for Violin, Piano and
Orchestra

Komorní Vety Pro Klavír, Klarinet A
Smycce
strings,pno&clar soli [12'] CESKY
HUD. (R106)

Sinfonietta
0.0.2.0. 2.2.0.1. strings [11']
CESKY HUD. (R107)

Sinfonietta No. 2
2.0.2.0. 1.2.0.1. strings [11']
CESKY HUD. (R108)

Symphony No. 3
3.0.0.0. 3.0.0.0. strings [18']
CESKY HUD. (R109)

Symphony No. 4
2.2.3.2. 4.3.3.1. timp,perc,vibra,
strings,B solo [24'] CESKY HUD.
(R110)

REICH, STEVE (1936- )
Duet
string orch,2vln soli [5'] BOOSEY-
ENG rent (R111)

REICHA, ANTON (1770-1836)
Adagio in A (from Concerto For
Violoncello)
(Thuri, F. X.) 0.2.0.0. 1.0.0.0.
strings,vcl solo CESKY HUD. (R112)

Árie Z Opery Sapphó
2.2.2.2. 2.0.0.0. harp,strings,S
solo CESKY HUD. (R113)

Aure Amiche
(Ondráček, Stanislav) 0.2.0.0.
2.0.0.0. strings,S solo [7']
CESKY HUD. (R114)

Rozloucení Jany Z Arku S Vlastí
2.2.2.2. 2.0.0.0. timp,strings,
speaking voice CESKY HUD. (R115)

Scéna, For English Horn And Orchestra
1.2.2.2. 2.0.0.0. strings,English
horn solo [7'] CESKY HUD. (R116)

REICHA, JOSEPH (1746-1795)
Concerto Concertant In D *Op.3
(Päuler) 2vln solo,2ob,2horn,string
orch KUNZELMANN ipa sc 10012A,
oct 10012 (R117)

Concerto for 2 Horns and Orchestra,
Op. 5
(Morgan) 2horn solo,orch KUNZELMANN
ipa sc 10088A, oct 10088 (R118)

Concerto for Oboe and Orchestra in B
flat
(Adamus) ob solo,orch KUNZELMANN
ipa sc 10250A, oct 10250 (R119)

Concerto for Oboe and Orchestra in F
(Renner) ob solo,orch KUNZELMANN
ipa sc 10078A, oct 10078 (R120)

REICHARDT, JOHANN FRIEDRICH (1752-1814)
Concerto for Piano and Strings in D
vln I,vln II,vla,vcl,db,pno solo
MÖSELER sc 40.144-00, solo pt
40.144-01, pts 40.144-02 TO 03,
set 40.144-09 (R121)

Sinfonia in B flat for Winds and
Strings
0.2.0.0. 2.0.0.0. vln I,vln II,vla,
vcl,db MÖSELER sc 40.149-00, pts
40.149-01 TO 02, set 40.149-09
(R122)

REIMANN, ARIBERT (1936- )
Chacun Sa Chimère
2(pic)+alto fl+bass fl.0.1+clar in
E flat+bass clar+contrabass
clar.0. 0.0.0.0. 6vcl,6db,T solo
[30'] (text by Charles
Baudelaire) SCHOTTS perf mat rent
(R123)

Concerto for Violin and Violoncello
1+pic+alto fl.1+English horn+
Heckelphone.1+clar in E flat+bass
clar.2+contrabsn. 4.3.2.1. timp,
perc,2harp,6db,vln solo,vcl solo
[25'] SCHOTTS perf mat rent
(R124)

Denn Bleiben Ist Nirgends
"First Duennese Elegy" 1+pic+alto
fl.1+English horn.1+clar in E
flat+bass clar.1+contrabsn.
4.2.2.1. timp,perc,harp,12vln I,
10vln II,8vla,6vcl,5db,speaking
voice [20'] (text by Rainer Maria
Rilke) SCHOTTS perf mat rent
(R125)

Finite Infinity
1+pic+alto fl.1+English horn.1+clar
in E flat+bass clar.1+contrabsn.
0.3.3.0. pno,harp,10vln I,8vln
II,6vla,6vcl,4db,S solo [35']
(text by Emily Dickinson) study
sc SCHOTTS ED 8497 perf mat rent
(R126)

First Duennese Elegy
see Denn Bleiben Ist Nirgends

Fragments From "Lear"
3(3pic)+alto fl.2+English
horn.2(clar in E flat)+bass
clar.2+contrabsn. 6.4.3.1. timp,
perc,2harp,24vln,10vla,8vcl,6db,
Bar solo [42'] (text by William
Shakespeare) SCHOTTS perf mat
rent (R127)

Invenzioni
1(pic,alto fl).1(English
horn).1(bass clar).1. 1.1.1.0.
strings [17'] SCHOTTS perf mat
rent (R128)

Neun Stücke Für Orchester
1+pic+alto fl.1+English horn.1+clar
in E flat+bass clar.1+contrabsn.
4.3.2.1. timp,3perc,pno,harp,
12vln I,10vln II,8vla,6vcl,5db
[23'] study sc SCHOTTS ED 8444
perf mat rent (R129)

REINE DE CHYPRE, LA: OVERTURE see
Halévy, Jacques

REINE INDIGO, LA: OVERTURE see Strauss,
Johann, [Jr.]

REINECKE, CARL (1824-1910)
Almansor *Op.124
2.2.2.2. 2.0.0.0. timp,strings,Bar
solo [8'] (concert aria)
BREITKOPF-W (R130)

Hindumädchen, Das *Op.151
2.2.2.2. 2.2.0.0. timp,strings,A/
Mez solo [8'] (concert aria)
BREITKOPF-W (R131)

Mirjams Siegesgesang *Op.74
2.2.2.2. 2.2.3.0. timp,harp,
strings,S solo [4'] (concert
aria) BREITKOPF-W (R132)

Romance (from König Manfred Op. 93)
2.0.2.2. 0.0.0.0. timp,strings,vln
solo [4'] BREITKOPF-W (R133)

Romance for Violin and Orchestra in A
minor, Op. 155
2.2.2.2. 2.0.0.0. timp,strings,vln
solo [8'] BREITKOPF-W (R134)

Sinfonia in A, Op. 79
2.2.2.2. 4.2.3.0. timp,strings
[28'] BREITKOPF-W (R135)

Vierjährige Posten, Der *Op.45,
Overture
2(pic).2.2.2. 4.2.0.0. timp,3perc,
strings [7'] BREITKOPF-W (R136)

Zenobia *Op.193, Overture
2.2.2.2. 4.2.3.0. timp,strings [7']
BREITKOPF-W (R137)

Zur Jubelfeier *Op.166, Overture
2.2.2.2. 4.2.3.1. timp,strings
[12'] BREITKOPF-W (R138)

REINER, KAREL (1910-1979)
Introdukce A Allegro
2.2.2.2. 4.3.3.1. timp,perc,strings
[10'] CESKY HUD. (R139)

Tri Symfonické Vety
3.3.3.3. 4.3.3.1. timp,perc,xylo,
vibra,harp,strings [19'] CESKY
HUD. (R140)

REINHOLD, OTTO (1899-1965)
Jugendmusik
strings [10'] BREITKOPF-W (R141)

REINTHALER, KARL (1822-1896)
Symphony in D, Op. 12
3.2.2.2. 4.2.3.0. timp.strings
[32'] BREITKOPF-W (R142)

REIS, DE see Havclaar, Anton

REISE, JAY (1950- )
Concertino Rhythmikosmos
1.1.1.0. 0.0.0.0. 2perc,pno,strings
MERION rent (R143)

REISER, JOACHIM
Rock For String Ensemble
vln I,vln II,vla,vcl,opt db (for
modern strings, number of players
in each part variable) sc,pts
SCHOTTS ED 7928 %H V 217.98.A
perf mat rent (R144)

REJDOVACKA see Trojan, Václav

REKASIUS, ANTANAS (1928- )
Concerto for Saxophone, Percussion
and Chamber Orchestra
see Saules Rezginai

Saules Rezginai (Concerto for
Saxophone, Percussion and Chamber
Orchestra)
strings,harp,pno,vibra solo,clar&
alto sax&tenor sax solo [10']
SIKORSKI perf mat rent (R145)

REKHIN, IGOR
Concerto for Mandolin and String
Orchestra
VOGT VF 1173 (R146)

REKKELIJKEN EN DE PRECIESEN, DE see
Meijering, Chiel

RELEASE see Malmlöf-Forssling, Carin

RELIEF NO. 2 see Hekster, Walter

RELIÉFY see Bárta, Jiri

REM: IMAGES FORMING AND DISSOLVING see
Sexton, Brian

REMEMBER KOLOZSVAR see Cornell, Klaus

REMEMBRANCE see Carter, Elliott Cook,
Jr. see Matsudaira, Yori-Aki

REMINISCENCE FOR 17 MUSICIANS see
Ostergaard, Edvin

REMINISCENCE OF SPACES see Ichiyanagi,
Toshi, Concerto for Piano, No. 1

REMINISCENCES FÜR ORCHESTER see
Erdmann, Dietrich

REMONTÉE D'ADANAC O, LE SALMO-SALAR, LA
see Bregent, Michel-Georges

RENAISSANCE SUITE see Rollin, Robert
Leon

RENATA see Lídl, Václav

RENESANCNÍ KONCERT see Rak, Stepán

RENS, JEAN-MARIE
Image-Temps
1.1.0.0. 0.1.1.0. 2perc,3vln,3vla,
3vcl,2db [15'] BELGE (R147)

Oppositions Multiples
string orch [18'] BELGE (R148)

RENSAKU "JO-MON" see Toyama, Yuzo

REPENTANT THIEF, THE see Tavener, John

REQUIEM see Takeuchi, Kenji, Str. Orch
N3 - II

REQUIEM PER LA MORTE DI UN POVERO see
Goormans, Raf

REQUIEM RENGA see Kasemets, Udo

RES MUSICA see Pentland, Barbara

RES SEVERA VERUM GAUDIUM see Reuter,
Willi Albrecht, Prologos

RES SONORAE see Kondo, Jo

RESEAUX FOR HARP AND ORCHESTRA see
Miroglio, Francis

RESIGNATION (GEISTLICHES LIED OHNE
WORTE) see Fitzenhagen, Wilhelm

RESONANCES see Haller, Hermann

RESPIGHI, OTTORINO (1879-1936)
Ancient Airs And Dances, Suite I
see Antiche Danze Ed Arie, Suite I

Antiche Danza Ed Arie Per Liuto
orch RICORDI-IT PR 1334 (R149)

Antiche Danze Ed Arie, Suite I
"Ancient Airs And Dances, Suite I"
BROUDE BR. (R150)

Belkis, Regina Di Saba
see Vetrate Di Chiesa

Feste Romane
see Fontane Di Roma

Fontane Di Roma
orch RICORDI-IT PR 1333 contains
also: Pini Di Roma; Feste Romane
(R151)

Pini Di Roma
see Fontane Di Roma

Trittico Botticelliano
see Uccelli, Gli

Uccelli, Gli
orch sc RICORDI-IT PR 1342 contains
also: Trittico Botticelliano
(R152)

Vetrate Di Chiesa
orch sc RICORDI-IT PR 1343 contains
also: Belkis, Regina Di Saba
(R153)

REST ETERNAL see Barab, Seymour

RESURRECION DE DON QUIJOTE, LA see
Román, José García

RESURRECTION see Burrell, Diana

RETROSPEKTIV METAMORFOS see Hansen,
Krister, Till Minnet

RETURN OF DEATH WITH A SLAP IN THE
FACE, THE see Horwood, Michael

REUTER, FRITZ (1896-1963)
Concerto for Cembalo and String
Orchestra
strings,timp,cembalo solo [26']
BREITKOPF-W (R154)

Concerto for Violin and Orchestra
2.2.2.2. 2.2.2.0. timp,strings,vln
solo [35'] BREITKOPF-W (R155)

REUTER, WILLI ALBRECHT
Prologos
"Res Severa Verum Gaudium" 3.2.2.2.
4.3.3.1. timp,perc,8vln I,7vln
II,6vla,5vcl,4db [8'] sc PETERS
03195 (R156)

Res Severa Verum Gaudium
see Prologos

REUTTER, HERMANN (1900-1975)
Concert Variations
2(pic).2(English horn).2.1+
contrabsn. 4.2.3.0. timp,2perc,
strings,pno solo [22'] SCHOTTS
perf mat rent (R157)

Concerto for Piano, No. 2, Op. 36
2.2.2.2. 4.2.3.0. timp,perc,
strings,pno solo [25'] SCHOTTS
perf mat rent (R158)

Concerto for Violin, Op. 39
2.2.2.2. 2.2.2.0. timp,perc,cel,
2vln,2vcl,2db,vln solo [20']
SCHOTTS perf mat rent (R159)

Drei Monologe Des Empedokles
2(pic).2(English horn).2(alto
sax).2(contrabsn). 2.2.2.0. timp,
perc,cel,pno,harp,strings,Bar
solo [18'] (text by Friedrich
Hölderlin) SCHOTTS perf mat rent
(R160)

Epitaph Für Ophelia
1.2(English horn).1.1. 1.0.0.0.
4vln I,4vln II,3vla,2vcl,db,vln
solo [22'] SCHOTTS perf mat rent
(R161)

REUTTER, JOHANN GEORG VON (1708-1772)
Concerto No. 1 in D for Trumpet,
Strings and Continuo
8vln I,7vln II,6vla,5vcl,4db,trp,
cont [12'] sc,solo pt PETERS
01142 (R162)
(Wojciechowski) [12'] PETERS (R163)

Concerto No. 2 in D for Trumpet,
Strings and Continuo
8vln I,7vln II,6vla,5vcl,4db,trp,
cont [12'] sc,solo pt PETERS
01143 (R164)
(Wojciechowski) [12'] PETERS (R165)

REVEALED TIME see Yuasa, Joji

RÉVEILLEZ-VOUS, BELLE ENDORMIE see
Canteloube de Malaret, Marie-Joseph

REVELATION see Chan, Ka Nin

REVELATION FOR ORCHESTRA (VERSION II)
see Chan, Ka Nin

REVELATION FOR ORCHESTRA (VERSION III)
see Chan, Ka Nin

REVELATION FOR ORCHESTRA (VERSION IV)
see Chan, Ka Nin

REVELRY see Liebermann, Lowell

REVERDY, MICHELE (1943- )
Concerto for Orchestra [19']
2.2.3.2. 1.1.1.1. 3perc,pno,3vln,
2vla,2vcl,db
BILLAUDOT (R166)

RÊVERIE D'HIVER see Tchaikovsky, Piotr
Ilyich, Symphony No. 1, Op. 13

REVISOR, DER see Eötvös, Jószef

REVIVAL OF THE DEAD see Sheriff, Noam,
Mechaye Hametim

RÉVOLUTIONS see Roscé, Francois

REVOLUTIONSPLATZ, DER see Müller-
Wieland, Jan

REVONTULET see Murto, Matti

REVUELTAS, SILVESTRE (1899-1940)
Pieza Para Orquesta
1+pic.0.2.2. 2.0.0.0. strings [3']
PEER rent (R167)

REYNOLDS, ROGER (1934- )
Myths
see Sinfonia

Odyssey
1.1.1.1. 1.1.2.0. 3perc,pno,
electronic tape,vln,vcl,db [50']
sc PETERS 04517 (R168)

Sinfonia
"Myths" 4.4.4.4. 4.4.4.1. 4perc,
pno,harp,8vln I,7vln II,6vla,
5vcl,4db [25'] sc PETERS 04665
(R169)

Watershed III
1.1.2.0. 1.1.1.0. pno,2vln,vla,vcl,
db,perc solo [21'] sc PETERS
04609 (R170)

REZÁC, IVAN (1924-1977)
Concerto for Viola, Cembalo and
String Orchestra
cembalo,strings,vla solo [13']
CESKY HUD. (R171)

REZNICEK, PETR (1938- )
Musica Festiva
2.2.2.2. 2.2.0.0. timp,strings [9']
CESKY HUD. (R172)

Sonatina
1.0.2.2. 2.2.1.0. timp,strings
[14'] CESKY HUD. (R173)

Svátecni Divertimento
[12'] CESKY HUD. (R174)

RHAPSODIA CARPATHIANA see Farkas,
Ferenc

RHAPSODIE EN RÊVE see Bauer, Robert

RHAPSODIE FLORIDIENNE see Delius,
Frederick, Quadroone, La

RHAPSODIE POUR VIOLON ET ENSEMBLE see
Werkman, Arne, Rhapsody for Violin
and Chamber Group, Op. 21

RHAPSODIE ROMANTIQUE see Godzinsky,
George De

RHAPSODIE SYMPHONIQUE see Stojowski,
Sigismund

RHAPSODIESCHE OUVERTÜRE see Tarp, Svend
Erik

RHAPSODY FOR COR ANGLAIS OR E FLAT
SAXOPHONE AND STRING ORCHESTRA see
Jacob, Gordon

RHAPSODY ON SOMERSET FOLK SONGS see
Redman, Reginald

RHEIN NIXEN, DIE: OVERTURE see
Offenbach, Jacques

RHYTHMIC BIRDS OF THE ANTIPODES see
Koehne, Graeme

RIBARY, ANTAL (1924- )
Sinfonia No. 1
3(pic).2.2.2. 4.3.3.1. 4timp,perc,
harp,cel,strings [12'] EMB rent
(R175)

RICE, THOMAS N. (1933- )
Festival Overture
2.2.2.2. 4.2.2.0. timp,2perc,
strings SEESAW (R176)

Pastoral Overture
2.2.2.2. 4.2.2.0. timp,2perc,
strings SEESAW (R177)

Toccata Overture
2.2.2.2. 4.2.2.0. timp,2perc,
strings SEESAW (R178)

RICHARD III: MONOLOGUE see Walton,
[Sir] William (Turner)

RICHARD III: PRELUDE see Walton, [Sir]
William (Turner)

RICHARD III: SHAKESPEARE SCENARIO see
Walton, [Sir] William (Turner)

RICHMOND GREEN see Amos, Keith

RICHMOND PRELUDE see Amos, Keith

RICHTER, FRANZ XAVER (1709-1789)
Sinfonia in A
2vln,vla,vcl,db [15'] ARTARIA AE124
(R179)

Sinfonia in B flat
2horn,2vln,vla,vcl,db [15'] ARTARIA
AE107 (R180)

Sinfonia in B flat, MIN 1
2vln,vla,vcl,db [16'] ARTARIA AE111
(R181)

Sinfonia in B flat, MIN 2
2vln,vla,vcl,db [12'] ARTARIA AE121
(R182)

Sinfonia in B flat, MIN 3
2vln,vla,vcl,db [8'] ARTARIA AE123
(R183)

Sinfonia in C
2vln,vla,vcl,db [15'] ARTARIA AE122
(R184)
2vln,vla,vcl,db [18'] ARTARIA AE127
(R185)

Sinfonia in C minor
2vln,vla,vcl,db [12'] ARTARIA AE113
(R186)

Sinfonia in D
2ob,2horn,2vln,vla,vcl,db [9']
ARTARIA AE129 (R187)

Sinfonia in E minor
2vln,vla,vcl,db [14'] ARTARIA AE125
(R188)

Sinfonia in F
2vln,vla,vcl,db [11'] ARTARIA AE112
(R189)

Sinfonia in F, MIN 1
2vln,vla,vcl,db [11'] ARTARIA AE114
(R190)

Sinfonia in F, MIN 2
2vln,vla,vcl,db [20'] ARTARIA AE115
(R191)

Sinfonia in F minor
2ob,2horn,2vln,vla,vcl,db [20']
ARTARIA AE128 (R192)

Sinfonia in G minor
2vln,vla,vcl,db [12'] ARTARIA AE126
(R193)

RICKARD, SYLVIA (1937- )
Chippewa: Chant To (T)He Firefly
see Four Indian Songs

Four Indian Songs
2(pic).2(English horn).2.2.
3.2.0.0. timp,perc,harp,strings,S
solo sc,solo pt CANADIAN
MV 1400 R539FO f.s.
contains: Chippewa: Chant To
(T)He Firefly; Kwakiutl: Prayer
To The Young Cedar; Nootka Love
Song; Ojibway: Drums Of My
Father (R194)

Kwakiutl: Prayer To The Young Cedar
see Four Indian Songs

Nootka Love Song
see Four Indian Songs

Ojibway: Drums Of My Father
see Four Indian Songs

RICONOSCENZA PER BERNARD HERRMANN see
Perna, Dana Paul

RICONOSCENZA PER JEAN MARTINON see
Perna, Dana Paul

RICONOSCENZA PER LEONARD BERNSTEIN see
Perna, Dana Paul

RICONOSCI IN QUESTO AMPLESSO see
Mozart, Wolfgang Amadeus

RICORDANZA see Hambraeus, Bengt

RICORDANZE 1 see Sárközy, Istvan,
Concerto Grosso

RID I NATT see Eyser, Eberhard

RIDDERSTRÖM, BO (1937- )
Chamber Music For 12 No. 1 'Clouds'
see Kammarmusik För 12 Nr 1 'Moln'

Kammarmusik För 12 Nr 1 'Moln'
"Chamber Music For 12 No. 1
'Clouds'" 1.1.1.1. 1.0.1.0. perc,
strings STIM (R195)

"RIDE OF THE VALKYRIES" AND OTHER
HIGHLIGHTS FROM THE RING see
Wagner, Richard

RIDOUT, GODFREY (1918-1984)
Ah! Si Mon Moine Voulait Danser!
see Folksongs Of Eastern Canada

Ballade for Viola and String
Orchestra
[10'] sc,solo pt CANADIAN
MI1612 R547BA2 (R196)

Concerto Grosso No. 2 for Brass
Quintet and Orchestra
2(pic).2.2.2. 2.2.0.0. timp,perc,
strings [15'] sc CANADIAN (R197)

Festal Overture
3(pic).3(English horn).3(bass
clar).2(contrabsn). 4.3.3.1.
timp,2perc,harp,strings [7'] sc
CANADIAN MI 1100 R547FE (R198)

Folksongs Of Eastern Canada
[Eng/Fr] 2.2.2.2. 2.2.0.0. perc,
strings,high solo/med solo sc
CANADIAN MV 1273 R547FO f.s.
contains: Ah! Si Mon Moine
Voulait Danser!; I'll Give My
Love An Apple; J'ai Cueilli La
Belle Rose; She's Like The
Swallow (R199)

I'll Give My Love An Apple
see Folksongs Of Eastern Canada

In Memoriam Anne Frank
2.2.2.2. 4.2.3.1. timp,perc,
strings,solo voice [8'] sc,solo
pt CANADIAN MV 1400 R547IN (R200)

J'ai Cueilli La Belle Rose
see Folksongs Of Eastern Canada

Kids' Stuff
2(pic).2.2.2. 2.2.3.1. timp,perc,
strings [5'] sc CANADIAN
MI 1100 R547KI (R201)

No Mean City: Scenes From Childhood
4(pic).3(English
horn).2.3(contrabsn). 4.4.3.1.
timp,perc,org&cel,strings [18']
(1. Introduction And The Twelfth
Of July 2. The Twenty-Fourth Of
May 3. The Eleventh Of November)
sc CANADIAN MI 1100 R547NO (R202)

She's Like The Swallow
see Folksongs Of Eastern Canada

RIEDLBAUCH, VACLAV (1947- )
Fantasy for Orchestra
see Vize

Pokušení A Cin
3.3.5.5. 4.3.3.1. perc,strings
[31'] CESKY HUD. (R203)

Povídka
3.3.3.3. 4.3.3.1. timp,perc,xylo,
strings [12'] CESKY HUD. (R204)

Príhoda
3.2.8.2.4sax. 4.8+2flügelhorn.3.5+
euphonium. 5perc,4db, 8 more
clarinets [11'] CESKY HUD. (R205)

Vize (Fantasy for Orchestra)
3.3.3.3.sax. 4.3.3.1. perc,strings
[19'] CESKY HUD. (R206)

RIETI, VITTORIO (1898-1994)
Album For Helena
hpsd solo,2.2.2.2. 4.3.0.0. timp,
strings [15'] SCHIRM.EC rent
(R207)

Cinquina Da Camera
fl,ob,clar,bsn,kbd,strings [10']
SCHIRM.EC rent (R208)

Concertina Novella
pno solo,fl,ob,clar,bsn,trp,kbd,
strings [12'] SCHIRM.EC rent (R209)

Concertino Pro San Luca
fl,ob,clar,bsn,trp,kbd,strings
[15'] SCHIRM.EC rent (R210)

RIETI, VITTORIO (cont'd.)
Concerto for Harpsichord and
Orchestra
hpsd solo,3.2.2.2. 2.2.2.0. timp,
perc,strings [15'] SCHIRM.EC rent
(R211)

hpsd solo,fl,ob,bsn,2horn,timp,
perc,strings [15'] SCHIRM.EC rent
(R212)

Concerto for Piano and Orchestra, No.
2
pno solo,3.2.2.2. 2.3.2.0. timp,
perc,strings [17'] SCHIRM.EC rent
(R213)

Concerto for Piano and Orchestra, No.
3
pno solo,3.2.2.2. 4.3.2.1. timp,
perc,strings [18'] SCHIRM.EC rent
(R214)

pno solo,2.1.2.1. 4.3.2.1. timp,
perc,strings [18'] SCHIRM.EC rent
(R215)

Concerto for String Quartet and
Orchestra
3.2.2.2. 2.2.3.1. timp,perc,strings
[15'] SCHIRM.EC rent (R216)

Concerto for Violoncello and
Orchestra, No. 2
vcl solo,2.2.2.2. 4.2.3.1. timp,
perc,strings [15'] SCHIRM.EC rent
(R217)

Concerto Gianetto
vln solo,2.2.2.2. 4.3.3.0. timp,
perc,strings [17'] SCHIRM.EC rent
(R218)

Concerto Triplo For Violin, Viola And
Piano
vln solo,vla solo,pno solo,2.2.2.
2.2.2.0. timp,strings [20']
SCHIRM.EC rent (R219)

Congedo (Farewell)
1.1.2.1. 0.1.0.0. kbd,string quar
[4'] SCHIRM.EC rent (R220)

Corale, Variazioni E Finale
3.2.2.2. 4.3.3.0. timp,perc,strings
[17'] SCHIRM.EC rent (R221)

Dittico (Diptych) For Violin And
Orchestra
vln solo,2.2.2.2. 2.0.0.0. timp,
perc,strings [6'] SCHIRM.EC rent
(R222)

Dodicetto
1.1.1.1. 2.0.0.0. kbd,strings [14']
SCHIRM.EC rent (R223)

Enharmonic Variations
"Variazione Enharmoniche" pno solo,
1.1.1.2. 0.1.0.0. kbd,strings
[10'] SCHIRM.EC rent (R224)

Enigma Sinfonico
2.2.2.2. 2.2.0.0. kbd,strings [12']
SCHIRM.EC rent (R225)

Fontaine, La (5 Fables)
see Suite for Orchestra

Improviso Tripartito
strings [12'] SCHIRM.EC rent (R226)

Indiana Ballet Suite
2.2.2.2. 4.3.3.0. timp,strings
[15'] SCHIRM.EC rent (R227)

Kaleidoscope, Ballet For Small
Orchestra
1.1.2.1. 2.1.1.0. perc,kbd,strings
[20'] SCHIRM.EC rent (R228)

Marchant Suite
1.1.1.1. 0.0.0.0. kbd,strings [13']
SCHIRM.EC rent (R229)

Pastoral Dream
3.2.2.2. 4.3.3.0. timp,perc,harp
[20'] SCHIRM.EC rent (R230)

Scenes Seen. Ballet Suite
3.2.2.2. 4.3.3.1. timp,perc,harp,
strings [20'] SCHIRM.EC rent
(R231)

Second Avenue Waltzes
1.1.1.1. 0.1.0.0. kbd,strings [15']
SCHIRM.EC rent (R232)

Sette Liriche Saffiche
"Seven Sapphic Lyrics" 2.0.2.1.
2.1.0.0. harp,kbd,strings,med
solo [8'] SCHIRM.EC rent (R233)

Seven Sapphic Lyrics
see Sette Liriche Saffiche

Sinfonia Breve
see Symphony No. 8

Sinfonietta
1.1.1.2. 2.2.2.0. timp,2perc,
strings [15'] SCHIRM.EC rent
(R234)

RIETI, VITTORIO (cont'd.)

Suite for Orchestra
"Fontaine, La (5 Fables)" 2.1.2.1.
2.2.2.0. timp,perc,harp,strings
[21'] SCHIRM.EC rent            (R235)

Symphony No. 2
3.3.3.3. 4.3.3.1. timp,2perc,
strings [17'] SCHIRM.EC rent   (R236)

Symphony No. 6
3.2.2.2. 4.2.3.1. timp,perc,strings
[25'] SCHIRM.EC rent           (R237)

Symphony No. 7
3.2.2.2. 4.3.3.1. timp,perc,strings
[18'] SCHIRM.EC rent           (R238)

Symphony No. 8
"Sinfonia Breve" 3.2.2.2. 4.3.3.0.
timp,perc,strings [10'] SCHIRM.EC
rent                           (R239)

Symphony No. 9
2.2.2.2. 4.2.3.0. timp,perc,strings
[14'] SCHIRM.EC rent           (R240)

Symphony No. 10
2.2.2.2. 4.3.3.0. timp,perc,harp,
strings [10'] SCHIRM.EC rent   (R241)

Symphony No. 11
2.2.2.2. 4.3.3.0. timp,2perc,harp,
strings [12'] SCHIRM.EC rent   (R242)

Tre Contrasti Sinfonici
2.2.2.2. 2.2.0.0. kbd,strings [8']
SCHIRM.EC rent                 (R243)

Tre Improvisi
1.1.1.1. 0.0.0.0. kbd,strings [9']
SCHIRM.EC rent                 (R244)

Variazione Enharmoniche
see Enharmonic Variations

Verdiana
1.1.1.1. 1.0.0.0. kbd,strings [20']
SCHIRM.EC rent                 (R245)

RIGI: IN MEMORIA A FRIEND see Douglas,
Paul M.

RIMÓN, JAN (1921-    )
Doubravka (Serenade)
2.2.2.2. 4.2.3.0. perc,harp,strings
[5'] CESKY HUD.                (R246)

Hra Svetla A Stínu
2.0.3.0. 3.3.3.0. perc,harp,gtr,
strings [4'] CESKY HUD.        (R247)

Humoreska
2.2.2.2. 4.2.3.1. perc,harp,strings
[5'] CESKY HUD.                (R248)

Intermezzo Scherzoso
2.2.2.2. 4.2.3.1. timp,perc,harp,
strings [4'] CESKY HUD.        (R249)

Kvetinové Scherzo
2.1.3.0. 3.3.3.0. harp,strings [4']
CESKY HUD.                     (R250)

Letní Vítr *Waltz
2.2.2.2. 4.3.3.1. perc,strings [5']
CESKY HUD.                     (R251)

Lyricky Pochod
2.2.2.2. 4.2.3.0. timp,perc,strings
[4'] CESKY HUD.                (R252)

Malování Pro Smycce
2.0.2.2. 4.0.0.0. perc,harp,strings
[5'] CESKY HUD.                (R253)

Pod Pyrenejemi
2.2.2.2. 4.2.3.0. perc,harp,strings
[4'] (paso doble) CESKY HUD.   (R254)

Serenade
see Doubravka

Tam, Kde Bydlíte
2.0.3.0. 1.3.3.0. perc,harp,3gtr,
strings,solo voice [4'] CESKY
HUD.                           (R255)

Vinohradsky Valcík
2.1.2.2. 4.2.3.0. perc,harp,strings
[4'] CESKY HUD.                (R256)

RIMSKY-KORSAKOV, NIKOLAI (1844-1908)
Allmächt'ger Zar
see Welikij Zar

Allmächtig Ist Natur
see Polna, Polna Tschudesj

Bataille De Kershenez (from Die
Legende Von Der Unsichtbaren
Stadt Kitesch)
3.2.3.2. 4.3.3.1. timp,perc,strings
[15'] PETERS                   (R257)

RIMSKY-KORSAKOV, NIKOLAI (cont'd.)

Legende Von Der Unsichtbaren Stadt
Kitesch, Die: Suite
3.3.3.3. 4.3.3.1. timp,perc,2harp,
cel,strings,opt balalaika [22']
study sc PETERS BEL 527        (R258)

Lied Vom Gefeiten Oleg
3.2.2.2. 4.2.3.1. timp,3perc,8vln
I,7vln II,6vla,5vcl,4db [5'] sc
BELAIEFF 01750                 (R259)

Mozart Und Salieri: Intermezzo Und
Fughue
1.1.1.1. 2.0.0.0. pno,8vln I,7vln
II,6vla,5vcl,4db [5'] BELAIEFF
01762                          (R260)

Polna, Polna Tschudesj (from
Schneeflöckchen)
"Allmächtig Ist Natur" 2.2.0.2.
0.0.0.0. strings,T solo,vcl solo
[3'] (kavatine des Zaren
Berendai) BREITKOPF-W          (R261)

Sadko: Lied Des Venezianischen
Kaufmanns
0.0.2.2. 0.1.0.0. timp,8vln I,7vln
II,6vla,5vcl,4db [5'] sc BELAIEFF
01770                          (R262)

Sadko: Lied Des Warägers
0.0.0.0. 4.3.3.1. timp,8vln I,7vln
II,6vla,5vcl,4db [5'] sc BELAIEFF
01771                          (R263)

Scheherazade
orch sc DOVER 24734-1          (R264)

Sonnwendnacht: Arie Der Oxana
3.2.3.2. 4.0.3.0. 8vln I,7vln II,
6vla,5vcl,4db [4'] sc BELAIEFF
01780                          (R265)

Sonnwendnacht: Tableaux VI-VII
3.2.3.2. 4.3.3.1. timp,5perc,harp,
8vln I,7vln II,6vla,5vcl,4db
[10'] sc BELAIEFF 01784        (R266)

Sonnwendnacht: Tableaux VIII
3.2.3.2. 0.0.0.0. timp,4perc,harp,
8vln I,7vln II,6vla,5vcl,4db
[10'] sc BELAIEFF 01785        (R267)

Terzett Op. 52 Bis
2.2.2.2. 0.0.0.0. 8vln I,7vln II,
6vla,5vcl,4db [4'] sc PETERS
01787                          (R268)

Welikij Zar (from Schneeflöckchen)
"Allmächt'ger Zar" 2+pic.2.2.2.
4.2.3.1. timp,2perc,harp,strings,
S solo [5'] (arioso of Snowflake)
BREITKOPF-W                    (R269)

Zarenbraut: Arie Der Ljuba
1.2.2.2. 4.0.0.0. 8vln I,7vln II,
6vla,5vcl,4db [3'] sc BELAIEFF
01792                          (R270)

RING see Boesmans, Philippe

RING OF FIRE see Larsen, Elizabeth B.
(Libby)

RINGING see Valkare, Gunnar

RIO CHICO
(Turba, Herbert) 2.1.2.1. 2.2.3.0.
timp,perc,pno,gtr,harp,4vln I,3vln
II,2vla,vcl,db [4'] (tango) SCHOTTS
perf mat rent                  (R271)

RISE see Wilson, Ian R.

RISING OF JOB, THE see Dodgson, Stephen

RITA JOE see Baker, Michael Conway

RITE NOW see Lindroth, Peter

RITE OF SPRING see Stravinsky, Igor

RITER: BALLET AND CONCERT SUITE see
Lidholm, Ingvar

RITORNELLI POI RITORNELLI see
Skrowaczewski, Stanislaw, Chamber
Concerto

RITORNELLO see Lidholm, Ingvar

RITORNO, IL see Tamas, Janos

RITUAL DANCE see Saygun, Ahmed Adnan,
Ayin Raksi

RITUAL FRAGMENT see Birtwistle,
Harrison

RITUEL DEC L'ESPACE see Morel, Francois
d'Assise

RIVER IN SUMMER, THE see Genge, Anthony

RIVER OF FOREST AND STARS, THE see
Suzuki, Yukikazu

RIVER OF LIFE, THE see Smirnov, Dmitri

RIVERRUN... see Koehne, Graeme

ROALD DAHL'S SNOW WHITE AND THE SEVEN
DWARFS see Alberga, Eleanor

ROANOKE RISING see Walker, Gwyneth

ROB-ROY: OVERTURE see Berlioz, Hector
(Louis)

ROBERT DER TEUFEL: ROBERT, ROBERT, MEIN
GELIEBTER see Meyerbeer, Giacomo

ROBERT LE DIABLE: BALLETMUSIC see
Meyerbeer, Giacomo

ROBERT LE DIABLE: OVERTURE AND
BACCHANALE see Meyerbeer, Giacomo

ROBERTSSON, KARL-OLOF (1918-    )
Bara Tusen Korta År
2.2.2.2. 2.2.2.0. timp,perc,strings
(orchestral suite from
Skådespelsmusiken) STIM        (R272)

ROBERTSSON, STIG (1940-    )
Variationer Över En Polska Fr
Medelpad
2.2(English horn).2(bass clar).2.
2.2.1.0. timp,strings sc,pts STIM
                               (R273)

ROBINSON CRUSOÉ: NO. 12 see Offenbach,
Jacques

ROCCA, LODOVICO (1895-1986)
Chiaroscuri  *Suite
3.3.3.2. 4.3.3.1. 3timp,perc,cel,
bells,harp,strings [17'] (A. On
danse au soleil B. À l'heure du
crépuscule C. Sabbat des
sorcières D. Calme lunaire) LEDUC
                               (R274)

Dittico  *Eng/Fr/Ger/It
4.4.4.4. 4.4.4.2. timp,3perc,harp,
strings [8'45"] LEDUC          (R275)

ROCHBERG, A. GEORGE (1918-    )
Concerto for Clarinet and Orchestra
3(pic).3(English
horn).0.3(contrabsn). 4.3.3.1.
timp,perc,cel,harp,strings [26']
PRESSER rent                   (R276)

ROCK FOR STRING ENSEMBLE see Reiser,
Joachim

RODELINDA: OVERTURE see Handel, George
Frideric

RODRIGO, DER: FÜNF ARIEN see Handel,
George Frideric

RODRIGO, JOAQUÍN (1902-    )
Cantico De La Esposa
1.1+English horn.0.1. 1.0.0.0.
3perc,strings,S solo [4'] (text
by San Juan De La Cruz) sc
SCHOTTS ED 8355 perf mat rent
                               (R277)

Concierto Andaluz
2(pic).2.2.2. 4.2.0.0. strings,4gtr
soli [25'] study sc SCHOTTS 8026
perf mat rent                  (R278)

Concierto Pastoral
0.1(English horn).1.0. 1.1.0.0.
strings,fl solo [25'] SCHOTTS
perf mat rent                  (R279)

Espera, La (from Villancicos Y
Canciones De Navidad)
fl,English horn,harp,strings,S solo
[3'] (text by Victoria Kamhi) sc
SCHOTTS ED 8351 perf mat rent
                               (R280)

Fantasia Para Un Gentilhombre
(Galway, James) 0.1.1.1. 1.1.0.0.
strings,fl solo [22'] SCHOTTS
perf mat rent                  (R281)

Piezas Infantiles, 5
3(pic).3(English horn).3(bass
clar).2. 4.3.3.1. timp,perc,cel,
harp,strings [12'] sc SCHOTTS
ED 8356 perf mat rent          (R282)

Preludio Para Un Poema A La Alhambra
2+pic.2+English horn.2.2. 4.3.3.1.
timp,perc,harp,strings [8'] sc
SCHOTTS ED 8365 perf mat rent
                               (R283)

Serranilla
1.1.1.1. 2.1.0.0. 2vln,vla,vcl,S
solo [3'] (text by Marqués De
Santillana) sc SCHOTTS ED 8355
perf mat rent                  (R284)

**RODRIGO, JOAQUÍN (cont'd.)**

Villancicos Y Canciones De Navidad
2(pic).1+English horn.0.0. 2.0.0.0.
timp,harp,strings,S solo [15']
SCHOTTS perf mat rent            (R285)

**ROGERS, BERNARD (1893-1968)**
Three Dance Scenes
2(pic).2.2.2+contrabsn. 4.2.3.1.
timp,perc,pno,harp,strings [14']
PEER rent                        (R286)

**ROGET, HENRIETTE PUIG (1910-1992)**
Montanyas Del Rosello
3.2.2.2. 4.2.3.0. 3timp,perc,glock,
strings [7'30'] LEDUC            (R287)

**ROHWER, JENS (1914-    )**
Kosmos
orch (orchestral version of the
choral work "Das Wort Heraklits")
MÖSELER                          (R288)

ROI CAROTTE: OVERTURE see Offenbach,
Jacques

ROI DE LAHORE, LE: 4 MORCEAUX see
Massenet, Jules

ROI D'YVETOT, LE: OVERTURE see Adam,
Adolphe-Charles

ROI S'AMUSE, LE: PASSEPIED (EXTRAIT NO.
6) see Delibes, Léo

ROKOKOVÁ SERENÁDA see Jonák, Zdenek

**ROLAND, CLAUDE ROBERT (1935-    )**
Indicatif 1  *Op.14
6vln,3vla,2vcl,db [8'] BELGE (R289)
7vln,2vla,2vcl,db [8'] BELGE (R290)

**ROLAND-MANUEL, ALEXIS (1891-1966)**
Tournoi Singulier, Le (Ballet En 1
Acte): Moria Blues
2.2.2.2. 2.2.1.0. timp,perc,harp,
pno,strings [7'] LEDUC        (R291)

**ROLIN, ÉTIENNE**
Sortilèges
string orch pts FUZEAU 1096 (R292)

**ROLLA, ALESSANDRO (1757-1841)**
Concerto for Basset Horn in F
basset horn solo,orch KUNZELMANN
ipr sc 10262A, oct 10262     (R293)

**ROLLIN, ROBERT LEON (1947-    )**
Concerto for Violin
2.2.2.2. 2.2.2.0. harp,2perc,
strings,vln solo SEESAW      (R294)

Renaissance Suite
2.2.2.2. 4.3.3.1. timp,3perc,harp,
strings SEESAW              (R295)

Seven Sound Images On Seven Stanzas
By A Child
2.2.2.2. 2.2.2.0. timp,2perc,kbd,
strings [9'] SCHIRM.EC rent
                             (R296)

**ROLNICK, NEIL B. (1947-    )**
Drones And Dances
2.2.2.2. 2.2.2.0. 2perc,
synthesizer,strings [15']
SCHIRM.EC rent              (R297)

Real Time
1.1.2.1. 1.1.1.0. perc,synthesizer,
strings [14'] SCHIRM.EC rent
                             (R298)

ROMA see Massenet, Jules

**ROMAN, JOHAN HELMICH (1694-1758)**
Concerto for Flute and Orchestra
fl,orch sc REIMERS 107024 rent
                             (R299)

Golovin Music, The
see Golovinmusiken

Golovinmusiken
(Bengtsson; Frydén) "Golovin Music,
The" strings,cont [50'] sc
REIMERS 107023 rent          (R300)

Golvin-musiken BeRI 1
"Musique Satt Till En Festin..."
string orch [49'5"] REIMERS
                             (R301)

Musique Satt Till En Festin...
see Golvin-musiken BeRI 1

Sinfonie 1-3
(Bengtsson, Ingmar) orch sc,min sc,
pts REIMERS f.s.
contains: Symphony No. 1;
Symphony No. 2; Symphony No. 3
                             (R302)

Symphony No. 1
see Sinfonie 1-3

Symphony No. 2
see Sinfonie 1-3

**ROMAN, JOHAN HELMICH (cont'd.)**

Symphony No. 3
see Sinfonie 1-3

**ROMÁN, JOSÉ GARCÍA**
Paseo De Los Tristes
EMEC 576-00759               (R303)
2.2.2.2. 2.2.0.0. timp,gtr,strings
[12'] perf sc EMEC f.s.      (R304)

Resurrecion De Don Quijote, La
string orch [20'] perf sc EMEC f.s.
                             (R305)

ROMAN CARNIVAL AND OTHER OVERTURES see
Berlioz, Hector (Louis)

ROMANCE A RONDO see Strniště, Jiri

ROMANCE DE LE CHATELIER see Hidalgo,
Manuel

ROMANCE DU VIN, LA see Hetu, Jacques

ROMANCE LETNÍHO DNE see Felix, Václav

ROMANCE O KARLU IV see Marík, A.F.

ROMANCE OF HSIAO AND CH'IN see Chen, Yi

ROMANCES AND INTERLUDES see Picker,
Tobias

ROMANS see Larsson, Folke

ROMANTIC READING: 2ND VERSION see
Vidovszky, Laszlo

ROMANTIC RHAPSODY, A see Mozetich,
Marjan

ROMANTICKÁ SUITA see Kratochvíl,
Jaromír

ROMANTIKUS OLVASMÁNY II: VÁLTOZAT see
Vidovszky, Laszlo, Romantic
Reading: 2nd Version

ROMANTISCHE BOTSCHAFTEN see Schut,
Vladislav

ROMANTISCHE SUITE see Koch, Friedrich
E.

ROMANTISCHE VARIATIONEN, FOR ORCHESTRA
see Petrov, Andrei P.

ROMANY VARIATIONS see Healey, Derek

ROMANZA see Matthews, David

ROMANZA ON THE NOTES OF THE FOURTH
PSALM see Goehr, Alexander

ROMANZE NACH EINEM GEDICHT VON
ALEXANDER PUSCHKIN see
Shostakovich, Dmitri

**ROMBERG, B.**
Concerto for Flute and Orchestra in B
minor, Op. 30
(Förster) fl solo,orch KUNZELMANN
10134 ipr                    (R306)

**ROMBERG, BERNHARD HEINRICH (1767-1841)**
Concertino for 2 Violoncelli and
Orchestra in A, Op. 72
1.0.2.2. 2.0.0.0. timp,strings,2vcl
soli [13'] (no score) BREITKOPF-W
                             (R307)

Concerto for Violoncello and
Orchestra in B minor
(Klengel, J.) 2.2.2.2. 2.2.0.0.
timp,strings,vcl solo [13'] (no
score) BREITKOPF-W           (R308)

ROMEO AND JULIET: JULIET'S ARIA see
Sutermeister, Heinrich

ROMEO AND JULIET OVERTURE AND CAPRICCIO
ITALIEN see Tchaikovsky, Piotr
Ilyich

ROMEO UND JULIA: OVERTURE see Bellini,
Vincenzo

**ROMERO, ALDEMARO**
Suite for Strings
string orch TONOS M-2015-3939-3
rent                         (R309)

**ROMERO, MANLY**
Concertino for Violin and Orchestra
set STILL MC001-CVO-S rent   (R310)

Legend Of Chung 'Ah, The
orch STILL MC001-LC1-S perf mat
rent                         (R311)

RONDE DES CAUSSES see Dijk, Jan van

RONDEL see Lutyens, Elisabeth

RONDINE see Dijk, Jan van

RONDO see Horwood, Michael

RONDO GIOCOSO see Koch, Erland von

RONDO NEUROICA see Nelson, Daniel

**RONELLI, BOB**
Prominadenflirt
"Sketch" 2.1.2.1. 2.3.3.0. perc,
gtr,harp,strings [2'50"] sc,set
BUSCH rent                   (R312)

Sketch
see Prominadenflirt

**RØNNES, ROBERT (1959-    )**
Concerto Da Requiem Pour Cor En Fa Et
Orchestre
2(pic).2(English horn).2(bass
clar).2(contrabsn). 4.3.3.1.
timp,2perc,harp,strings,horn solo
[43'] NORSKMI                (R313)

**RÖNTGEN, JULIUS (1855-1932)**
Liedchen Von Der See, Ein  *Op.45
2+pic.2.2.2+contrabsn. 4.3.3.1.
timp,4perc,harp,strings [10']
BREITKOPF-W                  (R314)

ROO see Svensson, Matthias

**ROOSENDAEL, JAN ROKUS VAN (1960-    )**
Heterophony
1.1.1.0. 1.1.1.0. 3perc,harp,cym,
pno,strings [15'] sc DONEMUS
                             (R315)

RÖRELSER I RUMMET see Bucht, Gunnar

**ROREM, NED (1923-    )**
Concerto for English Horn and
Orchestra
2(pic).2.2.2. 2.2.0.0. timp,4perc,
harp,pno&cel,strings,English horn
solo [24'] BOOSEY-ENG rent   (R316)

Concerto for Organ
2horn,trp,trom,timp,strings,org
solo [30'] BOOSEY-ENG rent   (R317)

Concerto for Piano Left-Hand and
Orchestra, No. 4
2(pic).2.2.2. 2.2.2.0. timp,3perc,
cel,harp,strings,pno left-hand
solo [25'] BOOSEY-ENG rent   (R318)

Concerto for Piano, No. 3
2+pic.3(English horn).3(clar in E
flat,alto sax).2+contrabsn.
4.3.3.1. timp,6-7perc,harp,cel,
strings,pno solo [23'] BOOSEY-ENG
rent                         (R319)

Concerto for Violin
1(pic).1.2.1. 0.1.0.0. timp,
strings,vln solo [22'] BOOSEY-ENG
rent                         (R320)

Fantasy
see Fantasy And Polka

Fantasy And Polka
BOOSEY-ENG f.s.
contains: Fantasy (2+pic.2+
English horn.3.2. 4.3.0.0.
strings) [5']; Polka (2+pic.2+
English horn.3.2. 4.3.3.1.
timp,perc,pno,strings) [3']
                             (R321)

Polka
see Fantasy And Polka

Quaker Reader, A  *Suite
2(pic).2(English horn).2.2.
2.1.1.0. strings [20'] BOOSEY-ENG
rent                         (R322)

Schuyler Songs, The
2(pic).2.2.2. 1.1.0.0. pno,strings,
solo voice [25'] (8 poems, text
by James Schuyler) BOOSEY-ENG
rent                         (R323)

Swords And Plowshares
3(pic).3(English horn).3.2.
4.3.3.1. timp,4perc,harp,pno&cel,
strings,SATB soli [48'] (text by
Rimbaud, Byron, Auden, Yeats,
MacLeish, Robinson, Dickinson,
Whitman, Leverton, and from Psalm
133) BOOSEY-ENG rent         (R324)

Triptych
2.2.2.2. 2.2.0.0. timp,strings
[10'] BOOSEY-ENG rent        (R325)

ROSA: OVERTURE see Andriessen, Louis

ROSATI, LES see Massenet, Jules

ROSE, DIE see Schubert, Franz (Peter)

ROSE LAKE, THE see Tippett, [Sir]
Michael

ROSE LATULIPPE: SUITE see Freedman, Harry

ROSEAUX AU VENT, LES see Whettam, Graham Dudley

ROSEBUD SUITE see Petitgirard, Alain

ROSEBUD (THE LAST FOREST) see Wagemans, Peter-Jan

ROSEINGRAVE
Orchestration Of Alec Rowley's "Pavan"
(Owens, David) 1.1.1.2. 2.0.0.0. strings [6'] (an organ piece arranged for chamber orchestra) ANDREA                    (R326)

ROSEN, ROBERT (1956- )
Concerto for Piano and Orchestra see From Silence

From Silence (Concerto for Piano and Orchestra)
2(pic).2.2.2. 2.2.3.0. timp,perc, strings,opt Mez solo,pno solo [25'] sc CANADIAN MI 1361 R813FR                    (R327)
Meditation No. 2
2.2.2.2. 2.0.0.0. perc,4vln I,4vln II,4vla,3vcl,2db [20'] sc CANADIAN MI 1200 R813ME2    (R328)
Sacre De Hephaestus, Le *Variations
2.2.2.2. 4.2.3.1. 2perc,strings [11'] sc CANADIAN MI 1100 R813SAC                    (R329)

ROSEN AUS DEM SÜDEN see Strauss, Johann, [Jr.]

ROSENFELD, GERHARD (1931- )
Architektonischer Entwurf
3.2.2.2. 3.3.3.0. timp,3perc,harp, 8vln I,7vln II,6vla,5vcl,4db [18'] sc PETERS 04408                    (R330)
Concerto for Flute, Percussion and Strings
3perc,17strings,fl solo [16'] sc, solo pt PETERS 03205    (R331)
Concerto for Organ and Orchestra
0.1.0.0. 3.3.3.0. timp,perc,8vln I, 7vln II,6vla,5vcl,4db [17'] sc, solo pt PETERS 03209    (R332)
Kleist-Briefe, Für Bariton Und Orchester
1.1.1.0. 3.3.3.1. timp,harp,8vln I, 6vla,5vcl,4db [15'] sc PETERS 03208                    (R333)
Reger-Variationen, Für Streichquartett Und Orchester
1.1.1.1. 1.3.3.1. timp,8vln I,7vln II,6vla,5vcl,4db,string quar soli [18'] sc PETERS 03206    (R334)

ROSENMAN, LEONARD (1924- )
Concerto No. 2 for Violin
2+pic.2+English horn.2+bass clar.2+ contrabsn. 4.3.3.1. timp,perc, pno&cel,harp,strings,SSAA soli, vln solo [28'] PEER rent    (R335)
Lorca Revisited: Prelude And Four Scenes
1(pic,alto fl).1(English horn).1(bass clar). 0.1.0.0. 2perc,harp,pno&cel,vln,vcl,db,S solo [21'] (text by F. Garcia Lorca) PEER rent    (R336)
Time Travel: Hugo Wolf To "Song At Sunset"
2+pic.2+English horn.2+bass clar.2+ contrabsn. 4.3.3.1. timp,perc, pno/cel,harp,strings,S solo [20'] PEER rent    (R337)

ROSES D'ISPAHAN, LES see Faure, Gabriel-Urbain

ROSETTI
Concerto for Clarinet and Orchestra in E flat
clar solo,orch KUNZELMANN ipa sc 10045A, oct 10045    (R338)
Concerto for Horn and Orchestra in E flat
(Päuler) horn solo,orch KUNZELMANN 10128 ipr    (R339)
Concerto No. 2 for Flute and Orchestra in F
fl solo/ob solo,orch KUNZELMANN ipa sc 10196A, oct 10196    (R340)
Sinfonia in G minor
fl,2ob,2horn,bsn,string orch sc KUNZELMANN EKB 30P ipa    (R341)

ROSETTI, FRANCESCO ANTONIO (1746-1792)
Sinfonia in F
(Burmeister) 1.2.0.1. 2.0.0.0. strings [20'] PETERS    (R342)
Sinfonia in G minor
1.2.0.1. 2.0.0.0. strings [20'] BREITKOPF-W    (R343)
Sinfonia Pastoralis
2.2.0.1. 2.0.0.0. strings [15'] BREITKOPF-W    (R344)

ROSEVINDUET: MUSIKK FOR 12 INSTRUMENTER OG RESITATØR see Kleiberg, Ståle

ROSIÈRE DU VILLAGE, LA see Tomasi, Henri

ROSLAVETZ, NICOLAS (1881-1944)
In Den Stunden Des Neumonds see V Casy Novolunija
V Casy Novolunija
"In Den Stunden Des Neumonds" 2+ pic.2+English horn.2+bass clar.2. 4.3.3.1. timp,perc,cel,harp, strings [15'] study sc SCHOTTS ED 8107 perf mat rent    (R345)

RÖSLER, P. GREGOR (1714-1775)
Sinfonia No. 3 in D
string orch COPPENRATH sc 16.043-01, pts 16.043-21 TO 28    (R346)

ROSSÉ, FRANCOIS (1945- )
F To Be
1.1.1.1. 0.1.0.0. 2perc,harp,vln I, vln II,vla,vcl,db,horn solo FUZEAU    (R347)
Force De Gris
2.2.2.2. 2.0+2trp in C.2.0. 2perc, 8vln I,6vln II,5vla,4vcl,2db [12'] pts FUZEAU 0960    (R348)
Ivy
2.2.2.2. 2.2.2.0. perc,6-8vln I,6-8vln II,4-6vla,4vcl,2db [7'] pts FUZEAU 1030    (R349)
Platonium
17inst FUZEAU sc 2159, pts 2628    (R350)
Révolutions
string orch [23'] pts FUZEAU 2995    (R351)
Sonorium d'Angers
orch [24'] pts FUZEAU 2746    (R352)

ROSSEM, ANDRIES VAN (1957- )
Strings And Harpsichord
string orch,hpsd solo [9'] sc DONEMUS    (R353)

ROSSINI, CARLO (1890-1957)
William Tell And Other Overtures
orch sc DOVER 28149-3    (R354)

ROSSINI, GIOACCHINO (1792-1868)
Aschenbrödel: Overture see Cenerentola, La: Overture
Belagerung Von Korinth, Die: Ouvertüre see Siège De Corinthe, Le: Ouverture
Cantata In Onore Dei Sommo Pontefice Pio Nono
(Bucaralli) orch RICORDI-IT GR 17    (R355)
Cenerentola, La: Overture
"Aschenbrödel: Overture" 2.2.2.1. 2.0.0.0. timp,strings [8'] (no score) BREITKOPF-W    (R356)
Ermione, Sinfonia With Chorus
3(pic).2.2.2. 4.2.3.0. timp,perc, strings,cor [10'] BOCCACCINI rent    (R357)
Gazza Ladra, La: Overture
"Thieving Magpie, The: Overture" BROUDE BR.    (R358)
Guillaume Tell: Ballet Music
"Wilhelm Tell: Ballettmusik" 1+ pic.2.2.2. 4.2.3.0. strings [15'] (no score) BREITKOPF-W    (R359)
Mohr Von Venedig, Der: Ouvertüre see Otello: Ouverture
Otello: Ouverture
"Mohr Von Venedig, Der: Ouvertüre" 2.2.2.2. 4.2.1.0. timp,strings [9'] (no score) BREITKOPF-W    (R360)
Scala Di Seta, La: Ouverture
"Seidene Leiter, Die: Ouvertüre" 2.2.2.1. 2.0.0.0. strings [6'] BREITKOPF-W    (R361)
Seidene Leiter, Die: Ouvertüre see Scala Di Seta, La: Ouverture

ROSSINI, GIOACCHINO (cont'd.)
Semiramide: Overture
BROUDE BR.    (R362)
Siège De Corinthe, Le: Ouverture
"Belagerung Von Korinth, Die: Ouvertüre" 2+pic.2.2.2. 4.2.3.0. timp,2perc,strings, serpent [9'] BREITKOPF-W    (R363)
Thieving Magpie, The: Overture see Gazza Ladra, La: Overture
Turco In Italia, Il: Ouverture
"Türke In Italien, Der: Ouvertüre" 2.2.2.2. 2.2.1.0. timp,perc, strings [8'] (no score) BREITKOPF-W    (R364)
Türke In Italien, Der: Ouvertüre see Turco In Italia, Il: Ouverture
Wilhelm Tell: Ballettmusik see Guillaume Tell: Ballet Music

RÖSSLER, FRANZ ANTON see ROSETTI, FRANCESCO ANTONIO

RÖSSLER-ROSSETTI, FRANTISEK ANTONIN (1746-1792)
Concerto for Oboe and Orchestra in C
(Koukal, Bohumír) 2.0.0.0. 2.0.0.0. strings,ob solo [21'] CESKY HUD.    (R365)
Concerto for Violin and Orchestra in D minor
(Koukal, Bohumír) 0.2.0.0. 2.0.0.0. strings,vln solo [23'] CESKY HUD.    (R366)
Parthia In D
2.2.2.1. 2.0.0.0. 3vcl,2db CESKY HUD.    (R367)
Parthia In F
2.2.2.1. 3.0.0.0. 4vcl,2db [18'] CESKY HUD.    (R368)

ROSSNES, DAGFINN (1975- )
Nebula
string orch [10'] NORSKMI    (R369)
O, Quae Mutatio Rerum
3(pic).3(English horn).3(bass clar).3(contrabsn). 4.3.3.1. 4timp,perc,strings [12'] NORSKMI    (R370)

ROSSUM, FREDERIC R. VAN (1939- )
Amnesty Symphony *Op.38
4.4.4.4. 4.4.4.1. 5perc,timp,harp, pno/cel,strings,S solo [40'] BILLAUDOT    (R371)
Blaue Reiter, Der *Op.23 [16']
3.3.3.3. 4.3.3.1. timp,3perc,pno/ cel,strings BILLAUDOT    (R372)
Concerto No. 1, Op. 37 [17']
3.3.3.3. 4.2.2.0. timp,3perc, harp,pno/cel,strings,vln solo BILLAUDOT    (R373)
Concerto No. 2, Op. 45 [35']
3.3.3.3. 4.3.3.1. timp,5perc, harp,pno,strings,vln solo BILLAUDOT    (R374)
Concerto, Op. 30 [28']
3.3.3.3. 4.3.3.0. timp,4perc,pno/ cel,harp,strings "Slovienska Duca" BILLAUDOT    (R375)
Divertimento, Op. 15
string orch [11'] BILLAUDOT    (R376)
Douze Miniatures *Op.13 [24']
3.3.3.3. 4.3.3.1. timp,4perc,pno/ cel,strings BILLAUDOT    (R377)
Eloquences *Op.39 [17']
3.3.3.3. 4.2.2.0. timp,2perc, harp,pno/cel,strings,horn solo BILLAUDOT    (R378)
Epitaphe *Op.25
string orch [13'] BILLAUDOT    (R379)
Lyrical Story *Op.50 [12']
3.3.3.3. 4.3.3.1. timp,7perc, harp,pno,strings BILLAUDOT    (R380)
Petite Suite Réactionnaire *Op.32 [12']
2.2.2.2. 2.2.2.0. timp,4perc,pno/ cel,harp,strings BILLAUDOT    (R381)
Polyptyque *Op.46 [22']
3.3.3.3. 4.3.3.1. timp,5perc,pno/ cel,harp,strings BILLAUDOT    (R382)

RYBA, JAN JAKUB SIMON (cont'd.)

Roztomily Slavícku *Pastorale
0.0.0.0. 2.0.0.0. org,strings,A
solo,vln solo [5'] CESKY HUD.
(R429)

Sinfonia in C
1.0.2.1. 2.0.0.0. strings [18']
CESKY HUD. (R430)

Spi, Spi Nevinátko (Pastorale in E
flat)
0.0.0.0. 2.0.0.0. org,strings,SA
soli [3'] CESKY HUD. (R431)

Symphony in C
0.0.2.0. 2.0.0.0. strings,fl&bsn
soli CESKY HUD. (R432)

Usni, Malé Poupátko (Pastorale in D)
0.0.0.0. 2.0.0.0. org,strings,solo
voice [3'] CESKY HUD. (R433)

RYBÁR see Smetana, Bedrich

RYELANDT, JOSEPH (1870-1965)
De Profundis *Op.75
2.2.2.2. 2.0.0.0. strings,A/B solo
[10'] BELGE (R434)

RYOANJI see Cage, John

RYPDAL, TERJE (1947- )
Adagio Von Mozart
1.0.2.2. 2.0.0.0. pno,strings
NORSKMI (R435)

Concerto For Electric Guitar,
Orchestra And Choir, Op.14b
4(4pic).2(English horn).0.0.
6.0.4.0. 4perc,strings without
vln,vla [15'-20'] NORSKMI (R436)

Double Concerto For Two Electric
Guitars And Symphony Orchestra
*Op.58
3(pic,alto fl).3(English
horn).3(bass clar).3. 4.3(bass
trp).3.0. cel/cembalo,2perc,
strings,2elec bass,2elec gtr soli
[26'] NORSKMI (R437)

Hvilket Skulle Bevises
see Q.E.D. [Quod Erat
Demonstrandum]

Largo for Guitar, Percussion and
Strings, Op. 55
[16'] NORSKMI (R438)

Q.E.D. [Quod Erat Demonstrandum]
*Op.52
"Hvilket Skulle Bevises" 1.0.1.1.
2.1.0.0. elec gtr,perc,2vln,2vla,
2vcl,db,elec bass NORSKMI (R439)

Symphony No. 5, Op. 50
3(pic).3(English horn).3(bass
clar).3(contrabsn). 4.3.3.1.
timp,perc,harp,pno,strings [47']
NORSKMI (R440)

RYTMEN AV EN RÖST see Rehnqvist, Karin,
Lamento

RYTTERKVIST, HANS (1926- )
Tre Pezzi Per Orchestra Da Camera
2(pic).2.3(bass clar).1. 1.1.1.0.
5vln I,5vln II,4vla,4vcl,4db
[28'] sc STIM (R441)

# S

(S)IRATÓ see Holliger, Heinz

SA ROBE FAIT FROU FROU see Offenbach,
Jacques

SACCHINI, ANTONIO (MARIA GASPARO
GIOACCHINO) (1730-1786)
O Quam Carae Et Quam Beatae Silvae
S solo,string orch,cont sc,pts
KUNZELMANN GM 1280 (S1)

SACHSE, HANS WOLFGANG (1899- )
Holzschnitte, 3 *Op.106
3.3.3.3. 4.3.3.1. timp,perc,8vln I,
7vln II,6vla,5vcl,4db [23'] sc
PETERS 03225 (S2)

SACHTY see Oborny, Vaclav

SACKMAN, NICHOLAS (1950- )
Concerto for Flute
6vln I,6vln II,4vla,4vcl,2db,fl&
pic&alto fl solo [20'] SCHOTTS
perf mat rent (S3)

Ellipsis
1(alto fl).0.1(clar in E
flat).0.soprano sax(tenor sax).
1.2.0.0. 3perc,prepared pno,elec
org,harp,vln,vla,2db,pno solo
[20'] SCHOTTS perf mat rent (S4)

Hawthorn
3.3+English horn.3.3+contrabsn.alto
sax. 6.4.3.1. timp,4perc,pno&cel,
harp,strings [26'] SCHOTTS perf
mat rent (S5)

SACRE DE HEPHAESTUS, LE see Rosen,
Robert

SACRED MONUMENTS: SYMPHONY NO. 1 see
Baley, Virko

SACRIFICE OF ISAAC, THE see Sheriff,
Noam, Akedah

SACRIFICIAL MUSIC TO THE SETTING SUN
see Dukay, Barnabás

SAD TUNED TALE, A see Conway, Joe

SADKO: LIED DES VENEZIANISCHEN
KAUFMANNS see Rimsky-Korsakov,
Nikolai

SADKO: LIED DES WARÄGERS see Rimsky-
Korsakov, Nikolai

SADLER, HELMUT (1921- )
Concertino
strings,clar solo SCHOTTS perf mat
rent (S6)

SAETTE D'AMOR see Salzedo, Leonard
(Lopes)

SAFRONOV, ANTON (1972- )
Espace De Sentiment Continu, L' [19']
3.3.3.3. 4.3.3.1. 4perc,harp,pno,
cel,strings
BILLAUDOT (S7)

SAGENHAFTES SOLOTHURN see Tamas, Janos

SAGRADA FAMILIA see Dijk, Jan van

SAGVIK, STELLAN (1952- )
Clushoes (Overture, Op. 187)
2(pic).3(English horn).3(bass
clar).2. 4.3.3.1. timp,perc,
strings [7'5"] STIM sc H-2965,
pts (S8)

Overture, Op. 187
see Clushoes

Paidsomenest *Op.141
3(pic).3(English horn).3(bass
clar).3(contrabsn). 4.3.3.1.
timp,4perc,harp,14vln I,12vln II,
12vla,10vcl,8db,elec bass,pno
[45'] (1. Paid; 2. Some nest; 3.
Aidsomen; 4. Pest; 5. Aid some)
sc STIM (S9)

SAHALI see Raminsh, Imant

SAHARA see Olias, Lothar

SAIDOKI (D-MON) see Ishii, Maki

ST. CECILIA RAG see Wilby, Philip

SAINT-GEORGES, CHEVALIER DE
see SAINT-GEORGES, JOSEPH BOULOGNE DE

SAINT-GEORGES, JOSEPH BOULOGNE DE
(1739-1799)
Six Concertos Pour Violon, Les
2ob,2horn,strings,vln solo, flute
obbligato BOIS (S10)

ST. JAGO (TRADITION IV (2) see
Schnebel, Dieter

SAINT-MARCOUX, MICHELINE COULOMBE
(1938-1985)
Luminance
2.2.2.2. 4.2.3.1. timp&perc,perc,
pno&perc,strings [14'] sc
CANADIAN MI 1100 S146LU (S11)

SAINT PAUL'S SUITE see Holst, Gustav

SAINT-SAËNS, CAMILLE (1835-1921)
Carnaval Des Animaux, Le
"Carnival Of The Animals" BROUDE
BR. (S12)
(Jost, Peter) "Karneval Der Tiere,
Der" BREITKOPF-W sc,pts
PB-OB 5321, study sc PB 5284
(S13)

Carneval Des Animaux
orch KUNZELMANN ipa sc 10076A, oct
10076 (S14)

Carnival Of The Animals
see Carnaval Des Animaux, Le

Concerto for Violoncello and
Orchestra in A minor, Op. 33
2.2.2.2. 2.0.0.0. timp,strings,vcl
solo [21'] PETERS (S15)

Karneval Der Tiere, Der
see Carnaval Des Animaux, Le

Morceau De Concert, Op. 154
harp,orch INTERNAT.S. sc,pts rent,
solo pt,pno red (S16)

Organ Symphony
see Symphony No. 3

Phaéton *Op.39
3.2.2.3. 4.2.3.1. timp,perc,2harp,
strings [8'] PETERS (S17)

Piano Concertos Nos. 2 And 4
orch,pno sc DOVER 28723-8 (S18)

Suite for Violoncello, Op. 16
2.2.2.2. 0.0.0.0. strings,vcl solo
[21'] LEDUC (S19)

Symphony No. 3
"Organ Symphony" orch sc DOVER
28306-2 (S20)

SAINTS, THE: THREE PIECES FOR ORCHESTRA
(WITH OPTIONAL AUDIENCE
PARTICIPATION) see Perera, Ronald
Christopher

SAISIR see Jaubert, Maurice

SÄKKIJÄRVEN-POLKA see Godzinsky, George
De

SALAL: AN IDYLL FOR ORCHESTRA see
Healey, Derek

SALBERT, DIETER
Quasi Una Sinfonia
orch MÖSELER pts 10.473.01 rent, sc
10.473.00 (S21)

SALIERI, ANTONIO (1750-1825)
Concerto for Piano and Orchestra in B
flat
2.2.0.0. 0.0.0.0. strings,pno solo
[20'] BOCCACCINI BS. 205 rent
(S22)
Concerto for Piano and Orchestra in C
2.2.0.0. 0.0.0.0. strings,pno solo
[20'] BOCCACCINI BS. 204 rent
(S23)

SALIERI, GIRAMOLO
Introduzione Con Variazioni
(Pojar) basset horn,string orch sc,
pts KUNZELMANN GM 1390 ipa (S24)

SALLEY GARDENS, THE (from Folk Songs)
(Britten, Benjamin) strings,high solo
[3'] BOOSEY-ENG rent (S25)

SALMANOV, VADIM (1912- )
Symphony No. 3
3(pic).2.2.2. 4.2.3.1. timp,perc,
strings [25'] SIKORSKI perf mat
rent (S26)

SALOME: INTRODUKTION UND TANZ see
Glazunov, Alexander Konstantinovich

SALPINX, THE see Forsyth, Malcolm

SALUTATION see Biggs, John

SALVADOR see Delerue, Georges

SALVADOR DALI: A SYMPHONIC PORTRAIT see
Madsen, Trygve, Salvador Dali: Et
Symfonisk Portrett

SALVADOR DALI: ET SYMFONISK PORTRETT
see Madsen, Trygve

SALVARE LA TERRA see Koch, Erland von,
Symfoni Nr 6

SALVATION CREEK WITH EAGLE see
Lumsdaine, David

SALVE REGINA see Gebhard, A.M.

SALVUM FAC POPULUM TUUM see Widor,
Charles-Marie

SALZEDO, LEONARD (LOPES)
Canzona
3.2.2.3. 4.2.3.0. timp,perc,strings
[12'] BMIC (S27)

Concerto for Violin and Orchestra
2.2.3.2. 4.3.3.0. timp,2perc,harp,
strings,vln solo [22'] BMIC (S28)

Pasacalle 1992
3.3.3.3. 4.4.3.1. timp,perc,harp,
strings [12'] BMIC (S29)

Saette D'amor
3.3.3.3. 4.4.3.0. timp,perc,harp,
strings,S solo BMIC (S30)

Variations
2.2.3.2. 4.2.3.1. timp,2perc,harp,
strings BMIC (S31)

SAMBA DA CAMERA see Josipovic, Ivo

SAMMARTINI, GIOVANNI BATTISTA
(1701-1775)
Sinfonia for 2 Oboes, 2 Horns and
Strings, No. 1, in G
(Zimpel) 2ob,2horn,strings
KUNZELMANN 10058 (S32)

Sinfonia for Strings, J-C 7, in C
(Ferrari, Daniele) hpsd,strings
[9'30"] SONZOGNO rent (S33)

Sinfonia for Strings, J-C 9, in C
minor
(Ferrari, Daniele) hpsd,strings
[12'30"] SONZOGNO rent (S34)

Sinfonia for Strings, J-C 14, in D
(Ferrari, Daniele) hpsd,strings
[7'] SONZOGNO rent (S35)

Sinfonia for Strings, J-C 15, in D
(Ferrari, Daniele) hpsd,strings
[6'] SONZOGNO rent (S36)

Sinfonia for Strings, J-C 23, in D
minor
(Ferrari, Daniele) hpsd,strings
[12'30"] SONZOGNO rent (S37)

Sinfonia for Strings, J-C 33, in F
(Ferrari, Daniele) hpsd,strings
[8'30"] SONZOGNO rent (S38)

Sinfonia for Strings, J-C 34, in F
(Ferrari, Daniele) hpsd,strings
[13'] SONZOGNO rent (S39)

Sinfonia for Strings, J-C 35, in F
(Ferrari, Daniele) hpsd,strings
[8'] SONZOGNO rent (S40)

Sinfonia for Strings, J-C 36, in F
(Ferrari, Daniele) hpsd,strings
[13'] SONZOGNO rent (S41)

Sinfonia for Strings, J-C 37, in F
(Ferrari, Daniele) hpsd,strings
[12'30"] SONZOGNO rent (S42)

Sinfonia for Strings, J-C 38, in F
(Ferrari, Daniele) hpsd,strings
[12'] SONZOGNO rent (S43)

Sinfonia for Strings, J-C 59, in G
minor
(Ferrari, Daniele) hpsd,strings
[9'] SONZOGNO rent (S44)

Sinfonia for Strings, J-C 64, in A
(Ferrari, Daniele) hpsd,strings
[7'30"] SONZOGNO rent (S45)

Sinfonia for Strings, J-C 65, in A
(Ferrari, Daniele) hpsd,strings
[11'30"] SONZOGNO rent (S46)

Sinfonia for Strings, J-C 66a, in B
(Ferrari, Daniele) hpsd,strings
[12'30"] SONZOGNO rent (S47)

Sinfonia for Strings, J-C 66b, in B
(Ferrari, Daniele) hpsd,strings
[9'30"] SONZOGNO rent (S48)

SAMMARTINI, GIOVANNI BATTISTA (cont'd.)

Sinfonia for Strings, J-C 67, in B
(Ferrari, Daniele) hpsd,strings
[9'30"] SONZOGNO rent (S49)

Sinfonia for Strings, J-C 88, in A
*Overture
(Ferrari, Daniele) hpsd,strings
[9'30"] (to Memet) SONZOGNO rent
(S50)

Sinfonia No. 1 in G
(Zimpel) 2fl,2ob,2horn,string orch
KUNZELMANN ipa sc 10058A, oct
10058 (S51)

Sinfonia No. 2 in G
(Zimpel) 2horn,string orch
KUNZELMANN ipa sc 10059A, oct
10059 (S52)

Sinfonia No. 3 in G
(Zimpel) 2fl,2ob,2trp,string orch
KUNZELMANN ipa sc 10057A, oct
10057 (S53)

SAMUELSSON, MARIE (1956-   )
Ahead
2.2.2.2. 2.2.2.0. 2perc,harp,
strings [10'] sc STIM (S54)

Rotationer
string orch sc,pts STIM (S55)

SAN see Xu, Shuya

SANDBERG, LARS
Diktan: Vers 1
2.1.2.2. 2.1.1.0. harp,strings
[11'] sc STIM (S56)

Efter-klang (ver ett fragment ur
Adagio h-moll KV 540 av W A
Mozart): Version 3
1(pic).0.1(bass clar).1. 1.1.0.0.
harmonium,2vln,vla,vcl,db [10']
sc,pts STIM (S57)

Efter-Klang: Version 4
3(pic).0.3(bass clar).2. 2.2.0.0.
12vln I,10vln II,8vla,6vcl,4db,
harmonium [10'] STIM sc H-2729B,
pts (S58)

Fljd: Fyra Orkesterskisser
2.2.2.2. 2.2.0.0. 6vln I,6vln II,
4vla,4vcl,2db sc,pts STIM (S59)

Grund-Drag: Vers 2
3(pic).2.3(bass clar).3(contrabsn).
4.2.3.1. 1 string [25'] sc STIM
(S60)

SANDBY, HERMAN (1881-1965)
Berceuse
harp,string orch sc,pts INTERNAT.S.
(S61)

SANDGREN, JOAKIM (1965-   )
Canon
strings [4'5"] STIM (S62)

False Tree, A
3(pic).0.3.3. 0.0.0.0. strings
[6'5"] sc STIM (S63)

Mad Horse, A
12vln I,12vln II,8vla,6vcl,4db [8']
sc STIM (S64)

SANDRED, ÖRJAN (1964-   )
[Ayas Ögal] Balettverk För Per
Jonsson: I Förspel Och 15 Bilder
string orch,4perc,org [65'] sc STIM
(S65)

Corona
4(pic).4(English horn).4(bass
clar).4(contrabsn). 4.3.3.1.
timp,2perc,strings [5'] STIM sc
H-2943, pts (S66)

First-Pieces *Overture
3.3.3.3. 4.3.3.1. timp,3perc,
strings [8'] STIM sc H-2874, pts
(S67)

Musik Till Facklorna: En Film I Tre
Avsnitt För TV
2.2.2.2. 4.2.3.0. timp,3perc,harp,
strings,pno sc STIM (S68)

Pieces Of Pieces
2.2.2.2. 2.2.2.1. 2perc,harp,
strings [17'] sc,pts STIM (S69)

Polykrom
1.1.1.1. 1.1.1.0. timp,perc,2vln,
vla,vcl,db [8'] sc,pts STIM (S70)

Symphonic Piece
4(pic).4.4(bass clar).4(contrabsn).
6.4.4.2. strings [25'] STIM sc
H-2870, pts (S71)

Three Movements
see Triptychos

SANDRED, ÖRJAN (cont'd.)

Triptychos
"Three Movements" 3(pic).3(English
horn).4(bass clar).3(contrabsn).
4.3.2.1. 3perc,harp,strings,pno
[14'] sc STIM H-2667 (S72)

Young Pieces
2.2.2.2. 2.2.2.0. perc,strings [8']
STIM sc H-2896, pts (S73)
string orch [8'] STIM sc H-2896,
pts (S74)

SANDSTRÖM, JAN (1954-   )
Acintyas
6vln I,6vln II,4vla,4vcl,2db [13']
sc NORDISKA (S75)

Emperor's Song
"Kejsarvisan" 2(pic).2.2.2.
4.2.3.1. perc,strings [8'] SUECIA
sc H-2776, pts (S76)

Kejsarvisan
see Emperor's Song

SANDSTRÖM, SVEN-DAVID (1942-   )
Concerto for Recorder, Harpsichord
and Strings
KMH (S77)

Fantasy No. 3
orch [19'] NORDISKA (S78)

SANGENS MAKT see Kvam, Oddvar S.

SÅNGER OM DÖDEN see Börtz, Daniel

ST. ALBERICI see Hirschberger,
Albericus, Concerto No. 2 in G

SANT' ELENA AL CALVARIRO: SINFONIA see
Leo, Leonardo (Ortensio Salvatore
de)

SANTOLIQUIDO, FRANCESCO (1883-1971)
Preghiera Per I Morti
orch FORLIVESI rent (S79)

Santuari Asiatici
3(pic).3(English horn).2.3.
4.3.4.0. timp,perc,harp,strings
[12'] SIKORSKI perf mat rent
(S80)

SANTUARI ASIATICI see Santoliquido,
Francesco

SAPFOS AVSKEDSSÅNG see Svensson,
Matthias

SAPPHO-GESÄNGE see Bose, Hans-Jurgen
Von

SAPPHO MONOLOGUES see Mills, Richard

SAPPORO see Ichiyanagi, Toshi

SARABANDE ESPAGNOLE DU XVIE SIÈCLE see
Massenet, Jules

SARAI, TIBOR (1919-   )
Sinfonia No. 3
3(pic).2+English horn.2+clar in E
flat.2+contrabsn. 4.3.3.1.
strings [22'] EMB rent (S81)

SARASATE, PABLO DE (1844-1908)
Carmen: Fantasy, For Violin And
String Orchestra *Op.25 (from
Bizet's Carmen)
(Dupin, Marc-Olivier) string orch,
vln solo [13'] BILLAUDOT (S82)

Malaguena, For Violin And Orchestra
(Barsov, Victor) 3(alto fl).0.2.1.
4.0.0.0. 3perc,harp,cel,strings,
vln solo [4'] SIKORSKI perf mat
rent (S83)

SARAZENEN, DIE; DIE SCHÖNE ALDA see
MacDowell, Edward Alexander

SARBA see Juchelka, Miroslav

SARDINE SARCOPHAGUS see Rabe, Folke,
Sardinsarkofagen

SARDINSARKOFAGEN see Rabe, Folke

SARGASMES see Moeschinger, Albert

SARJA JOUSIORKESTERILLE see Kyllönen,
Timo-Juhani

SÁRKÖZY, ISTVAN (1920-   )
Az If Júsághoz Nyitány
see To The Youth: Overture

Concerto Grosso
"Ricordanze 1" 2+pic.2.2.2.
4.3.2.1. 3timp,strings [16'] EMB
rent (S84)

SÁRKÖZY, ISTVAN (cont'd.)

Confessioni
2+pic.2+English horn.2+bass clar.2+
contrabsn. 4.4.2+bass trom.1.
3timp,perc,harp,strings,pno solo
[20'] EMB rent                    (S85)

Ricordanze 1
see Concerto Grosso

To The Youth: Overture
"Az If Júsághoz Nyitány"
2(pic).2.2.2. 4.3.3.1. 3timp,
perc,strings, tuba is optional
[8'] EMB rent                     (S86)

SARMATISCHE LIEDER see Matthus,
Siegfried

ŠAROUN, JAROSLAV (1943-    )
Illuminations
see Svetla

Svetla
"Illuminations" 1.1.1.1. 2.2.0.0.
timp,perc,harp,pno,strings [25']
CESKY HUD.                        (S87)

SARUYA, TOSHIRO (1960-    )
Fiber Of The Breath
string orch JAPAN                 (S88)

Mutual Recognition
orch [12'] JAPAN                  (S89)

SARY, LASZLO (1940-    )
Hyperions Song Of Destiny
"Hyperion Sorsdala" string orch.
(9, 7, 5, 3) [15'] EMB rent       (S90)

Hyperion Sorsdala
see Hyperions Song Of Destiny

Polyphonie For 28 Instruments
2.0.2.2. 0.2.2.0. 6vln,6vla,6vcl
[6'] EMB rent                     (S91)

SASONKIN, MANUS (1930-1992)
Concerto for Harpsichord and String
Orchestra
string orch,hpsd solo sc CANADIAN
MI 1662 S252CO                    (S92)

SATIE, ERIK (1866-1925)
Gymnopedie 1
orch EUR.AM.MUS. pts EA00389AS, set
EA00389BS, sc EA00389FS           (S93)

Gymnopedie 2
orch EUR.AM.MUS. pts EA00411AS, set
EA00411BS, sc EA00411FS           (S94)

Gymnopedie 3
orch EUR.AM.MUS. pts EA00412AS, set
EA00412BS, sc EA00412FS           (S95)

SATIE'S FACTION see Gastinel, Gérard

SATIRE see Laderman, Ezra

SATOH, SOMEI (1947-    )
Journey Through Sacred Time
2perc,2harp,8vln I,8vln II,6vla,
4vcl,2db, shô [14'] SCHOTTS perf
mat rent                          (S96)

SATOKO'S SONG see Stevens, James

SATSCHIDAO see Lagidse, Rewas

SATYR A DÍVKA see Novosad, Lubomir

SÄTZE FÜR KAMMERORCHESTER, 5 see
Wallborn,

SAUDEK, VOJTECH (1951-    )
Concerto for Flute and String
Orchestra
[20'] CESKY HUD.                  (S97)

Concerto for Piano and Orchestra
3.2.4.3. 4.3.3.1. timp,perc,harp,
cel,strings,pno solo [23'] CESKY
HUD.                              (S98)

Dve Písne
3.2.3.2. 4.3.3.1. timp,perc,harp,
cel,strings,S solo [12'] CESKY
HUD.                              (S99)

Sinfonietta
3.2.3.2. 2.2.0.0. perc,strings
[27'] CESKY HUD.                  (S100)

Symphony
3.3.4.3. 4.4.3.1. timp,perc,vibra,
harp,cel,strings [45'] CESKY HUD.
(S101)

Vylet Do Hor
1.1.1.1. 1.0.0.0. pno,strings,Mez&
speaking voice [11'] CESKY HUD.
(S102)

SAUGE FLEURIE see Indy, Vincent d'

SAUL AND THE WITCH OF ENDOR see
Glanville-Hicks, Peggy

SÄULEN DES MEMNON see Bürkholz, Thomas

SAULES REZGINAI see Rekasius, Antanas

SAUNDERS, REBECCA (1967-    )
Crimson
"Molly's Song 1" ob,bass clar&
contrabass clar,horn,trp in C&
piccolo trp,trom,harp,perc,2vln,
vla,vcl,db, metronomes, whistles,
and 3 music boxes [25'] set
PETERS rent                       (S103)

G And E On A
0+2pic.2.2(clar in E flat)+2bass
clar.2(contrabsn). 4.4(2piccolo
trp,flügelhorn).4.0. 3perc,pno,
harp,8vln I,8vln II,6vla,6vcl,
6db, 27 music boxes [22'] PETERS
(S104)

Molly's Song 1
see Crimson

SAURET, EMILE (1852-1920)
Concerto for Violin and Orchestra in
D minor, Op. 26
2.2.2.2. 4.2.3.0. timp,strings,vln
solo [30'] BREITKOPF-W    (S105)

SÄV, SÄV, SUSA see Sibelius, Jean

SAWER, DAVID
Byrnan Wood
4.4.4.4. 6.4.4.1. 5perc,2harp,
strings [25'] UNIVER.             (S106)

SAXTON, ROBERT (1953-    )
Concerto for Violoncello and
Orchestra
2.2.2.2. 4.3.3.1. timp,2perc,
strings,vcl solo CHESTER   (S107)

Psalm
see Song Of Ascents, A

Song Of Ascents, A (Psalm)
fl,ob,clar,bsn,horn,trp,trom,1perc,
strings [20'] CHESTER     (S108)

SAY SEA, TAKE ME! see Takemitsu, Toru,
Quotation Of Dream

SAYAT NOVA see Shoujounian, Petros,
Suite Concertante

SAYGUN, AHMED ADNAN (1907-1991)
Ayin Raksi
"Ritual Dance" 3.3.3.3. 4.3.3.1.
timp,4perc,harp,strings [10']
PEER rent                         (S109)

Concerto for Piano, No. 2
3.3.3.3. 4.3.3.1. timp,perc,harp,
strings,pno solo [17'] PEER rent
(S110)

Concerto for Viola
3.3.2.2. 4.3.3.0. timp,perc,cel,
harp,strings,vla solo [30'] PEER
rent                              (S111)

Concerto for Violoncello
3.3.3.3. 4.3.3.0. timp,perc,harp,
strings,vcl solo PEER rent (S112)

Deyis
"Dictum" string orch [17'] PEER
rent                              (S113)

Dictum
see Deyis

Ritual Dance
see Ayin Raksi

Seven Songs
2.2.2.2. 4.3.3.0. timp,perc,harp,
strings,B solo [21'25"] PEER rent
(S114)

Symphony No. 5
3.3.3.3. 4.3.3.1. timp,perc,pno&
cel,harp,strings [23'] PEER rent
(S115)

Variations for Orchestra
orch [14'] PEER rent              (S116)

SAYLOR, BRUCE (STUART) (1946-    )
Archangel
3.3.3.3. 4.3.4.1. timp,2perc,brass,
strings [6'] SCHIRM.EC rent
(S117)

Cantilena For String Orchestra
strings [6'] SCHIRM.EC rent (S118)

Symphony In Two Parts
2.2.2.2. 2.1.1.0. timp,2perc,harp,
strings [16'] SCHIRM.EC rent
(S119)

Turns And Mordents
fl solo,2.2.2.2. 2.2.0.0. timp,
perc,kbd,strings [13'] SCHIRM.EC
rent                              (S120)

SÁZENÍ HRUŠKY see Matoušek, Vlastislav

SCALA DI SETA, LA: OUVERTURE see
Rossini, Gioacchino

SCARF OF WHITE STREAM, A see Gifford,
Keith

SCARLATTI, ALESSANDRO (1660-1725)
Concerto Grosso in F minor for
Strings and Cembalo
(Schering) [9'] KAHNT     (S121)

Erminia: Rezitative Und Arie
cembalo,8vln I,7vln II,6vla,5vcl,
4db [8'] sc PETERS 01161  (S122)

SCARLATTI, DOMENICO (1685-1757)
Drei Sonaten  *CC3U
string orch/string quar MÖSELER
f.s. sc,pts 10.011-03, pts
10.011-01                         (S123)

Pastorale, K. 513
vln I,vln II,vla,vcl,db MÖSELER sc
40.153-00, pts 40.153-01, set
40.153-09                         (S124)

Sinfonia Tolomeo
(Blanchard) orch [4'] BOIS  (S125)

SCARLATTINE see Sheriff, Noam

SCENA see Lewis, Robert Hall see
Sibelius, Jean

SCÉNA, FOR ENGLISH HORN AND ORCHESTRA
see Reicha, Anton

SCENE see Bose, Hans-Jurgen Von

SCENES DE BALLET see Olthuis, Kees

SCÈNES DE FÉERIE see Massenet, Jules,
Suite for Orchestra, No. 6

SCÈNES DE LA LETTRE see Tchaikovsky,
Piotr Ilyich

SCÈNES FRANCISCAINES see Pierne,
Gabriel

SCENES FROM MER DE GLACE see Meale,
Richard

SCENES FROM SCHUMANN see Holloway,
Robin

SCENES FROM TETRALOGY "JOSEPH AND HIS
BROTHERS" BY THOMAS MANN see
Lendvay, Kamillo

SCENES FROM THE KINGDOM OF THE
DINAMITEN see Beltrami, Marco

SCÈNES HISTORIQUES I see Sibelius, Jean

SCÈNES HISTORIQUES II see Sibelius,
Jean

SCÈNES HONGROISES see Massenet, Jules,
Suite for Orchestra, No. 2

SCENES SEEN. BALLET SUITE see Rieti,
Vittorio

SCENT OF BLACK MANGO, THE see Xiaogang,
Ye

ŠČERBA
Concerto for Violin and Orchestra
2.2.2.2. 4.2.2.1. timp,perc,
strings,vln solo [15'] CESKY HUD.
(S126)

SCHAATHUN, ASBJØRN (1961-    )
Actions, Interpolations And Analyses:
Symphonies For Amplified Bass
Clarinet Solo, Large Ensemble (Of
Rewound Instruments), And
Electronics
2.2(English
horn).2.2(contrabsn).sax.
2.2.2.1. 2perc,harp,pno,cel,
synthesizer,strings,bass clar
solo NORSKMI                      (S127)

Doubleportrait For Concertante
Violin, 4 Instrumental Groups And
Live Electronics
2(pic,alto fl).1(English
horn).3(clar in E flat,bass
clar).1(contrabsn). 2.1.1.0.
timp,perc,harp,2synthesizer,2vln,
vla,vcl,db,electronic equipment,
vln solo [10'15"] NORSKMI  (S128)

Hypertrophies Pour Ensemble
1(pic).1(English horn).1(bass
clar).0. 1.0.1.0. perc,pno,vln,
vla,vcl, db NORSKMI               (S129)

SCHACHT, THEODOR VON (1748-1823)
Concerto for Clarinet and Orchestra
clar solo,orch KUNZELMANN ipa sc
10265A, oct 10265                 (S130)

SCHAEFERS, ANTON (1908-    )
Mädchen Ninette, Das: Scènes De
Ballet
2.2.2.2. 4.2.3.0. timp,perc,pno,
strings [27'] SIKORSKI perf mat
rent                              (S131)

SCHAFER, M.
see SCHAFER, R. MURRAY

SCHAFER, R. MURRAY (1933-    )
Concerto for Accordion and Orchestra
3(pic).2(English horn).2(bass
clar).2(contrabsn). 2.2.2.0.
3perc,strings,acord solo [26']
sc,solo pt CANADIAN
MI 1366 S296CO                    (S132)

Divan I Shams I Tabriz
3(pic).3(English horn).3(bass
clar).3(contrabsn). 4.3.3.1.
4perc,harp,Hamm,electronic tape,
strings,SSAATTBar soli [24'] sc
CANADIAN MV 5980 S296DI           (S133)

SCHAFFRATH, CHRISTOPH (1709-1763)
Sinfonia in A
(Schneider, M.) strings,cont [8']
BREITKOPF-W                       (S134)

SCHARF ABREISSEN see Padding, Martijn

SCHARWENKA, PHILIPP (1847-1917)
Concerto for Violin and Orchestra in
G, Op. 95
2.2.2.2. 2.2.0.0. timp,strings,vln
solo [36'] BREITKOPF-W            (S135)

Für Die Jugend  *Op.71
strings [7'] BREITKOPF-W          (S136)

SCHARWENKA, XAVER (1850-1924)
König Witichis' Werbung (from
Mataswintha)
3(pic).3(English horn).3(bass
clar).3(contrabsn). 4.3.3.1.
timp,3perc,harp,strings [7']
BREITKOPF-W                       (S137)

SCHATTEN FOR CHAMBER ORCHESTRA see
Ness, Jon Øivind

SCHATTENGESANG see Kirchner, Volker
David

SCHAUFELRAD see Holliger, Heinz

SCHAUSPIELMUSIK ZU SHAKESPEARES "KÖNIG
LEAR" see Shostakovich, Dmitri

SCHECK, HELMUT (1938-    )
Veni Redemptor Gentium (composed with
Scheidt, Samuel)  *Adv.hymn
strings,org/cembalo, violin iii may
replace viola BOHM                (S138)

SCHEFFER, RICKARD
Akrostikon
1(pic).1.1.1. 1.1.1.0. perc,2vln,
vla,vcl,db,pno [4'] sc STIM       (S139)

Chantant, En
3(pic).3(English horn).3(bass
clar).3(contrabsn). 4.3.3.1.
timp,2perc,harp,strings,cel [16']
STIM                              (S140)

SCHEHERAZADE see Rimsky-Korsakov,
Nikolai

SCHEIN, JOHANN HERMANN (1586-1630)
Intrada No. 20
strings, (viola divisi) [3']
BREITKOPF-W                       (S141)

Suite No. 10
strings, (viola divisi) [9']
BREITKOPF-W                       (S142)

Suite No. 14
strings, (viola divisi) [9']
BREITKOPF-W                       (S143)

Suite No. 19
strings, (viola divisi) [11']
BREITKOPF-W                       (S144)

Suite No. 22
strings, (viola divisi) [4']
BREITKOPF-W                       (S145)

SCHELOMO see Bloch, Ernest

SCHENKER, FRIEDRICH (1942-    )
Allemande
0.1+English horn.0.0. 0.0.1.0.
6perc,pno,vla,vcl,db,Bar solo sc
PETERS 03325 f.s. contains also:
Sonderschlosskonzert              (S146)

Ballade for Orchestra
see Fanal Spanien 1936

Concerto for Violin and Orchestra
2.0+English horn+ob
d'amore.0.0.tenor sax. 4.1.4.1.

SCHENKER, FRIEDRICH (cont'd.)
3perc,cembalo,harp,elec gtr,bass
gtr,8vln,4vla [33'] sc,solo pt
PETERS 03326                      (S147)

Concerto for Violoncello and
Orchestra
2.2.3.2.alto sax. 0.2.0.0. timp,
2perc,2pno,cel,6vcl,4db [45'] sc,
solo pt PETERS 03233              (S148)

Electrization
3.3.3.3. 4.3.3.1. timp,5perc,pno,
harp,8vln I,7vln II,6vla,5vcl,
4db, Beatgruppe: fl, a-sax, perc,
org, bass guitar [25'] sc PETERS
01318                             (S149)

Fanal Spanien 1936 (Ballade for
Orchestra)
4.3+ob d'amore.4.4. 5.4.4.1. timp,
4perc,2harp,acord,cembalo,pno,
strings [11'] PETERS              (S150)

Flötensinfonie
2.2.3.2. 4.3.3.1. 3perc,pno,cel,
harp,8vln I,6vln II,6vla,5vcl,4db,db solo
[37'] sc,solo pt PETERS 01343     (S151)

In Memoriam Paul Dessau (composed
with Bredemeyer, Reiner;
Goldmann, Friedrich)
15strings [4'] sc PETERS EP 10351 (S152)

5vln I,5vln II,3vla,2vcl,db [12']
sc PETERS 02634                   (S153)

Michelangelo-Sinfonie
4.4.4.4. 8.4.4.1. timp,5perc,harp,
org,cel,pno,strings, solo voices&
speaking voice,jr cor PETERS      (S154)

Sonata, Aria E Toccata Per Archi
5vln I,4vln II,3vla,2vcl,db [4'] sc
PETERS 03220                      (S155)

Sonderschlosskonzert
see Allemande

Stück Für Virtuosen I
3.3.4.3. 5.3.3.1. timp,5perc,pno,
15vln,6vla,5vcl,4db [16'] sc
PETERS 03229                      (S156)

Traum...Hoffnung...
4.3.3.3. 4.3.3.1. timp,6perc,pno,
cel,harp,15vln,6vla,5vcl,4db,vcl
solo [43'] sc PETERS 02171 (S157)

SCHERZINO FOR SMALL ORCHESTRA see
Simeonov, Blago

SCHERZO À LA RUSSE see Stravinsky, Igor

SCHERZO CAPRICCIOSO see Matthews, David

SCHERZO FANTASTIQUE see Gropp, Johann-
Maria

SCHERZO FOR BIDA see Jansson, Torbjörn

SCHERZO SINFONICO see Farkas, Ferenc

SCHERZO UND FINALE see Wolf, Hugo

SCHERZPARAPHRASEN see Zilcher, Heinz
Reinhardt

SCHIBBOLETH see Kirchner, Volker David

SCHIBLER, ARMIN (1920-    )
Concertino for Clarinet, Op. 49
clar solo,orch perf sc KUNZELMANN
ETP 1213 ipa                      (S158)

Concerto Breve  *Op.64
"Habisreutinger-Konzert" vcl solo,
string orch perf sc KUNZELMANN
ETP 1233 ipa                      (S159)

Concerto for Trumpet and Orchestra,
Op. 68
trp solo,orch sc KUNZELMANN GM 862
ipr                               (S160)

Concerto, Op. 76 for Percussion and
String Orchestra, No. 2
perc,orch min sc KUNZELMANN
ETP 1251 ipr                      (S161)

Habisreutinger-Konzert
see Concerto Breve

SCHICKELE, PETER (1935-    )
see also "BACH, P.D.Q."

see "BACH, P.D.Q."

Songlines
see Symphony No. 1

Symphony No. 1
"Songlines" 3.3.3.3. 4.3.3.1. timp,
4perc,harp,cel,pno,strings [27']
ELKAN-V rent                      (S162)

SCHIFFBRUECHIGE, DER see Kirkwood,
Antoinette

SCHILFROHR, SÄUSLE see Sibelius, Jean,
Säv, Säv, Susa

SCHILLING, HANS LUDWIG (1927-    )
Largo E Passacaglia Cromatica
strings MOSELER sc 10.470.00, pts
10.470.01, set 10.470.09  (S163)

SCHILLING, OTTO-ERICH (1910-1967)
Tänze Auf Der Kokosnuss
2.1.2.1.2sax. 0.3.3.0. perc,pno,
strings [15'] SIKORSKI perf mat
rent                              (S164)

SCHIMKE, CHRISTOPH ( ?  -1789)
Concerto for Viola and Orchestra in C
(Koukal, Bohumir) 0.2.0.0. 2.0.0.0.
strings,vla solo [22'] CESKY HUD.  (S165)

SCHIPIZKY, FREDERICK (1952-    )
Aurora Borealis
2.2.2.2. 2.2.1.0. timp,perc,strings
sc CANADIAN MI 1100 S336AU        (S166)

Aurora Fanfare (from Aurora Borealis)
2.2.2.2. 4.2.2.0. timp,2perc,
strings sc CANADIAN
MI 1100 S336AUF                   (S167)

Divertimento for String Orchestra
string orch [18'] sc CANADIAN
MI 1500 S336DI                    (S168)

From Under The Overture
3(pic).3(English horn).3(clar in E
flat,bass clar).3(contrabsn).
4.3.3.1. timp,3perc,harp,strings
[12'] sc CANADIAN MI 1100 S336FR  (S169)

Kleine Suite Für Streichorchester
(Suite for String Orchestra)
string orch [15'] (1. Preludium 2.
Fuga 3. Interludium 4. Finale) sc
CANADIAN MI 1500 S336KL           (S170)

Quiet Eve
3(pic).2.2.2. 4.3.3.1. timp,4perc,
synthesizer,strings,opt SATB [6']
sc CANADIAN MI 1100 S336QU        (S171)

Suite for String Orchestra
see Kleine Suite Für
Streichorchester

Symphonic Sketches
2(pic).2.2.2. 4.3(trp in C).3.1.
timp,3perc,harp,strings [14'] sc
CANADIAN MI 1100 S336SY           (S172)

SCHLAGSTÜCK 6 see Bredemeyer, Reiner

SCHLAGZEUGKONZERT SÜDEN-FEUER-SOMMER
see Ishii, Maki

SCHLEIERMACHER, STEFFEN
Concerto for Viola and Chamber
Orchestra
1.0.1.1. 0.1.0.0. perc,pno,strings,
vla solo [15'] PETERS             (S173)

SCHLEIMIGE LAST, DIE see Meijering,
Chiel

SCHLEMM, GUSTAV ADOLF (1902-    )
Fantasiestück
2.2.2.2. 2.2.0.0. strings,vcl solo
[5'] BREITKOPF-W                  (S174)

SCHLITTSCHUHLÄUFER, DIE see Waldteufel,
Emile

SCHLUMMERLIED DER MELUSINE see Perfall,
Karl

SCHMÄLE, SCHMÄLE, LIEBER JUNGE see
Mozart, Wolfgang Amadeus, Batti,
Batti, O Bel Masetto

SCHMELZER, JOHANN HEINRICH (1623-1680)
Ciaccona À 3 Chori
2S rec,bsn,trp,strings,cont (in
three instrumental choirs: I
strings II brass III woodwinds)
COPPENRATH sc 17.013-01, pts
17.013-21 TO 46                   (S175)

Sonata Per Chiesa E Per Camera
S rec,strings without db,cont
COPPENRATH sc 17.011-01, pts
17.011-21 TO 40                   (S176)

SCHMIDT, CHRISTFRIED (1932-    )
Concerto for Flute and Orchestra
0.0.0.0. 1.1.1.0. 2perc,cembalo,
strings,fl solo [20'] PETERS      (S177)

Concerto for Violin
3.3.3.3. 4.2.2.1. timp,3perc,pno,
strings,vln solo [25'] PETERS     (S178)

Orchestermusik II
3.0.3.3. 3.3.3.0. timp,3perc,
strings,ob&vcl&pno soli [25']

SCHMIDT, CHRISTFRIED (cont'd.)

BREITKOPF-W (S179)

SCHMIDT, HANSJÜRGEN
Farben Und Rhythmen
see Sinfonia No. 2

Parabel
3.3.3.3. 4.2.3.1. timp,3perc,pno,
cel,harp,8vln I,7vln II,6vla,
5vcl,4db [15'] sc PETERS 03240
(S180)

Sinfonia No. 2
"Farben Und Rhythmen" 2.2.2.2.
4.2.3.1. timp,3perc,harp,8vln I,
7vln II,6vla,5vcl,4db [14'] sc
PETERS 04437 (S181)

Taggedichte Und Nachtgesichte
3.3.2.3. 4.2.3.1. timp,perc,pno,
harp,8vln I,7vln II,6vla,5vcl,4db
[22'] sc PETERS 03238 (S182)

Triplum Harmonica
1.1.1.1. 1.1.0.0. 2perc,pno,2vln,
vla,vcl,db [16'] sc PETERS 03239
(S183)

Winterpastorale
2.2.2.2. 2.2.1.0. timp,3perc,pno,
cel,harp,8vln I,7vln II,6vla,
5vcl,4db [30'] sc PETERS 03236
(S184)

SCHNEBEL, DIETER (1930- )
Analysis
"Versuche I" timp,2perc,pno,harp,
2vln,2vla,2vcl [5'] SCHOTTS perf
mat rent sc ED 6541, study sc
ED 6336 (S185)

Canones
2(alto fl).2(English horn).2(bass
clar).2(contrabsn). 2.2.2.1.
timp,acord,marimba,harp,strings
[32'] SCHOTTS perf mat rent (S186)

Concerto for Piano
see Hymnus

Diapason
"Tradition I(2). Canon À 13" 0.2.2+
bass clar.2. 2(cornet).2.1+bass
trom.1. perc,cel,pno,vibra,
marimba,guitar,cel,gtr,12vln,8vla,
8vcl,4db,opt hpsd [9'] SCHOTTS
perf mat rent (S187)

Hymnus (Concerto for Piano) (from
Sinfonie X-II (3))
3(pic,alto fl).3.3.3.3.alto sax.
4.3.3.1. 3perc,acord,harp,Ondes
Martenot,14vln I,12vln II,10vla,
8vcl,6db,pno solo [18'] SCHOTTS
perf mat rent (S188)

Inter
2.2.2.2. 2.2.2.1. harp,strings
SCHOTTS perf mat rent (S189)

Janáček-Moment
0.3.3.0. 0.3.2.1. timp,perc,harp,
2vln,vla,vcl [2'] (Re-Visionen
II(1)) SCHOTTS perf mat rent
(S190)

Metamorphosen Des Ovid Oder Die
Bewegung Von Den Rändern Zur
Mitte Hin Und Umgekehrt
5vln,3vla,2vcl,db, solo voices
[120'] SCHOTTS perf mat rent
(S191)

Metamorphosenmusik
0+alto fl.0+English horn.1(bass
clar).0. 0.1.0.0. 5vln,3vla,2vcl,
db,Mez solo [35'] SCHOTTS perf
mat rent (S192)

Mozart-Moment
1.1.1.1. 2.0.0.0. 2perc,2-8vln I,2-
8vln II,2-6vla,2-4vcl,1-2db [1']
(Re-Visionen II(3)) SCHOTTS perf
mat rent (S193)
2.2.2.2. 2.0.0.0. 2perc,2-8vln I,2-
8vln II,2-6vla,2-4vcl,1-2db [1']
(Re-Visionen II(3)) SCHOTTS perf
mat rent (S194)

Orchestra: Symphonic Music For Mobile
Musician
3.3.2+bass clar.3. 6.3.3.1. timp,
perc,12vln I,12vln II,10vla,8vcl,
6db [75'] SCHOTTS perf mat rent
(S195)

St. Jago (Tradition IV (2)
0.0.1.0. 0.1.1.0. timp,perc,
synthesizer,harp,elec gtr,
strings,electronic tape,alto fl&
pic,bass clar&contrabass clar,3
speaking voices&SATB soli [85']
(Music and Pictures to Heinrich
von Kleist) SCHOTTS perf mat rent
(S196)

Schubert-Fantasie
3(2pic).3(English horn).3(clar in E
flat,bass clar).2+contrabsn.
4.(2Wagner tuba).3.3(2bass
trom).1. timp,perc,harp,strings,

SCHNEBEL, DIETER (cont'd.)

Orchestra II: 9vln I, 8vln II,
8vla, 4vcl, 2db [18'-25'] (Re-
Visionen I (5) for divided large
orchestra) SCHOTTS perf mat rent
(S197)

Sinfonia No. 10
3(2pic,alto fl).4(English
horn).4(2clar in E flat,bass
clar).0+3contrabsn. 5(3Wagner
tuba).4.3.1. timp,10perc,pno,
acord,harp,18vln I,12vln II,
14vla,10vcl,8db,electronic tape,
sax/bsn,A solo [156'] study sc
SCHOTTS ED 8326 perf mat rent
(S198)

Thanatos-Eros (Tradition III (1)
3(2pic,alto fl).0+2English horn.0+
2bass clar.3(contrabsn).
4(2tuba).3.3.1. timp,3perc,pno,
harp,12vln I,10vln II,10vla,8vcl,
6db,S/MezB/Bar soli [35']
(symphonic variations) SCHOTTS
perf mat rent (S199)

Tradition I(2). Canon À 13
see Diapason

Verdi-Moment
0+pic+alto fl.1+English horn.3.1+
contrabsn. 2.2.2.1. 2perc,strings
[3'] (Re-Visionen II (5)) SCHOTTS
perf mat rent (S200)
0+2pic+alto fl.2+English horn.3.2+
contrabsn. 4.3.3.1. 2perc,strings
[3'] (Re-Visionen II (5)) SCHOTTS
perf mat rent (S201)

Versuche I
see Analysis

SCHNEEWITTCHENSUITE see Bleyle, Karl

SCHNEIDER, ERNST (1939- )
Prelude for Orchestra
1.2.1.2. 2.1.0.0. strings [8'] sc
CANADIAN MI 1200 S358PR (S202)

SCHNEIDER, GEORG ABRAHAM (1770-1839)
Concerto for Basset Horn and
Orchestra
orch pno-cond sc KUNZELMANN 10276
(S203)
basset horn solo,orch KUNZELMANN
ipa sc 10276A, oct 10276 (S204)

SCHNELLPOLKA see Killmayer, Wilhelm,
Encore

SCHNITTKE, ALFRED (1934- )
Agonie: Suite
(Strobel, Frank) "Suite Aus Der
Filmmusik "Agonie""
3(pic).3.3(bass
clar).3(contrabsn). 4.4.4.1.
timp,2perc,2elec gtr,bass gtr,
harp,cel,pno,hpsd,org,strings,vln
solo [10'] SIKORSKI perf mat rent
(S205)

Concerto for Violin, Viola,
Violoncello and Strings
[16'] SIKORSKI min sc 1922 f.s.,
sc,pts perf mat rent (S206)

Concerto for Violoncello and
Orchestra, No. 2
3(pic,alto fl).3(English
horn).3(clar in E flat,bass
clar).3(contrabsn). 4.4.4.1.
7perc,harp,cel,pno,hpsd,strings,
vcl solo [32'] SIKORSKI sc 1878
f.s.,sc,pts perf mat rent (S207)

Concerto Grosso for Piano, Violin and
Orchestra, No. 5
3(pic,alto fl).3(English
horn).3(clar in E flat,bass
clar).3(contrabsn). 4.4.4.1. 3-
4perc,harp,cel/hpsd,strings,vln
solo, amplified piano solo [22']
SIKORSKI perf mat rent (S208)

Concerto Grosso for Piano, Violin and
Strings, No. 6
[15'] SIKORSKI sc 1932 f.s., sc,pts
perf mat rent (S209)

Concerto Grosso No. 3
2vln,chamber orch sc SCHIRM.G
SIK 1816 (S210)

Concerto Grosso No. 3 for 2 Violins,
Cembalo and Strings
strings,cembalo,2vln soli [21']
PETERS (S211)

Fünf Fragmente Zu Bildern Von
Hieronymus Bosch
vln,trom,hpsd,timp,strings,T solo
[21'] SIKORSKI min sc 1923 f.s.,
sc,pts perf mat rent (S212)

Für Liverpool
3(pic).3.3(clar in E flat,bass
clar).3. 4.3.3.1. 3perc,elec gtr,

SCHNITTKE, ALFRED (cont'd.)

bass gtr,harp,pno,synthesizer,
strings [15'] SIKORSKI min sc
1924 f.s., sc,pts perf mat rent
(S213)

Geschichte Eines Unbekannten
Schauspielers, Die: Suite
(Roschdestwenski, Gennadi) "Suite
Aus Der Filmmusik "Die Geschichte
Eines Unbekannten Schauspielers""
2.2.2.2. 4.3.3.1. timp,2perc,pno,
hpsd,strings [10'] SIKORSKI perf
mat rent (S214)

Gogol-Suite
1(pic).1(English horn).2(clar in E
flat,bass clar).2(contrabsn).
2.1.1.1. 5perc,elec gtr,bass gtr,
cel,pno,prepared pno,hpsd,org,
strings [37'] SIKORSKI min sc
1937 f.s., sc,pts perf mat rent
(S215)

Hommage À Grieg
3(pic).3.3(clar in E flat).2.
4.3.3.0. 2perc,harp,pno,strings
[5'] SIKORSKI perf mat rent
(S216)

In Memoriam
3.3.3.3. 4.4.4.1. timp,perc,harp,
elec gtr,cel,cembalo,pno,strings
[30'] (orchestral version of the
piano quintet) study sc PETERS
EP 5792 (S217)

Kleine Tragödien: Suite
(Kasparow, Juri) "Suite Aus Der
Filmmusik "Kleine Tragödien""
1.1.1.1. 1.1.1.0. 2perc,harp,cel,
pno,strings [20'] SIKORSKI perf
mat rent (S218)

Letzten Tage Von St. Petersburg, Die:
Suite
(Strobel, Frank) "Suite Aus Der
Filmmusik "Die Letzten Tage Von
St. Petersburg"" 1(pic).1(English
horn).1(clar in E flat,bass
clar).1. 1.1.1.0. 2perc,harp,pno,
strings,S solo,men cor [10']
SIKORSKI perf mat rent (S219)

Meister Und Margarita: Suite
(Strobel, Frank) "Suite Aus Der
Filmmusik "Meister Und
Margarita"" 2(pic).2.3(clar in E
flat,bass clar).3(contrabsn).
4.4.3.1. 5perc,elec gtr,harp,cel,
pno,hpsd,org,strings [14']
SIKORSKI perf mat rent (S220)

Music for Piano and Chamber Orchestra
1.0+bass clar.0. 1.1.0.0. perc,
strings [25'] UNIVER. perf mat
rent (S221)

Pianissimo, For Orchestra
3(2pic).3(English horn).3(clar in E
flat,bass clar).3(contrabsn).
4.4.3.1. 5perc,elec gtr,harp,cel,
2pno,hpsd,strings [9'] sc,pts
UNIVER. perf mat rent (S222)
3(2pic).3(English horn).3(clar in E
flat,bass clar).3(contrabsn).
4.4.3.1. 5perc,elec gtr,harp,cel,
2pno,hpsd,strings [9'] sc
SIKORSKI 6829 f.s. (S223)

Polyphonischer Tango
1.1.1.1. 1.1.1.0. 2perc,pno,strings
[5'] SIKORSKI perf mat rent
(S224)

Sinfonia No. 3
4.4.4.4. 6.4.4.1. timp,5perc,2harp,
elec gtr,bass gtr,org,cel,
cembalo,pno,16vln I,16vln II,
12vla,12vcl,10db [50'] PETERS
(S225)

Sinfonisches Vorspiel
4(2pic).3(English horn).3(clar in E
flat,bass clar).3(contrabsn).
4.3.3.1. 6perc,harp,pno,strings
[20'] SIKORSKI min sc 1926 f.s.,
sc,pts perf mat rent (S226)

Sonata for Violin and Chamber
Orchestra (from Sonata For
Violin, No. 1)
hpsd,strings,vln solo [23']
SIKORSKI perf mat rent (S227)

Sport, Sport, Sport: Suite
(Roschdestwenski, Gennadi) "Suite
Aus Der Filmmusik "Sport, Sport,
Sport"" 2.2.2.2. 4.3.3.1. timp,
3perc,cel,pno,strings [10']
SIKORSKI perf mat rent (S228)

Suite Aus Der Filmmusik "Agonie"
see Agonie: Suite

Suite Aus Der Filmmusik "Die
Geschichte Eines Unbekannten
Schauspielers"
see Geschichte Eines Unbekannten
Schauspielers, Die: Suite

SCHNITTKE, ALFRED (cont'd.)

Suite Aus Der Filmmusik "Die Letzten
Tage Von St. Petersburg"
see Letzten Tage Von St.
Petersburg, Die: Suite

Suite Aus Der Filmmusik "Die Toten
Seelen"
see Toten Seelen, Die: Suite

Suite Aus Der Filmmusik "Kleine
Tragödien"
see Kleine Tragödien: Suite

Suite Aus Der Filmmusik "Meister Und
Margarita"
see Meister Und Margarita: Suite

Suite Aus Der Filmmusik "Sport,
Sport, Sport"
see Sport, Sport, Sport: Suite

Sutartines
4perc,org,strings [4'] SIKORSKI
perf mat rent                (S229)

Symphony No. 6
3(2pic).3(English horn).4(clar in E
flat,bass clar).3(contrabsn).
4.4.4.1. 2perc,harp,pno,strings
[30'] SIKORSKI min sc 1901 f.s.,
sc,pts perf mat rent         (S230)

Symphony No. 7
3(pic,alto fl).3(English
horn).3(clar in E flat,bass
clar).3(contrabsn). 4.3.3.1.
3perc,harp,pno,hpsd,strings,vln
solo [24'] SIKORSKI min sc 1903
f.s., sc,pts perf mat rent (S231)

Symphony No. 8
3(pic).3(English horn).3(clar in E
flat,bass clar).3(contrabsn).
4.4.3.1. 3perc,2harp,cel/pno/
hpsd,strings [30'] SIKORSKI min
sc 1920 f.s., sc,pts perf mat
rent                         (S232)

Toten Seelen, Die: Suite
(Roschdestwenski, Gennadi) "Suite
Aus Der Filmmusik "Die Toten
Seelen"" 4(2pic).3(English
horn).4(clar in E flat,bass
clar).3(contrabsn). 4.4.4.1.
6perc,bass gtr,harp,cel,pno,hpsd,
org,strings [30'] SIKORSKI perf
mat rent                     (S233)

SCHNYDER, DANIEL
Colossus Of Sound
see Symphony No. 4

Miniaturen Für Streichorchester
string orch pno-cond sc KUNZELMANN
10281 ipr                    (S234)

Symphony No. 4
"Colossus Of Sound" orch sc
KUNZELMANN GM 505 ipr        (S235)

SCHOECK, OTHMAR (1886-1957)
Peregrina II *Op.17,No.4
(David, K.H.) med solo,2.2.2.2.
2.0.0.0. harp,timp,strings HUG
                             (S236)

SCHOENBERG, ARNOLD (1874-1951)
Chamber Symphony For 15 Solo
Instruments *Op.9
fl,ob,English horn,clar in D,clar
in A,bass clar,bsn,contrabsn,
horn,vln I,vln II,vla,vcl,db
[22'] BELMONT                (S237)

Five Orchestral Pieces & Pelleas Und
Melisande
orch sc DOVER 28120-5        (S238)

Sechs Kleine Klavierstücke *Op.19
(Wulff, Bernhard) 1+pic.1+English
horn.1+clar in A.0. 1.1.1.0.
2perc,harp,pno,vln,vla,vcl,db
[7'] BELMONT                 (S239)

SCHOENDLINGER, ANTON (1919-1983)
Concerto for Organ and String
Orchestra
strings,org solo [20'] BREITKOPF-W
                             (S240)

Partita (from Gesegn Dich Laub)
2.1.0.0. 0.0.0.0. strings [19']
BREITKOPF-W                  (S241)

Partita in B
2.2.2.2. 3.3.0.0. timp,strings
[19'] BREITKOPF-W            (S242)

Passacaglia for Organ and 2 String
Orchestras
strings,org solo [15'] BREITKOPF-W
                             (S243)

Prelude and Fugue
2.2.2.2. 4.3.3.0. timp,strings
[20'] BREITKOPF-W            (S244)

SCHOENE AUSSICHTEN see Heider, Werner

SCHON LACHT DER HOLDE FRÜHLING see
Mozart, Wolfgang Amadeus

SCHON STRECKT ICH AUS IM BETT DIE MÜDEN
GLIEDER see Wolf, Hugo

SCHÖNBERG, STIG GUSTAV (1933-    )
Concerto for Trombone and Orchestra,
Op. 144
1.1.0.1. 1.0.0.0. timp,perc,
strings,trom solo STIM       (S245)

SCHÖNE WELT, SCHÖNE WELT see Ospald,
Klaus

SCHOSTAKOWITSCH, DMITRI
see SHOSTAKOVICH, DMITRI

SCHRECKENSUTOPIEN see Dimitrakopoulos,
Apostolo

SCHREITENDE ALLEEN see Borisova-Ollas,
Victoria

SCHREYAHN see Platz, Robert

SCHRÖDER, KURT (1888-1962)
Film-Ouvertüre, Eine
2.2.2.1. 4.2.3.0. timp,perc,harp,
harmonium,strings [5'] SIKORSKI
perf mat rent                (S246)

SCHROYENS, DANIËL
Fresco
3.3.3.3. 4.3.4.0. timp,5perc,pno,
harp,strings [15'20"] BELGE  (S247)

SCHRYER, CLAUDE (1959-    )
Pensive Overture, A
2.2.2.2. 2.2.2.1. timp,perc,strings
[5'] sc CANADIAN MI 1100 S382PE
                             (S248)

SCHUBERT, FRANZ (PETER) (1797-1828)
An Den Mond "Füllest Wieder Busch Und
Tal" *D.296
(Reger, M.) 2.1.2.2. 2.0.0.0. timp,
strings,Mez solo [5'] BREITKOPF-W
                             (S249)

An Die Laute Op. 81, No. 2 *D.905
(Mottl, F.) 2.2.2.2. 2.0.0.0.
strings,solo voice [2']
BREITKOPF-W                  (S250)

An Schwager Kronos
see Four Songs

Auf Dem Wasser Zu Singen
(Cohen, Shimon) string orch,solo
voice [2'] PRESSER rent      (S251)

Biene, Die
(Thomas-Mifune, W.) vcl solo,string
orch sc,pts KUNZELMANN GM 1180
ipa                          (S252)

Four Songs
(Brahms, Johannes) 2.2.2.2.
4.0.0.0. strings perf sc set
OXFORD 3674971 sc,pts rent
contains: An Schwager Kronos;
Geheimes; Gruppe Aus Dem
Tartarus; Memnon              (S253)

Four Symphonies In Full Score
orch sc DOVER 23681-1        (S254)

Geheimes
see Four Songs

Grätzer Walzer *D.924
(Denissow, Edison) 1.1.1.1.
1.1.1.0. perc,harp,2vln,vla,vcl,
db [14'] SIKORSKI perf mat rent
                             (S255)

Gruppe Aus Dem Tartarus
see Four Songs

Konzertstück for Violin and Orchestra
in D, D. 345
0.2.0.0. 0.2.0.0. timp,strings,vln
solo [11'] BREITKOPF-W sc PB 977,
pts OB 1156L                 (S256)

Letzter Walzer *D.146
(Denissow, Edison) 1.1.1.1.
1.1.1.0. perc,2vln,vla,vcl,db
[20'] SIKORSKI perf mat rent
                             (S257)

Memnon
see Four Songs

Minuet in D, D. 86
strings [2'] BREITKOPF-W     (S258)

Overture in D, D. 590 *It
2.2.2.2. 2.2.0.0. timp,strings [8']
sc,pts BREITKOPF-W PB-OB 5141
                             (S259)

Rose, Die *D.745
(Mottl, F.) 2.2.2.2. 2.0.0.0.
strings,S solo [3'] BREITKOPF-W
                             (S260)

SCHUBERT, FRANZ (PETER) (cont'd.)

Salve Regina in A, Op. 153
S solo,string orch sc,pts
KUNZELMANN EKB 10 ipa        (S261)

Suleikas Zweiter Gesang *D.717
(Mottl, F.) 2.2.2.2. 2.0.0.0.
strings,S solo [4'] BREITKOPF-W
                             (S262)

Symphony No. 5 in B flat, D. 485
(Hauschild, Peter) 1.2.0.2.
2.0.0.0. strings [27'] sc,pts
BREITKOPF-W PB-OB 5205       (S263)

Symphony No. 8 in B minor, D. 759
(Gülke, P.) "Unfinished Symphony"
2.2.2.2. 2.2.3.0. timp,strings
[22'] study sc BREITKOPF-W
PB 5247                      (S264)

Symphony No. 8 in B minor, D. 759,
Scherzo *reconstruction
(Hollard) orch [7'] BOIS     (S265)

Symphony No. 8 in B minor, D. 759,
Scherzo, [arr.]
(Abraham) 2.2.2.2. 2.2.3.0. timp,
strings [6'] perf mat set OXFORD
3675021 sc,pts rent          (S266)

Thekla (Eine Geisterstimme) *D.595
(Mottl, F.) 2.2.2.2. 2.0.0.0. harp,
strings,solo voice [5'30"]
BREITKOPF-W                  (S267)

Unfinished Symphony
see Symphony No. 8 in B minor, D.
759

Wiegenlied Op. 98, No. 2 *D.498
(Mottl, F.) 1.0.1.0. 0.0.0.0.
strings,solo voice [3']
BREITKOPF-W                  (S268)

SCHUBERT, JOSEPH (1757-1837)
Concerto for Viola and Orchestra in C
vla solo,orch pno-cond sc
KUNZELMANN 10239             (S269)

SCHUBERT BIRDS, THE see Colgrass,
Michael (Charles)

SCHUBERT-FANTASIE see Schnebel, Dieter

SCHUBERTS "WINTERREISE" see Zender,
Hans

SCHUDEL, THOMAS (1937-    )
Concerto for Trombone
2(pic).2.2.2. 2.2.0.0. 2perc,
strings,alto trom solo [17'] sc
CANADIAN MI 1333 S384CO      (S270)

Symphony No. 2
2(pic).2(English horn).2.2.
4.3.2.1. timp,2perc,pno&cel,
strings [19'] sc CANADIAN
MI 1100 S384SY2              (S271)

Variations for Orchestra
2(pic).2.2.2. 2.2.0.0. timp,perc,
harp,strings [17'] sc CANADIAN
MI 1100 S384VA               (S272)

SCHUETZ, HEINRICH
see SCHÜTZ, HEINRICH

SCHULDIGKEIT DES ERSTEN GEBOTES, DIE
see Mozart, Wolfgang Amadeus

SCHULHOFF, ERWIN (1894-1942)
Concerto for Piano
1+pic.1+English horn.1(clar in E
flat)+bass clar.1+contrabsn.
2.1.0.0. timp,4perc,harp,8vln I,
8vln II,6vla,6vcl,6db,pno solo
[21'] SCHOTTS perf mat rent
                             (S273)

Eroica
see Symphony No. 7

Hot-Sonate
(Bensmann, Detlef) 2.2+English
horn.2+bass clar.1+contrabsn.
4.3.2.1. 2timp,3perc,cel,harp,
10vln I,8vln II,6vla,6vcl,3db,
alto sax solo [14'] SCHOTTS perf
mat rent                     (S274)

Suite for Chamber Orchestra
1(pic).1+English horn.1(clar in E
flat)+bass clar.1. 2.1.0.0.
4perc,harp,strings [20'] SCHOTTS
perf mat rent                (S275)

Symphony No. 7
(Brauel, Henning) "Eroica"
3(pic).2+English
horn.2.2(contrabsn). 4.3.3.1.
timp,3perc,strings,bass clar&clar
in A [45'] SCHOTTS perf mat rent
                             (S276)

SCHULLER, GUNTHER (1925-    )
Concerto for Orchestra, No. 3
see Farbenspiel

Farbenspiel (Concerto for Orchestra,
No. 3)
orch sc SCHIRM.G AMP-8050      (S277)

Music For Celebration
orch,opt audience sc SCHIRM.G
AMP8000                        (S278)

SCHULMEISTER, DER see Haydn, [Franz]
Joseph, Symphony No. 55 in E flat

SCHULTHEISS, ULRICH (1956-    )
Chatter-Box
2.2.2.2. 2.2.0.0. timp,perc,strings
[12'] PETERS                   (S279)
2.2.2.2. 2.2.0.0. timp,perc,8vln I,
7vln II,6vla,5vcl,4db [12'] sc
PETERS 02912                   (S280)

Poème (Sinfonia for Strings, No. 2)
[12'] PETERS                   (S281)
8vln I,7vln II,6vla,5vcl,4db [11']
sc PETERS 03833                (S282)

Sinfonia for Strings, No. 2
see Poème

Vergossen Und Vergessen
2.2.2.2. 2.2.2.1. timp,perc,strings
[13'] PETERS                   (S283)
2.2.2.2. 2.2.2.1. timp,2perc,2vln,
vla,vcl,db [13'] sc PETERS 02800
(S284)

SCHULTZE, NORBERT (1911-    )
Wandersuite
2.2.2.2. 3.3.3.1. timp,perc,harp,
pno,strings [40'] SIKORSKI perf
mat rent                       (S285)

SCHULWERK, OP. 4: 5PIECES4, NO. 4 see
Hindemith, Paul

SCHULWERK, OP. 44, NO. 2: 8 CANONS see
Hindemith, Paul

SCHULWERK, OP. 44, NO. 3: 8 PIECES see
Hindemith, Paul

SCHUMACHER, PAUL (1848-1891)
Symphony in D minor, Op. 8
2.2.2.2. 4.2.3.1. timp,2perc,
strings,vln&vcl soli [27']
BREITKOPF-W                    (S286)

SCHUMANN, CLARA (WIECK) (1819-1896)
Concerto for Piano and Orchestra in A
minor, Op. 7
(Klassen, J.) 2.2.2.2. 2.2.1.0.
timp,strings,pno solo [25'] study
sc BREITKOPF-W PB 5183         (S287)

Concerto for Piano in A minor
orch,pno solo sc,pts HILDEGARD
09205B rent                    (S288)

Konzertsatz f-Moll
(De Beenhouwer, J.; Nauhaus, G.)
2.2.2.2. 2.2.0.0. timp,strings,
pno solo [12'] study sc
BREITKOPF-W PB 5280            (S289)

SCHUMANN, GERHARD (1914-1976)
Kantate "Nacht Und Morgen": Adagio
Und Passacaglia
string orch [8'] HEINRICH      (S290)

Serenade for String Orchestra, Op. 62
[7'] HEINRICH                  (S291)

SCHUMANN, ROBERT (ALEXANDER)
(1810-1856)
Adagio And Allegro In A Flat Major
see Adagio Et Allegro En La-b
Majeur

Adagio Et Allegro En La-b Majeur
(Leloir, E.) "Adagio And Allegro In
A Flat Major" 2.2.2.2. 0.0.0.0.
strings,horn solo [12'] BILLAUDOT
(S292)
Braut Von Messina: Overture *Op.100
3.2.2.2. 2.2.3.0. timp,strings [9']
PETERS                         (S293)

Complete Symphonies By Schumann
orch sc DOVER 24013-4          (S294)

Concerto for Violoncello and
Orchestra in A minor, Op. 129
(Draheim, J.; Schiff, H.) 2.2.2.2.
2.2.0.0. timp,strings,vcl solo
[23'] BREITKOPF-W sc,pts
PB-OB 5283, pno red EB 8597    (S295)

Faust-Szenen: Overture
2.2.2.2. 4.2.3.0. timp,strings [8']
BREITKOPF-W                    (S296)

Frühlings-Symphonie
see Symphony No. 1 in B flat, Op.
38

SCHUMANN, ROBERT (ALEXANDER) (cont'd.)

Great Works For Piano And Orchestra
orch,pno sc DOVER 24340-0      (S297)

Lotusblume, Die
(Cohen, Shimon) string orch,solo
voice [2'] PRESSER rent        (S298)

Symphony No. 1 in B flat, Op. 38
(Draheim, J.) "Frühlings-Symphonie"
2.2.2.2. 4.2.3.0. timp,perc,
strings [32'] sc,pts BREITKOPF-W
PB-OB 5261                     (S299)

Symphony No. 2 in C, Op. 61
(Draheim, J.) 2.2.2.2. 2.2.3.0.
timp,strings [35'] sc,pts
BREITKOPF-W PB-OB 5262         (S300)

Symphony No. 4 in D minor, Op. 120
orch sc,pts BREITKOPF-W PB-OB 5264
(S301)

Träumerei *Op.15,No.7
(Herbeck, J.) strings,2horn soli
[3'] BREITKOPF-W               (S302)

SCHUT, VLADISLAV (1941-    )
Concerto for Bassoon and Orchestra
see Romantische Botschaften

Ex-Animo
3.3.3.3. 4.3.3.1. timp,5perc,harp,
strings [23'] BELAIEFF         (S303)
3.3.3.3. 4.3.3.1. timp,2perc,harp,
strings [27'] SIKORSKI perf mat
rent                           (S304)

Kammersinfonie Nr. 4
tam-tam,strings [18'] CHANT perf
mat rent                       (S305)

Largo-Sinfonie
1.1.1.1. 1.1.1.0. timp,2perc,cel/
hpsd,pno/org,strings [28']
SIKORSKI perf mat rent         (S306)

Romantische Botschaften (Concerto for
Bassoon and Orchestra)
fl,pno,strings,bsn solo [15']
SIKORSKI perf mat rent         (S307)

Sinfonia Da Camera No. 4
strings,tam-tam [26'] BELAIEFF
(S308)

Warum?
1.1.1.1. 1.1.1.0. 2perc,2vln,vla,
vcl,db [7'] SIKORSKI perf mat
rent                           (S309)

SCHÜTZ, HEINRICH (1585-1672)
Psalm No. 20
see Quatre Psaumes

Psalm No. 92
see Quatre Psaumes

Psalm No. 117
see Quatre Psaumes

Psalm No. 121
see Quatre Psaumes

Quatre Psaumes
(Jolas, Betsy) 2.2.2.2. 2.2.0.0.
timp,strings BILLAUDOT
contains: Psalm No. 20; Psalm No.
92; Psalm No. 117; Psalm No.
121                            (S310)

SCHÜTZ BIN ICH, EIN see Kreutzer,
Konradin

SCHUYLER SONGS, THE see Rorem, Ned

SCHUYLKILL see Hamburg, Jeff

SCHWANDA THE BAGPIPER: FURIANT see
Weinberger, Jaromir

SCHWANDA THE BAGPIPER: OVERTURE see
Weinberger, Jaromir

SCHWANDA THE BAGPIPER: SUITE see
Weinberger, Jaromir

SCHWANTNER, JOSEPH (1943-    )
And The Mountains Rising Nowhere
orch sc EUR.AM.MUS. EA00375FS
(S311)

Concerto for Percussion
3(pic).3(English horn).3(bass
clar).3(contrabsn). 4.3.3.1.
timp,3perc,pno/cel,harp,strings,
perc solo [20'] EUR.AM.MUS. perf
mat rent                       (S312)

Concerto for Piano
2(pic).2(English horn).2(bass
clar).2. 2.2.2.1. cel,2perc,
strings,pno solo [29'] study sc
EUR.AM.MUS. EA 698 perf mat rent
(S313)

Dreamcaller
1(alto fl).2(English horn).1(bass
clar).2. 2.1.0.0. perc,pno/cel,

SCHWANTNER, JOSEPH (cont'd.)

strings,S solo,vln solo [22']
(text by the composer) SCHOTTS
perf mat rent                  (S314)

Evening Land (Symphony)
orch sc EUR.AM.MUS. EA00781     (S315)

Freeflight
3(pic).3.3(bass clar).3(contrabsn).
4.3.3.1. timp,3perc,pno,harp,
strings [6'] (fanfares and
fantasy) study sc EUR.AM.MUS.
EA 736 perf mat rent           (S316)

From A Dark Millennium
orch sc EUR.AM.MUS. EA00470FS
(S317)

...From Afar
3(pic).3(English horn).3(bass
clar).3(contrabsn). 4.3.3.1.
timp,3perc,pno/cel,strings,gtr
solo [16'] SCHOTTS perf mat rent
(S318)

Music Of Amber
orch EUR.AM.MUS. EA00485        (S319)

Play Of Shadows, A
2(pic).2(bass clar).2. 2.1.1.0.
3perc,pno,harp,strings,fl solo
[15'] study sc EUR.AM.MUS. EA 715
perf mat rent                  (S320)

Sparrows
instrumental ensemble,S solo
EUR.AM.MUS. EA00450            (S321)

Symphony
see Evening Land

Toward Light
3(pic).3.3.3. 4.3.3.1. timp,3perc,
2pno,harp,strings [22'] study sc
EUR.AM.MUS. EA 701 perf mat rent
(S322)

SCHWARZE DOMINO, DER: OVERTURE see
Auber, Daniel-François-Esprit,
Domino Noir, Le: Overture

SCHWARZE VÖGEL see Katzer, Georg,
Concerto for Orchestra, No. 3

SCHWEDISCHE MINIATUREN see Peterson-
Berger, (Olof) Wilhelm

SCHWEINITZ, WOLFGANG VON (1953-    )
Dialog
see Wir Aber Singen

Stufengesang I
see Wir Aber Singen

Wir Aber Singen
BOOSEY-ENG f.s. symphonic cycle for
cello and orchestra on texts by
Hölderlin
contains: Dialog, "Einst Hab Ich
Die Muse Gefragt" Op.30 (timp,
12vln I,10vln II,8vla,6vcl,4db,
vcl solo) [8']; Stufengesang I,
"Was Bist Ferne Geblieben?"
Op.31a (2.3+English horn.3+bass
clar.3+contrabsn. 4.4.4(bass
trom).1. timp,perc,strings,vcl
solo) [5']; Zwölf Symphonische
Kanons, "Wenn Nemlich Hoher
Gehet Himmlischer Triumphgang",
Op.29 (2+2pic.4.3+clar in E
flat.3+contrabsn. 4.4.4.1.
4perc,strings,vcl solo) [9']
(S323)
Zwölf Symphonische Kanons
see Wir Aber Singen

SCHWEIZER, ALFRED (1941-    )
Concertino for Violin and Strings
3vln I,3vln II,2vla,2vcl,db MULL &
SCH rent                       (S324)
8vln I,6vln II,4vla,3vcl,2db MULL &
SCH rent                       (S325)

Concerto for Piano
2(pic).2(English horn).2(bass
clar).2(contrabsn). 2.2.2.0.
timp,2perc,3-6vln,2-4vla,3vcl,db
pno red MULL & SCH M&S 1208- rent
(S326)
Konzert Für Volksmusikinstrumente Und
Kammerorchester
2(pic).2.2.2. 2.2.0.0. timp,
synthesizer,pno,3vln I,3vln II,
3vla,3vcl,2db MULL & SCH rent
(S327)
Mantra Für Streichorchester Mit
"Violon Fou"
4vln I,4vln II,3vla,3vcl,db MULL &
SCH rent                       (S328)

Meta-Musik
perc,strings MULL & SCH rent   (S329)

Orchesterstück Nr. 1 "...Cielo
Azzurro..."
2(pic).2(English horn).2(bass
clar).2(contrabsn). 2.2.2.0.

SCHWEIZER, ALFRED (cont'd.)

 timp,perc,harp,synthesizer,8vln
 I,8vln II,4vla,4vcl,2db MULL &
 SCH rent (S330)

 Orchesterstück Nr. 2 "Danses"
 2(pic).2.2.2(contrabsn). 3.3.3.0.
 timp,perc,harp,synthesizer,10vln
 I,8vln II,4vla,6vcl,3db MULL &
 SCH rent (S331)

 Orchesterstück Nr. 3
 2.2.2.2. 2.2.2.0. timp,synthesizer,
 strings MULL & SCH rent (S332)

 Schwingungen Und Farben
 2.0.2.0. 0.0.0.0. strings MULL &
 SCH rent (S333)

SCHWEIZERISCHE-SYMPHONIE see Huber,
Hans

SCHWERINER SERENADE see Goldmann,
Friedrich

SCHWERTSIK, KURT (1935-    )
 Baumgesänge *Op.65
 "Tree Songs" 3(2pic).2(English
 horn).0+clar in E flat+2bass
 clar.3(contrabsn).soprano sax.
 4.3.3.1. timp,perc,harp,pno,
 strings [15'] BOOSEY-ENG rent
 (S334)
 Concerto for Double Bass, Op. 56
 "Empfindsames Konzert, Ein"
 2(pic).1.0+clar in E flat+bass
 clar.1+contrabsn. 0.0.1.1.
 strings,db solo [16'] BOOSEY-ENG
 rent (S335)

 Concerto for Timpani, Op. 54 (from
 Irdische Klänge)
 1+pic.1+English horn.1+clar in E
 flat+bass clar.2. 2.2.2.1. pno,
 strings,perc solo [20'] BOOSEY-
 ENG rent (S336)

 Empfindsames Konzert, Ein
 see Concerto for Double Bass, Op.
 56

 Märchen Von Fanferlieschen
 Schönefüsschen, Das:
 Verwandlungsmusik
 "Transformation-Scenes" 3.0.0+bass
 clar.0. 0.3.0.1. perc,pno,vln,
 4vcl,db [21'] BOOSEY-ENG rent
 (S337)
 Mit Den Riesenstiefeln *Op.60 (from
 Irdische Klänge)
 3(pic).3(English horn).3(bass
 clar).3(contrabsn). 4.3.3.1.
 timp,perc,harp,strings [6']
 BOOSEY-ENG rent (S338)

 Shâl-I-Mâr *Op.17
 [Ger] 1.1.0+bass clar.1. 1.1.0.0.
 timp,perc,harp,string quin,Bar
 solo [13'] (7 songs, text by H.
 C. Artmann) BOOSEY-ENG rent
 (S339)

 Transformation-Scenes
 see Märchen Von Fanferlieschen
 Schönefüsschen, Das:
 Verwandlungsmusik

 Tree Songs
 see Baumgesänge

 Uluru *Op.64
 3(pic).2.0+clar in E flat+2bass
 clar.3(contrabsn). 4.3.3.1. timp,
 perc,harp,pno,strings [12']
 BOOSEY-ENG rent (S340)

SCHWINGUNGEN UND FARBEN see Schweizer,
Alfred

SCIARRINO, SALVATORE (1947-    )
 Mozart A Nove Anni
 orch sc RICORDI-IT 136484 (S341)

SCIOSTAKOVIC, DMITRI
 see SHOSTAKOVICH, DMITRI

SCOTT, CYRIL MEIR (1879-1970)
 Two Pierrot Pieces
 (Coopersmith, J. M.) strings [8']
 BOOSEY-ENG rent (S342)

SCOTTISH SYMPHONY see Mendelssohn-
Bartholdy, Felix, Symphony No. 3 in
A minor, Op. 56

SCRIABIN, ALEXANDER (1872-1915)
 Andante for String Orchestra
 (Kirkor, Georgi) [5'] SIKORSKI perf
 mat rent (S343)

 "Poem Of Ecstasy" & "Prometheus"
 orch sc DOVER (S344)

 Symphonisches Poem
 3.2.3.2. 4.3.3.1. timp,perc,2harp,
 cel,strings [16'] (D min)

SCRIABIN, ALEXANDER (cont'd.)

 SIKORSKI perf mat rent (S345)

 Two Pieces, Op. 57a
 (Smirnov, Dmitri) 1.1.1.1. 1.1.1.0.
 perc,harp,cel,strings [7']
 (transcription for 15 players of
 op. 57) BOOSEY-ENG rent (S346)

SCRIABIN SETTINGS see Knussen, Oliver

SCULTHORPE, PETER [JOSHUA] (1929-    )
 Irkanda 4
 perc,strings,vln solo sc FABER
 50128 1 f.s. (S347)

 Kakadu
 orch sc FABER 51274 7 f.s. (S348)

 Lament For Strings
 strings sc FABER 50553 8 f.s.
 (S349)
 Mangrove
 brass,perc,strings sc FABER 50631 3
 f.s. (S350)

 Music For Japan
 orch sc FABER 50535 X f.s. (S351)

 Port Essington
 string orch, str trio sc FABER
 50579 1 f.s. (S352)

 Small Town
 chamber orch sc FABER 50274 1 f.s.
 (S353)
SCYLLA ET GLAUCUS: SUITE see Leclair,
Jean Marie

SE IL PADRE PERDEI see Mozart, Wolfgang
Amadeus

SEA CHANGE see Nicholson, George see
Pickard, John

SEA DRIFT see Carpenter, John Alden

SEA-SONG see Grainger, Percy Aldridge

SEANCE-HOMAGE A SIBELIUS see Picker,
Tobias

SEARCHING FOR ROOTS: HOMMAGE A SIBELIUS
see Tüür, Erkki-Sven

SEA'S STRONG VOICE, THE see Telfer,
Nancy

SEASIDE DANCES see Mills, Richard

SEASONS, THE see Blake, Michael

SECHS DEUTSCHE LIEDER, OP. 48 see
Grieg, Edvard Hagerup

SECHS DEUTSCHE TÄNZE see Mozart,
Wolfgang Amadeus

SECHS ETÜDEN, FOR ORGAN AND STRINGS see
Tchaikovsky, Boris

SECHS FANTASIEN see Purcell, Henry

SECHS FINNISCHE VOLKSLIEDER see
Godzinsky, George De

SECHS GEDICHTE VON ALEXANDER BLOK, OP.
9 see Smirnov, Dmitri

SECHS KLEINE KLAVIERSTÜCKE see
Schoenberg, Arnold

SECHS KONTRETÄNZE see Mozart, Wolfgang
Amadeus

SECHS LIEBESBRIEFE see Sutermeister,
Heinrich

SECHS MAILANNDER SINFONIEN: FOLGE 1 see
Mozart, Wolfgang Amadeus

SECHS MAILANNDER SINFONIEN: FOLGE 2 see
Mozart, Wolfgang Amadeus

SECHS MENUETTE see Beethoven, Ludwig
van

SECHS PRÄLUDIEN see Shostakovich,
Dmitri

SECHS PSALMODIEN see Raskatov,
Alexander

SECHS WEINACHTSLIEDER see Cornelius,
Peter

"66", FÜR SOPRAN UND 12 INSTRUMENTE see
Raskatov, Alexander

SECO DE ARPE, MANUEL (1958-    )
 Concerto Da Verona (Concierto De La
 Senda No. 3)
 ob solo,string orch [12'] perf sc
 EMEC f.s. (S354)

SECOND AVENUE WALTZES see Rieti,
Vittorio

SECOND CHANT DE NYANDARUA see Florentz,
Jean-Louis

SECOND FLIGHT OF THE MECHANICAL HEART
see Valkare, Gunnar

SECOND REGIMENT CONNECTICUT NATIONAL
MARCH see Anderson, Leroy

SECRET, LE see Faure, Gabriel-Urbain

SECRET INSTRUCTIONS see Altena, Maarten

SEDLÁCEK, BOHUSLAV (1928-    )
 Cas, Ten Nezastaviš
 sax,trp,trom,timp,perc,gtr,strings,
 solo voice [3'] CESKY HUD. (S355)

 Cervánky Nad Rekou
 2.0.3.0. 3.3.3.1. timp,perc,
 strings,harp solo [5'] CESKY HUD.
 (S356)
 Chvilka S Harfou
 2.0.3.0. 1.0.0.0. perc,gtr,strings,
 harp solo [5'] CESKY HUD. (S357)

 Elegy for Viola and Orchestra
 2.0.3.0. 3.0.3.1. timp,perc,harp,
 strings,vla solo [6'] CESKY HUD.
 (S358)
 Ješte Se Vrátím
 1.2.2.2. 3.3.3.0. harp,strings,solo
 voice [4'] CESKY HUD. (S359)

 Modlitba Za Vodu
 harp,strings,A solo [4'] CESKY HUD.
 (S360)
 Na Moravskou Notu
 2.2.2.2. 3.3.3.1. timp,perc,harp,
 strings [6'] CESKY HUD. (S361)

 Vonicka Milostného Kvítí
 2.0.2.0. 3.0.3.0. harp,strings,male
 solo [7'] CESKY HUD. (S362)

SEDMIDUBSKY, MILOSLAV (1924-    )
 Co Je Nejmilejší
 2.2.2.2. 2.3.3.0. timp,perc,strings
 [4'] CESKY HUD. (S363)

 Fugue for Strings
 (alla polka) CESKY HUD. (S364)

SEDMIKVÍTEK see Stedron, Milos

17. LOSTOPAD see Vacek, Miloš

ŠEDOMODRÉ NOKTURNO see Krízek, Zdenek

SEDUCED BY EVENING CICADAS see
Ninomiya, Tsuyoshi

SEEMORGH see Ranjbaran, Behzad

SEGRETA VOCE, LA see Puccini, Giacomo

SEIBER, MATYAS GYÖRGY (1905-1960)
 Transylvanian Rhapsody
 2(pic).2.2.2. 4.2.3.1. timp,perc,
 harp,strings [9'] BOOSEY-ENG rent
 (S365)
SEID UMSCHLUNGEN, MILLIONEN! see
Strauss, Johann, [Jr.]

SEIDENE LEITER, DIE: OUVERTÜRE see
Rossini, Gioacchino, Scala Di Seta,
La: Ouverture

SEKIAI, SATOSHI (1971-    )
 Concerto Grosso 3 X 3
 orch,9 soli JAPAN (S366)

SELBSTHENKER see Ruzicka, Peter

SELEN, REINHOLD
 Symphony No. 1
 3.3.3.3. 4.3.3.1. perc,strings
 [23'] sc DONEMUS (S367)

SELENE FOR ORCHESTRA see Kverndokk,
Gisle

SELF DELECTATIVE SONGS see Blake,
Michael

SELF PORTRAIT see Clarke, Jim

SELFISH GIANT see Barab, Seymour

SELFISH GIANT, THE: VISIONS OF PARADISE
see Koehne, Graeme

SELVA INCANTATA, LA see Henze, Hans
Werner

SEMAINE SAINTE À CUZCO see Tomasi,
Henri

SEMIRAMIDE: INTRODUCTION see Porpora,
Nicola Antonio

SEMIRAMIDE: OVERTURE see Rossini, Gioacchino

SEN O HOUSLÍCH see Flosman, Oldrich

SENHST - SENHST: LEK MED VIVALDI see Rehnqvist, Karin

SENKYR, AUGUSTIN (1736-1796)
Aria De Quovis Festo "Saevit Mare Surgunt Venti"
(Marušan, František) [Lat] 2horn, org.strings without vcl,B solo [7'] CESKY HUD. (S368)

Aria Pastoritia "Huc, Huc, Pastorculi"
(Marušan, František) [Lat] org, strings without vcl,S solo [9'] CESKY HUD. (S369)

Salve Regina
(Marušan, František) [Lat] 2horn, org,strings without vcl,SS soli [5'] CESKY HUD. (S370)

SENOHRABSKÁ POLKA see Smetácek, Václav

SENSE OF PLACE, A see Hall, Carl-Axel

SENTADO SOBRE UN GOLFO DE SOMBRA see De Paz, Xavier

SENTENCE see Gemrot, Jiri

SENTIERI MUSICALI see Baur, Jürg

SENTIMENTAL INTERLUDE see King, Reginald, Summer Haze

SENTIMENTAL JOURNEY: HOMMAGE À RINGO STARR see Johnson, Geir

SENTIMENTAL SEQUENCES see Raskatov, Alexander

SENTIMENTAL SONG see Still, William Grant

SENTIMENTALE SEQUENZEN see Raskatov, Alexander

SENTIMENTI DI CARL PHILIPP EMANUEL BACH, I see Henze, Hans Werner

SEPPUKU AND LULLABY see Stevens, James

SEPT BALLADES D'AMOUR see Machaut, Guillaume de

SEPT MAUPILLIERS, LES see Delerue, Georges

SEPT POÈMES DE RENÉ CHAR see Martinet, Jean-Louis

SEQUENZAS CONCERTANTE see Mills, Richard

SEQUOIA see Tower, Joan

SERAPHIC GAMES see Druckman, Jacob Raphael

SEREBRIER, JOSE (1938- )
Concerto for Violin
"Winter" 2(pic).2(opt English horn).2(bass clar).2. 4.2.3.1. timp,3perc,strings,vln solo [16'] PEER rent (S371)

Winter
see Concerto for Violin

SEREI, ZSOLT
Calyx
1.1.2+soprano clar in E flat+bass clar.1.soprano sax. 2.1.1.0. harp,6vln,4vla,3vcl,db [15'] EMB rent (S372)

SERENADE see Dijk, Jan van see Tomasi, Henri

SERENADE ESPAGNOLE OP. 20 see Glazunov, Alexander Konstantinovich

SERENADE FOR MEZZOSOPRAN OG STRYKERE see Hellan, Arne, Serenade for Solo Voice and Strings

SERENADE FOR SMALL ORCHESTRA see Dreyfus, George

SERENADE FRANÇAISE see Leoncavallo, Ruggiero

SERENADE NACH SCHWEDISCHEN MELODIEN see Bruch, Max, Serenade Nach Schwedischen Volksliedern

SERENADE NACH SCHWEDISCHEN VOLKSLIEDERN see Bruch, Max

SERENADE NAPOLITAINE see Leoncavallo, Ruggiero

SERENATA see Machonchy, Elizabeth see Still, William Grant

SERENATA, LA see Eklund, Hans, Symphony No. 7

SERENATA CONCERTATA see Pickard, John

SERENATA INCONSONANTE see Faltus, Leos

SERENATA PER ARCHI see Hvoslef, Ketil see Hvoslef, Ketil, Serenade for Strings

SERENATA PICCOLA see Zamecnik, Evzen

SERENATA SECCA CON OBBLIGATO see Kondo, Jo

SERENATE, 2 see Vivaldi, Antonio

SERENATI see Sluka, Luboš

SERGEJEWA, TATJANA (1951- )
Concerto, For Piano And Orchestra With Solo Trumpet
see Concerto for Piano and Orchestra, No. 2, Op. 18

Concerto for Piano and Orchestra, No. 2, Op. 18
"Concerto, For Piano And Orchestra With Solo Trumpet" 3.2(English horn).3.2.soprano sax.alto sax. 4.1.3.1. timp,2perc,strings [16'] SIKORSKI perf mat rent (S373)

SERLY, TIBOR (1900-1978)
Symphony in Three Movements
3+pic.2+English horn.3+bass clar.2+ contrabsn. 4.3.3.1. perc,cel, harp,strings PEER rent (S374)

SEROCKI, KAZIMIERZ (1922-1981)
Pianophonie
2.1.3.0. 2.2.2.0. 3perc,2harp, strings,pno [33'] MOECK rent sc 5207, pts (S375)

SEROTINOUS, THE see Kondo, Jo

SERPENT, THE see Hoiby, Lee

SERRANILLA see Rodrigo, Joaquín

SERVANTE AU BON TABAC, LA see Corrette, Michel

SERVIAN SONGS see Gal, Hans

SESSIONS, ROGER (1896-1985)
Black Maskers, The
orch sc SCHIRM.G 0000858 (S376)

Concerto for Piano and Orchestra
PRESSER 496-00019 (S377)

Symphony No. 3
orch sc SCHIRM.G 00008586 (S378)

Symphony No. 4
orch sc SCHIRM.G 00008587 (S379)

Symphony No. 5
orch sc SCHIRM.G 00008588 (S380)

ŠEST INVENCÍ see Tichy, Vladimir

ŠEST MALYCH PRELUDIÍ see Klusák, Jan

ŠEST RUSKYCH TANCU see Vodrazka, Karel

SEST VILLANEL see Stedron, Milos

ŠESTÁK, ZDENĚK (1925- )
Concerto for Viola and Orchestra
see Sokratovské Meditace

Concerto for Violin and Orchestra
see Sursum Corda

Concerto for Violin and Orchestra, No. 2
see Jan Houslista

Jan Houslista (Concerto for Violin and Orchestra, No. 2)
2.3.2.2. 4.3.3.0. timp,perc,harp, cel,strings,vln solo [25'] CESKY HUD. (S381)

Pamet *Variations
3.3.3.4. 4.3.4.1. timp,perc,strings [12'] CESKY HUD. (S382)

Sokratovské Meditace (Concerto for Viola and Orchestra)
2.2.2.2. 3.2.2.0. timp,strings,vla solo [23'] CESKY HUD. (S383)

Sursum Corda (Concerto for Violin and Orchestra)
3.3.4.4. 3.3.3.1. timp,perc,harp,

ŠESTÁK, ZDENĚK (cont'd.)
cel,vln solo [24'] CESKY HUD. (S384)

Zprítomnení Okamziku *Variations
3.3.3.3. 4.3.3.1. timp,perc,strings [17'] CESKY HUD. (S385)

SETKÁNÍ see Tichavsky, Radko

SETKÁNÍ VE SNECH see Malásek, Jiri

SETTE LIRICHE SAFFICHE see Rieti, Vittorio

SEUFZER see Wolf, Hugo

SEVCIK, OTAKAR (1852-1934)
Holka Modrooká
1.2.2.2. 2.2.0.0. timp,strings,vln solo [6'] CESKY HUD. (S386)

SEVEN CHORAL VARIATIONS TO SILENCE see Gondai, Atsuhiko

SEVEN DEADLY SINS, THE see Beaser, Robert

SEVEN MYSTERIES OF LIFE, THE see Doolittle, Quentin

SEVEN PARAPHRASES FOR ORCHESTRA see Holloway, Robin, Scenes From Schumann

SEVEN SAPPHIC LYRICS see Rieti, Vittorio, Sette Liriche Saffiche

SEVEN SHORT PIECES FOR ORCHESTRA see Paulus, Stephen Harrison

SEVEN SONGS see Saygun, Ahmed Adnan

SEVEN SOUND IMAGES ON SEVEN STANZAS BY A CHILD see Rollin, Robert Leon

SEVEN SPIRITUALS
(Ryan; Leon) 2(pic).1.1.1. 2.2.1.1. 2perc,pno,strings,Bar solo [20'] PEER rent (S387)

SEVENTEEN DIVERTIMENTI see Mozart, Wolfgang Amadeus

SEVENTEENTH CENTURY INSTRUMENTAL DANCE MUSIC IN UPPSALA UNIVERSITY LIBRARY
(Mrácek, Jaroslav Js) orch sc REIMERS 107006 (S388)

SEVENTY-FOUR see Cage, John

SÉVÉRAC see Dijk, Jan van

SEVERN CROSSING see Berkeley, Michael

SEVIUS, SVEN (1928- )
Arabesk
2.2.2.2. 2.2.2.1. timp,strings STIM (S389)

Burlesca Nr 2
string orch STIM (S390)

Humoresk
2.2.2.2. 2.2.1.1. perc,strings STIM (S391)

Väneridyll
1.1.1.1. 2.1.0.0. strings STIM (S392)

SEXTON, BRIAN (1953- )
Birdcage
string orch,fl solo [10'] sc CANADIAN MI 1621 S518BI (S393)

Line and texture
see Three Sketches

Newfie Bullet, The: A Newfoundland Journey
2.2(English horn).2.2. 3.3.3.1. timp,3perc,pno,strings, optional 4th horn [30'] sc CANADIAN MI 1100 S518NE (S394)

Parallelogy
see Three Sketches

REM: images forming and dissolving
see Three Sketches

Three Sketches
2(pic).2.2.2. 3.2.2.1. timp,2perc, harp,pno,strings sc,min sc CANADIAN MI 1100 S518TH f.s. contains: Line and texture; Parallelogy; REM: images forming and dissolving (S395)

SGAMBATI, GIOVANNI (1841-1914)
Berceuse-Réverie *Op.42,No.2
(Massenet) 2.0+English horn.1.1. 1.0.0.0. timp,harp,strings SCHOTTS perf mat rent (S396)

SGRAFFITO see Kruisbrink, Annette

SHADINGS see Silverman, Faye-Ellen

SHADOW OF THE NIGHT, A see Borisova-Ollas, Victoria

SHADOW PLAY see Hui, Melissa

SHADOWS see Singleton, Alvin

SHADOWS I: NEKUIA see Aitken, Robert

SHADOWS OF LIGHT see Brustad, Karsten

SHAHNAMA see Maw, Nicholas

SHAKESPEAREANA see Neef, Wilhelm

SHAKESPEARES STURM see Paine, John Knowles

SHAKESPEAROVSKÉ FRESKY see Válek, Jirí

SHÂL-I-MÂR see Schwertsik, Kurt

SHALOM see Pizzarro, Pablo

SHAM MAYIM see Feiler, Dror

SHANTI, SHANTI see Malmlöf-Forssling, Carin

SHAPE-NOTE SYMPHONY, A see Healey, Derek

SHAPE OF TIME, A see Kondo, Jo

SHAPERO, HAROLD SAMUEL (1920-    )
Chaconne After Monteverdi
see On Green Mountain

On Green Mountain
"Chaconne After Monteverdi"
2.2.2.2.alto sax.tenor sax.
2.3.3.1. timp,perc,vibra,elec
gtr,bass gtr,pno,harp,strings
[9'] PEER rent                    (S397)

Three Hebrew Songs
pno,string orch,T solo [21'] (texts
by S. Shalom, S. Tchernikovsky,
L. Goldberg) PEER rent           (S398)

SHAPEY, RALPH (1921-    )
Stonybrook Concerto
1.1.1.1. 1.1.1(bass trom).0. 2perc,
pno,vln,vcl [17'10] PRESSER rent  (S399)

SHARMAN, RODNEY (1958-    )
Concerto for Flute and Orchestra
1(pic).1.1.1. 0.0.0.0. timp&perc,
strings,fl solo sc CANADIAN
MI 1321 S531CO                    (S400)

In Transii
2.1.2(bass clar).2. 2.2.1.1. perc,
pno,6vln I,4vln II,4vla,3vcl,2db,
narrator [9'] sc CANADIAN
MV 1400 S531IN                    (S401)

Phantom Screen
2.2.2.2. 2.2.2.2. timp,harp,5vln I,
5vln II,4vla,4vcl,2db,S solo
[16'] sc CANADIAN MV 1400 S531PH
                                  (S402)

SHAWN, ALLEN
Autumnal Song
vln solo,2.2.2.2. 3.2.2.1. timp,
strings [15'] SCHIRM.EC rent     (S403)

Concertino for Flute and Strings
fl solo,strings [16'] SCHIRM.EC
rent                             (S404)

Concerto for Clarinet, Violoncello
and Chamber Orchestra
clar solo,vcl solo,2.2.1.2.
1.2.2.0. timp,perc,kbd,strings
[25'] SCHIRM.EC rent             (S405)

Midsummer Night's Dream (Incidental
Music)
1.1.0.1. 0.1.0.0. kbd,strings [45']
SCHIRM.EC rent                   (S406)

Nocturnes For Piano And Chamber
Orchestra
pno solo,1.1.1.1. 1.1.1.0. perc,
harp,strings [20'] SCHIRM.EC rent (S407)

Symphony In Three Parts
3.3.3.2. 4.2.3.1. timp,2perc,kbd,
strings [10'] SCHIRM.EC rent     (S408)

SHCHEDRIN, RODION (1932-    )
Bucklige Pferdchen, Das: Suite No. 1
3(pic).2(English horn).4(clar in E
flat,bass clar).3(contrabsn).
4.3.3.1. timp,perc,2harp,cel,pno,
strings [35'] SIKORSKI perf mat
rent                             (S409)

Concerto, For Piano And Orchestra
"Kreuztonarten" (Sharp Keys)
see Concerto for Piano and
Orchestra, No. 4

SHCHEDRIN, RODION (cont'd.)

Concerto for Piano and Orchestra, No.
4
"Concerto, For Piano And Orchestra
"Kreuztonarten" (Sharp Keys)"
3(pic).3(English
horn).2.3(contrabsn). 4.3.3.1.
timp,3perc,strings [22'] SIKORSKI
pno red 2375 f.s., sc,pts perf
mat rent                         (S410)

Concerto for Trumpet
3(pic,alto fl).3(English horn).2.2.
3.2.2.1. timp,2perc,16vln I,14vln
II,12vla,10vcl,8db,trp solo [20']
pno red SCHOTTS ED 8252 perf mat
rent                             (S411)

Concerto for Violoncello
"Sotto Voce Concerto" 3(pic,alto
fl)+rec.2+English horn.2.2+
contrabsn. 4.2.3.1. timp,3perc,
harp,16vln I,14vln II,12vla,
10vcl,8db,vcl solo [30'] pno red
SCHOTTS ED 8283 perf mat rent    (S412)

Concerto No. 3 for Orchestra
see Old Russian Circus Music

Concerto No. 4
see Khorovody-Reigen

Khorovody-Reigen (Concerto No. 4)
4(2pic,alto fl)+A rec.2+English
horn.3(clar in E flat,bass
clar).3. 4.3(bass trp).3.1. timp,
5perc,cel&pno,hpsd,harp,16vln I,
14vln II,12vla,10vcl,8db [23'] sc
SCHOTTS KIN 1003 perf mat rent   (S413)

Kristallene Gusli
2+pic.2.2.2. 3.3.3.1. 2perc,pno,
harp,16vln I,14vln II,12vla,
10vcl,8db [10'] SCHOTTS perf mat
rent                             (S414)

Möwe, Die: Suite
3(pic).2(English horn).4(clar in E
flat,bass clar).3(contrabsn).
4.3.3.1. timp,3perc,harp,cel,
hpsd,strings [20'] SCHIRM.G perf
mat rent                         (S415)

Music for Strings, 2 Oboes, 2 Horns
and Celesta
[22'] SIKORSKI sc 2374 f.s., sc,pts
perf mat rent                    (S416)

Old Russian Circus Music (Concerto
No. 3 for Orchestra)
4(2pic).2+English horn.4.2+
contrabsn. 4.3.3.1. timp,5perc,
pno&cel,16vln I,14vln II,12vla,
10vcl,8db [25'] sc SCHOTTS
ED 8182 perf mat rent            (S417)

Russische Photographien
strings sc SCHOTTS ED 8429 perf mat
rent                             (S418)

Shepherd's Pipes Of Vologda
ob,English horn,horn,strings [6']
SCHOTTS perf mat rent            (S419)

Songs Of Praise
see Velicanie

Sotto Voce Concerto
see Concerto for Violoncello

Stichira
4(pic,2alto fl).3(English
horn).3(clar in E
flat).3(contrabsn). 4.3.3.1.
timp,4perc,harp,cel/pno,strings
[25'] SIKORSKI sc 2371 f.s., sc,
pts perf mat rent                (S420)

Velicanie
"Songs Of Praise" strings [8']
SCHOTTS perf mat rent            (S421)

SHEBALIN, VISSARION (1902-1963)
Concertino for Horn and Orchestra,
Op. 142
2.2.2.2. 0.2.1.0. timp,perc,harp,
strings,horn solo [10'] SIKORSKI
perf mat rent                    (S422)

SHENG, BRIGHT
H'un (Lacerations): In Memoriam
orch sc SCHIRM.G ED3891          (S423)

SHEPHERD SONG see White, Andrew
Nathaniel

SHEPHERD'S PIPES OF VOLOGDA see
Shchedrin, Rodion

SHERIFF, NOAM (1935-    )
Akedah
"Sacrifice Of Isaac, The" 3.3.3.3.
4.3.3.1. timp,perc,harp,strings
[16'] PETERS                     (S424)

SHERIFF, NOAM (cont'd.)

Concerto for Piano and Orchestra
2.2.2.1. 2.1.1.0. timp,2perc,harp,
8vln I,7vln II,6vla,5vcl,4db,pno
solo [22'] sc PETERS 04397 (S425)
see Scarlattine

Concerto for Violoncello and
Orchestra
2.2.2. 2.1.0.0. 8vln I,7vln II,
6vla,5vcl,4db,vcl solo [18'] sc
PETERS 01745                     (S426)

Gomel Le'ish Hassid
"Hassid's Reward, The" strings,bass
clar [15'] PETERS                (S427)

Hassid's Reward, The
see Gomel Le'ish Hassid

Mechaye Hametim (Symphony)
"Revival Of The Dead" 3.3.3.3.
4.3.3.1. timp,4perc,harp,strings,
opt 3trom,TBar soli,jr cor&men
cor [55'] PETERS                 (S428)

Revival Of The Dead
see Mechaye Hametim

Sacrifice Of Isaac, The
see Akedah

Scarlattine (Concerto for Piano and
Orchestra)
2.2.2.1. 2.1.1.0. timp,2perc,harp,
8vln I,7vln II,6vla,5vcl,4db,pno
solo [22'] sc,solo pt PETERS
04682                            (S429)

Symphony
see Mechaye Hametim

Wenn Das Pendel Der Liebe Schwingt
2.2.2.1. 2.1.0.0. perc,harp,8vln I,
7vln II,6vla,5vcl,4db [15'] sc
PETERS 04559                     (S430)

SHERMAN, NORMAN (1926-    )
Canadian Summer
0.2(English horn).2(clar in E flat,
bass clar).1.alto sax. 3.2.2.0.
5perc,strings [6'] sc CANADIAN
MI 1100 S553CA                   (S431)

Events Of November 10, 1812, The
3(pic).2.2.1. 4.3.3.1. 4perc,
strings,narrator, optional cannon
[14'] sc CANADIAN MV 1400 S553EV
                                 (S432)

SHE'S LIKE THE SWALLOW see Ridout,
Godfrey

SHI, ZHEN-RONG
Hase Und Die Schildkröte, Der
1.1.1.1. 2.1.1.0. perc,pno,strings
[12'] PETERS                     (S433)

SHIKISOKUZEKUU II see Kaneta, Tchoji

SHIMODA MONOGATARI: DANCE SUITE see
Aoki, Nobuo

SHIMOYAMA, HIFUMI (1930-    )
Concerto for Violoncello and
Orchestra
[20'] JAPAN                      (S434)

Doubridge
5vln,3vla,2vcl,db [13'] JAPAN
                                 (S435)

20vln,9vla,6vcl,4db [13'] JAPAN
                                 (S436)

Zone For 16 Strings
16strings [8'] JAPAN             (S437)

SHINING BRIGHTLY: A CHRISTMAS FANTASIA
see Hazell, Chris

SHIRAY NESHAMA see Amram, David Werner,
Songs Of The Soul

SHO MYO KOKYO I see Ishii, Maki

SHO MYO KOKYO II see Ishii, Maki

SHOALHAVEN see Lumsdaine, David

SHOEMAKER FROM JERUSALEM, THE see
Grainger, Percy Aldridge

SHOG see Druckman, Jacob Raphael

SHORE, CLARE
July Remembrances
2.1.2.2. 2.0.0.0. perc,strings
[17'] SCHIRM.EC rent             (S438)

Trinity
1.0.0.1. 0.0.1.0. perc,kbd,vln,vla,
vcl,gtr [16'] SCHIRM.EC rent     (S439)

SHORT! see Surdin, Morris

SHORT ANIMATIONS WITH SYMPHONIC SOUNDS
see Yamamoto, Junnosuke, Tokochan
Chokkin 1.2.3

SHORT SKETCH ON A THEME see Holt,
Patricia Blomfield

SHORT SYMPHONY see Hagen, Daron,
Symphony No. 1

SHORT SYMPHONY NO. 1-2 see Brings,
Allen Stephen

SHOSTAKOVICH, DMITRI (1906-1975)
Abschied
see Vier Monologe Auf Verse Von
Puschkin

Adagio - Allegretto
(Sikorski, Christian) string orch
[8'] SIKORSKI min sc 2363 f.s.,
sc,pts perf mat rent          (S440)

Fragment
see Vier Monologe Auf Verse Von
Puschkin

Fünf Stücke Aus Der Filmmusik "König
Lear"
see King Lear: Five Pieces

Helle Bach, Der: Suite
(Titarenko, Konstantin) 3.2.3.3.
4.3.3.1. timp,perc,harp,strings
[17'] SIKORSKI          (S441)

Jahr 1917, Das
see Sinfonia No. 12, Op. 112

Junge Garde, Die: Suite
(Atowmjan, Lewon) "Suite Aus Der
Filmmusik "Die Junge Garde""
3.3.3.3. 6.6.3.1. timp,3perc,
harp,strings [22'] SIKORSKI perf
mat rent          (S442)

Kammersinfonie *Op.118a
(Barschai) strings [28'] BREITKOPF-
W          (S443)

Katerina Ismailowa
(Basner, Benjamin) 3.3.4.3.tenor
sax. 4.3+cornet.3.1. timp,5perc,
2harp,strings [45'] SIKORSKI perf
mat rent          (S444)

King Lear: Five Pieces *Op.137
"Fünf Stücke Aus Der Filmmusik
"König Lear"" 3.2.2.2. 4.3.3.1.
timp,perc,strings [12'] SIKORSKI
perf mat rent          (S445)

Kleine Sinfonie, Eine, Op. 49a (from
String Quartet No. 1)
(Barschai, Rudolf) string orch
[15'] SIKORSKI perf mat rent
          (S446)

Lady Macbeth Von Mzensk,
Zwischenspiele
3.3.4.3. 4.3.3.1. timp,5perc,2harp,
strings,band: 4cornetts,
2trumpets, 6flugelhorns, 2tubas
[15'] SIKORSKI perf mat rent
          (S447)

Lady Macbeth Von Mzensk: Sinfonische
Suite
(Conlon, James) 3.3.4.3. 4.3.3.1.
timp,4perc,2harp,strings [45']
SIKORSKI perf mat rent          (S448)

Märchen Vom Popen Und Seinem Knecht
Balda, Das: Suite
3.3.4.3.sax. 4.3.3.2. timp,perc,
gtr,harp,strings [20'] SIKORSKI
perf mat rent          (S449)

Mitschurin: Waltzes *Op.78
"Walzer Aus Der Filmmusik
"Mitschurin"" 3.2.2.2. 4.3.3.1.
timp,perc,harp,strings [4']
SIKORSKI perf mat rent          (S450)

Pirogow: Suite
(Atowmjan, Lewon) "Suite Aus Der
Filmmusik "Pirogow"" 3.3.3.3.
4.3.3.1. timp,perc,harp,strings
[25'] SIKORSKI perf mat rent
          (S451)

Prelude for Orchestra
(Kelemen) 1.1.1.1. 1.1.1.0. cel,
pno,strings [11'] study sc PETERS
EP 8072          (S452)

Requiem for String Orchestra, Op.
144a (from String Quartet No. 15,
Op. 144)
(Rachlewski, Mischa) [34'] SIKORSKI
perf mat rent          (S453)

Romanze Nach Einem Gedicht Von
Alexander Puschkin
(Roschdestwenski, Gennadi) [Russ]
4.2.3.3. 4.3.3.1. timp,perc,harp,
cel,pno,org,strings,B solo [5']
SIKORSKI perf mat rent          (S454)

SHOSTAKOVICH, DMITRI (cont'd.)

Schauspielmusik Zu Shakespeares
"König Lear" *Op.58a
[Russ] 2.1.1.2. 2.2.1.1. timp,perc,
pno,strings,MezBar soli [13']
SIKORSKI perf mat rent          (S455)

Scherzo in E flat, Op. 7
3.2.2.2. 4.2.3.1. timp,perc,pno,
strings [4'] SIKORSKI perf mat
rent          (S456)

Scherzo in F sharp minor, Op. 1
3.2.2.2. 4.2.3.1. timp,perc,strings
[5'] SIKORSKI perf mat rent
          (S457)

Sechs Präludien (from Opus 34)
(Poltorazki, Victor) string orch
[14'] (includes Nos. 6, 10, 13,
14, 17, 24) SIKORSKI perf mat
rent          (S458)

Sinfonia No. 12, Op. 112
"Jahr 1917, Das" 3.3.3.3. 4.3.3.1.
timp,perc,strings [40']
BREITKOPF-W          (S459)

Sinfonie Für Streicher
see Symphony for Strings

Sinfonie Für Streicher Und
Holzbläser, Op. 73a (from String
Quartet No. 3)
(Barschai, Rudolf) 1.2.1.1.
0.0.0.0. strings [33'] SIKORSKI
perf mat rent          (S460)

Sonata for Viola and String Orchestra
(from Sonata For Viola And Piano,
Op. 147)
(Mendelssohn, Vladimir) [30']
SIKORSKI perf mat rent          (S461)

Sonata for Violin and Orchestra (from
Sonata For Violin, Op. 134)
(Meyer, Krzysztof) 2.2.2.2.
2.0.0.0. perc,harp,strings [34']
SIKORSKI perf mat rent          (S462)

Streichersinfonie
see Symphony for Strings

Streichersinfonie, Op. 118a (Symphony
for Strings, Op. 118a) (from
String Quartet No. 10, Op. 118)
(Barschai, Rudolf) [23'] SIKORSKI
perf mat rent          (S463)

Suite Aus Der Filmmusik "Die Junge
Garde"
see Junge Garde, Die: Suite

Suite Aus Der Filmmusik "Pirogow"
see Pirogow: Suite

Symphony for Strings (from String
Quartet No. 4, Op. 83)
(Schmalenberg, Hilmar) "Sinfonie
Für Streicher" [25'] SIKORSKI
perf mat rent          (S464)
(Sitkovetsky, Dmitri)
"Streichersinfonie" string orch
[30'] SIKORSKI min sc 2382 f.s.,
sc,pts perf mat rent          (S465)

Symphony for Strings, Op. 118a
see Streichersinfonie, Op. 118a

Symphony No. 11, Op. 103
orch sc SCHIRM.G 00123413          (S466)

Symphony No. 14, Op. 135
orch sc SCHIRM.G 00123204          (S467)

Theme and Variations, Op. 3
3.2.2.2. 4.3.3.1. timp,perc,cel,
pno,strings [16'] SIKORSKI perf
mat rent          (S468)

Tief In Den Bergwerken Sibiriens
see Vier Monologe Auf Verse Von
Puschkin

Vier Monologe Auf Verse Von Puschkin
(Roschdestwenski, Gennadi) [Russ]
3.2.3.3. 4.3.3.1. timp,perc,harp,
cel,strings,B solo SIKORSKI perf
mat rent
contains: Abschied; Fragment;
Tief In Den Bergwerken
Sibiriens; Was Bedeutet Dir
Mein Name?          (S469)

Walzer Aus Der Filmmusik "Mitschurin"
see Mitschurin: Waltzes

Was Bedeutet Dir Mein Name?
see Vier Monologe Auf Verse Von
Puschkin

SHOUJOUNIAN, PETROS (1957-    )
Sayat Nova
see Suite Concertante

SHOUJOUNIAN, PETROS (cont'd.)

Suite Concertante
"Sayat Nova" 2(pic).2(English
horn).3(bass clar.clar in E
flat).2. 2.2.0.0. timp,perc,
strings,perc solo sc CANADIAN
MI 1340 S559SU          (S470)

SHULAMIT'S DREAM see Davidovsky, Mario

SHUT, VLADISLAV (1941-    )
Ex Animo
3.3.3.3. 4.3.3.1. timp,5perc,harp,
8vln I,7vln II,6vla,5vcl,4db
[23'] sc BELAIEFF 03538          (S471)

Serenade for Strings
8vln I,7vln II,6vla,5vcl,4db [14']
sc BELAIEFF 04502          (S472)

Sinfonia Da Camera
perc,8vln I,7vln II,6vla,5vcl,4db
[26'] sc BELAIEFF 03843          (S473)

SI J'ÉTAIS UNE PETITE HERBE see
Tchaikovsky, Piotr Ilyich

SI VA FACENDO NOTTE see Woolrich, John

SI VOUS CROYEZ QUE JE VAIS DIRE see
Offenbach, Jacques

SIBELIUS, JEAN (1865-1957)
All'Overtura
see Scènes Historiques I

An Der Zugbrücke
see Scènes Historiques II

Concerto for Violin in D minor, Op.
47
BROUDE BR.          (S474)

Dryade *Op.45,No.1
2+pic.2.2+bass clar.2. 4.3.3.1.
2perc,strings [6'] study sc
BREITKOPF-W PB 5193          (S475)

Festivo (Bolero)
see Scènes Historiques I

Flickan Kom Ifrån Sin Älsklings Möte
*Op.37,No.5
(Jalas, J.) "Mädchen Kam Vom
Stelldichein" 0.2.2+bass clar.2.
4.0.0.0. timp,strings [4']
BREITKOPF-W          (S476)

Hymn To The Earth
2.2.2.2. 4.2.3.0. timp,strings [8']
PEER rent          (S477)

Jagd, Die (Ouvertüre)
see Scènes Historiques II

Mädchen Kam Vom Stelldichein
see Flickan Kom Ifrån Sin Älsklings
Möte

Minnelied
see Scènes Historiques II

Säv, Säv, Susa *Op.36,No.4
(Borg, K.) "Schilfrohr, Säusle"
1.0.1.0. 1.0.0.0. strings,S/T
solo [3'] BREITKOPF-W          (S478)

Scena
see Scènes Historiques I

Scènes Historiques I *Op.25
study sc BREITKOPF-W PB 5196 f.s.
contains: All'Overtura (2.2.2.2.
4.3.3.0. perc,strings) [5'];
Festivo (Bolero) (2.2.2.2.
4.3.3.0. timp,3perc,strings)
[8']; Scena (2(pic).2.2.2.
4.3.3.0. timp,2perc,strings)
[5']          (S479)

Scènes Historiques II *Op.66
study sc BREITKOPF-W PB 5197 f.s.
contains: An Der Zugbrücke
(2.2.2.2. 4.0.0.0. timp,perc,
harp,strings) [7']; Jagd, Die
(Ouvertüre) (2.2.2.2. 4.0.0.0.
timp,strings) [8']; Minnelied
(2.2.2.2. 4.0.0.0. timp,harp,
strings) [5']          (S480)

Schilfrohr, Säusle
see Säv, Säv, Susa

Symphony No. 2 in D, Op. 43
BROUDE BR.          (S481)

Symphony Nos. 1-2
orch sc DOVER 27886-7          (S482)

Tone Poems By Sibelius (In Full
Score)
orch sc DOVER 26483-1          (S483)

SIBYLLE see Dmitriyev, Georgi

SIC, JAROSLAV (1908- )
Symphony, Op. 38
3.3.3.3. 4.4.4.1. timp,perc,harp,
cel,strings [35'] CESKY HUD.
(S484)

SIDE BY SIDE see Kitazume, Michio

SIDE BY SIDE (VERSION II) see Kitazume,
Michio

SIEBEN RAGTIMES FÜR STREICHORCHESTER:
HEFT 1
(Thomas-Mifune, W.) orch sc,pts
KUNZELMANN GM 776A f.s.
contains: Bohemia Rag (Lamb); Easy
Winners, The (Joplin); Slippery
Elm Rag (Woods) (S485)

SIEBEN RAGTIMES FÜR STREICHORCHESTER:
HEFT 2
(Thomas-Mifune, W.) orch sc,pts
KUNZELMANN GM 776B f.s.
contains: Agitation Rag (Hamton);
Chromatic Syncopations (Thomas-
Mifune); Heliotrope Bouquet
(Joplin); Sunburst Rag (Scott)
(S486)

SIEBEN STIMMUNGEN see Ledenjov, Roman

SIEBEN STÜCKE FÜR ORCHESTER see
Butting, Max, Stationen

SIEBER
Kleine Geschichte
(Morgenstern) S solo,orch
KUNZELMANN EES 440 (S487)

SIEBERT, FRIEDRICH (1906-1987)
Rondo
orch min sc KUNZELMANN GM 911P ipr
(S488)

SIÈGE DE CORINTHE, LE: OUVERTURE see
Rossini, Gioacchino

SIEGFRIED-IDYLL see Wagner, Richard

SIEGL, OTTO (1896-1978)
Pastoralouvertüre *Op.108
orch BÖHM (S489)

SIESTA see Groven, Sigmund

SIGNAL IN THE LAND, A see Kyr, Robert

SIGRANCIA BALLADE see Jolas, Betsy

SIGURD FAFNESBANE see Lundin, Dag

SIL JSEM PROSO see Trojan, Václav

SILENCE OF THE SAKYAMUNI, THE see
Xiaogang, Ye

SILHOUETTE see Wilson, Richard (Edward)

SILHOUETTEN see Cilensek, Johann

SILKEN SHOES see Delius, Frederick

SILOËL see Canat De Chizy, Edith

SILVANA: OVERTURE see Weber, Carl Maria
von

SILVANUS: SCENE, FOR ORCHESTRA see
Koerppen, Alfred

SILVER LADDERS see Tower, Joan

SILVERMAN, FAYE-ELLEN (1947- )
Bridges In Time
trp,db,perc,4vln,2vla,2vcl SEESAW
(S490)
Just For Fun
1.1.1.1. 1.1.1.0. perc,strings
SEESAW (S491)
Shadings
1.1.0.1.sax. 1.0.0.1. 2perc,vln,
vla,db SEESAW (S492)
Stirrings
1.1.1.1. 2.0.0.0. perc,strings
SEESAW (S493)

SILVESTROV, VALENTIN (1937- )
Cantata for Solo Voice and Chamber
Orchestra
1.1.0.0. 2.0.0.0. perc,harp,
cembalo,strings,S solo [16']
BELAIEFF (S494)
Exegi Monumentum (Symphony)
2.2.2.2. 2.4.3.1. 3perc,pno,cel,
2harp,8vln I,7vln II,6vla,5vcl,
4db [24'] sc BELAIEFF 03487 (S495)
2.2.2.2. 4.2.3.1. 3perc,2harp,cel,
pno,strings,Bar/Mez solo [20']
SIKORSKI perf mat rent (S496)
Intermezzo for Chamber Orchestra
1.1.1.0. 2.0.0.0. 2perc,opt 2elec
gtr,harp,pno,strings [8']

SILVESTROV, VALENTIN (cont'd.)
SIKORSKI perf mat rent (S497)
Meditation for Violoncello and
Orchestra
1.2.0.1. 2.0.0.0. perc,cel/cembalo,
strings,opt pno,vcl solo [33']
BELAIEFF (S498)
Meta-Music
2.2.2.2. 4.2.2.1. 3perc,harp,cel,
strings,pno solo [42'] BELAIEFF
(S499)
Postlude for Piano and Orchestra
2.2.2.2. 2.1.2.1. timp,perc,harp,
strings,pno solo [18'] PETERS
(S500)
Serenade for Strings
5vln I,5vln II,4vla,3vcl,2db [15']
sc BELAIEFF 03486 (S501)
Sinfonia No. 3 for Orchestra
4.4.4.4. 4.4.3.1. timp,3perc,2harp,
cel,pno,strings [22'] PETERS (S502)
Sinfonia No. 4
0.0.0.0. 4.2.3.1. strings [28']
BELAIEFF (S503)
Sinfonia No. 5
3.3.3.3. 4.3.3.1. timp,4perc,2harp,
cel,pno,strings [46'] BELAIEFF (S504)
Spektry
2.0.1.0. 1.1.1.0. 2perc,harp,pno,
strings [15'] BELAIEFF (S505)
Symphony
see Exegi Monumentum
Widmung
2.2.2.2. 4.2.3.1. 3perc,harp,cel,
pno,strings,vln solo [35']
BELAIEFF (S506)

SIMEONOV, BLAGO (1934- )
Scherzino For Small Orchestra
1.1.1.1. 2.0.0.0. strings [3'40"]
sc CANADIAN MI 1200 S589SC (S507)

SIMI see Kantscheli, Gija

ŠIMICEK, JAN (1942- )
Concerto for Piano and Orchestra, Op.
19
"Královéhradecky" 2.2.2.2. 4.3.3.1.
timp,perc,strings,pno solo [23']
CESKY HUD. (S508)
Královéhradecky
see Concerto for Piano and
Orchestra, Op. 19
Serenade for String Orchestra, Op. 14
[15'] CESKY HUD. (S509)

SIMON, LADISLAV (1929- )
Concerto for Piano and Orchestra
4.0.1.1.sax. 4.4.4.1. timp,perc,
strings without vln,pno solo
[25'] CESKY HUD. (S510)
Concerto for Saxophone and Orchestra
3.3.3.2. 4.3.3.1. timp,perc,
strings,soprano sax solo [25']
CESKY HUD. (S511)

SIMPLE CONCERTO see Yanov-Yanovsky,
Felix

SIMPLE SYMPHONY see Britten, [Sir]
Benjamin

SIMPSON, ROBERT
Concerto for Violoncello and
Orchestra
2.2.2.2. 4.2.3.0. timp,strings,vcl
solo [22'] LENGNICK (S512)
Symphony No. 11
2.2.2.2. 4.2.3.0. perc,harp,strings
[30'] LENGNICK (S513)

SIND SIE FORT? - WEHT LEISER, IHR WINDE
see Mozart, Wolfgang Amadeus, Dove
Son? - Soave Sia Il Vento

SINDING, CHRISTIAN (1856-1941)
Concerto No. 2 in D for Violin and
Orchestra, Op. 60
2.2.2.2. 4.2.0.0. timp,harp,8vln I,
7vln II,6vla,5vcl,4db [20'] sc,
solo pt PETERS 01178 (S514)

SINE NOMINE see Eklund, Hans, Sinfonia
10

SINEQUAN FORTE A see Kulenty, Hanna

SINEQUAN FORTE B see Kulenty, Hanna

SINFONIA see Flodin, Anders see
Kyllönen, Timo-Juhani

SINFONIA 3 see Forbes, Sebastian

SINFONIA 10 see Eklund, Hans

SINFONIA 12 see Eklund, Hans

SINFONIA ACCADEMICA see Hess, Ernst

SINFONIA AD FUGAM see Kenins,
Talivaldis

SINFONIA BELGICA see Uy, Paul

SINFONIA BREVE see Rieti, Vittorio,
Symphony No. 8 see Trexler, Georg

SINFONIA BREVIK see Brevik, Tor

SINFONIA BREVIS see Mateju, Zbynek

SINFONIA DA CAMERA see Brings, Allen
Stephen see Eliasson, Anders see
Shut, Vladislav

SINFONIA DA CAMERA NO. 4 see Schut,
Vladislav

SINFONIA DA CAMERA OP. 128 see Karkoff,
Maurice, Symphony No. 7, Op. 128

SINFONIA DA REQUIEM see Karlsen, Kjell
Mørk, Symphony No. 2, Op. 73

SINFONIA DALECARLICA see Koch, Erland
von, Symphony No. 2

SINFONIA D'AUTUNNO see Johansson, Sven
Eric

SINFONIA DELLA VITA see Karkoff,
Maurice, Symphony No. 11, Op. 202

SINFONIA DI SPERANZA see Panufnik,
Andrzej, Symphony No. 9

SINFONIA DIASPORA see Singleton, Alvin

SINFONIA DOS ORIXAS see Prado, Almeida
see Prado, José-Antonio (Almeida)

SINFONIA DRAMATICA see Whettam, Graham
Dudley

SINFONIA ESPANSIVA NR. 3 OP. 27 see
Nielsen, Carl

SINFONIA FUNEBRE, NO. 3 see Wittinger,
Robert

SINFONIA HUMANA, FOR PIANO AND STRING
ORCHESTRA see Pavlyenko, Sergei

SINFONIA IN LUOGHI APERTI see Sollima,
Giovanni

SINFONIA IN TRE MOVIMENTO see Kadosa,
Pal

SINFONIA INFERNALE see Neubert, Günter

SINFONIA INTROVERTITA see Eklund, Hans,
Symphony No. 9

SINFONIA KYOTO see Hirose, Ryohei

SINFONIA MORTIS ET VITAE see Slavicky,
Milan, Brunnen Des Lebens

SINFONIA NELLO STILE ANTICO see Heard,
Alan

SINFONIA NO.1 see Blum, Thomas

SINFONIA NO. 3 see Giron, Arsenio

SINFONIA PASTORALE see Mozart, Leopold

SINFONIA PASTORALE IN D see Stamitz,
Johann Wenzel Anton

SINFONIA PASTORALIS see Rosetti,
Francesco Antonio

SINFONIA PICCOLA see Drizga, Eduard see
Eklund, Hans, Symphony No. 10

SINFONIA PICCOLA FOR SMALL ORCHESTRA,
OP. 69 see Karlsen, Kjell Mørk

SINFONIA PICCOLA NO. 2 see Wenström-
Lekare, Lennart

SINFONIA QUODLIBET D-DUR see Wranitzky,
Paul

SINFONIA ROMANA see Szokolay, Sandor

SINFONIA ROMANTICA see Karlsen, Kjell
Mørk, Symphony No. 5

SINFONIA SEMPLICE see Karkoff, Maurice,
Symphony No. 12, Op. 206

SINFONIA SILVESTRICA see Smetácek,
Václav

SINFONIA SLOVACCA see Tausinger, Jan

SINFONIA STRETTA see Lokschin, Alexander, Symphony No. 4

SINFONIA SU UNA CANTILENA see Malek, Jan

SINFONIA TOLOMEO see Scarlatti, Domenico

SINFONICO see Fiala, George

SINFONIE 1-3 see Roman, Johan Helmich

SINFONIE CAPRICIEUSE see Berwald, Franz (Adolf)

SINFONIE FÜR STREICHER see Shostakovich, Dmitri, Symphony for Strings

SINFONIE FÜR STREICHER UND HOLZBLÄSER, OP. 73A see Shostakovich, Dmitri

SINFONIE GRACIEUSE OU L'APOTHÉOSE DE BERWALD see Bucht, Gunnar

SINFONIE "MAKRAMÉE" see Trojahn, Manfred, Symphony

SINFONIE NAÏVE see Berwald, Franz (Adolf)

SINFONIE NO. 3 see Tüür, Erkki-Sven, Symphony No. 3

SINFONIE (REQUIEM) see Lokschin, Alexander

SINFONIE SÉRIEUSE see Berwald, Franz (Adolf)

SINFONIE SINGULIÈRE see Berwald, Franz (Adolf)

SINFONIE "ZUM LICHT" see Uspensky, Vladislav

SINFONIETTA CAMERALIS see Spilka, Dalibor

SINFONIETTA FÜR SOLISTENENSEMBLE see Lampson, Elmar

SINFONIETTA ON HEBREW THEMES see Ma'ayani, Ami

SINFONIETTA PROVENÇALE see Tomasi, Henri

SINFONISCHE APHORISMEN see Stieber, Hans

SINFONISCHE FANTASIE see Andreae, Hans-Volkmar

SINFONISCHE INVENTIONEN see Thilman, Johannes Paul

SINFONISCHE KONTRASTE see Röttger, Heinz

SINFONISCHE TÄNZE, FOR PIANO AND ORCHESTRA see Jekimowski, Viktor

SINFONISCHE TRILOGIE see Stieber, Hans

SINFONISCHE VARIATIONEN see Franck, Cesar

SINFONISCHE WIDMUNG see Meyer, Ernst Hermann

SINFONISCHER PROLOG see Thilman, Johannes Paul

SINFONISCHES POEM see Ustvolskaya, Galina

SINFONISCHES VORSPIEL see Schnittke, Alfred

SING- UND SPIEL-MUSIKEN: EIN JÄGER AUS KURPFALZ see Hindemith, Paul

SINGLETON, ALVIN
After Fallen Crumbs
study sc EUR.AM.MUS. EA00626 (S515)
3.2+English horn.3.2+contrabsn.
4.3.2.1. timp,perc,harp,strings
[7'] study sc SCHOTTS EA 626 perf
mat rent (S516)

Again
1(pic).1.1(bass clar).1. 1.1.1.0.
perc,pno,2vln,vla,vcl,db [12']
SCHOTTS perf mat rent (S517)
strings [12'] SCHOTTS perf mat rent (S518)

Be Natural
(special order) sc EUR.AM.MUS.
EA00691X (S519)

SINGLETON, ALVIN (cont'd.)
Blows, 56
"Fifty-Six Blows" orch study sc
EUR.AM.MUS. EA00757 (S520)

Cara Mia Gwen
study sc EUR.AM.MUS. EA00745 (S521)
2.2.2(clar in E flat).2. 4.2.2.0.
strings [15'] SCHOTTS perf mat
rent (S522)

Durch Alles
3(pic,alto fl).3(English
horn).3(bass clar).3(contrabsn).
4.3.3.1. strings [15'] SCHOTTS
perf mat rent (S523)

Even Tomorrow
3(2pic).3.3(clar in E
flat).3(contrabsn). 4.3.3.1.
timp,4perc,pno&cel,harp,strings
[15'] SCHOTTS perf mat rent (S524)

Fifty-Six Blows
"Quis Custodiet Custodies?"
3(pic).3(English horn).3(bass
clar).3(contrabsn). 4.3.3.1.
3perc,pno,harp,strings [12']
study sc SCHOTTS EA 757 perf mat
rent (S525)
see Blows, 56

Idee Ist Ein Stueck Stoff, Eine
strings [10'] SCHOTTS perf mat rent (S526)

Quis Custodiet Custodies?
see Fifty-Six Blows

Shadows
EUR.AM.MUS. EA00670 (S527)
3(pic,alto fl).3(English
horn).3(clar in E flat,bass
clar).3(contrabsn). 4.3.3.1.
2timp,2perc,marimba,xylo,harp,
strings [20'] sc SCHOTTS EA 670
perf mat rent (S528)

Sinfonia Diaspora
(special order) EUR.AM.MUS.
EA00711X (S529)
3(pic).3(English horn).3(bass
clar).3(contrabsn). 4.3.3.1.
harp,strings [12'] sc SCHOTTS
EA 711X perf mat rent (S530)

SINIGAGLIA, LEONE (1868-1944)
Lamento *Op.38
2.2+English horn.2.2. 4.2.0.0.
timp,perc,harp,org,strings,vcl
solo [6'] BREITKOPF-W (S531)

SIQUEIRA, JOSE (1907- )
Sinfonia No. 3
3.3.3.3. 4.4.3.1. timp,perc,harp,
pno,cel,strings [22'] BREITKOPF-W (S532)

Toada
strings [8'] BREITKOPF-W (S533)

SIR CHARLES HIS PAVAN see Davies, [Sir] Peter Maxwell

SIRÉNA see Burian, Emil František

SIRENE, DER: OVERTURE see Auber, Daniel-François-Esprit, Sirène, La: Overture

SIRÈNE, LA: OVERTURE see Auber, Daniel-François-Esprit

SIRENENZAUBER see Waldteufel, Emile

SIRMEN, MADDALENA LOMBARDINI
Concerto No. 1 in B flat
see Three Violin Concertos

Concerto No. 3 in A
see Three Violin Concertos

Concerto No. 5 in B flat
see Three Violin Concertos

Three Violin Concertos
(Berdes, Jane L.) 0.2.0.0. 2.0.0.0.
vln I,vln II,vla,vcl/db,vln solo
set A-R EDN ISBN 0-89579-262-1
f.s. Appendix: Cadenzas by Robert
E. Seletsky
contains: Concerto No. 1 in B
flat; Concerto No. 3 in A;
Concerto No. 5 in B flat (S534)

SIS CANÇONS POPULARS CATALANES see Gerhard, Roberto, Six Catalan Folksongs

SISTE ULTRICEM DEXTERAM see Kopriva, Karel Blazej

SITSKY, LARRY (1934- )
Concerto for Orchestra
3.3.3.3. 4.3.3.1. timp,perc,harp,
pno,strings SEESAW (S535)

SITSKY, LARRY (cont'd.)
Concerto for Piano and Orchestra
3.3.3.3. 4.3.3.1. harp,perc,
strings,pno solo SEESAW (S536)

Concerto for Violin, No. 1
see Misterium

Concerto for Violoncello
see Sphinx

Misterium (Concerto for Violin, No.
1)
2.3.2.2. 4.3.3.1. perc,pno,harp,
strings,solo voice,vln solo
SEESAW (S537)

Sphinx (Concerto for Violoncello)
3.3.3.3. 4.3.3.1. timp,perc,harp,
strings,vcl solo SEESAW (S538)

SITT, HANS (1850-1922)
Concerto No. 1 for Violin and
Orchestra in D minor, Op. 11
2(pic).2.2.2. 4.2.3.0. timp,
strings,vln solo [35'] (no score)
BREITKOPF-W (S539)

SITUATIONEN, 3 see Stendel, Wolfgang

SIX BAGATELLES see Dijk, Jan van see Lutyens, Elisabeth

SIX BOHEMIAN SONGS AND DANCES see Weinberger, Jaromir

SIX BRANDENBURG CONCERTOS see Bach, Johann Sebastian

SIX CATALAN FOLKSONGS see Gerhard, Roberto

SIX CHROMOSOMES see Horwood, Michael

SIX CONCERTOS, OP.2 see Stanley, John

SIX CONCERTOS, OP.X see Stanley, John

SIX CONCERTOS POUR VIOLON, LES see Saint-Georges, Joseph Boulogne de

SIX DUKES WENT A-FISHIN' see Grainger, Percy Aldridge

SIX FABLES DE LA FONTAINE see Offenbach, Jacques

SIX GREAT OVERTURES see Beethoven, Ludwig van

SIX PIECES IN SEARCH OF A SEQUENCE see Surdin, Morris

SIX RAILROAD PRELUDES see Rathburn, Eldon

SIX SONGS, OP.17 see Ullmann, Viktor

SIX STUDIES IN ENGLISH FOLK SONG see Vaughan Williams, Ralph

SIX SYMPHONIES A PIÙ STRUMENTI, OPUS 4 see Maldere, Pierre van

SIXTH SYMPHONY FOR CHAMBER ORCHESTRA see Ward, Robert Eugene, Symphony No. 6 for Chamber Orchestra

SIXTY-EIGHT see Cage, John

"66", FOR SOPRANO AND 12 INSTRUMENTS see Raskatov, Alexander, "66", Für Sopran Und 12 Instrumente

SJÖBERG, JOHAN MAGNUS (1953- )
Rotate
orch STIM (S540)

Windows
chamber orch,electronic tape [7']
STIM (S541)

SJU DANSER see Eklin, Salomon

SJUTTONÅRSMELODIK see Blomberg, Erik

ŠKÁDLENÍ see Petr, Zdenek

SKANDINAVISCHES IDYLL see Landl, Ernst

SKARA see Uttini, Francesco Antonio B., Sinfonia in G

SKARECKY, JANA (1957- )
Aquamarine
2(pic).2.2.2. 2.2.2.1. timp&perc,
perc,strings sc CANADIAN
MI 1100 S626AQ (S542)

SKEMPTON
Concerto For Hurdy Gurdy And
Percussion
1.2.0.2. 2.0.0.0. timp,perc,
strings, hurdy gurdy solo, perc
solo [20'] OXFORD sc 3676524

SKEMPTON (cont'd.)

    f.s., perf sc set 3676524 sc,pts
    rent               (S543)

    Concerto for Oboe, Accordion and
    Strings
    [17'] perf sc set OXFORD 3676532
    sc,pts rent         (S544)

    Lento
    3.3+English horn.3.3+contrabsn.
    4.3.3.1. timp,strings [13']
    OXFORD sc 3676508 f.s., perf sc
    set 3676516 sc,pts rent (S545)

    Light Fantastic, The
    orch [13'] manuscript BMIC (S546)

SKETCH see Landl, Ernst,
    Skandinavisches Idyll see Okasaka,
    Keiki, Sobyo see Pütz, Johannes,
    Mexikanisches Pastell see Ronelli,
    Bob, Prominadenflirt

SKLENICKA, KAREL (1933-   )
    Sinfonietta for Chamber Orchestra
    1.2.0.1. 2.0.0.0. timp,perc,strings
    [17'] CESKY HUD.     (S547)

    Tre Scherzi
    0.0.0.0. 1.2.1.1. timp,strings
    [25'] CESKY HUD.     (S548)

SKOG, YLVA (1963-   )
    Modus Vivendi
    3(pic).3(English horn).3(bass
    clar).2(contrabsn). 4.2.2.1.
    timp,2perc,strings,pno/cel STIM
                   (S549)
    Sortie Et Entre
    1.1.1.1. 1.2.1.0. timp,perc,harp,
    strings,pno,harmonium/cel [5'] sc
    STIM              (S550)

SKOG I see Hultqvist, Anders

SKOG II see Hultqvist, Anders

SKOG III see Hultqvist, Anders

SKÖLD, BENGT-GÖRAN (1936-   )
    Concerto for Piano 4-Hands and
    Orchestra
    2.2.2.1. 0.2.2.0. timp,perc,
    strings,pno 4-hands solo STIM
                   (S551)
SKÖLD, SVEN (1899-1956)
    Gegen Herbst (Melody for Clarinet and
    String Orchestra)
    [2'40"] sc,pts BUSCH   (S552)

    Melody for Clarinet and String
    Orchestra
    see Gegen Herbst

SKORYK, MYROSLAV (1938-   )
    Huzulen-Triptychon
    3.3.3.3. 4.3.3.1. timp,perc,harp,
    pno,strings [12'] SIKORSKI perf
    mat rent         (S553)

    Melody for String Orchestra
    string orch [3'] sc,pts DUMA (S554)

SKOUEN, SYNNE (1950-   )
    Kjaere Mozart!
    2.2(pic).2.2(contrabsn). 2.2.2.0.
    timp,perc,strings [3'30"] NORSKMI
                   (S555)
SKRIN see Rehnqvist, Karin

SKRIVÁNEK see Broz, František

SKROUP, FRANTIŠEK (1801-1862)
    Columbus *Overture
    2.2.2.2. 2.2.3.1. timp,perc,strings
    [6'] CESKY HUD.     (S556)

    Fidlovacka *Overture
    2.2.2.2. 4.2.3.0. timp,strings [7']
    CESKY HUD.        (S557)

SKROUP, JAN NEPOMUK (1811-1892)
    Overture in E flat
    2.2.2.2. 4.2.3.0. timp,strings
    CESKY HUD.        (S558)

SKROWACZEWSKI, STANISLAW (1923-  )
    Chamber Concerto
    "Ritornelli Poi Ritornelli" 1+
    pic.2.1+bass clar.2. 3.1.0.0.
    perc,hpsd&cel,strings [24'] sc,
    pts JERONA rent    (S559)

    Concerto for Orchestra
    4.4.4.4. 4.4.3.1. timp,4perc,harp,
    pno&cel,strings [32'] sc,pts
    JERONA rent       (S560)

    Concerto for Violin and Orchestra
    3.2.3.3. 3.0.3.1. timp,3perc,cel,
    hpsd,harp,strings without vln.
    The harpsichord is amplified and
    the string section should be at
    least 0 0 10 10 8 [20'] sc,pts

SKROWACZEWSKI, STANISLAW (cont'd.)

    JERONA rent        (S561)

    Fanfare For Orchestra
    3.3.3.3. 4.3.3.1. timp,3perc,
    strings [5'] sc,pts JERONA rent
                   (S562)
    Gesualdo Di Venosa: Six Madrigals
    1.2.1.2. 3.1.0.0. strings [22'] sc,
    pts JERONA rent    (S563)

    Music At Night
    2+pic.2+English horn.2.2.alto sax.
    4.2.3.1. timp,2perc,harp,pno,
    strings [17'] sc,pts JERONA rent
                   (S564)
    Passacaglia Immaginaria
    3.3.3.3. 4.4.3.1. timp,4perc,cel&
    pno,harp,strings [28'] sc,pts
    JERONA rent       (S565)

    Ritornelli Poi Ritornelli
    see Chamber Concerto

    Triple Concerto
    3.0.0+bass clar.0. 3.2.3.0. timp,
    3perc,strings, amplified hpsd,
    clar&vln&pno soli [26'] sc,pts
    JERONA rent       (S566)

SLAGVERKSKONSERT see Hammerth, Johan

SLAPSTICK AND SWEET SORROWS see Lindh,
    Björn J.

SLAVICKY, MILAN (1947-   )
    Brunnen Des Lebens
    "Sinfonia Mortis Et Vitae" 3.3.3.3.
    5.4.4.1. perc,harp,cel,strings
    [31'] PETERS      (S567)

    Hamletiana
    see Zeme Lidí: Symfonicky Triptych

    Hommage À Saint Exupéry
    3.3.3.3. 4.3.3.1. perc,harp,cel,
    cembalo,strings [10'] PANTON
                   (S568)
    Land Of People, The
    (symphonic triptych) PANTON 082-90
                   (S569)
    Nadeje
    see Studna Zivota: Symfonicky
    Triptych

    Ozivená Krajina
    see Zeme Lidí: Symfonicky Triptych

    Sinfonia Mortis Et Vitae
    see Brunnen Des Lebens

    Studna Zivota
    see Studna Zivota: Symfonicky
    Triptych

    Studna Zivota: Symfonicky Triptych
    CESKY HUD. f.s.
    contains: Nadeje (3.3.3.2.
    4.3.2.1. timp,perc,harp,cel,
    strings) [9']; Studna Zivota
    (3.3.4.3. 4.5.4.1. timp,perc,
    xylo,harp,cel,strings) [9'];
    Triumf Smrti (3.3.4.3. 4.5.4.1.
    timp,perc,xylo,harp,strings)
    [11']            (S570)

    Triumf Smrti
    see Studna Zivota: Symfonicky
    Triptych

    Zeme Lidí
    see Zeme Lidí: Symfonicky Triptych

    Zeme Lidí: Symfonicky Triptych
    CESKY HUD. f.s.
    contains: Hamletiana (0.2.1.1.
    2.2.0.0. perc,cembalo,strings)
    [7']; Ozivená Krajina (2.2.4.2.
    6.4.0.0. perc,strings) [9'];
    Zeme Lidí (3.3.3.3. 4.3.3.1.
    timp,perc,strings) [8'] (S571)

SLAVNOSTI see Kašlik, Václav

SLAVNOSTI SNEZENEK see Podešva, Jaromír

SLAVNOSTNI see Felix, Václav, Symphony
    No. 4, Op. 70

SLAVNOSTNÍ FRESKA see Válek, Jirí

SLAVNOSTNÍ POCHOD see Berkovec, Jiri
    see Horky, Karel see Strniště, Jiří
    see Svehla, Antonín

SLAVNOSTNÍ POCHOD 6. PETILETKY see
    Juchelka, Miroslav

SLAVNOSTNÍ POCHOD NÁRODNÍ see Malat,
    Jan

SLAVNOSTNÍ PREDEHRA see Laburda, Jiri

SLAVNOSTNÍ PROLOG see Vacek, Miloš

SLAVONIC DANCES see Dvorák, Antonín

SLAWISCHE INTERMEZZI see Uhl, Edmund

SLAWISCHE SUITE see Liatoshinsky,
    Boris, Suite, Op. 68

SLAWISCHE TÄNZE see Dvorák, Antonín

SLEZAK, PAVEL (1941-   )
    Chvalozpevy Míru
    2.0.2.1. 2.1.1.1. perc,pno,strings,
    T solo [19'] CESKY HUD. (S572)

    Karpatsky Koncert
    3.2.3.2. 4.3.2.1. timp,perc,xylo,
    pno,strings,vln solo [21'] CESKY
    HUD.             (S573)

SLEZSKY TANEC C. 2 "KUNCICKY" see
    Ceremuga, Josef

SLEZSKY TANEC C. 3 "VÁNOCNÍ" see
    Ceremuga, Josef

SLIMÁCEK, JAN (1939-   )
    Partita Danzante
    [10'] CESKY HUD.    (S574)

    Poem for Orchestra
    see Zrozeni

    Quattro Intermezzi
    3.2.2.2. 4.3.3.1. timp,perc,xylo,
    harp,strings [15'] CESKY HUD.
                   (S575)
    Sinfonietta for String Orchestra
    [15'] CESKY HUD.    (S576)

    Sonatina for Strings
    [9'] CESKY HUD.     (S577)

    Zrozeni (Poem for Orchestra)
    2.2.2.2. 3.3.2.0. timp,perc,pno,
    strings [10'] CESKY HUD. (S578)

SLIMACEK, MILAN (1936-   )
    Fresky
    3.2.2.2. 4.3.3.1. timp,perc,harp,
    pno,strings CESKY HUD. (S579)

    Sonata for Oboe and String Orchestra
    [13'] CESKY HUD.    (S580)

SLIPPERY ELM RAG (WOODS) see Sieben
    Ragtimes Für Streichorchester: Heft
    1

SLOKY ODVAHY see Koštál, Arnošt

SLONIMSKY, SERGEY (1932-   )
    Concerto for Violin and String
    Orchestra
    "Concerto Primaverile, For Violin
    And String Orchestra" [16']
    SIKORSKI perf mat rent (S581)

    Concerto Primaverile, For Violin And
    String Orchestra
    see Concerto for Violin and String
    Orchestra

    Symphony No. 6
    3.2.3.2. 4.3.3.1. timp,4perc,
    strings [20'] SIKORSKI perf mat
    rent            (S582)

SLOVA see Kubik, Ladislav

SLOVANSKÁ RAPSODIE see Ullmann, Viktor

SLOVIENSKA DUCA see Rossum, Frederic R.
    van, Concerto, Op. 30

SLOW-MOBILE see Krebs, Joachim

SLUKA, LUBOŠ (1928-   )
    Cesta Uzdraveni *meditation
    2.2.2.2. 4.3.3.1. perc,pno,strings
    [12'] CESKY HUD.    (S583)

    Serenati
    [14'] CESKY HUD.    (S584)

    Vyznání
    strings,B solo [11'] CESKY HUD.
                   (S585)
    Vzpomínka
    2.2.2.2. 4.3.3.1. timp,perc,pno,
    strings [6'] CESKY HUD. (S586)

SLUNCI VSTRÍC see Vacek, Miloš

SLUNECNÁ SVITA see Bodorova, Sylvie

SLUNECNICE: SUITE see Petrova, Elena

SLYCHÁM O TVYCH OCÍCH see Sodomka,
    Karel

SMALL TOWN see Sculthorpe, Peter
    [Joshua]

SMEDEBY, SUNE (1934- )
Jajamen
string orch [3'] sc,pts STIM (S587)

SMÉKAL, MOJMIR (1920- )
Docela Prostá Písnicka
2.0.1.0. 3.2.3.0. perc,2gtr,harp,
strings,trp solo [3'] CESKÝ HUD.
(S588)

Povez Mi Má Lásko
5sax,trp,trom,perc,gtr,pno,kbd,
strings,solo voice [5'] CESKÝ
HUD. (S589)

SMET, RAOUL DE
Concerto
acord,strings,perc,alto sax solo
[17'] BELGE (S590)

SMETÁCEK, RUDOLF (1878-1946)
Football
see Kvapík Sportovcu

Kvapík Sportovcu
"Football" 2.1.2.1. 4.2.3.0. perc,
strings [3'] CESKÝ HUD. (S591)

Polka Slánskych Abiturientu
1.1.3.1. 4.4.4.0. perc,strings [3']
CESKÝ HUD. (S592)

Zaludská Polka
2.2.2.2. 4.2.3.0. perc,strings [3']
CESKÝ HUD. (S593)

SMETÁCEK, VÁCLAV (1906-1986)
Pochod
3.2.2.2. 4.2.3.0. perc,strings [3']
CESKÝ HUD. (S594)

Polka
see U Nás V Trešti

Senohrabská Polka
2.2.2.2. 4.2.3.0. perc,strings [3']
CESKÝ HUD. (S595)

Sinfonia Silvestrica
4.3.3.3. 4.4.3.1. timp,perc,strings
[15'] CESKÝ HUD. (S596)

Svatební Pochod
2.2.2.2. 4.3.3.1. timp,perc,harp,
strings [5'] CESKÝ HUD. (S597)

U Nás V Trešti (Polka)
2.2.2.2. 4.2.3.0. timp,perc,strings
[3'] CESKÝ HUD. (S598)

Vivat Olympia
2.2.2.2. 4.2.3.1. perc,strings [5']
PANTON (S599)

SMETANA, BEDRICH (1824-1884)
Baletní Hudba Z Opery Prodaná Nevesta
3.2.2.2. 4.2.3.0. timp,perc,strings
[12'] CESKÝ HUD. (S600)

Libušin Soud
2.2.2.2. 4.2.3.0. timp,strings
CESKÝ HUD. (S601)

Macbeth A Carodejnice
(Jeremiáš, O.; Hanuš, Jan) 3.3.3.3.
4.3.3.1. harp,strings CESKÝ HUD.
(S602)

Minuet in B flat
1.2.2.2. 4.2.0.0. perc,strings [2']
CESKÝ HUD. (S603)

"Moldau" And Other Works
orch sc DOVER 29252-5 (S604)

Pochod Národní Gardy
3.2.2.2. 4.2.3.1. timp,strings [3']
CESKÝ HUD. (S605)

Pochod Studentské Legie
3.2.2.2. 4.2.3.1. timp,strings [4']
CESKÝ HUD. (S606)

Rybár *Op.103
harp,harmonium,strings CESKÝ HUD.
(S607)

Valcíky
2.2.2.2. 4.2.3.1. timp,perc,strings
[7'] CESKÝ HUD. (S608)

SMETANA, RADIM (1950)
Obraz Pro Orchestr
2.2.2.2. 2.2.0.0. timp,perc,strings
[11'] CESKÝ HUD. (S609)

Sinfonia
3.2.2.2. 4.3.3.0. timp,perc,cel,
strings [17'] CESKÝ HUD. (S610)

ŠMIKOVANDA see Vodrazka, Karel

SMIRNOV, DMITRI (1948- )
Blake-Bild II
see Jakobsleiter, Die

Blake-Bild IV
see Fluss Des Lebens, Der

SMIRNOV, DMITRI (cont'd.)

Concerto for Violin and 13 Strings,
Op. 54
4vln I,3vln II,3vla,2vcl,db,vln
solo [20'] BOOSEY-ENG rent (S611)
[15'] SIKORSKI perf mat rent (S612)

Concerto for Violoncello and
Orchestra, Op. 74
3.3.3.3. 4.3.3.1. timp,perc,harp,
cel,strings,vcl solo [28']
BOOSEY-ENG perf mat rent (S613)

Fluss Des Lebens, Der *Op.66
"Blake-Bild IV" 1.1.1.1. 1.1.1.0.
2perc,2vln,vla,vcl,db [14'] BOIS
perf mat rent (S614)

Jacob's Ladder *Op.58
1.1.1.1. 1.1.1.0. 2perc,cel,harp,
2vln,vla,vcl,db [14'] BOOSEY-ENG
rent (S615)

Jakobsleiter, Die *Op.58
"Blake-Bild II" 1.1.1.1. 1.1.1.0.
2perc,harp,cel,2vln,vla,vcl,db
[14'] sc SIKORSKI 6864 f.s.
(S616)
"Blake-Bild II" 1.1.1.1. 1.1.1.0.
2perc,harp,cel,2vln,vla,vcl,db
[14'] sc,pts BOIS perf mat rent
(S617)

Mozart-Variationen, For Orchestra,
Op. 47 (Variations for Orchestra,
Op. 47)
1.2.2.2. 2.0.0.0. strings [14']
SIKORSKI perf mat rent (S618)

River Of Life, The *Op.66
1.1.1.1. 1.1.1.0. 2perc,2vln,vla,
vcl,db [14'] BOOSEY-ENG rent
(S619)

Sechs Gedichte Von Alexander Blok,
Op. 9
[Russ] 2.2.2.2. 2.1.1.0. perc,harp,
strings,solo voice [20'] SIKORSKI
perf mat rent (S620)

Thels Klagen: Prolog *Op.45a
1.1.1.1. 1.1.1.0. 2perc,harp,cel,
strings [8'] SIKORSKI perf mat
rent (S621)

Variations for Orchestra, Op. 47
see Mozart-Variationen, For
Orchestra, Op. 47

SMITH, MICHAEL (1938- )
Homage To Tbilisi
18vln,2vla,2vcl,2db [6'] sc STIM
(S622)

SMITH BRINDLE, REGINALD (1917- )
Concerto for Guitar
1.1.1.1. 0.0.0.0. perc,pno,elec
org,5vln I,4vln II,3vla,2vcl,db,
gtr solo [10'] SCHOTTS perf mat
rent study sc ED 11421, pts
ED 11421-01 (S623)

SMITH BRINDLE BORSI, REGINALD
see SMITH BRINDLE, REGINALD

SMOLKA, JAROSLAV (1933- )
Concerto for Violoncello and
Orchestra
see Jenom Ne Strach

Fugová Suita, 1. d-moll
string orch/string quar [14'] CESKÝ
HUD. (S624)

Jenom Ne Strach (Concerto for
Violoncello and Orchestra)
3.3.3.3. 4.3.3.1. timp,perc,xylo,
vibra,strings,vcl solo [18']
CESKÝ HUD. (S625)

Novoklasická Ouvertura
2.2.2.2. 2.2.0.0. timp,strings [5']
CESKÝ HUD. (S626)

Partita for Strings
[22'] CESKÝ HUD. (S627)

Pocta Václav Janu Stichovi Puntovi
(from Opera "Hra O Zuby") Suite
strings,cembalo&horn soli [12']
CESKÝ HUD. (S628)

Suite for Chamber Orchestra
see Ze Smetanova Zápisniku Motivu

Ze Smetanova Zápisniku Motivu (Suite
for Chamber Orchestra)
1.1.1.1. 0.0.0.0. strings/string
quar [15'] CESKÝ HUD. (S629)

SMOLKA, MARTIN (1959- )
Fantasy for Orchestra
see Vlnobití

Sinfonietta
4.0.3.0.sax. 2.2.2.0. perc,xylo,
2harp,prepared pno,electronic
tape,strings,S solo [30'] CESKY

SMOLKA, MARTIN (cont'd.)

HUD. (S630)

Vlnobití (Fantasy for Orchestra)
3.3.3.2.sax. 4.3.4.0. perc,strings
[11'] CESKÝ HUD. (S631)

SMUTECNÍ HUDBA see Pauer, Jirí

SMUTECNI MONODIE see Klusák, Jan

SMUTEK SLUŠÍ VIOLE see Obrovská, Jana

SMUTNY, JIRÍ (1932- )
Concertino Facile
trp,strings,pno 4-hands solo [10']
CESKÝ HUD. (S632)

Concertino for Cembalo and Chamber
Orchestra
1.1.1.1. 0.0.0.0. strings,cembalo
solo [18'] CESKÝ HUD. (S633)

Malé Etudy Pro Malého Dirigenta
1.1.1.1. 0.1.0.0. perc,pno,strings
[8'] CESKÝ HUD. (S634)

Sinfonietta for Orchestra and Piano
3.3.3.3. 4.3.3.1. timp,perc,
strings,pno solo [20'] CESKÝ HUD.
(S635)

Sonata Da Requiem
11strings,vln solo [15'] CESKÝ HUD.
(S636)

SNAKEBITE see Montague, Stephen

SNAP see Daugherty, Michael

SNOW WALKER see Colgrass, Michael
(Charles)

SNOW WHITE AND THE SEVEN DWARFS see
Alberga, Eleanor

SNOWMAM, THE: SUITE see Blake, Howard

SNUGGLEPOT AND CUDDLEPIE SUITE see
Mills, Richard

SO SEI'S! FÜR SEINEN FEIGEN WANKELMUT
see Wagner, Richard

SO WHAT? see Börjesson, Lars-Ove

SO WHEN THE GLITTERING QUEEN OF NIGHT
see Purcell, Henry

SOBYO see Okasaka, Keiki

SØDERLIND, RAGNAR (1945- )
Angst: Sinfonische Dichtung No. 2
Nach Bildern Von Edv. Munch
*Op.68
4(pic).3(English horn).3(bass
clar).3(contrabsn).soprano sax.
6.3.3(bass trom).1. timp,3perc,
2harp,strings [23'] NORSKMI
(S637)

Concerto for Violoncello and
Orchestra, Op. 54
3(pic).2.2.2. 4.2.3.1. timp,2perc,
harp,strings NORSKMI (S638)

Er Ei Slik Natt, Det
see Tvo Sanger Til Tekster Av Hans
Børli

Fanfare Regale *Op.63
3(2pic).2.3(bass
clar).2(contrabsn). 4.3.3.1.
timp,3perc,strings [1'45"]
NORSKMI (S639)

Kvitsunn
see Sinfonia No. 5, Op. 60

På Kveldshøgda
see Tvo Sanger Til Tekster Av Hans
Børli

Sinfonia No. 4, Op. 50
3(pic).3(English horn).3(bass
clar).3(contrabsn). 4.3.3.1.
3timp,2harp,strings [25'] NORSKMI
(S640)

Sinfonia No. 5, Op. 60
"Kvitsunn" 3(pic).2.2.2(contrabsn).
4.3.3.1. timp,2perc,harp,strings
[28'] NORSKMI (S641)

Tanz Des Lebens, Der *Op.57b
3.3(English horn).3(bass
clar).3(contrabsn).sax.
6.3.3(bass trom).1. timp,perc,
harp,strings [25'] NORSKMI (S642)

Tranströmer-Svit, Op. 52b
[Swed] string orch,2perc,pno,solo
voice [25'] NORSKMI (S643)

Tvo Sanger Til Tekster Av Hans Børli
*Op.55b
[Norw] 3(2pic).2(English
horn).3(2bass clar).2(contrabsn).
4.3.3.1. timp,2perc,harp,strings,

SØNSTEVOLD, GUNNAR (1912-1991)
Concertino for Harp and Orchestra
2.2.2.2(contrabsn). 4.2.2.1. timp,
perc,pno/cembalo,strings,harp
solo NORSKMI (S672)

SOPRONI, JOZSEF (1930-    )
Comments On A Theme By Handel
"Kommentárok Egy Handel-Témához"
3(pic).2+English horn.3(bass
clar).2+contrabsn. 4.3.3.1. timp,
perc,harp,pno,cel,strings [24']
EMB rent (S673)

Concerto for Violoncello and
Orchestra, No. 2
3(pic).2.3(bass clar).2. 4.3.3.1.
3timp,perc,harp,cel,pno,strings,
vcl solo EMB rent (S674)

Három Zenekari Darab
see Three Pieces For Orchestra

Kommentárok Egy Handel-Témához
see Comments On A Theme By Handel

Three Pieces For Orchestra
"Három Zenekari Darab"
3(pic).2.3(bass clar).2. 4.3.3.0.
timp,2perc,harp,pno,12vln I,10vln
II,8vla,8vcl,6db [20'] EMB rent (S675)

SORTIE ET ENTRE see Skog, Ylva

SORTILÈGE see Casken, John

SORTILÈGES see Rolin, Étienne

SOSEN, OTTO EBEL VON (1899-    )
Abendlied
1.2.2.0. 0.2.2.0. harmonium,8vln I,
7vln II,5vcl,4db,vln solo [10']
PETERS 02111 (S676)

SOSOSTRIS' ARIA see Tippett, [Sir]
Michael

SOSPIRI see Elgar, [Sir] Edward
(William)

SOTTILE see Ahlberg, Gunnar

SOTTO VOCE CONCERTO see Shchedrin,
Rodion, Concerto for Violoncello

SOUFFLE DE NÉMÉSIS, LE see Rossum,
Frederic R. van, Symphony No. 3,
Op. 48

SOUKUP, ONDREJ
Dál Nez Já
horn,perc,gtr,2pno,elec gtr,
strings,solo voice [4'] CESKY
HUD. (S677)

SOUKUP, VLADIMÍR (1930-    )
Concerto for Saxophone and Orchestra
2.2.2.2. 4.3.3.1. timp,perc,
strings,sax solo [18'] CESKY HUD.
(S678)
Concerto for Violin and Orchestra
2.2.2.2. 4.3.3.1. timp,perc,
strings,vln solo [23'] CESKY HUD.
(S679)

Symfonie Mládí
see Symphony No. 1

Symphony No. 1
"Symfonie Mládí" 2.2.2.2. 4.3.3.1.
timp,perc,strings [23'] CESKY
HUD. (S680)

SOUND CANVAS see Werder, Felix

SOUND FAME THY BRAZEN TRUMPET see
Purcell, Henry

SOUND OF MUSIC, THE see Tarenskeen,
Boudewijn

SOUND SCULPTURES FROM RATHENAU see
Dreyfus, George

SOUND SHIFT NO. 5 see Homma, Masao

SOUNDING: SILVER IN THE WAKE see
Lutzow-Holm, Ole

SOUNDS FROM IRELAND see Barrie, Stuart

SOUNDSCAPE see Jansson, Gunnar

SOUNDSCAPES FOR PERCUSSION AND
ORCHESTRA see Mills, Richard

SOUPER DES MONSIEUR PAPAGENOR, DAS see
Kirchner, Volker David

SOURIRE, UN see Messiaen, Olivier

SOUSA, JOHN PHILIP (1854-1932)
Liberty Bell March, The
"Monty Python's Flying Circus"
varied ensemble sc,pts FABER
51303 4 f.s. (S681)

SOUSA, JOHN PHILIP (cont'd.)

Monty Python's Flying Circus
see Liberty Bell March, The

SOUTHAM, ANN (1937-    )
Waves
string orch [10'] sc,pts CANADIAN
MI 1500 S726WA (S682)

SOUVENIR see Polgar, Tibor

SOUVENIR D'AIX-LES-BAINS see Offenbach,
Jacques

SOUVENIRS DE POLOGNE see Koprowski,
Peter Paul

SPACES I: THE RIVER see Symonds, Norman

SPACESCAPE FOR ORCHESTRA AND TAPE see
Bubalo, Rudolph

SPAHLINGER, MATHIAS (1944-    )
Furioso
0+pic.1(English horn).1(soprano
clar in E flat,contrabass clar)+
bass clar.1(contrabsn). soprano
sax.tenor sax. 0.1(piccolo
trp).1.0. harp,pno,vln I,vln II,
vla,vcl,db [20'] BREITKOPF-W
(S683)

Intermezzo
2.2.2.2. 4.2.2.0. perc,gtr,harp,
strings,pno solo [26'45"] PEER
rent (S684)

Passage
"Paysage" 4(pic,alto fl).4(English
horn).4(bass clar).4(contrabsn).
4.4.4.0. 6perc,2harp,gtr,2pno,
cel,16vln I,14vln II,11vla,9vcl,
8db [45'] study sc BREITKOPF-W
PB 5418 (S685)

Paysage
see Passage

ŠPANELSKY TANEC see Krízek, Zdenek

SPANILY, PETR (1941-    )
Kolonáda (Rhapsody for Piano and
Orchestra)
3.1.3.2. 4.3.3.0. timp,perc,harp,
strings,pno solo [7'] CESKY HUD.
(S686)
Rhapsody for Piano and Orchestra
see Kolonáda

SPANISCHE BILDER see Svetlanov, Evgeny,
Rhapsody No. 1

SPANNUNGEN EINGEGRENZT see Goldmann,
Friedrich

SPARAGMOS see Feiler, Dror

SPARKLING WAVES FOR 21 PLAYERS see
Nabeshima, Kaori

SPARROWS see Schwantner, Joseph

SPEAK ITS NAME! see Finnissy, Michael

SPECTRA see Lennon, John Anthony

SPECTRAL CANTICLE see Takemitsu, Toru

SPECTRUM see Burritt, Lloyd

SPEKTRY see Silvestrov, Valentin

SPEL see Erikson, Åke

SPELDOSAN: ETT UPPDRAGSVERK see
Burwick, Karin

SPELL FOR GREEN CORN see Davies, [Sir]
Peter Maxwell

SPENDIAROV, ALEXANDER (1871-1928)
Drei Palmen, Die *Op.10
3.3.3.3. 4.2.3.1. timp,perc,harp,
8vln I,7vln II,6vla,5vcl,4db
[18'] sc BELAIEFF 01810 (S687)

SPENNINGENS LAND see Nystedt, Knut

SPERGER, JOHANN M. (1750-1812)
Ankunftssinfonie
see Sinfonia in F

Concerto in G for Flute and Orchestra
0.2.0.0. 2.0.0.0. 8vln I,7vln II,
6vla,5vcl,4db,opt bsn,fl solo
[20'] sc,solo pt PETERS 02716
(S688)
Sinfonia in F
"Ankunftssinfonie" 2.2.0.2.
2.2.0.0. timp,cembalo,strings
[15'] sc PETERS 02453 (S689)

SPHINX see Sitsky, Larry

SPI, SPI NEVINÁTKO see Ryba, Jan Jakub
Simon

SPIEGARTI NON POSS'IO see Mozart,
Wolfgang Amadeus

SPIEGEL, DER see Kelemen, Milko see
Kempkens, Arnold

SPIEL DER ELFEN MIT DEN ZWÖLFEN see
Cornell, Klaus

SPILKA, DALIBOR (1931-    )
Sinfonietta Cameralis
2.2.2.2. 2.2.0.0. strings [15']
CESKY HUD. (S690)

SPINKS, CHARLES (1915-1992)
Dance Suite
strings,ob [7'40"] BARDIC (S691)

Variations On A Greek Folk-Song For
Piano & Orchestra
2+pic.2.2.2. 4.2.3.1. timp,perc,
strings,pno solo [10'15"] BARDIC
(S692)

SPIRAL see Aitken, Robert

SPIRAL TUNNEL BOOGIE see Rathburn,
Eldon

SPIRALGESANG see Trümpy, Balz

SPIRIT GARDEN see Takemitsu, Toru

SPIRITDANCE see Moravec, Paul

SPIRIT'S WHISPER, A: IN SWEDENBORG'S
GAZEBO see Nilsson, Bo

SPITTA, HEINRICH (1902-1972)
Concertante
vln I,vln II,vla,vcl,db,ob solo
MÖSELER sc 11.448-00, pts
11.448-01, set 11.448-09 (S693)

SPITZMUELLER, ALEXANDER (1894-1962)
Concerto for Piano, No. 2, Op. 40
2.2.2.2. 4.3.3.1. timp,strings,pno
solo [15'] BOOSEY-ENG rent (S694)

SPOHR, LUDWIG (LOUIS) (1784-1859)
Concertante A Für 2 Violinen Und
Orchester *Op.48
1.2.2.2. 2.0.0.0. 8vln I,7vln II,
6vla,5vcl,4db [20'] sc PETERS
02717 (S695)

Concertante For Harp, Violin &
Orchestra
INTERNAT.S. sc,pts rent, solo pt,
pno red (S696)

Concertante No. 1 In G
2.2.2.2. 2.0.0.0. timp,harp,
strings,vln solo,harp solo [25']
PETERS (S697)

Concertino No. 2 for Violin and
Orchestra in E, Op. 92
2.0.2.2. 2.2.0.0. timp,strings,vln
solo [10'] (no score) BREITKOPF-W
(S698)

Jessonda: Overture *Op.63
2(2pic).2.2.2. 4.2.3.0. timp,
strings [7'] BREITKOPF-W (S699)

SPOHR, MATHIAS
Hänschen Klein
2.1.2.1. 0.0.0.0. timp,perc,strings
MULL & SCH ESM 10'056 (S700)

Stück Für Röhrenglocken
1.0+English horn.0+bass clar.0+
contrabsn. 1.1.0+bass trom.0.
strings MULL & SCH ESM 10'055
(S701)

SPORT, SPORT, SPORT: SUITE see
Schnittke, Alfred

SPORTLERMARSCH see Rakov, Nikolai

SPRACHLANDSCHAFT see Dittrich, Paul-
Heinz

SPRING see Fortner, Jack

SPRING CAME DANCING see Grant, Stewart

SPRING IN FIALTA see Amos, Keith

SPRING INTO SUMMER see Kunz, Alfred

SPRING MUSIC see Maw, Nicholas

SPRING SONG see Connell, Adrian

SPRINGER, DER see Genzmer, Harald

SPRINT see Bach, Jan Morris

SPUREN see Müller, Thomas

SQUARE (VERSION FOR LARGE ORCHESTRA)
see Oosten, Roel van

SQUARE (VERSION FOR ORCHESTRA) see
Oosten, Roel van

SRNKA, JIŘÍ (1907-1982)
Lyrická Symfonie
[20'] CESKY HUD. (S702)

Nocturne No. 1
2.1.2.2. 2.1.0.0. perc,pno,strings
[10'] CESKY HUD. (S703)

Nocturne No. 2
harp,pno,strings [6'] CESKY HUD. (S704)

Preludio E Rondino Giocoso
harp,strings,vln solo [12'] CESKY
HUD. (S705)

ŠROM, KAREL (1904-1981)
Pro Orchestr *Rondo
3.3.3.3. 4.3.3.1. timp,perc,2harp,
pno,strings [10'] CESKY HUD. (S706)

Suite for Orchestra
3.3.3.3. 6.3.3.1. timp,perc,harp,
cel,pno,strings [30'] CESKY HUD. (S707)

Symphony
3.3.3.3. 6.3.3.1. timp,perc,harp,
pno,strings CESKY HUD. (S708)

STAALKAARTEN VOOR EEN HOBOCONCERT see
Geysen, Frans

STACCATO see Grandert, Johnny

STACHELSCHWEINE ZIEHEN UM, DIE see
Thomas-Mifune, Werner

STACHOWSKI, MAREK (1936- )
Sonata for String Orchestra
POLSKIE 514-02514 (S709)

STACKED TIME see Hove, Luc Van

STAD EN DE ENGEL, DE see Wagemans,
Peter-Jan

STADLMAIR, HANS (1929- )
Concerto Profano
strings,vln solo,vcl solo,pno/
cembalo solo [10'] PETERS (S710)

STAGE WORK NO. 3 see Becker, John,
Marriage With A Space, A

STAHMER, KLAUS H. (1941- )
Dedications
vln I,vln II,vla,vcl,db,harp solo,
vla solo MÖSELER sc 11.448-00,
pts 11.448-01, set 11.448-09, pno
red 11.448-08 (S711)

Rotations
chamber group [12'] sc HEINRICH
3529 (S712)

ŠTAIDL, LADISLAV (1945- )
Dialog
2sax,2trp,trom,perc,3gtr,strings,
elec pno CESKY HUD. (S713)

STALT VESSELIL see Grainger, Percy
Aldridge

STAMITZ
Symphony in D for Strings
(Petit, J.-L.) string orch BOIS (S714)

STAMITZ, ANTON (1750-ca. 1796)
Concerto for Clarinet and Orchestra
in B flat, MIN 1
clar solo,orch KUNZELMANN ipa sc
10267A, oct 10267 (S715)

Concerto for Clarinet and Orchestra
in B flat, MIN 2
clar solo,orch KUNZELMANN ipa sc
10269A, oct 10269 (S716)

Concerto for Viola and Orchestra in B
flat
(Koukal, Bohumír) 0.2.0.0. 2.0.0.0.
strings,vla solo [19'] CESKY HUD. (S717)

Konzertante Sinfonie In D
(Gronefeld) 2ob,2horn,strings,2fl
soli KUNZELMANN ipa sc 10141A,
oct 10141 (S718)

STAMITZ, CARL (1745-1801)
Concertante Quartet In B-Flat
*Op.14,No.5
2vln,vla,vcl&db [14'] ARTARIA AE020 (S719)

Concertante Quartet In G *Op.14,No.2
2vln,vla,vcl&db [15'] ARTARIA AE018 (S720)

Concerto for Clarinet and Orchestra
in E flat
clar solo,orch KUNZELMANN ipa sc
10268A, oct 10268 (S721)
(Opat, Bohumil) 0.2.0.0. 2.0.0.0.
strings,clar solo [20'] CESKY
HUD. (S722)

STAMITZ, CARL (cont'd.)
Concerto for Clarinet and Orchestra
in F
clar solo,orch KUNZELMANN ipa sc
10022A, oct 10022 (S723)

Orchestral Quartet In B-Flat *Op.1,
No.4
2vln,vla,vcl&db [9'] ARTARIA AE013 (S724)

Orchestral Quartet In C *Op.14,No.1
2vln,vla,vcl&db [14'] ARTARIA AE016 (S725)

2vln,vla,vcl&db [10'] ARTARIA AE010 (S726)

Orchestral Quartet In D *Op.1,No.6
2vln,vla,vcl&db [9'] ARTARIA AE015 (S727)

Orchestral Quartet In E-Flat *Op.1,
No.3
2vln,vla,vcl&db [9'] ARTARIA AE012 (S728)

Orchestral Quartet In F *Op.1,No.5
2vln,vla,vcl&db [9'] ARTARIA AE014 (S729)

Orchestral Quartet In F *Op.14,No.4
2vln,vla,vcl&db [19'] ARTARIA AE017 (S730)

Orchestral Quartet In G *Op.1,No.2
2vln,vla,vcl&db [13'] ARTARIA AE011 (S731)

Orchestrální Trio F-Dur *Op.21
(Suchy, František) 2.0.2.0.
2.0.0.0. timp,strings CESKY HUD. (S732)

Quartet In A *Op.14,No.6
2vln,vla,vcl&db [11'] ARTARIA AE021 (S733)

Quartet In D *Op.14,No.3
2vln,vla,vcl&db [11'] ARTARIA AE019 (S734)

Sinfonia Concertante for Violin,
Viola, 2 Horns and String
Orchestra
vln,vla,2horn,string orch
KUNZELMANN ipa sc 10274A, oct
10274 (S735)

STAMITZ, JOHANN WENZEL ANTON
(1717-1757)
Orchestral Trio In A *Op.1,No.2
2vln,vcl&db [16'] ARTARIA AE040 (S736)

Orchestral Trio In B-Flat *Op.1,No.5
2vln,vcl&db [15'] ARTARIA AE045 (S737)

Orchestral Trio In c *Op.4,No.3
2vln,vcl&db [15'] ARTARIA AE042 (S738)

2vln,vcl&db [17'] ARTARIA AE039 (S739)

2vln,vcl&db [12'] ARTARIA AE048 (S740)

Orchestral Trio In D *Op.1,No.4
2vln,vcl&db [15'] ARTARIA AE044 (S741)

Orchestral Trio In E *Op.5,No.3
2vln,vcl&db [16'] ARTARIA AE043 (S742)

Orchestral Trio In F *Op.1,No.3
2vln,vcl&db [16'] ARTARIA AE041 (S743)

Orchestral Trio In G *Op.1,No.6
2vln,vcl&db [13'] ARTARIA AE046 (S744)

2vln,vcl&db [17'] ARTARIA AE047 (S745)

Sinfonia in B flat, Op. 8, No. 5
0.0.0.0. 2.0.0.0. strings [22']
BREITKOPF-W (S746)

Sinfonia in D, Op. 5, No. 2
2.2.0.2. 2.0.0.0. strings [20']
BREITKOPF-W (S747)

Sinfonia, Op. 3, No. 1, in G
2ob,2horn,2vln,vla,vcl,db [15']
ARTARIA AE049 (S748)

Sinfonia, Op. 3, No. 3, in G
2ob,2horn,2vln,vla,vcl,db [15']
ARTARIA AE050 (S749)

Sinfonia, Op. 3, No. 4, in E flat
2horn,2vln,vla,vcl,db [9'] ARTARIA
AE051 (S750)

Sinfonia, Op. 3, No. 5, in A
2vln,vla,vcl,db [14'] ARTARIA AE052 (S751)

Sinfonia, Op. 3, No. 6, in F
2horn,2vln,vla,vcl,db ARTARIA AE053 (S752)

Sinfonia, Op. 4, No. 1, in F
2ob,2horn,2vln,vla,vcl,db [15']
ARTARIA AE002 (S753)

Sinfonia, Op. 4, No. 4, in E flat
2ob,2horn,2vln,vla,vcl,db [13']
ARTARIA AE004 (S754)

Sinfonia, Op. 4, No. 6, in E flat
2ob,2horn,2vln,vla,vcl,db [16']
ARTARIA AE005 (S755)

STAMITZ, JOHANN WENZEL ANTON (cont'd.)
Sinfonia, Op. 7, No. 2
2ob,2horn,2vln,vla,vcl,db [18']
ARTARIA AE110 (S756)

Sinfonia, Op. 7, No. 6, in D
2ob,2horn,2vln,vla,vcl,db [13']
ARTARIA AE109 (S757)

Sinfonia, Op. 8, No. 1, in D
2ob,2horn,2vln,vla,vcl,db [7']
ARTARIA AE103 (S758)

Sinfonia, Op. 8, No. 2, in E flat
2ob,2horn,2vln,vla,vcl,db [20']
ARTARIA AE104 (S759)

Sinfonia, Op. 8, No. 3, in G
2fl,2horn,2vln,vla,vcl,db [13']
ARTARIA AE105 (S760)

Sinfonia, Op. 8, No. 4, in D
2fl,2horn,2vln,vla,vcl,db [15']
ARTARIA AE106 (S761)

Sinfonia, Op. 8, No. 6, in D
2vln,vla,vcl,db [11'] ARTARIA AE108 (S762)

Sinfonia Pastorale In D *Op.4,No.2
2ob,2horn,2vln,vla,vcl,db [15']
ARTARIA AE003 (S763)

Symphony in C (from Trio In C Major,
Op. 1, No. 1)
(Suchy, František) 2.0.2.1.
2.0.0.0. timp,strings [12'] CESKY
HUD. (S764)

STANCE see Jolas, Betsy

STAND SWAYING, SLIGHTLY see Coulthard,
Jean

STÄNDCHEN EUCH ZU BRINGEN, EIN see
Wolf, Hugo

STANDING STONE see McCartney, Sir
[John] Paul

STANDPUNKTE see Globokar, Vinko

STANEK, PAVEL (1927- )
Bagatelle for Tuba and Orchestra
2.2.2.2. 4.3.3.0. timp,perc,
strings,tuba solo [6'] CESKY HUD. (S765)

Concertino Semplice
3.2.2.2. 4.3.3.1. timp,harp,
strings,tuba solo [13'] CESKY
HUD. (S766)

Jako Z Pohádky
2.2.2.2. 4.2.3.1. timp,perc,xylo,
harp,strings [6'] CESKY HUD. (S767)

STANFORD, [SIR] CHARLES VILLIERS
(1852-1924)
Concerto for Clarinet and Orchestra
2.2.0.2. 4.2.0.0. timp,strings,clar
solo CRAMER rent (S768)

Irische Rhapsodie Nr. 1 *Op.78
2(pic).2(English horn).2+bass
clar.2+contrabsn. 4.3.3.1. timp,
perc,harp,strings [14']
BREITKOPF-W (S769)

Serenade in G, Op. 18
2+pic.2.2.3. 4.2.0.0. timp,perc,
strings [25'] BOOSEY-ENG rent (S770)

Symphony, No. 5, in D
2.2.2.2. 4.2.3.0. timp,opt org,
strings [39'] (l'allegro ed il
pensieroso) sc,pts STAINER HL303
rent (S771)

STANISLAUS: SALVE POLONIA see Liszt,
Franz

STANLEY, JOHN (1713-1786)
Six Concertos, Op.2
(Caldwell) strings, org-hpsd-
fortepiano solo OXFORD sc 3676842
f.s., perf sc set 3676850 sc,pts
rent (S772)

Six Concertos, Op.X
(Gifford) strings, org-hpsd-
fortepiano solo perf sc set
OXFORD 3676990 sc,pts rent (S773)

STANZAS FOR CELLO AND CHAMBER ORCHESTRA
see Hagen, Daron

STANZAS X & IX see Werder, Felix

STAR-SHIP TWINKLE see Crawley, Clifford

STARE, IVAN (1919- )
Asyndeton
string orch [5'] sc,pts STIM (S774)

STARE, IVAN (cont'd.)

In Statu Nascendi
2fl,2clar,pno,strings [9'] sc,pts
STIM (S775)

STÁREK, JIRI (1952- )
Epická Ciaconna
3.3.3.3. 4.2.4.1. timp,perc,harp,
pno,strings [15'] CESKY HUD.
(S776)

Komorní Symfonie
2.2.2.2. 2.2.0.0. timp,strings
[20'] CESKY HUD. (S777)

Veta Pro Orchestr
0.0.0.0. 4.5.3.1. timp,perc,strings
[30'] CESKY HUD. (S778)

STARER, ROBERT (1924- )
Hudson Valley Suite
orch sc SCHIRM.G 00123581 (S779)

STARKE SCHEITE see Wagner, Richard,
Götterdämmerung: Schlussgesang Der
Brünnhilde

STARY BRUCOUN see Fucik, Julius

ŠTASTNOU CESTU see Myska, Rudolf

STATIONEN see Butting, Max

STAUB see Lachenmann, Helmut Friedrich

STEADFAST TIN SOLDIER, THE see Amos,
Keith

STEADFAST TIN SOLDIER, THE: SUITE NO. 1
see Amos, Keith

STEADFAST TIN SOLDIER, THE: SUITE NO. 2
see Amos, Keith

STEAM TRAIN PASSES, A see Dreyfus,
George

STEBBING, M. (1957- )
Concerto for Flute and String
Orchestra
6vln I,6vln II,4vla,4vcl,3db,tam-
tam,fl solo solo pt LEDUC rent
(S780)

STEDRON, MILOS (1942- )
Addio. Budva.
[7'] CESKY HUD. (S781)

Concerto for Violoncello and
Orchestra
3.2.2.2. 4.3.3.1. timp,perc,xylo,
vibra,harp,cel,pno,strings,vcl
solo CESKY HUD. (S782)

Sedmikvítek
2.2.2.2. 4.3.3.1. timp,perc,harp,
cel,cimbalom,strings,med solo
[13'] CESKY HUD. (S783)

Sest Villanel
string orch,vcl solo [8'] CESKY
HUD. (S784)

STEELHENGE see Rathburn, Eldon

STEFFANI, AGOSTINO (1654-1728)
Tassilone
0.2.0.1. 0.0.0.0. 8vln I,7vln II,
6vla,5vcl,4db sc PETERS 01237
(S785)

STEGET ÖVER TRÖSKELN see Nilsson,
Torsten

STEIN
Bird Named Byrd, A
2.0.2.0. 0.2.0.0. perc,vln I,vln
II,vla,vcl,db MÖSELER sc
10.476-00, pts 10.476-01 TO 02,
sets 10.476-08 TO 09 (S786)

STEINBERG, BEN (1930- )
Suite for String Orchestra
string orch [20'] sc CANADIAN
MI 1500 S819SU (S787)

STEINBRENNER, WILFRIED
Imago I
16vln I,16vln II,12vla,12vcl,8db,
vln solo [15'] SCHOTTS perf mat
rent (S788)

STEINE, FÜR ENSEMBLE see Eötvös, Pèter

STEINERNE GAST, DER: OVERTURE see
Dargomyzhsky, Alexander Sergeyevich

STELLAIRE see Delerue, Georges

STELLATIONS see Orton, Richard

STEMMER: SKETCH FOR ORCHESTRA see
Asheim, Nils Henrik

STENDEL, WOLFGANG
Concerto for Violoncello and
Orchestra
3.2.3.1. 4.3.3.1. timp,perc,8vln I,
7vln II,6vla,5vcl,4db [20'] sc
PETERS 03271 (S789)

Conoszena
3.0.3.0. 0.0.0.0. timp,perc,8vln I,
7vln II,6vla,5vcl,4db [15'] sc
PETERS 02058 (S790)

Gedanken
see Pensees

Pensees
"Gedanken" 4.3.3.3. 4.3.3.1. timp,
2perc,harp,8vln I,7vln II,6vla,
5vcl,4db sc PETERS 03273 (S791)

Situationen, 3
1.1.1.1. 1.1.1.0. 2perc,pno,harp,
2vln,vla,vcl,db [10'] sc PETERS
03399 (S792)

STEPANEK, JIRI (1917- )
Cestování Krajinou (Rondo for Violin
and Orchestra)
1.2.2.0. 0.2.1.0. perc,pno,strings,
vln solo [8'] CESKY HUD. (S793)

Concerto for Alto Saxophone and
Orchestra
2.2.2.2. 4.3.3.1. perc,pno,strings,
alto sax solo [20'] CESKY HUD.
(S794)

Mlécná Dráha
perc,strings [45'] CESKY HUD.
(S795)

Prelude for Piano and Orchestra
see Vridla

Promena
timp,perc,pno,strings [30'] CESKY
HUD. (S796)

Rondo for Violin and Orchestra
see Cestování Krajinou

Vridla (Prelude for Piano and
Orchestra)
2.2.2.2. 4.3.3.1. timp,perc,
strings,pno solo [12'] CESKY HUD.
(S797)

STEPHAN, RUDI (1887-1915)
Musik Für 7 Saiteninstrumente
(Lessing, G.E.) pno,harp,string
orch [25'] study sc SCHOTTS
ED 3463 perf mat rent (S798)

Symphonischer Satz
3(2pic).1+ob d'amore+English
horn.3+bass clar.3+contrabsn.
6.4.3.1. timp,perc,cel,harp,org,
strings [37'] SCHOTTS perf mat
rent (S799)

STEPKA, KAREL VACLAV (1909- )
Vita, Una
strings,cembalo solo [20'] CESKY
HUD. (S800)

STEPPENWOLF, DER see Betancur-Gonzalez,
Valentin

STEPPING OUT see Marsh, Roger

STEPS see Arteaga, Edward see Del
Tredici, David

STEPTOE, ROGER
Cheers!
2.1.2.2. 2.0.0.0. 1perc,strings
[6'] sc,pts STAINER HL299 rent
(S801)

Concerto for Clarinet and String
Orchestra
strings,clar solo [27'] sc,pts
STAINER HL285 rent (S802)

Concerto for Violoncello and
Orchestra
1.2.0.2. 2.2.0.0. timp,strings,vcl
solo [25'] pts STAINER HL293 rent
(S803)

STERNWALD, JIRÍ (1910- )
Na Pasekách
2.2.2.2. 2.2.1.0. timp,perc,harp,
pno,strings [6'] CESKY HUD.
(S804)

Nálady Z Plátna I
2.2.2.2. 2.2.1.0. perc,harp,gtr,db,
strings [4'] CESKY HUD. (S805)

Nálady Z Plátna II
1.1.2.1. 2.1.1.0. perc,harp,gtr,db,
strings [3'] CESKY HUD. (S806)

Nálady Z Plátna III
2.2.2.2. 2.2.1.0. perc,harp,gtr,db,
strings [5'] CESKY HUD. (S807)

STEVEN, DONALD (1945- )
For Madmen Only
2.2.2.2. 2.2.0.0. 2perc,harp,8vln
I,8vln II,6vla,6vcl,4db,vcl solo
[32'] sc CANADIAN MI 1313 S843FO
(S808)

That Other Side
strings without vln,vla,db solo sc
CANADIAN MI1614 S843TH (S809)

STEVENS, BERNARD GEORGE (1916-1983)
Mark Of Cain, The
(Williams, Adrian) 2.2.2.2.
4.3.3.1. timp,4perc,harp,strings
[9'-12'] BARDIC (S810)

Upturned Glass, The
(Williams, Adrian) 2.2.2.2.
4.3.3.1. timp,4perc,harp,strings
[12'30"] BARDIC (S811)

STEVENS, JAMES
Satoko's Song
2.2.2.2. 4.4.4.1. perc,harp,
strings,Mez solo manuscript BMIC
(S812)

Seppuku And Lullaby
2.2.2.2. 4.4.4.1. 2perc,harp,
strings,ABar soli manuscript BMIC
(S813)

STEZJUK, JEWGENI (1961- )
Symphony
4.3.3.3. 4.3.3.1. 4perc,cel,harp,
strings [15'] SIKORSKI perf mat
rent (S814)

STICHIRA see Shchedrin, Rodion

STICK ON STICK see Torstensson, Klas

STIEBER, HANS (1886-1969)
Sinfonische Aphorismen
1.2.2.1. 1.1.0.0. strings [25']
BREITKOPF-W (S815)

Sinfonische Trilogie
2.3.3.3. 4.3.3.1. timp,perc,strings
[30'] BREITKOPF-W (S816)

STILL see Ed, Fredrik

STILL, WILLIAM GRANT (1895-1978)
After You've Gone
2+pic.2+English horn.3.2.4sax.
4.4.4.1. timp,perc,harp,pno,
banjo,db,strings,opt solo voice
STILL (S817)

Alnados De España, Los
3(pic).2+English horn.3.2. 4.3.3.1.
timp,perc,harp,cel,strings
FISCHER,C f.s.
contains: Danza; Prologo Y
Narración; Serenata; Valle
Escondido, El (S818)

Captain Kidd, Jr.
see Pages From A Mother's Diary
(Little Red Schoolhouse)

Carmela
(Fine, Marshall) 2.2.2.2. 2.2.0.0.
timp,castanets,harp,pno,strings,
vla solo STILL (S819)

Colleen Bawn
see Pages From A Mother's Diary
(Little Red Schoolhouse)

Danza
see Alnados De España, Los

Dismal Swamp
3(pic).2+English
horn.4.3(contrabsn). 4.3.3.1.
timp,perc,strings,pno solo [15']
STILL (S820)

Egyptian Princess
see Pages From A Mother's Diary
(Little Red Schoolhouse)

Festive Overture
3(pic).2+English horn.3.2. 4.3.3.1.
timp,perc,harp,cel,strings [10']
FISCHER,C (S821)

Four Dances From Sahdji
pno,harp,strings STILL (S822)

From The Journal Of A Wanderer
3(pic).3(English horn)+English
horn.4.3(2contrabsn). 4.3.3.1.
timp,perc,harp,cel,strings [20']
pno-cond sc STILL (S823)

Little Conqueror
see Pages From A Mother's Diary
(Little Red Schoolhouse)

Little Song That Wanted To Be A
Symphony, The
2(pic).2(English horn).2.2.
3.3.2.1. timp,perc,harp,cel,
strings,narrator&opt 3S [19']
FISCHER,C (S824)

STILL, WILLIAM GRANT (cont'd.)

Pages From A Mother's Diary (Little
Red Schoolhouse)
2(pic).2(English horn).2(bass
clar).2. 3.3.2.1. timp,perc,harp,
cel,strings STILL f.s. an early
version of "Little Red
Schoolhouse"
contains: Captain Kidd, Jr.;
Colleen Bawn; Egyptian
Princess; Little Conqueror;
Petey                      (S825)

Petey
see Pages From A Mother's Diary
(Little Red Schoolhouse)

Prologo Y Narración
see Alnados De España, Los

Quit Dat Fool'nish
2.2.2.2.sax. 3.2.2.0. timp,harp,
strings [2'] (orchestration of
the piano work with the same
title) STILL                (S826)

Romance
2.2.2.2.sax. 2.0.2.0. harp,strings
[3'] (arrangement of a piece for
sax and piano with the same
title) STILL                (S827)

Sentimental Song
1.1.2.1. 2.1.2.0. harp,cel,strings
STILL                       (S828)

Serenata
see Alnados De España, Los

Songs: A Medley  *CC8L
clar,alto sax,tenor sax,trp,drums,
bongos,pno,gtr,banjo,strings,
conga drum STILL f.s.       (S829)

Sunday Symphony, The
see Symphony No. 3

Symphony In G-Minor, The
see Symphony No. 2 in G minor

Symphony No. 2 in G minor
"Symphony In G-Minor, The"
3(pic).2+English horn.4.2.
4.3.3.1. timp,perc,cel,harp,
strings [29'22"] FISCHER,C (S830)

Symphony No. 3
"Sunday Symphony, The" 3(pic).2+
English horn.3.2. 4.3.3.1. timp,
bells,triangle,tamb,drums,3tom-
tom,cym,cel,harp,strings [25']
FISCHER,C                   (S831)

Valle Escondido, El
see Alnados De España, Los

STILL LANDS see Goehr, Alexander

STILL MINE see Casken, John

STILLE DER NACHT see Hausegger,
Siegmund von see Weingartner,
(Paul) Felix von

STILLE NACHT FÜR ELEFANTEN see Thomas-
Mifune, Werner

STILLER, ANDREW
Periodic Table Of The Elements, A
1.1.1.1. 1.2.1.0. perc,2vln,vla,
vcl,db [8'] sc,pts KALLISTI
                           (S832)

STILLHET see Larsson, Folke

STILLNESS AT APPOMATTOX, A see Hagen,
Daron

STINKTIER DREHT DURCH, EINE see Thomas-
Mifune, Werner

STIRRINGS see Silverman, Faye-Ellen

STOCCASTA see Eyser, Eberhard

STÖCKIGT, MICHAEL (1957-    )
Concerto for Violin and Orchestra
3.2.3.3. 4.2.2.0. timp,perc,cel,
8vln I,7vln II,6vla,5vcl,4db
[11'] sc,solo pt PETERS 03274
                           (S833)

Orchestermusik I
4.3.3.3. 4.3.3.1. 2timp,8vln I,7vln
II,6vla,5vcl,4db [12'] sc PETERS
03276                      (S834)

Orchestermusik IV
3.2.2.3. 4.2.3.0. timp,3perc,8vln
I,7vln II,6vla,5vcl,4db [22'] sc
PETERS 04390               (S835)

STOCKMEIER, WOLFGANG (1931-    )
Concerto
org,string orch MÖSELER pts
11.458.01 rent, sc 11.458-00
                           (S836)

STOCKMEIER, WOLFGANG (cont'd.)

Credo for 15 Winds, WV 274
MÖSELER pts 10.475.01 rent, sc
10.475.00                  (S837)

Variations, WV 159
pno,orch,vln&vcl soli MÖSELER
11.444 rent                (S838)

STOJANTSCHEW, STOJAN
Capriccio for Orchestra
3.3.3.3. 4.3.3.0. timp,3perc,harp,
8vln I,7vln II,6vla,5vcl,4db,pno&
cel [15'] sc PETERS 04457  (S839)

STOJOWSKI, SIGISMUND (1870-1946)
Rhapsodie Symphonique  *Op.23
3.3.2.2. 4.1.3.0. timp,2perc,harp,
8vln I,7vln II,6vla,5vcl,4db
[14'] sc PETERS 02119      (S840)

STOKES, HARVEY J. (1957-    )
Lyric Symphony
3.2.2.2. 4.2.2.1. timp,2perc,
strings SEESAW             (S841)

Symphony No. 4
3.2.2.3. 4.3.3.1. timp,3perc,pno,
harp,strings SEESAW        (S842)

STONYBROOK CONCERTO see Shapey, Ralph

STORM, STAFFAN (1964-    )
TV Sets Glowing Blue In The Dusk:
Scenes
fl,ob,clar,trp,2perc,cel,string
quar [18'] sc STIM         (S843)
chamber group [18'] STIM   (S844)

STORY OF CATS AMD MICE, THE see Arima,
Reiko

STORY OF VASCO: SUITE NO.1 see Crosse,
Gordon

STØYVA, NJÅL GUNNAR (1948-    )
Fabel
2.1.2.1. 2.0.3.0. timp,2perc,
strings [15'] NORSKMI      (S845)

STR. ORCH N3 - II see Takeuchi, Kenji

STRAESSER, JOEP (1934-    )
Chamber Concerto No. 2
2.2.3.2. 2.2.0.0. timp,2perc,
strings,harp solo [14']
(symphonic variations on 4
different minor seconds) sc
DONEMUS                    (S846)

Chamber Concerto No. 3
0.1.1.1. 1.1.0.0. perc,strings,fl
solo [18'] sc DONEMUS      (S847)

STRAGANO see Eyser, Eberhard

STRAHOVSKY VALCÍK see Krízek, Zdenek

STRANDS OF BLUE see Freedman, Harry

STRASEK, EMIL (1927-    )
Duhovy Valcík
2.2.2.2. 4.2.3.0. perc,harp,strings
[4'] CESKY HUD.            (S848)

Jihoceskou Krajinou
2.2.2.2. 4.2.3.0. harp,strings [4']
CESKY HUD.                 (S849)

K Cíli Blíz
2.1.3.0. 4.3.3.0. perc,xylo,harp,
strings [4'] CESKY HUD.    (S850)

Klenovická Polka
2.2.2.2. 4.2.3.0. perc,strings [3']
CESKY HUD.                 (S851)

Krystaly  *Waltz
2.0.3.0. 3.3.3.0. perc,harp,bass
gtr,strings,acord solo [4'] CESKY
HUD.                       (S852)

Máme Zelenou
2.2.2.2. 3.2.2.0. perc,xylo,strings
[3'] CESKY HUD.            (S853)

Ohnivá Krev (Tarantelle)
2.2.2.2. 4.2.2.1. perc,harp,strings
[4'] CESKY HUD.            (S854)

Poetická Humoreska
2.2.2.2. 4.2.3.0. perc,strings [4']
CESKY HUD.                 (S855)

Prazské Promenády
2.2.2.2. 4.2.3.0. perc,strings [4']
CESKY HUD.                 (S856)

Radost Z Úspechu
2.2.2.2. 4.2.2.0. perc,harp,strings
[3'] CESKY HUD.            (S857)

Rozhoupany Valcík
2.2.2.2. 4.2.2.0. strings,perc [3']
CESKY HUD.                 (S858)

STRASEK, EMIL (cont'd.)

Rozmarné Nálady  *Waltz
2.2.2.2. 4.2.2.0. perc,strings [3']
CESKY HUD.                 (S859)

Svátek Radosti (Tarantelle)
2.0.3.0. 1.3.3.0. perc,harp,pno,
gtr,strings [4'] CESKY HUD. (S860)

Tarantelle
see Ohnivá Krev
see Svátek Radosti

Vzdušnou Carou
2.2.2.2. 4.3.3.1. perc,harp,strings
[4'] CESKY HUD.            (S861)

Zasnení
2.2.2.2. 4.2.2.0. harp,strings [5']
CESKY HUD.                 (S862)

STRATHCLYDE CONCERTO NO. 3 FOR HORN,
TRUMPET AND ORCHESTRA see Davies,
[Sir] Peter Maxwell

STRATHCLYDE CONCERTO NO. 4 see Davies,
[Sir] Peter Maxwell

STRATHCLYDE CONCERTO NO. 5 FOR VIOLIN,
VIOLA AND STRING ORCHESTRA see
Davies, [Sir] Peter Maxwell

STRATHCLYDE CONCERTO NO. 6 see Davies,
[Sir] Peter Maxwell

STRATHCLYDE CONCERTO NO. 7 FOR DOUBLE
BASS AND ORCHESTRA see Davies,
[Sir] Peter Maxwell

STRATHCLYDE CONCERTO NO. 8 see Davies,
[Sir] Peter Maxwell

STRATHCLYDE CONCERTO NO. 9 see Davies,
[Sir] Peter Maxwell

STRATHCLYDE CONCERTO NO.10 see Davies,
[Sir] Peter Maxwell

STRAUME, EGILS (1950-    )
Philippinisches Tagebuch
S rec,clar,soprano sax,perc,strings
[15'] SIKORSKI perf mat rent
                           (S863)

STRAUSS, JOHANN
Great Waltzes In Full Score
orch sc DOVER 26009-7      (S864)

STRAUSS, JOHANN, [JR.] (1825-1899)
Be Embraced, Ye Millions!
see Seid Umschlungen, Millionen!

Bons Vieux Temps, Les (Waltz, Op. 26)
(Kouzan) orch BOIS         (S865)

Cachucha Galop
(Kouzan) orch BOIS         (S866)

Chauve-Souris, La: Overture
see Fledermaus, Die: Overture

Csárdás (from Die Fledermaus)
orch min sc KUNZELMANN ETP 1345
                           (S867)
(Swarowsky) orch KUNZELMANN ipa
perf ETP 1345, oct ETP 1345A
                           (S868)

Fledermaus, Die: Overture
"Chauve-Souris, La: Overture"
2.2.2.2. 4.2.3.0. timp,perc,
strings [9'30"] LEDUC      (S869)

Frühlingstimmen  *Op.410
"Voices Of Spring" BROUDE BR.
                           (S870)

Galop Indien  *Op.111
(Kouzan) orch BOIS         (S871)

Geschichten Aus Dem Wienerwald
*Op.325
"Tales From The Vienna Woods"
BROUDE BR.                 (S872)

Lagunen-Walzer (from Eine Nacht In
Venedig, Op. 411)
2.2.2.2. 4.2.3.0. timp,perc,harp,
strings [11'] BREITKOPF-W  (S873)

Reine Indigo, La: Overture
2.2.1.1. 2.2.1.0. timp,perc,strings
[7'] LEDUC                 (S874)

Rosen Aus Dem Süden  *Op.388
1+pic.2.2.2. 4.2.3.0. timp,perc,
harp,strings [7'] BREITKOPF-W sc
PB 3286, pts OB 2756L      (S875)

Seid Umschlungen, Millionen! (Waltz,
Op. 443)
(Rubey, Norbert) "Be Embraced, Ye
Millions!" 2(pic).2.2(clar in
A).2. 4.2.3.0. timp,harp,4perc,
strings DOBLINGER DM 1037  (S876)

STRAUSS, JOHANN, [JR.] (cont'd.)

Tales From The Vienna Woods
see Geschichten Aus Dem Wienerwald

Voices Of Spring
see Frühlingsstimmen

Waltz, Op. 26
see Bons Vieux Temps, Les

Waltz, Op. 443
see Seid Umschlungen, Millionen!

Wiener Blut  *Op.354
2(pic).2.2.2. 4.2.3.0. timp,perc,
strings [8'] BREITKOPF-W sc
PB 3284, pts OB 2754L        (S877)

STRAUSS, JOSEF (1827-1870)
Faust-Quadrille, Op. 112
(Märzendorfer, Ernst) 1+pic.2.2.2.
4.2.1.1. timp,perc,2vln,vla,vcl,
db ARTARIA AE1-001        (S878)

STRAUSS, RICHARD (1864-1949)
Alpensinfonie, Eine & Symphonia
Domestica
orch sc DOVER 27725-9        (S879)

Aus Italien  *Op.16
3.2.2.3. 4.2.3.0. timp,perc,harp,
strings [47'] study sc PETERS
EP 10503        (S880)

Bourgeois Gentilhomme, Le  *Op.60,
incidental music
[Ger] 2.2.2.2. 2.1.1.0. timp,perc,
harp,pno,strings,opt SMez soli,
opt cor [75'] BOOSEY-ENG rent
(S881)

Capriccio: Closing Scene  *Op.85
3(pic).2+English horn.3+bass clar+
basset horn.3(contrabsn).
4.2.3.0. timp,2harp,16vln I,16vln
II,10vla,10vcl,6db,S solo [18']
BOOSEY-ENG rent        (S882)

Concert Overture In C Minor
2.2.2.2. 4.2.3.1. timp,strings
[13'] study sc SCHOTTS ETP 1135
perf mat rent        (S883)

Daphne: Closing Scene  *Op.82
3(pic).2+English horn.3+basset
horn+bass clar.3+contrabsn.
4.3.3.1. timp,perc,2harp,org,
16vln I,16vln II,12vla,10vcl,4db,
S solo [17'] BOOSEY-ENG rent
(S884)

Romance in E flat, Op. 61
0.2.0.2. 2.0.0.0. strings,clar solo
[10'] SCHOTTS perf mat rent study
sc ETP 1399, pno red KLB 35
(S885)

Symphony in D minor
2.2.2.2. 4.2.3.0. timp,strings
[34'] SCHOTTS perf mat rent
(S886)

Tone Poems, Series I
orch sc DOVER 23754-0        (S887)

Tone Poems, Series II
orch sc DOVER 23755-9        (S888)

STRAUSS, WOLFGANG (1927-   )
Sinfonia No. 5, Op. 80
3.2.2.2. 4.3.3.0. timp,3perc,pno,
harp,8vln I,7vln II,6vla,5vcl,
4db, 6 female voices behind the
stage [25'] sc PETERS 03272
(S889)

STRAUSSIANA see Korngold, Erich
Wolfgang

STRAVINSKY, IGOR (1882-1971)
Dumbarton Oaks
orch study sc SCHIRM.G ED3527
(S890)

Feu d'artifice  *Op.4, Fantasy
2+pic.2(English horn).3(bass
clar).2. 6.3.3.1. timp,perc,cel,
2harp,16vln I,14vln II,12vla,
10vcl,8db [4'] SCHOTTS perf mat
rent study sc ETP 1396-ETP 8039,
pno red ED 962        (S891)

Firebird
orch sc DOVER 25535-2        (S892)

Firebird-Ballet 1910
orch study sc EULENBURG ETP 8043
perf mat rent        (S893)

Jeu De Cartes
orch SCHIRM.G sc 50482126, study sc
50482127        (S894)

Petrushka
orch sc DOVER 25680-4        (S895)

Rite Of Spring
orch sc DOVER 25857-2        (S896)

STRAVINSKY, IGOR (cont'd.)

Scherzo À La Russe
(Flamm, Christoph) orch study sc
EULENBURG ETP 8035 perf mat rent
(S897)

STREAMLINE see Moravec, Paul

STREET MUSIC see Paulus, Stephen
Harrison

STREGHE, LE see Paganini, Niccolo

STREICHER, THEODORE (1874-1940)
Du Bist Es! Du!
2+pic.2.2.2. 4.2.3.1. timp,harp,
strings,S solo [2'] BREITKOPF-W
(S898)

Fonte Dos Amores "Um Inez Weinten"
1.1.2.1. 2.0.0.0. harp,strings,A
solo [3'] BREITKOPF-W        (S899)

Gedenken "Habe In Den Herbst Hinaus"
4.1.2.0. 0.0.0.0. 2perc,harp,
strings,S solo,2vln&vcl soli [3']
BREITKOPF-W        (S900)

Lied Der Tänzerin "Wecket Die Flammen
Auf"
3+pic.3+English horn.3+bass clar.3+
contrabsn. 4.2.3.1. timp,4perc,
2harp,strings,S solo [3']
BREITKOPF-W        (S901)

STREICHERSINFONIE see Shostakovich,
Dmitri, Symphony for Strings

STREICHERSINFONIE, OP. 118A see
Shostakovich, Dmitri

STREICHHOLZMÄDEL, DAS: OVERTURE see
Enna, August

STREJCOVSKY, JIRI (1928-   )
Concerto in C minor for Piano and
Strings
[22'] CESKY HUD.        (S902)

STRENUOUS LIFE, THE see Joplin, Scott

STRIDING FOLLY see Miller, Elma

STRIKKER, ERWIN
Thumoleï
1.1.1.1. 1.1.1.0. perc,pno,strings
[8'] sc DONEMUS        (S903)

STRINDBERG, HENRIK (1954-   )
Entymology
chamber orch [17'] study sc REIMERS
101186 rent        (S904)

Etymology
1(pic).1.1(bass clar).1.soprano
sax. 1.1.1.0. 2perc,harp,pno,
2vln,vla,vcl,db [16'] (Switch -
White - Shift; Pointers; Seed;
Define NIL; Strings) sc REIMERS
(S905)

I Träd
"Within Trees" 2(pic).2(English
horn).2(bass clar).2(contrabsn).
4.2.2.0. timp,4perc,harp,strings,
pno [14'] sc REIMERS ED.NR 101187
(S906)

Katsu
2(pic).2.2.2. 2.2.2.0. timp,3perc,
strings [7'] SUECIA sc H-2628,
pts        (S907)

Nattlig Madonna
"Nocturnal Madonna"
2(pic).2(English horn).2(bass
clar).2(contrabsn). 2.2.1.0.
timp,strings [8'] sc GEHRMANS
(S908)

Nocturnal Madonna
see Nattlig Madonna

Within Trees
see I Träd

STRINDBERG SUITE see Börtz, Daniel,
Strindbergsvit

STRINDBERGSVIT see Börtz, Daniel

STRING AROUND AUTUMN, A see Takemitsu,
Toru

STRING CASCADE see King, Reginald

STRING SYMPHONY see Qu, Xiao-Song

STRINGMUSIC see Gould, Morton

STRINGS see Hove, Luc Van

STRINGS AND HARPSICHORD see Rossem,
Andries van

STRINGS AND TIME III see Naito Akemi

STRINGS ON TOUR see Townsend, Jill

STRKROCK see Blomberg, Erik

STRNIŠTE, JIRÍ (1914-   )
Na Prátelství (Suite for Orchestra)
2.1.2.1. 3.3.2.0. timp,perc,strings
[18'] CESKY HUD.        (S909)

Nocturne for Strings
[3'] CESKY HUD.        (S910)

Romance A Rondo
strings,vcl solo [14'] CESKY HUD.
(S911)

Rumunsky Tanec
strings [8'] CESKY HUD.        (S912)

Slavnostní Pochod
2.2.2.2. 3.3.3.1. timp,perc,strings
[8'] CESKY HUD.        (S913)

Suite for Orchestra
see Na Prátelství

STROFE see Gullberg, Olof

STROM ZIVOTA see Burghauser, Jarmil

STROPHE see Xiaogang, Ye

STROPHES DE PETRARQUE, 2 see Glazunov,
Alexander Konstantinovich

STRUCTURES see Perna, Dana Paul

STRUENSEE: OVERTURE see Meyerbeer,
Giacomo

STRUENSEE: ZWEITER ENTREACT see
Meyerbeer, Giacomo

STRUKOW, WALERI (1937-   )
Concerto for Piano and Orchestra
2.2.2.2. 4.3.3.1. timp,perc,vibra,
harp,strings,pno solo [30']
PETERS        (S914)

STRUKTUREN see Engelmann, Hans Ulrich

STRYK see Ed, Fredrik

STSCHERBATCHEFF, NIKOLAI (1853-1929)
En Passant L'eau
see Zwei Idyllen

Étoile Du Berger, L'
see Zwei Idyllen

Serenade, Op. 33
3.2.2.2. 4.0.0.0. harp,strings
[10'] BELAIEFF        (S915)

Zwei Idyllen
3.2.2.2. 4.0.0.0. timp,perc,harp,
strings BELAIEFF f.s.
contains: En Passant L'eau;
Étoile Du Berger, L'        (S916)

STÜCK FÜR RÖHRENGLOCKEN see Spohr,
Mathias

STÜCK FÜR VIRTUOSEN I see Schenker,
Friedrich

STUCKY, STEVEN EDWARD (1949-   )
Concerto for 2 Flutes and Orchestra
0.2(English horn).2(clar in E flat,
bass clar).2. 2.2.1.0. timp,perc,
pno&cel,harp,strings,2fl soli
[17'] MERION rent        (S917)

Fanfare For Cincinnati
3(pic).3(English horn).3(bass
clar).3(contrabsn). 4.4.3(bass
trom).1. timp,2perc,pno,harp,
strings [2'] MERION rent   (S918)

Fanfare For Los Angeles
2.2.2(clar in E flat).2(contrabsn).
4.3.3.1. perc,harp,strings [2']
MERION rent        (S919)

Music For Saxophones And Strings
string orch,4sax soli [16'] MERION
rent        (S920)

Pinturas De Tamayo
3(2pic).3(English horn).3(clar in E
flat,bass clar).3(contrabsn).
4.3(piccolo trp).3.1. 3perc,pno,
harp,strings [18'] MERION rent
(S921)

STUDENT, THE see Pitfield, Thomas
Baron, Concerto for Piano, No. 2

STUDENT GLOSELUND see Kvam, Oddvar S.

STUDENTEN see Kaschlajew, Murad, Suite
No. 3

STUDENTSKÁ LÁSKA see Marsik, Emanuel

STUDENTSKÁ SUITA see Bartoš, Jan Zdenek

STUDIE PRO TRUBKU see Bazant, Jiri

STUDNA ZIVOTA see Slavicky, Milan

STUDNA ZIVOTA: SYMFONICKY TRIPTYCH see Slavicky, Milan

STUFENGESANG I see Schweinitz, Wolfgang von

STUMME VON PORTICI, DIE: OVERTURE see Auber, Daniel-François-Esprit, Muette Di Portici, La: Overture

STUMME VON PORTICI, DIE: TARANTELLE see Auber, Daniel-François-Esprit, Muette Di Portici, La: Tarantelle

STUNTZ, JOSEF HARTMANN (1793-1859)
Fantasy for Oboe and Orchestra (from I Capuleti E I Mentecchi (Bellini))
ob solo,orch KUNZELMANN ipa sc 10272A, oct 10272 (S922)

STURKOPF, DER (GUARACHA) see Thomas-Mifune, Werner

STYKKE MUSIKK TIL FEST OG ETTERTANKE, ET see Alterhaug, Bjorn

SU, CONG (1957- )
Variationen Über Ein Thema Aus "Der Letzte Kaiser"
1.1.1.1. 4.2.1.0. timp,2perc,pno, harp,electronic tape,8vln I,7vln II,6vla,5vcl,4db [13'] sc PETERS 02712 (S923)

SUBOTNICK, MORTON LEON (1933- )
Axolotl
1.0.2.0. 0.0.2.0. 2perc,pno,harp, 8vcl,4db,vcl solo [17'] SCHOTTS perf mat rent (S924)

Place
3.3.3.3. 5.3.3.1. timp,3perc,mand, cel,harp,strings [20'] SCHOTTS perf mat rent (S925)

SÜDBÖHMISCHE SUITE see Novak, Vitezslav

SUDDEN TIME see Benjamin, George

SUGÁR, M.
On The Snowy Hill Of The Rainbow "Szivárány Havasán"
3(2pic).3(English horn).0.3(contrabsn). 6.4.3.1. timp,perc,2harp,pno,cel,16vln I, 14vln II,12vla,10vcl,8db,3clar in A&bass clar [16'] EMB rent (S926)

Recontres
"Találkozások" 1.1.1.1. 1.2.0.0. strings [12'] EMB rent (S927)

Sinfonia
2.2.2.2. 2.2.1.0. timp,perc,harp, pno,strings [11'] EMB rent (S928)

Szivárány Havasán
see On The Snowy Hill Of The Rainbow

Találkozások
see Recontres

Venus
3.3.3.3. 4.3.3.1. timp,perc,harp, pno,strings [11'] EMB rent (S929)

SUGAR, REZSÖ (1919- )
Divertimento
strings [18'] EMB rent (S930)

SUITA ARCTICA see Helgason, Hallgrimur

SUITA CAPRICCIOSA PRO SMYCCE see Boháč, Josef

SUITA DANZA PER ARCHI see Domazlicky, Frantisek

SUITA RUSTICA see Lídl, Václav

SUITA SEMPLICE see Bartoš, Jan Zdenek

SUITE see Betancur-Gonzalez, Valentin

SUITE ANGLAISE see Milhaud, Darius

SUITE AUS DER FILMMUSIK "AGONIE" see Schnittke, Alfred, Agonie: Suite

SUITE AUS DER FILMMUSIK "DIE GESCHICHTE EINES UNBEKANNTEN SCHAUSPIELERS" see Schnittke, Alfred, Geschichte Eines Unbekannten Schauspielers, Die: Suite

SUITE AUS DER FILMMUSIK "DIE JUNGE GARDE" see Shostakovich, Dmitri, Junge Garde, Die: Suite

SUITE AUS DER FILMMUSIK "DIE LETZTEN TAGE VON ST. PETERSBURG" see Schnittke, Alfred, Letzten Tage Von

St. Petersburg, Die: Suite

SUITE AUS DER FILMMUSIK "DIE TOTEN SEELEN" see Schnittke, Alfred, Toten Seelen, Die: Suite

SUITE AUS DER FILMMUSIK "KLEINE TRAGÖDIEN" see Schnittke, Alfred, Kleine Tragödien: Suite

SUITE AUS DER FILMMUSIK "MEISTER UND MARGARITA" see Schnittke, Alfred, Meister Und Margarita: Suite

SUITE AUS DER FILMMUSIK "PIROGOW" see Shostakovich, Dmitri, Pirogow: Suite

SUITE AUS DER FILMMUSIK "SPORT, SPORT, SPORT" see Schnittke, Alfred, Sport, Sport, Sport: Suite

SUITE BURLESCA see Martinez, Miguel Angel Gomez

SVIT SUITE CHAMPTRE see Gullberg, Olof

SUITE CHORÉGRAPHIQUE see Gagnon, Alain

SUITE CONCERTANTE FOR GUITAR AND ORCHESTRA see Paisiello, Giovanni, Nocturnos De Andalucía

SUITE DAS ORIXÄS see Prado, José-Antonio (Almeida)

SUITE DE BALLET see Vlach-Vruticky, Josef

SUITE DE CABALLOS DE VAPOR see Chavez, Carlos

SUITE DE DANSE see DuBois, Pierre-Max

SUITE DREAMS see Wolfe, Lawrence

SUITE EN CONCERT see Kenins, Talivaldis

SUITE FOR SMALL ORCHESTRA see Pishny-Floyd, Monte Keene

SUITE FOR STRINGS LA MALINCHE see Barker, Paul

SUITE FROM "MARAT-SADE" see Peaslee, Richard

SUITE FROM SHAKESPEARE'S "THE MERRY WIVES OF WINDSOR" see Bazelon, Irwin Allen

SUITE LYRIQUE see Grieg, Edvard Hagerup

SUITE MIGNONNE see Nedbal, Oskar

SUITE NACH DEM NOTENBÜCHLEIN FÜR ANNA MAGDALENA BACH see Bach, Johann Sebastian

SUITE OF FABLES FOR NARRATOR AND ORCHESTRA see Lennon, John Anthony

SUITE OF SIX SONGS FROM "ORPHEUS BRITANNICUS" see Purcell, Henry

SUITE PARNASSIENNE see Massenet, Jules, Suite for Orchestra, No. 9

SUITE SYMPHONIQUE see Petitgirard, Laurent, Marathon, Le

SUITE THÉÂTRALE see Massenet, Jules, Suite for Orchestra, No. 8

SULEIKAS ZWEITER GESANG see Schubert, Franz (Peter)

SULYOK, IMRE (1912- )
Concerto for Organ and Orchestra
0.0.0.0. 4.3.3.0. timp,strings,org solo [31'] EMB rent (S931)

SUMERA, LEPO (1950- )
Music for Chamber Orchestra
fl,horn,strings [14'] SIKORSKI perf mat rent (S932)

SUMERKI 90 see Bäck, Sven-Erik

SUMMER DANCES see Maw, Nicholas

SUMMER DAYS, SUMMER NIGHTS see Buczynski, Walter

SUMMER HAZE see King, Reginald

SUMMER LIGHTNING see Druckman, Jacob Raphael

SUMMER NIGHT see Prokofiev, Serge

SUMMER NIGHT ON THE RIVER see Delius, Frederick

SUMMER NIGHTS see Kenessey, Stefania Maria de

SUMMER SOLSTICE see Dorff, Daniel Jay

SUN AND STEEL see Howard, Brian

SUN OF VENICE, THE see Osborne, Nigel

SUN WARRIOR see Alberga, Eleanor

SUNBURST see Dorff, Daniel Jay

SUNBURST RAG (SCOTT) see Sieben Ragtimes Für Streichorchester: Heft 2

SUNDAY SILENCE see Bazelon, Irwin Allen, Symphony No. 9

SUNDAY SYMPHONY, THE see Still, William Grant, Symphony No. 3

SUNDBØ, GEIR (1967- )
Abstraction For Orchestra *Op.7
3(pic).3.3(English horn).3(bass clar).3(contrabsn). 4.3.3.1. timp,perc,harp,strings [9'] NORSKMI (S933)

SUNDE, HELGE HAVSGAARD (1965- )
Ache For Orchestra
3.2(English horn,ob d'amore).3.2. 4.3.3.0. 2perc,kbd,strings [8'30"] NORSKMI (S934)

Mosaic, For Wind Quintet, Brass Quintet, String Quartet, Percussion And String Orchestra see Mosaikk

Mosaikk
"Mosaic, For Wind Quintet, Brass Quintet, String Quartet, Percussion And String Orchestra" 1.1.1.1. 2.2.1.1. perc,strings [12'] NORSKMI (S935)

SUNDIN, HAOKAN (1961- )
Hymn For Orchestra
2.2.2.2. 2.0.2.0. strings [10'] STIM (S936)

SUNES SOMMAR see Lindahl, Thomas

SUNES SOMMAR: EN NÄMNDEMANS DÖD see Lindahl, Thomas

SUNFLOWER see Lumsdaine, David

SUNRISE FABLE see Read, Thomas Lawrence

SUNSONG see Rehnqvist, Karin, Solsången

SUONATA VARSAVIA see Paganini, Niccolo

SUPER FLUMINA BABYLONIS see Hosokawa, Toshio

SUR LES RIVES DU TROP TARD see Bleuse, Marc

SURDIN, MORRIS (1914-1979)
Alteration I
see Six Pieces In Search Of A Sequence

Alteration II
string orch sc,pts CANADIAN MI 1500 S961AL (S937)
see Six Pieces In Search Of A Sequence

Andante
see Six Pieces In Search Of A Sequence

Berceuse
2.0.2.0. 0.0.0.0. cel,glock, strings,horn solo [6'] sc CANADIAN MI 1332 S961BE (S938)

Concerto for Mandolin and Strings
string orch,mand solo [23'] (I. Fantasia 2. Ostinato 3. Capriccio. sc,pno red CANADIAN MI 1630 S961CO (S939)

Concerto for Viola and Orchestra in Five Movements
2(pic).2(English horn).2.2. 4.2.3.0. timp,perc,harp,cel, strings,vla solo [24'] sc,pno red CANADIAN MI 1312 S961CO (S940)

Concerto No. 2 for Accordion, Percussion, Guitar and String Orchestra in Three Movements
acord,perc,elec gtr,string orch [24'] sc CANADIAN MI 9400 S726CO (S941)

Densities
see Six Pieces In Search Of A Sequence

SURDIN, MORRIS (cont'd.)

Five Shades Of Brass
2.2(English horn).2.2. 4.2.2.1.
perc,harp,strings,trp solo [25']
sc CANADIAN                    (S942)

Kleine "Hammer-Klapper" Musik, Eine:
Ein Musikalischer Spass
2(pic).2.2.2. 2.0.0.0. timp,perc,
strings [7'] (1. Eine kleine xylo
musik 2. Ein kleines glocken
spiel 3. Ein LOUD minuet!
(mostly) 4. Ein (who's got the
whistle?) march?) sc CANADIAN
MI 1200 S961EI              (S943)

Short!
see Six Pieces In Search Of A
Sequence

Six Pieces In Search Of A Sequence
sc CANADIAN MI 1750 S961SI f.s.
contains: Alteration I (string
orch,pic/vln/pno/acord solo);
Alteration II (string orch);
Andante (string orch,acord);
Densities (string orch,pno/
2pic/acord solo); Short!
(string orch,pno/acord/2vln
solo); Textures (string orch,
vln solo)                  (S944)

Softly As The Flute Blows (Suite for
Flute and Strings)
sc,pno red,solo pt CANADIAN
MI 1621 S961SO             (S945)

Suite for Flute and Strings
see Softly As The Flute Blows

Textures
see Six Pieces In Search Of A
Sequence

SURF AND SEAWEED: SUITE see Blitzstein,
Marc

SURFING see Boesmans, Philippe

SURGIR see Dufourt, Hugues

SURMA RITORNELLI, THE see Rouse,
Christopher

SURSUM CORDA see Korngold, Erich
Wolfgang, Symphonic Overture see
Šesták, Zdeněk

SURTEL, MAARTEN
...Del Amor Oscuro
0.0.0.2. 0.0.0.0. cym,2perc,
strings,vln&vla&vcl&horn soli
[10'] sc DONEMUS           (S946)

SURVIVAL see Lundquist, Torbjörn,
Symphony No. 9 in One Movement

SÜSSE LIED VERHALT, DAS see Wagner,
Richard

SÜSSE RACHE see Mozart, Wolfgang
Amadeus, Vendetta, Oh, La Vendetta,
La

SUTARTINES see Schnittke, Alfred

SUTER, ROBERT (1919-    )
Art Pour L'Art, L'
"Musik Für Orchester (1979)" 3(pic,
alto fl).3(English
horn).3(soprano clar in E flat,
bass clar).2. 4.3.3.1. gtr,harp,
strings [16'] HUG          (S947)

Concerto Grosso for Orchestra
2(pic).2(English horn).2(bass
clar).2(contrabsn). 3.2.1.0.
2perc,8vln I,6vln II,5vla,4vcl,
3db [15'] sc HUG GH 11466  (S948)

Conversazioni Concertanti
sax,vibra,string orch [19'] HUG
(S949)

Marcia Funebre
3(pic,alto fl).3(English
horn).3(bass clar).3. 6.4.4.1.
4perc,3harp,3gtr,strings,
electronic tape,SSS soli [25']
HUG                        (S950)

Music for Orchestra
3(pic,alto fl).3(English
horn).3(soprano clar in E flat,
bass clar).3(contrabsn). 6.3.4.0.
4perc,harp,gtr,strings [26'] HUG
(S951)

Musik Für Orchester (1979)
see Art Pour L'Art, L'

SUTERMEISTER, HEINRICH (1910-1995)
Aubade Pour Morges
2.2.2.2. 2.2.0.0. strings [11']
SCHOTTS perf mat rent      (S952)

SUTERMEISTER, HEINRICH (cont'd.)

Consolatio Philosophiae
3(pic).3(English horn).3(bass
clar).4.3.3.1.
timp,3perc,harp,strings,high solo
[18'] voc sc SCHOTTS ED 6817 perf
mat rent                   (S953)

Ich Reise Weit
see Romeo And Juliet: Juliet's Aria

Romeo And Juliet: Juliet's Aria
"Ich Reise Weit" 3(2pic).1+English
horn.2(clar in E flat,bass
clar).1+contrabsn. 4.3.3.1. timp,
2perc,strings [4'] SCHOTTS perf
mat rent                   (S954)

Sechs Liebesbriefe
2(pic).2.2.2. 4.2.0.0. timp,perc,
hpsd,harp,strings,S solo [20']
voc sc SCHOTTS ED 6913 perf mat
rent                       (S955)

Tambourin
pno/hpsd,perc,strings,opt gtr (2
suites) SCHOTTS perf mat rent sc
CON 149, pts CON 149-50-60 (S956)

SUTTON-ANDERSON, DAVID
Uffington Horse, The
1.1.1.1. 1.1.0.0. perc,strings
[12'] manuscript BMIC      (S957)

SUZUKI, HIDEAKI (1938-    )
Reflection II
string orch,pno [13'] JAPAN (S958)

SUZUKI, JUMMEI (1970-    )
Multiplicité
orch [14'] JAPAN           (S959)

SUZUKI, SEIYA
Fantasy
orch,pno [13'] JAPAN       (S960)

SUZUKI, YUKIKAZU (1954-    )
River Of Forest And Stars, The
orch, hichiriki JAPAN      (S961)

SVATEBNÍ POCHOD see Smetáček, Václav

SVÁTECNÍ DIVERTIMENTO see Reznicek,
Petr

SVÁTEK PÍSNE see Machek, Miloš

SVÁTEK RADOSTI see Strasek, Emil

SVATOJÁNSKÉ PROUDY see Rozkosny, Josef
Richard

SVATOS, VLADIMIR (1928-    )
Concertino for Piano and Strings
[15'] CESKY HUD.           (S962)

Concerto for Violin and Orchestra
3.2.2.3. 4.4.3.1. timp,perc,pno,
strings,vln solo [17'] CESKY HUD.
(S963)

Dramatická Predehra
4.2.2.2. 4.4.4.1. timp,perc,pno,
strings [10'] CESKY HUD.   (S964)

Malá Serenáda
[14'] CESKY HUD.           (S965)

Scherzo for Orchestra
3.2.2.2. 4.4.4.1. timp,perc,strings
[7'] CESKY HUD.            (S966)

Sinfonietta for Orchestra
4.2.2.3. 4.4.3.1. timp,perc,xylo,
pno,strings [22'] CESKY HUD.
(S967)

SVEDOMI SVETA see Vacek, Miloš

SVEHLA, ANTONIN (1921-    )
Cesky Tanec
2.2.2.2. 4.2.3.0. timp,perc,strings
[4'] CESKY HUD.            (S968)

Malá Procházka
2.0.1.0.2sax. 3.3.3.0. perc,harp,
3gtr,strings, polymoog [4'] CESKY
HUD.                       (S969)

Manuela
2.2.2.2. 4.2.3.1. timp,perc,harp,
strings [3'] CESKY HUD.    (S970)

Overture
see Predehra

Pekny Den
2.2.2.2. 4.2.3.0. timp,perc,harp,
strings [3'] CESKY HUD.    (S971)

Pojdte S Námi
2.2.2.2. 4.2.3.0. timp,perc,harp,
strings [3'] CESKY HUD.    (S972)

Predehra (Overture)
2.2.2.2. 4.3.3.1. timp,perc,harp,
strings [4'] CESKY HUD.    (S973)

SVEHLA, ANTONIN (cont'd.)

Scherzo
2.2.2.2. 4.3.3.1. timp,perc,strings
[5'] CESKY HUD.            (S974)

Serenade for Trumpet
2.2.2.2. 4.1.3.1. timp,perc,harp,
strings,trp solo [5'] CESKY HUD.
(S975)

Slavnostní Pochod
2.2.2.2. 3.2.3.1. timp,perc,vibra,
strings [4'] CESKY HUD.    (S976)

Vesely Príbeh
2.2.2.2. 4.2.3.1. timp,perc,strings
[4'] CESKY HUD.            (S977)

SVENSSON
Symphony No. 1
1.1.1.1. 1.1.1.1. strings [46'] sc
STIM                       (S978)

SVENSSON, MATTHIAS (1920-    )
Roo
string orch, (divisi) sc STIM
(S979)
string orch STIM           (S980)

Sapfos Avskedssång
3(pic).2(English horn).2(bass
clar).2(contrabsn). 3.2.2.1.
2perc,harp,strings,S solo STIM
(S981)

Suite No. 1 in G minor
see Tre Sviter F Strkar Ur Hans
Hakes Spelbcker

Suite No. 3 in D minor
see Tre Sviter F Strkar Ur Hans
Hakes Spelbcker

Suite No. 4 in B
see Tre Sviter F Strkar Ur Hans
Hakes Spelbcker

Tre Sviter F Strkar Ur Hans Hakes
Spelbcker
(Hedwall, Lennart) string orch sc
STIM f.s.
contains: Suite No. 1 in G minor;
Suite No. 3 in D minor; Suite
No. 4 in B                 (S982)

SVETEM MLÁDÍ see Ceremuga, Josef

SVETLA see Šaroun, Jaroslav

SVETLANOV, EVGENY (1928-    )
Poem for Violin and Orchestra
0.0.0.0. 4.0.3.1. timp,harp,strings
[16'] SIKORSKI perf mat rent (S983)

Rhapsody No. 1
"Spanische Bilder" 3(pic).3(English
horn).4(clar in E flat,bass
clar).3(contrabsn). 4.3.3.1.
timp,6perc,2harp,cel/pno,strings
[17'] SIKORSKI perf mat rent
(S984)

Rhapsody No. 2
3(pic).2.2.2. 4.3.3.1. 3perc,cel,
pno,2harp,strings [25'] SIKORSKI
perf mat rent              (S985)

Spanische Bilder
see Rhapsody No. 1

SVIT UR TOLV FRDMDA MN see Jeverud,
Johan

SWACK, IRWIN (1919-    )
Dance Episodes
0.1.2.0. 1.1.1.0. vla [18']
SCHIRM.EC rent             (S986)

Psalm No. 8
trp,kbd,strings,T solo [7']
SCHIRM.EC rent             (S987)

SWAFFORD, JAN (1946-    )
Chamber Sinfonietta
1.1.1.1. 1.1.1.0. perc,harp,pno,
strings [14'] PEER rent    (S988)

Late August
1(pic).2.2(clar in E flat).2.
2.0.0.0. perc,strings [8'] PEER
rent                       (S989)

SWEET ALCHEMY see Bourland, Roger

SWEET BAROQUE see Koprowski, Peter Paul

SWEET PROSPECT see Healey, Derek

SWEET WAS THE SONG THE VIRGIN SUNG see
Bergsma, William Laurence

SWORDS AND PLOWSHARES see Rorem, Ned

SYDEMAN, WILLIAM J. (1928-    )
Double Concerto
winds,strings,trp&trom soli SEESAW
(S990)

SYLPHIDE, LA see Løvenskjold, Herman Severin

SYLVIA: AN ADULT FAIRY TALE see Symonds, Norman

SYLVIA: LES PIZZICATI see Delibes, Léo

SYLVIA: PAS DES ESCLAVES see Delibes, Léo

SYLVIA: VALSE LENTE see Delibes, Léo

SYMFONI, EN see Jonsson, Reine

SYMFONI NR 6 see Koch, Erland von

SYMFONICKÁ FUGA see Flosman, Oldrich

SYMFONICKÁ SVITA see Gašparovicová, Marie

SYMFONICKÉ MATAMORFÓZY see Gregor, Cestmír

SYMFONICKÉ PRELUDIUM C. 1 see Tichy, Vladimir

SYMFONICKÉ PRELUDIUM C. 2 see Tichy, Vladimir

SYMFONICKÉ TANCE see Neumann, Veroslav

SYMFONICKÉ VETY see Návrat, Jaromír

SYMFONICKÉ VYPRÁVENÍ see Flosman, Oldrich

SYMFONICKY DIPTYCH see Zamecnik, Evzen

SYMFONIE BREVIS see Bartoš, Jan Zdenek, Symphony No. 7

SYMFONIE CHARAKTERISTICKÁ PRO MIR S REPUBLIKOU FRANCOUZSKOU see Wranitzky, Paul

SYMFONIE KOMORNÍ, 1. see Filas, Juraj

SYMFONIE KOMORNÍ, 2. see Filas, Juraj

SYMFONIE-KONCERT see Parsch, Arnost see Vrána, Jan

SYMFONIE MLÁDÍ see Soukup, Vladimír, Symphony No. 1

SYMFONIE PRO SMYCCOVÉ NÁSTROJE see Hrabánek, Pavel

SYMFONIETTA FESTIVA see Podešva, Jaromír

SYMFONISK DIKT BERGSLAGEN see Larsson, Folke

SYMFONISK INTRODUKSJON TIL EN SANG AV BRAHMS see Gaathaug, Morten

SYMFONISK SVIT see Hellman, Ivar

SYMFONISKA EPISODER see Liedbeck, Sixten

SYMFONY IN FREE STYLE see Harrison, Lou

SYMONDS, NORMAN (1920-    )
Big Lonely
3(pic).3(English horn).3(bass clar).3(contrabsn). 6.3.4.1. 4perc,harp,strings [35'] sc BOOSEY-CAN MI 1100 S988BI   (S991)

Concerto Grosso For Jazz Quintet And Orchestra
2(pic).3(English horn).2.2. 5.3.3.1. timp,perc,harp,strings, alto sax&trom&gtr&db&drums soli, (soli .. jazz quintet) [22'] sc CANADIAN MI 9400 S988CO   (S992)

Forest And Sky
2.2.2.2. 4.3.3.1. 3perc,harp, strings [12'] sc CANADIAN MI 1100 S988FO   (S993)

From The Eye Of The Wind
2(pic).2.2.2. 2.2.2.0. 3perc,pno, strings [21'] sc CANADIAN MI 1100 S988FR   (S994)

Gift Of Thanksgiving, The
3(pic).3(English horn).3(bass clar).3(contrabsn). 4.3.3.1. timp,4perc,harp,strings [18'] sc CANADIAN MI 1100 S988GI   (S995)

On An Emerald Sea
2(pic).2.2(bass clar).2. 2.2.0.0. timp,1-3perc,strings [18'] sc CANADIAN MI 1100 S9880N   (S996)

Spaces I: The River
string orch (1. The river 2. A moonlit pool 3. The bridge) sc CANADIAN MI 1500 S988SP   (S997)

SYMONDS, NORMAN (cont'd.)
Sylvia: An Adult Fairy Tale
orch,narrator, 2 or 3 jazz soloists [45'] CANADIAN MV 1300 S988SY   (S998)

SYMPHONIA CARMINUM see Vermeulen, Matthijs, Symphony No. 1

SYMPHONIA ROMANTICA see Connell, Adrian

SYMPHONIA SACRA see Widor, Charles-Marie

SYMPHONIA "VAMPA" see Filas, Juraj

SYMPHONIC DEDICATION see Meyer, Ernst Hermann, Sinfonische Widmung

SYMPHONIC ESSAY see Crossley, Lawrence

SYMPHONIC ETUDE see Heard, Alan

SYMPHONIC FRAGMENT see Albright, William H., Chasm

SYMPHONIC INTRODUCTION TO A SONG BY BRAHMS see Gaathaug, Morten, Symfonisk Introduksjon Til En Sang Av Brahms

SYMPHONIC MOVEMENT FOR PIANO AND ORCHESTRA see Orbon, Julian, Partita No. 4

SYMPHONIC MOVEMENT "KYOTO" see Ichiyanagi, Toshi

SYMPHONIC MUSIC 1957 see Kelemen, Milko

SYMPHONIC OVERTURE see Burritt, Lloyd see Korngold, Erich Wolfgang

SYMPHONIC PIECE see Sandred, Örjan

SYMPHONIC PIECE NO. 6 see Moevs, Robert Walter

SYMPHONIC POEM see Grandjany, Marcel

SYMPHONIC POEM, A see Okada, Shodai

SYMPHONIC POEM NO.1 see Wallace, William, Passing Of Beatrice

SYMPHONIC POEM "SHINANO" see Nagai, Akira

SYMPHONIC POEMS, HIROSHIMA see Tomotani, Koji

SYMPHONIC PRELUDE see Kraft, Leo Abraham

SYMPHONIC SCHERZO see Morawetz, Oskar

SYMPHONIC SKETCH see Zuckert, Leon

SYMPHONIC SKETCHES see Schipizky, Frederick

SYMPHONIC SUITE see Glass, Paul see Husa, Karel see Yuasa, Joji

SYMPHONIC VARIATIONS see Heard, Alan

SYMPHONIE À TRENTE see Beurden, Bernard van

SYMPHONIE ANTIQUE see Widor, Charles-Marie

SYMPHONIE CHEZ NOUS see Johansson, Sven Eric

SYMPHONIE DE CHAMBRE see Padilla, Antoine

SYMPHONIE DES DEUX CONTINENTS see Grippe, Ragnar

SYMPHONIE DU TIERS- MONDE see Tomasi, Henri

SYMPHONIE ESPAGNOLE see Lalo, Edouard

SYMPHONIE FANTASTIQUE & HAROLD IN ITALY see Berlioz, Hector (Louis)

SYMPHONIE PATHÉTIQUE see Tchaikovsky, Piotr Ilyich, Symphony No. 6 in B minor, Op. 74

SYMPHONIE RENDEZ-VOUS see Hundsnes, Svein

SYMPHONIE SÉRIEUSE (NR. 5) G-MOLL see Hamerik, Asger

SYMPHONIES NOS. 4 AND 7 see Bruckner, Anton

SYMPHONIQUE CONCERTO see Nakagawa, Toshio

SYMPHONISCHE BURLESKEN see Trexler, Georg

SYMPHONISCHE FESTMUSIK see Messner, Joseph

SYMPHONISCHE VARIATIONEN C-MOLL see Nicode, Jean Louis

SYMPHONISCHER PROLOG see Philipp, Franz

SYMPHONISCHER SATZ see Stephan, Rudi

SYMPHONISCHES POEM see Scriabin, Alexander

SYMPHONISK FANTASI NR 3 OP. 14 see Henke, Claes

SYMPHONY see Brings, Allen Stephen

SYMPHONY CONCERTANTE see Dahl, Ingolf

SYMPHONY DA PACEM DOMINE see Edwards, Ross

SYMPHONY "ET IN TERRA" see Grant, Stewart

SYMPHONY FOR CHORUS see Parchman, Gen Louis

SYMPHONY FOR ORCHESTRA & AUDIENCE see Tsubonoh, Katsuhiro

SYMPHONY FOR TWO WORLDS see Miki, Minoru, Kyu-No-Kyoku

SYMPHONY IN G-MINOR, THE see Still, William Grant, Symphony No. 2 in G minor

SYMPHONY IN RAGTIME see Zinn, William

SYMPHONY IN THE FORM OF PASSACAILLE see Kenins, Talivaldis, Symphony No. 7

SYMPHONY IN THREE PARTS see Shawn, Allen

SYMPHONY IN TWO PARTS see Saylor, Bruce (Stuart)

SYMPHONY NO. 3: LYRIC see Larsen, Elizabeth B. (Libby), Symphony No. 3

SYMPHONY NO. 3: THE INSCRUTABLE LIFE see Haug, Halvor, Symphony No. 3

SYMPHONY NO. 7 IN TWO PARTS see Bazelon, Irwin Allen

SYMPHONY NO. 8 AND HALF see Bazelon, Irwin Allen

SYMPHONY OF MEMORY, A see Maggio, Robert

SYMPHONY TO DANTEUS "DIVINA COMMEDIA", A see Liszt, Franz

SYMPHONY: WATER MUSIC see Larsen, Elizabeth B. (Libby), Symphony

SYMPOSION see Engström, Torbjörn

SYRÈNES, LES see Glière, Reinhold Moritzovich

SZABO, FERENC (1902-1969)
Ludas Matyi
2(pic).2(English horn).2(bass clar).2(contrabsn). 4.3.3.1. timp,perc,harp,cel,strings [28'] (Suite in 7 Movements) EMB rent   (S999)

Moldovan Rhapsody
2(pic).2.2+bass clar.2+contrabsn. 4.3.0.0. timp,perc,strings [17'] EMB rent   (S1000)

SZÉCHENYI CONCERTO see Hidas, Frigyes

SZEKELY, ENDRE (1912-    )
Concerto for Horn and Orchestra
3.0.3.0. 0.3.3.0. strings,horn solo [10'] (in memoriam Webern) EMB rent   (S1001)

Concerto for Piano, Percussion and Strings
string orch,perc,timp,cel,pno solo [20'] EMB rent   (S1002)

Concerto for Violin and Orchestra
2.2.2+bass clar.2. 4.3.3.1. timp, perc,harp,pno,strings,vln solo [13'] EMB rent   (S1003)

Duo Concertante
2horn,cel,harp,strings EMB rent   (S1004)

Fantasia Concertante
3.0.3.0. 2.0.0.0. timp,perc,harp, strings,vln solo EMB rent   (S1005)

SZEKELY, ENDRE (cont'd.)

Hullámmozgások
see Wave Motions

Rapsodia Concertante
3(pic).2.2.3(contrabsn). 4.2.3.1.
2timp,perc,harp,cel,strings,pno
solo [18'] EMB rent          (S1006)

Wave Motions
"Hullámmozgások" 4.3.3.3. 4.3.3.1.
timp,perc,harp,strings EMB rent
(S1007)

SZENEN FÜR KAMMERENSEMBLE see Zechlin,
Ruth

SZERVANSZKY, ENDRE (1911-    )
Merry March
"Vidám Induló" 2+pic.2.2.2.
4.3.3.1. timp,perc,strings [4']
EMB rent          (S1008)

Vidám Induló
see Merry March

SZIVÁRÁNY HAVASÁN see Sugár, M., On The
Snowy Hill Of The Rainbow

SZOKOLAY, SANDOR (1931-    )
Sinfonia Romana
strings [32'] EMB rent          (S1009)

SZÖLLÖSY, ANDRAS (1921-    )
Preludio, Adagio E Fuga
3.3.3(bass clar).3(contrabsn).
4.3.3.1(db tuba). 16vln I,16vln
II,12vla,10vcl,8db [18'] EMB rent
(S1010)
Pro Somno Igoris Stravinsky Quieto
0.1.0.1. 1.0.0.0. pno,strings [13']
(for chamber orchestra) EMB rent
(S1011)

SZÖLÖCSKE ÉS HALACSKA see Balassa,
Sándor, Little Grape And Little
Fish

SZÖNYI, ERZSEBET (ELIZABETH)
(1924-    )
Két Zenekari Darab
see Two Pieces For Orchestra

Preludio E Fuga
1.0.1.1. 0.0.0.0. timp,strings [7']
EMB rent          (S1012)

Two Pieces For Orchestra
"Két Zenekari Darab" 2(pic).2.2.2.
2.2.0.0. timp,perc,harp,strings
[9'] EMB rent          (S1013)

SZÓZAT AND HUNGARIAN HYMN see Liszt,
Franz

SZÓZAT ÉS MAGYAR HIMNUSZ see Liszt,
Franz, Szózat And Hungarian Hymn

# T

TABLE MUSIC see Farkas, Ferenc

TABLEAU see Lachenmann, Helmut
Friedrich

TABLEAU SYMPHONIQUE see Wanek,
Friedrich K.

TABLEAUX DES TROIS AGES see Casken,
John

TACHIHARA, ISAMU
Sinfonia for Orchestra
[14'] JAPAN          (T1)

TAFELMUSIK 1733, II-3 see Telemann,
Georg Philipp, Concerto for 3
Violins, Strings and Continuo in F

TAFELMUSIK 1733, III-1 see Telemann,
Georg Philipp, Concerto for 2
Oboes, Strings and Continuo in B
flat

TAG MEINES LEBENS see Ruzicka, Peter

TAGESGEBETE see Kantscheli, Gija

TAGGEDICHTE UND NACHTGESICHTE see
Schmidt, Hansjürgen

TAILLEFERRE, GERMAINE (1892-1983)
Concertino for Flute, Piano and
Chamber Orchestra
timp,harp,strings,fl solo,pno solo
[12'] BILLAUDOT rent          (T2)

Overture
2.2.1.1. 4.3.3.1. timp,3perc,xylo,
harp,hpsd,cel,strings [4'15"]
LEDUC          (T3)

TAKAHASHI, YUJI (1938-    )
Archipelago S.
1(alto fl).1(ob d'amore).2.1.
2.1.2.0. 2perc,cel,harp,2vln,
2vla,2vcl,db [14'] study sc
SCHOTTS SJ 1084 perf mat rent
(T4)

TAKE NOT A WOMAN'S ANGER see Purcell,
Henry

TAKEMITSU, TORU (1930-1996)
Alone On The Pacific  *Suite
orch [12'] SCHOTT,J          (T5)

Ceremonial
3(pic).3.3+bass clar.3. 4.3.3.0.
3perc,cel,harp,14vln I,12vln II,
10vla,8vcl,6db, shô solo [8'] (an
autumn ode) SCHOTTS perf mat rent
(T6)
Concerto Da Camera In D Major  *Op.33
2cornet,2horn,timp,string quin,fl
solo,vln solo [12'] SCHOTTS perf
mat rent          (T7)

Dodes'ka-Den
orch [5'] SCHOTT,J          (T8)

Family Tree
"Musical Verses For Young People"
3(pic,alto fl).2(English
horn).4(bass clar).3(contrabsn).
4.3.3.0. 3perc,harp,cel,acord,
14vln I,12vln II,10vla,8vcl,6db,
narrator [25'] (text by Shuntaro
Tanikawa) SCHOTTS perf mat rent
(T9)
Fantasma-Cantos
3(pic,alto fl).3(ob d'amore,English
horn).3(clar in E flat,bass
clar)+contrabass clar.2+
contrabsn. 4.3.3.0. 4perc,cel,
harp,14vln I,12vln II,10vla,8vcl,
6db,clar solo [18'] study sc
SCHOTTS SJ 1080 perf mat rent
(T10)
Fantasma-Cantos II
2(pic,alto fl).2(ob d'amore,English
horn).2(bass clar).2(contrabsn).
3.1.0.0. 2perc,harp,cel,6vln I,
6vln II,4vla,4vcl,2db,trom solo
[11'] SCHOTTS perf mat rent (T11)

Funeral Music
see Three Film Scores

How Slow The Wind
1(alto fl)+pic.2(English
horn).2(bass clar).2(contrabsn).
2.0.0.0. 2perc,pno&cel,harp,8vln
I,6vln II,4vla,4vcl,2db [11']
study sc SCHOTTS SJ1083 perf mat
rent          (T12)

Music Of Training And Rest
see Three Film Scores

TAKEMITSU, TORU (cont'd.)

Musical Verses For Young People
see Family Tree

Nami No Bon
orch [15'] SCHOTT,J          (T13)

Quotation Of Dream
"Say Sea, Take Me!" 3(pic,alto
fl).3(English horn).3(pic,bass
clar).3(contrabsn). 4.3.3.0.
4perc,cel,harp,12vln I,12vln II,
10vla,8vcl,6db,2pno soli [17']
SCHOTTS perf mat rent          (T14)

Say Sea, Take Me!
see Quotation Of Dream

Spectral Canticle
vln,gtr,orch [15'] SCHOTT,J    (T15)
3(pic,alto fl).3(English horn).3+
bass clar.3(contrabsn).soprano
sax. 4.3.3.0. 4perc,cel,harp,
14vln I,12vln II,10vla,8vcl,6db,
vln solo,gtr solo [15'] SCHOTTS
perf mat rent          (T16)

Spirit Garden
3(pic,alto fl).3(ob d'amore,English
horn).2+contrabsn.sax. 4.3.3.0.
5perc,2harp,cel,pno,14vln I,12vln
II,10vla,8vcl,6db [15'] SCHOTTS
perf mat rent          (T17)

String Around Autumn, A
3(pic,alto fl).3(ob d'amore,English
horn).3(clar in E flat,bass
clar)+contrabass clar.2+
contrabsn. 4.3.3.0. 4perc,pno&
cel,2harp,14vln I,12vln II,10vla,
8vcl,6db,vla solo [18'] study sc
SCHOTTS SJ 1064 perf mat rent
(T18)
Three Film Scores
string orch SCHOTTS f.s.
transcription of his music for
films
contains: Funeral Music (from
Black Rain); Music Of Training
And Rest (from Jose Torres);
Waltz (from Face Of Another)
(T19)
Treeline
1(alto fl).1.2(bass
clar).1(contrabsn). 2.1.1.0.
2perc,pno&cel,harp,2vln,vla,vcl,
db [12'] study sc SCHOTTS SJ 1058
perf mat rent          (T20)

Two Cine Pastrali
orch [7'] SCHOTT,J          (T21)

Visions
4(2pic,alto fl,bass fl).3(ob
d'amore,English horn).3(clar in E
flat,bass clar)+contrabass
clar.3(contrabsn). 4.3+bass
trp.3.0. 4perc,cel,pno,2harp,
16vln I,14vln II,12vla,10vcl,8db
[13'] study sc SCHOTTS SJ 1073
perf mat rent          (T22)

Waltz
see Three Film Scores

TAKEUCHI, KENJI (1942-    )
Academy Festival Music
orch [17'] JAPAN          (T23)

Requiem
see Str. Orch N3 - II

Str. Orch N3 - II
"Requiem" string orch,vln solo
[12'] JAPAN          (T24)

TAKOMIL see Kolberg, Kåre

TAKTAKISHVILI, OTAR (1924-1989)
Concerto for Violoncello and
Orchestra, No. 2
3.3.3.3. 4.3.3.1. timp,perc,harp,
cel,pno,strings [28'] SIKORSKI
perf mat rent          (T25)

TALÁLKOZÁSOK see Sugár, M., Recontres

TALE, A see Grahn, Ulf

TALE OF THE BIRD see Prevost, Andre,
Conte De L'Oiseau, Le

TALES FROM THE VIENNA WOODS see
Strauss, Johann, [Jr.], Geschichten
Aus Dem Wienerwald

TALES OF HOFFMANN see Offenbach,
Jacques

TALIN see Hovhaness, Alan

TALL STORY FOR ORCHESTRA, A see Moross,
Jerome

TALLIS see Ruzicka, Peter

TAM, KDE BYDLÍTE see Rimón, Jan

TAMAS, JANOS (1936-1995)
Ballade
2.2(English horn).2.2. 2.2.0.0.
timp,strings [20'] MULL & SCH
rent                              (T26)

Capriccio *ballet
orch [12'] MULL & SCH rent        (T27)

Concerto for Piano
orch,pno solo [18'] MULL & SCH rent
(T28)

Fest-Ouverture
orch [10'] MULL & SCH rent        (T29)

Larghetto
2.1(English horn).1(bass clar).1.
2.0.0.0. harp,strings,vln solo
[10'] MULL & SCH rent             (T30)

Overture for Orchestra
orch [9'] MULL & SCH rent         (T31)

Poem for Horn and Strings
[6'] MULL & SCH rent              (T32)

Poem for Viola and Strings
[6'] MULL & SCH rent              (T33)

Poem for Violin and Strings
MULL & SCH rent                   (T34)

Ritorno, Il
1.1.1.0. 1.0.0.0. strings [13']
MULL & SCH rent                   (T35)

Sagenhaftes Solothurn
chamber group [12'] MULL & SCH rent
(T36)

Serenade
orch min sc KUNZELMANN ETP 1326 ipr
(T37)

Suite for Orchestra
orch [15'] MULL & SCH rent        (T38)

TAMBERG, EINO (1930-   )
Concerto for Trumpet and Orchestra,
No. 2, Op. 100
"Drei Präludien Und Toccata" 0+alto
fl.0.3.0. 3.0.0.1. timp,4perc,
pno,strings,trp&flügelhorn solo
[18'] SIKORSKI perf mat rent      (T39)

Drei Präludien Und Toccata
see Concerto for Trumpet and
Orchestra, No. 2, Op. 100

TAMBOURIN see Gossec, François Joseph
see Sutermeister, Heinrich see
Tomasi, Henri

TAN, DUN
Death And Fire
"Dialogue With Paul Klee" orch sc
SCHIRM.G ED3935                   (T40)

Dialogue With Paul Klee
see Death And Fire

TAN, SU LIAN
Autumn Lute-Song
string orch,fl [14'] PRESSER rent
(T41)

TANCE A REFLEXE see Gemrot, Jiri

TANCE KEJKLÍRU see Kašlik, Václav

TANCE PRED BRANOU see Kašlik, Václav

TANCE PRO HARFU A SMYCCOVY ORCHESTR see
Flosman, Oldrich

TANCE VE STARÉM SLOHU see Vacek, Miloš

TANCRÈDE: SUITE INSTRUMENTALE see
Campra, André

TANCREDI see Henze, Hans Werner

TANECNÍ SCHERZO see Baier, Jiri

TANEJEW, S.
Canzone
(Thomas-Mifune) clar solo/vcl solo,
string orch pno-cond sc
KUNZELMANN 10238 ipr             (T42)

TANEYEV, SERGEY IVANOVICH (1856-1915)
Canzone, For Clarinet And String
Orchestra
[10'] SIKORSKI perf mat rent     (T43)

Symphony No. 2 in B flat
3(pic).3(English horn).2.2.
4.2.3.1. timp,strings [35']
SIKORSKI perf mat rent           (T44)

Symphony No. 3 in D minor
2.2.2.2. 2.2.1.0. timp,strings
[34'] SIKORSKI perf mat rent     (T45)

TANGIWA, TADIHIRO (1935-   )
Concerto for Violin, No. 2,First
Movement
see Parody From J.S. Bach

Parody From J.S. Bach (Concerto for
Violin, No. 2,First Movement)
strings,vln solo JAPAN           (T46)

TANN, HILARY
Adirondack Light
2.2.2.2. 2.2.0.0. timp,perc,
strings,narrator [18'] perf sc
set OXFORD 385922X sc,pts rent
(T47)

As Ferns
strings without db [9'] perf sc set
OXFORD 385869X sc,pts rent  (T48)

Here The Cliffs
2+pic.2.2(clar in E flat).2.
4.2.3.1. timp,2perc,harp,strings,
vln solo [16'] perf sc set OXFORD
3861224 sc,pts rent              (T49)

Through The Echoing Timber
2(pic).2.2.2. 4.3.3.1. timp,2perc,
strings [4'] perf sc set OXFORD
3859076 sc,pts rent              (T50)

Water's Edge
string orch [9'] perf sc set OXFORD
3859785 sc,pts rent              (T51)

With The Heather And Small Birds
2.2.2.2. 2.2.0.0. timp,perc,strings
[10'] perf sc set OXFORD 3859599
sc,pts rent                      (T52)

TANNER, DAVID (1950-   )
Veils And Images
3(pic,alto fl).2(English
horn).3(clar in E flat,bass
clar).2.soprano sax. 4.3.3.0.
timp,3perc,harp,pno,12vln I,12vln
II,8vla,8vcl,6db [14'] sc
CANADIAN MI 1100 T166VE          (T53)

TANNHÄUSER: OVERTURE see Wagner,
Richard

TANTUM ERGO, FOR SOLO VOICES AND
ORCHESTRA see Bellini, Vincenzo

TANZ DER NATIONALEN MINDERHEITEN see
Liu, Ties-Han

TANZ DES LEBENS, DER see Søderlind,
Ragnar

TANZ- UND SALONMUSIK, FROM "THE IDIOT"
see Henze, Hans Werner

TANZ VON RÜPELN, EIN see Mendelssohn-
Bartholdy, Felix

TÄNZE AUF DER KOKOSNUSS see Schilling,
Otto-Erich

TANZENDE FAUNE see Orff, Carl

TÄNZERISCHE SUITE see Voigtländer,
Lothar

TAPESTRY see Perna, Dana Paul

TAPRAY, JEAN-FRANÇOIS
Four Symphonies Concertantes For
Harpsichord And Piano With
Orchestra Ad Libitum
(Gustafson, Bruce) A-R ED
ISBN 0-89579-320-2 f.s. includes
a supplement containing op. 8 and
op. 9 arranged for unaccompanied
harpsichord and pno
contains: Symphonie Concertante
in C, Op. 13 (0.0.0.0. 2.0.0.0.
hpsd,pno,vln I,vln II,db);
Symphonie Concertante in D, Op.
8 (0.0.0.0. 2.0.0.0. hpsd,pno,
vln I,vln II,vla,db); Symphonie
Concertante in E flat, Op. 9
(0.0.0.0. 2.0.0.0. hpsd,pno,vln
I,vln II,vla,db,vln solo);
Symphonie Concertante in G, Op.
15 (vln I,vln II,db,hpsd,pno)
(T54)

Symphonie Concertante in C, Op. 13
see Four Symphonies Concertantes
For Harpsichord And Piano With
Orchestra Ad Libitum

Symphonie Concertante in D, Op. 8
see Four Symphonies Concertantes
For Harpsichord And Piano With
Orchestra Ad Libitum

Symphonie Concertante in E flat, Op.
9
see Four Symphonies Concertantes
For Harpsichord And Piano With
Orchestra Ad Libitum

Symphonie Concertante in G, Op. 15
see Four Symphonies Concertantes
For Harpsichord And Piano With

TAPRAY, JEAN-FRANÇOIS (cont'd.)

Orchestra Ad Libitum

TARANTELA-FANTAZIE see Bartoš, Jan
Zdenek

TARANTELLA see Thompson, Randall

TARANTELLA DI COMMEDIA see Sodomka,
Karel

TARANTELLA FESTIVA see Juchelka,
Miroslav

TARANTELLE. OVERTURE FOR ORCHESTRA see
Zaimont, Judith Lang

TARENSKEEN, BOUDEWIJN (1952-   )
Sound Of Music, The
4.4.4.4. 4.4.3.1. 4perc,2harp,pno,
strings [15'] sc DONEMUS        (T55)

TARNOPOLSKY, VLADIMIR (1955-   )
Atem Der Erschöpften Zeit, Der
4.3.5.3. 6.2.4.1. 6perc,harp,2elec
gtr,2synthesizer&pno&elec org,
strings [26'] sc PETERS 03534
(T56)

Brooklyn Bridge Oder Meine Entdeckung
Amerikas
[Russ] 1.1.2.1.3sax. 2.1.1.1.
4perc,harp,acord,strings,ST soli
[17'] SIKORSKI perf mat rent
(T57)

Eindruck-Ausdruck II: (Hommage) À
Kandinsky
1.1.2.1. 1.1.1.0. 2perc,harp,pno,
strings [15'] sc PETERS 02633
(T58)

Jesu, Deine Tiefen Wunden: Chorale
Prelude
1.1.2.1. 2.1.1.0. 2perc,8vln I,
6vla,5vcl,4db [10'] sc PETERS
04481                            (T59)

Jesu, Deine Tiefen Wunden:
Choralvorspiel
1.1.2.1. 2.1.1.0. 2perc,glock,
vibra/harp/cel,vln,vla,vcl,db
[11'] SIKORSKI perf mat rent
(T60)

Kassandra
1.1.2.1. 1.1.1.1. 2perc,harp,
synthesizer,pno,strings [30'] sc
PETERS 8838                      (T61)

Landschaft Nach Der Schlacht
1.1.2.1. 1.1.1.0. 2perc,pno,harp,
electronic tape,2vln,vla,vcl,db
[26'] sc PETERS 04396            (T62)

Punkte, Linien, Volumina
II...Kandinsky
1.1.2.1. 1.1.1.0. 2perc,pno,harp,
8vln I,7vln II,6vla,5vcl,4db
[15'] sc PETERS 03442            (T63)

Vent Des Mots Qu' L' N'a Pas Dits, Le
3.3.4.3. 4.2.2.0. 2perc,harp,10vla,
8vcl,6db,vcl solo [15'] sc PETERS
04672                            (T64)

TAROMIRS TID see Rehnqvist, Karin

TARP, SVEND ERIK (1908-   )
Overture
see Rhapsodiesche Ouvertüre

Rapsodisk Ouverture
see Rhapsodiesche Ouvertüre

Rhapsodiesche Ouvertüre (Overture)
"Rapsodisk Ouverture" 2.2.2.2.
2.2.2.0. timp,perc,strings [6']
sc,set BUSCH rent                (T65)

TARTINI, GIUSEPPE (1692-1770)
Concerto for Violin and String
Orchestra in G, Dounias 80
(Braun) vln solo,orch KUNZELMANN
ipa sc 10023A, oct 10023         (T66)

Concerto for Violin and String
Orchestra, No. 53, in E
(Scherchen, Hermann) [12'] HUG sc
GH 8883, pts,solo pt 8883-30, pno
red 8883A                        (T67)

Concerto for Violin, String Orchestra
and Continuo in B flat, Dounias
123
(Braun) vln solo,string orch,cont
KUNZELMANN ipa sc 10024A, oct
10024                            (T68)

Concerto for Violin, String Orchestra
and Continuo in E, Dounias 51
(Ney) vln solo,string orch,cont
KUNZELMANN ipa sc 10055A, oct
10055                            (T69)

Concerto for Violoncello and String
Orchestra in A
strings,cont,vcl solo [13']
BREITKOPF-W                      (T70)

TARTINI, GIUSEPPE (cont'd.)

Teufels-Triller, Der
(Becker, A.) 0.2.2.2. 2.0.0.0.
timp,strings,vln solo [14']
BREITKOPF-W                              (T71)

Trille Du Diable, Le
(Dupin, Marc-Olivier) string orch,
vln solo [12'] BILLAUDOT               (T72)

TASSILONE see Steffani, Agostino

TAUB, BRUCE J.H. (1948-    )
Of The Wing Of Madness
1.1.1.1. 1.1.1.0. 2-4perc,strings
[10'] sc PETERS EP 67283               (T73)

Often Fatal Malady, An
1.1.1.1. 1.1.1.0. 2perc,pno,strings
[18'] PETERS                           (T74)

TAUBERT, ERNST EDUARD
Suite for Strings, Op. 67
8vln I,7vln II,6vla,5vcl,4db [12']
sc KAHNT 01972                         (T75)

TAUSCH, FRANZ (1762-1817)
Concerto for Clarinet and Orchestra
in E flat
clar solo,orch KUNZELMANN ipa sc
10117A, oct 10117                      (T76)

TAUSINGER, JAN (1921-1980)
Sinfonia Slovacca
3.2.3.1. 3.3.3.0. timp,perc,xylo,
vibra,harp,pno,strings [16']
CESKY HUD.                             (T77)

TAVBA see Berkovec, Jiri

TAVENER, JOHN (1944-    )
Eternal Memory
strings,vcl solo [12'] CHESTER        (T78)

Repentant Thief, The
clar,timp,perc,strings [21']
CHESTER                                (T79)

Theophany
2.2.2.2. 3.3.2.1. timp,perc,
electronic tape,strings, bandic
drum [30'] CHESTER                     (T80)

TAYLOR, MATTHEW
Banquet And Invasion
4perc,strings [12'] BMIC              (T81)

Concerto for Piano and Orchestra
2.2.2.2. 4.2.0.0. timp,strings,pno
solo [33'] BMIC                        (T82)

TCHAIKOVSKY, ALEXANDER (1946-    )
Baschmet-Suite
string orch [26'] SIKORSKI perf mat
rent                                   (T83)

Concerto for Viola and Orchestra
3.3.3.3. 4.2.2.1. timp,perc,harp,
cel,strings,vla solo [25']
SIKORSKI perf mat rent                 (T84)

Concerto for Violin and Orchestra
2.2.2.2. 4.2.2.1. timp,perc,harp,
hpsd,strings,vln solo [33']
SIKORSKI perf mat rent                 (T85)

TCHAIKOVSKY, BORIS (1925-1996)
Capriccio for Orchestra
"Capriccio Über Englische Weisen"
3.3.2.2. 4.3.3.1. timp,perc,harp,
strings [7'] SIKORSKI perf mat
rent                                   (T86)

Capriccio Über Englische Weisen
see Capriccio for Orchestra

Sechs Etüden, For Organ And Strings
[26'] SIKORSKI perf mat rent          (T87)

TCHAIKOVSKY, PIOTR ILYICH (1840-1893)
Air De Lenski  *Op.24,No.17
2.2.2.2. 4.2.3.0. timp,strings,solo
voice [7'] BILLAUDOT                   (T88)

Air De Tatiana
see Scènes De La Lettre

Allegro In C, For Piano And String
Orchestra
pno solo,string orch KUNZELMANN ipa
sc,pts WW 907, sc WW 907P             (T89)

Andante Cantabile
(Serebrier, José) string orch
[7'30"] PEER rent                      (T90)

Andante Cantabile In B Flat (from
String Quartet, Op. 11)
string orch [7'30"] BREITKOPF-W
                                       (T91)

Arioso  *Op.60,No.5 (from Cantate De
Moscou)
2.2.2.2. 4.0.0.0. strings,Mez solo
[5'] BILLAUDOT                         (T92)

TCHAIKOVSKY, PIOTR ILYICH (cont'd.)

Chanson De La Bohémienne  *Op.60,No.7
0.2.2.2. 2.0.0.0. strings,solo
voice [3'] BILLAUDOT                   (T93)

Complete Piano Concertos
orch,pno solo sc DOVER 27385-7
                                       (T94)

Duo De Roméo Et Juliette
(Tanéiew, S.) [Fr/Russ] 2.2.2.2.
4.2.0.0. timp,harp,strings,ST
soli [12'] BILLAUDOT                   (T95)

1812 Overture, Marche Slave And
Francesca Da Rimini
orch sc DOVER 29069-7                  (T96)

1812 Overture
see Ouverture Solennelle Es-Dur,
Op. 49

Elegy for String Orchestra
string orch KUNZELMANN ipa sc
WW 908P, sc,pts WW 908                 (T97)

Fantaisie De Concert  *Op.56
3.2.2.2. 4.2.3.0. timp,perc,strings
[31'] BILLAUDOT                        (T98)

Jugendalbum: Suite No. 1
orch MÖSELER sc 10.009-00, pts
10.009-01 TO 02, set 10.009-09
                                       (T99)

Jugendalbum: Suite No. 2
orch MÖSELER sc 10.010-00, pts
10.010-01 TO 02, set 10.010-09
                                       (T100)

Largo & Allegro, For Flute And String
Orchestra
fl solo,string orch KUNZELMANN ipa
sc WW 906P, sc,pts WW 906             (T101)

Mazeppa: Air d'André (No. 16)
orch,solo voice BOIS                  (T102)

Meditation, Op. 42, No. 1
(Dupin, Marc-Olivier) string orch,
vln solo [9'] BILLAUDOT               (T103)

Mozartiana  *Op.61
2.2.2.2. 4.2.0.0. timp,perc,harp,
strings [25'] BILLAUDOT               (T104)

Nocturne for Violoncello and
Orchestra (from Klavierstück Op.
19, No. 4)
vcl solo,orch KUNZELMANN ipa sc
WW 901A, sc WW 901P, sc,pts
WW 901B                               (T105)

Nutcracker Suite
orch sc DOVER 25379-1                 (T106)

Ouverture Danoise  *Op.15
3.2.2.2. 4.2.2.1. timp,2perc,
strings [12'] BILLAUDOT               (T107)

Ouverture Solennelle Es-Dur, Op. 49
"1812 Overture" 2+pic.2+English
horn.2.2. 4.2+cornet.3.1. timp,
4perc,strings [16'] study sc
BREITKOPF-W PB 5284                   (T108)

Rêverie D'Hiver
see Symphony No. 1, Op. 13

Romeo And Juliet Overture And
Capriccio Italien
orch sc DOVER 25217-5                 (T109)

Scènes De La Lettre  *Op.24,No.9
"Air De Tatiana" 2.2.2.2. 4.2.3.0.
timp,harp,strings,solo voice
[14'] BILLAUDOT                       (T110)

Serenade, Op. 48, Nos. 2-3
string orch [11'] BILLAUDOT          (T111)

Si J'étais Une Petite Herbe  *Op.47,
No.7
2.2.2.2. 4.0.0.0. strings,solo
voice [5'] BILLAUDOT                  (T112)

Suite No. 1, Op. 43
4.2.2.2. 4.2.0.0. timp,perc,strings
[40'] BILLAUDOT                       (T113)

Symphonie Pathétique
see Symphony No. 6 in B minor, Op.
74

Symphony No. 1, Op. 13
"Rêverie D'Hiver" 3.2.2.2. 4.2.3.1.
timp,perc,strings [48'] BILLAUDOT
                                      (T114)

Symphony No. 2, Op. 17
3.2.2.2. 4.2.3.1. timp,perc,strings
[34'] BILLAUDOT                       (T115)

Symphony No. 3, Op. 29
3.2.2.2. 4.2.3.1. timp,strings
[40'] BILLAUDOT                       (T116)

TCHAIKOVSKY, PIOTR ILYICH (cont'd.)

Symphony No. 6 in B minor, Op. 74
"Symphonie Pathétique"
3(pic).2.2.2. 4.2.3.1. timp,perc,
strings [48'] study sc BREITKOPF-
W PB 3628                             (T117)

Symphony Nos. 1-3
orch sc DOVER 27050-5                 (T118)

Symphony Nos. 4-6
orch sc DOVER 23861-X                 (T119)

Tempête, La  *Op.18
3.2.2.2. 4.2.3.1. timp,perc,strings
[27'] BILLAUDOT                       (T120)

Valse De L'Opéra Eugène Onéguine
*Op.24,No.13
3.2.2.2. 4.2.3.0. timp,strings [6']
BILLAUDOT                             (T121)

TCHEREPNIN, ALEXANDER (1899-1977)
Concerto No. 5 for Piano and
Orchestra, Op. 96
3.2.3.2. 3.2.0.0. timp,perc,harp,
strings,pno solo [21'] PETERS
                                      (T122)

Serenade, Op. 97
string orch min sc KUNZELMANN
ETP 1337 ipr                          (T123)

Vivre D'Amour
2.2.2.2. 4.2.3.1. timp,pno,cel,8vln
I,7vln II,6vla,5vcl,4db [6'] sc
BELAIEFF 01890                        (T124)

TCHEREPNIN, IVAN ALEXANDROVITCH
(1943-    )
Concerto for Violin, Violoncello and
Orchestra
3.3.3.3. 4.3.3.1. timp,2perc,
marimba,xylo,harp,8vln I,7vln II,
6vla,5vcl,4db,vln solo,vcl solo
sc,solo pt BELAIEFF 04794            (T125)

TCHEREPNIN, NIKOLAY NIKOLAYEVICH
(1873-1945)
Bilder Zu Einem Russische Alphabet
3.3.2.2. 4.2.3.1. timp,perc,harp,
cel,strings [12'] PETERS             (T126)

Bilder Zu Einem Russischen Alphabet
3.3.2.2. 4.2.3.1. timp,perc,cel,
harp,8vln I,7vln II,6vla,5vcl,4db
[21'] sc BELAIEFF 03441              (T127)

TEARS OF NIGHT, THE see Lutyens,
Elisabeth

TED UZ VÍŠ see Wittmann, Max

TEDDY UND DIE TIERRE see Thomas-Mifune,
Werner

TELEGRAPHIST, THE: OVERTURE see Meyers,
Randall

TELEMANN, GEORG PHILIPP (1681-1767)
Concertino for Trumpet and Strings
vln I,vln II,vla,vcl,db,trp solo
MÖSELER sc 40.138-00, pts
40.138-01, set 40.138-09            (T128)

Concerto for Flute, String Orchestra
and Continuo in F
string orch,cont,fl solo KUNZELMANN
ipa sc 10219A, oct 10219            (T129)

Concerto for Flute, Strings and
Continuo in B minor
vln I,vln II,vla,vcl,db,fl solo
MÖSELER sc 40.150-00, pts
40.150-01, set 40.150-09            (T130)

Concerto for Flute, Strings and
Continuo in G
vln I,vln II,vla,vcl,db,fl solo
MÖSELER sc 40.156-00, pts
40.156-01, set 40.156-09            (T131)

Concerto for Oboe, String Orchestra
and Continuo in C minor
string orch,cont,ob solo KUNZELMANN
ipa sc 10243A, oct 10243            (T132)

Concerto for Oboe, Strings and
Continuo in E flat
vln I,vln II,vla,vcl,db,ob solo
MÖSELER sc 40.148-00, pts
40.148-01, set 40.148-09            (T133)

Concerto for 2 Oboes, Strings and
Continuo in B flat
"Tafelmusik 1733, III-1" strings,
cont,2ob soli [23'] BREITKOPF-W
                                     (T134)

Concerto for Recorder, Bassoon,
Strings and Continuo in F
(Angerhöfer, G.; Bernstein, W. H.)
strings,cont,rec&bsn soli [18']
BREITKOPF-W                          (T135)

**TELEMANN, GEORG PHILIPP** (cont'd.)

Concerto for 2 Trumpets and Strings
BOIS                                          (T136)

Concerto for Violin and Orchestra in
D
2ob,bsn,3horn,strings,cont,vln solo
KUNZELMANN ipa sc 10237A, oct
10237                                          (T137)

Concerto for 2 Violins and Orchestra
in D
(Schroeder) bsn,strings,cont,2vln
soli KUNZELMANN ipa sc 10061A,
oct 10061                                      (T138)

Concerto for 2 Violins, 2 Oboes,
Strings and Continuo in G
vln I,vln II,vla I/vln III,vla II,
vcl,db,cont,opt 2ob,2vln soli
MÖSELER sc 40.152-00, pts
40.152-01 TO 02, set 40.152-09
                                               (T139)

Concerto for 3 Violins, Strings and
Continuo in F
"Tafelmusik 1733, II-3" strings
without vln,cont,3vln soli [16']
BREITKOPF-W                                    (T140)

Concerto Grosso for 2 Flutes,
Bassoon, Strings and Continuo in
E minor
"Corona" 2fl/fl&ob,bsn,strings,cont
MÖSELER M 60.167                               (T141)

Concerto Grosso for 2 Flutes,
Bassoon, Strings and Continuo in
E minor, MIN 1
2fl/fl&ob,bsn,strings,cont MÖSELER
40.167                                         (T142)

Concerto in F
(Schroeder) rec,ob,bsn,2horn,
strings,cont KUNZELMANN ipa sc
10043A, oct 10043                              (T143)

Corona
see Concerto Grosso for 2 Flutes,
Bassoon, Strings and Continuo in
E minor

Konzertsuite A-Dur (Suite for Violin
and String Orchestra in A)
(Maertens, W.) strings,cont,vln
solo [18'] BREITKOPF-W                         (T144)

Suite for Flute and Strings
BOIS                                           (T145)

Suite for Trumpet, Strings and
Continuo
see Tromba, La

Suite for Violin and String Orchestra
in A
see Konzertsuite A-Dur

Tafelmusik 1733, II-3
see Concerto for 3 Violins, Strings
and Continuo in F

Tafelmusik 1733, III-1
see Concerto for 2 Oboes, Strings
and Continuo in B flat

Tromba, La (Suite for Trumpet,
Strings and Continuo)
vln I,vln II,vla,vcl,db,trp solo
MÖSELER sc 40.137-00, solo pt
40.137-01, pts 40.137-02, set
40.137-09                                      (T146)

**TELFER, NANCY** (1950-    )
Sea's Strong Voice, The
2(pic).2.2.2.  4.2.2.2.  timp&perc,
perc,strings,Mez solo [17'] (1.
With the ebb and flow 2. Slowly
3. Quickly 4. With intensity) sc
CANADIAN MV 1400 T271SE                        (T147)

**TELLEFSEN, THOMAS** (1823-1874)
Concerto for Piano and Orchestra, No.
2, in F minor, Op. 15
2.2.2.2.  2.2.0.0.  timp,strings,pno
solo NORSKMI                                   (T148)

TEMA MIT VARIATIONEN see Berwald, Franz
(Adolf)

TEMA PER 12 STRUMENTI see Donatoni,
Franco, Theme For 12 Instruments

TEMERARI - COME SCOGLIO see Mozart,
Wolfgang Amadeus

**TEML, JIRI** (1935-    )
Concerto for Violin and Orchestra
3.2.3.2.  4.3.3.1.  timp,perc,harp,
cel,pno,strings,vln solo [26']
CESKY HUD.                                     (T149)

Concerto for Violoncello, Strings,
Piano and Percussion
[18'] CESKY HUD.                               (T150)

**TEML, JIRI** (cont'd.)

Concerto Grosso for 2 Violins, Viola
and Chamber Orchestra
see Pocta Händlovi

Koncert-Fantazie Pro Housle, Harfu A
Orchestr
3.2.3.2.  4.3.3.1.  timp,perc,cel,
strings,vln&harp soli [17'] CESKY
HUD.                                           (T151)

Písecké Divertimento
2.2.2.2.  2.2.0.0.  timp,perc,pno,
2vln,vla,vcl,db [12'] CESKY HUD.               (T152)

Pocta Händlovi (Concerto Grosso for 2
Violins, Viola and Chamber
Orchestra)
2.2.2.2.  2.2.0.0.  timp,strings,
2vln&vla soli [10'] CESKY HUD.                 (T153)

Symphony No. 2
"Válka S Mloky" 3.3.3.3.  4.3.3.1.
timp,perc,harp,cel,pno,strings
[22'] CESKY HUD.                               (T154)

Tri Promenády
3.3.3.3.  4.3.3.1.  timp,perc,vibra,
harp,cel,pno,strings [22'] CESKY
HUD.                                           (T155)

Válka S Mloky
see Symphony No. 2

TEMPEST, THE: INCIDENTAL MUSIC see
Locke, Matthew

TEMPEST, THE: SUITE see Tippett, [Sir]
Michael

TEMPÊTE, LA see Tchaikovsky, Piotr
Ilyich

TEMPI PASSATI see Vea, Ketil

TEMPLE OF THE GOLDEN PAVILION, THE see
Howard, Brian

TEMPO, TEMPO see Hudec, Jirí

TEN CANADIAN FOLK SONGS see Turner,
Robert [Comrie]

TEN ITALIAN VIOLIN CONCERTOS FROM FONDS
BLANCHETON: PART I
(Hirshberg, Jehoash) orch,vln solo A-
R ED ISBN 0-89579-171-4 f.s.
contains: Alberti, Giuseppe Matteo,
Concerto No. 8 in G minor; Allay,
Maurin d', Concerto No. 15 in F
minor; Razetti, Carlo Alezio,
Concerto No. 12 in F minor;
Tessarini, Carlo, Concerto No. 21
in F                                           (T156)

TEN ITALIAN VIOLIN CONCERTOS FROM FONDS
BLANCHETON: PART II
(Hirshberg, Jehoash) orch,vln solo A-
R ED ISBN 0-89579-172-2 f.s.
contains: Salurini, Paulo, Concerto
No. 50 in B flat; Scaccia, Angelo
Maria, Concerto No. 23 in F;
Somis, Giovanni Battista,
Concerto No. 32 in G; Zanni,
Andrea, Concerto No. 31 in D;
Zuccarini, Carlo, Concerto No. 47
in G                                           (T157)

TENDER MERCIES see Dreyfus, George

TENEBRAE see Mills, Richard

TÉNÈBRES see Hetu, Jacques

TÉNÉRÉ-INCANTATION SUR UN VERSET
CORANIQUE see Florentz, Jean-Louis

**TENNEY, JAMES C.** (1934-    )
Clang
1+pic+alto fl.1+English horn.1+bass
clar.1+contrabsn.  2.2.2.1.  4perc,
pno,strings [15'] sc SMITH PUB
MI 1100 T298CL                                 (T158)

For Twelve Strings (Rising)
4vln,3vla,3vcl,2db sc SMITH PUB
MI 1500 T298FO                                 (T159)

TEO TORIATE see Fischer, Eduard

TER VELDHUIS, JACOB
see VELDHUIS, JACOB TER

**TERASHIMA, RIKUYA** (1964-    )
Concerto For Shakuhachi 20-Str. Koto
And Orchestra
orch, shaku, 20 gen [28'] JAPAN                (T160)

TERJE VIGEN see Guttormsen, Guttorm

**TERMOS, PAUL** (1942-    )
Concerto
2.2.2.2.  0.0.0.0.  strings,alto sax
solo [15'] sc DONEMUS                          (T161)

**TERMOS, PAUL** (cont'd.)

Concerto for Flute and Chamber
Orchestra
0.3.3.2.  2.0.0.0.  strings,fl solo
[15'] sc DONEMUS                               (T162)

TERPSICORE: SUITE see Handel, George
Frideric

TERRA LUCIDA see Clayton, Laura

TERRAIN see Powers, Anthony

TERZETT OP. 52 BIS see Rimsky-Korsakov,
Nikolai

**TESAR, MILAN**
Auf Einer Russischen Feier
17vln,pno,opt harp [5'] SIKORSKI
perf mat rent                                  (T163)

**TESSARINI, CARLO** (1690-ca. 1765)
Concerto for Violin and String
Orchestra, Op. 1, No. 4, in D
(Müller) vln solo,string orch
KUNZELMANN ipa sc 10073A, oct
10073                                          (T164)

TETRACHORDON see Liljeholm, Thomas

TEUFELS-TRILLER, DER see Tartini,
Giuseppe

TEUFELSTRILLER see Kasparov, Youri

TEXTURES see Surdin, Morris

THANATOS-EROS (TRADITION III (1) see
Schnebel, Dieter

THANKSGIVING SONG see Grainger, Percy
Aldridge

THARSIS VARIATIONS see Johansen, Bertil
Palmar

THAT OTHER SIDE see Steven, Donald

THAT QUICKENING PULSE see Druckman,
Jacob Raphael

THEATRE REPRESENTS A GARDEN AT NIGHT,
THE see Woolrich, John

THEKLA (EINE GEISTERSTIMME) see
Schubert, Franz (Peter)

THELS KLAGEN: PROLOG see Smirnov,
Dmitri

THEMA, VARIATIONEN UND FINALE FÜR
GROSSES ORCHESTER see Rozsa, Miklos

THEME FOR 12 INSTRUMENTS see Donatoni,
Franco

**THEODORAKIS, MIKIS** (1925-    )
Eros And Death
strings,solo voice BOIS                        (T165)

Lorca
orch,Mez solo,gtr solo (6 songs)
BOIS                                           (T166)

Phaedra
orch,MezBar soli [50'] (12 songs)
BOIS                                           (T167)

THEOPHANY see Tavener, John

THERE see Lloyd, Jonathan

THERE IS NO DARKNESS see Coulthard,
Jean

THERE WERE THREE FRIENDS see Grainger,
Percy Aldridge

THÉRÈSE: LA CHUTE DES FEUILLES see
Massenet, Jules

THESE PREMISES ARE ALARMED see Ades,
Thomas

THESIS FOR ORCHESTRA see Coles, Graham

**THIBAULT, ALAIN** (1956-    )
Paraboles Et Catastrophes
string orch,marimba solo sc
CANADIAN MI 1640 T425PA                        (T168)

**THIEL, WOLFGANG**
Media Vita
3.2.2.3.  4.2.0.0.  3perc,pno,8vln I,
7vln II,6vla,5vcl,4db,tuba solo
[15'] sc PETERS 03287                          (T169)

**THIELE, SIEGFRIED** (1934-    )
Hölderlin-Gesänge
3.0.2.0.  2.1.0.0.  timp,2perc,harp,
8vln I,7vln II,6vla,5vcl,4db,Bar
solo [18'] sc,pno-cond sc PETERS
03288                                          (T170)

THIEVING MAGPIE, THE: OVERTURE see
Rossini, Gioacchino, Gazza Ladra,
La: Overture

THILMAN, JOHANNES PAUL (1906-1973)
Concertino for Piano and Orchestra,
Op. 65
2.2.2.2. 2.2.0.0. timp,strings,pno
solo [14'] BREITKOPF-W        (T171)

Concerto for Violin and Orchestra,
Op. 59
2.2.2.2. 2.2.2.0. strings,vln solo
[25'] BREITKOPF-W             (T172)

Concerto Piccolo
1.0.2.0. 0.0.0.0. perc,strings,
cembalo solo [12'] BREITKOPF-W (T173)

Divertimento
2.2.2.2. 2.2.1.0. timp,perc,strings
[11'] BREITKOPF-W             (T174)

Festouvertüre Für Grosses Orchester
*Op.93
2.2.2.2. 4.2.2.0. timp,strings
[10'] BREITKOPF-W             (T175)

Impulse
2.3.3.2. 2.2.2.1. perc,harp,pno,
strings [15'] BREITKOPF-W     (T176)

Lichtenberger Konzert
strings,vln solo [18'] BREITKOPF-W
                              (T177)

Orchesterballade
2.2.3.2. 4.2.2.1. timp,perc,harp,
strings [20'] BREITKOPF-W     (T178)

Ornamente
2.2.3.2. 2.2.2.1. perc,pno,harp,
8vln I,7vln II,6vla,5vcl,4db
[16'] sc,study sc PETERS 03300
                              (T179)

Partita Piccola *Op.43
0.1.1.2. 2.1.1.0. strings [12']
BREITKOPF-W                   (T180)

Sinfonia No. 4 in D minor, Op. 64
2.2.2.2. 3.2.2.1. timp,strings
[25'] BREITKOPF-W             (T181)

Sinfonia No. 8 in C, Op. 101
2.2.2.2. 4.2.2.0. timp,perc,strings
[18'] BREITKOPF-W             (T182)

Sinfonische Inventionen *Op.77
2.2.3.2. 3.2.2.1. timp,perc,strings
[22'] BREITKOPF-W             (T183)

Sinfonischer Prolog *Op.94
2.3.3.2. 4.3.2.1. timp,perc,strings
[12'] BREITKOPF-W             (T184)

THIRD, THE see Decsenyi, Janos

THIRD ESSAY FOR ORCHESTRA see Barber,
Samuel see Kulesha, Gary, Midnight
Road, The

THIRD IDYLL: FROST AT MIDNIGHT see
Holloway, Robin

THIRIET, MAURICE (1906-1972)
Introduction, Chanson Et Ronde
2(pic).2(English horn).2.2.
2.2.2.0. timp,cel,perc,strings,
harp solo [23'15"] PEER rent
                              (T185)

THIRTEEN see Cage, John

THIRTEEN DREAMS AGO see Radulescu,
Horatio

13 VARIATIONS see Jeverud, Johan, 13
Variationer Over En Sonat Av
Scarlatti

THOMAS, AMBROISE (1811-1896)
Mignon: Ouvertüre
2.2.2.2. 4.2+cornet.3.0. timp,perc,
strings [8'] BREITKOPF-W      (T186)

THOMAS, AUGUSTA READ (1964-    )
Conquering The Fury Of Oblivion *ora
3.3.3.3. 4.3.3.1. 4perc,harp,pno,
strings,SATB&narrator,pic&English
horn&trp&vcl soli [35'] (text by
Leslie Dunton-Downer) PRESSER
rent                          (T187)

Five Haiku
2.2.2.0. 2.2.2.0. 2perc,harp,
strings,pno solo [17'] PRESSER
rent                          (T188)

Meditation for Trombone and Orchestra
2(pic).2.2(bass clar).2(contrabsn).
2.2.1.0. 2perc,pno,harp,strings,
trom solo [12'] PRESSER rent  (T189)

Sinfonia
1.1.2(bass clar,contrabass
clar).1(contrabsn).soprano sax.
1.1.1(alto trom,bass trom).0.
2perc,harp,strings [12'] PRESSER

THOMAS, AUGUSTA READ (cont'd.)
rent                          (T190)

THOMAS, KURT (1904-1973)
Concerto for Piano and Orchestra, Op.
30
2.2.2.2. 2.2.0.0. timp,strings,pno
solo [30'] BREITKOPF-W        (T191)

THOMAS-MIFUNE, WERNER
Argentina (Tango)
see Karikaturen Für
Streichorchester

Brasil (Samba)
see Karikaturen Für
Streichorchester

Deutschland (Stuben-Musi)
see Karikaturen Für
Streichorchester

Faule Krokodile (Blues)
see Vergnügliche Etüden Für
Streichorchester

Feuerwehr-Mambo
see Vergnügliche Etüden Für
Streichorchester

Figaro In Afrika
string orch sc,pts KUNZELMANN
GM 1733A f.s.
contains: Lokomotive Von Mombasa,
Die; Stachelschweine Ziehen Um,
Die; Stille Nacht Für
Elefanten; Stinktier Dreht
Durch, Eine; Vogel-Strauss-
Rally                         (T192)

Floh-Walzer (Samba)
see Vergnügliche Etüden Für
Streichorchester

Karikaturen Für Streichorchester
string orch sc,pts KUNZELMANN
GM 1686 f.s.
contains: Argentina (Tango);
Brasil (Samba); Deutschland
(Stuben-Musi); Turkiye
(Bauchtanz)                   (T193)

Lokomotive Von Mombasa, Die
see Figaro In Afrika

Stachelschweine Ziehen Um, Die
see Figaro In Afrika

Stille Nacht Für Elefanten
see Figaro In Afrika

Stinktier Dreht Durch, Eine
see Figaro In Afrika

Sturkopf, Der (Guaracha)
see Vergnügliche Etüden Für
Streichorchester

Teddy Und Die Tierre
string orch sc KUNZELMANN GM 1409B
ipa                           (T194)

Turkiye (Bauchtanz)
see Karikaturen Für
Streichorchester

Vergnügliche Etüden Für
Streichorchester
string orch sc,pts KUNZELMANN
GM 1685 f.s.
contains: Faule Krokodile
(Blues); Feuerwehr-Mambo; Floh-
Walzer (Samba); Sturkopf, Der
(Guaracha); Verliebter Kater
(Tango)                       (T195)

Verliebter Kater (Tango)
see Vergnügliche Etüden Für
Streichorchester

Vogel-Strauss-Rally
see Figaro In Afrika

THOMASS, EUGEN C. (1927-    )
Vier Sätze
vibra,marimba,strings MULL & SCH
ESM 10'006                    (T196)

THOMMESSEN, OLAV ANTON (1946-    )
...Eighth Author, The
2(pic).2(English horn).2(bass
clar).2. 4.3.3.1. timp,2perc,
harp,cel,strings,narrator NORSKMI
                              (T197)

Near The Comethead
see Ved Komethodet

To Instrumentale Madrigaler For
Sinfonietta
"Underholdningsmusikk For Tretten"
1(pic).1(English horn).1(bass
clar).1. 1.1.1.1. perc,vln,vla,
vcl,db NORSKMI                (T198)

THOMMESSEN, OLAV ANTON (cont'd.)
Underholdningsmusikk For Tretten
see To Instrumentale Madrigaler For
Sinfonietta

Uventede, Det: Åpningsmusikk For NRK-
P2
2(pic).2(English horn).2(bass
clar).2(contrabsn). 4.3.3.1.
timp,2perc,harp,pno,synthesizer,
strings [2'] NORSKMI          (T199)

Vaevet Af Staengler: A Symphonic Song
For Soprano And Strings
[23'] NORSKMI                 (T200)

Ved Komethodet
"Near The Comethead"
4(pic).4(English horn).5(bass
clar).4(contrabsn). 6.2.4.1.
timp,4perc,harp,cel&pno&
synthesizer,org,strings,vla solo,
A solo,SA [48'] NORSKMI       (T201)

THOMPSON, BRUCE A.
Venatic Chronicle
(Thompson, David B.)
2(pic).2(English horn).2+bass
clar.2+contrabsn. 4.2.3.1. timp,
4perc,harp,strings,horn solo THOM
ED OA1 f.s., perf mat rent    (T202)

THOMPSON, RANDALL (1899-1984)
Jazz Poem For Piano And Orchestra, A
pno solo,3.2.3.3. 4.3.3.1. timp,
3perc,strings [15'] SCHIRM.EC
rent                          (T203)

Nativity According To St. Luke:
Lullaby
fl,strings,S solo [8'] SCHIRM.EC
rent                          (T204)

Nativity According To St. Luke:
Magnificat
fl,ob,strings,S solo [4'] SCHIRM.EC
rent                          (T205)

Passenger, The
string orch,Bar solo SCHIRM.EC rent
                              (T206)

Tarantella
2.2.2.2. 4.2.0.0. timp,6perc,
strings [11'] SCHIRM.EC rent
                              (T207)

THOMSON, VIRGIL GARNETT (1896-1989)
Concertino for Harp, Strings and
Percussion
sc,set,pts INTERNAT.S.        (T208)

Thoughts For Strings
strings [4'] BOOSEY-ENG rent (T209)

THOREAU'S TRAIN see Rathburn, Eldon

THORESEN, LASSE (1949-    )
Carmel Eulogies
4(2pic).3(English horn).4(bass
clar).3(contrabsn). 4.3.3.1.
timp,5perc,harp,pno,synthesizer,
strings [26'] (symphonic poem in
2 movements inspired by
Bahā'u'llāh's Tablet of Carmel)
NORSKMI                       (T210)

THORNE, FRANCIS BURRITT (1922-    )
Concerto for Violoncello, No. 2
2.2.2.2. 2.2.2.0. timp,2perc,pno,
harp,strings,vcl solo [23']
MERION rent                   (T211)

Symphony No. 7
2.2.2.2. 4.2.3.1. timp,perc,pno,
harp,strings MERION rent      (T212)

THOSE SILENT AWE FILLED SPACES see
Somers, Harry Stewart

THOU TUNEST THE WORLD see Purcell,
Henry

THOUGHTS FOR STRINGS see Thomson,
Virgil Garnett

THREE see Lindroth, Peter

THREE A.M. ON CAPITOL SQUARE see
Chatman, Stephen

THREE BALLET PICTURES see Horusitzky,
Zoltan

THREE CANCIONES TORERAS see Gerhard,
Roberto

THREE CHRISTMAS PICTURES see Lane,
Philip

THREE CONCERTI FOR VIOLIN see Leclair,
Jean Marie

THREE-CORNERED HAT IN FULL SCORE see
Falla, Manuel de

THREE DANCE MINIATURES see Garall, Percival

THREE DANCE SCENES see Rogers, Bernard

THREE ENGLISH VERSES see Durko, Zsolt

THREE FILM SCORES see Takemitsu, Toru

THREE FOLK TALES see Conway, Joe

THREE FOR TWO TRUMPETS AND ORCHESTRA see Hobson, Bruce

THREE GREAT ORCHESTRAL WORKS see Debussy, Claude

THREE GRIEG SONGS see Berg, Olav, Tre Grieg-Sanger

THREE HARBOUR SKETCHES see Amos, Keith

THREE HEBREW SONGS see Shapero, Harold Samuel

THREE IMAGES BY THE POEMS OF BOCHO YAMAMURA see Ichinose, Tonika, Fukei Junginmozaiku From Soshite Ichimen No Nanohana

THREE IMAGES ON THE OTA RIVER see Tomotani, Koji, Symphonic Poems, Hiroshima

THREE INVENTIONS see Benjamin, George

THREE ISRAELI CHASSIDIC SONGS see Barnes, Milton

THREE JEWISH PORTRAITS see Duffy, John

THREE LYRIC PIECES OP. 12 (NOS. 2, 4 & 5) see Grieg, Edvard Hagerup

THREE MÉTIS SONGS FROM SASKATCHEWAN see Forsyth, Malcolm

THREE MOVEMENTS see Hidas, Frigyes see Sandred, Orjan, Triptychos

THREE MOVEMENTS FOR ORCHESTRA see Brady, Timothy see Dix, Robert

THREE MOVEMENTS ON A TWELVE-TONE SYSTEM see Fridolfson, Ruben

THREE NOCTURNES see Koehne, Graeme

THREE OCCASIONS FOR ORCHESTRA see Carter, Elliott Cook, Jr.

THREE ORCHESTRAL MOVEMENTS see Karkoff, Ingvar

THREE ORCHESTRAL WORKS BY BRAHMS see Brahms, Johannes

THREE PARTS OFF THE GROUND see Anderson, Julian

THREE PIECES FOR CLARINET AND STRINGS see Kunz, Alfred

THREE PIECES FOR ORCHESTRA see Behar, Gyorgy see Felder, David see Lazarof, Henri see Muldowney, Dominic see Soproni, Jozsef

THREE POEMS OF BYRON see Koehne, Graeme

THREE PRELUDES see Keuris, Tristan

THREE PRELUDES ON WELSH HYMN TUNES see Vaughan Williams, Ralph

THREE SACRED CONCERTOS see Henze, Hans Werner

THREE SCENES FROM GOETHE'S FAUST see Lokschin, Alexander

THREE SCREAMING POPES see Turnage, Mark-Anthony

THREE SERENADES see Buczynski, Walter

THREE SKETCHES see Sexton, Brian

THREE SONGS see Bose, Hans-Jurgen Von

THREE SONGS FOR SYLVIA see Barker, Paul

THREE SONGS FROM ECCLESIASTES see Pinkham, Daniel

THREE SONGS FROM "ORPHEUS BRITANNICUS" see Purcell, Henry

THREE SONGS IN CELEBRATION OF THE FAMILY FARM see Walker, Gwyneth

THREE SONGS OF LOVE AND WOE see Presser, William Henry

THREE SYMPHONIC PICTURES see Kalmar, Laszlo

THREE SYMPHONIC PIECES see Dijk, Jan van

THREE SYMPHONIC VERSIONS see Orbon, Julian, Tres Versiones Sinfonicas

THREE VIOLIN CONCERTI see Bach, Johann Sebastian

THREE VIOLIN CONCERTOS see Mysliveczek, Joseph

THREE VIOLIN CONCERTOS see Sirmen, Maddalena Lombardini

THRENI see Escaich, Thierry see Rossum, Frederic R. van

THRENODY see Morgan, David

THRENOS see Mathias, William

THRENOS II see Flender, Reinhard David

THROB see Jeths, Willem

THROUGH DARKNESS INTO LIGHT see Willan, Healey

THROUGH THE ECHOING TIMBER see Tann, Hilary

THROUGH THE GLASS see Matthews, Colin

THUMOLEÏ see Strikker, Erwin

THYRESTAM, GUNNAR (1900-1984)
Concerto for Organ, No. 2, in Three Movements
see Hymnus Organi

Hymnus Organi (Concerto for Organ, No. 2, in Three Movements)
[12'] BÜSCH HBM 036          (T213)

TI-NDE see Florentz, Jean-Louis

TICHAVSKY, RADKO (1959-    )
Setkání *Fantasy
4.3.4.3. 4.3.3.1. timp,perc,pno, strings [11'] CESKY HUD.   (T214)

Uvnitr *Fantasy
3.3.3.3. 4.3.3.1. timp,perc,strings [10'] CESKY HUD.          (T215)

TICHÉ PÍSNE see Fischer, Eduard

TICHY, VLADIMIR (1946-    )
Concerto for Violoncello and Orchestra
3.2.3.2. 2.0.0.0. timp,perc, strings,vcl solo [18'] PANTON          (T216)

Šest Invencí
1.2.2.2. 4.0.1.1. timp,perc,strings [12'] CESKY HUD.          (T217)

Symfonické Preludium c. 1
3.2.2.3. 4.3.3.1. timp,perc,strings [6'] CESKY HUD.          (T218)

Symfonické Preludium c. 2
3.2.3.3. 4.3.3.1. timp,perc,strings [9'] CESKY HUD.          (T219)

Symphony No. 2 for 15 Strings
[20'] CESKY HUD.          (T220)

Symphony No. 3
3.2.3.3. 4.3.3.1. timp,perc,pno, strings [25'] CESKY HUD.   (T221)

TIDDLES OF PADDINGTON see Rathburn, Eldon

TIDES see Lutyens, Elisabeth

TIDSMUSIK see Hansen, Krister

TIEF IN DEN BERGWERKEN SIBIRIENS see Shostakovich, Dmitri

TIENTOS see Krouse, Ian

TIFLISIANA see Djabadary, Heraclius

TILL-FLYKT see Mårtensson, Per

TILL MINNET see Hansen, Krister

TILL STRKORKESTERNS LOV see Lundin, Dag

TILLSTND - AVSTND see Isaksson, Madeleine

TILT see Mackey, Steven

TIMBER TIMBRE see Horwood, Michael

TIME AND AGAIN see Rea, John

TIME AND THE BELL see Hultqvist, Anders

TIME CURRENT see Ichiyanagi, Toshi

TIME FOR REMEMBRANCE see Duffy

TIME IN TEMPEST EVERYWHERE see Adler, Samuel Hans

TIME OF TAROMIR see Rehnqvist, Karin, Taromirs Tid

TIME OF THE HEATHEN: SUITE see Hiller, Lejaren Arthur

TIME SURROUNDING see Ichiyanagi, Toshi

TIME TRAVEL: HUGO WOLF TO "SONG AT SUNSET" see Rosenman, Leonard

TIMEDANCERS see Baker, Michael Conway

TIMELESS ENERGY see Åm, Magnar

TIME'S ARROW see Payne, Anthony

TIMOR see Hamary, Andräs

TIMPANI CONCERTANTE see Gutchë, Gene

TINEL, EDGAR (1854-1912)
Franziskus: Trauermarsch
2+pic.2.2.2. 4.3.3.1. timp,strings BREITKOPF-W          (T222)

TIPPETT, [SIR] MICHAEL (1905-    )
Byzantium
3(3pic).2+English horn.3(clar in E flat,3bass clar).2+contrabsn. 4.2.3.1. 7perc,cel,2harp,elec org,strings,S solo [25'] (text by William Butler Yeats) SCHOTTS perf mat rent study sc ED 12383, voc sc ED 12376          (T223)

Heart's Assurance, The
(Bowen, Meirion) 1.1.1.1. 4.1.0.0. perc,harp,3vln I,3vln II,2vla, 2vcl,db,high solo [17'] (text by Sydney Keyes, Alun Lewis) study sc SCHOTTS ED 12382 perf mat rent          (T224)

New Year Suite
3.2+English horn.2+bass clar.2+ contrabsn.alto sax.tenor sax. 4.4.3.1. 5perc,harp,2elec gtr, 4vln I,4vln II,4vla,4vcl,2db, electronic tape,baritone sax& soprano sax [30'] study sc SCHOTTS ED 12369 perf mat rent          (T225)

Rose Lake, The
3(pic).2+English horn.2+bass clar.2+contrabsn. 6.3.3.1. perc, 2harp,10vln I,10vln II,6vla,6vcl, 4db [25'] study sc SCHOTTS ED 12435 perf mat rent          (T226)

Sosostris' Aria (from The Midsummer Marriage)
2.2.2.2. 4.2.3.0. timp,perc,cel, harp,gtr,strings,S solo [11'] SCHOTTS perf mat rent          (T227)

Tempest, The: Suite
(Bowen, Meirion) 1(pic).0.1(bass clar).0. 1.1.1.0. perc,pno&cel, harp,2vln,vla,vcl,db,TBar soli [25'] (text by William Shakespeare) study sc SCHOTTS ED 12496 perf mat rent          (T228)

T'IS HOLIDAY see Purcell, Henry

TIŠE see Kalach, Jiri

TISHCHENKO, BORIS (1939-    )
Concerto for Piano and Orchestra, Op. 21
2(pic).1.1(clar in E flat).2. 2.0.0.0. timp,3-4perc,harp, strings,pno solo [24'] SIKORSKI perf mat rent          (T229)

Fliege Summ-Summ, Die
see Mucha-Zokotucha

Mucha-Zokotucha *Op.39
"Fliege Summ-Summ, Die" 3.3.4.2. 4.2.3.1. timp,perc,pno,strings [25'] SIKORSKI perf mat rent          (T230)

Requiem
[Russ] 3.3.3.3. 4.3.3.1. timp,perc, 2harp,pno/cel,strings,ST soli [60'] SIKORSKI perf mat rent          (T231)

Symphony No. 6, Op. 105
[Russ] 3.3.4.3. 6.3.3.1. 7perc, 2harp,cel,strings,SA soli [53'] SIKORSKI perf mat rent          (T232)

TITTLE, STEVE (1935- )
"...And It Always Will Be"
2(pic).2.2.2. 2.2.2.0. timp,harp,
strings,perc solo [8'] sc
CANADIAN MI 1340 T622AN (T233)

Dreams About Dancing
2.2.2.2. 2.2.1.0. timp,perc,pno,
strings,vcl solo sc CANADIAN
MI 1313 T622DR (T234)

Mourning The Loss Of Our Demons
2.2.2.2. 4.2.3.0. timp,2perc,pno,
strings [20'] sc CANADIAN (T235)

TITUS: JETZT, VITELLIA! SCHLÄGT DIE
STUNDE - NIE SOLL MIT ROSEN see
Mozart, Wolfgang Amadeus, Clemenza
Di Tito, La: Ecco Il Punto, O
Vitellia - Non Più Di Fiori

TITUS: SOLL DIE STRENGE, IHR GÜT'GEN
GÖTTER see Mozart, Wolfgang
Amadeus, Clemenza Di Tito, La: Se
All'Impero, Amici Dei!

TITUS: WIR BALD EIN LEISES LÜFTCHEN see
Mozart, Wolfgang Amadeus, Clemenza
Di Tito, La: Se Al Volto Mai Ti
Senti

TNK OM MAN HADE EN TIDSMASKIN see
Malmborg-Ward, Paula Af

TO COMPOSE WITHOUT ... see Matthews,
Colin

TO ECHO see Grainger, Ella

TO HIS SERVANT BACH, GOD GRANTS A FINAL
GLIMPSE: THE MORNING STAR see
Koehne, Graeme

TO INSTRUMENTALE MADRIGALER FOR
SINFONIETTA see Thommessen, Olav
Anton

TO JE MÁ ZEM see Juchelka, Miroslav

"...TO LIGHT ONE CANDLE..." see Miller,
Elma

TO MOTHER EARTH AND FATHER TIME see
Miller, Michael R., Sonata for
String Orchestra

TÖREDÉK see Maros, Rudolf, Fragment

TOREDÉKEK see Vidovszky, Laszlo,
Fragments

TO THE AIR OF A DREAM see Matsushita,
Isao

TO THE HEADLAND see Kondo, Jo

TO THE WIND'S TWELVE QUARTERS see
Grantham, Donald

TO THE YOUTH: OVERTURE see Sárközy,
Istvan

TOADA see Siqueira, Jose

TOCCATA see Bainbridge, Simon

TOCCATA, ARIA E FUGA see Farkas,
Ferenc, Musica Pentatonica

TOCCATA DE LA 5E SYMPHONIE see Widor,
Charles-Marie

TOCCATA E CANTO see Lidholm, Ingvar

TOCCATA ET PASSACAILLE POUR ORCHESTRE
see Badian, Maya

TOCCATA OSTINATA see Eklund, Hans

TOCCATA OVERTURE see Rice, Thomas N.

TOD DES HASEN, DER see Linke, Robert,
Kammermusik Nr. 8

TOD IM REBBERG see Cornell, Klaus

TOD UND VERKLÄRUNG see Wildberger,
Jacques

TODA, KUNIO (1915- )
Introduzione-Movimento-Rapido
strings JAPAN (T236)

TOKOCHAN CHOKKIN 1.2.3 see Yamamoto,
Junnosuke

TOLERANCE see Lloyd, Jonathan

TOLV FRDMDA MN: FILMMUSIKALISKA PORTRTT
see Jeverud, Johan

TOM-A-BEDLAM see Müller-Siemens, Detlev

TOM: ORCHESTRAL SUITE NO. 1 see
Diamond, David

TOM TWIST FOR NARRATOR AND ORCHESTRA
see Larsen, Elizabeth B. (Libby)

TOMASEK, VACLAV JAN KRTITEL (1774-1850)
Symphony in D, Op. 30
1.2.2.2. 2.2.0.0. timp,strings
CESKY HUD. (T237)

TOMASI, HENRI (1901-1971)
Ballade Écossaise
see Highland's Ballad

Ballade for Alto Saxophone
2.2.2.2. 2.2.2.0. 3timp,perc,glock,
harp,strings [14'] LEDUC (T238)

Cadences
see Pastorales Provençales

Chansons De Geishas
(Dumesnil, R.) 1.1.1.1. 1.0.0.0.
perc,gong,harp,cel,strings,med
solo [12'] (4 nos.) LEDUC (T239)

Chants Corses
1.1.1.1. 1.1.0.0. timp,perc,harp,
strings,low solo LEDUC f.s.
contains: Complainte; Lamentu D'u
Trenu; Nanna, Berceuse;
Sérénade; U Meru Pastore (T240)

Cinq Danses Profanes Et Sacrées
0.1.1.1. 1.0.0.1. timp,1-2perc,pno,
strings,ob solo,horn solo,tuba
solo,clar solo,bsn solo LEDUC
f.s.
contains: Danse Agreste; Danse
Guerrière; Danse Nuptiale;
Danse Profane; Danse Sacrée
(T241)

Complainte
see Chants Corses

Concert Asiatique
3.2.3.3.2alto sax.2tenor sax.opt
baritone sax. 4.4.3.1. 4timp,
perc,cel,glock,vibra,2xylo/pno,
2harp,pno,strings,opt 3marimba
[19'] (1. Invocation et danse
(timbales) 2. Scherzo (batterie)
3. Final (xylo obligé et vibra
adlib.)) LEDUC pno red
AL 19885 & AL 24969, solo pt
AL 21467 (T242)

Concertino for Flute in E
1.2.2.2. 2.2.1.0. 3timp,harp,
strings,fl solo [13'] LEDUC
(T243)

Concerto De Printemps
4timp,marimba,vibra,xylo&pno&cel,
6vln I,6vln II,3vla,3vcl,2db,opt
gtr,fl solo [25'] LEDUC (T244)

Concerto for Alto Saxophone
3.3.3.3. 4.3.3.1. 4timp,perc,glock,
xylo,harp,strings,alto sax solo
[18'30"] LEDUC (T245)

Concerto for Bassoon, Harp and
Strings
strings,harp/pno,bsn solo [15']
LEDUC (T246)

Concerto for Clarinet and String
Orchestra
8vln I,6vln II,4vla,3vcl,2db,opt
harp,clar solo [22'] LEDUC (T247)

Concerto for Flute in F
2.2.2.2. 4.3.3.0. 3timp,cel/pno,
glock,xylo,harp,strings,fl solo
[22'] LEDUC (T248)

Concerto for Horn
2.2(English horn).2.2. 0.1.0.0.
2timp,perc,cel/pno,glock,xylo,
harp,strings,horn solo [15']
LEDUC (T249)

Concerto for Oboe
pno,strings,opt clar,opt bsn,ob
solo [16'] LEDUC (T250)

Concerto for Trombone
2.2.2.2. 2.2.0.0. 2timp,perc,cel/
glock,vibra,xylo,harp,strings,
trom solo [14'] LEDUC (T251)

Concerto for Trumpet
3.3.2.2. 4.0.3.1. 2timp,perc,cel,
xylo,harp,strings,trp solo
[16'30"] min sc LEDUC AL 23539
(T252)

Concerto for Viola
2.2.2.2. 2.2.0.0. 3timp,harp/pno,
strings,opt snare drum,vla solo
[22'] LEDUC (T253)

Concerto for Violin
3.2(English horn).2.2. 4.3.3.0.
4timp,4perc,cel&pno,xylo,harp,
strings,vln solo [27'30"] min sc
LEDUC AL 23480 (T254)

TOMASI, HENRI (cont'd.)

Danse Agreste
see Cinq Danses Profanes Et Sacrées

Danse Guerrière
see Cinq Danses Profanes Et Sacrées

Danse Nuptiale
see Cinq Danses Profanes Et Sacrées

Danse Profane
see Cinq Danses Profanes Et Sacrées

Danse Sacrée
see Cinq Danses Profanes Et Sacrées

Divertimento Corsica
6vln I,5vln II,4vla,3vcl,2db,opt
harp,ob&clar&bsn soli [14']
(contains: . Paghiella. 2.
Cimetière marin. 3. Danse-
sérénade. 4. La Foire du Niolo.)
LEDUC sc AL 20967, solo pt
AL 20968, pts (T255)

Féerie Laotienne: Suite
3.2.3.3.2alto sax.2tenor sax.opt
baritone sax. 4.4.3.1. 4timp,
perc,cel,glock,vibra,2xylo/pno,
2harp,strings,opt 3marimba [20']
(symphonic suite: 1. Entrée. 2.
Invocation et danse. 3. Scherzo
pour une fête de nuit. 4.
Invocation à la lune, & 5. Final)
min sc LEDUC AL 20905 (T256)

Folies Mazarguaises, Les
2.2(English horn).2.2. 4.2.3.1.
4timp,perc,cel,glock,xylo,harp/
pno,strings [16'30"] (suite: 1.
Carnaval. 2. La Sainte-Cécile. 3.
Fête de la Saint-Éloi. 4. Idylle
À Sormiou. 5. Final) LEDUC (T257)

Highland's Ballad
harp,string orch,ob&clar&bsn soli
sc,solo pt,pno red INTERNAT.S.
(T258)
"Ballade Écossaise" ob,clar,bsn,
string orch,harp solo sc LEDUC
AL 23856 (T259)

Jabadao
3.4.3.3. 4.4.3.1. 4timp,perc,bells,
glock,vibra,xylo,2harp,strings
[16'] LEDUC (T260)

Lamentu D'u Trenu
see Chants Corses

Nanna, Berceuse
see Chants Corses

Noces De Cendres, Les
3.3.3.3. 4.3.3.1. 4timp,perc,glock,
bells,xylo,1-2harp,strings,opt
Ondes Martenot [20'] (symphonic
suite: Prélude (Le retour). Danse
triste. Scherzo fantastique (La
guerre). Lento (Plainte funèbre).
Andante (La jeune fille et la
mort).) min sc LEDUC AL 21372
(T261)

Nocturne
see Pastorales Provençales

Nuit Obscure De Saint Jean De La
Croix, La
3.3.3.3.alto sax. 4.3.3.1. 4timp,
perc,cel,glock,xylo,harp,strings,
Mez solo,opt cor [25'] LEDUC
(T262)

Nuits De Provence
2.2(English horn).2.2. 4.2.3.1.
4timp,perc,cel,bells,glock,xylo,
harp,strings [18'] (symphonic
evocations: Le Baux. Les Saintes-
Marie-de-la-Mer. Nuit de la
Saint-Éloi. Les Antiques. Nuit de
la Saint-Jean.) min sc LEDUC
AL 21372 (T263)

Pastorales Provençales
2gtr,fl,string orch,2vln soli solo
pt LEDUC AL 23748 f.s.
contains: Cadences; Nocturne;
Paysage; Tambourin (T264)

Paysage
see Pastorales Provençales

Rosière Du Village, La
3.2.2.2(contrabsn). 4.2.3.1. 3timp,
perc,cel,glock,xylo,harp,strings
[13'] (suite: Variation I.
Variation II. Tarantelle) min sc
LEDUC AL 20748 (T265)

Semaine Sainte À Cuzco
2harp,strings,opt 4timp,trp&trp in
C&piccolo trp solo [7'30"] LEDUC
(T266)

Sérénade
see Chants Corses

**TOMASI, HENRI (cont'd.)**

Sinfonietta Provençale
0+pic.1.0.1. 1.0.0.0. tamb,pno/
hpsd,4-8vln I,4-8vln II,3-6vla,2-
4vcl,1-3db,opt cel,opt vibra
[18'] LEDUC                         (T267)

Symphonie Du Tiers-Monde
3.2+English horn.2+bass clar.3. 4+
opt 2horn.3.3.1. 4timp,4perc,
bells,marimba,vibra,pno,harp,
strings,opt Ondes Martenot [22']
min sc LEDUC AL 23964              (T268)

Tambourin
see Pastorales Provençales

Trois Lettres De Mon Moulin
3.2(English horn).2.2. 4.3.3.0+opt
tuba. 4timp,perc,cel,bells,glock,
vibra,xylo,harp,strings [16'30"]
(images provençales, d'après
Alphonse Daudet: 1. Les trois
messes basses. 2. Le secret de
Maître Cornille. 3. L'élixir du
R. P. Gaucher.) min sc LEDUC
AL 21767                           (T269)

U Meru Pastore
see Chants Corses

Variations Grégoriennes Sur Un Salve
Regina
6vln I,4vln II,3vla,2vcl,2db,opt
2harp,trp/trp in C solo [7']
LEDUC                              (T270)

**TOMÁŠOVSKÁ POLKA see Paloucek, Alois**

**TOMBEAU DE LESTER PEARSON see Keane, David**

**TOMBEAU DE LIBERACE, LE see Daugherty, Michael**

**TOMBEAU DE NELLIGAN, LE see Hetu, Jacques**

**TOMOTANI, KOJI (1947-    )**
Symphonic Poems, Hiroshima
"Three Images On The Ota River"
orch,mix cor [32'] (the third
movement) JAPAN                   (T271)

Three Images On The Ota River
see Symphonic Poems, Hiroshima

**TON THAT, TIET (1933-    )**
Chu-Ky VII
1.1.2.1. 1.2.2.0. 2perc,pno,
strings,harp solo [20'] JOBERT
                                   (T272)

Dialogue Avec La Nature [18']
2.2.2.2. 2.1.1.0. perc,harp,
strings,gtr solo
BILLAUDOT                          (T273)

**TONAL LANDSCAPE - ISAWA see Homma, Masao**

**TONE POEMS BY SIBELIUS (IN FULL SCORE) see Sibelius, Jean**

**TONE POEMS, SERIES I see Strauss, Richard**

**TONE POEMS, SERIES II see Strauss, Richard**

**TONGEMÄLDE I: SLAGET VID LEIPZIG; ERNSTE UND HEITERE GRILLEN; ELFENSPIEL see Berwald, Franz (Adolf)**

**TOOVEY, ANDREW (1962-    )**
Concerto for Oboe and String
Orchestra
string orch,harp,ob solo [20']
manuscript BMIC                   (T274)

Mozart
10vln I,8vln II,6vla,4vcl,2db [6']
BOOSEY-ENG rent                   (T275)

**TOR ZUM VERLASSENEN GARTEN see Gullberg, Olof**

**TORKE, MICHAEL (1961-    )**
Brick
see Red

Bronze
3.3.3.3. 6.3.3.1. timp,strings,pno
solo [23'] BOOSEY-ENG rent (T276)

Cherry
see Red

Concerto for Piano
3(pic).2+English horn.2.2. 4.3.3.1.
3perc,strings,pno solo [30']
BOOSEY-ENG rent                   (T277)

**TORKE, MICHAEL (cont'd.)**

Concerto for Saxophone
1.1+English horn.2.0. 4.0.0+bass
trom.1. perc,strings [15']
BOOSEY-ENG rent                   (T278)

Crimson
see Red

Green (from Ecstatic Orange) ballet
"Verdant Music" 3(2pic).2+English
horn.2+bass clar.2. 4.3.3.1.
timp,3perc,harp,pno,strings [12']
BOOSEY-ENG rent                   (T279)

Monday And Tuesday
1.1.1.1. 1.1.1.0. 2vibra,pno,2vln,
vla,vcl,db [23'] BOOSEY-ENG rent
                                   (T280)

Red
2+pic.2+English horn.2+bass clar.2.
4.4.4.1. timp,4perc,harp,pno,
strings BOOSEY-ENG f.s.
contains: Brick [12']; Cherry
[12']; Crimson [5']           (T281)

Run
2+pic.2+English horn.2.2. 4.3.3.1.
timp,3perc,pno,strings [6']
BOOSEY-ENG rent                   (T282)

Verdant Music
see Green

**TORMIS, VELJO (1930-    )**
Overture No. 2
3.2.3.3. 4.3.3.1. timp,snare drum,
strings [10'] SIKORSKI perf mat
rent                              (T283)

**TORNQUIST, PETER (1963-    )**
Acalanto
3(pic).3(English horn).3(bass
clar).0. 4.3.3.1. 3perc,harp,pno,
strings [12'] NORSKMI             (T284)

**TORSTENSSON, KLAS (1951-    )**
Last Diary, The
0.0.2(bass clar).1(contrabsn).2sax.
1.0.1.1. 2perc,2vln I,2vln II,
2vla,2vcl,3db,elec gtr,pno [30']
sc DONEMUS                        (T285)

Stick On Stick
4(pic).4(English horn).4(bass
clar).4(contrabsn). 4.4.4.2.
5perc,harp,strings,pno,bass gtr
[21'] sc DONEMUS                  (T286)

**TORTOISE AND THE HARE, THE see Dorff, Daniel Jay**

**TOSTI, FRANCESCO PAOLO (1846-1916)**
Ideal Canzone, L'
(Corno, Filippo Del) string orch,T
solo [23'30"] (7 romances)
SONZOGNO rent                     (T287)

**TOTE METREN see Huber, Nicolaus A.**

**TOTEMISTISK SVIT see Winter, Tomas**

**TOTEN SEELEN, DIE: SUITE see Schnittke, Alfred**

**TOTENTANZ see Kirchner, Volker David, Symphony No. 1 see Nilsson, Ivo**

**TOTONAC RAIN DANCE see Amos, Keith**

**TOUCHINGS see Freedman, Harry**

**TOUR OF THE INSTRUMENTS OF THE ORCHESTRA, A see Arnold, Alan, Variations On An Elizabethan Ballad**

**TOURNAMENTS see Corigliano, John**

**TOURNOI SINGULIER, LE (BALLET EN 1 ACTE): MORIA BLUES see Roland-Manuel, Alexis**

**TOWARD LIGHT see Schwantner, Joseph**

**TOWARD THE BEGINNING see Lavista, Mario, Hacia El Comienzo**

**TOWARDS A NEW AGE see Downes, Andrew**

**TOWARDS SUMMER see Dijkstra, Lowell**

**TOWARDS THE END see Kvam, Oddvar S.**

**TOWER, JOAN (1938-    )**
Sequoia
orch sc SCHIRM.G AMP8020      (T288)

Silver Ladders
orch sc SCHIRM.G AMP-8017     (T289)

**TOWN see Freedman, Harry**

**TOWN FOX, THE see Davis, Carl**

**TOWNSEND, JILL**
Strings On Tour
strings CHESTER pts CH55719, sc
CH55718                           (T290)

**TOYAMA, YUZO (1931-    )**
Fantasia Sakaiminato
orch [10'] JAPAN                  (T291)

Ichi
orch [5'] JAPAN                   (T292)

Kamogawa
orch [17'] (symphonic poem) JAPAN
                                  (T293)

Rensaku "Jo-Mon"
orch [28'] JAPAN                  (T294)

Songs From The Poetry Of Kazue
Shinkawa
orch,Mez solo [18'] JAPAN     (T295)

**TRACES OF BECOMING see Dusatko, Tomas**

**TRADIDERUNT ME IN MANUS IMPIORUM II see Boudreau, Walter**

**TRADITION I(2), CANON À 13 see Schnebel, Dieter, Diapason**

**TRAFFORD, EDMUND (1948-    )**
Frescoes
1.1.1.0. 0.0.0.0. harp,pno,cel,
2vln,vla,vcl,db SEESAW       (T296)

**TRÄGEN VINNER see Eyser, Eberhard**

**TRAGIC PRELUDE see Kelen, H.**

**TRAGICOMEDY see Maggio, Robert**

**TRAGIKUS ELÖJÁTÉK see Kelen, H., Tragic Prelude**

**TRAIN MUSIC see Grainger, Percy Aldridge**

**TRAJECTOIRE see Morel, Francois d'Assise**

**TRAMONTO DELLA LUNA, IL see Howard, Brian**

**TRANCE POSITION see Zuidam, Rob**

**TRANSFIGURATION see Cherney, Brian**

**TRANSFORMATION-SCENES see Schwertsik, Kurt, Märchen Von Fanferlieschen Schönefüsschen, Das: Verwandlungsmusik**

**TRANSFORMATIONS OF THE HEART see Levi, Paul Alan**

**TRANSIT OF JUPITER, THE see Hamilton, Iain**

**TRANSITIO see Neidhöfer, Christoph**

**TRANSLUCENT LANDSCAPES see Paulus, Stephen Harrison**

**TRANSMUTATION see Apollyon, Nicolay**

**TRANSTRÖMER-SVIT, OP. 52B see Søderlind, Ragnar**

**TRANSYLVANIAN RHAPSODY see Seiber, Matyas György**

**TRAUERFARBENES LAND see Kantscheli, Gija**

**TRAUERMARSCH see Beethoven, Ludwig van**

**TRAUERODE see Heilmann, Harald**

**TRAUERODE: FÜR POSAUNE UND TIEFE STREICHER see Heilmann, Harald**

**TRAUM, EIN see Grieg, Edvard Hagerup**

**TRAUM DES STEPAN RASIN, DER see Ustvolskaya, Galina**

**TRAUM...HOFFNUNG... see Schenker, Friedrich**

**TRAUM IN DER CHRISTNACHT, EIN see Hiller, Ferdinand**

**TRÄUME see Zechlin, Ruth**

**TRÄUMEREI see Grimm, Julius Otto see Schumann, Robert (Alexander)**

**TRAUMTANZTANGO see Brandmüller, Theo**

**TRAUUNG, DIE: THREE FRAGMENTS see Kirchner, Volker David**

**TRAVAUX DE NUIT see Mather, Bruce**

TRAVELLING MUSICIANS, THE see Adaskin, Murray

TRAVESTIA, FOR 11 INSTRUMENTS see Lendvay, Kamillo

TRAVESTIES IN SAD LANDSCAPE see Bose, Hans-Jurgen Von

TRE BEVEGELSER FOR STRYKEORKESTER see Hellstenius, Henrik

TRE BOZZE see Hohensee, Wolfgang

TRE CANZONI DA SUONARE see Bodorova, Sylvie

TRE CANZONI SENZA PAROLE see Rands, Bernard

TRE CAPRICHOS see Moeschinger, Albert

TRE CONTRASTI SINFONICI see Rieti, Vittorio

TRE EPISODI see Jelinek, Stanislav

TRE GLOSELUND-SANGER, OP. 56C see Kvam, Oddvar S.

TRE GRIEG-SANGER see Berg, Olav

TRE IMPROVISI see Rieti, Vittorio

TRE INTERMEZZI: I. SEGNALI E CANTO see Gullberg, Olof

TRE INTERMEZZI: II. AUTUNNALE see Gullberg, Olof

TRE INTERMEZZI: III. SERENATA CON INTERRUZIONI see Gullberg, Olof

TRE ORKESTERSTYCKEN see Hallnäs, Eyvind

TRE PEZZI CONCERTANTE see Hanuš, Jan, Concerto for Violin and Orchestra, Op. 112

TRE PEZZI CONCERTANTI see Pfister, Hugo

TRE PEZZI PER ORCHESTRA DA CAMERA see Rytterkvist, Hans

TRE PRELUDI SINFONICI see De Grandis, Renato

TRE SCHERZI see Sklenicka, Karel

TRE SVITER F STRKAR UR HANS HAKES SPELBCKER see Svensson, Matthias

TREASURED PASTURE LEISURE PLEASURE see Chan, Ka Nin

TRÉBIZONDE: BRINDISI ET GALOP see Offenbach, Jacques

TREE OF SINGING NAMES see Gilbert, Anthony

TREE SONGS see Schwertsik, Kurt, Baumgesänge

TREELINE see Takemitsu, Toru

TREESTONE see Albert, Stephen Joel

TREIBMANN, KARL OTTOMAR (1936-    )
Concerto for Violin and Orchestra
3.2.3.2. 4.3.3.0. timp,2perc,harp,
8vln I,7vln II,6vla,5vcl,4db
[28'] sc,solo pt PETERS 03308
(T297)

Sinfonia No. 4
3.3.3.3. 4.3.3.1. timp,2perc,harp,
8vln I,7vln II,6vla,5vcl,4db
[30'] sc PETERS 02602      (T298)

Sinfonia No. 5
3.3.3.3. 4.3.3.1. timp,4perc,harp,
8vln I,7vln II,6vla,5vcl,4db
[24'] sc PETERS 04394      (T299)

TREMAIN, RONALD (1923-    )
Music for Violin and Strings
string orch,vln solo [6'] sc
CANADIAN MI1611 T789MU      (T300)

TREMBLAY, GILLES (1932-    )
Avec
3.3.3.3. 4.3.3.2. 6perc,pno,
strings,SB&narrator [45'] (wampun
symphonique) LEDUC      (T301)

TRES VERSIONES SINFONICAS see Orbon, Julian

TRÉSOR DES DIEUX, LE see Klein, Lothar

13 VARIATIONER ÖVER EN SONAT AV SCARLATTI see Jeverud, Johan

TREVELUA SUITE see Haworth, Frank

TREXLER, GEORG (1903-1979)
Concerto for Orchestra
2.2.2.2. 2.2.0.0. timp,perc,strings
[21'] BREITKOPF-W      (T302)

Concerto for Piano and Orchestra
2.2.2.3. 2.2.2.1. timp,perc,
strings,pno solo [18'] BREITKOPF-
W      (T303)

Concerto for Violoncello and Orchestra
2.3.2.3. 2.2.0.0. timp,strings,vcl
solo [18'] BREITKOPF-W      (T304)

Drei Gesänge
1.2.2.2. 2.0.0.0. timp,perc,
strings,S solo [16'] BREITKOPF-W
(T305)

Introduzione E Scherzo
2.2.2.2. 2.2.3.0. timp,perc,harp,
strings [12'] BREITKOPF-W  (T306)

Kleine Suite
1.1.1.1. 2.0.0.0. timp,strings
[15'] BREITKOPF-W      (T307)

Music for Oboe and Chamber Orchestra
2.0.0.2. 2.0.0.0. timp,strings,ob
solo [14'] BREITKOPF-W      (T308)

Music for Orchestra
2.2.2.3. 2.2.2.1. timp,strings
[25'] BREITKOPF-W      (T309)

Sinfonia Breve
2.2.2.3. 4.2.3.1. timp,perc,strings
[23'] BREITKOPF-W      (T310)

Symphonische Burlesken
3.3.2.3. 2.2.3.1. timp,perc,strings
[25'] BREITKOPF-W      (T311)

TRI DANTOVSKÁ PRELUDIA see Hanuš, Jan

TRI DUBY see Petr, Zdenek

TRI LIDOVÉ PÍSNE see Vodrazka, Karel

TRI MELODRAMY see Fiala, Jirí Julius

TRI OBELISKY see Kozeluha, Lubomir

TRI PÍSNE see Bláha, Oldrich

TRI PROMENÁDY see Teml, Jiri

TRI SCÉNY see Bachorek, Milan

TRI SYMFONICKÉ VETY see Reiner, Karel

TRI TANCE VE STARÉM SLOHU see Krcek, Jaroslav

TRI VETY see Bezdek, Jiri see Hruška, Jaromír Ludvík

TRI ZPEVY DOMOVA see Jirák, Karel Boleslav

TRIADE see Verbey, Theo

TRIADE DE TOUJOURS see Francaix, Jean

TRIAS see Engelmann, Hans Ulrich

TRIBULATION AND THE MORNING TRUMPET see Healey, Derek

TRIBUTE see Benjamin, George

TRIBUTE TO STAN KENTON see Amos, Keith

TRICHRUS MUSICA see Lowe, Wesley

TRICROMIA ARCANGELICA see Maeyer, Jan De

TRILLE DU DIABLE, LE see Kreisler, Fritz see Tartini, Giuseppe

TRINITY see Shore, Clare

TRIO GIOCOSO see Miller, Franz R.

TRIONFALE see Válek, Jirí, Symphony No. 14

TRIPELKAMMERVARIATIONEN see Jekimowski, Viktor

TRIPELKOCERT see Dubrovay, Laszlo

TRIPELKONZERT, FOR VIOLIN, VIOLONCELLO, PIANO & CHAMBER ORCHESTRA, OP. 27 see Lobanov, Vassily

TRIPLE CONCERTO see Skrowaczewski, Stanislaw see Zwilich, Ellen Taaffe

TRIPLE CONCERTO: A SONOROUS PATH see Ung, Chinary

TRIPLE MEASURE see Werder, Felix

TRIPLUM HARMONICA see Schmidt, Hansjürgen

TRIPPELKONSERT see Hvoslef, Ketil, Concerto for Violin, Violoncello, Piano and Orchestra

TRIPTIEK see Hove, Luc Van

TRIPTYCH see Bartoš, Jan Zdenek see Rorem, Ned

TRIPTYCHON see Geisthardt, Hans-Joachim

TRIPTYCHOS see Sandred, Örjan

TRIPTYQUE see Naoumoff, Emile

TRISTAN UND ISOLDE: VORSPIEL 3. AUFZUG see Wagner, Richard

TRISTESSA I see Karayev, Faradzh

TRISTIA see Artyomov, Vyacheslav

TRISTIUM see Kalabis, Viktor

TRITTICO BOTTICELLIANO see Respighi, Ottorino

TRIUMF SMRTI see Slavicky, Milan

TRIUMPHANT ALICE see Del Tredici, David

TROCHU, PIERRE (1953-    )
Fusion
2(pic)+alto fl.2(English
horn).2(bass clar,clar in E
flat).2(contrabsn). 2.2.2.1.
3perc,3vcl,db [20'] sc CANADIAN
MI 1100 T843FU      (T312)

Miracrose
1.1.1.1. 0.0.0.0. 2perc,2harp,vln,
vla,vcl,db [11'] sc,pts CANADIAN
MI 1200 T843MI      (T313)

Osmose
3(pic)+alto fl.3(English
horn).3(bass clar)+clar in E
flat.3(contrabsn). 4.4.4.1.
6perc,2harp,12vln I,12vln II,
10vla,8vcl,6db [24'] sc CANADIAN
MI 1100 T843OS      (T314)

TROIS CHANSONS see Ibert, Jacques

TROIS CHANTS see Migot, Georges

TROIS FOIS PASSERA see Panneton, Isabelle

TROIS LETTRES DE MON MOULIN see Tomasi, Henri

TROIS MÉLODIES see Gallois Montbrun, Raymond

TROIS MOUSQUETAIRES, LES: SUITE ÉPIQUE see Delerue, Georges

TROIS PIECES see Nadermann, Francois-Joseph

TROIS PIÈCES POUR ORCHESTRE À CORDES see Dijk, Jan van

TROIS PIECES POUR PIANO ET ORCHESTRE see Dijk, Jan van

TROIS POÈMES DE RENÉ CHAR see Martinet, Jean-Louis

TROJAHN, MANFRED (1949-    )
Sinfonie "Makramée"
see Symphony

Symphony
"Sinfonie "Makramée"" 3.3.3.3.
4.3.3.1. timp,4perc,harp,cel,
strings [13'] SIKORSKI sc 873
f.s., sc,pts perf mat rent (T315)

TROJAN, VÁCLAV (1907-1983)
Pastorale for Violin and Orchestra
see Sil Jsem Proso

Polka
see Rejdovacka

Rejdovacka (Polka)
1.2.2.3sax. 4.2.3.0. timp,perc,
strings CESKY HUD.      (T316)

Sil Jsem Proso (Pastorale for Violin
and Orchestra)
2.2.2.2. 2.2.0.0. timp,strings,vln
solo CESKY HUD.      (T317)

TROLLPOLSKA see Lovén, Birgitta, Holstamp

TROMBA, LA see Telemann, Georg Philipp

TROMBALCAZAR: TRIO see Offenbach, Jacques

TROMMER, JACK (1905-1990)
Abendläuten In Cordoba
see Charivari

Charivari
2(pic).2.2.0.baritone sax. 2.3.2.0.
perc,pno,strings,SAT soli
SIKORSKI perf mat rent
contains: Abendläuten In Cordoba;
Exzentrischen, Die; Ouverture;
Regen Über Paris;
Sonnenuntergang Und Abendlied
In Rom                          (T318)

Exzentrischen, Die
see Charivari

Ouverture
see Charivari

Regen Über Paris
see Charivari

Sonnenuntergang Und Abendlied In Rom
see Charivari

TROMMLER, DER see Genzmer, Harald

TROMPETEN IN TIROL see Godzinsky, George De

TRUMPET MAJOR, THE: FOUR SCENES see Hoddinott, Alun

TRUMPETS OF JERICO see Weinstangel, Sasha

TRÜMPY, BALZ (1946-    )
Nachtgesang
2(pic).2(English horn).2(bass
clar).2. 2.2.0.0. glock,vibra,
8vln I,6vln II,4vla,4vcl,2db [9']
HUG                             (T319)

Spiralgesang
2.2.2.2. 2.2.0.0. perc,strings
[12'] sc HUG GH 11516           (T320)

TRYTTEN, LORRE LYNN
Concerto for Violin
2.2.2.2. 2.2.1.0. 2perc,strings,vln
solo [15'] sc DONEMUS          (T321)

TSCHAIKIN, NIKOLAJ
Concerto, For Bajan (Accordion) And
Orchestra
see Concerto for Accordion and
Orchestra in B flat

Concerto for Accordion and Orchestra
in B flat
"Concerto, For Bajan (Accordion)
And Orchestra" 2.2.2.2. 4.2.1.0.
timp,perc,harp/pno,strings,
accordion or bajan solo [26']
SIKORSKI perf mat rent          (T322)

TSCHAIKOWSKY, PJOTR ILJITSCH
see TCHAIKOVSKY, PIOTR ILYICH

TSCHALAJEW, SCHIRWANI
Und Die Welt War Dazwischen
1.1.1.3. 2.3.0.1. perc,cel,pno,
strings,A solo [18'] (texts by
Emily Dickinson) SIKORSKI perf
mat rent                        (T323)

TSONTAKIS, GEORGE (1951-    )
Dove Descending, The
3(pic).3(English horn).3(bass
clar).3(contrabsn). 4.3.3.1.
timp,3perc,pno,harp,strings [15']
PRESSER rent                    (T324)

Other Echoes
3(pic).3(English horn).3(bass
clar).3. 4.3.3.1. timp,3perc,pno,
cel,strings,opt harp PRESSER rent
                                (T325)

TSUBONOH, KATSUHIRO (1947-    )
Symphony For Orchestra & Audience
orch,perc,mix cor [6'] JAPAN (T326)

TU, MÊME see Perrin, Glyn

TUBIN, EDUARD (1905-1982)
Symphony No. 7
2(pic).2(English horn).2(bass
clar).2. 2.2.0.0. timp,strings
[24'5] (Allegro moderato;
Larghetto; Allegro marciale) sc
NORDISKA                        (T327)

TULL, FISHER AUBREY (1934-    )
Dialogues
2(pic).2.2.2. 4.3.3(bass trom).1.
pno,strings,perc solo [17']
BOOSEY-ENG rent                 (T328)

TURANDOT see Brian, Havergal

TURCO IN ITALIA, IL: OUVERTURE see
Rossini, Gioacchino

TURINA, JOAQUIN (1882-1949)
Evangelio De Navidad *Op.12
2+pic.2+English horn.2+bass clar.2+
contrabsn. 4.3.3.1. timp,2perc,
harp,strings [15'] SCHOTTS perf
mat rent                        (T329)

TÜRKE IN ITALIEN, DER: OUVERTÜRE see
Rossini, Gioacchino, Turco In
Italia, Il: Ouverture

TURKIYE (BAUCHTANZ) see Thomas-Mifune,
Werner

TURN OF THE TIDE, THE see Davies, [Sir]
Peter Maxwell

TURNAGE, MARK-ANTHONY (1960-    )
Blood On The Floor
2(2alto fl).2(2English
horn).2(2bass
clar).2(2contrabsn). 2.2.2+
euphonium.1. 2perc,pno&elec pno&
cel,bass gtr&db,2vln I,2vln II,
2vla,2vcl,db,2soprano sax&2alto
sax,elec gtr solo,sax solo, jazz
kit solo [80'] SCHOTTS perf mat
rent                            (T330)

Dispelling The Fears
2(2alto fl).2(2English
horn).2(2bass
clar).2(2contrabsn).2soprano sax.
2.0.2+euphonium.1. 2perc,cel/pno,
harp,strings,2trp soli [20']
SCHOTTS perf mat rent           (T331)

Drowned Out
3(pic,2alto fl).3(English
horn).2(2bass clar).2+contrabsn.
4.4.3.1. 5perc,pno,harp,16vln I,
16vln II,12vla,12vcl,8db,2soprano
sax&2baritone sax [22'] study sc
SCHOTTS ED 12446 perf mat rent  (T332)

Greek-Suite
1(pic,alto fl).2(2English
horn).2(clar in E flat,2bass
clar).0. 2.1.1.0. 2perc,pno&elec
pno,harp,vla,2vcl,db,soprano sax&
alto sax&baritone sax,MezT soli,
most players double on perc [25']
(text by Steven Berkoff) SCHOTTS
perf mat rent                   (T333)

Kai
1(alto fl).0.1(bass
clar).1(contrabsn). 0.2.1.0.
perc,pno,harp,bass gtr,2vln&perc,
vla&perc,vcl,db,2alto sax&
2soprano sax,vcl solo [18'] study
sc SCHOTTS ED 12397 perf mat rent
                                (T334)

Momentum
3.3.3(clar in E flat,2bass
clar).3(contrabsn). 4.3.2+bass
trom.0. 2perc,pno,harp,16vln I,
14vln II,12vla,12vcl,8db,2alto
sax&soprano sax,opt bass gtr
[10'] study sc SCHOTTS ED 12416
perf mat rent                   (T335)

Some Days
0.0.3(clar in E flat,2bass
clar).3(2contrabsn). 0.0.0.0.
harp,12vln I,12vln II,8vla,8vcl,
4db,Mez solo [15'] study sc
SCHOTTS ED 12384 perf mat rent  (T336)

Three Screaming Popes
3(3pic,3alto fl).3(English
horn).3(clar in E flat,3bass
clar).3(contrabsn). 6.3.3+
euphonium.1. 4perc,cel,pno&elec
pno,harp,12vln I,12vln II,10vla,
10vcl,8db,2soprano sax&2alto sax
[15'] study sc SCHOTTS ED 12377
perf mat rent                   (T337)

Your Rockaby
3(2alto fl).3.2(bass clar)+
contrabass clar.2+contrabsn.
4.3.3.1. 5perc,cimbalom,pno&cel,
harp,16vln I,16vln II,12vla,
12vcl,8db,soprano sax solo [24']
study sc SCHOTTS ED 12448 perf
mat rent                        (T338)

TURNER, ROBERT [COMRIE] (1920-    )
From A Different Land
2(pic).2.2.2. 2.0.0.0. timp,2perc,
strings,brass quin soli [11'] sc
CANADIAN MI 1435 T951FR         (T339)

Gift From The Sea
see Symphony in One Movement

Group Of Seven, A
2(pic).2(English horn).2(bass
clar).2. 2.2.1.0. timp,perc,harp,
strings,narrator,vla solo [25']
(poems of love and nature) sc
CANADIAN MI 1312 T951GR         (T340)

TURNER, ROBERT [COMRIE] (cont'd.)
Johann's Gift To Christmas
3(pic).3(English horn).3(bass
clar).3(contrabsn). 4.3.3.1.
timp,2perc,harp,cel,strings,
narrator [44'] sc CANADIAN
MV 1400 T951JO                  (T341)

Manitoba Memoir
6vln I,6vln II,4vla,4vcl,2db [15']
(1. Of time and the river(s):
Pastorale 2. Ethnic celebration:
Folk dance 3. Prairies sunset:
Epilogue) sc CANADIAN
MI 1500 T951MA                  (T342)

Symphony in One Movement
"Gift From The Sea"
3(pic).3(English horn).3(bass
clar).3(contrabsn). 4.3.3.1.
timp,2perc,harp,strings [17'] sc
CANADIAN MI 1100 T951SY         (T343)

Symphony No. 3
2(pic).2(English horn).2(bass
clar).2. 4.3.3.1. timp,2perc,cel,
harp,strings [28'] sc CANADIAN
MI 1100 T951SY3                 (T344)

Ten Canadian Folk Songs
1(pic).1.2.1. 2.1.1.0. 1-2perc,
harp,strings,med solo [30'] sc
CANADIAN MV 1400 T951TE         (T345)

TURNS AND MORDENTS see Saylor, Bruce
(Stuart)

TUROK, PAUL HARRIS (1929-    )
Symphony in Two Movements
3.3.3.2. 4.2.3.1. 2perc,timp,pno,
strings SEESAW                  (T346)

TUTINO, MARCO (1954-    )
Concerto for Clarinet and Orchestra
see Piano Americano

Piano Americano (Concerto for
Clarinet and Orchestra)
2.2.0.2. 2.2.1.0. perc,pno,strings
[20'] SONZOGNO rent             (T347)

TUTTI, POUR GRAND ORCHESTRE see
Louvier, Alain

TUTU see Lindgren, Pär

TÜÜR, ERKKI-SVEN (1959-    )
Concerto for Violoncello and
Orchestra
1.1.1.1. 1.1.0.0. vibra,8vln I,7vln
II,6vla,5vcl,4db,vcl solo [20']
sc,solo pt PETERS 04687         (T348)

Crystallisatio
3.0.0.0. 0.0.0.0. glock,8vln I,7vln
II,6vla,5vcl,4db [12'] sc PETERS
04506                           (T349)

Insula Deserta
6vln I,5vln II,4vla,3vcl,db [9'] sc
PETERS 02529                    (T350)

Lighthouse
8vln I,7vln II,6vla,5vcl,4db sc
PETERS 02529                    (T351)

Searching For Roots: Hommage A
Sibelius
3.3.3.2. 6.3.3.0. timp,vibra,4perc,
6vln I,6vln II,5vla,4vcl,6db [8']
sc PETERS 02868                 (T352)

Sinfonie No. 3
see Symphony No. 3

Symphony No. 3
"Sinfonie No. 3" 2.2.2.2. 4.2.3.1.
timp,3perc,harp,8vln I,7vln II,
6vla,5vcl,4db [25'] sc PETERS
04767                           (T353)

TUURU see Kangro, Raimo

TV BALLADER see Jeverud, Johan

TV SETS GLOWING BLUE IN THE DUSK:
SCENES see Storm, Staffan

TVÅ SYMFONISKA ETYDER see Jeverud,
Johan

TVÁŘ. 4 BÁSNE FRANTIŠKA HALASE see
Klusák, Jan

TVEIT, SIGVALD (1945-    )
Xenos
string orch,vln solo NORSKMI (T354)

TVEITT, GEIRR (1908-1981)
Musik In Norwegischen Tonleitern Für
Orchester
see Prillar I G-Lydisk

TVEITT, GEIRR (cont'd.)

Prillar I G-Lydisk *Op.8
"Musik In Norwegischen Tonleitern
Für Orchester" 4(pic,alto
fl).2.3(bass clar).2. 4.4.3.1.
timp,strings [42'] NORSKMI (T355)

TVO SANGER TIL TEKSTER AV HANS BØRLI
see Søderlind, Ragnar

TWA, ANDREW (1919-   )
Oxford Sinfonia
string orch,string quar soli [18']
sc CANADIAN                     (T356)

TWENTY-EIGHT, TWENTY-SIX AND TWENTY-
NINE see Cage, John

TWENTY-NINE see Cage, John

TWENTY-SIX see Cage, John

TWENTY-THREE see Cage, John

TWENTY-THREE POEMS ABOUT HORSES see
Komorous, Rudolf

TWILIGHT ON THE WATERS see King,
Reginald

TWILIGHT TAPESTRY see Gellman, Steven

TWO A'MARVELL'S FOR WORDS see London,
Edwin

TWO ARE BETTER THAN ONE see "Bach,
P.D.Q." (Peter Schickele), Concerto
for 2 Pianos and Orchestra

TWO BALLADS see Jeverud, Johan, Tv
Ballader

TWO CINE PASTRALI see Takemitsu, Toru

TWO FANTASIAS see Ellis, David

TWO FANTASIES see Picker, Tobias

TWO HUNGARIAN DANCES see Farkas, Ferenc

TWO JEWISH DANCES see Duffy, John

TWO KEYBOARD CONCERTOS see Platti,
Giovanni Benedetto

TWO MEDITATIONS FOR STRINGS see
Binkerd, Gordon Ware

TWO MEXICAN SERENADES see Luening, Otto

TWO ORGANA see Knussen, Oliver

TWO PIECES FOR ORCHESTRA see Szönyi,
Erzsebet (Elizabeth)

TWO PIECES FOR VIOLIN AND ORCHESTRA see
Walton, [Sir] William (Turner)

TWO PIECES, OP. 57A see Scriabin,
Alexander

TWO PIERROT PIECES see Scott, Cyril
Meir

TWO PRELUDES FOUNDED ON WELSH HYMN
TUNES see Vaughan Williams, Ralph

TWO RONDOS see Kokai, Rezsö

TWO SCENES FOR TIMPANI AND STRINGS see
Klein, Lothar

TWO SIDES TO THE WIND see Hui, Melissa

TWO SKETCHES FOR SMALL ORCHESTRA see
Betts, Lorne M.

TWO SONGS FOR BASS-BARITONE AND
ORCHESTRA see Mather, Bruce

TWO SONGS OP. 5 see Kodály, Zoltán

TWO SONGS OP. 14, NOS. 1 & 3 see
Kodály, Zoltán

TWO STUDIES see Bose, Hans-Jurgen Von

TWO STUDIES IN STRINGS see Hayes, Gary

TWO SUITES FROM THE FAIRY QUEEN see
Purcell, Henry, Fairy Queen, The:
Two Suites

2000 PLUS ONE see Allen, Peter

TWO WORLDS see Norden, Maarten Van

TYCHE see Wilson, Lars

TYENDINAGA: LEGEND FOR ORCHESTRA see
Crawley, Clifford

TYMPAN see Keulen, Geert van

TZIGANE see Ravel, Maurice

# U

U LÉCIVÉHO VRÍDLA see Fryda, Jan

U MERU PASTORE see Tomasi, Henri

U NÁS V TREŠTI see Smetácek, Václav

ÜBER DIE WIESE ZIEHEN WIR see Rakov,
Nikolai

ÜBER ODER UND NEISSE see Malige, Fred

UCCELLI, GLI see Respighi, Ottorino

UDDA ELLER JÄMT? see Nilsson, Ivo

UF DEM ANGER see Orff, Carl

UFFINGTON HORSE, THE see Sutton-
Anderson, David

UHL, EDMUND (1853-1929)
Slawische Intermezzi *Op.17
3.2.2.2. 4.2.3.1. timp,perc,harp,
8vln I,7vln II,6vla,5vcl,4db
[25'] sc KAHNT 01973       (U1)

UHREN DER VERGANGENHEIT II see
Kutavicius, Bronius

ULLMANN, VIKTOR (1898-1944)
Concerto for Piano and Orchestra, Op.
25
3(pic).2+English horn.3(clar in E
flat)+bass clar.2+contrabsn.
4.3.3.1. timp,3perc,banjo,harp,
strings,pno solo [19'] SCHOTTS
perf mat rent              (U2)

Don Quixote Tanzt Fandango
(Wulff, Bernhard) 2(pic)+
pic.3(English horn).3(clar in E
flat,bass clar).3(contrabsn).
4.3.3.1. timp,3perc,hpsd,harp,
strings [15'] SCHOTTS perf mat
rent                       (U3)

Six Songs, Op.17
(Keulen, Geert Van)
2(pic).1(English horn).1+bass
clar.1. 1.0.0.0. cel,harp,
strings,S solo [14'] SCHOTTS perf
mat rent                   (U4)

Slovanská Rapsodie *Op.23
4.3.3.3. 4.2.3.1. timp,perc,2harp,
strings, obbligato sax CESKY HUD.
(U5)

Symphony No. 1, Op. 45
(Wulff, Bernhard) "Von Meiner
Jugend" 3(pic).3(English
horn).3(clar in E flat,bass
clar).3(contrabsn). 4.3.3.1.
timp,3perc,mand,cel,harp,strings
[19'] SCHOTTS perf mat rent (U6)

Symphony No. 2 in D
(Wulff, Bernhard) 3(2pic).3(English
horn).3(clar in E flat,bass
clar).3(contrabsn). 4.3.3.1.
timp,perc,hpsd,cel,harp,strings
[23'] SCHOTTS perf mat rent (U7)

Variations, Fantasy And Doublefugue
2(pic).1+English horn.2(bass
clar).2(contrabsn). 3.2.1.0.
timp,harp,strings [13'] (based on
a little piano piece, Op.5 by
Arnold Schoenberg) SCHOTTS perf
mat rent                   (U8)

Von Meiner Jugend
see Symphony No. 1, Op. 45

Weise Von Liebe Und Tod Des Cornet
Christoph Rilke, Die
(Brauel, Henning) 3(pic).2+English
horn.2+bass clar.2+contrabsn.
4.2.3.1. timp,3perc,pno&opt cel,
harp,strings,speaking voice [25']
SCHOTTS perf mat rent      (U9)

ULMANN, HELMUT VON (1913-1987)
Concerto Grosso for String Orchestra,
Op. 21
"Concerto Grosso Über Das Thema B-
A-C-H" [30'] SIKORSKI sc 1578
f.s., sc,pts perf mat rent (U10)

Concerto Grosso Über Das Thema B-A-C-
H
see Concerto Grosso for String
Orchestra, Op. 21

ULTIMA see Hermanson, Åke

ULURU see Schwertsik, Kurt

ULYSSES AWAKES see Woolrich, John

UNCHAINED MELODY see Koehne, Graeme

UND DER MOND HEFTET INS MEER EIN LANGES HORN AUS LICHT UND TANZ see Brandmüller, Theo

"...UND DIE ERD IST KALT..." see Ospald, Klaus

UND DIE WELT WAR DAZWISCHEN see Tschalajew, Schirwani

...UND FÜLLET DIE ERDE UND MACHET SIE EUCH UNTERTAN... see Wildberger, Jacques

UND FÜRCHTEN SIE NICHT DEN... see Jung, Helge

...UND VERSTREUT GEDICHTE... see Haselbach, Josef

UNDER EN BRO see Grainger, Percy Aldridge

UNDER NEONLIGHT 1 see Müller-Siemens, Detlev

UNDER THE GREENWOOD TREE see Walton, [Sir] William (Turner)

UNDERHILL, OWEN (1954-   )
Glimmer Broke
3(pic).3(English horn).3(bass clar).3(contrabsn). 4.2.3.1. timp,3perc,harp,15vln I,15vln II, 12vla,10vcl,8db [19'] sc CANADIAN MI 1100 U55GL          (U11)

Gray Glove
2.2.2.2. 2.2.1.1. timp&perc,perc, harp,strings,S solo [12'] sc CANADIAN MV 1400 U55GR          (U12)

UNDERHOLDNINGSMUSIKK FOR TRETTEN see Thommessen, Olav Anton, To Instrumentale Madrigaler For Sinfonietta

UNDERVEGETATION see Mårtensson, Per

UNDINE: BALLETMUSIK see Lortzing, (Gustav) Albert

UNDINE: HINWEG! HINWEG! ...MIR SCHIEN DER MORGEN AUFGEGANGEN see Lortzing, (Gustav) Albert

UNDINE: OVERTURE see Lortzing, (Gustav) Albert

UNFINISHED SYMPHONY see Schubert, Franz (Peter), Symphony No. 8 in B minor, D. 759

UNG, CHINARY (1942-   )
Desert Flowers Bloom
see Grand Spiral

Grand Spiral
"Desert Flowers Bloom" 3.3.5.3. 4.3.3.1. timp,3perc,pno,harp,8vln I,7vln II,6vla,5vcl,4db [12'] sc PETERS 04403          (U13)

Triple Concerto: A Sonorous Path
3.2.2.2. 1.0.0.0. timp,harp,8vln I, 7vln II,6vla,5vcl,4db,vcl&perc& pno soli [17'] sc PETERS 04405          (U14)

Water Rings
2.2.2.2. 2.2.2.0. timp,2perc,8vln I,7vln II,6vla,5vcl,4db [6'] sc PETERS 04406          (U15)

UNGVARI, TAMAS (1936-   )
Dis-Tanz
chamber orch sc,pts STIM          (U16)

UNISON see Marez Oyens, Tera de

UNIVERSE SYMPHONY see Ives, Charles

UNIVERSE SYMPHONY: PRELUDE, SECTION A, AND CODA OF SECTION C see Ives, Charles

UNOROVÁ PREDEHRA see Boháč, Josef

UNRUHE DER NACHT see Hausegger, Siegmund von see Weingartner, (Paul) Felix von

UNTER STERNEN see Hausegger, Siegmund von

UP AND AT IT! (CURTAIN RAISER) see Pinkham, Daniel

UP-FRONT CONCERTO, THE see Walker, Gwyneth

UPPLANDIA see Hudecek, Radovan

UPPLST FNSTER see Edlund, Mikael

UPPSTRÖM, TORE (1937-   )
Fem Orkesterstycken
2(pic).2.2.2. 3.2.1.0. timp,perc, harp,strings [16'] sc,pts STIM          (U17)

UPSTAIRS DOWNSTAIRS see Faris, Alexander

UPTURNED GLASS, THE see Stevens, Bernard George

URLAUBER, DER see Müller-Lampertz, Richard

URLIED see Raskatov, Alexander

USMEVAVÁ POLKA see Pravecek, Jindrich

ÚSMEVY A SLZY see Juchelka, Miroslav

USNI, MALÉ POUPÁTKO see Ryba, Jan Jakub Simon

USPÁVANKA PRO MARTÍNKU see Hudec, Jiri

USPENSKY, VLADISLAV (1937-   )
Monologe
1(pic).1.1.2. 2.1.1.0. 3perc,harp, strings,Mez solo [17'] SIKORSKI perf mat rent          (U18)

Sinfonie "Zum Licht"
2(pic).2.2.3(contrabsn). 4.3.3.1. timp,6perc,harp,cel/pno/hpsd, strings [20'] SIKORSKI perf mat rent          (U19)

USTVOLSKAYA, GALINA (1919-   )
Concerto for Piano, Timpani and String Orchestra
[20'] SIKORSKI perf mat rent          (U20)

Jesus, Messias, Errette Uns! see Symphony No. 3

Sinfonisches Poem
3.3.3.3. 6.3.4.1. perc,harp,cel, pno,strings [25'] SIKORSKI perf mat rent          (U21)

Suite for Orchestra
1.2.2.3. 4.3.3.1. timp,perc,harp, cel,pno,strings [21'] SIKORSKI perf mat rent          (U22)

Symphony No. 1
[Russ] 4.3.4.3. 3.4.1.1. timp,perc, harp,cel,pno,strings, amplified 2 boys soli [29'] (texts by Gianni Rodari) SIKORSKI perf mat rent          (U23)

Symphony No. 3
"Jesus, Messias, Errette Uns!" 0.5.0.0. 0.5.1.3. 3perc,pno,5db, solo voice [16'] SIKORSKI sc 1863 f.s., sc,pts perf mat rent          (U24)

Traum Des Stepan Rasin, Der
[Russ] 3.3.3.2. 4.3.3.1. timp,perc, harp,cel,strings,Bar solo [20'] SIKORSKI perf mat rent          (U25)

UTAH see Duffy

UTRPENÍ KNÍZETE STERNENHOCHA see Bulis, Jiri

UTSLÅTT see Germeten, Gunnar

UTSUROHI-NAGI see Hosokawa, Toshio

UTTINI, FRANCESCO ANTONIO B. (1723-1795)
Sinfonia in G
(Hedwall, Lennart) "Skara" strings, cont [6'] sc STIM          (U26)

Skara
see Sinfonia in G

UVENTEDE, DET: ÅPNINGSMUSIKK FOR NRK-P2 see Thommessen, Olav Anton

UVNITR see Tichavsky, Radko

UY, PAUL (1932-   )
Automnale
2.3.2.3. 4.2.2.1. timp,perc, strings,vln solo [12'15"] BELGE          (U27)
strings,vln solo [12'15"] (version II) BELGE          (U28)

Sinfonia Belgica
3.3.3.3. 4.4.3.1. timp,3perc, strings [16'] BELGE          (U29)

# V

V & V see Kantscheli, Gija

V CASY NOVOLUNIJA see Roslavetz, Nicolas

V HUDEBNÍ SÍNI see Myska, Rudolf

V KRAJINE VZPOMÍNÁNÍ see Kvech, Otomar

V LÁZENSKÉM PARKU see Myska, Rudolf

V MESTE KROMERÍZI see Petr, Zdenek

V POHODE see Bazant, Jiri

V STUDNI. MLADÁ LÁSKA see Blodek, Vilem (Wilhelm)

V STUDNI. PREDEHRA K OPERE see Blodek, Vilem (Wilhelm)

V STUDNI. SMES Z OPERY UPRAVIL J. MALY see Blodek, Vilem (Wilhelm)

V STUDNI. VSTUPNÍ ÁRIE VERUNY see Blodek, Vilem (Wilhelm)

V STUDNI. VYCHOD MESICE see Blodek, Vilem (Wilhelm)

V STUDNI. ZPEV JANKA see Blodek, Vilem (Wilhelm)

V TICHU PODVECERA see Deváty, Antonín

V ZADUMÁNÍ see Fryda, Jan

VAAGE, KNUT (1961-   )
Continue
3(pic).3(English horn).3(bass clar).3(contrabsn). 4.3.3.1. timp,2perc,pno,harp,strings [16'20"] NORSKMI          (V1)

VACANCES AU NÉVADA see Coiteux, Francis

VACEK, MILOŠ (1928-   )
Burleska
2.2.2.2. 4.2.0.0. timp,perc,strings [5'] CESKY HUD.          (V2)

Concerto for Trombone and Strings
[19'] CESKY HUD.          (V3)

Markyza De Pompadour
1.1.0.1. 2.0.0.0. org/cembalo, strings,narrator [20'] CESKY HUD.          (V4)

Mé Kamenici Nad Lipou (Suite for Orchestra)
3.2.2.2. 4.2.3.1. timp,perc,cel, strings [21'] CESKY HUD.          (V5)

November 17
see 17. Lostopad

Osamely Moreplavec
3.2.3.2. 4.3.4.1. timp,perc,xylo, vibra,harp,cel,pno,strings [18'] CESKY HUD.          (V6)

Pochod Prátelství
3.2.2.2. 4.3.4.1. timp,perc,strings [5'] CESKY HUD.          (V7)

17. Lostopad
"November 17" 3.2.3.2. 4.3.4.1. timp,perc,pno,strings [14'] CESKY HUD.          (V8)

Slavnostní Prolog
3.2.2.2. 4.3.4.1. timp,perc,harp, strings [9'] CESKY HUD.          (V9)

Slunci Vstríc
3.2.2.2. 4.3.4.1. timp,perc,strings [4'] CESKY HUD.          (V10)

Suite for Orchestra
see Mé Kamenici Nad Lipou

Svedomi Sveta
4.2.3.3. 4.4.4.1. timp,perc,harp, pno,strings (symphonic poem) CESKY HUD.          (V11)

Symphony No. 2
3.2.3.2. 4.3.4.1. timp,perc,pno, strings [31'] CESKY HUD.          (V12)

Tance Ve Starém Slohu
4.1.2.1. 2.0.0.0. cembalo,strings [17'] CESKY HUD.          (V13)

Vecny Duel
string orch,B solo [15'] CESKY HUD.          (V14)

VACKÁR, DALIBOR CYRIL (1906-1984)
Concerto Grosso for Saxophone,
Accordion, Guitar and Orchestra
1.1.0.0. 1.1.0.0. perc,strings,
soprano sax&acord&gtr soli [25']
CESKY HUD.                    (V15)

Extempore
2.2.2.2. 2.2.0.0. timp,perc,strings
[16'] CESKY HUD.              (V16)

Jubilejní
see Sinfonietta No. 2

Musica Concertante
"Musica Coucertante" 2.2.2.2.
4.2.0.0. timp,strings [16'] CESKY
HUD.                          (V17)

Musica Coucertante
see Musica Concertante

Oboe Concertante
2.0.2.2. 2.2.2.0. perc,pno,strings,
ob solo [26'] CESKY HUD.      (V18)

Príbeh O Peti Kapitolách
perc,strings,clar solo [20'] CESKY
HUD.                          (V19)

Pro Juventute
see Symphony No. 5

Sinfonietta No. 2
"Jubilejní" 2.2.2.2. 4.3.3.0. timp,
perc,pno,strings [20'] CESKY HUD.
                              (V20)

Symphony No. 5
"Pro Juventute" 2.2.2.2. 4.3.3.0.
timp,perc,xylo,vibra,pno,strings
[19'] CESKY HUD.              (V21)

VACKAR, TOMAS (1945-1963)
Concerto Recitativo
pno,strings,fl solo CESKY HUD.
                              (V22)

VACKRA DALKULLAN: DANSDRAMA KRING ETT
KVINNODE see Edn, Mats

VAEVET AF STAENGLER: A SYMPHONIC SONG
FOR SOPRANO AND STRINGS see
Thommessen, Olav Anton

VAGABUNDENLIEDER, OP. 36 see Mohler,
Philipp

VAINBERG, MOYSEY SAMUILOVITCH
(1919-1996)
Concerto for Clarinet and String
Orchestra, Op. 104
[24'] SIKORSKI perf mat rent   (V23)

Concerto for Violin and Orchestra,
Op. 67
3.2.3.3. 4.2.0.0. timp,perc,harp,
cel,strings,vln solo [26']
SIKORSKI perf mat rent         (V24)

Symphony No. 6, Op. 79
3.3.4.3. 6.4.3.1. timp,3perc,harp,
cel,strings,boy cor [45']
SIKORSKI perf mat rent         (V25)

Symphony No. 14, Op. 117
4.3.4.3. 6.4.4.0. timp,perc,cel,
pno,strings [20'] SIKORSKI perf
mat rent                       (V26)

VAIREY SUITE see Haworth, Frank

VAISSEAU D'OR, LE see Hetu, Jacques

VAJDA, JÁNOS
Holland Anziksz
see Picture Postcard From Holland

Picture Postcard From Holland
"Holland Anziksz" 1.1.1.1. 1.0.2.0.
strings [9'] EMB rent          (V27)

VAKEN HÄNRYCKNING see Naessen, Ray, In
Extasibus Vigilibus

VALAŠSKÉ INTERMEZZO see Petrov, Vadim

VALCÍK see Domazlicky, Frantisek see
Paloucek, Alois

VALCÍK PRO ORCHESTR see Fischer, Jan F.

VALCÍKY see Smetana, Bedrich

VÁLEK, JIRÍ (1923-    )
Concerto Burlesco
2.2.2.2. 2.1.0.0. timp,perc,
strings,English horn solo [22']
CESKY HUD.                     (V28)

Concerto Giocoso
1.2.2.2. 2.0.0.0. timp,perc,
strings,fl&harp&marimba soli
[20'] CESKY HUD.               (V29)

Hamlet, Náš Soucasník
3.2.2.3. 4.3.3.1. timp,perc,xylo,
harp,strings [20'] CESKY HUD.

VÁLEK, JIRÍ (cont'd.)

Katedrála                      (V30)
string orch,vln&vla soli [5'] CESKY
HUD.                           (V31)

Klasická
see Symphony No. 2

Shakespearovské Fresky
string orch,vln&vla soli [15']
CESKY HUD.                     (V32)

Slavnostní Freska
2.2.2.2. 4.3.3.1. timp,perc,xylo,
pno,strings [5'] CESKY HUD.    (V33)

Symphony No. 2
"Klasická" 2.2.2.2. 2.0.0.0. timp,
perc,cel/pno,strings [18'] CESKY
HUD.                           (V34)

Symphony No. 14
"Trionfale" 3.2.2.2. 4.3.3.1. timp,
perc,xylo,vibra,cel,strings,2pno
soli [18'] (double concerto)
CESKY HUD.                     (V35)

Trionfale
see Symphony No. 14

VALEN, FARTEIN (1887-1952)
Isla De Las Calmas, La *Op.21
2.2.2.2. 1.0.0.0. 8vln I,7vln II,
6vla,5vcl,4db [6'] sc,study sc
LYCHE                          (V36)

VALENTINI, GIOVANNI (1582-1649)
Sonata Per Tabula
S rec,A rec,T rec,strings without
db,cont COPPENRATH sc 17.004-01,
kbd pt 17.004-03, pts
17.004-21 TO 31                (V37)

VALENTINI, GIUSEPPE (ca. 1681-ca. 1740)
Weihnachts-Pastorale
(Schering) strings,cont [3'] KAHNT
                               (V38)

VÁLKA S MLOKY see Teml, Jiri, Symphony
No. 2

VALKARE, GUNNAR (1943-    )
Concerto for Accordion and String
Orchestra
see Viaggio

Intermedium 1: From Siefried-Idyll
(Wagner) To Konsert Op. 24
(Webern)
1.1.2.1. 2.1.1.0. timp,strings,pno,
electronic tape [4'] sc,pts STIM
                               (V39)

Intermedium 2: From Konsert Op.24
(Webern) till ur Histoire Du
Soldat (Stravinskij)
1.1.1.1. 1.1.1.0. timp,strings,pno
[2'5"] sc,pts STIM             (V40)

Kinema
3(pic).3.3(bass clar).3. 4.3.3.0.
3perc,harp,strings [11'] sc
REIMERS ED.NR 101176           (V41)

Play Next
2.2.2.2. 2.2.0.0. timp,perc,harp,
strings,cel sc STIM H-2744     (V42)

Ringing
8-36vln,8-36vla,8-36vcl,marimba
[20'] pts STIM                 (V43)

Second Flight Of The Mechanical Heart
1.1.1.1. 1.1.1.0. timp,strings,pno
[10'] sc STIM                  (V44)

Symphony No. 1
3(pic).3.3.3. 4.3.3.0. 2perc,
strings,cel [22'] SUECIA sc
H-2529, pts                    (V45)

Symphony No. 2,Finale
3(pic).3.3.3. 4.3.3.0. 4perc,harp,
strings sc STIM H-1896         (V46)

Viaggio (Concerto for Accordion and
String Orchestra)
string orch,acord solo STIM    (V47)

VALLE ESCONDIDO, EL see Still, William
Grant

VALLEE DES CLOCHES, LA see Ravel,
Maurice

VALLERAND, JEAN (1915-    )
Diable Dans Le Belfroi, Le
3(pic).3(English horn).3.3.
4.3.3.1. timp&perc,harp,strings
[12'] sc CANADIAN MI 1100 V184DI
                               (V48)

VALLEY OF A THOUSAND HILLS see Forsyth,
Malcolm

VALSE, LA see Ravel, Maurice

VALSE BOSTON see Kantscheli, Gija

VALSE BRILLANTE see Busch, Hans, Im
Walzerrausch

VALSE CONCERTANTE POUR PIANO ET
ORCHESTRE see Lauber, Anne

VALSE DE LA CIGARETTE see Lalo, Edouard

VALSE DE L'OPÉRA EUGÈNE ONÉGUINE see
Tchaikovsky, Piotr Ilyich

VALSE-FANTAISIE see Glinka, Mikhail
Ivanovich

VALSE MODERATO see Eisbrenner, Werner,
Vergessene Melodie

VALSE TRISTE see Korbar, Leopold

VAMPIR, DER: OVERTURE see Marschner,
Heinrich (August)

VAN DIJK, JAN
see DIJK, JAN VAN

VAN FEESTEN EN ANGSTEN see Bus, Jan

VAN ROOSENDAEL, JAN ROKUS
see ROOSENDAEL, JAN ROKUS VAN

VANDEVORST, TOON
Nachtvlinder
3.2.4.3. 4.4.4.1. 4perc,harp,
strings [9'] sc DONEMUS        (V49)

VANEK, STANISLAV (1954-    )
In Epicentrum
3.2.3.3. 4.2.3.1. timp,perc,strings
[10'] CESKY HUD.               (V50)

VÄNERIDYLL see Sevius, Sven

VANHAL, JOHANN BAPTIST
see WANHAL, JOHANN BAPTIST

VANHALL, JAN KRTITEL
see WANHAL, JOHANN BAPTIST

VANISHING POINTS: A TABLEAU FOR
ORCHESTRA see Rea, John

VANITAS see Davies, [Sir] Peter Maxwell

VANTUS, ISTVAN
Concerto Grosso
(Nella Notte) concertino: 1, 1, 1,
1, 0; ripieno: 1, 1, 1, 1 [8']
EMB rent                       (V51)

VARIACE A FUGA PRO MALY SMYCCOVY
ORCHESTR NA TÉMA NÁRODNÍ PÍSNE see
Iglo, Milan

VARIACE A KOLÁZE see Hanuš, Jan

VARIACE NA BAROKNÍ TÉMA see Dousa,
Eduard

VARIACE NA MORAVSKOU LIDOVOU PÍSEN see
Vodrazka, Karel

VARIACE NA RENESANCNÍ TÉMA see Ištvan,
Miloslav

VARIACE NA ROCKOVÉ TÉMA see Jirasek,
Jan

VARIACE NA STAROU FRANCOUZSKOU PÍSEN
see Flosman, Oldrich

VARIACE NA TÉMA ADAMA MICHNY see
Berkovec, Jiri

VARIACE NA TÉMA ALBANA BERGA see
Krízek, Milan

VARIACE NA TÉMA BOHUSLAVA MARTINU see
Zouhar, Zdenek

VARIACE NA TÉMA J. A. BENDY VE STARÉM
SLOHU see Berkovec, Jiri

VARIÁCIÓK ZENEKARRA OBLIGÁT ZONGORÁVAL
see Decsenyi, Janos, Variations For
Orchestra With Piano Obbligato

VARIACNÍ FANTAZIE NA TÉMA G. PH.
TELEMANNA see Fischer, Eduard

VARIACNÍ SYMFONIE see Sokola, Milos

VARIANTS see Brady, Timothy

VARIATIONEN AUF EINER SAITE NACH EINEM
THEMA VON ROSSINI see Paganini,
Niccolo

VARIATIONEN ÜBER EIN ALTES WIENER
STROPHENLIED see Eötvös, Jószef

VARIATIONEN ÜBER EIN EIGENES THEMA see Hruby, Victor see Rudorff, Ernst

VARIATIONEN ÜBER EIN RUSSISCHES THEMA see Glazunov, Alexander Konstantinovich

VARIATIONEN ÜBER EIN RUSSISCHES VOLKSLIED see Glazunov, Alexander Konstantinovich

VARIATIONEN ÜBER EIN THEMA AUS "DER LETZTE KAISER" see Su, Cong

VARIATIONEN ÜBER EIN THEMA VON CORELLI see Kreisler, Fritz

VARIATIONEN ÜBER EIN THEMA VON W.A. MOZART see Busch, Adolf

VARIATIONEN ÜBER EIN UKRAINISCHES VOLKSLIED see Knorr, Ivan

VARIATIONEN ÜBER EINE ENGLISCHE SCHULMUSIK see Wehding, Hans-Hendrik

VARIATIONEN UND FUGE ÜBER EIN THEMA VON J. ADAM HILLER see Reger, Max

VARIATIONEN UND FUGE ÜBER EIN THEMA VON MOZART see Reger, Max

VARIATIONER OCH INTERMEZZI see Börtz, Daniel

VARIATIONER ÖVER EN FRANSK FOLKMELODI see Elmehed, Rune

VARIATIONER ÖVER EN POLSKA FR MEDELPAD see Robertsson, Stig

VARIATIONS see Maw, Nicholas see Salzedo, Leonard (Lopes)

VARIATIONS D'CONCERTANTES see Montral, Pierre

VARIATIONS ET THÈME see Prevost, Andre

VARIATIONS, FANTASY AND DOUBLEFUGUE see Ullmann, Viktor

VARIATIONS FOR ORCHESTRA ON A. E. G. see Gayfer, James McDonald

VARIATIONS FOR ORCHESTRA WITH PIANO OBBLIGATO see Decsenyi, Janos

VARIATIONS FROM THE HEART see Baksa, Robert Frank

VARIATIONS GRÉGORIENNES SUR UN SALVE REGINA see Tomasi, Henri

VARIATIONS LIBRES POUR UN LIBRE PENSEUR MUSICAL see Delerue, Georges

VARIATIONS ON A GREEK FOLK-SONG FOR PIANO & ORCHESTRA see Spinks, Charles

VARIATIONS ON A LAPPISH MELODY see Koch, Erland von, Rauna

VARIATIONS ON A NURSERY SONG see Bennett, Richard Rodney

VARIATIONS ON A THEME BY HONEGGER see Eyerly, Scott

VARIATIONS ON A THEME BY RAICHL see Coles, Graham

VARIATIONS ON A THEME OF PAGANINI FOR TRUMPET AND ORCHESTRA see Proto, Frank, Capriccio Di Niccolo

VARIATIONS ON A WALTZ see Moross, Jerome

VARIATIONS ON AN ELIZABETHAN BALLAD see Arnold, Alan

VARIATIONS ON AN OLD AMERICAN MELODY see Proto, Frank, Voyage That Johnny Never Knew, The

VARIATIONS ON AN OLD FRENCH BALLADE see Gregor, Cestmír, Já Na Vojnu Se Dal

VARIATIONS ON AVE MARIS STELLA see Degazio, Bruno

VARIATIONS ON BERNSTEIN'S "NEW YORK, NEW YORK" see Druckman, Jacob Raphael

VARIATIONS POUR UNE TROMPETTE DE CAVALERIE see DuBois, Pierre-Max

VARIATIONS SUR LA TRAVIATA DE VERDI see Dupin, Marc-Olivier

VARIATIONS SUR LE THÈME DE "LA TRUITE" DE SCHUBERT see Natsuda, Masakazu

VARIAZIONE ENHARMONICHE see Rieti, Vittorio, Enharmonic Variations

VARIAZIONI CLASSICHE see Farkas, Ferenc

VARIAZIONI E ALLEGRO see Lang, Istvan

VARIAZIONI SUL CARNEVALE DI VENEZIA see Mortari, Virgilio

VÄRLDEN GENOM VÄRLDAR see Ekström, Lars

VASKS, PETERIS (1946-    )
Balsis
see Symphony for Strings

Concerto for English Horn
2(pic).2.2.2. 2.0.0.0. timp,perc, strings,English horn solo [20'] (available in USA & Canada through G. Schirmer) SCHOTTS perf mat rent                    (V52)

Concerto for Violoncello and Orchestra
2(alto fl)+pic.2.2.2. 4.3.3.1. timp,3perc,pno,cel,harp,strings, vcl solo [33'] SCHOTTS perf mat rent                    (V53)

Lauda
3(pic,alto fl).3.3(bass clar).3. 4.3.3.1. timp,4perc,pno,harp, strings [21'] SCHOTTS perf mat rent                    (V54)

Message
see Vestijums

Symphony for Strings
"Balsis" string orch [27'] study sc SCHOTTS ED 8032 perf mat rent                    (V55)

Vestijums
"Message" 4perc,2pno,strings [14'] (co-published with Sikorski) study sc SCHOTTS SIK. ED. 1826                    (V56)

VASS, LAJOS (1927-    )
Este A Táborban
see Evening In The Camp

Evening In The Camp
"Este A Táborban" 2.2(English horn).2(bass clar).2. 4.3.3.1. timp,perc,harp,strings [14'] EMB rent                    (V57)

Merry Music
"Vidám Zene" 2(pic).2(English horn).2.2. 4.3.3.1. timp,perc, harp,strings [13'] EMB rent (V58)

Vidám Zene
see Merry Music

VASSILENKO, SERGEY (1872-1956)
Concerto for Balalaika and Orchestra, Op. 63
2.2.2.2. 2.2.0.0. timp,perc,harp, strings,balalaika solo [22'] SIKORSKI perf mat rent                    (V59)

VATTEN see Hultqvist, Anders

VAUGHAN WILLIAMS, RALPH (1872-1958)
Fantasia On A Theme By Thomas Tallis
BROUDE BR.                    (V60)

Fantasia On "Greensleeves"
(Stone) 2fl/S rec&A rec,ob,2clar, bsn,2horn,gtr,pno/harp,strings [4'] OXFORD sc 3690551 f.s., set 380090X f.s.                    (V61)

London Symphony
orch sc DOVER 29263-0                    (V62)

March Past Of The Kitchen Utensils
orch sc FABER 51416 2 f.s.                    (V63)

Six Studies In English Folk Song
(Foster, Arnold) 2.1.2.2. 0.0.0.0. harp/pno,strings, solo instrument [9'] (solo parts available for sale: bashn, bsn, clar, engh, saxa, tba, vln, vla, vcl) sc,pts STAINER H301 rent                    (V64)
(Stanton, Robert) string quar/ string orch,English horn/alto sax [9'] (solo parts available for sale) STAINER rent sc H176, pt H166                    (V65)

Three Preludes On Welsh Hymn Tunes
2.1.2.2. 2.2.0.0. timp,perc,strings [15'] perf sc set OXFORD 3694514 sc,pts rent                    (V66)

Two Preludes Founded On Welsh Hymn Tunes
(Foster, Arnold) 2.2.2.2. 2.2.0.0. timp,strings [7'] ("Rhosymedre" &

VAUGHAN WILLIAMS, RALPH (cont'd.)

"Hyfrydol", may be performed with strings alone) pts STAINER HL297 rent                    (V67)

VCERA-DNES-ZÍTRA see Fiala, Jiri Julius

VEA, KETIL (1932-    )
Concerto for Tuba and Orchestra
3(pic).3(English horn).2.2. 4.3.3.0. timp,perc,glock,strings, tuba solo [21'] NORSKMI                    (V68)

Mjøsdronningen
2(pic).2.2.2. 4.3.2.0. timp,perc, strings,pno solo [9'] NORSKMI                    (V69)

Nordlandet For Sopran Solo, Resitasjon Og Orkester
[Norw] 2(pic).2.2(bass clar).2. 4.2.2.0. timp,perc,pno,strings [32'] (text by Kjell Sandvik) NORSKMI                    (V70)

Serenade
string orch,bsn solo [3'30"] NORSKMI                    (V71)

Tempi Passati
2.2.2.2. 4.2.2.1. timp,perc,strings [15'] NORSKMI                    (V72)

VECNE MLADÉ VENUŠE see Brabec, Jindrich

VECNY DUEL see Vacek, Miloš

VECNY NARAT see Petrzelka, Vilém

VÉCSEY, JENO (1909-1966)
Concert Symphonique; In Memoriam Gyula Krúdy
2+pic.2+English horn.2+bass clar.2+ contrabsn. 4.3.2.1. 3timp,perc, 2harp,cel,pno,strings [42'] EMB rent                    (V73)

VED KOMETHODET see Thommessen, Olav Anton

VEDRAI, CARINO see Mozart, Wolfgang Amadeus

VEILS AND IMAGES see Tanner, David

VEITSTANZ see Hiller, Wilfried

VELDHUIS, JACOB TER (1951-    )
Concerto for Piano and String Orchestra, Op. 63
[25'] sc DONEMUS                    (V74)

VELICANIE see Shchedrin, Rodion

VEM SOBRE OS MARES see Ketting, Otto, Kom, Over De Zeeën

VENATIC CHRONICLE see Thompson, Bruce A.

VENDETTA, OH, LA VENDETTA, LA see Mozart, Wolfgang Amadeus

VENETIAN MIRRORS see Clarke, Nigel

VENEZIA see Kálik, Vaclav

VENI REDEMPTOR GENTIUM see Scheck, Helmut

VENI SANCTE SPIRITUS see Dunstable, John

VENI SPONSA CHRISTI see Kopriva, Karel Blazej

VENI, VENI, EMMANUEL see Macmillan, James

VENT DES MOTS QU' L' N'A PAS DITS, LE see Tarnopolsky, Vladimir

VENTANA ABIERTA see Aponte-Ledee, Rafael

VENTRILOQUIST see Emmerik, Ivo Van

VENUS see Sugár, M.

VER TEMTO DNÚM see Jonák, Zdenek

VERA see Knaifel, Alexander

VERBESSELT, AUGUSTE (1919-    )
Concerto
marimba,vibra,strings,ob solo [17'] BELGE                    (V75)

Dubbel Concerto
3.2.0.2. 4.3.3.0. 3perc,cel,harp, strings,clar&bass clar soli [16'] BELGE                    (V76)

VERBEY, THEO (1959-    )
  Notturno
    0.1.0.0. 2.0.0.0. strings [12'] sc
    DONEMUS                        (V77)

  Pavane Oubliée
    string orch,harp [10'] sc DONEMUS
                                  (V78)
  Triade
    2.2.2.2. 2.0.0.0. perc,harp,strings
    [20'] sc DONEMUS              (V79)

VERBUGT, ERIC
  En Al Luisterend...
    1.1.1.1. 1.1.1.0. 2perc,harp,pno,
    strings [8'] sc DONEMUS       (V80)

VERDANT MUSIC see Torke, Michael, Green

VERDI, GIUSEPPE (1813-1901)
  Aïda, Act III: Air Du Nil
    3.1.2.1. 4.0.0.0. timp,strings,S
    solo LEDUC                    (V81)

  Aïda: Ô Céleste Aïda
    3.2.2.2. 3.2.3.0. strings,T solo
    [4'30"] LEDUC                 (V82)

  Giovanna D'Arco: Sinfonia
    2+pic.2.2.2. 4.2.3.1. perc,strings
    [12'] BOCCACCINI BS. 175 rent
                                  (V83)

VERDI-MOMENT see Schnebel, Dieter

VERDIANA see Rieti, Vittorio

VERETTI, ANTONIO (1900-1978)
  Fantasy for Clarinet
    1+pic.1+English horn.1+bass clar.1.
    1.1.1.1. timp,cel,vibra,xylo,
    harp,pno,strings,clar solo [14']
    LEDUC                         (V84)

VERGESSENE MELODIE see Eisbrenner,
  Werner

VERGINE DEL SOLE, LA see Cimarosa,
  Domenico

VERGNÜGLICHE ETÜDEN FÜR
  STREICHORCHESTER see Thomas-Mifune,
  Werner

VERGOSSEN UND VERGESSEN see
  Schultheiss, Ulrich

VERHAEGEN, MARC
  Concerto In Honorem Baldvini Regis
    2.1.2.1. 2.2.1.0. timp,perc,
    strings,vcl solo [21'] BELGE
                                  (V85)
  Concerto No. 2 for Piano and
    Orchestra
    2.2.2.2. 2.1.1.0. timp,perc,
    strings,pno solo [25'] BELGE
                                  (V86)

VERI see Lee, William Franklin

VERIFICAZIONE see Dubrovay, Laszlo

VERK see Lidholm, Ingvar

VERLIEBTER KATER (TANGO) see Thomas-
  Mifune, Werner

VERLOBUNG IN SAN DOMINGO, DIE see
  Eötvös, Jószef

VERLOR ICH DEN VATER see Mozart,
  Wolfgang Amadeus, Se Il Padre
  Perdei

VERMEULEN, MATTHIJS (1888-1967)
  Prélude À La Nouvelle Journée
    see Symphony No. 2

  Symphonia Carminum
    see Symphony No. 1

  Symphony No. 1
    "Symphonia Carminum" 3.3.5.3.
    4.4.3.1. timp,4perc,2harp,strings
    [26'] sc DONEMUS              (V87)

  Symphony No. 2
    "Prélude À La Nouvelle Journée"
    4.4.6.4. 4.6.3.1. timp,4perc,
    xylo,2harp,strings [23'] sc
    DONEMUS                       (V88)

VERNAL SHOWERS see Dillon, James

VERRA LA MORTE (ARIETTE NO.3) see
  Coria, Miguel Angel

VERS 210 MILLIARDS DE SOUVENIRS EN
  QUÊTE DE BOIS DE ROSE see Dion,
  Denis

VERS LES ÂMES see Badian, Maya

VERSCHWIEGENDE NACHTIGALL, DIE see
  Grieg, Edvard Hagerup

VERSCHWINDEN, DAS see Vustin, Alexander

VERSE TO THE TOREADOR SONG see Proto,
  Frank

VERSTELWERK see Janssen, Guus

VERSUCHE I see Schnebel, Dieter,
  Analysis

VERSUNKENE GLOCKE, DIE: PRELUDE TO ACT
  5 see Zöllner, Heinrich, Versunkene
  Glocke, Die: Rautendeleins Leid

VERSUNKENE GLOCKE, DIE: RAUTENDELEINS
  LEID see Zöllner, Heinrich

VERZAUBERTE SEE, DER see Liadov, Anatol
  Konstantinovich

VESELY PRÍBEH see Svehla, Antonin

VESTIJUMS see Vasks, Peteris

VETA PRO ORCHESTR see Stárek, Jiri

VETRATE DI CHIESA see Respighi,
  Ottorino

VIA DOLOROSA see Danev, Miroslav

VIACOLI IN OMBRA see Nieminen, Kai

VIAGGIO see Valkare, Gunnar

VICAR, JAN (1949-    )
  Cesta Ke Slunci
    3.2.2.3. 4.3.3.1. timp,perc,strings
    [12'] CESKY HUD.              (V89)

  Hudba Pro Smycce A Tympány (Music for
    Strings and Timpani)
    strings,timp [20'] CESKY HUD. (V90)

  Music for Strings and Timpani
    see Hudba Pro Smycce A Tympány

VICTOR see Korndorf, Nicolai

VID see Ed, Fredrik

VID EN VG: MUSIK see Larsson, Hokan

VIDÁM INDULÓ see Szervanszky, Endre,
  Merry March

VIDÁM KIS NYITÁNY see Vincze, Ottó,
  Merry Ouverture

VIDÁM ZENE see Kadosa, Pal, Merry Music
  see Vass, Lajos, Merry Music

VIDOVSZKY, LASZLO (1944-    )
  405
    1.1.1.1. 1.1.1.0. org,strings,pno
    solo [25'50"] EMB rent        (V91)

  Fragments
    "Toredékek" 2+pic.2+English
    horn.3(clar in E flat,bass
    clar).3(contrabsn). 4.3.3.1.
    timp,perc,harp,strings [5'] EMB
    rent                          (V92)

  Induló A Zászlók Bevonulásához
    see March To The Procession Of
    Flags

  March To The Procession Of Flags
    "Induló A Zászlók Bevonulásához"
    3.3.3.0. 4.3.3.1. perc,7vln I,
    6vln II,5vla,5vcl,4db [10'] EMB
    rent                          (V93)

  Music For Györ
    "Zene Györnek" 1+pic.1+English
    horn.2(bass clar).2(contrabsn).
    4.2.2.0. timp,perc,pno,strings
    [7'] EMB rent                 (V94)

  Romantic Reading: 2nd Version
    "Romantikus Olvasmány II: Változat"
    2.2(English horn).2(bass clar).1.
    2.0.0.0. strings, (2, 1, 1, 1)
    [10'] EMB rent                (V95)

  Romantikus Olvasmány II: Változat
    see Romantic Reading: 2nd Version

  Toredékek
    see Fragments

  Zene Györnek
    see Music For Györ

VIE PARISIENNE, LA: OVERTURE see
  Offenbach, Jacques

VIE PARISIENNE, LA: QUADRILLE see
  Offenbach, Jacques

VIEILLES CHANSONS see DuBois, Pierre-
  Max

VIENDRA L'AUBE see Gibbs, Alan

VIER BAUERNTÄNZE see Wolf, Hans

VIER CANZONEN see Custer, Laurenz

VIER GESÄNGE AUS BRECHTS "SCHWEYK" see
  Cornell, Klaus

VIER INVENTIONEN, FOR CHAMBER ORCHESTRA
  see Grabovsky, Leonid

VIER JAHRESZEITEN, DIE see Vivaldi,
  Antonio

VIER KONTRETÄNZE see Mozart, Wolfgang
  Amadeus

VIER MENUETTE see Mozart, Wolfgang
  Amadeus

VIER MONOLOGE AUF VERSE VON PUSCHKIN
  see Shostakovich, Dmitri

VIER ORCHESTERSTÜCKE see Bruckner,
  Anton

VIER SÄTZE see Thomass, Eugen C.

VIER SUITEN see Locke, Matthew

VIERGE, LA see Massenet, Jules

VIERJÄHRIGE POSTEN, DER see Reinecke,
  Carl

VIERTE NORDISCHE SUITE see Hamerik,
  Asger

VIISI HÄMÄLÄISTÄ KANSANLAULUA JOUSIORK
  see Raitio, Väinö

VIJF CONCERTPRELUDEN, OP. 44 see Coryn,
  R.

VILLA-LOBOS, HEITOR (1887-1959)
  Cancao Do Poeta Do Seculo XVIII
    "Song Of The 18th Century Poet"
    2.1(clar).2.0. 4.0.1.1. timp,
    harp,strings [3'] PEER rent (V96)

  Song Of The 18th Century Poet
    see Cancao Do Poeta Do Seculo XVIII

VILLANCICOS Y CANCIONES DE NAVIDAD see
  Rodrigo, Joaquín

VILLETTE, PIERRE (1926-1969)
  Poem
    clar,string orch [5'40"] LEDUC
                                  (V97)

VILLI, LE, TREGENDA see Puccini,
  Giacomo

VINCZE, IMRE (1926-1969)
  Sinfonia No. 1
    2(pic).2(English horn).2(bass
    clar).2. 4.3.3.1. timp,perc,harp,
    strings [25'] EMB rent        (V98)

  Sinfonia No. 2
    3(pic).3(English horn).2(bass
    clar).2. 4.3.3.1. timp,perc,
    strings [25'] EMB rent        (V99)

VINCZE, OTTÓ
  Merry Ouverture
    "Vidám Kis Nyitány" 2.2.2.2.
    4.2.0.0. timp,perc,harp,strings
    EMB rent                     (V100)

  Vidám Kis Nyitány
    see Merry Ouverture

VINGEL see Hedelin, Fredrik

VINGSLAG see Bohlin, Jonas

VINICNÉ ŠUMICE see Mojzis, Vojtech

VINOHRADSKY VALCÍK see Rimón, Jan

VINTERMUSIK see Larsson, Hokan

VINTERRESA see Jeverud, Johan

VINTERTRDGRDEN see Hultqvist, Anders

VIOLET, THE see Delius, Frederick

VIOLIN CONCERTI AND SINFONIA
  CONCERTANTE see Mozart, Wolfgang
  Amadeus

VIOLONCELLES, VIBREZ! see Sollima,
  Giovanni

VIRELAI see Cardy, Patrick

VIRTUE see Panufnik, Roxanna

VIRVELPOLSKA see Koch, Erland von

VISAGES OUBLIEES see Perna, Dana Paul

VISION AND A JOURNEY, A see Matthews, David

VISION AT THE CROSS ROAD see El-Dabh, Halim

VISION IN TWILIGHT see Nishimura, Akira

VISION OF PIERS THE PLOUGHMAN, THE: SUITE see Berkeley, Michael

VISIONEN see Hummel, Bertold see Kühnl, Claus

VISIONS see Brady, Timothy see Kelemen, Milko see Takemitsu, Toru

VISITATIO SEPULCHRI see Macmillan, James

VISKUP, ANTON (1953-    )
Koncertní Kus
2.2.2.2. 4.3.3.1. timp,perc,xylo, strings,clar solo [13'] CESKY HUD.                                    (V101)

VISMAN, BART
Orchestrales
3.3.3.3. 4.3.3.1. timp,6perc,harp, pno,strings [17'] sc DONEMUS                              (V102)

VITA, LA see Zechlin, Ruth

VITA, UNA see Stepka, Karel Vaclav

VITALI, TOMMASO ANTONIO (ca. 1663-1745)
Chaconne
(Dupin, Marc-Olivier) string orch, vln solo [11'] BILLAUDOT     (V103)

VITASEK, JAN AUGUST (1770-1839)
Minuet
2.2.2.2. 2.0.0.0. timp,strings [16'] CESKY HUD.              (V104)

Sinfonia in C
2.2.2.2. 2.2.0.0. timp,strings [31'] CESKY HUD.              (V105)

VÍTEZNÁ see Deváty, Antonín

VÍTEZNÁ PERLA see Vostrák, Zbynek

VIVA LUCERO see Proto, Frank

VIVALDI, ANTONIO (1678-1741)
Cantate Per Contralto
(Degrada) orch,A solo sc RICORDI-IT PR 1346                       (V106)

Cantate Per Soprano, Vol. 1
(Degrada) orch,S solo sc RICORDI-IT PR 1344                       (V107)

Cantate Per Soprano, Vol. 2
(Degrada; Heller) orch,S solo sc RICORDI-IT PR 1345           (V108)

Concerto
(Casella) INTERNAT.S.          (V109)

Concerto for Bassoon, Continuo and Strings in C minor, No. 40, RV 978
(Rønnes, Robert) string orch,cont, bsn solo NORSKMI          (V110)

Concerto for Bassoon, String Orchestra and Continuo in A minor, P. 72
(Hara) bsn solo,string orch,cont pno-cond sc KUNZELMANN 10021                            (V111)

Concerto for Flute, String Orchestra and Continuo in D, P. 205
(Braun) fl solo,string orch,cont pno-cond sc KUNZELMANN 10010                            (V112)

Concerto for Flute, Strings and Continuo in D, RV 783, F.VI no. 17
(Heller) sc RICORDI-IT PR 1339                              (V113)

Concerto for Oboe, Bassoon, String Orchestra and Continuo in G, Op. 42, No. 3
ob,bsn,string orch,cont KUNZELMANN 10011                        (V114)

Concerto for Oboe, RV 462, F.VII no. 19, in A minor
orch,ob solo study sc SCHIRM.G 50482439                       (V115)

Concerto for Oboe, String Orchestra and Continuo in C, P. 41
(Lampert) ob solo,string orch,cont pno-cond sc KUNZELMANN 10071                            (V116)

Concerto for Oboe, String Orchestra and Continuo in C, P. 44
(Károly) ob solo,string orch,cont pno-cond sc KUNZELMANN 10056                            (V117)

VIVALDI, ANTONIO (cont'd.)
Concerto for Oboe, String Orchestra and Continuo in F, P. 318
(Balla) ob solo,string orch,cont KUNZELMANN 10062            (V118)

Concerto for Oboe, Strings and Continuo in D, P. 187
(Braun) ob solo,strings,cont pno-cond sc KUNZELMANN 10032   (V119)

Concerto for 2 Oboes, String Orchestra and Continuo in C, P. 85
2ob,string orch,cont pno-cond sc KUNZELMANN 10074            (V120)

Concerto for String Orchestra in D minor, Op. 54, No. 1, P. 86 "Madrigalesco" string orch pno-cond sc KUNZELMANN 10049          (V121)

Concerto for Violin and Orchestra in G minor, RV 319
(Eller, R.) 0.2.0.1. 0.0.0.0. strings,cont,vln solo [11'] BREITKOPF-W                      (V122)

Concerto for Violin, Strings and Continuo, Op. 8, Nos. 1-4 "Quattro Stagioni, Le" pts RICORDI-IT 137301                       (V123)
(Everett; Talbot) "Quattro Stagioni, Le" sc RICORDI-IT 137300                       (V124)

Concerto for 2 Violins, String Orchestra and Continuo in A, Op. 3, No. 5, P. 212
(Eller) 2vln,string orch,cont pno-cond sc KUNZELMANN 10009  (V125)

Concerto for 2 Violins, String Orchestra and Continuo in B flat, P. 390
(Berlász) 2vln,string orch,cont KUNZELMANN 10037             (V126)

Concerto for 3 Violins, String Orchestra and Continuo in F, P. 278
(Károly) 3vln,string orch,cont KUNZELMANN 10036             (V127)

Concerto for 2 Violoncelli, String Orchestra and Continuo in G minor, P. 411
(Schroeder) 2vcl,string orch,cont KUNZELMANN 10060          (V128)

Concerto for Violoncello and String Orchestra
(Scheck, Helmut) "Concerto Nach Einer Violoncello-Sonate E-Moll" strings,cont,vcl solo BOHM    (V129)

Concerto for Violoncello, String Orchestra and Continuo in C, RV 399
vcl solo,string orch,cont KUNZELMANN ipa sc 10176A, oct 10176                         (V130)

Concerto for Violoncello, String Orchestra and Continuo in G, P. 120
(Fodor) vcl solo,string orch,cont pno-cond sc KUNZELMANN 10082                            (V131)

Concerto Grosso in B minor, Op. 3, No. 10, RV 580
strings,cont,4vln soli [10'] BREITKOPF-W                     (V132)

Concerto in A minor
see Deux Concertos Inédits P. Violon Et Cord

Concerto in E flat
see Deux Concertos Inédits P. Violon Et Cord

Concerto Nach Einer Violoncello-Sonate E-Moll
see Concerto for Violoncello and String Orchestra

Concerto No. 1
see Vier Jahreszeiten, Die

Concerto No. 2
see Vier Jahreszeiten, Die

Concerto No. 3
see Vier Jahreszeiten, Die

Concerto No. 4
see Vier Jahreszeiten, Die

Concerto, RV 761, in C minor
string orch,hpsd,vln solo (Amato Bene) perf sc set OXFORD 3679736 sc,pts rent                  (V133)

VIVALDI, ANTONIO (cont'd.)
Concerto, RV 780, in A
hpsd,strings [10'] sc OXFORD 3857693 f.s., ipa               (V134)

Deux Concertos Inédits P. Violon Et Cord
(Blanchard) strings,vln solo BOIS f.s.
contains: Concerto in A minor; Concerto in E flat, "De Naples"                     (V135)

Four Seasons
orch sc DOVER 28638-X          (V136)

Four Seasons, The
see Quattro Stagioni, Le

Madrigalesco
see Concerto for String Orchestra in D minor, Op. 54, No. 1, P. 86

Quattro Stagioni, Le
(Hogwood, Christopher) "Four Seasons, The" perf sc set OXFORD 3679698 sc,pts rent           (V137)
see Concerto for Violin, Strings and Continuo, Op. 8, Nos. 1-4

Serenate, 2
(Everett; Talbot) orch fac ed RICORDI-IT 136681              (V138)

Sinfonia in G
orch study sc SCHIRM.G 50482436                       (V139)

Sonata in E flat
(Guyot, D.) string orch,hpsd,2trp soli [11'] BILLAUDOT       (V140)

Vier Jahreszeiten, Die *Op.8
(Launchbury, Simon; Salter, Lionel) vln,string orch,cont sc,pno red, solo pt,pts SCHOTT ea.
contains: Concerto No. 1, "Frühling, Der"; Concerto No. 2, "Sommer, Der"; Concerto No. 3, "Herbst, Der"; Concerto No. 4, "Winter, Der"           (V141)

VIVANT WESTMANNIAE see Långström, Olle

VIVAT CARLSCRONA see Necksten, Gärt, Festmarsch

VIVAT OLYMPIA see Smetácek, Václav

VIVAT STUDENTES see Bartoš, Jan Zdenek

VIVIER, CLAUDE (1948-1983)
Deva Et Asura
1.1.1.1. 2.2.1.1. strings sc CANADIAN MI 1200 V862DE      (V142)

Orion
3(pic).3(English horn).3(clar in E flat).3. 4.2.2.1. 3perc,harp, 12vln I,10vln II,10vla,8vcl,6db [13'] sc CANADIAN MI 1100 V8620                         (V143)
3(pic).3(English horn).3(clar in E flat).3. 4.2.2.1. 3perc,16vln I, 14vln II,10vla,10vcl,8db sc CANADIAN MI 1100 V8620R   (V144)

VIVRE D'AMOUR see Tcherepnin, Alexander

VIXEN (A-VIXEN-A) see Hoyland, Victor

VIZE see Riedlbauch, Vaclav

VLACH-VRUTICKY, JOSEF (1897-1977)
Impromptu for Orchestra, Op. 56
3.2.2.2. 4.2.3.0. timp,perc,strings [10'] CESKY HUD.         (V145)

Moments Musicaux *Op.129
3.2.2.2. 4.2.3.0. timp,perc,strings [36'] CESKY HUD.         (V146)

Národní Tance I-XII
3.2.2.2. 4.2.3.0. timp,perc,strings [112'] CESKY HUD.        (V147)

Suite De Ballet *Op.61
3.2.2.2. 4.2.3.0. timp,perc,harp, strings CESKY HUD.         (V148)

VLNOBITÍ see Smolka, Martin

VOCALISE see Rachmaninoff, Sergey Vassilievich

VOCHT, LODEWIJK DE (1887-1977)
Concerto
2.2.2.2. 4.2.3.0. timp,strings,vcl solo [26'] BELGE          (V149)

Serenade
strings,vcl solo [4'20"] BELGE                              (V150)

VODRAZKA, KAREL (1904-1985)
Avignonsky Most
2.2.2.2. 4.2.3.0. perc,strings
CESKY HUD. (V151)

Blatácké Tance c. 1 a 2
2.2.2.2. 4.2.3.0. timp,perc,strings
[8'] CESKY HUD. (V152)

Ctyri Lidové Písne
2.2.1.2. 4.2.3.0. timp,perc,strings
CESKY HUD. (V153)

Detsky Valcík
2.2.2.1. 2.1.0.0. timp,perc,strings
[4'] CESKY HUD. (V154)

Dve Chodské Písne
2.2.1.2. 2.0.0.0. strings CESKY
HUD. (V155)

Dyz Sem (from Chodska)
2.2.2.2. 3.2.1.1. strings [2']
CESKY HUD. (V156)

Kašpárek
see Klaun

Klaun
"Kašpárek" 2.2.2.2. 3.2.1.0. perc,
strings CESKY HUD. (V157)

Na Tom Našem Dvore -- Husar
2.2.2.2. 4.2.3.0. timp,perc,strings
CESKY HUD. (V158)

Pochod
2.2.2.1. 3.2.1.0. perc,strings [4']
CESKY HUD. (V159)

Polka
see Šmikovanda

Prvosenka
2.2.2.2. 3.2.1.0. timp,perc,strings
[8'] CESKY HUD. (V160)

Ráda, Ráda
2.2.2.2. 3.2.1.0. timp,strings
CESKY HUD. (V161)

Šest Ruskych Tancu
2.2.2.1. 2.1.0.0. timp,perc,strings
[8'] CESKY HUD. (V162)

Šmikovanda (Polka)
2.2.2.2. 3.2.1.0. timp,strings
CESKY HUD. (V163)

Tri Lidové Písne
2.2.2.1. 2.1.0.0. timp,perc,
strings,Bar solo CESKY HUD. (V164)

Variace Na Moravskou Lidovou Písen
2.2.2.1. 3.1.1.0. timp,perc,strings
[9'] CESKY HUD. (V165)

VOGEL, W.
Concertino for Flute and String
Orchestra
fl solo,string orch sc,pts
KUNZELMANN GM 917 ipa (V166)

VOGEL-STRAUSS-RALLY see Thomas-Mifune,
Werner

VOICE LINES see Freedman, Harry

VOICE OF THE WINTER, THE see Meijering,
Cord

VOICES FROM THE ENVIRONMENT see
Ichiyanagi, Toshi

VOICES FROM THE GALLERY see Paulus,
Stephen Harrison

VOICES OF SPRING see Strauss, Johann,
[Jr.], Frühlingstimmen

VOICES: SKETCH FOR ORCHESTRA see
Asheim, Nils Henrik, Stemmer:
Sketch For Orchestra

VOICI LE NOTAIRES see Offenbach,
Jacques

VOIE LACTÉE Ô SOEUR LUMINEUSE see
Henze, Hans Werner

VOIGTLÄNDER, LOTHAR (1943- )
Concerto for Flute, Violin and
Orchestra
2.2.2.2. 1.3.3.0. timp,2perc,cel,
harp,8vln I,7vln II,6vla,5vcl,4db
[21'] sc PETERS 03318 (V167)

Harfensinfonie (Sinfonia No. 2)
3.3.3.3. 4.4.4.1. timp,3perc,pno,
cel,8vln I,7vln II,6vla,5vcl,4db,
harp solo [32'] sc PETERS 04030
(V168)

Memento: Hommage A Schostakowitsch
3.3.3.3. 4.4.4.1. timp,4perc,pno,
8vln I,7vln II,6vla,5vcl,4db
[12'] sc PETERS 01352 (V169)

VOIGTLÄNDER, LOTHAR (cont'd.)

Orgelsinfonie (Salzauer Sinfonie)
see Sinfonia No. 3

Overture
3.2.3.2. 3.3.3.0. timp,perc,harp,
pno,strings [7'] PETERS (V170)

Sinfonia No. 2
see Harfensinfonie

Sinfonia No. 3
"Orgelsinfonie (Salzauer Sinfonie)"
2.2.2.2. 3.3.3.1. 4timp,3perc,
cembalo,harp,8vln I,7vln II,6vla,
5vcl,4db,org solo [26'] sc PETERS
02207 (V171)

Tänzerische Suite
3.2.3.2. 3.3.3.0. timp,perc,pno,
harp,8vln I,7vln II,6vla,5vcl,4db
[21'] sc PETERS 04124 (V172)

VOILES see Debussy, Claude

VOKÁLNÍ POEMA see Bohác, Josef

VOKÁLNÍ SYMFONIE see Ištvan, Miloslav

VOLBACH, FRITZ (1861-1940)
Alt Heidelberg, Du Feine *Op.29
2+pic.2.2.2. 4.3.3.1. timp,3perc,
harp,strings [10'] BREITKOPF-W
(V173)
Es Waren Zwei Königskinder *Op.21
2+pic.2+English horn.2+bass clar.2.
4.3.3.1. timp,3perc,harp,strings
[17'] (symphonic poem) BREITKOPF-
W (V174)

VOLEJNICEK, DRAHOSLAV (1934- )
Kdyz Pláce Tráva
fl,sax,trp,perc,gtr,bass gtr,
strings,trom solo,elec pno,
polymoog [4'] (for jazz
orchestra) CESKY HUD. (V175)

VÖLKER, TONI
Nomos-Gegebild
1.0.1.1. 1.1.1.0. perc,harp,pno,
strings SEESAW (V176)

Nomos-Gegenbild
chamber orch TONOS M-2015-3975-1
(V177)

VOLKMANN, ROBERT (1815-1883)
Hungarian Sketches
(Buttykay) 2.2+English horn.2+bass
clar.2. 4.3.3.1. timp,perc,
strings EMB rent (V178)

Overture in C, Op. Posth.
2.2.2.2. 2.2.0.0. timp,strings [9']
BREITKOPF-W (V179)

VOLKSMELODIEN UND TÄNZE AUS FINNLAND
see Godzinsky, George De

VON MEINER JUGEND see Ullmann, Viktor,
Symphony No. 1, Op. 45

VON MENSCHLICHEN SCHWÄCHEN see Neubert,
Günter

VONICKA MILOSTNÉHO KVÍTÍ see Sedlácek,
Bohuslav

VOR BARNDOMS VENNER see Wellejus,
Henning, Freunde Aus Unsern
Kinderjahren

VOR DEM VERLASSEN see Kalson, Romuald

VORLOVÁ, SLÁVA (1894-1973)
Concerto for Bass Clarinet and
Strings, Op. 50
[22'] CESKY HUD. (V180)

Fantasy for Violoncello and
Orchestra, Op. 6
3.3.3.2. 4.2.3.1. timp,perc,harp,
cel,strings,vcl solo [14'] CESKY
HUD. (V181)

Korelace *Op.75
strings,bass clar&pno soli CESKY
HUD. (V182)

Symphony, Op. 18
3.3.3.2. 4.4.3.1. timp,perc,2harp,
strings [30'] CESKY HUD. (V183)

VOSÍ HNÍZDO see Jindra, Alfons

VOSTRÁK, ZBYNEK (1920-1985)
Concerto for Piano and Orchestra, Op.
66
see Vítezná Perla

Kapesní Vesmír *Op.62
strings,fl&cimbalom soli [16']
CESKY HUD. (V184)

VOSTRÁK, ZBYNEK (cont'd.)

Krystaly *Op.65
perc,strings,English horn solo
[13'] CESKY HUD. (V185)

Parabola Pro Orchestr *Op.55
3.3.3.3. 4.3.3.1. strings,
electronic tape [12'] CESKY HUD.
(V186)

Variations for Orchestra, Op. 61
5.3.4.2. 4.3.4.1. timp,perc,cel,
strings [30'] CESKY HUD. (V187)

Vítezná Perla (Concerto for Piano and
Orchestra, Op. 66)
3.2.3.2. 4.3.3.1. perc,strings,pno
solo [23'] CESKY HUD. (V188)

VOYAGE see Bailey, Judith

VOYAGE, THE see Barker, Paul

VOYAGE DANS LA LUNE, LE see Offenbach,
Jacques

VOYAGE DANS LA LUNE: OVERTURE see
Offenbach, Jacques

VOYAGE EN TORTILLARD see DuBois,
Pierre-Max

VOYAGE THAT JOHNNY NEVER KNEW, THE see
Proto, Frank

VOYAGEUR, LE see Faure, Gabriel-Urbain

VOYANTS see Kolb, Barbara

VRÁNA, JAN (1940- )
Concerto for Piano and Strings
CESKY HUD. (V189)

Symfonie-Koncert
2.2.0.2. 4.0.2.1. timp,perc,
strings,clar&trp&pno soli CESKY
HUD. (V190)

VRANICKY, ANTONÍN
see WRANITZKY, ANTON

VRANICKY, PAVEL
see WRANITZKY, PAUL

VRIDLA see Stepanek, Jiri

VRIEND, JAN N.M. (1938- )
Hallelujah I, A Symphony Of The North
4.4.4.4. 6.4.4.2. 2perc,strings,
bass clar solo [35'] sc DONEMUS
(V191)
Overture ... De Origen Volcánico
2.2.2.2. 4.2.3.0. 2perc,strings
[8'] sc DONEMUS (V192)

VUATAZ, ROGER (1898-1988)
Fantasy Nos. 1-3 for Harp and
Orchestra, Op. 123
INTERNAT.S. sc,pts rent, pno red
(V193)

VUSTIN, ALEXANDER (1943- )
Concerto for Percussion and Chamber
Orchestra
see Hommage À Beethoven

Fantasy for Violin and Orchestra
0.1.0.1. 1.1.0.0. 3perc,pno,
strings,vln solo [12'] SIKORSKI
perf mat rent (V194)

Heimkehr, Die
[Russ] horn,2perc,2pno,4vln,2vla,
2vcl, amplified baritone solo
[13'] (texts by Schtschedrowizki)
SIKORSKI perf mat rent (V195)

Hommage À Beethoven (Concerto for
Percussion and Chamber Orchestra)
1.1.1.1. 1.0.0.0. 7perc,opt
synthesizer,strings [20']
SIKORSKI perf mat rent (V196)

In Memoriam Boris Klusner
string orch,Bar solo [5'] SIKORSKI
perf mat rent (V197)

Verschwinden, Das
string orch,vln solo, bajan-
accordion solo [12'] SIKORSKI
perf mat rent (V198)

VYCHODOSLOVENSKÉ LIDOVÉ PÍSNE see
Hlaváč, Miroslav

VYHNA see Filas, Juraj, Symphonia
"Vampa"

VYLET DO HOR see Saudek, Vojtech

VYLETEL SOKOL see Petr, Zdenek

VYZNÁNÍ see Sluka, Luboš

VZDUŠNOU CAROU see Strasek, Emil

VZLÍNÁNI see Kurz, Ivan

VZPOMINKA see Bazant, Jiri see Sluka, Luboš

VZPOMÍNKA NA BALCIK see Krízek, Zdenek

VZPOMÍNKA NA J. M. see Popelka, Vladimir

VZPOMINKA NA JOSEFA HLINOMAZE see Chaun, František

# W

WA WA MOZART see Lloyd, Jonathan

WACHSENDE BEDROHUNG see Marti, Heinz

WACHTELSCHLAG, DER see Beethoven, Ludwig van

WAFFENSCHMIED, DER: BRINGT EILIG HUT UND MANTEL MIR see Lortzing, (Gustav) Albert

WAFFENSCHMIED, DER: MARIE'S ARIA see Lortzing, (Gustav) Albert, Waffenschmied, Der: Wir Armen, Armen Mädchen

WAFFENSCHMIED, DER: STADINGER'S ARIA see Lortzing, (Gustav) Albert, Waffenschmied, Der: Bringt Eilig Hut Und Mantel Mir

WAFFENSCHMIED, DER: WIR ARMEN, ARMEN MÄDCHEN see Lortzing, (Gustav) Albert

WAGEMANS, PETER-JAN (1952-    )
Draak, Het Huis, De Zon, De Boom En De Vijver, De
3.3.3.3. 4.3.3.0. 3perc,pno, strings,horn&trp&trom&tuba soli [24'] sc DONEMUS    (W1)

Dreams (What Did The Last Dinosaur Dream Of?)
3.3.3.3. 4.3.4.1. timp,2perc,cel, opt org,strings [16'] sc DONEMUS    (W2)

Muziek IV
1.1.1.1. 1.1.1.0. perc,2pno,strings [40'] sc DONEMUS    (W3)

Requiem
string orch,1-2perc,pno [12'] sc DONEMUS    (W4)

Rosebud (The Last Forest)
3.3.3.3. 2.3.3.1+2Wagner tuba. 5perc,strings [12'] sc DONEMUS    (W5)

Stad En De Engel, De
3.3.3.3. 4.2.3.1. 4perc,harp,pno, strings [14'] sc DONEMUS    (W6)

Walk On Water
1.1.1.1. 2.0.1.1. perc,pno,strings, piccolo trp solo [10'] sc DONEMUS    (W7)

WAGENAAR, DIDERIK
Lent, Vague, Indécis
1.1.2.1. 1.0.0.0. cel,harmonium, harp,strings [8'] sc DONEMUS (W8)

WAGENAAR, JOHAN (1862-1941)
Elverhöi, Symfonisch Gedicht  *Op.48
3.2.2.2. 4.3.3.0. timp,2perc,harp, strings [13'] sc DONEMUS    (W9)

WAGENSEIL, GEORG CHRISTOPH (1715-1777)
Concerto for Cembalo and Strings in D
strings without vla,cembalo solo [18'] BREITKOPF-W    (W10)

Concerto for Harp and Strings
solo pt,set,pts INTERNAT.S.    (W11)

WAGNER, J.
Concertino for Harp and Orchestra
INTERNAT.S. sc,pts rent, solo pt, pno red    (W12)

WAGNER, RICHARD (1813-1883)
Allmächt'ge Jungfrau (from Tannhäuser (WWV 70))
2.2.2+bass clar.2. 4.0.3.1. harp, vcl,S solo [4'] (prayer of Elisabeth) BREITKOPF-W    (W13)

Als Für Ein Fremdes Land (from Tristan Und Isolde (WWV 90))
0.2+English horn.2+bass clar.3. 4.0.3.0. timp,strings [2'] (Isolde's answer) BREITKOPF-W    (W14)

Atmest Du Nicht Mit Mir Die Süssen Düfte? (from Lohengrin (WWV 75))
2.2.2.3. 2.0.0.0. strings,T solo [3'] (Lohengrin's reprimand) BREITKOPF-W    (W15)

Du Ärmste Kannst Wohl Nie Ermessen (from Lohengrin (WWV 75))
2.2+English horn.2.2. 4.0.0.0. strings,S solo [2'] (Elsa's admonition to Ortrud) BREITKOPF-W    (W16)

Einzug Der Götter In Walhall (from Rheingold (WWV 86 A))
(Hutschenruyter, W.) 3+pic.3+ English horn.3+bass clar.3.

WAGNER, RICHARD (cont'd.)
4.3.4.5. 2timp,2perc,7harp, strings [10'] BREITKOPF-W    (W17)

Erhebe Dich, Genossin Meiner Schmach (from Lohengrin (WWV 75))
3(pic).3(English horn).3(bass clar).3. 4.3.3.1. timp,perc, strings,SBar soli [21'] (duet of Telramund & Ortrud) BREITKOPF-W    (W18)

Fantasy
(Schreiner, A.) 1.1.2.1. 2.2.1.0. timp,perc,pno,harmonium,strings [10'] BREITKOPF-W    (W19)

Fliegende Holländer, Der: Mit Gewitter Und Sturm
2+pic.2.2.2. 4.2.3.1. timp,perc, strings,T solo [6'] BREITKOPF-W    (W20)

Götterdämmerung: Schlussgesang Der Brünnhilde
"Starke Scheite" 3.2.2.2. 4.2.3.1. timp,2perc,harp,strings,S solo [20'] BREITKOPF-W    (W21)

Höchstes Vertraun Hast Du Mir Schon Zu Danken (from Lohengrin (WWV 75))
2.2+English horn.2+bass clar.3. 4.3.3.1. timp,strings,T solo [4'] (Lohengrin's admonition) BREITKOPF-W    (W22)

Kaiser-Marsch
2+pic.3.3.3. 4.3.3.1. timp,4perc, strings [10'] (WWV 104) BREITKOPF-W    (W23)

Konzertouvertüre C-Dur
2.2.2.2. 4.2.3.0. timp,strings [8'] (WWV 27) BREITKOPF-W    (W24)

Konzertouvertüre D-Moll
2.2.2.2. 4.2.0.0. timp,strings [5'] (WWV 20) BREITKOPF-W    (W25)

Mild Und Leise Wie Er Lächelt (from Tristan Und Isolde (WWV 90))
2+pic.2+English horn.2+bass clar.3. 4.3.3.1. timp,harp,strings,S solo [5'] (Isolde's transfiguration) BREITKOPF-W    (W26)

Nun Sei Bedankt, Mein Lieber Schwan (from Lohengrin (WWV 75))
[3'30"] (Lohengrin's arrival) BREITKOPF-W    (W27)

Overtures And Preludes
orch sc DOVER 29201-0    (W28)

Polonia: Overture
2+2pic.2.2.2. 4.4.3.1. timp,5perc, strings [12'] BREITKOPF-W    (W29)

"Ride Of The Valkyries" And Other Highlights From The Ring
orch sc DOVER 29375-0    (W30)

Siegfried-Idyll
(WWV. 103) BROUDE BR.    (W31)

So Sei's! Für Seinen Feigen Wankelmut (from Das Liebesverbot (WWV 38))
2+pic.2.2.2. 4.2.3.0. timp,perc, strings,S solo [3'] (scena and recitative of Isabella) BREITKOPF-W    (W32)

Sonata in B flat,Minuet
(Baselt, F.) 2.2.2.2. 3.2.0.0. strings [4'] BREITKOPF-W    (W33)

Starke Scheite
see Götterdämmerung: Schlussgesang Der Brünnhilde

Süsse Lied Verhalt, Das (from Lohengrin (WWV 75))
3.3(English horn).3(bass clar).3. 4.3.3.1. timp,perc,strings,ST soli [25'] (betrothal scene of Elsa & Lohengrin) BREITKOPF-W    (W34)

Tannhäuser: Overture
(WWV. 70) BROUDE BR.    (W35)

Tristan Und Isolde: Vorspiel 3, Aufzug
0.1+English horn.2.2. 4.0.0.0. strings [7'] BREITKOPF-W    (W36)

Waldweben "Dass Der Mein Vater Nicht Ist" (from Siegfried (WWV 86 C))
(Hutschenruyter, W.) 3.3.3.3. 4.3.3.0. timp,perc,strings,T solo [7'] BREITKOPF-W    (W37)

Wotans Abschied Und Feuerzauber (from Die Walküre (WWV 86 B))
3(pic)+pic.3+English horn.3+bass clar.3. 8.3+bass trp.4.1. timp, perc,6harp,strings,Bar solo [8']

WAGNER, RICHARD (cont'd.)

BREITKOPF-W (W38)

WAGNER NIGHTS see Holloway, Robin

WAHLBERG, RUNE (1910-    )
Amoroso
2fl,2clar,strings [3'5"] sc STIM
(W39)

WAHREN, KARL HEINZ (1933-    )
Auf Der Suche Nach Dem Verlorenen
Tango
2.2(English horn).2.2.alto sax.
4.4.4.0. 2perc,cel,pno,harp,
strings [21'] SCHOTTS perf mat
rent (W40)

WAL-BERG (1910-1994)
Concertino for Horn and Orchestra
2.2.2.2. 2.2.3.0. timp,2perc,harp,
strings,horn solo [12'] SIKORSKI
perf mat rent (W41)

Concertino for Piano and Orchestra
"2 Décembre" 2.2.3.2. 4.3.3.0.
timp,2perc,harp,strings,pno solo
[11'] SIKORSKI perf mat rent
(W42)

"2 Décembre" fl,bsn,3horn,strings,
pno solo [11'] (reduced version)
SIKORSKI perf mat rent (W43)

2 Décembre
see Concertino for Piano and
Orchestra

WALDTEUFEL, EMILE (1837-1915)
Dolores (Waltz, Op. 170) Op.17
(Steffen) 1.1.2.0.4sax. 0.3.2.0.
perc,gtr,acord,vln I,vln II,vcl,
db,vln solo [6'] PETERS 01396
(W44)
(Steffen, H.) 2.1.2(4sax).1.
2.3.2.0. perc,strings,opt gtr,opt
acord [6'] pts PETERS LICO 311
(W45)

España (Waltz, Op. 236)
(Schönherr, M.) 2.2.2(3sax).2.
4.2.3.0. perc,harp,strings,opt
gtr,opt acord [9'] pts PETERS
LICO 303 (W46)

Ganz Allerliebst (Waltz, Op. 159)
Op.159
(Schönherr) 1.1.2.0.3sax. 0.2.1.0.
perc,gtr,acord,vln,vcl,db,vln
solo [8'] PETERS 01399 (W47)
(Schönherr, M.) 2.2.2(3sax).2.
4.2.3.0. perc,harp,strings,opt
gtr,opt acord [8'] pts PETERS
LICO 302 (W48)

Goldregen (Waltz, Op. 160) Op.160
(Schönherr) 1.1.2.0.3sax. 0.2.1.0.
perc,gtr,acord,vln,vcl,db,vln
solo [9'] PETERS 02476 (W49)
(Schönherr, M.) 2.2.2(3sax).2.
4.2.3.0. perc,harp,strings,opt
gtr,opt acord [9'] pts PETERS
LICO 304 (W50)

Herbstweisen (Waltz, Op. 155) Op.155
(Schönherr) 1.1.2.0.3sax. 0.2.2.0.
timp,perc,gtr,acord,vln,vcl,db,vln
solo [15'] PETERS 01400 (W51)
(Schönherr) 2.2.2.2.3sax. 4.2.3.0.
timp,harp,gtr,acord,8vln I,7vln
II,6vla,5vcl,4db,vln solo [15']
PETERS 02731 (W52)
(Schönherr, M.) 2.2.2(3sax).2.
4.2.3.0. perc,harp,strings,opt
gtr,opt acord [15'] pts PETERS
LICO 306 (W53)

Immer Oder Nimmer (Waltz, Op. 156)
Op.156
(Schönherr) 1.1.2.0.3sax. 0.2.1.0.
timp,perc,gtr,acord,vln,vcl,db,vln
solo [10'] PETERS 01401 (W54)
(Schönherr, M.) 2.2.2(3sax).2.
4.2.3.0. perc,harp,strings,opt
gtr,opt acord [10'] pts PETERS
LICO 308 (W55)

Mitternachtspolka (Polka, Op. 168)
Op.168
(Mareczek) 1.1.1.1. 2.1.1.0. timp,
acord,2vln,vla,vcl,db [5'] PETERS
01402 (W56)
(Mareczek, F.) 2.2.2.2. 3.2.3.0.
perc,harp,acord,strings [5'] pts
PETERS LICO 316 (W57)

Polka, Op. 168
see Mitternachtspolka

Schlittschuhläufer, Die (Waltz, Op.
183) Op.183
(Schönherr) 2.2.2.2.3sax. 4.2.3.0.
perc,harp,gtr,acord,8vln I,7vln
II,6vla,5vcl,4db,vln solo [7']
PETERS 01403 (W58)
(Schönherr) 1.1.2.0.3sax. 0.2.1.0.
perc,gtr,acord,vln,vcl,db,vln
solo [7'] PETERS 01404 (W59)

WALDTEUFEL, EMILE (cont'd.)
(Schönherr, M.) 2.2.2(3sax).2.
4.2.3.0. perc,harp,strings,opt
gtr,opt acord [7'] pts PETERS
LICO 301 (W60)

Sirenenzauber (Waltz, Op. 154) Op.154
(Schönherr) 1.1.2.0.3sax. 0.2.1.0.
perc,gtr,acord,vln,vcl,db,vln
solo [10'] PETERS (W61)
(Schönherr, M.) 2.2.2(3sax).2.
4.2.3.0. perc,harp,strings,opt
gtr,opt acord [10'] pts PETERS
LICO 305 (W62)

Sommerabend, Ein (Waltz, Op. 188)
Op.188
(Steffen) 2.2.2.0.2alto sax.2tenor
sax. 2.2.2.0. perc,gtr,4vln,vla,
vcl,db [6'] PETERS 01406 (W63)
(Steffen, H.) 2.1.2(4sax).1.
2.3.2.0. perc,strings,opt gtr,opt
acord [6'] pts PETERS LICO 314
(W64)

Waltz, Op. 154
see Sirenenzauber

Waltz, Op. 155
see Herbstweisen

Waltz, Op. 156
see Immer Oder Nimmer

Waltz, Op. 159
see Ganz Allerliebst

Waltz, Op. 160
see Goldregen

Waltz, Op. 170
see Dolores

Waltz, Op. 183
see Schlittschuhläufer, Die

Waltz, Op. 188
see Sommerabend, Ein

Waltz, Op. 236
see España

WALDWEBEN "DASS DER MEIN VATER NICHT
IST" see Wagner, Richard

WALK ON WATER see Wagemans, Peter-Jan

WALK THE LINE see Kucharzyk, Henry

WALKER, GWYNETH (1947-    )
Bicentennial Suite
3.2.2.2. 4.3.3.1. perc,strings
[15'] SCHIRM.EC rent (W65)

Fanfare For The Family Farm
2.2.2.2. 4.2.3.1. 3perc,strings
[4'] SCHIRM.EC rent (W66)

Headless Horseman, The
3.2.2.2. 4.2.3.1. 3perc,strings
[7'] SCHIRM.EC rent (W67)

Light Of Three Mornings, The
1.1.1.1. 1.1.1.0. perc,harp,strings
[17'] SCHIRM.EC rent (W68)

Nocturne for Clarinet and String
Orchestra
clar solo,strings [17'] SCHIRM.EC
rent (W69)

Open The Door, Orchestral Overture
2.2.2.2. 4.2.3.1. timp,2perc,
strings [5'] SCHIRM.EC rent (W70)

Roanoke Rising
2.2.2.2. 4.2.2.1. timp,3perc,
strings [15'] SCHIRM.EC rent
(W71)

Three Songs In Celebration Of The
Family Farm
2.2.2.2. 4.2.3.1. perc,strings
[13'] SCHIRM.EC rent (W72)

Up-Front Concerto, The
1.1.1.1. 1.1.1.0. perc,strings,
solo hand drum [10'] SCHIRM.EC
rent (W73)

WALKER, ROBERT (1946-    )
My Dog Has Fleas
orch [9'] NOVELLO (W74)

WALKING WITH THE RIVER'S ROAR see Holt,
Simon

WALL, THE see Jager, Robert Edward

WALLACE, WILLIAM (1933-    )
Canticle For Orchestra
2.2(English horn).2.2. 3.2.1.0.
timp,perc,strings [17'] sc,pts
CANADIAN MI 1100 W195CA (W75)

WALLACE, WILLIAM (cont'd.)
Canticle II
string orch sc CANADIAN
MI 1500 W195CA (W76)

Cantilena For Strings
string orch [8'] sc CANADIAN
MI 1500 W195CAN (W77)

Introduction And Passacaglia
3(pic).2.2.1. 4.3.3.1. timp,2perc,
strings [8'] sc CANADIAN
MI 1100 W195IN (W78)

Luminations
2(pic).2.2.0. 3.2.1.0. timp,perc,
harp,synthesizer,strings [12'] sc
CANADIAN MI 1100 W195LU (W79)

Lyric Serenade
string orch/string quar,fl solo
[13'] sc,solo pt CANADIAN
MI 1621 W159LY (W80)

WALLACE, WILLIAM (1860-1940)
Passing Of Beatrice
"Symphonic Poem No.1" 2.2.2.2.
4.2.3.1. harp,strings [13']
SCHOTTS perf mat rent (W81)

Symphonic Poem No.1
see Passing Of Beatrice

WALLBORN,
Sätze Für Kammerorchester, 5
5vln I,4vln II,3vla,2vcl,db [20']
sc PETERS 04009 (W82)

WALLIN, PETER (1964-    )
Greetings To WK 89 The Democratic
Orchestra
12strings, all soloistic sc STIM
(W83)

Introduction And Funk
7vln,3vla,2vcl,db, all solo strings
[4'] sc,pts STIM (W84)

WALLIN, ROLF (1957-    )
Chi For Orchestra
3(pic,alto fl).3(English
horn).3(clar in E flat,bass
clar).3(contrabsn). 4.3.3.1.
timp,3perc,harp,pno/synthesizer,
strings [23'] NORSKMI (W85)

WALLS ARE QUIET NOW, THE see Glickman,
Sylvia

WALTHER, JOHANN GOTTFRIED (1684-1748)
Concerto in B minor
string orch,org solo COPPENRATH sc
60.111-01, pts 60.111-21 TO 29
(W86)

WALTON, [SIR] WILLIAM (TURNER)
(1902-1983)
Anon In Love
perc,harp,strings,T solo [10'] perf
sc set OXFORD 3468654 sc,pts rent
(W87)

As You Like It: Suite
(Davis) 1+pic.2.2.2. 4.2.0.0. timp,
3perc,hpsd,harp,strings [10']
perf sc set OXFORD 3681196 sc,pts
rent (W88)

Battle Of Britain Suite
2.2.2.2. 4.2.3.1. timp,2perc,harp,
strings [11'] perf sc set OXFORD
3681447 sc,pts rent (W89)

Christopher Columbus (Complete)
3+pic.2+English horn.2+bass clar.2+
contrabsn. 4.3.2.1. timp,3-4perc,
1-2harp,strings,TBar&2 speaking
voices,speaking cor [40'] perf sc
set OXFORD 3682249 sc,pts rent
(W90)

Christopher Columbus: Suite
(Palmer) 3.3.3.3. 4.3.3.1. timp,3-
4perc,2harp,strings,AT soli,SATB
[10'] OXFORD sc 368215X f.s.,
perf sc set 368215X sc,pts rent
(W91)

Concerto for Viola and Orchestra
(Wellington) (Walton Edition) sc
OXFORD 3681307 (W92)

Escape Me Never
2.2.2.2. 4.3.3.1. timp,3perc,harp,
strings [3'] perf sc set OXFORD
3681501 sc,pts rent (W93)

Escape Me Never: Suite
(Palmer) 3(2pic).2(English
horn).2(bass clar).2. 4.3.3.1.
timp,2perc,strings [12'] perf sc
set OXFORD 3681463 sc,pts rent
(W94)

Facade: Suite No.3
(Palmer) 2(pic).2(English
horn).2(bass clar).2. 4.2.1.1.
timp,3perc,pno/cel,strings [7']
perf sc set OXFORD 3681552 sc,pts
rent (W95)

WALTON, [SIR] WILLIAM (TURNER)
(cont'd.)

Five Bagatelles
(Russ) 2.2.2.2. 2.2.0.0. timp,
4perc,strings,gtr solo [14'] perf
sc set OXFORD 3681595 sc,pts rent
(W96)

Henry V; A Shakespeare Scenario
(Palmer) 3.3.3.2. 4.4.3.1. timp,4-
5perc,2harp,hpsd,pno,cel,opt org,
strings,speaking voice,mix cor&
boy cor [50'] (Walton Edition)
perf sc set OXFORD 3385317 sc,pts
rent                              (W97)

Introduction And National Anthem
2(pic).2+English horn.2+bass
clar.2+contrabsn. 4.3.3.1. timp,
2perc,2harp,strings [2'] perf sc
set OXFORD sc,pts rent        (W98)

March: History Of The English
Speaking Peoples
3+pic.2+English horn.2.1+contrabsn.
4.3.3.1. timp,2perc,harp,strings
[4'] perf sc set OXFORD 3682427
sc,pts rent                    (W99)

Miscellaneous Shorter Works
(Wright) (Walton Edition) sc OXFORD
3683652                       (W100)

Music For Children: Galop - Finale
(Palmer) 2(pic).2(English
horn).2.2. 4.2.3.1. timp,2perc,
harp,strings [14'] perf sc set
OXFORD 3682621 sc,pts rent (W101)

Orb And Sceptre: Coronation March
3(pic).2+English horn.3(bass
clar).2. 4.3.3.1. timp,4perc,
harp,opt org,strings [9'] OXFORD
study sc 3683024, perf sc set
3683016 sc,pts rent          (W102)

Quest, The: Complete Ballet Music
(Palmer) 3(2pic).2(English
horn).2.2. 4.3.3.1. timp,5perc,
pno/cel,2harp,strings [45'] perf
sc set OXFORD 3683571 sc,pts rent
(W103)

Richard III: Monologue
(Palmer) 2.2.2.3. 4.3.3.0. perc,
harp,hpsd,timp,perc,strings [4']
perf sc set OXFORD 3683997 sc,pts
rent                          (W104)

Richard III: Prelude
(Mathieson) 2.2(English horn).2(opt
bass clar).2. 4.2.3.1. opt timp,
2perc,harp,strings [8'] OXFORD
study sc 3683458 f.s., perf sc
set 3683466 sc,pts rent      (W105)

Richard III: Shakespeare Scenario
(Palmer) 3.3.3.3. 4.3.3.1. timp,
4perc,2harp,pno&hpsd/cel,strings
[40'] perf sc set OXFORD 3683989
sc,pts rent                   (W106)

Sinfonia Concertante
2+pic.2+English horn.2.2. 4.2.3.1.
timp,2perc,pno,strings [18']
(revised version) OXFORD study sc
3684063 f.s., perf sc set 368408X
sc,pts rent                   (W107)

Sonata for String Orchestra
[25'] sc OXFORD 3684276 f.s., ipa
(W108)

Sonata for Violin and Orchestra
(Palmer) 3(pic).2(English horn).2+
bass clar.2. 4.3.3.1. timp,2perc,
pno/cel,harp,strings [24'] perf
sc set OXFORD sc,pts rent    (W109)

Symphony No. 1
(Lloyd-Jones) 2(pic).2.2.2.
4.3.3.1. 2timp,2perc,strings
[43'] (Walton Edition) OXFORD sc
3684187, study sc 3684195, perf
sc set 3684195 sc,pts rent (W110)

Two Pieces For Violin And Orchestra
2.1.2.1. 2.1.0.0. perc,harp,strings
[5'] perf sc set OXFORD sc,pts
rent                          (W111)

Under The Greenwood Tree
2.1+English horn.2.2. 2.0.0.0.
harp,strings,solo voice [4'] perf
sc set OXFORD 3458675 sc,pts rent
(W112)

Wartime Sketchbook, A
3.2.3.2. 4.3.3.1. timp,3perc,harp,
pno,strings [20'] OXFORD sc
3685728 f.s., perf sc set 3685728
sc,pts rent                   (W113)

WALTZ see Takemitsu, Toru

WALTZER FÜR ORCHESTER see Eötvös,
Jószef

WALTZES see Gardner, R. Neil

WALZER AUS DER FILMMUSIK "MITSCHURIN"
see Shostakovich, Dmitri,
Mitschurin: Waltzes

WALZERIMPRESSION see Helbig, Michael,
Aurelia

WAN CHAI see Kaneko, Shin-Ichi

WANDERING ROCKS see Lutzow-Holm, Ole

WANDERSUITE see Schultze, Norbert

WANEK, FRIEDRICH K. (1929-1991)
Chamber Concerto
hpsd/elec pno,strings,trp solo
[17'] SCHOTTS perf mat rent
(W114)

Concerto for Harpsichord and
Orchestra
1.1.1.1. 1.0.0.0. strings,hpsd solo
SCHOTTS perf mat rent       (W115)

Divertimento
2.2.0.2. 2.1.0.0. strings [10']
SCHOTTS perf mat rent       (W116)

Due Sonetti
string orch,Mez solo [12'] SCHOTTS
perf mat rent               (W117)

Pièces Brèves, 4
string orch,4hpsd soli [10']
SCHOTTS perf mat rent       (W118)

Tableau Symphonique
2(2pic).2.2(bass
clar).2(contrabsn). 4.3.3.0.
timp,2perc,strings [11'] SCHOTTS
perf mat rent               (W119)

WANHAL, JOHANN BAPTIST (JAN KRTITEL)
(1739-1813)
Comista (Sinfonia in C)
2ob,2horn,2trp,timp,2vln,vla,vcl,db
[14'] ARTARIA AE057         (W120)

Concerto for 2 Bassoons
(Masier, Miloslav) 0.2.0.0.
2.0.0.0. cembalo,strings,2bsn
soli CESKY HUD.             (W121)

Concerto for 2 Bassoons and Orchestra
(Masier, Miloslav) 0.2.0.0.
2.0.0.0. cembalo,strings,2bsn
soli [24'] CESKY HUD.       (W122)

Concerto for Cembalo, No. 2
(Jirounek, Miloslav) cembalo,
strings, (without vcl & db) CESKY
HUD.                        (W123)

Concerto for Oboe and Strings in A
(Tausky) [12'] perf sc set OXFORD
3679604 sc,pts rent         (W124)

Concerto for Violoncello and
Orchestra in A
2horn,strings,vcl solo [26'] CESKY
HUD.                        (W125)

Concerto in C
0.2.0.0. 2.0.0.0. timp,strings,pno/
org solo CESKY HUD.         (W126)

Sinfonia in A
2ob,2trp,timp,2vln,vla,vcl,db [11']
ARTARIA AE101               (W127)

Sinfonia in B flat
2ob,2horn,2vln,vla,vcl,db [18']
ARTARIA AE096               (W128)

Sinfonia in C
see Comista

Sinfonia in C, MIN 1
2ob,2horn,2trp,2vln,vla,vcl,db [9']
ARTARIA AE097               (W129)

Sinfonia in D
2ob,2horn,2trp,timp,2vln,vla,vcl,db
[20'] ARTARIA AE054         (W130)

Sinfonia in D minor
2ob,5horn,2vln,vla,vcl,db [17']
ARTARIA AE055               (W131)

Sinfonia in G
fl,2ob,2horn,2vln,vla,vcl,db [26']
ARTARIA AE056               (W132)

Symphony in G
(Ryba, L.) 2.2.0.0. 2.0.0.0.
strings CESKY HUD.          (W133)

WANN WERDEN JE, IHR GÖTTER - VATER,
GESCHWISTER see Mozart, Wolfgang
Amadeus, Quando Avran - Padre,
Germani

WAR OF THE ELEMENTS, THE see Heinrich,
Anton Philip

WARD, ROBERT EUGENE (1917-    )
Claudia Legare: First Symphonic Set
2.2.2.2. 4.3.3.0. timp,perc,harp,
strings [18'] SCHIRM.EC rent
(W134)

Concert Music
3.2.2.2. 4.3.3.1. timp,3perc,kbd,
strings [8'] SCHIRM.EC rent
(W135)

Concerto for Saxophone and Orchestra
tenor sax solo,3.3.3.2. 4.3.3.1.
timp,perc,harp,strings [15']
SCHIRM.EC rent              (W136)

Dialogues For Violin, Cello And
Orchestra
vln solo,vcl solo,3.3.3.2. 4.3.3.1.
timp,2perc,strings [7'] SCHIRM.EC
rent                        (W137)

Festival Triptych For Narrator And
Orchestra
2.2.2.2. 4.3.3.1. timp,perc,harp,
strings,narrator [21'] SCHIRM.EC
rent                        (W138)

Five Times Five. 4 Variations On A
Five-Part Theme
2.2.2.2. 4.3.3.1. timp,2perc,
strings [12'] SCHIRM.EC rent
(W139)

Jubilation  *Overture
3.3.3.3. 4.3.3.1. timp,kbd,strings
[9'] SCHIRM.EC rent         (W140)

Lady From Colorado: Second Symphonic
Set
3.3.2.2. 4.3.3.1. timp,2perc,harp,
strings [19'] SCHIRM.EC rent
(W141)

Processional March
3.3.3.2. 4.3.3.1. timp,2perc,
strings [5'] SCHIRM.EC rent (W142)

Sixth Symphony For Chamber Orchestra
see Symphony No. 6 for Chamber
Orchestra

Sonic Structure
3.3.3.3. 4.3.3.1. timp,2perc,harp,
strings [11'] SCHIRM.EC rent
(W143)

Symphony No. 6 for Chamber Orchestra
"Sixth Symphony For Chamber
Orchestra" 1.1.1.1. 0.0.0.0. kbd,
strings [21'] SCHIRM.EC rent
(W144)

WARD-STEINMAN, DAVID (1936-    )
Cinnabar (Concerto for Viola,
Strings, Percussion and Piano)
strings,perc,pno/cel,vla solo [17']
MERION rent                 (W145)

Concerto for Viola, Strings,
Percussion and Piano
see Cinnabar

WARE, PETER (1951-    )
Latakia; By The Water's Edge
1.1.1.1. 2.1.0.0. timp,perc,harp,
strings sc CANADIAN
MI 1200 W271LA              (W146)

WARNER, SCOTT
Golden Heart
1.1.1.0. 1.1.0.1. perc,harp,strings
SEESAW                      (W147)

WARTIME SKETCHBOOK, A see Walton, [Sir]
William (Turner)

WARUM? see Schut, Vladislav

WARUM GABST DU BIS HEUTE NIE MEINEM
FLEHN GEHÖR? see Mozart, Wolfgang
Amadeus, Crudel! Perchè Finora
Farmi Languir Cosi

WAS BEDEUTET DIR MEIN NAME? see
Shostakovich, Dmitri

WAS IHR WOLLT see Paine, John Knowles

WATER COLOURS see Bauer, Robert

WATER IS WIDE, THE see O Waly, Waly

WATER MUSIC AND ROYAL FIREWORKS see
Handel, George Frideric

WATER RINGS see Ung, Chinary

WATERFRONT see Dreyfus, George

WATERHATCH, THE see Amos, Keith

WATERS AND WORTELEN - PART 2 see
Koolmees, Hans

WATER'S EDGE see Tann, Hilary

WATERSHED III see Reynolds, Roger

WAVE MOTIONS see Szekely, Endre

WAVES see Lerdahl, Fred see Southam, Ann

WAXMAN, DONALD (1925-    )
Overture To Serenade Concertante
1.1.1.1. 2.0.0.0. strings [11']
SCHIRM.EC rent                    (W148)

Quint Of Carols, A
3.2.2.2.bass sax. 3.2.3.1. timp,
2perc,strings [15'] SCHIRM.EC
rent                              (W149)

WAY TO CASTLE YONDER, THE see Knussen,
Oliver

WE WERE DREAMERS see Grainger, Percy
Aldridge

WEAVER'S SONG AND JIG see Larsen,
Elizabeth B. (Libby)

WEBBER, ANDREW LLOYD
see LLOYD WEBBER, ANDREW

WEBER, CARL MARIA VON (1786-1826)
Andante& Rondo Ungarese
vla solo/bsn solo,orch KUNZELMANN
10167                             (W150)

Concertino
(Klöcker) ob,fl,2clar,2bsn,2horn,
trp,trom,db KUNZELMANN 10161
                                  (W151)
Concerto for Piano and Orchestra in E
flat, Op. 32
2.0.2.2. 2.2.0.0. timp,strings,pno
solo [24'] BREITKOPF-W            (W152)

Drei Pintos: Arietta
2.2.2.2. 4.2.2.1. timp,perc,8vln I,
7vln II,6vla,5vcl,4db [5'] sc
KAHNT 02020                       (W153)

Freischütz, Der: Einst Träumte
2.0.2.2. 2.0.0.0. strings,S solo
[7'] (romance and aria of
Ännchen) BREITKOPF-W              (W154)

Freischütz, Der: Hier Im Ird'schen
Jammertal
2.2.0.2. 0.0.0.0. strings,B solo
[2'] (song of Kaspar) BREITKOPF-W
                                  (W155)
Freischütz, Der: Kommt Ein Schlanker
Bursch Gegangen
2.2.0.2. 2.0.0.0. strings,S solo
[5'] (arietta of Ännchen)
BREITKOPF-W                       (W156)

Freischütz, Der: Lied Des Caspar
2.2.0.2. 0.0.0.0. 8vln I,7vln II,
6vla,5vcl,4db [5'] sc PETERS
01389                             (W157)

Freischütz, Der: Nein, Länger Trag
Ich Nicht Die Qualen
2.2.2.2. 4.0.0.0. timp,strings,T
solo [7'] (aria of Max)
BREITKOPF-W                       (W158)

Freischütz, Der: Romanze Und Arie
2.0.2.2. 2.0.0.0. 8vln I,7vln II,
6vla,5vcl,4db [5'] sc PETERS
01390                             (W159)

Freischütz, Der: Und Ob Die Wolke
0.0.2.2. 2.0.0.0. strings,S solo,
vcl solo [6'] (cavatina of
Agathe) BREITKOPF-W               (W160)

Great Overtures By Weber In Full
Score
orch sc DOVER 25225-6             (W161)

Musik Zu Turandot *Op.37
(Schönzeler) orch KUNZELMANN 10120
ipr                               (W162)

Silvana: Overture
2.2.2.2. 2.2.1.0. timp,strings [7']
BREITKOPF-W                       (W163)

Theme and Variations for Viola and
Orchestra
(Drüner) vla solo,orch (J. 49)
KUNZELMANN 10123 ipr              (W164)

Variations for Viola and Orchestra
(Andreae) 1.2.0.2. 2.0.0.0.
strings,vla solo [5'] (on the
Austrian folksong "A Schüsserl
und a Reind'rl") study sc PETERS
EP 8320                           (W165)

WEDDING DAY AT TROLDHAUGEN see Grieg,
Edvard Hagerup

WEEP YOU NO MORE SAD FOUNTAINS see
Mann, Leslie

WEHDING, HANS-HENDRIK (1915-1975)
Variationen Über Eine Englische
Schulmusik
4.3.4.3.sax. 4.3.3.1. perc,harp,
pno,cel,strings [27'] BREITKOPF-W

WEHDING, HANS-HENDRIK (cont'd.)
                                  (W166)

WEIHNACHTS-PASTORALE see Valentini,
Giuseppe

WEIHNACHTSKONZERT see Locatelli, Pietro
see Manfredini, Francesco

WEIHNACHTSKONZERT, EIN see Baumann,
Herbert

WEIHNACHTSORATORIUM: NR. 7 see Wermann,
Oscar

WEILL, KURT (1900-1950)
Divertimento, Op. 5
(Drew, David; Shaw, Christopher)
0.0.1.1. 1.0.2.0. strings,men cor
[24'] EUR.AM.MUS.                 (W167)

Four Walt Whitman Songs
2.1.2(bass clar).1. 2.2.2.0. timp,
perc,harp,strings,solo voice
[18'] EUR.AM.MUS.                 (W168)

Huckleberry Finn: Five Songs
(Bennett, Robert Russell) 2.2.2.1.
4.2.3.1. timp,perc,pno,strings,
solo voice [20'] EUR.AM.MUS.      (W169)

Judgement Of Paris, The (from Die
Dreigroschenoper) ballet
(Tudor; Cooke) 1(pic).1.1(tenor
sax).1.alto sax(clar). 0.2.2.0.
perc,pno,strings [30']
EUR.AM.MUS. perf mat rent         (W170)

WEINBERGER, JAROMIR (1896-1967)
Beloved Voice, The: Overture
"Geliebte Stimme, Die: Overture"
3(pic).2(English horn).2.2.
4.3.3.1. timp,perc,harp,cel,
strings [9'] BOOSEY-ENG rent
                                  (W171)
Christmas
3(pic).2+English horn.2+bass
clar.2+contrabsn. 4.3.3.1. timp,
perc,2harp,cel,pno,strings [20']
BOOSEY-ENG rent                   (W172)

Dixie: Prelude And Fugue
3(pic).2.2.2. 4.3.3.1. timp,perc,
harp,opt org,strings, opt stage
band: 2horns, 2trp, 2trom, snare
drum [5'] BOOSEY-ENG rent         (W173)

Geliebte Stimme, Die: Overture
see Beloved Voice, The: Overture

Overture To A Knightly Play
1.1.1.1. 2.2.1.0. perc,pno,
harmonium,strings [10'] BOOSEY-
ENG rent                          (W174)

Overture To A Marionette Play
3(pic).2.2.2. 4.3.3.0. timp,perc,
harp,cel,strings [12'] BOOSEY-ENG
rent                              (W175)

Passacaglia for Organ and Orchestra
3.3.3.3. 6.4.4.1. timp,perc,
strings,org solo [30'] BOOSEY-ENG
rent                              (W176)
3.3.3.3. 4.3.3.1. timp,perc,
strings,org solo [30'] BOOSEY-ENG
rent                              (W177)

Schwanda The Bagpiper: Furiant
3.2.2.2. 4.3.3.1. timp,perc,harp,
cel,strings [3'] BOOSEY-ENG rent
                                  (W178)
Schwanda The Bagpiper: Overture
3.2.2.2. 4.3.3.1. timp,perc,2harp,
cel,strings BOOSEY-ENG rent
                                  (W179)
Schwanda The Bagpiper: Suite
3.2.2.2. 4.3.3.1. timp,perc,harp,
cel,strings [23'] BOOSEY-ENG rent
                                  (W180)
Six Bohemian Songs And Dances
2.2.2.2. 4.2.3.0. timp,perc,harp,
cel,strings [24'] BOOSEY-ENG rent
                                  (W181)
WEINER, LEO (1885-1960)
Divertimento No. 3, Op. 25
"Impressioni Ungheresi"
2(pic).2.2.2. 4.2.3.0. timp,perc,
harp,strings [14'] EMB rent
                                  (W182)
Impressioni Ungheresi
see Divertimento No. 3, Op. 25

WEINGARTNER, (PAUL) FELIX VON
(1863-1942)
Aus Fernen Welten *Op.39
2.2.2.2. 4.2.3.1. perc,harp,
strings,solo voice [18'] (1. Der
Born 2. Vöglein Schwermut 3.
Erdriese 4. Mondaufgang)
BREITKOPF-W                       (W183)

Deine Schönheit *Op.48,No.6
2.2.2.2. 4.2.0.0. timp,harp,
strings,solo voice [3']
BREITKOPF-W                       (W184)

WEINGARTNER, (PAUL) FELIX VON (cont'd.)
Des Kindes Scheiden *Op.36,No.2
2.2.2.2. 4.2.3.1. timp,harp,solo
2vla,2vcl.S/T solo [5']
BREITKOPF-W                       (W185)

Du Bist Ein Kind *Op.28,No.12
0.0.1.0. 0.0.0.0. strings,solo
voice [4'] BREITKOPF-W            (W186)

Er Weiss Es Besser *Op.36,No.1
2.2.2.2. 4.0.0.0. harp,strings,S/T
solo [5'] BREITKOPF-W             (W187)

Gefilde Der Seligen, Das *Op.21
3(pic).2+English horn.2+bass
clar.3+contrabsn. 4.4.3.1. timp,
4perc,2harp,strings [23']
BREITKOPF-W                       (W188)

Letzter Tanz *Op.36,No.3
2.2.2.2. 4.2.0.0. timp,perc,harp,
strings,S/T solo [3'] BREITKOPF-W
                                  (W189)
Lied Der Ghawaze *Op.25,No.5
2.2.2.2. 0.1.0.0. perc,strings,solo
voice [2'] BREITKOPF-W            (W190)

Stille Der Nacht *Op.35,No.2
2.2.2.2. 4.0.0.0. timp,strings,A/B
solo [5'] BREITKOPF-W             (W191)

Symphony No. 1 in G, Op. 23
3(pic).2.2.2. 4.2.3.0. timp,harp,
strings [30'] BREITKOPF-W         (W192)

Symphony No. 3 in E, Op. 49
4(pic).2(English horn).4+bass
clar.3+contrabsn+Heckelphone.
6.4.3.1. timp,perc,2harp,org&cel,
strings (no score) BREITKOPF-W
                                  (W193)
Unruhe Der Nacht *Op.35,No.1
2.2.2.2. 4.2.0.0. timp,strings,A/B
solo [5'] BREITKOPF-W             (W194)

WEINSTANGEL, SASHA (1947-    )
Concertino For Electric String
Quartet And String Orchestra
string orch, electric string
quartet [13'] sc CANADIAN
MI 1717 W424CO                    (W195)

Concerto for Orchestra
2(pic).2(English horn).2.2.
2.1.1.1. timp,2perc,pno,5vln I,
4vln II,3vla,3vcl,db [16'] sc
CANADIAN MI 1100 W424CO           (W196)

Hamilton Concerto
2string quar/string orch,pno,db,
perc, (players vocalize) [15'] sc
CANADIAN MI 1200 W424HA           (W197)

Trumpets Of Jerico
2(pic).2.2.2. 4.0.0.0. timp,2perc,
pno,strings,4trp soli,4trom soli
[10'] (fanfaric overture for two
brass groups and symphony
orchestra) sc CANADIAN
MI 1435 W424TR                    (W198)

WEINSTOCK, DER: ZYKLUS FÜR VIOLONCELLO
UND STREICHORCHESTER see Cornell,
Klaus

WEINZWEIG, JOHN (1913-    )
Barn Dance (Suite,Third Movement)
(from the ballet Red Ear Of Corn)
2(pic).2.2.2. 2.2.2.0. timp,3perc,
strings [7'] sc CANADIAN
MI 1100 W4245BA                   (W199)

Divertimento No. 3 for Bassoon and
String Orchestra
[18'] sc,pno red,solo pt CANADIAN
MI 1624 W245DI                    (W200)

Divertimento No. 7 for Horn and
String Orchestra
[20'] sc,solo pt CANADIAN
MI 1632 W4245DI                   (W201)

Divertimento No. 8
2(pic).2.2.2. 2.2.2.0. timp,perc,
strings,tuba solo [15'] sc
CANADIAN MI 1334 W4245DI          (W202)

Divertimento No. 9
3(pic).3(English horn).3(bass
clar).3(contrabsn). 4.3.3.1.
timp,3perc,harp,strings [24'] (1.
Fast 2. Agitated 3. Dialogues 4.
Blues 5. Fast) sc CANADIAN
MI 1100 W4245DI9                  (W203)

Divertimento No. 11
string orch,English horn solo sc,
solo pt CANADIAN MI 1622 W4245DIV
                                  (W204)
Music For Radio No. 1: Our Canada
(Suite for Orchestra)
2.2(English horn).2.2. 2.2.2.0.
timp,perc,strings [11'] (1. Wheat
2. Bonds Of Steel 3. The Land) sc

WEINZWEIG, JOHN (cont'd.)

    CANADIAN MI 1100 W4245MU    (W205)

  Suite,Third Movement
    see Barn Dance

  Suite for Orchestra
    see Music For Radio No. 1: Our
    Canada

WEIR, JUDITH (1954-    )
  Forest
    3.3.3.3. 4.4.3.1. 2perc,marimba,
    timp,strings [13'] CHESTER (W206)

  Heroic Strokes Of The Bow
    2.2.2.2. 2.2.0.0. timp,strings
    [15'] CHESTER            (W207)

  Music, Untangled
    2.2.2.2. 4.3.3.0. timp,cel,harp,
    strings [6'] CHESTER     (W208)

WEISE VON LIEBE UND TOD DES CORNET
  CHRISTOPH RILKE, DIE see Ullmann,
  Viktor

WEISGARBER, ELLIOTT (1919-    )
  As We Stood Then
    1(pic).1.1.1. 2.0.0.0. timp,perc,
    harp,strings,med solo [23'] (a
    sequence of poems by Thomas
    Hardy) sc CANADIAN MV 1376 W427AS
                             (W209)

  Concerto for Violin and Orchestra
    2.2.2.2. 2.0.0.0. harp,strings,vln
    solo [20'] sc,pno red CANADIAN
    MI 1311 W427CO           (W210)

  Northumbrian Elegy, A
    2.2(English horn) 2.2.1.0.
    timp,2perc,harp,strings [11'] sc
    CANADIAN MI 1100 W427NO  (W211)

WEISMANN, WILHELM (1900-1980)
  Concerto for Solo Voice, Chorus,
    Organ and Orchestra
    "Friedenslied" 2.2.2.2. 2.2.3.0.
    timp,8vln I,7vln II,6vla,5vcl,4db
    [5'] sc PETERS 04454     (W212)

  Friedenslied
    see Concerto for Solo Voice,
    Chorus, Organ and Orchestra

  Lieder Und Balladen
    (Zoephel, K.) 2.2.2.2. 2.2.1.0.
    timp,2perc,harp,8vln I,7vln II,
    6vla,5vcl,4db [13'] sc PETERS
    04451                    (W213)

WEISS, MANFRED (1935-    )
  Sinfonia No. 5
    3.3.3.3. 4.3.3.1. timp,3perc,cel,
    harp,8vln I,7vln II,6vla,5vcl,4db
    [25'] sc PETERS 03829    (W214)

WEISSE NÄCHTE IM NORDEN see Godzinsky,
  George De

WEISSE REQUIEM see Leistner-Mayer,
  Roland

WELCH EIN GESCHICK - MEINETWEGEN SOLL'T
  DU STERBEN see Mozart, Wolfgang
  Amadeus

WELCHE SCHRECKLICHE NACHT - ICH FINDE
  DEN VATER see Mozart, Wolfgang
  Amadeus, Ah Qual Gelido Orror - Il
  Padre Adorato

WELIKIJ ZAR see Rimsky-Korsakov,
  Nikolai

WELIN, KARL-ERIK (1934-1992)
  Prelude (from Suite Pour Piano)
    string orch [3'] sc STIM  (W215)

WELL MET see Jolas, Betsy

WELLEJUS, HENNING (1919-    )
  Freunde Aus Unsern Kinderjahren (from
    H. C. Andersen-Ballet "Der
    Schwan") Suite
    "Vor Barndoms Venner" 2(pic).2.2.2.
    2.2.1.0. timp,perc,strings [14']
    (in 9 Bildern) sc,set BUSCH rent
                             (W216)

  Master Jacob På Afveje
    see Meister Jakob Auf Abwegen

  Meister Jakob Auf Abwegen
    "Master Jacob På Afveje" 2.2.2.2.
    2.2.1.0. timp,perc,strings
    [2'45"] sc,set BUSCH rent (W217)

  Overture
    see Postwagen Rollt, Der

  Postvognen Ruller
    see Postwagen Rollt, Der

WELLEJUS, HENNING (cont'd.)

  Postwagen Rollt, Der (Overture)
    "Postvognen Ruller" 2.2.2.2.
    2.2.1.0. timp,perc,strings
    [2'40"] sc,set BUSCH rent (W218)

  Vor Barndoms Venner
    see Freunde Aus Unsern Kinderjahren

WELLERIANA see Soler, Enrique Llacer

WELLINGTONS SIEG see Beethoven, Ludwig
  van

WELSH SUITE see Hollyoak, Sidney

WEN-CHUNG, CHOU
  see CHOU, WEN-CHUNG

WENDELBOE, JENS (1956-    )
  Modus Vivendi
    2.2.2.2. 2.2.2.0. timp,2perc,harp,
    strings [4'] NORSKMI    (W219)

  Opposite Of One, The
    2.2.2.2. 4.3.3.0. timp,2perc,harp,
    pno,strings,vcl solo [22']
    NORSKMI                  (W220)

WENDLING, JOHANN BAPTIST
  (ca. 1720-1797)
  Concerto for Flute and String
    Orchestra in C
    HUG sc GH 11271, pts,solo pt
    11271-30, pno red 11727  (W221)

WENDLING FARM see Zappa, Enric

WENGLER, MARCEL
  Symphony No. 2
    3.3.3.3. 6.4.4.1. 3perc,pno,harp,
    strings SEESAW          (W222)

WENN DAS PENDEL DER LIEBE SCHWINGT see
  Sheriff, Noam

WENN DIE SANFTEN ABENDWINDE see Mozart,
  Wolfgang Amadeus, Che Soave
  Zefiretto

WENN DU MICH MIT DEN AUGEN STREIFST see
  Wolf, Hugo

WENSTRÖM-LEKARE, LENNART (1924)
  Sinfonia Piccola No. 2 (Symphony)
    1.1.2.1. 2.2.0.0. timp,strings sc
    STIM                     (W223)

  Symphony
    see Sinfonia Piccola No. 2

WENZEL, HANS JÜRGEN (1939-    )
  Bauhausmusik
    3.2.3.2. 4.3.3.1. timp,perc,pno,
    harp,elec gtr,8vln I,7vln II,
    6vla,5vcl,4db [35'] sc PETERS
    03335                    (W224)

  Concerto for Orchestra
    3.2.3.2. 4.3.3.1. timp,perc,harp,
    8vln I,7vln II,6vla,5vcl,4db
    [20'] sc PETERS 03333    (W225)

  Concerto for Organ and Orchestra
    3.3.4.3. 4.4.3.1. timp,perc,harp,
    elec gtr,8vln I,7vln II,6vla,
    5vcl,4db [24'] sc,solo pt PETERS
    03336                    (W226)

  Sinfonietta
    2.2.2.2. 3.3.3.0. timp,perc,8vln I,
    7vln II,6vla,5vcl,4db [20'] sc
    PETERS 03345             (W227)

WER EIN LIEBCHEN HAT GEFUNDEN see
  Mozart, Wolfgang Amadeus

WERDER, FELIX (1922-    )
  Sound Canvas  *Op.101
    2.2.2.2. 4.2.3.1. timp,perc,cel,
    strings ALLANS           (W228)

  Stanzas X & IX
    2.2.2.2. 4.2.2.0. timp,perc,strings
    ALLANS                   (W229)

  Triple Measure  *Op.110
    2.2.2.2. 2.2.2.0. timp,perc,harp,
    strings ALLANS           (W230)

WERDIN, EBERHARD (1911-1991)
  König Und Sein Floh
    1.0.0.0. 0.1.0.0. perc,8vln I,7vln
    II,6vla,5vcl,4db [70'] sc PETERS
    01418                    (W231)

  Konzertante Music: Für 2
    Instrumentalchöre
    strings,S rec,A rec/fl,T rec/ob,B
    rec/English horn, (Instrumental
    Chor I , Strings, Instrumental
    Chor II , Recorders) [9']
    HEINRICH                 (W232)

WERDIN, EBERHARD (cont'd.)

  Konzertante Musik
    strings,vln solo MÖSELER 11.446
    rent                     (W233)

WERKMAN, ARNE
  Overture, Op. 23, No. 1
    2.2.2.2. 4.2.3.0. timp,3perc,
    strings [11'] sc DONEMUS  (W234)

  Rhapsodie Pour Violon Et Ensemble
    see Rhapsody for Violin and Chamber
    Group, Op. 21

  Rhapsody for Violin and Chamber
    Group, Op. 21
    "Rhapsodie Pour Violon Et Ensemble"
    6vln,2vla,2vcl,db,hpsd,vln solo
    [17'] sc DONEMUS         (W235)

WERMANN, OSCAR
  Weihnachtsoratorium: Nr. 7
    0.0.0.0. 2.0.0.0. 8vln I,7vln II,
    6vla,5vcl,4db [6'] sc KAHNT 02026
                             (W236)

WERNER, JEAN-JACQUES (1935-    )
  Concerto
    string orch,tuba solo [18']
    BILLAUDOT                (W237)

  Concerto for Harp and String
    Orchestra [20']
    string orch,harp solo
    BILLAUDOT                (W238)

  Concerto for Horn and Orchestra
    see Quatre Bagatelles

  Concerto for Tuba and Strings
    [18'] BILLAUDOT rent     (W239)

  Quatre Bagatelles (Concerto for Horn
    and Orchestra)
    FUZEAU sc 1212, solo pt 2226, pts
    2229 TO 2233             (W240)

WERNER, RUDOLF
  Patchwork Für Klavier Und Orchester
    1(pic).1(English horn).1(bass
    clar).1. 1.0.0.0. strings,pno
    solo MULL & SCH ESM 10'012 (W241)

  Quislowck (Rondo)
    2.2.2.2. 3.2.3.1. timp,glock,harp,
    strings [20'] MULL & SCH
    ESM 10''11 rent          (W242)

  Rondo
    see Quislowck

WERNER, VLADIMIR (1937-    )
  Concerto for Oboe and Orchestra
    2.0.3.2. 4.2.3.0. timp,perc,pno,
    strings,ob solo [14'] CESKY HUD.
                             (W243)

  Symphony No. 2
    4.3.3.3. 4.3.3.1. timp,perc,harp,
    pno,strings [24'] CESKY HUD.
                             (W244)

WERNICK, RICHARD F. (1934-    )
  And A Time For Peace
    3(pic,alto fl).3(English
    horn).3(clar in E flat,bass
    clar).4(contrabsn). 4.3.4(bass
    trom).0. timp,3perc,pno&cel,harp,
    strings [15'] PRESSER rent (W245)

WERTHER-SZENEN: SUITE see Bose, Hans-
  Jurgen Von

WESSMAN, HARRI (1949-    )
  Concertino for Trombone and String
    Orchestra
    see Muumimaisuuksia

  Concertino for Trombone and Strings
    MODUS sc M97A, pts M97C  (W246)

  Muumimaisuuksia (Concertino for
    Trombone and String Orchestra)
    MODUS sc M61A, pts M61C   (W247)

WEST SIDE STORY: CONCERT SUITE NO. 1
  see Bernstein, Leonard

WEST SIDE STORY: CONCERT SUITE NO. 2
  see Bernstein, Leonard

WESTERLINCK, WILFRIED
  Landschappen 5
    6vln,3vla,2vcl,db,trp solo [8'20"]
    BELGE                    (W248)

  Landschappen II
    string orch [12'] BELGE   (W249)

WETTLAUF see Berwald, Franz (Adolf)

WHAT THE MONSTER SAW see Larsen,
  Elizabeth B. (Libby)

WHAT'S THAT SPELL? see Daugherty,
  Michael

WHEN THE WIND BLEW see Kondo, Jo

WHERE AM I? see Berg, Fred Jonny

WHERE THE BEE DANCES see Nyman, Michael

WHERE THE HEART IS PURE see Lewis,
Peter Scott

WHERE THE PALE MOONBEAMS LINGER see
Amos, Keith

WHETTAM, GRAHAM DUDLEY (1927-     )
Ballade Hébraïque
orch,vln solo MERIDEN 576-00767
(W250)

Concerto Ardente
string orch,horn solo MERIDEN
576-00773 (W251)

Concerto Conciso
string orch MERIDEN 576-00766
(W252)

Concerto for Clarinet, No. 2
string orch,clar solo MERIDEN
576-00769 (W253)

Hymnos
string orch MERIDEN 576-00774
(W254)

Idyll
fl,horn,harp,string orch MERIDEN
576-00765 (W255)

Introduction And Scherzo-Impetuoso-
Benvenuto Cellini
MERIDEN 576-00768 (W256)

Roseaux Au Vent, Les
2ob,English horn,string orch
MERIDEN 576-00771 (W257)
2ob,bsn,string orch MERIDEN
576-00772 (W258)
2ob,bsn,strings [17'] manuscript
BMIC (W259)

Sinfonia Dramatica
MERIDEN 576-00764 (W260)

WHIRL DANCE see Koch, Erland von,
Virvelpolska

WHIRLIGIG see Hewitt-Jones, Tony

WHITE, ANDREW NATHANIEL
Shepherd Song
orch (in two movements: 1.
pastorale 2. allegretto) ANDREW
42 rent (W261)

WHITE WHALE, THE. THEATER MUSIC see
Phillips, Barre

WHITMAN SETTINGS see Knussen, Oliver

WHITMAN TRIPTYCH see Bolcom, William
Elden

WHITTINGTON: NO. 25 see Offenbach,
Jacques

WHO'S HOT AND WHO'S NOT see Meijering,
Chiel

WHY SHOULD ME QUARREL see Purcell,
Henry

WIDMUNG see Silvestrov, Valentin

WIDOR, CHARLES-MARIE (1844-1937)
Salvum Fac Populum Tuum
2+pic.2.2.2. 4.4.3.1. timp,2perc,
strings [20'] LEDUC (W262)

Symphonia Sacra
0.1.1.0. 0.1.3.0. timp,strings,org
solo [17'] LEDUC (W263)

Symphonie Antique  *Op.83
2+pic.2+English horn.2.2. 4.4.3.1.
timp,triangle,drums,cym,bass
drum,glock,tam-tam,harp,org,
strings,cor LEDUC (W264)

Symphony, Op. 54
2+pic.2.0.2. 4.2.3.0. ophicleide,
timp,2cym,bass drum,strings LEDUC
(W265)

Toccata De La 5e Symphonie
(Delmotte, A.) 2.2.2.2. 4.2.3.1.
timp,perc,strings LEDUC (W266)

WIEDER AUFZUBLÜH'N WIRST DU GESÄT see
Chihara, Hideki

WIEGENLIED see Brahms, Johannes see
Karayev, Kara

WIEGENLIED OP. 98, NO. 2 see Schubert,
Franz (Peter)

WIENER BLUT see Strauss, Johann, [Jr.]

WIENHORST, RICHARD (1920-     )
Patterns Circus Patterns
3.2.2.2. 4.3.3.0. timp,perc,strings
[11'] SCHIRM.EC rent (W267)

WIERNIK, ADAM (1916-     )
Variations
2vln I,2vln II,2vla,2vcl,2db [11']
sc,pts STIM (W268)

WIESE, JAN (1953-     )
Pust, Et, For Oboe And Strings
string orch,ob solo NORSKMI (W269)

WIGGINS, CHRISTOPHER D.
Concerto for Strings
strings [19'] manuscript BMIC
(W270)

Song For Sam
strings [7'] manuscript BMIC (W271)

WILBY, PHILIP (1949-     )
Bird Fancyer's Delight, The
strings CHESTER pts CH55800, sc
CH55799 (W272)

Carol Singers
strings CHESTER pts CH55939, sc
CH55934 (W273)

Carols And Crackers  *Xmas,Suite
strings CHESTER pts CH55873, sc
CH55872 (W274)

Imagined Fable, An
fl/pic,ob&English horn,clar&bass
clar,bsn,2horn,trp,trom,2perc,
pno,strings [11'] CHESTER (W275)

St. Cecilia Rag
strings CHESTER pts CH55822, sc
CH55821 (W276)

Symphony No. 2
3.3.3.3. 4.3.3.1. timp,3perc,pno&
cel,harp,strings [27'] CHESTER
(W277)

WILD DECEMBERS see Lutyens, Elisabeth

WILDBERGER, JACQUES (1922-     )
An Die Hoffnung
3.3.3.3. 4.3.3.1. 3perc,cel,harp,
10vln I,10vln II,8vla,6vcl,4db,S&
narrator [18'] (text by
Hölderlin, J. Becker, and Erich
Fried) HUG (W278)

Concerto for Orchestra
see Dialoghi Attraverso Lo Spazio

Dialoghi Attraverso Lo Spazio
(Concerto for Orchestra)
4(bass fl,alto fl,pic).4(English
horn).4(basset horn,bass
clar).4(contrabsn). 7.6.4.1.
5perc,harp,cel, Strings A (10-5-
6-5-2) Strings B (6-9-6-5-5) HUG
(W279)

Du Holde Kunst
3.3(English horn).3(basset horn,
bass clar).3(contrabsn). 4.3.3.1.
harp,pno,cel,3perc,acord,gtr,
12vln I,10vln II,5vla,6vcl,4db,
vla solo,S&narrator [18'] (text
by Peter Weiss, Günter Eich,
Walter Benjamin, and Stéphane
Mallarmé) HUG (W280)

Konzertante Szenen
3(pic,alto fl).3(English
horn).3(bass clar).3(contrabsn).
4.4.4.0. 4perc,cel,harp,14vln I,
12vln II,10vla,8vcl,6db,sax solo
[19'] HUG (W281)

Tod Und Verklärung
Bar solo,0.0.1.1. 0.1.1.0. 3perc&
acord,cel,5vln I,4vln II,3vla,
3vcl,db (text by Novalis, Tepl,
Heine, and Zitate) HUG (W282)

...Und Füllet Die Erde Und Machet Sie
Euch Untertan...
3(pic,alto fl).3(English
horn).3(basset horn,bass clar,
contrabass clar).3(contrabsn).
4.3.3.1. 6perc,harp,cel,pno,12vln
I,10vln II,8vla,8vcl,6db [17']
HUG (W283)

WILDBIRD DREAMING see Howard, Brian

WILDERNESS see McCauley, William A.

WILDSCHÜTZ, DER: KOMM, LIEBES GRETCHEN,
BEKENNE FREI see Lortzing, (Gustav)
Albert

WILDSCHÜTZ, DER: TERZETT see Lortzing,
(Gustav) Albert, Wildschütz, Der:
Komm, Liebes Gretchen, Bekenne Frei

WILDWOOD SPIRIT'S CHANT, THE see
Heinrich, Anton Philip

WILHELM TELL: 3 LIEDER see Liszt, Franz

WILHELM TELL: BALLETTMUSIK see Rossini,
Gioacchino, Guillaume Tell: Ballet
Music

WILL YOU, WON'T YOU, WILL YOU, WON'T
YOU, WILL YOU JOIN THE DANCE? see
Crawley, Clifford

WILLAN, HEALEY (1880-1968)
Through Darkness Into Light
3(pic).3(English
horn).2.3(contrabsn). 4.3.3.1.
timp,perc,harp,org,strings [15']
(symphonic poem) sc CANADIAN
MI 1100 W689TH (W284)

WILLCOCKS, JONATHAN
Rainforest 3
2ob,2clar,2basset horn,2bsn,
contrabsn/db,4horn NOVELLO (W285)

WILLI, HERBERT (1956-     )
Concerto for Flute and Orchestra
2(pic,alto fl).2(English
horn).2(bass clar).2. 2.2.1.0.
timp,2perc,harp,strings,fl solo
[15'] SCHOTTS perf mat rent
(W286)

Concerto for Orchestra
3(3pic).3(English horn).2+bass
clar.3(contrabsn).soprano sax.
3.3.3.1. timp,3perc,harp,strings
[10'] study sc SCHOTTS ED 8348
perf mat rent (W287)

Für 16
1(pic).1.1+bass clar.1. 1.1.1.0.
2perc,pno,strings [12'] SCHOTTS
ED 8016 perf mat rent (W288)

Räume
2(2pic).1(English horn).3(2clar in
E flat,bass clar).0. soprano
sax(alto sax). 0.4.4.0. timp,
2perc,strings [10'] SCHOTTS perf
mat rent (W289)

WILLIAM TELL AND OTHER OVERTURES see
Rossini, Carlo

WILLIAMS, ADRIAN (1956-     )
Doubting Light, The
strings [10'] ESCHIG (W290)

Elegiac Serenade
strings [15'] ESCHIG (W291)

WILLIAMS, GRAHAM (1940-     )
Solstice Song
2.2.2.2. 2.2.0.0. 3perc,harp,
strings [20'] manuscript BMIC
(W292)

WILLIAMS, RALPH VAUGHAN
see VAUGHAN WILLIAMS, [SIR] RALPH

WILLIAMSON, MALCOLM (1931-     )
Au Tombeau Du Martyr Juif Inconnu
see Concerto for Harp and Strings

Concerto for Harp and Strings
"Au Tombeau Du Martyr Juif Inconnu"
[19'] BOIS (W293)

Concerto for Piano and String
Orchestra, No. 2
strings,pno solo [16'] BOOSEY-ENG
rent (W294)

WILMS, JOHANN WILHELM (1772-1847)
Sinfonia No. 4 in D minor, Op. 23
1.2.2.2. 4.2.0.0. timp,strings
[20'] sc DONEMUS (W295)

WILSON, CHARLES M. (1931-     )
Aubade And Nocturne
2.2.0.1. 2.2.2.0. timp,cym,strings,
clar solo,vibra solo [9'] sc
CANADIAN MI 1450 W747AU (W296)

Conductus
1.1.1.1. 2.2.1.1. perc,pno,2vln,
vla,vcl,db,pno solo [15'] sc
CANADIAN MI 1361 W747CO (W297)

WILSON, DONALD M. (1937-     )
Apotheosis
strings [6'] SCHIRM.EC rent (W298)

Dedication
strings [6'] SCHIRM.EC rent (W299)

WILSON, EUGENE (1937-     )
Concerto for Strings
string orch [22'] (The jam on
Gerry's rock -- She's like the
swallow -- The variations of Mr.
Webern -- The strawberry roan) sc
CANADIAN MI 1500 W747CO (W300)

WILSON, IAN R.
Rise
3.2.2.2. 4.2.3.1. timp,perc,strings
[11'] UNIVER. (W301)

WILSON, LARS (1952-   )
  Tyche
    fl,ob,clar,bsn,horn,3perc,2vln,vla,
    vcl,db [5'] STIM                    (W302)

WILSON, RICHARD (EDWARD) (1941-   )
  Agitations
    3(alto fl,pic).2+English horn.2+
    bass clar.3(contrabsn). 4.2.3.1.
    timp,3perc,pno,cel,harp,strings
    [12'] PEER rent                     (W303)

  Child's London, A
    2.2.2(clar in A).2. 2.2.0.0. timp,
    strings [12'] PEER rent             (W304)

  Concerto for Piano and Orchestra
    2.2.2.2(contrabsn). 4.2(bass
    trp).1.0. timp,harp,3perc,
    strings,pno solo [33'] PEER rent    (W305)

  Fantasy And Variations
    fl,clar,bsn,trp,trom,2perc,vln,vla,
    vcl,db [7'45"] PEER rent            (W306)

  Pamietam
    2.2.2.2. 2.2.0.0. timp,perc,
    strings,Mez solo [20'] PEER rent    (W307)

  Silhouette
    orch PEER min sc 61882-856 f.s.,
    pts rent                            (W308)

WILSON, THOMAS (1927-   )
  Carillon
    3.3.3.3. 4.3.2.1. timp,perc,harp,
    pno,cel,strings QUEENSGATE          (W309)

  Chamber Symphony
    fl,ob,clar,clar&bass clar,bsn,
    2horn,trp,2vln,vla,vcl,db
    QUEENSGATE                          (W310)

  Concerto for Guitar
    3vln I,3vln II,2vla,2vcl,db,perc,
    gtr solo, The percussion includes
    vibes and bongos. [20']
    QUEENSGATE                          (W311)

  Concerto for Trombone
    orch,trom solo QUEENSGATE           (W312)

  Concerto for Trumpet
    orch,trp solo QUEENSGATE            (W313)

  Concerto for Violin and Orchestra
    2.2.2.2. 4.3.3.1. timp,perc,pno&
    cel,harp,strings,vln solo [26']
    QUEENSGATE                          (W314)

WINDOWS see Sjöberg, Johan Magnus

WINDOWS AND CANOPIES see Dillon, James

WINDPRINTS see Harley, James

WINDS OF CHANGE see Rae, Allan,
  Symphony No. 2

WING see Lindgren, Pär

WINGLESS see Kantscheli, Gija,
  Flügellos

WINGS OF THE WIND see Borisova-Ollas,
  Victoria

WINTER see Serebrier, Jose, Concerto
  for Violin see Xiaogang, Ye

WINTER, TOMAS (1954-   )
  Arkieologisk Svit  *Op.152
    4(pic).3(English horn).4(bass
    clar).3(contrabsn). 2.2.2.1.
    timp,3perc,strings [21'] (1.
    Jägarfolk; 2. Trattbägarfolk
    (Blandad Kör); 3. Megalitfolk; 4.
    Gropkeramikfolk; 5. Båtyxfolk) sc
    STIM H-2837                         (W315)

  Hemligheter  *Op.165
    trp,trom,pno,strings [4'-5'] sc
    STIM                                (W316)

  Mälar-Öar
    string orch STIM                    (W317)

  Moder Jord  *Op.166
    1.1.0.1. 0.0.0.0. timp,perc,
    strings,pno [4'] sc STIM            (W318)

  Odin som schaman  *Op.156
    1(pic).0.1(bass
    clar).2(contrabsn).3sax. 1.0.1.1.
    timp,perc,vcl,db [5'] sc STIM       (W319)

  Totemistisk Svit  *Op.157
    3(pic).1.1.1. 1.2.2.1. timp,3perc,
    strings [23'] (1. Valen; 2.
    Björnen; 3. Älgen; 4. Vargen; 5.
    Lodjuret) sc STIM                   (W320)

  WINTER DANCE
    "Chamber Symphony No. 1" 1(pic).1.1+
    bass clar.1. 1.1.1.0. 2perc,pno&
    cel,harp,string quin,6vln I,5vln

II,4vla,4vcl,3db [15'] SCHOTTS perf
mat rent                              (W321)

WINTER MUSIC see Clarke, Nigel

WINTER OF THE WORLD, THE see Lutyens,
  Elisabeth

WINTER PORTRAIT see Ichiyanagi, Toshi,
  Concerto for Piano, No. 2

WINTERGARDEN, THE see Hultqvist,
  Anders, Vintertrdgrden

WINTERGEZICHT see Hamel, Micha

WINTERLUDE see Kunz, Alfred

WINTERNÄCHTE see Huber, Hans

WINTERPASTORALE see Schmidt, Hansjürgen

WIR ABER SINGEN see Schweinitz,
  Wolfgang von

WIR BETEN DICH UNENDLICH WESEN see
  Haydn, [Johann] Michael

WISHART, PETER (1921-1984)
  Concerto for Violin, No. 1
    0.2+English horn.0.2. 0.2.3.0. vln
    solo [17'] sc,pts STAINER HL249
    rent                                (W322)

  Symphony in E flat
    2(pic).2(English horn).2.2.
    2.0.0.0. strings [26'] sc,pts
    STAINER HL245 rent                  (W323)

WISHART, TREVOR
  Dance Music
    orch,electronic tape [17'] (suite
    of 4 pieces for orch. with click-
    tracks) sc UNIV.YORK 0075 f.s.      (W324)

  Dance Music 3
    3.3.2.2. 2.2.2.0. perc,pno,harp,
    strings manuscript BMIC             (W325)

  Dance Music 4
    6.2.2.2. 2.2.2.0. 2perc,pno,harp,
    strings manuscript BMIC             (W326)

  Kaleidoscope
    orch [20'] sc UNIV.YORK 0074 f.s.   (W327)

WITH THE HEATHER AND SMALL BIRDS see
  Tann, Hilary

WITHIN TREES see Strindberg, Henrik, I
  Träd

WITT, FRIEDRICH (1770-1836)
  Concertino in E for Horn and
  Orchestra
    0.2.0.0. 2.0.0.0. 8vln I,7vln II,
    6vla,5vcl,4db [21'] sc,solo pt
    PETERS 00208                        (W328)

  Sinfonia in A
    1.2.0.2. 2.0.0.0. strings [28']
    BREITKOPF-W                         (W329)

WITTINGER, ROBERT (1945-   )
  Concerto for Violin and Orchestra
    4.4.4.4. 6.4.4.1. 3perc,harp,pno,
    strings,vln solo [20'] MOECK sc
    5341 f.s., pts rent                 (W330)

  Concerto for Violoncello and
  Orchestra
    4.4.4.4. 6.4.4.1. 3perc,harp,pno,
    strings,vcl solo [20'] MOECK sc
    5351 f.s., pts rent                 (W331)

  Concerto Grosso, No. 1
    4.4.4.4. 4.3.3.1. timp,4perc,harp,
    cel,strings [20'] MOECK sc 5283
    f.s., pts rent                      (W332)

  Concerto Grosso, No. 2
    1.1.1.0. 1.1.1.0. perc,pno,strings
    [15'] MOECK sc 5359 f.s., pts
    rent                                (W333)

  Concerto No. 1, Op. 21
    see Montaggio

  Cronogramme 1
    perc,harp,pno,strings [17'] MOECK
    sc 5490 f.s., pts rent              (W334)

  Montaggio (Concerto No. 1, Op. 21)
    1(pic).1.1.0. 0.0.0.0. perc,pno,
    cembalo,cel,vla,vcl [14'] study
    sc BREITKOPF-W PB 4864              (W335)

  Sinfonia Funebre, No. 3
    4.4.4.4. 6.4.4.1. timp,3perc,harp,
    pno,strings [22'] MOECK sc 5270
    f.s., pts rent                      (W336)

  Sinfonia, No. 2
    4.4.4.4. 6.4.4.1. 5perc,2harp,cel,
    pno,strings [41'] MOECK sc 5202
    f.s., pts rent                      (W337)

WITTINGER, ROBERT (cont'd.)
  Sinfonia, No. 4
    1.1.1.1. 2.1.1.0. perc,pno,hpsd,
    strings [30'] MOECK sc 5448 f.s.
    pts rent                            (W338)

WITTMANN, MAX (1941-   )
  I Kdyby Se Rozplakaly Rimsy
    fl&tenor sax,clar&alto sax,trp,
    trom,perc,elec gtr,bass gtr,
    strings,solo voice, conga, piano
    fender, moog [5'] CESKY HUD.        (W339)

  Ted Uz Viš
    3sax,horn,3trp,3trom,gtr,bass gtr,
    strings,male solo&3 female soli,
    conga, moog [3'] CESKY HUD.         (W340)

WITZENMANN, WOLFGANG
  Sinfonia, No. 1
    3.3.3.3. 4.3.3.1. perc,harp,pno,
    strings [25'] MOECK sc 5475 f.s.
    pts rent                            (W341)

WOHL DENN, GEFASST IST DER ENTSCHLUSS
  see Nicolai, Otto

WOHLGEMUTH, GERHARD (1920-   )
  Divertimento for Piano and Orchestra
    see EU-Musik Nr. 1

  EU-Musik Nr. 1 (Divertimento for
  Piano and Orchestra)
    2.2.2.2. 3.2.2.0. timp,3perc,pno,
    cel,8vln I,7vln II,6vla,5vcl,4db
    [20'] sc,solo pt PETERS 03398       (W342)

  Sinfonia No. 3
    3.3.3.3. 4.4.3.1. timp,3perc,pno,
    cel,xylo,marimba,vibra,harp,8vln
    I,7vln II,6vla,5vcl,4db [27'] sc
    PETERS 03354                        (W343)

WOLF, HANS
  Vier Bauerntänze  *Op.7
    string orch BOHM                    (W344)

WOLF, HUGO (1860-1903)
  Concerto for Piano and Violin
    (Spitzer, Leopold) pno,vln,orch
    MUSIKWISS.                          (W345)

  Dein Liebesfeuer
    see Seufzer

  Du Denkst Mit Einem Fädchen
    (Cohen, Shimon) string orch,solo
    voice [1'] PRESSER rent             (W346)

  Mausfallen Sprüchlein
    (Cohen, Shimon) string orch,solo
    voice [1'] PRESSER rent             (W347)

  Nun Lass Uns Frieden Schliessen (from
    Italienisches Liederbuch)
    (Müller-Rehrmann) strings without
    db,solo voice [3'] PETERS           (W348)

  Penthesilea
    3.3.2.3. 4.4.3.1. timp,perc,harp,
    strings [35'] BREITKOPF-W           (W349)

  Scherzo Und Finale
    3.2.2.2. 4.3.3.1. timp,perc,strings
    [9'] BREITKOPF-W                    (W350)

  Schon Streckt Ich Aus Im Bett Die
    Müden Glieder (from Italienisches
    Liederbuch)
    (Müller-Rehrmann) 2.2.2.1. 3.0.0.0.
    strings,solo voice [3'] PETERS      (W351)

  Seufzer
    "Dein Liebesfeuer" 0.3.0.2.
    0.0.0.0. strings,solo voice [3']
    (text by Mörike) PETERS             (W352)

  Ständchen Euch Zu Bringen, Ein (from
    Italienisches Liederbuch)
    (Müller-Rehrmann) 1.1.2.2. 4.1.1.0.
    timp,strings,solo voice [3']
    PETERS                              (W353)

  Wenn Du Mich Mit Den Augen Streifst
    (from Italienisches Liederbuch)
    (Müller-Rehrmann) 1.0.1.2. 2.0.0.0.
    strings,solo voice [3'] PETERS      (W354)

WOLFE, LAWRENCE
  Concerto for Trumpet
    trp solo,3.2.2.2. 4.0.3.1. timp,
    perc,harp,strings [30'] SCHIRM.EC
    rent                                (W355)

  Fanfares
    3.2.2.2. 4.3.3.1. timp,3perc,
    strings [4'] SCHIRM.EC rent         (W356)

  Freefall  *Overture
    3.3.3.3. 4.3.2.1. timp,perc,harp,
    strings [8'] SCHIRM.EC rent         (W357)

  Suite Dreams (composed with Gerber,
    Stephen Edward)
    3.2.2.2. 4.3.3.1. timp,2perc,harp,

WOLFE, LAWRENCE (cont'd.)

    strings,narrator, optional actor
    [13'] SCHIRM.EC rent      (W358)

WOMEN OF TRACHIS see Horwood, Michael

WONDERFUL TOWN: SELECTIONS see
   Bernstein, Leonard

WOOD, GARETH (1950-    )
   Concerto for Double Bass and
     Orchestra
     3.3.3.2. 4.3.3.1. timp,3perc,harp,
     strings,db solo [27'] BMIC  (W359)

WOOD, HUGH BRADSHAW (1932-    )
   Concerto for Piano and Orchestra
     2.2.3.2. 2.2.1.1. timp,3perc,harp,
     strings,pno solo [33'] CHESTER
                         (W360)

WOODCUTS see Baley, Virko

WOOLRICH, JOHN
   Barber's Timepiece, The
     orch sc FABER 51261 5    (W361)

   Caprichos
     pic&alto fl,clar in E flat&bass
     clar,soprano sax,horn,trp,trom,
     perc,pno,vln,vla,vcl,db [7']
     FABER                   (W362)

   Concerto for Oboe and Orchestra
     3.3.3.3.soprano sax. 4.3.3.1. timp,
     4perc,strings,ob solo [22'] FABER
                         (W363)

   Concerto for Viola and Orchestra
     2.2.2.2. 2.2.0.0. 2perc,harp,
     strings,vla solo [20'] FABER
                         (W364)

   Curtain Tune, A *educ
     2.2.2.2. 2.2.0.0. timp,strings [5']
     FABER                   (W365)

   Ghost In The Machine, The
     3.3.3.3. 6.4.4.1. timp,4perc,harp,
     strings [15'] FABER     (W366)

   It Is Midnight, Dr. Schweitzer
     strings [12'] FABER     (W367)

   Music From A House Of Crossed Desires
     pic,ob,clar,clar in E flat,soprano
     sax,bass clar,contrabsn,horn,trp,
     trom,tuba,2perc,pno,vcl,db [8']
     FABER                   (W368)

   Si Va Facendo Notte
     clar,strings [20'] FABER   (W369)

   Theatre Represents A Garden At Night,
     The
     2.2.2.2. 2.0.0.0. strings [15']
     FABER                   (W370)

   Ulysses Awakes
     10strings,vla solo sc FABER 51289 5
                         (W371)

WORD, CRYSTAL CIRCLES AND THE WORLD see
   Ekström, Lars

WORD WITHOUT A WORD, THE see Friberg,
   Tomas

WORLDS see Hillborg, Anders

WOTANS ABSCHIED UND FEUERZAUBER see
   Wagner, Richard

WRANITZKY, ANTON (1761-1820)
   Omasis *Overture
     2.2.2.2. 4.2.0.0. timp,strings [9']
     CESKY HUD.           (W372)

WRANITZKY, PAUL (1756-1808)
   Sinfonia Quodlibet D-dur
     2.2.2.2. 2.2.0.0. timp,cembalo,
     strings [12'] CESKY HUD.  (W373)

   Symfonie Charakteristická Pro Mir S
     Republikou Francouzskou *Op.31
     [33'] CESKY HUD.      (W374)

   Symphony in C, Op. 11
     2.2.0.2. 4.2.0.0. timp,strings
     CESKY HUD.           (W375)

   Symphony in D, Op. 25
     1.2.0.2. 2.0.0.0. timp,strings
     [27'] CESKY HUD.     (W376)

WRATTNY, W.
   Concerto in B flat
     2ob,2horn,strings,clar solo
     KUNZELMANN 10264     (W377)

WUENSCH, GERHARD (1925-    )
   Concerto for Bassoon and Chamber
     Orchestra, Op. 69
     2.0.3(bass clar).0. 2.2.1.0.
     strings,bsn solo [25'] sc,solo
     pt,pno red CANADIAN
     MI 1324 W959CO      (W378)

WUENSCH, GERHARD (cont'd.)

   Concerto for Organ, 3 Trumpets,
     Timpani and Strings, Op. 76
     [27'] sc,solo pt CANADIAN
     MI 1750 W959CO      (W379)

   Concerto for 2 Pianos and Orchestra,
     Op. 81
     2(pic).2(English horn).2.2.
     4.3.3.0. timp,3perc,strings,2pno
     soli [27'] sc,pno red CANADIAN
     MI 1461 W959CO      (W380)

   Concerto Grosso, Op. 77
     string orch,acord solo [23'] sc
     CANADIAN MI 1666 W959CO  (W381)

WULLUR, SINTA
   Between Dreams And Fairy Tales
     1.1.2.1. 0.1.0.0. perc,pno,strings,
     electronic tape [17'] sc DONEMUS
                         (W382)

WUORINEN, CHARLES (1938-    )
   Another Happy Birthday
     3.2.3.3. 4.2.3.1. timp,perc,pno,
     8vln I,7vln II,6vla,5vcl,4db [2']
     sc PETERS 04315      (W383)

   Concerto for 4 Saxophones and
     Orchestra
     3.3.3.3. 4.3.3.1. timp,3perc,pno,
     harp,8vln I,7vln II,6vla,5vcl,
     4db,4sax soli [25'] sc PETERS
     02966                   (W384)

   Five: Concerto For Amplified Cello
     And Orchestra
     2.2.2.2. 4.2.3.1. timp,2perc,harp,
     8vln I,7vln II,6vla,5vcl,4db,
     amplified cello solo [21'] sc,
     solo pt PETERS 04334   (W385)

   Great Procession, The
     3.2.3.2. 4.2.3.1. timp,3perc,pno,
     harp,8vln I,7vln II,6vla,5vcl,4db
     [25'] sc PETERS 04603  (W386)

   Machault Mon Chou
     2.2.3.3. 4.2.3.1. timp,perc,harp,
     8vln I,7vln II,6vla,5vcl,4db
     [11'] sc PETERS 04338  (W387)

   Microsymphony
     4.3.3.3. 4.3.3.1. timp,3perc,pno,
     harp,8vln I,7vln II,6vla,5vcl,4db
     [11'] sc PETERS 04662  (W388)

WÜTHRICH-MATHEZ, HANS
   Netz-Werk 1
     4.4.4.4. 4.3.4.1. 4perc,harp,
     strings [12'] MOECK sc 5369 f.s.,
     pts rent              (W389)

   Netz-Werk 2
     4.2.4.2. 3.4.1.0. strings [10']
     MOECK sc 5370 f.s., pts rent
                         (W390)

   Netz-Werk 3
     3.2.2.2. 4.2.2.1. 4perc,harp,
     strings [25'] MOECK sc 5454 f.s.
     pts rent              (W391)

WYCK RISSINGTON GREEN see Amos, Keith

WYRE, JOHN (1941-    )
   Cloches Pour Michel
     string orch,harp,tuba,5perc soli
     [15'] sc CANADIAN MI 1750 W993CL
                         (W392)

   Connexus
     4(pic,alto fl).3(English
     horn).4(clar in E flat,bass
     clar).1(contrabsn). 4.4.3.1.
     3perc,harp,cel&perc,strings,6perc
     soli sc CANADIAN MI 1441 W993CO
                         (W393)

# X

XENIA see Raskatov, Alexander

XENOS see Tveit, Sigvald

XERXES: FRONDI TENERE see Handel,
   George Frideric

XERXES: OVERTURE AND SINFONIA see
   Handel, George Frideric

XIAOGANG, YE (1955-    )
   Last Paradise, The *Op.24
     3(pic).3(English horn).2.2+
     contrabsn. 5.3.3.1. 5perc,harp,
     strings,vln solo SCHOTTS  (X1)

   Purple Fog & White Poppy
     2.2.2.2. 4.3.3.1. 4perc,harp,
     strings,S solo [14'] SCHOTTS (X2)

   Scent Of Black Mango, The
     3.2.2.3. 4.3.3.1. 4perc,harp,
     strings,pno solo [17'] SCHOTTS
                         (X3)

   Silence Of The Sakyamuni, The *Op.29
     3(pic).2(English horn).2.2.
     4.3.3.1. timp,5perc,cel,harp,
     strings, shakuhachi solo SCHOTTS
                        (X4)

   Strophe
     1.1.1.1. 1.1.1.0. 2perc,pno,harp,
     strings [12'] SCHOTTS   (X5)

   Winter *Op.28
     3(pic).2.2.2. 4.2.3.1. 3perc,harp,
     strings SCHOTTS      (X6)

XU, SHUYA (1961-    )
   San
     1.1.1.0. 0.0.0.0. vln,vla,vcl,db,
     gtr,harp,pno,perc [14'] BILLAUDOT
                         (X7)

# Y

YAD VASHEM see Downey, John Wilham, For
Those Who Suffered

YAMAGISHI, MAO (1933- )
Prelude for Orchestra
[11'] JAPAN                              (Y1)

YAMAKAWA, KENICHI (1934- )
Concertino for Piano
string orch,pno solo [15'] JAPAN
(Y2)

Fantasy No. 2
string orch,db solo [12'] JAPAN
(Y3)

YAMAMOTO, JUNNOSUKE (1958- )
Doppel Konzert Für Shakuhachi Und
Kugo
orch, kugo, shaku [23'] JAPAN  (Y4)

Kou En
see Prominence

Prominence
"Kou En" orch, pipa [15'] JAPAN
(Y5)

Short Animations With Symphonic
Sounds
see Tokochan Chokkin 1.2.3

Tokochan Chokkin 1.2.3
"Short Animations With Symphonic
Sounds" chamber orch [15'] JAPAN
(Y6)

YAMAUCHI, MASAHIRO (1960- )
Sinfonia for Orchestra
[27'] JAPAN                              (Y7)

YANAGI, HIROSI (1932- )
Fukko Eno Inori
orch [8'] JAPAN                          (Y8)

YANOV-YANOVSKY, FELIX (1934- )
Concerto Grosso No. 2
see Simple Concerto

Simple Concerto (Concerto Grosso No.
2)
strings,vln&vla&vcl soli [14']
BOOSEY-ENG rent                     (Y9)

YASUMURA, YOSHIHIRO
Musical Flight
orch,pno [12'] JAPAN                 (Y10)

YASURAOKA, AKIO (1958- )
Antiphone
25strings [11'] JAPAN               (Y11)

Polifonia
orch,vla solo [19'] JAPAN           (Y12)

YE BANKS AND BRAES O'BONNIE DOON see
Grainger, Percy Aldridge

YEAR 1941, THE see Prokofiev, Serge

YELIEL see Galante, Carlo

YELL see Canat De Chizy, Edith

YNDIG OG FRYDEFULD SOMMERTID, EN see
Lindorff-Larsen, Eilert, Liebliche,
Heitere Sommerzeit, Die

YNGWE, JAN (1953- )
Queens Touché, The
3(pic).2.2.3(contrabsn). 4.4.4.1.
2timp,2perc,strings [0'5"]
(orchestral fanfare) STIM sc
H-2836, pts                         (Y13)

YOHEN see Kikuchi, Yukio

YOSHIOKA, TAKAYOSHI (1955- )
Concerto for Marimba, No. 1
orch,marimba solo [23'] JAPAN (Y14)

YOUNG PIECES see Sandred, Örjan

YOUNG PROMETHEUS, THE see Beethoven,
Ludwig van

YOUR ROCKABY see Turnage, Mark-Anthony

YOUTHFUL RAPTURE see Grainger, Percy
Aldridge

YOUTHFUL SUITE see Grainger, Percy
Aldridge

YUASA, JOJI (1929- )
Concerto for Violin
orch,vln solo [21'] JAPAN           (Y15)

Eye On Genesis II
3(alto fl,pic,bass fl).3(English
horn).4(clar in E flat,bass
clar).3(contrabsn). 4.3.3(bass
trom).1. 5perc,pno,cel,harp,

YUASA, JOJI (cont'd.)
strings [13'] SCHOTT,J perf mat
rent                                (Y16)

Hommage À Sibelius
"Midnight Sun, The" 3(pic,alto
fl).3(English horn).3(clar in E
flat,bass clar).3(contrabsn).
4.3.3(bass trom).0. cel,pno,harp,
2perc,strings [7'] SCHOTT,J perf
mat rent                            (Y17)

Midnight Sun, The
see Hommage À Sibelius

Narrow Road Into The Deep North;
Basho, The
orch [21'] (symphonic suite) JAPAN
(Y18)

see Symphonic Suite

Nine Levels By Ze-Ami
2.1.2.0. 1.1.1.0. 2perc,cel/elec
pno,pno,strings,electronic tape
solo [35'] SCHOTT,J perf mat rent
(Y19)

Requiem for Orchestra
3.3.3.3. 4.3.3.1. 5perc,cel,pno,
harp,strings [24'] SCHOTT,J perf
mat rent                            (Y20)

Revealed Time
3(3pic).2(English horn).3(clar in E
flat,bass clar).2(contrabsn).
4.3.3.0. 3perc,pno/cel,harp,
strings,vla solo [16'] study sc
SCHOTT,J SJ 1063 perf mat rent
(Y21)

Symphonic Suite
"Narrow Road Into The Deep North:
Bashõ, The" 3(pic,alto
fl).3(English horn).3(clar in E
flat,bass clar).3(contrabsn).
4.3.3.0. 4perc,harp,pno,cel,
strings [20'] SCHOTT,J perf mat
rent                                (Y22)

# Z

Z CESKYCH ZPEVU see Malat, Jan

Z POLABSKÉ KRAJINY see Myska, Rudolf

ZACH, JOHANN (JAN) (1699-1773)
Concerto in G for Flute and Orchestra
cembalo,strings without vla,fl solo
[11'] PANTON                        (Z1)

ZADOR, EUGENE (JENÖ) (1894-1977)
Five Contrasts
orch min sc KUNZELMANN ETP 1325 ipr
(Z2)

Fugue Fantasia Für Grosses Orchester
orch min sc KUNZELMANN ETP 1312 ipr
(Z3)

Music for Clarinet and String
Orchestra
clar solo,string orch KUNZELMANN
10027 ipr                           (Z4)

Suite for Horn, Percussion and String
Orchestra
horn,perc,string orch KUNZELMANN
10026 ipr                           (Z5)

ZAHRADNÍK, ZDENEK (1936- )
Monolog Julie
2.2.2.2. 2.2.0.0. timp,strings,S
solo [8'] CESKY HUD.               (Z6)

Monolog Julie II
2.2.2.2. 2.2.0.0. timp,perc,
strings,S solo [8'] CESKY HUD.
(Z7)

Pri Slunci A Jeho Jasu  *cant
3.3.3.3. 4.3.3.1. timp,perc,
strings,SBar&speaking voice [40']
CESKY HUD.                          (Z8)

ZAIMONT, JUDITH LANG (1945- )
Tarantelle. Overture For Orchestra
3.3.2.2. 4.2.3.1. timp,3perc,
strings [7'] SCHIRM.EC rent  (Z9)

ZALOBA PROTI NEZNÁMÉMU see Martinu,
Bohuslav (Jan)

ZALUDSKÁ POLKA see Smetácek, Rudolf

ZÁMECKÁ SERENÁDA see Juchelka, Miroslav

ZÁMECKÉ OZVENY see Myska, Rudolf

ZAMECNIK, EVZEN (1939- )
Concerto Grosso
2.2.2.2. 2.2.2.0. timp,perc,
strings,clar in E flat&clar&
flügelhorn&4trp&trom&tuba&
euphonium soli [18'] CESKY HUD.
(Z10)

Divertimento Semplice
[12'] CESKY HUD.                    (Z11)

Musica Lamentosa
3.2.3.3. 4.3.3.1. timp,perc,harp,
pno,strings [12'] CESKY HUD.
(Z12)

Preludio Deciso
3.2.2.2. 4.3.3.1. timp,perc,harp,
strings [11'] CESKY HUD.       (Z13)

Preludio Filarmonico
3.2.2.2. 4.3.3.1. timp,perc,harp,
strings [8'] CESKY HUD.       (Z14)

Preludium K Jubileu
2.2.2.2. 2.2.3.0. timp,perc,strings
[4'] CESKY HUD.                    (Z15)

Promenádní Predehra
1.1.1.1. 1.1.1.0. timp,perc,pno,
strings [9'] CESKY HUD.         (Z16)

Serenade in D
2.2.2.2. 2.2.1.1. timp,perc,strings
[14'] CESKY HUD.                   (Z17)

Serenata Piccola
[12'] CESKY HUD.                    (Z18)

Symfonicky Diptych
2.2.2.2. 4.2.3.0. timp,perc,harp,
strings,Bar solo [10'] CESKY HUD.
(Z19)

ZAMPA: OVERTURE see Herold, Louis-
Joseph-Ferdinand

ZANG VAN AQUARIUS, DE (VERSIE 2) see
Goeyvaerts, Karel, Aquarius, No. 2
(2nd Version)

ZANNATA FOR OBOE SOLO AND CHAMBER
ORCHESTRA see Meyers, Randall

ZAPF, HELMUT
Concertino No. 1 for Orchestra
2.1.1.2. 2.1.1.0. 2timp,3perc,pno,
harp,8vln I,7vln II,6vla,5vcl,4db
[8'] sc PETERS 02872 (Z20)

ZAPPA, ENRIC
Concerto for 4 Percussionists
2.2.2.2. 4.2.1.1. strings,4perc
soli SEESAW (Z21)

Wendling Farm
2.1.2.0. 3.0.0.0. timp,strings
SEESAW (Z22)

ZAR UND ZIMMERMANN: DARF EINE NIEDERE
MAGD ES WAGEN see Lortzing,
(Gustav) Albert

ZAR UND ZIMMERMANN: DUET OF MARIE AND
IWANOW see Lortzing, (Gustav)
Albert, Zar Und Zimmermann: Darf
Eine Niedere Magd Es Wagen

ZARATE, JOSÉ
Concerto for Piano and Chamber
Orchestra
1.1.1.1. 1.1.1.0. 2perc,strings,pno
solo [20'] perf sc EMEC f.s.
(Z23)

ZARENBRAUT: ARIE DER LJUBA see Rimsky-
Korsakov, Nikolai

ZÁRIVY DEN see Myska, Rudolf

ZASADIT STROM see Lukas, Zdenek

ZASNENÍ see Strasek, Emil

ZÁSNUBNÍ TANCE KARLA IV see Flosman,
Oldrich

ZATERDAGEDITIE, DE see Janssen, Guus

ZBINDEN, JULIEN-FRANÇOIS (1917- )
Lémanic 70 (Overture for Orchestra)
Op.48
2(pic).2(English
horn).2.2(contrabsn). 4.2.3.1.
timp,2harp,2perc,strings [12']
min sc HUG FF 8450 (Z24)

Overture for Orchestra
see Lémanic 70

ZBOJNICKÉ TANCE see Kašlik, Václav

ZE SMETANOVA ZÁPISNIKU MOTIVU see
Smolka, Jaroslav

ZEAMI see Nishimura, Akira

ZECHLIN, RUTH (1926- )
Concerto for Cembalo and Orchestra
see Kristalle

Concerto for Flute, Percussion and
Strings
see Dionysos Und Apollo

Concerto for Organ, No. 2
timp,perc,8vln I,7vln II,6vla,5vcl,
4db,org solo [16'] sc PETERS
02817 (Z25)

Dionysos Und Apollo (Concerto for
Flute, Percussion and Strings)
perc,strings,fl solo [12'] PETERS
(Z26)

Epitaph Und Polyphonie
see Musik Zu Bach

Hohelied
4.2.2.2. 4.4.4.0. timp,2perc,harp,
pno&cel,8vln I,7vln II,6vla,5vcl,
4db,T solo [20'] sc PETERS 02821
(Z27)

Kammersinfonie Nr. 2
1.1.1.0. 0.0.0.0. cel,cembalo,
vibra,8vln I,7vln II,6vla,5vcl,
4db [17'] sc PETERS 02814 (Z28)

Kanzone
1.1.0.0. 0.0.1.0. timp,8vln I,7vln
II,6vla,5vcl,4db,Bar solo [8'] sc
PETERS 03365 (Z29)

Konstellation Für Ballett
see Vita, La

Kristalle (Concerto for Cembalo and
Orchestra)
8vln I,7vln II,6vla,5vcl,4db,hpsd
solo [16'] sc PETERS 02818 (Z30)

Kristallisation
3.2.2.3. 0.4.2.1. 4perc,8vln I,7vln
II,6vla,5vcl,4db [13'] sc PETERS
02276 (Z31)

Linien
3+rec.0+English horn.1.0. 0.0.0.0.
2perc,cembalo,vln,4vcl,db [21']
sc PETERS 02273 (Z32)

ZECHLIN, RUTH (cont'd.)

Linien II
2+rec.0+English horn.1+bass clar.0.
0.0.0.0. perc,cembalo,2vln,vla,
vcl,db [11'] sc PETERS 02208
(Z33)

Musik Zu Bach
"Epitaph Und Polyphonie" 3.1.0.0.
0.0.3.0. timp,vibra,8vln I,7vln
II,6vla,5vcl,4db [22'] sc PETERS
01670 (Z34)

Portrait
1.1.1.0. 0.0.1.0. 3perc,vln,vla,
vcl,db [17'] sc PETERS 02274
(Z35)

Prager Vision
3.0.0.0. 0.0.3.1. perc,org,8vln I,
7vln II,6vla,5vcl,4db [22'] sc
PETERS 03367 (Z36)

Szenen Für Kammerensemble
fl,ob,English horn,trp,strings
[15'] PETERS (Z37)

Träume
3.2.2.3. 0.4.4.1. timp,3perc,vibra,
8vln I,7vln II,6vla,5vcl,4db
[21'] sc PETERS 02275 (Z38)

Vita, La
"Konstellation Für Ballett"
4.3.3.3. 3.3.3.1. timp,4perc,8vln
I,7vln II,6vla,5vcl,4db [55'] sc
PETERS 03366 (Z39)

ZEEKIP AHOY see Mengelberg, Misja

ZEELAND, CEES VAN
Opus Labyrinthum Lego
2.3.4.2. 4.2.2.0. perc,2harp,
strings [30'] sc DONEMUS (Z40)

ZEITZEICHEN see Muller-Weinberg, Achim,
Sinfonia No. 1

ZELENKA, IVAN (1941- )
Concertino for Oboe and Chamber
Orchestra
strings,ob solo [17'] CESKY HUD.
(Z41)

ZELTER, CARL FRIEDRICH (1758-1832)
Concerto for Viola and Orchestra
0.0.0.0. 2.0.0.0. cembalo,strings
[15'] PETERS (Z42)

Concerto for Viola and Orchestra in E
flat
(Beyer) vla solo,orch KUNZELMANN
10008 ipr (Z43)

ZEME LIDÍ see Slavicky, Milan

ZEME LIDÍ: SYMFONICKY TRIPTYCH see
Slavicky, Milan

ZEMEK, PAVEL (1957- )
Koncert-Symfonie
3vln I,2vln II,2vla,2vcl,db,clar
solo [17'] CESKY HUD. (Z44)

Symphony No. 1
3.3.3.3. 4.3.3.1. timp,perc,harp,
pno,strings [27'] CESKY HUD.
(Z45)

ZENDER, HANS (1936- )
Furin No Kyo
1(pic).1.1.1+contrabsn. 1.1.1.0.
2perc,harp,pno,3vln,vla,vcl,db,S
solo [18'] BREITKOPF-W (Z46)

Schuberts "Winterreise"
2(pic,harmonica).2(ob d'amore,
English horn).2(bass clar,soprano
sax).2(contrabsn,harmonica).
1.1(cornet).1.0. timp,3perc,
acord,harp,gtr,2vln,2vla,vcl,db,
3 wind machines [75'] (a
compositional interpretation for
tenor and ensemble) BREITKOPF-W
(Z47)

ZENE GYÖRNEK see Vidovszky, Laszlo,
Music For Györ

ZENITHS see Boudreau, Walter

ZENKL, MICHAL (1955-1983)
Concerto for Piano and Orchestra
2.2.2.2. 4.2.3.0. timp,perc,harp,
strings,pno solo [23'] CESKY HUD.
(Z48)

Symphony
3.3.3.3. 4.3.3.1. timp,perc,harp,
org,strings [30'] CESKY HUD.
(Z49)

Symphony No. 2
2.2.2.2. 2.2.1.0. perc,strings
[13'] CESKY HUD. (Z50)

ZENOBIA see Reinecke, Carl

ZES STUKKEN VOOR STRIJKORKEST see Dijk,
Jan van

ZEUGE DER LIEBE DIE BESIEGT D. TOD see
Zimmermann, Udo, Rozewicz-Gesänge

ZEUGE DER LIEBE DIE BESIEGT D. TOD, EIN
see Zimmermann, Udo

ZEUGE DER LIEBE DIE BESIEGT DEN TOD,
EIN see Zimmermann, Udo

ZHOU, LONG (1953- )
Peking Drum
2.2.2.2. 4.2.2.0. timp,3perc,
strings, pipa solo [15'] PRESSER
rent (Z51)

Poems From Tang
3(pic).3(English horn).3(bass
clar).2. 4.3.3.1. timp,4perc,
harp,12vln I,10vln II,8vla,8vcl,
6db [32'] PRESSER rent (Z52)

ZILCHER, HEINZ REINHARDT
Scherzparaphrasen
2.2.2.2. 3.3.3.1. timp,perc,8vln I,
7vln II,6vla,5vcl,4db sc PETERS
02129 (Z53)

ZILCHER, HERMANN (1881-1948)
Aus Dem Hohelied Salomonis *Op.38
pno,strings,ABar soli [20']
BREITKOPF-W (Z54)

Dance-Fantasy *Op.71
3.2.2.2. 4.3.3.1. timp,perc,cel,
harp,strings [16'] EULENBURG perf
mat rent (Z55)

Klage *Op.22
2.2.2.2. 2.2.0.0. timp,harp,
strings,vln solo [15'] BREITKOPF-
W (Z56)

Lustspielsuite *Op.54b
1(pic).1.1.1. 2.1.0.0. strings
[19'] BREITKOPF-W (Z57)

Musik Zu Shakespeares Wintermärchen
*Op.39
2.1.1.1. 2.1.0.0. 4perc,cel,pno,
harmonium,strings,SA soli [40']
BREITKOPF-W (Z58)

ZIMMERMANN, BERND ALOIS (1918-1970)
Alagoana (Caprichos Brasileiros
3(pic).2+English horn.0+clar in E
flat+bass clar.2+contrabsn.alto
sax.tenor sax. 3.3.2.1(db tuba).
2timp,5perc,pno,hpsd/cel,harp,
gtr,strings [29'] (ballet suite)
SCHOTTS perf mat rent (Z59)

Gelb Und Grün: Suite
1(pic).0.1(clar in D).1. 1.1.1(bass
trom).0. timp,2perc,pno/cel,hpsd,
harp,strings [9'] SCHOTTS perf
mat rent (Z60)

ZIMMERMANN, ROLF (1925- )
Serenade
strings,pno [14'] BREITKOPF-W (Z61)

ZIMMERMANN, UDO (1943- )
Rozewicz-Gesänge
"Zeuge Der Liebe Die Besiegt d.
Tod" 3.0.0.0. 3.3.0.0. 3perc,cel,
harp,7vla,5vcl,3db [15'] sc
PETERS 02954 (Z62)

Zeuge Der Liebe Die Besiegt d. Tod
see Rozewicz-Gesänge

Zeuge Der Liebe Die Besiegt d. Tod,
Ein
3.0.0.0. 3.3.0.0. 3perc,pno,cel,
harp,7vla,5vcl,3db [15'] sc
PETERS 01330 (Z63)

Zeuge Der Liebe Die Besiegt Den Tod,
Ein
3.0.0.0. 3.3.0.0. 3perc,harp,cel,
7vla,vcl,3db,S solo [15'] sc
PETERS EP 9632 (Z64)

ZINGARI see Lennon, John Anthony,
Concerto for Guitar and Orchestra

ZINN, WILLIAM
Concerto for Piccolo
3(pic).3(English horn).3(bass
clar).3(contrabsn). 4.3.3(bass
trom).1. timp,perc,cel,harp,
strings,pic solo [21'10"]
EXCELSIOR rent (Z65)

Hebraic Scenes
2.2.2.2. 4.0.0.0. timp,perc,harp,
strings,vln/vla/vcl/db solo
[26'50"] EXCELSIOR rent (Z66)

Symphony In Ragtime
3(pic).3(English horn).2.2.soprano
sax. 4.2.3(bass trom).1. timp,
perc,pno,harp,banjo,strings [31']
EXCELSIOR rent (Z67)

ZIPP, FRIEDRICH (1914-    )
Festliche Musik *Op.11a
vln.I,vln II,vla,vcl,pno solo
MÖSELER sc 11.445-00, pts
11.445-01, set 11.445-09    (Z68)

ZISKA, FRANZ
Concertino for Flute, Piccolo and
Orchestra
2.2.2.2.  4.2.3.0.  timp,perc,harp,
gtr,strings,fl&pic solo [10']
ČESKY HUD.    (Z69)

ZITTERN UND WAGEN see Killmayer,
Wilhelm

ZIVLY see Petrzelka, Vilém

ZOEK see Janssen, Guus

ZOEPHEL, KLAUS (1929-    )
Sinfonietta
1.0.0.1.  2.1.0.0.  timp,8vln I,7vln
II,6vla,5vcl,4db [10'] sc PETERS
02249    (Z70)

ZÖLLNER, HEINRICH (1854-1941)
Versunkene Glocke, Die: Prelude To
Act 5
see Versunkene Glocke, Die:
Rautendeleins Leid

Versunkene Glocke, Die: Rautendeleins
Leid
"Versunkene Glocke, Die: Prelude To
Act 5" 3.2+English horn.2+bass
clar.2.  4.2.3.1.  timp,2perc,harp,
strings [7'] BREITKOPF-W    (Z71)

ZONE FOR 16 STRINGS see Shimoyama,
Hifumi

ZOUHAR, ZDENEK (1927-    )
Blanenská Suita
[22'] ČESKY HUD.    (Z72)

Musica Giocosa
[13'] ČESKY HUD.    (Z73)

Variace Na Téma Bohuslava Martinu
2.3.2.2.  4.3.3.1.  timp,perc,harp,
strings [10'] ČESKY HUD.    (Z74)

ZPEV SLAVÍKA see Machek, Miloš

ZPEVY STARÉ C VINY see Buzek, Jan

ZPOD JAVORINY see Hudec, Jiří

ZPRÍTOMNENÍ OKAMZIKU see Šesták, Zdeněk

ZROZENI see Slimácek, Jan

ZROZENÍ CLOVEKA see Kohoutek, Ctirad

ZSCHOTZSCHER, JOHAN CHRISTIAN
(1741-1780)
Concerto in D
(Hedwall, Lennart) "Konsert D-Dur"
2fl,2horn,string orch [3'5"] sc
STIM    (Z75)

Konsert D-Dur
see Concerto in D

Sinfonia No. 1 in D
(Hedwall, Lennart) 2fl,2horn,string
orch sc STIM    (Z76)

Sinfonia No. 2 in D
(Hedwall, Lennart) chamber orch (1.
Allegro; 2. Adagio assai; 3.
Allegro) sc STIM    (Z77)

ZU HILFE, ZU HILFE see Mozart, Wolfgang
Amadeus

ZUCKERT, LEON (1904-1992)
Concerto for Bassoon and String
Orchestra
[21'] sc,pno red CANADIAN
MI 1624 Z94CO    (Z78)

Elegia (Elegy)
2.2.2.2.  3.2.3.0.  timp,perc,
strings, (3rd horn optional) [8']
sc CANADIAN MI 1100 Z94EL    (Z79)

Elegy
see Elegia

Escenas Granadinas: Suite De Ballet
Español
"Granada Scenes: Spanish Ballet
Suite" 3(pic).2.2.2.  4.3.3.1.
timp,perc,strings, (piccolo, 3rd
trumpet, and 3rd trombone
optional) [27'] (1. La Vega 2.
Les Jardines De La Alhambra 3. La
Torre De Las Infantas 4. La
Corrida Fatal 5. Las Exequias De
Torero 6. Sacromonte) sc CANADIAN
MI 1100 Z94ES    (Z80)

ZUCKERT, LEON (cont'd.)

Esquisse Symphonique
see Symphonic Sketch

Evening In A Russian Village
"Soirée Dans Un Village Russe"
1.1.2.0.  0.0.0.0.  acord,timp,
perc,strings, or mandolins &
mandolas [8'] (1. Spacious Chant
2. Lively Dance) sc CANADIAN
MI 1100 Z94EV    (Z81)

Granada Scenes: Spanish Ballet Suite
see Escenas Granadinas: Suite De
Ballet Español

Homage, A
"Hommage, Un" 2.2.2.0.  4.3.3.1.
timp,strings [7'] sc CANADIAN
MI 1100 Z94HO    (Z82)

Hommage, Un
see Homage, A

Lament
"Lamento" 2.2.2.0.  0.0.0.0.  timp,
perc,2acord,strings, or mandolins
[7'] sc CANADIAN    (Z83)

Lamento
see Lament

Preciosa And The Wind: Ballet On A
Theme By Federico Garcia Lorca
see Preciosa Y El Viento: Ballet
Sobre Un Tema De Federico Garcia
Lorca

Preciosa Y El Viento: Ballet Sobre Un
Tema De Federico Garcia Lorca
"Preciosa And The Wind: Ballet On A
Theme By Federico Garcia Lorca"
2.2.2.2.  2.2.3.0.  timp,perc,
strings [22'] sc CANADIAN
MI 1100 Z94PR    (Z84)

Soirée Dans Un Village Russe
see Evening In A Russian Village

Symphonic Sketch
"Esquisse Symphonique"
2(pic).2(English horn).2.2.
4.2.3.1.  timp,2perc,strings, (3rd
trombone optional) [14'] sc
CANADIAN MI 1100 Z94SY    (Z85)

ZUIDAM, ROB (1964-    )
G-String Mambo
string orch [9'] sc DONEMUS    (Z86)

Trance Position
3.3.3.3.  4.3.3.1.  4perc,harp,pno&
cel,strings [10'] sc DONEMUS    (Z87)

ZUR JUBELFEIER see Reinecke, Carl

...ZUR NÄHE-VORAN see Birkenkötter,
Jörg

ZUR ROSENZEIT see Grieg, Edvard Hagerup

ZUZANA VOJÍROVÁ see Pauer, Jiří

ZVEKE NUMMER TV see Hedelin, Fredrik

ZVONY see Blatny, Pavel

ZVONY Z CHATYNE see Kosut, Michal

"...ZWEI GEFÜHLE...", MUSIK MIT
LEONARDO see Lachenmann, Helmut
Friedrich

ZWEI IDYLLEN see Stscherbatcheff,
Nikolai

ZWEI KONZERTSTÜCKE, OP. 113 & 114 see
Mendelssohn-Bartholdy, Felix

ZWEI LIEDER see Holliger, Heinz

ZWEI LYRISCHE STÜCKE AUS OP. 68 see
Grieg, Edvard Hagerup

ZWEI ORCHESTERSTUECKE see Koenig,
Gottfried Michael

ZWEI PUSCHKIN-WALZER see Prokofiev,
Serge

ZWEI SONATEN FÜR ORCHESTER see Galuppi,
Baldassare

ZWEI STÜCKE, FOR STRINGS see Grabovsky,
Leonid

ZWEI STÜCKE, FÜR KAMMERORCHESTER see
Müller-Wieland, Jan

ZWEI STÜCKE, OP. 32 see Nicode, Jean
Louis

ZWEI VENI SPONSA CHRISTI see Jommelli,
Niccolo

ZWEI VERLORENEN TROMPETEN UND DAS
KONZERT, DIE see Leistner-Mayer,
Roland

ZWILICH, ELLEN TAAFFE (1939-    )
Jubilation
3(pic).3(English horn).3(bass
clar).3(contrabsn).  4.3.3.1.
timp,3perc,strings [6'] sc MERION
rent    (Z88)
orch PRESSER 446-41098    (Z89)

Triple Concerto
1.2.2.2.  2.2.0.0.  timp,strings,pno
solo,vln solo,vcl solo MERION
rent    (Z90)

ZWISCHEN RHONE UND RHEIN see Martin,
Frank

ZWÖLF CONTRETÄNZE see Beethoven, Ludwig
van

ZWÖLF DEUTSCHE TÄNZE see Beethoven,
Ludwig van

ZWÖLF GERSHWIN-IMPRESSIONEN see
Dressler, Rudolf

ZWÖLF MENUETTE see Beethoven, Ludwig
van

ZWÖLF MINIATUREN see Franck, Cesar

ZWÖLF SYMPHONISCHE KANONS see
Schweinitz, Wolfgang von

ZYTOVICH, VLADIMIR (1931-    )
Concerto for Guitar and Chamber
Orchestra
1.2.0.1.  0.1.0.0.  perc,strings,gtr
solo [22'] SIKORSKI perf mat rent    (Z91)

# EDUCATIONAL
# ORCHESTRAL MUSIC

# A

A LA BEGUINE see Charrosin, F.G.

ABBEY BY MOONLIGHT, THE see Humphries, F.

ABENDLIED see Schumann, Robert (Alexander)

ACADEMIC FESTIVAL OVERTURE see Brahms, Johannes

ADAGIETTO FOR STRINGS see Velke, Fritz

ADAGIO AND ALLEGRO see Handel, George Frideric

ADAGIO CANTABILE see Beethoven, Ludwig van

ADAM, ADOLPHE-CHARLES (1803-1856)
Cantique De Noel *educ
(Goldsmith, Owen) "O Holy Night"
string orch (med) CPP-BEL
BS09603, 029156199017 (A1)
(Niehaus) string orch,pno (gr. II)
KENDOR 8961 (A2)

O Holy Night
see Cantique De Noel

ADAMS, BRYAN
Everything I Do, I Do It For You
(composed with Lange, Robert;
Kamen, Michael) *film
(Cerulli, Bob) orch (med easy) CPP-
BEL 7155EB7X, 029156120387 (A3)

ADASKIN, MURRAY (1906- )
Meyerke My Son (Jewish Song)
see Three Tunes For Strings

Rankin Inlet (Eskimo Song)
see Three Tunes For Strings

Three Tunes For Strings *educ
string orch sc CANADIAN
MI 1500 A221TH f.s.
contains: Meyerke My Son (Jewish
Song); Rankin Inlet (Eskimo
Song); When The Iceworms Nest
Again (A4)

When The Iceworms Nest Again
see Three Tunes For Strings

ADELANTE! ADELANTE! see Elledge, Chuck

ADIRONDACK SLEIGHRIDE see Stephan, Richard

ADORATION see Borowski, Felix

ADVANCE MARCH, THE see Duthoit, W.J.

AHRENS, LYNN
Anastasia (A Medley For Orchestra)
(composed with Flaherty, Stephen)
*film
(Custer, Calvin) orch (med) WARNER
F09722, 029156668261 (A5)

Once Upon A December (composed with
Flaherty, Stephen)
(Cerulli, Bob) orch (med easy)
WARNER F09723, 029156668094 (A6)

AIDA: BALLET MUSIC see Verdi, Giuseppe

AIN'T MISBEHAVIN' see Waller, Thomas (Fats)

AIR AND DANCE see Daniels, Melvin L.

AIR FOR STRINGS see Scott, Paul

AIR WITH VARIATIONS see Handel, George Frideric

ALBINONI, TOMASO (1671-1750)
Adagio in G minor *educ
(Giazotto) string orch,pno (med
easy) pno-cond sc,pts BOSWORTH
1107 (A7)

ALBRIGHT FANTASY see Foster, Robert E.

ALETTER, WILLIAM
Rendezvous *educ
pno-cond sc,pts BOSWORTH 1099 from
SINGING STRINGS NO.3 (A8)

Rendezvous (Intermezzo Rococo) *educ
(Charrosin, F.G.) [3'50"] BOSWORTH
(A9)

Singing Strings No.3
see Rendezvous

ALGERIAN SCENE see Ketèlbey, Albert William

ALGIERS: THROUGH THE ARAB QUARTERS see Jalowicz, R.

ALI BABA see Engleman, Joseph

ALL I WANNA DO
(Cerulli, Bob) orch (med easy) CPP-
BEL F09515, 029156178975 (A10)

ALL I WANT FOR CHRISTMAS IS MY TWO
FRONT TEETH
(Cerulli, Bob) string orch (easy)
WARNER SO9611, 029156212860 (A11)

ALLA CUECA see Vinter, Gilbert

ALLA RUMBA see Vinter, Gilbert

ALLEGRETTO see Haydn, [Franz] Joseph
see Stamitz

ALLEGRO see Sammartini, Giovanni
Battista, Symphony in C

ALLEGRO FROM SONATA NO. 1 see Telemann,
Georg Philipp, Sonata No. 1,First
Movement

ALLEGRO GIOCOSO see Haydn, [Franz]
Joseph

ALLEGRO MAESTOSO see Handel, George
Frideric

ALLEGRO SPIRITOSO BY JEAN-BAPTISTE
SENAILLE
(Higgins, James) string orch (med
easy) CPP-BEL C000190, 029156114898
(A12)

ALLEGRO UND ANDANTE CON MOTO see
Schaper, Heinz-Christian

ALLELUJA SYMPHONY see Haydn, [Franz]
Joseph, Symphony No. 30

ALOUETTE see Suite Francaise

ALPINE HOLIDAY see Scott

ALSACE LORRAINE see Egerickx, A.

ALSHIN
Three Chinese Scenes *educ
string orch,pno,opt perc (gr. III)
KENDOR 9922 (A13)

AMERICA MARCHES see Barsotti, Roger

AMERICA, THE BEAUTIFUL see Ward, Samuel
Augustus

AMERICAN PORTRAIT, AN see Rocherolle,
Eugenie Ricau

AMERICAN SALUTE see Gould, Morton

AMERICANA RHAPSODY see Niehaus, Leonard

AMERICANA SUITE *educ
(Alshin, Harry A.) string orch (gr.
III, contains: "When Johnny Comes
Marching Home, " "In The Gloaming,
" & "Battle Hymn Of The Republic")
KENDOR 7887 (A14)

AMOS, KEITH
Catland For String Orchestra
string orch [7'30"] (med easy, 3
mvts.) set CMA 070 (A15)

Cheeky Larp, The
fl,ob,clar,opt bsn,horn,trp,trom,
strings,opt pno (easy, for junior
school orchestra, KS3 standard)
CMA 212 f.s. (A16)

Dance Of The Larp
fl,ob,clar,opt bsn,horn,trp,trom,
strings,opt pno (easy, for junior
school orchestra, KS3 standard)
CMA 214 f.s. (A17)

Dancers Theme: From The Steadfast Tin
Soldier
string orch (med easy, junior
string orch, 4 pts -3 vlns.&
cello) CMA 208 (A18)

Larp Visits The Albert Hall
fl,ob,clar,opt bsn,horn,trp,trom,
strings,opt pno (easy, for junior
school orchestra, KS3 standard)
CMA 216 f.s. (A19)

Louis Wain Suite
2.2.2.2. 2.2.0.0. timp,strings,clar
solo [9'] (med easy, 3 mvts.) CMA
set 093, sc 094 (A20)

Song Of The Larp
fl,ob,clar,opt bsn,horn,trp,trom,
strings,opt pno (easy, for junior
school orchestra, KS3 standard)

AMOS, KEITH (cont'd.)

CMA 213 f.s. (A21)

Steadfast Tin Soldier, The
narrator,orch (med easy, "junior
set", schools versions include
opt. recorders and classroom
percussion) CMA set 170, sc 164
(A22)
narrator,orch (med easy, "school
orchestra set", schools versions
include opt. recorders and
classroom percussion) CMA set
165, sc 163 (A23)

ANASTASIA (A MEDLEY FOR ORCHESTRA) see
Ahrens, Lynn

ANDANTE AND ALLEGRO *educ
LUDWIG LLE 47 (A24)

ANDANTINO see Boccherini, Luigi

ANDANTINO MARZIALE see Tchaikovsky,
Piotr Ilyich

ANDERSON, GERALD
Dorian Design
string orch (gr. I) KJOS pts
SO-110C, sc SO-110F (A25)

Merry Go Rondo
string orch (gr. II) KJOS pts
SO-73C, sc SO-73F (A26)

ANDERSON, LEROY (1908-1975)
Blue Tango
orch CPP-BEL 80121, 029156196245
(A27)
(Cerulli, Bob) string orch (easy)
CPP-BEL 3713BB4X, 029156005035
(A28)

Bugler's Holiday
orch (med) CPP-BEL 80161,
029156214949 (A29)

Christmas Festival, A
orch (med) CPP-BEL 80021,
029156095401 (A30)

Fiddle-Faddle
orch (med) CPP-BEL 80471,
029156133165 (A31)
(Applebaum, Samuel) string orch
(med easy) CPP-BEL BS000023,
029156095821 (A32)

Jazz Pizzicato
orch CPP-BEL 80651, 029156677706
(A33)
(Applebaum, Samuel) string orch
(concert level) CPP-BEL BS09707,
029156298888 (A34)

Leroy Anderson Favorites
(Custer, Calvin) orch (med) CPP-BEL
C0269B7X, 029156180275 (A35)

Lullaby Of The Drums
orch (med easy) CPP-BEL C000210,
029156005172 (A36)

Magic Of Leroy Anderson, The
(Cerulli, Bob) orch (easy, contains
Forgotten Dreams & Plink, Plank,
Plunk) CPP-BEL C0158B7X,
029156687910 (A37)

Plink, Plank, Plunk
string orch (med easy) CPP-BEL
87481, 029156635461 (A38)

Promenade
orch (med easy) CPP-BEL B000001,
029156019148 (A39)

Sleigh Ride
orch (med diff) CPP-BEL 81261,
029156104875 (A40)
(Applebaum, Samuel) string orch
(med easy) CPP-BEL BS000020,
029156043426 (A41)
(Cerulli, Bob) orch (med easy) CPP-
BEL 3742SB7X, 029156183900 (A42)
(Cerulli, Bob) string orch (very
easy) CPP-BEL 3742SB4X,
029156056884 (A43)

Suite Of Carols
string orch (med easy) CPP-BEL
87651, 029156107739 (A44)

Syncopated Clock, The
orch (med easy) CPP-BEL 81441,
029156635751 (A45)
(Cerulli, Bob) string orch (very
easy) CPP-BEL 8010SB4X,
029156671681 (A46)

Trumpeter's Lullaby, A
orch (med easy) CPP-BEL 81591,
029156671452 (A47)

ANDERSON, LEROY (cont'd.)

Waltzing Cat, The
orch CPP-BEL 81631, 029156616668
(A48)

ANDREW WITH STRINGS: VOLUME 1 "LITTLE
BAROQUE SUITE"
(White, Andrew) 3vln I,3vln II,2vla,
2vcl,2db,horn,trp,trom,alto sax
solo (med diff) sc,pts ANDREW f.s.
contains: Bach, Johann Sebastian,
Badinerie (from Second Orchestral
Suite In B Minor); Bach, Johann
Sebastian, Sinfonia (from Easter
Oratorio, The); Handel, George
Frideric, Adagio (from Third
Organ Concerto In G Minor, The,
Opus 4); Handel, George Frideric,
Sarabande (from Third Oboe
Concerto In G Minor, The)    (A49)

ANDREW WITH STRINGS: VOLUME 2 "A FRENCH
MEDLEY"
(White, Andrew) 3vln I,3vln II,2vla,
2vcl,2db,horn,trp,trom,alto sax
solo (med diff) sc,pts ANDREW f.s.
contains: From Shangh(A)I To
Bangkok; Girl Of The Night;
Lovers, The; Merry Christmas; My
Women; Say! When Are You Coming
Back?                         (A50)

ANDREW WITH STRINGS: VOLUME 3 "JAZZ IT
UP" *jazz
(White, Andrew) 3vln I,3vln II,2vla,
2vcl,2db,horn,trp,trom,alto sax
solo (med diff) sc,pts ANDREW f.s.
contains: Adamson, John, Everything
I Have Is Yours (composed with
Lane); Coltrane, John, Just For
The Love; Dameron, Tadd, Good
Bait; White, Andrew Nathaniel,
Keep On Dancin' Baby!; White,
Andrew Nathaniel, Three Hundred
Sixty One Degree Experience (A51)

ANGELS WE HAVE HEARD ON HIGH
(Del Borgo, Elliot) orch (med diff)
CPP-BEL BF09706, 029156606768 (A52)

ANIMANIACS (MAIN THEME)
(Cerulli, Bob) string orch (very
easy) CPP-BEL SO9504, 029156176940
(A53)

ANNABELLA see Vasata, Rudolph Leo

ANNIE LAURIE   *educ
(Hartley, Fred) [2'15"] BOSWORTH (A54)

ANOUSCHKA see Rais, M.

ANTIQUE DANCES AND AIRS see Respighi,
Ottorino

APACHE see Nunez, Carold

APOLLO 13, THEMES  *educ
(Del Borgo) string orch,opt combo
(gr. II) LEONARD-US 04490042 (A55)

APPALACHIAN SUNRISE see Gazda, Doris

APPALACHIAN WALTZ see Niehaus

APRIL DAY see Tattenhall, Barry

APRIL IN PARIS
(Sayre, Chuck) orch (med) WARNER
F09604, 029156200416        (A56)

ARDEN, HOLGER (1946-    )
Chinese Suite, For Youth Orchestra
see Kinesisk Suite, For
Ungdomsorkester

Kinesisk Suite, For Ungdomsorkester
"Chinese Suite, For Youth
Orchestra" 3.2.2.0. 1.1.0.0.
2timp,perc,strings [12'] NORSKMI
(A57)

ARIOSO see Bach, Johann Sebastian

ARISTOGATTI, GLI  *educ
(Short) [It/Eng] chamber orch sc,pts
RICORDI-IT 137282           (A58)

ARLEN, HAROLD (1905-    )
Over The Rainbow
(Cerulli, Bob) string orch (easy)
CPP-BEL T87850B4, 029156099287
(A59)

(Custer, Calvin) trom solo,string
orch (med) WARNER SO9509,
029156176964               (A60)

When You Wish Upon A Star  *educ
(Isaac) string orch BOURNE perf mat
rent                        (A61)

ARMANDOLA, JOSE
Blue Pavilion (Concert Tango)  *educ
BOSWORTH                    (A62)

Cowboys' Horsemanship (Galop)
see In The Circus


ARMANDOLA, JOSE (cont'd.)

Humpty Dumpty (Grotesque Intermezzo)
see In The Circus

In The Circus  *educ
BOSWORTH f.s.
contains: Cowboys' Horsemanship
(Galop) [2'30"]; Humpty Dumpty
(Grotesque Intermezzo) [3']; On
The Trapeze (Valse) [2'30"];
Rider In The Ring (Entrée) [3']
(A63)

On The Trapeze (Valse)
see In The Circus

Rider In The Ring (Entrée)
see In The Circus

ARTHUR, JOHN
Finger Drills For String Orchestra
string orch (64 patterns for
strength and skill) VELKE  (A64)

ARTIST'S LIFE see Strauss, Johann,
[Jr.]

ARTZA ALINU see Songs Of Israel

ASH GROVE, THE see Songs Of Celtic
Lands

ASHEIM, NILS HENRIK (1960-    )
Etyder Over Tiden
string orch [12'] NORSKMI   (A65)

ASHOKAN FAREWELL see Ungar, Jay

ASTON, WILLIAM
Christmas Medley  *educ
(Ketèlbey, A.W.) [3'] BOSWORTH
(A66)

Musical Jig-Saw, A: Potpourri  *educ
(Ketèlbey, A.W.) [11'] BOSWORTH
(A67)

AT THE GRASSHOPPER BALL see Meyer,
Richard

AT THE MIDNIGHT BALL (MIDNIGHT BELLS)
see Heuberger, Richard

AT THE THEATRE see Stuart, Graeme

AUBADE see Parker, Clifton

AUFZUG, OSTINATO UND KLEINES FINALE see
Schaper, Heinz-Christian

AUSTRALIAN FOLK SUITE see Stephan,
Richard

AUTRY, (ORVON) GENE (1907-1998)
Here Comes Santa Claus (Right Down
Santa Claus Lane) (composed with
Haldeman, Oakley)
(Cerulli, Bob) string orch (very
easy) WARNER SO9702, 029156607192
(A68)

AVENUE, THE see Redman, Reginald

AWAY IN A MANGER
(Ayars, Bo) 2.3(English horn).3(bass
clar).2. 4.3.3(bass trom).1. perc,
cel,harp,strings [2'35"] PRESSER
(A69)

AWAY IN A MANGER: A TRILOGY
(Kidd, Bryan) string orch (very easy)
CPP-BEL BS09711, 029156605525 (A70)

AXTON, HOYT
Joy To The World
(Cerulli, Bob) string orch (very
easy) CPP-BEL T4486JB4,
029156096996               (A71)


# B

BABES IN THE WOOD see Engleman, Joseph

BABES IN TOYLAND see Herbert, Victor

BABIANDAGAR see Bjurling, Björn

BACCHANALE FROM SAMSON & DELILAH see
Saint-Saëns, Camille

BACH, JOHANN SEBASTIAN (1685-1750)
Aria  *educ
(Wieloszynski) "Bist Du Bei Mir"
string orch,pno (gr. II) KENDOR
8905                        (B1)

Arioso
(Gearhart, Livingston) string orch,
vla solo (med easy) CPP-BEL
BS09506, 029156170757      (B2)

Bach Double Violin Concerto (Concerto
for 2 Violins in D minor) educ
(Muller, J. Frederick) (gr. IV)
KJOS pts 0-1014B, sc 0-1014F (B3)

Bach: Organ Chorale Suite  *educ
(Duffy) string orch BOURNE
augmented set 417680, set 417600,
sc 417604                   (B4)

Bist Du Bei Mir
see Aria

Chorale And Fugue
(Smith, Claude T.) string orch
WINGERT set 3030011, sc 3030012
(B5)

Concerto for 2 Violins in D minor
see Bach Double Violin Concerto

Concerto Italiano
see Italian Concerto

Do Thou Defend Us: Chorale Prelude
*educ
(Gordon, Philip) string orch BOURNE
augmented set 022680, set 022670
(B6)

Fugue in C
(Metcalf, Leon) string orch (easy)
CPP-BEL BS000051, 029156674217
(B7)

Fugue in G minor (from Sonata For
Solo Violin) educ
(Grant, Francis) "Little Fugue In G
Minor, The" string orch (med)
CPP-BEL BS09501, 029156180367
(B8)

(Levenson, David M.) (gr. IV) KJOS
pts 0-1059B, sc 0-1059F     (B9)

Fünf Instrumentalsätze
(Frotscher, Gotthold) 3-5strings,
cont,opt winds HUG f.s. from
cantatas
contains: Quodlibet (from Cantata
No. 212); Ritornell (from
Cantata No. 30); Sinfonia (from
Cantata No. 75, Part 2); Sonate
(from Cantata No. 182)      (B10)

Gavotte, Air And Gigue (from
Orchestral Suite No.3) educ
(Kaluza, G.) sc,pts BOSWORTH
BOE 4098                    (B11)

Italian Concerto  *educ
"Concerto Italiano" 2.2.0.2.
0.0.0.0. timp,strings sc,pts
BOSWORTH 4319               (B12)

Jesu, Joy Of Man's Desiring
(Del Borgo, Elliot) string orch
(med easy) CPP-BEL BS000095,
029156223200               (B13)

Little Fugue In G Minor, The
see Fugue in G minor

March
(Gibson, David) orch (easy) CPP-BEL
C000206, 029156671766      (B14)

March for 2 Violins, Viola and
Violoncello  *educ
(Wolpert) string orch sc,pts
HEINRICH 771                (B15)

Minuet for 2 Violins, Viola and
Violoncello  *educ
(Wolpert) string orch sc,pts
HEINRICH 770                (B16)

Musette, For 2 Violins, Viola And
Violoncello  *educ
(Wolpert) string orch sc,pts
HEINRICH 769                (B17)

BACH, JOHANN SEBASTIAN (cont'd.)

Quodlibet
see Fünf Instrumentalsätze

Ritornell
see Fünf Instrumentalsätze

Sinfonia
see Fünf Instrumentalsätze

Sinfonia No. 7 *educ
(Conley) string orch (gr. III)
KENDOR 9869                         (B18)

Sonate
see Fünf Instrumentalsätze

Three Bach Minuets *educ
(Muller, S. Frederick; Fink,
Lorraine) string orch,vln solo
(gr. III) KJOS pts SO-36C, sc
SO-36F                              (B19)

Wenn Wir In Höchsten Noten Sein:
Chorale Prelude *educ
string orch,pno (med diff) pno-cond
sc,pts BOSWORTH 1004                (B20)

BACH DOUBLE VIOLIN CONCERTO see Bach,
Johann Sebastian

BACH FAMILY, THE *educ
(Alshin, Harry A.) string orch (gr.
III, contains 5 movements) KENDOR
7905                                (B21)

BACH: ORGAN CHORALE SUITE see Bach,
Johann Sebastian

BAGATELLES FOR ORCHESTRA see Hartley,
Walter Sinclair

BAIN, JAMES LEITH MACBETH
Brother James' Air
(Hoffer, Marjorie) string orch
(very easy) CPP-BEL BSO00112,
029156102727                        (B22)

BALFE, MICHAEL WILLIAM (1808-1870)
Bohemian Girl: Overture [arr.] *educ
(Zeitlberger) [9'] BOSWORTH   (B23)

BALLADAIR see Erickson

BALLADS FOR STRINGS *educ
(Ryden) string orch sc BOURNE 411824
                                    (B24)

BALTIC DANCE see Mosier, Kirt N.

BAMBA, LA
(Custer, Calvin) orch (concert level)
WARNER F09714, 029156605242   (B25)

BANK HOLDIAY ('APPY 'AMPSTEAD) see
Ketèlbey, Albert William

BANK HOLIDAY ('APPY 'AMPSTEAD) see
Ketèlbey, Albert William

BANNERS OF VICTORY see Barsotti, Roger

BARBER OF SEVILLE, THE see Rossini,
Gioacchino

BAROQUE ANDANTE AND ALLEGRO see
Telemann, Georg Philipp

BAROQUE BAGATELLE, A see Goldsmith,
Owen

BARROSO, ARY
Brazil
(Gold, Marty) orch (med easy) CPP-
BEL 5776BB6X, 029156112542   (B26)

BARROW, P.
Dragonflies Wedding (Intermezzo)
*educ
(Ketèlbey, A.W.) [2'30"] BOSWORTH
                                    (B27)

BARSOTTI, ROGER
America Marches *educ
[6'] (contains musical fragments
from: The Liberty Bell,
Washington Post, Marching Through
Georgia, and others) BOSWORTH
                                    (B28)

Banners Of Victory *educ
[2'45"] BOSWORTH                    (B29)

Hurricane *educ
[2'45"] BOSWORTH                    (B30)

Jolly Shipmates *educ/medley
[3'30"] BOSWORTH                    (B31)

King's Colour, The *educ
(Gilbert, C.J.) [3'] BOSWORTH  (B32)

Mariquita (Tango Serenade) *educ
[3'5"] BOSWORTH                     (B33)

Mighty Malta (composed with Joyce,
Archibald) *educ
BOSWORTH                            (B34)

BARSOTTI, ROGER (cont'd.)

New Post Horn Galop, The *educ
[3'] BOSWORTH                       (B35)

Tenacity *educ
[3'45"] BOSWORTH                    (B36)

BARTLETT, VICTOR
Liberation *educ
[3'30"] BOSWORTH                    (B37)

BARTOK SUITE
(Clark, Larry) string orch (very
easy) CPP-BEL BSO9710, 029156604566
                                    (B38)

BASTIEN & BASTIENNE see Mozart,
Wolfgang Amadeus

BATMAN THEME see Hefti, Neal Paul

BATTLES AND BRAWLS see Huws Jones,
Edward

BAUERNSCHMIDT, ROBERT
Bear Mountain Polka *educ
orch SHAWNEE augmented set J 0119,
set JC 0459, sc JC 0457, pt
JC 0458                             (B39)

BEACH BOYS MEDLEY
(Custer, Calvin) orch (med) CPP-BEL
C0202B7X, 029156152708             (B40)

BEAR MOUNTAIN POLKA see Bauernschmidt,
Robert

BEATUS VIR: EXCERPTS see Vivaldi,
Antonio

BECCE, GIUSEPPE (1881-1973)
Souvenir De Capri (Serenata) *educ
orch,vln solo [4'] BOSWORTH   (B41)

BECKHAM, DWIGHT, SR.
Elegy
string orch WINGERT set 3030111, sc
3030112                             (B42)

BEETHOVEN, LUDWIG VAN (1770-1827)
Adagio Cantabile (from Piano Sonata
No. 8)
(Velke, Fritz) string orch (gr. IV)
VELKE                               (B43)

Bagatelle *educ
(Finno) string orch (gr. III)
KENDOR 9783                         (B44)

Für Elise
(Velke, Fritz) string orch (gr.
III) VELKE                          (B45)

Heavens Resound, The
(Smith, Claude T.) string orch
WINGERT set 3030101, sc 3030102
                                    (B46)

Ode To Joy
(Del Borgo, Elliot) string orch
(med) CPP-BEL BSO9607,
029156200454                        (B47)

Six German Dances *educ
(Alshin, Harry A.) string orch (gr.
II) KENDOR 8045                     (B48)

Symphony in E flat, No. 3, [excerpt],
[arr.]
(Goldsmith, Owen) orch (med easy)
CPP-BEL C000214, 029156110340      (B49)

Symphony No. 2,Second Movement,
[arr.]
see Symphony No. 2: Larghetto
[arr.]

Symphony No. 2: Larghetto [arr.]
(Symphony No. 2,Second Movement,
[arr.]) educ
(Dacblitz) [10'] BOSWORTH           (B50)

Symphony No. 5,Second Movement,
[excerpt]
(Velke, Fritz) string orch (gr. IV)
VELKE                               (B51)

Symphony No. 5, [excerpt], [arr.]
(Goldsmith, Owen) orch (med easy)
CPP-BEL C000204, 029156687880      (B52)

BEETHOVEN'S GREATEST HITS *educ
(Wieloszynski) string orch,pno (gr.
III) KENDOR 9792                    (B53)

BEGIN THE BEGUINE see Porter, Cole

BEGINNING BARTOK *educ
(Wieloszynski) string orch,pno (gr.
II, in 4 movements) KENDOR 8914
                                    (B54)

BEGINNING BEETHOVEN *educ
(Wieloszynski) string orch,pno (gr.
I, contains 3 movements) KENDOR
8175                                (B55)

BEGINNING BLUEGRASS *educ
(Wieloszynski) string orch,pno,opt
banjo&gtr (gr. II) KENDOR 8916 f.s.
contains: Boil The Cabbage Down;
Cajun Fiddlin'; Devil's Dream
                                    (B56)

BEIN' GREEN see Raposo, Joseph G.

BELIEVE ME IF ALL THOSE ENDEARING YOUNG
CHARMS see Casebow see Drewes,
[Captain] Barry

BELL, RICHARD
Tuning A-Round *educ
string orch (gr. I) KJOS pts
SO-119C, sc SO-119F                 (B57)

BELLA NOCHES CUBANOS (RUMBA) see Green,
Philip

BENDIX, T.
Butterfly *educ
[6'] BOSWORTH                       (B58)

BENSON, WARREN FRANK (1924-    )
Theme And Excursions
string orch WINGERT set 9042821, sc
9042822                             (B59)

BERCEUSE AND FINALE see Stravinsky,
Igor

BERCHE, R.A.
Glad Days (Entr'acte) *educ
BOSWORTH                            (B60)

BERGER, JEAN (1909-    )
Suite for Strings
string orch (gr. IV) KJOS pts
GSO-1C, sc GSO-1F                   (B61)

BERLIOZ, HECTOR (LOUIS) (1803-1869)
Hungarian March *educ
(Rokos, Kurt) string orch,pno pno-
cond sc,pts BOSWORTH 1005     (B62)

BERNARD, FELIX (1897-1949)
Winter Wonderland
(Cerulli, Bob) orch (med easy)
WARNER F09612, 029156213812   (B63)
(Cerulli, Bob) string orch (very
easy) WARNER WBS09411,
029156098679                        (B64)
(Custer, Calvin) orch WARNER
F09713, 029156605266          (B65)
(Rosenhaus, Steve) orch (med)
WARNER WBF09312, 029156061345
                                    (B66)

BERNSTEIN, ELMER (1922-    )
Magnificent Seven, The
(Cerulli, Bob) string orch (very
easy) CPP-BEL T0286MB4,
029156098693                        (B67)

BESTGEN, WILLY
Holiday In Switzerland *educ
[3'45"] BOSWORTH                    (B68)

BEWITCHED see Rodgers, Richard

BICK, H.
Bumble Bee's Wedding
see Visit To The Insect Zoo, A:
Suite

Butterfly's Lullaby
see Visit To The Insect Zoo, A:
Suite

Dreamy Shadows *educ
(Berlin, Ben) [3'] BOSWORTH   (B69)

Enigmatic Penguin
see Our Feathered Friends: Suite

Gossiping Sparrows
see Our Feathered Friends: Suite

Grasshopper's Holiday
see Visit To The Insect Zoo, A:
Suite

Hobgoblins *educ
(Berlin, Ben) [2'35"] BOSWORTH
                                    (B70)

Homesick Parrot
see Our Feathered Friends: Suite

Our Feathered Friends: Suite *educ
BOSWORTH f.s.
contains: Enigmatic Penguin
[2'45"]; Gossiping Sparrows
[1'45"]; Homesick Parrot
[2'45"]; Screeching Seagulls
[1'45"]                             (B71)

Screeching Seagulls
see Our Feathered Friends: Suite

Visit To The Insect Zoo, A: Suite
*educ
BOSWORTH f.s.
contains: Bumble Bee's Wedding
[2'20"]; Butterfly's Lullaby
[2'48"]; Grasshopper's Holiday
[2'45"]                             (B72)

BIDING YOUR TIME see Niehaus

BIG SPENDER see Coleman, Cy

BIRD SELLER, THE see Zeller, Carl,
Vogelhandler, Der

BIRTH OF A BUTTERFLY see Ives, M.

BIRTH OF THE BLUES see DeSylva, George
Gard (Buddy)

BIRTHDAY GREETING, A see Ketèlbey,
Albert William

BIRTHDAY SERENADE see Wolters,
Gottfried

BIST DU BEI MIR see Bach, Johann
Sebastian, Aria

BIZET, GEORGES (1838-1875)
Scenes From Carmen
(Alshin, Harry) string orch (med)
CPP-BEL BSO9507, 029156170887
(B73)

Scenes From Carmen (Suite No. 1)
(Alshin, Harry) orch (med) CPP-BEL
C000203, 029156216325      (B74)

Scherzo, [arr.] (from Symphony In C
Major)
(Goldsmith, Owen) orch (med) CPP-
BEL C000211, 029156045703    (B75)

BJURLING, BJÖRN (1966-    )
Babiandagar
3(pic).2.2.2. 4.2.3.0. 3perc,
strings [8'] STIM sc H-2800, pts
A-421                         (B76)

BLACK FOREST SUITE see Halen, Walter J.

BLACKMORE, GEORGE HENRY JAMES
(1921-    )
Knuckledust *educ
(Engleman, J.) [3'15"] BOSWORTH
(B77)

Spring Fever *educ
(Engleman, J.) [3'] BOSWORTH  (B78)

BLAKE, HOWARD (1938-    )
Snowman, The: Suite
"Snowman (Suite)" strings CRAMER
MUS sc,pts 51121 X, pts 58036 X
(B79)

Snowman (Suite)
see Snowman, The: Suite

BLUE BELLS OF SCOTLAND see Songs Of
Celtic Lands

BLUE BOUDOIR, THE see Engleman, Joseph

BLUE DANUBE, THE see Strauss, Johann,
[Jr.]

BLUE MOOD see Elledge, Chuck

BLUE PAVILION (CONCERT TANGO) see
Armandola, Jose

BLUE TANGO see Anderson, Leroy

BOCCHERINI, LUIGI (1743-1805)
Andantino
(Velke, Fritz) string orch (gr. IV)
VELKE                         (B80)

BOCK, JERRY (1928-    )
If I Were A Rich Man (from Fiddler On
The Roof)
(Rosenhaus, Steven) orch (med easy)
WARNER WBF09411, 029156112382
(B81)
Matchmaker (from Fiddler On The Roof)
(Cerulli, Bob) orch (easy) WARNER
WBF09407, 029156111873     (B82)

BODY AND SOUL
(Sayre, Chuck) orch (med) WARNER
F09605, 029156200492        (B83)
see Jirmal, Jiri

BOHEMIA see Joyce, Archibald

BOHEMIAN GIRL: OVERTURE [ARR.] see
Balfe, Michael William

BOIL THE CABBAGE DOWN see Beginning
Bluegrass

BONNIE GALLOWA' see Hornsby, G.F.

BOROWSKI, FELIX (1872-1956)
Adoration *educ
(Charrosin, F.G.) [4'30"] BOSWORTH
(B84)

BÖRSCHEL, ERICH (1907-    )
Jolly Trip (Galop) *educ
orch,xylo solo [2'] BOSWORTH (B85)
[2'] BOSWORTH                (B86)

Straussiana (composed with Strauss)
*educ
orch,pno solo [6'] (Strauss waltz

BÖRSCHEL, ERICH (cont'd.)

themes) BOSWORTH             (B87)

BOSWORTH'S ORCHESTRAL FOLIO *CC12L,
educ
pno-cond sc,pts BOSWORTH f.s.  (B88)

BOULOGNE, JOSEPH (CHEVALIER DE ST.-
GEORGES)
see SAINT-GEORGES, JOSEPH BOULOGNE DE

BOW-REGARD'S PARADE see Caponegro, John

BOWIE, GORDON
Then And Now
string orch (gr. III, 2 movements:
18th & 20th centuries contrasted)
VELKE                        (B89)

BOWING BAROQUE *educ
(McLeod) string orch,pno (gr. II)
KENDOR 8935 f.s.
contains: Handel, George Frideric,
Fughetta; Purcell, Henry, Theme
and Variations              (B90)

BOX AND COX see Fuchs, Hans

BOYS AND GIRLS COME OUT TO PLAY *educ
(Krein, Michael) BOSWORTH    (B91)

BRAHMS, JOHANNES (1833-1897)
Academic Festival Overture *Op.56,
educ
(Muller, J. Frederick) (gr. IV)
KJOS pts O-1030B, sc O-1030F (B92)
Brahms Hungarian Dances *educ/medley
(Charrosin, F.G.) [7'] (contains
Dances Nos. 6-3-5-1-4-5-2-14-6)
BOSWORTH                     (B93)

BRAHMS HUNGARIAN DANCES see Brahms,
Johannes

BRANDON
Suite Of Western European Music,
Movement 1: French Overture And
Bourreé *educ
string orch (gr. IV) KENDOR 9901
(B94)
Suite Of Western European Music,
Movement 2: Yorkshire Waltz &
Strathspey *educ
string orch (gr. IV) KENDOR 9902
(B95)
Suite Of Western European Music,
Movements 3 & 4: Dutch Polka;
Norwegian Folk Song *educ
string orch (gr. IV) KENDOR 9903
(B96)
Suite Of Western European Music,
Movement 5: Tarantella Napolitana
*educ
string orch (gr. IV) KENDOR 9904
(B97)

BRAVEHEART, THEMES *educ
(Conley) string orch,opt combo (gr.
II) LEONARD-US 04490043     (B98)

BRAZIL
(Custer, Calvin) string orch (med)
WARNER S09603, 029156213560  (B99)
see Barroso, Ary

BRAZILIAN IMAGES see Diniz, Paolo Braga

BRÉVAL, JEAN BAPTISTE (1756-1825)
Concerto for Orchestra
(Dalley, Orien) orch WINGERT set
9041351, sc 9041352        (B100)

BRIDGEWATER, ERNEST LESLIE (1893-    )
Dear Octopus *educ
[5'] BOSWORTH               (B101)

BRIDGMONT, LESLIE
Enchanting Eyes (Tango) *educ
(Charrosin, F.G.) [5'] BOSWORTH
(B102)
Moonlight Over Tahiti *educ
(Charrosin, F.G.) [4'10"] BOSWORTH
(B103)
Serenade To A Coquette (Caprice)
*educ
(Tattenhall, B.) [2'] BOSWORTH
(B104)

BRIGHTON HIKE see Joyce, Archibald

BRING A TORCH, JEANNETTE, ISABELLA!
(Ayars, Bo) "Flambeau, Jeanette,
Isabella!, Un" 3(pic).3(English
horn).3(bass clar).2. 4.3.3(bass
trom).1. timp,3perc,pno,harp,
strings [3'30"] PRESSER     (B105)

BRINKMANN, B.E.
Habanera, Für 2 Violinen, Viola,
Violoncello, Kontrabass *educ
string orch perf sc HEINRICH 3668
(B106)

BRISMAN, HESKEL (1923-    )
Carnival In Shushan *educ
string orch BOURNE perf mat rent
(B107)

BRITISH GRENADIERS *educ
(Caponegro) string orch,pno (gr. II)
KENDOR 8937                 (B108)

BRITT, BEN
see BRISMAN, HESKEL

BROOKS, GARTH
Garth: A Garth Brooks Medley
(Cerulli, Bob) orch (easy) CPP-BEL
C0344B7X, 029156111996     (B109)

BROOKS, RANDY
Grandma Got Run Over By A Reindeer
(Cerulli, Bob) orch (med easy) CPP-
BEL 5768GB7X, 029156687224 (B110)

BROTHER JAMES' AIR see Bain, James
Leith MacBeth

BRUBAKER, DALE
Concert Tunes For Beginning Strings:
Bass
db pt JLJ.MUSIC CT1-SB      (B111)

Concert Tunes For Beginning Strings:
Cello
vcl pt JLJ.MUSIC CT1-CO     (B112)

Concert Tunes For Beginning Strings:
Conductor's Score
vln,vla,vcl,db,pno sc JLJ.MUSIC
CT1-CS                      (B113)

Concert Tunes For Beginning Strings:
Viola
vla pt JLJ.MUSIC CT1-VA     (B114)

Concert Tunes For Beginning Strings:
Violin
vln pt JLJ.MUSIC CT1-VN     (B115)

Concert Tunes For Intermediate
Strings: Bass
db pt JLJ.MUSIC CT2-SB      (B116)

Concert Tunes For Intermediate
Strings: Cello
vcl pt JLJ.MUSIC CT2-CO     (B117)

Concert Tunes For Intermediate
Strings: Conductor's Score
vln,vla,vcl,db,pno sc JLJ.MUSIC
CT2-CS                      (B118)

Concert Tunes For Intermediate
Strings: Viola
vla pt JLJ.MUSIC CT2-VA     (B119)

Concert Tunes For Intermediate
Strings: Violin
vln pt JLJ.MUSIC CT2-VN     (B120)

Plaza De Toros
string orch (gr. I) set JLJ.MUSIC
SO 104                      (B121)

BRUBECK, DAVID (DAVE) WARREN
(1920-    )
It's About Time
(Sayre, Chuck) orch (med diff) CPP-
BEL F09512, 029156179866   (B122)

Take Five
(Custer, Calvin) string orch (med)
WARNER S09510, 029156177275
(B123)

BRUCKNER, ANTON (1824-1896)
Symphony No. 7,Third Movement, [arr.]
*educ
(Leidig, Vernon) (gr. IV) KJOS pts
WO-12B, sc WO-12F          (B124)

BRYANT, CURTIS
Theme and Variations *educ
string orch (gr. II) KJOS pts
GSO-30C, sc GSO-30F        (B125)

BUCZYNSKI, WALTER (1933-    )
Introduction Of Finger Three *educ
string orch [1'45"] (7th degr.) sc,
pts CANADIAN MI 1500 B926INT
(B126)
Last And Not Least Finger Four *educ
string orch [1'25"] (7th degr.) sc
CANADIAN MI 1500 B926LA    (B127)

Legend No. 1 (from Legends For String
Orchestra) educ
string orch [8'] sc CANADIAN
MI 1500 B926LE             (B128)

Legend No. 2 (from Legends For String
Orchestra) educ
string orch sc CANADIAN
MI 1500 B926LE2            (B129)

Legend No. 3 *educ
string orch [1'] sc CANADIAN
MI 1500 B926L3             (B130)

BUCZYNSKI, WALTER (cont'd.)

Legend No. 4 *educ
string orch sc CANADIAN
MI 1500 B926L4 (B131)

Legend No. 5 (from Legends For String
Orchestra) educ
string orch sc CANADIAN
MI 1500 B926LE5 (B132)

Legend No. 6 (from Legends For String
Orchestra) educ
string orch sc CANADIAN
MI 1500 B926LE6 (B133)

Legend No. 7 (from Legends For String
Orchestra) educ
string orch sc CANADIAN
MI 1500 B926LE7 (B134)

Legend No. 11 *educ
string orch sc CANADIAN
MI 1500 B926LE11 (B135)

Legend No. 12 *educ
string orch sc CANADIAN
MI 1500 B926LE12 (B136)

Open String, The *educ
string orch (7th degr.) sc CANADIAN
MI 1500 B9260P (B137)

BUDDHA'S FESTIVAL OF LOVE see
Kronberger-Marriott

BUGLER'S HOLIDAY see Anderson, Leroy

BUMBLE BEE'S WEDDING see Bick, H.

BURLESQUE see Young Bartok Suite, A

BUSY BUSINESS see Charrosin, F.G.

BUSY FINGERS see Rohlf, Earl A.

BUTTERFLIES IN THE RAIN see Myers,
Sherman

BUTTERFLY see Bendix, T.

BUTTERFLY'S LULLABY see Bick, H.

BY ROCK-BOUND COAST see Thiman, Eric
Harding

BY THE BLUE HAWAIIAN WATERS see
Ketèlbey, Albert William

BYE, FREDERICK (1901- )
Parade Of The Regiment *educ
[3'50"] BOSWORTH (B138)

# C

CABARET see Kander, John

CACAVAS
Dance Pavane *educ
string orch BOURNE augmented set
418480, set 418440, sc 418444 (C1)

CAJKOVSKIJ, PETR ILJIC
see TCHAIKOVSKY, PIOTR ILYICH

CAJUN FIDDLIN' see Beginning Bluegrass

CALEDONIA: FANTASIE IN MODERN SYMPHONIC
STYLE ON SCOTTISH AIRS see
Charrosin, F.G.

CALLER HERRIN' *educ
(Revel, Louis) string orch,pno,opt
org [4'30"] BOSWORTH (C2)

CAMBRIA: FANTASIE IN MODERN SYMPHONIC
STYLE ON WELSH AIRS see Charrosin,
F.G.

CAMERLOHER, PLACIDUS VON (1718-1782)
Sinfonia for String Orchestra and
Harpsichord in F *educ
string orch,opt cembalo sc,pts
HEINRICH 1164 (C3)

CAMPFIRE SUITE
(Arnold, Alan) string orch (easy,
elementary school level) HOLLOW (C4)

CAN CAN SELECTION see Charrosin, F.G.

CANDLEBERRY BAY see Niehaus

CANONIZED MELODY see Cechvala, Al

CANTIQUE DE NOEL see Adam, Adolphe-
Charles

CANTO MORUNO (PASO DOBLE) see Moscoso,
Tomas

CANZONETTA see Herbert, Victor see
Mendelssohn-Bartholdy, Felix

CAPER CAPRICCIOSO see Frost, Robert S.

CAPONEGRO, JOHN
Bow-Regard's Parade *educ
string orch,pno,opt perc (gr. I)
KENDOR 8180 (C5)

Fanfare And Celebration *educ
string orch (gr. III) KENDOR 9816 (C6)

Hanukkah Holiday *educ
string orch,pno (gr. I, includes
"Dreydle," "Tumbalalaika" &
"Hanukkah") KENDOR 8295 (C7)

Shoe Symphony *educ
string orch,pno (gr. I) KENDOR 8567 (C8)

Spirit Of Hanukkah, The *educ
string orch,pno,opt perc (gr. I)
KENDOR 8633 (C9)

CAPRICE PIANISTIQUE see Ketèlbey,
Albert William

CARAVELLE OVERTURE see Washburn, Robert
Brooks

CARDINAL'S SNUFF BOX see Rogers, F.M.

CAREFREE see Geller, Harold

CARLOSÉMA, BERNARD
Terra
youth orchestra [8'] FUZEAU sc
3701, perf sc set 3721 (C10)

CARMEN, CARMELA *educ/folk song,Mex
(Dardess) string orch,pno,opt perc
(gr. II) KENDOR 8957 (C11)

CARMICHAEL, HOAGY (1899-1981)
Georgia On My Mind
(Cerulli, Bob) string orch (easy)
CPP-BEL 1443GB4X, 029156005073 (C12)
(Custer, Calvin) trom solo,string
orch (med) WARNER S09609,
029156212921 (C13)
(Gold, Marty) orch (med easy) CPP-
BEL 1443GB6X, 029156112368 (C14)

Skylark (composed with Mercer,
Johnny)
(Gold, Marty) orch (med) WARNER
F09601, 029156197235 (C15)

CARNIVAL IN SHUSHAN see Brisman, Heskel

CARNIVAL NIGHTS see Groitzsch, G.

CAROL OF THE BELLS see Ukrainian Bell
Carol

CAROLL, HARRY
I'm Always Chasing Rainbows
(Cerulli, Bob) string orch (very
easy) CPP-BEL T3930IB4,
029156056907 (C16)

CAROLS FOR CHRISTMAS *educ/medley
(Dardess) string orch,pno,opt perc
(gr. II) KENDOR 8958 (C17)

CAROLS OF OLDE: SUITE NO. 1
(O'Neill, John) string orch CPP-BEL
BS09714, 029156605464 (C18)

CARROLL COUNTY see Niehaus

CARSON SUITE, THE see Missal, Joshua M.

CARTOON CAPERS
(Cerulli, Bob) orch (med easy) CPP-
BEL C0197B7X, 029156152425 (C19)

CASEBOW
Believe Me If All Those Endearing
Young Charms *educ
(Hartley, Fred) [2'25"] BOSWORTH (C20)

CASTILIAN REVELS see Charrosin, F.G.

CATLAND FOR STRING ORCHESTRA see Amos,
Keith

CATS AND DOGS see Stephan, Richard

CATS: SUITE NO. 1 see Lloyd Webber,
Andrew

CATS: SUITE NO. 2 see Lloyd Webber,
Andrew

CAVALLERIA RUSTICANA: INTERMEZZO see
Mascagni, Pietro

CAVALRY CALL see Hutchings, J.H.

CAVATINA see Myers, Stanley A.

CECHVALA, AL
Canonized Melody
string orch (gr. III) VELKE (C21)

CECHVALA, AL, EDITOR
Three Melodies From The British Isles
string orch (gr. III, contains 2
settings of "Drink To Me Only
With Thine Eyes" and "Londonderry
Air") VELKE (C22)

CELEBRATION see Cerulli, Bob see
Scheinberg, Art

CELEBRATION (A FOLK EVENT) see Dvořák,
Antonín

CELLO RONDO see Daniels, Melvin L.

CELTIC LILT see Vinter, Gilbert

CELTIC OVERTURE see Niehaus

CELTIC SUITE
(Fishburn, Kathy L.) string orch
WINGERT set 3030301, sc 3030302 (C23)

CEREMONIAL MARCH see Heilmann, Francis

CEREMONIAL OCCASION: A TRIBUTE TO HER
MAJESTY THE QUEEN see Friend,
Howard C.

CEREMONIAL PROCESSION see Washburn,
Robert Brooks

CERULLI, BOB
Celebration
orch CPP-BEL BF09703, 029156300376 (C24)

CHACONY see Purcell, Henry

CHADWICK, CECIL
Serenade To Moonlight *educ
[3'30"] BOSWORTH (C25)

CHAIKOVSKII, PETR IL'ICH
see TCHAIKOVSKY, PIOTR ILYICH

CHAL ROMANO see Ketèlbey, Albert
William

CHANSON TRISTE see Tchaikovsky, Piotr
Ilyich

CHANT AND JOYOUS DANCE see Del Borgo,
Elliot A.

CHANUKA CHAG YA'FE see Hanukkah
Favorites

CHAPLIN
Reel Chaplin, The *educ
(Knight) string orch BOURNE perf
mat rent                          (C26)

CHARIOTS OF FIRE see Vangelis

CHARLTON, DENNIS
Skitty Kitty *educ
[2'40"] BOSWORTH                   (C27)

CHARROSIN, F.G.
A La Beguine *educ
[2'40"] BOSWORTH                   (C28)

Busy Business *educ
[3'] BOSWORTH                      (C29)

Caledonia: Fantasie In Modern
Symphonic Style On Scottish Airs
*educ
[6'45"] BOSWORTH                   (C30)

Cambria: Fantasie In Modern Symphonic
Style On Welsh Airs *educ
[5'] BOSWORTH                      (C31)

Can Can Selection *educ
[4'30"] BOSWORTH                   (C32)

Castilian Revels *educ
[3'30"] BOSWORTH                   (C33)

Cheer Up Polka *educ
[4'30"] BOSWORTH                   (C34)

Cossack Life *educ
[5'30"] BOSWORTH                   (C35)

Cuban Lament *educ
[3'30"] BOSWORTH                   (C36)

Czibulka Memories *educ
[6'] BOSWORTH                      (C37)

Don Carlos (Paso Doble) *educ
[4'] BOSWORTH                      (C38)

Don José (Paso Doble) *educ
[3'] BOSWORTH                      (C39)

Festival In Seville *educ
[5'] BOSWORTH                      (C40)

Fireside Gypsies *educ
orch,vln solo [4'50"] BOSWORTH
                                  (C41)

Hibernia: Fantasie In Modern
Symphonic Style On Irish Airs
*educ
[7'] BOSWORTH                      (C42)

Ilonka *educ
[3'30"] BOSWORTH                   (C43)

Jubilation *educ
[5'] BOSWORTH                      (C44)

Juvenalia *educ
[6'] (contains nursery rhyme
selections) BOSWORTH              (C45)

Keep Moving *educ
[3'] BOSWORTH                      (C46)

Liszt Fantasie (composed with Liszt,
Franz) *educ
[10'] BOSWORTH                     (C47)

Nauticalia: Fantasy Of Sea Songs In
Modern Symphonic Style *educ
[6'] BOSWORTH                      (C48)

Old Salt, The *educ
[3'15"] BOSWORTH                   (C49)

Petals *educ
[3'] BOSWORTH                      (C50)

Playbox *educ
[4'30"] BOSWORTH                   (C51)

Russia Today *educ
[6'45"] (contains selection of
Soviet airs) BOSWORTH             (C52)

Sailors' Patrol *educ
[3'30"] BOSWORTH                   (C53)

Tricksy *educ
[3'10"] BOSWORTH                   (C54)

CHATSCHATURJAN, ARAM
see KHACHATURIAN, ARAM

CHATTANOOGA CHOO CHOO see Warren, Harry

CHEEKY LARP, THE see Amos, Keith

CHEER UP POLKA see Charrosin, F.G.

CHERRY RIPE *educ
(Hartley, Fred) [2'] BOSWORTH  (C55)
(Revel, Louis) string orch,pno,opt
org [4'] BOSWORTH               (C56)

CHEVALIER DE SAINT-GEORGES
see SAINT-GEORGES, JOSEPH BOULOGNE DE

CHILDREN OF THE REGIMENT see Fucik,
Julius

CHILDREN'S OVERTURE, A see Cohen,
Richard

CHILDREN'S PLAYTIME: SUITE see
Engleman, Joseph

CHILDREN'S SUITE see Schipizky,
Frederick

CHINESE SUITE, FOR YOUTH ORCHESTRA see
Arden, Holger, Kinesisk Suite, For
Ungdomsorkester

CHIQUI CHIQUI CHA (LA MULATA TOMASA)
see Quintero, L.

CHOPIN, FRÉDÉRIC (1810-1849)
Nocturne, Op. 9, No. 2
(Velke, Fritz) string orch (gr. IV)
VELKE                             (C57)

CHOPSTICKS *educ
string orch,pno,opt perc BOSWORTH
                                  (C58)
(Arnold, Alan) string orch, all
pizzicato (easy, elementary school
level) HOLLOW                     (C59)

CHORALE AND FUGUE see Bach, Johann
Sebastian

CHORUS OF HUNTSMEN see Weber, Carl
Maria von

CHRISTENSEN, JAMES HARLAN (1935-    )
Rondo And Round *educ
(gr. II) KJOS pts O-1063B, sc
O-1063F                           (C60)

CHRISTMAS BELLS *educ
(Caponegro) string orch,pno,opt perc
(gr. I, includes "Ding Dong Merrily
On High" & "Jingle Bells") KENDOR
8203                              (C61)

CHRISTMAS FESTIVAL, A see Anderson,
Leroy

CHRISTMAS GREETINGS
(Story, Michael) string orch (very
easy) CPP-BEL BS09717, 029156661064
                                  (C62)

CHRISTMAS MEDLEY see Aston, William

CHRISTMAS MUSIC FROM FRANCE (from Organ
Pieces By Guilmant And Gigout) educ
(Kaluza, G.) pno-cond sc,pts BOSWORTH
BOE 4094                          (C63)

CHRISTMAS OVERTURE, A
(Goldsmith, Owen) string orch (med)
CPP-BEL BS09712, 029156605723 (C64)

CHRISTMAS POLONAISE, A *carol/educ,
Polish
(Wieloszynski) string orch,pno (gr.
II) KENDOR 8987                   (C65)

CHRISTMAS REFLECTIONS
(Frost, Robert) string orch (gr. I)
KJOS pts SO-76C, sc SO-76F        (C66)

CHRISTMAS ROUND THE WORLD see Huws
Jones, Edward

CHRISTMAS SING-A-LONG TRADITIONAL
(Cerulli, Bob) orch (med easy) CPP-
BEL C0293B7X, 029156005059   (C67)

CHRISTMAS TRADITION, A
(Sayre, Chuck) orch (med) CPP-BEL
BF09607, 029156213799            (C68)

CHRISTMAS TRILOGY, A *educ
(Del Borgo) string orch (gr. II)
KENDOR 8992 f.s.
contains: Lully Lulay; O Come All
Ye Faithful; Rejoice And Be Merry
                                  (C69)

CHUCKERBUTTY, OLIPHANT
Fiesta Argentina *educ
(Charrosin, F.G.) [6'] (South
American descriptive work
featuring Paso Doble, Rumba &
Tango rhythms) BOSWORTH     (C70)

Pirouette *educ
(Charrosin, F.G.) orch,vln solo
[3'] BOSWORTH                     (C71)

Songe d'Extase *educ
orch,vln solo [4'] BOSWORTH   (C72)

Southern Night, A *educ
(Charrosin, F.G.) [6'45"] BOSWORTH
                                  (C73)

Souvenir D'Amour *educ
orch,vln solo [2'50"] BOSWORTH
                                  (C74)

CIAIKOVSKI, PIETRO
see TCHAIKOVSKY, PIOTR ILYICH

CIELITO LINDO
(Ayars, Bo) 3(pic).3(English
horn).3(bass clar).2. 4.3.3(bass
trom).1. timp,2perc,harp,strings
[1'52"] PRESSER                   (C75)
see South Of The Border Suite

CIGAR MAKERS see Green, Philip

CINDERELLA see Engleman, Joseph

CIRCUS, THE see Missal, Joshua M.

CITIZEN PATRIOT see Goodman

CLARK, LARRY
Torch Burns Bright, The
string orch (beginning level) CPP-
BEL BS09709, 029156603521   (C76)

CLARKE, JEREMIAH (ca. 1673-1707)
Let The Earth Resound (from Trumpet
Voluntary) educ
orch,pno,opt cor BOSWORTH 1042
                                  (C77)

CLARKSON CENTENNIAL OVERTURE see
Washburn, Robert Brooks

CLASSIC SINFONIA see Del Borgo, Elliot
A.

CLASSICAL CONTOURS see Frost, Robert S.

CLASSICAL OVERTURE see Mozart, Wolfgang
Amadeus

CLASSICAL SALZBURG SUITE see Mozart,
Leopold

CLEAVER, H. ROBINSON
Spotlight *educ
(Engleman, J.) [2'30"] BOSWORTH
                                  (C78)

CLOCK AND THE DRESDEN FIGURES see
Ketèlbey, Albert William

CLOCKWORK TWO-SEATER, THE see Engleman,
Joseph

CLOG DANCE see Del Borgo, Elliot A.

CLOWN, THE see Kabalevsky, Dmitri
Borisovich

CLOWN WITH A TAMBOURINE see Ewing,
Montague

COCKNEY LOVER see Ketèlbey, Albert
William

COCKNEY SUITE (CAMEOS OF LONDON LIFE)
see Ketèlbey, Albert William

COHEN, RICHARD
Children's Overture, A *educ
(gr. V) KJOS pts O-1066C, sc
O-1066F                           (C79)

Horns To The Hunt *educ
(gr. IV) KJOS pts O-1064B, sc
O-1064F                           (C80)

Pirate's Treasure March *educ
(gr. III) KJOS pts O-1065B, sc
O-1065F                           (C81)

Serenade Triste
string orch (gr. IV) KJOS pts
SO-125C, sc SO-125F               (C82)

COLEMAN, CY (1929-    )
Big Spender
(Cerulli, Bob) orch (easy) WARNER
WBF09303, 029156067767      (C83)

Hey, Look Me Over
(Cerulli, Bob) orch (intermediate
level) WARNER F09719,
029156609424                      (C84)

COLEMAN, TODD
To Remember
string orch (gr. III) set JLJ.MUSIC
SO 107                            (C85)

COLIN-MAILLARD see Lauber, Anne

COLOUR-SERGEANT, THE see Joyce,
Archibald

COLOURS OF LIBERTY see Kuhn, Wolfgang,
Editor

COME WHERE MY LOVE LIES DREAMING see
Foster, Stephen Collins

COMMEMORATION FANFARE & CHORALE see
Smith, Claude Thomas

CONCERT TUNES FOR BEGINNING STRINGS:
BASS see Brubaker, Dale

CONCERT TUNES FOR BEGINNING STRINGS: CELLO see Brubaker, Dale

CONCERT TUNES FOR BEGINNING STRINGS: CONDUCTOR'S SCORE see Brubaker, Dale

CONCERT TUNES FOR BEGINNING STRINGS: VIOLA see Brubaker, Dale

CONCERT TUNES FOR BEGINNING STRINGS: VIOLIN see Brubaker, Dale

CONCERT TUNES FOR INTERMEDIATE STRINGS: BASS see Brubaker, Dale

CONCERT TUNES FOR INTERMEDIATE STRINGS: CELLO see Brubaker, Dale

CONCERT TUNES FOR INTERMEDIATE STRINGS: CONDUCTOR'S SCORE see Brubaker, Dale

CONCERT TUNES FOR INTERMEDIATE STRINGS: VIOLA see Brubaker, Dale

CONCERT TUNES FOR INTERMEDIATE STRINGS: VIOLIN see Brubaker, Dale

CONCERTANTE see Mazas

CONCERTO ITALIANO see Bach, Johann Sebastian, Italian Concerto

CONCERTUS see Lonoce, Roberto

CONLEY
Holiday Sleigh Ride *educ
string orch,opt perc (gr. II)
KENDOR 9164            (C86)

COOTS, JOHN FREDERICK (1897-    )
For All We Know
(Custer, Calvin) string orch,
flügelhorn/trp solo (med) WARNER
S09610, 029156212945     (C87)

Santa Claus Is Comin' To Town
(Cerulli, Bob) orch (med easy) CPP-
BEL T0510SB7, 029156177879 (C88)

COPY CAT WALTZ & POTPOURRI POLKA see
Elledge, Chuck

CORELLI, ARCANGELO (1653-1713)
Folia, La *educ
(Alshin, Harry A.) string orch (gr.
III) KENDOR 9845          (C89)

Sonata da Chiesa No. 11 *educ
(Del Borgo) string orch (gr. III)
KENDOR 9878               (C90)

Three Corelli Dances
(Halen, Walter J.) string orch
WINGERT set 3033051, sc 3033052
(C91)

CORONATION MARCH see Del Borgo, Elliot A.

COSSACK LIFE see Charrosin, F.G.

COUNTERPOINT FOR CHRISTMAS *educ
(McLeod) string orch,pno (gr. II,
includes "We Wish You A Merry
Christmas" & "Deck The Halls")
KENDOR 9008               (C92)

COUNTRY DANCE MEDLEY *educ
(Hartley, Fred) [2'] BOSWORTH    (C93)
(Terry, Ray) [2'] BOSWORTH       (C94)

COWBOYS' HORSEMANSHIP (GALOP) see
Armandola, Jose

COWBOYS OVERTURE, THE see Williams,
John T.

CRAWLEY, CLIFFORD (1929-    )
Walkerville Suite, The *educ
string orch,opt kbd/gtr sc,pts
CANADIAN MI 3134 C911WA   (C95)

CROOKE, SIDNEY
Solo Flight *educ
[2'50"] BOSWORTH          (C96)

CROSSBOW OVERTURE see Niehaus

CROSSMAN, GERALD
Granada Mia (Paso Doble) *educ
[2'] BOSWORTH             (C97)

CROUDSON, HENRY
Pirouette *educ
[3'] BOSWORTH             (C98)

Serenade To The Moon *educ
[2'45"] BOSWORTH          (C99)

Up North: Phantasy *educ
[4'] BOSWORTH             (C100)

CRUELLA DE VIL *educ
(Conley) string orch,opt combo (gr.
II) LEONARD-US 04626066   (C101)

CRUSADERS! see Huws Jones, Edward

CUBAN LAMENT see Charrosin, F.G.

CUBAN SUITE see Green, Philip

CUCARACHA, LA *educ
(Wieloszynski) string orch,pno (gr.
II) KENDOR 9205           (C102)
see South Of The Border Suite

CUCURACHA, LA (RUMBA) see Green, Philip

CUMBANCHERO, EL
(Gold, Marty) orch (med) CPP-BEL
F09510, 029156173376      (C103)

CUOMO, R.
Gypsy Tambourin *educ
(Engleman, J.) orch,vln solo
[2'30"] BOSWORTH          (C104)

CZIBULKA, ALPHONS (1842-1894)
Hearts And Flowers (Intermezzo)
*educ
(Charrosin, F.G.) [5'30"] BOSWORTH
(C105)

Love's Dream *educ
(Geiger) BOSWORTH         (C106)

Love's Dream After The Ball
(Intermezzo) *educ
(Charrosin, F.G.) [3'15"] BOSWORTH
(C107)

CZIBULKA MEMORIES see Charrosin, F.G.

# D

DANCE see Prokofiev, Serge

DANCE IN D see Stephan, Richard

DANCE OF THE ANTILLESE GIRLS see
Prokofiev, Serge

DANCE OF THE FLIES see Young Bartok
Suite, A

DANCE OF THE LARP see Amos, Keith

DANCE OF THE MERRY MASCOTS see
Ketèlbey, Albert William

DANCE PAVANE see Cacavas

DANCE SUITE see Mozart, Wolfgang
Amadeus

DANCERS THEME: FROM THE STEADFAST TIN
SOLDIER see Amos, Keith

DANCING IN THE DARK see Schwartz,
Arthur

DANCING MOONBEAMS see Williams, A.

DANCING THE DAY AWAY see Mackey,
Percival

DANCLA, CHARLES (1817-1907)
Herald Quartet
(Klotman) string orch (med easy)
CPP-BEL 87241, 029156683394 (D1)

DANIELS
Rondo Caprice *educ
string orch,pno (gr. I) KENDOR 8553
(D2)

DANIELS, MELVIN L. (1931-    )
Air And Dance
string orch (gr. II) KJOS pts
WSO-8C, sc WSO-8F         (D3)

Cello Rondo
string orch (gr. II) KJOS pts
WSO-7C, sc WSO-7F         (D4)

Mourning Song *educ
(gr. III) KJOS pts WO-13C, sc
WO-13F                    (D5)

Night Beat
string orch (gr. IV) KJOS pts
WSO-6C, sc WSO-6F         (D6)

DANSE GAIE see Leggett, Ernest

DANSE MACABRE see Saint-Saëns, Camille

DANUBE LEGENDS see Fucik, Julius

DASHING AWAY WITH THE SMOOTHING IRON
*educ
(Hartley, Fred) [2'] BOSWORTH    (D7)

DAVIS, KATHERINE K. (1892-1980)
Little Drummer Boy, The (composed
with Onorati, Henry V.; Simeone,
Harry)
(Applebaum, Samuel) string orch
(med easy) CPP-BEL BS000021,
029156671711             (D8)
(Cerulli, Bob) string orch (easy)
CPP-BEL 2793LB4X, 029156174557
(D9)
(Cerulli, Bob) orch (easy) CPP-BEL
2793LB7X, 029156216332   (D10)

DAWN see North, Michael

DAY BEGINS, A see Mackey, Percival

DAY IN MAY, A (SUITE) see Mackey,
Percival

DAY OF THE DOLPHIN see Huws Jones,
Edward

DAYTIME see North, Michael

DE LATTRE, ROLAND
see LASSUS, ROLAND DE

DE ROSE, PETER (1900-1953)
Deep Purple
(Gold, Marty) orch (med) CPP-BEL
F09514, 029156179996      (D11)

DEAR OCTOPUS see Bridgewater, Ernest
Leslie

DEATH AND THE MAIDEN see Schubert,
Franz (Peter)

DEBUSSY, CLAUDE (1862-1918)
Girl With The Flaxen Hair, The
(Goldsmith, Owen) orch (med) CPP-
BEL BF09604, 029156202472    (D12)

Golliwog's Cakewalk  *educ
(Wieloszynski) string orch,pno (gr.
IV) KENDOR 9827           (D13)

Two Cakewalks By Claude Debussy
(Cerulli, Bob) string orch (med
easy) CPP-BEL BS000088,
029156696028             (D14)

DECLARATION OVERTURE see Smith, Claude
Thomas

DEEP PURPLE see De Rose, Peter

DEL BORGO, ELLIOT A. (1938-    )
Chant And Joyous Dance
orch (intermediate level) CPP-BEL
BF09704, 029156300338    (D15)

Classic Sinfonia  *educ
string orch,pno (gr. I) KENDOR 8213
                         (D16)

Clog Dance  *educ
string orch,pno (gr. I) KENDOR 8215
                         (D17)

Coronation March  *educ
string orch,pno (gr. I) KENDOR 8237
                         (D18)

Dorian Essay  *educ
string orch (gr. II) KENDOR 9043
                         (D19)

Étude in D  *educ
string orch,pno (gr. I) KENDOR 8258
                         (D20)

Fantasy for Strings
string orch (med easy) CPP-BEL
BS000080, 029156095371   (D21)

Highridge Overture  *educ
string orch,pno (gr. II) KENDOR
9162                     (D22)

New Horizons
string orch (med) CPP-BEL BS09605,
029156200430             (D23)

Oxford Overture
string orch (easy) CPP-BEL
BS000084, 029156671742   (D24)

Sinfonia in G  *educ
string orch (gr. II) KENDOR 9465
                         (D25)

Sonatina for Strings
string orch (very easy) CPP-BEL
BS09702, 029156299069    (D26)

Soundscape II  *educ
string orch (gr. III) KENDOR 9872
                         (D27)

String Scene  *educ
string orch,pno (gr. I) KENDOR 8675
                         (D28)

Tryptich For Strings  *educ
string orch (gr. II) KENDOR 9635
                         (D29)

Wexford Circle  *educ
string orch,pno (gr. I) KENDOR 8848
                         (D30)

DELIBES, LÉO (1836-1891)
Delibes Ballet Memories  *educ
(Geiger, I.) [13'30"] BOSWORTH
                         (D31)

Flower Duet (from Lakmé) educ
(Wieloszynski) string orch,pno (gr.
II) KENDOR 9108          (D32)

DELIBES BALLET MEMORIES see Delibes,
Léo see Geiger, I.

DEMUTH, NORMAN (1898-1968)
Overture For A Joyful Occasion  *educ
BOSWORTH sc rent, pts f.s.   (D33)

DESERT SHALL BLOOM AS THE ROSE, THE see
Hutchison, (David) Warner

DESMOND, PAUL
Take Five
(Cerulli, Bob) orch (easy) CPP-BEL
0134TB7X, 029156218510   (D34)

DESYLVA, GEORGE GARD (BUDDY)
(1895-1950)
Birth Of The Blues
(Custer, Calvin) clar solo,string
orch (med easy) WARNER SO9506,
029156179156            (D35)

DEVIL'S DREAM see Beginning Bluegrass

DI LASSO, ORLANDO
see LASSUS, ROLAND DE

DINIZ, PAOLO BRAGA
Brazilian Images
string orch (gr. III) KJOS pts
SO-128C, sc SO-128F      (D36)

DIVERTIMENTO FOR EASY STRINGS see Kunz,
Alfred

DO THOU DEFEND US: CHORALE PRELUDE see
Bach, Johann Sebastian

DO WAH DIDDY DIDDY
(Cerulli, Bob) orch (intermediate
level) WARNER F09712, 029156605778
                         (D37)

DOHM, ROBERT
Two Sea Songs
string orch (gr. I) set JLJ.MUSIC
SO 108                   (D38)

DOLL IN THE CRADLE, THE see Engleman,
Joseph

DOLL'S HOUSE: SUITE see Engleman,
Joseph

DOLLS ON PARADE see Engleman, Joseph

DON CARLOS (PASO DOBLE) see Charrosin,
F.G.

DON GIOVANNI: MELODIC MOMENTS see
Mozart, Wolfgang Amadeus

DON JOSÉ (PASO DOBLE) see Charrosin,
F.G.

DONIZETTI, GAETANO (1797-1848)
Quartet in D minor  *educ
(Storfer) string orch BOURNE
augmented set 413780, set 413720
                         (D39)

DON'T CRY FOR ME ARGENTINA; YOU MUST
LOVE ME see Lloyd Webber, Andrew

DOOLITTLE, QUENTIN (1925-    )
Sunrise - Sleighride  *educ/
incidental music
string orch sc CANADIAN
MI 1500 D691SU           (D40)

DORIAN DESIGN see Anderson, Gerald

DORIAN ESSAY see Del Borgo, Elliot A.

DOWLAND, JOHN (1562-1626)
Dowland On Strings  *educ
(Schwindt) string orch sc,pts
HEINRICH 3733            (D41)

DOWLAND ON STRINGS see Dowland, John

DOWN THE STREAM see Ketèlbey, Albert
William

DOWNS, HUGH
Elegiac Prelude In A Minor
orch WINGERT set 9041551, sc
9041552                  (D42)

DRAGONFLIES WEDDING (INTERMEZZO) see
Barrow, P.

DRDLA, FRANTIŠEK (FRANZ) ALOIS
(1868-1944)
Souvenir  *educ
(Hiess, K.) [2'50"] BOSWORTH  (D43)

DREAM FANTASY see Neville, Derek

DREAM OF A PRINCESS, THE see Gordon,
Harry

DREAM OF CHRISTMAS, A see Ketèlbey,
Albert William

DREAMS IN EXILE see King, Reginald

DREAMS OF YOU see Joyce, Archibald

DREAMY SHADOWS see Bick, H.

DREWES, [CAPTAIN] BARRY
Believe Me If All Those Endearing
Young Charms  *educ
(Terry, Ray) [2'25"] BOSWORTH (D44)

DRINK TO ME ONLY  *educ
(Revel, Louis) string orch,pno,opt
org [3'45"] BOSWORTH     (D45)

DUBINUSCHKA: POTPOURRI ON FAVORITE
RUSSIAN AND GYPSY AIRS see
Schirmann, A.

DUKE ELLINGTON (A MEDLEY FOR ORCHESTRA)
see Ellington, Edward Kennedy
(Duke)

DUPARLOIR
Rêve D'Enfant  *educ
BOSWORTH                 (D46)

DUSK see North, Michael

DUTHOIT, W.J.
Advance March, The  *educ
[2'15"] BOSWORTH         (D47)

DVORÁK, ANTONÍN (1841-1904)
Celebration (A Folk Event)
(Alshin, Harry) string orch (med)
CPP-BEL BS000076, 029156101720
                         (D48)

Furiant (from Symphony No. 6 In D)
(Goldsmith, Owen) orch (med) CPP-
BEL C000201, 029156679977   (D49)

Gypsy Songs  *Op.55,No.4,No.6
(Goldsmith, Owen) orch
(intermediate level) CPP-BEL
BF09702, 029156299939    (D50)

Humoreske
(Goldsmith, Owen) orch (med) CPP-
BEL BF09602, 029156199437   (D51)

Largo
(Heilmann, Francis) string orch/
orch HEILMAN            (D52)

New World Symphony (First Movement)
see Symphony, Op. 95, in E minor,
First Movement, [arr.]

Scherzo, [arr.] (from Symphony No. 7,
3rd Mvt.)
(Isaac, Merle) orch (med diff) CPP-
BEL C000158, 029156671667   (D53)

Symphony, Op. 95, in E minor,First
Movement, [arr.]
(Isaac, Merle) "New World Symphony
(First Movement)" orch (med) CPP-
BEL C000164, 029156668704   (D54)

# E

EASTER PARADE IN VIENNA see Stolz, Robert

ECCENTRIC COURTIER see Stuart, Graeme

ECHO CAROLE *educ
(Wieloszynski) string orch,pno (gr. I) KENDOR 8259                    (E1)

ECHO FANTASY see Lassus, Roland de (Orlandus)

ECSTASY see Gold, Marty

EDELWEISS see Komzak, Karl

EGERICKX, A.
Alsace Lorraine *educ
[3'30"] BOSWORTH                    (E2)

EIGHT LYRIC PIECES see Grieg, Edvard Hagerup

EIGHTEENTH CENTURY CHRISTMAS, AN *educ
(McLeod) string orch (gr. III) contains "O Tannenbaum" & "Jolly Old Saint Nicholas) KENDOR 9809
(E3)

EILENBERG, R.
March Of The Mountain Gnomes *educ
[5'] BOSWORTH                    (E4)

ELEGIAC PRELUDE IN A MINOR see Downs, Hugh

ELEGY see Ketèlbey, Albert William see Tchaikovsky, Piotr Ilyich, Serenade for Strings,Third Movement

ELFENTANZ see Jenkinson, Ezra, Elves' Dance

ELGAR, [SIR] EDWARD (WILLIAM) (1857-1934)
Pomp And Circumstance
(Del Borgo, Elliot) string orch (med diff) CPP-BEL BS09703, 029156299083                    (E5)
(Isaac) orch CPP-BEL C000110, 029156297881                    (E6)

Six Easy Pieces, Op. 22 *educ
string orch&pno/orch (easy) pno-cond sc,pts BOSWORTH 1009   (E7)

ELIZABETHAN DANCES see Hartley, Walter Sinclair

ELLEDGE, CHUCK
Adelante! Adelante!
string orch,opt perc (gr. V) KJOS pts GSO-29C, sc GSO-29F   (E8)

Blue Mood
string orch (gr. II) KJOS pts GSO-24C, sc GSO-24F                    (E9)

Copy Cat Waltz & Potpourri Polka
string orch (gr. I) KJOS pts GSO-22C, sc GSO-22F                    (E10)

Monument Valley
string orch (gr. I) KJOS pts GSO-28C, sc GSO-28F                    (E11)

Phantom Dance
string orch (gr. I) KJOS pts GSO-13C, sc GSO-13F                    (E12)

ELLINGTON, EDWARD KENNEDY (DUKE) (1899-1974)
Duke Ellington (A Medley For Orchestra)
(Custer, Calvin) orch (med) CPP-BEL C0270B7X, 029156181012   (E13)

I Got It Bad (And That Ain't Good)
(Gold, Marty) orch (med) WARNER F09602, 029156199093   (E14)

It Don't Mean A Thing (If It Ain't Got That Swing) (composed with Mills, Irving)
(Sayre, Chuck) orch (med) WARNER F09507, 029156177954   (E15)

Sophisticated Lady
(Gold, Marty) orch (med easy) CPP-BEL 4739SB6X, 029156112566   (E16)

ELVES' DANCE see Jenkinson, Ezra

EMBRACEABLE YOU see Gershwin, George

EMPEROR WALTZ see Strauss, Johann, [Jr.]

EMPIRE STRIKES BACK MEDLEY, THE see Williams, John T.

ENCHANTED CASTLE, THE see Glazunov, Alexander Konstantinovich

ENCHANTING EYES (TANGO) see Bridgmont, Leslie

ENESCO, GEORGES (ENESCU) (1881-1955)
Rumanian Rhapsody No. 1 *educ
(Alshin, Harry A.) string orch,opt perc (gr. III) KENDOR 9858   (E17)

ENGLEMAN, HARRY
Hammer And Tongs *educ
[2'] BOSWORTH                    (E18)

Leap Frog *educ
[2'30"] BOSWORTH                    (E19)

Speedway *educ
(Engleman, J.) [2'] BOSWORTH   (E20)

Spick And Span *educ
[2'] BOSWORTH                    (E21)

ENGLEMAN, JOSEPH
Ali Baba
see Tales From A Fairy Book: Suite

Babes In The Wood
see Tales From A Fairy Book: Suite

Blue Boudoir, The
see Doll's House: Suite

Children's Playtime: Suite *educ
BOSWORTH f.s.
contains: Hide And Seek (Valse Caprice) [3']; Marbles [1'25"]; Pick-A-Back [2'30"]; Ring O' Roses [2'45"]                    (E22)

Cinderella
see Tales From A Fairy Book: Suite

Clockwork Two-Seater, The
see Doll's House: Suite

Doll In The Cradle, The
see In A Toy Shop: Suite

Doll's House: Suite *educ
BOSWORTH f.s.
contains: Blue Boudoir, The [3']; Clockwork Two-Seater, The [3']; Green Baize Lawn, The [1'30"]; Miniature Piano, The [1']; Sleeping Doll, The [3']   (E23)

Dolls On Parade
see In A Toy Shop: Suite

Fiddler's Folly *educ
[2'15"] BOSWORTH                    (E24)

Green Baize Lawn, The
see Doll's House: Suite

Hide And Seek (Valse Caprice)
see Children's Playtime: Suite

Humoresque (Top Boot Dance)
see Three American Sketches: Suite

In A Toy Shop: Suite *educ
BOSWORTH f.s.
contains: Doll In The Cradle, The [2']; Dolls On Parade [2']; Pierrette On The Swing [2']; Rocking Horse, The [1']   (E25)

Ladies And Courtiers Of Lilliput, The (Valse Intermezzo)
see Voyage To Lilliput: A (Suite)

Lilliputian Army, The (Marche Grotesque)
see Voyage To Lilliput: A (Suite)

Marbles
see Children's Playtime: Suite

Miniature Piano, The
see Doll's House: Suite

Night Shade *educ
[2'15"] (pizzicato) BOSWORTH   (E26)

Paprika (Polka) *educ
orch,clar/vln solo [2'45"] BOSWORTH   (E27)

Pick-A-Back
see Children's Playtime: Suite

Pierrette On The Swing
see In A Toy Shop: Suite

Pizzicato Caprice *educ
BOSWORTH                    (E28)

Rêve d'Amour *educ
[4'] BOSWORTH                    (E29)
orch,vln solo [4'] BOSWORTH   (E30)

ENGLEMAN, JOSEPH (cont'd.)
Ride Him! Cowboy *educ
[2'30"] BOSWORTH                    (E31)

Ring O' Roses
see Children's Playtime: Suite

Riviera Express (Descriptive Interlude) *educ
[2'45"] BOSWORTH                    (E32)

Rocking Horse, The
see In A Toy Shop: Suite

Rope Dancers, The
see Voyage To Lilliput: A (Suite)

Rumpelstilskin
see Tales From A Fairy Book: Suite

Shores Of Lilliput, The (Prelude)
see Voyage To Lilliput: A (Suite)

Sleeping Doll, The
see Doll's House: Suite

Statue Of Liberty (Miniature Overture)
see Three American Sketches: Suite

Tales From A Fairy Book: Suite *educ
BOSWORTH f.s.
contains: Ali Baba [2'30"]; Babes In The Wood [2'30"]; Cinderella [3']; Rumpelstilskin [3'30"]   (E33)

Three American Sketches: Suite *educ
BOSWORTH f.s.
contains: Humoresque (Top Boot Dance) [1'45"]; Statue Of Liberty (Miniature Overture) [2'45"]; Yankee Doodle (Galop) [2']   (E34)

Voyage To Lilliput: A (Suite) *educ
BOSWORTH f.s.
contains: Ladies And Courtiers Of Lilliput, The (Valse Intermezzo) [4']; Lilliputian Army, The (Marche Grotesque) [4']; Rope Dancers, The [4']; Shores Of Lilliput, The (Prelude) [3']   (E35)

Wrens' Serenade *educ
[2'30"] BOSWORTH                    (E36)

Yankee Doodle (Galop)
see Three American Sketches: Suite

ENGLISH FOLKSONG, AN
(McQuilkin, Terry) string orch (gr. II) KJOS pts SO-102C, sc SO-102F
(E37)

ENGLISH SUITE
(Fishburn, Kathy L.) string orch WINGERT set 3030121, sc 3030122
(E38)

ENIGMATIC PENGUIN see Bick, H.

ENTERTAINER, THE see Joplin, Scott

ENTRANCE OF THE QUEEN OF SHEBA see Handel, George Frideric

ENTRY see Herbert, Victor

ERDLEN, HERMANN (1893-1972)
Winter Ist Vergangen, Der: Theme And Variations *educ
string orch sc,pts HEINRICH 1008
(E39)

ERICKSON
Air for Strings *educ
string orch BOURNE augmented set 416280, set 416200, sc 416204
(E40)

Balladair *educ
string orch BOURNE augmented set 416370, set 416380, sc 416384
(E41)

Toccata for Orchestra *educ
string orch BOURNE augmented set 416470, set 416460, sc 416464
(E42)

ERLEBACH, PHILIPP HEINRICH (1657-1714)
Overture for String Orchestra in A minor, No. 1 *educ
string orch,opt cont sc,pts HEINRICH 1168                    (E43)

Overture for String Orchestra in G minor, No. 6 *educ
string orch,opt cont sc,pts HEINRICH 1169                    (E44)

ESTEFAN, GLORIA
Gloria Estefan - Her Greatest Hits!
(Sayre, Chuck) orch (med diff) CPP-BEL C0321B7X, 029156061451   (E45)

Reach
(Custer, Calvin) orch (med) WARNER F09616, 029156220377   (E46)

ETYDER OVER TIDEN see Asheim, Nils Henrik

EVEILLE DE L'AMOUR see Scull, Harold [Thomas]

EVENING IN TOLEDO see Schmeling, M.

EVENING IN TOLEDO, AN see Schmeling, M.

EVENING ON THE RHINE see Richartz, Willy

EVENING PRAYER see Humperdinck, Engelbert

EVENSONG see Schumann, Robert (Alexander), Abendlied

EVERYTHING I DO, I DO IT FOR YOU see Adams, Bryan

EVITA: MUSIC see Lloyd Webber, Andrew

EWING, MONTAGUE
    Clown With A Tambourine  *educ
    [3'] BOSWORTH                        (E47)

    Lady Sergeant, The (March Intermezzo)
    *educ
    (Engleman, Joseph) [3'15"] BOSWORTH
                                         (E48)

    Over The Scottish Hills (March
    Intermezzo)  *educ
    (Harbury, J.) [3'30"] BOSWORTH       (E49)

    Phantom Piper, The  *educ
    (Franzel, A.) [4'20"] BOSWORTH       (E50)

    Sailormen All  *educ
    (Walker, F.) [4'25"] BOSWORTH        (E51)

    Whirling Leaves (Intermezzo) *educ
    (Walker, F.) [2'40"] BOSWORTH        (E52)

EXCERPTS FROM BEATUS VIR see Vivaldi, Antonio, Beatus Vir: Excerpts

EXCURSION TRAIN see Stuart, Graeme

EXSULTATE JUBILATE see Mozart, Wolfgang Amadeus

# F

FAIRY BALLET see Noack, Walter

FAIRY OF THE GLEN see Williams, A.

FAIRY ON THE CLOCK see Myers, Sherman

FAMOUS CZARDAS NO.1 see Michiels, G.

FANCY FIDDLES see Velke, Fritz

FANFARE AND CELEBRATION see Caponegro, John see Smith, Claude Thomas

FANFARE AND MARCH see Sullivan, [Sir] Arthur Seymour

FANFARE FOR STRINGS see Gazda, Doris

FANFARE FOR SYMPHONY ORCHESTRA see Larrick, Geary

FANFARE FOR THE THIRD see Wiggins, Christopher D.

FANFLAIRS see Niehaus

FANTAISIE SUR UN THÈME CONNU see Lauber, Anne

FANTASIA AND TOCCATA see Pachelbel, Johann

FANTASIA ON A SEVENTEENTH CENTURY TUNE see Stephan, Richard

FANTASY ON A KNOWN THEME see Lauber, Anne, Fantaisie Sur Un Thème Connu

FAREWELL ADAGIO see Haydn, [Franz] Joseph

"FAREWELL" SYMPHONY (FINALE) see Haydn, [Franz] Joseph, Symphony No. 45 in F sharp minor,Finale. [arr.]

FARIS, ALEXANDER
    Upstairs Downstairs (Waltz Theme)
    (Frazer, Alan) strings (opt. easy
    parts for vln & vcl) sc,pts
    CRAMER MUS 90437 f.s.             (F1)

FASCINATIN' RHYTHM see Gershwin, George

FAURE, GABRIEL-URBAIN (1845-1924)
    Morceau De Concours
    (Paget) strings,opt 3horn,opt harp,
    fl solo BOURNE augmented set
    417870, set 417860, sc 417864    (F2)

    Sicilienne (from Pelleas et
    Melisande)
    (Goldsmith, Owen) string orch (med)
    CPP-BEL BS000103, 029156045505   (F3)

FAUST, ACT II: WALTZ AND MARGARITA'S SONG see Gounod, Charles François

FESTIVAL see Nunez, Carold

FESTIVAL HOP  *educ
    (Jones) string orch BOURNE augmented
    set 040280, set 040240           (F4)

FESTIVAL IN ELYSIUM see Noack, Walter

FESTIVAL IN SEVILLE see Charrosin, F.G.

FESTIVAL PARTITA see Klein, Lothar

FESTIVAL SONG OF PRAISE see Mendelssohn-Bartholdy, Felix

FESTIVE RONDO see Frost

FESTIVITY MARCH see Hinton

FÊTE ORIENTALE see Noble, Harold

FETRAS, OSCAR
    Moonlight On The Alster  *educ
    [8'50"] BOSWORTH                 (F5)

FIDDLE FACTORY see Frost

FIDDLE-FADDLE see Anderson, Leroy

FIDDLE FEVER see Lowden

FIDDLER'S FANTASY see Sadlier, Ron

FIDDLER'S FOLLY see Engleman, Joseph

FIDDLER'S GREEN see Niehaus

FIESTA
    (Conley, Lloyd) string orch CPP-BEL
    BS09701, 029156275551            (F6)

FIESTA ARGENTINA see Chuckerbutty, Oliphant

FIESTA MEXICANA see Frost, Robert S.

FIESTA MEXICANA, LA see Reed, Herbert Owen

FIESTA MEXICANA S. QUAGENTI
    string orch CPP-BEL BS000044,
    029156671643                     (F7)

FIGHTING FOR FREEDOM see Ketèlbey, Albert William

FINALE (TARANTELLA) see Herbert, Victor

FINGER DRILLS FOR STRING ORCHESTRA see Arthur, John

FINGERNAIL MOON see Niehaus

FINLANDIA see Sibelius, Jean

FIRE ON THE HORIZON see Knorr, H.

FIRESIDE GYPSIES see Charrosin, F.G.

FIRST FLOWER see Wyre, John

FIRST WALTZ, THE see King, Reginald

FIVE FOR FOUR see Surdin, Morris

FIVE O'CLOCK TEA IN THE DOLL'S HOUSE see Rosen, W.

FLAGS IN THE SQUARE see Milner, Ch.

FLAMBEAU, JEANETTE, ISABELLA!, UN see Bring A Torch, Jeannette, Isabella!

FLEISCHER, H.
    Triptychon Für Streichorchester
    *Op.147,No.1, educ
    string orch HEINRICH sc 5539, pts
    5544-5544                        (F8)

FLEMING, ROBERT (1921-1976)
    Andante for String Orchestra  *educ
    string orch [20'] sc CANADIAN
    MI 1500 F598AN                   (F9)

    Gavotte And Mussette For Strings
    *educ
    string orch sc CANADIAN
    MI 1500 F598GA                   (F10)

    Invocation For String Orchestra
    *educ
    string orch [2'] sc CANADIAN
    MI 1500 F598IN                   (F11)

FLEMISH CAROL, A  *educ
    (Del Borgo) string orch (gr. II)
    KENDOR 9107                      (F12)

FLORENTINE MARCH see Fucik, Julius

FLOURISH, SONG AND TOCCATA see Smith, Claude Thomas

FLOWER DUET see Delibes, Léo

FLUTE SERENADE see Roland, M.

FODI, JOHN (1944-    )
    Suite For Junior String Orchestra
    *Op.81, educ
    string orch sc CANADIAN          (F13)

FOGGY DAY, A see Gershwin, George

FOLIA, LA see Corelli, Arcangelo

FOLK WALTZ, A  *educ
    (Alshin, Harry A.) string orch (gr.
    II) KENDOR 9109                  (F14)

FONES, A.F.
    Memory  *educ
    BOSWORTH                         (F15)

FOR ALL WE KNOW see Coots, John Frederick

FOSTER, DAVID
    Love Theme From St. Elmo's Fire
    see St. Elmo's Fire: Love Theme

    St. Elmo's Fire: Love Theme
    (Cerulli, Bob) "Love Theme From St.
    Elmo's Fire" orch (easy) CPP-BEL
    5231LB7X, 029156637717           (F16)

FOSTER, ROBERT E.
    Albright Fantasy
    string orch WINGERT set 303001, sc
    303002                           (F17)

FOSTER, STEPHEN COLLINS (1826-1864)
    Come Where My Love Lies Dreaming
    (Cechvala, Al) string orch (gr. II)
    VELKE                            (F18)

FOULDS, JOHN HERBERT (1880-1939)
Mendelssohn Fantasie *educ
[14'] (contains popular melodies by
Mendelssohn) BOSWORTH        (F19)

Schubert Fantasie *educ
[13'] (contains popular melodies by
Franz Schubert) BOSWORTH        (F20)

Tschaikowski Fantasie *educ
[15'] (contains popular melodies by
Tchaikovsky) BOSWORTH        (F21)

FRANCESCA DA RIMINI see Tchaikovsky,
Piotr Ilyich

FRANZEL (LANDLER) see Parker, Clifton

FREEDMAN, HARRY (1922-    )
Scales In Polytonality *educ
2+pic.2.3+bass clar.2.2alto
sax.tenor sax.baritone sax.
4.3.3+euphonium.1. timp,2perc,
strings sc,pts CANADIAN
MI 1100 F853SCA        (F22)

FRERE JACQUES see Suite Francaise

FRESCOBALDI, GIROLAMO (1583-1643)
Toccata *educ
(Higgins, James) string orch (gr.
III) KJOS pts SO-99C, sc SO-99F
(F23)
(Kindler) orch (med diff) CPP-BEL
81551, 029156184723        (F24)

FRIEND, HOWARD C.
Ceremonial Occasion: A Tribute To Her
Majesty The Queen *educ
(med diff) pno-cond sc,pts BOSWORTH
1012        (F25)

FROLIC SONG see Young Bartok Suite, A

FROLICSOME FRIDAY see Frost, Robert S.

FROM A DISTANCE see Gold, Julie

FROM AROUND THE WORLD *educ
(Alshin, Harry A.) string orch (gr.
II, contains 6 folk songs of
Hungary, Czechoslovakia, Israel,
Kenya & Greece) KENDOR 7937    (F26)

FROM SHANGH(A)I TO BANGKOK see Andrew
With Strings: Volume 2 "A French
Medley"

FROM THE COCKTAIL HOUR see Green,
Philip

FROST
Festive Rondo *educ
string orch,pno (gr. II) KENDOR
9065        (F27)

Fiddle Factory *educ
string orch,pno (gr. I) KENDOR 8263
(F28)

Kids Karnival *educ
string orch,pno (gr. II) KENDOR
9202        (F29)

Prelude And Dance *educ
string orch (gr. II) KENDOR 8015
(F30)

Red River Rapids *educ
string orch,pno (gr. II) KENDOR
9405        (F31)

Sunset Waltz *educ
string orch,pno (gr. I) KENDOR 8715
(F32)
Two Moods In The Morning *educ
string orch (gr. II) KENDOR 8085
(F33)
Variations A Comin' *educ
string orch (gr. II) KENDOR 8091
(F34)

FROST, ROBERT S. (1942-    )
Caper Capriccioso
string orch (gr. II) KJOS pts
SO-84C, sc SO-84F        (F35)

Classical Contours
string orch (gr. I) KJOS pts
SO-109C, sc SO-109F        (F36)

Fiesta Mexicana
string orch (gr. I) KJOS pts
SO-104C, sc SO-104F        (F37)

Frolicsome Friday
string orch (gr. II) KJOS pts
SO-108C, sc SO-108F        (F38)

Main Street March
string orch (gr. I) KJOS pts
SO-75C, sc SO-75F        (F39)

Pizzicato Pizazz
string orch (gr. I) KJOS pts
SO-90C, sc SO-90F        (F40)

FROST, ROBERT S. (cont'd.)

Theme and Variations *educ
string orch KJOS pts SO-85C, sc
SO-85F        (F41)

FROSTY FINGERS see Michaeloff, Mischa

FROU FROU see Joyce, Archibald

FUCHS, HANS
Box And Cox (composed with Hartmann,
Bruno) *educ
orch,clar&bsn soli/alto sax&tenor
sax soli [3'30"] BOSWORTH    (F42)

Happy Mood *educ
orch,2clar soli [4'] BOSWORTH    (F43)

FUCIK, JULIUS (1872-1916)
Children Of The Regiment *educ
[3'30"] BOSWORTH        (F44)

Danube Legends *educ
[9'] BOSWORTH        (F45)

Florentine March *educ
[5'] BOSWORTH        (F46)

Marinarella *Op.215, educ
[11'] BOSWORTH        (F47)

Trumpet Call *educ
[3'30"] BOSWORTH        (F48)

FUN, FUN, FUN see Wilson, Brian

FUNERAL MARCH OF A MARIONETTE see
Gounod, Charles François

FÜNF INSTRUMENTALSÄTZE see Bach, Johann
Sebastian

FÜR ELISE see Beethoven, Ludwig van

FURIANT see Dvořák, Antonín

# G

GALLANTRY (INTERMEZZO ROMANCE) see
Ketèlbey, Albert William

GANGE, KENNETH (1929-    )
Three Classical Pieces *educ
string orch,pno (easy) pno-cond sc,
pts BOSWORTH 1013        (G1)

GANNON, JAMES KIMBALL (KIM) (1900-1974)
I'll Be Home For Christmas
(Cerulli, Bob) string orch (very
easy) WARNER SO9704, 029156659351
(G2)
(Gold, Marty) orch WARNER FO9705,
029156300567        (G3)

GARNER, ERROLL (1923-1977)
Misty
(Custer, Calvin) clar solo,string
orch, rhythm section (med easy)
WARNER WBSO9413, 029156112849
(G4)
(Gold, Marty) orch (med) WARNER
WBF09305, 029156061284        (G5)
(Sayre, Chuck) orch (med) WARNER
FO9609, 029156209464        (G6)

GARTH: A GARTH BROOKS MEDLEY see
Brooks, Garth

GAVOTTE, AIR AND GIGUE see Bach, Johann
Sebastian

GAVOTTE AND MUSSETTE FOR STRINGS see
Fleming, Robert

GAY CARNIVAL see Geiger, I.

GAY PARADE see Schubert, Franz (Peter)

GAZDA, DORIS
Appalachian Sunrise
string orch (gr. II) KJOS pts
SO-122C, sc SO-122F        (G7)

Fanfare For Strings
string orch (gr. II) KJOS pts
SO-107C, sc SO-107F        (G8)

Suite On Numbers
string orch (gr. I) KJOS pts
SO-106C, sc SO-106F        (G9)

GEIGEN POLKA see Ritter, Helmut

GEIGER, I.
Delibes Ballet Memories *educ
[13'30"] (contains popular melodies
by Delibes) BOSWORTH        (G10)

Gay Carnival *educ
[12'] (contains a selection of
continental dances) BOSWORTH    (G11)

Master Melodies: Potpourri *educ
[15'] (contains melodies by Chopin,
Strauss, Liszt, Brahms, and
others) BOSWORTH        (G12)

Offenbach Memories *educ
[14'] (contains popular melodies by
Offenbach) BOSWORTH        (G13)

Strauss Selection *educ
(contains popular melodies by
Strauss) BOSWORTH        (G14)

Tango Cocktail, Part 1 *educ/medley
[4'] BOSWORTH        (G15)

Tango Cocktail, Part 2 *educ/medley
[3'] BOSWORTH        (G16)

Tango Cocktail, Part 3 *educ/medley
[3'30"] BOSWORTH        (G17)

Waltzing Thro' Old Vienna *educ
[7'] (contains melodies by Strauss)
BOSWORTH        (G18)

GEIGER, MAX
India Selection *educ/medley,India
[12'] BOSWORTH        (G19)

Russian Gypsies (composed with
Kessler) *educ/medley,Russ
[12'30"] BOSWORTH        (G20)

GELLER, HAROLD
Carefree *educ
[2'15"] BOSWORTH        (G21)

Rio Patrol *educ
[2'] BOSWORTH        (G22)

GENTLE ZEPHYRS [ARR.] see Jensen, Adolf

GEORGE M. COHAN MEDLEY  *educ
(Knight) string orch BOURNE perf mat
rent                                      (G23)

GEORGIA ON MY MIND see Carmichael,
Hoagy

GERSHWIN, GEORGE (1898-1937)
Embraceable You (composed with
Gershwin, Ira)
(Custer, Calvin) string orch,
flügelhorn solo, rhythm section
(med easy) WARNER WBS09405,
029156097818                              (G24)

Fascinatin' Rhythm (composed with
Gershwin, Ira)
(Custer, Calvin) string orch (med
easy) WARNER S09503, 029156177312
(G25)

Foggy Day, A (composed with Gershwin,
Ira)
(Sayre, Chuck) orch (med) WARNER
WBF09401, 029156112344                    (G26)

I Got Rhythm (composed with Gershwin,
Ira)
(Custer, Calvin) string orch (med)
WARNER S09602, 029156210750  (G27)
(Sayre, Chuck) orch WARNER F09708,
029156301953                              (G28)

Man I Love, The
(Gold, Marty) orch (med) WARNER
WBF09306, 029156061321                    (G29)

Porgy And Bess: Selections
(Sayre, Chuck) orch WARNER
WBRP4005, 029156088854                    (G30)

Prelude, No. 2 (from Preludes For
Piano)
(Gruselle, Carrie Lane) string orch
(med) CPP-BEL BS09610,
029156215960                              (G31)

Rhapsody In Blue
(Cerulli, Bob) orch (easy) WARNER
WBF09408, 029156112481                    (G32)

's Wonderful (composed with Gershwin,
Ira)
(Sayre, Chuck) orch (med) WARNER
WBF09404, 029156112504                    (G33)

Summertime
(Sayre, Chuck) orch (med) WARNER
F09502, 029156173284                      (G34)

GESU BAMBINO see Yon, Pietro Alessandro

GHOSTS OF BERKELEY SQUARE see May, Hans
von

GILBERT, C.J.
Spirit Of Youth  *educ
(Barsotti, R.) [3'] BOSWORTH  (G35)

GILLESPIE, HAVEN (1888-1975)
Santa Claus Is Coming To Town
(composed with Coots, John
Frederick)
(Cerulli, Bob) string orch (very
easy) CPP-BEL T0510SB4,
029156218404                              (G36)

GILLIS, DON E. (1912-1978)
Soliloquy For Strings
string orch WINGERT set 9042721, sc
9042722                                   (G37)

Strictly For Strads
string orch WINGERT set 9042751, sc
9042752                                   (G38)

GIPSY LAD see Ketèlbey, Albert William,
Chal Romano

GIRL I LEFT BEHIND ME, THE see Songs Of
Celtic Lands

GIRL OF THE NIGHT see Andrew With
Strings: Volume 2 "A French Medley"

GIRL WITH THE FLAXEN HAIR, THE see
Debussy, Claude

GLAD DAYS (ENTR'ACTE) see Berche, R.A.

GLAZUNOV, ALEXANDER KONSTANTINOVICH
(1865-1936)
Enchanted Castle, The
(Starr) string orch KJOS pts
SO-57B, sc SO-57F                         (G39)

GLOBETROTTER see Leopold, Bohuslav

GLORIA ESTEFAN - HER GREATEST HITS! see
Estefan, Gloria

GLORIA (IN EXCELSIS ARCO)  *educ
(Wieloszynski) string orch,pno (gr.
I) KENDOR 8285                            (G40)

GLORY OF ARNHEM see Stanley, Leo

GLORY OF LOVE
(Cerulli, Bob) orch (easy) CPP-BEL
3722GB7X, 029156636062                    (G41)

GLUCK, CHRISTOPH WILLIBALD, RITTER VON
(1714-1787)
Petite Valse (from Alceste)
(Gearhart, Livingston; Gearhart,
Fritz) string orch (med) CPP-BEL
BS09604, 029156199796                     (G42)

GO THE DISTANCE (from the film
"Hercules") educ
(Custer) string orch,opt combo (gr.
II) LEONARD-US 04626072                   (G43)

GOD HELP THE OUTCASTS (from the film
"The Hunchback Of Notre Dame") educ
(Del Borgo) string orch,opt combo
(gr. II) LEONARD-US 04626054   (G44)
(Higgins) string orch LEONARD-US
00864028                                  (G45)

GOD OF OUR FATHERS see Smith, Claude
Thomas

GOLD, JULIE
From A Distance
(Cerulli, Bob) orch (easy) CPP-BEL
5802FB7X, 029156152647                    (G46)

GOLD, MARTY
Ecstasy
orch (med easy) CPP-BEL F09511,
029156180022                              (G47)

Sound Around Us, The
orch (med) WARNER F09606,
029156204704                              (G48)

GOLDSMITH, OWEN
Baroque Bagatelle, A
string orch (med) CPP-BEL BS000078,
029156694901                              (G49)

Romanza
string orch (intermediate level)
CPP-BEL BS09705, 029156299311
(G50)

Tannenbaum Fantasia
orch CPP-BEL BF09705, 029156605747
(G51)

Ukrainian Sketches
string orch (med) CPP-BEL BS09606,
029156202458                              (G52)

Viva Vivaldi
string orch (easy) CPP-BEL
BS000057, 029156639643                    (G53)

GOLLIWOG'S CAKEWALK see Debussy, Claude

GOODMAN
Citizen Patriot  *educ
orch SHAWNEE augmented set J 0165,
set JC 0571, sc JC 0569, pt
JC 0570                                   (G54)

GORDON, HARRY
Dream Of A Princess, The  *educ
[3'30"] BOSWORTH                          (G55)

GOSSIPING SPARROWS see Bick, H.

GOULD, MORTON (1913-1996)
American Salute
orch (med diff) CPP-BEL 80061,
029156175066                              (G56)

GOUNOD, CHARLES FRANÇOIS (1818-1893)
Faust, Act II: Waltz and Margarita's
Song  *educ
(Alshin, Harry A.) string orch (gr.
III) KENDOR 9818                          (G57)

Funeral March Of A Marionette  *educ
(McLeod) string orch,pno (gr. III)
KENDOR 9824                               (G58)

GRAINGER, PERCY ALDRIDGE (1882-1961)
Over The Hills And Far Away
(Alshin, Harry) string orch (med
easy) CPP-BEL BS000114,
029156097856                              (G59)

GRANADA
(Sayre, Chuck) orch (med) WARNER
F09608, 029156204018                      (G60)

GRANADA MIA (PASO DOBLE) see Crossman,
Gerald

GRANADOS, ENRIQUE (1867-1916)
Spanish Dance, No. 5
(Velke, Fritz) string orch (gr. IV)
VELKE                                     (G61)

GRAND STROLL, THE
(McLeod, James "Red") string orch
(gr. III) KJOS pts GSO-26C, sc
GSO-26C                                   (G62)

GRAND STROLL NO. 2, THE
(McLeod, James "Red") string orch
(gr. III) KJOS pts GSO-27C, sc
GSO-27F                                   (G63)

GRANDMA GOT RUN OVER BY A REINDEER see
Brooks, Randy

GRASSHOPPER'S HOLIDAY see Bick, H.

GRAUPNER, CHRISTOPH (1683-1760)
Introduction And Allegro
(Clinesmith) string orch (3rd
degr.) WINGERT 3031601                    (G64)

GREAT ESCAPE MARCH, THE
(Sayre, Chuck) orch (concert level)
WARNER F09702, 029156298765              (G65)

GREAT GATE OF KIEV; WATCHMAN'S SONG see
Mussorgsky, Modest Petrovich

GREATEST LOVE OF ALL, THE
(Cerulli, Bob) orch (med easy) WARNER
F09613, 029156212846                      (G66)

GREEN, PHILIP
Bella Noches Cubanos (Rumba)  *educ
[3'15"] BOSWORTH                          (G67)

Cigar Makers
see Cuban Suite

Cuban Suite  *educ
BOSWORTH f.s.
contains: Cigar Makers [2'];
Itinerant Song Maker [3'20"];
Margo With The Brown Eyes
[2'50"]; Voodoo [4']             (G68)

Cucuracha, La (Rumba)  *educ
[2'50"] BOSWORTH                          (G69)

From The Cocktail Hour  *educ
BOSWORTH f.s.
contains: Sherry (Malaguena)
[2']; Tequila (Paso Doble) [2']
(G70)

Itinerant Song Maker
see Cuban Suite

Ladies Of Goya, The
see Maja De Goya, La

Maja De Goya, La  *educ
"Ladies Of Goya, The" [2'45"]
BOSWORTH                                  (G71)

Margo With The Brown Eyes
see Cuban Suite

Sherry (Malaguena)
see From The Cocktail Hour

Tequila (Paso Doble)
see From The Cocktail Hour

Voodoo
see Cuban Suite

GREEN BAIZE LAWN, THE see Engleman,
Joseph

GREETING OF THE BELLS, THE see
Ketèlbey, Albert William, Birthday
Greeting, A

GRIEG, EDVARD HAGERUP (1843-1907)
Eight Lyric Pieces  *educ
(Parfrey) string orch (gr. III)
KENDOR 9811                               (G72)

Norwegian Dance  *educ
(Finno) string orch (gr. IV) KENDOR
9852                                      (G73)

Norwegian Dances Nos. 2 & 3
(Isaac, Merle) orch (med) CPP-BEL
C000156, 029156680867                     (G74)

GROITZSCH, G.
Carnival Nights  *educ
BOSWORTH                                  (G75)

In The Arena  *educ
BOSWORTH                                  (G76)

Juggler, The  *educ
[2'] BOSWORTH                             (G77)

Monkey Tricks  *educ
[2'30"] BOSWORTH                          (G78)

Steeple Chase  *educ
[3'30"] BOSWORTH                          (G79)

GROUP OF SIX, A: FOR STRINGS IN FIRST
POSITION see Surdin, Morris

GROW: MUSIK OM OCH FÖR VÄXANDE see
Palmér, Catharina

**GUARALDI, VINCE**
Linus And Lucy
(Cerulli, Bob) string orch (very easy) CPP-BEL 2942LB4X, 029156098655 (G80)

GYPSY CARNIVAL see Krein, Yasha

GYPSY MOODS (RHAPSODY) see Paroni, T.

GYPSY SONGS see Dvořák, Antonín

GYPSY TAMBOURIN see Cuomo, R.

# H

HABANERA, FÜR 2 VIOLINEN, VIOLA, VIOLONCELLO, KONTRABASS see Brinkmann, B.E.

**HACKFORTH, NORMAN**
Summer Time In Fontainebleau *educ [4'45"] BOSWORTH (H1)

**HALEN, WALTER J. (1930- )**
Black Forest Suite
string orch (3rd degr.) WINGERT 3031201 (H2)

Meramec Polka
string orch WINGERT set 3032111, sc 3032112 (H3)

Rhineland Musical Scenes
string orch WINGERT set 3032211, sc 3032212 (H4)

Rumpelstiltskin's Dance
string orch WINGERT set 3033061, sc 3033062 (H5)

Tibetan Professional
string orch WINGERT set 3033071, sc 3033072 (H6)

**HALFERTY**
Mountain County Fiddle-In *educ
string orch,pno (gr. I) KENDOR 8467 (H7)

**HAMLISCH, MARVIN F. (1944- )**
Theme From Ice Castles
(Cerulli, Bob) "Through The Eyes Of Love" orch (easy) CPP-BEL 2625TB7X, 029156687194 (H8)

Theme From Ice Castles (Through The Eyes Of Love)
(Cerulli, Bob) "Through The Eyes Of Love" string orch (easy) CPP-BEL 2617TB4X, 029156636031 (H9)

Through The Eyes Of Love
see Theme From Ice Castles
see Theme From Ice Castles (Through The Eyes Of Love)

HAMMER AND TONGS see Engleman, Harry

HAMPTON COURT (MINUET) see Stuart, Graeme

**HANBY, B.R.**
Up On The Housetop And Icicles *educ
(Pinkston, Patricia; Baker, Myrian; Schliff, Mary Ann) (gr. II) KJOS pts GO-108B, sc GO-108F (H10)

**HANDEL, GEORGE FRIDERIC (1685-1759)**
Adagio And Allegro (from Sonata In F) educ
(Del Borgo) string orch (gr. III) KENDOR 9777 (H11)

Air With Variations *educ
(Wieloszynski) "Harmonious Blacksmith" string orch,pno (gr. IV) KENDOR 9778 (H12)

Allegro Maestoso *educ
(Del Borgo) "Processional March" string orch (gr. II) KENDOR 8897 (H13)

Chaconne *educ
(Del Borgo) string orch (gr. II) KENDOR 8964 (H14)

Entrance Of The Queen Of Sheba (from Solomon)
(Velke, Fritz) string orch (gr. IV) VELKE (H15)

Handel Celebration, A
(Isaac, Merle) orch (med easy) CPP-BEL C000178, 029156682281 (H16)

Harmonious Blacksmith
see Air With Variations

He Shall Feed His Flock (from Messiah) educ
(Wieloszynski) string orch,vln solo (gr. III) KENDOR 9835 (H17)

Music For The Royal Fireworks:
Overture *educ
(Johnson, Thor) KJOS pts O-1004B, sc O-1004F (H18)

Overture in B flat
(Frotscher, Gotthold) 4strings,2ob, opt bsn&cont HUG sc PE 853, pts PE 853-30 (H19)

**HANDEL, GEORGE FRIDERIC (cont'd.)**
Passacaglia in G minor *educ
(Wieloszynski) string orch,pno (gr. IV) KENDOR 9856 (H20)

Processional March
see Allegro Maestoso

See The Conquering Hero Comes
(Applebaum; Ployhar) orch CPP-BEL C000175, 029156672589 (H21)

Suite No. 3 in G
see Water Music: Suite No. 3 In G

Water Music: Suite No. 3 In G (Suite No. 3 in G)
(Anderson) string orch (gr. IV) KJOS pts SO-105C, sc SO-105F (H22)

HANDEL CELEBRATION, A see Handel, George Frideric

HANDEL WITH CARE *educ
(Wieloszynski) string orch,pno (gr. II, in 3 movements) KENDOR 9138 (H23)

HANG ON SLOOPY
(Cerulli, Bob) "My Girl Sloopy" orch (intermediate level) WARNER F09709, 029156604467 (H24)

HANGIN' OUT see Staudenmayer, Karin

**HANMER, RONALD (1917- )**
Lakeside *educ
[3'] BOSWORTH (H25)

Prayer At Sunset *educ
[3'30"] BOSWORTH (H26)

Song At Sunrise *educ
[3'15"] BOSWORTH (H27)

**HANNAH, RON (1945- )**
Divertimento for Strings *educ
string orch sc CANADIAN MI 1500 H243DI (H28)

HANSEL AND GRETEL: TWO MOVEMENTS see Humperdinck, Engelbert

HANUKKAH FAVORITES *educ
(Niehaus) string orch,pno,opt perc (gr. II) KENDOR 9139 f.s.
contains: Chanuka Chag Ya'Fe; Ner Li; Y'Me Hachanuka (H29)

HANUKKAH HOLIDAY see Caponegro, John

HAPPY-GO-LUCKY see Mills

HAPPY MOOD see Fuchs, Hans

HARLEQUIN'S FLIRTATION: ENTR'ACTE see Mordish, Louis

HARMONIOUS BLACKSMITH see Handel, George Frideric, Air With Variations

**HART, LORENZ**
My Funny Valentine (composed with Rodgers, Richard)
(Gold, Marty) orch (med) WARNER F09603, 029156202434 (H30)

**HARTLEY, WALTER SINCLAIR (1927- )**
Bagatelles For Orchestra
orch WINGERT set 3030041, sc 3030042 (H31)

Elizabethan Dances
orch WINGERT set 9041571, sc 9041572 (H32)

Fantasy for Tuba and Chamber Orchestra
string orch WINGERT set 3030071, sc 3030072 (H33)

HASKELL, BURT
see BRISMAN, HESKEL

HAVE YOURSELF A MERRY LITTLE CHRISTMAS see Martin, Hugh

**HAYDN, [FRANZ] JOSEPH (1732-1809)**
Allegretto (from Military Symphony) educ
(McLeod) string orch,pno (gr. II) KENDOR 8895 (H34)

Allegro Giocoso
(Halen, Walter J.) string orch WINGERT set 3030021, sc 3030022 (H35)

Alleluia Symphony
see Symphony No. 30

Farewell Adagio (from Symphony No. 45)
(Velke, Fritz) string orch (gr. III) VELKE (H36)

HAYDN, [FRANZ] JOSEPH (cont'd.)

"Farewell" Symphony (Finale)
see Symphony No. 45 in F sharp
minor,Finale, [arr.]

Haydn Trilogy, A *educ
(Finno) string orch,pno (gr. II)
KENDOR 9145                         (H37)

Minuet in E *educ
(Finno) string orch (gr. III)
KENDOR 9848                         (H38)

Sinfonietta in G, [arr.] *educ
(Bauernschmidt) orch SHAWNEE
augmented set J 0104, sc JC 0412,
pt JC 0413                          (H39)

Surprise Variations, The (from
Symphony No. 94, Mov't 2) educ
(Wieloszynski) string orch (gr. IV)
KENDOR 9906                         (H40)

Symphony No. 30
"Alleluja Symphony" 2.1.2+2clar in
C.1.S rec.A rec.T rec.B rec. 0.2+
2trp in C.1.0. 2glock,2vibra,
perc,timp,gtr,vln I,vln II,vla,
vcl,db MOSELER sc 43.514-00, pts
43.514-02 TO 06, augmented set
43.514-08, set 43.514-09    (H41)

Symphony No. 45 in F sharp minor,
Finale, [arr.] *educ
(Shapiro, Marsha Chusmir)
""Farewell" Symphony (Finale)"
(gr. III) KJOS pts O-1061B, sc
O-1061F                             (H42)

Two Minuets By Haydn *educ
(Caponegro) string orch,pno (gr. I)
KENDOR 8775                         (H43)

Zwei Kammerwerke *educ
(Kaisershot) string orch (gr. III)
KENDOR 9948                         (H44)

HAYDN SEEK *educ/medley
(Niehaus) string orch,pno,opt perc
(gr. I) KENDOR 8297                 (H45)

HAYDN TRILOGY, A see Haydn, [Franz]
Joseph

HAYWOOD,J.N.
Midnight Mood *educ
BOSWORTH                            (H46)

HE SHALL FEED HIS FLOCK see Handel,
George Frideric

HEADING FOR HOME see King, Reginald

HEARTS AND FLOWERS (INTERMEZZO) see
Czibulka, Alphons

HEAVENS RESOUND, THE see Beethoven,
Ludwig van

HECTIC OVERTURE, A see Lloyd, John

HEFTI, NEAL PAUL (1922-    )
Batman Theme
(Cerulli, Bob) orch (med easy) CPP-
BEL T1320BB7, 029156190021 (H47)
(Cerulli, Bob) string orch (very
easy) WARNER S09705, 029156659337
                                    (H48)

HEILMANN, FRANCIS
Ceremonial March
string orch/orch HEILMAN    (H49)

HEINICHEN, JOHANN DAVID (1683-1729)
Sinfonia in D
(Kerr, David) string orch WINGERT
set 3033081, sc 3033082     (H50)

HELLEM, MARK
Still, Still, Still
string orch (gr. III) KJOS pts
SO-96C, sc SO-96F           (H51)

HELP ME RHONDA see Wilson, Brian

HENLEY, LARRY
Wind Beneath My Wings, The (composed
with Silbar, Jeff)
(Rosenhaus, Steve) orch WARNER
WBRP4006, 029156116168      (H52)

HERALD QUARTET see Dancla, Charles

HERBERT, VICTOR (1859-1924)
Babes In Toyland
(McLeod) string orch (gr. III) KJOS
pts GSO-32C, sc GSO-32F     (H53)

Canzonetta (from Serenade Suite,
Op.12) educ
[2'] BOSWORTH               (H54)
see Serenade For Strings, Op. 12

Entry
see Serenade For Strings, Op. 12

HERBERT, VICTOR (cont'd.)

Finale (Tarantella)
see Serenade For Strings, Op. 12

Love Scene
see Serenade For Strings, Op. 12

Polonaise
see Serenade For Strings, Op. 12

Serenade For Strings, Op. 12 *educ
BOSWORTH f.s.
contains: Canzonetta [2']; Entry
[4'30"]; Finale (Tarantella)
[4']; Love Scene [7'20"];
Polonaise [4'15"]           (H55)

HERCULES: SELECTIONS *educ
(Custer) string orch,opt combo (gr.
II) LEONARD-US 04626070     (H56)

HERE COMES SANTA CLAUS (RIGHT DOWN
SANTA CLAUS LANE) see Autry,
(Orvon) Gene

HEROLD, LOUIS-JOSEPH-FERDINAND
(1791-1833)
Zampa Overture *educ
(McLeod, James "Red") string orch
(gr. IV) KJOS pts GSO-25C, sc
GSO-25F                     (H57)

HEUBERGER, RICHARD (1850-1914)
At The Midnight Ball (Midnight Bells)
(from The Opera Ball) educ
(Berlin, Ben) [2'] BOSWORTH (H58)

Im Chambre Separée (Midnight Bells)
*educ
[3'] BOSWORTH               (H59)

HEY, LOOK ME OVER see Coleman, Cy

HEYDAY see Tattenhall, Barry

HI-LILI, HI-LO see Kaper, Bronislaw

HIBERNIA: FANTASIE IN MODERN SYMPHONIC
STYLE ON IRISH AIRS see Charrosin,
F.G.

HIDE AND SEEK (VALSE CAPRICE) see
Engleman, Joseph

HIGHLAND FESTIVAL see Thiman, Eric
Harding

HIGHLAND SCENES (THREE PIECES) see
Thiman, Eric Harding

HIGHRIDGE OVERTURE see Del Borgo,
Elliot A.

HINTON
Festivity March *educ
[2'35"] BOSWORTH            (H60)

Sierra Blanca *educ
"White Mountains" [3'] BOSWORTH
                            (H61)

White Mountains
see Sierra Blanca

HIS AND HER MUSIC
(Cechvala, Al) string orch (gr. III)
VELKE f.s.
contains: Chaminade, Cécile, Scarf
Dance; Franz, Robert, In Autumn,
Op.17,No.6                  (H62)

HIS MASTER'S VOICE *educ
(Wieloszynski) string orch,pno (gr.
III, contains 3 baroque
masterworks) KENDOR 9837    (H63)

HOBGOBLINS see Bick, H.

HOFELDT, WILLIAM (1951-    )
Chaconne *educ
(gr. IV) KJOS pts O-1072C, sc
O-1072F                     (H64)

Song Of The Prairie *educ
(gr. IV) KJOS pts O-1070C, sc
O-1070F                     (H65)

Sunward Overture
string orch (gr. III) KJOS pts
SO-114C, sc SO-114F         (H66)

Toccatina *educ
string orch (gr. II) KJOS pts
SO-95C, sc SO-95F           (H67)

HOLIDAY FOR STRINGS see Rose, David

HOLIDAY GREETINGS *medley
(Swearingen, Jim) orch (med easy)
CPP-BEL FO9505, 029156172676 (H68)

HOLIDAY IN SWITZERLAND see Bestgen,
Willy

HOLIDAY POPS SING-ALONG
(Cerulli, Bob) orch (med easy) CPP-
BEL C0340B7X, 029156112092 (H69)

HOLIDAY SALUTE
(McLeod, James "Red") string orch
(gr. III) KJOS pts GSO-21C, sc
GSO-21F                     (H70)

HOLIDAY SLEIGH RIDE see Conley

HOLIDAY SOUNDS FOR STRINGS
(Smith, Robert W.) string orch (very
easy) CPP-BEL BS09715, 029156607000
                            (H71)

HOLLY JOLLY CHRISTMAS, A see Marks,
Johnny D.

HOLST, GUSTAV (1874-1934)
In The Bleak Midwinter
(Smith, Robert W.) orch CPP-BEL
BF09709, 029156659474      (H72)

HOME ALONE: THREE HOLIDAY SONGS see
Williams, John T.

HOME FOR THE HOLIDAYS
(Cerulli, Bob) orch (intermediate
level) WARNER FO9721, 029156617405
                            (H73)

HOMESICK PARROT see Bick, H.

HOPAK *educ,Russ
(Del Borgo) string orch,pno (gr. II)
KENDOR 9161                 (H74)

HORA PIZZICATO (DANSE PALESTINIENNE)
see Michaeloff, Mischa

HORNS TO THE HUNT see Cohen, Richard

HORNSBY, G.F.
Bonnie Gallowa' *educ
(Tattenhall, B.) [3'30"] BOSWORTH
                            (H75)

HOUR WITH THE GAME SHOWS, AN
(Cerulli, Bob) orch (med easy) CPP-
BEL C0159B7X, 029156700787 (H76)

HRÁBEK, J.
Suita Veneziana *educ
ob,hpsd,strings sc,pts,kbd pt
BOSWORTH 4318               (H77)

HUBAY, JENÖ (1858-1937)
Zephir *Op.30,No.5, educ
orch,vln solo [3'40"] BOSWORTH
                            (H78)

HUMORESKE see Dvořák, Antonín

HUMORESQUE (TOP BOOT DANCE) see
Engleman, Joseph

HUMPERDINCK, ENGELBERT (1854-1921)
Evening Prayer
(Del Borgo, Elliot) string orch
(very easy) CPP-BEL BS000108,
029156103830               (H79)

Hansel And Gretel: Two Movements
*educ
(Alshin, Harry A.) string orch (gr.
III) KENDOR 9832            (H80)

HUMPHRIES, F.
Abbey By Moonlight, The *educ
(Engleman, Joseph) [3'30"] BOSWORTH
                            (H81)

HUMPTY DUMPTY (GROTESQUE INTERMEZZO)
see Armandola, Jose

HUNCHBACK OF NOTRE DAME, THE:
SELECTIONS *educ
(Moss) string orch,opt combo (gr. II)
LEONARD-US 04626042         (H82)

HUNGARIAN MARCH see Berlioz, Hector
(Louis)

HUNGARIAN RHAPSODY NO. 2 see Liszt,
Franz

HUNT, HAROLD
Spirit Of The Toreador *educ
[3'30"] BOSWORTH            (H83)

HUPFELD, HERMAN (1894-1951)
As Time Goes By
(Cerulli, Bob) string orch (very
easy) WARNER WBSO9409,
029156098792               (H84)
(Custer, Calvin) string orch,alto
sax/tenor sax solo (med easy)
WARNER SO9505, 029156179767 (H85)

HURRICANE see Barsotti, Roger

HUSTLING THE POST (GALOP) see Merlin,
A.

HUTCHINGS, J.H.
Cavalry Call *educ
[2'45"] BOSWORTH            (H86)

HUTCHISON, (DAVID) WARNER (1930-    )
Desert Shall Bloom As The Rose, The
*educ
(gr. V) KJOS pts GO-109B, sc
GO-109F                              (H87)

HUWS JONES, EDWARD
Battles And Brawls
strings CRAMER MUS sc,pts 51246 1,
pts 51247 X                        (H88)

Christmas Round The World
strings CRAMER MUS sc,pts 51200 3,
pts 51215 1                        (H89)

Crusaders!
strings sc,pts CRAMER MUS 51277 1
(H90)

Day Of The Dolphin
strings sc,pts CRAMER MUS 51281 X
(H91)

# I

I FINALLY FOUND SOMEONE  *educ
(Wasson) string orch,opt combo (gr.
II) LEONARD-US 04626068        (I1)

I GET AROUND see Wilson, Brian

I GOT IT BAD (AND THAT AIN'T GOOD) see
Ellington, Edward Kennedy (Duke)

I GOT RHYTHM see Gershwin, George

I WILL ALWAYS LOVE YOU see Parton,
Dolly

I WONDER AS I WANDER
(Alshin, Harry) string orch (easy,
appalachian carol) CPP-BEL BS09508,
029156170825                   (I2)
(Ayars, Bo) 3(pic).3(English
horn).3(bass clar).3. 4.3.3(bass
trom).1. timp,3perc,pno&cel,strings
[3'30"] PRESSER                (I3)

IF I WERE A RICH MAN see Bock, Jerry

IL EST NÉ, LE DIVIN ENFANT
(Ayars, Bo) 3(pic).3(English
horn).3(bass clar).2. 4.3.3(bass
trom).1. timp,3perc,pno,harp,
strings [2'45"] PRESSER        (I4)

I'LL BE HOME FOR CHRISTMAS see Gannon,
James Kimball (Kim)

I'LL BE THERE FOR YOU
(Cerulli, Bob) orch (med easy) WARNER
F09607, 029156204315          (I5)

ILLUMINATED FÊTE, THE see Ketèlbey,
Albert William

ILONKA see Charrosin, F.G.

I'M ALWAYS CHASING RAINBOWS see Caroll,
Harry

IM CHAMBRE SEPARÉE (MIDNIGHT BELLS) see
Heuberger, Richard

IMPULSE 3 see Wallin, Peter

IN A CHINESE TEMPLE GARDEN see
Ketèlbey, Albert William

IN A PERSIAN MARKET see Ketèlbey,
Albert William

IN A ROMANY CAMP see Ketèlbey, Albert
William

IN A TOY SHOP: SUITE see Engleman,
Joseph

IN HOLIDAY MOOD (SUITE) see Ketèlbey,
Albert William

IN MY DREAM GARDEN (REVERIE) see
Rayners, Cecil

IN PARTY MOOD see Strachey, J.

IN THE ARENA see Groitzsch, G.

IN THE BLEAK MIDWINTER see Holst,
Gustav

IN THE CIRCUS see Armandola, Jose

IN THE HEATHER see Thiman, Eric Harding

IN THE MOONLIGHT see Ketèlbey, Albert
William

IN THE MYSTIC LAND OF EGYPT see
Ketèlbey, Albert William

INDIA SELECTION see Geiger, Max

INDIAN MOODS MARCH FOR BUDDING STRINGS
see Wolf, Artur

INTRODUCTION AND ALLEGRO see Graupner,
Christoph

INTRODUCTION OF FINGER THREE see
Buczynski, Walter

INTROSPECTION see Nunez, Carold

INVOCATION FOR STRING ORCHESTRA see
Fleming, Robert

INZANA, BARBARA
Washerwoman's Holiday
string orch (gr. III) VELKE    (I6)

IPPOLITOV-IVANOV, MIKHAIL MIKHAILOVICH
(1859-1935)
Procession Of The Sardar (from
Caucasian Sketches)
(Isaac, Merle) orch (med diff) CPP-
BEL C000157, 029156050295    (I7)

IRISH FIDDLER, THE see Mordish, Louis

IRISH LILT, AN see Songs Of Celtic
Lands

IRISH PASTORAL MELODY (ST. COLUMBA)
(Hoffer, Marjorie) string orch (very
easy) CPP-BEL BS000111,
029156102703                   (I8)

IRISH SOUVENIR, AN see Redman, Reginald

IRISH SUITE  *educ
(Del Borgo) string orch,pno (gr. II)
KENDOR 9175 f.s.
contains: Irish Washerwoman; Kerry
Dance; Lullaby             (I9)

IRISH WASHERWOMAN see Irish Suite

IT DON'T MEAN A THING (IF IT AIN'T GOT
THAT SWING) see Ellington, Edward
Kennedy (Duke)

ITALIAN CONCERTO see Bach, Johann
Sebastian

ITINERANT SONG MAKER see Green, Philip

IT'S ABOUT TIME see Brubeck, David
(Dave) Warren

IT'S CHRISTMASTIME
(Custer, Calvin) orch WARNER F09706,
029156300581                 (I10)

IT'S THE PIZZ.! see Washburn, Robert
Brooks

IVES, M.
Birth Of A Butterfly  *educ
[3'] BOSWORTH                 (I11)

# J

JACK ASHORE see Smith, Eric

JALOWICZ, R.
Algiers: Through The Arab Quarters
see Mediterranean Cruise, A

Mediterranean Cruise, A  *educ
BOSWORTH f.s.
contains: Algiers: Through The
Arab Quarters [3'30"]; Naples
(Serenade) [4']; Nice: Battle
Of Flowers [3'30"]; Shawl Dance
[4']                        (J1)

Naples (Serenade)
see Mediterranean Cruise, A

Nice: Battle Of Flowers
see Mediterranean Cruise, A

Shawl Dance
see Mediterranean Cruise, A

JAMES BOND THEME, THE
(Cerulli, Bob) orch (med easy) WARNER
F09611, 029156213584      (J2)

JARMAN, H.C.
Saucy Hat, The  *educ
[3'45"] BOSWORTH          (J3)

JAZZ CONCERTO, A: FOR ALTO SAXOPHONE
AND CHAMBER ORCHESTRA see White,
Andrew Nathaniel

JAZZ CONCERTO, A: FOR ALTO SAXOPHONE
AND SYMPHONY ORCHESTRA see White,
Andrew Nathaniel

JAZZ CONCERTO, A: FOR ALTO SAXOPHONE
AND YOUTH SYMPHONY ORCHESTRA see
White, Andrew Nathaniel

JAZZ PIZZICATO see Anderson, Leroy

JEANIE WITH THE LIGHT BROWN HAIR see
Songs Of Stephen Foster, Part 2

JEFFERIES, STANTON
Prunes And Prisms  *educ
[2'35"] BOSWORTH          (J4)

JENKINSON, EZRA
Elfentanz
see Elves' Dance

Elves' Dance  *educ
"Elfentanz" pno-cond sc,pts
BOSWORTH 1102 from SINGING
STRINGS NO.6             (J5)

Singing Strings No.6
see Elves' Dance

JENSEN, ADOLF (1837-1879)
Gentle Zephyrs [arr.]  *educ
(Charrosin, F.G.) [3'50"] BOSWORTH
                          (J6)

JEOPARDY THEME
(Gold, Marty) orch (med) CPP-BEL
F09508, 029156173390     (J7)

JESU, JOY OF MAN'S DESIRING see Bach,
Johann Sebastian

JIRMAL, JIRÍ
Body And Soul
(Custer, Calvin) string orch,tenor
sax/alto sax solo, rhythm section
(med easy) WARNER WBS09408,
029156098457             (J8)

JOHN ANDERSON see Songs Of Celtic Lands

JOHN PEEL  *educ
(Krein, Michael) [3'23"] BOSWORTH
                          (J9)

JOLLY OLD SAINT NICK
(Frost, Robert) string orch (gr. I)
KJOS pts SO-100C, sc SO-100F (J10)

JOLLY SHIPMATES see Barsotti, Roger

JOLLY TRIP (GALOP) see Börschel, Erich

JOPLIN, SCOTT (1868-1917)
Entertainer, The
(Buchtel) string orch (gr. III)
KJOS pts SO-37C, sc SO-37F (J11)

Ragtime Dance
(Higgins, James) string orch (med
easy) CPP-BEL BS000071,
029156696097            (J12)

Ragtimes, For Strings  *educ
(Sokoll) strings HEINRICH sc 3637,
pts 3638                 (J13)

JORDAN, HERBERTE
Pierrette's Wedding  *educ
[3'] BOSWORTH            (J14)

Salute To A Toy Hero  *educ
(Engleman, Joseph) [2'30"] BOSWORTH
                         (J15)

Toy Town Tattoo  *educ
[4'] BOSWORTH            (J16)

Wing Commander  *educ
[2'30"] BOSWORTH         (J17)

JOY OF CHRISTMAS, THE
(Cerulli, Bob) orch (easy, contains
Patapan & Gesu Bambino) CPP-BEL
2697CB7X, 029156060102  (J18)

JOY TO THE WORLD see Axton, Hoyt

JOYCE, ARCHIBALD
Bohemia  *educ
[5'] BOSWORTH            (J19)

Brighton Hike  *educ
[2'25"] BOSWORTH         (J20)

Colour-Sergeant, The  *educ
(Barsotti, Roger) BOSWORTH (J21)

Dreams Of You  *educ
[5'] BOSWORTH            (J22)

Frou Frou  *educ
[5'] BOSWORTH            (J23)

Mighty Malta (composed with Barsotti,
Roger)  *educ
BOSWORTH                 (J24)

Old Grenadier, The  *educ
(Barsotti, Roger) BOSWORTH (J25)

Phantom Of Salome, The  *educ
[4'] BOSWORTH            (J26)

Royal Standard  *educ
[2'25"] BOSWORTH         (J27)

Song Of The River  *educ
[5'] BOSWORTH            (J28)

JOYEUX NOEL
(Hellem, Mark) string orch (gr. III)
KJOS pts SO-88C, sc SO-88F (J29)

JUBILATION see Charrosin, F.G.

JUGGLER, THE see Groitzsch, G.

JUST ONE OF THOSE THINGS see Porter,
Cole

JUVENALIA see Charrosin, F.G.

# K

KABALEVSKY, DMITRI BORISOVICH
(1904-1987)
Clown, The  *educ
(Wieloszynski) string orch,pno (gr.
II) KENDOR 8995          (K1)

KABALEVSKY AND FRIENDS  *educ
(Alshin, Harry A.) string orch (gr.
III) KENDOR 7985 f.s.
contains: Bartók, Béla, Peasant
Song; Gretchaninoff, Bicycle
Ride; Kabalevsky, Dmitri
Borisovich, Fleet Fingers;
Kabalevsky, Dmitri Borisovich,
Waltz-Intermezzo; Miaskovsky,
Nikolai Yakovlevich, Dialogue
                         (K2)

KANDER, JOHN (1927)
Cabaret (composed with Ebb, Fred)
(Custer, Calvin) string orch (med)
WARNER S09507, 029156177299 (K3)

New York, New York (Theme)
(Sayre, Chuck) orch (med) WARNER
F09503, 029156173321     (K4)
(Whitney, John C.) orch (easy) CPP-
BEL T0450TB7, 029156208801 (K5)

Theme From New York, New York
(Cerulli, Bob) string orch (very
easy) CPP-BEL T0450TB4,
029156671698            (K6)

KAPER, BRONISLAW (1902-1983)
Hi-Lili, Hi-Lo
(Cerulli, Bob) string orch (very
easy) CPP-BEL T5360HB4,
029156097030            (K7)

KEEL ROW, THE  *educ
(Krein, Michael) [3'35"] BOSWORTH
                         (K8)

KEEP MOVING see Charrosin, F.G.

KELER-BELA (ADALBERT PAUL VON KELER)
(1820-1882)
Lustspiel  *educ
(Haensch) [5'] BOSWORTH  (K9)

KELL, FREDERICK
Sunset Serenade  *educ
[5'] BOSWORTH           (K10)

KENINS, TALIVALDIS (1919-    )
Sinfonietta  *educ
3(pic).2(English horn).2.2.
4.3.3.1. timp,4perc,strings [10']
sc CANADIAN MI 1100 K33SI (K11)

KERRY DANCE see Irish Suite

KETÈLBEY, ALBERT WILLIAM (1875-1959)
Algerian Scene  *educ
[4'30"] BOSWORTH         (K12)

Bank Holdiay ('Appy 'Ampstead) (from
Cockney Suite) educ
[2'30"] BOSWORTH        (K13)

Bank Holiday ('Appy 'Ampstead)
see Cockney Suite (Cameos Of London
Life)

Birthday Greeting, A  *educ
"Greeting Of The Bells, The" orch,
bells [4'] BOSWORTH     (K14)

By The Blue Hawaiian Waters  *educ
[8'] BOSWORTH           (K15)

Caprice Pianistique  *educ
orch,pno solo [3'30"] BOSWORTH
                        (K16)

Chal Romano  *educ
"Gipsy Lad" [7'] BOSWORTH (K17)

Clock And The Dresden Figures  *educ
orch,pno solo [4'] BOSWORTH (K18)

Cockney Lover
see Cockney Suite (Cameos Of London
Life)

Cockney Suite (Cameos Of London Life)
*educ
BOSWORTH f.s.
contains: Bank Holiday ('Appy
'Ampstead) [2'30"]; Cockney
Lover [2']; Elegy [4'30"];
Palais De Danse [3']; State
Procession [3']         (K19)

Dance Of The Merry Mascots  *educ
orch,pno solo [4'30"] BOSWORTH
                        (K20)

Down The Stream
see In Holiday Mood (Suite)

KETÈLBEY, ALBERT WILLIAM (cont'd.)

Dream Of Christmas, A *Xmas,carol/
educ
orch,opt org,cor (pantomime)
BOSWORTH (K21)
pno-cond sc,pts BOSWORTH 1101 from
SINGING STRINGS NO.5 (K22)

Elegy
see Cockney Suite (Cameos Of London
Life)

Fighting For Freedom *educ
[3'10"] BOSWORTH (K23)

Gallantry (Intermezzo Romance) *educ
BOSWORTH (K24)

Gipsy Lad
see Chal Romano

Greeting Of The Bells, The
see Birthday Greeting, A

Illuminated Fête, The
see In Holiday Mood (Suite)

In A Chinese Temple Garden *educ
[6'] BOSWORTH (K25)

In A Persian Market *educ
[7'] BOSWORTH (K26)

In A Romany Camp *educ
[7'30"] BOSWORTH (K27)

In Holiday Mood (Suite) *educ
BOSWORTH f.s.
contains: Down The Stream
[3'30"]; Illuminated Fête, The
[3'15"]; On The Promenade
[2'45"] (K28)

In The Moonlight *educ
[4'30"] BOSWORTH (K29)

In The Mystic Land Of Egypt *educ
[6'15"] BOSWORTH (K30)

Knights Of The King *educ
[4'30"] BOSWORTH (K31)

Love And The Dancer *educ
[3'30"] BOSWORTH (K32)

March Of The Pioneer Corps *educ
[2'35"] BOSWORTH (K33)

Mayfair Cinderella (Valse Brilliante)
*educ
BOSWORTH (K34)

On The Promenade
see In Holiday Mood (Suite)

Palais De Danse
see Cockney Suite (Cameos Of London
Life)

Pianistique Caprice *educ
orch,pno solo [3'30"] BOSWORTH
(K35)

Pictures In Melody, Part 1 *educ
[5'30"] (includes: In A Persian
Market, By The Blue Hawaiian
Waters, and others) BOSWORTH
(K36)

Pictures In Melody, Part 2 *educ
[5'6"] (includes: With Honour
Crowned, In A Romany Camp, and
others) BOSWORTH (K37)

Remembrance (Elegy) *educ
[3'15"] BOSWORTH (K38)

Sacred Hour, The *educ
orch,org,opt cor [6'] BOSWORTH
(K39)

Sanctuary Of The Heart *educ
orch,solo voice,opt cor [4'30"]
BOSWORTH (K40)
pno-cond sc,pts BOSWORTH 1098 from
SINGING STRINGS NO.2 (K41)

Singing Strings No.2
see Sanctuary Of The Heart

Singing Strings No.5
see Dream Of Christmas, A

State Procession
see Cockney Suite (Cameos Of London
Life)

Sunbeams And Butterflies *educ
orch,pno solo [2'40"] BOSWORTH
(K42)

Wedgwood Blue *educ
[4'] BOSWORTH (K43)

With Honour Crowned *educ
[4'] BOSWORTH (K44)

KEUNING, KEN
Meandering Gander, The
string orch (gr. I) KJOS pts
SO-91C, sc SO-91F (K45)

Royal Processional
string orch (gr. I) KJOS pts
SO-71C, sc SO-71F (K46)

Sailor's Song
string orch (gr. II) KJOS pts
SO-72C, sc SO-72F (K47)

Star Warriors
string orch (gr. II) KJOS pts
SO-116C, sc SO-116F (K48)

KHACHATURIAN, ARAM ILYICH (1903-1978)
Sabre Dance
(Frost, Robert) string orch (gr.
III) KJOS pts SO-35C, sc SO-35F
(K49)

KIDD, BRYAN
Latin And Lace
string orch (very easy) CPP-BEL
BS09708, 029156300413 (K50)

KIDS KARNIVAL see Frost

KINDLE THE HANUKKAH LIGHTS *educ/
medley
(Niehaus) string orch,pno,opt perc
(gr. II) KENDOR 9203 (K51)

KINESISK SUITE, FOR UNGDOMSORKESTER see
Arden, Holger

KING, BEN
Stand By Me (composed with Lieber,
Jerry; Stoller, Michael Endore)
(Custer, Calvin) orch WARNER
WBRP4002, 029156087253 (K52)
(Lowden, Bob) string orch WARNER
WBRP4001, 029156087260 (K53)

KING, REGINALD (1904- )
Dreams In Exile *educ
BOSWORTH f.s.
contains: Heading For Home
[3'15"]; Leafy Lanes Of England
[2'45"]; Those Far Away Hills
[3'30"] (K54)

First Waltz, The
see Youthful Days (Suite)

Heading For Home
see Dreams In Exile

Leafy Lanes Of England
see Dreams In Exile

Lullaby Land
see Youthful Days (Suite)

New Party Frock, A
see Youthful Days (Suite)

Those Far Away Hills
see Dreams In Exile

Up With The Lark
see Youthful Days (Suite)

Youthful Days (Suite) *educ
BOSWORTH f.s.
contains: First Waltz, The
[2'30"]; Lullaby Land [3']; New
Party Frock, A [2'30"]; Up With
The Lark [2'] (K55)

KING'S COLOUR, THE see Barsotti, Roger

KITCHEN PERCUSSION MARCH FOR 'SPECIAL
GUEST SOLOISTS' AND ORCHESTRA see
Rosenhaus, Steven L.

KLEIN, LOTHAR (1932- )
Festival Partita *educ
3(pic).2.2.2. 4.3.3.1. timp,4perc,
pno,strings [15'] (1. Preamble 2.
Play 3. Lyric 4. Trivial
Pursuits) sc CANADIAN
MI 1100 K64FE (K56)

Music For Kids *educ
2(pic).2.2.2. 2.2.0.0. perc,
strings,narrator,pno/pno 4-hands
[10'-12'] sc CANADIAN
MI 1361 K64MU (K57)

KLEINE SINFONIE FÜR MUSIKFREUNDE see
Mozart, Leopold

KLEINE TÄNZE GROSSER MEISTER *educ
(Deutschmann) string orch HEINRICH sc
8853, pts 8854 (K58)

KNAVE OF DIAMONDS see Steele, Henry

KNIGHTS OF THE KING see Ketèlbey,
Albert William

KNIGHTSBRIDGE SUITE see Washburn,
Robert Brooks

KNORR, H.
Fire On The Horizon *educ
[3'50"] BOSWORTH (K59)

KNUCKLEDUST see Blackmore, George Henry
James

KOMZAK, KARL
Edelweiss *educ
BOSWORTH (K60)

Storm Galop; Munich-Vienna Polka
*educ
BOSWORTH (K61)

Three Little Pieces *educ
BOSWORTH 1092 (K62)

KREIN, MICHAEL
Puck *educ
(Krein, Michael) orch,vln solo
[2'15"] BOSWORTH (K63)

KREIN, YASHA
Gypsy Carnival *educ
orch,vln solo [4'20"] BOSWORTH
(K64)

KROGSTAD, BOB
Power Of The Dream, The
cor,strings LEONARD-US 04626056
(K65)

KRONBERGER-MARRIOTT
Buddha's Festival Of Love *educ
[5'] BOSWORTH (K66)

KRUG,E.A.
When You Are With Me (Tango) *educ
BOSWORTH (K67)

KUHN, WOLFGANG, EDITOR
Colours Of Liberty *educ
BOSWORTH (K68)

KUNZ, ALFRED (1929- )
Divertimento For Easy Strings *educ
string orch sc,pts CANADIAN
MI 1500 K965DI (K69)

Six String Things *educ
string orch (easy) sc,pts CANADIAN
MI 1500 K965SI (K70)

Three Canadian Folk Songs *educ
string orch (easy) sc,pts CANADIAN
MI 1500 K965TH (K71)

# L

LADIES AND COURTIERS OF LILLIPUT, THE (VALSE INTERMEZZO) see Engleman, Joseph

LADIES OF GOYA, THE see Green, Philip, Maja De Goya, La

LADY SERGEANT, THE (MARCH INTERMEZZO) see Ewing, Montague

LAKESIDE see Hanmer, Ronald

LAMENTO see Vinter, Gilbert

LANDLER see Mozart, Wolfgang Amadeus

LARP VISITS THE ALBERT HALL see Amos, Keith

LARRICK, GEARY
Fanfare For Symphony Orchestra
winds,perc,strings (med) G & L (L1)

Symphony No. 3
strings,ob,timp (med) G & L (L2)

LASSO, ORLANDO DI
see LASSUS, ROLAND DE

LASSUS, ROLAND DE (ORLANDUS)
(1532-1594)
Echo Fantasy
(Klotman, Robert) 2string orch
WINGERT set 9041521, sc 9041522
(L3)

LAST AND NOT LEAST FINGER FOUR see Buczynski, Walter

LATIN AMERICA (SUITE) see Vinter, Gilbert

LATIN AND LACE see Kidd, Bryan

LAUBER, ANNE (1943- )
Colin-Maillard *educ
2.2.2.2. 2.2.2.1. timp,2perc,
strings,opt tuba [10'] sc
CANADIAN MI 1100 L366CO (L4)

Fantaisie Sur Un Thème Connu *educ
"Fantasy On A Known Theme" 2.2.2.2.
2.2.2.0. timp,perc,strings,pno
solo [11'] sc,pno red,pno-cond sc
CANADIAN MI 1361 L366FA (L5)

Fantasy On A Known Theme
see Fantaisie Sur Un Thème Connu

LEAFY LANES OF ENGLAND see King, Reginald

LEAP FROG see Engleman, Harry

LEGEND NO. 1 see Buczynski, Walter

LEGEND NO. 2 see Buczynski, Walter

LEGEND NO. 3 see Buczynski, Walter

LEGEND NO. 4 see Buczynski, Walter

LEGEND NO. 5 see Buczynski, Walter

LEGEND NO. 6 see Buczynski, Walter

LEGEND NO. 7 see Buczynski, Walter

LEGEND NO. 11 see Buczynski, Walter

LEGEND NO. 12 see Buczynski, Walter

LEGENDS OF THE FALL *educ
(Conley) string orch,opt combo (gr.
II) LEONARD-US 04626052 (L6)

LEGG, PAT
Let's Dance!
strings CRAMER MUS sc,pts 51177 5,
pts 51218 6 (L7)

Let's Dance Again!
strings CRAMER MUS pts 51219 4, sc,
pts 51178 3 (L8)

LEGGETT, ERNEST
Danse Gaie *educ
[3'30"] BOSWORTH (L9)

LEGIONS OF THE AIR see Thorton, R.S.

LEICHTE VORTRAGSSTÜCKE
string orch sc SCHOTTS ED8528 (L10)

LEOPOLD, BOHUSLAV (1888-1956)
Globetrotter *educ
[2'45"] BOSWORTH (L11)

LEROY ANDERSON FAVORITES see Anderson, Leroy

LET THE EARTH RESOUND see Clarke, Jeremiah

LET'S DANCE! see Legg, Pat

LET'S DANCE AGAIN! see Legg, Pat

LIBERATION see Bartlett, Victor

LIED AUF DEM DACH see Schaper, Heinz-Christian

LIFE'S LAUGHTER: A LITTLE OVERTURE see Rust, Friedrich Wilhelm

LIGHT AND SHADE see Raeburn, Hugh

LILLIPUTIAN ARMY, THE (MARCHE GROTESQUE) see Engleman, Joseph

LILY POND, THE see Redman, Reginald

LINUS AND LUCY see Guaraldi, Vince

LION, THE see Smith, H. Elliott

LISZT, FRANZ (1811-1886)
Hungarian Rhapsody No. 2
(Goldsmith, Owen) orch (med) CPP-
BEL C000207, 029156194241 (L12)

Liszt Fantasie *educ
(Charrosin, F.G.) [10'] BOSWORTH
(L13)

LISZT FANTASIE see Charrosin, F.G. see Liszt, Franz

LITTLE DRUMMER BOY, THE see Davis, Katherine K.

LITTLE FUGUE see Schumann, Robert (Alexander)

LITTLE FUGUE IN G MINOR, THE see Bach, Johann Sebastian, Fugue in G minor

LITTLE SYMPHONY see Nunez, Carold

LIVERPOOL SUITE see McCartney, Sir [John] Paul, Paul McCartney's Liverpool Suite

LLOYD, JOHN
Hectic Overture, A *educ
(gr. III) KJOS pts 0-1073C, sc
0-1073F (L14)

LLOYD WEBBER, ANDREW (1949- )
Cats: Suite No. 1
strings CRAMER MUS sc,pts 51163 5,
pts 51213 5 (L15)

Cats: Suite No. 2
strings CRAMER MUS sc,pts 51165 1,
pts 51214 3 (L16)

Don't Cry For Me Argentina; You Must
Love Me *educ
(Custer) string orch,opt combo (gr.
II) LEONARD-US 04490048 (L17)

Evita: Music *educ
(Custer) (gr. III) LEONARD-US
04490052 (L18)

Memory
varied ensemble sc,pts CRAMER MUS
51172 4 (L19)

You Must Love Me *educ
(Del Borgo) string orch,opt combo
(gr. II) LEONARD-US 04490045 (L20)

LOCH LOMOND *educ
(Hartley, Fred) [2'30"] BOSWORTH
(L21)

LONDON DAY, A (SUITE) see North, Michael

LONDONDERRY AIR *educ,Ir
(Goldsmith, Owen) string orch (easy)
CPP-BEL BS000096, 029156299380
(L22)

(Revel, Louis) string orch,pno,opt
org [3'45"] BOSWORTH (L23)

LONDONDERRY SUITE see Washburn, Robert Brooks

LONOCE, ROBERTO
Concertus *educ
chamber orch sc,pts RICORDI-IT
137602 (L24)

LOOK MA - NO BOW! *educ
(Del Borgo) string orch,pno (gr. I,
based on "Early One Morning")
KENDOR 8397 (L25)

LOST CHORD, THE see Sullivan, [Sir] Arthur Seymour

LOST MELODY, THE see Österling, Fredrick

LOUIS WAIN SUITE see Amos, Keith

LOVE, HENRY
When The Violins Are Playing (Tango)
*educ
[4'] BOSWORTH (L26)

LOVE AND THE DANCER see Ketèlbey, Albert William

LOVE AND THE TRUMPETER see Mainzer, H.

LOVE SCENE see Herbert, Victor

LOVE THEME FROM ST. ELMO'S FIRE see Foster, David, St. Elmo's Fire: Love Theme

LOVERS, THE see Andrew With Strings: Volume 2 "A French Medley"

LOVE'S AWAKENING see Scull, Harold [Thomas], Eveille De L'Amour

LOVE'S DREAM see Czibulka, Alphons

LOVE'S DREAM AFTER THE BALL (INTERMEZZO) see Czibulka, Alphons

LOWDEN
Fiddle Fever *educ
string orch,pno (gr. II) KENDOR
9075 (L27)

LUBLYANKA (TREPAK RUSSE) see Michaeloff, Mischa

LUDWIG'S CELEBRATION!
(Custer, Calvin) orch WARNER F09720,
029156617566 (L28)

LULLABY see Irish Suite

LULLABY LAND see King, Reginald

LULLABY OF THE DRUMS see Anderson, Leroy

LULLY, JEAN-BAPTISTE (LULLI)
(1632-1687)
Overture To L'Amour Malade
(Goldsmith, Owen) orch (med easy)
CPP-BEL C000212, 029156045680
(L29)

LULLY LULAY see Christmas Trilogy, A

LUPITA (PASO DOBLE) see May, Hans von

LUSTSPIEL see Keler-Bela (Adalbert Paul von Keler)

# M

MAASZ, GERHARD (1906-1984)
Sinfonietta Facile
S rec,A rec,ob,clar,trp in C,trp,
glock,perc,pno,vln I,vln II,vln
III,vla,vcl MOSELER sc 10.464-00,
pts,kbd pt 10.464-01 TO 3, sets
10.464-08 TO 9                         (M1)

MACARTHUR PARK see Webb, Jimmy Layne

MCBROOM, AMANDA
Rose, The
(Cerulli, Bob) orch (easy) WARNER
WBF09410, 029156109276        (M2)
(Custer, Calvin) orch WARNER
F09703, 029156298901          (M3)

MCCARTNEY, SIR [JOHN] PAUL (1942-    )
Liverpool Suite
see Paul McCartney's Liverpool
Suite

Paul McCartney's Liverpool Suite
(Davis, Carl) "Liverpool Suite"
strings sc,pts CRAMER MUS 51348 4
(M4)

PAUL MCCARTNEY'S LIVERPOOL SUITE see
McCartney, Sir [John] Paul

MACK THE KNIFE see Weill, Kurt

MACKEY, PERCIVAL
Dancing The Day Away
see Day In May, A (Suite)

Day Begins, A
see Day In May, A (Suite)

Day In May, A (Suite) *educ
BOSWORTH f.s.
contains: Dancing The Day Away
[3'33"]; Day Begins, A [2'];
May Mood [1'45"]              (M5)

May Mood
see Day In May, A (Suite)

With Gambolling Gait *educ
[2'15"] BOSWORTH                (M6)

MCLEOD
Staccato Pizzicato *educ
string orch,pno (gr. II) KENDOR
9488                           (M7)

Stomp And Fiddle *educ
string orch,pno (gr. II) KENDOR
9489                           (M8)

MCQUILKIN, TERRY
Salisbury Overture
string orch (gr. II) KJOS pts
SO-113C, sc SO-113F            (M9)

MAGIC FLUTE, THE: SUITE [ARR.] see
Mozart, Wolfgang Amadeus

MAGIC OF LEROY ANDERSON, THE see
Anderson, Leroy

MAGNIFICENT SEVEN, THE see Bernstein,
Elmer

MAHLER, GUSTAV (1860-1911)
Song Of A Wayfarer
(Goldsmith, Owen) string orch (med)
CPP-BEL BS000079, 029156696035
(M10)
MAIN STREET MARCH see Frost, Robert S.

MAINZER, H.
Love And The Trumpeter *educ
orch,2trp soli/trp&trom soli
[3'30"] BOSWORTH               (M11)

Merry Musicians *educ
orch,2clar soli [2'30"] BOSWORTH
(M12)
MAJA DE GOYA, LA see Green, Philip

MAN I LOVE, THE see Gershwin, George

MANCINA, MARK
Twister
(Custer, Calvin) orch (med) WARNER
F09617, 029156267693          (M13)

MANCINI, HENRY (1924-1994)
Mancini Magic
(Brubaker, Jerry) orch (concert
level) WARNER F09715,
029156607239                  (M14)

Mancini Memories
(Gold, Marty) orch (med easy)
contains Breakfast At Tiffany's,
Baby Elephant Walk) CPP-BEL
C0261B6X, 029156201024        (M15)

MANCINI, HENRY (cont'd.)
Peter Gunn
(Custer, Calvin) orch (med easy)
CPP-BEL 1470PB6X, 029156679588
(M16)
Pink Panther, The
(Cerulli, Bob) orch (easy) CPP-BEL
2766PB7X, 029156200546        (M17)
(Cerulli, Bob) string orch (very
easy) CPP-BEL 2739PB4X,
029156056853                  (M18)
(Custer, Calvin) orch (med easy)
CPP-BEL 2739PB6X, 029156151794
(M19)
Tribute To Henry Mancini, A
(Custer, Calvin) orch (med) CPP-BEL
C0343B7X, 029156102178        (M20)

MANCINI MAGIC see Mancini, Henry

MANCINI MEMORIES see Mancini, Henry

MANDEL, JOHNNY ALFRED (1925-    )
Shadow Of Your Smile, The
(Cerulli, Bob) orch (easy) CPP-BEL
T0410SB7, 029156111309        (M21)
(Custer, Calvin) string orch (med)
WARNER S09605, 029156214185   (M22)
(Sayre, Chuck) orch (med) CPP-BEL
T0410SB6, 029156671391        (M23)

MARBLES see Engleman, Joseph

MARCH FROM LOVE FOR THREE ORANGES see
Prokofiev, Serge

MARCH OF THE MOUNTAIN GNOMES see
Eilenberg, R.

MARCH OF THE PIONEER CORPS see
Ketèlbey, Albert William

MARCH TRIUMPHANT see Rusch, Harold W.

MARCHISIO, G.
Matador *educ
BOSWORTH                       (M24)

MARGO WITH THE BROWN EYES see Green,
Philip

MARINA, CRISTIAN (1965-    )
Concertino for Violin, Violoncello
and Strings
STIM                           (M25)

MARINARELLA see Fucik, Julius

MARIQUITA (TANGO SERENADE) see
Barsotti, Roger

MARKS, JOHNNY D. (1909-1985)
Holly Jolly Christmas, A
(Cerulli, Bob) string orch (easy)
WARNER S09615, 029156219272 (M26)

Rudolph The Red-Nosed Reindeer
(Cerulli, Bob) string orch (very
easy) CPP-BEL T8840RB4,
029156208306                  (M27)

MARLAND, BERT
Piccadilly Prelude *educ
(Engleman, Joseph) [3'30"] BOSWORTH
(M28)
MARRIAGE OF FIGARO, THE: OVERTURE see
Mozart, Wolfgang Amadeus, Overture
To The Marriage Of Figaro

MARSCH UND FREMDLÄNDISCHES LIED see
Schaper, Heinz-Christian

MARSTON COURT (SUITE) see Redman,
Reginald

MARTELL ERIC
Sailors' Holiday *educ
(Charrosin, F.G.) [2'40"] BOSWORTH
(M29)
MARTIN, HUGH (1914-    )
Have Yourself A Merry Little
Christmas (composed with
Hunsecker, Ralph Blane)
(Cerulli, Bob) orch (med easy) CPP-
BEL T1720HB7, 029156180107  (M30)
(Custer, Calvin) string orch (med)
WARNER S09601, 029156210736 (M31)
(Gold, Marty) orch (med easy) CPP-BEL
T1720HB6, 029156671704      (M32)

MASCAGNI, PIETRO (1863-1945)
Cavalleria Rusticana: Intermezzo
(Goldsmith, Owen) orch (med easy)
CPP-BEL BF09503, 029156171273
(M33)
MASSENET, JULES (1842-1912)
Meditation, [arr.] (from Thaïs) educ
(Arnold, Alan) (med diff) pno-cond
sc,pts BOSWORTH 1105          (M34)

MASTER MELODIES: POTPOURRI see Geiger,
I.

MASTERPIECE see Nolan, Kenny

MATADOR see Marchisio, G.

MATCHMAKER see Bock, Jerry

MATTHEWS, MICHAEL (1950-    )
Three Echoes *educ
string orch [5'] sc CANADIAN
MI 1500 M441TH                (M35)

MAY, HANS VON (1913-    )
Ghosts Of Berkeley Square *educ/film
[7'30"] BOSWORTH               (M36)

Lupita (Paso Doble) *educ
[2'30"] BOSWORTH               (M37)

Night Of Romance, A *educ
[4'20"] BOSWORTH               (M38)

Shadow Serenade (from Ghosts Of
Berkeley Square) educ
orch,vln solo [2'30"] BOSWORTH
(M39)
MAY DAY CAROL *folk song,Eng
(Hoffer, Marjorie) string orch (med)
CPP-BEL BS09602, 029156184297 (M40)

MAY MOOD see Mackey, Percival

MAYFAIR CINDERELLA (VALSE BRILLIANTE)
see Ketèlbey, Albert William

MAYFAIR PARADE see Strachey, J.

MAYPOLE DANCE see Young Bartok Suite, A

MAZAS
Concertante *educ
(Del Borgo) string orch (gr. III)
KENDOR 9797                   (M41)

MEANDERING GANDER, THE see Keuning, Ken

MECHANICA
2.2.2.1. 4.2.2.0. timp,strings [9']
STIM sc H-2952, pts A-454     (M42)

MEDITERRANEAN CRUISE, A see Jalowicz,
R.

MEET, THE see Redman, Reginald

MEET MR. JOPLIN see Searle, Leslie

MEMORY see Fones, A.F. see Lloyd
Webber, Andrew

MENDELSSOHN-BARTHOLDY, FELIX
(1809-1847)
Canzonetta
(Goldsmith, Owen) string orch (med)
CPP-BEL BS09510, 029156170801
(M43)
Festival Song Of Praise *educ
(Harris) string orch BOURNE
augmented set 040480, set 040400
(M44)
Mendelssohn Fantasie *educ
(Foulds, John H.) [14'] BOSWORTH
(M45)
MENDELSSOHN FANTASIE see Foulds, John
Herbert see Mendelssohn-Bartholdy,
Felix

MENUET SUR LE NOM D'HAYDN see Ravel,
Maurice

MERAMEC POLKA see Halen, Walter J.

MERLIN, A.
Hustling The Post (Galop) *educ
orch,opt xylo solo [2'30"] BOSWORTH
(M46)
[2'30"] BOSWORTH               (M47)

MERRILY WE ROLL ALONG
(Cerulli, Bob) string orch (easy)
WARNER S09614, 029156219258  (M48)

MERRY CHRISTMAS see Andrew With
Strings: Volume 2 "A French Medley"

MERRY GO RONDO see Anderson, Gerald

MERRY-GO-ROUND BROKE DOWN, THE
(Cerulli, Bob) string orch (very
easy) WARNER S09703, 029156607215
(M49)
MERRY MUSICIANS see Mainzer, H.

MEXICAN HAT DANCE
(Ayars, Bo) 3(pic).3(English
horn).3(bass clar).2. 4.3.3(bass
trom).1. timp,2perc,harp,strings
[4'16"] PRESSER                (M50)

MEXICAN PROMENADE see Mordish, Louis

MEYER, H.-E.
Spaziergang Im Zoo *educ
orch,narrator HEINRICH sc 2140, kbd
pt 2141, pts                   (M51)

MEYER, RICHARD
  At The Grasshopper Ball
    string orch (gr. I) KJOS pts
    SO-112C, sc SO-112F                    (M52)

MEYERKE MY SON (JEWISH SONG) see
  Adaskin, Murray

MIAMI SOUND MACHINE MEDLEY, THE
  (Cerulli, Bob) orch (med easy,
    contains Coming Out Of The Dark &
    Seal Our Fate) CPP-BEL C0276B7X       (M53)

MICHAELIS
  Turkish Patrol, The *educ
    (Charrosin, F.G.) [4'20"] BOSWORTH    (M54)

MICHAELOFF, MISCHA
  Frosty Fingers *educ
    [4'20"] BOSWORTH                       (M55)

  Hora Pizzicato (Danse Palestinienne)
    *educ
    [3'30"] BOSWORTH                       (M56)

  Lublyanka (Trepak Russe) *educ
    [2'30"] BOSWORTH                       (M57)

  Polka Polonaise *educ
    [4'] BOSWORTH                          (M58)

MICHIELS, G.
  Famous Czardas No.1 *educ
    BOSWORTH                               (M59)

MIDNIGHT MOOD see Haywood,J.N.

MIGHTY MALTA see Barsotti, Roger see
  Joyce, Archibald

MILLENNIUM see Niehaus

MILLER, (ALTON) GLENN (1904-1944)
  Moonlight Serenade
    (Cerulli, Bob) orch (med easy) CPP-
    BEL FO9509, 029156173208              (M60)

MILLS
  Happy-Go-Lucky *educ
    string orch BOURNE augmented set
    053030, set 053020                     (M61)

MILNER, CH.
  Flags In The Square *educ
    [3'15"] BOSWORTH                       (M62)

MINIATURE PIANO, THE see Engleman,
  Joseph

MISSAL, JOSHUA M. (1915-    )
  Carson Suite, The
    string orch (gr. III) KJOS pts
    GSO-18C, sc GSO-18F                    (M63)

  Circus, The
    string orch (gr. III) KJOS pts
    GSO-31C, sc GSO-31F                    (M64)

  Romeo And Juliet: Three Episodes
    *educ
    (gr. III) KJOS pts GO-107B, sc
    GO-107F                                (M65)

  Short Overture, A *educ
    (gr. III) KJOS pts GO-111C, sc
    GO-111F                                (M66)

MISSION: IMPOSSIBLE THEME *educ
  (Del Borgo) string orch,opt combo
    (gr. II) LEONARD-US 04626050          (M67)

MISTY see Garner, Erroll

MODERN STRING QUARTET: VOL. 1 *educ
  vln I,vln II,vla,vcl sc,pts SCHOTTS
    ED 7676 f.s. the number of
    performers in each part variable
    contains: Morris, Stevland (Stevie
    Wonder), Sir Duke; Widmoser,
    Jörg, That's New                       (M68)

MODERN STRING QUARTET: VOL. 2 *educ
  vln I,vln II,vla,vcl sc,pts SCHOTTS
    ED 7677 f.s. the number of
    performers in each part variable
    contains: Davis, Miles, All Blues;
    Hecker, Jost H., Joey's Rock          (M69)

MODERN STRING QUARTET: VOL. 3 RAGTIMES
  FOR STRING ENSEMBLE see Searle,
  Leslie

MOMENT MUSICAL see Schubert, Franz
  (Peter)

MONK, THELONIUS
  'Round Midnight (composed with
    Williams, Charles Melvin
    (Cootie))
    (Custer, Calvin) string orch,
    flügelhorn/trp solo (med) WARNER
    SO9501, 029156177008                  (M70)

MONKEY TRICKS see Groitzsch, G.

MONTY'S FOXHOUNDS see Plater, D.J.

MONUMENT VALLEY see Elledge, Chuck

MONY, MONY
  (Cerulli, Bob) string orch (very
    easy) WARNER SO9707, 029156661309     (M71)

MOONGLOW
  (Custer, Calvin) clar solo,string
    orch (med) WARNER SO9606,
    029156214123                          (M72)

MOONLIGHT MELODY see Rogers, F.M.

MOONLIGHT ON THE ALSTER see Fetras,
  Oscar

MOONLIGHT OVER TAHITI see Bridgmont,
  Leslie

MOONLIGHT SERENADE see Miller, (Alton)
  Glenn

MOORE, JOHN W.
  Twisted Keel *educ
    (Barry, M.) [4'] BOSWORTH             (M73)

MORAWETZ, OSKAR (1917-    )
  Railway Station, The *educ
    3+pic.3+English horn.3+bass clar.3+
    contrabsn. 4.3.3.1. timp,3perc,
    harp,strings [12'] sc CANADIAN
    MI 1100 M831RA                         (M74)

MORCEAU DE CONCOURS see Faure, Gabriel-
  Urbain

MORDISH, LOUIS
  Harlequin's Flirtation: Entr'acte
    *educ
    [3'] BOSWORTH                          (M75)

  Irish Fiddler, The *educ
    orch,vln solo [2'55"] BOSWORTH        (M76)

  Mexican Promenade *educ
    BOSWORTH                               (M77)

MORELLE, MAX
  Romany Serenade *educ
    (Charrosin, F.G.) orch,vln solo
    [3'] BOSWORTH                          (M78)

MORGAN, J.
  Romany Revels: Fantasy *educ
    [5'30"] BOSWORTH                       (M79)

MORGAN, RUSS (1904-1969)
  Shadow Song, The *educ
    (Tattenhall, B.) orch,vln solo
    [2'30"] BOSWORTH                       (M80)

MORRIS, STEVLAND (STEVIE WONDER)
  (1950-    )
  You Are The Sunshine Of My Life
    (Custer, Calvin) string orch,fl
    solo (med) WARNER SO9607,
    029156214147                          (M81)

MOSCOSO, TOMAS
  Canto Moruno (Paso Doble) *educ
    [2'40"] BOSWORTH                       (M82)

MOSCOW NIGHTS see Soloviev-Sedoy,
  Vassily Pavlovich

MOSIER, KIRT N.
  Baltic Dance
    string orch (gr. IV) KJOS pts
    SO-129C, sc SO-129F                   (M83)

  Overture To The Wind
    string orch (gr. V) KJOS pts
    SO-89C, sc SO-89F                     (M84)

  Prophet's Dance *educ
    (gr. V) KJOS pts O-1071C, sc
    O-1071F                                (M85)

MOT-STYCKE: SJU VARIANTER
  2.2.2.2. 2.2.0.0. timp,strings [6']
    sc STIM                                (M86)

MOUNTAIN COUNTY FIDDLE-IN see Halferty

MOURANT
  Preamble To The Constitution Of The
    United States *educ
    orch,cor BOURNE perf mat rent          (M87)

MOURNING SONG see Daniels, Melvin L.

MOUSSORGSKY, MODEST PETROVITCH
  see MUSSORGSKY, MODEST PETROVICH

MOZART, LEOPOLD (1719-1787)
  Classical Salzburg Suite
    (Halen, Walter J.) string orch
    WINGERT set 3030501, sc 3030502       (M88)

  Kleine Sinfonie Für Musikfreunde
    *educ
    (Höckner, W.) string orch pts
    HEINRICH 6032                          (M89)

MOZART, WOLFGANG AMADEUS (1756-1791)
  Andante (from Concerto No. 21, 2nd
    Mvt.)
    (Goldsmith, Owen) string orch
    (easy) CPP-BEL BS000117,
    029156103854                          (M90)

  Aria (from Marriage Of Figaro) educ
    (Gordon, Philip) string orch BOURNE
    augmented set 107480, set 107410      (M91)

  Bastien & Bastienne
    (Smith, Steven) string orch (gr.
    II) set JLJ.MUSIC SO 103              (M92)

  Classical Overture
    (Applebaum, Samuel; Ployhar, James)
    orch (med easy) CPP-BEL CO00180,
    029156671759                          (M93)

  Concerto for Piano and Orchestra in
    A, No. 23, K. 488,First Movement
    (Velke, Fritz) string orch,pno solo
    (gr. IV, cadenza provided) VELKE      (M94)

  Concerto No. 3, K. 216, in G,First
    Movement
    (Velke, Fritz) string orch,vln solo
    (gr. IV) VELKE                        (M95)

  Dance Suite
    (Johnson, Thor) string orch (gr.
    III) KJOS pts SO-20C, sc SO-20F       (M96)

  Don Giovanni: Melodic Moments *educ
    (Arnold, Alan) (med diff) pno-cond
    sc,pts BOSWORTH 1106                  (M97)

  Exsultate Jubilate
    (Goldsmith, Owen) string orch
    (easy) CPP-BEL BS000097,
    029156045383                          (M98)

  Landler *educ
    (Caponegro) string orch,pno (gr. I)
    KENDOR 8356                           (M99)

  Magic Flute, The: Suite [arr.] *educ
    (Carter) string orch (med easy) sc,
    pts BOSWORTH 1030                     (M100)

  Marriage Of Figaro, The: Overture
    see Overture To The Marriage Of
    Figaro

  Minuet (from Clarinet Quintet In A
    Major, K.581) educ
    (Niehaus) string orch,pno (gr. III)
    KENDOR 9849                           (M101)

  Overture To The Marriage Of Figaro
    (Isaac, Merle) "Marriage Of Figaro,
    The: Overture" orch (med diff)
    CPP-BEL C000163, 029156218138         (M102)

  Sonatina in C
    (Halen, Walter J.) string orch
    WINGERT set 3033091, sc 3033092       (M103)

  Symphony in G minor,First Movement,
    [arr.]
    (Isaac, Merle) orch (med) CPP-BEL
    C000161, 029156151732                 (M104)

  Symphony No. 29,First Movement *educ
    (Frost) string orch (gr. IV) KENDOR
    9907                                   (M105)

  Symphony No.41 In C, Part 1: Allegro
    Vivace (from Jupiter Symphony)
    educ
    (Daeblitz) [8'30"] BOSWORTH           (M106)

  Symphony No.41 In C, Part 2: Andante
    Cantabile (from Jupiter Symphony)
    educ
    (Daeblitz) [7'30"] BOSWORTH           (M107)

  Symphony No.41 In C, Part 3: Menuetto
    (from Jupiter Symphony) educ
    (Daeblitz) [3'] BOSWORTH              (M108)

  Symphony No.41 In C, Part 4: Molto
    Allegro (from Jupiter Symphony)
    educ
    (Daeblitz) [7'] BOSWORTH              (M109)

  Table Music *educ
    (Del Borgo) string orch (gr. II)
    KENDOR 9515                           (M110)

MUSETTE, FOR 2 VIOLINS, VIOLA AND
  VIOLONCELLO see Bach, Johann
  Sebastian

MUSIC FOR KIDS see Klein, Lothar

MUSIC FOR THE ROYAL FIREWORKS: OVERTURE
  see Handel, George Frideric

MUSIC SCHOOL RAG see Searle, Leslie

MUSICAL JIG-SAW, A: POTPOURRI see
  Aston, William

MUSIK ZU EINEM MÄRCHENSPIEL see
Schäfer, K.

MUSSORGSKY, MODEST PETROVICH
(1839-1881)
Great Gate Of Kiev; Watchman's Song
*educ
(Herfurth, C. Paul) string orch
BOURNE augmented set 050370, set
050390                          (M111)

MY FUNNY VALENTINE see Hart, Lorenz see
Rodgers, Richard

MY GIRL SLOOPY see Hang On Sloopy

MY WOMEN see Andrew With Strings:
Volume 2 "A French Medley"

MYERS, SHERMAN
Butterflies In The Rain *educ
(Engleman, Joseph) [2'30"] BOSWORTH
(M112)

Fairy On The Clock *educ
(Engleman, Joseph) [4'] BOSWORTH
(M113)

Pierrot Comes To Town *educ
(Grant, C.) [3'] BOSWORTH    (M114)

MYERS, STANLEY A. (1908-1994)
Cavatina (from the film "The
Deerhunter")
(Frazer, Alan) 2.1.2.1. 2.0.0.0.
perc,harp/pno,strings sc,pts
CRAMER MUS 90436 f.s.       (M115)

# N

NAPLES (SERENADE) see Jalowicz, R.

NAUTICALIA: FANTASY OF SEA SONGS IN
MODERN SYMPHONIC STYLE see
Charrosin, F.G.

NEAPOLITAN SERENADE see Winkler,
Gerhard

NELLY BLY see Songs Of Stephen Foster,
Part 2

NER LI see Hanukkah Favorites

NEVILLE, DEREK
Dream Fantasy *educ
[4'15"] BOSWORTH              (N1)

NEW CENTURY MARCH see Steele, Henry

NEW ENGLAND HOLIDAY see Washburn,
Robert Brooks

NEW HORIZONS see Del Borgo, Elliot A.

NEW PARTY FROCK, A see King, Reginald

NEW POST HORN GALOP, THE see Barsotti,
Roger

NEW WORLD SYMPHONY (FIRST MOVEMENT) see
Dvořák, Antonín, Symphony, Op. 95,
in E minor,First Movement, [arr.]

NEW YORK, NEW YORK (THEME) see Kander,
John

NICE: BATTLE OF FLOWERS see Jalowicz,
R.

NIEHAUS
Appalachian Waltz *educ
string orch,pno,opt perc (gr. I)
KENDOR 8145                  (N2)

Biding Your Time *educ
string orch,pno,opt perc (gr. I)
KENDOR 8177                  (N3)

Candleberry Bay *educ
string orch,pno (gr. II) KENDOR
8955                         (N4)

Carroll County *educ
string orch,pno,opt perc (gr. II)
KENDOR 8962                  (N5)

Celtic Overture *educ
string orch,pno,opt perc (gr. II)
KENDOR 8963                  (N6)

Crossbow Overture *educ
string orch,pno,opt perc (gr. III)
KENDOR 9802                  (N7)

Fanflairs *educ
string orch,pno,opt perc (gr. I)
KENDOR 8261                  (N8)

Fiddler's Green *educ
string orch,pno,opt perc (gr. II)
KENDOR 9105                  (N9)

Fingernail Moon *educ
string orch,pno,opt perc (gr. I)
KENDOR 8267                  (N10)

Millennium *educ
string orch,pno,opt perc (gr. II)
KENDOR 9255                  (N11)

Quixotic Sketch *educ
string orch,pno,opt perc (gr. I)
KENDOR 8533                  (N12)

String Bouquet *educ
string orch,pno,opt perc (gr. II)
KENDOR 9495                  (N13)

Stringtide *educ
string orch,pno,opt perc (gr. I)
KENDOR 8692                  (N14)

Tableau Vivant *educ
string orch,pno,opt perc (gr. I)
KENDOR 8722                  (N15)

Whiskers *educ
string orch,pno,opt perc (gr. I)
KENDOR 8854                  (N16)

NIEHAUS, LEONARD
Americana Rhapsody *educ
(gr. IV) KJOS pts JO-2000B, sc
JO-2000F                     (N17)

NIGHT AND DAY see Porter, Cole

NIGHT BEAT see Daniels, Melvin L.

NIGHT IN RIO, A see Romero,R.

NIGHT OF ROMANCE, A see May, Hans von

NIGHT SHADE see Engleman, Joseph

NIGHTINGALE'S GREETING see Recktenwald,
F.

NINETTE AT COURT see Saint Amans, Louis

NO MAN IS AN ISLAND *educ
(Cacavas, John) string orch set
BOURNE 090310                (N18)

NOACK, WALTER (1900-    )
Fairy Ballet *educ
[10'] BOSWORTH               (N19)

Festival In Elysium *educ
[9'] BOSWORTH                (N20)

NOBLE, HAROLD (1903-    )
Fête Orientale *educ
[2'30"] BOSWORTH             (N21)

NOBODAY KNOWS DE TROUBLE I'VE SEEN
(Heilmann, Francis) string orch/orch
HEILMAN                      (N22)

NOLAN, KENNY
Masterpiece
(Cerulli, Bob) orch (med easy) CPP-
BEL 0438MB7X, 029156671599   (N23)

NORTH, MICHAEL
Dawn
see London Day, A (Suite)

Daytime
see London Day, A (Suite)

Dusk
see London Day, A (Suite)

London Day, A (Suite) *educ
BOSWORTH f.s.
contains: Dawn [1'30"]; Daytime
[1'45"]; Dusk [2'30"]       (N24)

NORWEGIAN DANCE see Grieg, Edvard
Hagerup

NORWEGIAN DANCES NOS. 2 & 3 see Grieg,
Edvard Hagerup

NUNEZ, CAROLD
Apache
string orch (gr. I) KJOS pts
SO-98C, sc SO-98F            (N25)

Festival
string orch KJOS pts SO-80C, sc
SO-80F                       (N26)

Introspection
string orch (gr. III) KJOS pts
SO-127C, sc SO-127F          (N27)

Little Symphony
string orch (gr. I) KJOS pts
SO-121C, sc SO-121F          (N28)

Suite for Strings
string orch (gr. IV) KJOS pts
SO-87C, sc SO-87F            (N29)

NUTCRACKER, THE: THEMES see
Tchaikovsky, Piotr Ilyich

NUTCRACKER BALLET, SET 1 see
Tchaikovsky, Piotr Ilyich

NUTCRACKER BALLET, SET 2 see
Tchaikovsky, Piotr Ilyich

# O

O COME ALL YE FAITHFUL see Christmas Trilogy, A

O COME, O COME, EMANUEL
(Ayars, Bo) 3(pic).3(English horn).3(bass clar).2. 4.3.3(bass trom).1. timp,2perc,pno,harp, strings [3'30"] PRESSER    (O1)

O HOLY NIGHT see Adam, Adolphe-Charles, Cantique De Noel

O MIO BABBINO CARO see Puccini, Giacomo

ODE TO JOY see Beethoven, Ludwig van

OFFENBACH, JACQUES (1819-1880)
Offenbach Memories *educ
(Geiger, I.) [14'] BOSWORTH    (O2)

OFFENBACH MEMORIES see Geiger, I. see Offenbach, Jacques

OLD GRENADIER, THE see Joyce, Archibald

OLD SALT, THE see Charrosin, F.G.

OLD TIME ROCK 'N ROLL
(Cerulli, Bob) string orch (easy)
CPP-BEL 37380B4X, 029156671650    (O3)

OLYMPIC SPIRIT, THE see Williams, John T.

ON BROADWAY *educ
(Lavender) string orch,opt combo (gr. II) LEONARD-US 04626060    (O4)

ON THE DNIEPER see Portnoff, Leo

ON THE PROMENADE see Ketèlbey, Albert William

ON THE TRAPEZE (VALSE) see Armandola, Jose

ONCE UPON A DECEMBER see Ahrens, Lynn

O'NEILL
Our Land, Our Home
(Moss) cor,winds,opt strings
LEONARD-US 04490054    (O5)

O'NEILL, JOHN
Rootbeer Barrel Polka, The
string orch,pno,perc (easy) CPP-BEL BS000090, 029156001655    (O6)

OPEN STRING, THE see Buczynski, Walter

ÖSTERLING, FREDRICK (1966-   )
Lost Melody, The
string orch, in 3 groups for children STIM    (O7)

OUR FEATHERED FRIENDS: SUITE see Bick, H.

OUR LAND, OUR HOME see O'Neill

OVER THE HILLS AND FAR AWAY see Grainger, Percy Aldridge

OVER THE RAINBOW
(Gold, Marty) orch WARNER F09701, 029156298963    (O8)
see Arlen, Harold

OVER THE SCOTTISH HILLS (MARCH INTERMEZZO) see Ewing, Montague

OVERTURE FOR A CELEBRATION see Smith, Claude Thomas

OVERTURE FOR A JOYFUL OCCASION see Demuth, Norman

OVERTURE TO L'AMOUR MALADE see Lully, Jean-Baptiste (Lulli)

OVERTURE TO THE MARRIAGE OF FIGARO see Mozart, Wolfgang Amadeus

OVERTURE TO THE WIND see Mosier, Kirt N.

OXFORD OVERTURE see Del Borgo, Elliot A.

# P

PACHELBEL, JOHANN (1653-1706)
Fantasia And Toccata *educ
(Conley) string orch (gr. IV)
KENDOR 9819    (P1)

PALAIS DE DANSE see Ketèlbey, Albert William

PALMÉR, CATHARINA (1963-   )
Grow: Musik Om Och För Växande orch STIM    (P2)

PALOMA, LA see Yradier, Sebastian

PAPRIKA (POLKA) see Engleman, Joseph

PARADE OF THE REGIMENT see Bye, Frederick

PARKER, CLIFTON (1905-   )
Aubade *educ
chamber orch [2'15"] BOSWORTH    (P3)

Franzel (Landler) *educ
[2'45"] BOSWORTH    (P4)

PARONI, T.
Gypsy Moods (Rhapsody) *educ
[3'] BOSWORTH    (P5)

PARTON, DOLLY
I Will Always Love You
(Cerulli, Bob) orch (easy) CPP-BEL 7426IB7X, 029156061475    (P6)

PAVANE FOR A DEAD PRINCESS see Ravel, Maurice, Pavane Pour Une Infante Defunte

PAVANE POUR UNE INFANTE DEFUNTE see Ravel, Maurice

PEACHES AND SKIM MILK see Velke, Fritz

PENNYCOOK, BRUCE (1949-   )
Symphony For Youth Orchestra *educ
3(pic).2.2.1. 4.3.3.1. timp,perc, pno,strings sc CANADIAN
MI 1100 P416SY    (P7)

PEPIN, CLERMONT (1926-   )
Three Miniatures For Strings *educ
string orch pts CANADIAN
MI 1500 P422TH    (P8)

PERPETUAL MOTION
(Higgins) string orch (easy) CPP-BEL C000189    (P9)

PETALS see Charrosin, F.G.

PETER GUNN see Mancini, Henry

PETITE VALSE see Gluck, Christoph Willibald, Ritter von

PETTERSEN, NANCY
Meditation for String Orchestra
string orch (med easy) CPP-BEL BS000109, 029156103816    (P10)

Symphonic Tribute
orch (med) CPP-BEL C000202, 029156687897    (P11)

PEZZO see Tchaikovsky, Piotr Ilyich, Serenade for Strings,First Movement

PHANTOM DANCE see Elledge, Chuck

PHANTOM OF SALOME, THE see Joyce, Archibald

PHANTOM PIPER, THE see Ewing, Montague

PHILLIPS, BURRILL (1907-1988)
Three Easy Pieces
string orch WINGERT set 9042851, sc 9042852    (P12)

PIANISTIQUE CAPRICE see Ketèlbey, Albert William

PICARDY VARIATIONS *Fr
(Hoffer, Marjorie) string orch (med)
CPP-BEL BS09601, 029156184310    (P13)

PICCADILLY PRELUDE see Marland, Bert

PICK-A-BACK see Engleman, Joseph

PICTURES IN MELODY, PART 1 see Ketèlbey, Albert William

PICTURES IN MELODY, PART 2 see Ketèlbey, Albert William

PIERRETTE ON THE SWING see Engleman, Joseph

PIERRETTE'S WEDDING see Jordan, Herberte

PIERROT COMES TO TOWN see Myers, Sherman

PINK CHAMPAGNE see Strachey, J.

PINK PANTHER, THE see Mancini, Henry

PIRATE'S TREASURE MARCH see Cohen, Richard

PIROUETTE see Chuckerbutty, Oliphant see Croudson, Henry

PIZZICATO CAPRICE see Engleman, Joseph

PIZZICATO PIZAZZ see Frost, Robert S.

PLATER, D.J.
Monty's Foxhounds *educ
[3'] BOSWORTH    (P14)

Tank Town *educ
[2'30"] BOSWORTH    (P15)

PLAYBOX see Charrosin, F.G.

PLAZA DE TOROS see Brubaker, Dale

PLINK, PLANK, PLUNK see Anderson, Leroy

POET see Schumann, Robert (Alexander)

POLDINI, EDE (EDUARD) (1869-1957)
Valse Serenade
(Cechvala, Al) string orch (gr. II)
VELKE    (P16)

POLKA DOTS see Rudge, H.

POLKA FOR BUDDING STRINGS see Wolf, Artur

POLKA POLONAISE see Michaeloff, Mischa

POLONAISE see Herbert, Victor

POMP AND CIRCUMSTANCE see Elgar, [Sir] Edward (William)

PORGY AND BESS: SELECTIONS see Gershwin, George

PORTER, COLE (1892-1964)
Begin The Beguine
(Custer, Calvin) string orch (med easy) WARNER WBSO9402, 029156112030    (P17)

Just One Of Those Things
(Custer, Calvin) string orch (med easy) WARNER WBSO9406, 029156111712    (P18)

Night And Day
(Custer, Calvin) string orch (med)
WARNER S09604, 029156214208    (P19)
(Rosenhaus, Steven L.) orch (med easy) WARNER WBF09412, 029156112405    (P20)

PORTNOFF, LEO
On The Dnieper *educ
(Charrosin, F.G.) "Russian Fantasy No.4" [2'] BOSWORTH    (P21)

Russian Fantasy No.4
see On The Dnieper

POWER OF THE DREAM, THE *educ
(Custer) string orch,opt combo (gr. II) LEONARD-US 04626058    (P22)
(Higgins) string orch LEONARD-US 00864030    (P23)
see Krogstad, Bob

PRAYER AT SUNSET see Hanmer, Ronald

PREAMBLE TO THE CONSTITUTION OF THE UNITED STATES see Mourant

PRELUDE ALLA MARCIA see Rachmaninoff, Sergey Vassilievich

PRELUDE AND DANCE see Frost

PRELUDE ON AN EARLY AMERICAN FOLK HYMN see Smith, Claude Thomas

PRESTO see Stamitz, Carl, Symphony in D

PRIZE SONG see Wagner, Richard

PROCESSION OF THE SARDAR see Ippolitov-Ivanov, Mikhail Mikhailovich

PROCESSIONAL MARCH see Handel, George Frideric, Allegro Maestoso

PROKOFIEV, SERGE (1891-1953)
Dance
see Romeo And Juliet: Two Dances

Dance Of The Antillese Girls
see Romeo And Juliet: Two Dances

March From Love For Three Oranges
(McLeod) string orch (gr. IV) KJOS
pts GSO-4C, sc GSO-4F        (P24)

Romeo And Juliet: Two Dances  *educ
(Berlin, Ben) BOSWORTH f.s.
contains: Dance [2'5"]; Dance Of
The Antillese Girls [2'5"]
(P25)

Troika (from Lt. Kije) educ
(Wieloszynski) string orch,pno,opt
perc (gr. III) KENDOR 9926  (P26)

PROMENADE see Anderson, Leroy

PROPHET'S DANCE see Mosier, Kirt N.

PRUNES AND PRISMS see Jefferies,
Stanton

PUCCINI, GIACOMO (1858-1924)
O Mio Babbino Caro (from Gianni
Schicchi)
(Heilmann, Francis) string orch
HEILMAN                      (P27)

Un Bel Di, Vedremo (from Madame
Butterfly)
(Alshin, Harry) string orch (med
easy) CPP-BEL BS000115,
029156097870                (P28)

PUCK see Krein, Michael

PUNWAR, KATHERINE
Tintinabulations  *educ
(gr. III) KJOS pts O-1057B, sc
O-1057F                      (P29)

PURCELL, HENRY (1658 or 59-1695)
Chacony  *educ
(Ryden) string orch BOURNE
augmented set 415870, set 415880,
sc 415884                   (P30)

Sonata in F
(Klotman, Robert) string orch (med
easy, "The Glorious") CPP-BEL
BS000059, 029156671735      (P31)

Trumpet Voluntary
(Heilmann, Francis) orch/string
orch HEILMAN                (P32)

Two Seventeenth Century Dances  *educ
(Frost, Robert) string orch (gr.
II) KJOS pts SO-77C, sc SO-77F
(P33)
Variations On A Ground Bass Theme
(Washburn, Robert) string orch
(med) CPP-BEL BS09609,
029156203776                (P34)

PUSZTA ROMANCE see Rogez, S.

# Q

QUEEN NOOR SUITE see Washburn, Robert
Brooks

QUINTERO, L.
Chiqui Chiqui Cha (La Mulata Tomasa)
*educ
[2'45"] BOSWORTH            (Q1)

QUIXOTIC SKETCH see Niehaus

QUODLIBET see Bach, Johann Sebastian

# R

RACHMANINOFF, SERGEY VASSILIEVICH
(1873-1943)
Prelude Alla Marcia (from Opus 23)
educ
(Alshin, Harry A.) string orch,opt
perc (gr. III) KENDOR 9861  (R1)

Vocalise
(Alshin, Harry) string orch (med)
CPP-BEL BS000098, 029156045529
(R2)
RAEBURN, HUGH
Light And Shade  *educ
[4'] BOSWORTH              (R3)

Twinkle-Toes  *educ
[3'] BOSWORTH              (R4)

RAGAMUFFIN (SPITZBUB) see Rixner, Josef

RAGTIME DANCE see Joplin, Scott

RAGTIMES, FOR STRINGS see Joplin, Scott

RAILWAY STATION, THE see Morawetz,
Oskar

RAINY DAY MEDLEY, A
(Gold, Marty) orch (med easy) CPP-BEL
C0319B6X, 029156056488     (R5)

RAIS, M.
Anouschka  *educ
"Valse Appassionata" [3'] BOSWORTH
(R6)
Valse Appassionata
see Anouschka

RANKIN INLET (ESKIMO SONG) see Adaskin,
Murray

RAPLEY, FELTON
Twilight Rapture  *educ
"Valse Lent" [2'30"] BOSWORTH  (R7)

Valse Lent
see Twilight Rapture

RAPOSO, JOSEPH G. (1937-1989)
Bein' Green
(Cerulli, Bob) string orch (easy)
WARNER S09613, 029156215571  (R8)

Sing (from Sesame Street)
(Cerulli, Bob) string orch (easy)
WARNER S09612, 029156216011  (R9)

RASPA, LA see South Of The Border Suite

RAVEL, MAURICE (1875-1937)
Menuet Sur Le Nom D'Haydn  *educ
(Finno) string orch (gr. III)
KENDOR 9847                (R10)

Pavane For A Dead Princess
see Pavane Pour Une Infante Defunte

Pavane Pour Une Infante Defunte
(Goldsmith, Owen) "Pavane For A
Dead Princess" string orch CPP-
BEL BS09713, 029156605501   (R11)
(Goldsmith, Owen) "Pavane For A
Dead Princess" orch (med) CPP-BEL
BF09502, 029156170863      (R12)

Two French Miniatures (composed with
Satie, Erik)
(Goldsmith, Owen) string orch (med)
CPP-BEL BS09608, 029156200478
(R13)
RAYNERS, CECIL
In My Dream Garden (Reverie)  *educ
(Engleman, Joseph) [3'] BOSWORTH
(R14)
RE LEONE, IL  *educ
(Short) [Eng/It] chamber orch sc,pts
RICORDI-IT 137281          (R15)

REACH see Estefan, Gloria

RECKTENWALD, F.
Nightingale's Greeting  *educ
orch,pic/xylo solo [3'] BOSWORTH
(R16)
RED CARPET, THE see Wiggins, Arthur M.

RED RIVER RAPIDS see Frost

REDMAN, REGINALD (1892-    )
Avenue, The
see Marston Court (Suite)

Irish Souvenir, An  *educ
[3'] BOSWORTH              (R17)

Lily Pond, The
see Marston Court (Suite)

REDMAN, REGINALD (cont'd.)

Marston Court (Suite) *educ
    BOSWORTH f.s.
        contains: Avenue, The [2'30"];
        Lily Pond, The [3'30"]; Meet,
        The [2'30"]; Tudor Music Room,
        The [2'] (R18)

Meet, The
    see Marston Court (Suite)

Tudor Music Room, The
    see Marston Court (Suite)

REED, HERBERT OWEN (1910-    )
Fiesta Mexicana, La
    orch CPP-BEL BF09605, 029156220452
                                    (R19)

REEL CHAPLIN, THE see Chaplin

REJOICE AND BE MERRY see Christmas
Trilogy, A

REMEMBRANCE (ELEGY) see Ketèlbey,
Albert William

RENAISSANCE SUITE
    (Del Borgo, Elliot) string orch (very
    easy) CPP-BEL BS000116,
    029156103793 (R20)

RENDEZVOUS see Aletter, William

RENDEZVOUS (INTERMEZZO ROCOCO) see
Aletter, William

RESPIGHI, OTTORINO (1879-1936)
Antique Dances And Airs *educ
    (Alshin, Harry A.) string orch (gr.
    III, in 5 movements) KENDOR 9791
                                    (R21)

RÊVE D'AMOUR see Engleman, Joseph

RÊVE D'ENFANT see Duparloir

REYNOLDS, WYNFORD
Stringing Along *educ
    (Charrosin, F.G.) [3'] BOSWORTH
                                    (R22)

RHAPSODY IN BLUE see Gershwin, George

RHINELAND MUSICAL SCENES see Halen,
Walter J.

RHYTHM & BLUES see Schaum, W.

RICHARDSON, CLIVE
White Cliffs *educ
    [5'] BOSWORTH (R23)

RICHARTZ, WILLY (1900-1972)
Evening On The Rhine *educ
    [6'] BOSWORTH (R24)

Valse Capricieuse *educ
    BOSWORTH (R25)

RIDE HIM! COWBOY see Engleman, Joseph

RIDER IN THE RING (ENTRÉE) see
Armandola, Jose

RING O' ROSES see Engleman, Joseph

RING RING THE BANJO see Songs Of
Stephen Foster, Part 2

RIO PATROL see Geller, Harold

RITORNELL see Bach, Johann Sebastian

RITTER, HELMUT
Geigen Polka *educ
    orch,opt vln/acord solo [2'20"]
    BOSWORTH (R26)

RIVIERA EXPRESS (DESCRIPTIVE INTERLUDE)
see Engleman, Joseph

RIXNER, JOSEF (1902-1973)
Ragamuffin (Spitzbub) *educ
    [3'] BOSWORTH (R27)

ROCHEROLLE, EUGENIE RICAU (1936-    )
American Portrait, An (composed with
    Elledge, Chuck)
    string orch (gr. V) KJOS pts
    GSO-23C, sc GSO-23F (R28)

ROCK MASTERPIECES
    (Cerulli, Bob) orch (med easy,
    contains Joy To The World & Proud
    Mary) CPP-BEL C0292B7X,
    029156003444 (R29)

ROCKING HORSE, THE see Engleman, Joseph

RODGERS, RICHARD (1902-1979)
Bewitched
    (Custer, Calvin) string orch (med
    easy) WARNER WBS09415,
    029156111675 (R30)

RODGERS, RICHARD (cont'd.)

My Funny Valentine
    (Custer, Calvin) string orch (med
    easy) WARNER WBS09403,
    029156111699 (R31)

ROGERS, F.M.
Cardinal's Snuff Box *educ
    [3'30"] BOSWORTH (R32)

Moonlight Melody *educ
    (Engleman, Joseph) [3'] BOSWORTH
                                    (R33)

ROGEZ, S.
Puszta Romance *educ
    (Carod, F.) orch,vln solo [3']
    BOSWORTH (R34)

ROHLF, EARL A.
Busy Fingers
    string orch WINGERT set 9041181, sc
    9041182 (R35)

ROLAND, M.
Flute Serenade *educ
    orch,fl solo [3'] BOSWORTH (R36)

ROMANY REVELS: FANTASY see Morgan, J.

ROMANY SERENADE see Morelle, Max

ROMANZA see Goldsmith, Owen

ROMEO AND JULIET see Tchaikovsky, Piotr
Ilyich

ROMEO AND JULIET: THREE EPISODES see
Missal, Joshua M.

ROMEO AND JULIET: TWO DANCES see
Prokofiev, Serge

ROMERO,R.
Night In Rio, A *educ
    [2'15"] BOSWORTH (R37)

RONDO AND ROUND see Christensen, James
Harlan

RONDO CAPRICE see Daniels

ROOTBEER BARREL POLKA, THE see O'Neill,
John

ROPE DANCERS, THE see Engleman, Joseph

ROSAMUNDE: OVERTURE see Schubert, Franz
(Peter)

ROSE, DAVID (1919-1990)
Holiday For Strings
    (Custer, Calvin) string orch (med
    easy) WARNER WBS09404,
    029156112801 (R38)
    (Gold, Marty) orch (concert level)
    WARNER F09704, 029156300086 (R39)

ROSE, THE see Mcbroom, Amanda

ROSE BOUQUET, A *educ
    (Wieloszynski) string orch,pno (gr.
    III, contains pieces by Brahms,
    MacDowell, & Schubert) KENDOR 9857
                                    (R40)

ROSEN, W.
Five O'clock Tea In The Doll's House
    *educ
    [4'45"] BOSWORTH (R41)

ROSENHAUS
Shojo-Ji *educ
    string orch BOURNE augmented set
    419670, set 419680, sc 419684
                                    (R42)

ROSENHAUS, STEVEN L.
Kitchen Percussion March For 'Special
    Guest Soloists' And Orchestra
    orch (med) WARNER F09615,
    029156215991 (R43)

ROSSINI, GIOACCHINO (1792-1868)
Barber Of Seville, The
    (McLeod) string orch (gr. IV) KJOS
    pts GSO-16C, sc GSO-16F (R44)

ROUND AND ROUND AND ROUND *educ
    (Wieloszynski) string orch,pno (gr.
    I, contains: "Are You Sleeping?"
    "Scotland's Burning" &
    "Kookaburra") KENDOR 8557 (R45)

'ROUND MIDNIGHT see Monk, Thelonius

ROUND THE SHOPS see Stuart, Graeme

ROVING FANCIES see Wood, Haydn

ROYAL PROCESSIONAL see Keuning, Ken

ROYAL STANDARD see Joyce, Archibald

RUDGE, H.
Polka Dots *educ
    (Charrosin, F.G.) orch,pic/xylo
    solo [2'30"] BOSWORTH (R46)

RUDOLPH THE RED-NOSED REINDEER see
Marks, Johnny D.

RUMANIAN RHAPSODY NO. 1 see Enesco,
Georges (Enescu)

RUMPELSTILSKIN see Engleman, Joseph

RUMPELSTILTSKIN'S DANCE see Halen,
Walter J.

RUNDTANZ UND FINALE see Schaper, Heinz-
Christian

RUSCH, HAROLD W. (1908-    )
March Triumphant
    (Spinosa) string orch (gr. II) KJOS
    pts SO-61C, sc SO-61F (R47)

RUSSIA TODAY see Charrosin, F.G.

RUSSIAN FANTASY NO.4 see Portnoff, Leo,
On The Dnieper

RUSSIAN GYPSIES see Geiger, Max

RUST, FRIEDRICH WILHELM (1739-1796)
Life's Laughter: A Little Overture
    *educ
    [4'] BOSWORTH (R48)

RUTHENIAN SONG see Young Bartok Suite,
A

# S

'S WONDERFUL see Gershwin, George

SABRE DANCE see Khachaturian, Aram Ilyich

SACRED HOUR, THE see Ketèlbey, Albert William

SADLIER, RON
Fiddler's Fantasy
string orch (gr. II) set JLJ.MUSIC
SO 101                               (S1)

SAILORMEN ALL see Ewing, Montague

SAILORS' HOLIDAY see Martell Eric

SAILOR'S HORNPIPE *educ
(Hartley, Fred) [3'15"] BOSWORTH (S2)
(Krein, Michael) [4'] BOSWORTH    (S3)
(Terry, Ray) BOSWORTH             (S4)

SAILORS' PATROL see Charrosin, F.G.

SAILOR'S SONG see Keuning, Ken

SAINT AMANS, LOUIS
Ninette At Court *Classical
(Cechvala, Al) string orch (gr.
III) VELKE                        (S5)

ST. ELMO'S FIRE: LOVE THEME see Foster, David

SAINT-GEORGES, CHEVALIER DE
see SAINT-GEORGES, JOSEPH BOULOGNE DE

SAINT-GEORGES, JOSEPH BOULOGNE DE
(1739-1799)
Sinfonia in D *educ
(Levenson, David M.) (gr. IV) KJOS
pts 0-1067C, sc 0-1067F          (S6)

SAINT-SAËNS, CAMILLE (1835-1921)
Bacchanale From Samson & Delilah
(Isaac, Merle) orch (med) CPP-BEL
C000166, 029156133141            (S7)

Danse Macabre *educ
(Alshin, Harry) string orch (med
easy) CPP-BEL BS000106,
029156097832                     (S8)
(McLeod) string orch,vln solo (gr.
III) KENDOR 9807                 (S9)

SAKURA, SAKURA
(Del Borgo, Elliot) string orch
(intermediate level) CPP-BEL
BS09704, 029156299106            (S10)

SALISBURY OVERTURE see McQuilkin, Terry

SALUTE TO A TOY HERO see Jordan, Herberte

SALUTE TO IRVING BERLIN *educ
(Custer) string orch,opt combo (gr.
II) LEONARD-US 04626062          (S11)

SALUTE TO THE BIG APPLE, A
(Custer, Calvin) orch (med) WARNER
F09610, 029156208528            (S12)

SALUTE TO THE BIG BANDS, A
(Custer, Calvin) orch (med diff) CPP-
BEL F09506, 029156178791        (S13)

SAMMARTINI, GIOVANNI BATTISTA
(1701-1775)
Allegro
see Symphony in C

Symphony in C
(Smith, Steven) "Allegro" string
orch (gr. III) set JLJ.MUSIC
SO 105                           (S14)

SANCTUARY OF THE HEART see Ketèlbey, Albert William

SANTA CLAUS IS COMIN' TO TOWN see Coots, John Frederick

SANTA CLAUS IS COMING TO TOWN see Gillespie, Haven

SASCHINKA: POTPOURRI ON RUSSIAN GYPSY DANCE AIRS see Schirmann, A.

SAUCY HAT, THE see Jarman, H.C.

SAUNDERS, MAX
With Blue Brocade And Dainty Shoe
*educ
orch/string orch&pno [2'20"]
BOSWORTH                         (S15)

SAY! WHEN ARE YOU COMING BACK? see Andrew With Strings: Volume 2 "A French Medley"

SCALES IN POLYTONALITY see Freedman, Harry

SCARBOROUGH FAIR
(Tiffault, Leighton) string orch (med
easy, traditional) CPP-BEL BS09509,
029156172300                    (S16)

SCENES FROM CARMEN see Bizet, Georges

SCENES FROM CARMEN (SUITE NO. 1) see Bizet, Georges

SCHÄFER, K.
Musik Zu Einem Märchenspiel *educ
fl,string orch,opt perc sc,pts
HEINRICH 7002                   (S17)

Spielmusik Für Stabspieler Und
Streicher *educ
strings,perc sc,pts HEINRICH 779 (S18)

SCHAPER, HEINZ-CHRISTIAN (1927-    )
Allegro Und Andante Con Moto
2.1.2+2clar in C.1.S rec.A rec.T
rec.B rec. 0.2+2trp in C.1.0.
2glock,2vibra,perc,timp,gtr,vln
I,vln II,vla,vcl,db MOSELER sc
43.507-00, pts 43.507-02 TO 06,
augmented set 43.507-08, set
43.507-09                        (S19)

Aufzug, Ostinato Und Kleines Finale
2.1.2+2clar in C.1.S rec.A rec.T
rec.B rec. 0.2+2trp in C.1.0.
2glock,2vibra,perc,timp,gtr,vln
I,vln II,vla,vcl,db MOSELER sc
43.509-00, pts 43.509-02 TO 06,
augmented set 43.508, set
43.509-09                        (S20)

Lied Auf Dem Dach
2.1.2+2clar in C.1.S rec.A rec.T
rec.B rec. 0.2+2trp in C.1.0.
2glock,2vibra,perc,timp,gtr,vln
I,vln II,vla,vcl,db MOSELER sc
43.505-00, pts 43.505-02 TO 06,
augmented set 43.505-08, set
43.505-09                        (S21)

Marsch Und Fremdländisches Lied
2.1.2+2clar in C.1.S rec.A rec.T
rec.B rec. 0.2+2trp in C.1.0.
2glock,2vibra,perc,timp,gtr,vln
I,vln II,vla,vcl,db MOSELER sc
43.506-00, pts 43.506-02 TO 06,
augmented set 43.506-08, set
43.506-09                        (S22)

Rondo for 2 Violins and Orchestra
2.1.2+2clar in C.2.S rec.A rec.T
rec.B rec. 0.2+2trp in C.1.0.
2glock,2vibra,perc,timp,gtr,vln
I,vln II,vla,vcl,db,2vln/vln&vla
soli MOSELER sc 43.503-00, solo
pt 43.503-01, pts
43.503-02 TO 06, augmented set
43.503-08, set 43.503-09        (S23)

Rundtanz Und Finale
2.1.2+2clar in C.1.S rec.A rec.T
rec.B rec. 0.2+2trp in C.1.0.
2glock,2vibra,perc,timp,gtr,vln
I,vln II,vla,vcl,db MOSELER sc
43.508-00, pts 43.508-02 TO 06,
augmented set 43.508-08, set
43.508-09                        (S24)

SCHAUM, W.
Rhythm & Blues *educ
BOSWORTH BOE 4102               (S25)

SCHEINBERG, ART
Celebration
string orch (gr. I) set JLJ.MUSIC
SO 102                           (S26)

SCHERZO PIZZICATO see Tchaikovsky, Piotr Ilyich

SCHIPIZKY, FREDERICK (1952-    )
Children's Suite *educ
strings without db/string orch sc
CANADIAN MI 3134 S336CH         (S27)

SCHIRMANN, A.
Dubinuschka: Potpourri On Favorite
Russian And Gypsy Airs *educ/
medley
[14'] BOSWORTH                  (S28)

Saschinka: Potpourri On Russian Gypsy
Dance Airs *educ
[14'] BOSWORTH                  (S29)

SCHMELING, M.
Evening In Toledo *educ
BOSWORTH f.s.
contains: Serenade; Spanish Dance
(S30)

SCHMELING, M. (cont'd.)
Evening In Toledo, An *educ
"Serenade And Spanish Dance"
BOSWORTH                        (S31)

Serenade
see Evening In Toledo

Serenade And Spanish Dance
see Evening In Toledo, An

Spanish Dance
see Evening In Toledo

SCHUBERT, FRANZ (PETER) (1797-1828)
Death And The Maiden *educ
(Harris) string orch BOURNE
augmented set 031480, set 031410
(S32)

Gay Parade *educ
(Harris) string orch BOURNE
augmented set 045270, set 045290
(S33)

Moment Musical *Op.94,No.3, educ
(Haensch) [2'30"] BOSWORTH      (S34)

Rosamunde: Overture *educ
(Haensch) [11'] BOSWORTH        (S35)

Schubert Fantasie *educ
(Foulds, John H.) [13'] BOSWORTH
(S36)

Symphony in B minor, No. 7,
[excerpt], [arr.]
(Goldsmith, Owen) orch (med) CPP-
BEL BF09601, 029156199130      (S37)

SCHUBERT FANTASIE see Foulds, John Herbert see Schubert, Franz (Peter)

SCHUBERT SAMPLER *educ
(McLeod) string orch,pno (gr. III)
KENDOR 9866                     (S38)

SCHUMANN, ROBERT (ALEXANDER)
(1810-1856)
Abendlied *educ
"Evensong" BOSWORTH f.s. contains
also: Traumerei, "Dreaming" (S39)

Evensong
see Abendlied

Little Fugue
(Cechvala, Al) string orch (gr.
III) VELKE                      (S40)

Poet *educ
string orch (also contains: "Hail
Star Of Heaven by Grieg) BOURNE
augmented set 103780, set 103770
(S41)

Scherzo, [arr.] (from Symphony No. 4
In D Minor)
(Goldsmith, Owen) orch (med) CPP-
BEL BF09501, 029156170900      (S42)

Traumerei
see Abendlied

SCHWARTZ, ARTHUR (1901-1984)
Dancing In The Dark
(Sayre, Chuck) orch (med) WARNER
WBF09402, 029156112863         (S43)

SCOTT
Alpine Holiday *educ
string orch,pno,opt perc (gr. I)
KENDOR 8115                     (S44)

SCOTT, PAUL
Air For Strings
string orch (gr. IV) KJOS pts
SO-97C, sc SO-97F               (S45)

SCOTTISH FANTASY see Washburn, Robert Brooks

SCREECHING SEAGULLS see Bick, H.

SCULL, HAROLD [THOMAS] (1898-    )
Eveille De L'Amour *educ
(Engleman, Joseph) "Love's
Awakening" [4'30"] BOSWORTH     (S46)

Love's Awakening
see Eveille De L'Amour

SEARLE, LESLIE
Meet Mr. Joplin
see Modern String Quartet: Vol. 3
Ragtimes For String Ensemble

Modern String Quartet: Vol. 3
Ragtimes For String Ensemble
*educ
vln I,vln II,vla,vcl,opt db sc,pts
SCHOTTS ED 8454 f.s. the number
of performers in each part
variable
contains: Meet Mr. Joplin; Music
School Rag                      (S47)

SEARLE, LESLIE (cont'd.)

Music School Rag
  see Modern String Quartet: Vol. 3
  Ragtimes For String Ensemble

SEASONS OF LOVE (from Rent) educ
  (Del Borgo) string orch,opt combo
  (gr. II) LEONARD-US 04626064     (S48)

SEE THE CONQUERING HERO COMES see
  Handel, George Frideric

SERENADE see Schmeling, M.

SERENADE AND SPANISH DANCE see
  Schmeling, M., Evening In Toledo,
  An

SERENADE FOR ROSEMARY see Velke, Fritz

SERENADE FOR STRINGS, OP. 12 see
  Herbert, Victor

SERENADE IN BLUE see Warren, Harry

SERENADE TO A COQUETTE (CAPRICE) see
  Bridgmont, Leslie

SERENADE TO MOONLIGHT see Chadwick,
  Cecil

SERENADE TO THE MOON see Croudson,
  Henry

SERENADE TRISTE see Cohen, Richard

SERENATA see Vasata, Rudolph Leo,
  Annabella

SHADOW OF YOUR SMILE, THE see Mandel,
  Johnny Alfred

SHADOW SERENADE see May, Hans von

SHADOW SONG, THE see Morgan, Russ

SHAFTESBURY AVENUE see Strachey, J.

SHALOM CHAVARINE
  (Del Borgo, Elliot) orch (med) CPP-
  BEL BF09603, 029156202502     (S49)

SHAPIRO, MARSHA CHUSMIR
  Simple Gifts  *educ
    (gr. II) KJOS pts 0-1056B, sc
    0-1056F     (S50)

SHAWL DANCE see Jalowicz, R.

SHE'LL BE COMIN' ROUND THE MOUNTAIN
  (Ayars, Bo) 3(pic).3(English
  horn).3(bass clar).2. 4.3.3(bass
  trom).1. timp,2perc,harp,strings
  [2'17"] PRESSER     (S51)

SHENANDOAH
  (Ayars, Bo) 3(pic).3(English
  horn).3(bass clar).2. 4.3.3(bass
  trom).1. timp,2perc,harp,strings
  [4'17"] PRESSER     (S52)
  (Goldsmith, Owen) string orch (easy,
  traditional) CPP-BEL BS000118,
  029156102680     (S53)

SHERRY (MALAGUENA) see Green, Philip

SHOE SYMPHONY see Caponegro, John

SHOJO-JI see Rosenhaus

SHORES OF LILLIPUT, THE (PRELUDE) see
  Engleman, Joseph

SHORT OVERTURE, A see Missal, Joshua M.

SIBELIUS, JEAN (1865-1957)
  Finlandia
    (Goldsmith, Owen) orch CPP-BEL
    BF09701, 029156300543     (S54)

SICILIENNE see Faure, Gabriel-Urbain

SIERRA BLANCA see Hinton

SILENT NIGHT
  (Sample, Steve) string orch (med
  easy) CPP-BEL BS000105,
  029156061437     (S55)

SIMPLE GIFTS see Shapiro, Marsha
  Chusmir

SINFONIA see Bach, Johann Sebastian

SINFONIETTA FACILE see Maasz, Gerhard

SING see Raposo, Joseph G.

SINGING STRINGS NO.2 see Ketèlbey,
  Albert William

SINGING STRINGS NO.3 see Aletter,
  William

SINGING STRINGS NO.4 see Squire,
  William Henry

SINGING STRINGS NO.5 see Ketèlbey,
  Albert William

SINGING STRINGS NO.6 see Jenkinson,
  Ezra

SINGING STRINGS NO.8 see Winkler,
  Gerhard

SIR ROGER DE COVERLEY  *educ
  (Krein, Michael) [2'30"] BOSWORTH
       (S56)

SIX EASY PIECES, OP. 22 see Elgar,
  [Sir] Edward (William)

SIX GERMAN DANCES see Beethoven, Ludwig
  van

SIX STRING THINGS see Kunz, Alfred

SKITTY KITTY see Charlton, Dennis

SKYLARK see Carmichael, Hoagy

SLEEPING BEAUTY WALTZ see Tchaikovsky,
  Piotr Ilyich

SLEEPING DOLL, THE see Engleman, Joseph

SLEIGH RIDE see Anderson, Leroy

SLUMBER SONG see Squire, William Henry

SMITH, CLAUDE THOMAS (1932-    )
  Commemoration Fanfare & Chorale
    orch WINGERT set 3030031, sc
    3030032     (S57)

  Declaration Overture
    orch WINGERT set 3030051, sc
    3030052     (S58)

  Fanfare And Celebration
    orch WINGERT set 3030061, sc
    3030062     (S59)

  Flourish, Song And Toccata
    orch WINGERT set 3030081, sc
    3030082     (S60)

  God Of Our Fathers
    orch WINGERT set 3030091, sc
    3030092     (S61)

  Overture For A Celebration
    orch WINGERT set 3032021, sc
    3032022     (S62)

  Prelude On An Early American Folk
  Hymn
    string orch WINGERT set 3033031, sc
    3033032     (S63)

  Suite for String Orchestra
    string orch WINGERT set 3033041, sc
    3033042     (S64)

SMITH, ERIC
  Jack Ashore  *educ
    (Barsotti, Roger) [3'50"] BOSWORTH
       (S65)

SMITH, H. ELLIOTT
  Lion, The  *educ
    [4'] BOSWORTH     (S66)

  Squirrel Dance, The  *educ
    [2'15"] BOSWORTH     (S67)

SMITH, ROBERT W.
  Tangents For Strings
    string orch (very easy) CPP-BEL
    BS09716, 029156609400     (S68)

  Tempest, The
    orch CPP-BEL BF09707, 029156656893
       (S69)

  Where The Black Hawk Soars
    orch CPP-BEL BF09708, 029156656879
       (S70)

SNOW WHITE FANTASY  *educ
  (Herfurth, C. Paul) string orch
  augmented set BOURNE 119610     (S71)

SNOW WHITE (SYMPHONIC SELECTIONS)
  *educ
  (Knight) string orch BOURNE perf mat
  rent     (S72)

SNOWMAN, THE: SUITE see Blake, Howard

SNOWMAN (SUITE) see Blake, Howard,
  Snowman, The: Suite

SOLILOQUY FOR STRINGS see Gillis, Don
  E.

SOLO FLIGHT see Crooke, Sidney

SOLOVIEV-SEDOY, VASSILY PAVLOVICH
  (1907-1979)
  Moscow Nights  *educ
    (Punwar, Katherine W.) (gr. IV)
    KJOS pts 0-1062B, sc 0-1062F

SOLOVIEV-SEDOY, VASSILY PAVLOVICH
  (cont'd.)
       (S73)

SOMERS, HARRY STEWART (1925-    )
  Variations  *educ
    string orch [4'] (for junior high
    string orchestra) sc CANADIAN
    MI 1500 S694VA     (S74)

SONATE see Bach, Johann Sebastian

SONG AT SUNRISE see Hanmer, Ronald

SONG OF A WAYFARER see Mahler, Gustav

SONG OF THE LARP see Amos, Keith

SONG OF THE PRAIRIE see Hofeldt,
  William

SONG OF THE RIVER see Joyce, Archibald

SONGE D'EXTASE see Chuckerbutty,
  Oliphant

SONGS OF CELTIC LANDS  *educ
  (Alshin, Harry A.) string orch (gr.
  II) KENDOR 8055 f.s.
    contains: Ash Grove, The; Blue
    Bells Of Scotland; Girl I Left
    Behind Me, The; Irish Lilt, An;
    John Anderson; When Love Is Kind
       (S75)

SONGS OF ISRAEL  *educ
  (Frost, Robert) string orch (gr. II)
  KENDOR 8057 f.s.
    contains: Artza Alinu; Tzena, Tzena
       (S76)

SONGS OF STEPHEN FOSTER, PART 2  *educ
  (Caponegro) string orch,pno,opt perc
  (gr. I) KENDOR 8616 f.s.
    contains: Jeanie With The Light
    Brown Hair; Nelly Bly; Ring Ring
    The Banjo     (S77)

SOPHISTICATED LADY see Ellington,
  Edward Kennedy (Duke)

SOUND AROUND US, THE see Gold, Marty

SOUNDS FROM HOLLYWOOD (A MEDLEY FOR
  ORCHESTRA)
  (Gold, Marty) orch (med easy) CPP-BEL
  C0302B6X, 029156019575     (S78)

SOUNDSCAPE II see Del Borgo, Elliot A.

SOUTH OF THE BORDER  *educ
  string orch,pno,opt perc BOSWORTH
       (S79)

SOUTH OF THE BORDER SUITE
  (Arnold, Alan) string orch (easy)
  HOLLOW f.s. elementary school level
    contains: Cielito Lindo; Cucaracha,
    La; Raspa, La     (S80)

SOUTHERN NIGHT, A see Chuckerbutty,
  Oliphant

SOUVENIR see Drdla, František (Franz)
  Alois

SOUVENIR D'AMOUR see Chuckerbutty,
  Oliphant

SOUVENIR DE CAPRI (SERENATA) see Becce,
  Giuseppe

SOUVENIR DE MONTE CARLO see Tattenhall,
  Barry

SPANISH DANCE see Schmeling, M.

SPANISH DANCE, NO. 5 see Granados,
  Enrique

SPAZIERGANG IM ZOO see Meyer, H.-E.

SPEEDWAY see Engleman, Harry

SPICK AND SPAN see Engleman, Harry

SPIELMUSIK FÜR STABSPIELER UND
  STREICHER see Schäfer, K.

SPIRIT OF HANUKKAH, THE see Caponegro,
  John

SPIRIT OF THE TOREADOR see Hunt, Harold

SPIRIT OF YOUTH see Gilbert, C.J.

SPOTLIGHT see Cleaver, H. Robinson

SPRING FEVER see Blackmore, George
  Henry James

SQUIRE, WILLIAM HENRY (1871-1963)
  Singing Strings No.4
    see Slumber Song

  Slumber Song  *educ
    orch,vcl solo BOSWORTH     (S81)
    pno-cond sc,pts BOSWORTH 1100 from
    SINGING STRINGS NO.4     (S82)

SQUIRREL DANCE, THE see Smith, H. Elliott

STACCATO PIZZICATO see McLeod

STAMITZ
Allegretto *educ
(Del Borgo) string orch (gr. III)
KENDOR 9779 (S83)

STAMITZ, CARL (1745-1801)
Presto
see Symphony in D

Symphony in D
(Smith, Steven) "Presto" string
orch (gr. III) set JLJ.MUSIC
SO 106 (S84)

STAND BY ME see King, Ben

STANLEY, LEO
Glory Of Arnhem *educ
BOSWORTH (S85)

STAR WARRIORS see Keuning, Ken

STAR WARS see Williams, John T.

STAR WARS (MAIN THEME) see Williams, John T.

STATE PROCESSION see Ketèlbey, Albert William

STATUE OF LIBERTY (MINIATURE OVERTURE) see Engleman, Joseph

STAUDENMAYER, KARIN
Hangin' Out *jazz
string orch (gr. IV) VELKE (S86)

STEADFAST TIN SOLDIER, THE see Amos, Keith

STEELE, HENRY
Knave Of Diamonds *educ
[3'] BOSWORTH (S87)

New Century March *educ
[4'] BOSWORTH (S88)

STEEPLE CHASE see Groitzsch, G.

STEPHAN, RICHARD
Adirondack Sleighride
string orch (gr. II) KJOS pts
SO-94C, sc SO-94F (S89)

Australian Folk Suite
string orch (gr. IV) KJOS pts
SO-123C, sc SO-123F (S90)

Cats And Dogs
string orch (gr. II) KJOS pts
SO-74C, sc SO-74F (S91)

Dance In D
string orch (gr. I) KJOS pts
GSO-93C, sc SO-93F (S92)

Fantasia On A Seventeenth Century Tune
string orch (gr. IV) KJOS pts
SO-124C, sc SO-124F (S93)

Two German Folksongs *educ
string orch (gr. II) KJOS pts
SO-118C, sc SO-118F (S94)

Vanguard Overture *educ
string orch (gr. II) KJOS pts
SO-101C, sc SO-101F (S95)

STILL, STILL, STILL see Hellem, Mark

STIRLING CASTLE see Thiman, Eric Harding

STOLZ, ROBERT (1880-1975)
Easter Parade In Vienna (Waltz, Op. 837) educ
[3'35"] BOSWORTH (S96)

Waltz, Op. 837
see Easter Parade In Vienna

STOMP AND FIDDLE see McLeod

STORM GALOP; MUNICH-VIENNA POLKA see Komzak, Karl

STORY, MICHAEL
Triptych
string orch (very easy) CPP-BEL
BS09718, 029156661101 (S97)

STRACHEY, J.
In Party Mood *educ
[3'15"] BOSWORTH (S98)

Mayfair Parade *educ
[3'15"] BOSWORTH (S99)

STRACHEY, J. (cont'd.)
Pink Champagne *educ
[3'30"] BOSWORTH (S100)

Shaftesbury Avenue *educ
[3'40"] BOSWORTH (S101)

Variety Cavalcade *educ
[3'25"] BOSWORTH (S102)

STRAUSS
Straussiana *educ
(Börschel, Erich) orch,pno solo
[6'] BOSWORTH (S103)

STRAUSS, JOHANN, [JR.] (1825-1899)
Artist's Life *Op.316, educ
(Muller, J. Frederick) (gr. IV)
KJOS pts 0-1037B, sc 0-1037F
(S104)

Blue Danube, The *educ
(Halferty) string orch (gr. II)
KENDOR 8933 (S105)

Emperor Waltz
(Applebaum, Samuel; Ployhar, James)
orch (easy) CPP-BEL C000183,
029156225945 (S106)

Strauss Selection *educ
(Geiger, I.) BOSWORTH (S107)

STRAUSS SELECTION see Geiger, I. see Strauss, Johann, [Jr.]

STRAUSSIANA see Börschel, Erich see Strauss

STRAVINSKY, IGOR (1882-1971)
Berceuse And Finale (from Firebird Suite)
(Isaac, Merle) orch (med easy) CPP-BEL C000137, 029156214451 (S108)

STRICTLY FOR STRADS see Gillis, Don E.

STRING BOUQUET see Niehaus

STRING ROCK BLUES *educ
string orch,pno,opt perc BOSWORTH
(S109)
see Ward, Norman

STRING SCENE see Del Borgo, Elliot A.

STRINGING ALONG see Reynolds, Wynford

STRINGTIDE see Niehaus

STUART, GRAEME
At The Theatre
see Up For The Day (Suite)

Eccentric Courtier *educ
orch,opt 2pno [4'] BOSWORTH (S110)

Excursion Train
see Up For The Day (Suite)

Hampton Court (Minuet)
see Thames Castles (Suite)

Round The Shops
see Up For The Day (Suite)

Thames Castles (Suite) *educ
BOSWORTH f.s.
contains: Hampton Court (Minuet)
[3']; Tower Beefeaters, The
[4']; Windsor Castle (March)
[4'] (S111)

Tower Beefeaters, The
see Thames Castles (Suite)

Up For The Day (Suite) *educ
BOSWORTH f.s.
contains: At The Theatre [3'];
Excursion Train [2']; Round The
Shops [3'] (S112)

Windsor Castle (March)
see Thames Castles (Suite)

SUITA VENEZIANA see Hrábek, J.

SUITE FOR BUDDING STRINGS see Wolf, Artur

SUITE FOR JUNIOR STRING ORCHESTRA see Fodi, John

SUITE FRANCAISE *educ
(Del Borgo) string orch,pno (gr. I)
KENDOR 8705 f.s.
contains: Alouette; Frere Jacques;
Sur Le Pont D'Avignon (S113)

SUITE OF CAROLS see Anderson, Leroy

SUITE OF WESTERN EUROPEAN MUSIC, MOVEMENT 1: FRENCH OVERTURE AND BOURREE see Brandon

SUITE OF WESTERN EUROPEAN MUSIC, MOVEMENT 2: YORKSHIRE WALTZ & STRATHSPEY see Brandon

SUITE OF WESTERN EUROPEAN MUSIC, MOVEMENTS 3 & 4: DUTCH POLKA; NORWEGIAN FOLK SONG see Brandon

SUITE OF WESTERN EUROPEAN MUSIC, MOVEMENT 5: TARANTELLA NAPOLITANA see Brandon

SUITE ON NUMBERS see Gazda, Doris

SULLIVAN, [SIR] ARTHUR SEYMOUR (1842-1900)
Fanfare And March *educ
(Leidig, Vernon) (gr. III) KJOS pts
WO-7B, sc WO-7F (S114)

Lost Chord, The *educ
(Alshin, Harry A.) string orch (gr. II) KENDOR 9226 (S115)

SUMMER TIME IN FONTAINEBLEAU see Hackforth, Norman

SUMMERTIME see Gershwin, George

SUMMON THE HEROES see Williams, John T.

SUNBEAMS AND BUTTERFLIES see Ketèlbey, Albert William

SUNRISE - SLEIGHRIDE see Doolittle, Quentin

SUNSET SERENADE see Kell, Frederick

SUNSET WALTZ see Frost

SUNWARD OVERTURE see Hofeldt, William

SUR LE PONT D'AVIGNON see Suite Francaise

SURDIN, MORRIS (1914-1979)
Five For Four *educ
string orch/strings without db, (strings in first position) sc
CANADIAN (S116)

Group Of Six, A: For Strings In First Position *educ
string orch sc CANADIAN
MI 1500 S961GR (S117)

Who's On Bass *educ
string orch sc CANADIAN
MI 1500 S961WH (S118)

SURPRISE VARIATIONS, THE see Haydn, [Franz] Joseph

SWAN-LAKE BALLET see Tchaikovsky, Piotr Ilyich

SWAN LAKE: THEMES see Tchaikovsky, Piotr Ilyich

SWEET BETSY see Wolf, Artur

SWEET BETSY FROM PIKE
(Ayars, Bo) 3(pic).2(English horn).3(bass clar).2. 4.3.3(bass trom).1. timp,2perc,harp,strings
[4'25"] PRESSER (S119)

SWEET CHARITY *medley
(Holcombe) orch CPP-BEL C0135B6X
(S120)

SWEET DAY, SO COOL *educ
(Revel, Louis) string orch,pno,opt org [4'30"] BOSWORTH (S121)

SYMPHONIC TRIBUTE see Pettersen, Nancy

SYMPHONY FOR YOUTH ORCHESTRA see Pennycook, Bruce

SYMPHONY NO. 2: LARGHETTO [ARR.] see Beethoven, Ludwig van

SYMPHONY NO.41 IN C, PART 1: ALLEGRO VIVACE see Mozart, Wolfgang Amadeus

SYMPHONY NO.41 IN C, PART 2: ANDANTE CANTABILE see Mozart, Wolfgang Amadeus

SYMPHONY NO.41 IN C, PART 3: MENUETTO see Mozart, Wolfgang Amadeus

SYMPHONY NO.41 IN C, PART 4: MOLTO ALLEGRO see Mozart, Wolfgang Amadeus

SYNCOPATED CLOCK, THE see Anderson, Leroy

# T

TABLE MUSIC see Mozart, Wolfgang Amadeus

TABLEAU VIVANT see Niehaus

TAKE FIVE see Brubeck, David (Dave)
Warren see Desmond, Paul

TALES FROM A FAIRY BOOK: SUITE see Engleman, Joseph

TANGENTS FOR STRINGS see Smith, Robert W.

TANGO COCKTAIL, PART 1 see Geiger, I.

TANGO COCKTAIL, PART 2 see Geiger, I.

TANGO COCKTAIL, PART 3 see Geiger, I.

TANK TOWN see Plater, D.J.

TANNENBAUM FANTASIA see Goldsmith, Owen

TÄNZE DER RENAISSANCE  *educ
  (Schwindt) string orch sc,pts
  HEINRICH 3667                    (T1)

TATTENHALL, BARRY
  April Day  *educ
  [2'30"] BOSWORTH                 (T2)

  Heyday  *educ
  [2'40"] BOSWORTH                 (T3)

  Souvenir De Monte Carlo  *educ
  [2'50"] BOSWORTH                 (T4)

TCHAIKOVSKY, PIOTR ILYICH (1840-1893)
  Andantino Marziale (from Symphony No.
    2 In C Minor, first Mvt.)
    (Goldsmith, Owen) string orch (med
    easy) CPP-BEL BS000072,
    029156695984                   (T5)

  Chanson Triste
    (Cechvala, Al) string orch (gr.
    III) VELKE                     (T6)

  Elegy
    see Serenade for Strings,Third
    Movement

  Francesca Da Rimini  *educ
    (Muller, J. Frederick) (gr. V) KJOS
    pts O-1022B, sc O-1022F        (T7)

  Nutcracker, The: Themes  *educ
    (McLeod, James "Red") string orch
    KJOS pts GSO-8C, sc GSO-8F     (T8)

  Nutcracker Ballet, Set 1
    (Isaac, Merle) orch (med diff,
    contains Dance Of The Sugar Plum
    Fairy & Waltz Of The Flowers)
    CPP-BEL C000154, 029156197914  (T9)

  Nutcracker Ballet, Set 2
    (Isaac, Merle) orch (med diff,
    contains March Of The Nutcracker
    & Trepak) CPP-BEL C000155,
    029156174595                   (T10)

  Pezzo
    see Serenade for Strings,First
    Movement

  Romance
    (Goldsmith, Owen) orch (easy) CPP-
    BEL C000218, 029156109788      (T11)

  Romeo And Juliet  *educ
    (Muller, J. Frederick) (gr. IV)
    KJOS pts O-1019B, sc O-1019F   (T12)

  Scherzo Pizzicato
    (Frost, Robert) string orch (gr.
    IV) KJOS pts SO-41C, sc SO-41F (T13)

  Serenade for Strings,First Movement
    *educ
    (Del Borgo) "Pezzo" string orch
    (gr. III) KENDOR 9873          (T14)

  Serenade for Strings,Second Movement
    *educ
    (Del Borgo) "Waltz" string orch
    (gr. III) KENDOR 9874          (T15)

  Serenade for Strings,Third Movement
    *educ
    (Del Borgo) "Elegy" string orch
    (gr. III) KENDOR 9875          (T16)

  Serenade for Strings,Fourth Movement
    *educ
    (Del Borgo) "Tema Russo" string
    orch (gr. III) KENDOR 9876     (T17)

TCHAIKOVSKY, PIOTR ILYICH (cont'd.)
  Sleeping Beauty Waltz
    (Isaac, Merle) orch (med diff) CPP-
    BEL C000165, 029156301151      (T18)

  Swan-Lake Ballet  *educ
    (Charrosin, F.G.) [7'] BOSWORTH
                                   (T19)

  Swan Lake: Themes  *educ
    (Halferty) string orch (gr. II)
    KENDOR 9555                    (T20)

  Tema Russo
    see Serenade for Strings,Fourth
    Movement

  Tschaikowski Fantasie  *educ
    (Foulds, John H.) [15'] BOSWORTH
                                   (T21)

  Waltz
    see Serenade for Strings,Second
    Movement

TELEMANN, GEORG PHILIPP (1681-1767)
  Allegro From Sonata No. 1
    see Sonata No. 1,First Movement

  Baroque Andante And Allegro (from Six
    Canonic Sonatas) educ
    (Del Borgo) string orch (gr. III)
    KENDOR 9787                    (T22)

  Chaconne, [arr.]  *educ
    (Bauernschmidt, Robert) orch
    SHAWNEE augmented set J 0105, sc
    JC 0415, pt JC 0416            (T23)

  Overture in G  *educ
    orch SHAWNEE augmented set J 0113,
    sc JC 0439, pt JC 0440         (T24)

  Sonata No. 1,First Movement
    (Mosier) "Allegro From Sonata No.
    1" string orch KJOS pts SO-126C,
    sc SO-126F                     (T25)

TEMA RUSSO see Tchaikovsky, Piotr
  Ilyich, Serenade for Strings,Fourth
  Movement

TEMPEST, THE see Smith, Robert W.

TENACITY see Barsotti, Roger

TEQUILA
  (Sayre, Chuck) orch WARNER F09711,
  029156605587                     (T26)

TEQUILA (PASO DOBLE) see Green, Philip

TERRA see Carloséma, Bernard

THAMES CASTLES (SUITE) see Stuart, Graeme

THEME AND EXCURSIONS see Benson, Warren Frank

THEME FROM ICE CASTLES see Hamlisch, Marvin F.

THEME FROM ICE CASTLES (THROUGH THE
  EYES OF LOVE) see Hamlisch, Marvin
  F.

THEME FROM NEW YORK, NEW YORK see
  Kander, John

THEMES FROM 007 (A MEDLEY FOR
  ORCHESTRA)
  (Custer, Calvin) orch (med) CPP-BEL
  C0156B7X, 029156134841           (T27)

THEN AND NOW see Bowie, Gordon

THIMAN, ERIC HARDING (1900-1975)
  By Rock-Bound Coast
    see Highland Scenes (Three Pieces)

  Highland Festival
    see Highland Scenes (Three Pieces)

  Highland Scenes (Three Pieces)  *educ
    BOSWORTH f.s.
    contains: By Rock-Bound Coast
    [3']; Highland Festival
    [1'45"]; In The Heather [2'45"]
                                   (T28)

  In The Heather
    see Highland Scenes (Three Pieces)

  Stirling Castle  *educ
    [6'] BOSWORTH                  (T29)

THIS IS IT (from The Bugs Bunny Show)
  (Cerulli, Bob) string orch (very
  easy) CPP-BEL SO9511, 029156179392 (T30)

THORTON, R.S.
  Legions Of The Air  *educ
  [3'30"] BOSWORTH                 (T31)

THOSE FAR AWAY HILLS see King, Reginald

THREE AMERICAN SKETCHES: SUITE see
  Engleman, Joseph

THREE BACH MINUETS see Bach, Johann
  Sebastian

THREE CANADIAN FOLK SONGS see Kunz,
  Alfred

THREE CHINESE SCENES see Alshin

THREE CLASSICAL PIECES see Gange,
  Kenneth

THREE CORELLI DANCES see Corelli,
  Arcangelo

THREE DANCES see Wiggins, Christopher
  D.

THREE EASY PIECES see Phillips, Burrill

THREE ECHOES see Matthews, Michael

THREE LITTLE PIECES see Komzak, Karl

THREE MELODIES FROM THE BRITISH ISLES
  see Cechvala, Al, Editor

THREE MINIATURES FOR STRINGS see Pepin,
  Clermont

THREE SONGS FOR CHANUKAH  *educ
  (Shapiro, Marsha Chusmir) string orch
  (gr. II) KJOS pts SO-68C, sc SO-68F
                                   (T32)

THREE TUNES FOR STRINGS see Adaskin,
  Murray

THROUGH THE EYES OF LOVE see Hamlisch,
  Marvin F., Theme From Ice Castles
  see Hamlisch, Marvin F., Theme From
  Ice Castles (Through The Eyes Of
  Love)

TIBETAN PROFESSIONAL see Halen, Walter
  J.

TICO-TICO
  (Gold, Marty) orch WARNER F09710,
  029156603927                     (T33)

TIGER RAG  *educ
  (McLeod) string orch,pno (gr. III)
  KENDOR 9923                      (T34)

TIME OF MY LIFE (I'VE HAD THE)
  (Cerulli, Bob) orch (easy) CPP-BEL
  2874TB7X, 029156687187           (T35)

TINTINABULATIONS see Punwar, Katherine

TO REMEMBER see Coleman, Todd

TOCCATINA see Hofeldt, William

TORCH BURNS BRIGHT, THE see Clark,
  Larry

TOWER BEEFEATERS, THE see Stuart,
  Graeme

TOY TOWN TATTOO see Jordan, Herberte

TRANSLATEUR, S.
  Wedding In Lilliput  *educ
  [4'15"] BOSWORTH                 (T36)

TRAUMEREI see Schumann, Robert
  (Alexander)

TRIBUTE TO HENRY MANCINI, A see
  Mancini, Henry

TRIBUTE TO THE THREE B'S, A  *educ
  (Anderson, Gerald) string orch (gr.
  I) KJOS pts SO-103C, sc SO-103F  (T37)

TRICKSY see Charrosin, F.G.

TRIPTYCH see Story, Michael

TRIPTYCHON FÜR STREICHORCHESTER see
  Fleischer, H.

TROIKA see Prokofiev, Serge

TROLL
  2.2.2.2.alto sax. 4.4.3.1. timp,
  2perc,strings [5'] STIM sc H-2782,
  pts A-408                        (T38)

TRUMPET CALL see Fucik, Julius

TRUMPET VOLUNTARY see Purcell, Henry

TRUMPETER'S LULLABY, A see Anderson,
  Leroy

TRYPTICH FOR STRINGS see Del Borgo,
  Elliot A.

TSCHAIKOWSKI FANTASIE see Foulds, John
  Herbert see Tchaikovsky, Piotr
  Ilyich

TSCHAIKOWSKY, PJOTR ILJITSCH
see TCHAIKOVSKY, PIOTR ILYICH

TUDOR MUSIC ROOM, THE see Redman,
Reginald

TUNING A-ROUND see Bell, Richard

TURKISH PATROL, THE see Michaelis

TWILIGHT RAPTURE see Rapley, Felton

TWINKLE-TOES see Raeburn, Hugh

TWIST AND SHOUT
(Cerulli, Bob) string orch (very
easy) WARNER S09706, 029156659412
(T39)

TWISTED KEEL see Moore, John W.

TWISTER see Mancina, Mark

TWO CAKEWALKS BY CLAUDE DEBUSSY see
Debussy, Claude

TWO FRENCH MINIATURES see Ravel,
Maurice

TWO GERMAN FOLKSONGS see Stephan,
Richard

TWO IRISH REELS  *educ
(Hartley, Fred) [2'30"] BOSWORTH
(T40)
(Terry, Ray) BOSWORTH          (T41)

TWO LATE ROMANTIC PIECES
(Cechvala, Al) string orch (gr. III)
VELKE f.s.
contains: Fibich, Zdenek (Zdenko),
Poem; Scriabin, Alexander,
Prelude, Op. 11, No. 6      (T42)

TWO MINUETS BY HAYDN see Haydn, [Franz]
Joseph

TWO MOODS IN THE MORNING see Frost

TWO PIECES FOR YOUNG ORCHESTRA (RONDO
AND COUNTRY DANCE
(Applebaum, Samuel) orch (easy) CPP-
BEL C000186, 029156695953    (T43)

TWO SEA SONGS see Dohm, Robert

TWO SEVENTEENTH CENTURY DANCES see
Purcell, Henry

TWO SONGS OF PRAISE  *educ
(Alshin, Harry A.) string orch (gr.
III) KENDOR 9932          (T44)

TZENA, TZENA see Songs Of Israel

## U

UKRAINIAN BELL CAROL  *educ
(Caponegro) "Carol Of The Bells"
string orch,pno,opt perc (gr. I)
KENDOR 8803                (U1)

UKRAINIAN SKETCHES see Goldsmith, Owen

UN BEL DI, VEDREMO see Puccini, Giacomo

UNGAR, JAY
Ashokan Farewell
(Custer, Calvin) string orch WARNER
WBS09401, 029156080421    (U2)

UP FOR THE DAY (SUITE) see Stuart,
Graeme

UP NORTH: PHANTASY see Croudson, Henry

UP ON THE HOUSETOP AND ICICLES see
Hanby, B.R.

UP WITH THE LARK see King, Reginald

UPSTAIRS DOWNSTAIRS (WALTZ THEME) see
Faris, Alexander

## V

VALENTINI
Concerto for String Orchestra in G,
Op. 7, No. 6  *educ
string orch,opt cont sc,pts
HEINRICH 1163              (V1)

VALSE APPASSIONATA see Rais, M.,
Anouschka

VALSE CAPRICIEUSE see Richartz, Willy

VALSE LENT see Rapley, Felton, Twilight
Rapture

VALSE SERENADE see Poldini, Ede
(Eduard)

VANGELIS
Chariots Of Fire  *educ
(Jennings) string orch,opt combo
(gr. II) LEONARD-US 04626046 (V2)

VANGUARD OVERTURE see Stephan, Richard

VARIATIONS A COMIN' see Frost

VARIATIONS ON A GROUND BASS THEME see
Purcell, Henry

VARIATIONS ON A WELL-KNOWN SEA CHANTEY
*educ
(Stephan, Richard) string orch (gr.
III) KJOS pts SO-86C, sc SO-86F
(V3)

VARIETY CAVALCADE see Strachey, J.

VASATA, RUDOLPH LEO
Annabella  *educ
(Leopold, B.) "Serenata" [4']
BOSWORTH                   (V4)

Serenata
see Annabella

VELKE, FRITZ
Adagietto For Strings
string orch (gr. IV) VELKE    (V5)

Fancy Fiddles
string orch (gr. III) VELKE   (V6)

Peaches And Skim Milk
string orch (gr. III) VELKE   (V7)

Serenade For Rosemary
string orch (gr. IV) VELKE    (V8)

Suite for String Orchestra
string orch (gr. V, in 4 movements)
VELKE                      (V9)

VERDI, GIUSEPPE (1813-1901)
Aida: Ballet Music
(Isaac, Merle) orch (med diff) CPP-
BEL C000159, 029156044027  (V10)

Viva Verdi
(Goldsmith, Owen) orch (med easy)
CPP-BEL C000217, 029156112948
(V11)

VINTER, GILBERT (1909-1969)
Alla Cueca
see Latin America (Suite)

Alla Rumba
see Latin America (Suite)

Celtic Lilt  *educ
[4'] BOSWORTH              (V12)

Lamento
see Latin America (Suite)

Latin America (Suite)  *educ
BOSWORTH f.s.
contains: Alla Cueca [2']; Alla
Rumba [3']; Lamento [3'] (V13)

VISIT TO THE INSECT ZOO, A: SUITE see
Bick, H.

VIVA VERDI see Verdi, Giuseppe

VIVA VIVALDI see Goldsmith, Owen

VIVALDI, ANTONIO (1678-1741)
Beatus Vir: Excerpts  *educ
(Daniels) "Excerpts From Beatus
Vir" string orch (gr. III) KENDOR
9815                       (V14)

Excerpts From Beatus Vir
see Beatus Vir: Excerpts

VOCALISE see Rachmaninoff, Sergey
Vassilievich

VOGELHANDLER, DER see Zeller, Carl

VOODOO see Green, Philip

VOSS, CARL
Divertimento in C *educ
(Gr. VI) KJOS pts O-1068C, sc
O-1068F                    (V15)

VOYAGE TO LILLIPUT: A (SUITE) see
Engleman, Joseph

# W

WABASH CANNON BALL
(Gillespie) string orch LEONARD-US
00864026                    (W1)

WAGENSEIL, GEORG CHRISTOPH (1715-1777)
Sinfonia for String Orchestra and
Continuo, WV 7, in A
LIENAU sc RL 40340, pts
RL 40341-44, kbd pt RL 40345 (W2)

Sinfonia for String Orchestra and
Continuo, WV 16, in D
LIENAU sc RL 40350, pts
RL 40351-54, kbd pt RL 40355 (W3)

WAGNER, ALFRED (1918-    )
Overture *educ
0.0.0.0. 0.3.3.0. 8vln I,7vln II,
6vla,5vcl,4db,opt timp [5'] sc
PETERS 03330                (W4)

WAGNER, RICHARD (1813-1883)
Prize Song (from Die Meistersinger
Von Nürnberg) educ
(Gold) [5'] BOSWORTH        (W5)

WALKERVILLE SUITE, THE see Crawley,
Clifford

WALLER, THOMAS (FATS) (1904-1943)
Ain't Misbehavin' (composed with
Razaf, Andy (Andrea Paul
Razafkeriefo); Brooks, Harry)
(Cerulli, Bob) orch (easy) CPP-BEL
2758AB7X, 029156111279     (W6)
(Custer, Calvin) string orch (med)
WARNER SO9502, 029156177336 (W7)

WALLIN, PETER (1964-    )
Impulse 3
marimba,string orch,horn solo STIM
                           (W8)

WALT DISNEY *educ
(Short) [Eng/It] chamber orch sc,pts
RICORDI-IT 137283          (W9)

WALTZ see Tchaikovsky, Piotr Ilyich,
Serenade for Strings,Second
Movement

WALTZ IN A MAJOR
(Goldsmith, Owen) string orch (med
diff) CPP-BEL BS09706, 029156298949
                           (W10)

WALTZING CAT, THE see Anderson, Leroy

WALTZING THRO' OLD VIENNA see Geiger,
I.

WARD, NORMAN
String Rock Blues
string orch (easy, elementary
school level) HOLLOW       (W11)

WARD, SAMUEL AUGUSTUS
America, The Beautiful *educ
(Scott, Paul) (gr. IV) KJOS pts
O-1069B, sc O-1069F        (W12)

WARREN, HARRY (1893-1981)
Chattanooga Choo Choo
(Cerulli, Bob) orch (med easy)
WARNER FO9614, 029156215298 (W13)

Serenade In Blue
(Gold, Marty) orch (med easy)
WARNER WBFO9413, 029156109801
                           (W14)

WASHBURN, ROBERT BROOKS (1928-    )
Caravelle Overture
orch (med easy) CPP-BEL C000215,
029156112191               (W15)

Ceremonial Procession
orch (med) CPP-BEL BFO9504,
029156171297               (W16)

Clarkson Centennial Overture
orch (med) CPP-BEL BFO9606,
029156204766               (W17)

It's The Pizz.!
string orch (med easy) CPP-BEL
BS09502, 029156170849      (W18)

Knightsbridge Suite
string orch (med) CPP-BEL BS000100,
029156048810               (W19)

Londonderry Suite
string orch (med easy) CPP-BEL
BS000107, 029156097795     (W20)

New England Holiday
orch (med diff) CPP-BEL C000209,
029156005158               (W21)

WASHBURN, ROBERT BROOKS (cont'd.)
Queen Noor Suite
string orch (med diff) CPP-BEL
BS000089, 029156001631     (W22)

Scottish Fantasy
orch (med) CPP-BEL C000213,
029156049916               (W23)

WASHERWOMAN'S HOLIDAY see Inzana,
Barbara

WATER MUSIC: SUITE NO. 3 IN G see
Handel, George Frideric

WEBB, JIMMY LAYNE (1946-    )
Macarthur Park
(Cerulli, Bob) string orch (easy)
CPP-BEL 0414MB4X, 029156003055
                           (W24)

WEBBER, ANDREW LLOYD
see LLOYD WEBBER, ANDREW

WEBER, CARL MARIA VON (1786-1826)
Chorus Of Huntsmen (from Der
Freischütz) educ
(Gordon, Philip) string orch BOURNE
augmented set 022880, set 022830,
sc 022834                  (W25)

WEDDING IN LILLIPUT see Translateur, S.

WEDGWOOD BLUE see Ketèlbey, Albert
William

WEILL, KURT (1900-1950)
Mack The Knife (from The Threepenny
Opera) educ
string orch,pno,opt perc BOSWORTH
                           (W26)
(Arnold, Alan) string orch (easy,
elementary school level) HOLLOW
                           (W27)
(Cerulli, Bob) orch (med easy) CPP-
BEL FO9513, 029156179361   (W28)
(Sayre, Chuck) orch (med diff)
WARNER WBFO9307, 029156070194
                           (W29)

WEINACHTSWEISEN *CC20U,Xmas,educ
(Majewski) vln I,vln II,vla/vln III,
vcl,opt pno sc,pts HEINRICH 6083
f.s.                       (W30)

WELTLICHE STÜCKE: THREE SUITES see
Witzendorff, H.

WENN WIR IN HÖCHSTEN NOTEN SEIN:
CHORALE PRELUDE see Bach, Johann
Sebastian

WEXFORD CIRCLE see Del Borgo, Elliot A.

WHAT CHILD IS THIS?
(Cerulli, Bob) orch (intermediate
level) WARNER FO9716, 029156607178
                           (W31)

WHAT'S NEW?
(Custer, Calvin) string orch,tenor
sax/alto sax solo (med) WARNER
SO9608, 029156213836       (W32)
(Gold, Marty) orch (med) CPP-BEL
FO9504, 029156173352       (W33)

WHEN LOVE IS KIND see Songs Of Celtic
Lands

WHEN SHADOWS FALL see Williams, A.

WHEN THE ICEWORMS NEST AGAIN see
Adaskin, Murray

WHEN THE VIOLINS ARE PLAYING (TANGO)
see Love, Henry

WHEN YOU ARE WITH ME (TANGO) see Krug,
E.A.

WHEN YOU WISH UPON A STAR see Arlen,
Harold

WHERE THE BLACK HAWK SOARS see Smith,
Robert W.

WHIRLING LEAVES (INTERMEZZO) see Ewing,
Montague

WHISKERS see Niehaus

WHITE, ANDREW NATHANIEL
Jazz Concerto, A: For Alto Saxophone
And Chamber Orchestra
1.1.1.1. 1.1.1.1. timp,perc,3vln I,
3vln II,2vla,2vcl,2db,alto sax
solo [25'] (med diff) set,sc,pts,
solo pt,pno red ANDREW 41C (W34)

Jazz Concerto, A: For Alto Saxophone
And Symphony Orchestra
2.2.2.2. 4.3.3.1. timp,3perc,5vln
I,5vln II,4vla,4vcl,3db,alto sax
solo [25'] (med diff, in three
movements: 1. Cool And Spiffy 2.
Dream Boogie 3. Slow Down,
Sweetie!) set,sc,pts,solo pt,pno
red ANDREW 41A             (W35)

WHITE, ANDREW NATHANIEL (cont'd.)

Jazz Concerto, A: For Alto Saxophone And Youth Symphony Orchestra 2.2.2.2. 4.3.3.1. timp,3perc,5vln I,5vln II,4vla,4vcl,3db,alto sax solo [25'] (med diff, in three movements: 1. Cool And Spiffy 2. Dream Boogie 3. Slow Down, Sweetie!) set,sc,pts,solo pt,pno red ANDREW 41B (W36)

WHITE BLUE see Zeller-Bauckner

WHITE CLIFFS see Richardson, Clive

WHITE MOUNTAINS see Hinton, Sierra Blanca

WHO'S ON BASS see Surdin, Morris

WIGGINS, ARTHUR M. (1920-    )
Red Carpet, The
orch (med diff) CPP-BEL C000194
(W37)

WIGGINS, CHRISTOPHER D.
Fanfare For The Third  *educ
(gr. III) KJOS pts GO-106B, sc
GO-106F (W38)

Three Dances  *educ
string orch (gr. I) KJOS pts
GSO-14C, sc GSO-14F (W39)

WILLIAMS, A.
Barcarolle
see When Shadows Fall

Dancing Moonbeams  *educ
orch,opt xylo solo [2'30"] BOSWORTH
(W40)

Fairy Of The Glen  *educ
(Engleman, Joseph) [3'] BOSWORTH
(W41)

When Shadows Fall (Barcarolle) educ
[3'] BOSWORTH (W42)

WILLIAMS, JOHN T. (1932-    )
Cowboys Overture, The
LEONARD-US pts 04490060, sc
04490061 (W43)

Empire Strikes Back Medley, The
(Whitney, John) orch (concert
level) WARNER F09718,
029156609387 (W44)

Home Alone: Three Holiday Songs
LEONARD-US pts 04490038, sc
04490039 (W45)

Olympic Spirit, The  *educ
LEONARD-US pts 04490040, sc
04490041 (W46)
(Lavender) string orch,opt combo
(gr. II) LEONARD-US 04626044
(W47)
Star Wars
LEONARD-US pts 04490056, sc
04490057 (W48)

Star Wars (Main Theme)
(Sayre, Chuck) orch (concert level)
WARNER F09717, 029156607840 (W49)

Summon The Heroes  *educ
LEONARD-US pts 04490036, sc
04490037 (W50)
(Custer) (gr. III) LEONARD-US
04490034 (W51)
(Custer) string orch,opt combo (gr.
II) LEONARD-US 04626048 (W52)
(Higgins) string orch LEONARD-US
00864024 (W53)

WILLOW WEEP FOR ME
(Custer, Calvin) string orch,fl solo
(med easy) WARNER S09512,
029156179958 (W54)

WILSON, BRIAN
Fun, Fun, Fun (composed with Love,
Mike)
(Cerulli, Bob) string orch (very
easy) CPP-BEL 6730FB4X,
029156679960 (W55)

Help Me Rhonda
(Cerulli, Bob) orch (easy) CPP-BEL
1567HB7X, 029156111392 (W56)

I Get Around
(Cerulli, Bob) string orch (easy)
CPP-BEL 2013IB4X (W57)

WILSON, THOMAS (1927-    )
Concerto for Violin
2.2.2.2. 4.3.3.1. timp,3perc,pno/
cel,harp,strings [26'] (for youth
orchestra) QUEENSGATE (W58)

WIND BENEATH MY WINGS, THE see Henley,
Larry

WINDSOR CASTLE (MARCH) see Stuart,
Graeme

WING COMMANDER see Jordan, Herberte

WINKLER, GERHARD
Neapolitan Serenade  *educ
[3'30"] BOSWORTH (W59)
pno-cond sc,pts BOSWORTH 1104 from
SINGING STRINGS NO.8 (W60)

Singing Strings No.8
see Neapolitan Serenade

WINTER IST VERGANGEN, DER: THEME AND
VARIATIONS see Erdlen, Hermann

WINTER WONDERLAND see Bernard, Felix

WITH BLUE BROCADE AND DAINTY SHOE see
Saunders, Max

WITH GAMBOLLING GAIT see Mackey,
Percival

WITH HONOUR CROWNED see Ketèlbey,
Albert William

WITZENDORFF, H.
Weltliche Stücke: Three Suites  *educ
(Roos) string orch,cont HEINRICH
sc,pts 2123, pts 2123A (W61)

WIZARD OF OZ, THE
(Sayre, Chuck) orch WARNER F09707,
029156300000 (W62)

WIZARD OF OZ, THE: TWO SELECTIONS
(Cerulli, Bob) orch (med easy,
contains Over The Rainbow & We're
Off To See The Wizard) CPP-BEL
C0198B7X, 029156218169 (W63)

WOLF, ARTUR
Indian Moods March For Budding
Strings
string orch VELKE (W64)

Polka For Budding Strings
string orch VELKE (W65)

Suite For Budding Strings
string orch (in 3 movements) VELKE
(W66)
Sweet Betsy
string orch (variation for each
instrument) VELKE (W67)

WOLTERS, GOTTFRIED (1910-1989)
Birthday Serenade  *educ
pno-cond sc,pts BOSWORTH BOE 4067
(W68)

WONDER, STEVIE
see MORRIS, STEVLAND

WOOD, HAYDN (1882-1959)
Roving Fancies  *educ
[3'45"] BOSWORTH (W69)

WRENS' SERENADE see Engleman, Joseph

WYRE, JOHN (1941-    )
First Flower  *educ
2.2.2.2. 2.2.3.1. timp,3perc,pno,
harp,strings sc CANADIAN
MI 1100 W993NY (W70)

# Y

YANKEE DOODLE (GALOP) see Engleman,
Joseph

YE BANKS AN' BRAES  *educ
(Revel, Louis) string orch,pno,opt
org [3'45"] BOSWORTH (Y1)

YELLOW ROSE OF TEXAS, THE  *educ
(Ayars, Bo) 3(pic).3(English
horn).3(bass clar).2. 4.3.3(bass
trom).1. timp,2perc,harp,strings
[3'17"] PRESSER (Y2)
(Klotman, Robert) (gr. I) KJOS pts
GO-110C, sc GO-110F (Y3)
(McLeod) string orch,pno (gr. III)
KENDOR 9943 (Y4)

Y'ME HACHANUKA see Hanukkah Favorites

YON, PIETRO ALESSANDRO (1886-1943)
Gesu Bambino  *educ
(Wieloszynski) string orch,pno,vln&
vcl soli (gr. III) KENDOR 9826
(Y5)

YOU ARE THE SUNSHINE OF MY LIFE see
Morris, Stevland (Stevie Wonder)

YOU DO SOMETHING TO ME
(Sayre, Chuck) orch (med diff) WARNER
F09501, 029156173307 (Y6)

YOU MUST LOVE ME see Lloyd Webber,
Andrew

YOUNG BARTOK SUITE, A  *educ
(Alshin, Harry A.) string orch (gr.
II) KENDOR 8095 f.s.
contains: Burlesque; Dance Of The
Flies; Frolic Song; Maypole
Dance; Ruthenian Song (Y7)

YOUNG MOZART, THE  *educ
(Alshin, Harry A.) string orch (gr.
II) KENDOR 9776 (Y8)

YOUTHFUL DAYS (SUITE) see King,
Reginald

YRADIER, SEBASTIAN (1809-1865)
Paloma, La  *educ
(Charrosin, F.G.) [4'] BOSWORTH
(Y9)

YULETIDE CAROLS  *educ
(Williamson, Richard) string orch
(gr. III) KJOS pts SO-79C, sc
SO-79F (Y10)

# Z

ZAMPA OVERTURE see Herold, Louis-
    Joseph-Ferdinand

ZELLER, CARL (1842-1898)
  Bird Seller, The
    see Vogelhandler, Der

  Vogelhandler, Der  *educ
    "Bird Seller, The" [10'] BOSWORTH
                            (Z1)

ZELLER-BAUCKNER
  White Blue (from The Birdseller) educ
    [5'] BOSWORTH          (Z2)

ZEPHIR see Hubay, Jenö

ZWEI KAMMERWERKE see Haydn, [Franz]
    Joseph

# Publisher Directory

The list of publishers which follows contains the code assigned for each publisher, the name and address of the publisher, and U.S. agents who distribute the publications. This is the master list for the Music-in-Print series and represents all publishers who have submitted information for inclusion in the series. Therefore, all of the publishers do not necessarily occur in the present volume.

This list is organized by publisher code. When a name and code are not listed in their usual or expected places, cross references are provided to easily locate the publisher. Since publishers may have addresses in several different countries, those addresses are located under a single publisher code.

| Code | Publisher | U.S. Agent |
|------|-----------|------------|
| A COEUR JOIE | Éditions A Coeur Joie<br>Les Passerelles, BP 9151<br>24 avenue Joannés Masset<br>F-69263 Lyon cédex 09<br>France | |
| A MOLL DUR | A Moll Dur Publishing House | |
| A-R ED | A-R Editions, Inc.<br>801 Deming Way<br>Madison, WI 53717 | |
| AAP | Edition AAP (Audio Attic Productions)<br>Aas-Wangsvei 8<br>N-1600 Fredrikstad<br>Norway | |
| ABC | ABC Music Co. | BOURNE |
| ABERBACH | The Aberbach Group<br>988 Madison Avenue<br>New York, NY 10021 | |
| ABERDEEN | Aberdeen Music, Inc.<br>170 N.E. 33rd Street<br>Fort Lauderdale, FL 33334 | PLYMOUTH |
| ABINGDON | Abingdon Press<br>P.O. Box 801<br>Nashville, TN 37202 | |
| ABRSM | Associated Board of the Royal<br>Schools of Music<br>14 Bedford Square<br>London WC1B 3JG<br>England | PRESSER |
| ACADEMIA | Academia Music Ltd.<br>16-5, Hongo 3-Chome<br>Bunkyo-ku<br>Tokyo, 113<br>Japan | KALMUS,A |
| ACCORDO | Edizioni Accordo | CURCI |
| ACCURA | Accura Music<br>P.O. Box 4260<br>Athens, OH 45701-4260 | |
| ACSB | Antigua Casa Sherry-Brener, Ltd.<br>of Madrid<br>3145 West 63rd Street<br>Chicago, IL 60629 | |
| ADAMS | D. Adams Music<br>P.O. Box 8371<br>Asheville, NC 28814 | |

| Code | Publisher | U.S. Agent |
|------|-----------|------------|
| ADD.-WESLEY | Addison-Wesley Publishing Co., Inc.<br>2725 Sand Hill Road<br>Menlo Park, CA 94025 | |
| ADDINGTON | Addington Press | ROYAL |
| AEOLUS | Aeolus Publishing Co.<br>60 Park Terrace West<br>New York, NY 10034 | |
| AGAPE | Agape | HOPE |
| AGEHR | American Guild of English Handbell<br>Ringers, Inc. | LORENZ |
| AHLINS | Ahlins Musikförlag<br>Box 26072<br>S-100 41 Stockholm<br>Sweden | |
| AHN | Ahn & Simrock<br>Sonnenstraße 19<br>D-8 München<br>Germany | |
| AKAD.D&V | Akademische Druck- und<br>Verlagsanstalt<br>Schönaugasse 6<br>A-8010 Graz<br>Austria | |
| AKADEMISKA | Akademiska Musikförlaget<br>Sirkkalagatan 7 B 41<br>SF-20500 Abo 50<br>Finland | |
| ALBERSEN | Muziekhandel Albersen & Co.<br>Groot Hertoginnelaan 182<br>NL-2517 EV Den Haag<br>Netherlands | DONEMUS |
| ALBERT | J. Albert & Son Pty. Ltd.<br>139 King Street<br>Sydney 2000, N.S.W.<br>Australia<br><br>J. Albert & Son - U.S.A.<br>1619 Broadway<br>New York, NY 10019 | |
| ALCOVE | Alcove Music | WESTERN |
| ALEXANDRIA | Alexandria House<br>see BRENTWOOD | |
| ALFRED | Alfred Publishing Co.<br>16380 Roscoe Blvd.<br>P.O. Box 10003<br>Van Nuys, CA 91410-0003 | |

| Code | Publisher | U.S. Agent |
|------|-----------|------------|
| ALKOR | Alkor Edition | FOR.MUS.DIST |
| ALLAIRE | Allaire Music Publications<br>93 Gooseneck Point Road<br>Oceanport, NJ 07757 | |
| ALLANS | Allans Music Australia Ltd.<br>P.O. Box 4072<br>Richmond East<br>Victoria 3121<br>Australia | PRESSER |
| ALLEN | William Allen Music, Inc.<br>P.O. Box 790<br>Newington, VA 22122-0790 | |
| ALLIA | Alliance Publications, Inc.<br>9171 Spring Road<br>Fish Creek, WI 54212-9619 | |
| ALLOWAY | Alloway Publications<br>P.O.Box 25<br>Santa Monica, CA 90406 | |
| ALMITRA | Almitra | KENDOR |
| ALMO | Almo Publications | WARNER |
| ALPEG | Alpeg | PETERS |
| ALPHENAAR | W. Alphenaar<br>Kruisweg 47-49<br>NL-2011 LA Haarlem<br>Netherlands | |
| ALPUERTO | Editorial Alpuerto<br>Caños del Peral 7<br>28013 Madrid<br>Spain | |
| ALSBACH | G. Alsbach & Co.<br>P.O. Box 338<br>NL-1400 AH Bussum<br>Netherlands | |
| ALSBACH&D | Alsbach & Doyer | |
| AM.COMP.ALL. | American Composers Alliance<br>170 West 74th Street<br>New York, NY 10023 | |
| | American Guild of English Handbell<br>Ringers, Inc.<br>see AGEHR | LORENZ |
| AM.INST.MUS. | American Institute of Musicology | FOSTER |
| AM.MUS.ED. | American Music Edition<br>263 East Seventh Street<br>New York, NY 10009 | PRESSER<br>(partial) |
| AMADEUS | Amadeus Verlag<br>Bernhard Päuler<br>Am Iberghang 16<br>CH-8405 Winterthur<br>Switzerland | FOR.MUS.DIST. |
| | American String Teachers Association<br>see ASTA | |

| Code | Publisher | U.S. Agent |
|------|-----------|------------|
| AMICI | Gli Amici della Musica da Camera<br>Via Bocca di Leone 25<br>Roma<br>Italy | |
| AMP | Associated Music Publishers | LEONARD-US<br>(sales)<br>SCHIRM.G<br>(rental) |
| AMPHION | Éditions Amphion<br>12, rue Rougement<br>F-75009 Paris<br>France | |
| AMS | AMS Press, Inc.<br>56 East 13th Street<br>New York, NY 10003 | |
| AMSCO | AMSCO Music Publishing Co. | MUSIC |
| AMSI | Art Masters Studios, Inc.<br>3706 East 34th Street<br>Minneapolis, MN 55406-2702 | |
| ANDEL | Edition Andel<br>Madeliefjeslaan, 26<br>B-8400 Oostende<br>Belgium | |
| ANDERSSONS | Anderssons Musikförlag<br>Sodra Forstadsgatan 6<br>Box 17018<br>S-200 10 Malmö<br>Sweden | |
| ANDRÉ | Johann André Musikverlag<br>Frankfurterstraße 28<br>Postfach 141<br>D-6050 Offenbach-am-Main<br>Germany | |
| ANDREA | Andrea Press<br>75 Travis Road<br>Holliston, MA 01746 | |
| ANDREU | Andreu Marc Publications<br>611 Broadway, Suite 615<br>New York, NY 10012 | MUSIC SC. |
| ANDREW | Andrew's Music<br>4830 South Dakota Avenue, N.E.<br>Washington, D.C. 20017 | |
| ANERCA | Anerca Music<br>35 St. Andrew's Garden<br>Toronto, Ontario M4W 2C9<br>Canada | |
| ANFOR | Anfor Music Publishers<br>(Div. of Terminal Music Supply)<br>1619 East Third Street<br>Brooklyn, NY 11230 | MAGNA D |
| ANGLO | Anglo-American Music Publishers<br>P.O. Box 161323<br>Altamonte Springs<br>Orlando FL 32716-1323 | |
| | Annie Bank Muziek<br>see BANK | |

| Code | Publisher | U.S. Agent |
|------|-----------|------------|
| ANTARA | Antara Music Group<br>see INTRADA | |
| ANTICO | Antico Edition<br>P.O. Box 1, Moretonhampstead<br>Newton Abbot<br>Devon TQ13 8UA<br>England | BOSTON EMC |
| | Antigua Casa Sherry-Brener, Ltd. of Madrid<br>see ACSB | |
| APM | Artist Production & Management | VIERTMANN |
| APNM | Association for Promotion of New Music<br>2002 Central Avenue<br>Ship Bottom, NJ 08008 | |
| APOGEE | Apogee Press | WORLD |
| APOLLO | Apollo-Verlag Paul Lincke<br>Weihergarten 5<br>6500 Mainz<br>Germany | SCHOTT |
| ARCADIA | Arcadia Music Publishing Co., Ltd.<br>P.O. Box 1<br>Rickmansworth<br>Herts WD3 3AZ<br>England | |
| ARCANA | Arcana Editions<br>Indian River<br>Ontario K0L 2B0<br>Canada | |
| ARCO | Arco Music Publishers | WESTERN |
| ARGENTINA | Editorial Argentina de Musica &<br>    Editorial Saraceno<br>Buenos Aires<br>Argentina | PEER |
| ARIADNE | Ariadne Buch- und Musikverlag<br>Schottenfeldgasse 45<br>A-1070 Wien<br>Austria | |
| ARION | Coleccion Arion | MEXICANAS |
| ARION PUB | Arion Publications, Inc.<br>4964 Kathleen Avenue<br>Castro Valley, CA 94546 | |
| ARISTA | Arista Music Co.<br>8370 Wilshire Blvd<br>Berverly Hills, CA 90211 | WARNER |
| ARNOLD | Edward Arnold Series | NOVELLO |
| ARS FEM | Ars Femina Ensemble<br>P.O. Box 7692<br>Louisville, KY 40257 | |
| ARS NOVA | Ars Nova Publications<br>121 Washington<br>San Diego, CA 92103 | PRESSER |
| ARS POLONA | Ars Polona<br>Krakowskie Przedmies cie 7<br>Skrytka pocztowa 1001<br>PL-00-950 Warszawa<br>Poland | |

| Code | Publisher | U.S. Agent |
|------|-----------|------------|
| ARS VIVA | Ars Viva Verlag<br>Weihergarten<br>D-6500 Mainz 1<br>Germany | EUR.AM.MUS |
| ARSIS | Arsis Press<br>1719 Bay Street SE<br>Washington D.C. 20003 | PLYMOUTH |
| | Art Masters Studios, Inc.<br>see AMSI | |
| ARTARIA | Artaria Editions<br>P.O. Box 9836<br>Te Aro, Wellington<br>New Zealand | |
| ARTHUR | J. Arthur Music<br>The University Music House<br>4290 North High Street<br>Columbus, OH 43214 | |
| ARTIA | Artia Prag<br>Ve Smeckkách 30<br>Praha 2<br>Czech Republic | |
| | Artist Production & Management<br>see APM | |
| ARTRANSA | Artransa Music | WESTERN |
| ASCHERBERG | Ascherberg, Hopwood & Crew Ltd.<br>50 New Bond Street<br>London W1A 2BR<br>England | |
| ASHBOURNE | Ashbourne Publications<br>425 Ashbourne Road<br>Elkins Park, PA 19117 | |
| ASHDOWN | Edwin Ashdown Ltd. | BRODT |
| ASHLEY | Ashley Publications, Inc.<br>P.O. Box 337<br>Hasbrouck Heights, NJ 07604 | |
| ASPEN | Aspen Grove Music<br>P.O. Box 977<br>North Hollywood, CA 91603 | |
| ASSMANN | Hermann Assmann, Musikverlag<br>Franz-Werfel-Straße 36<br>D-60431 Frankfurt<br>Germany | |
| | Associated Board of the Royal Schools of Music<br>see ABRSM | |
| | Associated Music Publishers<br>see AMP | |
| | Association for Promotion of New Music<br>see APNM | |
| ASTA | American String Teachers Association<br>1806 Robert Fulton Dr. Suite 300<br>Reston, VA 20191 | PRESSER |
| ATV | ATV Music Publications<br>6255 Sunset Boulevard<br>Hollywood, CA 90028 | CHERRY |

| Code | Publisher | U.S. Agent |
|------|-----------|------------|
| | Audio Attic Productions<br>see AAP | |
| AUG-FOR | Augsburg Fortress Publishers<br>426 South Fifth Street<br>P.O. Box 1209<br>Minneapolis, MN 55440 | |
| AULOS | Aulos Music Publishers<br>P.O. Box 54<br>Montgomery, NY 12549 | |
| AUREOLE | Aureole Editions | PARACLETE |
| AUSTRALIAN | Australian Music Center<br>PO Box N690<br>Grosvenor Place NSW 2000<br>Australia | |
| AUTOGRAPHUS | Autographus Musicus<br>Ardalavägen 158<br>S-124 32 Bandhagen<br>Sweden | |
| AUTRY | Gene Autry's Publishing Companies | WARNER |
| AVANT | Avant Music | WESTERN |
| BAGGE | Jacob Bagge | STIM |
| BANK | Annie Bank Muziek<br>P.O. Box 347<br>1180 AH Amstelveen<br>Netherlands | HARMONIA |
| BANKS MUS | Banks Music Publications<br>The Old Forge<br>Sand Hutton<br>York YO4 1LB<br>England | INTRADA |
| BARDIC | Bardic Edition<br>6 Fairfax Crescent, Aylesbury<br>Buckhamshire, HP20 2ES<br>England | BRAZIN |
| BÄREN. | Bärenreiter Verlag<br>Heinrich Schütz Allee 31-37<br>Postfach 100329<br>D-3500 Kassel-Wilhelmshöhe<br>Germany | FOR.MUS.DIST. |
| BARNHOUSE | C.L. Barnhouse<br>205 Cowan Avenue West<br>P.O. Box 680<br>Oskaloosa, IA 52577 | |
| BARON | M. Baron Co.<br>P.O. Box 149<br>Oyster Bay, NY 11771 | |
| BARRY | Barry & Cia<br>Srl Lavalle 1145 4A<br>1048 Buenos Aires<br>Argentina | BOOSEY |
| BARTA | Barta Music Company | JERONA |
| BASART | Les Éditions Internationales Basart | GENERAL |

| Code | Publisher | U.S. Agent |
|------|-----------|------------|
| BASEL | Musik-Akademie der Stadt Basel<br>Leonhardstraße 6<br>CH-4051 Basel<br>Switzerland | |
| BASSOON | Bassoon Heritage Editions<br>P.O. Box 4491<br>Fort Lauderdale, FL 33338 | |
| BAUER | Georg Bauer Musikverlag<br>Luisenstraße 47-49<br>Postfach 1467<br>D-7500 Karlsruhe<br>Germany | |
| BAVARIATON | Bavariaton-Verlag<br>München<br>Germany | ORLANDO |
| | Bay Publications, Mel<br>see MEL BAY | |
| BEACON HILL | Beacon Hill Music | LILLENAS |
| BEAUDOIN | Stuart D. Beaudoin<br>629 Queen Street<br>New Market, Ontario<br>Canada L3Y 2J1 | |
| BEAUTIFUL | Beautiful Star Publishing, Inc.<br>4040 West 70th Street<br>Minneapolis, MN 55435 | |
| BECKENHORST | Beckenhorst Press<br>P.O. Box 14273<br>Columbus, OH 43214 | |
| BEECHWOOD | Beechwood Music Corporation<br>1750 Vine Street<br>Hollywood, CA 90028 | WARNER |
| BEEKMAN | Beekman Music, Inc. | PRESSER |
| BEETHOVEN | Casa Beethoven Publicacions<br>Sepúlveda, 130 1R. 3A<br>08002 Barcelona<br>Spain | |
| BEIAARD | Beiaard School<br>Belgium | |
| BELAIEFF | M.P. Belaieff<br>Kennedyallee 101<br>D-6000 Frankfurt-am-Main 70<br>Germany | PETERS |
| BELGE | CeBeDeM<br>Centre Belge de Documentation<br>  Musicale<br>rue d'Arlon 75-77<br>B-1040 Bruxelles<br>Belgium | |
| BELLA | Bella Roma Music<br>1442A Walnut Street<br>Suite 197<br>Berkeley, CA 94709 | |
| BELMONT | Belmont Music Publishers<br>P.O. Box 231<br>Pacific Palisades, CA 90272 | |

| Code | Publisher | U.S. Agent |
|------|-----------|-----------|
| BELWIN | see WARNER | |
| BENJAMIN | Anton J. Benjamin<br>Werderstraße 44<br>Postfach 2561<br>D-2000 Hamburg 13<br>Germany | PRESSER |
| BENNY | Claude Benny Press<br>1401 1/2 State Street<br>Emporia, KS 66801 | |
| BENSON | John T. Benson<br>see BRENTWOOD | |
| BERANDOL | Berandol Music, Ltd.<br>110A Sackville Street<br>Toronto, Ontario M5A 3E7<br>Canada | |
| BERBEN | Edizioni Musicali Berben<br>Via Redipuglia 65<br>I-60122 Ancona<br>Italy | PRESSER |
| BERGMANS | W. Bergmans | BANK |
| BERKLEE | Berklee Press Publications | LEONARD-US |
| BERLIN | Irving Berlin Music Corp.<br>29 W. 46 Street<br>New York, NY 10036 | |
| BERNOUILLI | Ed. Bernouilli | DONEMUS |
| BESSEL | Éditions Bessel & Cie | BREITKOPF-W |
| BETECA | Beteca Music | MAA |
| BETTONEY | Cundey Bettoney Co. | FISCHER,C |
| BEUSCHER | Éditions Paul Beuscher Arpège<br>29, Boulevard Beaumarchais<br>F-75180 Paris<br>France | |
| BEZIGE BIJ | De Bezige Bij | DONEMUS |
| BIBGT | Biblioteca De La Guitarra<br>Postfach 18<br>7953 Bad Schussenried<br>Germany | |
| BIELER | Edmund Bieler Musikverlag<br>Thürmchenswall 72<br>D-5000 Köln 1<br>Germany | |
| BIG3 | Big Three Music Corp | WARNER |
| BILLAUDOT | Éditions Billaudot<br>14, rue de l'Echiquier<br>F-75010 Paris<br>France | PRESSER |
| BIRCH | Robert Fairfax Birch | PRESSER |
| BIRNBACH | Richard Birnbach Musikverlag<br>Aubinger Straße 9<br>D-8032 Lochheim vor München<br>Germany | |

| Code | Publisher | U.S. Agent |
|------|-----------|-----------|
| BIZET | Bizet Productions and Publications | PRESSER |
| BLOOM | The Robert Bloom Collection<br>University Towers<br>100 York Street #15D<br>New Haven, CT 06511 | |
| BMG RICORDI | BMG Ricordi S.P.A.<br>Via Salamone, 77<br>I-20138 Milano<br>Italy | |
| BMI | Broadcast Music, Inc.<br>320 West 57th Street<br>New York, NY 10019 | |
| BMIC | British Music Information Center<br>10 Stratford Place<br>London W1N 9AE<br>England | |
| BOCCACCINI | Boccaccini & Spada Editori<br>Via Francesco Duodo, 10<br>I-00136 Roma<br>Italy | PRESSER |
| BOCK | Fred Bock Music Co.<br>P.O. Box 333<br>Tarzana, CA 91356 | INTRADA |
| BODENSEE | Bodensee-Edition<br>Fabrikstrasse 16A<br>D-78224 Singen<br>Germany | |
| BODENSOHN | Edition Ernst Fr. W. Bodensohn<br>Dr. Rumpfweg 1<br>D-7570 Baden-Baden 21<br>Germany<br>see also ERST | |
| BOEIJENGA | Boeijenga Muziekhandel<br>Kleinzand 89<br>NL-8601 BG Sneek<br>Netherlands | |
| BOELKE-BOM | Boelke-Bomart Music Publications | JERONA |
| BOETHIUS | Boethius Press<br>3 The Science Park<br>Aberystinyth<br>Dyfed SY23 3AH<br>Wales | |
| BÖHM | Anton Böhm & Sohn<br>Postfach 110369<br>Lange Gasse 26<br>D-86028 Augsburg 11<br>Germany | |
| BOILEAU | Casa Editorial de Musica Boileau<br>Provenza, 287<br>08037 Barcelona<br>Spain | |
| BOIS | Bureau De Musique Mario Bois<br>19 Rue De Rocroy<br>F-75010 Paris<br>France | |
| BOMART | Bomart Music Publications | BOELKE-BOM |
| BONART | Bonart Publications | CANADIAN |

| Code | Publisher | U.S. Agent |
|------|-----------|------------|
| BONGIOVANNI | Francesco Bongiovanni<br>Via Rizzoli 28 E<br>I-40125 Bologna<br>Italy | |
| BOONIN | Joseph Boonin, Inc. | EUR.AM.MUS. |
| BOOSEY | Boosey & Hawkes, Inc.<br>35 East 21st Street<br>New York, NY 10010-6212 | |
| BOOSEY-CAN | Boosey & Hawkes Ltd.<br>279 Yorkland Boulevard<br>Willowdale, Ontario M2J 1S7<br>Canada | BOOSEY |
| BOOSEY-ENG | Boosey & Hawkes Music Publishers<br>Ltd.<br>295 Regent Street<br>London W1R 8JH<br>England | BOOSEY |
| BORNEMANN | Éditions Bornemann<br>15 rue de Tournon<br>F-75006 Paris<br>France | KING,R<br>PRESSER |
| BOSSE | Gustav Bosse Verlag<br>Von der Tann Straße 38<br>Postfach 417<br>D-8400 Regensburg 1<br>Germany | EUR.AM.MUS. |
| BOSTON | Boston Music Co.<br>172 Tremont Street<br>Boston, MA 02111-1001 | |
| BOSTON EMC | Boston Early Music Center | |
| BOSWORTH | Bosworth & Company, Ltd.<br>14-18 Heddon Street, Regent Street<br>London W1R 8DP<br>England | BRODT |
| BOTE | Bote & Bock<br>Hardenbergstraße 9A<br>D-10623 Berlin<br>Germany | PRESSER |
| BOURNE | Bourne Co.<br>5 W. 37th Street<br>New York, NY 10018-6232 | |
| BOWDOIN | Bowdoin College Music Press<br>Department of Music<br>Bowdoin College<br>Brunswick, ME 04011 | |
| BOWMASTER | Bowmaster Productions<br>3351 Thornwood Road<br>Sarasota, FL 33581 | |
| BRADLEY | Bradley Publications<br>80 8th Avenue<br>New York, NY 10011 | WARNER |
| BRANCH | Harold Branch Publishing, Inc.<br>95 Eads Street<br>West Babylon, NY 11704 | |

| Code | Publisher | U.S. Agent |
|------|-----------|------------|
| BRANDEN | Branden Press, Inc.<br>17 Station Street<br>P.O. Box 843<br>Brookline Village, MA 02147 | |
| BRASS PRESS | The Brass Press<br>136 8th Avenue North<br>Nashville, TN 37203-3798 | |
| BRATFISCH | Musikverlag Georg Bratfisch<br>Hans-Herold-Str. 23<br>D-8650 Kulmbach<br>Germany | PRESSER |
| BRAUER | Les Éditions Musicales Herman Brauer<br>30, rue St. Christophe<br>B-1000 Bruxelles<br>Belgium | |
| BRAUN-PER | St. A. Braun-Peretti<br>Dreieck 16<br>Postfach 1309<br>5300 Bonn 1<br>Germany | |
| BRAVE | Brave New Music | SON-KEY |
| BRAZIN | Brazinmusikanta Publications<br>73 Ireland Place<br>Suite #108<br>Amityville, NY 11701 | |
| BREITKOPF | Breitkopf & Härtel | |
| BREITKOPF-L | Breitkopf & Härtel (Leipzig) | |
| BREITKOPF-W | Breitkopf & Härtel<br>Walkmühlstraße 52<br>Postfach 1707<br>D-65195 Wiesbaden<br>Germany | SCHIRM.G<br>(rental) |
| BRENNAN | John Brennan Music Publisher<br>Positif Press Ltd.<br>130 Southfield Road<br>Oxford OX4 1PA<br>England | ORGAN LIT |
| BRENT | Michael Brent Publications, Inc.<br>P.O. Box 1186<br>Port Chester, NY 10573 | CHERRY |
| BRENTWOOD | Brentwood-Benson Music Publishing<br>365 Great Circle Road<br>Nashville, TN 37228 | |
| BRIDGE | Bridge Music Publishing Co.<br>1350 Villa Street<br>Mountain View, CA 94042 | |
| BRIGHT STAR | Bright Star Music Publications | WESTERN |
| BRITISH | British and Continental Music<br>Agencies Ltd. | EMI |

British Music Information Center
    see BMIC

Broadcast Music, Inc.
    see BMI

| Code | Publisher | U.S. Agent |
|---|---|---|
| BROADMAN | Broadman Press<br>127 Ninth Avenue, North<br>Nashville, TN 37234 | |
| BRODT | Brodt Music Co.<br>P.O. Box 9345<br>Charlotte, NC 28299-9345 | |
| BROEKMANS | Broekmans & Van Poppel B.V.<br>van Baerlestraat 92-94<br>NL-1071 BB Amsterdam<br>Netherlands | |
| BROGNEAUX | Éditions Musicales Brogneaux<br>73, Avenue Paul Janson<br>B-1070 Bruxelles<br>Belgium | |
| BROLGA | Brolga Music | LUDWIG |
| BROOK | Brook Publishing Co.<br>4047 Meadowbrook Blvd.<br>University Heights, OH 44118-3836 | |
| BROUDE,A | Alexander Broude, Inc. | PLYMOUTH |
| BROUDE BR | Broude Brothers Ltd.<br>141 White Oaks Road<br>Williamstown, MA 01267<br><br>Broude Brothers Ltd.-Rental Dept.<br>170 Varick St.<br>New York, NY 10013 | |
| BROWN | Brown University Choral Series | BOOSEY |
| BROWN,R | Rayner Brown<br>2423 Panorama Terrace<br>Los Angeles, CA 90039 | WESTERN<br>COMP.LIB |
| BROWN,WC | William C. Brown Co.<br>2460 Kerper Boulevard<br>Dubuque, IA 52001 | |
| BRUCKBAUER | Musikverlag M. Bruckbauer<br>"Biblioteca de la Guitarra"<br>Postfach 18<br>D-7953 Bad Schussenried<br>Germany | |
| BRUCKNER | Bruckner Verlag<br>Austria | PETERS<br>(rental) |
| BRUZZICHELLI | Aldo Bruzzichelli, Editore<br>Borgo S. Frediano, 8<br>I-50124 Firenze<br>Italy | MARGUN |
| BUBONIC | Bubonic Publishing Co.<br>706 Lincoln Avenue<br>St. Paul, MN 55105 | |
| BUDAPEST | Editio Musica Budapest (Kultura)<br>Vörösmarty tér 1<br>H-1051 Budapest<br>Hungary<br>    see also EMB | BOOSEY<br>PRESSER<br>(partial) |
| BUDDE | Rolf Budde Musikverlag<br>Hohenzollerndamm 54A<br>D-1000 Berlin 33<br>Germany | |

| Code | Publisher | U.S. Agent |
|---|---|---|
| BUGZY | Bugzy Bros. Vocal Athletics<br>P.O. Box 1900<br>Orem, UT 84059 | MUSICART |
| BUSCH | Hans Busch Musikförlag<br>Mariehällsvägen 35<br>P.O. Box 20504<br>S-16102 Bromma<br>Sweden | |
| BUSCH,E | Ernst Busch Verlag<br>Schlossstrasse 43<br>D-7531 Neulingen-Bauschlott<br>Germany | |
| BUTZ | Dr. J. Butz Musikverlag<br>Postfach 3008<br>D-53739 Sankt Augustin<br>Germany | |
| CAILLARD | Edition Philippe Caillard<br>5 bis rue du Château-Fondu<br>78200 Fontenay-Mauvoisin<br>France | |
| CAILLET | Lucien Caillet | SOUTHERN |
| CAMBIATA | Cambiata Press<br>P.O. Box 1151<br>Conway, AR 72032 | |
| CAMBRIA | Cambria Records & Publishing<br>P.O. Box 374<br>Lomita, CA 90717 | |
| CAMBRIDGE | Cambridge University Press<br>The Edinburgh Building<br>Shaftesbury Road<br>Cambridge CB2 2RU<br>England | |
| CAMDEN | Camden Music<br>19a North Villas<br>Camden Square<br>London NW1 9BJ<br>England | PRESSER |
| CAMERICA | Camerica Music<br>535 Fifth Avenue, Penthouse<br>New York, NY 10017 | WARNER |
| CAMPUS | Campus Publishers<br>713 Ellsworth Road West<br>Ann Arbor, MI 48104 | |
| CANADIAN | Canadian Music Centre<br>20 St. Joseph Street<br>Toronto, Ontario M4Y 1J9<br>Canada | |
| CAN.MUS.HER. | Canadian Musical Heritage Society<br>Patrimoine Musical Canadien<br>P.O. Box 262, Station A<br>Ottawa, Ontario K1N 8V2<br>Canada | |
| CANAAN | Canaanland Publications | WORD |

| Code | Publisher | U.S. Agent |
|------|-----------|------------|
| CANTATE | Cantate Domino<br>Editions de musique<br>Rue du Sapin 2a<br>C.P. 156<br>2114 Fleurier<br>Switzerland | |
| CANTANDO | Cantando Forlag<br>Bj. Bjornsonsgt. 2 D<br>N-4021 Stavanger<br>Norway | |
| CANTORIS | Cantoris Music<br>P.O. Box 162004<br>Sacramento, CA 95816 | |
| CANYON | Canyon Press, Inc.<br>P.O. Box 447<br>Islamorada, FL 33036 | KERBY |
| CAPELLA | Capella Music, Inc. | BOURNE |
| CAPITAL | Capital Press | PODIUM |
| CARABO | Carabo-Cone Method Foundation<br>1 Sherbrooke Road<br>Scarsdale, NY 10583 | |
| CARISCH | Carisch S.P.A.<br>see NUOVA CAR. | |
| CARLANITA | Carlanita Music Co. | LEONARD-US<br>(sales)<br>SCHIRM.G<br>(rental) |
| CARLIN | Carlin Publications<br>P.O. Box 2289<br>Oakhurst, CA 93644 | |
| CARLTON | Carlton Musikverlag | BREITKOPF-W |
| CARUS | Carus-Verlag<br>Wannenstrasse 45<br>D-70199 Stuttgart<br>Germany | FOSTER |
| CATALANA | Catalana D'Edicions Musicals<br>Laietana, 23 1r.-D<br>08003 Barcelona<br>Spain | |
| CATALUNYA | Biblioteca de Catalunya<br>Hospital, 56<br>08001 Barcelona<br>Spain | |
| CATENA | Catena Press<br>67 Marlborough Ave.<br>Glenfield, Auckland 1310<br>New Zealand | |
| CATHEDRAL | Cathedral Music<br>Maudlin House<br>Westhampnett<br>Chichester<br>West Sussex PO18 0PB<br>England | INTRADA |

Catholic Conference
  see U.S. CATH

| Code | Publisher | U.S. Agent |
|------|-----------|------------|
| CAVATA | Cavata Music Publishers, Inc. | PRESSER |
| CAVELIGHT | Cavelight Music<br>P.O. Box 85<br>Oxford, NJ 07863 | |
| CCMP | Colorado College Music Press<br>14 E. Cache La Poudre<br>Colorado Springs, CO 80903 | |
| CDMC | Centre de Documentation de la<br>  Musique Contemporaine<br>225 Avenue Charles De Gaulle<br>F-92521 Nevilly-Sur-Seine<br>France | |
| CELESTA | Celesta Publishing Co.<br>P.O. Box 560603, Kendall Branch<br>Miami, FL 33156 | |
| CENTORINO | Centorino Productions<br>P.O. Box 4478<br>West Hills, CA 91308 | |

Centre Belge de Documentation Musical
  see BELGE

Centre de Documentation de la Musique Contemporaine
  see CDMC

| Code | Publisher | U.S. Agent |
|------|-----------|------------|
| CENTURY | Century Music Publishing Co.<br>263 Veterans Boulevard<br>Carlstadt, NJ 07072 | ASHLEY |
| CENTURY PR | Century Press Publishers | |
| CESKY HUD. | Cesky Hudebni Fond<br>Parizska 13<br>CS-110 00 Praha 1<br>Czech Republic | BOOSEY<br>(rental)<br>NEW WORLD |
| CHAMBER | Chamber Music Library<br>84 Jefferson St. #2-C<br>Hoboken, NJ 07050 | |
| CHANT | Éditions Le Chant du Monde<br>31/33, rue Vandrezanne<br>F-75013 Paris<br>France | |
| CHANTERELLE | Éditions Chanterelle S.A.<br>Postfach 103909<br>D-69 Heidelberg<br>Germany | BÄREN. |
| CHANTRAINE | Éditions Chantraine<br>S.A., 7, Avenue Henri-Paris<br>B-7500 Tournai<br>Belgium | |
| CHANTRY | Chantry Music Press, Inc.<br>c/o Augsburg Fortress Publishers<br>426 South Fifth Street<br>P.O. Box 1209<br>Minneapolis, MN 55440 | AUG-FOR |
| CHAPLET | Chaplet Music Corp. | PARAGON |
| CHAPPELL | Chappell & Co., Inc.<br>1290 Avenue of the Americas<br>New York, NY 10019 | LEONARD-US |

| Code | Publisher | U.S. Agent |
|------|-----------|------------|
| CHAPPELL-CAN | Chappell Music Canada Ltd.<br>85 Scarsdale Road, Unit 101<br>Don Mills, Ontario M3B 2R2<br>Canada | LEONARD-US |
| CHAPPELL-ENG | Chappell & Co. Ltd.<br>Printed Music Division<br>60-70 Roden Street<br>Ilford, Essex IG1 2AQ<br>England | LEONARD-US |
| CHAPPELL-FR | Chappell S.A.<br>25, rue d'Hauterville<br>F-75010 Paris<br>France | LEONARD-US |
| CHARING | Charing Cross Music, Inc.<br>1619 Broadway, Suite 500<br>New York, NY 10019 | |
| CHARNWOOD | Charnwood Music Publishing Co.<br>12 Barrington Road<br>Leicester LE2 2RA<br>England | |
| CHARTER | Charter Publications, Inc.<br>P.O. Box 850<br>Valley Forge, PA 19482 | PEPPER |
| CHENANGO | Chenango Valley Music Press<br>P.O. Box 251<br>Hamilton, NY 13346 | |
| CHERITH | Cherith Publishing Co. | INTRADA |
| CHERRY | Cherry Lane Music Co.<br>10 Midland Avenue<br>Port Chester, NY 10573 | WARNER |
| CHESTER | Chester Music<br>8-9 Frith Street<br>London W1V 5TZ<br>England | SCHIRM.G |
| CHILTERN | Chiltern Music<br>see CATHEDRAL | |
| CHOIR | Choir Publishing Co.<br>564 Columbus Street<br>Salt Lake City, UT 84103 | |
| CHORAGUS | Choragus<br>Box 1197<br>S-581 11 Linköping<br>Sweden | |
| CHORISTERS | Choristers Guild<br>2834 West Kingsley Road<br>Garland, TX 75041 | LORENZ |
| CHOUDENS | Édition Choudens<br>38, rue Jean Mermoz<br>F-75008 Paris<br>France | PETERS |
| CHRISTOPHER | Christopher Music Co.<br>380 South Main Place<br>Carol Stream, IL 60188 | PRESSER |

| Code | Publisher | U.S. Agent |
|------|-----------|------------|
| CHRISTOPHORUS | Christophorus-Verlag Herder<br>Hermann-Herder-Straße 4<br>D-7800 Freiburg Breisgau<br>Germany | |
| CHURCH | John Church Co. | PRESSER |
| CLARION | Clarion Call Music | SON-KEY |
| CLARK | Clark and Cruickshank Music<br>Publishers | BERANDOL |
| CLASSIC | Classic Artists Publishing | LAURENDALE |
| CLASSIC.V | Classical Vocal Reprints<br>P.O. Box 20263<br>Columbus Circle Station<br>New York, NY 10023 | |
| CLIVIS | Clivis Publicacions<br>C-Còrsega, 619 Baixos<br>Barcelona 25<br>Spain | |
| CMA | CMA Publications<br>10 Avenue Road<br>Kingston upon Thames<br>Surrey KT1 2RB<br>England | FISCHER,C |
| CMP | CMP Library Service<br>MENC Historical Center/SCIM<br>Music Library/Hornbake<br>University of Maryland<br>College Park, MD 20742 | |
| CNRS | CNRS Editions<br>20-22 rue Saint-Armand<br>F-75015 Paris<br>France | SMPF |
| CO-OP | Co-op Press<br>RD2 Box 150A<br>Wrightsville, PA 17368 | |
| COBURN | Coburn Press | PRESSER |
| CODERG | Coderg-U.C.P. sàrl<br>42 bis, rue Boursault<br>F-75017 Paris<br>France | |
| COLE | M.M. Cole Publishing Co.<br>919 North Michigan Avenue<br>Chicago, IL 60611 | |
| COLEMAN | Dave Coleman Music, Inc.<br>P.O. Box 230<br>Montesano, WA 98563 | |
| COLFRANC | Colfranc Music Publishing Corp. | KERBY |
| COLIN | Charles Colin<br>315 West 53rd Street<br>New York, NY 10019 | |
| COLLERAN | Colleran Associates<br>Flat 6 York House<br>12 Berners Street<br>London W1T 3AF<br>England | |

| Code | Publisher | U.S. Agent |
|------|-----------|------------|
| COLOMBO | Franco Colombo Publications | WARNER<br>PRESSER<br>(rental) |
| Colorado College Music Press<br>  see CCMP | | |
| COLUM UNIV | Columbia University Music Press<br>562 West 113th Street<br>New York, NY 10025 | ECS |
| COLUMBIA | Columbia Music Co. | PRESSER |
| Columbia Pictures Publications<br>  see WARNER | | |
| COMBRE | Consortium Musical, Marcel Combre<br>  Editeur<br>24, Boulevard Poissonnière<br>F-75009 Paris<br>France | KING,R |
| COMP.FAC. | Composers Facsimile Edition | AM.COMP.AL. |
| COMP.GR. | Composer's Graphics<br>5702 North Avenue<br>Carmichael, CA 95608 | |
| COMP.LIB. | Composer's Library Editions | PRESSER |
| COMP-PERF | Composer/Performer Edition<br>2101 22nd Street<br>Sacramento, CA 95818 | |
| COMP.PR. | The Composers Press, Inc. | OPUS |
| CON B | Edition Con Brio<br>Box 7457<br>S-103 22 Stockholm<br>Sweden | STIM |
| CONCERT | Concert Music Publishing Co.<br>c/o Studio P-R, Inc.<br>16333 N.W. 54th Avenue<br>Hialeah, FL 33014 | WARNER |
| CONCERT W | Concert Works Unlimited | SHAWNEE |
| CONCORD | Concord Music Publishing Co. | ELKAN,H |
| CONCORDIA | Concordia Publishing House<br>3558 South Jefferson Avenue<br>St. Louis, MO 63118-3968 | |
| CONGRESS | Congress Music Publications<br>100 Biscayne Boulevard<br>Miami, FL 33132 | |
| CONSEJO | Consejo Superior de Investagaciones<br>  Cientificas<br>Servicio de Publicaciones<br>Vitruvio, 8<br>28006 Madrid<br>Spain | |
| CONSOL | Consolidated Music Publishers, Inc.<br>33 West 60th Street<br>New York, NY 10023 | |

| Code | Publisher | U.S. Agent |
|------|-----------|------------|
| CONSORT | Consort Music, Inc.<br>  (Division of Magnamusic Distributors)<br>Sharon, CT 06069 | |
| CONSORT PR | Consort Press<br>1755 Monita Drive<br>Ventura, CA 93001 | |
| CONSORTIUM | Consortium Musical | PRESSER |
| Consortium Musical, Marcel Combre Editeur<br>  see COMBRE | | |
| CONTE | Contempart Verlag<br>Goldschmiedgasse 10/3<br>A-1010 Wien<br>Austria | |
| CONTINUO | Continuo Music Press, Inc. | PLYMOUTH |
| COPPENRATH | Musikverlag Alfred Coppenrath<br>Postfach 11 58<br>D-84495 Altötting<br>Germany | |
| COR PUB | Cor Publishing Co.<br>67 Bell Place<br>Massapequa, NY 11758 | |
| CORDA | Corda Music Publications<br>183 Beech Road<br>St. Albans, Herts AL3 5AN<br>England | GSP |
| CORMORANT | Cormorant Press<br>P.O. Box 169<br>Hallowell, ME 04347 | PLYMOUTH |
| CORONA | Edition Corona-Rolf Budde<br>Hohenzollerndamm 54A<br>D-1 Berlin 33<br>Germany | |
| CORONET | Coronet Press | PRESSER |
| COROZINE | Vince Corozine Music Publishing Co.<br>6 Gabriel Drive<br>Peekskill, NY 10566 | |
| COSTALLAT | Éditions Costallat<br>60 rue de la Chaussée d'Antin<br>F-75441 Paris Cedex 09<br>France | PRESSER |
| COVENANT | Covenant Press<br>3200 West Foster Avenue<br>Chicago, IL 60625 | |
| COVENANT MUS | Covenant Music<br>1640 East Big Thompson Avenue<br>Estes Park, CO 80517 | |
| CPP-BELL | see WARNER | |
| CRAMER | Cramer Music<br>23 Garrick Street<br>London  WC2E 9AX<br>England | BOOSEY |

| Code | Publisher | U.S. Agent |
|------|-----------|------------|
| CRANZ | Éditions Cranz<br>30, rue St.-Christophe<br>B-1000 Bruxelles<br>Belgium | |
| CREAGHAN | Creaghan Publications<br>P.O. Box 11211<br>Edmonton, Alberta<br>Canada T5J 3K5 | |
| CREATIVE | Creative Jazz Composers, Inc.<br>1240 Annapolis Road<br>Odenton, MD 21113 | |
| CRES.-NETH | Uitgeverij Crescendo | DONEMUS |
| CRESCENDO | Crescendo Music Sales Co.<br>P.O. Box 395<br>Naperville, Il 60540 | FEMA |
| CRESPUB | Crescendo Publications, Inc.<br>6311 North O'Connor Road<br>#112<br>Irving, TX 75039-3112 | |
| CRITERION | Criterion Music Corp.<br>P.O. Box 660<br>Lynbrook, NY 11563 | |
| CROATIAN | Croatian Music Institute | DRUS.HRVAT.<br>SKLAD. |
| CRON | Edition Cron Luzern<br>Zinggentorstraße 5<br>CH-6006 Luzern<br>Switzerland | |
| CROWN | Crown Music Press | BRASS PRESS<br>(partial) |

Cundey Bettoney Co.
  see BETTONEY

| Code | Publisher | U.S. Agent |
|------|-----------|------------|
| CURCI | Edizioni Curci<br>Galleria del Corso 4<br>I-20122 Milano<br>Italy | |
| CURTIS | Curtis Music Press | KJOS |
| CURWEN | J. Curwen & Sons | LEONARD-US<br>SCHIRM.G<br>(rental) |
| CZECH | Czechoslovak Information<br>  Centre<br>Besedni 3<br>CS-118 00 Praha 1<br>Czech Republic | BOOSEY<br>(rental) |
| DA CAPO | Da Capo Press, Inc.<br>233 Spring Street<br>New York, NY 10013 | |
| DANE | Dane Publications<br>1657 The Fairway, Suite 133<br>Jenkintown, PA 19046 | |

Dansk Musik, Samfundet til udgivelse at
  see SAMFUNDET

| Code | Publisher | U.S. Agent |
|------|-----------|------------|
| DANTALIAN | Dantalian, Inc.<br>Eleven Pembroke Street<br>Newton, MA 02458-2122 | |
| DAVID | E. Henry David Music Publishers | PRESSER |
| DAVIMAR | Davimar Music<br>M. Productions<br>159 West 53rd Street<br>New York, NY 10019 | |
| DAYBREAK | Daybreak Productions | BRENTWOOD |
| DE MONTE | De Monte Music<br>F-82240 Septfonds<br>France | |
| DE SANTIS | Edizioni de Santis<br>Viale Mazzini, 6<br>I-00195 Roma<br>Italy | |
| DEAN | Roger Dean Publishing Co.<br>345 West Jackson Street, #B<br>Macomb, IL 61455-2112 | LORENZ |
| DEIRO | Pietro Deiro Publications<br>133 Seventh Avenue South<br>New York, NY 10014 | |
| DELRIEU | Georges Delrieu & Cie<br>Palais Bellecour B<br>14, rue Trachel<br>F-06000 Nice<br>France | ECS |
| DENNER | Erster Bayerischer Musikverlag<br>Joh. Dennerlein KG<br>Beethovenstraße 7<br>D-8032 Lochham<br>Germany | |
| DESCANT | Descant Publications | INTRADA |
| DESERET | Deseret Music Publishers<br>P.O. Box 900<br>Orem, UT 84057 | MUSICART |
| DESHON | Deshon Music, Inc. | WARNER<br>PRESSER<br>(rental) |
| DESSAIN | Éditions Dessain<br>Belgium | |
| DEUTSCHER | Deutscher Verlag für Musik<br>Walkmühlstr. 52<br>D-6200 Wiesbaden 1<br>Germany | BREITKOPF-W |
| DEWOLFE | DeWolfe Ltd.<br>80-88 Wardour Street<br>London W1V 3LF<br>England | DONEMUS |
| DI MUSIC | D.I. Music<br>13 Bank Square<br>Wilmslow<br>Cheshire SK9 1AN<br>England | |

| Code | Publisher | U.S. Agent |
|------|-----------|------------|
| DIAPASON | The Diapason Press<br>Dr. Rudolf A. Rasch<br>P.O Box 2376<br>NL-3500 GJ Utrecht<br>Netherlands | |
| DIESTERWEG | Verlag Moritz Diesterweg<br>Wachterbacher Strasse 89<br>D-60386 Frankfurt-am-Main<br>Germany | |
| DILIA | Dilia Prag | BÄREN. |
| Diputacion Provincal de Barcelona<br>Servicio de Bibliotecas<br>   see DPBSB | | |
| DITSON | Oliver Ditson Co. | PRESSER |
| DOBERMAN | Les Éditions Doberman-Yppan<br>C.P. 2021<br>St. Nicholas, Quebec G0S 3L0<br>Canada | BOOSEY |
| DOBLINGER | Ludwig Doblinger Verlag<br>Dorotheergasse 10<br>A-1011 Wien I<br>Austria | |
| DOMINIS | Dominis Music Ltd.<br>Box 11307, Station H<br>Ottawa<br>Ontario K2H 7V1<br>Canada | |
| DONEMUS | Donemus Foundation<br>Paulus Potterstraat 14<br>NL-1071 CZ Amsterdam<br>Netherlands | PRESSER |
| DOORWAY | Doorway Music<br>2509 Buchanan Street<br>Nashville, TN 37208 | |
| DORABET | Dorabet Music Co.<br>170 N.E. 33rd Street<br>Ft. Lauderdale, FL 33334 | PLYMOUTH |
| DÖRING | G.F. Döring Musikverlag<br>Hasenplatz 5-6<br>D-7033 Herrenburg 1<br>Germany | |
| DORN | Dorn Publications, Inc.<br>P.O. Box 206<br>Medfield, MA 02052 | |
| DOUBLEDAY | Doubleday & Co., Inc.<br>1540 Broadway<br>New York, NY 10036 | |
| DOUGLAS,B | Byron Douglas | WARNER |
| DOVEHOUSE | Dovehouse Editions<br>32 Glen Avenue<br>Ottawa, Ontario K1S 2Z7<br>Canada | |
| DOVER | Dover Publications, Inc.<br>31 East 2nd Street<br>Mineola, NY 11501 | ALFRED |

| Code | Publisher | U.S. Agent |
|------|-----------|------------|
| DOXOLOGY | Doxology Music<br>P.O. Box M<br>Aiken, SC 29802 | |
| DPBSB | Diputacion Provincial de Barcelona<br>Servicio de Bibliotecas<br>Carmen 47<br>Barcelona 1<br>Spain | |
| DRAGON | Dragon Music Co.<br>28908 Grayfox Street<br>Malibu, CA 90265 | |
| DREIKLANG | Dreiklang-Dreimasken Bühnenund<br>   Musikverlag<br>D-8000 München<br>Germany | ORLANDO |
| DRK | DRK Music Co.<br>111 Lake Wind Rd.<br>New Canaan, CT 06840 | |
| DRUS.HRVAT.<br>SKLAD. | Drustvo Hrvatskih Skladatelja<br>Berislavićeva 9<br>Zagreb<br>Croatia | |
| DRUSTVA | Edicije Drustva Slovenskih<br>   Skladateljev<br>Trg Francoske Revolucije 6<br>Ljubljana<br>Slovenia | NEW WORLD |
| DRZAVNA | Drzavna Zalozba Slovenije<br>   see DRUSTVA | |
| DUCHESS | Duchess Music Corp. | MCA<br>PRESSER<br>(rental) |
| DUCKWORTH | Gerald Duckworth & Co., Ltd.<br>43 Gloucester Crescent<br>London, NW1<br>England | |
| DUMA | Duma Music Inc.<br>580 Alden Street<br>Woodbridge, NJ 07095 | |
| DUNSTAN | Dunstan House<br>P.O. Box 1355<br>Stafford, VA 22555 | INTRADA |
| DUNVAGEN | Dunvagen Music Publishers, Inc. | SCHIRM.G |
| DURAND | Durand & Cie<br>215, rue du Faubourg St.-Honoré<br>F-75008 Paris<br>France | PRESSER |
| DUTTON | E.P. Dutton & Co., Inc.<br>201 Park Avenue South<br>New York, NY 10003 | |
| DUX | Edition Dux<br>Arthur Turk<br>Beethovenstraße 7<br>D-8032 Lochham<br>Germany | DENNER |

| Code | Publisher | U.S. Agent |
|---|---|---|
| DVM | DVM Productions<br>P.O. Box 399<br>Thorofare, NJ 08086 | |
| | E.C. Schirmer Music Co.<br>see ECS | |
| EAR.MUS.FAC. | Early Music Facsimiles<br>P.O. Box 711<br>Columbus, OH 43216 | |
| EARTHSONGS | Earthsongs<br>220 N.W. 29th<br>Corvallis, OR 97330 | |
| | East West Publications<br>see EWP | |
| EASTMAN | Eastman School of Music | FISCHER,C |
| EBLE | Eble Music Co.<br>P.O. Box 2570<br>Iowa City, IA 52244 | |
| ECK | Van Eck & Zn. | DONEMUS |
| ECOAM | Editorial Cooperativa Inter-Americana<br>de Compositores<br>Casilla de Correa No. 540<br>Montevideo<br>Uruguay | PEER |
| ECS | ECS Publishing<br>138 Ipswich Street<br>Boston, MA 02215-3534 | |
| EDI-PAN | Edi-Pan | DE SANTIS |
| ED.SEV | Edition 7<br>Lasserstrasse 6<br>A-5020 Salzburg<br>Austria | CHENANGO |
| | Éditions du Centre Nationale de la Recherche Scientifique<br>see CNRS | |
| | Editorial Cooperativa Inter-Americana de Compositores<br>see ECOAM | |
| | Editorial de Musica Española Contemporanea<br>see EMEC | |
| EDUTAIN | Edu-tainment Publications<br>(Div. of the Evolve Music Group)<br>P.O. Box 20767<br>New York, NY 10023 | |
| EERSTE | De Eerste Muziekcentrale<br>Flevolaan 41<br>NL-1411 KC Naarden<br>Netherlands | |
| EGAN | Randall M. Egan & Associates,<br>Publishers, Inc.<br>2024 Kenwood Pkwy.<br>Minneapolis, MN 55405 | |
| EGTVED | Edition EGTVED<br>P.O. Box 20<br>DK-6040 Egtved<br>Denmark | FOSTER |

| Code | Publisher | U.S. Agent |
|---|---|---|
| EHRLING | Thore Ehrling Musik AB<br>Box 21133<br>S-100 31 Stockholm<br>Sweden | |
| EIGEN UITGAVE | Eigen Uitgave van de Componist<br>(Composer's Own Publication) | DONEMUS |
| ELITE | Elite Edition | SCHAUER |
| ELKAN,H | Henri Elkan Music Publisher | |
| ELKAN&SCH | Elkan & Schildknect<br>Vastmannagatan 95<br>S-113 43 Stockholm<br>Sweden | |
| ELKAN-V | Elkan-Vogel, Inc.<br>Presser Place<br>Bryn Mawr, PA 19010 | |
| ELKIN | Elkin & Co., Ltd | PRESSER |
| EMB | Editio Musica Budapest<br>Vörösmarty tér 1<br>H-1051 Budapest<br>Hungary<br>see also BUDAPEST | BOOSEY<br>PRESSER |
| EMC | European Music Centre (Holland)<br>Ambacktsweg 42,<br>1271 AM Huizea | |
| EMEC | Editorial de Musica Española<br>Contemporanea<br>Ediciones Quiroga<br>Alcalá, 70-28009<br>Madrid 9<br>Spain | |
| EMERSON | Emerson Edition<br>Windmill Farm<br>Ampleforth<br>York YO6 4HF<br>England | EBLE<br>KING,R<br>WOODWIND<br>PRESSER |
| EMI | EMI Music Publishing Ltd.<br>127 Charing Cross Road<br>London WC2H 0EA<br>England | INTER.MUS.P. |
| ENGELS | Musikverlag Carl Engels Nachf.<br>Auf dem Brand 3<br>D-5000 Köln 50 (Rodenkirchen)<br>Germany | |
| ENGSTROEM | Engstroem & Soedering<br>Borgergade 17<br>DK-1300 Kobenhavn K<br>Denmark | PETERS |
| ENOCH | Enoch & Cie<br>193 Boulevard Pereire<br>F-75017 Paris<br>France | PRESSER<br>SCHIRM.G<br>(rental-partial) |
| ENSEMB.M.PR. | Ensemble Music Press | FISCHER,C |
| ENSEMBLE | Ensemble Publications<br>P.O. Box 98, Bidwell Station<br>Buffalo, NY 14222 | |

| Code | Publisher | U.S. Agent |
|------|-----------|------------|
| EPHROS | Gershon Ephros Cantorial Anthology Foundation, Inc. | TRANSCON. |
| ERDMANN | Rudolf Erdmann, Musikverlag<br>Adolfsallee 34<br>D-62 Wiesbaden<br>Germany | |
| ERES | Edition Eres Horst Schubert<br>Hauptstrasse 35<br>Postfach 1220<br>D-2804 Lilienthal/Bremen<br>Germany | |
| ERICKSON | E.J. Erickson Music Co.<br>606 North Fourth Street<br>P.O. Box 97<br>St. Peter, MN 56082 | |
| ERIKS | Eriksforlaget AB<br>Bigarråvägen 4<br><br>11421 Stockholm<br>Sweden | |
| ERST | Erstausgaben Bodensohn<br>see also BODENSOHN | |
| ESCHENBACH | Eschenbach Editions<br>28 Dalrymple Crescent<br>Edinburgh, EH9 2NX<br>Scotland | PRESSER |
| ESCHIG | Éditions Max Eschig<br>215 rue du Faubourg Saint-Honoré<br>F-75008 Paris<br>France | PRESSER |
| ESSEX | Clifford Essex Music | MUSIC-ENG |
| ESSO | Van Esso & Co. | DONEMUS |
| ETHOS | Ethos Publications<br>P.O. Box 2043<br>Oswego, NY 13126 | |
| ETOILE | Etoile Music, Inc.<br>Publications Division<br>Shell Lake, WI 54871 | MMB |
| EUGANEA | Euganea Editoriale Comunicazioni<br>Via Roma 82<br>I-35122 Padova<br>Italy | |
| EULENBURG | Edition Eulenburg | EUR.AM.MUS.<br>(miniature<br>scores) |
| EUR.AM.MUS. | European American Music Corp.<br>P.O. Box 850<br>Valley Forge, PA 19482 | |
| | European Music Center (Holland)<br>see EMC | |
| EVANGEL | Evangel Press | AMSI |
| EWP | East West Publications | MUSIC |

| Code | Publisher | U.S. Agent |
|------|-----------|------------|
| EXCELLENT | Excellent Music Holland<br>Postbus 347<br>1180 AH Amstelveen<br>Netherlands | HARMONIA |
| EXCELSIOR | Excelsior Music Publishing Co. | PRESSER |
| EXPOSITION | Exposition Press<br>325 Kings Highway<br>Smithtown, NY 11787 | |
| FABER | Faber Music Ltd.<br>3 Queen Square<br>London WC1N 3AU<br>England | LEONARD-US<br>(sales)<br>FOR.MUS.DIST.<br>(rental) |
| FAIRFIELD | Fairfield Publishing, Ltd. | PRESSER |
| FAITH | Faith Music | LILLENAS |
| FALLEN LEAF | Fallen Leaf Press<br>P.O. Box 10034-N<br>Berkeley, CA 94709 | |
| FAR WEST | Far West Music | WESTERN |
| FARRELL | The Wes Farrell Organization | LEONARD-US |
| FASE | Foundation for the Advancement<br>of String Education<br>P.O. Box 610215<br>Newton Highlands, MA 02161 | |
| FAZER | Musik Fazer<br>P.O. Box 169<br>SF-02101 Espoo<br>Finland | PRESSER |
| FEEDBACK | Feedback Studio Verlag<br>Gentner Strasse 23<br>D-5 Köln 1<br>Germany | BÄREN. |
| FEIST | Leo Feist, Inc. | PRESSER |
| FEJA | Musik - und Buchverlag Werner Feja<br>An Der Dorfkirche 1D<br>D - 1000 Berlin 48<br>Germany | |
| FELDMAN,B | B. Feldman & Co., Ltd. | EMI |
| FEMA | Fema Music Publications<br>P.O. Box 395<br>Naperville, IL 60566 | |
| FENETTE | Fenette Music Ltd. | BROUDE,A |
| FENTONE | Fentone Music Ltd.<br>Fleming Road, Earlstrees<br>Corby, Northants  NN17 2SN<br>England | PRESSER |
| FEREOL | Fereol Publications<br>Route 8,  Box 510C<br>Gainesville, GA 30501 | |
| FEUCHTINGER | Feuchtinger & Gleichauf<br>Niedermünstergasse 2<br>D-8400 Regensburg 11<br>Germany | |

| Code | Publisher | U.S. Agent |
|------|-----------|------------|
| FIDDLE | Fiddle & Bow<br>7 Landview Drive<br>Dix Hills, NY 11746 | HOLLOW |
| FIDELIO | Fidelio Music Publishing Co.<br>39 Danbury Avenue<br>Westport, CT 06880-6822 | |
| FIDULA | Fidula-Verlag Johannes Holzmeister<br>Ahornweg, Postfach 250<br>D-56154 Boppard/Rhein<br>Germany | HARGAIL |
| FILLMORE | Fillmore Music House | FISCHER,C |
| FINE ARTS | Fine Arts Press<br>2712 W. 104th Terrace<br>Leawood, KS 66206 | BRENTWOOD |
| FINNISH.MIC | Finnish Music Information Center<br>Runeberginkatu 15 A<br>SF-00100 Helsinki 10<br>Finland | |
| FISCHER,C | Carl Fischer, Inc.<br>62 Cooper Square<br>New York, NY 10003 | |
| FISCHER,J | J. Fischer & Bro. | WARNER<br>PRESSER<br>(rental) |
| FISHER | Fisher Music Co. | PLYMOUTH |
| FITZSIMONS | H.T. FitzSimons Co., Inc.<br>18345 Ventura Boulevard<br>P.O. Box 333, Suite 212<br>Tarzana, CA 91356 | INTRADA |
| FLAMMER | Harold Flammer, Inc. | SHAWNEE |
| FMA | Florilegium Musicae Antiquae | HÄNSSLER |
| FOETISCH | Foetisch Frères<br>Rue de Bourg 6<br>CH-1002 Lausanne<br>Switzerland | ECS |
| FOG | Dan Fog Musikforlag<br>Grabrodretorv 7<br>DK-1154 Kobenhavn K<br>Denmark | |
| FOLEY,CH | Charles Foley, Inc. | FISCHER,C<br>PRESSER<br>(rental) |
| FOR.MUS.DIST. | Foreign Music Distributors<br>13 Elkay Drive<br>Chester, NY 10918 | |
| FORBERG | Rob. Forberg-P. Jurgenson<br>Musikverlag<br>Mirbachstraße 9<br>D-5300 Bonn-Bad Godesberg<br>Germany | PETERS |
| FORLIVESI | A. Forlivesi & C.<br>Via Roma 4<br>50123 Firenze<br>Italy | |

| Code | Publisher | U.S. Agent |
|------|-----------|------------|
| FORNI | Arnaldo Forni Editore<br>Via Gramsci 164<br>I-40010 Sala Bolognese<br>Italy | OLD |
| FORSTER | Forster Music Publisher, Inc.<br>216 South Wabash Avenue<br>Chicago, IL 60604 | |
| FORSYTH | Forsyth Brothers Ltd.<br>126 Deansgate<br>Manchester M3 2GR<br>England | |
| FORTEA | Biblioteca Fortea<br>Fucar 10<br>Madrid 14<br>Spain | |
| FORTISSIMO | Fortissimo Musikverlag<br>Margaretenplatz 4<br>A-1050 Wien<br>Austria | |
| Fortress Press<br>see AUG-FOR | | |
| FOSTER | Mark Foster Music Co.<br>28 East Springfield Avenue<br>P.O. Box 4012<br>Champaign, IL 61820-1312 | |
| Foundation for New American Music<br>see NEWAM | | |
| Foundation for the Advancement of String Education<br>see FASE | | |
| FOUR STAR | Four Star Publishing Co. | WARNER |
| FOX, S | Sam Fox Publishing Co.<br>5276 Hollister Avenue<br>Suite 251<br>Santa Barbara, CA 93111 | PLYMOUTH<br>(sales)<br>PRESSER<br>(rental) |
| FRANÇAIS | Éditions Françaises de Musique | PRESSER |
| FRANCE | France Music | AMP |
| FRANCIS | Francis, Day & Hunter Ltd. | WARNER |
| FRANGIPANI | Frangipani Press | ALFRED |
| FRANK | Frank Music Corp. | LEONARD-US<br>SCHIRM.G<br>(rental-partial) |
| FRANTON | Franton Music<br>4620 Sea Isle<br>Memphis, TN 38117 | |
| FREDONIA | Fredonia Press<br>3947 Fredonia Drive<br>Hollywood, CA 90068 | SIFLER |
| FREEMAN,H | H. Freeman & Co., Ltd. | EMI |
| FREELAND | Freeland Publications<br>2718 Russell Street<br>Berkeley, CA 94705 | |

| Code | Publisher | U.S. Agent |
|------|-----------|------------|
| FROG | Frog Peak Music<br>Box 1052<br>Lebanon, NH 03766 | |
| FRÖHLICH | Friedrich Wilhelm Fröhlich Musikverlag<br>Ansbacher Straße 52<br>D-1000 Berlin 30<br>Germany | |
| FUJIHARA | Fujihara | |
| FURORE | Furore Verlag<br>Johannesstrasse 3<br>3500 Kassel<br>Germany | TONGER |
| FÜRSTNER | Fürstner Ltd. | BOOSEY |
| FUZEAU | Editions Fuzeau<br>B.P. 6<br>79440 Courlay<br>France | |
| GABRIEL | Gene Gabriel Publications, Ltd.<br>P.O. Box 1959<br>Cathedral Station<br>New York, NY 10025 | |
| GAF | G.A.F. and Associates<br>1626 E. Williams Street<br>Tempe, AZ 85281 | |
| GAITHER | Gaither Music Company | BRENTWOOD |
| G & L | G and L Publishing<br>2337 Jersey Street<br>Stevens Point, WI 54481-3123 | |
| GALAXY | Galaxy Music Corp. | ECS |
| GALLEON | Galleon Press<br>17 West 60th St.<br>New York, NY 10023 | BOSTON |
| GALLERIA | Galleria Press<br>170 N.E. 33rd Street<br>Fort Lauderdale, FL 33334 | PLYMOUTH |
| GALLIARD | Galliard Ltd.<br>Queen Anne's Road<br>Southtown, Gt. Yarmouth<br>Norfolk<br>England | GALAXY |
| GARLAND | Garland Publishing, Inc.<br>19 Union Sq. W. FL8<br>New York, NY 10003-3304 | |
| GARZON | Éditions J. Garzon<br>13 rue de l'Échiquier<br>F-75010 Paris<br>France | |
| GEHRMANS | Carl Gehrmans Musikförlag<br>Odengatan 84<br>Box 6005<br>S-102 31 Stockholm<br>Sweden | BOOSEY |

| Code | Publisher | U.S. Agent |
|------|-----------|------------|
| GEMINI | Gemini Press<br>Music Div. of the Pilgrim Press<br>Box 390<br>Otis, MA 01253 | PRESSER |
| GENERAL | General Music Publishing Co., Inc.<br>145 Palisade Street<br>Dobbs Ferry, NY 10522 | BOSTON |
| GENERAL WDS | General Words and Music Co. | KJOS |
| GENESIS | Genesis | PLYMOUTH |
| GENTRY | Gentry Publications<br>P.O. Box 570567<br>Tarzana, CA 91357 | INTRADA |
| GERIG | Musikverlage Hans Gerig<br>Drususgasse 7-11 (AM Museum)<br>D-5000 Köln 1<br>Germany | BREITKOPF-W |
| GIA | GIA Publications<br>7404 South Mason Avenue<br>Chicago, IL 60638 | |
| GILBERT | Gilbert Publications<br>4209 Manitou Way<br>Madison, WI 53711 | |
| GILLMAN | Gillman Publications<br>P.O. Box 155<br>San Clemente, CA 92672 | |
| GILPIN | Gilpin-McPheeters Publishing | INTRADA |
| GLOCKEN | Glocken Verlag Ltd.<br>12-14 Mortimer Street<br>London W1N 8EL<br>England | EUR.AM.MUS. |
| GLORY | Glory Sound<br>Delaware Water Gap, PA 18327 | SHAWNEE |
| GLOUCHESTER | Glouchester Press<br>P.O. Box 1044<br>Fairmont, WV 26554 | HEILMAN |
| GM | G & M International Music Dealers<br>1225 Candlewood Hill Road<br>Box 2098<br>Northbrook, IL 60062 | |
| GOLDEN | Golden Music Publishing Co.<br>P.O. Box 383<br>Golden, CO 80402-0383 | |
| GOODLIFE | Goodlife Publications | WARNER |
| GOODWIN | Goodwin & Tabb Publishing, Ltd. | PRESSER |
| GORDON | Gordon Music Co.<br>Box 2250<br>Canoga Park, CA 91306 | |
| GORNSTON | David Gornston | FOX,S |
| GOSPEL | Gospel Publishing House<br>1445 Boonville Avenue<br>Springfield, MO 65802 | |

| Code | Publisher | U.S. Agent |
|---|---|---|
| GRAHL | Grahl & Nicklas<br>Braubachstraße 24<br>D-6 Frankfurt-am-Main<br>Germany | |
| GRANCINO | Grancino Editions<br>15020 Burwood Dr.<br>Lake Mathews, CA 92370 | |
| | Grancino Editions<br>2 Bishopswood Road<br>London N6 4PR<br>England | |
| | Grancino Editions<br>Schirmerweg 12<br>D-8 München 60<br>Germany | |
| GRAS | Éditions Gras<br>36 rue Pape-Carpentier<br>F-72200 La Flèche (Sarthe)<br>France | SOUTHERN |
| GRAV | Editions Gravis<br>Adolfstrasse 71<br>Postfach 1107<br>D-6208 Bad Schwalbach 1<br>Germany | |
| GRAY | H.W. Gray Co., Inc. | WARNER<br>PRESSER<br>(rental) |
| GREENE ST. | Greene Street Music<br>354 Van Duzer Street<br>Stapleton, NY 10304 | |
| GREENWOOD | Greenwood Press, Inc.<br>88 Post Road West<br>P.O. Box 5007<br>Westport, CT 06881 | WORLD |
| GREGG | Gregg International Publishers, Ltd.<br>1 Westmead, Farnborough<br>Hants GU14 7RU<br>England | |
| GREGGMS | Gregg Music Sources<br>P.O. Box 868<br>Novato, CA 94947 | |
| Gregorian Institute of America<br>see GIA | | |
| GROEN | Muziekuitgeverij Saul B. Groen<br>Ferdinand Bolstraat 6<br>NL-1072 LJ Amsterdam<br>Netherlands | |
| GROSCH | Edition Grosch<br>Phillip Grosch<br>Postfach 1736<br>D-82145 Planegg Bei<br>München<br>Germany | THOMI-BERG |
| GROVENS | Eivind Grovens Institutt for<br>Reinstemming<br>Ekebergveien 59<br>N-1181 Oslo 11<br>Norway | |

| Code | Publisher | U.S. Agent |
|---|---|---|
| GSP | Guitar Solo Publications<br>514 Bryant Street<br>San Francisco, CA 94107-1217 | |
| GUARANI | Ediciones Musicals Mundo Guarani<br>Sarmiento 444<br>Buenos Aires<br>Argentina | |
| GUILYS | Edition Guilys<br>Case Postale 90<br>CH-1702 Fribourg 2<br>Switzerland | |
| GUNMAR | Gunmar Music, Inc.<br>see MARGUN | JERONA |
| HA MA R | Ha Ma R Percussion Publications, Inc.<br>333 Spring Road<br>Hutington, NY 11743 | BOOSEY |
| Hal Leonard Music<br>see LEONARD-US | | |
| HAMBLEN | Stuart Hamblen Music Co.<br>26101 Ravenhill Road<br>Canyon Country, CA 91351 | |
| HAMELLE | Hamelle & Cie<br>175 rue Saint-Honoré<br>F-75040 Paris Cedex 01<br>France | KING,R<br>PRESSER<br>SOUTHERN |
| HAMPE | Adolf Hampe Musikverlag<br>Hohenzollerndamm 54A<br>D-1000 Berlin 33<br>Germany | BUDDE |
| HAMPTON | Hampton Edition | MARKS |
| HANSEN-DEN | Wilhelm Hansen Musikforlag<br>Bornholmsgade 1,1<br>1266 Copenhagen K<br>Denmark | SCHIRM.G |
| HANSEN-ENG | Hansen, London<br>see CHESTER | |
| HANSEN-FIN | Edition Wilhelm Hansen<br>Helsinki | SCHIRM.G |
| HANSEN-GER | Edition Wilhelm Hansen, Frankfurt | SCHIRM.G |
| HANSEN-NY | Edition Wilhelm Hansen-Chester<br>Music New York Inc.<br>New York, NY | SCHIRM.G |
| HANSEN-SWED | Edition Wilhelm Hansen<br>see NORDISKA | SCHIRM.G |
| HANSEN-US | Hansen House Publications, Inc.<br>1870 West Avenue<br>Miami Beach, FL 33139-9913 | |
| HÄNSSLER | Hänssler-Verlag<br>Röntgenstrasse 15<br>Postfach 1230<br>D-7312 Kirchheim/Teck<br>Germany | |
| HAPPY | Happy Music<br>P.O. Box 2842<br>San Anselmo, CA 94960 | |

| Code | Publisher | U.S. Agent |
|------|-----------|------------|
| HARGAIL | Hargail Music Press<br>P.O. Box 118<br>Saugerties, NY 12477 | WARNER |
| HARMONIA | Harmonia-Uitgave<br>P.O. Box 210<br>NL-1230 AE Loosdrecht<br>Netherlands | FOR.MUS.DIST. |
| HARMS,TB | T.B. Harms | WARNER |
| HARMUSE | Harmuse Publications<br>529 Speers Road<br>Oakville, Ontario L6K 2G4<br>Canada | |
| HARP PUB | Harp Publications<br>3437-2 Tice Creek Drive<br>Walnut Creek, CA 94595 | |
| HARRIS | Frederick Harris Music Co., Ltd.<br>529 Speers Road<br>Oakville, Ontario L6K 2G4<br>Canada | HARRIS-US |
| HARRIS,R | Ron Harris Publications<br>22643 Paul Revere Drive<br>Woodland Hills, CA 91364 | BRENTWOOD<br>INTRADA |
| HARRIS-US | Frederick Harris Company, Ltd.<br>340 Nagel Drive<br>Buffalo, NY 14225-4731 | |
| HART | F. Pitman Hart & Co., Ltd. | BRODT |
| HARTH | Harth Musikverlag<br>PSF 467<br>D-04004 Leipzig<br>Germany | |
| HAS | Edition HAS Publishing Co.<br>P.O. Box 1753<br>Maryland Heights, MO 63043 | HENLE |
| HASLINGER | Verlag Carl Haslinger<br>Tuchlauben 11<br>A-1010 Wien<br>Austria | FOR.MUS.DIST. |
| HASTINGS | Hastings Music Corp. | WARNER |
| HATCH | Earl Hatch Publications<br>5008 Aukland Ave.<br>Hollywood, CA 91601 | |
| HATIKVAH | Hatikvah Publications | TRANSCON. |
| HAWK | Hawk Music Press<br>668 Fairmont Avenue<br>Oakland, CA 94611 | |
| HAYMOZ | Haydn-Mozart Presse | EUR.AM.MUS. |
| HAZAMIR | Hazamir Publications<br>35 Garland Road<br>Newton, MA 02159 | |

Hebrew Union College Sacred Music Press
see SAC.MUS.PR.

| Code | Publisher | U.S. Agent |
|------|-----------|------------|
| HEER | Joh. de Heer & Zn. B.V.<br>Muziek-Uitgeverij en Groothandel<br>Rozenlaan 113, postbus 3089<br>NL-3003 AB Rotterdam<br>Netherlands | |
| HEIDELBERGER | Heidelberger | BÄREN. |
| HEILMAN | Heilman Music<br>P.O. Box 1044<br>Fairmont, WV 26554 | |
| HEILMANN | Heilmann Publications<br>P.O. Box 18180<br>Pittsburgh, PA 15236 | |
| HEINRICH | Heinrichshofen's Verlag<br>Liebigstraße 16<br>Postfach 620<br>D-26354 Wilhelmshaven<br>Germany | PETERS |
| HELBLING-AUS | Edition Helbling<br>Kaplanstraße 9<br>A-6021 Neu-Rum b. Innsbruck<br>Austria | |
| HELBLING-SW | Helbling Edition<br>Pffäfikerstraße 6<br>CH-8604 Voketswil-Zürich<br>Switzerland | |
| HELICON | Helicon Music Corp. | EUR.AM.MUS. |
| HELIOS | Editio Helios | FOSTER |
| HENDON | Hendon Music | BOOSEY |
| HENKLE | Ted Henkle<br>5415 Reynolds Street<br>Savannah, GA 31405 | |
| HENLE | G. Henle Verlag<br>Forstenrieder Allee 122<br>Postfach 71 04 66<br>D-81454 München<br>Germany | |
| | G. Henle USA, Inc.<br>P.O. Box 1753<br>2446 Centerline Industrial Drive<br>St. Louis, MO 63043 | |
| HENMAR | Henmar Press | PETERS |
| HENN | Editions Henn<br>8 rue de Hesse<br>Genève<br>Switzerland | |
| HENREES | Henrees Music Ltd. | EMI |
| HERALD | Herald Press<br>616 Walnut Avenue<br>Scottdale, PA 15683 | |
| HERITAGE | Heritage Music Press | LORENZ |
| HERITAGE PUB | Heritage Music Publishing Co. | CENTURY |

| Code | Publisher | U.S. Agent |
|------|-----------|------------|
| HEUGEL | Heugel & Cie<br>175 rue Saint-Honoré<br>F-75040 Paris Cedex 01<br>France | KING,R<br>PRESSER<br>SOUTHERN |
| HEUWEKE | Edition Heuwekemeijer & Zoon<br>Postbus 289<br>NL-1740 AG Schagen<br>Netherlands | PRESSER |
| HEYN | Verlag Johannes Heyn<br>Friedensgasse 23<br>A-9020 Klagenfurt<br>Austria | |
| HIEBER | Musikverlag Max Hieber KG<br>Postfach 330429<br>D-80064 München<br>Germany | |
| HIGHER GR. | Higher Ground Music Publishing | |
| HIGHGATE | Highgate Press | ECS |
| HIGHLAND | Highland/Etling Music Co.<br>1344 Newport Avenue<br>Long Beach, CA 90804 | |
| HILDEGARD | Hildegard Publishing Co.<br>Box 332<br>Bryn Mawr, PA 19010 | |
| HINRICHSEN | Hinrichsen Edition, Ltd. | PETERS |
| HINSHAW | Hinshaw Music, Inc.<br>P.O. Box 470<br>Chapel Hill, NC 27514 | |
| HINZ | Hinz Fabrik Verlag<br>Lankwitzerstraße 17-18<br>D-1000 Berlin 42<br>Germany | |
| HIRSCHS | Abr. Hirschs Forlag<br>Box 505<br>S-101 26 Stockholm<br>Sweden | GEHRMANS |
| HISPAVOX | Ediciones Musicales Hispavox<br>Cuesta Je Santo Domingo 11<br>Madrid<br>Spain | |
| HLH | HLH Music Publications<br>611 Broadway, Suite 615<br>New York, NY 10012 | MUSIC SC. |
| HNH | HNH International Ltd.<br>6th Floor, Sino Industrial Plaza<br>9 Kai Cheung Road, Kowloon<br>Hong Kong | |
| HOA | HOA Music PUblisher<br>756 S. Third Street<br>Dekalb, IL 60115 | |
| HOFFMAN,R | Raymond A. Hoffman Co.<br>c/o Fred Bock Music Co.<br>P.O. Box 333<br>Tarzana, CA 91356 | INTRADA |

| Code | Publisher | U.S. Agent |
|------|-----------|------------|
| HOFMEISTER | VEB Friedrich Hofmeister, Musikverlag,<br>Leipzig<br>Karlstraß 10<br>D-701 Leipzig<br>Germany | |
| HOFMEISTER-W | Friedrich Hofmeister Musikverlag,<br>Taunus<br>Ubierstraße 20<br>D-6238 Hofheim am Taunus<br>Germany | |
| HOHLER | Heinrich Hohler Verlag | SCHNEIDER,H |
| HOLLOW | Hollow Hills Press<br>7 Landview Drive<br>Dix Hills, NY 11746 | |
| HOLLY-PIX | Holly-Pix Music Publishing Co. | WESTERN |
| HONG KONG | Hong Kong Music Media Publishing<br>Co., Ltd.<br>Kai It Building, 9th Floor<br>58 Pak Tai Street<br>Tokwawan, Kowloon<br>Hong Kong | |
| HONOUR | Honour Publications | WESTERN |
| HOPE | Hope Publishing Co.<br>380 South Main Place<br>Carol Stream, IL 60188 | |
| HORNPIPE | Hornpipe Music Publishing Co.<br>400 Commonwealth Avenue<br>P.O. Box CY577<br>Boston, MA 02215 | |
| HUEBER | Hueber-Holzmann<br>Pädagogischer Verlag<br>Krausstraße 30<br>D-8045 Ismaning, München<br>Germany | |
| HUG | Hug & Co. Musikverlage<br>Limmatquai Postfach 28-30<br>CH-8022 Zürich<br>Switzerland | EUR.AM.MUS. |
| HUGUENIN | Charles Huguenin & Pro-Arte<br>Rue du Sapin 2a<br>CH-2114 Fleurier<br>Switzerland | |
| HUHN | W. Huhn Musikalien-Verlag<br>Jahnstraße 9<br>D-5880 Lüdenshied<br>Germany | |
| HULLENHAGEN | Hullenhagen & Griehl Verlage<br>Ringstrasse 52<br>D-22145 Hamburg<br>Germany | |
| HULST | De Hulst<br>Kruisdagenlaan 75<br>B-1040 Bruxelles<br>Belgium | |
| HUNTZINGER | R.L. Huntzinger Publications | WILLIS |

| Code | Publisher | U.S. Agent |
|------|-----------|-----------|
| HURON | Huron Press<br>P.O. Box 2121<br>London, Ontario N6A 4C5<br>Canada | |
| ICELAND | Iślenzk Tónverkamiðstöd<br>Iceland Music Information Centre<br>Sidumuli 34<br>108 Reykjavik<br>Iceland | |
| IISM | Istituto Italiano per la Storia della<br>  Musica<br>Academia Nazionale di Santa Cecilia<br>Via Vittoria, 6<br>I-00187 Roma<br>Italy | |
| IMB | Internationale Musikbibliothek | BÄREN. |
| IMC | Indiana Music Center<br>322 South Swain<br>P.O. Box 582<br>Bloomington, IN 47401 | |
| IMPERO | Impero-Verlag<br>Liebigstraße 16<br>D-2940 Wilhelmshavn<br>Germany | PRESSER<br>(partial) |
| INDEPENDENT | Independent Publications<br>P.O. Box 162<br>Park Station<br>Paterson, NJ 07513 | |
| INDIANA | Indiana University Press<br>601 N. Morton Street<br>Bloomington, IN 47404-3797 | |

Indiana Music Center
  see IMC

| INST ANT | Instrumenta Antiqua, Inc.<br>P.O. Box 2804<br>Menlo Park, CA 94026-2804 | |
| INSTRUMENTAL | The Instrumentalist<br>200 Northfield Road<br>Northfield, IL 60093-3390 | |

Institute Of Stringed Instruments,
  Guitar & Lute
    see ISI

| INTER.MUS.P. | International Music Publications<br>Woodford Trading Estate<br>Southend Road<br>Woodford Green, Essex IG8 8HN<br>England | WARNER |
| INTERLOCHEN | Interlochen Press | CRESCENDO |
| INTERNAT.S. | International Music Service<br>133 W. 69th Street<br>New York, NY 10023 | |
| INTERNATIONAL | International Music Co.<br>5 W. 37th Street<br>New York, NY 10018 | |

Internationale Musikbibliothek
  see IMB

| Code | Publisher | U.S. Agent |
|------|-----------|-----------|
| INTRADA | Intrada Music Group<br>P.O. Box 1240<br>Anderson, IN 46015 | |
| IONA | Iona Music Publishing Service<br>P.O. Box 8131<br>San Marino, CA 91108 | |
| IONE | Ione Press | ECS |
| IRIS | Iris Verlag<br>Hernerstraße 64A<br>Postfach 100.851<br>D-4350 Recklinghausen<br>Germany | |
| IROQUOIS | Iroquois Press<br>P.O. Box 2121<br>London, Ontario N6A 4C5<br>Canada | |
| ISI | Institute Of Stringed Instruments,<br>  Guitar & Lute<br>Poststraße 30<br>4 Düsseldorf<br>Germany | |

Isle-de-France, Aux Presses d'
  see PRESSES

Islenzk Tónverkamiðstöd
  see ICELAND

| ISR.MUS.INST. | Israel Music Institute<br>P.O. Box 3004<br>61030 Tel Aviv<br>Israel | PRESSER |
| ISR.PUB.AG. | Israel Publishers Agency<br>7, Arlosoroff Street<br>Tel-Aviv<br>Israel | |
| ISRAELI | Israeli Music Publications, Ltd.<br>25 Keren Hayesod<br>Jerusalem 94188<br>Israel | PRESSER |

Istituto Italiano per la Storia della Musica
  see IISM

| J.B. PUB | J.B. Publications<br>404 Holmes Circle<br>Memphis, TN 38111 | |
| J.C.A. | Japan Composers Association<br>3-7-15, Akasaka<br>Minato-Ku<br>Tokyo<br>Japan | |
| JACKMAN | Jackman Music Corp.<br>P.O. Box 1900<br>Orem, UT 84059 | MUSICART |
| JAPAN | Japan Federation of Composers<br>307 5th Sky Bldg.<br>3-3-8 Sendagaya<br>Shibuya-Ku<br>Tokyo 151<br>Japan | |

| Code | Publisher | U.S. Agent |
|------|-----------|------------|
| | Japan Composers Association<br>see J.C.A. | |
| JAREN | Jaren Music Co.<br>9691 Brynmar Drive<br>Villa Park, CA 92667 | |
| JASEMUSIIKKI | Jasemusiikki Ky<br>Box 136<br>SF-13101 Håmeenlinna 10<br>Finland | |
| JAYMAR | Jaymar Music, Ltd.<br>Box 2191, Stn.B<br>London, Ontario N6A 4E3<br>Canada | |
| JAZZ ED | Jazz Education Publications<br>P.O. Box 802<br>Manhattan, KS 66502 | |
| JEANNETTE | Ed. Jeannette | DONEMUS |
| JEHLE | Jehle | HÄNSSLER |
| JENSON | Jenson Publications, Inc.<br>7777 W. Bluemound Road<br>Milwaukee, WI 53213 | LEONARD-US |
| JERONA | Jerona Music Corp.<br>P.O. Box 671<br>Englewood, NJ 07631 | |
| JEWISH | Jewish Music Publications<br>2500 NE 135 Street, #111<br>N. Miami, FL 33181-3554 | |
| JLJ MUSIC | JLJ Music Publishing<br>P.O. Box 41183<br>Mesa, AZ 85274-1183 | |
| JOAD | Joad Press<br>4 Meredyth Road<br>London SW13 0DY<br>England | FISCHER,C<br>(rental-partial) |
| JOBERT | Editions Jean Jobert<br>76, rue Quincampoix<br>F-75003 Paris<br>France | PRESSER |
| JOED | Joed Music Publications<br>234 Stanley Park Road<br>Carshalton Beeches<br>Surrey, SM5 3JP<br>England | |
| JOHNSON | Johnson Reprint Corp.<br>757 3rd Avenue<br>New York, NY 10017 | |
| JOHNSON,P | Paul Johnson Productions<br>P.O. Box 2001<br>Irving, TX 75061 | |
| JOSHUA | Joshua Corp. | SCHIRM.G |
| JOY | Joy Music Press | INTRADA |
| JRB | JRB Music Education Materials<br>Distributor | PRESSER |

| Code | Publisher | U.S. Agent |
|------|-----------|------------|
| JUNNE | Otto Junne GmbH<br>Sendinger-Tor-Platz 10<br>D-8000 München<br>Germany | |
| JUS-AUTOR | Jus-Autor<br>Sofia, Bulgaria | BREITKOPF-W |
| JUSKO | Jusko Publications | WILLIS |
| KAHNT | C.F. Kahnt, Musikverlag<br>Kennedyallee 101<br>6000 Frankfurt 70<br>Germany | PETERS |
| KALLISTI | Kallisti Music Press<br>810 South Saint Bernard Street<br>Philadelphia, PA 19143-3309 | |
| KALMUS | Edwin F. Kalmus<br>P.O. Box 5011<br>Boca Raton, FL 33431 | WARNER<br>(string and<br>miniature<br>scores) |
| KALMUS,A | Alfred A. Kalmus Ltd.<br>38 Eldon Way, Paddock Wood<br>Tonbridge, Kent TN12 6BE<br>England | EUR.AM.MUS. |
| KAMMEN | J. & J. Kammen Music Co. | CENTURY |
| KAPLAN | Ida R. Kaplan<br>1308 Olivia Avenue<br>Ann Arbor, MI 48104 | |
| KARTHAUSE | Karthause Verlag<br>Panzermacherstrasse 5<br>D-5860 Iserlohn<br>Germany | |
| KAWAI | Kawai Gafuku | JAPAN |
| KAWE | Edition Kawe<br>Brederodestraat 90<br>NL-1054 VC Amsterdam 13<br>Netherlands | KING,R |
| KAY PR | Kay Press<br>612 Vicennes Court<br>Cincinnati, OH 45231 | |
| KELTON | Kelton Publications<br>1343 Amalfi Drive<br>Pacific Palisades, CA 90272 | |
| KENDALE | Kendale Company<br>6595 S. Dayton Street<br>Englewood, CO 80111 | |
| KENDOR | Kendor Music Inc.<br>Main & Grove Streets<br>P.O. Box 278<br>Delevan, NY 14042 | |
| KENSINGTON | Kensington Music Service<br>P.O. Box 471<br>Tenafly, NJ 07670 | |
| KENYON | Kenyon Publications | LEONARD-US |

| Code | Publisher | U.S. Agent |
|------|-----------|------------|
| KERBY | E.C. Kerby Ltd.<br>198 Davenport Road<br>Toronto, Ontario  M5R IJ2<br>Canada | LEONARD-US<br>BOOSEY<br>(rental) |
| KEYS | The Keys Press<br>66 Clotilde Street<br>Mount Lawley<br>Western Australia 6050<br>Australia | |
| KIMMEL | Kimmel Publications, Inc.<br>P.O. Box 1472<br>Decatur, IL 62522 | HOPE |
| KINDRED | Kindred Press | HERALD |
| KING,R | Robert King Sales, Inc.<br>Shovel Shop Square<br>28 Main Street, Bldg. 15<br>North Easton, MA 02356 | |
| KING'S | King's Music<br>Redcroft, Bank's End<br>Wyton, Huntingdon<br>Cambridgeshire  PE17 2AA<br>England | |
| KIRKLAND | Kirkland House | LORENZ |
| KISTNER | Fr. Kistner & C.F.W. Siegel & Co.<br>Adrian-Kiels-Straße 2<br>D-5000  Köln 90<br>Germany | CONCORDIA |
| KJOS | Neil A. Kjos Music Co.<br>4382 Jutland Drive<br>Box 178270<br>San Diego, CA  92117-0894 | |
| KLAVARSKRIBO | Klavarskribo<br>Postbus 39<br>2980 AA Ridderkerk<br>Holland | |
| KLIMENT | Musikverlag Johann Kliment<br>Kolingasse 15<br>A-1090  WIEN 9<br>Austria | |
| KMH | KMH Förlaget | |
| KNEUSSLIN | Edition Kneusslin<br>Amselstraße 43<br>CH-4059 Basel<br>Switzerland | FOR.MUS.DIST.<br>PETERS |
| KNOPF | Alfred A. Knopf<br>201 East 50th Street<br>New York, NY 10022 | |
| KNUF | Frits Knuf Uitgeverij<br>Rodeheldenstraat 13<br>P.O. Box 720<br>NL-4116 ZJ Buren<br>Netherlands | PENDRAGON |
| KODALY | Kodaly Center of America, Inc.<br>15 Denton Road<br>Wellesley, MA  02181 | SUPPORT |
| KON BOND | Kon. Bond van Chr. Zang- en<br>Oratoriumverenigingen | DONEMUS |
| KONINKLIJK | Koninklijk Nederlands<br>Zangersverbond | DONEMUS |
| KÖPER | Musikverlag Karl-Heinz Köper<br>Schneekoppenweg 12<br>D-3001 Isernhagen NB/Hannover<br>Germany | |
| KRENN | Ludwig Krenn Verlag<br>Neulerchenfelderstr. 3-7<br>A-1160  Wien<br>Austria | |
| KROMPHOLZ | Krompholz & Co.<br>Spitalgasse 28<br>CH-3001  Bern<br>Switzerland | |
| KRONOS | Kronos Press<br>25 Ansdell Street<br>London W8 5BN<br>England | |
| KRUSEMAN | Ed. Philip Kruseman | DONEMUS |
| KUNZELMANN | Edition Kunzelmann<br>Grutstrasse 28<br>CH-8134  Adliswil<br>Switzerland | FOR.MUS.DIST. |
| KYSAR | Michael Kysar<br>1250 South 211th Place<br>Seattle, WA  98148 | |
| LAABER | Laaber Verlag<br>Regensburgstrasse 19<br>D-8411  Laaber<br>Germany | |
| LABATIAZ | Editions Labatiaz<br>Case Postale 112<br>CH-1890  St. Maurice<br>Switzerland | |
| LAGOS | Editorial Lagos<br>Talachuano 638 P.B."H"<br>1013  Buenos Aires<br>Argentina | |
| LAKE STATE | Lake State Publishers<br>P.O. Box 1593<br>Grand Rapids, MI  49501 | |
| LAMP | Latin-American Music Pub. Co. Ltd.<br>8 Denmark Street<br>London<br>England | |
| LAND | A. Land & Zn. Musiekuitgevers | DONEMUS |
| LANDES | Landesverband Evangelischer<br>Kirchenchöre in Bayern | HÄNSSLER |
| LANG | Lang Music Publications<br>P.O. Box 11021<br>Indianapolis, IN 46201 | |

| Code | Publisher | U.S. Agent |
|------|-----------|------------|
| LÄNSMAN | Länsmansgarden<br>PL-7012<br>S-762 00 Rimbo<br>Sweden | |
| LARK | Lark Publishing | INTRADA |
| Latin-American Music Pub. Co. Ltd.<br>see LAMP | | |
| LATINL | The Latin American Literary<br>Review Press<br>2300 Palmer St.<br>Pittsburgh, PA 15218 | |
| LAUDAMUS | Laudamus Press | INTRADA |
| LAUDINELLA | Laudinella Reihe | FOSTER |
| LAUMANN | Laumann Verlag<br>Alter Gartenweg 14<br>Postfach 1360<br>D-4408 Dülmen<br>Germany | |
| LAUREL | Laurel Press | LORENZ |
| LAURENDALE | Laurendale Associates<br>15035 Wyandotte Street<br>Van Nuys, CA 91405 | |
| LAVENDER | Lavender Publications, Ltd.<br>Borough Green<br>Sevenoaks, Kent TN15 8DT<br>England | |
| LAWSON | Lawson-Gould Music Publishers, Inc.<br>250 W. 57th St., Suite 1005<br>New York, NY 10107 | ALFRED |
| LEA | Lea Pocket Scores<br>P.O. Box 138, Audubon Station<br>New York, NY 10032 | EUR.AM.MUS. |
| LEAWOOD | Leawood Music Press | INTRADA |
| LEDUC | Alphonse Leduc<br>175 rue Saint-Honoré<br>F-75040 Paris Cedex 01<br>France | KING,R<br>PRESSER<br>(rental) |
| LEE | Norman Lee Publishing, Inc.<br>Box 528<br>Oskaloosa, IA 52577 | BARNHS |
| LEEDS | Leeds Music Ltd.<br>MCA Building<br>2450 Victoria Park Avenue<br>Willowdale, Ontario M2J 4A2<br>Canada | MCA<br>PRESSER<br>(rental) |
| LEMA | LEMA Musikförlag<br>Vetevägen 24<br>S-691 48 Karlskoga<br>Sweden | |
| LEMOINE | Henry Lemoine & Cie<br>17, rue Pigalle<br>F-75009 Paris<br>France | PRESSER |

| Code | Publisher | U.S. Agent |
|------|-----------|------------|
| LENGNICK | Alfred Lengnick & Co., Ltd.<br>Purley Oaks Studios<br>421a Brighton Road<br>South Croydon, Surrey CR2 6YR<br>England | |
| LEON S | Stanley Leonard Publications<br>551 Sandrae Drive<br>Pittsburgh, PA 15243 | |
| LEONARD-ENG | Leonard, Gould & Bolttler<br>60-62 Clerkenwell Road<br>London EC1M 5PY<br>England | |
| LEONARD-US | Hal Leonard Music<br>7777 West Bluemound Road<br>Milwaukee, WI 53213 | |
| LESLIE | Leslie Music Supply<br>P.O. Box 471<br>Oakville, Ontario L6J 5A8<br>Canada | BRODT |
| LEUCKART | F.E.C. Leuckart<br>Nibelungenstraße 48<br>D-8000 München 19<br>Germany | |
| LEUPOLD | Wayne Leupold Editions<br>8510 Triad Drive<br>Colfax, NC 27235 | ECS |
| LEXICON | Lexicon Music<br>P.O. Box 2222<br>Newbury Park, CA 91320 | BRENTWOOD |
| LIBEN | Liben Music Publications<br>1191 Eversole Road<br>Cincinnati, OH 45230 | |
| LIBER | Svenska Utbildningsförlaget Liber AB<br>Utbildningsfölaget, Centrallagret<br>S-136 01 Handen<br>Stockholm<br>Sweden | |
| LIBIT | Libitum Musik<br>Box 81<br>S-371 21 Karlskrona<br>Sweden | |
| LICHTENAUER | W.F. Lichtenauer | DONEMUS |
| LIED | VEB Lied der Zeit Musikverlag<br>Rosa-Luxemburg-Straße 41<br>D-102 Berlin<br>Germany | |
| LIENAU | Robert Lienau Musikverlag<br>Hildegardstr. 16<br>D-10715 Berlin<br>Germany | |
| LIGA | Liga de Compositores de Musica de<br>Concierto de Mexico, A.C.<br>Mayorazgo No. 129<br>Col. Xoco<br>03330, Mexico, D.F.<br>Mexico | |
| LIGHT | Light of the World Music | INTRADA |

| Code | Publisher | U.S. Agent |
|------|-----------|------------|
| LILLENAS | Lillenas Publishing Co.<br>P.O. Box 419527<br>Kansas City, MO 64141 | |
| LINDSAY | Lindsay Music<br>23 Hitchin Street<br>Biggleswade, Beds SG18 8AX<br>England | PRESSER |
| LINDSBORG | Lindsborg Press<br>P.O. Box 737<br>State Road 9 South<br>Alexandria, VA 46001 | INTRADA |
| LINGUA | Lingua Press<br>c/o 1st Natl. Bank<br>310 S. Hamel Road<br>Los Angeles, CA 90048-3844 | |
| LISTER | Mosie Lister | LILLENAS |
| LITOLFF | Henry Litolff's Verlag<br>Kennedy Allee 101<br>Postfach 700906<br>D-6000 Frankfurt 70<br>Germany | PETERS |
| LITURGICAL | Liturgical Music Press<br>St. Johns Abbey<br>Collegeville, MN 56321 | |
| LLUQUET | Guillermo Lluquet<br>Almacen General de Musica<br>Avendida del Oeste 43<br>Valencia<br>Spain | |
| | London Pro Musica Edition<br>see LPME | |
| LONG ISLAND | Long Island Music Publishers | BRANCH |
| LOOP | Loop Music Co. | KJOS |
| LORENZ | Lorenz Corporation<br>501 East Third Street<br>P.O. Box 802<br>Dayton, OH 45401-9969 | |
| LOVE | Edition Love<br>Love Kustannus Oy<br>Hämeentie 6 A 4<br>00530 Helsinki<br>Finland | |
| LPME | The London Pro Musica Edition<br>15 Rock Street<br>Brighton BN2 1NF<br>England | MAGNAMUSIC |
| LUCKS | Luck's Music Library<br>P.O. Box 71397<br>Madison Heights, MI 48071 | |
| LUDWIG | Ludwig Music Publishing Co.<br>557-67 East 140th Street<br>Cleveland, OH 44110-1999 | |
| LUNDÉN | Edition Lundén<br>Bromsvagen 25<br>S-125 30 Alvsjö<br>Sweden | |

| Code | Publisher | U.S. Agent |
|------|-----------|------------|
| LUNDMARK | Lundmark Publications<br>811 Bayliss Drive<br>Marietta, GA 30067 | SUPPORT |
| LUNDQUIST | Abr. Lundquist Musikföflag AB<br>Katarina Bangata 17<br>S-116 25 Stockholm<br>Sweden | |
| LYCHE | Harald Lyche<br>Postboks 2171 Stromso<br>N-3003 Drammen<br>Norway | WALTON<br>(partial) |
| LYDIAN ORCH | Lydian Orchestrations<br>31000 Ruth Hill Road<br>Orange Cove, CA 93646 | SHAWNEE |
| LYNWOOD | Lynwood Music Photo Editions<br>2 Church St. West Hagley<br>West Midlands DY9 0NA<br>England | |
| LYRA | Lyra Music Co.<br>133 West 69th Street<br>New York, NY 10023 | |
| MAA | Music Associates of America<br>224 King Street<br>Englewood, NJ 07631 | |
| MAAS | Kurt Maas<br>Postfach 710267<br>D-8 München 71<br>Germany | |
| MACNUTT | Richard Macnutt Ltd.<br>Hamm Farm House<br>Withyham, Hartfield<br>Sussex TN7 4BJ<br>England | |
| | Mac Murray Publications<br>see MMP | |
| MAGNAMUSIC | Magnamusic Distributors, Inc.<br>P.O. Box 338<br>74 Amenia Union Road<br>Sharon, CT 06069 | |
| MALCOLM | Malcolm Music Ltd. | SHAWNEE |
| MANNA | Manna Music, Inc.<br>22510 Stanford Avenue<br>Suite 101<br>Valencia, CA 91355 | |
| MANNHEIMER | Mannheimer Musikverlag<br>Kunigundestraße 4<br>D-5300 Bonn 2<br>Germany | |
| MANUSCRIPT | Manuscript Publications<br>see CO OP | |
| MAPA MUNDI | Mapa Mundi - Music Publishers<br>72 Brewerey Road<br>London N7 9NE<br>England | ECS |

| Code | Publisher | U.S. Agent |
|------|-----------|------------|
| MARBOT | Edition Marbot Gmbh<br>Mühlenkamp 43<br>D-2000 Hamburg 60<br>Germany | PEER |
| MARCHAND | Marchand, Paap en Strooker | DONEMUS |
| MARGUN | Margun/Gunmar Music, Inc.<br>167 Dudley Road<br>Newton Centre, MA 02159 | JERONA |
| MARI | E. & O. Mari, Inc.<br>38-01 23rd Avenue<br>Long Island City, NY 11105 | |
| MARK | Mark Publications | CRESPUB |
| MARKS | Edward B. Marks Music Corp.<br>1619 Broadway<br>New York, NY 10019 | LEONARD-US<br>(sales)<br>PRESSER<br>(rental) |
| MARSEG | Marseg, Ltd.<br>18 Farmstead Road<br>Willowdale, Ontario M2L 2G2<br>Canada | |
| MARSH | Marsh Publications<br>P.O. Box 635, Astor Station<br>Boston, MA 02123 | |
| MARTIN | Editions Robert Martin<br>B.P. 502<br>106, Grande rue de la Coupée<br>F-71009 Charnay-les-Macon<br>France | PRESSER |
| MASTER | Master Music | CRESPUB |
| MASTERS | Masters Music Publications<br>P.O. Box 810157<br>Boca Raton, FL 33481-0157 | |
| MAURER | J. Maurer<br>Avenue du Verseau 7<br>B-1200 Brussel<br>Belgium | |
| MAURRI | Edizioni Musicali Ditta R. Maurri<br>Via del Corso 1 (17R.)<br>Firenze<br>Italy | |
| MAYHEW | Kevin Mayhew Ltd.<br>Rattlesden<br>Bury St. Edmunds<br>Suffolk IP30 0SZ<br>England | BRODT |
| MCA | MCA and Mills/MCA Joint Venture<br>Editions<br>1755 Broadway, 8th Floor<br>New York, NY 10019 | LEONARD-US<br>(sales)<br>PRESSER<br>(rental) |
| MCAFEE | McAfee Music Corp. | WARNER |
| MCGIN-MARX | McGinnis & Marx<br>236 West 26th Street, #11S<br>New York, NY 10001 | |
| MDV | Mitteldeutscher Verlag<br>Thalmannplatz 2, Postfach 295<br>D-4010 Halle-Saale<br>Germany | PETERS |

| Code | Publisher | U.S. Agent |
|------|-----------|------------|
| MEDIA | Media Press<br>P.O. Box 250<br>Elwyn, PA 19063 | |
| MEDICI | Medici Music Press<br>5017 Veach Road<br>Owensboro, KY 42301-9643 | |
| MEDIT | Mediterranean | GALAXY |
| MEL BAY | Mel Bay Publications, Inc.<br>P.O. Box 66<br>Pacific, MO 63069 | |
| MELE LOKE | Mele Loke Publishing Co.<br>Box 7142<br>Honolulu, Hawaii 96821 | HIGHLAND<br>(continental<br>U.S.A.) |
| MELODI | Casa Editrice Melodi S.A.<br>Galleria Del Coroso 4<br>Milano<br>Italy | |
| MEMPHIS | Memphis Music Craft Publications<br>4096 Blue Cedar<br>Lakeland, TN 38002 | |
| MENC | Music Educators National Conference<br>Publications Division<br>1902 Association Drive<br>Reston, VA 22091 | |
| MENTOR | Mentor Music<br>13205 Indian School Road<br>Albequerque, NM 87112 | |
| MERCATOR | Mercator Verlag & Wohlfahrt (Gert)<br>Verlag<br>Stresemannstrasse 20-22<br>Postfach 101461<br>D-4100 Duisberg 1<br>Germany | |
| MERCURY | Mercury Music Corp. | PRESSER |
| MERIDEN | Meriden Music<br>The Studio Barn Silverwood House<br>Woolasten Nr. Lidney<br>Gloucestershire GL15 6PJ<br>England | PRESSER |
| MERIDIAN | Les Nouvelles Éditions Meridian<br>5, rue Lincoln<br>F-75008 Paris 8<br>France | |
| MERION | Merion Music, Inc. | PRESSER |
| MERRYMOUNT | Merrymount Music, Inc. | PRESSER |
| MERSEBURGER | Merseburger Verlag<br>Motzstraße 13<br>D-3500 Kassel<br>Germany | |
| METRO | Metro Muziek<br>Uilenweg 38<br>Postbus 70<br>NL-6000 AB Weert<br>Netherlands | |

| Code | Publisher | U.S. Agent |
|------|-----------|------------|
| METROPOLIS | Metropolis Music Publishers<br>Jan Van Rijswijcklaan 7<br>B-2018 Antwerpen<br>Belgium | |
| MEULEMANS | Arthur Meulemans Fonds<br>Charles de Costerlaan, 6<br>2050 Antwerpen<br>Belgium | |
| MEXICANAS | Ediciones Mexicanas de Musica<br>Avenida Juarez 18<br>Mexico City<br>Mexico | PEER |
| MEZ KNIGA | Mezhdunarodnaya Kniga<br>39, Dimitrov St.<br>Moscow 113095<br>Russia | |
| MIDDLE | Middle Eight Music | WARNER |
| MILL CREEK | Mill Creek Publications<br>P.O. Box 556<br>Mentone, CA 92359 | |
| MILLER | Miller Music Corp. | WARNER |
| MILLS MUSIC | Mills Music Jewish Catalogue | TRANSCON.<br>PRESSER<br>(rental) |
| MINKOFF | Minkoff Reprints<br>8 rue Eynard<br>CH-1211 Genève 12<br>Switzerland | OLD |
| MIRA | Mira Music Associates<br>199 Mountain Road<br>Wilton, CT 06897 | |
| Mitteldeutscher Verlag<br>  see MDV | | |
| MJQ | M.J.Q. Music, Inc.<br>1697 Broadway #1100<br>New York, NY 10019 | FOX,S |
| MMB | MMB Music, Inc.<br>Contemporary Arts Building<br>3526 Washington Avenue<br>St. Louis, MO 63103-1019 | |
| MMME | Modern Musical Methods<br>P.O. Box 245<br>90 South Demarest Ave.<br>Bergenfield, NJ 07621 | |
| MMP | Mac Murray Publications | MUS.SAC.PRO. |
| MOBART | Mobart Music Productions | JERONA |
| MOD ART | Modern Art Music | SON-KEY |
| MODERN | Edition Modern<br>Rhodter Strasse 26<br>D-76185 Karlsruhe<br>Germany | |
| Modern Musical Methods<br>  see MMME | | |

| Code | Publisher | U.S. Agent |
|------|-----------|------------|
| MODUS | Mödus Musiikki Oy<br>PL 82, 57101 Savonlinna<br>Finland | |
| MOECK | Moeck Verlag<br>Postfach 3131<br>D-29231 Celle<br>Germany | EUR.AM.MUS.<br>MAGNAMUSIC |
| MOLENAAR | Molenaar's Muziekcenrale<br>Industrieweg 23<br>Postbus 19<br>NL-1520 AA Wormerveer<br>Netherlands | GM |
| MONDIAL | Mondial-Verlag KG<br>8 rue de Hesse<br>Genève<br>Switzerland | |
| Monte Music, De<br>  see DE MONTE | | |
| MONTEVERDI | Fondazione Claudio Monteverdi<br>Via Ugolani Dati, 4<br>I-26100 Cremona<br>Italy | |
| MONUMENTA | Monumenta Musica Svecicae | STIM |
| MORNING STAR | Morning Star Music Publishers<br>1727 Larkin Williams Rd.<br>Fenton, MO 63026-2024 | |
| MOSAIC | Mosaic Music Corporation | BOSTON |
| MÖSELER | Karl Heinrich Möseler Verlag<br>Hoffman-von-Fallersleben-Straße 8-10<br>Postfach 1661<br>D-3340 Wolfenbüttel<br>Germany | |
| MOSER | Verlag G. Moser<br>Kirschweg 8<br>CH-4144 Arlesheim<br>Switzerland | |
| MOWBRAY | Mowbray Music Publications<br>Saint Thomas House<br>Becket Street<br>Oxford OX1 1SJ<br>England | PRESSER |
| MSM | MSM Music Publishers | BRODT |
| MT.SALUS | Mt. Salus Music<br>710 Dunton Rd.<br>Clinton, MS 39056 | |
| MT. TAHOMA | Mt. Tahoma | BROUDE,A |
| MULL & SCH | Müller & Schade AG Musikhaus<br>Kramgasse 50<br>CH-3011 Bern<br>Switzerland | |
| MÜLLER | Willy Müller,Süddeutscher Musikverlag<br>Marzgasse 5<br>D-6900 Heidelberg<br>Germany | |
| MUNSTER | Van Munster Editie | DONEMUS |

| Code | Publisher | U.S. Agent |
|------|-----------|------------|
| MURPHY | Spud Murphy Publications | WESTERN |
| MUS.ANT.BOH | Musica Antiqua Bohemica | SUPRAPHON |
| MUS.ART | Music Art Publications<br>P.O. Box 1744<br>Chula Vista, CA 92010 | |
| MUS.PERC. | Music For Percussion, Inc.<br>170 N.E. 33rd Street<br>Fort Lauderdale, FL 33334 | |
| MUS. RARA | Musica Rara<br>Le Traversier<br>Chemin de la Buire<br>F-84170 Monteux<br>France | |
| MUS.SAC.PRO | Musica Sacra et Profana<br>P.O. Box 7248<br>Berkeley, CA 94707 | |
| MUS.SER.BUR | Music Service Bureau<br>1645 Harvard St. NW<br>Washington, D.C. 20009-3702 | |
| MUS.SUR | Musica del Sur<br>Apartado 5219<br>Barcelona<br>Spain | |
| MUS.VERA | Musica Vera Graphics & Publishers<br>350 Richmond Terrace 4-M<br>Staten Island, NY 10301 | ARISTA |
| MUS.VIVA | Musica Viva<br>262 King's Drive<br>Eastbourne<br>Sussex BN21 2XD<br>England | |
| MUSIA | Musia | PETERS |
| MUSIC | Music Sales Corp. Executive Offices<br>257 Park Avenue South, 20th Fl<br>New York, NY 10010 | |
| | Music Sales Corp. (Rental)<br>5 Bellvale Road<br>Chester, NY 10918 | |
| Music Associates of America<br>see MAA | | |
| MUSIC BOX | Music Box Dancer Publications Ltd. | PRESSER |
| Music Educators National Conference<br>see MENC | | |
| MUSIC-ENG | Music Sales Ltd.<br>Newmarket Road<br>Bury St. Edmunds<br>Suffolk IP33 3YB<br>England | MUSIC |
| MUSIC INFO | Muzicki Informativni Centar-ZAMP<br>Ulica 8 Maja 37<br>P.O. Box 959<br>Zagreb<br>Croatia | BREITKOPF-W |

| Code | Publisher | U.S. Agent |
|------|-----------|------------|
| MUSIC SC. | Musical Score Distributors<br>611 Broadway, Suite 615<br>New York, NY 10012 | |
| MUSIC SEV. | Music 70, Music Publishers<br>170 N.E. 33rd Street<br>Fort Lauderdale, FL 33334 | |
| Musica Russica<br>see RUSSICA | | |
| MUSICART | Musicart West<br>P.O. Box 1900<br>Orem, UT 84059 | |
| MUSICIANS PUB | Musicians Publications<br>P.O. Box 7160<br>West Trenton, NJ 08628 | |
| MUSICO | Musico Muziekuitgeverij | DONEMUS |
| MUSICPRINT | Musicprint Corporation<br>P.O. Box 20767<br>New York, NY 10023 | |
| MUSICUS | Edition Musicus<br>P.O. Box 1341<br>Stamford, CT 06904 | |
| Musik-Akademie der Stadt Basel<br>see BASEL | | |
| MUSIKALISKA | Musikaliska Konstföreningen<br>Aarstryck, Sweden | WALTON |
| MUSIKHOJ | Musikhojskolens Forlag ApS | EUR.AM.MUS |
| MUSIKINST | Verlag das Musikinstrument<br>Klüberstraße 9<br>D-6000 Frankfurt-am-Main<br>Germany | |
| MUSIKK | Musikk-Huset A-S<br>P.O. Box 822 Sentrum<br>0104 Oslo 1<br>Norway | |
| MUSIKWISS. | Musikwissenschaftlicher Verlag Wien<br>Dorotheergasse 10<br>A-1010 Wien 1<br>Austria | FOR.MUS.DIST<br>(Bruckner &<br>Wolf) |
| Muzicki Informativni Centar-Zamp<br>see MUSIC INFO | | |
| MUZYKA | Muzyka Publishers<br>14 Neglinnaya Street<br>103031 Moscow<br>Russia | |
| MYRRH | Myrrh Music | WORD |
| MYRTLE | Myrtle Monroe Music<br>2600 Tenth Street<br>Berkeley, CA 94710 | |
| NAGELS | Nagels Verlag | |
| NAKAS | H. Nakas-C. Papagrigoriou Co.<br>39 Panepistimiou Str.<br>105 64 Athens<br>Greece | |

| Code | Publisher | U.S. Agent |
|------|-----------|------------|
| NATIONAL | National Music Publishers<br>16605 Townhouse<br>Tustin, CA 91680 | |
| NEUE | Verlag Neue Musik<br>An der Kolonnade 15<br>Postfach 1306<br>D-1080 Berlin<br>Germany | FOR.MUS.DIST |
| NEW HORIZON | New Horizon Publications | TRANSCON. |
| New Music Edition<br>see NME | | |
| NEW MUSIC WEST | New Music West<br>1437 Crest Dr.<br>Altadena, CA 91001 | |
| NEW VALLEY | New Valley Music Press of Smith<br>College<br>Sage Hall 49<br>Northampton, MA 01063 | |
| NEW WORLD | New World Enterprises of Montrose,<br>Inc.<br>2 Marisa Court<br>Montrose, NY 10548 | |
| NEWAM | Foundation for New American Music | LUCKS |
| NGLANI | Edition Nglani<br>Box 871<br>Merrifield, VA 22116-2871 | |
| NIEUWE | De Nieuwe Muziekhandel | DONEMUS |
| NIPPON | Nippon Hosu | PRESSER |
| NL | NL Productions Inc. | PLUCKED ST |
| NLS | NLS Music | LAUREN |
| NME | New Music Edition | PRESSER |
| NO.AM.LIT. | North American Liturgy Resources<br>Choral Music Department<br>10802 North 23rd Avenue<br>Phoenix, AZ 85029 | |
| NOBILE | Nobile Verlag<br>Aixheimer Straße 26<br>D-7000 Stuttgart 75<br>Germany | |
| NOETZEL | Noetzel Musikverlag<br>Liebigstraße 16<br>Postfach 620<br>D-26354 Wilhelmshaven<br>Germany | PETERS |
| NOMOS | Edition Nomos | BREITKOPF-W |
| NOORDHOFF | P. Noordhoff | DONEMUS |
| NORDISKA | AB Nordiska Musikförlaget<br>Nybrogatan 3<br>S-114 34 Stockholm<br>Sweden<br>see also HANSEN-SWEDEN | |

| Code | Publisher | U.S. Agent |
|------|-----------|------------|
| NORK | Norske Komponisters Forlag<br>Gjernesvegen 24<br>N-5700 Voss<br>Norway | |
| NORRUTH | Norruth Music Publishers | MMB |
| NORSK | Norsk Musikforlag AS<br>Karl Johansgaten 39<br>P.O. Box 1499 Vika<br>N-0116 Oslo 1<br>Norway | WALTON |
| Norske Komponisters Forlag<br>see NORK | | |
| NORSKMI | Norsk Musikkinformasjon<br>Toftesgatan 69<br>N-0552 Oslo 5<br>Norway | |
| North American Liturgy Resources<br>see NO.AM.LIT. | | |
| NORTHLIGHT | Northlight Music Inc. | SCHIRM.G |
| NORTHRIDGE | Northridge Music, Inc.<br>7317 Greenback Lane<br>Citrus Heights, CA 95621 | WARNER |
| NORTON | W.W. Norton & Co., Inc.<br>500 Fifth Avenue<br>New York, NY 10003 | |
| Norwegian Music Information Center<br>see NORSKMI | | |
| NOSKE | A.A. Noske | DONEMUS |
| NOTA | Nota Bene Music<br>PO Box 29-125<br>Christchurch<br>New Zealand | |
| NOTENBOOM | De Notenboom<br>Dever 10<br>2550 Kontich<br>Belgium | |
| NOTERIA | Noteria<br>S-590 30 Borensberg<br>Sweden | STIM |
| NOTON | Noton<br>Kolltjernvn. 11<br>P.O. Box 1014<br>N-2301 Hamar<br>Norway | |
| NOVA | Nova Music Ltd.<br>Goldsmid Mews<br>15a Farm Road<br>Hove<br>Sussex BN3 1FB<br>England | ECS |
| NOVELLO | Novello & Co., Ltd.<br>8/9 Frith Street<br>London W1V 5TZ<br>England | SHAWNEE MUSIC (sales)<br>SCHIRM.G (rental) |

| Code | Publisher | U.S. Agent |
|------|-----------|------------|
| NOW VIEW | Now View | PLYMOUTH |
| NUOVA CARISH | Nuova Carisch s.r.l.<br>Via M.F. Quintiliano, 40<br>20138 Milano<br>Italy | |
| NYMPHENBURG | Edition Nymphenburg<br>Unterföhring, Germany | PETERS |
| OAK | Oak Publications | MUSIC |
| OCTAVA | Octava Music Co. Ltd. | WEINBERGER |
| OECUMUSE | Oecumuse<br>52a Broad St.<br>Ely, CB7 4AH<br>England | CANTORIS |
| OERT | Johannes Oertel Musikverlag<br>Ainmillerstr. 42<br>D-80801 Mu"nchen<br>Germany | |
| OISEAU | Éditions de L'Oiseau-Lyre<br>Les remparts<br>Boite Postale 515<br>MC-98015 Monaco Cedex | MAGNAMUSIC<br>OLD |
| OJEDA | Raymond J. Ojeda<br>98 Briar Road<br>Kentfield, CA 94904 | |
| OKRA | Okra Music Corp. | SEESAW |
| OLD | OMI - Old Manuscripts & Incunabula<br>P.O. Box 6019, FDR Station<br>New York, NY 10150 | |
| OLIVIAN | Olivian Press | ARCADIA |
| OLMS | G. Olms Verlag<br>Hagentorwall 7<br>D-3200 Hildesheim<br>Germany | |
| ONGAKU | Ongaku-No-Tomo Sha Co. Ltd.<br>Kagurazaka 6-30, Shinjuku-ku<br>Tokyo 162<br>Japan | PRESSER |
| OPUS | Opus Music Publishers, Inc.<br>1318 Chicago Avenue<br>Evanston, IL 60201 | |
| OPUS-CZ | Opus<br>Ceskoslavenske Hudobne<br>  Vydaratelstro<br>Mlynske nivy 73<br>827 99 Bratislava<br>Slovakia | BOOSEY<br>(rental) |
| OR-TAV | Or-Tav Music Publications<br>P.O. Box 1126<br>Kfar Sava 44110<br>Israel | |
| OREGON | Oregon Catholic Press<br>5536 NE Hassalo<br>Portland, OR 97213 | |
| ORGAN | Organ Music Co. | WESTERN |

| Code | Publisher | U.S. Agent |
|------|-----------|------------|
| ORGAN LIT | Organ Literature Foundation<br>45 Norfolk Road<br>Braintree, MA 02184 | |
| ORGANMASTER | Organmaster Music Series<br>282 Stepstone Hill<br>Guilford, CT 06437 | |
| ORION MUS | Orion Music Press<br>P.O. Box 145, University Station<br>Barrien Springs, MI 49104 | OPUS |
| ORLANDO | Orlando Musikverlag<br>Kaprunerstraße 11<br>D-8000 München 21<br>Germany | |
| ORPHEE | Editions Orphee, Inc.<br>1240 Clubview Blvd. N.<br>Columbus, OH 43235-1226 | |
| ORPHEUM | Orpheum Music<br>10th & Parker<br>Berkeley, CA 94710 | |
| OSTARA | Ostara Press, Inc. | WESTERN |
| ÖSTERREICH | Österreichischer Bundesverlag<br>Schwarzenberg Platz 5<br>A-1010 Wien<br>Austria | |
| OSTIGUY | Editions Jacques Ostiguy Inc.<br>12790 Rue Yamaska<br>St. Hyacinthe, Quebec<br>Canada J2T 1B3 | |
| OSTNORSK | Ostnorsk Musikkforlag<br>Nordre Langgate 1 B<br>N-9950 Vardo<br>Norway | |
| OTOS | Otos Edizioni Musicali<br>Via Marsillo Ficino, 10<br>I-50132 Firenze<br>Italy | |
| OUVRIÈRES | Les Éditions Ouvrières<br>12, Avenue Soeur-Rosalie<br>F-75621 Paris Cedex 13,<br>France | KING,R |
| OXFORD | Oxford University Press<br>Walton Street<br>Oxford OX2 6DP<br>England<br><br>Oxford University Press<br>198 Madison Avenue<br>New York, NY 10016 | |
| PACIFIC | Pacific Publications | INTRADA |
| PAGANI | O. Pagani & Bro, Inc.<br>c/o P. Deiro Music<br>289 Bleeker Street<br>New York, NY 10014 | |
| PAGANINIANA | Paganiniana Publications, Inc.<br>1 T.F.H. Plaza<br>3rd & Union Avenue<br>Neptune City, NJ 07753 | |

| Code | Publisher | U.S. Agent |
|------|-----------|------------|
| PAIDEIA | Paideia Editrice | BÄREN |
| PALLMA | Pallma Music Co. | KJOS |
| PAN | Editions Pan<br>Schaffhauserstraße 280<br>Postfach 176<br>CH-8057 Zürich<br>Switzerland | PRESSER |
| PAN AM | Pan American Union | PEER |
| PAN FIN | Edition Pan of Finland<br>Vihertie 56C<br>01620 Vantaa<br>Finland | |
| PANTON | Panton<br>Radlická 99<br>CS-150 00 Praha 5<br>Czech Republic | NEW WORLD |
| PARACLETE | Paraclete Press<br>P.O. Box 1568<br>Hilltop Plaza, Route 6A<br>Orleans, MA 02653 | |
| PARAGON | Paragon Music Publishers | CENTURY |
| PARAGON ASS. | Paragon Associates | BRENTWOOD |
| PARIS | Uitgeverij H.J. Paris | DONEMUS |
| PARKS | Parks Music Corp. | KJOS |
| PASTORALE | Pastorale Music Company<br>235 Sharon Drive<br>San Antonio, TX 78216 | |
| PASTORINI | Musikhaus Pastorini AG<br>Kasinostraße 25<br>CH-5000 Aarau<br>Switzerland | |
| PATERSON | Paterson's Publications, Ltd.<br>8-10 Lower James Street<br>London W1R 3PL<br>England | MUSIC |
| PATHWAY | Pathway Music<br>P.O. Box 2250<br>Cleveland, TN 37320 | |
| | Patrimoine Musical Candien<br>see CAN.MUS.HER. | |
| PAVANE | Pavane Publishing<br>321 Railroad Avenue<br>Myrtle Point, OR 97458 | INTRADA |
| PAXTON | Paxton Publications<br>Sevenoaks, Kent<br>England | PRESSER |
| PECKTACKULAR | Pecktackular Music<br>3605 Brandywine Drive<br>Greensboro, NC 27410 | |
| PEDAGOGUE | Pedagogue Press<br>PO Box 141215<br>Columbus, OH 43214 | |

| Code | Publisher | U.S. Agent |
|------|-----------|------------|
| PEER | Peer Southern Concert Music<br>810 Seventh Avenue<br>New York, NY 10019 | PRESSER |
| PEER MUSIK | Peer Musikverlag GmbH<br>Muhlenkamp 43<br>Postfach 602129<br>D-2000 Hamburg<br>Germany | PEER |
| PEGASUS | Pegasus Musikverlag<br>Liebig Straße 16<br>Postfach 620<br>D-2940 Wilhelmshaven<br>Germany | PETERS |
| PELICAN CAY | Pelican Cay Publications | PLYMOUTH |
| PELIKAN | Musikverlag Pelikan | EUR.AM.MUS. |
| PEMBROKE | Pembroke Music Co., Inc. | FISCHER,C |
| PENADÉS | José Penadés<br>En Sanz 12<br>Valencia<br>Spain | |
| PENDRAGON | Pendragon Press<br>R.R. 1, Box 159<br>Stuyvesant, NY 12173-9720 | |
| PENGUIN | Penguin Books<br>120 Woodbine Street<br>Bergenfield, NJ 07621 | |
| PENN STATE | Penn State Press<br>The Pennsylvania State University<br>Barbara Building, Suite C<br>University Park, PA 16802-1003 | |
| PENOLL | Penoll<br>Goteberg<br>Sweden | STIM |
| PEPPER | J.W. Pepper And Son, Inc.<br>P.O. Box 850<br>Valley Forge, PA 19482 | |
| PERF.ED | Performer's Editions | BROUDE BR |
| PERFORM | Perform Our Music<br>Leuven<br>Belgium | PEER |
| PERMUS | Permus Publications<br>P.O. Box 02033<br>Columbus, OH 43202 | |
| PETER | Peters Edition Ltd.<br>Bach House<br>10-12 Baches Street<br>London N1 6DN<br>England | |
| PETERER | Edition Melodie Anton Peterer<br>Brunnwiesenstraße 26<br>Postfach 260<br>CH-8409 Zürich<br>Switzerland | |

| Code | Publisher | U.S. Agent |
|---|---|---|
| PETERS | Edition Peters<br>C.F. Peters Corp.<br>373 Park Avenue South<br><br>New York, NY 10016<br><br>Edition Peters<br>Postfach 746<br>D-7010 Leipzig<br>Germany<br><br>C.F. Peters Musikverlag<br>Postfach 700851<br>Kennedyallee 101<br>D-6000 Frankfurt 70<br>Germany | |
| PETERS,K | Kermit Peters<br>1515 90th Street<br>Omaha, NE 68124 | |
| PETERS,M | Mitchell Peters<br>3231 Benda Place<br>Los Angeles, CA 90068 | |
| PFAUEN | Pfauen Verlag<br>Adolfsallee 34<br>Postfach 471<br>D-6200 Wiesbaden<br>Germany | |
| PHILHARMONIA | Philharmonia | EUR.AM.MUS.<br>(miniature<br>scores) |
| PHILIPPO | Editions Philippo | ELKAN-V |
| PHOEBUS | Phoebus Apollo Music Publishers<br>1126 Huston Drive<br>West Mifflin, PA 15122 | |
| PIEDMONT | Piedmont Music Co. | PRESSER<br>(rental) |
| PILES | Piles Editorial de Musica<br>Archena 33y Yatova, 4<br>Apartado 8.012<br>E-46080 Valencia<br>Spain | |
| PILLIN | Pillin Music | WESTERN |
| PILLON | Pillon Press | THOMAS |
| PIONEER | Pioneer Music Press | MUSICART |
| PIPER | Piper Music Co.<br>P.O. Box 1713<br>Cincinnati, OH 45201 | LIBEN |
| PIZZ | Pizzicato Edizioni Musicali<br>Via M. Ortigara 10<br>33100 UDINE<br>Italy | |
| PLAINSONG | Plainsong & Medieval Music Society<br>Catherine Harbor, Hon.Sed.<br>c/o Turner<br>72 Brewery Road<br>London N7 9NE<br>England | |

| Code | Publisher | U.S. Agent |
|---|---|---|
| PLAYER | Player Press<br>139-22 Caney Lane<br>Rosedale, NY 11422 | |
| PLENUM | Plenum Publishing Corp.<br>233 Spring Street<br>New Jork, NY 10013 | DA CAPO |
| PLESNICAR | Don Plesnicar<br>P.O. Box 4880<br>Albuquerque, NM 87106 | |
| PLOUGH | Plough Publishing House<br>Rifton, NY 12471 | |
| PLUCKED STR | Plucked String<br>P.O. Box 11125<br>Arlington, VA 22210 | |
| PLYMOUTH | Plymouth Music Co., Inc.<br>170 N.E. 33rd Street<br>P.O. Box 24330<br>Fort Lauderdale, FL 33334 | |
| PODIUM | Podium Music, Inc.<br>360 Port Washington Boulevard<br>Port Washington, NY 11050 | |
| POLSKIE | Polskie Wydawnictwo Muzyczne<br>Al. Krasinskiego 11a<br>PL31-111 Krakow<br>Poland | PRESSER |
| POLYPH MUS | Polyphone Music Co. | ARCADIA |
| POLYPHON | Polyphon Musikverlag | BREITKOPF-W |
| PORT.MUS. | Portugaliae Musicae<br>Fundaçao Calouste Gulbenkian<br>Avenida de Berna 45<br>P-1093 Lisboa Codex<br>Portugal | |
| Positif Press Ltd.<br>see BRENNAN | | |
| POSTHORN | Posthorn Press | INTRADA |
| POWER | Power and Glory Music Co.<br>6595 S. Dayton St.<br>Englewood, CO 80111 | SON-KEY |
| PRAEGER | Praeger Publications<br>383 Madison Avenue<br>New York, NY 10017 | |
| PRB | PRB Productions<br>963 Peralta Avenue<br>Albany, CA 94706-2144 | |
| PREISSLER | Musikverlag Josef Preissler<br>Postfach 521<br>Bräuhausstraße 8<br>D-8000 München 2<br>Germany | |
| PRELUDE | Prelude Publications<br>150 Wheeler Street<br>Glouchester, MA 01930 | |
| PRENTICE | Prentice-Hall, Inc.<br>Englewood Cliffs, NJ 07632 | |

| Code | Publisher | U.S. Agent |
|------|-----------|------------|
| PRESSER | Theodore Presser Co.<br>1 Presser Place<br>Bryn Mawr, PA 19010 | |
| PRESSES | Aux Presses d'Isle-de-France<br>12, rue de la Chaise<br>F-75007 Paris<br>France | |
| PRICE,P | Paul Price Publications<br>470 Kipp Street<br>Teaneck, NJ 07666 | |
| PRIMAVERA | Editions Primavera | GENERAL |
| PRINCE | Prince Publications<br>1125 Francisco Street<br>San Francisco, CA 94109 | |
| PRO ART | Pro Art Publications | WARNER |
| PRO MUSICA | Pro Musica Verlag<br>Postfach 467<br>D-04004 Leipzig<br>Germany | |
| PRO.MUS.INT | Pro Musica International<br>130 Bylor<br>P.O. Box 1687<br>Pueblo, CO 81002 | |
| PROCLAM | Proclamation Productions, Inc.<br>Orange Square<br>Port Jervis, NY 12771 | |
| PROGRESS | Progress Press<br>P.O. Box 12<br>Winnetka, IL 60093 | |
| PROPRIUS | Proprius Musik AB<br>Vartavagen 35<br>S-115 29 Stockholm<br>Sweden | |
| PROSVETNI | Prosvetni Servis | DRUSTVA |
| PROVIDENCE | Providence Music Press<br>251 Weybosset St.<br>Providence, RI 02903 | |
| PROVINCETOWN | Provincetown Bookshop Editions<br>246 Commercial Street<br>Provincetown, MA 02657 | |
| PROWSE | Keith Prowse Music Publishing Co.<br>138-140 Charing Cross Road<br>London, WC2H 0LD<br>England | INTER.MUS.P |
| PRUETT | Pruett Publishing Co.<br>2928 Pearl<br>Boulder, CO 80301-9989 | |
| PSALTERY | Psaltery Music Publications<br>P.O. Box 111325<br>Dallas, TX 75223 | KENDALE |
| PSI | PSI Press<br>P.O. Box 2320<br>Boulder, CO 80306 | |

| Code | Publisher | U.S. Agent |
|------|-----------|------------|
| PTM | PTM Music Manuscripts<br>6004 Candlewood Ct.<br>Brooklyn Park, MN 55443 | |
| PURIFOY | Purifoy Publishing<br>P.O. Box 30157<br>Knoxville, TN 37930 | JENSEN |
| PUSTET | Verlag Friedrich Pustet<br>Gutenbergstraße 8<br>Postfach 339<br>D-8400 Regensburg 11<br>Germany | |
| PYRAMINX | Pyraminx Publications | ACCURA |
| QUEENSGATE | Queensgate Music<br>120 Dowanhill Street<br>Glasgow G12 9DN<br>Scotland | |
| QUIROGA | Ediciones Quiroga<br>Alcalá, 70<br>28009 Madrid<br>Spain | PRESSER |
| RADIANT | Radiant Music<br>1445 Boonville Avenue<br>Springfield, MO 65802 | |
| RAHTER | D. Rahter<br>Werderstraße 44<br>D-2000 Hamburg 13<br>Germany | SCHAUER |
| RAMSEY | Basil Ramsey Publisher of Music | INTRADA |
| RARITIES | Rarities For Strings Publications<br>50 Bellevue Ave.<br>Bristol, CT 06010 | |
| RAVEN | Raven Press<br>1185 Avenue of the Americas<br>New York, NY 10036 | |
| REAL | Real Musical Publicaciones y<br>  Ediciones, S.A.<br>CTRA, C-501, KM9, 300<br>APDO, De Correos No. 27<br>28670 Villaviciosa De Odón Madrid,<br>Spain | |
| RECITAL | Recital Publications, Ltd.<br>P.O. Box 1697<br>Huntsville, TX 77342-1697 | |
| REGENT | Regent Music Corp.<br>488 Madison Avenue<br>5th Floor<br>New York, NY 10022 | LEONARD-US |
| REGINA | Regina Verlag<br>Schumannstraße 35<br>Postfach 6148<br>D-6200 Wiesbaden 1<br>Germany | |
| REGUS | Regus Publisher<br>10 Birchwood Lane<br>White Bear Lake, MN 55110 | |

| Code | Publisher | U.S. Agent |
|------|-----------|------------|
| REIMERS | Edition Reimers AB<br>Box 15030<br>S-16115 Bromma<br>Sweden | PRESSER |
| REINHARDT | Friedrich Reinhardt Verlag<br>Missionsstraße 36<br>CH-4055 Basel<br>Switzerland | |
| RENAISSANTES | Les Editions Renaissantes | EUR.AM.MUS. |
| RENK | Musikverlag Renk "Varia Edition"<br>Herzog-Heinrich-Straße 21<br>D-8000 München 2<br>Germany | |
| RESEARCH | Research Publications, Inc.<br>Lunar Drive<br>Woodbridge, CT 06525 | |
| RESOURCE | Resource Publications, Inc.<br>160 E. Virginia Street, #290<br>San Jose, CA 95112-5876 | |
| RESTORATION | Restoration Press | THOMAS |
| REUTER | Reuter & Reuter Förlag AB<br>Box 26072<br>S-100 41 Stockholm<br>Sweden | |
| RHODES,R | Roger Rhodes Music, Ltd.<br>P.O. Box 1550, Radio City Station<br>New York, NY 10101 | |
| RICHMOND | Richmond Music Press, Inc.<br>P.O. Box 465<br>Richmond, IN 47374 | |
| RICHMOND ORG. | The Richmond Organization<br>11 W. 19th St., Suite 711<br>New York, NY 10011<br>    see also TRO | PLYMOUTH |
| RICORDI-ARG | Ricordi Americana S.A.<br>Cangallo, 1558<br>1037 Buenos Aires<br>Argentina | LEONARD-US<br>BOOSEY<br>(rental) |
| RICORDI-BR | Ricordi Brasileira S.A.<br>R. Conselheiro Nebias 773<br>1 S-10-12<br>Sao Paolo<br>Brazil | LEONARD-US<br>BOOSEY<br>(rental) |
| RICORDI-CAN | G. Ricordi & Co.<br>Toronto<br>Canada | LEONARD-US<br>BOOSEY<br>(rental) |
| RICORDI-ENG | G. Ricordi & Co. Ltd.<br>The Bury, Church Street<br>Chesham, Bucks HP5 1JG<br>England | LEONARD-US<br>BOOSEY<br>(rental) |
| RICORDI-FR | Société Anonyme des Éditions<br>    Ricordi | LEONARD-US<br>BOOSEY<br>(rental) |
| RICORDI-GER | G. Ricordi & Co.<br>Postfach 114<br>D-85618 Feldkirchen Bei München<br>Germany | LEONARD-US<br>BOOSEY<br>(rental) |
| RICORDI-IT | G.Ricordi & Co.<br>    see BMG RICORDI | LEONARD-US<br>BOOSEY<br>(rental) |
| RIDEAU | Les Éditions Rideau Rouge<br>24, rue de Longchamp<br>F-75116 Paris<br>France | PRESSER<br>SCHIR.G |
| RIES | Ries & Erler<br>Charlottenbrunner Straße 42<br>D-4193 Berlin (Grunewald)<br>Germany | |
| RILEY | Dr. Maurice W. Riley<br>Eastern Michigan University<br>512 Rossevelt Boulevard<br>Ypsilanti, MI 48197 | |
| ROBBINS | Robbins Music Corp. | WARNER<br>PRESSER<br>(rental) |
| ROBERTON | Roberton Publications<br>The Windmill, Wendover<br>Aylesbury, Bucks, HP22 6JJ<br>England | PRESSER |
| ROBERTS,L | Lee Roberts Music Publications, Inc.<br>P.O. Box 225<br>Katonah, NY 10536 | |
| ROBITSCHEK | Adolf Robitschek Musikverlag<br>Graben 14 (Bräunerstraße 2)<br>Postfach 42<br>A-1011 Wien<br>Austria | |
| ROCHESTER | Rochester Music Publishers, Inc.<br>358 Aldrich Road<br>Fairport, NY 14450 | ACCURA |
| RODEHEAVER | Rodeheaver Publications | WORD |
| ROLLAND | Rolland String Reasearch Associates<br>#101 W. Windsor Road #3114<br>Urbana, IL 61801 | BOOSEY |
| RONCORP | Roncorp, Inc.<br>P.O. Box 724<br>Cherry Hill, NJ 08003 | |
| RONGWEN | Rongwen Music, Inc. | BROUDE BR |
| ROSSUM | Wed. J.R. van Rossum | ZENGERINK |
| ROUART | Rouart-Lerolle & Cie | SCHIRM.G |
| ROW | R.D. Row Music Co. | FISHER,C |
| ROYAL | Royal School of Church Music<br>Addington Palace<br>Croydon, Surrey CR9 5AD<br>England | |
| | Royal Schools of Music, Associated Board of the<br>    see ABRSM | |
| ROYAL TAP. | Royal Tapestry<br>50 Music Square West<br>Suite 500A<br>Nashville, TN 37203 | BRENTWOOD |

| Code | Publisher | U.S. Agent |
|------|-----------|------------|
| ROZSAVÖLGI | Rozsavölgi & Co. | BUDAPEST |
| RUBANK | Rubank, Inc.<br>16215 N.W. 15th Avenue<br>Miami, FL 33169 | LEONARD-US |
| RUBATO | Rubato Musikverlag<br>Hollandstraße 18<br>A-1020 Wien<br>Austria | DONEMUS |
| RUH,E | Emil Ruh Musikverlag<br>Zürichstraße 33<br>CH-8134<br>Adliswil - Zürich<br>Switzerland | |
| RUMAN.COMP. | Uniunea Compozitorilor din<br>R.S. România<br>(Union of Rumanian Composers)<br>Str. C. Escarcu No. 2<br>Bucuresti, Sector 1<br>Rumania | |
| RUNDEL | Musikverlag Rundel<br>Postfach 61<br>D-88428 Rot an der Rot<br>Germany | |
| RUSSICA | Musica Russica<br>27 Willow Lane<br>Madison, CT 06443 | |
| RUTGERS | Rutgers University Editions | JERONA |
| RYDET | Rydet Music Publishers<br>P.O. Box 477<br>Purchase, NY 10577 | |
| SAC.MUS.PR. | Sacred Music Press of Hebrew Union<br>College<br>One West Fourth Street<br>New York, NY 10012 | TRANSCON. |
| SACRED | Sacred Music Press | LORENZ |
| SACRED SONGS | Sacred Songs, Inc. | WORD |
| SALABERT | Francis Salabert Éditions<br>22 rue chauchat<br>F-75009 Paris<br>France | LEONARD-US<br>(sales)<br>SCHIRM.G<br>(rental) |
| SAMFUNDET | Samfundet til udgivelse af Dansk<br>Musik<br>Valkendorfsgade 3<br>DK-1151 Kobenhavn<br>Denmark | PETERS |
| SAN ANDREAS | San Andreas Press<br>3732 Laguna Avenue<br>Palo Alto, CA 94306 | |
| SANJO | Sanjo Music Co.<br>P.O. Box 7000-104<br>Palos Verdes Peninsula, CA 90274 | |
| SANTA | Santa Barbara Music Publishing<br>P.O. Box 41003<br>Santa Barbara, CA 93140 | |

| Code | Publisher | U.S. Agent |
|------|-----------|------------|
| | Santis, Edizioni de<br>see DE SANTIS | |
| SAUL AVE | Saul Avenue Publishing Co.<br>4172 Fox Hollow Drive<br>Cincinnati, OH 45241-2939 | |
| SAVGOS | Savgos Music Inc.<br>P.O. Box 279<br>Elizabeth, NJ 07207 | |
| SCARECROW | The Scarecrow Press, Inc.<br>4720 Boston Way<br>Lanham, MD 20706 | |
| SCELTE | Studio per Edizioni Scelte<br>Lungarno Guicciardini 9R<br>I-50125 Firenze<br>Italy | |
| SCHAUER | Richard Schauer, Music Publishers<br>67 Belsize Lane, Hampstead<br>London NW3 5AX<br>England | PRESSER |
| SCHAUM | Schaum Publications, Inc.<br>2018 East North Avenue<br>Milwaukee, WI 53202 | |
| SCHEIDT | Altonaer Scheidt-Ausgabe | HÄNSSLER |
| SCHERZANDO | Muziekuitgeverij Scherzando<br>Lovelingstraat 20-22<br>B-2000 Antwerpen<br>Belgium | |
| SCHIRM.EC | E.C. Schirmer Music Co.<br>see ECS | |
| SCHIRM.G | G. Schirmer, Inc. (Executive Offices)<br>257 Park Avenue South, 20th Floor<br>New York, NY 10010<br><br>G.Schirmer Rental Performance Dept.<br>P.O. Box 572<br>5 Bellvale Road<br>Chester, NY 10918 | LEONARD-US<br>(sales) |
| SCHMIDT,H | Musikverlag Hermann Schmidt<br>Berliner Straße 26<br>D-6000 Frank-am-Main 1<br>Germany | |
| SCHMITT | Schmitt Music Editions | WARNER |
| SCHNEIDER,H | Musikverlag Hans Schneider<br>Mozartstraße 6<br>D-8132 Tutzing<br>Germany | |
| SCHOLA | Editions Musicales de la Schola<br>Cantorum<br>Rue du Spain 2A<br>CH-2114 Fleurier<br>Switzerland | |
| SCHOTT | Schott & Co. Ltd.<br>Brunswick Road<br>Ashford, Kent TN23 1DX<br>England | EUR.AM.MUS. |

| Code | Publisher | U.S. Agent |
|------|-----------|------------|
| SCHOTT-FRER | Schott Frères<br>30 rue Saint-Jean<br>B-1000 Bruxelles<br>Belgium | EUR.AM.MUS. |
| SCHOTT,J | Schott & CO.<br>Kasuga Bldg., 2-9-3 Iidabashi,<br>Chiyoda-ku<br>Tokyo 102<br>Japan | EUR.AM.MUS. |
| SCHOTTS | B. Schotts Söhne<br>Weihergarten 5<br>Postfach 3640<br>D-6500 Mainz<br>Germany | EUR.AM.MUS. |
| SCHROTH | Edition Schroth<br>Kommandatenstrasse 5A<br>D-1 Berlin 45<br>Germany | BÄREN. |
| SCHUBERTH | Edward Schuberth & Co., Inc. | CENTURY |
| SCHUBERTH,J | J. Schuberth & Co.<br>Marienstrasse 13<br>D-99817 Eisenach<br>Germany | |
| SCHULTHEISS | Carl L. Schultheiß<br>Postfach 1736<br>D-82145 Planegg Bei München<br>Germany | |
| SCHULZ.FR | Blasmusikverlag Fritz Schulz<br>Am Märzengraben 6<br>D-7800 Freiburg-Tiengen<br>Germany | |
| SCHUP | Schuppanzigh Press<br>P.O. Box 10436<br>Alexandria, VA 22310 | |
| SCHWANN | Musikverlag Schwann | PETERS |
| SCHWEIZER | Schweizericher Kirchengesangbund<br>Musik Lipp AG<br>Kasinostraße 25<br>Postfach<br>CH-5001 Aarau<br>Switzerland | FOSTER |
| SCIENTIA | Scientia<br>Verlag und Antiquariat<br>Postfach 1660<br>Alderstrasse 65<br>D-7080 Aalen 1<br>Germany | |
| SCOTT | G. Scott Music Publishing CCo. | WESTERN |
| SCOTT MUSIC | Scott Music Publications | ALFRED |
| SCOTUS | Scotus Music Publications, Ltd. | ESCHENBACH |
| SCREEN | Screen Gems<br>Columbia Pictures | WARNER |
| SDG PR | SDG Press<br>170 N.E. 33rd Street<br>Ft. Lauderdale, FL 33334 | PLYMOUTH |
| SEAMONT | Seamont International | INTRADA |

| Code | Publisher | U.S. Agent |
|------|-----------|------------|
| SEESAW | Seesaw Music Corp.<br>2067 Broadway<br>New York, NY 10023 | |
| SEIFERT | Studio-Verlag Rudi Seifert<br>Eugenstraße 11<br>D-88045 Friedrichshafen<br>Germany | |
| SELAH | Selah Publishing Co.<br>P.O. Box 3037<br>Kingston, NY 12401 | |
| SELMER | Selmer Éditions<br>18, rue de la Fontaine-au-Roi<br>F-75011 Paris<br>France | |
| SEMI | Société d'Editions Musicales<br>Internationales | PEER |
| SENART | Ed. Maurice Senart<br>22 rue Chauchat<br>F-75009 Paris<br>France | SCHIRM.G |
| SEPTEMBER | September Music Corp.<br>250 W. 57th Street<br>New York, NY 10019 | |
| SERENUS | Serenus Corp.<br>145 Palisade Street<br>Dobbs Fery, NY 10522 | |
| SERV M | Servant Music | INTRADA |
| SERVANT | Servant Publications<br>P.O. Box 8617<br>840 Airport Boulevard<br>Ann Arbor. MI 48107 | |
| SESAC | Sesac, Inc.<br>10 Columbus Circle<br>New York, NY 10019 | |
| SHALL-U-MO | Shall-U-Mo Publications<br>P.O. Box 2824<br>Rochester, NY 14626 | |
| SHAPIRO | Shapiro, Bernstein & Co., Inc.<br>10 East 53 Street<br>New York, NY 10022 | PLYMOUTH |
| SHATTINGER | Shattinger Music Co.<br>1810 S. Broadway<br>St. Louis, MO 63104 | |
| SHAWNEE | Shawnee Press, Inc.<br>49 Waring Drive<br>Delaware Water Gap, PA 18327-1099 | MUSIC |
| SHEPPARD | John Sheppard Music Press | EUR.AM.MUS. |
| | Sherry-Brener, Ltd., Antigua Casa<br>see ACSB | |
| SIDEMTON | Sidemton Verlag | BREITKOPF-W |
| SIFLER | Paul J. Sifler<br>3947 Fredonia Drive<br>Hollywood, CA 90068 | |

| Code | Publisher | U.S. Agent |
|---|---|---|
| SIGHT & SOUND | Sight & Sound International<br>3200 South 166th Street<br>Box 27<br>New Berlin, WI 53151 | |
| SIJN | D. van Sijn & Zonen<br>Banorstraat 1<br>Rotterdam<br>Netherlands | |
| SIKORSKI | Hans Sikorski Verlag<br>Johnsallee 23<br>Postfach 132001<br>D-2000 Hamburg 13<br>Germany | LEONARD-US |
| SIMROCK | Nicholas Simrock<br>Lyra House<br>37 Belsize Lane<br>London NW3 5AX<br>England | PRESSER |
| SINGSPIR | Singspiration Music<br>The Zondervan Corp.<br>1415 Lake Drive S.E.<br>Grand Rapids, MI 49506 | |
| SIRIUS | Sirius-Verlag | PETERS |
| SKANDINAVISK | Skandinavisk Musicforlag<br>Gothersgade 9-11<br>DK-1123 Kobenhavn K.<br>Denmark | |
| SLATKINE | Slatkine Reprints<br>5 rue des Chaudronniers<br>Case 765<br>CH-1211 Genève 3<br>Switzland | |
| SLOV.AKA | Slovenska Akademija Znanosti in<br>  Umetnosti<br>Trg Francoske Revolucije 6<br>Ljubljana<br>Slovenia | |
| SLOV.HUD.FOND. | Slovenský Hudobny Fond<br>Fucikova 29<br>811 02 Bratislava<br>Slovakia | BOOSEY<br>(rental) |
| SLOV.MAT | Slovenska Matica | DRUSTVA |
| SMITH,D. | David E. Smith Publications<br>4826 Shabbona Road<br>Deckerville, MI 48427 | |
| SMITH PUB | Smith Publications-Sonic Art Editions<br>2617 Gwynndale Avenue<br>Baltimore, MD 21207 | |
| SMPF | SMPF, Inc.<br>16 E. 34th St., 7th Floor<br>New York, NY 10016 | |
| SOC.FR.MUS. | Société Française de Music | TRANSAT. |
| SOC.PUB.AM. | Society for the Publication<br>  of American Music | PRESSER |

Société d'Éditions Musicales Internationales
  see SEMI

| Code | Publisher | U.S. Agent |
|---|---|---|

Society for the Preservation & Encouragement of
  Barber Shop Quartet Singing in America
    see SPEBSQSA

Society of Finnish Composers
    see SUOMEN

| Code | Publisher | U.S. Agent |
|---|---|---|
| SODENKAMP | Rieks Sodenkamp<br>P.O. Box 10<br>NL 6200 AA Maastricht<br>Netherlands | |
| SOLAR | The Solar Studio<br>178 Cowles Road<br>Woodbury, CT 06798 | |
| SOLID F | Solid Foundation Music | SON-KEY |
| SOMERSET | Somerset Press | HOPE |
| SON-KEY | Son-Key, Inc.<br>P.O. Box 31757<br>Aurora, CO 80041 | |
| SONANTE | Sonante Publications<br>P.O. Box 74, Station F<br>Toronto, Ontario M4Y 2L4<br>Canada | |
| SONIC ARTS | Sonic Arts | |
| SONOS | Sonos Music Resources, Inc.<br>P.O. Box 1510<br>Orem, UT 84057 | |
| SONSHINE | Sonshine Productions | LORENZ |
| SONZOGNO | Casa Musicale Sonzogno<br>Via Bigli 11<br>I-20121 Milano<br>Italy | PRESSER |
| SOUNZ | SOUNZ New Zealand<br>Level 3<br>15 Brandon Street<br>PO Box 10042<br>Wellington<br>New Zealand | |
| SOUTHERN | Southern Music Co.<br>1100 Broadway<br>P.O. Box 329<br>San Antonio, TX 78292 | |
| SOUTHRN PUB | Southern Music Publishing Co., Pty.<br>  Ltd.<br>Sydney, Australia | PEER |
| SOUTHWEST | Southwest Music Publications<br>Box 4552<br>Santa Fe, NM 87502 | |
| SPAN.MUS.CTR. | Spanish Music Center, Inc.<br>4 Division Street<br>P.O. Box 132<br>Farmingville, NY 11738 | |
| SPEBSQSA | Society for the Preservation &<br>  Encouragement of Barber Shop<br>  Quartet Singing in America, Inc.<br>6315 Third Avenue<br>Kenosha, WI 53143-5199 | |

| Code | Publisher | U.S. Agent |
|------|-----------|-----------|
| SPIRE | Spire Editions | FISHER,C WORLD |
| SPRATT | Spratt Music Publishers 17 West 60th Street, 8th Fl. New York, NY 10023 | PLYMOUTH |
| ST.GREGORY | St. Gregory Publishing Co. 64 Pineheath Road High Kelling, Holt Norfolk, NR25 6RH England | ROYAL |
| ST.MARTIN | St. Martin Music Co., Inc. | ROYAL |
| STAFF | Staff Music Publishing Co., Inc. 170 N.E. 33rd St. Ft. Lauderdale, FL 33334 | PLYMOUTH |
| STAINER | Stainer & Bell Ltd. P.O. Box 110, Victoria House 23 Gruneisen Road London N3 1DZ England | ECS HOPE |
| STAMON | Nick Stamon Press 4280 Middlesex Drive San Diego, CA 92116 | |
| STAMPS | Stamps-Baxter Music Publications Box 4007 Dallas, TX 75208 | SINGSPIR |
| STANDARD | Standard Music Publishing, Inc. | |
| STANGLAND | Thomas C. Stangland Co. P.O. Box 19263 Portland, OR 97280 | |
| STEINGRÄBER | Edition Steingräber Auf der Reiswiese 9 D-6050 Offenbach/M. Germany | |
| STILL | William Grant Still Music 22 S. San Francisco Street Suite 422 Flagstaff, AZ 86001-5737 | |
| STIM | STIMs Informationcentral för Svensk Musik Sandhamnsgatan 79 Box 27327 S-102 54 Stockholm Sweden | |
| STOCKHAUSEN | Stockhausen-Verlag Kettenberg 15 D-51515 Kürten Germany <br><br> Stockhausen-Verlag, U.S. 2832 Maple Lane Fairfax, VA 22030 | |
| STOCKTON | Fred Stockton P.O. Box 814 Grass Valley, CA 95945 | |
| STRONGHOLD | Stronghold Publications | BRENTWOOD |
| STUD | Studio 224 | STUDIO |

| Code | Publisher | U.S. Agent |
|------|-----------|-----------|
| STUDIO | Studio P/R, Inc. | WARNER |
| STYRIA | Verlag Styria Schönaugasse 64 Postfach 435 A-8011 Graz Austria | |
| SUECIA | Edition Suecia | STIM |
| SUISEISHA | Suiseisha Editions | ONGAKU |
| SUMMA | Summa Productions | AMSI |
| SUMMIT | Summit Music Ltd. 38 North Row London W1R 1DH England | |
| SUMMY | Summy-Birchard Co. | WARNER |
| SUNSHINE | Sunshine Music Distribution Co., Inc. 407 North Grant Ave., Suite 400 Columbus, OH 43215-2157 | |
| SUO.TM | Suomen Tyovaen Musiikkiliitto Hameenpuisto 33 B SF-33200 Tampere 20 Finland | |
| SUOM | Suomen Laulajien JA Soittajien Liitto Fredrikinkatu 61 FIN-00100 Helsinki Finland | |
| SUOMEN | Suomen Säveltäjät ry (Society of Finnish Composers) Runeberginkatu 15 A SF-00100 Helsinki 10 Finland | |
| SUPPORT | Support Services 79 South Street P.O. Box 478 Natick, MA 01760 | |
| SUPRAPHON | Supraphon Palckeho 1 CS-112 99 Praha 1 Czech Republic | FOR.MUS.DIST (rental) NEW WORLD |
| SVENSKA | Svenska Utbildningsförlaget Liber AB see LIBER | |
| SVERIGES | Sveriges Körföbund Walton Rosenlundsgatan 54 S-116 53 Stockholm, Sweden | |
| SVERR | Sveriges Radios Musikbibliotek S-105 10 Stockholm Sweden | |
| SWAN | Swan & Co. P.O. Box 1 Rickmansworth, Herts WD3 3AZ England | ARCADIA |
| SWAND | Swand Publications 120 North Longcross Road Linthicum Heights, MD 21090 | |
| | Swedish Music Information Center see STIM | |

| Code | Publisher | U.S. Agent |
|------|-----------|------------|
| SYMPHONIA | Symphonia Verlag | WARNER |
| TARA | Tara Publications<br>29 Derby Ave.<br>Cedarhurst, NY 11516 | |
| TAUNUS | Taunus | HOFMEISTER-W |
| TCA PUB | TCA Publications<br>Teacher-Composer Alliance<br>P.O. Box 6428<br>Evanston, IL 60204 | |
| TECLA | Tecla Editions<br>Soar Chapel<br>Penderyn<br>South Wales CF 44 9JY<br>United Kingdom | |
| TEESELING | Muziekuitgeverij van Teeseling<br>Buurmansweg 29B<br>NL-6525 RV Nijmegen<br>Netherlands | |
| TEMPLETON | Templeton Publishing Co., Inc. | SHAWNEE |
| TEMPO | Tempo Music Publications<br>3773 W. 95th Street<br>Leawood, KS 66206 | BRENTWOOD |
| TEMPO P | Tempo Praha | PRESSER |
| TEN TIMES | Ten Times A Day<br>P.O. Box 230<br>Deer Park, L.I., NY 11729 | |
| TENUTO | Tenuto Publications<br>see also TRI-TEN | PRESSER |
| TETRA | Tetra Music Corp. | PLYMOUTH<br>WESLEYAN<br>(rental) |
| THAMES | Thames Publishing<br>14 Barbly Road<br>London W10 6AR<br>England | |
| THINGS FS | Things For Strings Publishing Co.<br>P.O. Box 9263<br>Alexandria, VA 22304 | |
| THOM ED | Thompson Edition, Inc.<br>231 Plantation Road<br>Rock Hill, SC 29732-9441 | |
| THOMA COM. | Thoma CompuGraphics | |
| THOMAS | Thomas House Publications<br>P.O. Box 1423<br>San Carlos, CA 94070 | INTRADA |
| THOMI-BERG | E. Thomi-Berg Musikverlag<br>Postfach 1736<br>D-82145 Planegg Bei München<br>Germany | |
| THOMPSON | Thompson Music House<br>P.O. Box 12463<br>Nashville, TN 37212 | |

| Code | Publisher | U.S. Agent |
|------|-----------|------------|
| THOMP.G | Gordon V. Thompson Music<br>see WAR | |
| THORPE | Thorpe Music Publishing Co. | PRESSER |
| TIEROLFF | Tierolff Muziek Centrale<br>P.O. Box 18<br>NL-4700 AA Roosendaal<br>Netherlands | |
| TISCHER | Tischer und Jagenberg Musikverlag<br>Nibelungenstraße 48<br>D-8000 München 19<br>Germany | |
| TOA | Toa Editions | ONGAKU |
| TONGER | P.J. Tonger, Musikverlag<br>Postfach 501818<br>50978 Köln<br>Germany | |
| TONIC | Tonic Publishing<br>c/o RSCM Music Supplies<br>The Royal School of Church Music<br>Cleveland Lodge<br>West Humble<br>Dorking RH5 GWB<br>England | |
| TONOS | Tonos Musikverlags GmbH<br>Holzhofallee 15<br>D-64295 Darmstadt<br>Germany | SEESAW |
| TOORTS | Muziekuitgeverij De Toorts<br>Nijverheidsweg 1<br>Postbus 576<br>NL-2003 RN Haarlem<br>Netherlands | |
| TRANSAT. | Éditions Musicales Transatlantiques<br>151, avenue Jean-Jaures<br>F-75019 Paris<br>France | PRESSER<br>GENERAL<br>(rental) |
| TRANSCON. | Transcontinental Music Publications<br>838 Fifth Avenue<br>New York, NY 10021 | |
| TREKEL | Joachim-Trekel-Verlag<br>Postfach 620428<br>D-2000 Hamburg 62<br>Germany | |
| TRI-TEN | Tritone Press and Tenuto<br>Publications<br>P.O. Box 5081, Southern Station<br>Hattiesburg, MS 39401 | PRESSER |
| TRIGON | Trigon Music Inc. | LORENZ |
| TRINITY | Trinity House Publishing | CRESPUB |
| TRITON | Editions du Triton<br>Rue du Sapin 2 a<br>CH-2114 Fleurier<br>Switzerland | |
| TRIUNE | Triune Music, Inc. | LORENZ |

| Code | Publisher | U.S. Agent |
|------|-----------|------------|
| TRN | TRN Music Publishers<br>111 Torreon Loop<br>P.O. Box 1076<br>Ruidoso, NM 88345 | |
| TRO | TRO Songways Service, Inc.<br>11 W. 19th St., Suite 711<br>New York, NY 10011<br>see also RICHMOND ORG. | PLYMOUTH |
| TROPPE | Troppe Note Publishing, Inc.<br>1932 Howard Ave.<br>Las Vegas, NV 89104 | |
| TROY | Troy State University Library<br>Troy, AL 36081 | |
| TUSCANY | Tuscany Publications | PRESSER |
| TUSKEGEE | Tuskegee Institute Music Press | KJOS |
| TVAR | Themes & Variations<br>39 Danbury Ave.<br>Westport, CT 06880-6822 | |
| TWO-EIGHTEEN | Two-Eighteen Press<br>P.O. Box 218, Village Station<br>New York, NY 10014 | |
| U.S. CATH | United States Catholic Conference<br>Publications Office<br>1312 Massachusetts Avenue N.W.<br>Washington, D.C. 20005 | |
| UBER,D | David Uber<br>Music Department<br>Trenton State College<br>Trenton, NJ 08625 | |
| UFATON | Ufaton-Verlag | ORLANDO |
| UNC JP | UNC Jazz Press<br>University of Northern Colorado<br>Greeley, CO 80639 | |
| UNICORN | Unicorn Music Company, Inc. | BOSTON |
| UNION ESP. | Union Musical Ediciones<br>Carrera de San Jeronimo 26<br>Madrid 14<br>Spain | SCHIRM.G |
| | Union Musical Española<br>see UNION ESP. | |
| UNISONG | Unisong Publishers | PRESSER |
| UNITED ART | United Artists Group | WARNER<br>PRESSER<br>(rental) |
| UNITED MUS. | United Music Publishers Ltd.<br>42 Rivington Street<br>London EC2A 3BN<br>England | PRESSER |
| UNIV.ALA | University of Alabama Press<br>Box 870380<br>Tuscaloosa, AL 35487-0380 | |

| Code | Publisher | U.S. Agent |
|------|-----------|------------|
| UNIV.CAL | University of California Press<br>2120 Berkeley Way<br>Berkeley, CA 94720 | |
| UNIV.CH | University of Chicago Press<br>5801 South Ellis Avenue<br>Chicago, IL 60637 | |
| UNIV.CR | University College - Cardiff Press<br>P.O. Box 78<br>Cardiff CF1 1XL, Wales<br>United Kingdom | |
| UNIV.EVAN | University of Evansville Press<br>P.O. Box 329<br>Evansville, IN 47702 | |
| UNIV.IOWA | University of Iowa Press<br>Iowa City, IA 52242 | |
| UNIV.MIAMI | University of Miami Music<br>Publications<br>P.O. Box 8163<br>Coral Gables, FL 33124 | PLYMOUTH |
| UNIV.MICRO | University Microfilms<br>300 North Zeeb Road<br>Ann Arbor, MI 48106 | |
| UNIV.MINN | University of Minnesota Press<br>2037 University Avenue S.E.<br>Minneapolis, MN 55455 | |
| UNIV.MO | University of Missouri Press<br>2910 Lemone Boulevard<br>Columbia, MO 65201 | |
| UNIV.MUS.ED | University Music Editions<br>P.O. Box 192-Ft. George Station<br>New York, NY 10040 | |
| UNIV.NC | University of North Carolina Press<br>P.O. Box 2288<br>Chapel Hill, NC 27514 | |
| UNIV.OTAGO | University of Otago Press<br>P.O. Box 56<br>Dunedin<br>New Zealand | |
| UNIV.TEXAS | University of Texas Press<br>P.O. Box 7819<br>Austin, TX 78712 | |
| UNIV.UTAH | University of Utah Press<br>Salt Lake City, UT 84112 | |
| UNIV.WASH | University of Washington Press<br>Seattle, WA 98105 | |
| UNIV.YORK | University of York Music Press<br>Department of Music<br>University of york<br>Heslington, York YO1 5DD<br>England | |
| UNIVER. | Universal Edition<br>Bösendorfer Straße 12<br>Postfach 130<br>A-1015 Wien<br>Austria | EUR.AM.MUS. |

| Code | Publisher | U.S. Agent |
|------|-----------|------------|
| UNIVER. (Cont.) | Universal Edition (London) Ltd.<br>2/3 Fareham Street, Dean Street<br>London W1V 4DU<br>England | EUR.AM.MUS. |
| UNIVERH | Universal Songs Holland<br>Postbus 305<br>1200 AH Hilversum<br>Netherlands | GM |
| UNIVERSE | Universe Publishers<br>P.O. Box 1900<br>Orem, UT 84059 | PRESSER |
| UP WITH | Up With People<br>3103 North Campbell Avenue<br>Tucson, AZ 85719 | LORENZ |
| VAAP | VAAP<br>6a, Bolshaya Bronnaya St.<br>Moscow 103670,GSP<br>Russia | SCHIRM.G |
| VALANDO | Valando Music, Inc. | PLYMOUTH |
| VAMO | Musikverlag Vamö<br>Leebgasse 52-25<br>Wien 10<br>Austria | |
| VAN NESS | Van Ness Press, Inc. | BROADMAN |
| VANDEN-RUP | Vandenhoeck & Ruprecht<br>Theaterstrasse 13<br>Postfach 3753<br>D-3400 Göttingen<br>Germany | |
| VANDERSALL | Vandersall Editions | EUR.AM.MUS. |
| VANGUARD | Vanguard Music Corp.<br>357 W. 55th Street<br>New York, NY 10019 | |
| VELDE | Editions Van De Velde<br>La Petite Plaine, BP 22<br>Fondettes<br>F-37230 Luynes<br>France | |
| VER.HUIS | Vereniging voor Huismuziek<br>Utrechtsestraat 77<br>Postbus 350<br>NL-3041 CT ljsselstein<br>Netherlands | |
| VER.NED.MUS. | Vereniging voor Nederlandse<br>Muziekgeschiedenis<br>Postbus 1514<br>NL-3500 BM Utrecht<br>Netherlands | |
| VEST-NORSK | Vest-Norsk Musikkforslag<br>Postboks 4016, Dreggen<br>N-5023 Bergen<br>Norway | |
| VIENNA | Vienna Masterworks<br>Margaretenstrasse 125/15<br>A-1050 Vienna<br>Austria | |

| Code | Publisher | U.S. Agent |
|------|-----------|------------|
| VIERTMANN | Viertmann Verlag<br>Lübecker Straße 2<br>D-5000 Köln 1<br>Germany | |
| VIEWWEG | Chr. Friedrich Viewweg, Musikverlag<br>Nibelungenstrße 48<br>D-8000 München 19<br>Germany | LEONARD-US<br>SCHIRM.G<br>(rental) |
| VIKING | Viking Press, Inc<br>P.O. Box 4030<br>Church Street Station<br>New York, NY 10261-4030 | |
| VIOLA | Viola World Publications<br>2 Inlander Road<br>Saratoga Springs, NY 12866 | |
| VIVACE | Vivace Press<br>NW 310 Wawawai Road<br>Pullman, WA 99163 | |
| VOGGEN | Voggenrieter Verlag<br>Viktoriastraße 25<br>D-5300 Bonn<br>Germany | |
| VOGT | Musikverlag Vogt & Fritz<br>Friedrich-Stein-Straße 10<br>D-8720 Schweinfurt<br>Germany | |
| VOICE | Voice of the Rockies<br>P.O. Box 1043<br>Boulder, CO 80306-1043 | |
| VOLK | Arno Volk Verlag | BREITKOPF-W |
| VOLKWEIN | Volkwein Brothers, Inc. | WARNER |
| WADSWORTH | Wadsworth Publishing Co.<br>10 Davis Street<br>Belmont, CA 94002 | |
| WAGENAAR | J.A.H. Wagenaar<br>Oude Gracht 109<br>NL-3511 AG Utrecht<br>Netherlands | ELKAN,H |
| WAI-TE-ATA | Wai-te-ata Press<br>Dept. of Music<br>Victoria University of Wellington<br>P.O. Box 600<br>Wellington, New Zealand | |
| WALKER | Walker Publications<br>P.O. Box 61<br>Arnold, MD 21012 | |
| WALK.MUS.PRO | Walker Music Productions<br>643 Oenoke Ridge<br>New Canaan, CT 06840 | |
| WALTON | Walton Music Corp.<br>170 N.E. 33rd Street<br>Ft. Lauderdale, FL 33334 | |
| WARCH AUS | Warner/Chappell Music<br>1 Cassins Avenue<br>North Sidney NSW 2060<br>Australia | |

| Code | Publisher | U.S. Agent |
|------|-----------|------------|
| WARNER | Warner Brothers Publications, Inc.<br>15800 NW 48th Avenue<br>Hialeah, FL 33014<br><br>Warner-Chappell Music<br>810 Seventh Avenue<br>New York, NY 10119<br><br>Warner-Chappell Music<br>Ratapihantie 11<br>PL 126 * 00521 Helsinki<br>Finland | |
| WATERLOO | Waterloo Music Co. Ltd.<br>3 Regina Street North<br>Waterloo, Ontario N2J 4A5<br>Canada | |
| WEHMAN BR. | Wehman Brothers, Inc.<br>Ridgedale Avenue<br>Morris County Mall<br>Cedar Knolls, NJ 07927 | |
| WEINBERGER | Josef Weinberger Ltd.<br>12-14 Mortimer Street<br>London W1N 7RD<br>England<br><br>Weinberger, Josef<br>Oeder Weg 26<br>D-60318 Frankfurt<br>Germany | BOOSEY<br>CANTORIS<br>BOCK |
| WEINTRAUB | Weintraub Music Co. | SCHIRM.G<br>(rental) |
| WELT | Welt Musik<br>Josef Hochmuth Verlage<br>Hegergasse 21<br>A-1160 Wien<br>Austria | |
| WESLEYAN | Wesleyan Music Press<br>P.O. Box 1072<br>Fort George Station<br>New York, NY 10040 | |
| WESSMANS | Wessmans Musikforlag<br>S-620 30 Slite<br>Sweden | STIM |
| WESTEND | Westend | PETERS |
| WESTERN | Western International Music, Inc.<br>3707 65th Avenue<br>Greeley, CO 80634 | |
| WESTMINSTER | The Westminster Press<br>925 Chestnut Street<br>Philadelphia, PA 19107 | |
| WESTWM | West Wind Music<br>3072 S. Laredo Cir.<br>Aurora, CO 80013-1806 | |
| WESTWOOD | Westwood Press, Inc.<br>3759 Willow Road<br>Schiller Park, IL 60176 | WORLD |
| WHITE HARV. | White Harvest Music Publications<br>P.O. Box 1144<br>Independence, MO 64051 | |

| Code | Publisher | U.S. Agent |
|------|-----------|------------|
| WIDE WORLD | Wide World Music, Inc.<br>Box B<br>Delaware Water Gap, PA 18327 | |
| WIEN.BOH. | Wiener Boheme Verlag GmbH<br>Sonnenstraße 19<br>D-8000 München 2<br>Germany | |
| WIENER | Wiener Urtext Edition | EUR.AM.MUS. |
| WILDER | Wilder | MARGUN |
| WILHELMIANA | Wilhelmiana Musikverlag<br>see HANSEN-GER | |
| | William Grant Still Music<br>see STILL | |
| WILLIAMS | Williams School of Church Music<br>The Bourne<br>Harpenden<br>England | |
| WILLIAMSON | Williamson Music, Inc. | LEONARD-US |
| WILLIS | Willis Music Co.<br>7380 Industrial Road<br>Florence, KY 41042 | |
| WILLSHIRE | Willshire Press Music Foundation, Inc. | WESTERN |
| WILSHORN | Wilshorn | HOPE |
| WILSON | Wilson Editions<br>13 Bank Square<br>Wilmslow SK9 1AN<br>England<br>see DI MUSIC | |
| WIMBLEDON | Wimbledon Music Inc.<br>1888 Century Park East<br>Suite 10<br>Century City, CA 90067 | |
| WIND MUS | Wind Music, Inc.<br>153 Highland Parkway<br>Rochester, NY 14620 | KALMUS,A |
| WINGERT | Wingert-Jones Music, Inc.<br>11225 Colorado<br>Kansas City, MO 64137-2502 | |
| WISCASSET | Wiscasset Music Publishing Company<br>Box 810<br>Cambridge, MA 02138 | |
| WOITSCHACH | Paul Woitschach Radio-Musikverlag<br>Grosse Friedberger Strasse 23-27<br>D-6000 Frankfurt<br>Germany | |
| WOLF | see WOLFLAND | WESTERN |
| WOLFLAND | Wolfland Music Publishing<br>7949 Belton Drive<br>Los Angeles, CA 90045 | |
| WOLLENWEBER | Verlag Walter Wollenweber<br>Schiffmannstrasse 4<br>Postfach 1165<br>D-8032 Gräfelfing vor München<br>Germany | FOR.MUS.DIST<br>PETERS |

| Code | Publisher | U.S. Agent |
|------|-----------|-----------|
| WOODBURY | Woodbury Music Co.<br>33 Grassy Hill Road<br>P.O. Box 447<br>Woodbury, CT 06798 | PRESSER<br>(rental<br>-partial) |
| WOODWARD | Ralph Woodward, Jr.<br>1033 East 300 South<br>Salt Lake City, UT 84102 | |
| WOODWIND | Woodwind Editions<br>P.O. Box 457, Station K<br>Toronto, Ontario<br>Canada M4P 2G9 | |
| WORD | Word, Incorporated<br>3319 West End Avenue<br>Suite 200<br>Nashville, TN 37203 | |
| WORD GOD | The Word of God Music | SERVANT |
| WORLD | World Library Publications, Inc.<br>3825 Willow Road<br>P.O. Box 2703<br>Schiller Park, IL 60176 | |
| WORLDWIDE | Worldwide Music Services<br>P.O. Box 995, Ansonia Station<br>New York, NY 10023 | |
| WWILD | Edition Walter Wild<br>Seestrasse 73<br>CH-8712 Stäfa-Zürich<br>Switzerland | |
| WYE | WYE Music Publications | EMERSON |
| WYNN | Wynn Music Publications<br>P.O. Box 739<br>Orinda, CA 94563 | |
| XYZ | Muziekuitgeverij XYZ<br>P.O. Box 338<br>NL-1400 AH Bussum<br>Netherlands | SUNSHINE |
| YAHRES | Yahres Publications<br>1315 Vance Avenue<br>Coraopolis, PA 15108 | |
| YBARRA | Ybarra Music<br>P.O. Box 665<br>Lemon Grove, CA 92045 | |
| YORKE | Yorke Editions<br>31 Thornhill Square<br>London N1 1BQ<br>England | ECS |
| YOUNG WORLD | Young World Publications<br>10485 Glennon Drive<br>Lakewood, CO 80226 | |
| Yugoslavian Music Information Center<br>  see MUSIC INFO | | |
| ZALO | Zalo Publications & Services<br>P.O. Box 913<br>Bloomington, IN 47402 | FRANGIPANI |

| Code | Publisher | U.S. Agent |
|------|-----------|-----------|
| ZANIBON | G. Zanibon Edition<br>Piazza dei Signori, 44<br>I-35100 Padova<br>Italy | |
| ZEN-ON | Zen-On Music., Ltd.<br>3-14 Higashi Gokencho<br>Shinjuku-ku<br>Tokyo 162<br>Japan | EUR.AM.MUS<br>MAGNAMUSIC |
| ZENEM. | Zenemukiado Vallalat | BOOSEY<br>GENERAL |
| ZENGERINK | Herman Zengerink<br>Urlusstraat 24<br>NL-3533 SN Utrecht<br>Netherlands | |
| ZERBONI | Edizioni Suvini Zerboni<br>Via Quintiliano 40<br>I-20138 Milano<br>Italy | BOOSEY<br>(rental) |
| ZIMMER.PUBS | Oscar Zimmerman Publications<br>4671 State Park Highway<br>Interlochen, MI 49643-9527 | |
| ZIMMERMANN | Musikverlag Zimmermann<br>Gaugrafenstraße 19-23<br>Postfach 940183<br>D-6000 Frankfurt-am-Main<br>Germany | |
| ZINNEBERG | Zinneberg Musikverlag | LEUCKART |
| Zondervan Corp., The<br>  see SINGSPIR | | |
| ZÜRCHER | Zurcher Liederbuchanstalt<br>Postfach 279<br>8056 Zurich<br>Switzerland | |
| ZURFLUH | Éditions Zurfluh<br>73, Boulevard Raspail<br>F-75006 Paris<br>France | PRESSER |

# Advertisements

## Index to Advertisers

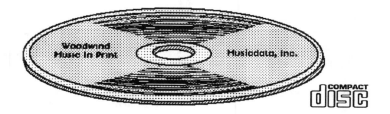

# *Publishers to the performing arts*

**RHINEGOLD PUBLISHING**

www.rhinegold.co.uk

## YEARBOOKS

### British & International Music Yearbook
Britain's most comprehensive and accurate directory of the classical music industry
*Published each December*
*£28.45 (to Europe); £36.95 (outside Europe)*

### British Performing Arts Yearbook
The guide to performing companies, venues, suppliers, services, festivals, education and support organisations
*Published each June*
*£28.45 (to Europe); £36.95 (outside Europe)*

### Music Education Yearbook
A guide for parents, teachers, students and musicians
*Published each May*
*£19.50 (to Europe); £23.50 (outside Europe)*

### Musicians' Union National Directory 1999/2000
The first complete national guide to MU members
*Published June*
*£28.50 (to Europe); £37.00 (outside Europe)*

## OTHER PUBLICATONS

### The Musician's Handbook
41 chapters of advice for aspiring and established professional musicians
*(hardback)*
*£19.95 (to Europe); £25.95 (outside Europe)*

### Healthy Practice for Musicians
An expertly written self-help guide covering the whole spectrum of a musician's physical and mental well-being
*(hardback)*
*£21.45 (to Europe); £25.95 (outside Europe)*

### Arts Marketing
The definitive guide to audience-building through effective marketing
*(hardback)*
*£17.00 (to Europe); £18.50 (outside Europe)*

### Analysis Matters 2000/01
A students' revision guide to the Group 2 London Board A-Level Music Papers for 2000/01
*(paperback)*
*£12.50 (to Europe); £13.50 (outside Europe)*

## MAGAZINES

### Classical Music
The magazine of the classical music profession
*Fortnightly £2.95*
*Annual Subscription £66.00 (Airmail)*

### Music Teacher
Respected and enjoyed by music teachers for more than 90 years
*Monthly £2.95*
*Annual Subscription £44.00 (Airmail)*

### The Singer
For amateur and professional singers of every persuasion – from cabaret to grand opera
*Bi-monthly £2.40*
*Annual Subscription £18.00 (Airmail)*

### Piano
The magazine for performers and enthusiasts of classical, jazz and blues piano
*Bi-monthly £2.40*
*Annual Subscription £18.00 (Airmail)*

### Early Music Today
Britain's brightest early music news magazine
*Bi-monthly £2.40*
*Annual Subscription £18.00 (Airmail)*

### Opera Now
The international magazine for opera professionals and enthusiasts
*Bi-monthly £4.95*
*Annual Subscription £39.00 (Airmail)*

## INTERNET

### www.classicalsearch.com
The most comprehensive classical music search engine on the Web. Updated and validated on an almost daily basis with links to tens of thousands of music industry websites worldwide. Try it now.

### www.operadata.co.uk
Provides access to performance details, cast lists, dates and booking information for all the world's major opera houses, up to two years ahead, plus archive access going back four years and an exclusive up-to-the-minute on-line opera news service. Only available to *Opera Now* subscribers.

### www.rhinegold.co.uk
Read all about our magazines, yearbooks, supplements and other publications on the frequently-changing Rhinegold website. Contents summaries from the current, previous and forthcoming issues of all our magazines plus the ability to order books and magazine subscriptions on-line and pay by credit card or invoice.

---

**Rhinegold Publishing Limited**
241 Shaftesbury Avenue
London WC2H 8EH
England
**Tel:** +44 207 333 1721 **Fax:** +44 207 333 1769
**Email:** book.sales@rhinegold.co.uk
**Website:** www.rhinegold.co.uk

**R·**

# An essential resource for string teachers and players

AMERICAN STRING TEACHERS ASSOCIATION
WITH
NATIONAL SCHOOL ORCHESTRA ASSOCIATION

# AMERICAN STRING TEACHER

*Official quarterly publication of the American String Teachers Association WITH National School Orchestra Association*

The *American String Teacher* journal is the only magazine to serve teachers and players of all stringed instruments across the United States and in some twenty-five countries worldwide.

An Editorial Committee review process ensures that each issue contains solid, seminal information by prestigious members of the profession.

In addition to five to seven full-length articles pertinent to today's string teacher and player, each issue of *AST* contains:

- Announcements of upcoming national symposia, summer workshops, and conferences of importance to the string world.

- Reviews of books and music, competition announcements, new product information, and other news of interest to string teachers and players.

- Information about publications and other benefits available to ASTA WITH NSOA members.

- A "My Turn" editorial article, often controversial in nature, a regular Teaching Tips column, and "Preprofessional Perspectives" especially for students members.

- A regular Master Class column, featuring the pearls of wisdom of national ASTA and NSOA award winners.

## No library is complete without a subscription to *AST*.

**Active memberships $54**          **Library/Schools: $75**

For more information, contact the ASTA WITH NSOA National Office, 1806 Robert Fulton Dr., Suite 300, Reston, VA 20191.
Tel: 703-620-3484; Fax 703-476-1317; Email: asta@erols.com; Web site: www.astaweb.com

# The time is now!
## Reserve your copy of the Millennium Edition of Musical America today!

Praised by professionals around the world for its accurate, comprehensive and up-to-date marketplace information, **Musical America International Directory of the Performing Arts** puts the names, organizations, addresses, phone and fax numbers, and E-mail addresses of everyone who's anyone in the performing arts right at your fingertips! With detailed information on festivals, orchestras, choral groups and dance companies, music schools and departments, record companies, music magazines, and radio and TV stations, as well as scores of artists and attractions, **Musical America** is a one-stop guide to the performing arts industry.

Don't miss your chance to own a copy of the performing arts industry's authoritative resource!

**Call (800) 221-5488, ext. 7783 or (609) 371-7783**

Fax: **(609) 371-7718**
E-mail:
**info@musicalamerica.com**

www.musicalamerica.com

A Publication of **PRIMEDIA Directories**
10 Lake Drive, Hightstown, NJ 08520-5397

# Revista de Música Latino Americana

# Latin American Music Review

**Editor: Gerard Béhague, University of Texas at Austin**

**Latin American Music Review** explores the historical, ethnographic, and socio-cultural dimensions of Latin American music. Each issue contains film, record and video reviews and appear in English, Spanish, or Portuguese.

". . . **LAMR** is one of a few interdisciplinary core titles essential to a music research and education collection."
—**Magazines for Libraries, 1997**

## FALL/WINTER 1998, Vol 19:2

The Song of the Snake: Silvestre Revueltas' Sensemayá
RICARDO ZOHN-MULDOON

Play It Con Filin!: The Swing and Expression of Salsa
CHRISTOPHER WASHBURNE

Apropiaciones y estrategias políticas: una interpretación sobre la dinámica de cambio musical en contexto ritual
IRMA RUIZ

Conversión religiosa y cambio musical
MIGUEL A. GARCÍA

La Plaza Tomada: Proceso histórico y etnogénesis musical entre los Chiriguano de Bolivia
WALTER SÁNCHEZ C.

Consideraciones teórico-metodológicas en el estudio semiológico y contextual de la danza Yu'pa
ANGEL ACUÑA DELGADO

**Subscription rates (one year):**
Individual $25, Institution $42; Canada/Mexico, add $5 for postage,
other foreign, add $8 for postage (airmail).
**Single copy rates:**
Individual $15, Institution $26; foreign postage, add $4.

 **University of Texas Press, Journals Division, Box 7819,
Austin, Texas 78713-7819**

Phone # 512-471-4531, Fax # 512-320-0668, *journals@uts.cc.utexas.edu*

# Guide to
# www.**schirmer**.com

The web site of G. Schirmer and Associated Music Publishers

---

## Anniversaries
http://www.schirmer.com/**composers/anniv.html**

## Biographies
http://www.schirmer.com/**composers.html**

## Catalogues
### music in stores
http://www.schirmer.com/**S/sale.htm**

### manuscript and rental editions
http://www.schirmer.com/**catalogs.html#rent**

### Schirmer's Library of Musical Classics
http://www.schirmer.com/**S/library.htm**

## Music for Young People
http://www.schirmer.com/**repertoire/young_people.html**

## New Publications
http://www.schirmer.com/**S/new.htm**

## News
http://www.schirmer.com/**news.html**

## Performances
http://www.schirmer.com/**calendars.html**

## Questions
http://www.schirmer.com/**mail.html**

## Repertoire
http://www.schirmer.com/**repertoire.html**

---

G. Schirmer, Inc. and Associated Music Publishers, Inc.
257 Park Avenue South, 20th Floor
New York, NY 10010

phone: 212-254-2100
fax: 212-254-2013
E-mail: schirmer@schirmer.com

285

# *Are you up to date ?*

# The Music-In-Print Series

### Sacred Choral Music In Print

Vols. 1a,b. 2nd Ed. (1985) 2-volume set
Vol. 1c. 2nd Ed.: Arranger Index (1987)
Vol. 1s. 1988 Supplement
Vol. 1t. 1992 Supplement
Vol. 1u. 1996 Supplement
Vol. 1x. Master Index 1996

### Organ Music In Print

Vol. 3. 2nd Edition (1984)
Vol. 3s. 1990 Supplement
Vol. 3t. 1997 Supplement
Vol. 3x. Master Index 1997

### Orchestral Music In Print

Vol. 5. 1st Edition (1979)
Vol. 5s. 1983 Supplement
Vol. 5t. 1994 Supplement
Vol. 5u. 1999 Supplement

### Classical Guitar Music In Print

Vol. 7. 1st Edition (1989)
Vol. 7s. 1998 Supplement

### Secular Choral Music In Print

Vols. 2a,b. 2nd Ed. (1987) 2-volume set
Vol. 2c. 2nd Ed.: Arranger Index (1987)
Vol. 2s. 1991 Supplement
Vol. 2t. 1993 Supplement
Vol. 2u. 1996 Supplement
Vol. 2x. Master Index 1996

### Classical Vocal Music In Print

Vol. 4. 1st Edition (1976) (out of print)
Vol. 4s. 1985 Supplement
Vol. 4t. 1995 Supplement
Vol. 4x. Master Index 1995

### String Music In Print

Vol. 6. 2nd Edition (1973)
Vol. 6s. 1984 Supplement
Vol. 6t. 1998 Supplement

### Woodwind Music In Print

Vol. 8. 1st Edition (1997)

### Music-In-Print Master Index

Vols. XCa,b. Master Composer Index 1999
Vol. XT. Master Title Index 1999

Stay up to date with a **STANDING ORDER** for the Music-In-Print Series.

A Standing Order is a subscription to all future Music-In-Print volumes as published. Standing Orders receive a special discount. Your subscriiption may be customized, revised or cancelled at any time.

**MUSICDATA, INC.**
P.O. Box 12380
Philadelphia, PA 19119 U.S.A.

TEL:(215)248-3530   FAX:(215)248-3531
email: musicdat@voicenet.com
www.voicenet.com/~musicdat